Child Development
Context, Culture, and Cascades

FIRST EDITION

Catherine S. Tamis-LeMonda

Carefully scratch off the silver coating to see your personal redemption code.

This code can be redeemed only once.

Once the code has been revealed, this access card cannot be returned to the publisher.

Access can also be purchased online during the registration process.

The code on this card is valid for two years from the date of first purchase. Complete terms and conditions are available at learninglink.oup.com

Access Length: 6 months from redemption of the code.

OXFORD
UNIVERSITY PRESS

Your OUP digital course materials can be delivered several different ways, depending on how your instructor has elected to incorporate them into his or her course.

BEFORE REGISTERING FOR ACCESS, be sure to check with your instructor to ensure that you register using the proper method.

VIA YOUR SCHOOL'S LEARNING MANAGEMENT SYSTEM

Use this method if your instructor has integrated these resources into your school's Learning Management System (LMS)—Blackboard, Canvas, Brightspace, Moodle, or other.

Log in to your instructor's course within your school's LMS.

When you click a link to a resource that is access-protected, you will be prompted to register for access.

Follow the on-screen instructions.

Enter your personal redemption code (or purchase access) when prompted.

VIA OXFORD learning link

Use this method if you are using the resources for self-study only. **NOTE**: *Scores for any quizzes you take on the OUP site will not report to your instructor's gradebook.*

Visit www.oup.com/us/ tamis-lemonda1e

Select the edition you are using, then select student resources for that edition.

Click the link to upgrade your access to the student resources.

Follow the on-screen instructions.

Enter your personal redemption code (or purchase access) when prompted.

VIA OXFORD learning cloud

Use this method only if your instructor has specifically instructed you to enroll in an Oxford Learning Cloud course. **NOTE**: *If your instructor is using these resources within your school's LMS, use the Learning Management System instructions.*

Visit the course invitation URL provided by your instructor.

If you already have an oup.instructure.com account you will be added to the course automatically; if not, create an account by providing your name and email.

When you click a link to a resource in the course that is access-protected, you will be prompted to register.

Follow the on-screen instructions, entering your personal redemption code where prompted.

For assistance with code redemption, Oxford Learning Cloud registration, or if you redeemed your code using the wrong method for your course, please contact our customer support team at **learninglinkdirect.support@oup.com** or 855-281-8749.

Child Development
Context, Culture, and Cascades

CHILD DEVELOPMENT

CONTEXT, CULTURE, AND CASCADES

Catherine S. Tamis-LeMonda

OXFORD
UNIVERSITY PRESS

NEW YORK   OXFORD
OXFORD UNIVERSITY PRESS

Library of Congress Cataloging-in-Publication Data

Names: Tamis-LeMonda, Catherine S. (Catherine Susan), 1958- author.
Title: Child Development : Context, Culture, and Cascades / Catherine S. Tamis-LeMonda.
Description: New York, NY : Sinauer Associates/Oxford University Press, [2022] |
        Includes bibliographical references and index.
Identifiers: LCCN 2021034546 (print) | LCCN 2021034547 (ebook) |
        ISBN 9780190216900 (paperback) | ISBN 9780190216979 (epub)
Subjects: LCSH: Child development. | Child psychology.
Classification: LCC HQ767.9 .T36 2022 (print) | LCC HQ767.9 (ebook) |
        DDC 305.231--dc23
LC record available at https://lccn.loc.gov/2021034546
LC ebook record available at https://lccn.loc.gov/2021034547

Printing number: 9 8 7 6 5 4 3 2 1
Printed by LSC Communications, United States of America

I dedicate this book to Brittany, Christopher, and Michael.
Watching you develop from infancy through adulthood each and every day
has been the most inspiring, fulfilling part of my life.
Thank you for opening my eyes to the true wonders and complexities of child development.

Brittany

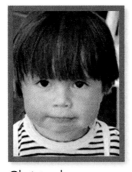

Christopher

Michael

Preface: The Power of Change

Changing People

The Greek philosopher Heraclitus famously stated that "the only constant in life is change." Indeed, Heraclitus's writings highlight a critical distinction between the words "being" and "becoming." Being implies that people and things are fixed: the idea that we have somehow arrived at a destination, and who we are remains constant over time and space. Conversely, becoming signifies something much more exciting and brimming with potential, but perhaps disrupting as well: the idea that people, animals, nature, the world, are in constant flux. Nothing ever is. But everything is always becoming. Change is the norm.

The principle of change lies at the core of developmental science. Developmental researchers seek to understand how change occurs and why, especially over the years spanning conception to adolescence, when the body and mind rapidly transform. Our bodies change in size, shape, and capacity, with billions of cells dying each day to be replaced by billions of new ones. Our states and emotions are in constant flux over the course of a day, as we transition from alertness to fatigue, hunger to satiety, and joy to anger. Change likewise defines our perceptual experiences. As we move about and interact with our environments, what we see, hear, feel, smell, and sense. Change characterizes our thinking as we gain new knowledge and memories and revise our beliefs day to day and year to year. And relationships continually evolve as the people in our lives embark on new life paths. The parent-infant relationship, as one example, looks markedly different than the parent-adolescent relationship.

Changing Environments

Notably, developmental scientists extend the study of change to the contexts of everyday life. People do not exist in vacuums. Rather, they interact with objects, spaces, and people in their family, school, community, and so on. Their interactions affect and are affected by changes in those settings. For example, children who experience supportive relationships with friends and teachers at school not only change in their own attitudes and behaviors—they also positively affect the people around them and the climate of the school community. As a result, the classroom that children depart in June is quite different from the one they enter in September. Indeed, Heraclitus also observed that "no person ever steps in the same river twice." The river (a metaphor for environment) is always flowing and ever changing. In short, to understand how children develop requires understanding the inseparable connection between person and context.

Personal Changes

Like all people, I continue to change in my relationships to others and as a developmental researcher. Over 30 years ago, I embarked on my PhD in Developmental Psychology and, a few years later, gave birth to Brittany. Christopher arrived in August, when I was a newly hired Assistant Professor at New York University. I began teaching two weeks later, because there was no maternity leave at the time, and we could not afford to forego my salary. Michael came along when my professional career was a bit more stable and my lab was bustling with research on infant learning and development. Over the years, I followed the path forged by millions of women as I attempted to master the art of juggling career and home life—research, cooking, grant writing, homework, teaching, soccer games, conferences, babysitters. Fortunately, my children had a highly involved father, who learned the art of juggling as well. He changed diapers, cooked meals, did laundry, cleaned, and taught our children how to play tennis and ski while working in the NYC Fire Department. The rivers of life were forever changing, yet for the most part, we managed to ride the waves.

But then on the morning of September 11, 2001, my husband responded to a call to help at the Twin Towers in New York City after terrorists had crashed planes into the buildings. He ushered people out of the towers that day as many of his friends and fellow firefighters perished. He dug out fragments of bodies and burnt badges for months on end, attended countless funerals, and suffered lung disease that forced him to retire at a young age. Our children also faced their share of tragedies, losing adolescent friends to prison, drug overdoses, and car crashes.

As I look back, I realize that the fascination of studying children was a source of strength that helped me to navigate rough waters. I accepted the fact that my children, my husband, and I were always becoming. The river we stepped in when our first child was born had long washed away, to be replaced by new waters, sometimes stormy, sometimes calm, but forever changing. And so, my goal in writing this book is to give back to others what the field of child development has offered me: an appreciation and understanding of the sources and consequences of life changes.

Understanding Change

In *Child Development: Context, Culture, and Cascades*, I seek to convey the wonder and awe of child development. In addition, I aim to inspire students to understand the process of change and to think about change through the eyes of a developmental scientist.

To appreciate child development requires understanding the basics: What is changing and why? Accordingly, each chapter describes changes in a select domain of development at a specific time in childhood (the what) and considers the many forces that spur changes in children (the how). Within and across chapters, students will learn about interactions between biology and environment; the role of contexts (e.g., family, school, community, and other contexts) in development; and how cultural views and practices infuse children's everyday lives. Finally, because the path of a river is affected by the flowing waters that preceded it, students will come to appreciate how small changes can exert downstream effects on development in the process of developmental cascades. Changing children swim in ever-changing waters that spill into the future.

However, beyond providing the fundamentals of child development, the ultimate message of this book runs much deeper than words on a page. Students will see that answers to the "whats" and "hows" of change are both fundamental to science and hold a key to improving the lives of children and families around the world.

What Makes this Book Unique?

Child Development: Context, Culture, and Cascades stands apart in the landscape of child development textbooks. Many otherwise excellent books were crafted years ago and, even if updated, are not systematically organized around topics at the forefront of developmental science: the roles of context and culture in development and developmental cascades. Furthermore, many texts glaze over research methods or relegate them to a highlighted box, rather than systematically incorporating research methods into core material so that students understand how scientists arrive at the conclusions they do. Finally, as someone who has long been fascinated by the study of how infants enter the world of communication through interactions with others, this book showcases the critical area of language development in a dedicated chapter, rather than burying it under another domain.

Context and Culture

Children develop in multiple interrelated contexts—the intrauterine environment and the contexts of family, peers, childcare, school, and neighborhood—all of which are subject to important cultural influences. In addition, biological context is integral to developmental processes—for example, brain asymmetry channels language input to the left hemisphere from the start of life, and the universal and individual experiences of children cause the brain to develop in ways that make all children alike and each child unique. This theme—that development is the product of multiple interacting contexts—is systematically integrated into every chapter of *Child Development: Context, Culture, and Cascades*. Students will learn that there is no such thing as development devoid of context or culture and that contexts are nested within other contexts: an infant regularly held in its father's arms is next to a warm body in rooms that are more or less noisy and cluttered, and these nested contexts work together to affect the baby's development.

Similarly, culture infuses all aspects of development. Children from communities across the globe show striking variations in their experiences and development while also following many shared developmental paths. However, most of developmental psychology is grounded in a small subset of the world's population of children. For example, popular motor milestone charts, based on the research of Arnold Gesell decades ago, draw from a handful of U.S. children; the literature on language acquisition is grounded in monolingual children learning English; and most of what is known about children's social skills (from attachment to peer relationships) is based on children from North America raised in nuclear families.

In contrast, *Child Development: Context, Culture, and Cascades* includes many examples of the impressive range of human variation—communities where infants begin to walk at eight months of age or not until later in the second year; communities where children as young as four years care for siblings; and communities where schooling is rare—with attention to the views and practices that contribute to such differences. At the same time, students are reminded of the balance between unique cultural practices and universal developmental processes. That is, most children babble before they produce their first words; most children transition from being wobbly to proficient walkers though the strength and postural control that come from practice in upright postures; and supportive and loving caregivers benefit the social development of all children, regardless of where they are raised. This presentation of cultural breadth invites students to reflect on what is "universal" about human development, yet recognize that many assumptions about child development are rooted in their own experiences.

Many child development texts place the important topics of context and culture in separate chapters, where they remain isolated from critical material on developmental processes, or include the information as tag-on sentences buried in the main text. In contrast, *Child Development: Context, Culture, and Cascades* showcases the themes of context and culture in every chapter, with subheadings that underscore how family, peer groups, school, culture, and other influences contribute to developmental processes.

Developmental Cascades

The concept of a developmental cascade captures the idea that changes in one domain of development can reverberate across other domains and time. The theme of developmental cascades is woven into the fabric of *Child Development: Context, Culture, and Cascades* through dedicated sections in each chapter that illustrate such interconnections. For example, changes in motor development, such as the ability to walk, spill over to domains of cognitive, language, and social development, as infants develop new ways of navigating their environments, expand their interactions with people around them, and begin to hear new sentences, such as "Don't touch that!" Similarly, the developmental timing of puberty can affect adolescents' interactions with peers and parents, sexual behaviors, and attitudes toward school. Thus, this book rejects artificial distinctions among skills and embraces the idea of a "whole child."

Child Development: Context, Culture, and Cascades addresses developmental cascades in a major heading at the end of most chapters, with subsections offering illustrative examples of how changes in the area of development discussed in the chapter reverberate across other domains and time. This approach contrasts with existing books that either omit critical material around developmental cascades or provide limited coverage.

Research Methods

Most developmental textbooks present research methods in an opening chapter on measurement and study design before offering students mere snapshots of methods in later chapters. *Child Development: Context, Culture, and Cascades*, in contrast, includes a dedicated chapter on foundations, theories, and methods and also provides chapter-specific overviews of the methods that researchers use to study different areas of development at different periods of development. For example, the chapter on infant cognitive development describes looking-time studies (e.g., habituation); explains why such studies are a cornerstone of infancy research (because babies can't tell researchers what they know or remember); and tackles questions about how much researchers should infer about infant understanding from looking behaviors. The goal is to arm students with a thorough understanding of how to do research, and to then apply that knowledge to exercises at the end of chapters that ask students to design their own studies (for example) to address hypothetical questions. By learning and doing, students will come to appreciate how to tackle critical development questions with an eye toward age-appropriate measures and methods relevant to the domain of interest.

Dedicated Chapter on Language Development in Infancy

The path to language is one of the most inspiring and frequently studied topics in child development. Typing the words "language" and "development" into scholarly search engines yields over 4 million hits (equivalent to hits for cognitive, social, and emotional development). Moreover, a plurality of talks at professional conferences are dedicated to language development, and funding agencies have entire departments that review proposals to support such research. Perhaps most centrally, language skills spill over to all domains (think about the language required to engage with school material, foster friendships, and negotiate conflicts with parents). However, language remains the lonely stepchild in textbooks to date, typically subsumed under cognitive development. In contrast, *Child Development: Context, Culture, and Cascades* includes a dedicated chapter that showcases the rapid changes to language during infancy and toddlerhood—as the cooing and babbling of young infants evolve into the words and sentences of toddlers. By delving deeply into key aspects of early language development, how researchers measure such skills, how language abilities change, and cascading influences to other domains, readers are equipped with foundational knowledge that scaffolds a deeper appreciation of the language topics that are systematically expanded on in later chapters.

Features

Scope and Organization

Like many other texts, *Child Development: Context, Culture, and Cascades* adopts a chronological organization, with 16 chapters discussing specific "domains of development" under each "period of development" (language development in infancy, emotional development in early childhood, physical development in adolescence, and so on). This organization facilitates student learning by providing digestible, targeted information; ensures balance of coverage across age periods; facilitates coverage of key themes (context, culture, cascades); and introduces students to research methods specific to each domain and age (e.g., measures used to assess infant cognitive development versus adolescent cognitive development). As noted, however, *Child Development: Context, Culture, and Cascades* goes beyond the traditional chronological organization by incorporating dedicated sections to reciprocal effects of development across different domains and reverberating effects of development over time. Thus, *Child Development: Context, Culture, and Cascades* balances chronological and topical approaches.

Learning Tools

Child Development: Context, Culture, and Cascades takes a serious approach to its subject matter, at a level appropriate for most undergraduates, even for those who have not taken introductory psychology. Topics and key terms are introduced and clearly defined, so students can build on solid foundations as they progress through the text. Consistency in terminology, topics, and subheadings across chapters (such as repeated "context" sections of family, school, and neighborhood) reinforce take-home messages and allow students to draw connections among chapters.

Beyond the strong focus on clarity, readability, and consistency, all chapters include an array of learning tools designed to support and extend student learning.

Chapter-Opening Tools

- Chapter outline: Shows main headings and first-level subheadings to give students an overview of the chapter organization before they start reading.

- Chapter introduction: Introduces a brief story, case study, or description of current research encapsulating some of the major themes of the chapter, segueing into an overview of the chapter.

Midchapter Tools

- Learning Objectives: Connect to the major subheadings of the chapter and cue students to what they should be able to know and/or do after reading.
- Check Your Understanding questions: Test students' understanding of content related to Learning Objective sections (answers are available to Instructors on Oxford Learning Link).
- Key terms and marginal glossaries: Bolded terms denote important topics and subtopics, research methods, and a wide range of specialized concepts, with each term clearly and explicitly defined when introduced.
- Figures and tables: Provide strong visual and organizational support in the form of graphs, diagrams, charts, illustrations, and photos, accompanied by informative captions reinforcing key points and ideas.

End-of-Chapter Tools

- The Developmentalist's Toolbox: Recaps the research methods discussed in the chapter, briefly describing the method and its purpose, to reinforce students' research understanding.
- Bulleted chapter summary: Summarizes the contents of main sections.
- Thinking Like a Developmentalist questions: Present students with hypothetical situations (e.g., design a study to address a research question) to engage students in the application of chapter information.

The Oxford Digital Difference

The Oxford Digital Difference is the flexibility to teach your course the way that you want to. At Oxford University Press, content comes first. We create high-quality, engaging, and affordable digital material in a variety of formats and deliver it to you in the way that best suits the needs of you, your students, and your institution.

Oxford Insight Courseware

Child Development: Context, Culture, and Cascades is available powered by Oxford Insight. Oxford Insight delivers the trusted and student-focused content of *Child Development: Context, Culture, and Cascades* within powerful, data-driven courseware designed to optimize student success. Developed with a foundation in learning science, Insight enables instructors to deliver a personalized and engaging learning experience that empowers students by actively engaging them with assigned reading. This adaptivity, paired with real-time actionable data about student performance, helps instructors ensure that each student is best supported along their unique learning path. Features of Oxford Insight include:

- A dynamically personalized learning experience for each student, based on their own learning needs. Oxford Insight delivers adaptive practice sessions that function much like a human tutor for students. The content and focus of these sessions is based on student interaction with formative assessment that they encounter as they work through course content.

- Improved reading retention with chapter content broken down into smaller "chunks" of content that are centered on specific Learning Objectives and accompanied by Formative Assessment activities. As students progress through chapter reading, they are periodically required to answer formative questions, allowing the platform to collect information along the way and adapt a personalized plan to help improve their learning. The practice plan is followed by a summative quiz to demonstrate learning, turning students from passive readers to engaged problem solvers.

- A clear, customizable, query-based Learning Dashboard that displays powerful and actionable, real-time data on student performance. With the query-based Learning Dashboard, instructors can quickly answer questions like:
    - Which students are having difficulties?
    - Which objectives are my students having difficulties with?
    - How often are my students visiting the course?

- Developed with a learning-science-based course design methodology. Powered by Acrobatiq by VitalSource, a leading provider of adaptive learning solutions, Oxford Insight builds on years of research at Carnegie Mellon's Open Learning Initiative that was aimed at discovering how best to optimize online learning for both students and instructors.

Oxford Insight for *Child Development: Context, Culture, and Cascades* includes the following resources:

- Research in Action videos: These short videos explore classic and current research in child development. They are accompanied by multiple choice questions that can be assigned (2–4 videos per chapter | ~2–5 minutes in length, although some are longer).

- Concepts in Action videos: These short videos highlight important concepts in child development, bringing methods and concepts to life. They are accompanied by multiple choice questions that can be assigned (1–2 videos per chapter | ~2–3 minutes in length).

- Cascades videos: These short videos, featuring the author, complement end-of-chapter sections on Developmental Cascades, emphasizing key points related to these important concepts (1 video per chapter | 3–5 minutes in length).

- Context and Culture videos: These short videos, featuring the author, complement selected context and culture sections in chapters to emphasize key points (1–2 videos per chapter | ~3 minutes in length).

- Data in Action: These interactive graphs enable students to manipulate independent and dependent variables relevant to chapter topics to see associations change in real time. For example, students will see side-by-side bar graphs representing 2 children high or low on an independent variable, with bar values rising or falling for the dependent variable of academic performance. Then, students can manipulate variables such as "motivation" or "stereotype threat," which will change values on academic performance in line with the selected variable (e.g., bars representing performance will be high for the group high in motivation but low for those low in motivation). After observing effects, students will respond to multiple choice questions that can be assigned.

Ancillaries for Instructors

An extensive and thoughtful ancillary program offers instructors everything they need to prepare their course and lectures and to assess student progress, including suggested answers to the book's Check Your Understanding questions, an instructor's manual, lecture slides, figure slides, concepts in action clicker slides, and a test bank in Word, Respondus, and Common Cartridge formats.

Oxford Learning Link

Oxford Learning Link is your central hub for a wealth of engaging digital learning tools and resources to help you get the most of your Oxford University Press course material.

Available online exclusively to adopters, the Oxford Learning Link includes all of the instructor resources that accompany *Child Development: Context, Culture, and Cascades* 1e.

Suggested Answers to "Check Your Understanding" Questions

These PDFs provide suggested answers from the author for all of the "Check Your Understanding" questions included at the end of learning objective subsections in the book.

Instructor's Manual

The Instructor's Manual, written by the author and based on her experience teaching the course, includes chapter outlines, descriptions of classroom activities/lecture launchers, and suggested video clips and descriptions.

Lecture PowerPoints

Complete lecture outlines for each chapter are available and ready for use in class. These include coverage of all important facts and concepts presented in each chapter.

Figure PowerPoints

These include all of the figures presented in each chapter.

Concepts in Action Real-Time Class Participation Activities

To solve the problem of engaging students in large lecture classes, various questions, exercises, and activities are available that engage students, asking them to respond in real time to prompts of various kinds (including knowledge and understanding checks). Professors will be able to use identifiers to track student responses and to see how they responded in real-time to facilitate discussion. Some activities enable students to experience research studies first-hand, such as by responding to Stroop Task items or Implicit Association Tests of stereotypes, to see how their reaction times change on such tasks and to better understand the research material in chapters. Several activities are accompanied by Concepts in Action videos that more thoroughly explain the activities and concepts under discussion.

Test Bank

A complete test bank provides instructors with a wide range of test items for each chapter, including multiple choice, fill-in-the-blank, true/false, matching, short answer, and essay questions.

Acknowledgements

First and foremost, I am indebted to my children, Brittany, Christopher, and Michael, who forever are the inspiration behind my fascination with child development. Through them, I came to understand first-hand that each child follows a unique developmental path. And I am deeply proud of the paths they each took—and continue to take—some straightforward and others marked by challenging detours that define life and change. I am grateful to my husband, Richard, who has supported my career for decades; joined me in our co-juggling of family and career; and encouraged my dream to (finally) write a textbook. He put up with many headaches as I confronted the reality of how to find time to actually get words on the page (or 1,200 pages to be exact). Even when we took a vacation, Rich was beside me on a lounge chair at the beach or looking out at the woods, as I perched my laptop on my knees to write whenever I could steal a few minutes. And as someone of Italian and Greek heritage, I have a very large family to thank. They all cheered me on even though they had no idea why I was taking so long: my wonderful sisters, Lisa, Jacqueline, and AnneMarie; brothers- and sisters- in-law; and nieces and nephews. My mother, who kept asking, "When in the world will your book finally be done?" passed away just before its completion, but I know her pride lives on, as does my father's.

I am indebted and forever thankful to two people who have been central to my professional development. Marc H. Bornstein, my doctoral mentor and continued colleague, introduced me to the awe of child development. Thank you for all you have done to encourage my thinking. And my dearest friend and colleague, Karen Adolph, has been by my side for over 20 years and shares with me a passion for understanding developmental processes. She continues to inspire me to think deeply about discovery science, the importance of description, and developmental cascades. Indeed, it takes a true friend and brilliant scholar to spend countless hours reading nearly every chapter, even while vacationing in Maine, and offering feedback that always bettered the science. To the extent that certain messages come alive in this book, Karen can be credited as a source of their energy.

Of course, I had the fortune of working with the greatest team of supporters, the many talented individuals at Oxford University Press who were instrumental in ensuring the book's rigor, innovation, and successful completion. Thank you to Jane Potter, who persistently tracked me down at conferences to convince me to write this book. Although she hinted at the huge time drain the book would entail, she did not warn me enough. Still, it got done. That's because the team at Oxford expected nothing short of excellence. I could not have been luckier landing the opportunity to work with Senior Development Editor Lisa Sussman, whose input each step of the way, across multiple chapter drafts, helped me to strike just the right balance of research depth, breadth, and readability. (Lisa, thank you for pushing me to explain complicated ideas in straightforward ways.) Thank you as well to Executive Editor Jessica Fiorillo; Media Editor Lauren Elfers; Production Editor Stephanie Nisbet; freelance copyeditor Danna Niedzwiecki Lockwood; Editorial Assistants Ryan Amato and Malinda Labriola; Marketing Manager Joan Lewis-Milne; Marketing Assistant Ashendri Wickremasinghe; Production Manager Joan Gemme; Production Specialist and Book Designer Donna DiCarlo; Photo Research Editor Mark Siddall; Senior Production Editor Peter Lacey; Senior Production Editor of art Johannah Walkowicz; Freelance Development Editor Carol Pritchard-Martinez; Permissions Supervisor Michele Beckta; Proofreader Jennifer S. Jefferson; and Tonia Cristofaro with help on various features of the book. Although I constantly lost track of who was doing what along the way, each person at Oxford displayed impressive professionalism and openness to new ideas that raised the caliber of the final product.

Finally, I want to acknowledge the thousands of families and children who have participated in research at my lab at New York University and those who participate each and every day in developmental research around the world. It is an understatement to say that they are the source of every line in this book. Everything we know about children and the contexts of their development can be credited to the time that parents and children generously contributed to the science of child development. Thank you for paying it forward. I hope that the knowledge generated by our work continues to support children and families everywhere.

Reviewers
for *Child Development: Context, Culture, and Cascades*

Gina Abbott, *Quinnipiac University*

Karen E. Adolph, *New York University*

Jacobose Victor Ammons, *Kansas City Kansas Community College*

Laura Anaya, *Gonzaga University*

Adrienne Armstrong, *Lone Star College*

Vanessa Bailey, *College of the Sequoias*

Marie Balaban, *Eastern Oregon University*

Patricia Berezny, *Caldwell University*

Marilyn Bisberg, *Fordham University*

Katrin Blamey, *DeSales University*

Louisa Egan Brad, *Bryn Mawr College*

Gina Brelsford, *Penn State–Harrisburg*

Sarah Brenner, *Central Michigan University*

Dawn Browder, *Eastern New Mexico University*

Judy Bryant, *University of South Florida*

Holly Buckley, *University of La Verne*

Rebecca Bulotsky-Shearer, *University of Miami*

Allison Butler, *Bryant University*

Julie Campbell, *Illinois State University*

Barbara Carl, *Penn State University*

Jennifter Chaiyakal, *Orange Coast College*

Tess Nicole Chevalier, *Wake Forest University*

E. Namisi Chilungu, *Georgia State University*

Alison Colbert, *Eastern Michigan University*

Jessamy Comer, *Rochester Institute of Technology*

Suzanne Cox, *Beloit College*

Salvador Cuellar, *Hudson County Community College*

Carmen Culotta, *Wright State University*

Andrew Cummings, *University of Nevada–Las Vegas*

Amy Dexter, *Roosevelt University*

Rosanne Dlugosz, *Scottsdale Community College*

Stacey Doan, *Boston University*

Dawn Dugan, *Hunter College*

Naomi Ekas, *Texas Christian University*

Susan Engel, *Williams College*

Flora Farago, *Stephen F. Austin State University*

Michael Figuccio, *Farmingdale State College*

Lisa Fozio-Thielk, *Waubonsee Community College*

Sarah Frantz, *Lehman College/CSI/CUNY Graduate Center*

Malinda Freitag, *University of Utah*

Dale Fryxell, *Chaminade University*

Debra Garcia, *CSULA*

Nathan George, *Adelphi University*

Karla Gingerich, *Colorado State University*

Peggy Goldstein, *Florida Atlantic University*

Karen Groth, *Macomb Community College*

Miles Groth, *Wagner College*

Maria Guarneri-White, *University of Texas–Arlington*

Oh-Ryeong Ha, *University of Missouri–Kansas City*

Catherine Haden, *Loyola University*

Phillip Hamid, *CUNY Hunter College*

Shanta Hattikudur, *Temple University*

Stephen Hill, *Nazareth College*

Jameson Hirsch, *East Tennessee State University*

Wendy Hope, *St. Joseph's College*

Donna Hoskins, *Bridgewater College*

Julie Ivey, *Baylor University*

Virginia Johnson, *Biola University*

Maya Khanna, *Creighton University*

Dennis Kirchen, *Dominican University*

Nicholas Koberstein, *Keuka College*

Lisa Anna Kovach, *University of Toledo*

Kevin Ladd, *Indiana University South Bend*

Kirsten Li-Barber, *High Point University*

Caitlin Lombardi, *University of Connecticut*

Donna Hayman Long, *University of Maryland Eastern Shore*

Rebecca Lorentz, *Marquette University*

Julie Markant, *Tulane University*

April Masarik, *Boise State University*

Nicole McAninch, *Baylor University*

Robert McDermid, *Missouri State University*

Brianna McMillan and spring 2021 students, *Smith College*

Danielle Mead-Nykto, *San Jose State University*

Darcy Mitchell, *Colby-Sawyer College*

Robert Moeller, *Middlebury College*

Cathy Neimetz, *Eastern University*

Judith Newman, *Penn State University*

Simone Nguyen, *University of North Carolina–Wilmington*

Annette Nolte, *Tarrant County College–Northwest*

Tim Oblad, *Texas A&M University–Kingsville*

Grace Paradis, *California State University–Stanislaus*

Evelyn Paz-Durocher, *Los Angeles Community College*

Tiffany Pempek, *Hollins University*

Debra Pierce, *Ivy Tech Community College of Indiana*

Michelle Potter, *Santa Rosa Junior College*

Elizabeth Purnell, *Northern Virginia Community College*

Meenal Rana, *Humboldt State University*

Martha Ravola, *Alcorn State University*

Maggie Renken, *Georgia State University*

Chatee Richardson, *Spelman College*

Leslie Rollins, *Christopher Newport University*

Karl Rosengren, *Northwestern University*

Alison Sachet, *Williams College*

Cindy Salfer, *Ridgewater College*

Yoshie Sano, *Washington State University*

Tanya Sharon, *Mercer University*

Rebecca Shearer, *University of Miami*

Karen Singer-Freeman, *State University of New York–Purchase*

Jay Slosar, *Chapman University*

Patrick Smith, *Thomas Nelson Community College*

Dante Spetter, *Harvard University*

Joan Steidl, *Kent State University*

Amy Strimling, *Sacramento City College*

Lisa Tafuro and spring 2021 students, *Saint Joseph's College of New York*

Susan Talley, *Utah State University*

Peggy Thelen, *Alma College*

Ingrid Tiegel, *Carthage College*

Marilyn Toliver, *John A. Logan College*

Beth Venzke, *Concordia University Chicago*

Jennifer Vu, *University of Delaware*

Kristin Walker, *University of Memphis*

Shawn Ward, *Le Moyne University*

Elsa Weber, *Perdue Northwest*

Karl Wheatley, *Cleveland State University*

Lisa White, *Athens Technical College*

Karen Yanowitz, *Arkansas State University*

William Yerger, *Eastern University*

Sonia Yoshizasw, *East Tennessee State University*

About the Author

Catherine S. Tamis-LeMonda is Professor of Developmental Psychology in the Department of Applied Psychology at the Steinhardt School of Culture, Education, and Human Development at New York University, where she directs the Play & Language Lab (https://wp.nyu.edu/catherinetamislemonda/). She is a Fellow of the American Psychological Society and has served in various capacities (past and current) such as President of the International Congress of Infant Studies; member of the Governing Council of the Society for Research on Child Development; associate editor of Infancy and Journal of Experimental Psychology: General; and reviewer on editorial boards of several journals and panels of federal and foundation funding agencies. Tamis-LeMonda's research focuses on infant and child language, communication, object play, literacy, and motor skill, and the roles of language input, home experiences, parenting, and culture in infant learning and development across domains. Tamis-LeMonda's research has been funded by the National Science Foundation, National Institute of Child Health and Human Development, National Institute of Mental Health, Administration for Children, Youth and Families, the LEGO Foundation, Ford Foundation, and the Robinhood Foundation. She has over 200 publications in peer-reviewed journals and books and co-edited the volumes *Child Psychology: A Handbook of Contemporary Issues*, 1st, 2nd, and 3rd editions (Psychology Press, 1999, 2006, 2016); *Handbook of Father Involvement: Multidisciplinary Perspectives* (Psychology Press, 2002; 2013); *The Development of Social Cognition and Communication* (Psychology Press, 2005); and the *Handbook of Infant Development* (Cambridge University Press, 2020). Her husband, Richard; children, Brittany, Christopher, and Michael; grandchildren, Lila and Zoe; and dog, Lucy, are a constant source of joy and a continual reminder to always find the time to take a break, go for a walk, host a holiday, do some cooking, and relish time with family.

Brief Table of Contents

Contents

PART 1: FOUNDATIONS

PART 2: INFANCY AND TODDLERHOOD

PART 3: EARLY CHILDHOOD

PART 4: MIDDLE CHILDHOOD

PART 5: ADOLESCENCE

14 | Physical Development and Health in Adolescence   547

15 | Cognitive Development in Adolescence   587

Goals, Theories, and Methods

Drawing by Minxin Cheng from a photo by Karen Adolph

Everyone is intrigued by developmental psychology, whether they are aware of it or not. Consider conversations you might hear at a family get-together. Uncle John declares, "You better watch out—you're about to experience the terrible twos!" Aunt Jane wonders about her niece's choice of a college major, "Whatever made her decide to go into *theater* as a career?" and follows up with the witty observation, "Well, even as a child she was a *drama queen*!" Cousin Matt reflects on his high-school friend Roy's substance use, "It's just a phase. He's confused and needs to find himself." In response Matt's mother declares, "Given Roy's parents, it's no wonder he's so confused. The apple doesn't fall far from the tree," and Matt's father adds, "It's all in the genes!"

What is common across these excerpts of small talk is the focus on the grand questions of human development: How do people change? Why do they change? What are the sources and consequences of those changes? In essence, the participants in this family get-together feel compelled to discuss, interpret, and understand the origins and consequences of human behavior and development.

Also common across these excerpts are the shared cultural norms and expectations of participants. Uncle John warns of the impending negativity of the "terrible twos," and everyone nods in agreement. However, the idea of "terrible twos" is rooted in U.S. and Western cultures. Children in many cultures smoothly transition from being dependent infants to cooperative toddlers. Aunt Jane similarly interprets her niece's career choice through a cultural lens that portrays emotional girls as "drama queens." Interestingly, "drama kings" don't exist. What about Cousin Matt's comment? Notice that he does not proclaim Roy to be a "total mess," but rather appeals to the cultural stereotype of adolescence as a time of confusion and a search for one's unique identity. However, in many communities around the world, children take on adult roles after they transition to puberty. There is no adolescent confusion. There may not even be a word for adolescence. Finally, Matt's mother and father assume the role of armchair psychologists as they take on the nature-nurture debate. They question whether Roy's behavior is due to poor upbringing or poor genes. In short, the conversations at this family gathering illustrate how questions core to the field of child development permeate our everyday lives.

The goal of this book is to transform you—the inquisitive student observer—into an inquisitive scientist who will come to understand the intriguing process of child development in context: how development unfolds, the forces that affect development, and how developmental processes are integrally bound to context, including the culture in which children are reared. You will read about the questions that inspire developmental science, the methods used to tackle those questions, the theoretical perspectives that frame the study of development, and how developmental findings have informed policies and practices around critical social issues.

■ *The Goals of Developmental Science*

People often consider developmental psychology to hold the key to changing the world. Parents read books about child development to promote positive behaviors in their children. Educators read about effective teaching practices that support child learning. Practitioners rely on the latest developmental findings to inform interventions aimed at helping children from disadvantaged backgrounds, such as children living in poverty. Journalists turn to developmental science to understand why adolescents are passionate about social issues and volunteer hundreds of hours for community organizations. The heart of developmental science rests on describing and explaining why people do what they do and identifying ways to promote positive developmental paths. In essence, three aims frame the work of developmental science:

- *Describe:* to document what development looks like. For example, how do the vocal and language skills of infants change as they transition from babbling babies to talkative toddlers?

- *Explain:* to understand the multiple factors that underpin developmental change. For example, what factors in the infants' biology and environment support the transition from babbling to talking?

- *Apply:* to translate research findings into practices, programs, and policies that can improve the lives of children and families. For example, how can scientists take what they know about infant language development to help children with language delays?

Of course, a single person can't do everything. Consequently, some developmental scientists dedicate their energies to describing and explaining developmental processes, whereas others focus on application—a distinction referred to as basic versus applied science. At one end of the continuum, scientists engage in **basic developmental science**. These scientists dedicate their time to describing and explaining learning and development. For example, a researcher interested in children's mathematical understanding might study strategies and reasoning that children apply to math problems at different ages. At the other end of the continuum, scientists engage in **applied developmental science**. These scientists seek ways to effectively apply scientific principles and knowledge to real-life problems. Applied researchers who are interested in children's mathematical understanding might test the effectiveness of different math curricula, and train teachers to implement effective strategies.

basic developmental science
An approach in developmental psychology that focuses on description and explanation of basic learning and developmental processes

applied developmental science
An approach in developmental psychology that focuses on the application of scientific principles and knowledge to real-life problems

Keep in mind, however, that the basic-applied distinction is not clear cut. Many researchers combine basic and applied questions, and the two approaches reciprocally inform one another. Specifically, programs and policies that serve children and families should be grounded in research evidence, just as what happens in the real world should inform theories and science and generate new questions for researchers to solve. Thus, when things go right, advances in basic science lead to improved applications, and the results of those applications propel further scientific knowledge (**FIGURE 1.1**). You will be exposed to many concrete examples of intersections between basic and applied developmental science throughout the book.

Describing Development

Developmental scientists are first and foremost committed to describing what development looks like: What developmental changes occur across childhood? Are those changes abrupt or slow? What are the ultimate skills that children attain in different areas, and how much do those skills vary from child to child?

Quantitative vs. Qualitative Change: Coral Reef Fish or Frogs?

LEARNING OBJECTIVE 1.1 Distinguish between quantitative and qualitative changes in development.

Are humans like coral reef fish or frogs? Coral reef fish and frogs exhibit strikingly different patterns of growth (**FIGURE 1.2**). The growth of coral reef fish is incremental: The fish gradually increase in weight and length. In contrast, the frog's growth is characterized by unique stages. When the frog egg hatches, it is a tadpole that swims, feeds on algae, and travels in schools just like fish. But unlike fish, the tadpole transforms into a very different looking and functioning organism—a frog that leaves the water to feed on dead insects and plants, and which breathes air. The contrasting growth patterns of coral reef fish and frogs illustrate the distinction between quantitative and qualitative change. Is child development characterized by **quantitative change**, like coral reef fish, with children exhibiting gradual changes in the amount, frequency, or degree of their behaviors, or is it characterized by **qualitative change**, like frogs, with children progressing through a sequence of distinct stages in their thinking and acting?

The answer is that the distinction between quantitative and qualitative change is not clear-cut. Sometimes, changes in children's vocabulary appear to be quantitative, as children gradually acquire new words. Yet, vocabulary shows sharper increases at some points than at other times, suggesting that even adding words to one's language is far from incremental. Perhaps, the transition from crawling to walking can be viewed as qualitative. Infants are now upright, their visual vantage point on the world has changed, their hands are free to carry things, and they can get to lots of places much faster than before

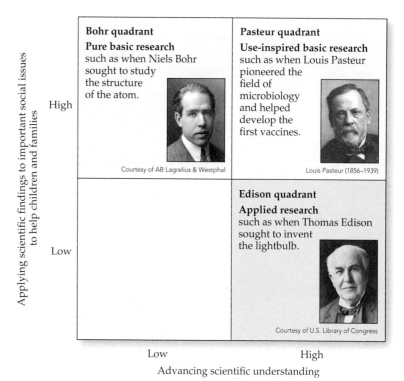

FIGURE 1.1 Basic versus applied research. As represented in the upper left quadrant, pure basic research advances science, but it is conducted without a goal of real-life application. The lower right quadrant represents the explicit aim of scientific application. The upper right quadrant, Pasteur's quadrant, is driven by the dual goals of advancing scientific understanding and achieving real-life application. Like Pasteur's quadrant, the science of developmental psychology represents the integration of basic and applied science. (Based on a diagram from M. E. Smith. Publishing Archaeology [blog]. May 19, 2011. http://publishingarchaeology.blogspot.com/2011/05/is-there-archaeology-in-pasteurs.html; D. E. Stokes. 1997. *Pasteur's Quadrant*. Brookings Institution Press: Washington, D.C.)

quantitative change Gradual changes over time in the amount, frequency, or degree of children's behaviors

qualitative change Progression through a sequence of distinct stages in children's thinking and acting

(A)

(B)

FIGURE 1.2 Coral reef fish or frogs. (A) Coral reef fish and (B) frogs exhibit strikingly different patterns of growth that can be conceptualized as "quantitative" or "qualitative."

(Adolph & Tamis-LeMonda, 2014). Again, however, what appears to be a qualitative change on the face of it, shows gradual incremental change if you look closely enough. For example, walking doesn't appear overnight, and infants go through a period of transitioning from crawling to walking day to day, gradually, sometimes reverting back and forth. Nonetheless, despite the complexity of characterizing developmental change, certain researchers emphasize qualitative change—viewing children to be much like frogs—whereas others emphasize quantitative change—viewing children to be much like coral reef fish.

✓ **CHECK YOUR UNDERSTANDING 1.1**

1. What is a way in which child development is quantitative?
2. What is a way in which child development is qualitative?

Differences among Children in Development

LEARNING OBJECTIVE 1.2 List three ways that children differ in their course of development.

Much of developmental psychology focuses on averages—namely when children as a group acquire certain skills. But developmental scientists also recognize that children vary enormously in their course of development. Each child follows a unique developmental path that veers off, sometimes slightly and other times markedly, from the group average. Developmental scientists therefore seek to describe **individual differences**—the spread or variability among children in various aspects of development, including age onsets, rates of change, and the forms that skills take (Adolph, Karasik, & Tamis-LeMonda, 2010).

Developmental onset refers to the approximate age when specific skills emerge, such as first words, first steps, first signs of puberty, and so forth. Developmental onsets are characterized by large individual differences among

individual differences The spread or variability among children in various aspects of development, including age onsets, rates of change, and the forms that skills take

developmental onset Approximate age when specific skills emerge, such as first words, first steps, and first signs of puberty

rate of change Course of change over time, including how fast children progress in their skills

the form of skills The form that a specific behavior takes in children from different communities, such as learning to use chopsticks or forks as implements for eating

stability Consistency in the rank-ordering of children on a specific behavior or skill, such as when children who are relatively high or low on a particular behavior or characteristic at a certain point in time are also relatively high or low on the same behavior or characteristic at later times children in basically everything that scientists study. For example, children generally express their first words at around 12 months of age and put their first two words together during the latter half of the second year. However, some children achieve such language milestones many months earlier and others many months later (Fenson et al., 1994; Frank et al., 2017). Such differences may be due to the language inputs and responsiveness that children experience from their caregivers (**FIGURE 1.3**). Similarly, children from cultures across the globe differ in when they acquire certain motor skills. For example, in cultures where infants are intentionally exercised, motor skills such as sitting and walking occur several months earlier than in U.S. samples (Adolph, Karasik, & Tamis-LeMonda, 2010). Puberty is another example (Ullsperger & Nikolas, 2017). Some girls experience a growth spurt and breast development as young as 8 years of age, and others many years later, due to nutrition and other factors.

Rate of change refers to the course of change over time, including how fast children progress in their skills. Returning to the example of language development, some children show rapid growth in the number of words in their vocabularies across infancy and toddlerhood, whereas others show slower but steady growth.

The form of skills refers to what behavior looks like in children with diverging experiences. Striking differences exist for skills that people often assume to be universal, such as counting. For example, the Pirahã people, who live in the rainforest of Brazil, have no number words in their language, and consequently seem to lack a concept of number (Gordon, 2004) (**FIGURE 1.4**). Pirahã adults' number knowledge is limited to the concept of one, two, and three, and even with extensive training, adults are unable to count to ten because their unique developmental experiences make counting a completely foreign concept. In contrast, in technological societies, high mathematical proficiency is expected of children who must learn how to function in a commerce economy. As a result, individuals who attend school for many years show dramatically different skills in their mathematical development than do the Pirahã.

✓ CHECK YOUR UNDERSTANDING 1.2

1. Provide an example of a way that children might differ in a developmental onset, in a developmental rate of change, and in the form of a skill.

Developmental Stability

LEARNING OBJECTIVE 1.3 Explain and contrast developmental stability and developmental plasticity.

Do a child's early skills matter in the long run? A primary motivation for studying child development is to understand and possibly predict future development based on current development. And so, individual differences in children's development naturally spark questions about **stability**— that is, whether children who are relatively high or low on a particular behavior or characteristic at a certain point in time are also relatively high or low on the same behavior or characteristic at later times. Stability is

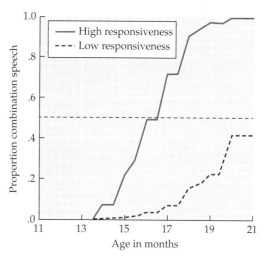

FIGURE 1.3 Age of onset. Age of onset refers to the age at which children attain a specific milestone in development. Consider differences among children in when they first display combinatorial speech—that is, when they put two or more words together in a simple sentence. This is a milestone that is shaped by infants' experiences at home (here, how responsive mothers are to infants' vocalizations and play). A subgroup of children with highly responsive mothers first displayed combinatorial speech on average around 17 months, with all children doing so by 21 months. In contrast, by 21 months, only 40% of children with low responsive caregivers put two words together. (After C. Tamis-LeMonda et al. 2001. *Child Dev* 72: 748–767. © 2001 by the Society for Research in Child Development, Inc. All rights reserved.)

FIGURE 1.4 Differences in the form of skills. Differences in the form of skills also exist for skills that are often assumed to be universal, such as counting. The Pirahã people do not have number words in their language. Developmental researcher Peter Gordon tested adults on arrays with different numbers of objects, for example asking them to match the number of objects to the objects he laid out (as shown in this image). The Pirahã succeeded only when tested with small quantities. Essentially, the experience of not using number words in everyday life made such a concept foreign to them.

the rule in most areas of development, with individuals roughly maintaining a consistent level on a specific measure relative to their peers over time. For example, children with difficulties regulating their emotions in infancy display difficulties regulating emotions years later (e.g., Perry et al., 2018).

Nonetheless, changes in environmental or biological circumstances can lead to instability. And instability can be a good thing. It reveals humans' **plasticity**—the impressive capacity to adapt to changing environments and experiences—a concept we expand on in Chapter 2. For example, adoption studies reveal remarkable malleability in child development. Analysis of nearly 300 adoption studies showed that children who were adopted out of impoverished environments caught up to their peers who had never been in impoverished environments (van IJzendoorn & Juffer, 2006). However, we will also learn about limits to plasticity, such as the case of children living in orphanages who were not adopted until after 18 months of age and continued to experience behavioral problems that were difficult to reverse for many years (e.g., McCall et al., 2019). Thus, although stability is the norm, early expressions of development in no way completely determine where a child will go. And so, developmental scientists seek to understand *why* people change—that is, what forces drive change—a theme we review next.

✓ CHECK YOUR UNDERSTANDING 1.3

1. Which is more common in most areas of development: instability or stability? Give examples.

Explaining Development

Descriptive data are sometimes limited in what they reveal about development, just as knowing that a baseball player has a batting average of .350 does little to explain *why* he is so talented. Thus, the second aim of developmental psychology is to identify the factors that explain developmental change in children as a group, such as the transition from babbling to talking, and in individual differences, such as why one infant speaks first words months before another.

Genes and Environment: The Nature-Nurture Seesaw

LEARNING OBJECTIVE 1.4 Understand the main arguments that characterize the nature-nurture debate in developmental psychology.

You may be familiar with the popular nature-nurture debate in psychology (**FIGURE 1.5**). Do our genes explain who we are? Do our experiences? Do both genes and experiences contribute? These questions about the origins of behavior date back centuries.

Nature refers to a child's biological endowment, in particular the genes inherited from parents. This genetic inheritance includes biological characteristics shared across humans (arms, legs, eyes, etc.) and unique characteristics of people such as physical appearance (eye color, height, hair color, etc.) and personality (extraversion, agreeableness, openness, etc.) (e.g., Asbury & Plomin, 2013; Rothbart & Bates, 2007). **Nurture** refers to the range of environmental contexts and experiences that influence development. These influences begin with the fetal environment and extend to the various settings that shape people's formation from birth to death, including family, childcare, school, neighborhood, and culture.

As introduced at the start of this chapter, people often appeal to nature or nurture when they talk about children. You may have heard parents speak about their children's "inborn" behaviors or temperaments. Parents may describe one child as having been calm and quiet from birth and another as active and fussy, assuming that nature, not nurture, explains newborns' distinct

---

plasticity The capacity to adapt and change in response to changing environments and experiences

nature Influences on learning and development arising from a child's genetic inheritance and other biological factors

nurture Influences on learning and development that arise from life experiences and environmental contexts

©Naf/CartoonStock

"So, how do you want to play this? Nature, nurture, or a bit of both?"

FIGURE 1.5 The nature-nurture seesaw. The nature-nurture debate goes back centuries.

behaviors. However, nature alone does not explain development: A person's genes interact with environmental experiences to explain development, as we will see in Chapter 2. The nine months that a fetus spends in the womb, for example, constitute critical, early environmental influences on development. Before birth, the developing fetus is exposed to an environment that is affected by multiple forces, including maternal nutrition and health, maternal stress, and sometimes harmful substances such as alcohol and toxins that can interfere with healthy development.

Conversely, you may have heard people talk about environmental influences on children's behaviors, or nurture, such as when a person blames a child's tantrums on overindulgent parents. Yet, just as biological explanations are limited, so too is the idea that environmental factors *alone* explain child behavior. Many children who experience "poor parenting" (whatever that means) do not throw temper tantrums when they get frustrated.

Scientists tend to lean toward either nature or nurture in their theories and studies. That is, much like a seesaw moves up and down, developmental researchers sometimes place more weight on nature (genes) and other times place more weight on nurture (environmental contexts) (Fausto-Sterling, 2014). Yet, even if a scientist largely studies one side of the nature-nurture debate, all developmental scientists agree that development is the product of a complex, continual interplay between biology and environment.

✓ CHECK YOUR UNDERSTANDING 1.4

1. What might you study if you were interested in the role of nature in development? Nurture?
2. What is a criticism of focusing only on nature or only on nurture in the nature-nurture debate?

Developmental Cascades

LEARNING OBJECTIVE 1.5 Define a developmental cascade and discuss how cascading influences can be seen across domains and across developmental time.

A useful way to think about the complexity of child development, namely how multiple factors work together to affect change over time, is from the perspective of **developmental cascades**—the idea that changes of one kind can have cascading effects, setting other kinds of changes in motion, both immediately and at later ages. Developmental cascades can be positive or negative and typically exert spillover effects across different areas of development (Bornstein, Hahn, & Suwalsky, 2013; Masten & Cichetti, 2010) (**FIGURE 1.6**). Thus, although researchers typically specialize in a specific **developmental domain** or area of child development—such as motor development (related to physical growth, movement, and action), perceptual development (related to the senses), cognitive development (related to thought processes), language development (related to communication), social development (related to interaction with others), or emotional development (related to understanding and expressing feelings)—all researchers share an interest in understanding cross-domain connections in the form of developmental cascades.

An appreciation of cascading influences among different domains and experiences reflects a "whole child" approach to development. For example, a child's reaction to a friend being bullied will depend on emotional, cognitive, and social factors. The emotions the child experiences, including the intensity of those emotions, will influence how the child thinks about the incident and how the child reacts, such as whether the child helps the friend or freezes due to fear. The child's responses to the situation, in turn, will result in changed social relationships and a new understanding of oneself, victim, and bully.

developmental cascades The idea that changes of one kind can have cascading effects, setting other kinds of changes in motion, both immediately and at later ages; developmental cascades may be positive or negative and typically exert spillover effects across different areas of development

developmental domain Area of child development such as motor development (related to physical growth, movement, and action), perceptual development (related to the senses), cognitive development (related to thought processes), language development (related to communication), social development (related to interaction with others), or emotional development (related to understanding and expressing feelings)

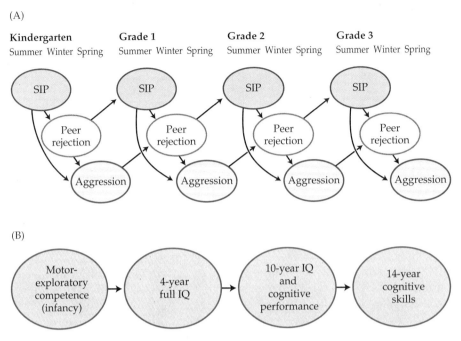

FIGURE 1.6 Development cascades. Developmental cascades occur within time and across time and can be negative or positive. (A) In a negative developmental cascade, poor social information processing (SIP—how a child understands and interprets social information) can spill over to peer rejection, which leads to aggression, with the cascading cycle continuing from kindergarten through third grade. (B) In a positive developmental cascade, infants' motor competence at 5 months of age predicts children's intelligence at preschool, which then relates to children's math and literacy skills in adolescence (A after J. E. Landsford et al. 2010. *Dev Psychopathol* 22: 593–602. Reproduced with permission. B after M. H. Bornstein et al. 2013. *Psychol Sci* 24: 1906–1917.)

Cascades within Time

Developmental cascades within time occur during a specific period in development. These "concurrent" influences can occur across different domains and/or between the developing child and the child's environment and experiences. For example, you may have heard parents say "use your words" as their children scream in frustration. Clearly, children can only use their words if they have the language skills to express what they want. Thus, developmental researchers might ask how children's language skills play out in their emotional regulation—an example of a within-time, cross-domain cascade.

And as children develop in their skills, they affect their environments in ways that further feed into their development. For example, as infants learn how to crawl and then to walk, their world broadens, and they may even discover forbidden places and things, like electrical sockets (Campos et al., 2000). These discoveries might elicit reprimands from parents, leading to infants' understanding of the word "NO!" This example shows a cascading effect from locomotion to environmental exploration to language exposure to learning words.

Cascades over Time

Developmental cascades over time occur when changes at one period in development lead to changes at a later period, either in the same domain or different domains. For instance, children who experience low-quality parenting in early childhood (including neglect or harsh punishment such as hitting) are at heightened risk for later academic and social problems at school and for associating with peers who encourage and reinforce antisocial behavior (Dodge et al., 2008). As children fall behind in their schoolwork and gravitate toward problem peers, they may limit their future educational chances and thus career opportunities. In this example, what happened during early childhood harmed later occupational choices in adulthood through a process of developmental cascades.

✓ **CHECK YOUR UNDERSTANDING 1.5**

1. Give examples of cascading influences across domains within time and across developmental time.

Applying Developmental Science

Many of the studies that you will read about in this book might, at first glance, seem interesting but only loosely connected to the issues that you care about. We'll learn that developmental scientists have a lot of clever methods in their "toolboxes." They observe infants crawling or walking down slopes or over gaps; place marshmallows in front of preschoolers with instructions to not eat them; ask children to nominate their most and least favorite classmates; measure children's attention to faces of different races; observe how teenagers act when told their friend is watching them from a nearby room, and so on. But how do these methods inform us about everyday life? And, why do we care?

Beyond scientific value, developmental science has social and practical significance, addressing topics spanning parenting, school readiness, bullying, stress, racism and discrimination, and so forth. The findings of developmental science have implications for intervention and prevention programs for children and families at risk, educational curricula and teacher training, health and economic policies, books and training materials for soon-to-be parents, local and national investments in childcare and schooling, and even the types of toys, clothes, and paraphernalia that manufacturers market to children and parents. Let's consider two examples of how developmental science affects the everyday lives of children and families. You will become familiar with many more throughout the course of this book.

Raising Children

LEARNING OBJECTIVE 1.6 Compare how early philosophers' advice to parents about raising children differs from current advice to parents.

Everyone is invested in figuring out ways to raise competent, happy children. The interest in child-rearing has a long history and likely even longer future. The Chinese philosopher Confucius (551–479 BC) viewed parents as responsible for "cultivating" virtues such as benevolence, righteousness, propriety, wisdom, and sincerity in their children so that children could attain future success. Similarly, the early Greek philosophers Plato (427–347 BC) and Aristotle (384–322 BC) advised that children would become unruly and rebellious in the absence of proper upbringing.

Centuries later, the English philosopher John Locke (1632–1704) and the French philosopher Jean-Jacques Rousseau (1712–1778) offered opposing views about how parents and society should support child development. Locke viewed the child as a *tabula rasa*, or "blank slate," on which parents should build positive character traits by setting good examples, not overindulging their children, and remaining firm in discipline. Rousseau, in contrast, believed that parents should give children the freedom to explore their interests and to learn from their unrestricted interactions with the world. According to Rousseau, children should not begin formal education until 12 years of age when they could evaluate the merits of what they read and were told.

(A)

(B)

(C)

FIGURE 1.7 Book reading and children. Developmental findings on the importance of book reading for children's development and learning have sparked many local and national initiatives to foster parent involvement in book reading and young children's interest in books. (A) The mission of Texas's Curiosity Cruiser program is to provide free books to children to improve the quality of life for children living in areas of Texas. (B) In Nicaragua, The Flying Book is a mobile library program designed to educate children in urban and rural communities. (C) Reach Out and Read is a U.S. nonprofit organization that partners with pediatric clinicians to encourage parents to read to children. They distribute more than 7 million books per year to more than 4.5 million children across the U.S.

How do the messages of philosophers differ from those of contemporary developmental scientists? Most centrally, early philosophers offered advice that was philosophically rather than scientifically driven. Today, messages about raising children and children's capacities at different ages are based on replicable research from the labs of developmental scientists.

Parents and caregivers look to developmental science for answers to questions about what to do and when to do it with their children. They want to know how they can help their children to talk, read, count, and share with other children. They want to know which forms of discipline are acceptable: "How long is long enough for a time-out?" and "Is it okay to lightly spank a misbehaving child?" They want to know how to avoid raising a teenager who gets involved in drinking, using drugs, or having unprotected sex. Essentially, parents, educators, clinicians, and policy makers want to know the science. Fortunately, you will learn that developmental science offers insight into many important questions around raising children.

✓ CHECK YOUR UNDERSTANDING 1.6

1. Brittany and Mike just brought their infant Lila home from the hospital and want to provide the best support for Lila's development. Which philosopher would tell them to be firm in their discipline and to not overindulge their baby? How does this advice differ from the advice of a developmental scientist today?

Programs and Policies

LEARNING OBJECTIVE 1.7 List ways that developmental science has affected programs and policies for young children.

A main goal of developmental science is to inform the design, implementation, and evaluation of programs and policies that affect children and families. For example, an understanding of how children learn language has the potential to inform interventions with children at risk for language delay; educational policies around early language curricula; and programs for children who are learning more than one language. Take book reading as a case in point.

Current views on the importance of book reading are grounded in developmental findings: Book reading has the potential to expose infants and toddlers to a greater variety of words than children would otherwise encounter during other activities. Exposure to new words, in turn, facilitates growth in vocabulary that sets children on a path toward academic success. Today, educators, interventionists, and practitioners who work with low-income families encourage parents to read books to their children. Local programs, such as Texas's Curiosity Cruiser, and national programs, such as The Flying Book in Nicaragua and Reach Out and Read in the United States, provide books to families with few resources (**FIGURE 1.7**). Publication companies in the United States produce books in Spanish and other languages to provide reading opportunities to parents and children from various cultural backgrounds.

Awareness of developmental cascades has likewise raised consciousness about the importance of early timing in intervention initiatives. Learning disparities, behavior problems, and various kinds of psychopathology snowball over time and have far-reaching consequences for other domains of development. Scientists now recognize that early childhood interventions, such as high-quality preschool programs, more effectively mitigate such negative cascades, and thus have a higher rate of return, than do interventions that begin later in childhood (Brooks-Gunn, Markman-Pithers, & Rouse, 2016; Heckman, 2006; Magnuson & Duncan, 2016; Reynolds et al., 2019) (**FIGURE 1.8**). Moreover, interventions that help children in certain domains can have positive cascading effects on other domains (Cicchetti & Gunnar, 2008; Masten et al., 2010). As one example, interventions that help children learn how to regulate their emotions support children's learning and school performance (Ursache, Blair, & Raver, 2012).

Finally, developmental science informs local, state, and federal policies and initiatives that affect families and children. Maternity and paternity leave policies, child and family welfare laws, health care initiatives, programs such as Head Start (which provide quality childcare and support to poor families), and even laws about the legal ages for smoking and drinking present noteworthy examples of areas that are grounded in the findings of developmental science.

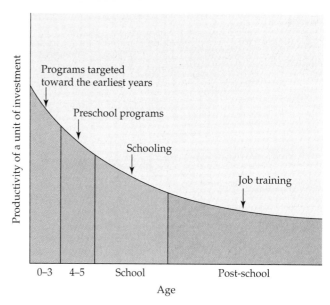

FIGURE 1.8 Heckman equation. Many scientists, including Nobel-prize winning economist James Heckman, show that investments in children's development at early ages yield greater benefits than investments at later ages. Here, for example, the relative rates of return or benefits for investments made for families and children early on (pink bar) are greater than those made post-schooling (latter blue bar). (After J. J. Heckman. 2008. *Econ Inq* 46: 289–324.)

✓ CHECK YOUR UNDERSTANDING 1.7

1. List areas where the findings of developmental science have made a difference in the lives of families and children.

2. Describe an initiative that has grown out of developmental research on the benefits of book reading for children.

■ *Theoretical Orientations*

Whether a developmental scientist engages in basic or applied research, the work should be guided by a **theory**—a set of interconnected statements that explain a set of observable events (Miller, 2002). Without a theory, research findings may be uninterpretable and directions for application remain fuzzy.

Developmental psychology is guided by different theoretical orientations to describing and explaining change (**TABLE 1.1**). In terms of describing development, theories differ in their emphasis on quantitative versus qualitative change; how they explain development; and their relative emphases on nature versus nurture. Theories also differ in how active they view children to be in the developmental process and, relatedly, whether they view development as a top-down versus bottom-up process. Top-down explanations focus on biologically driven abilities that are largely influenced by the brain and considered to be innate. Bottom-up explanations focus on the role of experience, largely reflecting how children build knowledge through their everyday interactions with people, places, and objects in the environment. Finally, theories differ in their scope—that is, whether they address a narrow or wide range of developmental topics. Some theories are considered to be "grand theories," meaning they aim to explain many developmental phenomena across a broad range of child ages. Other theories are based on narrower principles or topics, such as theories about how children come to

theory A set of interconnected statements or general principles that explain a set of observable events

TABLE 1.1 ■ Theoretical Orientations

Theoretical Orientation	Theory Description	Theorist (Classic Example)
Evolutionary Theory	Evolutionary theorists recognize the importance of learned behaviors but consider learned behaviors to be the product of innate biological tendencies that serve human survival.	Charles Darwin
Psychodynamic Theory	Psychodynamic theorists focus on the development of personality, which is viewed as a product of conscious and unconscious forces, with individuals progressing through a series of stages as they attempt to resolve certain conflicts.	
	Psychosexual Stage Theory considers the goals of survival and reproduction to be the main catalysts for behavior and development. Children are seen as progressing through five stages as they learn to satisfy survival and reproduction drives in ways that are socially and psychologically acceptable.	Sigmund Freud
	Psychosocial Stage Theory focuses on the conflicts that individuals encounter as they struggle to answer the question "Who am I?" Individuals pass through eight stages, in each of which they experience a conflict about their identity. If they resolve the conflict positively, they can move on to the next stage; otherwise, their personality will be negatively affected.	Erik Erikson
Behaviorism/Learning Theory	*Behaviorism* views learning as a change in observable behaviors as a result of environmental influences, thus placing full weight on the nurture end of the nature-nurture continuum.	
	Classical Conditioning refers to a situation in which a stimulus can take on a new significance when paired with other, personally meaningful stimuli; it applies to many types of everyday learning.	John B. Watson
	Operant Conditioning refers to a situation in which the forms and frequencies of behaviors depend on how behaviors are rewarded or punished; versions of operant conditioning are applied to studies of infant learning and memory.	B. F. Skinner
Constructivism	*Constructivism* underscores children's active role in learning and development. The originator of constructivism, Piaget, stated that children progress through four qualitatively distinct, universal, and invariant stages. At each stage, children have schemas that provide them with a way of organizing information and understanding and acting on their environments. Children move through the stages by the processes of assimilation, disequilibrium, and accommodation.	Jean Piaget
Nativist Theories	*Nativist theories* propose that innate core capacities, essential for human adaptation, evolved over time in the form of modules or structures wired in the brain. Features of evolutionary theory can be seen in nativist approaches to development.	Elizabeth Spelke
Social Learning Theory	*Social Learning Theory* extends the principles of operant conditioning to the study of how children learn the social behaviors that society expects of them, including through observational learning and vicarious reinforcement.	Albert Bandura
Information Processing Theory	*Information Processing Theory* draws an analogy between the human mind and a computer, emphasizing the mind's "hardware" (brain structures and neural connections) and "software" (rules and strategies for dealing with information). An information processing model of memory involves: a sensory register; short-term memory; long-term memory.	Robert Kail
Developmental Systems Theory	*Developmental Systems Theory* views human behavior as the product of a complex, ever-changing system, where developmental changes occur in response to many different kinds of factors. New behaviors emerge out of complex interactions between children's bodies and actions in the environment.	Linda Smith and Esther Thelen
Bioecological Theories	*Bioecological theories* focus on the effects of environment on human development, where environment includes factors internal and external to the child, such as each child's psychological and behavioral characteristics and socio-cultural contexts. Bronfenbrenner advanced a comprehensive theory that conceptualized development as nested within five systems along with a biological dimension.	Urie Bronfenbrenner
Sociocultural Theories	*Sociocultural theories* focus on the social and cultural contexts of child development, particularly how social partners influence children's learning and how culture infuses everyday experiences and children's interactions with people, objects, and spaces of their environments. Sociocultural theorists, originating with the writings of Vygotsky, advance the concepts of a cultural learning environment and developmental niche.	Lev Vygotsky, Beatrice and John Whiting, and Charles Super and Sara Harkness

understand what other people feel or think. An important characteristic of all scientific theories is that they must be testable—researchers must be able to gather evidence for or against them. In the sections that follow, we consider early foundational theories that continue to shape developmental psychology today, and then describe recent approaches that have enriched and extended the study of how children learn and develop.

Foundational Theories

Many theories of developmental psychology can be traced to the writings of philosophers and scientists from the nineteenth and twentieth centuries. Here we examine key tenets of five influential perspectives: evolutionary theory, psychodynamic theory, behaviorism, constructivism, and sociocultural theory.

Evolutionary Theory

LEARNING OBJECTIVE 1.8 Explain how environmental experiences can shape biologically rooted behaviors in adaptive ways.

Many of you are familiar with Charles Robert Darwin (1809–1882), the naturalist and biologist whose expeditions and scientific observations led to his pioneering book *On the Origins of Species*. According to Darwin's evolutionary account, individuals with physical and behavioral traits that are well suited to their environments have an increased chance of surviving and reproducing (Buss, 2012). These adaptive traits are selected to be passed on to subsequent generations in what is referred to as **natural selection**. The well-known phrase *survival of the fittest* asserts that the odds of survival are greater for better-adapted individuals, who will pass on advantageous traits to future generations (**FIGURE 1.9**).

At first glance, Darwin's theory of evolution might appear to be unrelated to the topic of developmental psychology. After all, evolutionary change occurs over a span of at least a million years, whereas a child's development roughly spans only two decades. Still, many developmental researchers seek to understand human behavior through a Darwinian lens of adaption, claiming that specific behaviors in children confer evolutionary benefits. An evolution-based interpretation of human development might help explain, for example, why infants cry and cling to caregivers; why teens seek excitement and take risks around the time of puberty, and so forth. Furthermore, Darwin's focus on adaptive behaviors helps explain why individual children differ in their developmental paths. Specifically, children attempt to adapt to their unique circumstances, which is why different environments produce different behaviors in children. In fact, at the heart of evolutionary theory is the idea that a child's environment modifies otherwise universal, biological tendencies.

Take infant attachment, for example. Infants everywhere form attachments to their primary caregivers—a clear survival-related adaptation—and engage in behaviors that signal their connection to loved ones. Attachment-related behaviors are seen when an infant crawls over to mom or dad or gets upset if a caregiver leaves the home. But individual infants develop different attachment styles based on the type of caregiving they receive. For example, infants whose parents are unable

natural selection Individuals with physical and behavioral traits that are well suited to their environments have an increased chance of surviving and reproducing, thereby passing these adaptive traits on to subsequent generations, an observation first advanced by Charles Darwin

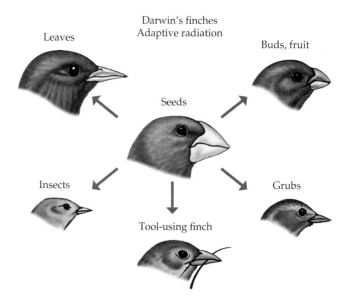

FIGURE 1.9 Evolutionary theory. Darwin observed how species develop traits that allow them to adapt to their environments through the process of survival of the fittest. Here, the beaks of finches have evolved to shapes ideally suited to the environments they encounter and what they eat. (After D. Futuyma and M. Kirkpatrick. 2017. *Evolution.* 4th ed. Sinauer/Oxford University Press: Sunderland, MA.)

to care for them adequately—maybe because of a scarcity of food or the caregiver being under enormous stress—may increase their clinginess to obtain whatever meager attention or resources are available to them (Chisholm, 1996; Miller, 2002).

Bullying illustrates how children's behaviors might change to fit environmental circumstances. You might wonder why bullying is so common if it appears to harm everyone involved. Perhaps, for children who feel powerless at home, aggressive behaviors enable them to cope with adversity and gain attention or resources from their victims. Bullying can lead to a sense of empowerment and feeling of control that allows children to cope in an environment they perceive to be hostile. Therefore, although a bully's behaviors make little sense to an outsider, they may yield adaptive benefits for the aggressor.

✓ CHECK YOUR UNDERSTANDING 1.8

1. Give an example of how harsh environmental circumstances can lead to behaviors that appear to be negative, yet might benefit a child's adaptation.

Psychodynamic Theories

LEARNING OBJECTIVE 1.9 Distinguish between Freud's psychosexual stage theory and Erikson's psychosocial stage theory.

One of the earliest psychological approaches to the study and treatment of personality originated with **psychodynamic theories**, a set of theories that consider personality to be a product of conscious and unconscious forces. Here, we consider the two most prominent theorists in this tradition, Sigmund Freud (1856–1939) and Erik Erikson (1902–1994), who shared the view that children progress through a series of stages as they cope with and attempt to resolve certain conflicts.

Freud's Psychosexual Stage Theory

Sigmund Freud was trained as a neurologist, yet made theoretical contributions to the field of psychology that continue to influence contemporary thought and popular culture. Many of Freud's patients suffered from phobias, anxiety, and emotional trauma, which Freud believed could be treated by delving into patients' unresolved childhood problems. On the basis of his clinical data, Freud developed a **psychosexual stage theory** of personality that emphasized the central role of children's biological drives, particularly the sex drive.

Influenced by Darwinian theory, Freud claimed that even the behaviors of infants and young children could be explained by a motivation to satisfy the sex drive, an idea that shocked his contemporaries. According to Freud, children progressed through five stages (**FIGURE 1.10**). Although Freud's psychosexual stage theory emphasized biology as a primary force in development, it also pointed to social influences (Miller, 2002, p. 137). For instance, how well children satisfied their drives depended on the behaviors that their parents or other authorities allowed. Children therefore had to learn how to satisfy their drives in ways that were socially and psychologically acceptable.

A major part of Freud's psychosexual theory focused on the tensions that people experience among three parts of their personality: the id, ego, and superego. The **id** refers to the primitive biological drives that are present from birth. The rational component of personality, the **ego**, begins to emerge in early childhood and helps keep inappropriate thoughts, impulses, and desires from rising to consciousness and being acted upon. The later-developing **superego** functions as a conscience to ensure that children behave in morally acceptable ways and uphold family and community standards and expectations. Of course, the three parts of personality are often in conflict, such as when the id seeks to fulfill

psychodynamic theories A set of theories that consider personality to be a product of conscious and unconscious forces; Sigmund Freud and Erik Erikson were two prominent theorists of this tradition

psychosexual stage theory A theory developed by Sigmund Freud that emphasized the central role of children's biological drives, particularly the sex drive, in behavior

id According to Sigmund Freud, a part of one's personality comprised of the primitive biological drives that are present from birth

ego According to Sigmund Freud, the rational component of personality that helps keep inappropriate thoughts, impulses, and desires from rising to consciousness and being acted upon

superego According to Sigmund Freud, a part of one's late-developing personality that functions as a conscience to ensure that children behave in morally acceptable ways and uphold family and community standards and expectations

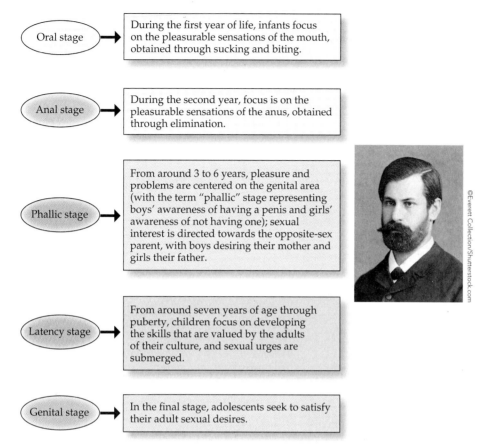

FIGURE 1.10 Freud's psychosexual stage theory.   On the basis of his clinical data, Freud developed a psychosexual stage theory of personality that emphasized the central role of five stages—oral, anal, phallic, latency, and genital—in children's personality development. (After S. A. McLeod. Simply Psychology. July 18, 2019. https://www.simplypsychology.org/psychosexual.html.)

an immediate desire and the superego imposes demands of parents and society. According to Freud, children's attempts to resolve these unpleasant internal conflicts propel development forward.

Erikson's Psychosocial Stage Theory

Inspired by Freud, Erik Erikson also devised a stage theory to characterize development. Erikson's **psychosocial stage theory** proposed that people confront specific challenges in their search for an identity at different stages in the life course. According to Erikson, at each of eight psychosocial stages (**FIGURE 1.11**) people experience a unique internal conflict about their identity—in essence "Who am I?" A person must in some way resolve the conflict to move on to the next stage in a healthy way (Erikson, 1963, 1968). For example, children might work on resolving psychosocial conflicts through play by acting out society's demands and expectations, such as when a child pretends an adult doll scolds a child doll for not cleaning her room. According to Erikson, how well a person deals with each of the psychosocial crises gradually comes to shape that person's personality.

psychosocial stage theory
A theory, developed by Erik Erikson, positing that people's search for an identity presents developmental challenges throughout the life course; at each of eight psychosocial stages, people experience a unique internal conflict about their identity that they must resolve to move on to the next stage in a healthy way

✓ CHECK YOUR UNDERSTANDING 1.9

1. List and define the three parts of personality described by Freud.
2. List the eight psychosocial stages proposed by Erikson and the major challenge of each.

FIGURE 1.11 Erikson's psychosocial stage theory. According to Erikson, at each of eight psychosocial stages people experience an internal conflict about their identity—in essence "Who am I?" Successfully resolving the conflict at each stage results in a healthy personality. (After E. H. Erikson. 1976. *Daedalus* 105: 1–28.)

Older adult

Integrity vs despair (65+ years)
Older adults are able to look back on their past and see a life that has been meaningful, or they feel despair over missed opportunities.

Middle-age adult

Generativity vs stagnation (~40 to 65 years)
Adults experience a sense of productivity in their lives and work and are willing to contribute to the next generation, or they experience a sense of stagnation.

Young adult

Intimacy vs isolation (~18 to 40 years)
Young adults form close and committed relationships with others, or they risk loneliness and isolation.

Teenager

Identity vs role confusion (~12 to 18 years)
Adolescents establish a sense of personal identity, or they become confused about who they are and what they want to do in life.

Grade schooler

Industry vs inferiority (~5 to 12 years)
Children learn to be effective and capable in the activities that are valued by members of their community, or they experience a sense of inferiority.

How individuals resolve earlier psychosocial conflicts around identity will affect how they resolve later psychosocial conflicts

Pre-schooler

Initiative vs guilt (~3 to 5 years)
Children learn to take initiative to achieve their goals; if children are prevented from taking initiative, they experience guilt over the failure of their efforts to become independent.

Toddler

Autonomy vs shame and doubt
(~18 months to 3 years)
Children learn to be autonomous and in control or feel shame because they doubt their abilities to do things by themselves.

Infant

Trust vs mistrust (~0 to 18 months)
Infants learn to either trust or mistrust the people who tend to their basic needs.

©Ted Streshinsky Photographic Archive/Corbis/Getty Images

Behaviorism

LEARNING OBJECTIVE 1.10 Compare and contrast the learning theories of classical conditioning and operant conditioning.

The scientific approach of **behaviorism** emerged in the early twentieth century with the goal of explaining how people learn new behaviors based on their experiences. Behaviorism arose from a harsh critique of the focus of psychodynamic theory on underlying, unobservable conflicts, and the inability of psychodynamic theory to test predictions through rigorous experimental methods.

But why the term *behaviorism*? In 1913, American psychologist John B. Watson stated that the studies in psychology should be based on observable human *behaviors* and discovering the ways to predict those behaviors. Watson believed that behavior was entirely the product of the social environment, and that any behavior could be conditioned or produced in any child. Watson's famous quote (1926) underscores this idea:

> *Give me a dozen healthy infants, well-formed, and my own specified world to bring them up in and I'll guarantee to take any one at random and train him to become any type of specialist I might select—doctor, lawyer, artist, merchant-chief, and, yes, even beggar-man and thief, regardless of his talents, penchants, tendencies, abilities, vocations, and race of his ancestors.*

Watson's emphasis on behavior revolutionized the field of psychology by sparking inquiry into different types of learning, with classical conditioning and operant conditioning being two primary examples. Today, scientists refer to "learning theories" rather than behaviorism when studying environmental influences on children's learning.

Classical Conditioning

In a famous study—that today would be considered unethical—Watson demonstrated that he could instill extreme fear in an otherwise calm baby, known today as "Little Albert" (although Albert was later found to not be the infant's real name) (Watson & Rayner, 1920). Specifically, Watson presented 9-month-old Albert with various stimuli in the laboratory—a white rat, a rabbit, a dog, a monkey with masks, cotton wool, and so forth—none of which elicited fear in the baby. Watson stated, "No one had ever seen him [Albert] in a state of fear and rage. The infant practically never cried" (Watson & Rayner, 1920, p. 313). Watson soon changed that. To alarm Albert, Watson paired the white rat with a loud noise by striking a hammer on a steel bar. Albert cried loudly, apparently out of fear. After several pairings of the rat and the noise, Albert began reacting with fear to the rat alone, in the absence of the noise. Then, Watson showed that Albert's fear generalized to other white objects as well. Thus, by pairing an initially harmless stimulus (the rat) with a frighteningly loud noise, Watson had conditioned fear in Albert in what is referred to as **classical conditioning** (**FIGURE 1.12**).

Notably, much of everyday learning follows principles of classical conditioning, when a neutral stimulus takes on new significance after being paired with meaningful experiences. An infant will turn her head and open her mouth as soon as her mother sits with her in a certain chair, having associated the specific chair with eating. A child will begin to salivate in response to the tune of an ice-cream truck that often passes by his house. And you might experience a quickened heartbeat in response to the scent of someone to whom you are attracted.

Operant Conditioning

American psychologist B. F. Skinner (1904–1990) advanced the idea of **operant conditioning**—that behaviors increase or decrease depending on whether they are rewarded or punished. Skinner placed animals, mostly pigeons and rats,

behaviorism A scientific approach that emerged in the early twentieth century that explained people's behaviors as learned through conditioning (experiences)

classical conditioning A learning process that occurs when a neutral stimulus takes on new significance after being paired with another meaningful stimulus

operant conditioning A learning process that leads to an increase or decrease in behaviors depending on whether the behaviors are rewarded or punished

Before conditioning

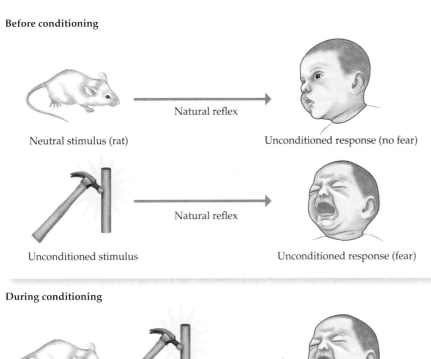

During conditioning

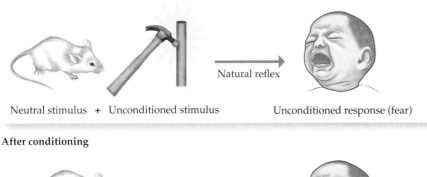

After conditioning

FIGURE 1.12 Watson and classical conditioning. John Watson paired a neutral stimulus (white rat) with an unconditioned stimulus (loud noise) to elicit an unconditioned response (fear) in "Little Albert." After several presentations of this pairing, Little Albert showed a conditioned response (fear) at the presentation of the white rat in the absence of the loud noise. (After J. Watson and R. Rayner. 1920. *J Exp Psychol: General* 3: 1–14.)

Skinner box An operant conditioning chamber, originally used by B.F. Skinner, in which animals learn to increase or decrease specific behaviors to obtain food, water, or other types of reinforcement

positive reinforcement The introduction of a desirable or pleasant stimulus to reward and encourage a particular behavior

negative reinforcement The presentation of an aversive stimulus that involves some type of discomfort (e.g., car alarm) to strengthen a target behavior (e.g., fastening a seat belt)

in a chamber that became known as a **Skinner box**. He then reinforced specific behaviors to see if he could get the animals to increase or decrease their behaviors (**FIGURE 1.13**). For example, the chamber might contain a tray for food and a lever that dispensed food into the tray when pressed. The animal would at first accidently hit the lever and receive a food pellet, an example of **positive reinforcement**. Over time, the animal increased its lever pressing to receive food pellets. A parallel in everyday life is seen when teachers reward children with stickers for completion of school assignments, hoping to encourage children's continued behavior. In contrast, **negative reinforcement** is when something unpleasant is removed in response to a behavior. Ivan Pavlov (1849–1936) conducted experiments of negative reinforcement in which he subjected animals to mild electric shocks via the chamber floor. Animals quickly learned how to press a lever to stop the shocks. Car manufacturers rely on the principles of negative reinforcement to get you to buckle up—a loud and annoying alarm continues until you fasten your seatbelt. You will see that developmental scientists sometimes use operant conditioning to study infant learning, such as by rewarding infants with music or pictures for certain behaviors to test what infants know and remember.

FIGURE 1.13 Skinner and operant conditioning.   American psychologist B. F. Skinner advanced the idea of operant conditioning—that behaviors increase or decrease depending on whether they are rewarded or punished. He placed animals in what became known as a Skinner box and then reinforced certain behaviors to see if he could get the animal to increase or decrease behaviors.

✓ **CHECK YOUR UNDERSTANDING 1.10**

1. Describe the work of Albert Watson that illustrated the phenomenon of classical conditioning.
2. Give examples of positive reinforcement and negative reinforcement in your daily life.

Constructivism: Piaget's Stage Theory

LEARNING OBJECTIVE 1.11 Explain key features of Piaget's constructivist theory and how it contrasts with behaviorism.

Jean Piaget (1896–1980) was perhaps the most influential theorist in the history of developmental psychology. Piaget rejected behaviorism's sole emphasis on observable behaviors, which he felt left out a critical piece of the story—what went on in a child's mind. Without considering how children think, it is nearly impossible to explain why two children might respond in entirely different ways to identical situations. For example, a young boy might refuse to play with someone who accidentally broke a toy. However, a teenager will give the benefit of the doubt to a peer who accidentally did something wrong. Piaget attributed such differences to changes in children's understanding about other people's intentions. In this example, the young child is unable to reason that a peer did not mean to break the toy, whereas the teenager can.

Piaget therefore advanced a **constructivist theory** of development that spotlighted children's active role in learning and development. According to Piaget, children actively construct knowledge as they engage with their environments. At the same time, children's maturing brains and bodies place constraints on how they think and what they can do. Thus, Piaget viewed the interaction between nature, the developing brain and body, and nurture, a child's everyday experiences, as jointly explaining development. For example, a young child might not understand why a friend doesn't want to play the same video game that the child does. That's because the child's immature brain and limited social experiences result in an egocentric view of the world, and this viewpoint prevents the child

constructivist theory A theory of development proposed by Jean Piaget that spotlights children's active role in learning and development from taking a friend's perspectives. With development, the child moves beyond egocentrism and understands that different people think and feel differently. Piaget's focus on the active child shifted attention away from environmental reinforcement to detailed descriptions of children's developmental stages.

Qualitative Stages

Piaget viewed development as comprising four qualitatively distinct stages (sensorimotor, preoperational, concrete operational, and formal operational), each representing a different way of organizing knowledge and understanding and acting on the world (**FIGURE 1.14**). Piaget believed that children everywhere advance through the four stages in an orderly progression, without skipping stages or regressing to earlier stages. Additionally, Piaget claimed that children engage in a unified way of thinking and behaving at each stage that cuts across different problems and situations. For example, children who are unable to reason logically about one type of problem will be unable to reason logically about a different type of problem. He noted, however, that children on the cusp of a more advanced stage display thinking that bounces between the less advanced and more advanced stage.

Schemas

schemas Basic units of information, as posited by Jean Piaget, that are cognitive representations of the world; Piaget believed that schemas determine how children of different ages organize and understand information

In Piaget's theory, children have **schemas**, cognitive structures that provide them with a way to organize information and understand the world (Inhelder & Piaget, 1969). Newborns' very first schemas are seen in reflexes, such as when newborns automatically turn their head toward a stimulus and make sucking movements that aid breastfeeding. As children interact with the world their schemas change, leading to advances in development. For instance, the rooting reflex of newborns becomes increasingly differentiated as infants place different objects in their mouth, such as their own fingers and toes, rattles, blankets, and house keys. Then, as children transition from the sensorimotor stage to the next ("preoperational") stage, they are able to mentally represent the things they have experienced—for example, the word "ball" is a mental schema or symbol for round, bouncy toys. At even older ages, schemas extend to mental operations, such as when children use schemas for addition,

STAGE 1	STAGE 2	STAGE 3	STAGE 4	
Sensorimotor period	**Preoperational period**	**Concrete operational period**	**Formal operational period**	
Infants' schemas—cognitive structures that organize information and guide understanding of and actions in the world—are limited to sensory experiences and motor actions.	Children are capable of mental representation or the interalization of thought, as seen in the growth of language, symbolic play, deferred imitation, and understanding of object permanence.	Children develop logical, flexible, organized, and rational thinking; however, their thinking is limited to concrete experiences.	Children are capable of abstract and hypothetical thinking, in which logical reasoning and problem solving move beyond concrete information and experiences.	
Birth to 2 years	**2 to 7 years**	**7 to 11 years**	**11 years through adulthood**	

© CSU Archives/Everett Collection/Alamy Stock Photo

FIGURE 1.14 Piaget and constructivist theory. Piaget advanced a constructivist theory of development that underscored children's active role in learning and development. Piaget viewed development as comprising four qualitatively distinct stages —sensorimotor, preoperational, concrete operational, and formal operational—that all children progress through in order. (After B. J. Wadsworth. 2003. *Piaget's Theory of Cognitive and Affective Development: Foundations of Constructivism.* 5th ed. Pearson: London, United Kingdom.)

subtraction, multiplication, and division to manipulate numbers mentally and think abstractly and hypothetically.

Moving through the Stages

How do children move from one stage to the next? Piaget claimed that several related processes propel development: assimilation, equilibration versus disequilibrium, and accommodation. **Assimilation** refers to the incorporation of new experiences into an existing schema. Assimilating new experiences that fit with an existing schema can strengthen the schema. Children achieve **equilibration** when there is a cognitive balance or alignment between new information and existing knowledge. However, when new experiences do not fit a schema, the attempt to assimilate can produce **disequilibrium**—an imbalance between the schema and reality. Disequilibrium, in turn, leads to **accommodation**, or children's modification of a schema to fit reality.

To understand these concepts, consider Brittany, who, on her first day of preschool, observes that only girls are in the dollhouse corner and only boys are playing with the toy trucks and cars. If Brittany has a schema about gender that includes the idea that boys never play with dolls, then assimilating this new experience will strengthen her schema further; she experiences equilibration. What happens, however, on Brittany's second day of preschool, when two boys ask to play with the dollhouse? This experience—boys asking to play with dolls—no longer fits Brittany's schema about gender, causing her to experience disequilibrium. Brittany might attempt to assimilate the experience by reasoning that the boys didn't really want to play with the dolls and her classmates were just being nice. Alternatively, Brittany might resolve the disequilibrium through accommodation—that is, she might modify her schema to include the more complex idea that *some* boys play with dolls, or that boys *sometimes* play with dolls. Note, however, that Brittany would be unlikely to modify her schema to fully embrace the idea that boys in general like to play with dolls. This example illustrates Piaget's claims that incremental, quantitative change occurs within stages as children gradually accommodate their schemas to align with their experiences.

✓ CHECK YOUR UNDERSTANDING 1.11

1. Describe Piaget's stages of cognitive development.
2. Distinguish accommodation from assimilation and give an example of each.

Lev Vygotsky and the Origins of Sociocultural Theory

LEARNING OBJECTIVE 1.12 Describe Vygotsky's main theoretical contribution to developmental science.

Soviet psychologist Lev Vygotsky (1896–1934) agreed with many aspects of Piaget's theory, but he believed that Piaget overlooked the critical role of social interactions in learning and development. Vygotsky stated that children learn through interacting with knowledgeable adults, such as parents and teachers, and in doing so master more challenging tasks than they would when acting alone. Furthermore, children learn best when caregivers adjust their input to be slightly above the child's current or "actual" level of understanding. A child's **zone of proximal development** refers to the distance between what a child can achieve independently versus with the support of a social partner (**FIGURE 1.15**). Information that falls within the zone of proximal development supports learning; whereas, information that is too easy or too hard relative to a child's current understanding yields few if any benefits.

For example, a preschooler may be able to count aloud by reciting numbers, but still find it difficult to count the crayons in a box. If a teacher simply states aloud "1, 2, 3, 4, 5," it may not help the child count a larger set (or, if the box

---

assimilation Incorporation of new experiences or information into an existing schema that move children from one stage to the next according to Piaget

equilibration A cognitive balance or alignment between existing knowledge and new information

disequilibrium When new experiences do not fit a schema, creating an imbalance between the schema and reality; Jean Piaget posited that disequilibrium moves children from one stage to the next through the process of accommodation

accommodation Children's modification of a schema to fit reality that is the result of disequilibrium

zone of proximal development The distance between what a child can achieve independently versus with the guidance of a more knowledgeable or skilled social partner. Vygotsky proposed that children learn best when caregivers adjust their input to be slightly above the child's current or "actual" level of understanding

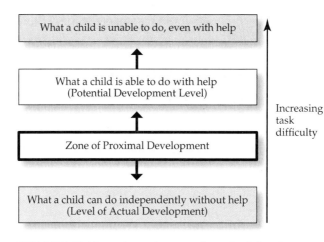

FIGURE 1.15 Vygotsky and zones of proximal development. Soviet psychologist Lev Vygotsky stated that children learn through interacting with knowledgeable adults, such as parents and teachers, and master more challenging tasks through this interaction than they would when acting alone. Furthermore, children learn best when information provided by caregivers falls within children's zone of proximal development—that is, input is neither too easy nor too difficult relative to a child's current understanding. (After L. S. Vygotsky. 1978. *Mind in Society: The Development of Higher Psychological Processes*, M. Cole et al. [Eds.] Harvard University Press: Cambridge, MA.)

contains 64 crayons that a teacher counts aloud, that won't help either). However, if the teacher guides the child to count a set of 10 crayons one by one, gesturing to each crayon while reciting its number, the child will begin to grasp that counting objects means connecting numbers to a specific set of objects. Although Vygotsky died at a young age, his theoretical contributions on social influences permeate contemporary sociocultural theories and research, as you will see in subsequent sections throughout this chapter and book.

✓ CHECK YOUR UNDERSTANDING 1.12

1. What did Vygotsky mean by the zone of proximal development? Give an example.

Contemporary Theories

Evolutionary theory, behaviorism/learning theories, psychodynamic theory, Piaget's constructivist theory, and Vygotsky's sociocultural theory continue to influence developmental psychology today. Indeed, contemporary science stands on the shoulders of giants while making significant theoretical and methodological strides.

Nativist Approaches

LEARNING OBJECTIVE 1.13 Explain how a nativist approach to core capacities aligns with evolutionary perspectives of human development.

Darwin's evolutionary theory sparked many questions about the early origins of behavior—what capacities are innately available as foundations to human development? This question underlies the nativist approach to learning and development. A **nativist approach** asserts that people are born with innate, or core, capacities that are essential for human adaptation (Spelke, 2016). For example, a nativist approach to language development claims that children acquire the rules of grammar with impressive speed because a device or module in the brain is specialized for language (Chomsky, 1965).

nativist approach An approach to development that asserts people are born with innate, or core, capacities that are essential for human adaptation

Nativist interpretations have been applied to a wide range of behaviors that are considered to be building blocks of development. For example, young babies distinguish between large and small quantities of objects, even though they've never learned math. Nativists attribute infants' behaviors to a core "number sense" that paves the way to later mathematical understanding (Starr, Libertus, & Brannon, 2013; Feigenson, Dehaene, & Spelke, 2004). Certainly, being able to discriminate among large and small quantities may have been critical to human survival—you'd have a lot more food to eat if you chose a bush with a lot of berries compared to a bush with just a few.

✓ CHECK YOUR UNDERSTANDING 1.13

1. Provide an example of an infant behavior that is thought to reflect an innate, core capacity.

Social Learning Theory

LEARNING OBJECTIVE 1.14 Explain the principles of social learning theory, and how Bandura's research illustrated these principles.

Social learning theory echoes some of the principles of behaviorism regarding learning through reinforcement, yet advances on those principles in key ways. A social learning theorist might ask how children respond to positive or negative feedback about acceptable and unacceptable behaviors. Consider the case of a boy who plays with dolls and is teased by his peers. The negative feedback might cause him to abandon dolls and act in ways that align with social expectations of gender roles. By conforming to gender stereotypes in his play, he increases his future chances of being accepted by his peers.

However, according to social learning theory, children don't necessarily have to be rewarded or punished to figure out how to act. Children also learn by simply watching other people, what is referred to as **observational learning**. The boy who plays with dolls might begin to gravitate toward trucks and blocks as he observes other boys in the classroom doing so. He has learned gender stereotypes simply by watching his classmates.

Albert Bandura and his doctoral student Richard Walters (1963) demonstrated the power of observational learning in their famous Bobo doll experiment. Children watched an adult aggressively hit and verbally assault an inflated "Bobo doll" while shouting "Sock him!" "Kick him!" A second group of children observed the adult play non-aggressively with other toys in the room (Bandura & Walters, 1963). When later placed in the playroom with the Bobo doll, children who had watched the aggressive adult were more likely to act physically aggressive toward the Bobo doll than were those who had watched the nonaggressive adult (**FIGURE 1.16**).

Observational learning also takes the form of **vicarious reinforcement**, in which children learn how to behave by watching others get rewarded or punished. For example, if children see a teacher scolding a classmate for talking in class, children might remain quiet despite not having been punished themselves.

The principles of social learning theory extend to many common behaviors and situations, such as when younger siblings imitate the behaviors of older siblings and when high school freshmen mimic the clothes, expressions, and attitudes of their senior classmates. Yet, a child's thinking also comes into play in each of these situations. That is, building on Bandura's famous Bobo study, social learning theory considers how children's cognitive development affects who they imitate, when, and why (Martin & Ruble, 2010). A cognitive perspective explains why young girls might closely attend to and imitate the fairy princesses in movies, whereas female adolescents might choose to imitate the behaviors of successful and powerful women. In both cases, the girls and teens hold views

social learning theory An approach to development that echoes some of the principles of behaviorism regarding learning through reinforcement, yet advances on those principles in key ways; social learning theory also emphasizes how children learn new behaviors by imitating others

observational learning A form of learning in which children figure out how to act by watching and modeling other people; Albert Bandura first demonstrated the importance of children's observational learning

vicarious reinforcement A form of observational learning in which children learn how to behave by watching others get rewarded or punished

From Bandura et al. 1963. J. of Abnormal and Social Psychology 66: 1, 3–11. ©1963, American Psychological Association

Courtesy of Albert Bandura/CC BY-SA 4.0

FIGURE 1.16 Bandura and observational learning. Albert Bandura demonstrated the power of observational learning in a seminal study in which children watched an adult attack an inflated "Bobo doll." The children were then taken into a playroom that contained a Bobo doll and other toys. Children who had watched the adult display aggression toward the Bobo doll were more likely to be physically aggressive toward the doll than were those who had watched the nonaggressive adult.

about their social group membership and differ in their flexibility around what they consider to be female roles. These cognitions, or understandings, around gender motivate them to observe and emulate esteemed role models.

✓ CHECK YOUR UNDERSTANDING 1.14

1. Give one example of observational learning and one of vicarious reinforcement.

Information Processing Theories

LEARNING OBJECTIVE 1.15 Explain how information processing theories draw connections between humans and computers.

information processing theories
Theories that focus on the flow of information (in the forms of sounds, sights, and smells) through the mind; information is perceived, manipulated, stored, retrieved, and acted on, much like a computer manipulates and stores information

Information processing theories focus on how children attend to, manipulate, process, store, and retrieve information (from sensory input in the forms of sounds, sights, smells, and so on), much like a computer manipulates and stores information. Children perceive, manipulate, store in memory, and retrieve incoming sensory information (such as sounds, sights, and smells) much like a computer manipulates and stores information (Munakata, 2007) (**FIGURE 1.17**). For example, consider a child watching an unfamiliar animal, a giraffe, while visiting a zoo. Suppose the child's father points to the animal and says, "giraffe." The child must attend to and integrate incoming sensory information—the sound of the word "giraffe" and the visual image of the giraffe—to learn its name. If the child connects the word and sight of the animal (the word "giraffe") and takes time to process the word, the image of the animal and its name might be stored in memory for future use.

The information processing approach gained prominence as developmental scientists began to test components of the model in children of different ages. As children get older, they become faster at processing information, less likely to become distracted, and better able to use strategies to remember material and solve problems (Bjorklund & Causey, 2017; Kail, 2003).

✓ CHECK YOUR UNDERSTANDING 1.15

1. What would information processing theorists focus on in the study of children's cognitive development?

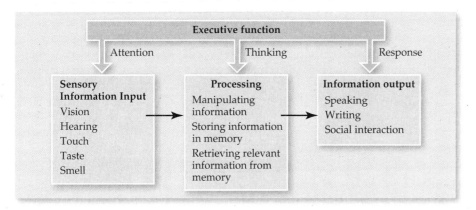

FIGURE 1.17 Information processing. The focus of information processing theories is on how children attend to, process, store, and retrieve information as they engage with their environments. From a developmental perspective, information processing researchers examine how children improve over age and with experience in aspects of cognitive development such as attention, speed of processing information, memory for material, and the strategies they deploy to solve problems, remember material, and so on. (After C. Lytridis et al. 2019. In *International Joint Conference SOCO'18-CISIS'18-ICEUTE'18*, M. Graña et al. [Eds.], pp. 562-570. Springer: Cham, Switzerland. https://doi.org/10.1007/978-3-319-94120-2_55.)

Developmental Systems Theory

LEARNING OBJECTIVE 1.16 Explain how developmental systems theorists conceptualize development.

Developmental systems theorists view human behavior to be the product of a complex, ever-changing system, in which many factors produce developmental change. From this perspective, developmental change *is not* the product of a top-down process that is orchestrated by the brain or by biological maturation. Further, developmental systems theory rejects the nativist idea of innate, core capacities. Rather, developmental change occurs because behaviors "self-organize" in response to experience: New behaviors emerge out of complex interactions between children's genes, their bodies, their actions in the environment, and the broader context of their lives.

On first glance, developmental systems' focus on body and environment interactions may appear to be quite similar to that of Piaget. However, developmental systems theorists go a few steps further. The systems piece of the theory recognizes that *many* intersecting forces, or systems—including body size and strength, brain development, motivation, social inputs, environmental layouts, and so forth—spur development and affect children's behaviors at any point in time. The *developmental* piece of the theory recognizes that those many systems are in constant flux. Children might therefore differ in how they act and think at any point in time, depending on environmental circumstances and supports (**FIGURE 1.18**).

Consider, for example, the complex forces that give rise to a behavior as straightforward as walking. Most people think that babies just get up and walk somewhere around their first birthday. Perhaps, the brain acts as a kind of clock that tells the body when it is time to walk. However, walking is a lot more complicated than that. Infants must be sufficiently motivated to walk; willing to abandon their fairly effective means of crawling; and their body dimensions must change from the top-heavy shape of young infants to an elongated, cylindrical shape (Thelen, 1984). Furthermore, infants

developmental systems theorists Theorists who posit that human behavior is the product of a complex, ever-changing system, in which multiple factors affect developmental change; this approach highlights the shared contributions of genes and environment on development and rejects the nativist approach of innate core capacities

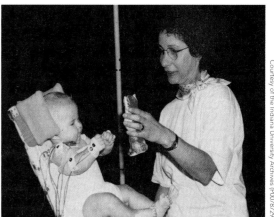

FIGURE 1.18 Esther Thelen and developmental systems theorists. Developmental scientist Esther Thelen (shown) documented the ways that infants generate solutions to motor challenges such as reaching for objects. Individual infants vary in how they ultimately succeed at reaching, depending on many factors, including their current posture, strength, skills at controlling their arms, motivation to get an object, and so on.

must have sufficient muscle strength and postural control to lift their legs off the ground, support their bodies, and maintain balance on one leg while the other leg is in motion (Adolph & Robinson, 2015). And social experiences shape when infants walk. In cultural communities where caregivers encourage infant movement through exercise and other forms of stimulation, walking onsets are accelerated by many months relative to Western norms (Adolph, Karasik, & Tamis-LeMonda, 2010).

✓ CHECK YOUR UNDERSTANDING 1.16

1. How might a developmental systems theorist explain why one baby learns to walk at a younger age in development than another?

Bioecological Theories

LEARNING OBJECTIVE 1.17 Describe Bronfenbrenner's bioecological theory of development.

Just as biologists might focus on how environmental conditions such as temperature, oxygen levels, and the availability of water and nutrients affect the growth of bacteria, theorists working from the **bioecological perspective** focus on the way that the environment affects human development. Notably, bioecological theorists fall under the broader umbrella of developmental systems theories in their emphasis on children's active role in development and the reciprocal influences among children's biology, behaviors, and the multiple environments in which children develop. That is, children influence their environments just as their environments influence them (Sameroff & Chandler, 1975). For example, children may increase their negative behaviors over time in response to unsupportive, abusive, or neglectful parenting. Children's growing negativity will then lead to even more negative parenting, and potentially feed into a downward spiral of poor social interactions with peers, teachers, and other people.

Urie Bronfenbrenner (1917–2005), one of the most influential bioecological theorists, conceptualized development as the product of nested environmental "systems" (Bronfenbrenner 2000, 2004; Bronfenbrenner & Morris, 1998). Bronfenbrenner placed the child's biological characteristics at the center, with the surrounding "systems" working together with child characteristics to guide development (**FIGURE 1.19**):

- *Biology.* The personal characteristics of individuals that affect their social interactions and experiences, including physical attributes such as age, sex, and appearance; unobservable characteristics, such as intelligence; and aspects of personality, including temperament, motivation, and persistence.

- *Microsystem.* An immediate, or proximal, environment in which individuals interact directly. The most widely studied microsystems include family/home, school, peer groups, and neighborhood.

- *Mesosystem.* The connections among two or more microsystems, such as family/home and school. For instance, if a child's parents expect the child to be respectful and obedient and to speak to adults only when spoken to, the child might have difficulties in a classroom where teachers expect active participation.

- *Exosystem.* The environments in which the child does not participate, but that affect the child through their influences on one or more microsystems. Exosystems might include parent work environments and healthcare systems. For example, if a child's parent works long hours at a stressful job, she might be short-tempered and less responsive in the family/home microsystem.

bioecological perspective Theory, proposed by Uri Bronfenbrenner, that focuses on how the environment affects human development; this approach highlights development as the product of different nested environmental "systems" (microsystem, mesosystem, exosystem, macrosystem, and chronosystem) and biology

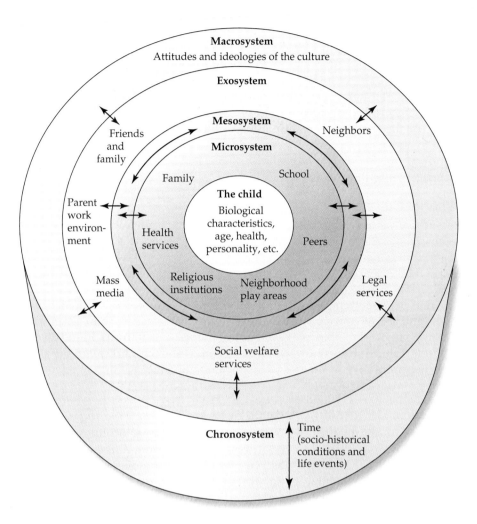

FIGURE 1.19 Bronfenbrenner and the bioecological theory of human development. Bronfenbrenner advanced a comprehensive theory in which he conceptualized development as the product of nested environmental "systems," with the child (including the child's biological characteristics) at the center. (After J. W. Santrock. 1992. *Child Development: An Introduction*, 5th ed. Wm. C. Brown: Dubuque, IA. Republished with permission of McGraw-Hill LLC; permission conveyed through Copyright Clearance Center, Inc.)

- *Macrosystem.* A culture's broad system of beliefs, values, resources, and institutions, including economic and governmental institutions, which can affect one or more microsystems. The macrosystem can be viewed as a cultural blueprint that influences the ways that children are raised. For example, cultural communities differ in views around gender equality, which may affect how boys and girls are treated at home and school.

- *Chronosystem.* Changes in the life events that affect development across the lifespan and historical time. An example of a changing life event would be a parent's death, which will affect children differently at different periods during their lifespan. Events such as the Great Depression of the 1930s and World War II (1939–1945) represent historical events that affected child nutrition and health and parental psychological functioning and employment.

Many current developmental researchers apply Bronfenbrenner's bioecological theory to their science and practice (e.g., Lerner, 2019). Thus, developmentalists investigate multiple contextual influences in their research and target multiple contexts when designing interventions and programs for children and families.

✓ CHECK YOUR UNDERSTANDING 1.17

1. What are the five systems of Bronfenbrenner's theory? Give examples of each.

sociocultural theories Theories that build on the foundational work of Lev Vygotsky that focus on the contexts of child development, placing much weight on the nurture end of the nature-nurture seesaw and assigning a very central role to culture

culture The shared physical, behavioral, and symbolic features of a community

cultural learning environment A concept introduced by Beatrice and John Whiting that encompasses the consistent elements of daily living, including a "physically defined space, a characteristic group of people, and norms of behavior"

developmental niche A concept introduced by Charles Super and Sara Harkness that encompasses the physical and social settings of children's lives, the customs of childcare and child-rearing, and the beliefs and views of caregivers

FIGURE 1.20 The Whitings and the study of culture. Beatrice and John Whiting conducted a seminal study of culture in which they observed children from India, Japan, Kenya, Mexico, the Philippines, and the United States in their homes and communities. Their research highlighted dramatic cultural differences in the nature of children's experiences.

Sociocultural Theories

LEARNING OBJECTIVE 1.18 Understand the components of culture and how culture affects children's experiences and development.

Like bioecological theories, **sociocultural theories** focus on the contexts of child development, building on the work of Lev Vygotsky, and thus placing much weight on the nurture end of the nature-nurture seesaw. However, sociocultural theories assign a very central role to culture. Whereas Bronfenbrenner situated culture at the outermost circle of his model (the macrosystem), sociocultural theorists view culture as infusing all aspects of children's lives.

What Is Culture?

You may wonder what exactly *is* culture? The concept of culture is sometimes so abstract that it is nearly impossible to put a finger on it when you see it. Yet, most theorists agree that **culture** refers to the shared physical, behavioral, and symbolic features of a community (Cole, Cole, & Lightfoot, 2005; Rogoff et al., 2007). This definition encompasses the countless subtle features of culture that people often take for granted. Culture is expressed in how we talk, move, and act; what we believe and think; the skills we learn; how we engage with the people and objects of our environments; and so forth. In the case of children, culture shapes how, when, and from whom children learn the skills of their community so that they can become valued contributors to society (Weisner et al., 2005).

Children's Cultural Environment

If culture infuses all of children's experiences, how do sociocultural scientists go about understanding the experiences of children from different communities? Sometimes, they simply observe everyday life and document what they see. In one of the most influential descriptions of children's cultural experiences, Beatrice and John Whiting observed children from communities in India, Japan, Kenya, Mexico, the Philippines, and the United States (Whiting, 1963; Whiting & Whiting, 1975) (**FIGURE 1.20**). Children's experiences differed dramatically from community to community in the amount and quality of contact with immediate family members, other relatives, and unrelated children; the time children and family members spent in work and play; how and where children ate and slept; the type and level of education children received; and so on. Based on their observations, the Whitings introduced the concept of a **cultural learning environment**—the consistent elements of daily living, including a "physically defined space, a characteristic group of people, and norms of behavior" (Whiting, 1980, p. 97; Pope et al., 2010).

Charles Super and Sara Harkness further expanded on the Whitings' notion of a cultural learning environment based on their observations of family life in Bangladesh, India, Kenya, Malaysia, and the United States. They introduced the concept of a **developmental niche** to describe the physical and social settings of children's lives, the customs of childcare and child-rearing, and the beliefs and views of caregivers (Super & Harkness, 1986, 1999) (**FIGURE 1.21**). Today, most sociocultural theorists emphasize three components of culture that correspond Super and Harkness's developmental niche:

- *Physical features: materials and the use of space.* Members of a cultural community share the physical features of daily living, including how space is used and the material objects available to members of the community. Children from different communities are exposed to different tools, such as chopsticks or forks and spoons for eating; to different learning materials, such as books and puzzles versus toys made from natural materials; and different symbolic tools such as maps, artwork, diagrams, and charts.

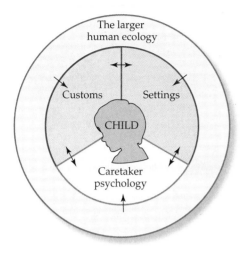

FIGURE 1.21 The developmental niche. Charles Super and Sara Harkness introduced the concept of a developmental niche to describe the physical and social settings of children's lives, the customs of childcare and child rearing, and the psychology of caregivers, namely their beliefs and views. (After M. J. Packer. 2018. In *The SAGE Encyclopedia of Lifespan Human Development*, M. H. Bornstein [Ed.], pp. 582–583. SAGE Publications, Inc.: Thousand Oaks, CA.)

Moreover, the physical features of a culture—such as mats or chairs for sitting, books for reading, rivers for swimming—determine whether children sit or squat, read, swim, and so on.

- *Behavioral features: cultural practices and routines.* Members of a cultural community share practices, or ways of doing things, including how they structure their days. For example, children from many communities spend most of their daytime hours in school, whereas children in other communities spend their daytime hours in the fields helping their parents harvest food. Opportunities to participate in drawing and writing activities support children's readiness for school, whereas opportunities to fish with older peers support learning to provide for the village. Behavioral features also include how people interact, including their use of gestures to communicate, whether they talk over and interrupt each other or wait their turn, and whether they express emotions flamboyantly or keep emotions restrained.

- *Symbolic features: cultural beliefs and views.* Members of a cultural community share views and ways of thinking—including attitudes, beliefs, values, and expectations. For example, adults from different cultural communities differ in their views about the proper ways to raise children and the behaviors they expect from their children. Parents in some cultures endorse independence and assertiveness, expecting children to speak their minds, make independent choices, and move out of the house to attend college, or at least move out by early adulthood. Parents in other cultures endorse humility, deference to authority (rather than speaking one's mind), and respect and responsibility for elders, which may include living with and supporting elderly parents as an adult.

As we will learn, components of culture are intertwined. Physical settings and caregiver views affect customs of child-rearing, just as child-rearing customs reciprocally affect views and how caregivers arrange physical materials and space. For example, parents in cultures that endorse the importance of literacy will showcase books throughout the house and engage children in book reading at early ages. As children learn to read, they reinforce parents' views about the importance of literacy.

FIGURE 1.22 Children everywhere are recipients and change agents in their cultures. Children's interactions with technology and social media have led to the proliferation of new e-books, platforms, apps, and tools.

Cultural Universals

Throughout this book, you will learn about the striking variability that characterizes life in cultures around the world. At the same time, cultural differences should in no way detract from appreciating the universal aspects of child development. Humans have a shared biology and evolutionary history that provide nearly all children with capacities to adapt to their environments (Keller & Kärtner, 2013). Humans in all cultures perform the universal tasks of constituting families, raising children, and passing on the norms, values, skills, knowledge, and dispositions that will enable children to survive and thrive (Whiting & Whiting, 1975). Moreover, children everywhere are recipients and agents of change in their cultures. They not only internalize shared views and practices but also change those views and practices as they participate in social interactions (Gauvain & Nicolaides, 2015).

For example, children's interactions with technology and social media have led to the proliferation of new e-books, platforms, apps, and tools (**FIGURE 1.22**). These new technologies then get propagated throughout society at a pace that would likely never have occurred if only older generations interacted with technology. (Consider how your own skills with technology compare to that of your parents or grandparents!) In essence, cultural learning and change are universal processes: Children learn how to fit in with their environments at the same time that they modify the environments in which they live.

✓ CHECK YOUR UNDERSTANDING 1.18

1. List and define the three components of the developmental niche.
2. What is meant by a cultural universal? Give an example.

■ Research in Developmental Science

Every developmental study is unique. One researcher may ask about infant language learning, another about children's friendships, and yet another about adolescent risk taking. And, even when researchers study the same thing, they may do so in very different ways depending on their theoretical orientation. Yet, all researchers follow steps that take them from the kernels of an idea to the final conclusions about what they have learned.

Notably, the research enterprise in developmental psychology is unique from other disciplines in important ways. The sheer variety of approaches that researchers take to address their questions swamps all other disciplines. Moreover, the focus of developmental science—children—entails enormous flexibility and openness in how researchers ask questions and design their studies.

Studying children also raises the bar on ethical issues, because researchers must vigilantly ensure that the potential benefits of their work—on naive participants who require parental consent—outweigh any potential risks. In the following sections, we review the steps involved in conducting research and the ways that developmental scientists attempt to ensure rigor and integrity in their methods, measures, and findings.

Conducting Research

Sometimes, a developmental researcher begins with a question that involves a precise idea about what the researcher expects to find, what is characterized as **hypothesis-driven research**. That is, the research study is guided by a clear **hypothesis**—an assumption or proposed explanation that is based on limited or no evidence. The researcher's goal is to test whether sufficient evidence exists to support the starting hypothesis. Upon conclusion of the study, the researcher might accept the hypothesis as supported, or reject the hypothesis as not having evidence to back its claims.

Other times, a developmental researcher aims to discover and understand what children do and what development looks like without any presuppositions about what might be found; this is characterized as **discovery-based science**. Here, the researcher's goal is to learn from what the data reveal in an effort to advance a fuller understanding of development than was previously possible. Regardless of whether a study is hypothesis-driven or discovery-based, researchers must attend carefully to issues around sampling, choice of methods, measurement, and research design.

Hypothesis-Driven Research and the Scientific Method

LEARNING OBJECTIVE 1.19 Understand the steps involved in the scientific method.

Imagine that a researcher learns about statistics on adolescent risk taking—that adolescents show relatively high rates of risky behaviors such as drug use, drinking and driving, and unprotected sexual encounters that decline in early adulthood. In attempting to understand this pattern the researcher might hypothesize that adolescents know less than do adults about the negative consequences of risk-taking behaviors. The researcher proposes that with age, adolescents become increasingly knowledgeable about such risks, and their growing knowledge causes a decline in risk taking between adolescence and adulthood. If this hypothesis is correct, an effective way to prevent adolescent risk taking would be to mount educational campaigns on social media and in schools, youth groups, and other points of contact with teenagers to warn them about the dangers of risk-taking behaviors.

However, to justify the costs of mounting an educational campaign, the researcher must find evidence that teenagers lack awareness about the dangers of risk-taking behaviors. Without such evidence, the explanation remains merely a hypothesis. Thus, the researcher would have to conduct a study to test the hypothesis. (Actual researchers have in fact tested the hypothesis that knowledge explains adolescent risk taking, as we will review in Chapter 16, and the results may surprise you!). In this example, the researcher followed the steps of the **scientific method** (**FIGURE 1.23**):

1. *Identifying a question*: "Why do adolescents engage in more risk-taking behaviors than adults?"

2. *Formulating a hypothesis that answers the question*: "Adolescents are less knowledgeable than adults about risks."

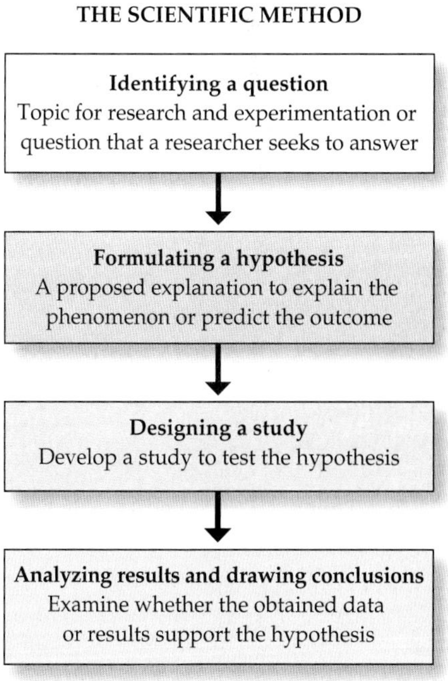

hypothesis-driven research Research that seeks to examine a specific and measurable question along with specified hypotheses

hypothesis An assumption or proposed explanation that is based on limited or even no evidence

discovery-based science Research that seeks to discover principles of children's learning and development without presuppositions about what might be found

scientific method Steps that scientists use to test hypotheses: identifying a question; formulating a hypothesis that answers the question; testing the hypothesis with a research study; and analyzing study results and drawing conclusions

THE SCIENTIFIC METHOD

Identifying a question
Topic for research and experimentation or question that a researcher seeks to answer

↓

Formulating a hypothesis
A proposed explanation to explain the phenomenon or predict the outcome

↓

Designing a study
Develop a study to test the hypothesis

↓

Analyzing results and drawing conclusions
Examine whether the obtained data or results support the hypothesis

FIGURE 1.23 The steps of the scientific method.

3. *Testing the hypothesis with a research study*: Researchers must design and conduct a valid and reliable research study that would generate the necessary data on adolescent and adult knowledge and risk-taking behaviors (terms discussed later in this chapter) to gather necessary data.

4. *Analyzing the results of the study and drawing conclusions*: Statistical analysis of the data, such as comparisons of adolescent and adult knowledge about risk taking, would help answer the researchers' question. Findings may support the hypothesis, indicate that the hypothesis is incorrect, or fall somewhere in between.

✓ CHECK YOUR UNDERSTANDING 1.19

1. A researcher wishes to test whether a particular curriculum would better support children's math learning than the current curriculum being used in a school. Apply the steps of the scientific method to the researcher's goal of studying the effectiveness of the proposed curriculum.

Discovery-Based Science

LEARNING OBJECTIVE 1.20 Compare discovery-based research to the traditional scientific method.

Not all developmental science begins with a hypothesis. Indeed, developmental science is unique in its widespread use of discovery-based science—research that is guided by one or more questions, but without specific hypotheses. Many of the most important findings in developmental psychology were discoveries made by researchers who simply observed children or family life, or asked questions without starting assumptions about what they'd find. For example, the study of infant attachment to caregivers (see Chapter 7) arose because British psychologist John Bowlby noticed in his clinic that infants became extremely distressed when separated from their caregivers for prolonged periods of time. Similarly, Piaget's discoveries arose out of watching the behaviors of his children and meticulously documenting how they responded to specific problems. Today, much of our current understanding around infant motor skill development, language experiences, peer relationships, adolescent sexuality, and so on, is based on careful, detailed descriptions of what children do, feel, and believe at different ages, across different domains, in different settings, and in different cultures.

Continuing with the example of adolescent risk taking, a discovery-based researcher might wish to better understand the situations under which adolescents engage in risk taking. The researcher might ask some open-ended questions, conduct informal observations, or analyze the text messages that adolescents share with their friends. Whatever approach the researcher takes, the goal is to understand what adolescents do and why, rather than seeking to generate confirmatory evidence around a specific hypothesis.

✓ CHECK YOUR UNDERSTANDING 1.20

1. Under which conditions might a researcher rely on discovery-based science rather than following the hypothesis-driven steps of the scientific method?

Sampling

LEARNING OBJECTIVE 1.21 Understand the decisions involved in determining the participants or sample to be included in a research study.

Whether hypothesis-driven or discovery-driven, decisions about sampling are critical to research. The term **sample** includes the number of people who participate in a study (**sample size**) and most centrally, the characteristics

sample size The number of people who participate in a study of participants. In the adolescent risk-taking example, the researcher must decide which adolescents (and perhaps adults) to study, considering factors such as age, education, ethnicity, etc. Decisions about a sample will affect confidence in the study findings and generalizability of findings.

Generalizability refers to the degree to which research findings and conclusions based on a specific study and sample extend to the population at large. A general rule of thumb is that the larger a study sample, the greater the chance that findings are generalizable. Clearly, more trust can be placed in findings that are based on 1,000 adolescents and 1,000 adults than on findings based on 10 adolescents and 10 adults.

However, sample size alone does not guarantee generalizability. A sample that includes people from a range of backgrounds and locations is preferable to one based on a narrow group of participants. Sometimes, researchers recruit participants into a study based on how easy it is to get them, such as the students in a researcher's class or children in the local community, which is referred to as **convenience sampling.** Samples of convenience may bias findings, because the sample might not be representative—that is, it might differ in significant ways from the **population** to which the researcher wishes to generalize (**FIGURE 1.24**). Suppose, for example, that in the risk-taking study example, the researcher recruited adolescents from an elite private school where adolescents scored in the 99th percentile on a standardized test. The findings of the study would probably be biased, because teenagers at the private school certainly differ from the entire population of teenagers on their knowledge about risk taking and risk-taking behaviors.

Attention to sampling is especially important when comparing two or more groups of participants who might differ on characteristics unrelated to the **variables**, or factors of interest. For example, imagine that a researcher sampled adults from a faith-based organization in the suburbs and adolescents from a progressive school in the city to test hypotheses about risk taking. Any differences in adolescent and adult responses might be explained by factors other than age. Thus, to the extent possible, participants should be matched on characteristics that may affect findings.

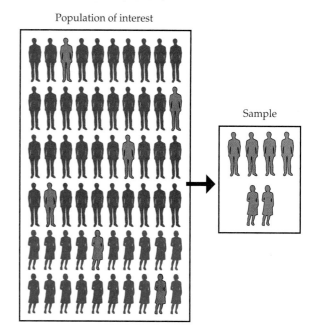

Population of interest

Sample

FIGURE 1.24 Sampling.   When researchers conduct a study, participants only represent a small and select group of the overall population of interest. The smaller a sample size, the less likely the data are to be generalizable. The problem of generalization is most pronounced when researchers rely on convenience sampling. (After L. Musu-Gillette. NCES Blog [blog]. April 5, 2016. https://nces.ed.gov/blogs/nces/post/statistical-concepts-in-brief-how-and-why-does-nces-use-sample-surveys.)

✓ **CHECK YOUR UNDERSTANDING 1.21**

1. Explain why a small sample of children from a local preschool in southern Florida might be problematic for researchers who wish to investigate what young U.S. children understand about temperature changes across the four seasons.

Methods: Gathering Data

LEARNING OBJECTIVE 1.22 Compare and contrast the various approaches or methods developmental scientists use to gather data.

Research method refers to *how* data are gathered. The choice of which methods to use depends on the question under study, the researcher's theoretical orientation, the age of participants, and even the resources available to conduct the study. Four types of methods dominate much of the research that you will learn about in this book: interviews, surveys, observations of behavior (under naturalistic or structured settings), and physiological assessments (**TABLE 1.2**).

generalizability The degree to which research findings and conclusions based on a specific study and sample extend to the population at large

convenience sampling The recruitment of participants into a study based on ease of access to them, such as the students in a researcher's class or children in the local community

population The target sample to which a researcher aims to generalize findings based on a specific study sample

variables Factors of interest in a study (such as a child's sex); a characteristic or something that can be examined in relation to something else (i.e., another variable), such as whether a child's sex relates to the type of play children display

research method How data are gathered to test predictions and interpret results

TABLE 1.2 ■ Methods for Gathering Data

Type of Method	Examples	Benefits	Drawbacks
Interviews	Structured interview, unstructured interview	Yields data from the perspective of participants on their behaviors, feelings, thoughts, beliefs, and so on. Also allows researchers to gather information on infrequent behaviors or events that are unlikely to be observed in a single study session.	Participants can be biased in their reporting, and prone to social desirability or answering in ways that they assume researchers expect. Participants may selectively disclose only certain information to hide negative behaviors or feelings.
Written Surveys	Paper, online	Participants can respond without speaking directly to a researcher, which may minimize social desirability effects.	Literacy demands may be a concern, which makes surveys inappropriate for young children and individuals with low education.
Observations	Naturalistic observation, structured observation, direct assessment	Allows researchers to directly observe or assess behaviors of interest, oftentimes in ecologically valid naturalistic contexts such as at a child's home or school.	Can be costly time wise, and may require later coding of behaviors from videorecordings. Participant behavior may be affected by a researcher's presence.
Physiological Assessments	Brain activation, heart rate, blood pressure, eye movements, measurement of hormones	Can assess how participants react and respond to stimuli and different situations physiologically, offering a unique lens into the unobservable aspects of learning and development.	Many such techniques can be costly in the required technology and training. Some methods cannot be used with young children. Behavioral measures may be needed to interpret the meaning of physiological data, which can be noisy and affected by time of day (such as in hormone measurement) and other factors that cause loss of data and messiness of data.

interview Questions asked of participants face-to-face or via phone

survey Questions asked of participants through written format

social desirability bias When participants answer questions in a way they believe is desired or "correct," rather than truthfully

structured interview Interview in which researchers ask specific, close-ended questions; for example, a structured interview may ask an adolescent about specific risk behaviors

unstructured interview Interview in which researchers ask open-ended questions to elicit more information from participants than would be possible with close-ended questions; unstructured interviews are a part of qualitative research

qualitative research An approach in which researchers explore in depth a phenomenon without a set of specific hypotheses; qualitative research may include unstructured interviews

Interviews and Surveys

Developmental scientists frequently ask participants about their opinions, beliefs, and attitudes ("Should parents have the right to impose a curfew on their teenagers?"), feelings and emotions ("How often do you feel anxious?"), preferences ("Would you rather play with a doll or a truck?), behaviors ("Do you smoke, and if so how often?"), and so on. Researchers may ask these questions face-to-face or by telephone in an **interview**, or in written form as a **survey**.

Whether to use an interview or survey format depends on the research question. For instance, returning to the example of adolescent risk taking, a survey would be used if the researcher believed that adolescents are less likely to admit to certain risk-taking behaviors in a face-to-face interview than when filling out an anonymous survey. Surveys can minimize **social desirability bias**, which occurs when participants answer questions in a way they believe is desired or "correct," rather than truthfully. Another consideration is the literacy skills of participants. For example, young children can't fill out questionnaires, and so interviews or observations (described next) may make more sense.

If researchers decide to gather data through interviews, an additional consideration is the form that those interviews will take. During a **structured interview** the researcher asks specific, close-ended questions, for example by asking an adolescent about specific risk behaviors. In contrast, during an **unstructured interview** an examiner asks open-ended questions to elicit more information from participants than would be possible with close-ended questions. Unstructured interviews fall under the broad umbrella of **qualitative research**, an approach in which researchers explore in depth a phenomenon without a set of specific hypotheses. For example, researchers may want to understand adolescents' perspectives about risk taking, including the reasons for such behaviors, and so would ask a few open-ended questions and then listen to what teens have to say.

Sometimes, researchers use unstructured interviews to explore understudied topics or populations. For example, if you wanted to learn about parent involvement in a small hunting-gathering village, you would likely not ask "How often do you read to your child?" You would likely ask parents to talk about family life in the village, and based on their responses, design a culturally sensitive measure of parent involvement. Furthermore, you might couple your informal interviews with observations of village life and note taking (which we describe next) to obtain a first-hand sense of life in the community.

Observations

Researchers often rely on **observations** to study developmental phenomena, by watching what children do in a controlled laboratory setting or in natural settings such as home or school. In **structured observations**, researchers observe participants performing a specific activity—for example, interacting with peers during a game, or viewing images on screen, typically in a laboratory setting. Sometimes, researchers test children on a specific task or test, what is referred to as **direct assessment.** For example, researchers might assess children's vocabulary by pointing to pictures in a test booklet and asking children to name the pictures. They might assess children's spatial skills by asking children to nest shapes in shape sorters. Or they might assess moral reasoning by asking children how they would respond to a dilemma, such as if a friend stole items from a store.

In **naturalistic observations**, researchers observe participants in everyday settings, such as at home, school, or on playgrounds. Researchers attempt to remain unobtrusive by remaining at a distance and not interacting with participants. For example, a researcher who is interested in developmental changes in child peer friendships might observe children of different ages during lunch breaks or recess. A researcher might observe classrooms to compare how teachers talk to boys versus girls in a study of gender stereotypes. And a researcher interested in children's early language learning might observe parent-child language interactions at home.

Physiological Assessments

Observational studies focus on overt behaviors. But, researchers can also learn a lot by studying what can't be seen with the naked eye. Developmental psychology has witnessed a surge in **physiological assessments**—measurements of the functioning of different parts of the body including brain activation, heart rate, blood pressure, eye movements, limb movements, and even the hormones people produce in response to stress. Noninvasive research techniques can identify areas of the brain involved in processing specific types of information, such as areas that are activated when infants hear speech (Kuhl, 2010). Researchers might gauge changes in heart rate, for example, to assess infant memory and attention (Reynolds & Richards, 2019), fear (LoBue, Kim, & Delgado, 2019), or even how children respond to social situations (van Rijn, Urbanus, & Swaab, 2019).

observation Watching what participants do in a controlled laboratory setting or in natural settings such as home or school

structured observations Observations in which researchers observe participants performing a specific activity—for example, interacting with peers during a game—typically in a laboratory setting

direct assessment A specific task or test that researchers administer to children

naturalistic observations Observations of participants in everyday settings, such as at home, school, or on playgrounds

physiological assessments Measures of the functioning of different parts of the body including brain activation, heart rate, blood pressure, eye movements, and even the hormones people produce in response to stress

✓ CHECK YOUR UNDERSTANDING 1.22

1. Describe and compare various research methods, including (a) surveys and interviews; (b) naturalistic and structured observations; and (c) physiological assessments.

2. Give examples of when you might choose to use each of the three research methods and why.

Study Designs

LEARNING OBJECTIVE 1.23 Compare and contrast the benefits and limitations of the different study designs used in developmental science.

study design A specific plan for conducting a study that allows the researcher to test a study's hypotheses

A **study design** is a specific plan for conducting a study that allows the researcher to test a study's hypotheses. Here, we consider several common study designs (**TABLE 1.3**). Bear in mind that study designs and research methods are distinct. For example, a researcher might design a longitudinal study—one that follows children over time—that includes interviews, naturalistic observations, physiological assessments, or a combination of these.

Correlational Studies

correlational study A study that tests associations between two or more variables without manipulating any variables

A **correlational study** tests associations between two or more variables, but without manipulating any of the variables. For example, a researcher might ask children to report on how often they play violent video games and then observe their aggressive behaviors toward peers. The researcher might find a relation (i.e., a correlation) between the number of hours children spend playing violent video games and their aggression toward peers. However, the drawback of correlational studies is their limited ability to disentangle cause-and-effect associations. The researcher could not convincingly assert that playing violent video games causes aggression because the alternative direction of causality is equally plausible—that children who enjoy playing violent video games might already be socially aggressive; in other words, aggressiveness may predict playing violent video games, rather than the reverse.

TABLE 1.3 ■ Study Designs

Type of Study	How It Works	Benefits	Drawbacks
Correlational Studies	Test associations between two or more variables but without manipulating the variables	Easy to implement. Researchers can capitalize on naturally occurring situations or behaviors, without manipulating variables	Limited ability to disentangle cause-and-effect associations
Longitudinal Studies	Follow the same participants over time, typically across months or years	Allows researchers to test stability and prediction over developmental time	Costly time-wise, as researchers must follow the same children over time; can suffer from attrition as participants drop out of the study
Cross-sectional Studies	Compare children of different ages at roughly the same point in time	Less costly than longitudinal studies	Do not permit a test of stability or prediction
Cohort Sequential Studies	Follow two or more groups of children of different ages over time, thus providing a mix of longitudinal and cross-sectional designs	Allows for testing of stability and prediction in subsets of children, but takes less time to cover a wide age span than would longitudinal designs	Still require more time than a cross-sectional study that would see participants only once, and there is risk once more of participant attrition
Microgenetic Studies	Involve frequent, closely spaced observations of children and/or detailed observations of learning in real time	Rich descriptive information about the process of change	Take a lot of time to code behaviors at frequent intervals or frame-by-frame; may lack generalizability, because most microgenetic studies rely on small samples
Behavioral Genetic Studies	Include twin studies, adoption studies, and genome-wide association studies	Especially useful for assessing genetic contributions to development	Require large samples that may take much effort to recruit (such as MZ and DZ twins); certain types of analyses, such as those based on genetic similarities, require thousands of participants

Moreover, a "third variable" or **confounding variable** may relate to both independent and dependent variables, and thus explain the association between the two. To illustrate with an absurd example: shoe size is correlated to the size of children's vocabulary, but larger feet do not cause growth in vocabulary. Rather, older children have more exposure to language than do younger children, and they also have larger feet. Thus, experience with language helps account for the correlation between shoe size and vocabulary size.

Experiments

An **experiment** is a study designed to directly test a hypothesis about a cause-and-effect relation between two (or more) variables, one or more independent variable(s) and one or more dependent variable(s). The **independent variable** is manipulated to see whether changes follow in the **dependent variable**. Typically, the participants in an experiment are divided into an **experimental group**—those who receive the "treatment," or the experimental manipulation—and a **control group**—those who do not receive the treatment.

For instance, a researcher might hypothesize that playing violent video games (the independent variable) causes aggressiveness (the dependent variable) in children (**FIGURE 1.25**). To test this hypothesis, the researcher might divide the study participants into an experimental group of children who receive the treatment of playing a violent video game and a control group of children who play a neutral video game. Children from the two groups might then be observed in a contrived situation in which another person—perhaps

confounding variable A "third variable" that relates to both the independent and dependent variables and can thus affect the outcome of a study

experiment A research method that tests a hypothesis about a cause-and-effect relation between two (sometimes more) variables, an independent variable, and a dependent variable

independent variable A variable that is manipulated to see whether changes follow in the dependent variable, or in non-experimental studies, a variable that is thought to explain another variable

dependent variable A variable whose value depends on another (independent) variable(s)

experimental group The participants who receive the "treatment" in an experimental manipulation

control group The participants who do not receive the "treatment" in an experimental manipulation

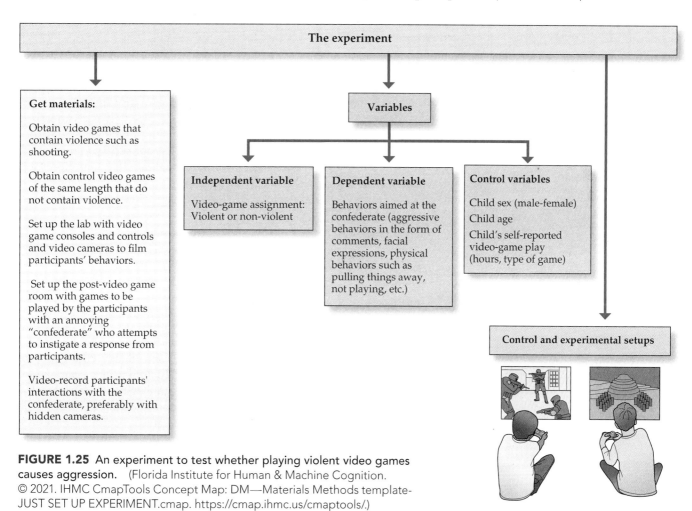

FIGURE 1.25 An experiment to test whether playing violent video games causes aggression.   (Florida Institute for Human & Machine Cognition. © 2021. IHMC CmapTools Concept Map: DM—Materials Methods template-JUST SET UP EXPERIMENT.cmap. https://cmap.ihmc.us/cmaptools/.)

confederate An actor who pretends to be a participant in a research study but actually works for the researcher

a research **confederate,** an actor who pretends to be a participant but actually works for the researcher—makes insulting comments such as, "I got more points than you did!" If children in the experimental group respond more aggressively to the confederate than do those in the control group, the hypothesis would be supported.

Although experimental studies purportedly test cause-and-effect relations, confounding variables could also create problems of interpretation if researchers are not careful in their study design. For example, imagine if the experimenter let children choose whether they'd like to play the violent video game or the neutral one, and assigned children to treatment and control based on children's choices. (In reality, experimenters would not do this!) Perhaps, the more aggressive children enjoy playing violent video games and chose to be in that group. If so, the child's predisposition toward aggressiveness is a confounding variable that biases findings toward the hypothesis.

random assignment The use of chance procedures, such as flipping a coin or using a random-number table, to assign participants to treatment or control; these procedures ensure that every person in the study has the same opportunity to be assigned to one or the other group

Thus, researchers typically control for confounding variables in experimental studies through a process of random assignment. **Random assignment** refers to the use of chance procedures, such as flipping a coin or using a random-number table to assign participants to treatment or control, to ensure that every person in the study has the same opportunity to be assigned to one or the other group. Random assignment helps ensure an even distribution of confounding variables between the groups. In essence, by randomly assigning participants to groups, the researcher can be somewhat confident that any observed differences between treatment and control are due to receiving the treatment or not.

Longitudinal Studies

longitudinal study A study that follows the same participants over time, typically across months or years

A **longitudinal study** follows the same participants over time, typically across months or years (**FIGURE 1.26**). Longitudinal studies enable researchers to examine stability, which refers to consistency over time in the ordering of individuals on a particular measure. For this reason, longitudinal studies are necessary to test developmental cascades over time: Repeated assessments of the same children are required to investigate whether and how skills (or experiences) at one point in time affect the same or different skills at later times. For example, to test whether children's ability to regulate their emotions and behaviors in early childhood has cascading effects on school performance in childhood and then delinquency in adolescence the researcher must follow the same children over several years.

mediator An intervening, explanatory variable that explains the association between the dependent and independent variable

Longitudinal designs also enable researchers to investigate whether a variable at time 1 relates to a variable at time 2 because of an association with an intervening, explanatory variable called a **mediator.** Suppose, for example, that a longitudinal study shows that toddlers who experienced relatively high levels of harsh parental discipline are more likely to be rejected by their peers in childhood than are those who experienced less harsh parental discipline as toddlers. This long-term connection, however, does not explain *why* harsh parental discipline predicts childhood rejection by peers. The researcher, therefore, designs a second longitudinal study to test the hypothesis that a mediator—child aggressiveness—explains the connection. That is, the researcher hypothesizes that harsh parental discipline in toddlerhood predicts aggressiveness in preschool, which then predicts peer rejection in later

FIGURE 1.26 Longitudinal studies. These studies follow the same participants over months or years.

years. In this study design, parental discipline is assessed in toddlerhood, child aggressiveness is assessed in preschool, and child popularity is assessed in third grade. If the researcher finds that harsh parental discipline predicts high levels of aggression in preschool, which in turn predicts low popularity in third grade, the meditation hypothesis would be supported.

Despite the many benefits of longitudinal studies, they are costly, take a great deal of time to conduct, and can suffer from **attrition**—participants dropping out of the study. A study that aims to examine connections between harsh punishment during early childhood and delinquency in adolescence, for example, would require a researcher to follow children and families at multiple times across 10 or more years. Attrition is especially problematic if participants who drop out of the study differ in meaningful ways from those who remain. For example, if children with parents who are high on harsh punishment are more difficult to follow over time than are those with parents who are low on harsh punishment, the study may no longer include a sufficient number of children from highly punitive homes to test the hypothesis.

attrition The dropping out of participants from a research study

Cross-Sectional Studies

A **cross-sectional study** compares children of different ages at roughly the same point in time (**FIGURE 1.27**). Cross-sectional designs avoid the time and cost of longitudinal studies, while still enabling researchers to investigate age-related differences in a particular phenomenon. And, attrition is no longer a problem because the researcher can recruit participants as needed and only has to see them once. For example, a researcher might compare 3-, 5-, and 7-year-olds on how long they can wait for a desired reward, such as a tasty cupcake, to study developmental changes in children's self-regulation skills. The researcher might find that 3- and 5-year-olds are unable to sit still and avoid eating the cupcake, whereas 7-year-olds can wait because they distract themselves by playing games. Still, cross-sectional designs do not permit tests of stability or cascading influences over time. That is, the researcher cannot ask whether 3-year-olds

cross-sectional study A study that compares children of different ages at roughly the same point in time to enable researchers to explore age-related differences in a certain phenomenon

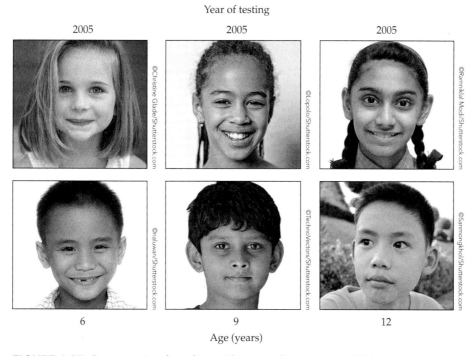

FIGURE 1.27 Cross-sectional studies.   These studies compare children of different ages at roughly the same point in time.

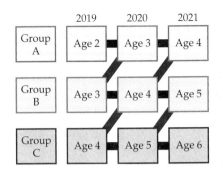

FIGURE 1.28 Cohort-sequential designs.   Cohort-sequential designs follow two or more groups of children of different ages over time, thus providing a mix of longitudinal and cross-sectional designs. Red lines represent the researcher's ability to compare children of the same age who were born at different times; black lines represent the ability to follow children over age.

cohort sequential design A study that follows two or more groups of children of different ages over time, creating a mixture of longitudinal and cross-sectional designs

microgenetic study A study that involves frequent, closely spaced observations of children, for instance, daily or weekly tracking of child learning and/or detailed observations of learning in real time

who are low in self-regulation remain low relative to their peers years later, or whether early self-regulation has cascading effects on later school performance.

Sometimes, researchers test children of a single age to inquire into children's skills at that specific time in development—a form of cross-sectional design that does not compare across age groups. Clever variations of single-age cross-sectional studies contrast children of the same age who differ on a variable of interest—such as asking how 13-month-olds who walk versus those who still crawl interact with their caregivers (Karasik, Tamis-LeMonda, & Adolph, 2011).

Cohort-Sequential Studies

Cohort-sequential studies follow two or more groups of children of different ages over time (referred to as cohorts), thus providing a mix of longitudinal and cross-sectional designs. For example, a researcher may test groups of 2-, 3-, and 4-year-olds at the start of the study, which allows for age-based comparisons in the cross-sectional nature of the study. The researcher may then follow the children for 2 additional years, allowing for longitudinal analyses within each group of children. In essence, the researcher has data available across a 4-year age span from only 2 years of data gathering (2-year-olds from the study's start and from 6-year-olds at the study's end). These cohort-sequential designs enable the researcher to examine stability and change in behaviors of interest (**FIGURE 1.28**).

Microgenetic Studies

Cross-sectional, longitudinal, and sequential studies may be limited in their ability to describe the *process* of change, because they offer only snapshots of behaviors at typically widely spaced ages (Adolph & Robinson, 2011; Siegler, 1995). That is, none of the designs capture change as it occurs. In contrast, a **microgenetic study** involves frequent, closely spaced observations of children, for instance, daily or weekly tracking of child learning, and/or detailed observations of learning in real time, such as in a single experimental session in which researchers document children's changing behaviors from second to second.

Microgenetic studies take a "data-dense" approach that yields rich descriptive information about the process of change, but generally include fewer children than would be seen in cross-sectional and longitudinal studies. For example, the relative growth charts posted in medical offices and online suggest that growth across the first 2 years of life follows a relatively smooth trajectory, which is certainly the case if you sample a child's height every 6 months or so. However, when researchers charted infants' growth weekly from 0 to 21 months, they found that babies showed bursts of growth in 1 week (up to 2.5 cm, nearly an inch) followed by long intervals of up to a month when children showed no measurable growth (Lampl et al., 1992).

Developmentalist Robert Siegler championed the value of a microgenetic approach in his studies of children's mathematical reasoning and problem solving. Siegler showed that within a session and across closely spaced observational periods, children's use of certain strategies gradually declined while their use of other strategies increased. Siegler described changes in children's strategies as resembling overlapping waves, rather than abrupt movement from one to another strategy (**FIGURE 1.29**).

In one of his original studies, Siegler followed a small group of 4- to 5-year-old children every week for an 11-week period to assess changes in children's strategies for solving addition problems (Siegler, 1987; Siegler & Jenkins, 1989). Children showed gradual shifts from less advanced strategies to more advanced strategies. For example, to solve the problem 5 + 2, young children would count their fingers first up to 5 and then count 2 more, to reach 7. Older children would automatically start with the larger number 5, and then add 2 more to get to 7. Still older children might retrieve the number fact from memory. Because observations were frequent, Siegler could track the process of discovery as children learned that problems they had successfully solved in the past using a less advanced strategy could be solved in a different, more efficient way. However, even when children had discovered new strategies, they did not completely abandon their less advanced strategies. Rather, they relied on multiple strategies to solve the problems at each session. Sometimes a child would guess an answer, sometimes count every number, sometimes add the smaller to the larger number, and sometimes retrieve the answer from memory. Children's variability in strategies in a single session challenged Piaget's view that children display a unified and consistent way of thinking and solving problems at each developmental stage.

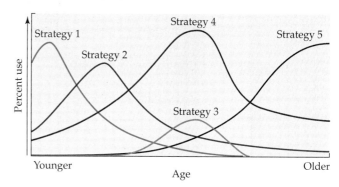

FIGURE 1.29 Microgenetic studies.   Robert Siegler used a microgenetic approach to study changes in children's mathematical reasoning and problem solving. His closely spaced observations showed how the use of certain strategies increased and others declined with children's experience and age. Siegler described changes as resembling a series of overlapping waves. (After R. S. Siegler. 1996. *Emerging Minds: The Process of Change in Children's Thinking.* Oxford University Press: New York, NY.)

When designing microgenetic studies, researchers must decide how frequently to sample children's behavior to accurately chart the developmental trajectory of a specific skill. For some behaviors, frequent sampling intervals may be necessary to describe variability of behaviors from day to day, especially during periods of rapid change, such as the transition from crawling to walking. Indeed, daily sampling of motor skills reveals a prolonged period of time when infants' behaviors fluctuate day to day: Infants might walk one day, but crawl the next, then revert back to walking, and so on, until they settle on walking as the preferred mode of locomotion (e.g., Adolph et al, 2008). Larger intervals of weeks or months would mask such fluctuations and cloud the picture of what infants actually do as they acquire new skills.

Behavioral Genetic Studies

Behavioral genetic studies tackle questions about genetic influences on development by measuring the degree of behavioral similarity among people who vary in genetic relatedness (Plomin & von Stumm, 2018). Twin studies, adoption studies, and genome-wide association tests fall under this broad umbrella.

Twin studies test whether genetic similarity relates to behavioral similarity. Identical twins have nearly the same genetic makeup, whereas fraternal twins are no more genetically alike than any two non-twin siblings. Suppose that similarity on a given behavior tends to be greater between identical twins than between fraternal twins; this would support the hypothesis that genetics contribute to the target behavior. The genetic basis of behaviors can also be investigated using an **adoption study**, in which researchers investigate whether adopted children are more similar to their biological parents and siblings (who have a similar genetic makeup) or to their adoptive parents and siblings (who share their home environment but are dissimilar genetically).

Both twin and adoption studies indicate that greater genetic relatedness predicts greater similarity on characteristics such as intelligence, antisocial behavior, attention-deficit/hyperactivity disorder, substance abuse, and personality. However, a common criticism of twin and adoption studies is that they fail to consider the potential effects of how parents treat children. Suppose, for instance, that an adopted child and a biological child living in the same home environment have different personalities. It is tempting to conclude that genetic differences account for their personality differences. However, this reasoning does not consider the fact that parents tend to treat their children differently, which could affect children's behaviors.

behavioral genetic study Studies that address questions about genetic influences on development by measuring the degree of behavioral similarity among people who vary in genetic relatedness

twin study A study that tests whether genetic similarity relates to behavioral similarity

adoption study A study that tests whether adopted children are more similar to their biological parents and siblings (who have a similar genetic makeup) or to their adoptive parents and siblings (who share their home environment but are dissimilar genetically)

genome-wide association tests
Tests that analyze massive amounts of DNA information across thousands of participants and then relate people's DNA composition to specific outcomes

DNA The carrier of genetic information on chromosomes

Genome-wide association tests offer a third approach to testing genetic inheritance. Such tests analyze massive amounts of **DNA** information—the carrier of genetic information on chromosomes—across thousands of participants and then relate people's DNA composition to specific outcomes. For example, researchers might ask whether a person's DNA corresponds to their intelligence. The researcher would gather information on the intelligence and DNA from participants and then use powerful computers to process the resulting information. If similarity in people's intelligence increases in line with the resemblance of their DNA, genetics can be considered to play a role (Plomin & von Strumm, 2018).

✓ **CHECK YOUR UNDERSTANDING 1.23**

1. Consider a developmental question for which you might decide to use each of the following study designs: (a) experiment; (b) correlational study; (c) longitudinal study; (d) cross-sectional study; (e) microgenetic study; (f) behavioral genetic study. Explain your choices.

Ensuring Scientific Rigor and Integrity

After researchers have settled on an approach for gathering information from study participants, it is important to ensure that research measures are reliable and valid, to promote confidence in the accuracy of the study's findings. In addition, over the past several years, researchers have recognized the importance of **replication** of research findings (Shrout & Rodgers, 2018). That is, all things being equal (although in reality nothing is ever entirely equal from lab to lab), other scientists should be able to obtain similar findings if they were to use the same methods and measures on a similar population as in the original study.

replication The ability of other scientists to obtain similar findings if they were to use the same methods and measures on a similar population as in the original study

Validity

LEARNING OBJECTIVE 1.24 Distinguish among the different types of validity and explain why they are crucial to the quality of research.

validity The degree to which a test (which can be an actual test, questionnaire, and so forth) measures what it is supposed to measure; there exist different forms of validity

Validity refers to the degree to which a test or task (which can be an actual test, questionnaire, and so forth) measures what it is supposed to measure. For example, imagine that developmental scientists wish to test whether punitive disciplinary practices (such as hitting) lead to child aggression. They ask parents to answer questions about their disciplinary practices with the goal of relating parents' answers to children's observed aggression in the classroom. The questionnaire contains 20 questions asking parents whether they engage in certain types of discipline (hitting, yelling, giving children "time out," ignoring misbehavior, etc.), and the researchers create a composite score of "discipline" from parents' answers. A first step to testing the hypothesized connection between discipline and child aggression is to examine various types of validity in parents' discipline scores (**TABLE 1.4**):

face validity The degree to which the purpose of a test is clear to people who look it over

- **Face validity** simply means that the purpose of the test (here questions around discipline) is clear to people who look it over (Nevo, 1985). In the example of punitive discipline, most people would agree that asking parents what they do when their child misbehaves, followed by various options (hit, yell, and time out), has strong face validity. In contrast, if the researchers claimed that the same items assessed parents' love for their children, you might be more skeptical.

construct validity The extent to which a test measures what it purports to measure

- **Construct validity** is the extent to which a test measures what it purports to measure. For example, if researchers developed a test of "intelligence,"

TABLE 1.4 ■ Types of Validity	
Type of Validity	Explanation
Face Validity	The purpose of the measure is clear to people who look it over
Concurrent Validity	Reflects the degree to which a measure corresponds to another measure that tests the same phenomenon at the same point in time
Predictive Validity	Reflects the degree to which a measure predicts a criterion to be measured at a future point in time
External Validity	Refers to the extent to which a measure can be applied across different settings or different groups of people

construct validity would refer to the extent that the test accurately measures a person's intelligence.

- **Concurrent validity** reflects the degree to which scores on a test correspond to those on another test of the same construct at the same point in time. For example, if researchers developed a new intelligence test that they claimed could assess a child's intelligence in a fraction of the time it takes to conduct the commonly used test, concurrent validity would be shown if children's scores on the new test correlated strongly with their scores on the standard test.

- **Predictive validity** reflects the degree to which scores on a test at one point in time predict scores on a similar or related test or criterion (often over time). In the intelligence example, predictive validity would be demonstrated if the new intelligence test predicted intelligence years later or predicted SAT scores later in high school.

- **External, or ecological, validity** refers to the extent to which a test can be applied across different settings or groups of people. A test's external validity is especially challenging in cross-cultural investigations, in which items developed to assess one population might not apply to a different population. For example, researchers testing memory might ask children to remember a list of words taken from various categories (vehicles, movies, school subjects), but the words may be unfamiliar to children living in a remote farming village in South America, where children don't encounter many vehicles, attend movies, or go to school. The researchers will have to modify their list to include words that are more familiar to children, such as the names of farm tools and crops.

✓ CHECK YOUR UNDERSTANDING 1.24

1. Define face validity, construct validity, concurrent validity, predictive validity, and external validity.

Reliability

LEARNING OBJECTIVE 1.25 Define different forms of reliability.

The **reliability** of a test or a task refers to the consistency of scores for participants across different observers or over time. There are two common types of reliability:

- **Interobserver reliability** refers to the extent to which different observers using a test arrive at the same results. (Again the term "test" can refer

concurrent validity The degree to which scores on a test correspond to those on another test of the same construct at the same point in time

predictive validity The degree to which scores on a test at one point in time predict scores on a similar or related test or criterion (often over time)

external, or ecological, validity The degree to which a test can be applied across different settings or groups of people

reliability The consistency of scores for participants across different observers or over time; two common types of reliability are interobserver reliability and test-retest reliability

interobserver reliability The degree to which different observers using a test arrive at the same results to different things, such as the frequencies of behaviors based on observations, scores on an instrument or questionnaire, and so forth.) For example, imagine that two researchers collaborate on a study of how 3-year-old children regulate their behaviors. They place children in a room full of tempting toys, and tell the children not to touch the toys. The researchers then independently score children's behaviors from video recordings of the session. One researcher scores a child as high in behavioral regulation and the second researcher scores the same child as low in behavioral regulation. Their lack of agreement indicates that the test of behavioral regulation may need to be modified and/or one or both researchers may need further training before the study can proceed.

test-retest reliability The degree to which an individual receives the same score (or at least a close score) when tested at different times under similar conditions

- **Test-retest reliability** is seen when an individual receives the same score (or at least a close score) when tested at different times under similar conditions. In the example of behavioral regulation, if children's scores on a second assessment were not consistent with their scores on a first assessment, it would be impossible to determine which score (if either) accurately measured the children's true ability to regulate behaviors. Furthermore, if children's self-regulation scores are inconsistent across two assessments, it is unlikely that the scores will predict other measures of self-regulation at the same point in time or later in development.

✓ CHECK YOUR UNDERSTANDING 1.25

1. Which type of reliability is violated if a child's aggression in the classroom on the first week of school does not relate to the same child's aggression a week later?
2. Which type of reliability is violated if two observers do not agree on how positive children are in their emotions while playing a game with peers?

Scientific Replicability and Transparency

LEARNING OBJECTIVE 1.26 Explain the concepts of replication and transparency in research, and why transparency is vital to replication.

replicability The degree to which the findings of a study are confirmed when repeated using the identical procedures applied in the original study with a new sample

Scientific **replicability** refers to the degree to which the findings of a study are confirmed when repeated using the identical procedures applied in the original study with a new sample. In 2005, John Ioannidis, a professor at Stanford University's School of Medicine, published an article entitled "Why Most Published Research Findings Are False" in which he showed that medical research studies mostly failed to replicate either the size or even the existence of the findings in the previous studies. This article, and other similar critiques that followed, generated a lot of discussion among scientists about the "replication crisis," and what could be done to address the issue (**FIGURE 1.30**).

Researchers can adopt several strategies to raise the bar of scientific integrity. One strategy revolves around scientific transparency, or complete openness, about all steps of the scientific enterprise. Indeed, recommendations around **open science** encourage researchers to fully document and share information on a study's procedures, recruitment methods, participant characteristics, measures, raw data, analyses, and funding sources (Gilmore et al., 2017; Nosek, 2017; Gennetian, Tamis-LeMonda, & Frank, 2020) (**FIGURE 1.31**).

open science A movement that encourages researchers to fully document and share information on a study's procedures, recruitment methods, participant characteristics, measures, raw data, analyses, and funding sources

To illustrate the connection between transparency (openness) and replication, consider what might happen if a researcher provided insufficient documentation about study procedures. This would certainly make it difficult for other researchers to accurately replicate what was done. And sometimes, even when researchers provide critical information about a study, findings may not replicate for unforeseen reasons. Imagine, for example, if two researchers wanted to examine children's spatial skills by asking children to fit shapes into

Courtesy of Maki Naro – https://thenib.com/repeat-after-me/

FIGURE 1.30 **The purported replication crisis.** Replicability refers to the degree to which the findings of a study are confirmed when repeated using the identical procedures applied in the original study. An article published in 2005 by Professor John Ioannidis indicated that the medical findings of many studies could not be replicated. The article sparked concern about the failure to replicate science and led to various suggestions about how to address the potential "replication crisis."

shape sorters. Both researchers use the same materials, test children of the same age, and apply the same trial lengths, but they differ in something as basic as where they position the shapes relative to the child. One experimenter lays the shapes out in front of the child, making each shape easy to identify. The other researcher dumps the shapes in a pile. If the children in these two studies differ in their performance, the lack of replication might be due to minor methodological differences that could easily have been avoided had the researchers shared information about where to place the shapes. Of course, it is difficult to communicate every little step of a research study, and so full transparency of procedures is not easy to achieve. However, one way to ensure transparency is to video record procedures to share with the scientific community on platforms designed for video sharing (Gilmore & Adolph, 2017).

✓ **CHECK YOUR UNDERSTANDING 1.26**

1. What are some steps a researcher can take to ensure transparency and optimize the chances of a study being replicated?

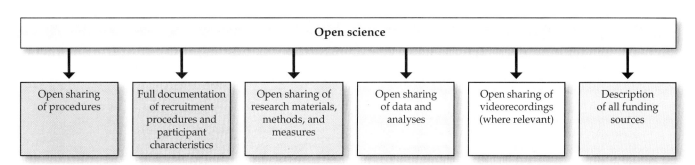

FIGURE 1.31 **Open science framework.** Open science refers to scientific transparency and openness about all pieces of the scientific enterprise.

Ethics in Research

LEARNING OBJECTIVE 1.27 Explain why developmental research must adhere to ethical guidelines and the process used to ensure the ethical treatment of children.

In 1961, when German Nazi Adolf Eichmann was being tried in court for his criminal acts, psychologist Stanley Milgram designed a study to examine the bounds of people's obedience to authority figures (**FIGURE 1.32**). Milgram wondered whether Eichmann and others involved in the Holocaust were "just following orders." Would people physically harm other people because they felt obligated to obey the commands of a perceived authority figure?

In what has become a highly controversial set of studies, Milgram instructed participants to press a button to give electric shocks to a person in another room every time the person in the other room answered incorrectly, with the shocks increasing in intensity over the course of the session. In reality, no shocks were delivered—the person in the other room was a confederate (or actor)—but participants did not know this. Despite the agonized screams and pleas faked by the confederate in the other room, participants followed the experimenter's orders. They continued to inflict pain just because Milgram told them to do so.

Milgram's experiment produced subsequent psychological harm to some of the participants, who reported damage to self-image and trust in others after they realized that they had been deceived (Baumrind, 1980). And, the study's disturbing findings raised an ethical debate about how far an experimenter should be permitted to go in the name of science. John B. Watson's inducing of extreme anxiety and fear in Little Albert, discussed earlier in this chapter, raises similar ethical concerns and would be unacceptable today.

To avoid such ethical violations, various organizations, including the American Psychological Association and the Society for Research on Child Development (SRCD), have formulated codes of ethical conduct for researchers to follow (**FIGURE 1.33**). The guidelines follow the same requirements that universities and the federal government expect of researchers who study children, and include (but are not limited to) the following:

- The research must *not harm participants* in any way.
- Participation in research must be *voluntary*. Participants should sign documents giving their informed consent to participate. Children who cannot read may be asked to provide verbal assent, and when children are too young to give consent, legal guardians must provide informed consent.
- Participants have the *right to withdraw* from the study at any time and to not participate in procedures that make them feel uncomfortable.
- Participants must be assured of *confidentiality* of all the information they provide. For example, participant data should be stored in locked closets and/or in password-protected computerized formats, and identifiers such as names and social security numbers should not be connected to individual data.
- Participants must be *debriefed after any study deception*. For example, if an experimenter asks a child to solve a puzzle that is impossible to solve, resulting in a high level of frustration for the child, debriefing would try to mitigate the negative effects of that frustration.

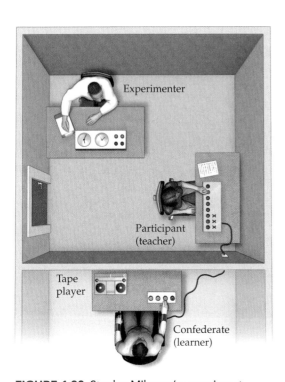

FIGURE 1.32 Stanley Milgram's experiment. In 1961, psychologist Stanley Milgram designed a study to examine the extent to which people would engage in harmful behaviors toward others out of obedience to authority figures. His research was motivated by the heinous actions of German Nazi Adolf Eichmann, who was being tried in court for his criminal acts at the time. (After S. Milgram. 1974. *Obedience to Authority: An Experimental View*. Harper & Row: New York, NY.)

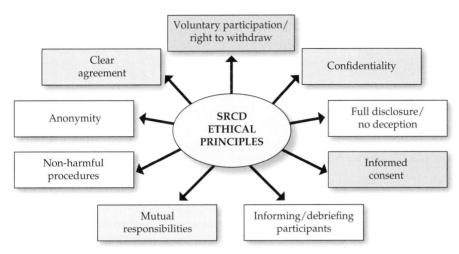

FIGURE 1.33 Ethical research principles.   In response to ethical concerns, various organizations including the Society for Research on Child Development formulated codes of ethical conduct that developmental scientists must follow to protect the rights of participants in research studies.

- Researchers should evaluate the *risk-benefit ratio* to ensure that the potential benefits of a research study outweigh the potential risks. For example, if a researcher of children's learning believes that a certain improved curriculum would facilitate math learning, and knows from other research that a prior tested curriculum was ineffective, it would be unethical to randomly assign children to be taught with the "ineffective" curriculum.

   To ensure that researchers adhere to ethical guidelines, they must obtain approval from their institution's **scientific review board** by submitting a written application of their research plans. The membership of scientific review boards typically includes scientists from disciplines across a university or institution whose research involves human subjects, and also might include legal representatives, university staff, and community members with no affiliation to the university. After reading the application, the review board may ask for changes in aspects of a study, and the researcher cannot begin the study until the study receives approval.

scientific review board A university board that reviews research study plans to ensure they are ethical and well designed; the board is usually comprised of scientists from multiple disciplines and also might include legal representatives, university staff, and community members with no affiliation to the university

✓ CHECK YOUR UNDERSTANDING 1.27

1. List the ethical guidelines that researchers must follow when studying children.

◼ CLOSING THOUGHTS

Setting the Stage

This first chapter was intended to introduce you to the core goals of developmental psychology and the theories and scientific approach that researchers take to study developmental change. In Chapter 2, you will read about the foundations for development, including the role of heredity in different domains of development; the functions, structures, and changes of the living brain; and how a person's genes and brain interact with environmental experiences to affect development. Chapter 3 will discuss environmental and genetic influences at the start of life, including how the growing fetus is influenced by and engages with its intrauterine environment in preparation for life outside the womb. The remaining chapters will examine development during infancy, early childhood, middle childhood, and adolescence. Within each age period, you will learn about changes in core developmental domains—health and physical development, perceptual and cognitive development, language development, and emotional and social development.

Throughout this book, you will be exposed to two core principles of development that together underscore the importance of taking a "whole child" approach to development. First, *development occurs in context*. You will come to appreciate that a child's environment, ranging from home to school to neighborhood to culture, powerfully influences developmental change, much like the contexts of soil, sun, nutrients, and water determine a plant's growth. Second, *development has cascading effects*. That is, in line with what you've learned about developmental cascades, changes in one area of development reverberate throughout the system, affecting multiple domains of functioning within and across developmental time. These two cross-cutting themes—development in context and developmental cascades—are woven throughout each chapter as a continual reminder that development is much more than fleeting change in a child.

■ Chapter Summary

The Goals of Developmental Science

- The three goals of developmental science are to describe change, explain change, and apply research findings to practices, programs, and policies.
- Research in basic developmental science is aimed at describing and explaining development by unearthing fundamental laws of learning and development.
- Research in applied developmental science is aimed at applying scientific principles and knowledge to real-life problems.
- The distinction between basic and applied developmental science is not absolute—advances in basic science lead to improved applications, and the outcomes of those applications feed back into scientific advances.

Describing Development

- Developmental change is both quantitative and qualitative, but the distinction is not always clear, and different developmentalists emphasize one or the other.
- Children show enormous variability in development, including in developmental onsets, rates of change, and the forms that skills take. The forms that skills take are especially pronounced among individuals from different cultural backgrounds.
- Research indicates that stability is the rule in most areas of development. However, environmental influences can result in instability, reflecting the plasticity of human development.

Explaining Development

- Development is the product of a complex interaction between "nature" (e.g., genes) and "nurture" (e.g., environment and experiences), but individual developmental scientists tend to emphasize one or the other in their theories and research.

- Developmental cascades occur when changes in one area of development instigate changes within and across domains at the same point in time or at a later time in development. The effects of cascades can be positive, neutral, or negative.

Applying Developmental Science

- Developmental studies have implications for knowledge about child-rearing and practices, programs, and policies that affect children and families.
- Programs such as Reach Out and Read, federal programs for children such as Head Start, and policies on parental leave are examples that reflect the translation of basic research findings to application.

Theoretical Orientations

- A scientific theory is a set of interconnected statements that explains a set of observable events.
- Each theoretical orientation in developmental science takes a unique perspective on describing and explaining change.
- Theoretical orientations also differ in the scope—the domains of development they study and the research methods they use.

Foundational Theories

- Evolutionary theory describes human behavior as evolutionarily adaptive, thereby building on Charles Darwin's writings about species survival.
- Individuals with adaptive traits have an increased chance of surviving and reproducing, and thus passing the adaptive traits on to future generations, a process called natural selection.
- Evolutionary theorists recognize the importance of learned behaviors but consider learned behaviors to be the product of innate biological tendencies.

- Psychodynamic theories focus on the development of personality, which is viewed as a product of conscious and unconscious forces, with individuals progressing through a series of stages as they attempt to resolve certain conflicts.

- Sigmund Freud's psychosexual stage theory considers the goals of survival and reproduction to be the main catalysts for behavior and development. Children are seen as progressing through five stages as they learn to satisfy survival and reproduction drives in ways that are socially and psychologically acceptable.

- Erik Erikson's psychosocial stage theory focuses on the conflicts that individuals encounter as they struggle to answer the question "Who am I?" Erickson views individuals as passing through eight stages, in each of which they experience a conflict about their identity. If they resolve the conflict positively, they can move on to the next stage; otherwise, their personality will be negatively affected.

- Behaviorism is based on the idea that the sole focus of psychology should be on observable human behavior, not on unobservable mental states.

- Behaviorism views learning as a result of environmental influences, thus placing full weight on the nurture end of the nature-nurture continuum.

- Classical conditioning—in which a stimulus can take on a new significance when paired with other, personally meaningful stimuli—applies to many types of everyday learning.

- Operant conditioning—in which the form and frequency of a behavior depend on how the behavior is rewarded or punished—is often used in studies of infant learning and memory.

- Jean Piaget advanced a constructivist theory that underscored children's active role in learning and development, which he viewed as the product of both nature and nurture.

- Piaget viewed development as a process comprising four qualitatively distinct, universal, and invariant stages. At each stage, children have schemas that provide them with a way of organizing information and understanding and acting on the world.

- Piaget claimed that children move through stages by the processes of assimilation, disequilibrium, and accommodation.

- Vygotsky's sociocultural theory emphasized the zone of proximal development and the role of social interactions in children's learning. According to Vygotsky, children can master more challenging tasks when interacting with knowledgeable adults (e.g., parents and teachers) than when acting alone.

Contemporary Theories

- Nativist theories propose that innate, core capacities, essential for human adaptation, evolved over time in the form of modules or structures wired in the brain. Features of evolutionary theory can be seen in nativist approaches to development.

- Social learning theory extends the principles of operant conditioning to the study of how children learn the social behaviors that society expects of them, including through observational learning and vicarious reinforcement.

- Information processing theories focus on how children attend to, process, and remember information in their environments, drawing an analogy between the human mind and a computer.

- Developmental systems theories view human behavior as the product of a complex, ever-changing system, where developmental changes occur in response to many different kinds of factors. New behaviors are seen as emerging out of complex interactions between children's bodies and actions in the environment.

- Bioecological theories (a form of developmental systems theory) focus on the effects of multiple environmental contexts on human development, including how children's biology and behaviors affect development. Urie Bronfenbrenner advanced a comprehensive theory that conceptualized development as the result of five nested systems along with a biological dimension.

- Sociocultural theories focus on the contexts of child development but assign a more central role to culture than do other theories. Sociocultural theorists advanced the concepts of a cultural learning environment and developmental niche.

- Culture is defined as the shared physical, behavioral, and symbolic aspects of a community that are learned and passed on through social interactions.

Conducting Research

- Developmental research can be hypothesis driven or discovery driven. Hypothesis-driven research follows the scientific method: identifying a question, formulating a hypothesis to answer the question, testing the hypothesis with a research study, and analyzing the results of the study and drawing conclusions. Discovery–driven science approaches a question without pre-formulated hypotheses.

- Sampling refers to the characteristics of the participants in a study. Convenience sampling can lead to biased findings, because the sample might not be representative. Sampling is especially important when comparing two or more groups of participants on a variable.

- A research method is the approach taken to gathering data for a study. Methods include: interviews, surveys, structured and naturalistic observations, and physiological assessments.

- A study design is a specific plan for conducting a study, a plan that will allow the investigator to directly address the research questions. Study designs include experiments, correlational studies, longitudinal studies, cross-sectional studies, cohort-sequential studies, microgenetic studies, and behavioral genetic studies.

- In an experiment, the independent variable is manipulated to see whether that causes a change in the dependent variable. Typically, the participants in an experiment are divided into an experimental group (participants who receive the experimental manipulation) and a control group (participants who do not receive the experimental manipulation). Experimenters must exercise careful control over possible confounding variables, which can create problems in interpreting the results of the experiment.

- A longitudinal study follows the same participants over time, allowing researchers to test stability and prediction. However, longitudinal studies can suffer from attrition.
- A cross-sectional study compares children of different ages at roughly the same point in time. Cross-sectional studies are less costly than longitudinal studies, but do not permit a test of stability or prediction.
- In cohort-sequential designs researchers follow two or more groups of children of different ages over time. Such designs contain a mix of longitudinal and cross-sectional designs, thus offering the benefits of studying stability and prediction but over shorter time frames than typical in longitudinal designs.
- Microgenetic studies involve frequent, closely spaced observations of children and/or detailed observations of learning in real time, yielding rich descriptive information about the process of change.
- Behavioral genetic studies include twin studies, adoption studies, and genome-wide association studies. Such study designs are especially useful for assessing genetic contributions to development.

Ensuring Scientific Rigor and Integrity
- The scientific adequacy of studies depends on their satisfying the criteria of validity, reliability, and replicability.

- Various types of validity include face validity, construct validity, concurrent validity, predictive validity, and external validity.
- Validity refers to the degree to which a measure assesses what it is supposed to measure.
- Reliability reflects the degree to which a measure yields consistent scores for participants, as assessed either by different observers or at different points in time. Test-retest reliability and interobserver reliability are two types of reliability.
- Replicability refers to the degree to which the findings of a study are confirmed when the study is repeated using the exact methods of the original study in a new sample.
- Scientific transparency refers to openness about all features of a study, including procedures, recruitment methods, participant characteristics, and so forth. Transparency is vital for replication, and video recordings can help to ensure transparency.
- Researchers of child development must follow an ethical code of conduct that includes not harming participants in any way; voluntary participation and informed consent in research by children and families; and confidentiality of data.
- To ensure adherence to ethical guidelines, researchers must present their work to a scientific review board for approval.

Thinking Like a Developmentalist

1. You wonder whether young children's viewing of programs that involve characters engaged in helping and sharing behaviors might prompt young children to likewise share and help peers. What kind of study would you implement, and why? What decisions would you need to make as you develop your study?

2. You have an interest in studying adolescents' social development, and in particular the quality of their relationships with other people. You wish to develop a new observational measure to assess positive and negative interactions between teens and their peers. How would you go about developing the measure? What sample would you recruit into your

study? What behaviors would you observe? What would you need to do to evaluate the different types of validity and reliability in your new measure?

3. In your study of adolescent relationships with peers, you believe that high-quality peer interactions influence teens' relationships with teachers and ultimately affect adolescents' grade point average (GPA) and psychological well-being through the later high school years. What type of study would you design to test this hypothesis? What concept did you learn about that captures your hypotheses on the influences of teen peer relationships on later outcomes?

Heredity, Environment, and the Brain

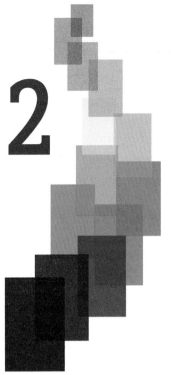

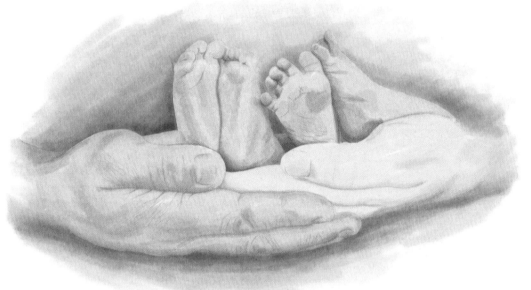

Drawing by Minxin Cheng from a photo by Fallon Michael on Unsplash

M ark Twain once stated that truth is often stranger than fiction. Psychiatrist Peter Neubauer's unethical experiment to test the role of genetics and environment in development offers a riveting confirmation of Twain's observation. Neubauer worked at an agency in the United States that matched Jewish orphans with adoptive families. Unknown to anyone, he manipulated the placement of three sets of twins and one set of triplets. The families had no idea that their single adoptees were twins or triplets. Neubauer merely told them that he wanted to study the development of adopted children. In reality, his goal was to track genetically identical siblings who were raised under experimentally controlled circumstances. How would the children turn out? Would genetics or environment reign?

Identical triplets David Kellman, Eddy Galland, and Bobby Shafran were victims of Neubauer's scheme (**FIGURE 2.1**). The three brothers were born to a single mother in 1961, given up for adoption at 6 months of age, and placed by Neubauer into selected adoptive homes—one with a blue-collar family of limited economic means; one with a middle-class family of moderate means; and one with a wealthy family of high economic means. After 19 years of separation, two of the brothers met by happenstance while attending the same college; the third united with his brothers after news of the reunion hit the media.

At first, the triplets noticed many similarities: they looked identical, shared behavioral quirks, and struggled with depression. Gradually, however, their differences surfaced, including differences in personality traits, abilities to cope with stress, and social relationships and careers, revealing the power of environmental forces.

FIGURE 2.1 Identical triplets David Kellman, Eddy Galland, and Bobby Shafran.   The brothers were victims of Peter Neubauer's experiment to test the role of genetics and the environment in development. The three brothers were born to a single mother in 1961 and placed into different adoptive homes at 6 months of age. After 19 years of separation, two of the brothers met while attending the same college; the third united with his brothers once news of the reunion hit the media.

As the brothers investigated the circumstances surrounding their separation, the unethical backstory eventually came to light, and out of fear of the consequences, Neubauer never published the results of his experiment. Information about the 13 children whose lives he manipulated like puppets on a string remain legally sealed in a Yale archive until 2065. However, the triplet's story became the focus of a highly acclaimed 2018 documentary, *Three Identical Strangers*, which premiered at the Sundance Film Festival and was in contention for an Academy Award.

This story illustrates the longstanding fascination of scientists and the public with genetically identical individuals. Researchers long believed that the study of twins might offer a foolproof way to distinguish biological from environmental influences in human development. They reasoned that by comparing twin siblings who were genetically matched (that is, identical, or monozygotic) versus those who were partially matched on their genetics (fraternal twins, or dizygotic twins) they would finally determine the heritability of human behaviors and traits such as substance use, sexual orientation, mood and anxiety disorders, intelligence, personality, and so on. However, the story of development is not that simple. Twin and adoption studies alone do not hold the key to the heritability of human behaviors and traits. Rather, genes interact with environmental influences in highly complex ways. Everyday experiences drive the expression of genes, and development itself is a context for gene expression.

The goal of this chapter is to shed light on the complex intertwining of biology and environment in human development. You will learn about the methods that scientists use to study genetics, brain, and behavior, and the scientific insights that new technologies offer on learning and development. By the chapter's end, you will appreciate the inseparable effects of genetics, environment, and brain—how a person's changing biology and experiences reciprocally affect one another and shape how people interact in their environments. You will come to understand the critical need to put all the pieces together to understand the forces that underpin developmental change.

■ *Genetics and the Environment*

Before Neubauer sought to manipulate people's lives in a quest to understand the role of genetics in development, Austrian monk Gregor Mendel (1822–1884) made a fascinating discovery while tending his monastery garden. Mendel observed that some of the traits of parent pea plants, such as yellow seed color, appeared disproportionately in daughter plants, and hypothesized that underlying factors—what we now call genes—determined the traits. Moreover, some factors occurred more often than others. For example, the factor determining yellow seed color seemed to occur more often than the factor determining green seed color. As Mendel crossbred his pea plants, he observed the patterns of inheritance shown in **FIGURE 2.2**. In a similar vein, Neubauer could not force crossbreeding on humans, but he still engaged in unethical "cross-raising" of children, while keeping genetics constant.

As you will learn, scientists today have valuable technologies at their disposal that allow them to delve into the mysteries of **genetics**—the study of genes and heredity—and environmental influences. And you will see that the study of animals offers unique insights into human development.

genetics The study of genes and heredity and how genes affect an individual's characteristics, such as personality and physical appearance

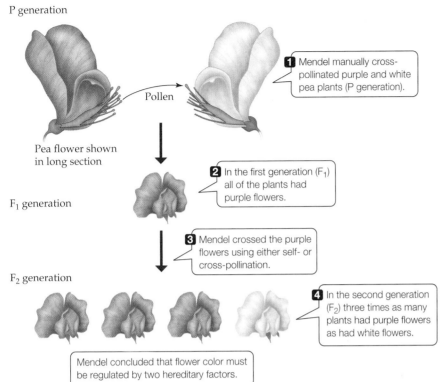

P generation

Pollen

Pea flower shown
in long section

1 Mendel manually cross-
pollinated purple and white
pea plants (P generation).

F_1 generation

2 In the first generation (F_1)
all of the plants had
purple flowers.

3 Mendel crossed the purple
flowers using either self- or
cross-pollination.

F_2 generation

4 In the second generation
(F_2) three times as many
plants had purple flowers
as had white flowers.

Mendel concluded that flower color must
be regulated by two hereditary factors.

FIGURE 2.2 Mendel's pea plants. Gregor Mendel conducted a series of experiments in which he crossbred pea plants in his monastery garden and observed the resulting patterns of inheritance.

Genetic Foundations

Development begins well before birth. In fact, the path that leads genes to interact with environmental influences begins even before sexual reproduction. It starts with the behaviors of mothers and fathers, and even their own parents, who collectively establish conditions that will play out in complex and cascading ways to shape the development of a new human. For simplicity, here we begin with conception, and show that development is a constantly evolving process. Mutations may occur along the way, and environmental forces ranging from the microorganisms of the womb to the fetus's own activity affect gene expression and developmental paths.

Chromosomes, DNA, and Genes

LEARNING OBJECTIVE 2.1 Explain the connection among chromosomes, DNA, and genes.

Chromosomes—structures found in the nucleus of living cells—carry genetic information (**FIGURE 2.3**). Each chromosome is a single molecule of **DNA** (**deoxyribonucleic acid**). And each DNA molecule consists of a long sequence of four chemical subunits called **bases**. James Watson and Francis Crick determined the exact structure of DNA—the famous double helix—in 1953 (**FIGURE 2.4**). This led to the discovery of the **genetic code**, the set of rules by which particular sequences of bases produce the proteins that govern the workings of living cells.

As you can see in Figure 2.4, the DNA double helix consists of two threadlike strands that spiral around one another. Each strand is made up of a backbone of alternating sugar and phosphate groups. One of the four bases— guanine (G), cytosine (C), thymine (T), and adenine (A)—is attached to each sugar group of the backbone. The bases in the two strands pair up to form

chromosomes Threadlike structures found in living cells that carry genetic information; human cells have 23 pairs of chromosomes

DNA (deoxyribonucleic acid) A nucleic acid that is the main constituent of chromosomes; DNA contains the genetic information for the development of living organisms

bases Long sequences of chemical subunits that make up each DNA molecule

genetic code A set of rules by which particular sequences of bases create the proteins that govern the workings of living cells

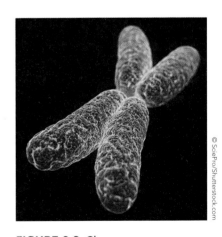

© SciePro/Shutterstock.com

FIGURE 2.3 Chromosomes. Chromosomes are structures found in the nucleus of living cells—they are the carriers of genetic information.

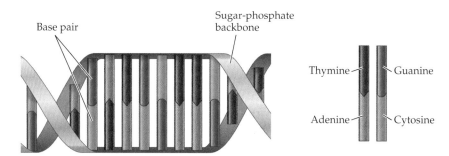

FIGURE 2.4 DNA double helix. The DNA double helix consists of two threadlike strands that wind around one another like a twisted ladder. Each strand contains a backbone of alternating sugar and phosphate groups. One of the four bases guanine—(G), cytosine (C), thymine (T), and adenine (A)—is attached to each sugar group. The bases in the two strands pair up to form base pairs. (After S. M. Breedlove. 2015. *Principles of Psychology*. Sinauer/Oxford University Press: Sunderland, MA.)

gene A small segment of DNA that codes for the production of a particular protein and specifies the sequence of base pairs in the DNA segment; a unit of heredity that is passed on from parent to offspring; hundreds to thousands of genes exist in each human chromosome

gametes Sex cells or an organism's reproductive cells; female gametes are called ova or egg cells and male gametes are called sperm; gametes have only 23 chromosomes each

fertilization The process in which gametes join together to form a zygote

zygote The cell that is created when gamete cells (ovum and sperm) are joined; the zygote has 46 chromosomes in 23 pairs

meiosis The process in which a single human cell divides twice to create four cells that contain half the amount of the original genetic information

mitosis The process in which the zygote's chromosome replicates, resulting in two identical cells with 23 chromosome pairs, which replicate and divide to create four cells containing the identical 46 chromosomes in 23 pairs; this process repeats and every cell keeps the identical genetic information

sex chromosomes A type of chromosome that is involved in sex determination; one of the 23 pairs of chromosomes in the zygote is made up of the sex chromosomes; sex chromosomes have two forms: X or male and Y or female

X chromosome One of two sex chromosomes; females have two X chromosomes in their cells

base pairs—the rungs of a twisted ladder-shaped molecule. G always pairs with C, and T always pairs with A, but the sequence of pairs can occur in any order along the ladder (e.g., G–C, G–C, T–A, A–T, C–G, T–A, and so on). A **gene** is a small segment of DNA that codes for the production of a particular protein and specifies the sequence of base pairs in the DNA segment. Each human chromosome contains hundreds to thousands of genes. Those genes hold much of the story about who we are.

✓ CHECK YOUR UNDERSTANDING 2.1

1. Define the terms chromosome, DNA, and gene.

From Gametes to Human Beings

LEARNING OBJECTIVE 2.2 Explain the process that leads from the fertilization of a zygote to the expression of a sex-linked trait.

Human cells contain 46 chromosomes. However, the **gametes**, or sex cells—ova (in females) and sperm (in males)—contain only 23 chromosomes each. The reason for the 23 chromosomes initially in the gametes is that human cells divide through the process called **meiosis** (**FIGURE 2.5**). Gamete cells join in a process called **fertilization**, resulting in a **zygote** of 46 chromosomes in 23 pairs—one member of each pair inherited from the father and one from the mother.

The zygote then undergoes a process called **mitosis** (**FIGURE 2.6**), in which the chromosomes first replicate (making 46) and then sort themselves into two sets of 23 pairs before the cell divides, yielding two identical cells with 23 pairs each. The two resulting cells then replicate and divide to produce four cells, each containing the identical 46 chromosomes in 23 pairs. The process of mitosis keeps repeating, with every cell retaining the identical genetic information. Note, however, that even when DNA starts out in the same place, as in the case of identical twins, by the time they are born, their experiences in utero (including possible mutations to the genes of one twin and not the other) will result in different gene expressions that will shape future development (e.g., Van Dongen et al., 2012). We return to this point later in the chapter under the topic of epigenetics.

Sex Chromosomes

One of the 23 pairs of chromosomes in the zygote is made up of the **sex chromosomes**, which can take two forms: the female **X chromosome** and the male

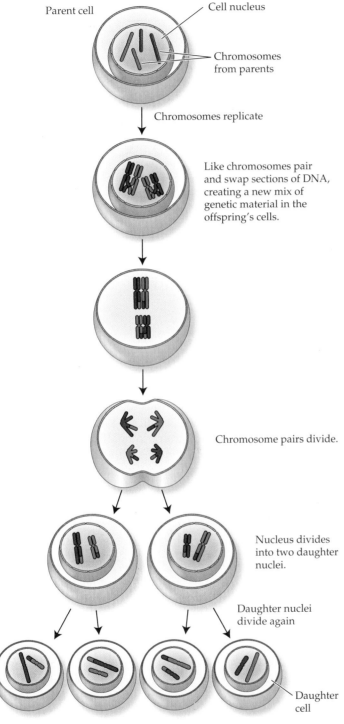

Parent cell

Cell nucleus

Chromosomes from parents

Chromosomes replicate

Like chromosomes pair and swap sections of DNA, creating a new mix of genetic material in the offspring's cells.

Chromosome pairs divide.

Nucleus divides into two daughter nuclei.

Daughter nuclei divide again

Daughter cell

Daughter nuclei have single chromosomes and a new mix of genetic material.

FIGURE 2.5 Meiosis and fertilization.   Most normal human cells include 46 chromosomes. Fertilization (the joining of the gamete cells [ova and sperm] from each parent) results in a zygote that contains the usual 46 chromosomes in 23 pairs, with one member of each pair inherited from the father and one from the mother. (After D. M. Hillis et al. 2020. *Life: The Science of Biology*. 12th ed. Sinauer/ Oxford University Press: Sunderland, MA.)

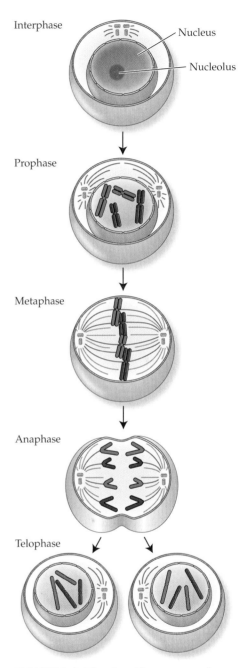

Interphase

Nucleus

Nucleolus

Prophase

Metaphase

Anaphase

Telophase

FIGURE 2.6 Mitosis.   The process of mitosis occurs when chromosomes first replicate (making 46) and then sort them- selves into two sets of 23 pairs before the cell divides, yielding two identical cells with 23 pairs each. The two resulting cells then replicate and divide to produce four cells, each containing the identical 46 chromo- somes in 23 pairs. The process of mitosis keeps repeating, with every cell retaining the identical genetic information. (After D. M. Hillis et al. 2020. *Life: The Science of Biology*. 12th ed. Sinauer/Oxford University Press: Sunderland, MA.)

Chromosomes in the cell nuclei for males and females

Male

Female

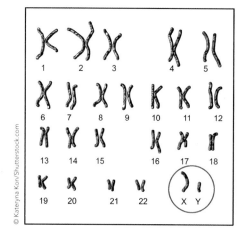
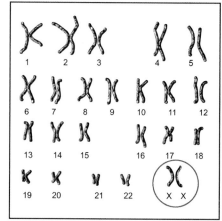

FIGURE 2.7 Sex chromosomes. Photos of the set of chromosomes of two individuals show the sex chromosomes (circled). Sex chromosomes can take two forms: the female X chromosome and the male Y chromosome. An XX zygote will develop into a female, and an XY zygote will develop into a male.

Y chromosome One of two sex chromosomes; males have one X chromosome and one Y chromosome in their cells

alleles Different versions or forms of a gene; the various forms are on a particular location on a chromosome

dominant allele A variation of a gene that will create a phenotype even while other alleles are present

recessive allele A variation of a gene that needs to be homozygous when inherited to create a phenotype

phenotype A set of outward, observable characteristics of an individual; these characteristics result from the interaction between the individual's genotype and the environment

genotype The gene or set of genes that determines an individual's traits; the genotype may be considered an individual's genetic makeup

Y chromosome (**FIGURE 2.7**). A zygote with two X chromosomes (referred to as XX) will develop into a female, and a zygote with one X chromosome and one Y chromosome (referred to as XY) will develop into a male. Because males are XY, meiosis results in half of a father's sperm containing X chromosomes and half of his sperm containing Y chromosomes. In contrast, because females are XX, all of a mother's ova contain an X chromosome. If a sperm with an X chromosome fertilizes an ovum, the zygote will be XX and will develop into a female. But if fertilization involves a sperm with a Y chromosome, the zygote will be XY and will develop into a male, with a gene on the Y chromosome triggering the production of testes. The X chromosome is much larger than the Y chromosome and contains many more genes.

Alleles, Phenotypes, and Genotypes

In the other 22 pairs of chromosomes, the members of the pair are similar in size and contain matching genes, but the matching genes are not necessarily identical—genes can occur in different versions called **alleles**. For example, in Mendel's pea plants the gene for flower color had two alleles, a **dominant allele** for purple flower color (P) and a **recessive allele** for white flower color (p). That is, white flowers appeared only in the plants in which both members of the chromosome pair contained the recessive allele. The four possible combinations of dominant and recessive alleles—dominant-dominant (PP), dominant-recessive (Pp), recessive-dominant (pP), and recessive-recessive (pp)—mean that a 3:1 ratio of purple flowers to white flowers could be expected, and that was, in fact, the ratio that Mendel observed (**FIGURE 2.8**).

The example of pea plant color illustrates the concepts of phenotype and genotype. A **phenotype** refers to the outward appearance of a particular trait, whereas a **genotype** refers to the gene or set of genes that determines the trait. Thus, in Mendel's pea plants, the phenotype of purple flower color could be the result of three different genotypes: dominant-dominant (PP), dominant-recessive (Pp), and recessive-dominant (pP). However, the phenotype of white flower color results from only one genotype (recessive-recessive, pp).

© Kateryna Kon/Shutterstock.com

FIGURE 2.8 Dominant and recessive alleles. The flower color gene in Mendel's pea plants had two alleles. The dominant allele for purple flower color is denoted P and the recessive allele for white flower color is denoted p. F_1 generation flowers all had the same genetic makeup, Pp, and are purple, because P is the dominant allele. F_2 generation flowers had four possible combinations of the dominant and recessive alleles—PP, Pp, pP, and pp—which gives a 3:1 ratio of purple flowers to white flowers.

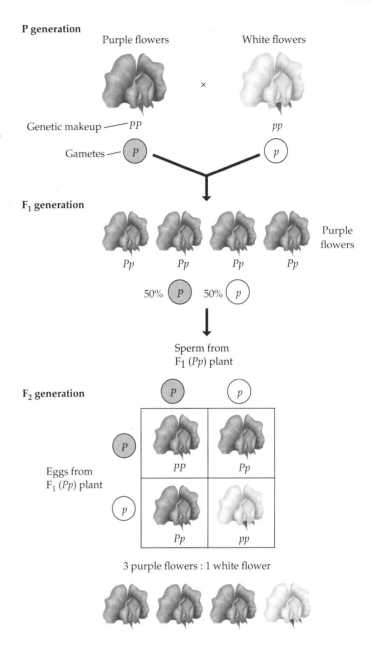

You can see from this example that individuals with mixed genotypes, either dominant-recessive or recessive-dominant, do not outwardly express the trait corresponding to the recessive allele. However, they are carriers of that allele and can therefore pass it on to their offspring.

Although humans are more complex than pea plants, certain characteristics generally follow Mendel's rules around recessive and dominant traits:

- hair color (brown hair color is dominant over blond)
- hair texture (curly hair is dominant over straight)
- facial dimples (dimples are dominant over no dimples)
- eye color (brown eye color is dominant over blue and green, although researchers now know that eye color is affected by multiple genes)
- blood types (A and B blood types are dominant over O, and Rh-positive blood type is dominant over Rh-negative).

Differences in the sex chromosomes produce exceptions to the general rule that a recessive allele will not be expressed unless present on both members of a chromosome pair. These exceptions almost always affect males rather than females. To see why, consider what happens when a female has a recessive allele on one of her X chromosomes. The likelihood is that her other X chromosome will not have the same recessive allele, so the recessive allele will not be expressed. Now consider what happens when a male has a recessive allele on his X chromosome. His Y chromosome, with many fewer genes, is unlikely to have a matching dominant allele, which means that the recessive allele on his X chromosome is not blocked. Because the Y chromosome contains relatively few genes, it is unlikely for a recessive allele to appear on the Y chromosome with no corresponding dominant allele on the X chromosome.

Sex-linked traits result from the expression of an allele found on just one of the sex chromosomes, and as we just saw, most sex-linked traits are determined by an allele on the X chromosome. As a result, disorders such as hemophilia, muscular dystrophy, and color blindness—all of which are X-linked traits—are more likely to affect males than females, because females are usually protected from the recessive alleles that cause these disorders by having a dominant, normal allele on their other X chromosome (**TABLE 2.1**).

sex-linked traits Traits in which a gene is located on a sex chromosome; the majority of sex-linked traits are located on the X chromosome

TABLE 2.1 ■ Example sex-linked disorders.

Disorder	Description	Dominant/ Recessive	Frequency among human births
Tay-Sachs disease	A metabolic disorder in which certain lipids accumulate in the brain, eventually leading to death in childhood	Recessive	1/3,600 live births (Ashkenazi Jews)
Cystic fibrosis	A condition in which the individual experiences breathing and digestive difficulties due to large amounts of thick secretions in the lungs, liver, and pancreas	Recessive	1/3,200 (Whites)
Hemophilia	An X-linked disorder in which blood does not clot normally, leading to internal bleeding and tissue damage	Recessive	Hemophilia A: 1/5,000 males; hemophilia B: 1/25,000 males
Phenylketonuria (PKU)	A condition in which the individual cannot metabolize the amino acid phenylalanine, which adversely affects cognition and can lead to a shortened life span	Recessive	1/13,500–1/19,000
Sickle-cell anemia	A potentially fatal disorder in which a mutated form of hemoglobin distorts red blood cells into a crescent shape at low oxygen levels	Recessive	1/300–1/500 African Americans
Huntington's disease	A disease characterized by degeneration of nerve cells in the brain that leads to progressive dementia; usually symptoms do not appear until after about 35 years of age	Dominant	1/24,000
Muscular dystrophy	A group of diseases that lead to progressive weakness and loss of muscle mass	Recessive	1/3,500 males
Color blindness	A condition characterized by the inability to distinguish one or several colors	Recessive	1/12 males

Sources: National Human Genome Research Institute (https://www.genome.gov/For-Patients-and-Families/Genetic-Disorders); National Organization for Rare Diseases (https://rarediseases.org/?s=H&post_type=rare-diseases)

✓ CHECK YOUR UNDERSTANDING 2.2

1. Explain how a person's genotype (including whether a specific trait is recessive or dominant) comes to be expressed in a person's phenotype. Provide an example.

Mutations

LEARNING OBJECTIVE 2.3 Distinguish among neutral, positive, negative, and mixed mutations.

mutation An alteration in the structure of an individual's DNA that arises from an error in chromosomal replication or from exposure to environmental factors such as radiation, toxic chemicals, or other toxins; mutations vary in size, from a single DNA building block to a large part of a chromosome with multiple genes

genetic mutation A gene mutation that occurs in a germ cell or gamete and is a permanent alteration in the DNA sequence making up a gene; the hereditary mutations are inherited from a parent

In most cases, the trillions of cells of our bodies work together in just the right ways for development to follow a typical path. However, sometimes DNA is altered. A **mutation** is an alteration in the structure of an individual's DNA arising from an error during chromosomal replication or from exposure to radiation, toxic chemicals, or other toxins. Alterations can be as small as a change in a single base in the DNA sequence, such as when an A replaces a G, or deletion or insertion of a single base. Other times, the alteration is larger, such as when a deletion, insertion, or rearrangement affects longer sequences of bases (**FIGURE 2.9**). A **genetic mutation**—a mutation that occurs in a germ cell, a cell that creates a gamete, or the gamete itself—can be passed on to the next generation.

As we will see, genetic mutations are not necessarily harmful in a population. Mutations can be neutral, positive, negative, or can have mixed effects.

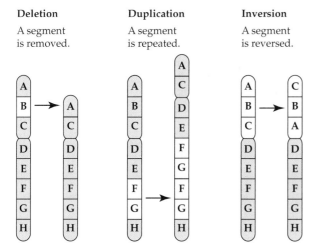

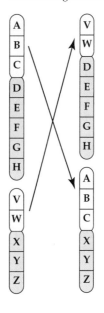

Deletion
A segment is removed.

Duplication
A segment is repeated.

Inversion
A segment is reversed.

Translocation
A segment moves from one chromosome to a nonhomologous one.

FIGURE 2.9 Mutations. A mutation is an alteration in the structure of an individual's DNA arising from an error during chromosomal replication or from exposure to radiation, toxic chemicals, or other toxins. Alterations can be as small as a change in a single base in the DNA sequence, such as when an A replaces a G or a single base is deleted or inserted. Other times, the alteration is larger, such as when a deletion, insertion, or rearrangement affects longer sequences of bases. (After D. M. Bozzone and D. S. Green. 2014. *Biology for the Informed Citizen.* Oxford University Press: New York, NY.)

Neutral Mutations

Mutations that have no effect are called **neutral mutations** or silent mutations. For example, a mutation that changes the base sequence AAA to AAG has no effect because AAA and AAG code the same amino acid (the building blocks of proteins).

neutral mutations Silent mutations in DNA that have no effect on an individual's phenotype

Positive Mutations

Positive mutations enhance the adaptability of the population when passed on. For example, human populations thousands of years ago lost the ability to digest milk past infancy. The loss of this ability did not much matter until about 10,000 years ago, when populations of humans began herding milk-producing animals. When a mutation that let adults retain the ability to digest milk appeared in those populations, individuals with the mutation, who could consume milk and dairy products, had a better chance of being well nourished and surviving to have children. Those individuals then passed along the mutation to their children, who likewise had better chances to survive. And so, the ability to consume dairy was passed along to subsequent generations (Curry, 2013; Gerbault et al., 2011).

positive mutations Beneficial mutations in DNA that have a positive effect on the individual, leading to new versions of proteins that enable organisms to better adapt to changes in their environment

Many positive mutations have occurred over the course of evolution. Positive mutations confer immediate adaptive advantages, like the ability to digest milk, while expanding the genetic variability of a population. By expanding genetic variability, the chances of survival heighten. Suppose, for example, that a fatal disease emerges in a population. If genetic variability has produced individuals who happen to have a gene that allows them to resist the disease, they will survive and can pass on the gene and protect the population from extinction.

Normal red blood cells

Cross section of RBC

Normal hemoglobin

Normal red blood cell

Sickled (abnormal) red blood cells

Cross section of sickled cell

Abnormal hemoglobin

Rigid and pointy sickle cell

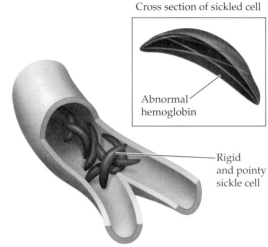

■ Normal allele (*A*)
■ Dysfunctional allele

AS
Father, carrier

AS
Mother, carrier

AA
Normal

AS
Carrier for sickle cell anemia

AS
Carrier for sickle cell anemia

SS
Sickle cell anemia

FIGURE 2.10 Sickle cell anemia. Sickle cell anemia is an example of a mixed mutation. It is a potentially fatal disease caused by a mutation of the gene that helps produce the protein hemoglobin, which carries oxygen in red blood cells. The mutated allele is recessive, meaning an individual must inherit two copies of the allele to develop the disease. Positive effects of the sickle cell mutation occur in individuals with only one copy of the allele who live in malaria-prone areas: They are resistant to malaria, because the parasites that cause malaria cannot live inside the sickled shape of the red blood cells. (From D. M. Bozzone and D. S. Green. 2014. *Biology for the Informed Citizen*. Oxford University Press: New York, NY; after S. M. Breedlove. 2015. *Principles of Psychology*. Sinauer/Oxford University Press: Sunderland, MA.)

negative mutations Harmful mutations in DNA that have a negative effect on the individual, leading to adverse, even lethal, consequences; negative mutations may be inherited or occur randomly during the formation of reproductive cells

Negative Mutations

Some mutations have adverse, even lethal, effects. Some **negative mutations** result in early miscarriage (Coulam et al., 2006). Others cause developmental abnormalities. In most instances, the harmful consequences of negative mutations manifest when individuals have inherited two recessive alleles. That's because negative mutations transmitted through dominant alleles are unlikely to be passed on to the next generation: Individuals with dominant mutations are often unlikely to live long enough to reproduce.

However, exceptions exist. When a person with a dominant mutation lives long enough to pass it along, the mutation survives. Huntington's disease, which is characterized by lethal degeneration of the nerve cells in the brain, is one example. Usually, symptoms do not appear until after about 35 years of age, leaving enough time for individuals to reproduce and pass the dominant gene to offspring. Table 2.1 includes some examples of conditions resulting from the inheritance of two recessive alleles with negative mutations.

Some negative mutations are not inherited, but occur randomly during the formation of reproductive cells (eggs and sperm). **Klinefelter syndrome** is a random mutation that results in an extra copy of the X chromosome in males (thus, XXY, rather than XY). Affected males have small testes and produce low amounts of testosterone, which leads to infertility. Because features of Klinefelter syndrome may be mild, up to 75 percent of affected males are never diagnosed. **Turner syndrome** represents another random negative mutation, leading to a partial or missing X chromosome in females. Affected females may have medical and developmental problems including failure of the ovaries, short stature, and heart defects.

Mixed Mutations

Other mutations—termed **mixed mutations**—have positive effects under certain conditions but negative effects under other conditions. Consider, for example, sickle cell anemia, a potentially fatal disease caused by a mutation of the gene that helps produce hemoglobin, a protein that carries oxygen in red blood cells (**FIGURE 2.10**). The mutated allele is recessive, which means that an individual must inherit two copies of the allele to develop the disease. Individuals with only one copy of the allele are resistant to malaria, because the parasites that cause malaria are killed inside the altered red blood cells. That is, the recessive allele alters blood cells to be immune to malaria. (Note that the altered blood cells are sickle shaped, hence the name of the disease.) Resistance to malaria is adaptive for people living in regions of the world where the risk of malaria is high, such as parts of Africa, India, the Caribbean, and the Middle East. However, in regions where malaria is not prevalent, the danger of producing offspring with two copies of the recessive allele is not offset by any protective advantage, so the effects of the mutation are largely negative. Sickle cell anemia thus illustrates how environmental context can determine whether a specific genetic inheritance is adaptive or not.

✓ CHECK YOUR UNDERSTANDING 2.3

1. Explain why sickle cell anemia is considered to be a mixed mutation.

Decoding the Genome

LEARNING OBJECTIVE 2.4 Illustrate how the Human Genome Project and current advances in the science of genetics may create ethical challenges for society.

About two decades after Watson and Crick's 1953 discovery of the structure of DNA, scientists developed laboratory techniques to determine the exact sequence of bases in any given sample of DNA. Then, in 1990, an international effort known as the **Human Genome Project** undertook the complete decoding of the human genome, determining the sequence of base pairs and identifying all the genes in the DNA of each of the 23 pairs of human chromosomes. The Human Genome project armed researchers with new tools to investigate the genetic underpinnings of human physical and behavioral characteristics. It also

Klinefelter syndrome A random negative mutation or chromosomal abnormality resulting in an extra copy of the X chromosome in males (XXY, not XY); males with Klinefelter syndrome have small testes and produce low amounts of testosterone, leading to infertility

Turner syndrome A random negative mutation or chromosomal abnormality resulting in a missing or partially missing X chromosome in females (X, not XX); females with Turner syndrome may have different medical and developmental challenges (e.g., failure of the ovaries)

mixed mutations Mutations with either positive or negative effects under various conditions

Human Genome Project An international research program (1990–2003) to map and understand all the genes of humans in an effort to explore the genetic foundations of human physical and behavioral characteristics and to create new strategies for identifying and treating disorders

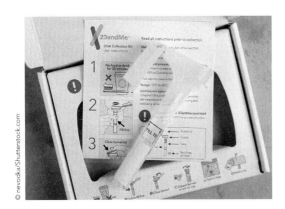

© nevodka/Shutterstock.com

FIGURE 2.11 23andMe personal ancestry. DNA test kits include items for collecting DNA. When the kit is sent to a lab, scientists isolate cells and analyze genes. The kits are inexpensive, and results are obtained within a short period of time.

gene therapy An experimental technique using genes to prevent or treat diseases

microbiome Genetic material or microbes that have many times the number of genes as identified in the human genome; in utero, mothers pass on microbes to the fetus and, by the end of their first year, infants have a distinct microbiome that continues to develop until about age 3

sought to develop new strategies for the diagnosis, treatment, and prevention of diseases and disorders.

Scientists completed decoding the genome in 2003. Beyond mapping the genome, the project spawned several technological advances that enabled researchers to quickly read the entire genetic blueprint of any individual at low cost. Locating a gene thought to be involved in an inherited disease can now be done quite cheaply in just a few days, compared to the costly process that once took several years (**FIGURE 2.11**). The Human Genome Project spurred a revolution in biotechnology innovation around the world, with the United States at the forefront. Researchers now have a much firmer estimate of the approximate number of human genes (about 20,500, surprisingly fewer than previous estimates of 50,000 to 140,000), and know a lot about the locations of specific genes and their functions. The project has fueled discovery of over 1,800 genes implicated in disease, and over 2,000 tests are now available to assess people's genetic risk for specific diseases. Research into **gene therapy** is also advancing, with the potential to provide the necessary knowledge and tools to prevent or cure diseases by replacing harmful gene versions with normal ones.

Still, as scientists increasingly identify how a person's genotype may shape developments in mental health, intelligence, personality, height and weight, it will become increasingly important to think about what this means for society. How far should scientists go in altering the natural conditions and variations of human development? Ethical, legal, and social implications of new discoveries will remain at the forefront of scientific research for years to come.

✓ CHECK YOUR UNDERSTANDING 2.4

1. Contrast the benefits of gene therapy with its potential risks.

The Microbiome

LEARNING OBJECTIVE 2.5 Explain the role of the microbiome in health.

As scientists mapped the human genome, they discovered additional genetic material that lives in and on the human body, such as bacteria, fungi, and viruses, or what is referred to as the **microbiome**. The microbiome has many times the number of genes as identified in the human genome. And development of a child's microbiome, which begins in utero, can have far-reaching consequences.

In utero, mothers transfer microbes to the fetus through the prenatal environment, with the process of labor further affecting the newborn's microbiome. Then, by the end of the first year, infants have a distinct microbiome, which continues to develop until around 3 years of age when it is mostly established. Thus, the first years of life may be a critical time in development for establishing a healthy microbiome through healthy nutrition of first the pregnant mother and then the feeding infant (Rodriguez, Murphy, & Collado, 2015). Notably, a healthy microbiome underpins many biological processes vital to health, including digestion, development of the immune system, and defense against infection. Imbalance in the microbiome has been connected to diseases including asthma, inflammatory bowel disease, and type 1 diabetes (Moore & Townsend, 2019; Tanaka & Nakayama, 2017).

✓ CHECK YOUR UNDERSTANDING 2.5

1. What is the microbiome? Which aspects of health has it been shown to affect?

Contexts of Environmental Influences on Gene Expression

Few human traits are determined in the same way as the colors of Mendel's pea plants. For most traits, the path from genotype to phenotype is much more complex. In some instances, a single gene affects multiple traits. But, more commonly several genes contribute to a trait in what scientists refer to as **polygenic inheritance**. Human skin color is a well-known example of a trait influenced by multiple genes (Ganesan et al., 2008).

Furthermore, environmental influences shape how a person's genetic inheritance expresses itself in a person's traits. **Phenotypic plasticity** refers to the degree to which environmental factors affect a given trait (Pigliucci, 2001). Some traits have little phenotypic plasticity. For example, eye color is largely genetically determined. A child's eye color will not change based on where or how the child is raised, although certain environmental experiences, like face trauma, can disturb the tissue that produces eye color and cause change. **Canalization** refers to phenotypes that remain unchanged or are difficult to change regardless of environmental variability.

In contrast, many other human traits display relatively high plasticity. Physical traits such as height and behavioral traits such as shyness and aggression show high plasticity. That is, the same genotype can lead to a range of phenotypes, depending on the environment. For example, the same person can grow to different heights or weights depending on household nutrition. The range of possible phenotypes for a given genotype is termed the **norm of reaction**.

How Do Genes and Environment Interact?

LEARNING OBJECTIVE 2.6 Explain the various ways that genes and environment work together to affect human development.

Genes and environment interact to affect development. But, the question is how? Research in the exciting field of **epigenetics** reveals the complex and dynamic processes through which environments shape the expression of the genetic code (Champagne, 2020; Noble, 2015; Waddington, 1942). The term epigenetics contains the Greek prefix *epi* meaning "above" to highlight that many variables *above* heredity guide the course of development. Indeed, genes and environment work together to affect development in four fundamental ways:

- *Environmental factors can affect whether genes are switched on or off*. During development, genes turn on and off for varying periods of time. Regulator genes typically control gene activation and inactivation. But, environmental factors can also influence the process of turning a gene on or off. Consider, for example, the case of thalidomide, an over-the-counter drug that was marketed to pregnant women in the late 1950s to prevent nausea and morning sickness. No one knew at the time that the presumed safe drug thalidomide could shut off the activation of certain genes. Specifically, thalidomide interfered with the activation of genes responsible for arm and hand development during a certain period of prenatal development. Its use resulted in the birth worldwide of about 10,000 infants with malformed arms, and only half of those infants survived (**FIGURE 2.12**).

- *Environmental factors can alter the magnitude of genetic effects on development*. For example, the effects of the recessive allele that causes phenylketonuria (PKU), a disorder in which an individual cannot metabolize

polygenetic inheritance An occurrence when one characteristic is controlled by two or more genes; height, weight, skin color, and eye color are examples of polygenetic inheritance

phenotypic plasticity The degree to which environmental factors affect a given trait; the ability of one genotype to create more than one phenotype in different environments, or the ability of an organism to change in response to stimuli from the environment

canalization The ability of a genotype to produce the same phenotype regardless of environmental variability

norm of reaction The range of possible phenotypes for a given genotype; the norm of reaction may be viewed as a curve that relates variation in the environment to phenotypic variation

epigenetics The complex, dynamic process through which environments shape the expression of the genetic code; the term was originally used to illustrate gene-environment interactions

Thalidomide

FIGURE 2.12 Thalidomide infant. Thalidomide, marketed to pregnant women in the late 1950s to prevent nausea and morning sickness, resulted in the birth worldwide of about 10,000 infants with malformed arms, only half of which survived.

evocative effects The effects of a person's traits or characteristics on the environment, which may heighten those traits and characteristics

the amino acid phenylalanine, range from severe intellectual disability to relatively normal intelligence, depending on children's nutritional environment. Children with PKU who eat a normal diet display impaired brain development. But when placed on a proper diet as infants (a diet with no phenylalanine), the brain of children with PKU develops normally.

- *Gene expression can affect how people respond to children, thus further affecting children's behaviors.* A child's genetic makeup is expressed in the child's personality, physical appearance, and so forth. Such traits then affect the child's environment by eliciting certain kinds of responses from other people, what researchers refer to as **evocative effects** (Deater-Deckard & O'Connor, 2000; Scarr & McCartney, 1983). For example, a child who is high in negativity because of her genetic makeup may elicit more discipline and greater punishment from adults than a less negative child. Adult responses, in turn, will further influence how the child acts—the child may become withdrawn or perhaps escalate in negativity in response to a caregiver's punishment.

- *A person's genotype affects the environments the person chooses to experience.* Sometimes, genotypes lead to phenotype differences that determine which environments a person selects. The person's choices then strengthen the development of certain traits. For example, an inhibited child might habitually revert to a quiet corner at a party or avoid peers in the classroom. By choosing to be away from peers, the child creates few opportunities for social interactions, making interactions with others even more intimidating than before. As a result, the child's self-induced isolation escalates.

✓ CHECK YOUR UNDERSTANDING 2.6

1. Provide examples of gene-environment interactions in: (a) how environment can switch genes on and off; (b) how environment can alter a genetic effect; (c) evocative effects; and (d) a person's self-selection into specific environments.

Epigenetic Principles: From Animals to Humans

LEARNING OBJECTIVE 2.7 Describe the unique value of animal research in both the testing of gene-environment interactions and also its application to studies of human development.

The various ways that environments and genes co-shape a person's development are theoretically clear. But how can researchers experimentally test theories about gene-environment interactions without slipping into the unethical territory of manipulating a person's genes or environment? The study of animals offers a valuable approach.

Over half a century ago, researchers observed that rats differ in the genetically inherited trait of cognitive ability and that those differences were stable across a rat's life span. That is, rats who were able to navigate complex mazes early in infancy tended to be strong at navigating mazes as adults (Cooper & Zubek, 1958). And, because rats' cognitive ability is inherited, researchers could breed "maze-dull" and "maze-bright" rats, by mating bright rats with other bright rats and dull rats with other dull rats over several generations, something they couldn't do with humans. After breeding bright and dull rats, researchers placed them in environments that were either enriched or impoverished in stimulating materials such as running wheels (Cooper & Zubek, 1958) (**FIGURE 2.13**). They found that maze-dull rats who were reared in enriched environments were better

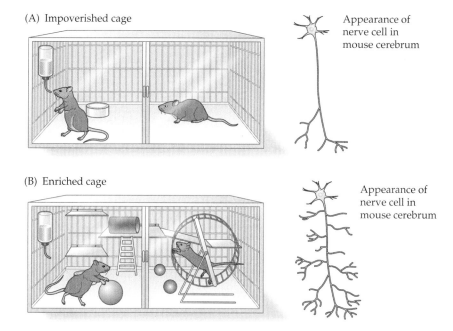

(A) Impoverished cage

Appearance of nerve cell in mouse cerebrum

(B) Enriched cage

Appearance of nerve cell in mouse cerebrum

FIGURE 2.13 Animal research provides insights into environmental influences. Researchers can manipulate the experiences of animals to test the bounds of environmental and genetic influences. For example, researchers Cooper and Zubek found that maze-dull rats who were reared in enriched environments were better at navigating complex mazes than maze-dull rats reared in regular environments. And, maze-bright rats reared in impoverished environments were worse at navigating complex mazes than maze-bright rats reared in regular environments. Thus, environmental influences altered the inherited characteristic of cognitive ability, showing that genes alone do not determine destiny. In later research, scientists have shown that experiences of deprivation versus enrichment alter the brain development of rats. (After S. M. Breedlove. 2015. *Principles of Psychology*. Sinauer/Oxford University Press: Sunderland, MA.)

at navigating complex mazes than maze-dull rats reared in regular environments. And, maze-bright rats reared in impoverished environments were worse at navigating complex mazes than maze-bright rats reared in regular environments. Thus, environmental influences altered the inherited characteristic of cognitive ability, showing that genes alone do not determine destiny. But, can environments actually *alter* how a person's genes express themselves?

Current advances in science allow researchers today to directly test how modifications to an animal's environment produce changes to gene expression (Champagne, 2020). Studies of rat licking offer a compelling example of epigenetics. Specifically, mother rats vary in how much they lick their pups, and those differences can be traced to genetic differences that mothers then pass off to their offspring. So, what would happen if you placed a high-licking rat mom with the offspring of a low-licking rat mom? Would the offspring be affected by their experiences? Would they turn out to be low-lickers (their biology) or high-lickers (their experience) with their own offspring? Frances Champagne's intriguing work shows that as mothers lick their rat pups, they actually alter the expression of their offspring's genomes. Specifically, different amounts of licking affect how offspring's genes are one day expressed and how their offspring ultimately behave (Champagne & Meaney, 2006).

The same principles of gene-environment interactions observed in animals apply to human development (LaFreniere & MacDonald, 2013). In fact, epigenetic processes that have already begun in the womb account for why "identical" twins, even at birth, are not identical in their expressions of genes, and will increasingly diverge in their phenotypes as genes interact with environments. And for all infants, whether twin or not, prenatal experiences affect the expression of genes. For example, prenatal exposure to harmful substances, such as maternal intake of drugs, alcohol, or smoking, can instigate changes in DNA (Shorey-Kendrick et al., 2017) that may lead to later problems in hyperactivity (Melchior et al., 2015), conduct disorder (Talati et al., 2017), and even substance use in adolescence (Cecil et al., 2016). Epigenetic changes in the developing fetus have also been connected to maternal obesity, stress, and depression during pregnancy (Cicchetti et al., 2016; Kertes et al., 2017; Sharp et al., 2017).

In short, a general rule of thumb is that genes and environment work together in just about anything that developmentalists study. Consider breastfeeding. Some studies have shown that breastfeeding confers an intellectual advantage for children (Mortensen et al., 2002), which is one reason that pediatricians encourage the practice. However, only some children benefit from breastfeeding, and their gains depend on their genetics. Children with a specific gene responsible for processing fatty acids show higher intelligence if they had also been breastfed than do children who had not been breastfed. However, children without the gene who are breastfed show no superiority of intelligence to non-breastfed children (Caspi et al., 2007).

✓ CHECK YOUR UNDERSTANDING 2.7

1. Describe an animal study that supports the idea that the environment can change the expression of a gene. Draw parallels to the human experience of being breastfed.

Summing Up: The Library Metaphor

LEARNING OBJECTIVE 2.8 Apply a library metaphor to explain gene-environment interactions.

The study of epigenetics in rats and humans has illuminated how genes and environment interact. Throughout this book, you will learn about many such interactions. Most centrally, such work reveals that genetic inheritance is by no means deterministic: Many genes require specific environmental circumstances to be expressed, and many genes are never expressed. In fact, a useful "library" metaphor highlights current views:

> *Think of an individual's DNA as books in a library that have been ordered and arranged very precisely by a meticulous librarian. These books contain a wealth of knowledge and the potential to inspire whoever should choose to read them. Asking what DNA does is like asking what a book in this library does. Books sit on a shelf waiting to be read. Once read, the information in those books can have limitless consequences. Likewise, DNA sits in our cells and waits to be read.… The reading, or expression, of DNA can, like the books in our library, have limitless consequences. However, without the active process that triggers such expression, this potential may never be realized. Importantly, it is the environment around the DNA that contains those critical factors that make it possible to read the DNA.*

(Champagne & Mashoodh, 2009, p. 128)

✓ CHECK YOUR UNDERSTANDING 2.8

1. Connect the library metaphor on gene-environment interactions to a concrete example in animal or human research.

■ *The Brain*

The human brain is a source of what makes all people similar and each person unique. Our brains share basic structures and connections that enable us to see the colors of a rainbow, relish the flavors of food, and feel the rain and wind. We can reflect on the past, attend to the present, and imagine the future. These human capacities emerge from the unceasing flow of electrical and chemical signals among the roughly 100 billion neurons, or nerve cells, in the human brain. Yet, against a backdrop of human similarities, the precise patterns of connections among regions of the brain and between brain and body vary from person to person. Our unique brain enables us to think unique thoughts, feel unique emotions, remember unique experiences, and act in unique ways—that is, our brain is intimately involved in who we are.

Knowledge about the brain's structures and functions is expanding at an astounding rate, largely driven by advances in neuroscience and new techniques for imaging the brain. In the sections that follow, you will learn about the brain's architecture, scientific advances in the study of the brain, developmental changes in brain processes and structures, and reciprocal influences among brain development, behavior, and experience.

Brain Anatomy and Function

The average adult brain weighs a mere 3 pounds, yet its exquisite anatomy allows people to engage in the many complex activities of everyday life. The brain is divided into two hemispheres, a left hemisphere and a right hemisphere, separated by a deep groove and connected by the **corpus callosum**, a dense tract of nerve fibers that facilitates communication between the hemispheres. Each hemisphere has an outer layer called the **cerebral cortex** that surrounds a large number of subcortical structures that sit below the cortex. The brain also divides into forebrain, midbrain, and hindbrain. Researchers refer to the anatomy of the brain as brain "structure," and the brain's role in regulating our body and mind as brain "function" (**FIGURE 2.14**).

corpus callosum A dense tract of nerve fibers, beneath the cerebral cortex, which facilitates communication between the left and right hemispheres of the brain as it stretches across the midline of the brain

cerebral cortex The layer of gray matter that covers the left and right hemispheres, consisting of folds of axons and neurons; the cerebral cortex is involved in higher functions of the nervous system, including language and memory; the cortex has four lobes in each hemisphere

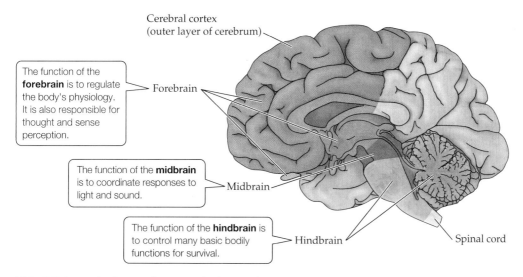

Cerebral cortex (outer layer of cerebrum)

The function of the **forebrain** is to regulate the body's physiology. It is also responsible for thought and sense perception.

Forebrain

The function of the **midbrain** is to coordinate responses to light and sound.

Midbrain

The function of the **hindbrain** is to control many basic bodily functions for survival.

Hindbrain

Spinal cord

FIGURE 2.14 The human brain. The human brain can be divided into three overarching structures, each with specific functions. (After S. M. Breedlove and N. V. Watson. 2019. *Behavioral Neuroscience*. 9th ed. Sinauer/Oxford University Press: Sunderland, MA.)

FIGURE 2.15 Cerebral cortex and other structures of the forebrain. The forebrain, the largest part of the human brain, consists of the cerebral cortex and various subcortical structures. (After S. M. Breedlove. 2015. *Principles of Psychology*. Sinauer/Oxford University Press: Sunderland, MA; after S. M. Breedlove and N. V. Watson. 2019. *Behavioral Neuroscience*, 9th ed. Sinauer/Oxford University Press: Sunderland, MA)

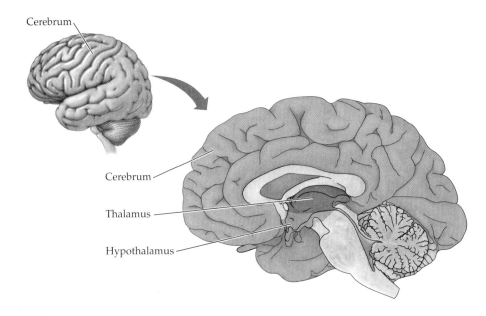

forebrain The largest part of the human brain that consists of the cerebral cortex and subcortical structures; the forebrain controls such functions as body temperature, reproductive functions, eating, and emotions

occipital lobe One of the four lobes of the brain in the rearmost area of the brain; the occipital lobe is involved in processing visual information

temporal lobe One of the four lobes of the brain that is located closest to the ear; the temporal lobe is involved in processing emotional and auditory information, memory, and visual recognition

parietal lobe One of the four lobes of the brain located in the back of the brain, divided into two hemispheres; the parietal lobe is involved in processing spatial information, integrating information from other modalities, connecting information with memory, and interpreting visual information and processing such as for language and mathematics

frontal lobe One of the four lobes of the brain located at the front of the cerebral hemispheres that contains the primary motor cortex; the frontal lobe, or the "executive" area of the brain, is involved in reasoning, planning, impulse control, attention, and goal-directed behaviors

association areas Parts of the cerebral cortex that receive input from different areas and which form connections between sensory and motor areas of the brain; association areas process information from the lobes to create meaningful experiences

Forebrain

LEARNING OBJECTIVE 2.9 Describe the structures of the forebrain and the functions of each.

The **forebrain**, the largest part of the human brain, consists of the cerebrum and various subcortical structures (**FIGURE 2.15**). The cerebrum accounts for over 80% of the volume of the total human brain, a far larger proportion than that of other species. Consequently, it is the part of the brain that separates humans from other animals (Kolb & Whishaw, 1998).

Four Lobes

Structurally, the cerebrum is divided into two hemispheres and contains 4 lobes in each hemisphere (**FIGURE 2.16**). Each lobe serves unique functions:

- The **occipital lobe** is involved in processing visual information.
- The **temporal lobe** is involved in processing emotional and auditory information, memory, and visual recognition.

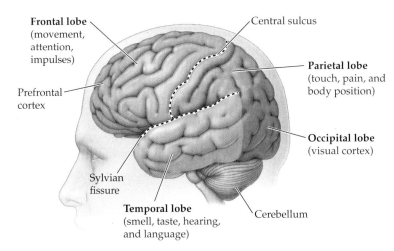

FIGURE 2.16 Four lobes of the cerebral cortex.   The cerebral cortex includes four lobes: occipital, temporal, parietal, and frontal. (After S. M. Breedlove. 2015. *Principles of Psychology*. Sinauer/Oxford University Press: Sunderland, MA.)

- The **parietal lobe** is involved in processing spatial information, integrating sensory information from different modalities (e.g., visual and auditory information), and connecting that information with memory.
- The **frontal lobe**, the "executive" area of the brain, is involved in reasoning, planning, impulse control, attention, and goal-directed behaviors.

In addition, **association areas**—networks connecting the lobes—process and integrate information from the lobes to produce meaningful perceptions and experiences.

Specialized Functions in the Right and Left Hemispheres

Regions in the right and left hemispheres likewise have specialized functions, a phenomenon referred to as **cerebral lateralization**. The left hemisphere is largely involved in language, and regions in the right hemisphere are largely involved in processing social and emotional information, including nonverbal information about other people's emotions. However, most complex functions are not completely lateralized. In language, for example, information from regions in both hemispheres must be integrated for speech to be meaningfully produced and understood (e.g., Atallah, Frank, & O'Reilly, 2004; Can, Richards, & Kuhl, 2013; Fedorenko et al., 2010; Hickok & Poeppel, 2007).

The brain also exhibits **contralateral organization**—that is, the left hemisphere processes sensory information from the right side of the body and controls movements of the right side, and vice versa. For example, if you close your left eye, the right side of your brain will send signals causing your left eyelid to close, and your open right eye will send signals from the continued visual inputs to your left hemisphere for processing.

Subcortical Structures

Subcortical structures in the forebrain serve a variety of functions. Three of these structures—the hippocampus, amygdala, and cingulate cortex—comprise the **limbic system**, which is involved in emotions and memory (**FIGURE 2.17**). The **hippocampus** is a memory center, sending information to the cerebral cortex for storage and retrieval. The **amygdala** plays a pivotal role in the "fight or flight" response and memory. The **cingulate cortex** receives and relays information from and across regions of the brain and is also involved in emotion formation and memory.

The **hypothalamus** is an important center involved in the experience of emotions such as happiness, sadness, anger, and exhilaration. The **thalamus** relays

cerebral lateralization A phenomenon referring to the specialized functions of regions in the right and left hemispheres; the left hemisphere is largely involved in language and the right hemisphere is largely involved in processing social and emotional information, although both hemispheres are involved in mostly all processes

contralateral organization The physical body control of the brain; the right brain controls the left side of the body and the left brain controls the right side of the body

limbic system The collection of brain structures involved in emotions and memory; the limbic system consists of the hippocampus, amygdala, and cingulate cortex

hippocampus The part of the brain located in the inner region of the temporal lobe that is involved in regulating emotions and supports children's memory, spatial understanding, and executive functioning

amygdala A region of the brain that is a part of the limbic system and involved in emotion processes, particularly fear and the fight-or-flight response

cingulate cortex A region of the brain that is a part of the limbic system that communicates with different regions of the brain and is involved in emotion processes

hypothalamus The part of the brain located below the thalamus and involved in the experience of emotions such as happiness and sadness; the hypothalamus is also involved in such behaviors as eating and drinking

thalamus The part of the brain located above the brainstem and between the cerebral cortex and midbrain; the thalamus relays information to and from the spinal cord and between the two hemispheres

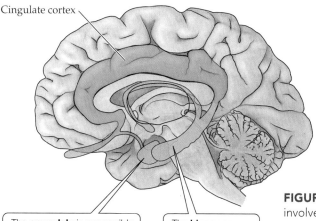

Cingulate cortex

The **amygdala** is responsible for emotions, such as fear and anxiety.

The **hippocampus** is responsible for memory.

FIGURE 2.17 Limbic system. The limbic system is involved in emotions and memory and comprises the hippocampus, the amygdala, and the cingulate cortex. (After D. Purves et al. 2011. *Neuroscience*, 5th ed. Sinauer/Oxford University Press: Sunderland, MA.)

basal ganglia A cluster of nerve cells that surrounds the hypothalamus and is involved in movement/motor control and the coordination of automatic behaviors

information to and from the spinal cord and between the two hemispheres. Both the hypothalamus and thalamus communicate with the hippocampus through a tract of nerve cells. Finally, the **basal ganglia**, a cluster of nerve cells, surrounds the hypothalamus and is involved in movement. Parkinson's disease, which is characterized by tremors, muscular rigidity, and imprecise movements, is associated with degeneration of the basal ganglia.

✓ CHECK YOUR UNDERSTANDING 2.9

1. Explain the brain's contralateral organization.
2. Which subcortical structures are found in the forebrain, and what are their functions?

Midbrain and Hindbrain

midbrain The uppermost region of the brainstem that controls reflex actions and is involved in vision, hearing, movements, and sleep-wake cycles

brainstem The part of the brain consisting of the midbrain, the pons, and the medulla oblongata; the brainstem controls the messages between the brain and the rest of the body

hindbrain The central core of the brain that includes the rest of the brainstem, the cerebellum, the pons, and the medulla oblongata; the hindbrain controls automatic functions such as breathing and digestion

LEARNING OBJECTIVE 2.10 Explain why the midbrain and hindbrain may be found in all animals.

Whereas our cerebral cortex makes us uniquely human, the midbrain and hindbrain are found in all animals, serving critical functions in dealing with sensory input and directing basic bodily functions (**FIGURE 2.18**). The **midbrain**, the uppermost region of the **brainstem**, controls some reflex actions and is involved in vision, hearing, movements, and sleep-wake cycles.

The **hindbrain** includes the rest of the brainstem, the cerebellum, the pons, and the medulla. The hindbrain portion of the brainstem controls automatic

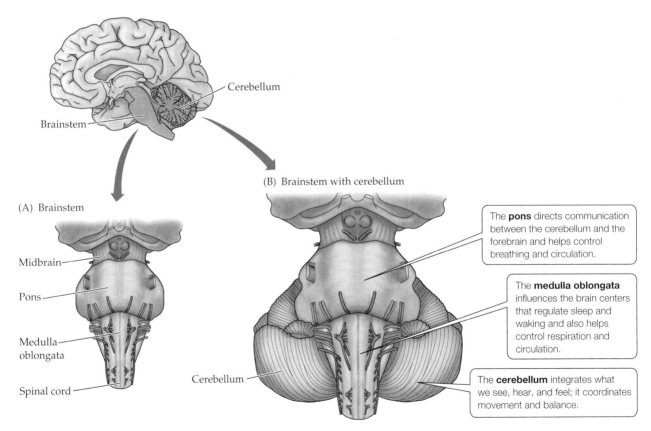

Cerebellum

Brainstem

(A) Brainstem

Midbrain

Pons

Medulla oblongata

Spinal cord

(B) Brainstem with cerebellum

The **pons** directs communication between the cerebellum and the forebrain and helps control breathing and circulation.

The **medulla oblongata** influences the brain centers that regulate sleep and waking and also helps control respiration and circulation.

The **cerebellum** integrates what we see, hear, and feel; it coordinates movement and balance.

Cerebellum

FIGURE 2.18 Midbrain and hindbrain. (A) The midbrain, the uppermost region of the brainstem, controls some reflex actions and is involved in vision, hearing, movements, and sleep–wake cycles. (B) The hindbrain includes the rest of the brainstem, the cerebellum, the pons, and the medulla. The hindbrain portion of the brainstem controls automatic functions such as breathing, digestion, heart rate, and blood pressure. (After D. Purves et al. 2011. *Neuroscience*, 5th ed. Sinauer/Oxford University Press: Sunderland, MA.)

functions such as breathing, digestion, heart rate, and blood pressure. The **cerebellum** coordinates movement, including rote movements such as walking. The **pons** helps relay messages between the cortex and the cerebellum and is central to sleep. Along with the brainstem, the **medulla oblongata** helps regulate vital functions such as blood pressure and breathing.

✓ CHECK YOUR UNDERSTANDING 2.10

1. Identify parts of the hindbrain, along with their functions.

Neurons and Glial Cells

LEARNING OBJECTIVE 2.11 Describe the main parts of neurons.

The various structures in the brain must communicate with one another and receive and relay information to other parts of the body. The approximately 100 billion **neurons** in the brain are key to these communications and form complex networks that direct the complex functions of human life. As shown in **FIGURE 2.19**, neurons are structured in three main parts:

- The **cell body** contains a nucleus with genetic information, proteins and enzymes necessary to the cell's functioning, and **neurotransmitters**, chemical substances involved in communication between neurons.

- The **axon** is a long, threadlike fiber that extends out from the cell body. Electrical impulses travel down the axon from the cell body to **axon terminals**, where neurotransmitters are released to send signals to other neurons.

- **Dendrites** are fibers that receive signals from other neurons and transmit signals to the cell body and down the axon.

Neurons send signals to one another through the flow of neurotransmitters across **synapses**, microscopic separations between axon terminals and dendrites. A signal can activate or suppress the receiving neuron. An activated neuron fires—that is, it sends an electrical impulse down its axon. The moving electrical impulse results in the release of neurotransmitters, which then continue the chain of neural communications. An activated neuron communicates

cerebellum The brain structure that coordinates movement, such as walking and balancing, and that is involved in memory, cognition, and emotion

pons The brain structure located above the medulla that regulates sleep, arousal, consciousness, and sensory processes; the pons has nerve fibers that connect the cerebrum and cerebellum

medulla oblongata The brain structure that is responsible for vital functions such as blood pressure, breathing, and heart rate

neurons Specialized cells that transmit chemical and electrical signals in the brain; neurons are structured in three main parts: cell body, axon, and dendrites

cell body The spherical portion of a neuron that contains the nucleus and connects to dendrites; the cell body controls all of the cell functions

neurotransmitters Chemical substances that are involved in communication between neurons

axon A long threadlike fiber that extends out from the cell body; electrical impulses travel down the axon from the cell body to axon terminals

axon terminals The parts of the nerve cell that create synaptic connections with other cells; axon terminals release neurotransmitters to send signals to other neurons

dendrites Fibers or branched extensions of a nerve cell that receive signals from other neurons and transmit signals to the cell body and down the axon

synapses Microscopic separations between axon terminals and dendrites; neurons send signals to each other through a flow of neurotransmitters across synapses

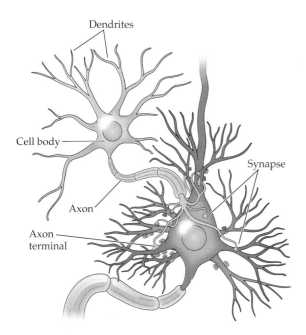

FIGURE 2.19 A typical neuron and neural communication. Neurons are divided into three main parts: cell body, axon, and dendrites. Cells communicate through signals that are sent from neuron to neuron by the flow of neurotransmitters across synapses. (After S. M. Breedlove and N. V. Watson. 2019. *Behavioral Neuroscience*. 9th ed. Sinauer/Oxford University Press: Sunderland, MA.)

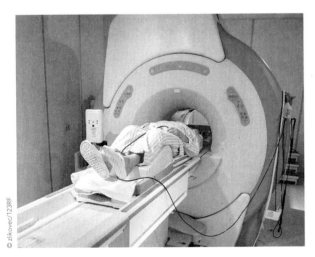

FIGURE 2.20 Glial cells.   Glial cells surround and protect neurons and are involved in a number of vital brain functions.

glial cells Nonneuronal cells that surround and protect neurons and are involved in a number of important functions, including the strengthening of synapses

by firing. A suppressed neuron is inhibited from firing, breaking the chain.

Glial cells surround and protect neurons and are involved in a number of vital brain functions (**FIGURE 2.20**). Glial cells not only communicate among themselves, but also influence communication among neurons by helping in the formation and strengthening of synapses.

✓ CHECK YOUR UNDERSTANDING 2.11

1. Explain the process of neuronal communication.

New Ways to Study the Brain

LEARNING OBJECTIVE 2.12 Describe different technologies used in the study of the human brain, and contrast their benefits and limitations.

How do scientists study changes in brain architecture and function across development? The past two decades have seen record growth in noninvasive methods for studying the human brain. These methods offer a much clearer picture of the associations between brain processes and people's thoughts and actions than was possible in the past.

Functional Magnetic Resonance Imaging (fMRI)

A person lies motionless inside a scanner that magnetically detects regions of increased blood flow and oxygen metabolism in the brain while the person processes certain stimuli or engages in other mental activity (**FIGURE 2.21**). The scanner records images that can be used to analyze the timing and location of human brain activity with high precision. Imaging with fMRI is suitable for adults and older children, but not for children younger than 5 or 6, who have trouble remaining still in the scanner.

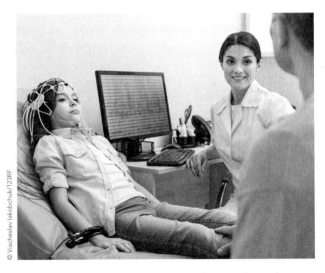

FIGURE 2.21 Functional magnetic resonance imaging. This technique is a method for mapping and measuring brain activity. A person lies motionless inside the scanner, and as the individual processes particular stimuli or engages in other mental activity, the scanner magnetically detects regions of increased blood flow and oxygen metabolism in the brain.

FIGURE 2.22 Electroencephalography.   In this technique, a person wears a head cap with embedded electrodes that are connected to a recording device with wires. EEG records electrical activity of the brain and enables analysis of the stability, organization, and timing of brain wave patterns.

FIGURE 2.23 Magnetoencephalography. In this technique, the person's head is partially enclosed in a scanner that records the magnetic fields produced by electrical activity in the brain.

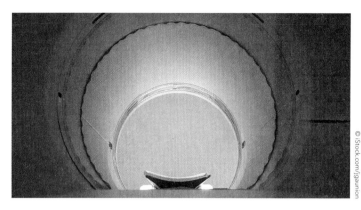

FIGURE 2.24 Positron emission tomography.   In this technique, a person is injected with or inhales a radioactive substance that then circulates in the blood. The person then lies on an apparatus with a radiation-detecting scanner, enabling measurement of changes in blood flow in areas of the brain in response to specific stimuli.

Electroencephalography (EEG)

A person is outfitted with a head cap with embedded electrodes that record electrical activity from the surface of the scalp (Luck, 2014) (**FIGURE 2.22**). EEG enables analysis of the stability, organization, and timing of brain wave patterns. Event-related potentials (ERPs) refer to the brain activity information that EEG records. EEG allows even more precise measurement of the timing of brain activity—to millisecond precision—than does fMRI. However, it lacks fMRI's precision about the location of brain activity. Also, EEG can be used with infants, to observe how their brain responds to pictures, music, words, and so forth.

Magnetoencephalography (MEG)

A person's head is partially enclosed in a scanner that records the magnetic fields produced by electrical activity in the brain (**FIGURE 2.23**). Like EEG, MEG enables analysis of activity in the cerebral cortex and can be used with infants. MEG offers more precision than EEG in establishing the location of brain activity.

Positron Emission Tomography (PET)

A person is injected with or inhales a radioactive substance that then circulates in the blood. The person then lies on an apparatus with a radiation-detecting scanner, enabling measurement of changes in blood flow in areas of the brain in response to specific stimuli (**FIGURE 2.24**). As with fMRI, the outcome of a PET scan is a computerized moving image of brain activity, but the timing of activity is determined much less precisely than with fMRI. Given the invasiveness of the procedure and the need to lie still during the scan, PET is not appropriate for children younger than 5 or 6 years of age. Also, it is expensive.

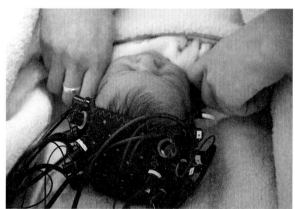

FIGURE 2.25 Near-infrared spectroscopy.   In this technique, very thin, flexible optical fibers are attached to a person's scalp, and invisible, infrared light is beamed at the outer surface of the brain.

Near-Infrared Spectroscopy (NIRS)

Very thin, flexible optical fibers are attached to a person's scalp, and invisible, infrared light is beamed at the outer surface of the brain (**FIGURE 2.25**). As the brain responds to stimuli, blood flow and oxygen metabolism changes in the brain provide a computerized, moving picture of the brain's active areas. NIRS can be used with infants and young children, who can move within a limited range during testing, but NIRS (like EEG) is relevant to understanding brain activity in the cerebral cortex, whereas fMRI can be used to assess activity throughout the brain (Aslin, Shukla, & Emberson, 2015).

✓ CHECK YOUR UNDERSTANDING 2.12

1. Which technologies would you use to study brain activity in a 1-year-old infant, and why?
2. How could you extend the study of brain functioning in older children?

Brain Development

What have new methods told us about the developing brain? Scientists understand that the brain is a living organ that changes throughout life, from the prenatal period through late adulthood. And, these changes allow people to think and act in new ways at different times in the life course.

How the Brain Changes

LEARNING OBJECTIVE 2.13 Describe five processes involved in brain growth.

Brain growth involves several types of changes: neurogenesis, migration, synaptogenesis, myelination, and pruning.

Neurogenesis

neurogenesis The process in which new neurons are formed in the brain through cell division or mitosis; neurogenesis begins during the third or fourth week of prenatal life

Neurogenesis refers to the proliferation of neurons through cell division (mitosis). Neurogenesis begins around the third or fourth week of prenatal life. As many as 250,000 new neuron cells are created every minute during the period between about weeks 5 and 25. By week 18, the number of brain neurons almost matches the approximately 100 billion neurons of the adult brain (Rakic, 1995; Stiles, 2017).

Migration

migration The movement of new neurons to locations within the brain where they will serve their ultimate, final functions; during the process of migration, some cells become nerve cells and others become different types of cells, such as muscle cells and skin cells

Migration is the movement of new neurons to locations within the brain where they will serve their ultimate functions. In the process of neuron migration, some cells become nerve cells that form the nervous system. Others become muscle cells, skin cells, and so on, with each type of tissue and body system developing and integrating with the others until forming a new human.

Synaptogenesis

synaptogenesis The process by which neurons form synapses with each other; one neuron may form multiple synapses with thousands of other neurons; synaptogenesis begins prenatally and is quite rapid before and after birth

arborization The growth and branching of dendrite "trees" and the creation of spines on the branches; arborization enables extensive synaptogenesis

Synaptogenesis is the process by which neurons form synapses with each other. A single neuron can form multiple synapses with thousands of other neurons, resulting in trillions of inter-neural connections. **Arborization**—the growth and branching of dendrite "trees"—makes extensive synaptogenesis possible and enhances a neuron's capacity for forming synapses. Synaptogenesis begins prenatally and is especially rapid before and after birth, although the timing and rate of synaptogenesis differs across brain regions.

Myelination

myelination The formation of an insulating myelin sheath around the axons of neurons that allows signals to travel down the axon more quickly

Myelination refers to the formation of an insulating myelin sheath around the axons of neurons that allows signals to travel down the axon more quickly (**FIGURE 2.26**). Myelination of different regions of the brain occurs at different times in development; for example, the prefrontal cortex does not become fully myelinated until adolescence or early adulthood.

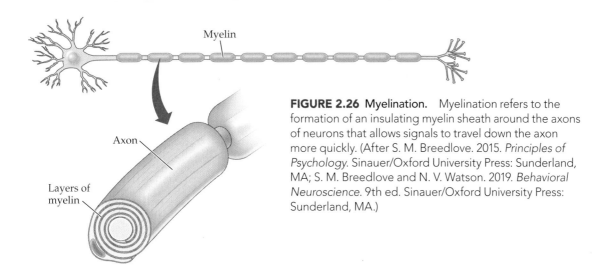

FIGURE 2.26 Myelination.   Myelination refers to the formation of an insulating myelin sheath around the axons of neurons that allows signals to travel down the axon more quickly. (After S. M. Breedlove. 2015. *Principles of Psychology*. Sinauer/Oxford University Press: Sunderland, MA; S. M. Breedlove and N. V. Watson. 2019. *Behavioral Neuroscience*. 9th ed. Sinauer/Oxford University Press: Sunderland, MA.)

Synaptic Pruning

Synaptic pruning is the process by which synapses are pruned, or eliminated, to increase the efficiency of neural communication (**FIGURE 2.27**). Synaptic pruning is vital because neurogenesis and synaptogenesis result in "hyperconnectivity"—that is, many more synapses than can be used or are needed. The brain's hyperconnectivity must be fixed if development is to proceed normally (Huttenlocher, 1994; Rakic, 1995). For example, early in development, synapses form between neurons in areas involved in hearing and vision, and neurons in both of these areas become hyperconnected to neurons in areas involved in taste and smell. About 40% of these superfluous connections are pruned by **apoptosis**, the death of neurons, and the consequent elimination of their synapses. Researchers refer to the "use it or lose it" selection process of synaptic

synaptic pruning The process in which synapses are eliminated to increase the efficacy of neural communication

apoptosis The death of neurons as part of development; about 40% of excess connections are eliminated by apoptosis

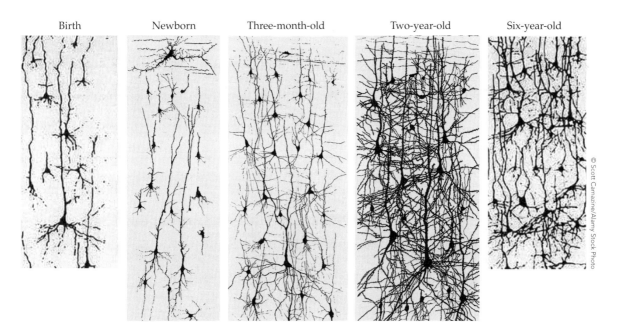

Birth   Newborn   Three-month-old   Two-year-old   Six-year-old

FIGURE 2.27 Synaptic pruning.   Synaptic pruning is the process by which some of the synapses formed by synaptogenesis are pruned, or eliminated, to increase the efficiency of neural communication. (From J. L. Conel. 1939–1967. *The Postnatal Development of the Human Cerebral Cortex*: Vols. 1–8. Harvard University Press: Cambridge, MA.)

pruning as "neural Darwinism" (Edelman, 1987). Synaptic pruning continues for years after birth, and, like synaptogenesis, proceeds at different rates and at different times depending on brain region.

✓ **CHECK YOUR UNDERSTANDING 2.13**

1. Contrast synaptogenesis and pruning.
2. Define arborization and apoptosis.

Periods of Brain Development

LEARNING OBJECTIVE 2.14 Explain how developments in the brain differ in the first years of life compared to later periods in the life course.

Brain development can be roughly categorized into five major periods, each with unique patterns of change: the prenatal period, first two years of life, age two years through early adolescence, young and middle adulthood, and late adulthood. Brain development is most rapid during the prenatal period and the first two years of postnatal life, with the prenatal brain undergoing neurogenesis followed by rapid synaptogenesis during infancy (**FIGURE 2.28**). Because the brain is rapidly creating new connections every day, it already achieves 80% of its adult size by 2 years of age (Lyall et al., 2016).

The brain's volume gradually increases over childhood through the process of synaptogenesis, before leveling off during adolescence. But synaptogenesis alone is insufficient to allow children to learn the things they need to learn. The brain becomes increasingly selective over the course of childhood through the process of pruning. As the brain responds to each child's individual experiences and environmental conditions, it prunes away synapses that are unused between childhood and adolescence. At the same time, the neurons of axons undergo myelination to allow signals to travel faster (Richards & Conte, 2020). Finally, during adulthood, brain changes are much more gradual. In fact, brain volume remains relatively stable until the 50s, after which it shows gradual decline over later adulthood (Sowell et al., 2004).

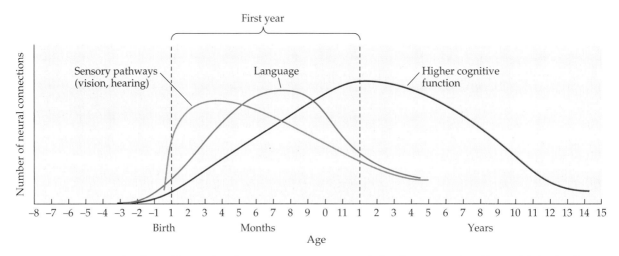

FIGURE 2.28 Periods of rapid brain development. Major developments in the brain occur during the first years of life. The rapid early growth in specific regions of the brain supports specific functions such as vision, hearing, language, and more advanced forms of thinking. (After Center on the Developing Child at Harvard University. 2007. The Science of Early Childhood Development [InBrief]. https://developingchild.harvard.edu/resources/inbrief-science-of-ecd/. Republished with permission of Center on the Developing Child at Harvard University; permission conveyed through Copyright Clearance Center, Inc. Data from C. A. Nelson. 2000. In *From Neurons to Neighborhoods: The Science of Early Childhood Development*, J. Shonkoff and D. Phillips [Eds.]. National Academy Press: Washington, DC.)

1. How might myelination of the brain help children with learning in school?

Contexts and the Brain

Why does the human brain follow a roundabout developmental course by producing excessive neurons and synapses and then pruning them? And how does the brain know which neurons and synapses to eliminate and which to retain? Brain plasticity, also known as neuroplasticity, provides answers to these questions. Recall, we learned about genetic plasticity earlier in the chapter. **Brain plasticity** is the brain's capacity to be shaped by experience. In line with the notion of gene-environment interactions, both genetics and environmental experiences influence the creation of new neurons in the brain and also guide the establishment, modification, and termination of neural connections throughout the life course (Greenough, Black, & Wallace, 1987; Stiles, 2017). Genes only need to specify a small proportion of the full complement of neurons and connections that an individual will eventually develop. Experience does the rest of the work, thanks to brain plasticity. Specifically, as children engage with the environment, their experiences lead to further specification in brain wiring. As you will see next, brain plasticity takes two fundamental forms: experience-expectant plasticity and experience-dependent plasticity.

brain plasticity The ability of the brain to change and adapt due to experience; two main forms of brain plasticity are experience-expectant plasticity and experience-dependent plasticity

Experience-Expectant Plasticity

LEARNING OBJECTIVE 2.15 Identify situations in which a person's brain development may diverge from its typical course in line with experience-expectant plasticity.

Almost all humans share a general set of experiences that affect the wiring of the brain, including everyday sensory stimulation—seeing, hearing, smelling, tasting, touching, and moving. Specific sensory inputs activate certain regions of the brain more than others. As sensory inputs get channeled to select brain regions, the brain becomes increasingly specialized by fine-tuning its neural connections. The ability of the brain to adapt in response to sensory information is referred to as **experience-expectant plasticity** (Greenough, Black, & Wallace, 1987).

Sometimes, however, things go awry. When a person does not receive specific "expected" inputs, regions of the brain that would otherwise develop in response to those inputs veer from their usual path. Children born blind or deaf, for example, show diverging patterns of brain development. Even children who are born with cataracts—clouded lenses in the eyes that obscure vision—show altered brain development if their cataracts are not removed in infancy. Children whose cataracts are removed later in development suffer from visual impairments, including an inability to see clearly or to recognize faces because the synapses that support these functions are pruned (LeGrand et al., 2003; Maurer, 2020).

experience-expectant plasticity A form of brain plasticity in which the brain adapts in response to sensory information; much research demonstrates how everyday, common, universal, and "expected" experiences affect brain development

Visual Stimulation and Experience-Expectant Plasticity

In the 1960s and 1970s, David Hubel and Torsten Wiesel demonstrated experience-expectant plasticity in their groundbreaking research with kittens (Hubel & Wiesel, 1963, 1979; Hubel & Weisel, 1965) (**FIGURE 2.29**). Hubel and Wiesel manipulated the visual experiences of kittens by raising them in artificial environments or suturing shut one or the other eye at different periods in development. They then documented how the kitten's visual cortex responded to altered visual inputs. (Note: The visual cortex, located in the

(A)

FIGURE 2.29 Experience-expectant plasticity.
(A) In the 1960s and 1970s, David Hubel and Torsten Wiesel demonstrated experience-expectant plasticity in their groundbreaking research with kittens.
(B) Compared to kittens with no deprivation of visual experiences (left panel), suturing of kittens' eye early on resulted in disruption to development of brain regions typically associated with visual processing (middle panel). In contrast, deprivation in adulthood did not lead to disrupted visual processing (right panel). (B after D. H. Hubel and T. N. Wiesel. 1962. *J Physiol* 160: 106–154; D. H. Wiesel and T. N. Hubel. 1963. *J Neurophysiol* 26: 1003–1017; D. H. Hubel and T. N. Wiesel. 1970. *J Physiol* 206: 419–436.)

(B)

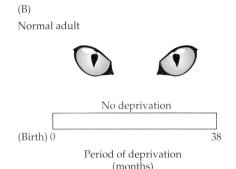

Normal adult

No deprivation

(Birth) 0   38

Period of deprivation
(months)

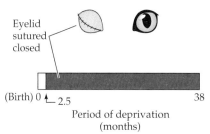

Monocular deprivation in kitten

Eyelid sutured closed

(Birth) 0   2.5   38

Period of deprivation
(months)

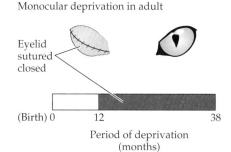

Monocular deprivation in adult

Eyelid sutured closed

(Birth) 0   12   38

Period of deprivation
(months)

occipital lobe, is the primary area of the cerebral cortex that is involved in vision.) They found, for example, that the area of visual cortex that normally receives input from the sutured eye started responding to input from the other eye. And, kittens did not develop areas of the visual cortex that normally receive input from both eyes.

Language Exposure and Experience-Expectant Plasticity

Research on brain plasticity, initially with kittens and later with other animals and humans, provides unequivocal evidence that everyday experiences change the way brains are wired (Blakemore & Cooper, 1970). Consider, for example, the way brain structures develop in response to language exposure. As noted earlier, certain regions in the left hemisphere become specialized for language, particularly areas of the brain that are capable of processing the rapid changes in sound found in human speech. In infants, certain dense areas of the brain are, in effect, "expecting" or waiting for speech. As speech input is channeled to select brain regions, the specialization of those brain areas and pathways strengthens (Johnson, 1999). As brain pathways strengthen and new neurons form, children acquire the building blocks for continued language development.

Brain Development in Atypical Populations

Interestingly, regions of the brain specialized for experience-expectant plasticity are not necessarily locked into their "expected" paths of development. Brain development in atypical populations, such as children born deaf or blind, illustrates this point. For instance, regions of the brain that are specialized for auditory processing in hearing children become specialized for visual processing in children who are deaf (Neville, 1995). Similarly, in congenitally blind individuals, regions of the occipital lobe that would otherwise be devoted to vision are recruited to support other functions, including language processing and memory (Pasqualotto & Proulx, 2012).

Because the very young brain displays high plasticity, infants who experience lesions to the brain (i.e., damage due to trauma, infection, stroke, genetics, etc.) in the left hemisphere, which is typically involved in language, do not show the same impairments as do adults with injuries, as long as the damage is not major (Bates, 2014; Trauner et al., 2013; Vicari et al., 2000). That's because other parts of the developing brain take over the functions that these areas would otherwise control—a phenomenon that illustrates the impressive plasticity of the brain to reorganize by arranging its neurons in alternative ways (Johnson, 1999; Stiles, 2000). Moreover, effects of early brain lesions on language development do not differ for left or right hemisphere damage, which similarly counters the idea that the brain is "hardwired" from the start for left-hemispheric language lateralization (Trauner et al., 2013).

✓ CHECK YOUR UNDERSTANDING 2.15

1. Provide an example of adaptations in the brain's development in response to atypical experiences.

Experience-Dependent Plasticity

LEARNING OBJECTIVE 2.16 Explain the type of experiences that may shape the brain development of individual children in line with experience-dependent plasticity.

In contrast to experience-expectant plasticity, in which brain wiring depends on nearly universal, "expected" experiences, **experience-dependent plasticity** refers to changes in brain wiring that occur in response to a person's unique personal experiences. For example, brain wiring develops differently in children raised in high-stress, low-stimulation environments than in children raised in low-stress, high-stimulation environments (e.g., Merz et al., 2019), a theme we return to throughout the book.

experience-dependent plasticity A form of brain plasticity in which changes in brain wiring occur in response to an individual's unique personal experiences and life circumstances

It would be unethical to conduct experiments with children to test how impoverished environments alter brain development. However, animal research once more indicates that animals raised in complex environments have brains with more synapses, a thicker cortex, and more glial cells. Of course, the reverse is seen for animals raised in impoverished environments. For instance, rats reared in enriched versus impoverished environments are not only quicker to learn mazes, as described earlier, but also show changes in their visual cortex and in the synaptic connections of their brains (Greenough & Volkmar, 1973; Juraska, Henderson, & Müller, 1984; Rosenzweig, Bennett, & Diamond, 1972).

Correlational studies on children's home environments further support experience-dependent brain plasticity in humans, although causality cannot be directly tested (see Chapter 1). For example, the brain surface area of over 1,000 typically developing children and adolescents between 3 and 20 years of age differed in line with their parents' socioeconomic status (SES)—that is, their parents' income and education (Noble et al., 2015). As parents' SES increased, so did the surface areas of certain brain regions in children, including regions involved in language and cognitive functions. Moreover, associations between poverty and children's brain development intensify with child age and the extent of poverty (Hackman & Farah, 2009; Hanson et al., 2013; Jensen, Berens, & Nelson, 2017) (**FIGURE 2.30**).

✓ CHECK YOUR UNDERSTANDING 2.16

1. Define experience-dependent brain plasticity and provide an example.

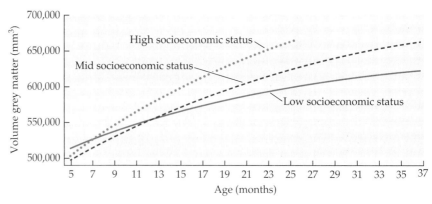

FIGURE 2.30 Poverty can affect brain development. Children from low, middle, and high socioeconomic status (SES) households show different patterns of growth in the gray matter of their brains. As a result, children living in low-SES households also show poorer neurocognitive outcomes than children from more resourced homes, with associations intensifying with child age and the extent of poverty. For example, although infants from low- and high-SES families had similar overall brain volume to start, they showed a widening of differences in gray matter volumes after their second year. (After J. L. Hanson et al. 2013. *PLOS ONE* 8: e0146434. https://doi.org/10.1371/journal.pone.0080954. © 2013 Hanson et al. CC BY 3.0, https://creativecommons.org/licenses/by/3.0/.)

Timing of Experience

LEARNING OBJECTIVE 2.17 Illustrate with examples how the developmental timing of experiences matters for brain development.

Experience-expectant and experience-dependent plasticity stimulate questions about timing: When in development do experiences most affect the developing brain? Is the brain always open to change, or is it more receptive to experience at certain ages than at others?

Critical Periods versus Sensitive Periods in Brain Development

critical periods Times when specific experiences result in permanent changes in a child's brain that cannot be altered

For many years, scientists claimed that there were so-called **critical periods** in brain development, times when specific experiences would result in permanent changes in the brain that could never be altered. For example, Hubel and Wiesel's experiments with kittens demonstrated that cortical plasticity of the visual cortex in kittens was time bound: Suturing a kitten's eye shut during a specific time window early in development resulted in changes to the visual cortex, whereas suturing before or after that period did not produce change. Critical periods in brain development also have been documented in birds, cats, dogs, monkeys, and humans, and largely exist during early development (Johnson, 2005; Michel & Tyler, 2005).

However, critical periods may not be as strictly timed or irreversible as was once believed (Bolhuis, 1991). In fact, most scientists today use the term **sensitive periods** to refer to times in development when the brain is most susceptible to experiences, but changes are still reversible (Johnson, 2005). In particular, the first years of life might be a sensitive period in development, when the brain undergoes dramatic changes as a function of experiences. But, although plasticity is markedly reduced at the end of the sensitive period, it is not entirely eliminated. Experiences continue to affect the brain after the period has passed and to alter the changes produced by earlier experiences.

sensitive periods Times in development when the brain is most susceptible to experiences, but changes are still reversible

Reasons for Sensitive Periods

Why might the brain be most susceptible to environmental experiences in the first years of life? Three general explanations have been put forth (Johnson, 2005).

First, different regions of the brain may follow genetically fixed timetables in their development, with automatic reduction in plasticity occurring after a certain period. For example, during the first year of life regions of the brain responsible for processing language input are especially sensitive to the sounds of a language, with sensitivity markedly reduced after that period (Werker & Tees, 2005).

Second, learning itself may produce brain changes that reduce the brain's plasticity. As children naturally experience different types of stimulation—seeing the sights around them, hearing the sounds of their language, and so on—regions of the brain naturally become increasingly specialized, more sensitive to the commonly occurring types of sensory inputs, and less attuned to other types. Indeed, once a region of the brain is committed to a specific function, it becomes difficult, although not impossible, to change that commitment (Thomas & Johnson, 2008).

Finally, sensitive periods may occur simply because experiences become increasingly stable over the course of development, thereby leading to consistent brain responses. For example, as infants gain control of their torso and head, they become better able to hold their head steady and maintain visual focus on the world around them. As a consequence, the visual input to the brain and the brain's responses to visual input stabilize. Such developmental changes might create an impression of decreased plasticity after a sensitive period when in fact the brain's plasticity remains unchanged (Johnson, 2005).

Flexibility of Sensitive Periods

Notably, although the early years of life may be a sensitive period in brain development, the timing of brain plasticity appears to flexibly adjust in line with human experience. Such flexibility can serve to accelerate or delay the opening of a sensitive period, and perhaps even "re-open" a seeming critical period (Werker & Hensch, 2015). In essence, the window of opportunity for learning can sometimes "stretch," as though the brain were patiently waiting for the appropriate type of sensory stimulation (Johnson, 2005). For example, surgery on infants born with cataracts in both eyes is typically done when infants are between 1 and 9 months of age. Immediately after surgery, the infant displays the visual acuity (sharpness) of a newborn, but after only 1 hour of unimpaired vision, visual acuity improves to that of a 6-week-old, and after a month visual acuity approaches that of age-matched peers born with normal vision. Moreover, whether an infant undergoes surgery at 1 month or 9 months of age, the infant shows similar gains to vision, indicating that the sensitive period for the development of visual acuity early in infant life can extend to a much later time (Lewis & Maurer, 2005).

The presence, flexibility, and duration of sensitive periods have important social and practical implications. For example, does a sensitive period in language learning exist? What might this mean for children who are learning more than one language? Would learning be enhanced if children were exposed to a second language within a specified time window? Should interventions be designed to build children's language and cognitive skills early in life? What about children born with disabilities? Would training in a specific skill at a specific age make a difference in children's ultimate skill level? What about infants who lack loving caregivers? Can a child's early deprivation of attachment and emotional bonds ever be overcome? Answers to such questions have powerful potential to inform educational policy and shape interventions for children with physical or mental impairments or inadequate supports in their social environments.

✓ CHECK YOUR UNDERSTANDING 2.17

1. Define sensitive periods in terms of brain plasticity and the timing of experience.

Looking to the Future

LEARNING OBJECTIVE 2.18 Reflect on the clinical applications of new initiatives and research on the brain, including potential improvements to human development.

The current, unprecedented pace of breakthroughs in developmental neuroscience can largely be credited to new methods for studying the structures and activities of the brain. In fact, in response to the extraordinary potential of these new methods the U.S. government launched the BRAIN Initiative in 2013 (braininitiative.nih.gov), calling on scientists to develop the tools and knowledge needed to better understand the brain in action: how people think, learn, and remember (**FIGURE 2.31**).

In terms of the first two goals of developmental science reviewed in Chapter 1—to describe and explain processes of change—the BRAIN initiative aims to provide scientists with opportunities to map brain circuits, measure patterns of electrical and chemical activity in those circuits, and understand how brain processes in children affect and are affected by their emerging skills. In terms of the third main goal of developmental psychology—to apply scientific discovery to pressing social issues—research into healthy brain functioning is fundamental to understanding the etiology, prognosis, and treatment of many neurological and psychiatric disorders that affect children, including depression, posttraumatic stress disorder, epilepsy, and autism spectrum disorder. As one of many examples, scientists now understand that unstable neural communication in the brain can lead to the uncontrolled excitations and brain seizures seen in epilepsy. New technologies may soon help scientists pinpoint abnormal circuits, predict when seizures are likely to occur, and develop treatments to stabilize brain activity. Advances in knowledge about the brain may help children with traumatic brain or spinal cord injury control prosthetic limbs and regain skills. And improved understanding of how to regulate neurotransmitters such as dopamine and serotonin may help in the diagnosis and treatment of mood disorders such as depression.

However, breakthroughs in developmental neuroscience can also come at a cost and spotlight critically important ethical and social concerns. Ethical and social concerns mirror those raised by genetics research, as discussed earlier in the chapter, such as whether scientists should one day alter brains or genes to make an individual smarter. Can research on the brain ultimately reach the point where scientists are able to intervene in the development of individual children's health and in the development of their intellectual, cognitive, language, emotional, and social skills? If so, under which conditions would developmental interventions be appropriate, under which conditions might interventions overstep important human boundaries, and who ultimately will determine whether, how much, and when to intervene?

✓ CHECK YOUR UNDERSTANDING 2.18

1. Provide examples of promising future breakthroughs sparked by the BRAIN initiative and new findings about the brain's functions and structures.

Courtesy of Jeff Lichtman - Harvard Center for Brain Science

FIGURE 2.31 BRAIN Initiative 2013. The Brain Initiative identified a set of goals, including characterizing all the cell types in the nervous system and developing tools to record, mark, and manipulate neurons in the brain. An example of new methods is Brainbow transgenes. This technology, developed by researchers at Harvard University, uses genetic methods to label individual nerve cells in different colors to identify and track axons and dendrites over long distances. Shown here is the dentate gyrus of the mouse hippocampus.

Developmental Cascades

Advances in research on genetics, the brain, and environmental influences have yielded a rich understanding of why children differ in their developmental paths, including their abilities to overcome obstacles and meet challenges. For example, we've seen that a person's genetic makeup affects how that person responds to the environment and in turn how the environment responds to the person. Interactions between genes and environment, coupled with the remarkable plasticity of the human brain, result in powerful cascading influences over children's development, affecting behaviors ranging from an infant's interactions with caregivers to the risks that an adolescent is willing to take. In the following sections, we offer examples of how genes and environment work together in areas of addiction and maltreatment.

Responding to Experiences: Dandelions and Orchids

Genetics can establish conditions that affect how children respond to their experiences. That is, the same experience can exert dramatically different impacts on children, depending on their biological constitution and genetic inheritance. An apt plant metaphor distinguishes between hardy **dandelion children**, who seem able to flourish despite adverse environmental conditions, and vulnerable **orchid children**, who seem to wilt in the face of any environmental challenge (Boyce & Ellis, 2005). Developmental scientists often use the term **resilience** to refer to differences among children in their responses to adversity (Luthar, Doernberger, & Zigler, 1993; Labella et al., 2019). Dandelion children are highly resilient, whereas orchid children show limited resilience. Of course, resilience is best viewed along a continuum, with most children falling somewhere in the middle. And typically, children show resilience at certain points in time or in certain areas, but not others. Nevertheless, although no child is in reality a "dandelion" or an "orchid," the metaphor is useful.

Importantly, the influence of environmental factors on children classified as orchids or dandelions can be good or bad, depending on the quality of the environment. That is, children who are susceptible to environmental influences—orchids—do very well in environments with rich social, emotional, and cognitive supports. Resilient children—dandelions—also flourish in richly supportive environments. However, in negative environments, children who are more susceptible (orchids) may do much worse than children who are more resilient (dandelions) (**FIGURE 2.32**).

What might account for these differences? A child's genetically determined level of biological reactivity, namely how the body responds to challenge or threat, may be crucial (Boyce & Ellis, 2005). From an evolutionary perspective, some degree of biological reactivity is necessary for people to adapt to changes in the environment. For example, the "flight-or-fight" response mobilizes the body to deal with threats quickly and effectively. However, high biological reactivity necessarily places stress on the individual. As a result, frequent exposure to stressful environmental conditions can cascade to long-lasting physical and mental health problems, especially in children who display high reactivity, namely those who lean toward being orchids. Conversely, in supportive environments, children with high reactivity may be especially energized to take advantage of the opportunities offered by their environments (Boyce & Ellis, 2005).

dandelion children "Resilient" children who are able to cope with stress and flourish despite adverse environmental conditions; drawn from a metaphor used by Dr. Thomas Boyce on the resilience of children

orchid children Children characterized by "low resilience," who seem to wilt in the face of environmental challenges, drawing from a metaphor used by Dr. Thomas Boyce on the resilience of children

resilience Differences among children in their responses to adversity or the process of adapting to challenges, stress, or trauma; it is important to view resilience along a continuum, with most children falling somewhere in the middle of the continuum

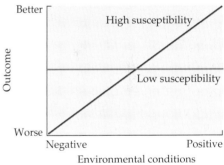

FIGURE 2.32 Differential susceptibility to environmental influences. Children vary in their susceptibility to environmental influences. Children who have high susceptibility to environmental influences do very well in environments rich with social, emotional, and cognitive supports; however, they may be more vulnerable to negative environments, and thus do worse than children who have low susceptibility to environmental influences. (After M. Del Giudice and B. Ellis. 2016. *In Developmental Psychopathology, Vol. 2: Developmental Neuroscience*, 3rd ed. D. Cicchetti [Ed.], pp. 1–58. Wiley: Hoboken, NJ. Copyright © 2016 by John Wiley & Sons, Inc. All rights reserved. NJ: Wiley.)

Differences among people in their biological reactivity and outward emotional reactions to situations emerge very early in life, and researchers often attribute such differences to temperament (which we review in depth in later chapters). Indeed, twin and adoption studies lend support to the role of genetics in infant emotional development and temperament. Comparisons of monozygotic ("identical") and dizygotic ("fraternal") twins reveal that heredity helps explain at least some of the variation among infants in temperament. Similarities in infant temperament were greater for monozygotic than for dizygotic twins based on parents' reports on the temperament of their twin pairs when children were 14, 20, 24, and 36 months of age (Saudino, 2005). Researchers have also documented genetic similarities in temperamental characteristics such as fear, anger, pleasure, interest/persistence, and activity (Auerbach et al., 2001). As you will learn in later chapters, early differences in temperament reverberate across developmental domains, for example by affecting children's interactions with other people, including parents, peers, and teachers.

Susceptibility to Addiction

Some people show high susceptibility to addiction relative to others. And, temptations that fuel susceptibility peak at certain points in the life course. Specifically, adolescence is a time of heightened risk taking in which some teens indulge in addictive substances, ranging from alcohol to drugs. Can genetic differences explain why some teens, but not others, fall into a spiral of escalating use that ultimately cascades to addiction? Twin studies provide a lens into the role of genetics in such behaviors. A meta-analytic study that combined findings across tens of thousands of twin pairs revealed relatively high heredity estimates for alcohol and tobacco use (Polderman et al., 2015). Of course, however, heredity interacts with environmental circumstances to determine whether susceptibility to substance use is expressed.

Animal studies offer another way to test genetic cascades, because researchers can experimentally manipulate rats' exposure to substances. When experimenters breed rodents to have a particular genetic makeup, the rodents exhibit addiction-like behavior, choosing to self-administer a preferred drug despite its harmful consequences. In contrast, rodents with other genetic makeups do not exhibit such behavior (e.g., Crabbe, 2008; Crabbe & Harris, 2013; McClearn & Rodgers, 1959).

In humans, like rodents, brain circuits regulate a person's responses to naturally rewarding substances such as food and water. For example, circuits that are activated by the neurotransmitter dopamine may be involved in responses to cocaine and other stimulants (Nestler & Landsman, 2001). Drugs may stimulate these brain circuits in people to different degrees depending on a person's genetic makeup; this would account for differences in people's vulnerability to drug abuse. Here again, the interaction between genetic factors (the level of response to dopamine) and environmental factors (exposure to drugs and family and peer contexts that heighten the likelihood of use) shift the odds that a person will develop a particular behavioral trait like drug addiction. Thus, genetic variations may account for why some teenagers "experiment" with drugs and alcohol without serious consequences, whereas others become dangerously derailed by the same experiences. In essence, genetics can instigate cascading influences from environmental exposures and pressures. The current U.S. crisis around opioids highlights the vital role that research plays in understanding the origins and treatment of adolescents and young adults who confront addiction. In addition, the Substance Abuse and Mental Health Services Administration (SAMHSA) of the government offers valuable resources for information and help (www.samhsa.gov).

Response to Maltreatment

Genetic differences may also affect children's reactions to abusive parenting (Kim-Cohen & Gold, 2009). Heredity helps to explain why some children who experience severe maltreatment show cascading effects to depression, violence, and antisocial behaviors, whereas others do not. For example, an X-linked gene known as *MAOA* (monoamine oxidase A) affects the production of brain chemicals associated with aggression. A groundbreaking study showed that maltreated children who carried a low-activity allele of the gene had difficulty suppressing aggression and displayed high levels of antisocial behavior in adolescence and adulthood (Caspi et al., 2002). In contrast, maltreated children who carried the high-active allele were less likely to develop such traits (**FIGURE 2.33**). As is common with other X-linked alleles, this gene-environment interaction was especially evident for boys: Men who had been severely maltreated as children and had the low-active allele were 10 times more likely to have been convicted of a violent crime than were men who had been maltreated but had the high-active allele.

A few years later, researchers identified another gene, known as *5-HTT*, as being involved in the association between child maltreatment and later mental health problems. The *5-HTT* gene has a "short" allele and a "long" allele, and individuals who had been maltreated as children or otherwise experienced extreme stresses as children *and* who had one or two copies of the short allele had more depressive symptoms, higher rates of diagnosable depression, and more suicidal tendencies than did individuals who had undergone similar childhood experiences but had two copies of the long allele (Caspi & Moffitt, 2006). The risk of depression was especially high for maltreated children who also carried the low-active *MAOA* allele and had experienced multiple types of maltreatment, for example children who had experienced a combination of physical abuse, neglect, and emotional abuse (Caspi et al., 2002; Cicchetti, Rogosch, & Sturge-Apple, 2007).

Perhaps most significant, the presence of the short allele alone, in the absence of early maltreatment, did not lead to adverse outcomes. The lack of a genetics-alone effect further spotlights the importance of gene-environment interactions. A genetic predisposition is not necessarily sufficient to cause later psychological problems; rather, certain childhood environmental factors must also be present. Moreover, maltreated children who are genetically at risk may be protected against developing mental health problems if they later experience a supportive relationship with an adult (Kaufman et al., 2006).

Again, studies with animals shed light on the precise ways in which early life experiences affect gene expression and, in turn, cascade to long-term outcomes. Let's return once more to the example of the licking of rat pups by rat mothers to illustrate these cascades. We saw that genetics explains how much licking rat pup mothers display. In addition, stress also changes rates of licking. Rat mothers exposed to daily stress display low levels of licking their offspring, and their offspring in turn are low in licking their own offspring (Weaver et al., 2004). Furthermore, the influence of stress on rat pup care across generations could be explained by the way that maternal licking, or the lack of it, affects the expression of genes in the rat pups that then influences their own maternal care behavior (Champagne & Meaney, 2006). Moreover, the quality of the later environment further alters the way in which genes influence the maternal behavior

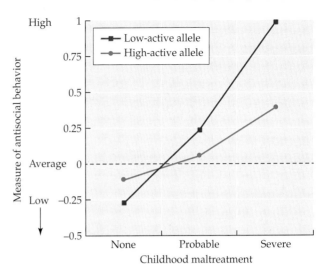

FIGURE 2.33 The effects of childhood maltreatment depend on genetics. Maltreated children who carried a low-active allele of the gene MAOA had difficulty suppressing aggression and displayed high levels of antisocial behavior in adolescence and adulthood. In contrast, maltreated children who carried the high-active allele were less likely to develop these traits. (After A. Caspi et al. 2002. *Science* 297: 851–854. Reprinted with permission from AAAS. https://doi.org/10.1126/science.1072290.)

of rodents. If rodents beyond the pup stage are subjected to stress and prolonged separation from their peers, they will later, as adults, display reductions in maternal care that are passed on to subsequent generations (Champagne & Meaney, 2006, 2007). And so, we see that environmental stress and genetics together can play out in the care of offspring across multiple generations. Such animal models have important implications for humans, and we will see many parallels throughout the book, in topics ranging from children's experiences of abuse and neglect to adolescent sexuality.

■ CLOSING THOUGHTS
Dismantling the Nature-Nurture Controversy

Chapter 1 introduced you to the nature-nurture controversy. However, in this chapter you learned that answers to what drives development are not neat and simple. In fact, the debate is basically obsolete, because nature and nurture are so intertwined. Multiple factors and cascading influences among genes, brain, and environment underpin developmental change. This chapter aimed to open your eyes to the fascinating and deep revelations that come with studying gene-environment interactions.

Let me end with NASA's twin studies as further food for thought. In 2015, NASA sent astronaut Scott Kelly into space for a year while his identical twin brother Mark, also an astronaut, remained on earth (Scott, 2016). When Scott returned to Earth, he was a remarkably changed person. Changes were not merely seen in how he thought about life and the planet we call Earth, but rather extended to his physical and genetic self. Upon return, 7% of Scott Kelly's genes were expressed differently than his brother Mark's. His gene expression affected his immune system, bone formation, eye health, cell repair and aging, and the ways he responded to oxygen and carbon dioxide in the environment (Brodwin, 2018; Hu, 2018). He was even 2 inches taller! (Although, stretching of his spine, rather than changes to his genes produced his height change). When researchers sequenced Scott's and Mark's DNA, they identified differences in over 200,000 molecules!

Although a fascinating story, and one that diverges from anyone's everyday experiences, by now you should recognize that separating identical twins fails to reveal the complexity of human development. In reality, according to principles of epigenetics, Scott and Mark may have differed in their gene expression already at birth, despite being identical twins. Moreover, their individual life experiences likely continued to shape their gene expression. Thus, any observed molecular and genetic differences after Scott's year in space may have been attributable to the natural evolution of human development.

In 2018, NASA sent 20 mice into space, while their twins remained on Earth. One day, the mice-in-space studies may shed some light on how environmental factors influence gene expression, and which genes are most affected. In the meantime, the developmental researchers who remain here on Earth will continue to make enormous strides in understanding the not-so-simple science of human development, and certainly raise appropriate skepticism about the limits of what a twin mouse (or human) in space can truly reveal.

■ Chapter Summary

Genetic Foundations

- Genetics is the study of genes and heredity.
- Chromosomes are the carriers of genetic information.
- Each chromosome is a single molecule of DNA, which consists of a long sequence of paired bases structured in the famous double helix.
- The genetic code is the set of rules by which particular sequences of bases are used to produce proteins in living cells.
- A gene is a small segment of DNA that codes for the production of a particular protein.
- The normal number of chromosomes in human cells is 46 (in 23 pairs), but gametes (ova and sperm) have only 23 (one member from each pair).
- Gametes are formed by meiosis.
- When an ovum and a sperm merge during fertilization, a zygote is formed, with 46 chromosomes. The zygote then divides by mitosis, and the daughter cells then divide by mitosis, and so on, ultimately developing into a new human being.
- The sex chromosomes (the female X chromosome and the male Y chromosome) are one of the 23 pairs.
- A zygote with two X chromosomes will develop into a female, and a zygote with one X and one Y chromosome will develop into a male. The X chromosome is much larger than the Y chromosome and contains many more genes.
- Genes can occur in different versions, called alleles, which can be dominant or recessive.
  - Organisms with different combinations of dominant and recessive alleles (i.e., different genotypes) can have the same observed traits (i.e., the same phenotype).
  - Generally, recessive alleles are not expressed unless both members of a chromosome pair have that allele, but the sex chromosomes can produce exceptions to this rule, typically in males when a recessive allele on the X chromosome has no matching dominant allele on the Y chromosome.
  - Traits that result from the expression of an allele on just one of the sex chromosomes (usually, the X chromosome) are called sex-linked traits.
- A mutation is an alteration in the structure of an individual's DNA.
  - A genetic mutation (i.e., a mutation that occurs in a germ cell or a gamete) can be passed on to the next generation.
  - Genetic mutations can be neutral, positive, negative, or mixed, according to their effects on the adaptiveness of the population.
- The Human Genome Project—the decoding of the human genome—was completed in 2003, spurring a revolution in biotechnology, including research into gene therapy and in epigenetics. The ethical, legal, and social implications of new discoveries in these areas will remain at the forefront in how we evaluate research.
- The microbiome develops in utero and is established in the first years of life and is maintained throughout life. The microbiome refers to genetic material that lives in or on the human body, such as bacteria, fungi, and viruses, and is critical to many aspects of health, including digestion, development of the immune system, and defense against infection. Imbalance in the microbiome has been connected to diseases including asthma, inflammatory bowel disease, and type 1 diabetes.

Contexts of Environmental Influences on Gene Expression

- Some traits are determined in a straightforward dominant-recessive way, but most traits are determined by the interactions of multiple genes, termed polygenic inheritance.
- Some traits show high phenotypic plasticity, reflecting strong environmental influence on phenotypes, whereas other traits remain unchanged in the presence of environmental variation, referred to as canalization.
- Epigenetics is the study of how environments shape the expression of genes.
- Genes and environment interact in four main ways:
  - Environmental factors can affect whether genes are switched on or off.
  - Environmental factors can influence the effects of activated genes on development.
  - The way genes are expressed can affect the environment, which can then affect child behaviors.
  - A person's genotype can affect the environments they choose to experience.
- Animal studies have contributed greatly to our understanding of gene-environment interactions.

Brain Anatomy and Function

- The brain is divided into left and right hemispheres connected by the corpus callosum.
  - The outer layer of each hemisphere is the cerebral cortex.
  - The forebrain includes the cerebral cortex, which is divided into four lobes in each hemisphere—occipital lobe, temporal lobe, parietal lobe, and frontal lobe.
  - The brain exhibits cerebral lateralization and contralateral organization.
  - Subcortical structures in the forebrain include the limbic system, the hypothalamus, the thalamus, the hippocampus, and the basal ganglia.
  - The midbrain is the uppermost region of the brainstem.
  - The hindbrain includes the rest of the brainstem, the cerebellum, the pons, and the medulla.
- The approximately 100 billion neurons in the brain form complex neural circuits.
- Neurons are structured in three main parts:
  - the cell body, which contains a nucleus and neurotransmitters
  - the axon, a long fiber that carries electrical impulses to axon terminals, where neurotransmitters are released to send signals to other neurons
  - dendrites, fibers that receive signals from other neurons

- Signals are sent between neurons via the release of neurotransmitters into synapses (microscopic separations between axon terminals and dendrites).
- Glial cells influence communication among neurons by strengthening synapses and through their involvement in myelination (the formation of myelin sheaths around axons, speeding the transmission of signals).
- Functional magnetic resonance imaging (fMRI), electroencephalography (EEG), magnetoecnephalagraphy (MEG), positron emission tomography (PET), and near-infrared spectroscopy (NIRS) are five techniques for studying the human brain.

Brain Development

- Four key types of changes are seen in brain development:
  - neurogenesis, the proliferation of neurons through division by mitosis
  - migration, the movement of new neurons to their ultimate locations
  - synaptogenesis, the formation of synapses among neurons, supported by arborization
  - synaptic pruning, the elimination of unused or under-used synapses, mostly by the process of apoptosis
- From the prenatal period through adulthood, the brain is constantly changing and developing, with development especially striking in the prenatal period and the first years of life.

Contexts and the Brain

- Brain plasticity is the capacity of the brain to be shaped by experience.
- Experience-expectant plasticity refers to brain development in response to nearly universal, "expected" experiences, such as early visual experiences and early experiences with language. When, in atypical cases, such experiences don't occur, the brain areas that would otherwise develop in response to those experiences are recruited to support other functions.

- Experience-dependent plasticity refers to brain development in response to individuals' unique experiences throughout life, as seen in differences in maze-learning ability among rats raised in enriched environments versus impoverished environments and in differences in cortical surface area in the brains of children raised in different environments.
- Both types of plasticity raise the question of the timing of experience: Is the brain more receptive to experience at certain periods in development than at others?
- There is evidence both for and against the existence of such periods, termed sensitive periods. It may be that reduction in brain plasticity is a result of learning itself, or it may be that plasticity is not really reduced, but that the stabilizing of experience over time produces changes that look like a reduction in plasticity.
- The BRAIN Initiative promises to provide scientists with opportunities to map brain circuits, measure activity in those circuits, and understand how brain processes in children affect and are affected by their emerging skills. Such research is fundamental to understanding and treating a wide range of disorders that affect children, but it also raises significant ethical and social questions.

Developmental Cascades

- Cascading genetic influences on responses to the environment are apparent in the differences between so-called dandelion children (who can flourish under adverse environmental circumstances) and orchid children (who wilt in the face of environmental challenges).
- A key factor in these differences is the child's genetically determined level of biological reactivity—the body's reaction to challenge or threat.
- Differences among individuals in their responses to environmental influences occur across many areas, including the risk for addiction and reactions to maltreatment.

Thinking Like a Developmentalist

1. Scientists have discovered a gene "Gene S" in humans that may be associated with a person's reactions to stress. The presence of "Gene S" is associated with a person showing high reactivity to stress. The same gene exists in rodents. You are an animal researcher who studies gene-environment interactions, and you believe that a rodent's early experiences (being licked and nurtured by mother versus being isolated without such experiences) will determine how rodents with Gene S react to stress. What experiment might you design to test the interaction between Gene S and a rodent's early experiences? What would be your independent and dependent variables? What would the study of rodents allow you to do that could not be done with humans?

How would you apply your findings to understanding the role of Gene S in human reactions to stress?

2. You are a scientist who studies children's brain development. You are asked to talk with a group of parents of newborns, whose babies were born with cataracts in both eyes. Some parents in the group state that they want to wait until their infants are much older (2 years of age) to remove the cataracts, to not upset their "too young" infants. Others in the group want to remove the cataracts right away, but worry that their infants will not acquire normal vision. How would you respond to the two groups of parents? What advice would you give, and what research evidence would you use to back up your statements?

Prenatal and Postnatal Health and Physical Development

3

Drawing by Minxin Cheng from a photo by Catherine S. Tamis-LeMonda

There is nothing quite as important as the health of a newborn. People around the world engage in behaviors they hope will lead to timely conception, a healthy pregnancy, and a birth free of complications. Indeed, members of every cultural community share a set of practices passed down through generations and guided by shared information and beliefs about "the right way to do things" or the "expected way to do things." Baby showers, gender-reveal parties, waiting to announce a pregnancy until the 3-month mark, visits to obstetricians, naming rituals, and rites around circumcision, baptism, and other religious ceremonies are practices that many U.S. parents follow.

Similarly, villagers in the province of Moldova, Romania follow traditional customs dating from the 1800s to ensure healthy conception and birth (Hulubaş, 2011). Women who want children drink tea from special plants to stimulate pregnancy, and they drink bath water that has been poured over a pregnant woman's navel to enhance their fertility. Midwives rinse women with the water taken from a newborn's bath, or make women sit on a container where a newborn had experienced a first bath. These customs are thought to help women who want children to have them.

In countries around the world, hopeful parents-to-be often eliminate harmful habits such as smoking, drinking, late nights, and fast foods. In essence, whether passed down through tradition or rooted in scientific evidence, the welcoming of a new child spans an extended period of time before, during, and after pregnancy.

In this chapter, you will learn about the marvelous and universal experiences of conception, pregnancy, and birth. We begin by describing the biological processes of human life, from the union of egg and sperm to the cell divisions and specifications that result in the fully developed infant. We next review the influence of the uterine environment (mother's womb) on the developing fetus and how the mother's stress, nutrition, and exposure to toxic substances come to define the first living environment. We then examine the processes of infant birth and health, ranging from nutrition to sleep. Throughout the chapter, we consider contextual influences and cultural variations in beliefs and practices around pregnancy, birth, and infant health and development. We end the chapter by highlighting developmental cascades that arise from circumstances surrounding the **perinatal period**—the weeks that precede and follow an infant's birth, specifically, the period between 22 weeks of gestation and seven days after birth.

■ *Conception and Prenatal Development*

Conception initiates the start of a unique human life when a sperm fertilizes an egg to produce a **zygote** that contains all of the genetic information required for development. After the genetic blueprint has been established, the **fetus,** or unborn offspring, undergoes remarkable and rapid structural and functional changes over the next 40 weeks, while simultaneously interacting with the sensory-rich uterine environment. Together, biology and experience lay a critical foundation for life outside the womb.

Conception

The reproductive process begins when a woman's egg launches from one of her ovaries into a fallopian tube. The egg releases a chemical substance that attracts a man's sperm as the sperm makes a 6-hour journey from vagina to uterus to fallopian tube. When a sperm's head penetrates the outer membrane of the egg, a chemical reaction seals the membrane so that other sperm cannot enter. The zygote has a full complement of human genetic material—23 chromosomes from mother and 23 from father—the blueprint for becoming a genetically unique person.

On rare occasions, the ovary simultaneously releases two eggs that two different sperm fertilize. This leads to the development of **dizygotic twins**—two genetically unique individuals sometimes referred to as fraternal twins. Sometimes, the zygote splits in half soon after conception, which leads to the development of **monozygotic twins**—two nearly genetically identical individuals sometimes referred to as identical twins (**FIGURE 3.1**).

perinatal period The time that precedes and follows an infant's birth, specifically, the period between 22 weeks of gestation and seven days after birth

zygote A cell that results from a sperm fertilizing an egg; a zygote contains all the genetic information needed for development

fetus An unborn offspring; from the end of the eighth week after conception until birth in humans

dizygotic twins Two separate fertilized eggs, also referred to as fraternal twins, which typically develop two separate amniotic sacs and placentas; dizygotic twins have genetically unique material

monozygotic twins Identical twins resulting from the fertilization of a single egg that splits in two; monozygotic twins share all their genes and are of the same sex

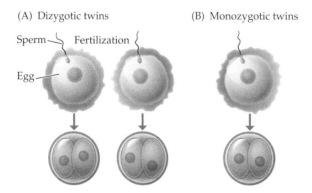

FIGURE 3.1 Twins. (A) Dizygotic twins occur when the ovary releases two eggs and each egg is fertilized by a different sperm. This results in two genetically different individuals. (B) Sometimes, a zygote splits in half soon after conception, which leads to the development of monozygotic twins. (After S. M. Breedlove. 2015. *Principles of Psychology.* Sinauer/Oxford University Press: Sunderland, MA.)

Influences on Conception

LEARNING OBJECTIVE 3.1 Discuss factors that influence the likelihood of conception.

Conception depends on many factors, including a man's reproductive health, a woman's reproductive health, and timing. Sometimes, medical technology can assist with pregnancy when an individual or couple is unable to conceive.

Man's Reproductive Health

Although millions of sperm enter the vagina, only a small fraction (about 200) make it to the egg. Some sperm remain in the vagina and others may be prevented from propelling forward to reach and fertilize the egg because of genetic or other defects. Approximately one-third of infertility problems that couples face occur because of problems in male fertility (Fronczak, Kim, & Barqawi, 2013). Many factors determine a man's reproductive health (i.e., the physical, social, and psychological factors that affect reproduction), including the quality of sperm, stress levels, sleep disturbances, depression, nutrition, and exposures to environmental pollutants and toxins (Pressman, Hernandez, & Sikka, 2018). Additionally, illicit drugs such as steroids, opiates, marijuana, cocaine, and methamphetamines place men at risk of low fertility (Fronczak et al. 2013), and high alcohol consumption can reduce sperm volume (Ricci et al., 2017; Beitawi et al., 2017).

The sperm that make it through the fallopian tube and reach the egg are the healthiest. Because strong sperm reach the egg before weak ones, odds increase that a healthy sperm will fertilize the egg (**FIGURE 3.2**). Sometimes, however, a mutated sperm fertilizes the egg—a possibility that increases with a man's age—which can lead to a genetic disorder in the offspring. Achondroplasia, which is characterized by short stature and bone deformities, is one such mutation (Tiemann-Boege et al., 2002).

Woman's Reproductive Health

Women must have healthy reproductive systems to ensure ovulation and the descent of eggs through the fallopian tubes. The woman's body releases hormones that stimulate the production of mucus to facilitate the sperm's travels through the cervix and uterus. Additionally, a thick layer of cells in the uterus, called the endometrial lining, allows the zygote to implant in the uterine wall.

With age, women are less likely to conceive. This is because women are born with a finite set of eggs, and eventually those eggs run out. The likelihood of conception is about 20%–25% per menstrual cycle for young, healthy women but declines to only 1%–3% by the time a woman is about 45 years of age.

Maternal age also increases the likelihood of abnormalities in the developing fetus, because older eggs are subject to chromosomal error during cell division. The likelihood of a chromosomal abnormality increases from a low of around 1 in nearly 400 for a 30-year-old woman to 1 in 66 for a 40-year-old woman (Creasy & Resnik, 1999). A defect involving chromosome 21 causes **Down syndrome** (trisomy-21), a disorder that leads to cognitive impairment and physical abnormalities in the child, including short stature and a broad facial profile. Although women of any age can have an infant with Down syndrome, risk increases with age (**FIGURE 3.3**). The chance of a woman giving birth to a child with Down syndrome is around 1 in 900 for women at age 30 years, and rises to about 1 in 100 by the time a woman reaches age 40. Miscarriage also increases with a woman's age. In the United States, about 15%–20% of pregnancies end in miscarriage, with rates for older women being

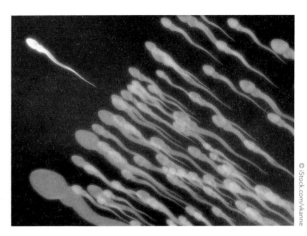

FIGURE 3.2 Sperm.   Strong sperm reach the egg before weak ones, increasing the odds that a healthy sperm will fertilize the egg.

Down syndrome A genetic disorder coming from a defect in chromosome 21, usually an extra copy (trisomy-21), resulting in intellectual impairment and physical abnormalities, such as short stature and flat facial features

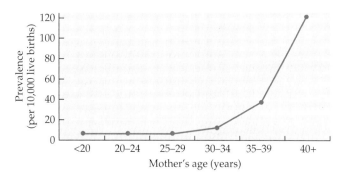

FIGURE 3.3 The risk of Down syndrome, or trisomy 21, increases with maternal age. (After Down Syndrome. Medical Home Portal. Accessed 2021. https://www.medicalhome-portal.org/diagnoses-and-conditions/down-syndrome; based on E. Alberman. 2002. *J Med Screen* 9: 97–98.)

substantially higher than rates for younger women (Centers for Disease Control and Prevention, 2010).

Timing

The timing of a woman's menstrual cycle and intercourse determine the likelihood of conception. The egg is released each month, typically on day 14 of a woman's 28-day menstrual cycle. However, because women vary in their menstrual cycles, ovulation can occur as early as day 6 or as late as day 30. After it is released, the egg only survives 12–24 hours, and the sperm survives about 3 days. Therefore, a sperm is likely to fertilize an egg if it is already in the fallopian tube when the ovary releases the egg.

✓ CHECK YOUR UNDERSTANDING 3.1

1. What factors in men's and women's reproductive health influence the likelihood of conception?

Fertility Treatments

LEARNING OBJECTIVE 3.2 Describe options that are open to individuals who wish to have children, but may not be able to for various reasons.

Science continues to push the frontiers on options for people who find it difficult to conceive or are unable to naturally conceive. Years ago, adoption was the only option available. Today, it is not uncommon for single women or men, gay couples, and couples having difficulty getting pregnant to achieve parenthood through **assisted reproduction**—a variety of procedures that make use of technology to aid with pregnancy. In 2016 alone, individuals in the United States reported nearly 200,000 assisted reproductive procedures, with around 3,000 procedures performed per 1 million women (Sunderam et al., 2019) (**FIGURE 3.4**). These techniques include:

assisted reproduction The use of various medical techniques to aid with pregnancy, from conception to the birth of a child

intrauterine insemination (IUI) An assisted reproductive technique/fertility treatment involving placing sperm inside a woman's uterus to enable fertilization

- **Intrauterine insemination (IUI)**—the placement of a man's sperm into a woman's uterus using a long, narrow tube. This treatment may be effective for infertility caused by scarring on a woman's cervix or when a man has

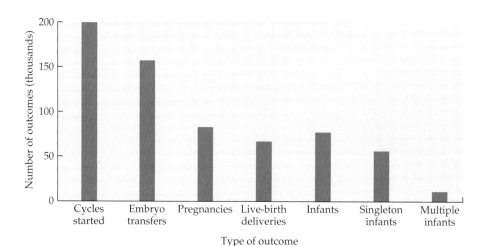

FIGURE 3.4 Assisted reproduction. Outcomes of assisted reproductive procedures reported to the CDC in 2016 for the United States and Puerto Rico. (After S. Sunderam et al. 2019. *MMWR Surveill Summ* 68: 1–23.)

low sperm count or motility. Success depends on several factors, including a woman's age, and can reach a high of 20% per menstrual cycle.

- **In vitro fertilization (IVF)**—the process of incubating eggs and sperm in a laboratory dish to produce an embryo. The process entails a woman taking medication to stimulate the production of multiple eggs, removal of the eggs from the ovaries, and the placement of sperm and eggs in a dish that is left in an incubator. Fertilization can occur on its own or through direct injection of the sperm into the egg. The embryo is then implanted into the woman's uterus using a long, thin tube. If the embryo implants into the uterus lining after 6–10 days, it leads to pregnancy.

- **Third-party assisted reproduction**—situations in which an outside male or female donates sperm or eggs to assist with pregnancy. When a man is unable to produce any sperm, produces insufficient sperm, or has a genetic disease, couples can turn to donated sperm, which are then used together with IUI or IVF. Similarly, if a woman does not produce healthy eggs or has health obstacles to egg production, such as ovary removal or exposure to chemotherapy or radiation therapy, third-party egg donation can be used. Eggs are retrieved from the donor using the same procedure as in IVF, fertilized by the sperm of the male partner, and the resulting embryo is placed in the woman's uterus. A surrogate mother relies on donor sperm, and is typically the biological mother. A gestational carrier, in contrast, is a form of surrogacy that involves *both* donated sperm and egg. In this case, the carrier is implanted with an embryo that has no biological relation to her. The embryo can use donated egg and sperm or the egg and sperm of the couple hoping to have a child.

in vitro fertilization (IVF) An assisted reproductive technique/fertility treatment involving incubating eggs and sperm outside a woman's body (such as in a laboratory dish) to create an embryo

third-party assisted reproduction The use of eggs, sperm, or embryos that have been donated by a third person to enable an infertile individual or couple to become parents

✓ CHECK YOUR UNDERSTANDING 3.2

1. Describe three forms of assisted reproduction.

Prenatal Development

If conception occurs and all goes well, over the next 9 months the fetus will develop the necessary biological structures and functions for life outside the womb. The **prenatal period**, the time from conception to birth, divides into three key periods: germinal period, embryonic period, and fetal period.

prenatal period The period from conception to birth that divides into three key periods or stages: germinal, embryonic, and fetal

Germinal Period

LEARNING OBJECTIVE 3.3 Describe changes to the zygote during the germinal period.

The approximately 2-week **germinal**, or **zygotic period** lasts from the time of conception until the zygote implants in the uterine wall (Jones, 2006). During the germinal period, the zygote begins cell division as it travels down the fallopian tube to the uterus. Within 12 hours of fertilization, the zygote divides into two parts, each containing a full complement of genetic materials. Every 12 hours thereafter, the zygote doubles its number of cells: the two parts divide into four, the four into eight, eight into sixteen, and so forth.

germinal/zygotic period A 2-week prenatal period from conception until the zygote implants in the uterine wall; the organism starts cell division and growth during this time

Blastocyst

One week after conception, a ball of 100 cells called the **blastocyst** becomes firmly embedded in the lining of the uterus in the process of **implantation.** By the end of the second week, the blastocyst is completely embedded in the uterine wall. Less than half of zygotes successfully implant due to chromosomal problems that cause cell division to slow down or stop (Johnson, 2008). Once implantation occurs, the embryo depends on the mother for sustenance.

blastocyst A ball of 100 cells that becomes firmly embedded in the lining of the uterus one week after conception; forms a structure with two layers

implantation The attachment of the blastocyst to the wall of the uterus; by the end of the second week after conception, the blastocyst is embedded in the uterine wall completely

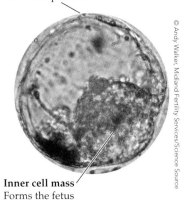

Trophecdoderm
Forms the placenta

Inner cell mass
Forms the fetus

FIGURE 3.5 Embryonic disk and trophoblast.   The blastocyst forms into a structure that contains two layers. The inner layer is called the embryonic disk and it becomes the embryo. The outer layer is called the trophoblast and it forms the placenta.

embryonic disk The inner layer or flattened inner cell mass at the end of the blastocyst stage that becomes the embryo

trophoblast The outer layer of the blastocyst that becomes the environment holding and protecting the developing fetus; the trophoblast forms the main part of the placenta and comprises three structures: amniotic sac, placenta, and umbilical cord

amniotic sac A membrane developing out of the trophoblast that has a clear, watery fluid in which the fetus floats; the amniotic fluid protects the fetus

placenta An organ developing out of the trophoblast that enables the exchange of substances between the fetus and mother through the bloodstream

umbilical cord A flexible cordlike structure developing out of the trophoblast that connects the placenta and embryo and contains blood vessels running between the two

embryonic period The period between the third and eighth week of pregnancy during which cells of the embryo start to differentiate into specialized cells and brain regions; three layers make up the mass of inner cells: ectoderm, mesoderm, and endoderm

ectoderm The outer layer of the embryo that develops into the nervous system, sensory organs, nails, teeth, and the outer surface of the skin

Embryonic Disk and Trophoblast

The blastocyst forms into a structure that contains two layers. The inner layer, the **embryonic disk**, becomes the embryo, and the outer layer, the **trophoblast**, becomes the environment that will hold, nourish, and protect the developing fetus (**FIGURE 3.5**). Sometimes, the inner cell mass of the blastocyst splits in half, which results in the formation of monozygotic twins as described previously. Three structures develop out of the trophoblast:

- The **amniotic sac** is a membrane that contains a clear, watery fluid in which the fetus floats. The buoyancy, cushioning, and consistent temperature of the amniotic fluid protects the fetus and allows it to move about without the effects of gravity.

- The **placenta** is an organ that permits the exchange of substances between the fetus and its mother through the bloodstream. The placenta contains a network of blood vessels that would cover a surface area of approximately 10 square yards if spread out.

- The **umbilical cord** connects the placenta and the embryo and contains blood vessels that run between the two.

✓ CHECK YOUR UNDERSTANDING 3.3

1. What structures develop out of the inner and outer layers of the blastocyst during the germinal period?

Embryonic Period

LEARNING OBJECTIVE 3.4 Describe changes to the embryo during the embryonic period of development.

The **embryonic period** spans the time of implantation to about the eighth week of pregnancy. During the embryonic period, cells of the embryo (the inner cell mass called the embryonic disk) begin to differentiate into specialized cells and brain regions that take on different forms and serve unique functions. The mass of cells folds into three layers (**FIGURE 3.6**):

- The outer layer or **ectoderm** develops into the nervous system, sensory organs, the nails, teeth, and the outer surface of the skin.

- The middle layer or **mesoderm** develops into muscles, bones, the circulatory system, inner layers of the skin, and other internal organs.

- The inner layer or **endoderm** develops into the digestive and respiratory systems.

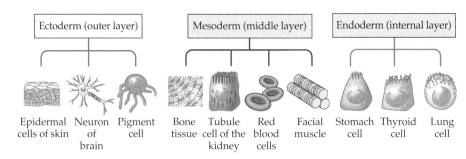

FIGURE 3.6 Ectoderm, mesoderm, and endoderm.   During the embryonic period, cells of the embryo fold into three layers which will each take on unique forms and serve different purposes: the endoderm, mesoderm, and ectoderm. The figure shows a few of the cell types that form in each layer. (After M. J. F. Barresi and S. F. Gilbert. 2019. *Developmental Biology*. 12th ed. Sinauer/Oxford University Press: Sunderland, MA.)

The Growing Embryo

The various systems that develop from the ectoderm, mesoderm, and endoderm do so at different times in the embryo's growth. The nervous system develops first and fastest (Johnson, 2008). By the end of week 3 post conception, part of the ectoderm forms the neural tube that begins producing neurons—the cells of the nervous system—at an astounding rate of over 250,000 per minute. One end of the tube develops into the brain, and the rest of the tube becomes the spinal cord. By around 5 weeks after conception, the spinal cord looks like a tail, and by week 8 it resembles a spinal cord.

In the fourth week, the ribs, muscles, and digestive tract develop. From this point forward, the embryo grows rapidly. Areas near the head develop earlier than those farther down, in a pattern referred to as **cephalocaudal development**—head before body; arms before legs. The shape of the head becomes apparent, and the eyes, nose, mouth, and ears begin to form. Embryonic growth also is characterized by **proximodistal development**, with areas near the center of the body developing before areas toward the periphery (**FIGURE 3.7**). Thus, the spinal cord develops before the arms, the forearms before fingers, and so forth. Small buds off the torso become the arms and legs of the embryo in week 5, the heart begins to beat in week 6, and by week 8 the hands and feet lose their webbed appearance and fingers and toes appear.

By the end of the eighth week, all the main body parts and organs of the embryo have formed. Although the embryo is just 1 inch long (2.5 cm) and 0.03 ounces (1 gram), it looks distinctly human (Johnson, 2008). The embryo now moves and responds to touch (Moore & Persaud, 2003). At around the eighth week after conception, the testes (in what will become males) produce the hormone testosterone, which determines the sex of the child. Male sex organs will develop if testosterone is present, and female sex organs will develop in the absence of testosterone.

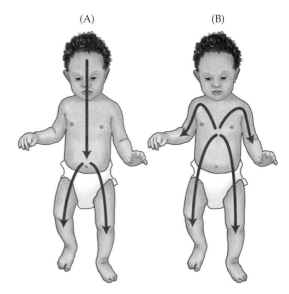

FIGURE 3.7 Principles of fetal growth and development.   Fetal development follows the principles of (A) cephalocaudal development—head before body, arms before legs, and (B) proximodistal development, areas near the center of the body develop before areas toward the periphery. These principles continue into infancy and beyond as children grow and develop. (After E. Polan and D. Taylor. 2003. *Journey across the Life Span: Human Development and Health Promotion.* F. A. Davis: Philadelphia, PA.)

From Stem Cells to Specialized Cells

The term **cell specialization** refers to the changes in cell shape, structure, and composition that enable cells to carry out specific functions in the body. Initially, all embryonic cells, referred to as **stem cells**, are equivalent and interchangeable. However, after several cell divisions these originally "open" stem cells develop into specific types of cells—the cells of muscles, eyes, ears, bones, brain, heart, liver, and so forth—which each performs unique, vital functions.

What determines the ultimate destiny of a stem cell? Cell specialization is an intriguing process, given that all cells in the human body contain identical genetic information. The specific functions of cells therefore depend on the subset of genes that are switched on and thus expressed in that cell. Proteins that bind to specific sequences of DNA regulate this expression of genes by making sure that only the genes appropriate to the specific cell type are turned on. The control of gene expression determines whether a cell becomes a neuron, lung cell, or red blood cell, for example (**FIGURE 3.8**). A stem cell's location in the body also influences its ultimate destiny, with neighboring cells affecting the function and structure of a stem cell (Wolpert, 2011). For example, if a region of a frog embryo that was normally destined to become an eye is grafted onto a frog's trunk region early in development, before the eye cells become specialized, the transplanted cells will develop normally into a part of the frog's trunk. However, if grafted eye cells are relocated later in development, after becoming specialized, they will develop into an eye in their new location (Wolpert, 2011). Thus, the timing of cell specialization illustrates the idea of a critical period as described in Chapter 2.

mesoderm The middle layer of the embryo between the ectoderm and endoderm that develops into muscles, bones, the circulatory system, inner layers of the skin, and other internal organs

endoderm The inner layer of the embryo that develops into the digestive and reproductive systems

cephalocaudal development The growth pattern of organisms in which areas near the head develop earlier than areas farther down (i.e., head before body, arms before legs)

proximodistal development The growth pattern of organisms in which areas near the center of the body develop before areas near the periphery (i.e., forearms before fingers)

cell specialization Cell differentiation or changes in cell shape, structure, and composition to enable cells to carry out specific bodily functions

stem cells Embryonic cells from the undifferentiated mass of cells of a human embryo; cells from which cells with specialized functions grow

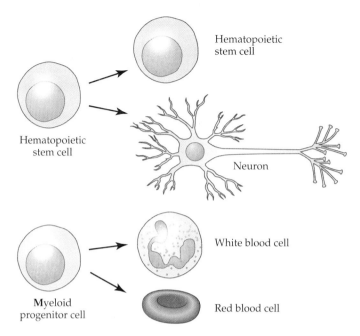

FIGURE 3.8 Cell specialization.   The cells of the human body contain identical genetic information. Genes that switch on are expressed in the cell, thereby determining the specific functions of the cell. Such gene expression is regulated by proteins that bind to specific sequences of DNA and ensure that only the genes appropriate to the specific cell type are turned on. The control of gene expression determines the final destiny of a cell as a neuron, white blood cell, red blood cell, and so on. For example, hematopoietic stem cells can develop into all types of blood cells, and myeloid progenitor cells are the precursors of red blood cells and white blood cells. (After T. Winslow. 2001. *Stem Cells: Scientific Progress and Future Research Directions.* National Institutes of Health: Washington, DC; S. Juris. 2022. *Immunology*, 1st ed. Sinauer/Oxford University Press: Sunderland, MA; S. M. Breedlove. 2020. *Behavioral Neuroscience*, 9th ed. Sinauer/Oxford University Press: Sunderland, MA.)

✓ **CHECK YOUR UNDERSTANDING 3.4**

1. Explain how cells of the embryo differentiate into different layers, and describe the systems associated with those layers.
2. How do stem cells become specialized cells?

Fetal Period

LEARNING OBJECTIVE 3.5 Describe changes to the fetus during the fetal period of development.

The fetal period lasts from about the ninth week of pregnancy to birth, and involves impressive changes in fetus size, brain development, sensory capacities, and learning (**FIGURE 3.9**). Growth in size and organ function enables the developing fetus to learn from and engage with the environment of the womb. In fact, the fetal period marks the beginning of learning as we know it. The fetus's experiences with movement, sleep-wake cycles, breathing, swallowing, and hearing set the stage for life outside the womb.

Fetal Growth and Brain Development

By the start of the fetal period, the sex organs have formed, and will eventually release hormones that influence brain organization and body size. As the fetus continues to develop, it displays a tremendous growth in sheer size: The fetus adds over 5 pounds to its weight and many inches to its stature to reach

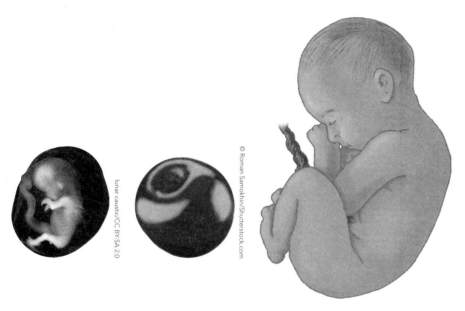

FIGURE 3.9 Fetal development.   Fetal development begins the ninth week of pregnancy, when the fetus is less than an ounce (as big as a cherry), through birth at 40 weeks, when the average U.S.-born infant is 7.5 pounds. (From D. M. Bozzone and D. S. Green. 2014. *Biology for the Informed Citizen*. Oxford University Press: New York, NY.)

an average of 7.5 pounds and 20 inches at the time of birth. **Vernix**—a slimy, white substance—covers the skin of the fetus to protect it from the amniotic fluid. Downy hair called lanugo helps the vernix to adhere to the skin. **Skeletal ossification**—the process of bone formation—unfolds rapidly from week 13, and can be observed on an X-ray by week 16. At this point, the lower limbs of the fetus are well defined and the ears have migrated to each side of the head. The genitals for boys and girls become differentiated by the fourth month. Over the subsequent months, the lungs continue to develop, the eyes open and respond to light, and the brain undergoes a process of gyrification, or convolution, in which cortical folding results in greater surface area and capacities.

During the fetal period, the brain rapidly develops neurons that form layers within the cortex and establish critical pathways to other neurons in brain organization. During the final two months of the fetal period, brain growth accelerates, with the brain and head eventually achieving a size that matches the size of the birth canal (DeSilva & Lesnik, 2008).

Fetal Movement

Researchers track the extensive repertoire of fetal movements using **ultrasonography**, an imaging technique that uses ultrasound to visualize the body structure and movements of the developing fetus (Birnholz, 1984; Rayburn, 1982). By around 7–8 weeks post-conception, the fetus moves spontaneously. At first the fetus moves by simply bending its head and spine, but in just a few weeks displays increasingly complex and varied movements (De Vries, Visser, & Prechtl, 1982). The fetus expands its movements to include moving arms and legs, wiggling fingers, grasping the umbilical cord, moving head and eyes, hiccupping, yawning, sucking its thumb, and changing body position through a kind of backward flip (Adolph & Robinson, 2015).

While moving, the fetus's hands come in contact with other parts of its body, with more than half of arm movements at 19–35 weeks resulting in contact between hand and mouth (Myowa-Yamakoshi & Takeshita, 2006). A fetus will open its mouth before rather than after its hand arrives to the mouth, indicating

vernix A slimy, white substance that covers the skin of a fetus as a form of protection from the amniotic fluid

skeletal ossification The process of bone formation or laying of new bone material by cells

ultrasonography An imaging technique using echoes of ultrasound pulses to visualize the body structure and movements of the developing fetus

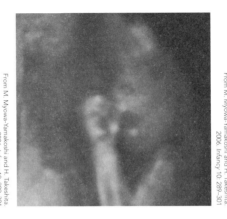
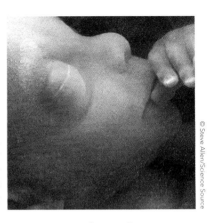

From M. Myowa-Yamakoshi and H. Takeshita. 2006. Infancy 10: 289–301

From M. Myowa-Yamakoshi and H. Takeshita. 2006. Infancy 10: 289–301

© Steve Allen/Science Source

FIGURE 3.10 Hand to mouth movements and anticipation.   A fetus will open its mouth before its hand arrives to the mouth, indicating that it anticipates that the hand is approaching the mouth.

that it anticipates that the hand is approaching the mouth rather than another part of the body (Myowa-Yamakoshi & Takeshita, 2006; Reissland et al., 2014). After the hand arrives at the mouth, the fetus often sucks its thumb in what may be considered the first goal-directed actions of human development (Adolph & Robinson, 2015) (**FIGURE 3.10**).

As the fetus grows, it occupies an increasingly large space in the amniotic sac, has less space to move, and often bumps against the walls of the uterus. By term, the fetus occupies the entire volume of the amniotic sac (Smotherman & Robinson, 1996). And by the last trimester the frequent body and limb movements of the first two trimesters decline to a small fraction of the day (DiPietro et al., 1998).

Sleep-Wake Cycles

Over the course of pregnancy, fetal daytime activity begins to differ from nighttime activity. As a result, daily **circadian rhythms**—the biological 24-hour cycle that regulates physiological functioning such as when people sleep, wake, and eat, much like an internal 24-hour clock—become apparent. The fetus's circadian rhythm develops in response to signals from the mother, whose body releases the hormone melatonin when regulating sleep (Mark et al., 2017). Thus, pregnant mothers who go to sleep and wake up at consistent hours support circadian adaptations in their fetuses (Mark et al., 2017; Reiter et al., 2014).

Indeed, fetuses who display fairly regular periods of sleeping and waking are more likely to have regular sleep times as newborns and fewer sleep and behavior problems as infants than fetuses with disrupted circadian rhythms (DiPietro, Costigan, & Pressman, 2002; Reiter et al., 2014). And so, pregnant mothers should try to avoid shift work and exposure to bright lights late at night, especially in late pregnancy, to prevent disruptions to their fetuses' developing circadian rhythms.

Breathing, Swallowing, Taste, and Smell

As early as 10 weeks after conception, the fetus moves its chest wall in and out as a sign of breathing, which helps with lung development. In the process of fetal breathing, small amounts of amniotic fluid enter the lungs and are then expelled. The breathing in of amniotic fluid promotes normal lung development and aids survival during the **postnatal period** (after birth). Because the lungs are the last major organ to fully develop, a baby born prematurely may require a respirator to assist with breathing until the baby can breathe independently.

circadian rhythms The biological 24-hour cycle ("internal clock") regulating physiological functioning, such as when individuals sleep, wake, and eat

postnatal period The time right after birth typically defined by the first six weeks after childbirth

The fetus also swallows amniotic fluid regularly. The swallowed amniotic fluid passes through the fetus's stomach and intestines, which helps the digestive system function at birth. And, just as breathing helps with lung development, fetal practice with the tongue movements and muscle contractions involved in drinking and swallowing provide continuity to postnatal life (Adolph & Robinson, 2015).

Swallowing also promotes learning about tastes, because the amniotic fluid contains many flavors (Maurer & Maurer, 1988). The fetus can detect and prefers some tastes, particularly sweet flavors, to others. In the first study of fetal taste preference, physician K. De Snoo (1937) documented a "sweet tooth" in human fetuses by modifying the taste of amniotic fluid. He injected saccharin, an artificial sweetener, into the amniotic fluid of a group of pregnant women and injected a dye without saccharin into the fluid of a control group. Fetuses who received the saccharin injection increased their swallowing, revealing their preference for the sweetener.

Hearing

The uterine environment is brimming with sounds. Over three decades ago, scientists used microphones to record the intrauterine fetal environment (Querleu, Renard, & Crépin, 1981). The microphones picked up maternal and placental vascular sounds, maternal intestinal noises, and external sounds such as the mother's voice. Scientists soon wondered whether the fetus could hear those sounds, and if so, when? We now know that by 5–6 months postconception, the fetus responds to sound (Abrams, Gerhardt, & Antonelli, 1998), and by 6–7 months, the fetus reacts when sounds change (Draganova et al., 2007).

Moreover, infants appear to remember the sounds they heard prenatally. DeCasper and colleagues were the first to test infants' memory for sounds experienced during the prenatal period. DeCasper and Fifer (1980) compared the sucking response of 3-day-old newborns to 25 minutes of recorded speech by their mother or by an unfamiliar female. They used a **contingent reinforcement paradigm**, in which a specific behavior (in this case, sucking on a pacifier) produces a reward (in this case, hearing a voice). Newborns modified their rate of sucking to hear the recording of their mother's voice relative to that of an unfamiliar female, suggesting that prenatal experience of hearing the mother's voice led to a postnatal preference.

However, an alternative possibility was that postnatal exposure to mother's voice, even if limited to 2–3 days, explained infants' preference. Thus, in a subsequent study, pregnant women were asked to read select passages from Dr. Seuss's *The Cat in the Hat* twice a day during the last 6 weeks of pregnancy (DeCasper & Spence, 1986). After birth, infants who had been exposed to the passages prenatally demonstrated different sucking responses to the familiar passages compared to infants who had not been exposed to the passages or had been exposed to different passages. Because infants' preference for a specific passage could not be attributed to their postnatal experiences, DeCasper concluded that infants remembered what they had heard in the womb. Of course, fetuses are not learning the words or the story line. But they do learn the distinctive rhythms and intonation patterns of the passages—"We looked! Then we saw him step in on the mat! We looked! And we saw him! The cat in the hat! And he said to us, 'Why do you sit there like that?'" (DeCasper & Spence, 1986).

Researchers have since confirmed that infants do indeed remember what they have heard in utero, even beyond the mother's voice. For example, fetuses changed their movements in response to music that researchers applied to the maternal abdomen, and they responded differently to that familiar music later as newborns when compared to newborns who had not been exposed to the music prenatally (James, Spencer, & Stepsis, 2002). When researchers sought to identify precisely *when* fetuses are capable of hearing, they found that the

contingent reinforcement paradigm The delivery of positive reinforcement in response to specific behaviors, such as by presenting a recording of the mother's voice in response to infant sucking majority of fetuses of 35–37 weeks showed increased heart rate to low intensity (soft) sounds held above pregnant women's abdomens, then decreased heart rate once they became accustomed to the sound, then increased heat rate when researchers introduced a new sound. In contrast, fetuses of 32–34 weeks did not show this pattern of heart rate changes (Morokuma et al., 2008).

✓ CHECK YOUR UNDERSTANDING 3.5

1. What physical changes occur during the fetal period of development, including changes to bones, genitals, and the fetal brain?
2. Explain how a fetus's experiences in the womb set the stage for life outside the womb. Provide examples of fetal movement, sleep-wake cycles, breathing, swallowing, and hearing.

Contextual Influences on Prenatal Development

The building blocks for development are established well before a child is born. Just as the hardiness of crops on a farm begins with the tilling and fertilizing of soil, planting of seeds, and watering and nourishing of the budding plants, many forces affect the health and development of the newborn: parent age, health, genetics, behaviors of the parents-to-be, prenatal nutrition and care, and the experiences of the developing fetus while in the womb. Each of these forces unfolds within a broader, cultural context that shapes beliefs and practices around childbearing and parenting.

Identifying the ingredients to newborn health is vital to the functioning of society. Indeed, societal goals for infant health have a long history. For example, at the turn of the twentieth century, Britain experienced a noticeable decline in its population due to a low birth rate and high **infant mortality rate**—the number of infant deaths that occur before one year of age per number of live births (Barker, 1998). In response to the crisis, one British county enlisted midwives to assist pregnant women during and after their pregnancies to hopefully improve the health of mothers and children. Detailed records of women's life histories and pregnancies were combined with national health records to form the basis of the "developmental origins of disease model," or Barker hypothesis, named after the English physician and epidemiologist David Barker (Glynn & Sandman, 2011). Barker's work indicated that fetal and early infant conditions can permanently affect the body's metabolism and lead to chronic conditions later in life (Barker & Thornburg, 2013).

But, *how* do early experiences affect the developing fetus, and what can be done to alter potentially harmful effects? In the sections following, you will learn about several influences on fetal health including exposure to toxic substances that cross the placenta and maternal nutrition and exercise, prenatal care, and psychological functioning.

Teratogens

LEARNING OBJECTIVE 3.6 Explain how the semipermeability of the placenta causes the growing fetus to be vulnerable to a variety of harmful substances.

The placental membrane allows certain vital elements, including oxygen, nutrients, minerals, and some antibodies from the mother's circulating blood to pass through the placenta and enter the fetal blood system. The fetus uses what it needs and excretes waste products that pass back through the placenta into the mother's bloodstream to later be excreted by the mother. The placenta also acts as a barrier that prevents many toxins and infectious agents in the mother's body from reaching the fetus.

---

infant mortality rate The number of infant deaths out of live births that occur before age one year

Unfortunately, however, the semipermeability of the placenta means that harmful substances can also reach the fetus. **Teratogens**, a word that derives from the Greek word *teras* or "monster," are external agents that can produce physical malformation and negative psychological and behavioral effects on the developing embryo and fetus. The sedative **thalidomide** is an often-cited teratogen that had alarming adverse effects on the developing fetus (see Chapter 2) with malformed limbs, such as stumps for arms or legs (see Figure 2.12).

Teratogens may reach the fetus by directly passing through the mother's body to the fetus, as seen in the case of radiation, or passing through the blood and placental membrane. Three key factors determine the magnitude of a teratogen's effects (Lovely et al., 2017):

- *Genetic makeup of the organism.* For example, although thalidomide was tested on animals and found to be safe, the unique genetics of humans made fetuses susceptible to its negative effects.

- *Timing of exposure.* Teratogens affect the organs that are developing at the time of exposure, and may have no effects at all during certain prenatal periods. For example, the zygote period is relatively resistant to some teratogens because the fluids of the zygote do not mix with those of the mother. After uterine attachment occurs, substances in the mother's blood can pass to the fetus and affect developing organs. If an organ is already formed, teratogens can result in slowed growth or tissue damage.

- *Dosage.* The amount of the harmful substance that reaches the fetus will determine the extent of abnormal development, which can range from no effect at all to fetal death.

Scientists continue to identify substances that are harmful to the developing fetus, including illegal drugs, legal but harmful substances such as cigarettes and alcohol, environmental hazards, and infectious diseases.

Illicit Drugs

Illegal drugs that harm adults also harm the developing fetus. Crack, heroine, and methadone cause slowed growth, premature birth, and withdrawal symptoms in the newborn, such as trembling, irritability, vomiting, and continual crying. Infants exposed to heroin prenatally are 10 times more likely to die of **sudden infant death syndrome** (**SIDS**)—the unexplained death, usually while sleeping, of a seemingly healthy infant younger than 1 year of age—than are infants not exposed (March of Dimes, 2005). Cocaine affects the fetus by reducing maternal blood flow to the uterus, which compromises fetal access to nutrients and oxygen. It also affects chemical nerve transmitters in the brain. Heavy use of lysergic acid diethylamide (LSD) and marijuana by pregnant women likewise results in premature birth and slowed growth and sometimes chromosomal breakage. The ingesting of illegal drugs during pregnancy can also cause medical complications such as the placenta pulling away from the uterus and causing extensive bleeding.

Nonetheless, the long-term outcomes of illicit drug use during pregnancy remain somewhat unclear. That is, the associations between various drugs and difficulties in child attention regulation and impulsivity may be explained by other factors associated with drug use during pregnancy, rather than the drug itself. For example, women who use cocaine while pregnant are also likely to smoke, drink, and use other drugs, to live in chaotic environments, to experience poverty, and to be in poor physical and mental health, making it difficult to pinpoint precisely which of these many risk factors explains the negative effects on the developing fetus (Lester et al., 2000).

Still, findings on the long-term harmful consequences of certain drugs, including marijuana, are robust. In a longitudinal study in Canada, children

teratogens External agents that can produce physical malformation and negative psychological and behavioral effects on the developing embryo and fetus

thalidomide A drug that pregnant mothers took to treat morning sickness that was marketed as harmless but led to malformed limbs in children

sudden infant death syndrome (SIDS) A situation in which a seemingly healthy infant under age 1 dies while sleeping due to an apparent stop to breathing

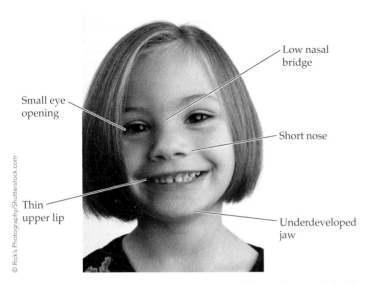

Low nasal bridge

Small eye opening

Short nose

Thin upper lip

Underdeveloped jaw

© Rick's Photography/Shutterstock.com

FIGURE 3.11 Fetal alcohol syndrome. Children born with fetal alcohol syndrome may have unique facial features such as a low nasal bridge, small eye openings, short nose, underdeveloped jaw, and thin upper lip. They may also display feeding difficulties as infants, brain and heart damage, slowed growth, failure to thrive, limb and facial malformations, anomalies in genital development, poor attention, motor-performance limitations, intellectual disabilities, and learning disabilities.

fetal alcohol syndrome (FAS)
A set of fetal problems caused by a mother's alcohol consumption during pregnancy; FAS is associated with unique physical features (e.g., small eye openings, thin upper lip), sleep and feeding difficulties, brain and heart damage, and failure to thrive

microcephaly A condition in which the head is smaller than normal; microcephaly may be caused by genetic abnormalities or fetal exposure to toxins, drugs, alcohol, or infectious disease

exposed prenatally to marijuana were followed into childhood and adolescence (Fried, 2002). Infants born to mothers who had used marijuana more than 6 times per week during pregnancy had abnormalities in the spacing of their eyes and shape of their eyelids and difficulties learning visual stimuli; they also displayed motor tremors and exaggerated and prolonged startle responses—extreme reactions to stimuli through sudden movements and high expressions of fear. Later in development, children had problems with attention, controlling impulses, and persisting at tasks such as reading.

Alcohol

Pregnant women who ingest large amounts of alcohol put the developing fetus at risk for physical and mental problems. **Fetal alcohol syndrome (FAS)**—the unique set of fetal problems caused by mothers' alcohol consumption—afflicts approximately 10% of infants born to mothers who abuse alcohol (Mayes & Fahy, 2001). Fetal alcohol syndrome is associated with unique facial features including a small forehead, small eye openings, short nose, and thin upper lip (**FIGURE 3.11**). Additionally, problems associated with FAS include sleep and feeding difficulties during infancy, brain and heart damage, slowed growth, failure to thrive, limb and facial malformations, anomalies in genital development, poor attention, motor-performance limitations, intellectual disabilities, and learning disabilities (Larsson, Bohlin & Tunell, 1985; Streissguth & Connor, 2001).

Environmental Teratogens

A woman's exposure to environmental hazards can heighten her odds of miscarriage or of having an infant with physical or mental abnormalities. Environmental teratogens include maternal exposure to:

- mercury, which can result in abnormal head and brain growth, infant problems with motor coordination, and intellectual disabilities;
- lead, which is associated with anemia and developmental delays;
- radiation, which can result in miscarriage or stillbirth, leukemia and other cancers, abnormal brain and body growth, and genetic alterations;
- pesticides, which have been linked to leukemia and other cancers and abnormal reproductive development; and
- X-rays, which can stunt prenatal growth, eye growth, and cause **microcephaly**—an abnormally small head and brain.

Infectious Disease

Pregnant women who contract infectious diseases have increased odds of miscarrying or having infants with birth defects, physical anomalies, and mental health problems. Zika virus, traced to mosquitoes in Brazil, is an infectious agent that affected pregnant women and caused vision problems and microencephaly in infants exposed in utero (de Paula Freitas et al., 2016). Sexually transmitted diseases represent infectious diseases that may result in fetal problems, including infant death. Acquired immune deficiency syndrome (AIDS) is associated with birth defects and vulnerability to infections; herpes is associated with infant mortality, eye damage, and intellectual disabilities; and syphilis is associated with miscarriage, infant death, blindness, deafness, and intellectual disabilities.

✓ CHECK YOUR UNDERSTANDING 3.6

1. What factors may determine the effects of a teratogen on the fetus?
2. Provide examples of specific teratogens found to harm the developing fetus.

Maternal Exercise and Nutrition

LEARNING OBJECTIVE 3.7 State ways that lack of physical activity or poor maternal nutrition may harm the developing fetus.

Staying healthy during pregnancy is important. Remaining active and consuming nutritious foods (including a diet rich in plant foods and healthy proteins) benefit mothers and infants.

Exercise

Remaining active is important for health at all times in the life course, and pregnancy is no exception. Sedentary behaviors place individuals at risk for obesity, diabetes, cardiovascular disease, and even premature death. A review of 26 studies found that pregnant women spent over half their time in sedentary behaviors such as reading, watching TV, spending time in front of a computer, resting, and lying down (Fazzi et al., 2017). Furthermore, the time that women spent in sedentary behaviors related to their cholesterol levels, the newborn's stomach circumference, and the risk of delivering **macrosomic infants** (i.e., infants born much larger than average). Thus, a comprehensive focus on women's health during pregnancy should include encouragement of daily activity.

macrosomic infants Infants who are born much larger than average

Nutrition and Fetal Development

The effects of nutrition on conception and fetal development were well documented during World War II, when many European nations suffered from a lack of food supplies that resulted in low rates of conception and increased miscarriages, stillbirths, and congenital malformations. Since that time, researchers have made great strides in understanding how maternal malnutrition may compromise fetal development.

Because the developing fetus relies on the mother for nutrients, inadequate diet during pregnancy can cause premature birth and problems in physical and cognitive areas (Bauerfeld & Lachenmeyer, 1992). A meta-analysis that combined the findings of several studies revealed that infants born to underweight women were at greater risk for prematurity and low birth weight than were infants born to women of normal weight (Han et al., 2011). Analysis of the weight statuses of two cohorts of women pregnant between 2003 and 2018 (a total of 20,000 women) found the highest rates of premature delivery for women who were underweight compared to normal, overweight, and obese women (Grove et al., 2019) (**FIGURE 3.12**).

The harmful effects of malnutrition on fetal development are specific. That is, deficiencies in specific vitamins and minerals in a woman's diet are associated with particular impairments in the fetus and infant. For example:

anencephaly A neural tube defect resulting in the absence of a major portion of the brain, skull, and scalp during embryonic development, usually between days 23 and 26 after conception; a mother's folic acid deficiencies may be a factor

spina bifida A birth defect of the spine causing paralysis and mental disability when the spine and spinal cord do not form correctly; a mother's folic acid deficiencies may be a factor

• Folic acid deficiencies can produce neural tube defects that cause **anencephaly**, a defect that results in the absence of a major portion of the brain, skull, and scalp, or **spina bifida**, a defect of the spine that can cause paralysis and mental disability.

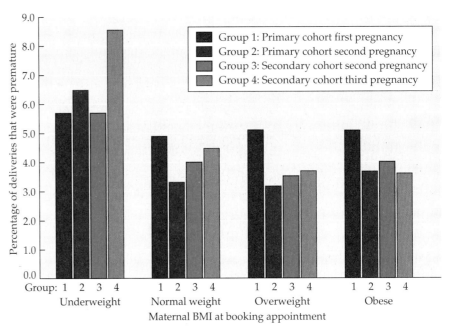

FIGURE 3.12 Weight of the mother and premature birth. Women who were underweight during pregnancy were more likely to give birth prematurely than those who were normal weight, overweight, or obese. (After G. Grove et al. 2019. *PLOS ONE* 14: e0225400. doi: 10.1371/journal.pone.0225400. © 2019 Grove et al. CC BY 4.0. https://creativecommons.org/licenses/by/4.0/)

- Iron deficiency is associated with anemia in infancy.
- Iodine deficiency is associated with thyroid deficiency in children, which can lead to physical stunting and low cognitive functioning.

A particular form of fatty acid found in fish oil (DHA) may also contribute to fetal brain development. DHA is a primary structural component of the human brain, skin, and retina, and pregnant and nursing women are often encouraged to eat foods high in DHA. Developmental scientist John Colombo assessed mothers' and infants' DHA at delivery and infant attention, exploratory play, and how quickly babies learned a picture at 4, 6, 8, 12, and 18 months. Compared to infants of mothers who had low DHA, infants of mothers who consumed high DHA showed advantages on visual attention and processing speed and were advanced in their object exploration in the second year (Colombo et al., 2004).

Notably, although "malnutrition" suggests a lack of food, the term also applies to conditions when a person does not eat enough of the right types of foods, eats too much, and/or lacks a balanced diet. Women who are overweight or obese may be overfed but undernourished, and obesity during pregnancy can negatively impact fetal growth and result in preterm birth and neonatal mortality (Castro & Avina, 2002; McDonald et al., 2011).

Adaptive Response?

In Chapter 1, you were introduced to evolutionary approaches to development, which posit that certain human behaviors may be adaptive to the survival of the individual. Some researchers interpret slowed fetal growth and low birth weight to be an adaptive response to maternal malnourishment (Bateson, et al., 2004). That is, if a mother consumes insufficient food, her "starvation" signals to the fetus that food is likely to be scarce in the future. This leads to a modified metabolism in the fetus—a kind of natural acclimation to receiving little food—and corresponding small body weight. The small body weight helps the infant cope in the future

active movement of abdominal muscles further accelerates the fetus's descent. The fetus's skull bones are still flexible and immature, and so show a temporary molding in their shape as they settle low in the mother's pelvis, which allows the fetus to more easily pass through the birth canal. Moreover, as contractions squeeze the fetus, they force the intake and release of amniotic fluid from the lungs, which helps with breathing after birth.

The second stage may last from a few minutes to several hours. The fetus's head is tucked down into the chest, and the first to emerge. In 4% of births, the fetus is in **breech** position, which causes feet or buttocks to emerge before the head. Breech position can lead to complications, and thus a decision may be made to remove the infant surgically in a **caesarean birth** (also known as **C-section**). Caesarean births are common when pregnancy complications arise and vaginal delivery would place the infant or mother at risk. Circumstances that lead to caesarean birth include problems with the placenta or umbilical cord; changes to infant heartbeat; mother carrying multiple children; and mother having health problems such as heart or brain conditions.

Third Stage of Labor

The **third stage of labor** starts right after the birth of the infant and ends with delivery of the placenta. A few minutes after infant birth, the uterus contracts again to separate the placenta from the uterine wall. The placenta and other fetal membranes (the afterbirth) are usually delivered in 5–10 minutes.

breech A bottom-first or feet-first position of the baby right before birth

caesarean birth (C-section) A surgical procedure used to deliver a baby through incisions in the abdomen and uterus, in contrast to a vaginal delivery; C-sections may be advised if there are complications during labor (such as breech position)

third stage of labor The shortest stage of labor occurring right after the birth of the infant and ending with the delivery of the placenta

✓ **CHECK YOUR UNDERSTANDING 3.10**
1. What changes occur during each stage of labor to propel forward the infant's birth?
2. Why are contractions important?

Neonatal Health

LEARNING OBJECTIVE 3.11 Identify measures used to assess newborn health.

The newborn infant is immediately assessed for its health to determine whether it needs further intervention. For example, a premature infant may have difficulty breathing, and an assessment would indicate the need for the infant to be placed in an incubator—an enclosed crib that provides a controlled, protected environment for the infant in temperature, oxygen, and so forth.

The **Apgar scale** represents the most common assessment of newborn health (Apgar, 1952), and is typically conducted at 1 minute and then at 5 minutes after the infant's birth. The Apgar is based on ratings of newborn appearance, pulse, grimace, activity, and respiration (**FIGURE 3.14**). It provides a quick and easy way for doctors to evaluate newborn health based on five criteria: skin color, heart rate, reflex irritability, muscle tone, and respiration, which are each scored at 0, 1, or 2 points, with 2 being the highest score. For example, under the criterion of skin color, an infant with normal color (including hands and feet) would receive 2 points; a newborn with hands and feet that are bluish-grey 1 point; and a newborn with a bluish-gray color all over, 0 points. Doctors then sum the five scores for a total score.

Apgar scale The most common assessment of newborn health typically conducted by a nurse or doctor at 1 minute and then at 5 minutes after the infant's birth; the Apgar scale is based on ratings of neonate appearance, pulse, grimace, activity, and respiration

	Indicator	0 points	1 point	2 points
A	Activity (muscle tone)	Absent	Flexed arms and legs	Active
P	Pulse	Absent	Below 100 beats per minute	Over 100 beats per minute
G	Grimace (reflex irritability)	Floppy	Minimal response to stimulation	Prompt response to stimulation
A	Appearance (skin color)	Blue, pale	Pink body, blue extremities	Pink
R	Respiration	Absent	Slow and irregular	Vigorous cry

FIGURE 3.14 The Apgar scale. This tests a newborn's **a**ppearance, **p**ulse, **g**rimace, **a**ctivity, and **r**espiration and is the most common assessment of newborn health, conducted at 1 minute and then at 5 minutes after the infant's birth. Each aspect of infant health is scored at 0, 1, or 2 points, with 2 being the highest score. (After V. Apgar et al. 1958. *JAMA* 168: 1985–1988.)

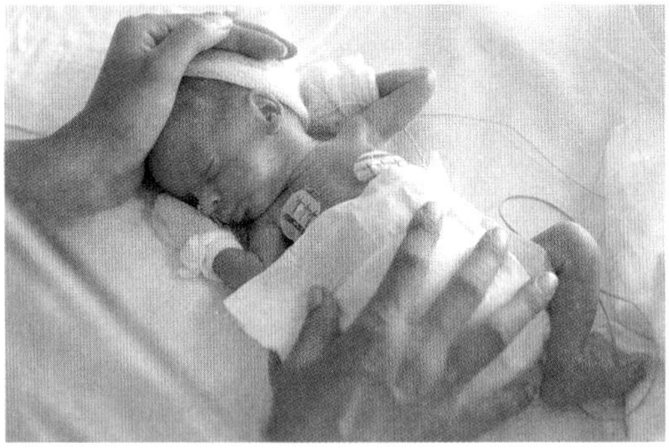

FIGURE 3.15 Premature birth. Premature birth occurring before 37 weeks is the most common reason for a baby being low birth weight or very low birth weight. Various problems can arise from prematurity, including problems in attention, language development, brain and neurological functioning, cognitive development, motor coordination, and health.

gestational age The time that passes from conception to the infant's birth; term newborns are born between 37 and 41 weeks of pregnancy

premature birth A birth that occurs more than three weeks before the infant's estimated due date (before week 37 of pregnancy), which may lead to medical challenges at and after birth

small-for-date infants Infants who weigh less than expected at birth based on the time they spent in the womb; they may have experienced inadequate nutrition in the womb

anoxia A situation in which infants experience an inadequate supply of oxygen during labor or after birth; prolonged minutes without breathing may result in brain damage

Newborns with scores of 7–10 points are considered to be in good to excellent health; those with scores of 4–6 points are considered to be low in health; and newborns scoring 3 points or below likely require immediate medical attention. The duration of scores also matters. Sometimes newborns with initially low scores rebound by the second assessment; those who do not rebound may have neurological damage or other serious health problems.

Gestational age, the time that passes from conception to the infant's birth, offers another measure of newborn health. Term newborns are born between 37 and 41 weeks, whereas a **premature birth** occurs before 37 weeks (**FIGURE 3.15**). After birth, post-birth assessment of gestational age is determined by a newborn's neuromuscular and physical characteristics. For example, a newborn's posture at rest is one indicator of gestational age. A healthy newborn has legs and arms that are moderately flexed, while a less healthy preterm newborn may display less flexion.

✓ CHECK YOUR UNDERSTANDING 3.11
1. Explain the purpose of an Apgar score.

Birth Complications

LEARNING OBJECTIVE 3.12 Describe possible birth complications.

Fortunately, birth complications are relatively rare, although rates increase substantially for women with a history of prenatal problems or poor health. Low birth weight and oxygen deprivation are two serious birth complications that can cause long-term developmental problems.

Birth Weight

Newborns average about 7.5 pounds (3.2 kg). Newborns weighing fewer than 5 pounds, 8 ounces (2.5 kg) are classified as low birth weight (LBW), and those weighing 3.5 pounds (1.5 kg) or less are classified as very low birth weight (VLBW), regardless of gestational age. At the other extreme, infants weighing more than 8 pounds, 13 ounces (4 kg) have high birth weight.

Premature birth is the most common reason for a baby being LBW or VLBW. However, some infants born at term are **small-for-date infants** because their weight is less than would be expected based on the time they spent in the womb. Infants born prematurely who are also small-for-date are especially at risk. Small-for-date infants likely experienced inadequate nutrition while in the womb due to their mothers' poor eating habits, defects in placenta functioning that interfered with nutrients passing from mother to infant, or biological defects that interfered with proper growth.

Oxygen Deprivation

Sometimes infants experience an inadequate supply of oxygen during birth, a situation referred to as **anoxia**. Anoxia can occur during labor or after birth if an infant fails to breathe within a few minutes. Typically, brief interruptions to breathing do not cause harm, but extended minutes without breathing can cause brain damage (Kendall & Peebles, 2005). The duration and severity of problems depend on the extent of oxygen deprivation. Babies who suffer from high levels of oxygen deprivation have compromised cognitive and language performance through childhood (Hopkins-Golightly, Raz, & Sander, 2003).

Anoxia during labor can be caused by a baby being in the breech position, because breech causes the umbilical cord to be squeezed, leading to oxygen disruption. In about 1% of births, the placenta prematurely separates, which can cause oxygen deprivation so severe it can lead to infant death. Thus, obstetricians immediately deliver the baby by C-section if placental separation occurs.

Preterm infants are also at risk of oxygen deprivation because their lungs are not yet mature enough for them to breathe on their own. As a result, babies who are premature may experience **respiratory distress syndrome (RDS)**, a breathing disorder in which fluid collects in the air sacs of lungs, depriving the newborn of oxygen, and potentially resulting in infant death (Marseglia et al., 2019).

respiratory distress syndrome (RDS) A breathing disorder in newborns that occurs when fluid collects in the air sacs of lungs, depriving newborns of oxygen and resulting in breathing challenges

✓ **CHECK YOUR UNDERSTANDING 3.12**

1. Describe two serious birth complications.

Contextual Influences on Infant Mortality and Birth Weight

LEARNING OBJECTIVE 3.13 Describe historical trends in infant mortality.

The economic circumstances of families and communities affect rates of infant mortality in the United States and globally, in part due to differences in the quality of healthcare available to families. Indeed, improvements in health care and living standards at a national level account for gains in newborn health over historical time. In the United States, improvements in nutrition, access to health care, monitoring of disease, clinical medicine, access to clean water, and standards of living and education over the twentieth century have led to massive declines in infant and mother mortality rates (Cutler & Miller, 2005). For example, at the turn of the twentieth century, approximately 100 infants died before 1 year of age for every 1,000 live births, and 6–9 women died of pregnancy-related complications (Loudon, 1992) (**FIGURE 3.16**). The infant mortality rate declined

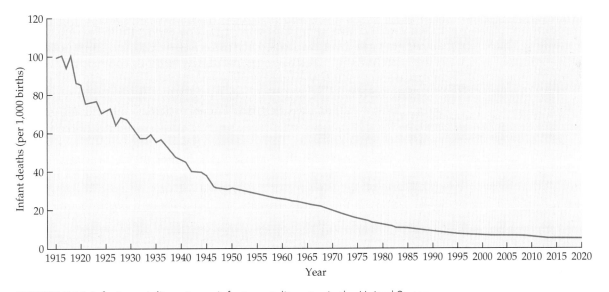

FIGURE 3.16 Infant mortality rates. Infant mortality rates in the United States showed huge declines over the twentieth century, due to improved health, clean water, and improved standards of living. (Data sources: 1915-1949: R. D. Grove and A. M. Hetzel. 1968. Vital Statistics Rates in the United States 1940-1960, Public Health Service Pub. No. 1677, p. 206. U.S. Dept of Health, Education and Welfare/National Center for Health Statistics: Washington, DC; 1950-2020: https://www.macrotrends.net/countries/USA/united-states/infant-mortality-rate, based on United Nations - World Population Prospects https://population.un.org/wpp/.)

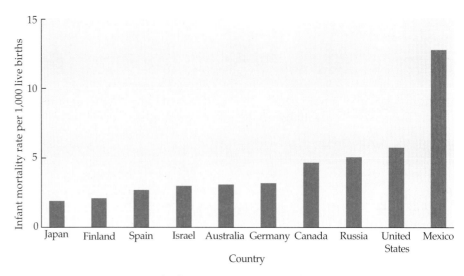

FIGURE 3.17 Comparison of infant mortality rates. Infant mortality rate in the United States is higher than many other developed countries. (Infant mortality rates [indicator]. OECD. 2021 [Accessed on 24 February 2021]. doi: 10.1787/83dea506-en)

90% between 1915 and 1997, to 7.2 infants for every 1,000 births (Hoyert, Kochanek, & Murphy, 1992). In 2018, infant mortality was down to 5.9 deaths per 1,000 live births (United Health Foundation, 2018). Although these declines are impressive, the United States falls behind a number of other wealthy countries. For example, an infant born in the United States is three times more likely to die in the first year than is a baby born in Finland, Japan, Norway, Luxembourg, Sweden, Iceland, and a few other countries (**FIGURE 3.17**).

What accounts for disparities in infant mortality rates across countries, and the relatively high rate of the United States? Country-level differences in what qualifies as an infant mortality is one explanation. An infant born extremely preterm in the United States is considered to be a live birth, and thus, is included in rates of infant mortality. In other countries, an infant of extreme prematurity might be classified as a miscarriage or stillbirth, a classification difference that leads to inflated U.S. mortality rates relative to those countries. When classification differences across countries are considered, 40% of the U.S. disadvantage in infant mortality is eliminated (Chen, Oster, & Williams, 2014).

However, even after such corrections, the United States continues to have a high infant mortality rate relative to rates in several other wealthy nations. Conditions associated with poverty contribute to disparities in infant mortality. Infants in the United States who are born to parents with low levels of education, single women, and Black women have much higher mortality risks than do infants from other groups. For example, the mortality rate for infants born to non-Hispanic Black women in 2013 was 11.11 per 1,000 live births, compared to 5.06 deaths for infants born to non-Hispanic White mothers (Mathews, MacDorman, & Thoma, 2015). Infant mortality and prematurity rise with poverty because of low maternal nutrition during pregnancy, lack of health care access and prenatal care, high stress, and exposure to environmental hazards (Lorenz et al., 2016).

✓ CHECK YOUR UNDERSTANDING 3.13

1. Explain the factors that may contribute to country-level differences in infant mortality rates.

Infant Brain Development

LEARNING OBJECTIVE 3.14 Review how rapid changes to the infant brain support learning and development.

Newborns enter a world of new sights, sounds, smells, tastes, and touches. Infants' sensory experiences propel brain development, and the developing brain facilitates new learning.

Growth in the Brain

Across the first two years of life, the infant brain forms extensive neural connections and nearly doubles its volume to achieve roughly the size, shape, and cortical thickness of the adult brain (Lyall et al., 2016). The cortex, in particular, forms more synapses than at any other time in the life span (Richards, 2020). In fact, the human infant produces an overabundance of neuronal connections that the brain will prune at later periods in development (see Figure 2.27).

The cerebellum, which is involved in the development of motor and cognitive skills, triples in size in the first year (see Figure 2.16). Preterm birth or prenatal lesions that damage specific cerebellar regions of the brain can lead to motor impairments and long-term cognitive disruption (Stoodley & Limperopoulos, 2016). Developments in the prefrontal cortex (located in the front portion of the frontal lobe in both hemispheres of the brain) help infants to plan and control their actions (Cuevas et al., 2012; Werchan et al., 2016). The visual cortex (located in the occipital lobe in both hemispheres of the brain) likewise develops rapidly in the first months of postnatal life, aiding infants' binocular vision (Knickmeyer et al., 2008).

Bidirectionality and Brain Specialization

Brain development is a bidirectional process. The infant brain grows in response to experience, and changes in the brain allow infants to act and think in new ways. With age and experience, regions of the brain become increasingly specialized, taking on the functions necessary for human survival.

Language development offers an apt illustration of brain-experience bidirectionality and specialization: The brain's structure supports infant language development, and reciprocally, exposure to language chisels the neural circuitry of the brain (e.g., Romeo et al., 2018). But how does this occur? To start, the infant brain is structurally asymmetrical. Regions of the left hemisphere are densely packed with neurons, making them especially suited for processing speech (Boemio et al., 2005; Zatorre & Belin, 2001). When 2-month-olds listened to the speech of their mother or a stranger, the left hemisphere activated. But, when they listened to music, which does not contain the rapid sound transitions of speech, the brain activated in both hemispheres (Dehaene-Lambertz et al., 2010).

Over time, as speech is channeled to the densely packed regions of the left hemisphere, those areas become dedicated to language. For example, **Broca's area** is associated with language production, and lesions to Broca's area in adults result in problems speaking, pronouncing words, and producing complex grammatical structures (Benson & Ardila, 1996). **Wernicke's area**, a region slightly to the rear of Broca's area, is involved in understanding spoken and written language (Démonet et al., 1992). Adults with a lesion to Wernicke's area produce sentences that are relatively grammatical (Harpaz, Levkovitz, & Lavidor, 2009), but they are unable to understand other people's speech or written words or to repeat what other people have said (**FIGURE 3.18**). However, infants with lesions to these areas do not show the same impairments as do adults. Thus, although infants are not born with Broca's or Wernicke's areas, early brain structure, coupled with high brain plasticity (see Chapter 2), guides the specialization of brain functions in these areas.

Broca's area A region in the frontal lobe of the left hemisphere that is involved in such activities as speech and language production

Wernicke's area A region to the rear of Broca's area, in the temporal lobe in the left hemisphere of the brain, which is involved in understanding spoken and written language

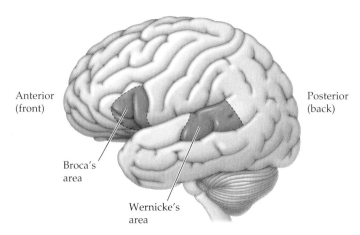

Anterior (front)

Posterior (back)

Broca's area

Wernicke's area

FIGURE 3.18 Broca's area and Wernicke's area. These areas of the brain are located in the left hemisphere. Broca's area is involved in language production and Wernicke's area is involved in language understanding. These areas develop over time as infants experience language input, demonstrating the plasticity of brain development. Lesions to these areas will compromise language in adults but not infants. (After S. M. Breedlove and N. V. Watson. 2019. *Behavioral Neuroscience*. 9th ed. Sinauer/ Oxford University Press: Sunderland, MA.)

neonates Infants who are less than four weeks of age; neonates typically spend over 16 hours a day sleeping

REM (rapid eye movement) A type or stage of active sleep that involves dreaming and is characterized by quick, erratic eye movements under closed lids, frequent body movements, a distinct pattern of brain activity, and irregularity in breathing and heart rate

✓ **CHECK YOUR UNDERSTANDING 3.14**

1. Illustrate bidirectional influences between brain and development with the example of language.

Infant Sleep and Nutrition

As we saw, infants require stimulation, such as language and social interactions, to grow their brains. Additionally, healthy infant development depends on the basics: Infants require sleep, and they require nutrients to feed their bodies and brains.

Sleep

LEARNING OBJECTIVE 3.15 Analyze why sleep supports infant development.

All animals, from fruit flies to humans, sleep. Sleep's universality signals its importance for survival (Tononi & Cirelli, 2006). Sleep is especially important in the healthy development of newborns. As all new parents learn, newborns spend much of the day and night sleeping. Indeed, **neonates**—babies less than 4 weeks of age—spend over 16 hours a day sleeping, about 8–9 hours during the day and about 8 hours during the night. Infant sleep time only tapers slightly to 15 hours in the second month and to 14 hours by about the fourth month (Thoman & Whitney, 1989). Newborns sleep extensively because sleep serves important developmental functions. In the next sections, we review types of sleep, the sleep-wake cycles of newborns, and the functions of sleep in development.

Types of Sleep

Infants spend many hours sleeping and proportionately more time in **rapid eye movement (REM)** sleep than do children and adults. REM sleep is an active form of sleep that involves dreaming. REM sleep contains quick, erratic eye movements under closed lids, frequent body movements, a distinct pattern of brain activity, and irregularity in heart rate and breathing. In contrast, during non-REM sleep, dreaming, eye movements, and motor activity are absent; sleep is very deep; and brain waves, breathing, and heart rate are slow and regular.

The amount of time spent in REM sleep declines across the first years of life. For example, newborns spend about 50% of their sleep time in REM and 50% in non-REM sleep, compared to young children who spend only 20% of their sleep time in REM sleep. Newborns' high amount of time in REM sleep allows them to remain vigilant to internal and external cues that might require them to awaken. In fact, problems awakening from sleep may place infants at risk of sudden infant death syndrome.

Sleep-Wake Cycles

For the most part, older children, adolescents, and adults settle down for an extended, single bout of sleep at night and are awake during the day. Newborns have very different sleep-wake cycles: They transition between sleep and wake states several times in a 24-hour period, with periods of sleep lasting a few minutes to a few hours (Whitney & Thoman, 1994). Newborns' relatively small stomachs help explain why they do not remain asleep for extended periods. Thus, although they spend the majority of the 24-hour period sleeping, they wake up every 3 hours to feed and replenish their systems. Over the first year of life, infants gradually can ingest larger amounts of food and so develop mature patterns of nighttime sleep and begin to converge on the sleep-wake schedules of adults (Jenni, Deboer, & Achermann, 2006).

Functions of Sleep

Why do people need sleep? This question is particularly interesting when considering the relative costs of sleep versus wakefulness: When asleep, people are disconnected from the world, generally immobile, and in a state that prevents them from participating in the activities on which survival depends; sleep also leaves people prey to unknown dangers (Kurth et al., 2015). Clearly, there must be biological benefits to allowing the brain to periodically "go offline" as happens in sleep. Indeed, scientists have identified several important functions of sleep, especially as they pertain to infants:

- *Sleep reduces energy expenditure in the brain.* The everyday maintenance of brain synapses demands a lot of energy, as seen in how much oxygen the brain uses during awake hours (Tononi & Cirelli, 2006). During sleep, the strength of synaptic connections lowers, reducing the burden on neurons and cells (Kurth et al., 2015). Infants' higher density of synapses and lower myelin content relative to children and adults may explain their need for a lot of sleep.

- *Important metabolic housekeeping takes place during sleep.* Cells produce chemical byproducts that the body must eliminate. Cells of the brain are no exception, and many of the waste products that accumulate in the awake brain are removed during sleep (Xie et al., 2013).

- *Sleep aids the development of the visual system.* The high brain activity and eye movements during REM sleep may facilitate early development of the visual system and compensate for the low level of visual stimulation during the fetal period (Roffwarg, Muzio, & Dement, 1966). Indeed, sleep is associated with changes in synapse number, size, and connections, especially in the developing visual cortex (Kurth et al., 2010; Wilhelm et al., 2014).

- *Sleep supports the sensorimotor system.* REM sleep may be vital to motor development. Sleeping newborns often appear to be restless, frequently "twitching" their arms, hands, torsos, legs, and feet. Twitching is a highly structured form of movement that may help infants learn about their bodies and how to control their limbs, joints, and muscles. While sleeping, newborn rat pups exhibit hundreds of thousands of twitches in a 24-hour period, a "practice regimen" that relays enormous information about limbs, joints, and muscles to the spinal cord and brain (Blumberg, Marques, & Iida, 2013).

- *Sleep facilitates the consolidation and learning of information.* Sleep facilitates the consolidation of information acquired during the day (Wilhelm, Diekelmann, & Born, 2008). Moreover, infants learn while sleeping. Researchers presented sleeping newborns with recordings of different speech sounds and monitored their brain waves. Newborns could distinguish among the different speech sounds while sleeping, as revealed by changes to brain activation patterns (Cheour et al., 2002; Sambeth et al., 2008). Newborns can also form memories about events that occur during sleep. Newborns who heard a tone that was coupled with a puff of air directed to their eyelids while sleeping were four times as likely as a control group of newborns to move or blink their eyes in response to the tone *without* the puff of air; thus, they had learned and remembered that the puffs and sounds belonged together (Fifer et al., 2010). By 6 to 8 months of age, infants presented with novel words showed stronger brain responses to those words (suggesting learning) after a nap compared to infants who did not nap (Freidrich et al., 2017) (**FIGURE 3.19**). The capacity to consolidate and learn material

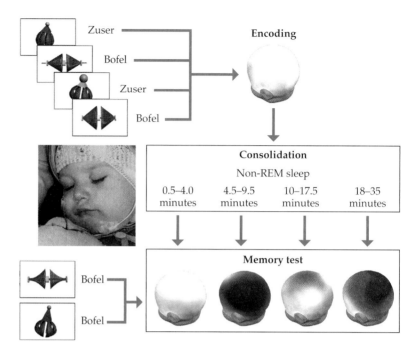

FIGURE 3.19 Learning and sleep. Researchers are able to study infant brain responses to words that are presented to infants while they sleep. Brain activation patterns indicate that already by 6 months of age, infants are able to store information about language in long-term memory. Researchers presented "novel words" to awake infants, along with the images the words were meant to represent. Infants were given a memory test an hour later, as shown in the bottom panel. When infants took a nap after the first presentation (middle panel), the longer amount of time they spent in non-REM sleep, the better they remembered what they had learned for the words presented before the nap, suggesting they were consolidating the information during sleep. White represents no reactivity in the brain on hearing the novel words; blue represents brain activity that is weak and late; red represents early and strong brain activity to hearing the novel words. (From M. Freidrich et al. 2017. *Curr Biol* 27: 2374–2380.E3.)

during sleep may be unique to young infants because of their high brain plasticity. As sleep patterns mature, opportunities to learn during sleep may diminish (Fifer et al., 2010).

✓ CHECK YOUR UNDERSTANDING 3.15

1. Distinguish REM sleep from non-REM sleep.
2. List the functions of sleep.

Cultural Context of Infant Sleep

LEARNING OBJECTIVE 3.16 Explain how and why cultures may differ in infant co-sleeping practices and perspectives.

Cultural practices infuse all aspects of infant life, including how parents structure their newborn's days around sleep and co-sleeping. In many cultural communities, infant sleep is thought to reflect the new baby's adjustment to family life. In the United States, it is common practice to ask parents of a new baby: "How is your baby sleeping? Does your baby sleep through the night? Does your baby sleep alone or with you?" Indeed, sleeping through the night is a shared, although implicit, milestone in infant development. Countless authors have made a lot of money selling books about how parents might get their babies to sleep over the nighttime hours, and there is no shortage of parents who aim to get their infants' sleep patterns to fit with their own.

Sleeping through the Night

A gold standard does not exist for when in development an infant should "sleep through the night." Most infants in the United States sleep through the night by about 4 months of age, if not sooner, largely because their parents actively attempt to ensure nighttime sleep. Parents refer to websites and professionals about ways to best handle infant crying and resistance. (An online search for "steps to get a baby to sleep alone" yields nearly 5 million results!). Parents may choose to adopt a CIO (cry it out) approach, in which they ignore infants' cries and believe that infants will eventually learn to comfort themselves and fall asleep alone. Other parents follow an "attachment" approach, adopting responsive, infant-centered strategies to achieve infant self-sleeping. Other parents turn to grandparents, relatives, or their pediatricians for advice.

In many cultural communities around the world, the U.S. obsession with getting infants to sleep through the night may appear to be bizarre. Anthropologist Charles Super and developmentalist Sara Harkness were the first to illustrate the cultural context of sleeping patterns by studying Kipsigi infants in rural Kenya (Harkness & Super, 1995; Super & Harkness, 1986). In the Kipsigi community, infant sleep received little attention, and infants' sleep patterns diverged substantially from infants in U.S. non-Hispanic White families. Rather than sleeping for long stretches of time at night, Kipsigi infants took many naps and woke up several times a night to nurse. Infants spent nearly all of their time in close proximity to their mothers. Mothers carried their infants on their backs for much of the day as they went about their daily chores. At night, infants slept with their mothers in skin-to-skin contact and were allowed to nurse whenever they wished.

Co-sleeping

Cultural goals around infants' sleeping through the night go hand in hand with cultural practices around **co-sleeping**, the sharing of a bed with one or two parents. In many U.S. families, infants typically sleep in their own crib, which is often in the same room as their parents, as soon as they arrive home from the hospital. A few short months later, infants move to a different room, where they continue to sleep apart from their parents throughout childhood (McCoy et al., 2004; Smith et al., 2016; Willinger et al., 2003). The U.S. avoidance of co-sleeping partly results from the American Academy of Pediatrics' recommendation for infants not to share a bed with parents, caregivers, or other children to minimize the risk of sudden infant death syndrome.

In contrast, co-sleeping is widespread in cultural communities around the world (Super & Harkness, 2013). Bed sharing is the norm in Mayan families in Northern Guatemala (Morelli et al., 1992); and in the Caribbean island of Barbados, about half of infants under 6 months of age slept in bed with their mother (Galler, Harrison, & Ramsey, 2006). Even after moving to the United States, Mexican immigrant mothers in Dallas reported higher rates of co-sleeping than did U.S. non-Hispanic White parents (Nie et al., 2010). The majority (70%) of mothers with two foreign-born Hispanic parents practiced co-sleeping with their infant compared to only 10% of mothers with two U.S.-born parents (Duzinski et al., 2013).

Why do cultures differ in their practices around co-sleeping? Many variables contribute to cultural differences, including economic status, housing arrangements, cultural values, and health concerns. In general, co-sleeping is more common in families from low- and middle-income countries compared to high-income countries, such as the United States (Bornstein, 2002; Miller & Commons, 2010; Owens, 2004). However, cultural values also come into play. Mayan families believe that co-sleeping fosters closeness between infants and parents. In contrast, U.S. non-Hispanic White parents may encourage

co-sleeping Caregivers' sharing of a bed with an infant or child; cultural practices and cultural goals often inform parents' views and practices around co-sleeping children to sleep alone to support independence and ensure that infants learn how to sleep at night to align with adult work schedules (Morelli et al., 1992). In fact, cultural expectations that infants sleep alone are so strong in U.S. European American families that mothers who co-sleep with their infants after 6 months report being criticized, feeling depressed, and having concerns about their infants' sleep, despite the fact that they had chosen such sleeping arrangements (Shimizu & Teti, 2018).

Notably, the consequences of co-sleeping also differ by cultural context. For example, a multi-national study on sleep problems in nearly 30,000 families from predominantly non-Hispanic White and predominantly Asian communities, found that co-sleeping resulted in *more* nighttime sleep by Asian children but *less* nighttime sleep in non-Hispanic White children (Mindell et al., 2010). Similarly, co-sleeping between children and Dutch mothers of Northern European descent more strongly predicted child restless behavior, night waking, and sleep problems than did co-sleeping in Turkish, Caribbean, and Moroccan immigrant mothers in the Netherlands (Luijk et al., 2013). In contrast, in communities such as the Kipsigi (described previously), the practice of keeping infants close at night and maintaining skin-to-skin contact may have adaptive benefits, given high rates of infant mortality. Body contact helps regulate infants' temperature and glucose levels and is associated with high rates of head growth in preterm infants (e.g., Rojas et al., 2003). In short, cultural differences in patterns of co-sleeping suggest that there is no one-size-fits-all mandate about what works and what does not.

✓ CHECK YOUR UNDERSTANDING 3.16

1. If you were a pediatrician, what would you tell a mother who asks about when her infant should sleep through the night, and whether it is okay to let her young infant sleep in bed with her? Why?

Nutrition and Breastfeeding

LEARNING OBJECTIVE 3.17 Discuss the benefits of breastfeeding.

Infants require nutrients and vitamins to support healthy development. And breast milk is considered the best choice for providing adequate nutrients and vitamins. However, when breastfeeding is not possible, iron-fortified formulas offer an alternative that contains all the nutrients that infants will need in the first months of life (Butte et al., 2004).

Breastfeeding Benefits

Mothers who are able and willing to breastfeed offer their infants many health benefits. Breastfeeding ensures that infants obtain the proteins, fats, and vitamins that are critical for brain and body development. Breast milk also contains carbohydrates, enzymes, and hormones that promote intestinal health and biochemical balance, and immune boosters that protect infants from illness. Furthermore, breast milk is easy to digest and absorb.

Beyond its nutritional benefits, breastfeeding may help prevent sudden infant death syndrome, infections, asthma, childhood leukemia, and high blood pressure, obesity, and diabetes later in life (Hauck et al., 2011; Horta & Victora, 2013; Robinson & Fall, 2012). Moreover, breastfeeding relates to children's cognitive development and intelligence (Horta & Victora, 2013; Kramer et al., 2008). And, many mothers find breastfeeding to be a rewarding experience that helps them bond with their infants.

Challenges to "Breast is Best"

Despite the dominant health message that "breast is best," decisions to breastfeed are highly personal, and new parents should not feel that they are harming their infants' futures by not breastfeeding. In fact, research on the benefits of breast milk has been critiqued as overstated and possibly explained by other confounding factors (Colen & Ramey, 2014; Wolf, 2013). Because it is unethical to conduct an experimental study on breastfeeding, the positive outcomes associated with breastfeeding remain correlational. Perhaps other attributes distinguish families who breastfeed versus those who do not, and account for differences seen in children. In fact, when researchers compared siblings where one child was breastfed and the other was not, thus controlling for family factors, many of the benefits of breastfeeding became statistically insignificant (Evenhouse & Reilly, 2005). Similarly, researchers find little or no effect of breastfeeding on infants' intelligence after mothers' intelligence and other factors related to breastfeeding are considered in analyses (Der, Batty, & Dreary, 2006). Relatedly, a comprehensive study of breastfeeding showed no effects of breastfeeding on the intelligence of over 11,000 twins in the United Kingdom who were followed through adolescence (Von Stumm & Plomin, 2015). Therefore, although breast milk is nutritious and may confer health benefits for infants, the long-term impact of breastfeeding on child development remains an open question.

✓ CHECK YOUR UNDERSTANDING 3.17

1. Debate the importance of breastfeeding. Offer evidence in support of the idea that "breast is best," and provide some challenges.

Context and Culture in Breastfeeding

LEARNING OBJECTIVE 3.18 Describe factors that may contribute to the likelihood of a woman breastfeeding.

The prevalence of breastfeeding differs across income and education groups in the United States. Women with higher family incomes, higher education levels, partners with higher education levels, and women who hold or whose partners hold professional occupations are more likely to breastfeed than were their counterparts who are low in income, education, and/or occupation. When multiple factors are considered together, the strongest predictor of breastfeeding is maternal and paternal education (Heck et al., 2006).

Ethnic and racial differences also exist in the practice of breastfeeding. The Centers for Disease Control and Prevention (CDC, 2010) monitored state-specific progress in the start and duration of breastfeeding among different racial/ethnic groups based on data from the National Immunization Survey for children who had been born between 2003 and 2006. In all but two states, non-Hispanic Blacks were less likely to breastfeed than were non-Hispanic Whites. The National Health and Nutrition Examination study identified similar disparities in breastfeeding by ethnicity and race (McDowell, Wang, & Kennedy-Stephenson, 2008) (**FIGURE 3.20**). Furthermore, foreign-born Hispanic women were the most likely to breastfeed their infants than are women from other racial or ethnic groups (Heck et al., 2006). When researchers interviewed Mexican immigrant U.S. mothers during pregnancy and at various times during their infants' first year, they found that the likelihood of breastfeeding decreased and that mothers breastfed for shorter durations with mothers' increasing years in the United States (Harley, Stamm, & Eskenazi, 2007). Women who lived in the United States for 5 years or fewer breastfed their infants 2 months on average; mothers who lived in the United States for 6–10 years breastfed their infants for 1 month on average; and those who lived in the United States for 11 years or more breastfed their infants for less than a week.

Cross-national comparisons of breastfeeding indicate that answers to the question of "who breastfeeds and for how long" likewise differs enormously across countries. For example, ethnic/racial differences in breastfeeding in

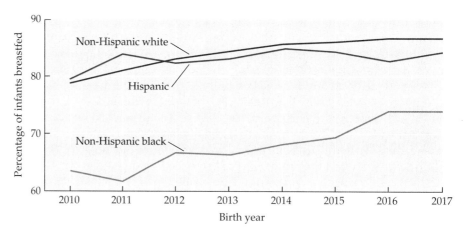

FIGURE 3.20 Breastfeeding.   Within the United States, rates of breastfeeding are higher in Mexican American immigrants and non-Hispanic Whites than in non-Hispanic Blacks, although rates of breastfeeding have risen in all groups. (After CDC. 2020. National Immunization Survey, Breastfeeding Rates by Socio-demographics. Centers for Disease Control and Prevention, Department of Health and Human Services: Washington, DC.)

the United Kingdom counter trends in the United States. A national study of over 17,000 mothers of singleton infants in the United Kingdom found that Indian, Pakistani, Bangladeshi, Black Caribbean, and Black African mothers were more likely to initiate breastfeeding and more likely to continue breastfeeding their 3-, 4-, and 6-month-old infants compared to White mothers (Kelly, Watt, & Nazroo, 2006). This contrasts with the generally high rates of breastfeeding in U.S. non-Hispanic White mothers. Differences in breastfeeding patterns across countries and states in the United States suggest that campaigns that promote breastfeeding may need to be tailored to specific populations (Kelly, Watt, & Nazroo, 2006).

✓ CHECK YOUR UNDERSTANDING 3.18

1. Describe factors associated with low breastfeeding in the United States.
2. Explain how statistics on breastfeeding in the United States may differ from observations in other countries.

Developmental Cascades

The term "butterfly effect" refers to the idea that small initial differences can produce strikingly large differences later. The term originated with the research of mathematician and meteorologist Edward Lorenz, whose predictions of weather patterns changed drastically when he modified a value in his calculations from 0.506 to 0.506127. Lorenz was stunned that a minor numerical adjustment made such a huge difference, and so he used the butterfly metaphor to communicate his message: Something as small as the flapping of a butterfly's wings could cause changes in the atmosphere and lead to cascading effects on something as large as the timing of a tornado.

The concept of developmental cascades mirrors the butterfly effect. If the tiny flap of a butterfly's wings can cause a downstream tornado, imagine the powerful cascading effects on development that are rooted in behaviors around conception, the prenatal period, and infants' birth experiences. Small (and sometimes quite large) differences in the behaviors of future fathers and mothers; choices around when to have children; a mother's nutritional intake during pregnancy; the fetus's own behaviors in the womb, and so on may produce cascading influences on development. Here, we offer select examples of how pre-birth experiences reverberate across domains of learning and development.

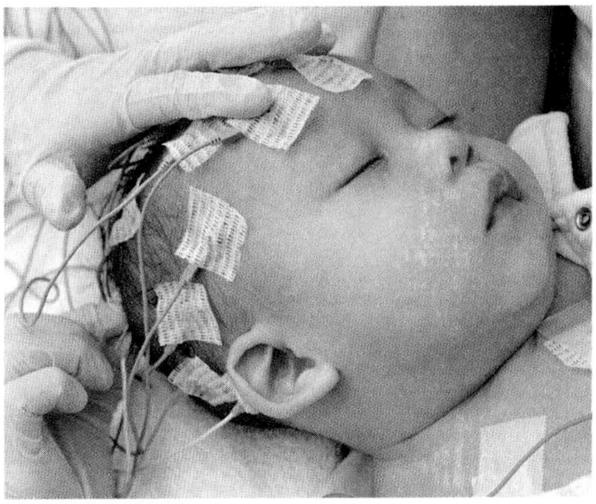

Cascades from Fetal Movement

You learned that the fetus is continually active and moving. Fetal movements are central for shaping brain development and preparing for life outside the womb (Hepper, 2003). Most movements that are present at birth appear by 3–4 months prenatally (De Vries, Visser, & Prechtl, 1982). As the fetus moves, it generates feedback that leads to improved motor coordination, which is important for later motor development (e.g., Robinson, 2016). Experimental evidence further reinforces the importance of fetal movement for postnatal development. When researchers experimentally disrupted fetal movement in rats, physical development did not proceed normally (Moessinger, 1983). Thus, something as simple as the ability to move in the womb has cascading effects for body and brain development that plays out in post-birth behaviors.

FIGURE 3.21 Prenatal auditory experience. When researchers tested infant brain activation postnatally for words the infants had been exposed to prenatally, brain responses indicated that infants recognized the words they heard prenatally.

Cascades from Fetal Auditory Experiences

Just as fetal movement paves the way for postnatal motor development, auditory experiences during the prenatal period provide a springboard for later language development. For example, we saw that infants recognize familiar voices and passages that they heard during their time in the womb, as seen in their responses to passages from *The Cat in the Hat*. Additionally, auditory experiences in the womb lead to post-birth recognition of familiar language(s) (e.g., Byers-Heinlein, Burns, & Werker, 2010).

For example, researchers asked expectant mothers to play a recording of a made-up word ("tatata") several times a week during the last trimester of pregnancy. By the time of birth, fetuses had been exposed to the word over 25,000 times! When researchers tested brain responses postnatally (**FIGURE 3.21**), the activation patterns of infants who had been exposed to the recording in the womb differed from the activation patterns of infants not exposed to the words. Thus, infants appeared to recognize the words they'd heard prenatally (Partanen, Kujala, Näätänen, Liitola, Sambeth, & Huotilainen, 2013). Such findings indicate that infants enter the world with months of prenatal auditory experience that allow them to recognize the sounds of their language.

Cascades from Maternal Stress

Recall that high maternal stress causes elevated cortisol levels and that cortisol can reach the fetus through the placenta. Thus, the connection between maternal stress and child development begins in utero, and studies indicate that such effects may even spill over to childhood and adolescence (de Kloet et al., 2005). Specifically, elevated maternal prenatal stress relates to the behavior problems, emotional disturbances, depression, and aggression of children and adolescents (e.g., Glynn & Sandman, 2011; Talge, Neal, & Glover, 2007). Maternal stress during pregnancy may also affect fetal and child brain development. Expectant women who felt anxious about their pregnancy and their fetuses' health had children with lower brain volume at 6–9 years of age (**FIGURE 3.22**). As women's pregnancy anxieties increased, children's gray matter volume reduced in brain regions associated with reasoning, planning, attention, memory, and

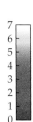
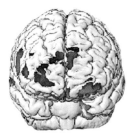
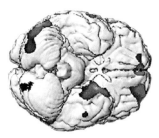
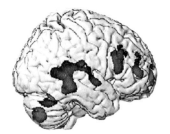
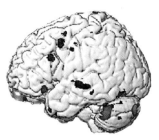

FIGURE 3.22 Anxiety and brain volume. Expectant women who experienced high anxiety at 19 weeks of pregnancy had children with lower brain volume at 6–9 years of age. Red regions represent areas in the brain where gray matter volume was reduced, specifically representing regions involved in reasoning, planning, attention, memory, language, and social and emotional processing (After C. Buss et al. 2010. *Psychoneuroendocrinol* 35: 141–153.)

language. Thus, the experiences of pregnant women cascade to the cognitive skills of their children (Buss et al., 2010).

Cascades from Infant Birth Weight

We've seen that poor prenatal nutrition and exposure to toxins such as alcohol can cause low birth weight and premature birth. Preterm birth accompanied by oxygen deprivation poses added risk for infant health and development and may even threaten survival. Infants of low or very low birth weight have disproportionately high problems in attention, language development, brain and neurological functioning, cognitive development, motor coordination, and health, with compromised development sometimes persisting into adolescence and even adulthood (Aarnoudse-Moens et al., 2009).

Many researchers have confirmed the harmful cascading influences of low birth weight on children's later health status. For example, lower infant birth weight related to attention-deficit disorder, developmental disabilities, cerebral palsy, intellectual disabilities, seizures, stuttering, and the use of special education services in a nationally representative U.S. sample (Boulet, Schieve, & Boyle, 2011). Similarly, 34% of children in a sample of 6,198 who had been born extremely low birth weight, 0.9–2 pounds (0.4–1 kg), had severe disabilities (Mercier et al., 2010). And a review of 16 articles showed that prematurity and very low birth weight led to disorders in motor coordination in childhood (Edwards et al., 2011).

Cascades from Parenting and Protective Factors

Developmental cascades from low birth weight do not occur in a vacuum. Many factors, including an infant's caregiving environment, contribute. Indeed, the negative cascading effects of prematurity are pronounced in the context of poor parenting. And unfortunately, preterm infants who are sick at birth may be less likely to be held close, touched, and gently talked to than their healthy term peers. They may be more likely to experience pokes, commands, and other intrusive behaviors from their parents (Barratt, Roach, & Leavitt, 1996; Feldman, 2007). Additionally, preterm infants are more likely to be high in negative reactivity or irritability than are term infants, which may place added stress on parents. As a result, the combination of preterm birth and poor-quality parenting may have rippling effects into childhood.

However, negative cascades are not a foregone conclusion. And for most infants, even for those born of low birth weight or prematurely, rates of impairment in children are relatively low. And most children thrive in the presence of loving family members because supportive environments can buffer the harmful effects of low birth weight and other birth complications on development. Indeed, preterm infants who experience warm, sensitive parenting, in which caregivers lovingly respond to infant cries and other behaviors, have low rates of later behavior problems compared to preterm infants who experience insensitive parenting (Poehlmann et al., 2011). Parents in stable situations with strong social support are better positioned to care for their preterm infants and sensitively interact with them. Even preterm babies who are very sick at birth have a high likelihood of catching up to their term-at-birth peers by middle childhood when relationships with caregivers are positive (Ment et al., 2003). The healthy outcomes of infants who otherwise confront risks during the perinatal period demonstrate how supportive early environments can disrupt the potential for negative developmental cascades.

■ CLOSING THOUGHTS
The Dynamics of Development

The journey that takes a single-celled zygote to a walking, talking, thinking child is nothing short of remarkable. How can something so simple evolve into something so complex? Perhaps, biology holds the answer? Are changes from zygote, to fetus, to newborn, to infant, to child hardwired into the system? Chapter 2 tells us that this is not the case. Human development is dynamic and self-organizing and only "softly assembled" from the genetic blueprint (Thelen & Smith, 1998). What does that mean?

At every point in development, living organisms, whether a cell or a child, fluidly and flexibly adapt to the demands of a changing environment. A stem cell changes its function in response to its location, eventually forming eyes, ears, nose, torso, limbs, liver, heart, and so on. A fetus changes its size to adjust to available nutrition, sometimes exiting the womb prematurely when risks are high. The growing brain achieves just the right size to fit through the birth canal. And, soon after the infant is welcomed into the world, it learns to adapt to the expectations of its environment, for example by self-organizing its sleep patterns to align with family routines. Thus, although the butterfly effect highlights cascading influences, those influences remain probabilistic. Development is neither predetermined nor linear: Many factors contribute along the way. And so, let me end with an excerpt from a metaphor that beautifully captures the dynamics of development—Esther Thelen's analysis of development as a mountain stream (Thelen, 2005, p. 259):

> *A mountain stream is moving all the time in continuous flow and continuous change. … But the stream also has patterns. We can see whirlpools, eddies, and waterfalls, places where the water is moving rapidly and places where it is still. …The patterns arise from the water and natural parts of the stream and the environment, such as the streambed, the rocks, the flow of the water, the current temperature and wind. The patterns … also reflect the history of the whole system, including the snowfall on the mountain last winter, the conditions on the mountain last summer, and the entire geological history of the region…. In addition, the stream also carves the rocks and the soil and creates its own environment, which then constrains and directs the water. It is not possible to say what directly causes what, because the whole system is so mutually embedded and interdependent.*

In later chapters, we will learn about the mountain streams of development. We will see that children leverage new opportunities as they grow and learn and interact with the objects, places, and people of their social worlds. And we will come to understand how children actively carve their own path in development while continually being shaped by the paths carved out by the people and circumstances around them.

■ Chapter Summary

Conception

- A zygote is formed when a sperm fertilizes an egg. The zygote contains 23 chromosomes from mother and 23 from father.
- A male's age, stress levels, sleep disturbances, depression, nutrition, and exposures to environmental pollutants and toxins can affect male reproductive health and the quality of sperm.
- As maternal age increases, the likelihood of fetal abnormalities increases as well, including the likelihood of trisomy-21 or Down syndrome.
- Timing of intercourse relative to when an egg is released determines the chance of pregnancy.
- Various types of assisted reproduction can aid individuals unable to naturally conceive, including intrauterine insemination (IUI), in vitro fertilization (IVF), and third-party assisted reproduction.

Prenatal Development

- The prenatal period spans three key periods: germinal period, embryonic period, and fetal period.
- The germinal period lasts from the time of conception until the 100-cell blastocyst becomes firmly implanted in the lining of the uterus.
- The blastocyst forms into two layers. The inner layer, or embryonic disk, becomes the embryo, and the outer layer, the trophoblast, becomes the environment that will hold, nourish, and protect the developing fetus.
- During the embryonic period, cells of the embryo separate into three layers: The outer layer, or ectoderm, develops into the nervous system, sensory organs, the nails, teeth, and the outer surface of the skin. The middle layer, or mesoderm, develops into the muscles, bones, the circulatory system, the inner layers of the skin, and other internal organs. The inner layer, or endoderm, develops into the digestive and respiratory systems.
- Growth of the embryo is characterized by principles of cephalocaudal and proximodistal development.
- Initially, all cells in the embryo are equivalent, but such "stem cells" develop into specific cells with specialized functions.
- The fetal period lasts from the ninth week of pregnancy until birth, and involves impressive changes in size, brain development, sensory capacities, and learning.
- The fetus engages in a rich repertoire of movements that help shape brain development and prepare the fetus for life outside the womb.
- The fetus develops a circadian rhythm that is affected by the mother's circadian rhythm and that is stable into postnatal life.
- The fetus gains experience in breathing, swallowing, tastes, and smell and is able to hear sounds from within and outside the uterus.

Contextual Influences on Prenatal Development

- The semipermeability of the placenta means that the fetus is vulnerable to harmful substances, or teratogens. The effects of teratogens depend on the genetics of the individual, the timing of exposure, and dosage of the harmful substances.
- Mothers' ingestion of illicit drugs, tobacco, and alcohol are teratogens that can affect the growing fetus. Environmental teratogens include radiation, lead, and pesticides.
- The developing fetus relies on the mother for nutrients. A mother's inadequate diet during pregnancy can cause premature birth and problems in physical and cognitive areas. However, it is difficult to isolate the effects of a mother's nutrition from other variables, including an infant's postnatal experiences.
- Prenatal care is key to supporting a healthy pregnancy. Women who seek and receive regular prenatal care are less likely to give birth to preterm or underweight infants and are less likely to experience birth complications than are those who do not receive such care.
- Maternal depression and stress can place the developing fetus at risk for later physical and behavioral problems, with stress in particular relating to reduced gray matter volume in children's brains.

Labor and Birth

- Labor can be divided into three stages: beginning with contractions; moving to the pushing stage; and finally, the birth of the infant when the placenta and other fetal membranes, or afterbirth, are expelled.
- Neonatal health at birth is typically assessed with the Apgar scale; gestational age is another measurement of neonatal health.
- Birth complications include low and very low birth weight, premature birth, and oxygen deprivation. However, positive home environments and care can buffer the risks associated with birth complications.
- Across the first two years of life, the infant brain forms extensive neural connections and nearly doubles its volume to achieve roughly the size, shape, and cortical thickness of the adult brain. Regions of the brain develop in response to environmental stimulation, such as when language input feeds into the development of Broca's and Wernicke's areas.
- National and international disparities exist in infant mortality rates, with many such disparities being the result of poverty.

Infant Sleep and Nutrition

- Newborn infants spend over 16 hours a day sleeping. Time spent in REM sleep is proportionally higher in newborns and young infants than in children and adults.
- Over the first months of life, infants gradually develop mature patterns of nighttime sleep.

- Sleep serves a variety of functions, including reducing energy expenditure in the brain; eliminating waste products that accumulate in the brain; aiding the development of the visual system; supporting development of the sensorimotor system; and facilitating the consolidation and learning of information.
- Cultural views and practices, including the idea that infants should sleep alone and through the night, affect infant sleep experiences around co-sleeping and nighttime sleep durations.
- Breast milk confers many health benefits because of its unique composition and easy digestibility. Breastfeeding may also support health and cognitive development across a range of outcomes.
- However, research that supports the claim that the "breast is best" has been critiqued as potentially ignoring other relevant factors (such as family economic status or mother's own intelligence) that may explain associations to long-term outcomes in children.

- Rates of breastfeeding differ across ethnic/racial groups in the United States and between nations.

Developmental Cascades

- Fetal movement supports motor coordination, and thus is critical to prenatal motor development.
- Auditory experiences in the womb lead to later recognition and preferences of the "familiar" language by infants.
- Maternal stress can affect the fetus through cortisol passing through the placenta, with evidence of long-term cascading influences to behavior problems in childhood and adolescence.
- Preterm birth, low birth weight, and associated complications can cascade to problems in attention, language, motor coordination, health, and so on into adolescence and even adulthood.
- Supportive early environments can buffer infants who were born prematurely or low birth weight from later negative cascades.

Thinking Like a Developmentalist

1. You are asked to present a workshop to pregnant women about behaviors associated with a healthy pregnancy and parenting practices that promote infant health after an infant's birth. List the topics you would cover and suggestions to parents under each. (Note: One mother states that she is concerned that she will be unable to breastfeed her infant. What do you respond?)

2. During the COVID-19 pandemic, a group of obstetricians asks you to give a "remote" presentation on the potential risks to infants who are born to pregnant women who are quarantined and expressing high levels of anxiety. What points would you touch on in your presentation regarding potential negative cascades to later behaviors for those infants born to those women?

3. You are participating in a debate on the roles of genetics and environment in conception, birth, brain development, and early infant health. Your position highlights environmental influences on development. You review information on the role of prenatal experiences on fetal development and postnatal experiences on early infant development. What points do you present in your debate? How do you refute your opponent's claims that genes determine development and that the brain (not experience) drives development?

Perceptual and Motor Development in Infancy and Toddlerhood

Drawing by Minxin Cheng, based on a photo by Catherine S. Tamis-LeMonda

Infants are little explorers. They may not fit the common conception of an explorer—someone who uses a machete to swath a path through the jungle to study rare birds—but they are explorers nonetheless, and pretty good ones at that. They try out new things (what happens when I throw my plate on the floor?), gather evidence (it makes a loud bang), and then engage in new behaviors based on the results (let me try throwing a cup). They are tireless in their quest to learn about their environments, flexible in their approach to the world, and quick to modify their actions when their attempts are unsuccessful.

If you remain unconvinced, watch a baby. Closely. As a developmental researcher, and mother of three, I've done so for 30 years. I've watched thousands of babies in the laboratory and home environment as they looked at pictures, listened to sounds, cried and grunted, spoke their first words, interacted with caregivers, navigated their environments, and played with toys. I've observed the countless discoveries of my own children. I remember visiting my sister, baby in tow, well before she had children. I commented in admiration when my daughter removed tissues from the tissue box and crumpled them up into a ball for play. My sister was unimpressed, even after I explained that Brittany, my little explorer, had noticed the tissues, discovered that they were pliable, and creatively solved the problem of what to play with in the absence of toys.

My sister's "so what?" reaction is typical. Infants are given little credit for their discoveries. Although parents may consider certain infant achievements, such as a baby's first steps, to be worthy of social media posts, most new motor and perceptual skills go unnoticed. Yet, even the seemingly straightforward act of picking up a toy requires a lot of exploration and hard work. Infants must accurately gauge a toy's distance relative to the length of their arms and their ability to keep balance, because reaching for something far away, for example, will result in a fall. If the toy is beyond reach, infants must lean forward or crawl to it, adjust their posture and maintain balance in the new position, reassess the toy's distance, direct their arms to the toy, and ramp up or slow down their reach as their hand approaches the goal. With impending contact, infants must open their hands just the right amount, close their hands to grip the toy, and control the grip to maintain possession.

In this chapter, you will learn about infants' quest to understand the sights, sounds, smells, and tastes around them, and how infants integrate information across their sensory systems to engage with their worlds. You will learn how perception works together with changing motor skills to allow infants to move about and engage with people and objects in new ways.

■ *Perceptual Development*

The market for baby products is a multi-billion-dollar industry. Parents, family members, and friends invest enormous amounts of money on the latest gadgets, toys, and home decor to engage infants' attention and stimulate learning, much to the delight of manufacturers. Parents cover infants' walls with pictures to encourage babies to visually explore their surroundings. They provide infants with colorful toys of different types to entice infants to play; and they situate small mirrors in infants' cribs so infants can examine their own faces. They play audio tracks of classical music and infant-geared songs. And they mount mobiles on cribs so that infants may track dangling, moving objects. Such purchases assume that infants have the capacities to explore these many opportunities. Do they? In the sections that follow, you will learn about infants' developing abilities in perception and what this means for infants' learning and development across domains. Later in the chapter, we will expand our focus to infant motor skills and action—how infants actually engage with the world around them.

The Study of Perception in Infants

Imagine that you are sitting in front of a computer screen viewing these graphics:

What do you see? Most of you would report seeing a square, triangle, and hexagon rather than four lines, three lines, and six lines. That's because you perceive the shapes as wholes—rather than merely sensing visual input (the lines), you perceive the input as meaningful (the shapes). **Sensation** begins when a stimulus in the environment activates receptors in the sensory organs (eyes, ears, nose, mouth, and skin). Receptors are neurons that convert the stimulus into signals that are sent to the brain. For example, light activates electromagnetic receptors in the eyes that then transmit information to the brain about the visible environment. Similarly, airborne molecules activate chemoreceptors in the nose that signal about odors (**FIGURE 4.1**). Infants' sensory organs enable them to detect and discriminate among the sights, sounds, tastes, smells, and touches of their environments. Infants then organize and interpret sensory information in the process of **perception**.

sensation The process of sensing the environment, beginning with a stimulus activating receptors in the sensory organs (i.e., eyes, ears, nose, mouth, and skin); receptor neurons convert the stimulus into signals that are sent to the brain

perception The psychological process of organizing and interpreting sensory information

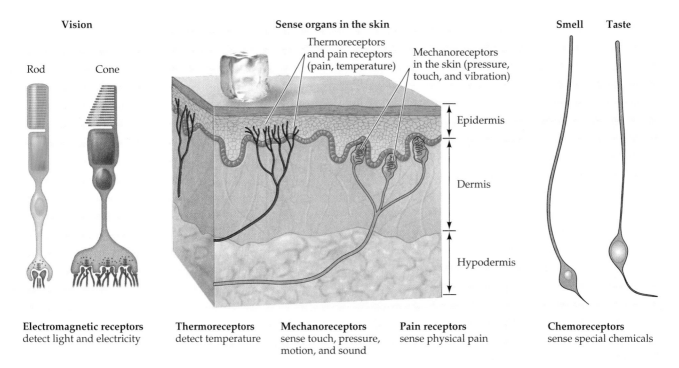

FIGURE 4.1 Sensory receptors. Receptors are neurons that convert sensory stimuli into signals that they send to the brain. For example, electromagnetic receptors in the eyes are activated by light and send visual information to the brain; thermoreceptors detect and relay information about temperature; mechanoreceptors relay information about touch and pressure; pain receptors relay information about pain; and chemoreceptors relay information about taste and smell. (After J. Wolfe et al. 2021. *Sensation and Perception*, 6th ed. Sinauer/Oxford University Press: Sunderland, MA; S. M. Breedlove and N. V. Watson. 2021. *The Mind's Machine: Foundations of Brain and Behavior*, 4th ed. Sinauer/Oxford University Press: Sunderland, MA; R. W. Hill et al. 2017. *Animal Physiology*, 4th ed. Sinauer/Oxford University Press: Sunderland, MA.)

Most of us rarely reflect on the origins and development of our perceptual capacities. We largely take for granted the automatic ways that our sensory systems translate light, sound, and pressure into meaningful perceptions. When a person moves towards us, we perceive that person's size as constant, even though the image of the person expands on the retina (in our eyes) as the distance decreases. When people talk, we connect their words to the mouth movements producing those words. That is why when we watch a foreign movie dubbed into a different language, the experience can be oddly disconcerting—the visual and auditory worlds do not match up.

Questions about when and how perceptual capacities develop underpin much of developmental research. Are they products of experience? Do infants perceive line drawings of squares, triangles, and hexagons as coherent shapes? Do they perceive moving mouths and the sounds as a single event? How do researchers attempt to answer such questions, given infants cannot verbally report their experiences?

Early Theories

LEARNING OBJECTIVE 4.1 Describe early theories on infants' perceptual capacities.

Theories about the origins of infant perceptual capacities are fraught with controversy. Like all developmental phenomena, initial debates about the perceptual capacities of human infants revolved around the nature-nurture controversy.

Some theorists credited infants with innate perceptual capacities to perceive the world as stable and coherent. German psychologists Max Wertheimer (1890–1943), Kurt Koffka (1886–1941), and Wolfgang Kohler (1887–1967) claimed that infants are innately equipped with abilities to make adultlike perceptual sense of their experiences. They advanced the **Gestalt theory of perception** describing how humans spontaneously and naturally organize visual stimuli into meaningful patterns. Your perception of the whole shapes of square, triangle, and hexagon—rather than isolated lines—illustrates the organizational principles of Gestalt theory.

However, other theorists emphasized the limited skills of infants, claiming that perceptual learning gradually develops as infants attempt to make sense of the sensory overload that results from a largely chaotic environment. For example, American philosopher and psychologist William James (1842–1910) considered infants to be "blank slates," claiming that the constant bombardment of sights, sounds, and smells makes the infant's world a "great blooming, buzzing, confusion" (1890, Vol. 1, p. 488, as cited in Slater et al., 2010). Canadian psychologist Donald Hebb (1904–1985) believed that infants require months of learning to perceive objects in the same ways as do adults, emphasizing the role of experience or nurture in development (Hebb, 1968). Similarly, Jean Piaget claimed that basic perceptual skills, such as perceiving shapes, sizes, positions, and distances, precede the understanding that objects and people *maintain* their size and shape over time and space (Piaget, 1969; Slater et al., 2010).

In the context of theoretical divides, however, perspectives on perceptual development commonly focused on infants' understanding of basic, mostly static visual images like shapes. With the exception of Piaget, researchers tended to ignore infants' active role in learning—how infants' own behaviors in the moment shape their perceptual experiences. For example, a simple turn of the head causes the visual world to sweep to the left or right, and simply pulling a toy to the mouth expands the object's image on the retina. And so, perception and action cannot be separated—bodies, environments, and perceptual systems must be considered together to fully appreciate how infants learn to navigate their worlds.

✓ CHECK YOUR UNDERSTANDING 4.1

1. Contrast views of early perception that emphasize infants' innate versus limited capacities.
2. How did Gestalt's theory challenge James's characterization of the infant as a "blank slate"?

The Ecological Theory of Perception

LEARNING OBJECTIVE 4.2 Explain the core principles of the Gibsons' ecological theory of perception.

Today, research on infant perception highlights co-dependencies between perception and action, building on the **ecological theory of perception** advanced by American psychologists James Gibson (1904–1979) and Eleanor Gibson (1910–2002). The ecological theory of perception emphasizes the evolutionary roots of human perceptual capacities and the direct connections between perception and action (e.g., J. J. Gibson, 1979; Gibson & Pick, 2000). Three main tenets define this approach: (1) environments are dynamic and rich, containing all the information needed for adaptive action; (2) perceptual systems have evolved to detect and use environmental information; and (3) learning entails gauging affordances for action—learning which actions are possible and which actions are not based on perceptual information.

Environments Contain an Abundance of Information

James and Eleanor Gibson challenged William James's view that the infant's world is a "blooming, buzzing, confusion." Similarly, they shunned the notion of an impoverished environment that lacks the necessary information for perceptual learning. Rather, they said, the environment provides rich information for all the

Gestalt theory of perception
Principles or laws of human perception that describe humans' spontaneous and natural organization of visual stimuli into meaningful patterns, such as perceiving objects as whole

ecological theory of perception
A theory of development posited by Eleanor Gibson and James Gibson that highlights the evolutionary foundations of human perceptual abilities and the connections between perception and action

senses—information that is constantly changing as people move around and act on their worlds. Visual information, for example, is not static as in a photograph, but rather changes over time and space as people turn their heads to look in different directions. Thus, the infant's task is to piece together already existing, dynamic perceptual information to effectively interact with their environments.

Perceptual Systems and Bodies Have Evolved to Use Sensory Input

Although information available to the senses is rich and accessible, infants must perceive the information to use it. Sensory systems have evolved over millions of years, equipping humans (and other animals) with the biological architecture to perceive all of the sounds, sights, tastes, and so on available to them. Moreover, the bodies and sensory systems of different species are uniquely designed to adapt to the environments that they inhabit. For example, people walk on firm surfaces, but spiders' bodies allow them to walk on water.

Gauging Affordances for Action

The evolutionary basis for an ecological theory of perception does not discount the role of learning. Infants must learn which information is relevant to engage in specific actions in specific environments. But doing so takes time. For example, young infants initially look at objects, reach for them, and typically miss their aim. However, infants' actions generate perceptual information that allows them to see and feel what went wrong and modify their reaches the next time around. Eventually, after hundreds of reaches per day, infants hone their attention and begin to perceive detailed, relevant information—such as how far an object is, how large it is, and so on—information that was always available in the environment but not yet used. The **perception-action feedback loop** refers to the continuous cycle that connects perception and action as people perceive, act, and adjust their actions in response to an ever-changing environment (J. J. Gibson, 1979) **(FIGURE 4.2)**.

perception-action feedback loop The continuous cycle that connects perception and action as individuals perceive, act, and adjust their actions in response to an environment that changes

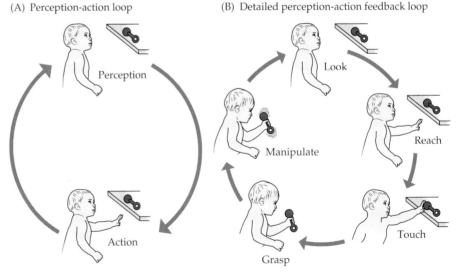

FIGURE 4.2 Perception-action feedback loop. (A) Depiction of a simple perception-action feedback loop. (B) An example of a perception-feedback loop in which an infant looks at a toy, reaches, touches, grasps, and manipulates the toy. The feedback from each step in the sequence leads to new actions and alters the infant's perceptions as what the baby sees and touches continually changes. (After D. Corbetta et al. 2018. In *Studying the Perception-Action System as a Model System for Understanding Development*, J. M. Plumert [Ed.], Advances in Child Development and Behavior 55, pp. 1–29. Academic Press: London.)

As infants learn to attend to relevant details in the environment, their targeted perceptions allow them to determine which actions are possible and which are not—what researchers refer to as **gauging affordances for action.** Returning to the example of reaching, the infant who now perceives critical cues to distance will not reach for objects far away. Notably, the ability to gauge affordances for action is fundamental to every motor skill at every age (J. J. Gibson, 1979; E. J. Gibson, 2000). A rock climber gradually learns to attend to small details such as the stability of crevices to guide safe ascent, just as an expert skier perceives subtle cues to friction in the shine of icy spots and the shading of moguls. We will return to reciprocal connections between perception and action later in the chapter.

gauging affordances for action
An individual's interpretation of which actions are possible and which are not possible based on their perceptions, as in when infants determine they can walk on a flat surface

✓ CHECK YOUR UNDERSTANDING 4.2

1. What are the three main tenets of the ecological theory of perception?
2. What is the perception-action feedback loop? Provide an example.
3. Explain the concept of gauging affordances for action.

Methods for Studying Infant Perception

LEARNING OBJECTIVE 4.3 Discuss common methods for studying infant perception and how those methods have yielded new insights into what infants know and understand.

As a first step toward understanding connections between perception and action, it's critical to determine what infants perceive in their environments across each of the senses, and how those perceptions change. Clearly, infants' perceptual capacities cannot be studied in the same way that researchers study older children and adults. For example, if you were interested in whether older children and adults perceive hues of green as differing from hues of blue, you might present different shades of green and blue and ask them to name the color or categorize colors into different groups by tapping on screens or sorting cards (**FIGURE 4.3**). Similarly, you could test children's or adults' hearing by playing sounds through headphones and asking them to raise a hand when they hear a sound or when the sound changes. With minor adjustments, you could study children's and adults' senses of taste, smell, and touch.

In contrast, testing infants is not straightforward. Infants cannot answer questions about the difference between color hues. They cannot follow directions to raise hands, touch screens, or sort cards. To accommodate the limited reporting abilities of infants, researchers have developed ingenious methods for asking questions—preferential looking, habituation-recovery, and contingent reinforcement. Such methods have yielded important insights into what infants perceive and understand.

preferential-looking test
A research method to study infant perceptual development introduced by Robert Fantz to determine whether young infants discriminate between two stimuli by looking more to one image than the other

Preferential-Looking Tests

In 1961, American developmental scientist Robert Fantz (1925–1981) introduced the **preferential-looking test** to ask whether young infants are able to discriminate among different visual images. He placed infants in front of two side-by-side screens and observed them through a peephole located between the screens, noting how long infants looked at each image (**FIGURE 4.4**). If infants looked significantly longer at the image on one of the screens, it signaled that they had discriminated between the two.

To ensure that an infant's bias to look to the right or left did not explain looking time, Fantz randomly presented stimuli on left and right screens. Using this procedure, he documented infants' tendencies to look more at complex patterns over simple ones (such

FIGURE 4.3 Testing powers of perception in infants and children. If you were interested in whether older children and adults categorized hues of green and blue in the same way, you might show them different shades of green and blue and ask them to name the color.

(A)   (B)

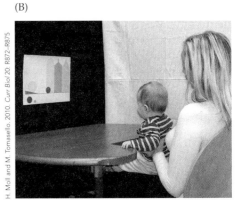

From D. Y. Teller and J. A. Movshon. 1986. Vis Res 26: 1483–1506.

H. Moll and M. Tomasello. 2010. Curr Biol 20: R872–R875

FIGURE 4.4 Robert Fantz's preferential-looking test.   (A) In early versions of the preferential-looking test, an examiner placed the infant in front of two side-by-side screens, observed the infant through a peephole located between the screens, and recorded how long the infant looked at each screen. (B) Today, computer-mounted eye-trackers enable assessment of infant looking time, with no need for an observer looking through a peephole.

as black-and-white stripes versus a gray patch), solid objects over comparable flat objects (such as a sphere versus a disc), facelike images over non-facelike images, and so on (e.g., Fantz, 1961, 1963).

Today, computer-mounted eye-trackers enable fine-grain assessment of infant looking time and scan patterns, with no need for an observer looking through a peephole (Oakes, 2020). Moreover, as we will learn, developmental scientists continue to debate *why* infants look longer at one stimulus compared to another. Although Fantz used the term "preferential looking," infants' longer looks do not imply that they *prefer* one stimulus to another. Perhaps infants find the image to be more attention grabbing, pleasurable to look at, surprising, complicated, or puzzling. The jury is still out about what looking-time studies reveal about infant understanding.

Habituation-Recovery Tests

habituation-recovery test
A research method that involves presenting infants with a stimulus until infants habituate; researchers then present a new stimulus to which infants typically recover or rebound attention

Habituation-recovery tests involve presenting infants with a stimulus until they *habituate* or decrease their attention to the stimulus. When researchers then present infants with a new stimulus, infant attention might *recover* or *rebound* to its initial level. Infants' rebound of attention is thought to offer a window into how infants perceive and remember different stimuli.

For example, an infant might be shown a picture of a face on a computer screen until the infant looks away for some time, which signals habituation. At that point, the infant is presented with a picture of a *different* face and the picture of the familiar face. If the infant looks a lot at the novel face, but relatively less at the familiar face, the infant has demonstrated **novelty preference**, which suggests that the infant discriminates between the two faces and remembers having seen the familiar face (Colombo, 1993) (**FIGURE 4.5**). Most habituation-recovery studies show that infants look longer at novel compared to familiar stimuli, although inconsistencies exist across some studies.

novelty preference Seen when an infant looks longer at a novel stimulus relative to a familiar stimulus, suggesting that the infant discriminates between the two and remembers having experienced the familiar stimulus

Contingent Reinforcement Studies

contingent reinforcement studies
Techniques used by researchers to test whether infants increase a specific behavior in response to certain stimuli; for example, researchers may test infants' sucking behaviors in response to hearing their mothers' voice

Contingent reinforcement studies follow the learning principles of operant conditioning (see Chapter 1). Researchers test whether infants increase a specific behavior, such as sucking a pacifier or turning their head, in response to certain stimuli, such as hearing the mother's voice. Contingent reinforcement is sometimes used in conjunction with habituation-recovery to examine decreases

Familiar

Camera

Novel

FIGURE 4.5 Habituation-recovery tests.   These tests involve presenting infants with a stimulus until they habituate or decrease their attention to the stimulus (habituation phase). Infants are then presented with the familiar stimulus (here a face) and a novel stimulus (here a new face). Infants' rebound of attention to the novel stimulus is thought to indicate that they distinguish between the two stimuli and remember the familiar one. (After J. S. DeLoache and V. LoBue. 2009. *Dev Sci* 12: 201–207.)

and then increases in the rewarded behavior. For example, an infant might learn to suck on a pacifier to hear music. After some time, the infant habituates to the music and the sucking subsides. At that point, researchers introduce a new stimulus, such as the sound of birds chirping. Infants' rebound in sucking indicates that they can discriminate between the old and the new sounds.

New Methods, New Insights

The advent of preferential-looking, habituation-recovery, and contingent reinforcement methods led to new insights into infant perception. As findings from these research methods poured in, they suggested that infants perceive sounds, sights, and tastes in meaningful ways. By the late 1960s, developmental scientists advanced the idea of a "competent infant" who meaningfully organizes perceptions from the first days of life (Slater et al., 2010). Still, infants' early perceptual capacities continue to develop over many months (and in most cases over months and years!), in line with the ecological theory of development. That is, as the body and brain mature and grow, and with each new motor skill, perceptions zero in on relevant information, expanding opportunities to interact with the world in increasingly adaptive, competent ways.

✓ CHECK YOUR UNDERSTANDING 4.3

1. What do preferential-looking studies say about infants' abilities to distinguish between different stimuli? What are some alternative interpretations for infants' looking time?

2. Give an example of how a researcher might use habituation-recovery and contingent reinforcement tasks to study infant perception.

Tasting and Smelling

The very first perceptions of the world begin with taste and smell. Recall that the fetus swallows amniotic fluid, and thus is exposed to the flavors ingested by mother (see Chapter 3). Postnatally, infants continue to expand their repertoires of taste and smell as they encounter new foods and odors. Taste perceptions result from stimulation of receptors on the tongue by molecules in substances that enter the mouth. Similarly, odor perceptions result from airborne molecules stimulating receptors in the nose.

FIGURE 4.6 Taste preferences. Infants pucker lips to sour tastes, open mouths widely to expel bitter tastes, and suck when presented with sweet flavors.

Taste and Odor Preferences

LEARNING OBJECTIVE 4.4 Describe infant reactions to different tastes and odors.

Newborns distinguish among different tastes and odors and exhibit behaviors that communicate their taste and odor preferences. For example, infants just 2 hours old respond to sour and bitter tastes and noxious odors. They pucker their lips to sour tastes, which stimulates saliva production and dilutes the sourness of the substance (**FIGURE 4.6**). In response to bitter tastes, which characterize toxic substances, infants expel the potentially harmful stuff by widely opening their mouths. And in response to unpleasant odors, infants wrinkle their noses, which reduces contact with the smells by narrowing the nasal passages (Rosenstein & Oster, 1988).

In contrast, newborns like sweet tastes and odors, such as the taste and smell of breast milk. They suck when given sweet flavors. They smile to sugary odors, and only minutes after birth turn their head toward maternal breast odors (Porter & Winberg, 1999). When researchers lightly pricked infants on their heels with a needle for a standard blood test, infants who had just swallowed sugar water cried and grimaced less, showed less brain activation, and experienced a shorter duration of elevated heart rate than did infants who received plain water (Fernandez et al., 2003).

Infants continue to learn about tastes across the first years of life. They grow in their ability to distinguish between sweet and bitter tastes between birth and 6 months of age; decline in their acceptance of bitter substances; and increase their acceptance of salty tastes between 4 and 24 months (Beauchamp, Cowart, & Moran, 1986; Schwartz, Issanchou, & Nicklaus, 2009). Experiences with foods contribute to infants' changing taste preferences, as we will see next.

✓ CHECK YOUR UNDERSTANDING 4.4

1. Give an example of evidence of early infant taste preferences.

Contexts of Taste Perception

LEARNING OBJECTIVE 4.5 Explain the role of context in infant taste preferences.

Exposure to different tastes shapes infant taste preferences. It is striking how soon in development such influences begin. As discussed, the amniotic fluid constitutes the first flavors of life, and then immediately after birth, breast-feeding mothers transmit the taste and odor of foods they eat to their infants through breast milk (Menella et al., 2020). Because breastfeeding infants come to prefer familiar flavors, infants from different cultures and communities may acquire different tastes depending on the foods that their mothers consume (Mennella, Jagnow, & Beauchamp, 2001).

Contextual influences on infant taste preferences are especially evident when experimenters manipulate mothers' eating habits and observe effects on infants. In one study, mothers consumed either carrot juice or water 2–3 hours before breastfeeding so that infants ingested either carrot-flavored breast milk or breast milk without added flavor. All the infants were then fed cereal flavored with carrot juice. Infants who had been exposed to the unflavored breast milk grimaced when fed the carrot-flavored cereal and spent less time eating it than did infants exposed to carrot-flavored breast milk (Mennella, Jagnow, & Beauchamp, 2001).

Do early taste experiences set the stage for food choices and preferences later on? Early diets rich in salt produce greater acceptance of salty tastes that persists into childhood, just as exposure to sour-tasting juices and bitter vegetables can prompt acceptance of such flavors (Beauchamp & Menella, 2009; Menella & Beauchamp, 2002; Stein, Cowart, & Beauchamp, 2012). Interventions that modify the eating habits of breastfeeding mothers to be healthier may lead to later acceptance of healthy foods by their children. Similarly, exposing infants to a variety of flavors at the transition to solid foods may result in expanded palates later in development, a topic we will return to in later chapters.

✓ CHECK YOUR UNDERSTANDING 4.5

1. What is the evidence that early taste experiences set the stage for later food choices?

Looking

Infant "looking" is the most studied behavior in infant perception. Much early work on infant visual perception investigated development of the visual system. Over the first months of life, infants improve in their abilities to see fine details, perceive contrasts in brightness and differences in color, and judge the relative distances of objects. Physical maturation of the eye explains some of these developments.

However, vision is not just seeing. Infants actively look, move their heads to track objects and people, and recognize familiar and loved faces. And, the visual world changes as infants develop. For example, the entire body affects what infants look at and experience: Newborns, who spend hours on their backs, will look at different things than will walking infants who view the world from an upright position. In the sections following, you will learn about the many co-developing factors that lead to changes in infants' visual world.

Acuity and Contrast

LEARNING OBJECTIVE 4.6 Describe improvements in infant visual acuity and contrast sensitivity across the first months of life.

Development of the eyes supports a number of visual abilities in infants. These include the abilities to discern fine details and perceive an image against its background (i.e., contrast sensitivity).

Visual Acuity

Physical maturation of the eyes aids infants' **visual acuity**, the ability to see fine detail. The newborn's **fovea**—the central portion of the retina, where light rays fall from objects at which the eye is pointed—is structurally immature, lacking the density of receptors found in the foveas of older children and adults (Slater et al., 2010). But, as the number of receptors increases, so does infants' visual acuity.

visual acuity The ability to see fine detail including the clearness and sharpness of a visual image; physical maturation of the eye facilitates visual acuity

fovea The central portion of the retina where the field of vision is focused; the fovea contains a high density of cones (cells that respond to color wavelengths), thus allowing for sharp central vision

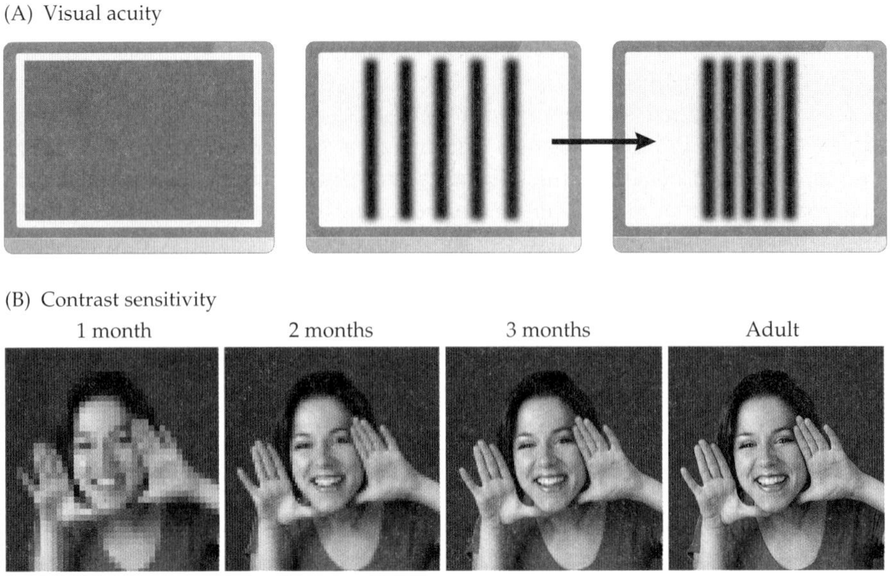

(A) Visual acuity

(B) Contrast sensitivity

FIGURE 4.7 Testing visual acuity and contrast sensitivity in infants. (A) Visual acuity experiment. To test visual acuity, researchers may present babies with a gray panel on one screen and black and white stripes on the other. The black and white stripes were moved progressively closer together, which tended to make the stripes blend visually so the striped panel increasingly resembled the gray panel. (B) To test contrast sensitivity, researchers test infants' ability to detect an image against its background (by varying the contrast between the two); here, the contrast sensitivity of infants of different ages are simulated relative to the sensitivity of adults. (A after J. Atkinson et al. 1974. *Nature* 247: 403–404.)

How do developmental scientists test infant visual acuity? A slightly modified preferential-looking experiment offers one approach. For example, researchers present infants with two screens, one containing a solid gray panel and the other a panel of black and white stripes. When the black and white stripes move progressively closer together, the stripes blend visually until the striped panel resembles the gray panel (black and white blend to make gray) (**FIGURE 4.7A**). A researcher (who doesn't know which side contains the striped pattern) decides on each trial whether the striped panel was on the left or the right based on infant looking and other behaviors. The assumption is that infants will look longer at the striped panel or gray panel when they perceive a difference between the two (Dobson & Teller, 2012). Such studies show that infants' visual acuity starts out relatively poor and improves through 6 months of age. Details that adults see clearly at a distance of 180 meters (591 feet) must be within 6 meters (20 feet) to be seen clearly by infants younger than 6 months of age (e.g., Maurer & Lewis, 2001; Teller, 1997).

Contrast Sensitivity

Infants also improve in their **contrast sensitivity**, the minimum difference in brightness between an image and its background that infants can perceive (**FIGURE 4.7B**). The contrast between a black image on a white background or vice versa is the greatest possible difference in brightness; whereas, the contrast between a gray image on a darker or lighter gray background is less of a difference. Young infants display low contrast sensitivity, again due to biological immaturity of the eye (Brown & Lindsey, 2009; Peterzell et al., 1996).

contrast sensitivity The minimum difference in brightness between an image and its background that infants can perceive; infants' contrast sensitivity improves as their eyes mature

✓ **CHECK YOUR UNDERSTANDING 4.6**

1. How might a researcher test infants' visual acuity and contrast sensitivity?

Perceiving Colors

LEARNING OBJECTIVE 4.7 Describe evidence that infants discriminate among different colors and group those colors in ways similar to adults.

How does color vision develop, and do infants perceive colors in ways similar to adults? Development of the eye and visual cortex, located in the occipital lobe of the brain (see Figure 2.16), leads to improvements in infants' color vision over the first months of life. A study conducted more than 40 years ago showed that 2-month-olds have some form of color vision (Peeles & Teller, 1975). By 4 months, infants perceive the full range of colors perceived by adults and can discriminate among different hues of the same color category, such as a green object on a green background (Franklin, Pilling, & Davies, 2005).

But just because infants can distinguish among different colors doesn't necessarily mean that they categorize colors like adults. For instance, if you went into a store and told the salesperson you wanted a blue shirt, you would probably be shown a variety of different hued shirts, all of which you would call blue. If you then said that maybe you would like to see a green shirt, you would be shown shirts of still other hues, and likely would call those green. Do infants similarly categorize different hues of blue and green and so on?

One of the first tests of whether infants categorize color into the basic adult categories of blue, green, yellow, and red used a habituation procedure (Bornstein, Kessen, & Weiskopf, 1976). On each trial, the infants viewed a stimulus of a particular color, such as a shade of blue, until they habituated. Infants were then shown either an identical stimulus, a stimulus from the same adult color category—such as a different shade of blue—or a stimulus from a different category like green. Four-month-old infants increased their attention when they were presented with a new color category, but not when presented with a color from the same category as before. Other studies later showed that infants categorize color hues in line with how colors are named in the world's different languages (Franklin, Pilling, & Davies, 2005; Skelton et al., 2017).

size constancy The perception of an object having a constant size despite changes in the size of the retinal image

shape constancy The perception of an object having a constant shape despite changes to the retinal image

✓ CHECK YOUR UNDERSTANDING 4.7

1. How might a researcher test if an infant had color categories for yellow versus orange?

Size and Shape Constancy

LEARNING OBJECTIVE 4.8 Define size and shape constancy.

When we look at things in the environment, images are projected onto the retinas in our eyes. As we move about, the size and shape of retinal images change. That is, as the distance to an object decreases, the retinal image enlarges; as the distance to an object increases, the retinal image shrinks (**FIGURE 4.8**); and as the viewing angle changes, the retinal image alters its shape. Yet despite changes to retinal images, our perception of an object remains unchanged. The perception of an object as having a constant size despite changes in the size of the retinal image is called **size constancy**. Similarly, the perception of an object as having a constant shape despite changes to the retinal image is referred to as **shape constancy**. In the

Different retinal image sizes for the same object at different distances

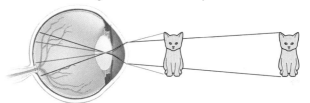

Same retinal image sizes for different objects at different distances

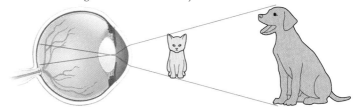

FIGURE 4.8 Perception of size constancy. Retinal image size varies not only as a function of the size of an object, but also as a function of the distance of the object from the viewer. For any particular object, the closer the object is to the viewer, the larger the image will be of the object on the retina. (A) The retinal image of the closer kitten is larger than that of the kitten farther away. (B) The closer small kitten and the farther large dog can have the same retinal image size at a particular distance. Red lines represent the size of the retinal image for the close kitten, and the blur lines the size of the retinal image for the farther kitten. (After I. Sperandio and P. A. Chouinard. 2015. *Multisens Res* 28: 253–283; J. Wolfe et al. 2021. *Sensation and Perception*, 6th ed. Sinauer/Oxford University Press: Sunderland, MA.)

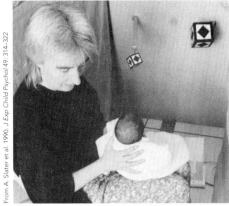

FIGURE 4.9 Size constancy experiment. In Alan Slater's size constancy experiment, infants were presented with two cubes of two different sizes. The smaller cube (on the left) was placed closer to the infant than the larger cube (on the right). Although the cubes were different sizes, their retinal image was identical. Still, infants perceived the larger cube as different in size from the smaller one, despite equivalence in retinal image size.

good continuation A Gestalt principle of organization claiming an innate tendency for individuals to view objects or stimuli as continuous, as when an infant perceives a rod to be whole even when part of the rod is hidden by another object

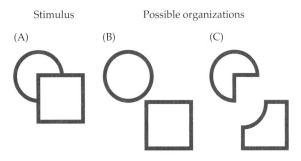

FIGURE 4.10 The Quinn experiment testing the Gestalt principle. Quinn habituated infants to (A) Stimulus: An image of what adults would perceive as a square overlapping with a circle. Then, in test trials, he presented infants with (B) whole shapes and (C) pacman-like versions of the images. Infants looked longer at the pacman-like shapes, as though they had perceived the original images as representing "whole" or complete circles and squares. (After P. C. Quinn et al. 1997. *Infant Behav Dev* 20: 35–46.)

absence of size and shape constancy, the world would be a confusing place: People and objects would seem to grow and shrink and change shapes like blobs of goo. Do infants perceive these constancies? It appears that they do.

In a preferential-looking experiment on size constancy, Alan Slater and colleagues showed newborns either a large cube or a small cube and then presented the two cubes simultaneously but at different distances, so infants' retinal images were the same size (Slater, Mattock, & Brown, 1990). Despite the same-size retinal images, the infants looked more at the cube that differed in size from the one they had first seen—that is, infants who had first been shown the small cube looked longer at the large cube, and vice versa. Newborns had perceived the cubes' true difference in size, regardless of the size of the cubes' retinal images (**FIGURE 4.9**)

Newborns also perceive the shape of an object as remaining constant despite changes in orientation. Researchers presented infants with a either a square or a trapezoid in various orientations, followed by a square and a trapezoid together at unfamiliar orientations (Slater & Morison, 1985). Infants who had viewed the square looked longer at the trapezoid and vice versa.

✓ CHECK YOUR UNDERSTANDING 4.8

1. Describe an experiment that shows that infants have size and shape constancy.

Perceiving Objects as "Whole"

LEARNING OBJECTIVE 4.9 Explain evidence that supports the Gestalt principle that infants perceive objects as whole.

Recall the graphics at the start of the chapter—a square, triangle, and hexagon. You perceived them to be whole shapes rather than disconnected lines. Your tendency to perceive coherent shapes aligns with Gestalt principles: You experience the world as organized and stable rather than fragmented and disconnected. Do Gestalt principles apply to infants' visual perceptions?

Gestalt psychologists asserted that infants, like adults, perceive a coherent visual world, and so will infer for example, that two pieces of a rod sticking out from either end of a box in front of the rod form a single rod. That's because infants perceive an object as whole when part of the object is occluded (hidden) by another object, what is referred to as **good continuation**.

Habituation studies offer evidence that infants perceive good continuation. Paul Quinn and colleagues habituated 3- and 4-month-olds to a square overlapping with a circle, as illustrated in **FIGURE 4.10A**, and then showed infants a picture of the two complete shapes separated (**FIGURE 4.10B**) or "pacman-like images" that represented divided shapes, yet could be alternative representations of what infants viewed (**FIGURE 4.10C**) (Quinn, Brown, & Streppa, 1997). Infants looked longer at the divided images than at the complete shapes, suggesting that they perceived the divided images as unfamiliar and the complete circle and square shapes as familiar and what they had seen during habituation.

Similarly, 2- and 4-month-old infants treated an occluded rod as though it were a single object, even though they only saw the bottom and top parts of the rod peeking out from behind the occluder, as illustrated in **FIGURE 4.11A** (Kellman & Spelke, 1983). After habituating infants to a moving, occluded rod, the experimenter presented infants with either the bottom and top parts of the rod moving back and forth (**FIGURE 4.11B**)—which matched what they had actually seen during habituation—or a complete rod moving back and forth

(FIGURE 4.11C). Infants attended more to the two separated rod pieces than to the complete rod, suggesting that they had perceived the rod as a complete object despite the occlusion, thus viewing the broken rod as novel.

✓ **CHECK YOUR UNDERSTANDING 4.9**

1. What is the Gestalt principle of good continuation?
2. How can we tell if an infant perceives objects according to the principle of good continuation?

Tracking Motion and Actions

LEARNING OBJECTIVE 4.10 Describe changes in infants' visual tracking across the first months of life.

The visual world is dynamic: Objects move and people move and turn their heads. Thus, things in the environment are in constant flux. To maintain a stable perception of the world, we must be able to visually track the movement of objects relative to us and to each other. Researchers often assess infants' eye movements and patterns of visual fixation using **eye-trackers**, devices built into computer monitors (see Figure 4.4B) or worn on a participant's head (**FIGURE 4.12**).

Infants move their heads in response to moving stimuli from birth (Braddick & Atkinson, 2011; Hainline, 1993). However, they produce jerky eye movements when tracking moving objects until about 2 months of age (Hainline & Abramov, 1985). Infants' ability to smoothly track moving targets continues to develop through 4 or 5 months of age, with infants tracking increasingly faster moving objects as they gain control of their eye movements and head (e.g., Aslin, 1981). But infants do not display **anticipatory eye movements**—shifting the eyes before something occurs, as though predicting what will happen next—until around 6 months of age (Johnson, Amso, & Slemmer, 2003). Anticipatory eye movements develop through experience and growth of the motor system and facilitate social interactions because infants can now reliably look where others look (Gredebäck & Falck-Ytter, 2015). In fact, infants who failed to orient and attend to moving stimuli were likely to be diagnosed with autism at 3 years of age (Falck-Ytter et al., 2018).

Notably, infants appear to infer meaning about the motion of living things even from randomly moving dots. For example, infants detect the structural features of biological motion (e.g., a person "walking") when presented with moving dots that resemble walking! Infants 7- to 8-months old showed activation in brain regions involved in the analysis of biological motion when they viewed moving dots that resembled a walking human, but did not show such activation for dots moving randomly (Lisboa et al., 2020).

✓ **CHECK YOUR UNDERSTANDING 4.10**

1. What is the difference between smoothly tracking objects and showing anticipatory eye movements?

Perceiving Depth

LEARNING OBJECTIVE 4.11 Distinguish between monocular and binocular cues to depth perception.

Depth perception refers to the ability to perceive vertical distance from a top surface or space to a bottom one. (Note: distance refers to the space between two points, which can be horizontal or vertical). Without depth and distance perception, we would be unable to move about without bumping into things or recognize the dangers of a train platform, balcony, or mountain cliff.

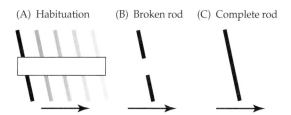

(A) Habituation   (B) Broken rod   (C) Complete rod

FIGURE 4.11 The infant perception of object unity. (A) Infants were habituated to a rod moving laterally behind an occluder. They were then shown a (B) broken rod moving laterally and (C) a complete rod moving laterally. Infants attended more to the broken rod moving laterally, indicating they perceived the rod in (A) to be a complete object. (After P. J. Kellman and E. S. Spelke. 1983. *Cog Psych* 15: 483–524.)

eye-trackers Devices that researchers use to assess infant eye movements and patterns of visual fixation; eye-trackers are built into computer monitors or worn on a participant's head

anticipatory eye movements Eye movements that occur before something occurs in anticipation of a stimulus's movement direction

depth perception The ability to perceive vertical distance from a top surface or space to a bottom one

From Franchak et al. 2011. *Child Dev* 82: 1738–1750

FIGURE 4.12 Eye-trackers. Eye-trackers, devices that are either built into computer monitors or worn on a participant's head, are often used to assess infant eye movements and patterns of visual fixation.

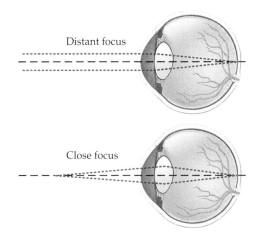

Distant focus

Close focus

FIGURE 4.13 Visual accommodation. The lens accommodates to the distance of the object being viewed. (After S. M. Breedlove and N. V. Watson. 2013. *Biological Psychology: An Introduction to Behavioral, Cognitive, and Clinical Neuroscience*, 7th ed. Oxford University Press/Sinauer: Sunderland, MA; J. Wolfe et al. 2020. *Sensation and Perception*, 6th ed. Oxford University Press/Sinauer: Sunderland, MA.)

visual accommodation A physical process in which the lens of the eyes changes shape to focus on objects of different distances

binocular cues Depth perception cues develop from two eyes that signal depth and distance; binocular cues develop because the two eyes send different signals to the brain

FIGURE 4.14 The original Gibson and Walk (1960) visual cliff experiment. Infants crossed the visual cliff when the floor below was raised up and the drop-off appeared to be very shallow. But, when the floor was lowered, and the drop-off appeared to be steep, infants refused to cross.

In the process of looking at objects of different distances or depths, the lens of the eyes automatically changes shape—this is referred to as **visual accommodation**. When focusing on nearby objects, the lens is relatively thick and round, but when focusing on distant objects, the lens flattens (**FIGURE 4.13**). Between birth and 2 months of age, infants improve in their focus on objects of different distances because of improvements in accommodation. In fact, newborns most clearly see objects at a distance of about 30 centimeters (12 inches), which approximates the distance from an infant's eyes to the mother's face during breastfeeding (Hainline et al., 1992).

Depth and distance are signaled by cues from two eyes—**binocular cues**, and also from one eye—**monocular cues**. Binocular cues arise because the two eyes have different views of the world and thus send different signals to the brain. Monocular cues also provide information about depth and distance through information about visual angles: Distant objects produce smaller angles and smaller objects on the retina relative to close objects. **Motion parallax** is a monocular cue that arises from the relative velocities of objects at different distances as they move across the retina. For example, if you look out a train window, houses nearby move across the retina more quickly than those that are far away.

Binocular and monocular cues show different developmental timelines. To illustrate, researchers placed infants aged 5–7 months in front of two objects of different sizes at equal distances. They covered one of the infants' eyes in the monocular condition and left both eyes uncovered in the binocular condition. Older infants used monocular clues to figure out the object's distance and whether they should reach for it, but 5-month-olds required binocular cues to estimate distance (Yonas, Granrud, & Pettersen, 1985). Of course, relying solely on monocular cues for reaching is more difficult than obtaining visual information from both eyes.

The **visual cliff** is perhaps the most famous experiment used to study infant depth perception. Over half a century ago, Eleanor Gibson and Richard Walk designed a visual cliff to test whether infants would avoid a large drop-off (Gibson & Walk, 1960). They placed infants in a crawling position on a starting platform that abutted an apparent drop-off or "cliff" of 90 cm (3 feet) (**FIGURE 4.14**). In reality, the cliff was covered with Plexiglas to ensure infants' safety. In the "shallow" condition, the floor was placed right under the glass, thus signaling it was safe to cross. Infants crawled across the shallow side but did not crawl when the drop-off was deep, suggesting that depth cues informed their behaviors.

✓ CHECK YOUR UNDERSTANDING 4.11

1. Explain what is meant by binocular and monocular cues to depth.
2. Describe the visual cliff experiment and how it informed research on infant depth perception.

Face Perception

LEARNING OBJECTIVE 4.12 Describe evidence that faces are special to infants.

Infants' world is populated with faces. And faces especially pervade the visual field of very young infants, who spend much of their time lying down because they don't have the posture control to sit up and look around. At least through 2 months of age, nearly half the time that infants are awake, their visual field contains one or more faces, whether near or far (Jayaraman, Fausey, & Smith, 2015) (**FIGURE 4.15**).

(A) Head camera system

(B) Frames from head camera video

FIGURE 4.15 What do infants see most? (A) Researchers mounted head cameras on infants, to "see what babies see." (B) When the researchers then analyzed the images taken from infants' viewpoint, they found that much of young infants' visual world is filled with faces.

Infants' frequent exposure to faces may explain their seeming preference to look at faces over other stimuli. Robert Fantz's looking-time studies (discussed earlier) provided the first evidence that infants look longer at human faces than other visual stimuli (Fantz, 1961, 1963). Even newborns, who have as yet no experience with faces, look longer at a normal face than one that is distorted and thus no longer appears face-like (Goren, Sarty, & Wu, 1975).

But why do newborns look longer at faces if they have such limited social experience? Structures in the brain that bias visual attention toward stimuli that contain many features may account for newborns' looking patterns (Morton & Johnson, 1991). Consider that faces have lots of features to examine—eyes, eyebrows, nose, hairline, mouth, and so forth. Moreover, infants display more attention to the upper portion of faces than the lower portion, perhaps because the upper half contains more visual features. In fact, newborn infants are drawn to images that contain top-heavy features generally, which may help explain their early bias to look at faces (e.g., Macchi, Turati, & Simion, 2004) (**FIGURE 4.16**). Early biases toward face-like patterns, together with infants' daily experiences

monocular cues Depth perception cues from one eye that signal depth and distance to figure out an object's distance; monocular cues provide information about visual angles

motion parallax A monocular depth perception cue that results from the relative velocities of objects at different distances as they move across the retina

visual cliff A test developed by Eleanor Gibson and Richard Walk, which involves an apparatus with an apparent drop-off or cliff, to determine if infants perceive depth; the famous visual cliff experiment showed that infants crawled across the shallow side of the cliff but not the deep side, indicating perception of depth

Experiment 1

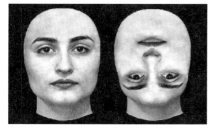

Upright face   Upside-down face

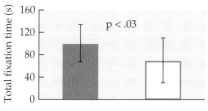

Experiment 2

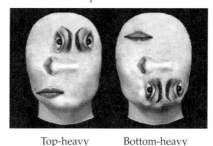

Top-heavy configuration   Bottom-heavy configuration

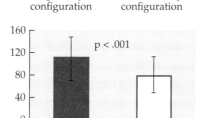

Experiment 3

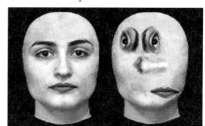

Upright face   Top-heavy configuration

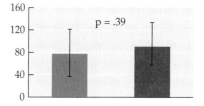

FIGURE 4.16 Newborns may look at faces because of their top-heavy features. Infants' early tendency to look at faces may be explained by a bias to look at things that contain a density of features in the top half. When researchers compared newborns' looking to faces configured in different ways, babies spent more time looking at upright than upside down faces (Experiment 1) and to top-heavy scrambled faces than bottom-heavy scrambled faces (Experiment 2). However, they did not differ in their looking time at upright faces versus faces with scrambled features that were top heavy (Experiment 3). (After V. Macchi Cassis et al. 2004. *Psychol Sci* 15: 379–383.)

interacting with people, may lead to development of specialized regions of the brain dedicated to face processing (de Haan, Johnson, & Halit, 2003).

Infants also look longer at attractive faces than unattractive ones. Infants as young as 3 days old showed an **attractiveness effect** by looking longer at faces that adults rated attractive over faces rated as less attractive (Slater et al., 2000). Perhaps, attractive faces tend to look like a "prototypic face"—the average face that would result from combining a large set of different faces. In fact, when researchers digitally blend the faces of many people of the same gender, ethnicity, and age, the result is a face that people rate as more attractive than the individual faces used to create it (e.g., Langlois & Roggman, 1990). And so, through experiences with many different faces, infants may come to prefer attractive faces simply because they map to the "average" facial prototype. Alternatively, infants may be biased towards the greater symmetry of attractive faces relative to unattractive ones (Langlois & Roggman, 1990; Quinn & Slater, 2003).

attractiveness effect
The phenomenon that infants look longer at attractive faces than unattractive ones, perhaps because attractive faces map to the "average" facial prototype or contain symmetry

✓ CHECK YOUR UNDERSTANDING 4.12

1. How might attention biases explain infants' preference for faces?
2. What might explain infants' preferences for attractive faces?

Contexts of Face Perception

LEARNING OBJECTIVE 4.13 Define and provide examples of perceptual narrowing for faces.

Experience powerfully affects infant face perception. As infants interact with parents, siblings, relatives, and caregivers they increasingly come to prefer faces that resemble the faces of familiar people. This is a good thing, because infants gravitate toward the people they love and know. But, preferences for familiar faces can also come at a cost. As infants attend to familiar faces, their ability to differentiate among unfamiliar types of faces may decline. That is, infants display **perceptual narrowing** for faces—a diminished ability to distinguish among stimuli because of a lack of experience with them. Faces associated with a person's sex and race illustrate the phenomenon of perceptual narrowing.

perceptual narrowing
A developmental process characterized by a diminished ability to distinguish among stimuli because of a lack of experience with them; infants display perceptual narrowing for faces as they attend to familiar faces, such as faces of a specific sex or race

Male and Female Faces

Infants show an early preference for their mother's face and female faces and are better able to distinguish among the faces of women than men in habituation-recovery studies (Quinn et al., 2002). Perhaps the fact that a majority of primary caregivers are still women may influence infants' preferences and abilities to better discern among female faces. In fact, infants with male primary caregivers displayed a visual preference for male faces (Quinn et al., 2002). And, experiences with both male and female caregivers reduces perceptual narrowing for male faces (Rennels et al., 2017).

Race

Most infants regularly interact with people of a specific race. As a result, infants look longer at faces that match the racial appearance of the people around them (Bar-Haim et al., 2006; Kelly et al., 2007; Kelly et al., 2005). In turn, infants' experiences with faces of generally the same race diminish their ability to distinguish among faces of other races—a type of perceptual narrowing that is referred to as the **other-race effect** (Kelly et al., 2007; Quinn et al., 2008). In fact, younger infants are actually *better* at differentiating among other-race faces than are older infants.

But why would the ability to differentiate among faces of other races decline? A bias in infant attention is the likely reason. When infants frequently

other-race effect A type of perceptual narrowing in which infants have a reduced ability to distinguish among faces of other races due to their experiences with faces of generally the same race look at certain types of faces, they may selectively attend to those faces. As a result, they scan the finer details of familiar faces and thus process those faces in greater depth relative to other-race faces (Markant & Scott, 2018). (Infants' heightened attention to details in the process of perceptual learning illustrates Gibsons' ecological theory of perception at the start of the chapter).

Notably, exposing infants to other-race faces reduces the same-race face bias (Anzures, et al., 2012; Fair, et al., 2012; Heron-Delaney, et al., 2011; Spangler, et al., 2013). When researchers cued infants to attend to faces of different races, by presenting a yellow ring on the left or right of a panel to signal where to look, 9-month-old infants who were White and who attended to the face on the side of the cue could subsequently identify the face that they attended to, regardless of the race (Markant, Oakes, & Amso, 2015) **(FIGURE 4.17)**.

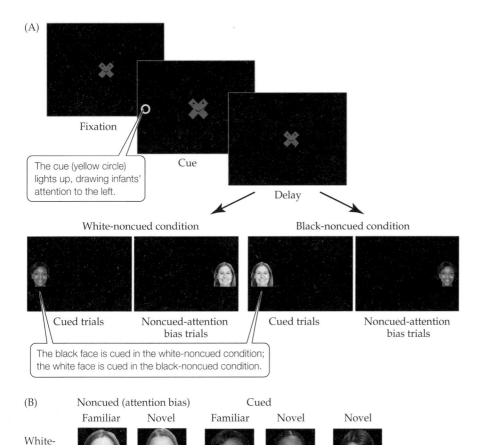

A & B from J. Markant et al. 2015. *Dev. Psychobiol* 58: 355–365

FIGURE 4.17 Distinguishing faces of different races. Infants were presented with photographs of faces of different races. (A) Before test trials, infants were presented with a yellow circle that prompted them where to look (left or right). When they looked to that location, they were presented with a face of a specific race (see figure for Black-cue condition and White-cue condition). (B) During test trials, infants were better able to discriminate between faces of the same race if they had been cued to attend to that specific race first. Thus, even brief experience with faces of a specific race can aid face identification by affecting infant attention.

Indeed, biracial infants and infants who regularly encounter people from different racial groups in their community show less of an other-race effect compared to infants who are not biracial and infants who have limited opportunities to look at faces of other races (Ellis et al., 2017; Gaither, Pauker, & Johnson, 2012).

✓ CHECK YOUR UNDERSTANDING 4.13

1. How might being cared for solely by a mother and grandmother (two women) affect infants' perceptions of male faces?
2. How might infants' racial context affect their attentional bias toward faces of different races?

Hearing

The fetus can hear sounds, and soon after birth infants can distinguish voices, music, and passages they heard while in the womb from those they did not (see Chapter 3). Still, infants improve in their abilities to hear soft sounds, distinguish among sounds of different loudness and pitch, and even to detect changes to beat and melodies over the first year of life. Infants also display a strong preference for the human voice, which paves the way for language.

Loudness and Pitch

LEARNING OBJECTIVE 4.14 Distinguish absolute and relative thresholds in infants' perception of sounds that differ along dimensions of loudness and pitch.

Sounds vary in loudness and pitch: A shout is louder than a whisper, and thunder is lower pitched than a referee's whistle. Perception of loudness and pitch can be defined by two thresholds: absolute and relative. A person's **absolute threshold** is the minimum sound level required to detect a sound. A person's **relative threshold** is the minimum difference in loudness or pitch needed to distinguish between two sounds.

Because infants cannot report whether they hear a sound, a typical approach to testing infants' hearing is to present tones of different pitch and loudness through earphones. Infants will turn their heads, change their activity, and widen their eyes if they are able to detect the sound or changes in the pitch or loudness of sounds (Cone & Whitaker, 2013).

Across the first postnatal year, infants' absolute threshold progresses toward adult levels, although adultlike thresholds are not achieved until well past the preschool years (Jensen & Neff, 1993). For example, for 3-month-old infants a medium-pitched sound has to be about as loud as a humming refrigerator to be detectable; for 6- and 12-month-olds, about as loud as a whisper; and for adults, about as loud as rustling leaves (Olsho, Koch, Carter, Halpin, & Spetner, 1988). The ability to discriminate among pitches continues to develop for several years (Jensen & Neff, 1993; Soderquist & Moore, 1970).

✓ CHECK YOUR UNDERSTANDING 4.14

1. Do children hear as well as adults? On what measures (e.g., loudness, pitch, relative threshold) can infants' hearing be tested?

Perceiving Music

LEARNING OBJECTIVE 4.15 Describe evidence that infants are sensitive to different features of music.

Infants display uncanny sensitivity to features of music, including pitch and rhythmic patterns. Perhaps, social interactions facilitate infants' learning about

absolute threshold The minimum sound level of a stimulus required to detect a sound; absolute threshold is one way to define perception of loudness and pitch

relative threshold The minimum difference in loudness or pitch needed to distinguish between two sounds; relative threshold is one way to define perception of loudness and pitch music. Indeed, parents around the world sing to infants and tailor their songs to meet their infants' developing capacities (Trehub & Gudmundsdottir, 2015).

Yet, exposure to songs does not fully account for young infants' keen music perceptions. Even newborns reliably react to music pitch and structure. Newborn brains respond to variations in absolute pitch, differences in the pitch between notes, and changes in pitch or rhythmic structure of music and tempo sequences (Cirelli & Trehub, 2020; Winkler et al., 2009).

Infants can also reliably detect temporal characteristics of music (just as for speech), such as pauses (e.g., Háden et al., 2015). For example, researchers presented 4- to 7-month-old infants with Mozart minuets that contained either pauses placed between natural segments in the composition or pauses that interrupted natural segments. Infants preferred to listen to minuets that contained pauses between natural segments, based on contingent reinforcement procedures (Krumhansl & Jusczyk, 1990).

Toward the middle to end of the first year, infants detect differences in rhythmic patterns. For example, 8-month-old infants can distinguish between dancing that is synchronized to a beat from dancing that is not synchronized (Hannon, Schachner, & Nave-Blodgett, 2017). Moreover, infants move rhythmically to music, but don't do so to speech, suggesting they distinguish the unique features of each (Zentner & Eerola, 2010). Already between 1 and 2 years, infants begin to sing familiar songs with recognizable pitch and contours (Gudmundsdottir & Trehub, 2018).

With experience, infants come to learn the music of their cultures. Four-month-old infants prefer to listen to music with simple structures that are characteristic of Western or Turkish music, depending on whether they were raised in Western or Turkish cultures (Soley & Hannon, 2010). Infant preferences in turn result in perceptual narrowing. By around 12 months of age, infants have difficulty with foreign metrical structures, but not with familiar ones (Hannon & Trehub, 2005).

✓ CHECK YOUR UNDERSTANDING 4.15

1. What evidence exists to show infants are sensitive to features of music?
2. How does infants' perception for music change with experience?

Perceiving Speech

LEARNING OBJECTIVE 4.16 Identify the sounds that research shows newborns and infants prefer.

Most people would agree that language contains the most important sounds in our lives. That is why **speech perception**, the hearing and interpretation of the sounds of language, is the most frequently studied topic in infant auditory development. Here, we briefly introduce infant speech perception to illustrate infants' early ability to discriminate speech sounds from nonspeech sounds. Chapter 6 presents further elaboration.

Developmental scientists Athena Vouloumanos and Janet Werker (2004) investigated whether infants distinguish novel speech sounds from nonspeech sounds by allowing infants to control the sounds they heard by looking at a monitor. When infants looked at the monitor, the sounds played, and when they looked away the sounds stopped. When infants looked back to the monitor, researchers presented a different sound. Although researchers matched nonspeech sounds with speech sounds on critical features, such as pitch, infants as young as 2 months attended longer to the speech sounds than to the nonspeech sounds. In a subsequent study, neonates younger than 4 days old preferred speech sounds to nonspeech sounds (Vouloumanos & Werker, 2007). Such preferences make sense considering evidence that the developing fetus already begins to process the sounds of speech in the womb (see Chapter 3).

speech perception
The interpretation of sounds of language; infants show speech perception by discriminating speech from nonspeech sounds

Interestingly, young infants' bias toward speech sounds may initially extend beyond human vocalizations. Newborns show no preference for human speech over monkey vocalizations, although they prefer human and monkey vocalizations to inanimate sounds. But, by 3 months of age, infants prefer human to animal vocalizations, revealing a sharpened preference for species-specific vocalizations (Vouloumanos et al., 2010). Infants' early preferences for human speech lay the groundwork for learning language because infants are motivated to attend to and make meaning of what people say.

✓ CHECK YOUR UNDERSTANDING 4.16

1. Which sounds do infants prefer to listen to as newborns and then a few months later?

From Perception to Meaning: Integration and Categorization

Humans (and other animals!) do not experience visual, auditory, and other sensory inputs as isolated perceptions. Rather, they create meaning out of experiences in two key ways. First, people combine information across the senses in a process of integration, and second, people group perceptually similar things together in a process of categorization. Here, we examine perceptual integration and categorization in infants, and demonstrate how these processes help infants learn about their environments.

Perceptual Integration

LEARNING OBJECTIVE 4.17 Evaluate evidence that the temporal synchrony of visual and auditory inputs helps infants integrate information across senses.

Imagine that you see a ball land on a surface with a thump, then bounce up, fall again, rise again, and so on, creating a sound each time it lands. Without thinking, you automatically connect the thumping sound with the ball's contact with the surface, experiencing a single event—a bouncing ball. Such an experience illustrates the idea of **intermodal perception**—perceiving information from objects or events that are available to multiple senses simultaneously. Do infants show intermodal perception as well? Does the breastfeeding infant who sees mother's face, hears mother's voice, feels mother's touch, smells mother's scent, and tastes mother's milk unify these sensations into a single experience of being fed by mother?

According to J. J. Gibson (1979), the nervous system evolved to enable infants to integrate different types of perceptual information based on **temporal synchrony**, the occurrence of different sensations at the same time—for example, hearing a voice while seeing a person's lips move. Temporal synchrony is considered to be the glue that binds perceptions together in the process of intermodal perception, with infants attending longer to temporally synchronous, multimodal information (e.g., Bahrick & Lickliter, 2014; Curtindale, et al., 2019; Lewkowicz, 1996).

How do researchers study infant intermodal perception? A standard procedure is to contrast infants' behaviors to temporally synchronous stimuli, such as time-locked sounds and sights, with temporally asynchronous stimuli. For example, researchers habituated 2- to 8-month-old infants to a display of a bouncing disk coupled with a sound that occurred every time the disk bounced (Lewkowicz, 1996). Then infants were shown the same display with the sound occurring shortly before or after the disk bounced, so the sound and sight were no longer synchronous. Infants looked longer to the asynchronous display, if the sound and sight were sufficiently far apart in time, as though they found the misalignment to be odd.

intermodal perception
The process in which an individual perceives and connects information that is available to multiple senses simultaneously

temporal synchrony When different types of perceptual information occur at the same time, creating a unitary perceptual experience

The powerful pull of temporal synchrony means that infants are exquisitely sensitive to mismatches between words and moving mouths, even if the language spoken is foreign! Experimenters habituated 8-month-old infants to a video of a person speaking either a familiar or an unfamiliar language. They then presented infants with the same video with the sound track out of sync. Infants looked longer at the strange asynchronous video regardless of the language (Pons & Lewkowicz, 2014).

✓ **CHECK YOUR UNDERSTANDING 4.17**

1. What is temporal synchrony and how is it thought to be involved in intermodal perception?

Categorization

LEARNING OBJECTIVE 4.18 Describe how infants categorize perceptions and integrate information across the senses.

People create order out of all of the small bits of sensory information they encounter each day by grouping similar objects, people, and events into broad categories such as "green things," "faces," and "animals"; and narrower categories such as "green vegetables," "my friends' faces," and "birds." Adult categories are typically elaborate, complex, and interconnected (Rakison & Oakes, 2003). People also create hierarchically organized categories: Snakes are reptiles, reptiles are animals, and animals are living things.

Do infants categorize their perceptions similarly to adults? Habituation-recovery procedures help address this question. Researchers typically habituate infants to examples from a single category and then show a new example from the same category and an example from a different category. For instance, researchers may present infants with pictures from the category of "animals," such as a cat, dog, and horse. Then, they may present infants with a rabbit and a truck, an example from the same category of "animals" and an example from a different category of "vehicles." When this is done, infants attend more to the truck than the rabbit, suggesting that they grouped the cat, dog, and horse into a single category, and perceived the rabbit, but not the truck, as belonging to that same category. Categorization studies reveal that young infants form categories for animals, vehicles, spatial relations, geometric forms and patterns, speech sounds, gender, and human voices (e.g., Oakes & Kovack-Lesh, 2013; Oakes, 2020; Quinn, 2016; Rakison & Oakes, 2003).

Infant categories, however, differ from adult categories in that infants often group things together based on their physical appearance (perceptual categories) rather than their use, what they do, or how you use them (conceptual categories) (Mandler, 2000). A habituation-recovery study of 7- to 11-month-olds illustrates the distinction between perceptual and conceptual categorization (Mandler & McDonough, 1993). When researchers habituated 7-month-old infants to pictures of birds, infants did not rebound their attention when shown pictures of airplanes (or the reverse). Infants appeared to treat birds and airplanes as members of the same category. Why? They did so because birds and airplanes are similar in physical appearance—both have elongated bodies and wings. In contrast, 9- and 11-month-olds distinguished birds from airplanes, grouping them by their conceptual categories (**FIGURE 4.18**).

As infants' conceptual understanding of the world develops, they increasingly treat members of the same category similarly. For example, 14-month-old infants watched an adult play with

FIGURE 4.18 Perceptual versus conceptual categories. In categorization tasks based on habituation, 7-month-olds treat airplanes and birds as though they belong to the same category, drawing connections that are based on shape. In contrast, 9- to 11-month-olds distinguish the category of birds from airplanes, thus grouping them based on conceptual categories.

toy animals and toy vehicles in different ways. The adult fed the animals and put them to bed; they gave dolls rides on the vehicles; and they put keys into doors. Researchers then gave infants similar and dissimilar examples of the two types of toys. For example, children who had watched the adult play with a dog, were given a similar animal like a cat and a dissimilar animal like a fish. If they had watched the adult play with a car, they would be given a similar vehicle like a bus and a dissimilar vehicle like an airplane. Although the new objects differed in physical appearance, infants extended their "animal" and "vehicle" categories to the new examples. They fed a fish and put it to bed and gave a doll a ride on an airplane. Thus, the developmental story indicates that infants first form categories based on visually salient features such as shape, later form categories based on conceptual criteria, and then extend their understanding about a specific category, such as what to do with it, to multiple examples within the category (Mandler, 2004).

✓ CHECK YOUR UNDERSTANDING 4.18

1. What is the difference between perceptual categorization and conceptual categorization?

■ *Motor Development*

As any parent can attest, infant motor development is thrilling to watch. Infants' bodies and motor skills change so quickly that it is hard to keep track of the new actions babies do each day and the potential dangers that await them. Years ago, I was preparing dinner, and our 8-month-old daughter Brittany, who could not yet crawl, was upstairs safely asleep in her crib (or so I assumed). My mindless chopping was interrupted by a thunderous crash followed by ear-piercing shrieks. Brittany had managed to climb out of her crib and make her way to the staircase landing where she plummeted down a flight of stairs. Fortunately, there was little damage. However, the incident reminded me firsthand of a fundamental law of motor development: Experience matters. Error rates are high when infants acquire new motor skills, and conversely, practice (almost) makes perfect. Infants' first attempts to reach and grasp yield empty hands. Novice sitters topple over. Inexperienced crawlers and walkers lose balance and fall (or worse, plunge down staircases). Yet, as a result of massive hours of practice, novices become experts who can move about and act on their environments with impressive skill.

If experience matters, then understanding motor development requires understanding infants' everyday experiences: What opportunities do infants have to practice new skills? And how might culture and context influence the skills that infants acquire and when those skills emerge? The sections that follow describe pioneers in the study of motor development followed by contemporary research on infant posture, sitting, reaching, grasping, tool use, and locomotion. We investigate the role of environment in infant skill acquisition and learn about striking variations in cultural practices that challenge Western assumptions about the ages and stages of infant motor development.

The Study of Motor Development in Infants

The study of child development began as a science of description, and motor development is no exception. Scientifically inspired parents conducted the first studies of child development through elaborate descriptions of their infants' motor skills. One of the first parent pioneers, English physiologist William Thierry Preyer (**FIGURE 4.19**), systematically documented changes in his son's motor skills from birth to 3 years of age. He was particularly fascinated by parallels between his son's behaviors and the behaviors of animals. Preyer proposed that

prehension The action of reaching and grasping an object a common, universal sequence of motor development can be seen in children and other species. His book, *The Soul of a Child* (1881) joined the writings of his contemporaries Darwin and Perez (*The First Three Years of Childhood*, 1878) to mark the beginning of the study of child development (Byford, 2013).

Gesell and the Concept of Motor Milestones

LEARNING OBJECTIVE 4.19 Explain the theoretical position of Arnold Gesell and his contribution to the understanding of motor development.

Several decades later, American child psychologist, educator, and pediatrician Arnold Gesell carried out an intensive study at the Yale Clinic of Child Development from the late 1910s through the 1930s. Gesell closely tracked the motor behaviors and physical growth of 107 infants ages 4–56 weeks. He filmed 51 of those infants during natural situations, and categorized their skills in **prehension** (approach, grasp, and release of objects), posture (lying face-down, lying face-up, or sitting), and locomotion (rolling, crawling, and walking) (Gesell, Thompson, & Amatruda, 1934) (**FIGURE 4.20A**).

Gesell's observations culminated in a set of "developmental schedules," later referred to as the Gesell scales, that described infants' progression through various milestones with accompanying illustrations, photographs, and line drawings (**FIGURE 4.20B**). For instance, a developmental schedule of motor skills at 4

FIGURE 4.19 William Thierry Preyer. Preyer was a pioneer in the study of infant motor development. He systematically documented behaviors and developmental changes based on his observations of his son, from when his son was born to 3 years of age.

© Herbert Gehr/The LIFE Picture Collection/Shutterstock.com

FIGURE 4.20 Arnold Gesell. (A) Gesell studied infant prehensile skills. (B) Gesell's careful documentation of the ages and order in which children progress through motor milestones inspired new assessments of infant developmental status. Gesell's motor development scales have become a gold standard in the assessment of infant motor (and mental) development. Pediatricians, physical therapists, and other professionals use Gesell's charts of infant motor milestones to assess infant progress, advise parents, and guide treatment plans. However, such milestones do not capture the range of experiences and skills in infants around the world. (B after W. K. Frankenburg et al. 1992. *Pediatrics* 89: 91–97, based on data in A. Gesell. 1925. *The Mental Growth of the Pre-school Child: A Psychological Outline of Normal Development from Birth to the Sixth Year, Including a System of Developmental Diagnosis*. Macmillan: New York, NY.)

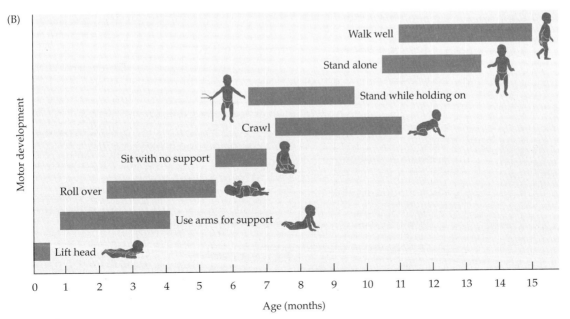

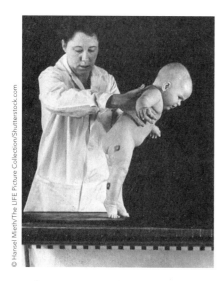

FIGURE 4.21 Myrtle McGraw's work. Myrtle McGraw's experiment with twins Johnny and Jimmy showed that it is possible to train infants to excel at specific motor skills, such as diving into pools or descending high pedestals. Johnny was trained daily on various motor skills while Jimmy remained in a crib in the laboratory.

maturation A genetically determined process that controls and preserves the order of behaviors and skills as children develop

FIGURE 4.22 Jimmy and Johnny older. Jimmy (left) and Johnny (right)—Although Jimmy was a bit taller, Johnny was leaner and more muscular and showed greater motor skills as an adult.

months included descriptions of posture, balance, and movement, such as "prefers to lie on back, tries to raise self by lifting head and shoulders, can roll side to back (or back to side), holds head erect when carried, lifts head when prone, and pushes with feet against the floor when held" (Gesell, 1925, p. 378).

Gesell claimed that infants were highly consistent in their developing motor behaviors because of **maturation**—a genetically determined process that controls and preserves the order of developmental events. To test his maturation hypothesis, Gesell conducted a "co-twin" study on stair climbing in identical twin girls (Gesell & Thompson, 1929). One twin was trained on stair climbing beginning at 46 weeks of age for 10 minutes a day for 6 weeks. At the end of the first twin's training, the second twin was trained on stair climbing for 2 weeks. Despite an abbreviated practice period, the second twin performed as well as her sister, leading Gesell to conclude that experience was secondary to maturation in motor development.

Although Gesell is best known for documenting the progression of motor milestones, he was keenly aware that infants vary substantially in what they can do at different ages because of differences in biology and experiences. As you will see, cross-cultural studies of motor development reveal that group averages and norms can be misleading because they fail to capture the wide age range for any given skill.

✓ **CHECK YOUR UNDERSTANDING 4.19**

1. Why did Arnold Gesell propose a maturational explanation for motor development?

Myrtle McGraw and Motor Practice

LEARNING OBJECTIVE 4.20 Explain how McGraw's study of Johnny and Jimmy contributed to an understanding of the role of experience in motor development.

While Gesell was busy establishing developmental norms for specific motor milestones, Myrtle McGraw was immersed in theoretical and experimental work aimed at understanding how experience may alter developmental paths. She engaged in a controversial and highly provocative study with twin boys, Johnny and Jimmy, decades before universities established ethical guidelines for human research (**FIGURE 4.21**). McGraw selectively intervened with one twin (Johnny) but not the other (Jimmy), showing that it was possible to change the time course and levels of proficiency in motor skills by modifying experience.

Beginning when he was 21 days old and continuing until he was 22 months old, Johnny was extensively exercised for 2 hours a day. His twin Jimmy, in contrast, was restricted to a crib in the laboratory. Johnny's exercises over nearly 2 years included practice swimming and diving, roller skating, and climbing and descending slopes of various inclines and pedestals of different heights. Johnny developed remarkable motor skills because of his extensive practice and outperformed his twin on every exercised skill. For example, Johnny swam by 16 months, roller skated proficiently by 15 months, walked up and down steep slopes by 15 months, climbed up and down slopes of 70 degrees (nearly vertical) in crawling and backing positions at 21 months, and jumped off and backed down pedestals of several feet by 14–15 months. However, the boys did not differ on skills that all children typically acquire, such as crawling and walking. Johnny continued to exhibit superior motor coordination compared to Jimmy into adulthood (McGraw, 1935) (**FIGURE 4.22**).

✓ **CHECK YOUR UNDERSTANDING 4.20**

1. What does McGraw's Jimmy and Johnny study tell us about the role of experience in motor development?
2. How do her findings challenge those of Gesell?

Esther Thelen and Dynamic Systems

LEARNING OBJECTIVE 4.21 Describe how Esther Thelen's research challenged longstanding brain-based interpretations of newborn stepping and led to a theory of the multiple factors that affect development.

A dynamic systems approach to motor development considers the many interacting forces that influence infant motor skills, including an infant's opportunities to practice specific motor skills; changes in body size, strength, and balance; characteristics of the physical environment; and social and cultural pressures.

Newborn stepping—a phenomenon in which newborns demonstrate spontaneous, coordinated "stepping" movements by lifting one leg and then the other when held over a surface—presents a starting point for understanding how something as seemingly simple as body weight can affect the expression of a behavior (**FIGURE 4.23A**).

Curiously, infants' stepping movements disappear by 2 months of age and then reappear toward the end of the first year when they begin learning to walk. A graph of the presence, disappearance, and reappearance of stepping movements has a characteristic shape known as a U-function. For many years, scientists attributed the U-shaped progression of stepping to maturation of the brain. Scientists hypothesized that lower brain centers controlled newborn stepping. Newborn stepping was thought to allow infants to practice movement patterns before higher brain centers were sufficiently mature to control intentional walking (Peiper, 1963). Then, as higher brain centers matured, they inhibited the behavior, leading to the disappearance of stepping movements until further brain maturation ushered in "true" walking.

American psychologist Esther Thelen (Thelen et al., 1982; Thelen, Fisher, & Ridley-Johnson, 1984), however, proposed that changes in infants' bodies might explain why 2-month-olds no longer stepped when upright: Infants had insufficient strength to lift their increasingly chubby legs against gravitational forces. To test her hypothesis that leg strength was involved in stepping, Thelen and colleagues sought to make infants with heavy legs lighter by holding infants upright in an aquarium filled with water, which reduced the pull of gravity on infants' legs. In the context of buoyancy, infants increased their stepping as soon as their feet touched the bottom of the tank (**FIGURE 4.23B**). Reciprocally, when lighter infants were outfitted with tiny leg weights that simulated them being 4–6 weeks older, they reduced their stepping.

Thelen's research was revolutionary in that it revealed the role of developmental factors that had been previously ignored: Something as straightforward as infant weight and muscle mass could affect something as complex as walking. Today, developmental scientists aim to understand the many experiential and individual factors that contribute to infants' changing motor skills, as we will see in the next sections.

(A)   (B)

J.P. Spencer et al 2006. *Child Dev* 77: 1521–1538

FIGURE 4.23 Newborn stepping. (A) Newborns demonstrate spontaneous, coordinated "stepping" movements by lifting one leg and then the other when held over a surface. However, such spontaneous stepping then disappears, which led some researchers to attribute the disappearing "reflex" to changes in brain control over stepping. Esther Thelen's experiments of stepping, however, suggested infants stopped stepping because their legs were chubbier and heavier. (B) When she held infants upright in an aquarium filled with water, the pull of gravity on their legs decreased, and their stepping increased as soon as their feet touched the bottom of the tank.

newborn stepping A phenomenon in which newborns demonstrate spontaneous and coordinated "stepping" movements by lifting one leg and then the other leg when held over a surface

✓ CHECK YOUR UNDERSTANDING 4.21

1. Describe Esther Thelen's study of newborns' stepping behavior. What did she find? What did those findings suggest?

Developments in Infant Motor Skill

Infants make steady progress in their motor skills from day to day. Somehow, order arises out of chaos. Babies' random and unintentional movements give way to organized ways of acting in the world. What enables infants to advance in their motor skills? Changes in strength and coordination, along with lots of practice moving parts of the body are key ingredients.

Each new motor skill, however, takes time to develop, bringing to mind the familiar saying of "two steps forward and one step back." But the end result pays off. Each motor skill—sitting, reaching, grasping, crawling, cruising, and walking—opens up a world of opportunities for infants to engage in new ways with the people and objects of their environments. Furthermore, advances in each motor skill pave the way for advances in others. Infants cannot reach for objects unless they can steady their head, fixate their gaze, and keep their balance while extending an arm. Being able to sit changes infants' view of the world, and with hands free, infants can eye, reach for, and then manipulate nearby objects. And, crawling and walking allow infants to get to things across the room. Therefore, although each motor skill is described separately, keep in mind that all motor skills are intertwined. Indeed, the concept of developmental cascades—which we return to later in the chapter—aptly captures how new motor skills cascade to other motor skills.

Posture

LEARNING OBJECTIVE 4.22 Describe the cross-cutting role of posture in motor skills.

posture The position in which a person holds their head and body

Critical to motor skill development is **posture**, or the position in which a person holds their head and body. Posture controls what infants see, touch, and where they go. Posture must be sufficiently stable for infants to look around, reach for objects, move from place to place, and so on (e.g., Adolph & Franchak, 2017).

Stable posture *facilitates* action, as when an experienced sitter smoothly reaches for objects without toppling over and a walking infant darts across the room without falling. Conversely, unstable posture *impedes* action.

The importance of posture in motor action spotlights contextual influences as well. Very young infants depend on adults to prop their heads up for support so they can see what is in front of them, whereas somewhat older infants have the capacity to move their heads as they look around to track things of interest.

✓ CHECK YOUR UNDERSTANDING 4.22

1. What is the role of posture in motor action? Give an example.

Sitting

LEARNING OBJECTIVE 4.23 Explain the requirements for independent sitting.

As with all skills, infants can only sit if they are able to maintain their posture. And for this to happen, the body must be sufficiently strong. Sitting requires muscles to gradually strengthen in the neck, torso, legs, and hips so that infants may balance (Adolph & Berger, 2006). Before infants successfully sit alone, they accumulate hours of practice with various types of supported sitting—being held in their caregivers' arms, propped up with pillows, and secured in contraptions such as infant seats, swings, car seats, and high chairs. After a few months of externally supported sitting, infants figure out ways to support themselves with their hands to maintain a seated position, such as by placing their hands on the floor between their legs, which they spread out in a V formation to help keep balance (Adolph & Berger, 2006).

Between 5 and 7 months of age, infants begin to sit independently (Rochat & Goubet, 1995). Still, they remain shaky in their first weeks of unsupported sitting, especially when trying to play with objects around them. If infants turn to the side or reach too far, they tumble over. By around 9 months of age, the muscles in the trunk and hips are sufficiently developed such that infants can reach for objects, turn their torso, lean over, and transition between sitting and crawling without losing balance (Adolph & Berger, 2006; von Hofsten, 1991). When researchers seat infants at the edge of gaps of different sizes and tempt them with treats, experienced sitters avoid reaching over large gaps for treats, but reach when the gap is within the bounds of their abilities (Adolph, 2000; Adolph, Kretch, Lobue, 2014) (**FIGURE 4.24**).

✓ **CHECK YOUR UNDERSTANDING 4.23**

   1. What are the key events leading to an infant's ability to sit without assistance?

Reaching, Grasping, and Tool Use

LEARNING OBJECTIVE 4.24 Describe developmental changes in infants' reaching, grasping, and use of objects as tools, and the skills infants must acquire to successfully implement these actions.

Over the course of a day, we reach and grasp hundreds of objects. With each reach and grasp we spontaneously modify our actions to accommodate the varying distances, dimensions, textures, and functions of objects (think of how you hold a cup versus a pencil versus a spoon). Although adults smoothly reach, grasp, and manipulate objects, infants require months of practice to achieve on-target reaches and effective grasps. Early reaches are jerky and early grasps are imprecise. Perception and action come together to result in successful reaches and grasps.

Judging Distance

Infants must learn how to modify their actions and body position to reach objects near and far (Adolph & Robinson, 2015) (**FIGURE 4.25**). With researchers supporting their heads and torsos, infants between 3 and 5 months of age successfully contact objects (Adolph & Berger, 2006; Clifton et al., 1993; Hopkins & Rönnqvist, 2002). Yet, figuring out whether and how far to reach and planning

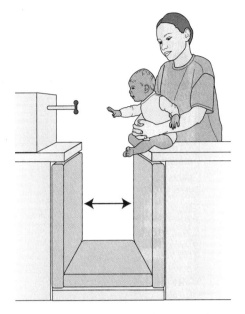

FIGURE 4.24 Sitting. When seated at the edge of a gap and presented with a tempting lure such as toy or cheerios in front of them at varying distances, experienced sitters accurately avoid reaching over risky gaps, but reach when the gap is within the range of their abilities. Here, a new (inexperienced) sitter reaches over to get the object far away, which would lead to falling over. (After K. E. Adolph. 2000. *Psych Sci* 11: 209–295.)

(A)
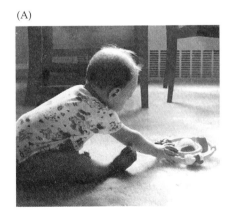

(B)

(C)
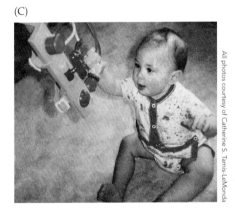

All photos courtesy of Catherine S. Tamis-LeMonda

FIGURE 4.25 Reaching. An action as basic as reaching for an object draws on many emerging motor skills, including the control of posture and balance. Infants must learn how to modify their actions and body position and maintain balance to reach for and grasp objects located (A) in front of them, (B) on their side, or (C) up in the air to avoid falling over.

to reach takes several more weeks. When researchers placed 4- and 5-month-old infants in an infant seat, with toys *within* reach that did not require leaning forward, 5-month-olds rarely leaned, whereas 4-month-olds still did. When the toy was *slightly beyond* the infants' arm length, both 5- and 4-month-old infants leaned forward to reach. And, when the toy was *beyond* reach, 5-month-old infants were less likely than 4-month-olds to continue attempts to reach the object (Yonas & Hartman, 1993). Some months later, infants lean forward even before attempting to grasp distant objects, in anticipation of their grasp. For example, 8-, 10-, and 12-month-old infants simultaneously reached and leaned forward to reach far objects, rather than reaching first, failing to grasp the object, and then leaning in. Infants' ability to plan their reaches continues to improve with age. By 14 months of age, they modify how fast or slow they move their arms based on the distance and size of objects. Reaching for something that is far away and quite small, for example, requires slowing down the arm movement to ensure success (Gottwald et al., 2017).

Controlling Hands

Reaching for an object does not guarantee a successful grasp. Grasping requires infants to control their hands to accommodate the sizes, shapes, and textures of objects (Adolph & Robinson, 2015). But, 3- and 4-month-old infants have limited hand control, which renders imprecise grips and dropped objects (Von & Rönnqvist, 1988).

Grips improve by about 5 months of age when infants alter their hand configuration to match the shapes and sizes of objects (Newell et al., 1989). By 9 months of age, infants display **prospective control** in their grasps—they open their hands to match an object size *before* grasping, and begin to close the hand in anticipation of contact (von Hofsten & Rönnqvist, 1988).

Toward the end of the first year, infants' well-developed hand control allows them to grasp small objects between the index finger and thumb using a **pincer grasp** (Schum, Jovanovic, & Shwarzer, 2011). Infants also improve at estimating how much distance they will need between their two hands to pick up large objects (van Wermeskerken et al., 2011). Accuracy at estimating distances and prospective control means that infants can even catch moving objects (van der Meer, van der Weel, & Lee, 1994; van Hof et al., 2005).

Everyday experience explains developmental changes in infant reaches and grasps. Developmental scientist Amy Needham designed a clever "Sticky Mittens" study to test whether infants' practice picking up objects aids manual skill (**FIGURE 4.26**). She outfitted 3-month-old infants—who cannot yet pick up objects—with sticky mittens that had adhesive on them, which allowed infants to reach, grasp, and manipulate toys (Needham, Barrett, & Peterman, 2002). After 10 minutes of daily practice for 2 weeks, infants who wore the sticky mittens looked at objects, swatted, put them in their mouths to suck, and alternated between looking and mouthing more often than did a control group of infants without the mittens. As infants gain experience reaching for and manipulating objects, they come to understand which objects are graspable and which objects are not (Libertus et al., 2013).

Play and Tool Use

Reaching and grasping are only first steps in the use of objects. What infants do with those objects changes in fundamental ways over the course of development.

Much of infant object interactions falls under the broad category of play. In the early months of object play, infants learn about objects by putting things in their mouths and manipulating them (fingering, banging, rotating). During the latter half of the first year, infants discover the designed features of objects, and their play zeroes in on object functions: Infants

prospective control The ability to act adaptively in an anticipatory manner, such as when an infant opens the hands to match an object's size before grasping the object

pincer grasp The coordination of an infant's index finger and thumb to grasp small objects, usually developed toward the end of the first year of life

FIGURE 4.26 The Needham Sticky Mittens study. Three-month-old infants were outfitted with sticky mittens (which contained an adhesive so that they could reach, grasp, and manipulate toys).

Courtesy of Amy Needham

push buttons, turn knobs, and spin the wheels of toy vehicles (**FIGURE 4.27**). Moreover, infants increasingly relate objects to other objects to produce new effects, such as banging to produce sounds, or inserting blocks into shape-sorters and pegs into boards (Lockman & Tamis-LeMonda, 2021; Tamis-LeMonda & Lockman, 2020).

Tools are objects that help humans carry out actions in ways that would not be possible by using the body alone. Spoons, chopsticks, hammers, crayons, combs, shovels, zippers, buttons, and can openers are examples of tools (although research on tool use is limited to infants' use of spoons and sometimes hammers for banging). Tool use differs from other forms of object engagements in that the infant must detect the possible relations of objects to one another and then act on those possibilities (Lockman, 2000). For example, when eating, the infant must understand that one object (spoon) can be related to another object (food) to serve a practical function (transporting food to the mouth), and then use the spoon accordingly.

The multiple steps involved in tool use develop over time as infants learn how to manipulate objects and improve in their planning and execution of actions (e.g., Lockman & Kahrs, 2017). Young infants may recognize that two or more objects are related, but still have difficulties acting on them. For example, they may realize that two objects can be banged together to produce a sound, and yet still fail to bang them together. To illustrate, researchers presented 6- to 10-month-old infants with two cubes, each composed half of wood and half of sponge. Infants were able to rotate a single cube to bang it against a table to make noise but did not yet bang the wood side of the two cubes together (Lockman, 2000). By around 14 months of age, however, infants displayed efficient straight up-down movements as they banged objects against surfaces. Infants' control of such manual actions paves the way to hammering and other forms of percussive tool use (Kahrs, Jung, & Lockman, 2012).

The use of spoons further illuminates developmental changes in tool use (McCarty, Clifton, & Collard, 2001). Infants must grip the spoon with one hand, position the hand in the right place and angle, keep the spoon steady and at a proper angle so the food doesn't spill out, and open the mouth in anticipation of the food (e.g., Gesell & Ilg, 1937; Keen, Lee, & Adolph, 2014). It takes at least a couple of years for infants to demonstrate full control of the sequence. For instance, 9-month-old infants may grasp a spoon by the cupped end rather than the handle or grasp the handle upside down and then have to rotate their hand to eat the food. With practice, by around 18 months of age, infants grasp the correct side of the spoon (**FIGURE 4.28**).

FIGURE 4.27 Infants spend much of their awake hours exploring the features of objects, including toys.

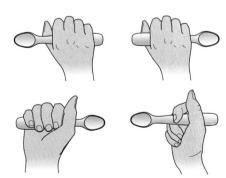

FIGURE 4.28 Using spoons.   Infants understand the function of spoons before they are able to plan their actions and use them correctly. They may grasp the handle upside down and then have to rotate their hand to eat the food. With practice, by around 18 months of age, infants grasp the correct side of the spoon. (After R. Keen et al. 2014. *Ecol Psych* 26: 108–198. Taylor & Francis Ltd, http://www.tandfonline.com)

Between 2 and 3 years of age, children begin to appreciate that different tools can be used to carry out different actions. When 3-year-old children were presented with different tools—such as pencils and paintbrushes—to draw on surfaces that were rough, nonrigid, and bumpy, the tool they selected depended on the properties of the surface (Lockman, 2000). Around this same time in development, children begin to successfully implement highly specific actions that objects require for their use—such as twisting the cap of a bottle; turning the knob of a cabinet or faucet; zipping a sweater, and so on (Rachwani et al., 2020).

✓ CHECK YOUR UNDERSTANDING 4.24

1. How do each of the following affect infants' abilities to reach and grasp objects: (a) keeping balance, (b) controlling arms, (c) judging distance, and (d) controlling hands?
2. What makes "tools" unique from other objects? Give an example of how infants' use of tools improves over time.

Locomoting: Crawling, Cruising, Walking

LEARNING OBJECTIVE 4.25 Describe the different forms of infant locomotion and the role of experience in infants' proficiency with each skill.

Infants are highly motivated to move their bodies through space. Long before infants crawl or walk, they roll and pivot their torsos to change positions or reach for enticing objects. Parents must remain on high alert to ensure that their lively infants don't fall from changing tables or roll off couches and beds. As infants become stronger, and their actions more coordinated and intentional, they get around by crawling, cruising, and then walking, and they improve in the speed, smoothness, and flexibility of their motor behaviors.

Crawling

On the developmental path to hands-and-knees crawling, infants generate unique solutions for getting about (Adolph & Franchak, 2017; Adolph, Vereijken, & Denny, 1998): They bum-shuffle along the floor from a seated position; use their arms to propel themselves forward while dragging their legs behind; "swim" across the floor with all four limbs moving; or "inchworm" crawl by pushing their chests off the floor and propelling themselves forward on their bellies. By around 8 months of age, most U.S. infants settle on the relatively efficient strategy of hands-and-knees crawling, although some infants entirely skip crawling (Adolph et al., 1998) (FIGURE 4.29).

Practice with crawling allows infants to accurately estimate if different surfaces are safe or risky to crawl across, including whether it is safe to cross a

FIGURE 4.29 Infants find creative ways to get around.
As infants begin to locomote, they may take several weeks before showing the classic "hands-and-knees" crawling. Rather, infants generate unique solutions for moving about. Sometimes they scoot on their bottoms; sometimes they use their arms to pull their bodies along the floor; or they may propel themselves forward by lifting their bellies and "swimming" forward.

glass-covered visual cliff as described earlier in the chapter (Bertenthal, Campos, & Barrett, 1984; Campos, Hiatt, Ramsay, Henderson, & Svejda, 1978). When researchers tested infants on a veritable cliff (without the protective glass used in the original cliff studies), 12-month-old infants' locomotor experience predicted their attempts to cross (Kretch & Adolph, 2013) (**FIGURE 4.30**). Specifically, experienced 12-month old crawlers refused to cross risky cliffs, but crossed safe ones; whereas, novice 12-month-old walkers repeatedly walked over the edge of steep cliffs, only to be rescued by an experimenter who stood alongside. Notably, although experienced crawlers were the same age as novice walkers, infants' experience with crawling helped them to accurately perceive cues in the environment, indicating their abilities at gauging affordances for action in their skilled posture.

Cruising

Infants are not content to remain on all fours. And so, they eventually abandon crawling in favor of upright locomotion. At around 7–13 months, infants use furniture, walls, and other supports to pull themselves up to a standing position and "cruise" sideways while holding on (Bly, 1994). The common observer views cruising as an early form of walking because cruising, on the surface, looks so much like walking. However, despite the visual parallels to walking, cruising is functionally more similar to crawling than to walking. Both cruisers and crawlers heavily rely on their arm muscles for support and balance, whereas walkers rely on their legs.

Developmental scientist Karen Adolph illustrated the similarities between crawling and cruising in a clever study in which she placed cruising infants on a walkway that had a railing for them to hold on (Adolph et al., 2011). On some trials, the handrail was interrupted by a gap. The gap in the handrail ranged from being small enough to permit infants to reach the rail on the other side of the gap and continue cruising to being so large that it prevented infants from continuing their sideways journey without hand support. On other trials, a gap was placed in the floor, with the floor gap also varying in width from trial to trial. As the gap to the handrail became larger, cruisers modified their behaviors, for example by crawling instead of cruising, indicating they recognized their reliance on arm support for moving. But when the gap in the floor was large, they continued to cruise and stepped right into the gap, requiring rescue by the experimenter. Cruisers apparently had not yet learned the importance of a floor to support their moving bodies (**FIGURE 4.31**).

Walking

Somewhere around their first birthday, infants let go (literally) of their physical safety nets to locomotion: They liberate themselves of holding onto floors, walls, and furniture. During the first weeks of walking, balance is precarious and falls are frequent (Adolph et al., 2012). Moreover, infants display tiny steps, spread their legs wide apart for stability and balance, and keep both feet planted on the floor between steps for as long as possible (e.g., Adolph et al., 2012; Ledebt, van Wieringen, & Savelsbergh, 2004).

With experience, infants become more proficient at walking, based on step length, step speed, and step width. Researchers can measure walking proficiency using a **gait-mat procedure**, in which they encourage infants to walk across a portable, flexible mat or walkway that contains pressure sensors that record the length of footsteps and how long it takes the infant to walk the length of the mat. And sometimes researchers use high-speed motion tracking

FIGURE 4.30 Real cliff study. The role of experience in infant response to a visual cliff has also been tested with a real cliff that did not contain protective plexiglas. The cliff could be adjusted in its depth, so that the drop off, and therefore risk to falling, varied trial to trial. Experimenters stood alongside the infant, ready to save infants from falls. (After K. E. Adolph. 2000. *Psych Sci* 11: 209–295.)

gait-mat procedure A technique used by researchers to examine infants' walking proficiency; infants are encouraged to walk across a portable, flexible mat or walkway with pressure sensors that record the length of footsteps and how long it takes

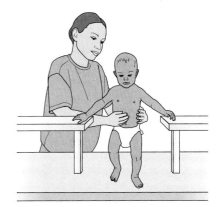

FIGURE 4.31 Cruising. When the gap in the handrail became too large for cruisers to reach the rail on the opposite side, they modified their behaviors, for example by discontinuing their cruising, indicating they were aware of the need for arm support for moving. (After K. Adolph et al. 2011. *Dev Sci* 14: 306–318. © 2011 John Wiley & Sons Ltd.)

to assess infant walking. Although infant age and body dimensions predict walking proficiency, walking experience is by far the strongest predictor of proficiency (Adolph, Vereijken, & Shrout, 2003).

Gait mats offer useful information on infant walking skill, but they typically require infants to walk straight paths, which is far from how infants walk spontaneously—in curved paths and in all directions, frontwards, backwards, and side to side (Lee et al., 2018). Spontaneous walking, therefore, requires infants to flexibly adjust to changing directions and environments as they walk around obstacles, on slippery floors versus rugs, and on flat versus sloped surfaces. Once again, experience is key to flexibility in walking. When researchers present infants with various obstacles to walking, new walkers fall into wide gaps in the floor or plunge off slopes that are too steep for walking. In contrast, experienced 18-month-old walkers avoid drop-offs beyond their skill and adopt creative strategies to descend steep slopes: They take small, slow steps to safely walk down moderately steep slopes and sit and back down steep, unmanageable slopes (e.g., Gill, Adolph, Vereijken, 2009). In fact, 18-month-old experienced walkers are so competent at identifying risky surfaces for walking that they refuse to walk down slopes that are beyond their ability, even when enthusiastically encouraged to walk by a caregiver (Tamis-LeMonda et al., 2008).

✓ CHECK YOUR UNDERSTANDING 4.25

1. What is cruising? What evidence is there that cruisers are more like crawlers than walkers?
2. How might experienced walkers differ from novice walkers when encountering a risky slope or a high drop-off? What actions might the infant take to reduce the risk of falling?

Contexts of Motor Development

Practice, practice, practice. That's the take-home message on motor development. Experience with a motor skill influences when an infant will display a specific skill and how proficient the infant will be at a given age. And, because context and culture determine the opportunities that infants have to practice new skills, we return full circle to the work of Arnold Gesell, and the strides that scientists have made in understanding differences among infants in motor skills. Today, researchers recognize the commanding role of social and cultural experiences in every motor skill.

Home Context of Motor Development

LEARNING OBJECTIVE 4.26 Provide examples of caregiving practices at home that affect infant motor development.

Infants develop and refine their motor skills primarily in the home context. The opportunities that caregivers provide and how they physically organize space and materials in the home shape the skills infants practice, where infants practice those skills, and how often. Sometimes, parents' role in motor development is obvious, such as when they prop infants up with pillows to encourage sitting; position enticing toys within reach to encourage toy play; or place gates on stair landings and strap infants into high chairs to ensure their safety. Other times, parents are unaware of how seemingly insignificant parenting behaviors affect infant motor development. As two cases in point, let's consider practices around sleep and variations in the physical characteristics of homes.

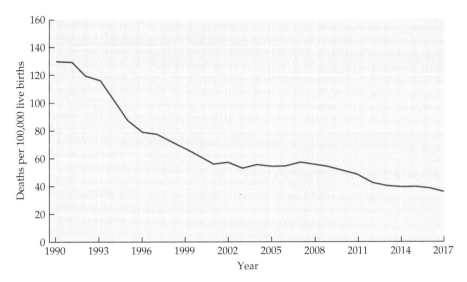

FIGURE 4.32 Belly sleeping and the incidence of SIDS.   The AAP Back to Sleep Campaign successfully reduced the rate of SIDS. (After CDC. 2021. NCHS, NVSS, Mortality Files. CDC: Washington, DC. https://www.cdc.gov/sids/data.htm)

Back Sleeping

The Back to Sleep campaign (now called the Safe to Sleep campaign), implemented in 1994, provides one of the most compelling illustrations of the unforeseen consequences of parenting practices on motor development. Prior to the campaign, and for most of the twentieth century, most infants slept on their stomachs. But in 1992 the American Academy of Pediatrics (AAP) sought to reduce the incidence of sudden infant death syndrome (SIDS), the unexplained death of healthy infants while asleep. SIDS was the leading cause of death among U.S. infants between 1 month and 1 year of age (Hauck & Tanabe, 2017). The AAP responded to the crisis by warning parents against the dangers of a prone (stomach) sleeping posture. Parents paid attention, positioning their infants on their backs or sides for sleep. As a result, prone sleeping declined from 70% to 13% from 1992 to 2004 (Kattwinkel et al., 2005), and the rates of SIDS reduced by 50% (American Academy of Pediatrics, 2016) (**FIGURE 4.32**).

Nonetheless, the Back to Sleep campaign led to delays in certain motor skills. Back sleepers, compared to belly sleepers, were slower to roll over, sit supported, crawl, and stand up, largely because belly sleepers have more opportunity than back sleepers to exercise their arms and trunk by pushing up from a prone position. Indeed, some of the milestones on Gesell's charts, established well before the Back to Sleep campaign, were delayed by weeks or months! As a result, campaigns began to spread the importance of "tummy time" to give infants opportunities to strengthen their torsos, which supports motor development in infants around the globe (Hewitt et al., 2020) (**FIGURE 4.33**).

Physical Layouts of Homes

Homes differ in physical layouts and the materials available for infant exploration—factors that affect opportunities for movement and manual action. As infants engage with specific objects—including toys, writing instruments, and eating utensils—they develop the requisite fine motor skills to use those objects effectively. Similarly, differences in physical environments affect the motor skills that infants develop and the relative timing of those

FIGURE 4.33 Tummy time. Caregivers are encouraged to give their infants time to be on their stomachs so that infants gain experience pushing up and crawling.

skills. For example, infants who live in multi-floor homes climb up and down stairs sooner in development than do infants in homes without stairs (Berger, Theuring, & Adolph, 2007). And, although research on home layouts is scarce, many potential influences on motor development come to mind. Infants living in the suburbs versus a small apartment in the city will navigate very different spaces, such as large expanses of open rooms versus the confined quarters of many urban apartments; and infants in different home environments traverse different surfaces, including grass, sand, cement, wood floors, and carpets, that feed into the practice they experience in moving about.

✓ CHECK YOUR UNDERSTANDING 4.26

1. How did the Back to Sleep campaign affect infant motor development? Why does this finding challenge a maturational view of motor development?

2. How might the layout of a home affect an infant's motor development?

Cultural Context of Motor Development

LEARNING OBJECTIVE 4.27 Describe the types of cultural practices shown to facilitate and delay infant motor skill development.

Cultural studies offer compelling evidence on how infants' everyday experiences shape motor development. Infants reared in different parts of the world encounter profoundly different opportunities to practice motor skills such as sitting and walking, which play out in the timing and course of their motor development (Adolph, Karasik, & Tamis-LeMonda, 2010). In fact, to put cultural variation in perspective, onset ages for a seemingly basic motor skill such as sitting ranges from 3.8 months to 9.2 months in infants around the world, as documented by the World Health Organization (de Onis et al., 2006).

The history of cultural comparisons can be traced to Geber's intriguing descriptions of motor development in Ugandan infants in Africa (Geber, 1958, 1962; Geber & Dean, 1957). Geber reported that Ugandan infants surpassed U.S. infants in head control and limb extension as newborns. On average, Ugandan infants could sit independently at 4 months (compared to 6 months for U.S. infants), stand upright at 7 months (compared to 11 months), and walk proficiently by 10 months (compared to about 12 months). Other researchers corroborated the accelerated motor onsets of infants from several countries in Africa and infants of African descent for sitting, standing, and walking relative to Western norms (e.g., Hopkins & Westra, 1989, 1990; Kilbride, Robbins, & Kilbride, 1970).

Studies of African infants' motor skills were highly controversial because they suggested a genetically determined racial advantage. One way to test whether motor skill disparities were "inborn" was to ask whether cultural differences were evident from birth. However, comparisons of newborns from different African countries (Zambia, Uganda, Kenya) with U.S. newborns provided mixed results. Sometimes African newborns lagged behind Western norms (Brazelton, Koslowski, & Tronick, 1976). Sometimes there were no differences (Warren & Parkin, 1974). And sometimes African newborns were relatively advanced (Keefer et al., 1982). It soon became apparent that infant experience might have explained differences across studies, and that specific cultural practices facilitate or hinder motor development.

Cultural Practices That Facilitate Motor Skills

Culture-specific practices, including formal exercise routines in certain African and Caribbean communities, accelerate the development of infant motor skills (Adolph, Karasik, & Tamis-LeMonda, 2010). For example, to promote sitting, mothers hold newborns on their laps and support them around the waist (e.g., Kilbride & Kilbride, 1975). In some cultural communities, mothers placed infants in a hole in the ground or in a mound of sand, wrapped cloth around infants' hips, or used cushions to prop infants up when they are as young as 3 months of age (Ainsworth, 1967; Konner, 1977; Super, 1976).

During everyday home routines, 5-month-old infants from six cultures— United States, Korea, Italy, Argentina, Kenya, and Cameroon—had substantially different opportunities to practice sitting. Infants in Kenya and Cameroon had more experience with sitting than did infants in the other cultures, including sitting on high furniture while their mothers went about their daily chores (Karasik et al., 2015). In turn, cultural practices around sitting accelerate infants' sitting skill. For example, Kenyan and Cameroon infants sat without support for up to 30 minutes at a time, which far exceeds the brief bouts of sitting (a few seconds) observed in infants from the other cultural communities.

Cultural differences are seen in infant practice with crawling and standing as well. Teso Ugandan infants crawled on average at 5.5 months of age, in line with their mothers' intentional teaching of crawling (Super, 1976). Similarly, in cultural communities where infant walking onsets occur earlier than the Gesell norms, caregivers engage in various practices to encourage walking. Mothers propped their infants against stools and held their infants' hands to stimulate walking, often luring infants with food (Hopkins, 1976; Konner, 1977). In Bali, infants practiced taking independent steps by holding a bamboo rail built by caregivers (Mead & Macgregor, 1951).

A clever quasi-experimental investigation of Jamaican immigrants to England suggests that cultural practices *cause* changes in infant motor skill, rather than merely being correlational. Some Jamaican mothers continued exercises to promote infant sitting and walking after immigrating to England, whereas others did not. Infants whose mothers continued the practices of their home culture showed better head control at 1 month of age and sat and walked at earlier ages than did infants whose mothers did not exercise those skills (Hopkins & Westra, 1988, 1990).

Cultural Practices That Hinder Motor Skills

Cultural studies illuminate the consequences of restricted movement on motor development in the otherwise loving context of family life. For example, certain cradling practices in Central Asia constrain infant movement in ways that may impede motor skill development. Mothers in Tajikistan use a *gahvora* to cradle, toilet, put infants to sleep, and contain infants throughout the day (Karasik et al., 2018) (**FIGURE 4.34**). While in the gahvora, infants' upper and lower limbs are bound tightly, inhibiting movement, and a draping is placed over the top and sides of the cradle, preventing visual exploration. Mothers remove the draping to feed their infants, which takes place while the infant is lying face up in the cradle. An external catheter is placed on the infant, and a hole underneath the infant's buttocks catches waste. Gahvora cradling has been carried on for centuries and serves important functions for life in Tajikistan. In the absence of electricity and heat, the gahvora keeps infants warm during winter; safe from insects and other creatures; and away from the dirt and stone floors of homes. Mothers are able to go about their chores without worrying about their infants. Still, infants have limited occasions to gain practice and proficiency with motor skills, which may

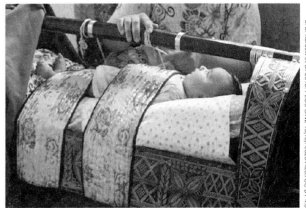

FIGURE 4.34 Gahvora for sleeping, toileting, and containing infants throughout the day.   In Central Asia, many infants are cradled in a gahvora, where their limbs are swaddled and bound to the cradle.

contribute to their later average walking age relative to norms established by the World Health Organization, which do not include infants from Central Asia (Karasik et al., 2018).

Other cultural practices also may hamper infant movement, sometimes for safety and economic reasons. For example, the Ache—a foraging society of Eastern Paraguay—travel for extended trips through dangerous forests. To ensure that their children do not get into trouble, mothers rarely put their infants down or let them venture more than a meter (3 feet) away. Consequently, Ache infants do not begin walking until about 2 years of age, a full year behind the walking age documented by Gesell (Kaplan & Dove, 1987).

Interpreting Cultural Differences

Several observations around cultural differences warrant attention. Although people may be biased toward using terms such as "advanced" or "delayed" when describing the motor skills of infants from different cultures, such terms are misguided. "Delayed" or "advanced" relative to whom? The developmental ages seen in Western infants? By switching cultural lenses, definitions of delay and advancement change as well. It is just as reasonable (or unreasonable) to describe Cameroon infants as "advanced" in sitting relative to U.S. norms as it is to describe U.S. infants as "delayed" relative to Cameroon infants (Adolph & Robinson, 2015).

Furthermore, although gahvora cradles may be viewed as confining infant movement, many parents in the United States keep infants strapped into highchairs, strollers, car seats, and infant seats for hours a day, yet the effects of such practices remain unexamined.

Finally, researchers know little about the long-term impacts of cultural practices around motor development. Short-term restrictions on infant movement, for example, may have little bearing on what children do years later, given that many intervening experiences equip children with the motor skills necessary to become integral members of their cultural communities. For example, although Ache infants do not walk until around 2 years of age, by 8–10 years of age Ache children climb trees of nearly 8 meters (24 feet) and adeptly use machetes and sharp knives for cutting and chopping—skills that are highly valued in their community.

✓ CHECK YOUR UNDERSTANDING 4.27

1. Give an example of a cultural practice that "promotes" crawling or walking and one that "hinders" motor development.

Developmental Cascades

Perceptual and motor development are the engines that drive learning and development. They underpin everything infants do, and they touch on every domain of functioning. As infants perceive, they act. As infants act, perceptions change. And, as perceptions change and motor skills expand, infants' interactions with people and objects are forever altered. Perception-action feedback loops and cascading influences lie at the heart of developmental science.

Cascades from Perceptual Development

Developmental cascades are seen when changes in one area affect changes in others. It is intriguing to consider how something as basic as perceptual development affects other areas of functioning, including social and emotional development. Perceptual biases and preferences affect where infants look, the speech sounds they discriminate, the foods they prefer, the people with whom they interact, and so forth.

How might early perceptual biases and perceptual narrowing spill over to infants' interactions with caregivers? As you learned, infants enjoy looking at the dynamic, talking faces around them, and come to prefer those familiar faces to unfamiliar ones (Quinn, 2016). Infants' early social preferences then influence the formation of attachments. When infants communicate with their caregivers through looks and vocalizations, caregivers respond with touches, smiles, and talk, which heightens the bond between infants and caregivers. Furthermore, infants' bias toward the human voice and early capacities for intermodal perception establish a foundation ripe for language learning.

The long-term implications of perceptual narrowing are intriguing to consider as well. For example, what is the impact of perceptual narrowing toward the speech sounds of one's language on second language learning? Do infants in bilingual households show different patterns of perceptual narrowing around language given that they are exposed to a wider variety of speech sounds? Similarly, might perceptual narrowing in infant face perception affect how people from different ethnic groups interact? Is it possible to minimize infants' same-race preferences and thus encourage openness to human differences? We examine the ways that developmental scientists tackle these socially significant questions in later chapters.

Cascades from Motor Development

New motor skills enable infants to engage with their environments in new ways. Indeed, gains in motor development affect the objects infants access, how they play, where they go, how quickly they get there, and even what they see (e.g., Adolph & Tamis-LeMonda, 2014). Let's consider the cascading effects of sitting, manual skills, and locomotion for infant perception, cognition, and social relationships.

Sitting and Manual Skills

Sitting represents a vital piece of the developmental cascade in how infants engage with their environments. As infants learn to sit independently, their hands free up to grasp and manipulate objects. In turn, hands-on experiences help infants learn about the properties of objects and engage in new forms of social interaction.

Sitting promotes learning about objects because infants can more easily explore objects manually, orally, and visually when sitting than when lying face-up or face-down (Soska & Adolph, 2014). In turn, manual exploration teaches infants that objects look different from different orientations—what researchers refer to as "mental rotation" (Frick & Möhring, 2013). To illustrate the developmental cascade from sitting to manual action to object perception, developmental scientist Kasey Soska observed 4.5- to 7.5-month-old infants who varied in sitting skills (Soska, Adolph, & Johnson, 2010). Parents reported on their infants' sitting experience, and researchers coded infants' manual interactions with novel objects from video recordings. A habituation-recovery task tested infants' understanding of the three-dimensional (3D) features of objects. In the habituation task, infants were first exposed to a single view of an object that did not contain information about its backside (imagine seeing a cube from one angle only). In subsequent test trials, infants watched two videos of a version of the 3D object rotating: one rotating object contained a backside and one was backless (imagine observing the rotated cube with an unexpected hollow back versus its complete 3D form) (**FIGURE 4.35**).

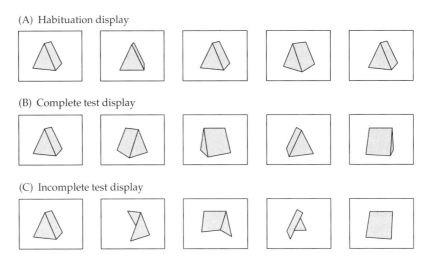

(A) Habituation display

(B) Complete test display

(C) Incomplete test display

FIGURE 4.35 Motor skill acquisition facilitates 3D object perception. Infants' 3D perceptual understanding of objects was examined in a habituation task. (A) In the habituation task, infants were first exposed to an object that partially rotated, but without showing any information about its backside. In subsequent test trials, they were shown videos of two versions of the same object rotating. (B) One video of the object showed a backside as it rotated, thus reflecting what the object would look like from different angles. (C) The other video presented an image of the object rotating, but without a backside. Infants looked longer at the rotated backless form than the complete form display. (After K. C. Soska et al. 2010. *Dev Psychol* 46: 129–138. © 2010 by American Psychological Association. Reproduced with permission.)

In line with a developmental cascade hypothesis, infants who could sit unassisted better understood the three-dimensionality of objects compared to infants who needed support. They looked longer at the "odd" backless objects than did non-sitters. Moreover, infants who more frequently rotated, fingered, and transferred objects between their hands performed better on the 3D habituation-recovery task than infants who did not display such manual actions (Soska, Adolph, & Johnson, 2010).

Manual exploration of objects also helps infants to identify similarities among objects, which supports categorization (Woods & Wilcox, 2013). For example, by rolling and bouncing balls, infants learn that balls belong in a special class of round things that can be played with and are distinct from oranges, plums, rocks, cotton balls, and other round objects. Two-year-old infants who were encouraged to move objects up and down later categorized objects that shared this movement characteristic. Similarly, when infants moved objects side to side, they grouped objects together that moved sideways (Smith, 2005) (**FIGURE 4.36**).

Gains in manual and sitting skills also alter how infants interact with other people. As an example, Klaus Libertus and Amy Needham (2010) showed that the development of manual skills heightened infants' attention to other people's faces. They divided 3-month-old infants into two groups—a group they trained to actively manipulate objects for 2 weeks and a group that passively touched objects that were placed on their hands. They then compared the two groups of infants on their attention to faces and objects. Infants who practiced actively manipulating objects attended more to faces than did infants subjected to the passive experience. Furthermore, infants who were trained on picking up objects with the sticky mittens described previously were more attentive to other people and objects during interactions than infants who merely observed others acting on objects (Libertus & Needham, 2010).

Why might object exploration affect infants' attention to people? Perhaps as infants manipulate objects, they seek to share their experiences with other

(A)   (B)

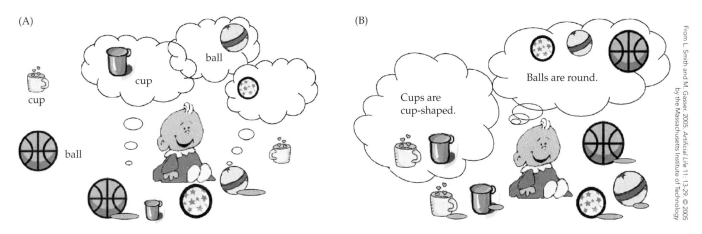

From L. Smith and M. Gasser, 2005. *Artificial Life* 11: 13-29 © 2005 by the Massachusetts Institute of Technology

FIGURE 4.36 Object exploration promotes categorization skills.   As infants manipulate objects, they learn about object features and functions and what makes certain objects similar to others of the same kind. Thus, object manipulation facilitates categorization, as infants learn (for example) that (A) cups are similar and balls are similar, but (B) the two categories differ from one another.

people. Additionally, the more infants reach for and manipulate objects, the more they understand that other people also intentionally reach for and manipulate objects (Libertus & Needham, 2010). Indeed, 12-month-old infants who were encouraged to place objects in containers were quick to attend to objects that another person placed in containers, suggesting that their own actions helped them anticipate what the other person was going to do next (Cannon et al., 2012).

Infants' interactions with objects also open the doors to learning language. When infants play with objects and then hold those objects out to share, caregivers often respond by talking about the objects of infant attention—"That's a soft, blue bunny"—which supports infant growth of vocabulary (Tamis-LeMonda, Kuchirko, & Song, 2014). We return to the role of social interactions in language development in Chapter 6.

Locomotion

Locomotion is the quintessential example of how changes in one domain of development spill over to other domains. In an article aptly entitled, "Travel Broadens the Mind," developmental scientist Joseph Campos and colleagues described the many changes that followed the onset of crawling (2000). Locomoting infants can actively explore a larger landscape than they had before, thereby learning about spatial relations among objects, including object locations (Campos et al., 2000; Newcombe, 2002; Sheya & Smith, 2010). In fact, the primary way that people learn about the layout of an environment is by traveling through different spaces.

To illustrate the cascading influence of locomotion on infants' understanding of location, novice and expert crawling and walking infants were placed inside an "arena" encircled by a curtain. Their mothers were inside with them, but then stepped outside behind the curtain at a specific location. Infants' task was to find their mother by crawling or walking to the location where she had disappeared. Infants with fewer than 6 weeks of experience either crawling or walking could not find their mother, but infants with more locomotor experience, regardless of posture, were successful. In addition, infants with little locomotor experience had difficulty locating their mother even when a landmark was placed next to the place where she had disappeared (Clearfield, 2004) (**FIGURE 4.37**).

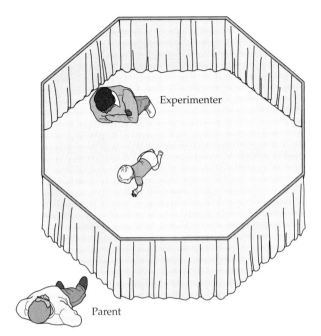

FIGURE 4.37 Spatial arena from Clearfield study. Researchers placed an infant in an "arena" surrounded by a curtain with a parent. The parent then exited the arena at one location, leaving the infant inside the arena with an experimenter. The infant had to identify the location where the parent exited by crawling or walking to that section of the arena. Infants with more crawling or walking experience were able to locate their parent better than those with little experience. (After M. W. Clearfield. 2004. *J Exp Child Psychol* 89: 214–241.)

Walking in particular transforms infants' interactions with their environments. As an infant begins to walk, the visual world changes dramatically. Crawling infants mostly see the floor as they move around, but walking infants see the entire room, including objects in the distance and people (Kretch, Franchak, & Adolph, 2014). Walking also allows infants to carry objects to share with others (Karasik, Tamis-LeMonda, & Adolph, 2011). Indeed, 13-month-old walkers are more likely than 13-month-old crawlers to retrieve objects that are out of reach and to carry those objects to their mothers for play. Crawlers, in contrast, play with objects that are nearby and share objects from a stationary, typically seated position. Mothers, in turn, respond differently to the play bids of their walkers and crawlers. Mothers of walkers more frequently respond with action directives or verb phrases as infants carry things over for play ("Open it," "Read the book,"), whereas, mothers of crawlers are twice as likely to ignore their infants' largely stationary bids for play (Karasik, Tamis-LeMonda, & Adolph, 2014).

The cascading influence of infant motor skills on social interactions may explain why the onset of walking is associated with growth in infant productive vocabulary (Oudgenoeg-Paz, Volman, & Leseman, 2012; West et al., 2019), and why motor skills in infancy predict intelligence and cognitive skills at 4, 10, and 14 years of age (Bornstein, Hahn, & Suwalsky, 2013). Getting around faster and getting to more objects in the environment generates new information about the world and fresh opportunities to hear words for objects and events that are the target of infant attention.

■ CLOSING THOUGHTS
The Engines of Learning and Development

As noted at the chapter opening, infant development is thrilling to watch. Parents document their baby's first steps on cell phones and surround infants with colorful, visually appealing toys that contain lots of small pieces for infants to finger, rotate, and twist. Few things are as meaningful as when infants smile at the people they love, orient to familiar voices, or toddle over to share toys with a sibling or caregiver. Each of these behaviors is rooted in perceptual and motor abilities that open the floodgates for participation in a wider social world. In the rare instances when developmental problems arise because of disabilities or disorders—such as when infants fail to orient to certain sounds or sights or lag in their motor capacities to sit, crawl, walk, and so on—identifying risk early on may help avert problems down the road.

In short, perceptual and motor development represent much more than a checklist of infant milestones. Rather, they have profound importance from a clinical perspective; are central to researchers' quest to understand developmental change; assume enormous significance for parents and caregivers; and lay a foundation for every developmental achievement that we will examine in the upcoming chapters. Essentially, perceptual and motor skills reflect the most fundamental (yet sometimes overlooked) engines of learning and development.

The Developmentalist's Toolbox

Method	Purpose	Description
Measuring infant perceptual development		
Preferential-looking tests	To test infants' abilities to discriminate between visual stimuli and preferences for specific visual stimuli over others	Infants are presented with two stimuli—for example, side-by-side pictures. Greater attention to one stimulus over the other indicates that infants distinguish between the stimuli, and possibly prefer one to the other.
Habituation-recovery tests	Used to assess how quickly infants encode specific stimuli or a set of related stimuli (e.g., female faces), and whether they distinguish familiar from novel stimuli; used to examine infant memory and categorization skills	Infants are presented with a stimulus (or set of related stimuli; e.g., female faces) for a fixed amount of time or until their attention wanes (habituation phase). They are then presented with a novel stimulus and a familiar stimulus (either together or serially). Attention to the novel stimulus indicates infants recall seeing the familiar stimulus, can tell the difference between the two, and perceive the novel stimulus to be different. To test categorization, infants' attention to a stimulus from a novel category (e.g., male faces) is compared to attention to a stimulus from a familiar category (e.g., a new female face).
Contingent reinforcement studies	Used to determine if infants can distinguish between two stimuli and whether infants prefer one stimulus to the other	Infants are trained to engage in a particular behavior to receive a "reward" (such as sucking on a pacifier to hear mother's voice). Differences in infant behaviors in the presence of different stimuli (such as sucking more to hear mother's voice than a stranger's voice) indicate infants can tell the difference between the two stimuli and may prefer one to the other.
Eye tracking	Used to assess precisely where a child is looking and for how long	Infants view displays on computer monitors that are outfitted with eye-trackers to assess quick eye movements, blinks, and areas and patterns of fixation. Eye-trackers can also be mounted on an infant's head to assess where they are looking as they engage with people and objects in their environments.
Intermodal perception studies	To test whether infants integrate information from different senses (such as vision and sound; vision and touch, etc.)	Infants are presented with a stimulus in one sensory modality (e.g., they are given the opportunity to touch a round object) and at the same time or subsequently are presented with the same stimulus along with a different stimulus, in a different modality (e.g., they are shown both the round object and a square object). Differences in attention to matching versus nonmatching stimuli suggest recognizing commonalities of information across the senses.
Measuring infant motor development		
Naturalistic observations	To assess infants' motor skills in natural situations	Examiners observe infants during naturalistic free play or at home during their everyday routines to assess their everyday motor experiences and motor skills, including opportunities to engage in specific actions.
Gait-mat procedure	To measure the maturity of infants' walking gait	Researchers measure walking proficiency by encouraging infants to walk across a portable and flexible mat or walkway that contains pressure sensors that record length of footsteps and how long it takes the infant to walk the length of the mat.
Cross-cultural research	To discover how variations in cultural practices affect motor development	Comparisons are made of infants' everyday motor experiences and skill across cultural communities with widely disparate caregiving practices and opportunities to practice specific motor skills.

▧ Chapter Summary

The Study of Perception in Infants

- Perceptual systems discriminate, organize, and interpret sensory information.

- Philosophers and scholars historically debated the origins of infant perceptual capacities: Some advocated that perception is innately endowed (a product of nature), whereas others argued that perception arises from experience (a product of nurture). Gestalt theorists highlighted infants' natural abilities to perceive continuities in sensory input.

- James and Eleanor Gibson's ecological approach takes an evolutionary approach to highlighting interconnections between perception and action. The body and biological architecture of humans and animals evolved to use the rich sensory information available in the environment in the service of action.

- Movements generate perceptual information, which in turn guides motor actions in a perception-action feedback loop.

- Learning in the domain of perception entails learning to gauge affordances for action by learning to attend to details in the environment that will inform what actions are possible.

- Psychologists have developed several methods to figure out the bounds of infants' sensory and perceptual capacities, including the preferential-looking test, the habituation-recovery test, the contingent reinforcement procedure, and eye-tracking experiments.

Tasting and Smelling

- Newborns (and fetuses) can distinguish among different tastes and odors, and communicate their preferences by puckering to sour tastes, wrinkling their noses in response to unpleasant odors, smiling to sugary odors, and opening their mouths widely to spit out bitter substances.

Looking

- Over the first months of postnatal life, the eye matures. Coupled with visual experiences, infants become increasingly better able to focus on objects at a distance, discriminate fine details (visual acuity) and contrasts in a scene (contrast sensitivity), and distinguish colors.

Hearing

- Early speech perception is central to emerging skills in language, and very young infants show an early preference for speech-like sounds over non-speech-like sounds.

- Infants' ability to hear is present from birth (and prenatally), although sensitivity to sound and an ability to detect frequency changes in pitch continue to improve across the first years.

From Perception to Meaning: Integration and Categorization

- Infants group similar things together in a process referred to as perceptual categorization. Examples include categorization of colors, animals, vehicles, spatial relations, geometric forms, patterns, gender, and human voices. Infants shift from categorizing objects based on

perceptual features such as shape to categorizing objects based on conceptual meaning and function (such as what can be done with an object). Intermodal perception refers to the process of integrating information across the senses (modalities). Auditory-visual integration is the most frequently studied type of intersensory integration.

- Infants' everyday experiences shape the types of perceptual information to which they are exposed, and in turn their preferences and abilities to discriminate among specific sights, sounds, tastes, and so forth.

- Infants show a preference for voices to which they are frequently exposed and their experience with speech sounds leads to perceptual narrowing, a decline in the ability to discriminate among stimuli because of a lack of experience with them.

- Fetal experiences around taste and smell, and later the flavors to which breastfed infants are exposed, differ depending on what their mothers consume, and later food preferences might be based on these early experiences.

The Study of Motor Development in Infants

- Arnold Gesell developed motor milestone norms in areas of prehension, posture (such as sitting), and locomotion (crawling, cruising, walking). He advanced a maturational account of motor skill development.

- In contrast to Gesell's maturational explanation, the Jimmy and Johnny experiment of Myrtle McGraw highlighted the role of practice and experience in the development of specific motor skills.

- Esther Thelen's dynamic systems theory emphasized that multiple factors affect infants in the course of motor development, and her research on newborn spontaneous stepping behaviors refuted the idea that the course of motor development is prewired in the brain.

Developments in Infant Motor Skill

- Postural control is critical to all motor actions.

- Stable posture allows infants to engage in actions such as looking, sitting, reaching, moving, and so on.

- Manual skills, such as reaching, grasping, play, and tool use, improve over the first months of life, with improvements in infants' abilities to maintain balance, control the arms and hands, judge distance, and gauge opportunities for actions.

- Independent sitting is seen in U.S. infants around 5–7 months of age, but it takes a couple more months of experience before infants can coordinate sitting and grasping by reaching for objects all around them without losing balance.

- With experience crawling, cruising, and walking, infants become better able to figure out what their bodies can do in specific situations (e.g., to flexibly adjust their actions to accommodate obstacles in their path, different surfaces for walking, and so forth). The visual cliff is a famous experiment used to study the effects of locomotor experience on infants' ability to make such adjustments.

Contexts of Motor Development

- Cross-cultural investigations of infant motor development indicate that infants' experiences at home, including opportunities to engage in specific actions, home layout (such as having stairs or not), parenting practices (such as placing infants to sleep on their backs, or exercising infants' posture and limbs), have powerful influences on motor skill onsets and infant motor skill proficiency. Home experiences can both facilitate or impede infant progress.

Developmental Cascades

- Infant motor skill development has widespread implications for other domains, including social interactions with other people, play with objects and object perception, spatial cognition, memory, and language.

- Perceptual narrowing for faces and speech sounds of different languages can affect infants' preferences for different people and social interactions.
- Sitting allows infants to manually explore objects; helps infants learn about the 3D properties of objects and how objects fit within specific categories (e.g., balls); and fosters social interactions and infants' attention to others' faces.
- Locomotion in the forms of crawling, cruising, and walking allows infants to get to and explore new places independently and supports infants' understanding about spatial layouts.
- Walking allows infants to carry objects over for sharing, elicits new language forms from caregivers, and is accompanied by growth in language.

Thinking Like a Developmentalist

1. Perception: You are the owner of a music company that wants to market a collection of new song recordings for infants. Before doing so, you want to figure out (a) which songs infants would like the most; (b) whether infants prefer to listen to their songs more than the songs of their competitors; and (c) whether infants can remember the tunes of songs after hearing them a few times. What might you do to answer these questions?

2. Motor development: You are a cultural anthropologist who has documented that toddlers in one cultural community live in huts with uneven, dirt surfaces and are free to wander outside where the ground has rocks, grass, roots, and other uneven surfaces. Toddlers in the neighboring cultural community live in homes with smooth, flat, hardwood flooring and rarely wander outside. You wonder if these different experiences have affected toddlers' skills at gauging opportunities for walking. What might you do to test this idea across the two communities?

5

Cognitive Development in Infancy and Toddlerhood

Drawing by Minxin Cheng from a photo by Catherine S. Tamis-LeMonda

The media and public often display frenzied interest in the astounding things that infants can do. Their interest is gratifying because developmental scientists hope to convey science to the public so that knowledge can benefit children, parents, educators, practitioners, and policy makers. However, it is also troubling because the complexity of the research often gets lost in translation.

Infant cognitive development is especially prey to flashy headlines and sound bites. Sometimes the popular media (and unfortunately, even the academic press) grossly simplifies findings, proclaiming that infants understand space and gravity; can count, add, and subtract; can judge moral character and evaluate others' intentions; and even read minds (a British headline announced: "Babies Can Read Your Mind! Research Shows One-Year-Olds Can Guess Thoughts Through Empathy"). Headlines like these spur changes in parents' interactions with infants and have led to the development of "educational" toys and apps that promise to promote infants' intelligence and improve their chances of one day getting into an Ivy League college.

But the study of infant cognitive development is not as straightforward as the popular press would lead you to believe. Do infants look more at a display of one versus two versus three objects—after objects have been manually "added" or "subtracted" from the array—because infants can (sort of) count or because they are attracted to the perceptual features of the display? How much do infants truly understand? Such questions frame much of the research covered in this chapter and have spurred many debates.

The study of infant cognition began with the seminal work of Jean Piaget, the Swiss psychologist and philosopher whose constructivist theory of development was presented in Chapter 1. In this chapter, we provide an overview of Piaget's findings and examine various theoretical and empirical challenges to Piaget's position. You will learn why nativists assert that babies know much more than Piaget thought. You will consider how developmental systems theorists discovered that simple changes to Piagetian tasks can dramatically alter infant performance. You will see how information processing theorists extended an understanding of infant cognition to aspects of learning that Piaget overlooked, such as the speed with which infants process new information. By the end of the chapter, you will see that questions about infant cognitive development have spilled over to the study of infants' social understanding—whether and how infants reason about other people's goals and intentions.

■ *Learning about the Physical World*

Countless nuggets of understanding about the physical world enable people to function in their environments. Humans intuitively grasp the laws of physics—principles that apply to matter, motion, space, time, energy, and force. For instance, we recognize that solid objects take up space, that when objects move out of view they continue to exist, and that if we let go of our coffee mug it will fall and potentially break. Infants, however, have little understanding of the physical world at birth. How do infants come to understand that releasing a toy in mid-air will cause it to fall to the ground? Or that if a block is placed into an empty box and two more blocks are added, three blocks will be in the box? What and how much do infants understand about the physical world, and how do they gain this understanding? In the sections that follow, you will read about different theoretical approaches to these questions and the provocative findings that new scientific methods have yielded on infants' emerging cognitive skills.

Piaget's Theory of Cognitive Development

Jean Piaget's careful testing and observations of children of different ages—including his son and two daughters—led to his constructivist theory of development (see Chapter 1). Key to his theory was the idea that children play an active role in learning and thus "construct" or build an understanding of the world. The concept of *schemas* was among the central tenets of Piaget's theory. Recall from Chapter 1 that Piaget considered schemas—defined as cognitive representations of the world that determine how children of different ages organize and understand information—as a basic unit of information (Piaget & Inhelder, 1969). Here we examine changes that occur in what Piaget called the **sensorimotor stage** of development, the time spanning birth to approximately 18 months, when schemas are limited to sensory experiences and motor actions.

According to Piaget, infants cannot yet mentally represent the world. Nonetheless, infants actively engage with the world in ways that promote learning and development. Babies hear and produce sounds, look at people and things around them, and feel their bodies move and make contact with objects, surfaces, and people. These everyday experiences, together with infants' maturing brains and bodies, drive the changes that lead from the spontaneous, unintentional actions of newborns to the intentional behaviors of toddlers.

Piaget divided the sensorimotor stage into six substages reflecting progressive cognitive change during this time (**TABLE 5.1**). In the sections that follow, we follow the infant's development through each of these substages, culminating in the achievements that mark the final substage known as mental representation.

sensorimotor stage The earliest stage in Piaget's cognitive theory of development that spans between birth to about 18 months of age when schemas are limited to sensory experiences and motor actions; the sensorimotor stage is divided into six substages

TABLE 5.1 ■ The six substages of the sensorimotor period according to Piaget

Stage	Age	Description
Reflexes	Birth to 1 month	Newborns display movements including sucking and grasping and produce a variety of spontaneous and rhythmic actions by moving their fingers, limbs, heads, and torsos.
Primary circular reactions	1–4 months	Infants begin to repeat their actions. They combine actions into recurring behaviors organized around the immediate environment of their bodies. For example, infants will repeatedly suck their thumbs or kick their legs.
Secondary circular reactions	4–8 months	Infants enjoy watching the effects their actions have on the world, and they often attempt to recreate events by repeating their actions with objects. For example, a baby might swipe at a mobile, watch the dangling parts move, and then swipe again and again to reproduce the effort.
Coordination of secondary circular reactions	8–12 months	Infants' actions now appear to be "goal directed" and intentional. Infants coordinate and combine several actions to accomplish a goal. For example, the infant might try to move a pillow aside to get a toy that is behind it.
Tertiary circular reactions	12–18 months	Infants are capable of means-end analysis and can search for new solutions to solve problems. Infants display increased flexibility and creativity, often engaging in trial-and-error experiments to explore the consequences of their actions with objects.
Mental representation	18–24 months	Infants are able to mentally represent and manipulate objects and events in their minds, as seen in the use of language, symbolic play, and deferred imitation (such as imitating another person's action of pulling a mitten off a stuffed animal).

Sensorimotor Substages 1–5

LEARNING OBJECTIVE 5.1 Describe the first five substages of the sensorimotor period.

Reflexes and Spontaneous Movements: Birth to 1 Month

According to Piaget, the first substage, from birth through about 1 month, involves reflexive schema and spontaneous movements. Newborns are in constant motion, but their actions are far from deliberate (**FIGURE 5.1A**). Newborns display a rich variety of behaviors, including sucking and grasping, and produce spontaneous and rhythmic actions by wiggling their fingers, flailing their arms, kicking their legs, and rocking their heads and torsos. Piaget viewed these early, seemingly random movements to be building blocks to the mature actions of later substages. As an example, consider infant sucking. When a nipple is placed in infants' mouths, babies tend to suck. This newborn behavior initially serves an adaptive function of feeding, but later extends to infants sucking their thumb and objects they bring to their mouth. (Note, however, that although Piaget referred to infants' spontaneous behaviors as "reflexes," behaviors such as sucking and spontaneous stepping (see Chapter 4) are not reflexes in the sense of being automatic, instantaneous, and always occurring, as when you automatically withdraw a hand after touching a hot stove.)

Primary Circular Reactions: 1–4 Months

During the second substage, infants begin to repeat their actions. They combine actions into recurring (or "circular") behaviors organized around the immediate (or "primary") environment of their bodies (**FIGURE 5.1B**). For example, infants repeatedly suck their thumb, or kick their legs. As infants extend their

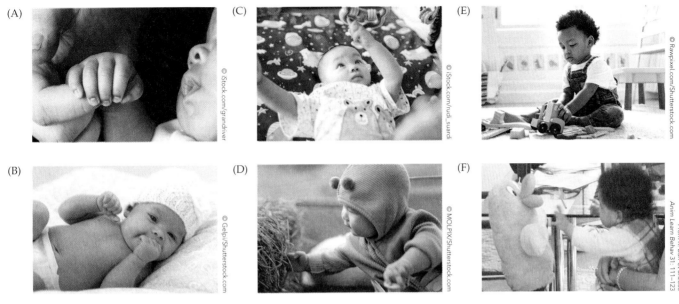

FIGURE 5.1 **The six substages of the sensorimotor stage.**   Piaget divided the sensorimotor stage into six substages according to developments in infants' actions and schema. (A) Reflexes. (B) Primary circular actions. (C) Secondary circular actions. (D) Coordination of secondary circular actions. (E) Tertiary circular actions. (F) Mental representation.

behaviors in new ways, they eventually display simple **motor habits**. Infants modify motor habits in response to environmental demands, as when they suck on a fist versus a thumb versus the mother's nipple.

Secondary Circular Reactions: 4–8 Months

During substage 3, at about 4 months of age, infants extend their actions to objects rather than only their own bodies (hence, the term secondary). Infants now enjoy watching the effects their actions have on the world and often attempt to recreate their actions with objects (**FIGURE 5.1C**). For example, infants may bang their hands against their highchair tray and then bang again and again to recreate the satisfying sound. Infants are now forming connections between their own actions and the consequences in the world.

Coordination of Secondary Circular Reactions: 8–12 Months

By substage 4, something special occurs in infants' interactions with their environments. Actions now appear to be goal directed and intentional (**FIGURE 5.1D**). That is, infants coordinate and combine several actions to accomplish a goal. For example, infants might crawl across the room to get a desired object or push aside an object that's in the way to reach a toy for play. Piaget considered infants' coordinated sequences to be foundational to problem solving. To solve problems, infants must engage in **means-end analysis**—the ability to identify and execute the necessary actions (the means) to achieve a specific goal (the end).

Tertiary Circular Reactions: 12–18 Months

As infants pass their first birthday and enter the fifth substage, they are capable of means-end analysis and can search for new solutions to solve problems, often through trial-and-error experiments in which they repeat actions to explore

motor habits Movements individuals make with their bodies without having to think about them; during the second substage of the sensorimotor stage (primary circular reactions), infants will display simple motor habits as they extend their behaviors in new ways

means-end analysis The ability to identify and execute the necessary actions or means to attain a specific goal or end; by the fourth substage of the sensorimotor stage (coordination of secondary circular reactions), infants engage in goal-directed behaviors to solve problems, such as how to get a desired toy their consequences. For example, an infant might accidentally drop a spoon to the ground, and upon hearing the loud clang, throw down a plate and then cup and so on to repeat the experience. Means-end analysis can be seen in Piaget's description (p. 11) of a child figuring out how to access an object that was on top of a rug but out of reach (**FIGURE 5.1E**): "The child, after trying in vain to reach the object directly may eventually grasp one corner of the rug and then observe a relationship between the movements of the rug and those of the object." The child had to generate a new, unfamiliar solution of pulling on a rug to get the object. However, according to Piaget, although infants can now solve a variety of problems and attempt to find new solutions to achieve their goals, they cannot yet represent actions in their minds.

✓ CHECK YOUR UNDERSTANDING 5.1

1. List the first five substages of the sensorimotor stage identified by Piaget and provide an example of each.

Mental Representation (Sensorimotor Substage 6): 18–24 Months

LEARNING OBJECTIVE 5.2 Identify the hallmarks of mental representation.

Infants' progress through the sensorimotor period leads to the achievement of mental representation, the sixth and final substage. Piaget described **mental representation** as infants' ability to "hold" and "manipulate" objects and events in their minds, for example by planning behaviors and predicting outcomes before acting. Piaget observed (p. 12): "A child is confronted by a slightly open matchbox containing a thimble and tries to open the box by physically groping, but upon failing, he presents an altogether new reaction: he stops the action and attentively examines the situation, after which he suddenly slips his finger into the crack and thus succeeds in opening the box." In this example, the infant's failure to open the matchbox was followed by a pause during which the infant appeared to think of—mentally represented—a new solution.

Toddlers can now think about the goals they wish to achieve and about what they must do to achieve those goals. For instance, a toddler might realize that her dad has hidden a treat somewhere in the kitchen, and even though the treat is out of view, she displays various searching behaviors to find it. These skills in mental representation, in turn, enable children to engage in deferred imitation, language, and symbolic play, and to understand the permanence of objects (**FIGURE 5.1F**).

Deferred Imitation

Imitation is copying another person's actions, and **deferred imitation** refers to the reproduction of another person's actions hours or days later. Piaget claimed that deferred imitation is not seen until sometime during the second year, because it requires storing and then retrieving a memory of what had been observed. Thus, deferred imitation calls upon **memory recall**—memory for a past experience in the absence of the stimulus. As we will see later in the chapter, researchers often study deferred imitation to probe infants' memory skills, including how long infant memories last.

Language and Symbolic Play

Language and symbolic play both require children to use symbols to represent objects and events they have experienced in the past. Piaget considered both to mark children's attainment of mental representation.

In language, words are symbols that refer to objects, people, and events. In particular, **displaced reference**—children's ability to understand and use words

mental representation The ability to hold and manipulate objects and events in the mind; according to Jean Piaget, toddlers achieve this ability during the sixth substage of the sensorimotor stage (mental representation)

imitation The act of copying another person's actions

deferred imitation Copying another person's actions hours or days later

memory recall Memory for a past experience in the absence of the stimulus; deferred imitation requires memory recall

displaced reference A major symbolic accomplishment in which children understand and use words to refer to things that are not present to refer to things that are *not present*—is a major symbolic accomplishment. For instance, a toddler may go into another room to retrieve an object when asked, "Where's your teddy?," recognizing the word "teddy" refers to a favorite toy that is not immediately visible. Similarly, displaced reference is seen when toddlers point to a patch of grass and say "doggie" as they remember petting a dog there the previous day.

In symbolic play, children use actions and words in a pretend mode, such as by putting a spoon to a doll's mouth and making eating sounds as if the doll were eating (**FIGURE 5.2**). Children might then pretend to burp the doll, and then lay the doll down to sleep. Essentially, children are telling a story through play by reenacting what is known about babies being fed and put to sleep. Notably, toddlers first engage in pretend play about the time when they express their first words, and they first engage in combinations in play, such as stirring imaginary food in a toy bowl and then feeding a doll, about the time when they combine words into simple sentences (McCune, 1995; Quinn, Donnelly, & Kidd, 2018). These similarities in how toddlers play and talk at different points in development support Piaget's claim that language and symbolic play reflect a common ability to mentally represent the world.

Object Permanence

Perhaps the most important and frequently studied example of mental representation is **object permanence**—the understanding that objects continue to exist independent of one's immediate perceptual experiences. For example, a toddler who has achieved object permanence might search the house for a favorite teddy, knowing that it still exists somewhere out there for cuddling. Toddlers who have not yet achieved object permanence would not imagine and search for a favorite teddy, but instead would play with whatever stuffed animal is in view. Piaget considered object permanence to be central to the achievement of mental representation, and he therefore devoted much time to observing how infants acquire this understanding.

To test infants' understanding of object permanence, Piaget hid objects in different locations—covering a toy with a cloth or putting a toy behind a box—as babies watched him, and then he observed infants' responses. In the first two substages, infants failed to search for objects that were partially visible (e.g., toy poking out from the cloth covering), and in substage 3, they failed to search if the object was completely hidden. In these early substages, infants looked away as if they no longer believed that the toy existed. Not until substage 4, around 8 months of age, did infants search for objects that were fully hidden, seeming to understand that objects continued to exist even when not visible. However, infants' understanding of object permanence was not yet complete.

When Piaget changed the location of a hidden object, in what is commonly referred to as the **A-not-B task**, infants in substage 4 failed to change their search behaviors based on the object's new location. Specifically, Piaget repeatedly hid a toy under a cloth at location A, and infants eagerly retrieved it. Piaget then hid the toy at location B, under an identical cloth several inches from the cloth still resting in location A. Infants around 8–12 months continued to search for the object in location A after watching it moved to location B, rather than searching in location B (**FIGURE 5.3**).

Piaget referred to infants' unsuccessful, repeated searches at location A as the **A-not-B error**. He attributed infants' failure in this task to their limited cognitive reasoning about the continued existence of objects. That is, at substage 4, infants successfully pull off the cloth to reveal the object when it was hidden at location A failing to understand that the object's location had changed. At substage 5 (at about 12 months of age) infants begin to consider the object might be in location B, but only if they see the object being visibly moved. Finally, in the sixth

FIGURE 5.2 Symbolic play. In symbolic play, children use actions and words in a pretend mode, such as "feeding" a stuffed toy or doll by putting a spoon to its mouth and making slurping and chewing sounds as if the toy or doll were eating, or pretending to talk on a toy phone using mannerisms of an adult.

Courtesy of Catherine S. Tamis-LeMonda

object permanence The understanding that objects continue to exist independent of one's immediate perceptual experiences

A-not-B task A test used to study infants' understanding of object permanence in which a researcher hides an object at location A while the infant watches; the infant retrieves the toy from location A; and then the researcher hides the object at location B after one or several trials

A-not-B error Infants' repeated and unsuccessful searches for hidden objects at location A, not B; Jean Piaget suggested that infants' repeated errors indicate limited reasoning about objects and a lack of object permanence

FIGURE 5.3 A-not-B Task. When an examiner hides an object at location A, the baby retrieves the object at that location. However, after several trials, if the examiner now hides the object at location B, the infant will continue reaching toward and searching at location A.

substage of mental representation, at about 18–24 months, toddlers search for hidden objects without watching the hiding event. At this stage, toddlers use various strategies to locate objects after multiple, invisible displacements. For example, toddlers might pick up a cushion to find an object, find an unexpected cloth under the cushion, and then pick up the cloth to locate the object underneath. As adults, we might think we parked a car in a specific row, but when it's not there, search other rows for the car, knowing the car still exists (and hoping that it was not stolen). According to Piaget, at substage 6, toddlers are now capable of mentally representing the continued existence of objects, although not until early childhood do children fully reason about objects.

✓ CHECK YOUR UNDERSTANDING 5.2

1. How might toddlers demonstrate their attainment of mental representation?
2. What is the concept of object permanence, and how does the A-not-B task examine infants' understanding of this concept?

Challenges to Piaget That Inspired New Theoretical Orientations

LEARNING OBJECTIVE 5.3 List observations that challenge Piagetian theory.

Piaget's legacy continues to this day. He presented a rich and detailed account of changes in infant cognition across the first 2 years of life while developing clever methods to test infants who cannot yet use words to tell us what they know. In addition, Piaget spotlighted infant behavior as a valuable window into children's minds, and he inspired countless studies and theoretical debates about how infants learn and what they understand at different ages. But, notwithstanding Piaget's major contributions to the field of cognitive development, aspects of Piaget's theory and findings have been challenged, opening the door to new theoretical and research directions. Indeed, three theoretical perspectives arose out of critiques of Piaget's work:

1. The nativist view asserts that Piaget underestimated infants' cognitive ability and that infants understand a lot more than Piaget assumed. In particular, nativists claim that babies are capable of mental representation at younger ages than Piaget described. As one example, researchers present compelling evidence that infants display an understanding of object permanence and abilities to solve various problems that appear to depend on mental representation by 4–5 months of age! Furthermore, Piaget claimed that infants are incapable of deferred imitation until they achieve mental representation. However, some researchers find that newborns and infants less than 1 month old imitate tongue protrusions and facial and manual behaviors 15 seconds (and sometimes longer) after observing a model, which has been interpreted as a natural, biological tendency to connect with other people (Meltzoff & Moore, 1977; Meltzoff, 2017). Note, however, that skeptics of infant imitation argue

that infants' imitation may reflect arousal or involuntary actions rather than deferred imitation (Jones, 2007; Oostenbroeck et al., 2016).

2. The developmental systems view critiques Piaget's emphasis on mental representation rather than in-the-moment contextual influences on cognitive performance. Scientists who follow a developmental systems approach argue that Piaget placed too much emphasis on internal, brain-governed schema, which ignored the many factors that combine to affect cognitive performance. For example, developmental systems researchers show that infants' errors in the A-not-B task depend on many in-the-moment contextual influences, rather than a fixed ability to mentally represent objects.

3. The information processing view takes issue with Piaget's description of abrupt, qualitative, stagelike change, suggesting that changes in cognitive skills occur gradually. Scientists who follow an information processing approach reject what they view to be abstract, hard-to-study concepts, such as Piaget's description of "schema." Instead, they propose that cognitive development can be explained by quantifiable changes in basic cognitive skills such as attention and memory.

We examine each of these alternative theoretical orientations and their research contributions in the sections that follow.

✓ **CHECK YOUR UNDERSTANDING 5.3**
1. List three critiques of Piaget's theory along with their alternative accounts.

Nativist Tests of Infant Core Capacities

Nativists claim that infants know much more than Piaget credited. They assert that infants are born with various **core capacities**—innate, mental capabilities that serve as building blocks to cognitive development and allow infants to make sense of their environments (e.g., Baillargeon et al., 2010; Spelke & Kinzler, 2007). These core capacities involve distinct areas of knowledge that have evolved over time through natural selection. Because of their core capacities, infants enter the world equipped to understand and learn certain things, including being able to reason about the physical world. Object permanence is a prime example.

Nativists reason that infants may fail Piagetian tasks, including tests of object permanence, because of the methods that Piaget used rather than because of cognitive limitations. If young infants don't yet have the motor control and skills to actively search for things, for example, then researchers should adopt other methods to inquire into infants' understanding. Indeed, looking-time tasks offer a promising method because infants can control their eyes from a very young age (see Chapter 4). Thus, nativists often rely on tests of infants' differential looking to certain stimuli rather than tests of active search behaviors as studied by Piaget to study infants' understanding of concepts such as object permanence, object solidity, gravity, and cause-effect relations.

Infant Understanding of Object Permanence

LEARNING OBJECTIVE 5.4 Identify neo-nativist studies that suggest babies understand the permanence of objects at much younger ages than Piaget claimed.

T. G. R. Bower was one of the first to test whether infants have a core capacity for understanding that objects continue to exist even when not visible (although some of Bower's findings were not replicated). Bower conducted a study of young infants' physiological reactions to object "disappearance" by presenting 3-month-old infants with an object that was hidden behind a screen but then removed, unknown to infants (Bower, 1971). That is, infants could not see the examiner remove the object from behind the screen. The screen then lifted to

core capacities Innate, mental capacities that are building blocks to cognitive development and allow infants to make sense of the environment; nativists claim that infants are born with core capacities, including object permanence reveal no object. Infants' heart rates changed upon seeing nothing behind the screen, which Bower interpreted to mean that babies were surprised to see that the object seemingly "disappeared" and had thus formed a mental representation of the object. Recall, Piaget found that it was not until at least 8 months of age that babies searched for fully hidden objects on Piagetian A-not-B tasks, and not until 18–24 months that toddlers reliably searched across multiple locations.

Today, researchers use infant looking as a window into infants' cognitive capacities. Many such studies rely on the **violation-of-expectation paradigm**, in which researchers compare how long infants look to certain events compared to other events. Sometimes, the contrasting events depict "possible" versus "impossible" situations. Possible events are consistent with adultlike expectations, such as when an object is placed behind a screen, the screen is raised, and the object is still there. Impossible events are inconsistent with expectations, such as when an object is no longer there when the screen is raised. Researchers interpret longer looking time to the impossible or inconsistent event (relative to the possible/consistent one) as evidence that infants hold an expectation that objects still exist even when not seen and thus look longer when the expectation is violated.

Renee Baillargeon and colleagues were among the first to test looking time to "possible" versus "impossible" events with infants as young as 3.5–5.5 months (Baillargeon, 1987; Baillargeon, Spelke, & Wasserman, 1985). Would infants' looking behaviors indicate they had a concept of object permanence? To test this, Baillargeon presented infants with a moving screen that began in an upright position and rotated down to a flat position like a drawbridge. The examiner then placed a box behind the screen so that infants saw the placement but could no longer see the box once it was behind the screen. In test trials, researchers presented infants with possible and impossible events. In the possible event, the screen stopped rotating halfway, as though the box behind it had interrupted its rotation. In the impossible event, the screen completed its rotation to a flat position, as if the box behind it did not exist. Infants looked longer at the impossible event than at the possible event, which Baillargeon interpreted as showing that infants were surprised or puzzled to see a screen pass through a box. Infants seemed to understand the box continued to exist even though it was blocked by the screen and was out of sight (**FIGURE 5.4**).

violation-of-expectation paradigm
A looking technique, based on a habituation and dishabituation procedure that compares infant looking at certain events (such as "impossible" events or "unexpected outcomes") compared to other events (such as "possible" events or "expected outcomes")

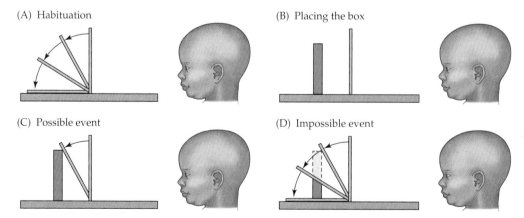

(A) Habituation   (B) Placing the box

(C) Possible event   (D) Impossible event

FIGURE 5.4 A violation-of-expectation experiment. (A) In the habituation stage, infants watched a moving screen that began in an upright position and rotated down to a flat position. (B) Infants then watched as the examiner placed a box behind the screen. (C) In the *possible* event, the screen stopped rotating before coming to a flat position, as though the box behind it interrupted its rotation. (D) In the *impossible* event, the screen rotated to a flat position, as if the box behind it did not exist. (After R. Baillargeon. 1987. *Cog Dev* 2: 179–200. Copyright 1987. Reprinted with permission from Elsevier; D. T. Benton and D. H. Rakison. 2018. In *SAGE Research Methods Cases Part 2*, p. 9. SAGE Publications Ltd.: London.)

Numerous follow-up studies have shown that infants look longer to events in which objects seemingly disappear—behind screens, in train tunnels, and so forth. And beyond understanding that objects continue to exist, nativists propose that infants seem to understand that objects retain their physical properties, such as height, an innate understanding referred to as the **principle of persistence** (Baillargeon, 2008).

In one such study based on a habituation task, the "disappearing carrot top," 3.5-month-old infants were familiarized with two events: a tall carrot or a short carrot moving behind a screen (Baillargeon & DeVos, 1991) (**FIGURE 5.5**). In test trials, infants saw the same moving carrots as in the familiarization trials except the screen changed color and had a window (opening) on the upper half. In the possible event, the short carrot passed behind the screen without its top showing up in the window. This event was possible because the short carrot was shorter than the bottom of the window. In the impossible event, the tall carrot passed behind the screen without appearing in the window. Infants looked longer at the impossible event than at the possible event, indicating that they expected the tall carrot to be visible through the window and were surprised when it did not appear. They did not respond with longer looking to the shorter carrot. Infants seemingly understood that the carrot still existed when it was behind the screen. Furthermore, the disappearing carrot study suggests that infants kept in mind information about the constant features of the carrot, namely its height—the principle of persistence defined previously—as they tracked the carrot's movement.

principle of persistence As claimed by nativists, an innate understanding that objects retain their physical properties, such as height

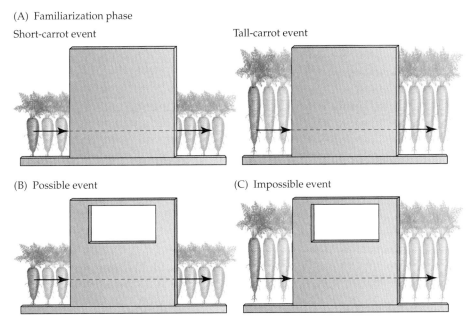

(A) Familiarization phase

Short-carrot event

Tall-carrot event

(B) Possible event

(C) Impossible event

FIGURE 5.5 Testing infants' understanding of object persistence: the disappearing carrot top.   Baillaregeon and DeVos (1991) conducted a test of infants' violated expectations about the physical properties of objects (in this case, an object's height). (A) During a familiarization phase, infants watched a tall or short carrot move along a path behind a screen and then reappear on the other side. (B, C) On later test trials, infants saw the short carrot or long carrot move along the same path, but this time the screen had an opening on the upper half. Infants looked longer at the impossible event—the tall carrot moving behind the screen but its top not appearing in the opening—than at the possible event—the short carrot moving behind the screen and not appearing in the opening. Infant looking time suggested that they understood that objects persist through space—that is, infants appeared to expect the tall carrot to be visible through the window and looked longer when it was not. (After R. Baillargeon and J. DeVos. 1991. *Child Dev* 62: 1227–1246. © 1991 by the Society for Research in Child Development, Inc. All rights reserved.)

Infants' longer looking time to disappearing objects, and their understanding of the constant properties of objects, challenge Piaget's notion that young infants lack the ability to mentally represent objects that are no longer visible. According to nativists then, infants understand the permanence of objects, and this understanding reflects infants' core knowledge about objects.

✓ CHECK YOUR UNDERSTANDING 5.4

1. How have findings from violation-of-expectation paradigms and other looking-time studies such as infant response to possible and impossible events challenged Piaget's idea that children do not achieve object permanence until 18 months?

Infant Understanding of Solidity and Substance

LEARNING OBJECTIVE 5.5 Describe evidence that infants understand object properties of solidity and substance.

Children and adults would be quite surprised to see someone walk through a chair or through solid obstacles in their path. We reach around objects to get to other objects, because we understand that we would otherwise knock over the object in between. In essence, people know that objects take up space and two things can't be in the same place at once. We also understand that we can put our arms through water, but not a concrete wall. That's because we recognize the physical properties of different substances. Do infants also understand object solidity and substance? According to Piaget, children should not display an understanding of object solidity until they have achieved mental representation (at 18–24 months).

Nativists, however, propose that infants have a core capacity to understand object solidity. The rotating screen study described earlier offers evidence to that effect (Baillargeon Spelke, & Wasserman, 1985) (see Figure 5.4). Other tests of infants' understanding of solidity have yielded similar findings. For example, Baillargeon (1986) presented infants with a train that moved along a track after a box had been placed either on the track, where it would block the train's passage, or behind the track, where it would not block passage. An examiner then lowered a screen, covering the portion of the track that contained the obstacle. Infants looked longer when the train continued its path when the box was on the track compared to when the train continued its path but the box was behind the track. Again, infant looking time was interpreted as an understanding that trains cannot pass through obstacles.

Beyond knowing objects can't move through other objects, infants may understand that some substances, such as liquids and sand, are loosely bound and can move around and pass through grids and small crevices (Anderson, Hespos, & Rips, 2018; Hespos et al., 2016). Susan Hespos and colleagues showed that when infants watched a glass of sand being tilted and rotated, their looking times suggested that they expected the sand in the glass to pass through a sieve, whereas when small balls like marbles were in the glass, they did not.

✓ CHECK YOUR UNDERSTANDING 5.5

1. How might you test whether infants understood that water but not ice cubes could pass through a screen?

Infant Understanding of Gravity and Support

LEARNING OBJECTIVE 5.6 Describe evidence that infants have a core capacity around object support.

If you drop an object, you expect it to fall to the floor. This is why magicians who levitate things mesmerize audiences who are stunned to see objects floating in the air. Do infants also expect objects to fall to surfaces below them? Nativists show that infants may indeed understand rules governing object support

(A) Possible event

(B) Impossible event

FIGURE 5.6 The Needham & Baillargeon (1993) experiment on object support. Infants 4–5 months of age look longer at impossible events than possible events, suggesting they are surprised by the violation of their expectations. (A) A possible event, when a hand places a box on a platform, and (B) an impossible event, when the hand places the box beyond the platform, leaving the box "floating" in the air without support. (After A. Needham and R. Baillargeon. 1993. *Cognition* 47: 121–148.)

(Baillargeon & Dejong, 2017). In one of the earliest such studies, Needham and Baillargeon presented 4.5-month-old infants with a possible event in which a hand put a box on a platform, and an impossible event, in which the hand pushed the box beyond the edge of the platform, leaving the box "floating" in the air without support, as well as two control events, in which the hand never released the box (**FIGURE 5.6**). Infants looked longer at the floating box than at the box placed on the platform, suggesting that they expected the box to fall and were surprised when it did not (Needham & Baillargeon, 1993).

✓ CHECK YOUR UNDERSTANDING 5.6

1. According to the research of Needham and Baillargeon, how would an infant respond to a box that seemingly floated in the air?

Testing Core Capacity for Understanding Number

LEARNING OBJECTIVE 5.7 What is an "approximate number system" (ANS) and what does it enable infants to do?

In 1992, developmental scientist Karen Wynn made headlines. Her research suggested that 5-month-old infants could perform simple calculations of addition and subtraction, such as 1 + 1 or 2 − 1. The press reacted with unbridled excitement about the miraculous talents of babies. But, are infants truly little mathematicians? What evidence supports this claim? Again, violation-of-expectation studies help to address such questions.

Wynn presented babies with a figure of Mickey Mouse, lowered a screen to hide the figure, and then, as the infant watched, placed another figure behind the screen. When the screen was removed, infants looked longer to the "wrong" mathematical answers of 1 Mickey Mouse or 3 Mickey Mouse figures compared to the "correct" answer of 2 Mickey Mouse figures. In variations of the problem, such as removing a Mickey Mouse figure, infants also looked longer to incorrect mathematical answers. And, infants' number representations become more precise with age. Nine-month-old infants can distinguish additions or subtractions of 4 objects from additions or subtractions of 6 objects, but 6-month-old infants cannot (Wood & Spelke, 2005).

Wynn concluded that infants have a core capacity to understand numbers that paves the way for later mathematical understanding. Wynn carefully tested alternative interpretations of her findings—for instance, by asking whether number understanding persisted when researchers manipulated the spacing and patterns of object configurations, such as clustering or spreading out objects. Under various experimental conditions, infants still appeared to detect additions and subtractions of objects.

Of course, it would be wrong to conclude that infants were "counting" the objects in an array similarly to a child or adult. Perhaps instead babies display a general sensitivity to the approximate number of items in an array rather than an exact count of the items. For example, if an examiner presents a baby with an array of 3 objects followed by an array of 6 objects, the baby might be able to detect the difference between the arrays because one has half the amount as the first, a ratio of 1:2, *not* because the baby attended to the absolute difference and somehow knows that 3 + 3 = 6.

Indeed, infants appear to distinguish among displays with different numbers of entities by roughly comparing the magnitudes of each. To illustrate, researchers habituated 6-month-old infants to a series of pictures that contained the same number of elements but differed in features such as color or configuration. They then presented infants with a new array containing a changing number of elements. Infants looked longer to the changing number array if the two numbers differed by a ratio of 1:2 or 1:3. However, infants were unable to discriminate between arrays that had a 2:3 ratio until they were about 9 months old (Starr, Libertus, & Brannon, 2013) (**FIGURE 5.7**).

Thus, infants appear to have an **approximate number sense** (**ANS**), a cognitive system that enables them to estimate the magnitude of items in a set without having to rely on counting (e.g., Feigenson, Dehaene, & Spelke, 2004;

approximate number sense (ANS) Infants' ability to estimate the approximate magnitude of items in a set without relying on counting (e.g., an infant choosing a pile of 18 cheerios versus a pile of 6 cheerios)

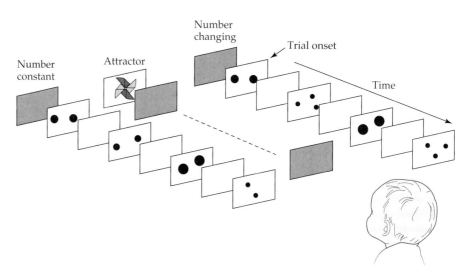

FIGURE 5.7 Testing infants' "approximate number sense." Infants view a series of pictures of two arrays of numbers, one to the left and one to the right. One array (here, the left side) presents images with the same number of dots each time. The second (here, the right side) presents images with changing numbers. If infants look longer to the array that changes numbers, they perceive the number differences and have an approximate number sense. However, 6-month-old infants are unable to discriminate arrays when changes in the ratios of numbers across arrays is small. So, for example, arrays that change between 1 and 2 dots or 5 and 10 dots (ratios of 1:2) are easier to discriminate than arrays that change between 2 and 3 or 4 and 6 dots (ratios of 2:3). Nine-month-old infants were able to discriminate arrays with ratios of 2:3 (shown in the figure). (After A. B. Starr et al. 2013. *Infancy* 18: 927-941; based on M. E. Libertus and E. M. Brannon. 2010. *Dev Sci* 13: 900-906. © 2010 Blackwell Publishing Ltd.)

Starr, Libertus, & Brannon, 2013; Wang, Libertus, & Feigenson, 2018). The ANS explains why an infant might spontaneously choose a pile of 18 cheerios over a pile with only 3 cheerios (a ratio of 6:1), even though they can't yet count.

✓ **CHECK YOUR UNDERSTANDING 5.7**

1. Describe studies on infants' abilities in "math" and the approximate number sense (ANS).

Challenges to Nativism

LEARNING OBJECTIVE 5.8 Explain counter-arguments to the nativist view on core knowledge.

As stated previously, nativists assert that infants are hardwired with core capacities that allow them to reason about the permanence of objects at much younger ages than Piaget claimed. Yet, just as Piaget was criticized for underestimating the cognitive abilities of infants, nativists are criticized for overestimating babies' abilities and for their overreliance on looking-time studies. Skeptics argue that infant looking-time patterns may instead be explained by infants' attention to the perceptual features of arrays and immense hours of experience acting in the world (Blumberg, 2005; Haith, 1998; Kagan, 2008).

To illustrate the role of attention and perception during looking-time studies, let's revisit the "disappearing carrot top" study for a moment. Bogartz and colleagues speculated that infants attended to the interesting top halves of the tall and short carrots (Bogartz, Shinskey, & Speaker, 1997). Recall that the test trials introduced a window in the upper half of the screen. In the test trial with the short carrot, infants' attention would be focused on the lower half of the screen. Infants would therefore not notice the introduction of the window in the top half of the screen. In the test trial with the tall carrot, however, infants' attention would be focused on the *top half* of the screen and therefore lead them to see the new window that appeared. Thus, longer looking times in the impossible condition (the tall carrot not showing up) might be explained by infants' interest in the novelty of the window in test trials (a perceptual interpretation) rather than by an understanding that the carrot continued to exist and that its top should be taller than the window (a cognitive interpretation). Similarly, critics argue that infants' seemingly hard-wired understanding of number, gravity, and so on might be explained by basic perceptual processes.

Nativist accounts have also been critiqued for not considering the hours of experience infants accumulate while interacting in and learning about their worlds. Recall, for example, that 4.5-month-olds look longer to objects that are dropped yet "float" in the air compared to objects that fall to a surface below, which some researchers attribute to an innate understanding of gravity. An alternative account is that 4.5-month-olds have learned quite a lot about the laws of physics during their approximately 1,500 hours of awake time as they watch objects fall and land on other objects, including the objects they themselves drop and manipulate.

Despite skepticism about infant core capacities, nativists spawned vigorous and much-needed debate about whether infants are naturally hard-wired to understand certain concepts, and if so, what those concepts are and how they develop further with experience and maturation. Moreover, nativists acknowledge that core capacities are only primitive building blocks. Through their experiences in the environment, infants eventually achieve the complex and logical thinking of children and adolescents (Baillargeon et al., 2010; Hespos & Anderson, 2020; Spelke, 2013).

✓ **CHECK YOUR UNDERSTANDING 5.8**

1. Give an example of an alternative interpretation for infant looking in the disappearing carrot study that does not require core knowledge.

Developmental Systems Insights into Cognitive Performance

Developmental systems theorists focus on the multiple forces, inside and outside the child, that give rise to children's thoughts and actions. Developmental systems theorists reject Piaget's idea of top-down mental "schema" determining what babies understand and can do. Rather, from a developmental systems perspective, many factors influence an infant's performance on a given task in a given moment. Let's consider some findings that support a dynamic system's approach to cognitive development.

Modifying the A-not-B Task

LEARNING OBJECTIVE 5.9 Explain why follow-up research on Piaget's A-not-B task challenges Piaget's claims of mental representation.

Developmental systems theorists showed that infants' performance on Piaget's A-not-B task depends on how researchers present the task. When examiners slightly modify Piaget's traditional A-not-B task, they change infants' success. For example, if a researcher increases the number of times an object is hidden at location A before switching to location B, infants are more biased to search and reach for the object at location A than at the new location B. This is because with each successful search at location A infants experience positive feedback that reinforces their reaching. Consequently, infants are less likely to search for the object at location B after several successful searches at A than they are after fewer successful searches at A (Spencer, Smith, & Thelen, 2001).

In fact, 10-month-old infants who initially fail A-not-B tasks can perform as well as 12-month-old infants when researchers vary the problem, such as extending the time between A and B trials, standing infants up between the A and B trials, or putting a glittery sleeve on infants' arms—all of which lead to a decline in erroneous reaches to location A. In short, if altering a task can change the outcome, then the claim that object permanence resides in an infant's brain rests on thin ice. It is not simply what a baby knows or does not know that determines success, but rather many overlooked in-the-moment influences, including sensory feedback from one's actions, affect performance on any given cognitive task.

✓ CHECK YOUR UNDERSTANDING 5.9
1. List modifications to the A-not-B task that lead to changes in infant success.
2. Why do those changes improve or harm infant performance?

Changing Sensory Feedback

LEARNING OBJECTIVE 5.10 Explain why manipulations to infants' posture and hand weights might alter performance on A-not-B tasks.

We saw that repeated reaches to a given location when searching for an object may reinforce a simple motor habit. The sensory feedback from repeated reaches intensifies the habit, such that reaching in a specific way to a specific location becomes automatic. If so, then changing an infant's posture or even how heavy an arm feels should also alter sensory feedback from reaches and perhaps diminish the tendency of infants to search repeatedly in the wrong location.

Indeed, when researchers manipulated infants' posture between the two phases of the task, performance improved. Infants were first encouraged to find an object hidden at location A while sitting and were then prompted to find the object at location B in a standing posture. When experimenters switched infants' posture between the A and B trials, infants were less likely to make the A-not-B error compared to infants whose posture was not switched by experimenters

From L. B. Smith and E. Thelen, 2003. *Trends Cog Sci 7*, 343–348

FIGURE 5.8 In-the-moment contextual influences on cognitive performance. Infants were tested in the A-not-B task, but with a minor change. Examiners changed infants' posture between A and B trials. When this was done, infants no longer perseverated to location A when the hidden object was switched to location B.

(Smith et al., 1999) (**FIGURE 5.8**). Similarly, placing small weights on infants' wrists made them less likely to continue to search at location A when the object was hidden at location B compared to infants who did not receive the arm weights (Smith, 2005). In both studies, disruption to the motor habit aided infant performance.

Sensory feedback continues to affect behavior and performance throughout our lives, such as when you leave your watch at home but keep checking your arm throughout the day out of habit. And, when context changes, so does behavior. In a classic study (that has been replicated many times!) adults were better able to remember information when they were tested in the same setting in which the material was originally learned than in a new setting (Godden & Baddeley, 1975). This explains why you are likely to do better on a test if you take it in the same chair and same room in which you originally learned the material!

✓ **CHECK YOUR UNDERSTANDING 5.10**

1. Why does changing infants' posture diminish the tendency to search for an object at location A?

Information Processing: Attention in Cognition

Like Piagetian theory, information processing approaches to cognitive development highlight children's active role in learning (see Chapter 1). Children have goals that lead them to seek out and attend to relevant information in their environments, and they develop strategies to manipulate and process that information (Klahr, 1978). Moreover, just as Piaget attributed changes in cognitive development to children's mental schema, information processing theorists investigate how growth in children's knowledge base (the mind's vast store of information) affects learning. For example, infants who have knowledge about oranges, apples, and balls, might throw or roll a ball never seen before, attempt to bite into an apple, but hold out the orange for dad to peel. Infants' knowledge allows them to express distinct actions toward otherwise similarly spherical objects.

Information processing researchers emphasize gradual rather than stagelike changes in cognitive structures and cognitive processes. **Cognitive structures** are regions of the brain involved in cognition and connections among neurons in the brain. Information processing theory likens cognitive structures in the human brain to hardware components of computers such as the computer's hard drive. Children's growing knowledge base results in changes to the brain's

cognitive structures Regions and neural connections in the brain involved in cognitive processes such as memory and comprehension

cognitive processes Mental processes, such as attention and perception, involved in cognition

hardware expressed through the complexity and specificity of neuronal connections in the brain. **Cognitive processes** are reflected in mental activities involved in deploying attention and using rules and strategies to achieve goals, much like a computer's software. Developmental improvements in attention are an example of cognitive processes.

Phases of Attention

LEARNING OBJECTIVE 5.11 Explain the phases of attention and their connection to learning new information.

Attention is a process rather than a fixed state because people continually shift among phases of attention, sometimes keenly focusing on a task, and other times being distracted and unfocused. And, attention is vital to learning. Infants must attend to specific things in their environments to learn about them.

How do developmental scientists know if infants are attending? Gaze is one indicator of attention, but not the only one. In fact, a baby may appear to be looking at something, but that doesn't mean the infant is actually processing information. Indeed, infants often "blank stare" at things around them without attending to the material in a meaningful way. Thus, physiological measures such as heart rate or patterns of brain activity from electroencephalography (EEG) recordings (see Chapter 3) offer another way to test whether infants are attending. EEG patterns change in reliable ways as infants transition among phases of attention (Xie, Mallin, & Richards, 2018). Similarly, when researchers present infants with stimuli, such as sounds or sights, babies' heart rates change in line with four phases of attention (**FIGURE 5.9**):

automatic response The first phase of attention, characterized by the detection of a stimulus before orienting to it

1. Infants first show an **automatic response**, in which they detect a stimulus presence even before orienting to it, as indicated by accelerated heart rate.

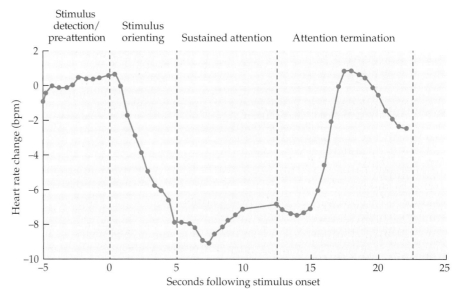

FIGURE 5.9 Phases of attention. Infant heart rate changes (in beats per minute) as infants transition among phases of attention. Detection of a stimulus (pre-attention) causes infants to orient to a stimulus; they then enter a phase of sustained attention where heart rate slows. Heart rate rebounds when infants stop attending. Researchers show that infants best learn stimuli that researchers present during the period of sustained attention. (After J. E. Richards and B. J. Casey. 1991. *Psychophysiology* 28: 43–53. © Society for Psychophysiological Research.)

2. During **orientation**, the infant turns head and eyes to a picture, and heart rate rapidly slows down.

3. During **sustained attention**, the infant starts to process the stimulus and learning occurs (Courage, Reynolds, & Richards, 2006). The brain is alert, and heart rate is slow.

4. During **attention termination**, the infant no longer processes the stimulus information. Heart rate returns to a baseline level.

To illustrate the connection between attention and learning, researchers presented infants with a Sesame Street clip (*Follow That Bird*). As infants viewed the clip, researchers briefly superimposed a computer-generated pattern (such as a flashing checkerboard or moving shapes) at different phases of infant attention (**FIGURE 5.10**). When the stimulus was presented during the sustained attention phase, infant learning was observed—as indicated by their longer looking times to a novel stimulus. However, if the stimulus was presented during the other phases of attention, infants did not differ in their looking times to the novel versus familiar stimuli (Richards, 1997). Thus, infants may be unlikely to learn about objects, people, and events in their environments unless they sustain attention to those stimuli.

Consider next how recordings of brain activity (see Chapter 3) provide evidence for learning during the sustained attention phase (Xie et al., 2018). Researchers presented infants of 4.5, 6.0, and 7.5 months of age with the Sesame Street clip with brief exposures to stimuli overlaid on the clip. EEG measurements showed active arousal in infants' brain only during sustained attention. During other phases of attention, even if infants were looking at the stimulus, the brain was not actively processing the information. Additionally, the brain regions that responded to the stimuli varied with age. Event-related potentials (ERPs) from the 4.5-month-old infants showed brain responses scattered over a wide region of the prefrontal cortex, whereas ERPs of the 7.5-month-olds were concentrated in a specific region of the prefrontal cortex. Studies spanning a wider age range of infants, from 6 to 12 months, additionally revealed that brain areas associated with sustained attention become more organized, less widely scattered, and more efficient across the period of infancy, which helps account for developmental improvements in infant learning.

✓ CHECK YOUR UNDERSTANDING 5.11

1. What are the four phases of attention?
2. In what phase does learning take place?

Selective Attention

LEARNING OBJECTIVE 5.12 Explain how cognitive processes such as selective attention and working memory are measured in infants.

As we saw, infants learn by attending, with learning occurring during the phase of sustained attention. But which of the many stimuli in the environment are worthy of an infant's attention? How does the young infant, with limited experience and knowledge about the world, allocate attention to competing environmental stimuli such as mother talking, people conversing in the background, sounds from the TV, or a car honking outside? Infants must direct their attention to aspects of the environment that are relevant to their goals, while ignoring irrelevant information—a process referred to as **selective attention**. Researchers agree that features of the stimulus (an influence from outside infants) and infants' ability to focus on certain stimuli and ignore others (influences from within infants) instigate selective attention (Craik et al., 1996).

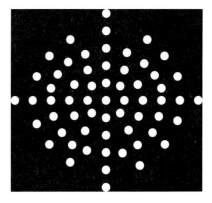

FIGURE 5.10 Learning during sustained attention. As babies viewed a *Sesame Street* clip, researchers briefly superimposed a computer-generated pattern (similar to the one shown in this figure) at different phases of infant attention. When the stimulus was presented during the sustained attention phase only, infant learning was observed. In fact, infants who experienced only 5 seconds of exposure to the stimulus during the sustained attention phase learned it as well as infants who were shown the stimulus for 20 seconds during other phases of attention. (After J. E. Richards. 2018. Media Exposure and Child Development, NIH. January 2018. https://www.nichd.nih.gov/sites/default/files/2018-03/RichardsAttentionDevVideo.pdf.)

orientation The second phase of attention, characterized by turning head and eyes to a picture, object, or person

sustained attention The third phase of attention when an individual begins to process a stimulus, during which learning occurs

attention termination The fourth phase of attention when an individual no longer processes the stimulus information

selective attention The process of directing attention to relevant information in the environment while ignoring irrelevant information

stimulus salience The features (e.g., brightness, different sounds) of an object that characterize how attractive, prominent, and noticeable it is

intersensory redundancy hypothesis A hypothesis that attention is recruited and learning is enhanced in the presence of multi-modal stimuli (such as sight and sound)

visual search tasks Perceptual tasks in which a target stimulus is embedded in a background of distractors and infants' attention to the target is measured as they look at the target

Stimuli that Elicit Attention

Stimulus salience refers to how prominent and noticeable something is. As you learned in Chapter 4, infants are biased to attend to certain things relative to others—and salience makes a difference. Infants prefer, for example, to listen to speech over nonspeech sounds and to look at moving faces over static displays. Temporally coordinated inputs across multiple senses (multimodal) such as the sight and sound of clapping hands, are likewise salient to infants. Indeed, infants are biased to attend to stimuli that offer repetitive and complementary information across multiple senses, and learn more from such stimuli than those based in a single sensory input (e.g., Bahrick, Lickliter, & Flom, 2004; Bahrick et al., 2019).

The **intersensory redundancy hypothesis** refers to the enhanced learning that occurs in the presence of multimodal stimuli (Bahrick et al., 2004). When 3-month-olds are presented with synchronized audio and visual information, such as hearing and seeing a toy hammer tapping, they are more able to discriminate a change in tempo than when researchers present them with auditory or visual input only (Bahrick, Flom, & Lickliter, 2002). In essence, multimodal stimuli effectively draw infants' attention and result in learning.

Infant Control of Attention

A person's selective attention to environmental stimuli also depends on internal control of attention, not just on features of the stimulus itself. We often must attend to less appealing material rather than more appealing possibilities, which requires us to take charge of our attention. To illustrate, you are currently reading this section of your textbook, rather than surfing social media, despite such interesting possibilities vying for your attention. To do so, you must selectively attend to the written words and ignore distractors to avoid bouncing your attention from one thing to the next.

Infants too must selectively attend to certain stimuli over others, because responding on the basis of how salient something is alone would impede learning (Amso & Johnson, 2006). Because infants have less control of their attention and more limited attention resources than do older children and adults, selective attention is challenging. Infants often flit from one thing to another, and find it difficult to focus on any given stimulus while ignoring others.

However, over the course of development infants' selective attention improves, as seen in **visual search tasks**—tasks in which a target stimulus is embedded in a background of distractors and infants' attention to the target is measured (Atkinson et al., 1992; Dannemiller, 2000). For instance, researchers presented infants aged 7–21 weeks with a moving target embedded in an array of nonmoving, colorful distractors on the left and right sides of a display (Dannemiller, 2000). Infants of all ages looked to the target stimulus at above chance levels; yet, infants still improved in their selective attention with increasing age.

Is Infants' Lack of Selective Attention Adaptive?

On first glance, infants' early lack of selective attention may seem to be a liability. However, such an interpretation may be flawed. That is, very young infants' seeming "distractibility" likely reflects an early, adaptive strategy and openness to learning everything possible about the world. Young infants' high exuberant activity, as seen in their rapid switching from object to object in play or during laboratory search tasks, allows them to notice many things and form associations among those entities during a period of rapid brain growth and learning (Herzberg et al., 2021; Rovee-Collier & Giles, 2010). Specifically, as infants shift attention from one thing to another, they come to learn about the functions of objects and what they can do with those objects, and thereby create rich opportunities for social interactions with other people.

1. What two factors affect an infant's ability to demonstrate sustained attention?
2. What is the intersensory redundancy hypothesis?

Processing Information

LEARNING OBJECTIVE 5.13 Illustrate how selectively attending to information leads to the processing and encoding of that information.

Selective attention allows infants to learn new information. Developmental researchers often use habituation-recovery experiments, such as those you read about in Chapter 4, to examine infants' processing of information. For example, in a standard habituation-recovery experiment, infants view a picture on a computer monitor until attention diminishes. After infants reach a pre-established criterion of low attention, they are said to have "habituated." The assumption is that habituation occurs because infants sufficiently encoded the visual information and are no longer interested in it. With this assumption in mind, developmental scientists consider the time it takes for infants to habituate, the **habituation rate**, as a measure of processing speed (Colombo et al., 1987). Following the habituation phase of an experiment, an examiner presents the baby with test trials, in which the familiar stimulus and a novel stimulus are presented side-by-side or consecutively on a computer screen. When infants rebound their attention to the novel stimulus—**novelty preference**—researchers infer that they have sufficiently processed the familiar stimulus and can differentiate it from the novel one.

With increasing age, infants typically take less time to habituate to the same stimulus, indicating faster encoding of information (Slater & Morison, 1985). However, infants who are at risk for cognitive delay may take longer. One of the earliest studies of infant habituation found that infants born at term readily habituated to stimuli, whereas infants born prematurely did not (Field et al., 1979). Physical problems associated with preterm birth, such as infants' poor eye control, may contribute to their slowed habituation rates (Downes et al., 2018; White-Traut et al., 2009).

habituation rate The time it takes for a decrease in infants' response to a stimulus after repeated exposures to the stimulus, which is thought to measure how long infants require to process the stimulus information

novelty preference The rebounding of infant attention to a novel stimulus relative to a familiar stimulus experienced previously

1. How might a preterm infant who has experienced medical complications differ from a term infant without complications in habituation?

Memory

LEARNING OBJECTIVE 5.14 Explain the three methods that researchers use to study infant memory.

Infants can't report what they remember to researchers. And so, researchers must rely on innovative procedures to test infant memory, some based on infants' looking behaviors and others based on infants' actions. As you will see, despite methodological differences, studies converge on a consistent developmental story. Between birth and around 2.5 years of age, infants improve in how long they remember information, their ability to retrieve information from memory in new situations, and the number of details they remember.

Habituation-Recovery Studies

For the most part, infants prefer to look at things that are new. And even fetuses habituate to a repeated stimulus and then rebound to a new one, showing how early in development such learning occurs (see Chapter 3). Infant looking time is one way that researchers determine whether infants remember having seen something in the past. Specifically, infants' rebound of attention to a novel stimulus

recognition memory Recognition that a specific stimulus had been experienced in the past; it is thought to be seen when infants rebound attention to a new stimulus relative to a familiar stimulus following experience with the familiar stimulus

conjugate mobile experiment A test used to study infant memory in which the infant's leg is tied to a mobile, with kicking causing the mobile to move; when the tie is removed, infants later kick in response to the familiar mobile, indicating they remembered that their kicking elicited a response

relative to a familiar one, as observed in habituation-recovery studies, is a form of **recognition memory**—recognition that a specific stimulus had been experienced previously. The logic is that after infants have formed a memory of the stimulus, such as the details of a picture, they can now turn their attention to something new (Sokolov, 1963). With age, infants improve in their recognition memory, just as they improve in their rate of habituation. Furthermore, full-term infants show stronger novelty preference than do preterm infants, even when exposed to a stimulus for the same amount of time (Rose, 1983; Rose, Feldman, & Jankowski, 2002).

Conjugate Mobile Experiments

Researchers also assess infants' memory by testing how long infants recall actions that produce rewarding feedback. In a **conjugate mobile experiment**, introduced by developmental researcher Carolyn Rovee-Collier (who in fact credited Piaget with the initial idea), infants who were taught to "kick" to cause a mobile to jiggle remembered to kick in the presence of the same mobile hours, days, and even weeks later (**FIGURE 5.11**).

Rovee-Collier placed infants in a crib and tied a ribbon to their foot. She then counted the number of times infants kicked at the start of the study as a measure of the baseline kicking. Then she attached the other end of the ribbon to a mobile that hung over the crib, so that the mobile moved when infants kicked. After infants learned that their kicking caused the mobile to move, they increased their kicking. To test infants' memory, Rovee-Collier then removed the mobile for a period of time—minutes, days, or weeks—and later reintroduced infants to the mobile, without attaching the ribbon. If infants displayed a high rate of kicking when reintroduced to the mobile, it suggested that they remembered the connection between kicking and the moving mobile.

(A)

(B)

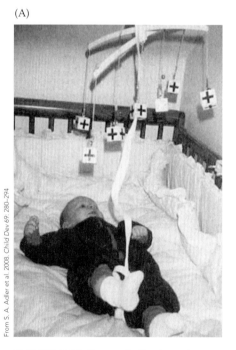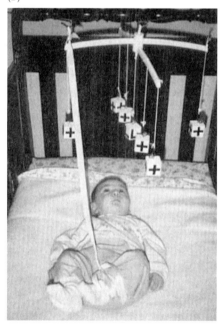

From S. A. Adler et al. 2008. *Child Dev 69*: 280–294

FIGURE 5.11 Rovee-Collier's conjugate mobile experiment. To test infant memory, Carolyn Rovee-Collier tied a ribbon to infants' feet and attached the other end to a mobile. Infants learned that their movement caused the mobile to move and so they increased their kicking. When placed back in the crib hours, days, and sometimes even weeks later, infants (A) increased their kicking in the presence of the same mobile but (B) did not kick to a different mobile. Such findings indicate that infants remembered the experience of moving a specific mobile.

Conjugate mobile studies revealed that infant memory increases with age: Two-month-olds remembered the connection between the kicking and the mobile for 1 day; 3-month-olds remembered for 8 days; and 6-month-olds remembered for two weeks (e.g., Rovee-Collier & Barr, 2001; Sullivan, Rovee-Collier, & Tynes, 1979). Moreover, infants not only remembered that their kicking caused the mobile to move, they also remembered specific details about the mobile, such as the colors and shapes of the dangling objects and the patterned bumpers along the sides of their crib. That is, infants only increased kicking to mobiles that were the same in appearance as the original.

Deferred Imitation Tasks

Deferred imitation tasks, introduced earlier in the chapter, offer a third approach to testing infant memory. In deferred imitation tasks, researchers test whether infants can later reproduce the actions of other people based on live interactions or what they see on screens. By 6 months of age, infants can imitate a sequence of novel actions a day after they watch an adult perform the actions (Barr, Marrott, & Rovee-Collier, 2003) (**FIGURE 5.12**). The fact that even 6-month-olds can later recall a sequence of actions challenges Piaget's claim that children only achieve mental representation in the second year of life.

Older infants can recall more complex sequences of behaviors and for longer periods of time than younger infants (Lukowski & Bauer, 2014). For example, when experimenters extended the length of delays from 1 month to 12 months,

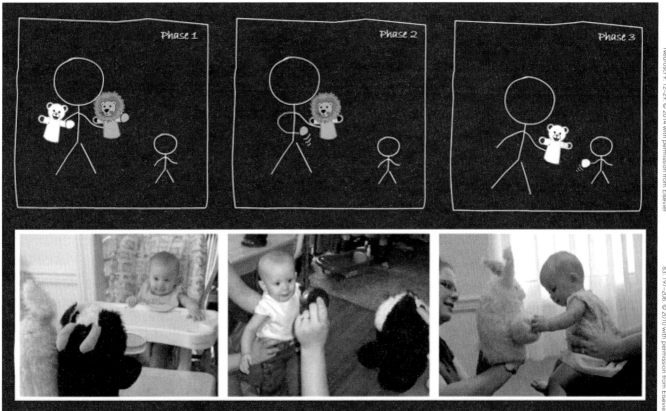

From S. L Mulally and E. A. Maguire, 2014, Dev Cog Neurosci 9: 12–29. © 2014 with permission from Elsevier

From C. Rovee-Collier and A. Giles, 2010, Behav Proc 83: 197–206. © 2010 with permission from Elsevier

FIGURE 5.12 **Imitative actions by infants.** By 6 months, infants can imitate novel action sequences a day after they watch an adult perform the actions. For example, infants will repeat the sequence of removing a mitten from a puppet, shaking the mitten to ring a bell that is inside, and replacing the mitten on the hand of the puppet (Barr, Marrott, & Rovee-Collier, 2003). Sometimes, the task is made even more complicated by pairing a different puppet with the first and testing if the infant generalizes imitation to the associated puppet.

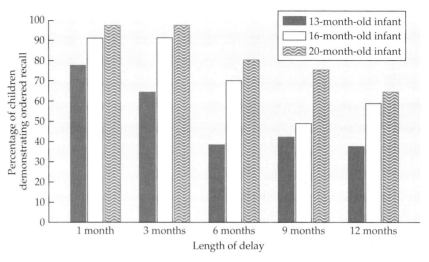

FIGURE 5.13 Deferred imitation tasks. Older infants can recall more complex sequences of behaviors and for longer periods of time than can younger infants. For example, over the second year, infants grow in their ability to repeat a series of behaviors in a precise order (e.g., Lukowski & Bauer, 2014). However, the duration of memory differs with infant age. When experimenters extended the length of delays from 1 month to 12 months, older infants (20-month-olds and some 16-month-olds) but not younger infants (13-month-olds) showed robust memories: most continued to imitate sequences after long delays (Bauer et al., 2000). (After P. J. Bauer. 2002. *Curr Dir Psychol Sci* 11: 137–141; data from P. J. Bauer et al. 2000. *Monogr Soc Res Child Dev* 65: i–213.)

the percentage of infants who imitated decreased. However, most older infants (20-month-olds and some 16-month-olds) continued to imitate at long delays of up to 12 months, whereas most 13-month-olds did not (Bauer, 2002, 2007) (**FIGURE 5.13**). However, infants are better at imitating actions they observed during live interactions than those seen on screens such as television, computers, or apps. That's because infants have difficulties transferring what they learn from the two-dimensional (2D) display to the three-dimensional (3D) world (Barr, 2013).

✓ CHECK YOUR UNDERSTANDING 5.14

1. How would you test infant memory using a (a) habituation-recovery study; (b) conjugate mobile study; (c) deferred imitation study?

Contexts of Cognitive Development

Infants spend most of their awake hours in the home, where they learn through interactions with objects and people. And, infants' home contexts are economically and culturally situated. Thus, family resources—such as whether infants live in an impoverished household—and shared cultural views and practices of community members—such as beliefs about how infants learn—shape the everyday experiences of infants.

Home Context of Cognitive Development

LEARNING OBJECTIVE 5.15 Describe the Home Observation for the Measurement of the Environment (HOME).

Primary caregivers create opportunities for infant learning. These opportunities include how caregivers organize the home environment and structure infant activities and how they directly interact with their infants.

Measuring the Home Environment

Researchers often observe the home environment to objectively measure infants' experiences. Developmental researchers Betty Caldwell and Robert Bradley created a widely used assessment of children's home environments called the **Home Observation for the Measurement of the Environment** (**HOME**), which continues to be a gold standard instrument today (Bradley, 2016; Bradley & Caldwell, 1979). The HOME is a checklist of factors that reflect children's home experiences, including the quality and quantity of support and stimulation caregivers provide their children, family organization and routines, and the involvement of family members in children's lives (**FIGURE 5.14**).

The Infant-Toddler version of the HOME, which is used for children from birth through 3 years, requires a home visit lasting about 1 hour, during which researchers interview caregivers about the home environment and directly observe how caregivers interact with the target infant or toddler. These observations and interviews yield measures of caregiver responsiveness, caregiver acceptance including discipline strategies, caregiver involvement, the organization of the environment, play/learning materials, and the variety of daily stimulation. The HOME has undergone various modifications over its 30-plus year history, including changes to make it appropriate across different cultural communities within and outside the United States.

What have researchers learned from the HOME? Most centrally, the homes of infants and toddlers vary enormously at every socio-economic level and in communities across the globe. Within any given sample, infants range from experiencing very low-quality environments to very high-quality environments, with the HOME predicting individual differences in cognitive functioning across many domains concurrently and later in development (Bradley & Corwyn, 2005, 2016; Niklas et al., 2016). Home environments characterized by high parental responsiveness, acceptance, and involvement, and those that are organized to be safe and offer children a variety of stimulation, relate positively to infants' and toddlers' cognitive skills (Linver, Martin, & Brooks-Gunn, 2004).

Parent-Infant Interactions

Whereas the HOME measures many aspects of infants' and toddlers' home environments, parenting quality deserves to be spotlighted as perhaps the strongest influence on infants' cognitive development. Parenting quality is typically seen in caregivers' sensitivity toward infants, involvement with infants, language stimulation, engagement of infants in learning activities such as book sharing, and the provision of age-appropriate materials for play and learning (Rodriguez & Tamis-LeMonda, 2011). These positive features of parenting support infants' abilities in just about every cognitive area reviewed thus far.

As one example, consider the role parents play in helping infants understand 2D information on television, computer screens, and tablet and phone apps. Recall that infants and toddlers have difficulty imitating actions observed on 2D screens because they fail to grasp the connection between the 2D experience and its 3D referent in the real world (Barr, 2010, 2013). Yet, parents can help make the 2D-to-3D cognitive challenge a bit more manageable. For example, when mothers provide high quality interactions with their infants through verbal elaborations, gestures, and by drawing connections

High-Quality HOME Environment

LEARNING MATERIALS

Child has toys that teach colors, sizes, and shapes.	✔
Child has 3 or more puzzles.	
Child has a tablet or other device to play music.	
Child has toys or games permitting free expression.	✔
Child has toys or games requiring refined movement.	✔
Child has toys or games which help teach numbers.	
Child has at least 10 children's books.	✔
At least 10 books are visible in the apartment or home.	✔
Family buys or reads a daily newspaper.	
Family subscribes to at least one magazine.	
Child is encouraged to learn shapes.	✔

FIGURE 5.14 HOME. Developmental researchers Betty Caldwell and Robert Bradley created a widely used assessment of children's home environments called the Home Observation for the Measurement of the Environment (HOME), which researchers continue to use today. Researchers visit children's homes and fill out a series of checklists that assess children's experiences, such as their access to learning materials like puzzles and books (shown here). (After B. M. Caldwell and R. H. Bradley. 2016. Home Observation for Measurement of the Environment: Administration Manual. Family & Human Dynamics Research Institute, Arizona State University: Tempe, AZ. [FIGURE: HOME Inventory, adapted.])

Home Observation for the Measurement of the Environment (HOME) A widely used assessment of children's home environments based on observations of the quantity and quality of caregiver support and stimulation; family organization and routines; and family involvement in children's lives to everyday experiences while viewing 2D videos, infants do better at interpreting and imitating the 2D videos than do infants without high-quality interactions (Zack & Barr, 2016). In fact, infants show a 20-fold increase in imitation of actions observed on 2D monitors when their mothers scaffold their learning. Thus, although infants and toddlers are unlikely to learn from screen time when left alone, positive interactions with caregivers can facilitate learning in this context.

✓ **CHECK YOUR UNDERSTANDING 5.15**

1. What is the purpose of the Home Observation for the Measurement of the Environment (HOME)?
2. What might a parent do when interacting with a toddler around apps to support learning?

Socioeconomic Context of Cognitive Development

LEARNING OBJECTIVE 5.16 Discuss examples of intervention programs aimed at supporting infants and parents living in poor households.

When considering caregiving influences on infants' cognitive development, it's important to recognize that parents are likewise affected by the contexts of their lives. Poverty is a critically important context. Many children from low socioeconomic households are at risk of not achieving their full cognitive potential due to poor nutrition, inadequate home environments, and low access to learning materials and activities (Blair & Raver, 2016; Chaudry & Wimer, 2016). Fortunately, developmental science can guide programs and policies that seek to level the playing field for infants living in poverty so that early cognitive disparities don't snowball over time.

Carolina Abecedarian Project
One of the most widely cited intervention programs for children growing up in poverty; children between infancy and five years attended full-time day care with activities focused on cognitive stimulation, language development, and social growth, and showed sustained academic and cognitive achievements years later compared to individuals who did not receive the intervention

The **Carolina Abecedarian Project** is one of the most often-cited intervention efforts to promote long-term development of infants living in poverty. Infants born between 1972 and 1977 were selected to participate based on a number of risk factors, including low family socioeconomic status, father absence in the home, and low maternal IQ (i.e., an "intelligence quotient" that is a score obtained through standardized testing). Children in the treatment group (randomly assigned to the intervention) attended a full-time daycare center between the ages of 6 months and 5 years where they received the attention and cognitive stimulation needed to thrive. Mothers in the treatment group received training in child development, and families in both the treatment and control groups received nutritional supplements and quality health care.

The Abecedarian program yielded impressive, long-lasting results. Children who received the intervention exceeded those in the control group on measures of IQ and academic achievement years after the program ended: They had higher scores in math and reading than did those in the control group based on assessments at 12 and 15 years, and were less likely than children in the control group to be held back in school or placed in special education classes. At 21 years, adults who had been in the program as infants and toddlers had IQ scores that averaged 5 points higher than those who had been in the control group, with the benefits of the intervention being highest for those who had low birth weights and mothers with low education levels (Campbell et al., 2001; Ramey & Ramey, 2004). The Carolina Abecedarian project continues to stand out as a remarkable success story in terms of children's cognitive development and academic performance.

Evaluations of other interventions with socioeconomically disadvantaged infants produced mixed findings. Some programs do not affect cognitive development and others yield early effects that fade over time. Nonetheless, there continues to be promising evidence that early intervention programs, such as the federally funded Early Head Start initiative, which began in 1995 and serves thousands of low-income families with infants and toddlers throughout the country, can avert negative developmental trajectories in infants at risk (Chazan-Cohen et al., 2015). Early Head Start helps parents to engage in positive and sensitive interactions with infants, while also providing direct services to infants, such as quality daycare, to support their cognitive development and later school readiness. In a national evaluation of the impacts of Early Head Start, by 3 years of age, children who participated in the program performed better than did children in a matched, randomly assigned control group in cognitive and language development and sustained attention during play (Love et al., 2005). They also were more engaged with their parents relative to the control group, and their parents were more emotionally supportive, provided more language and learning stimulation, and read to their children more often than did parents in the control group.

✓ CHECK YOUR UNDERSTANDING 5.16

1. What was the Carolina Abecedarian Project and what did it demonstrate?

Cultural Context of Cognitive Development

LEARNING OBJECTIVE 5.17 Describe the ways that cultural context might affect infant cognitive development.

Most of the studies you read about thus far were conducted with infants from white, middle-income households in the United States or Europe, a reality that has aptly been critiqued as narrowly focusing on children from WEIRD (*W*hite, *e*ducated, *i*ndustrialized, *r*ich, *d*emocracies) populations (Henrich, Heine, & Norenzayan, 2010). This limitation does not necessarily compromise the validity and relevance of findings on early cognitive development because many of the developmental processes involved in learning and cognition are universal. Infants everywhere learn about the properties of objects through active engagements with the environment. Children everywhere grow in their abilities to selectively attend to relevant environmental information and inhibit attention to distractors. And children everywhere benefit from an increasingly elaborate knowledge base, are able to process new information more efficiently over time, and show steady gains in their abilities to remember information.

Nevertheless, infants from different cultural communities experience unique physical and social environments and as a result learn culture-specific information. Sociocultural theorist Lev Vygotsky (1978), whom you read about in Chapter 1, wrote extensively about the ways that culture defines the materials of children's environments, such as toys for play and tools of everyday life, and the symbols used in communication, such as the content and forms of language. For example, children living in the United States quickly learn that a pencil is for writing, keys are for opening, and spoons and forks are for eating. These lessons are unique to U.S. children's cultural context, even though children in the United States learn how to use these specific tools in the same way that learning occurs everywhere—through practice, observation, and the continual progress made across all areas of development.

The interplay between cultural universals and cultural specificity was illustrated by Pierre Dasen (1979, 1984), a student of Jean Piaget, who embarked on one of the first cross-cultural investigations of cognitive development. Dasen tested West African (Baoule) and French infants on their actions with objects and object permanence. (Recall that Piaget's six substages of the sensorimotor period are distinguished by the sophistication of infants' engagements with objects). The Baoule infants behaved much as the French infants did—except when tested on objects that were unfamiliar (e.g., objects that required rotation, such as toy cars, or that required sliding, such as drawers). Not surprisingly, the

French infants surpassed the Baoule in their goal-directed actions associated with these familiar objects. They knew which actions were required and could thus implement them. What infants experienced, and therefore what they could do, was culturally bound. Researchers today continue the quest to understand cultural similarities and differences in cognitive development, as we will see throughout chapters on early childhood, middle childhood, and adolescence.

✓ **CHECK YOUR UNDERSTANDING 5.17**

1. What did Dasen's research on the object permanence of French and Baoule infants reveal?

■ *Learning about the Social World*

As social beings, adults are profoundly interested in what drives human behavior—the psychological states, thoughts, goals, and intentions that motivate everyday life. Why did that person do what they did? What does a romantic partner really want out of the relationship? People are not content to merely interact with others, but rather they continually reflect, mull over, and reason about social affairs of the heart and mind.

The subfield of child psychology that examines how children process, store, and apply information about people and social situations is referred to as **social cognition**. This subfield is relatively new, because psychologists have traditionally separated the study of "cognitive" development from that of "social" development. However, just as children grow in their cognitive skills at representing the physical world, they grow in their cognitive representation of the social world. It therefore makes sense to place the study of social cognition under the broad umbrella of cognitive development.

Infants have a long way to go before they can reason fully about people's beliefs, thoughts, goals, and intentions. The study of infant social cognition, therefore, is a study of building blocks, with researchers debating whether building blocks exist; if so, what are they and how do they change across the first years—questions that mirror those pertaining to infants' understanding of the object world. For instance, nativists ask whether infants are innately equipped with core capacities to understand other people. Developmental systems theorists, in contrast, focus on how infants' interactions in their environments might help them to understand others' actions, such as whether an infant who can now reach for toys better understands why other people reach. Questions such as these offer an intriguing picture of how early social cognitive skills pave the way for the mature forms of social understanding that we will learn about in later chapters.

Understanding Others' Attention

Something as straightforward as where a person looks can be quite informative. Looks can reveal whether someone is attracted to someone else, curious about a situation, intending to head in a certain direction, or planning to prepare a certain food for dinner. And so, humans are compelled to figure out what other people are looking at, and why.

Social psychologist Stanley Milgram and his colleagues demonstrated the powerful influence of gaze over half a decade ago in a study entitled the *Wisdom of Crowds* (Milgram, Bickman, & Berkowitz, 1969). Milgram placed men on a street corner and instructed them to look up at an empty sky for a minute. A substantial number of pedestrians stopped to see what the men were looking at by gazing up at the sky themselves. As the number of confederate (fake) "sky

social cognition The processing, storing, and application of information about people and social situations gazers" increased, so did the number of pedestrians who stopped to figure out what the excitement was all about. Although Milgram sought to document the role of crowds in social behavior, he serendipitously illustrated the power of gaze in social cognitive understanding. We follow gaze because we understand that people look at things that they consider to be interesting or important.

What does any of this have to do with infants? Recall that earlier in the chapter you learned that attention is a first step to learning. Infants learn about people by watching them, and over the course of infancy they come to recognize, just as Milgram demonstrated in the sky-gazer study, that where a person looks reveals something about that person's goals or interests. And so, a logical question is to ask when and how do babies recognize that people purposefully look at things. In essence, when do infants learn that attention is intentional?

Gaze Following and Joint Attention

LEARNING OBJECTIVE 5.18 Distinguish among different interpretations of infant joint attention and gaze following.

The early precursors to infants' understanding of attention emerge in the first months of life. Between 3 and 6 months of age, infants follow the gaze direction of other people (D'Entremont, Hains, & Muir, 1997; Scaife & Bruner, 1975). If a person looks at an object at the far right of the room, infants move their heads in the same direction. But just because infants look at the same object does not imply that they interpret peoples' attention as *intentional*. Over the next several months, infants' gaze following becomes more accurate. By 9–10 months of age, infants respond to people's shifts in gaze, head turns, and points to objects by looking at the specific object or event (Baldwin & Moses, 1996; Moore & Corkum, 1994), and infants 12 months of age and older regularly share attention to the same objects as other people, which researchers refer to as **joint attention** (Adamson & Bakeman, 1984; Tomasello & Farrar, 1986; Yu, Suanda, & Smith, 2019). At younger ages, before 6–9 months, infants simply look at people or objects of interest, without engaging in joint attention.

By the end of the first year, infants seem to understand the role of the eyes in signaling a person's interests and behaviors. When an examiner turned toward an object with eyes open and eyes closed in different experimental conditions, 10- and 11-month-olds looked in the same direction when the examiner's eyes were open but not when they were closed. In contrast, 9-month-olds turned regardless of the examiner's eyes being open or closed, responding to the body's orientation, but not yet appreciating that people are visually connected to the world (Brooks & Meltzoff, 2005) (**FIGURE 5.15**).

How should researchers interpret infants' ability to engage in joint attention with other people? Do 9- to 10-month-olds recognize the intentionality of attention? A generous interpretation of joint attention credits infants with understanding that people intentionally look at things they find interesting or important. On this intentionality argument, infants have a rudimentary understanding of the psychological motivations for people's attention. Alternatively, infants may merely associate fun or interesting things with the direction of a person's head orientation or eye gaze, much like when people look in the location of a spotlight that is shone at the center of a stage.

Debate about the age at which infants fully appreciate the intentions behind attention continues. However, it's safe to say that between 12 and 18 months of age, infants understand that people look certain places for a reason. For instance, 12- to 14-month-old infants crawl several meters to look behind a barrier after an adult

joint attention The shared attention of two individuals on the same object or event; shifts in gaze, head turning, and pointing are ways that infants engage in joint attention

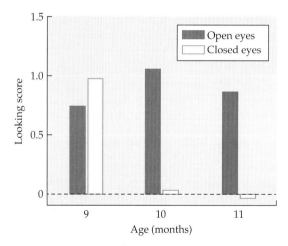

FIGURE 5.15 Role of eyes in signaling interest. Infants 10 and 11 months of age appreciate that the eyes signal a person's interests. Nine-month old infants orient in the direction of a person's body movement whether the person's eyes are open or closed. However, 10- and 11-month-old infants only orient when the person's eyes are open. (After R. Brooks and A. N. Meltzoff. 2005. *Dev Sci* 8: 535–543. © Blackwell Publishing Ltd. 2005.)

looks that way, indicating that they understand that the adult saw something interesting (Moll & Tomasello, 2007).

✓ **CHECK YOUR UNDERSTANDING 5.18**

1. Distinguish between the gaze following of a 3-month-old and the gaze following of a 14-month-old.

Pointing

LEARNING OBJECTIVE 5.19 Explain the significance of infant pointing in the study of social cognition.

Like gaze, pointing signals to other people where to look. Infants' points can be regarded as an effort to elicit another person's attention. It's as though infants desire to establish joint attention with others (Bates et al., 1979; Butterworth, 2003; Carpenter, Akhtar, & Tomasello, 1998). But, do infants truly intend to share attention with others when they point? Perhaps infants simply point because they are excited about something.

To test these alternatives, researchers presented 12- to 14-month-old infants with puppets that appeared from behind a screen and moved to the far side of the room (Liszkowski et al., 2004). Infants eagerly and spontaneously pointed whenever the puppets appeared. Then, in an experimental manipulation, the researcher responded to the infant's pointing by engaging in joint attention with the infant about the puppet (for example by looking at the puppet and infant and talking about the puppet), or not engaging in joint attention (for example, by interacting with the infant but not looking at the puppet).

Infants were only satisfied when the experimenter responded to their points with joint attention. For example, infants eventually stopped pointing when the experimenter responded in any other way. When experimenters pretended to "misunderstand" what infants were pointing at, by trying to engage in joint attention around a different object, infants persistently pointed at the original object as though saying, "No! I want to show you something else!" (Liszkowski, Carpenter, & Tomasello, 2008). Thus, at least by the start of the second year, infants use gestures like pointing to establish joint attention with others around interesting things.

✓ **CHECK YOUR UNDERSTANDING 5.19**

1. What evidence suggests that infants point because they want to share attention with other people?

Understanding Others' Actions, Knowledge, and Beliefs

We've seen that infants eventually understand that people look at objects and events in the world for a reason. What about infants' interpretations of other behaviors, such as reaching or manipulating objects? Do infants understand that other people display certain actions intentionally? Do they reason about others' actions, knowledge, and beliefs?

Interpreting Actions

LEARNING OBJECTIVE 5.20 Describe evidence that suggests infants interpret people's actions as intentional.

If you reach across the kitchen table, your friends might assume that you want something, and would likely hand you the salt or some other object. By around 5–6 months of age, infants likewise attribute goals to people's actions. They understand, for example, that people reach to get something they desire (Robson & Kuhlmeier, 2016; Woodward, 2009).

Developmental scientist Amanda Woodward was the first to document infants' understanding of goal-directed reaching (Woodward, 1998). Woodward habituated 6-month-old infants to a scene in which a person reached for one of two toys followed by test trials in which the person reached for the original toy or a different toy. At test trials, infants looked longer when the person reached for a different toy than when the person reached for the original toy, as though they were surprised the person no longer wanted the toy that had been originally preferred. In fact, infants looked longer to the different toy reach even when the locations of the toys were swapped and the direction of the reach changed. If infants had not understood the intentionality of the original reach—that it was directed at a specific object rather than a just a movement in a certain direction—they should have looked longer instead at the salient changed direction of the reach. Moreover, infants interpreted object-directed goals to be unique to humans: They looked longer at reaches to the new object only when a human engaged in the goal-directed action, and not when a mechanical claw did the "reaching" (**FIGURE 5.16**).

By around 9 months of age, infants distinguish intentional from accidental actions. Consider an adult who does not give an infant a toy because (1) the adult is *unwilling* to give the toy to the infant, or (2) the adult is *unable* to give the toy to the infant because it has accidentally been dropped. In both situations, the infant does not get the toy—but for different reasons. Nine-month-old infants displayed patience and did not get upset if the adult dropped the toy, but were less patient and became more upset when the adult was unwilling to give them the toy (Behne et al., 2005). Infants seemed to understand that the adult had *intended* to give the toy in one situation but to keep the toy away in the other. In contrast, 6-month-olds did not distinguish between the adult's intentional and unintentional actions.

Even more impressive, 9-month-old infants seem to draw conclusions about how two people will interact based on whether people share the same goals or interests, for example, the desire to eat or avoid a specific food (Liberman,

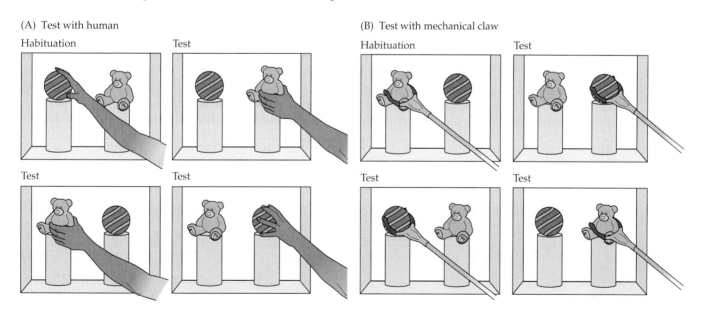

FIGURE 5.16 Interpreting goal-directed reaching.
Infants interpret object-directed goals to be unique to humans. (A) After seeing a human hand reach for a specific object (the ball, top left panel), infants looked longer during a test phase when the human hand reached for a new object (the teddy, top right and lower left panels) versus the same object (the ball, lower left panel). Such a finding suggests that infants expected the human to attempt to get the same toy again. (B) However, when the same procedure was shown with a mechanical claw, infants did not differ in their looking times to the claw's grasping of the ball or teddy. (After A. L. Woodward. 1998. *Cognition* 69: 1–34.)

FIGURE 5.17 Infant understanding of other people's interactions. Infants expect two adults to interact positively if they like the same things, such as food, but not if they disagree. (From Z. Liberman et al. 2014. *J Exp Psychol* 143: 966–971.)

Kinzler, & Woodward, 2014). Infants observed two actors comment on and treat food favorably or with disgust. The actors then greeted one another either positively by smiling and saying "hi" or negatively by turning away and grunting under their breath. Infants looked longer at the actors who disagreed on their evaluations of the food, yet interacted positively compared to actors who agreed in their evaluations and acted positively to one another (**FIGURE 5.17**). Infants appeared to use their social cognitive understanding of other people's intentions to figure out how those individuals would socially interact.

✓ CHECK YOUR UNDERSTANDING 5.20

1. How might you test whether an infant understands that people reach for things because they wish to obtain those objects?

Imitating Actions

LEARNING OBJECTIVE 5.21 Distinguish infant imitation during the newborn period from later forms of imitation.

Earlier in the chapter we saw that Piaget considered deferred imitation to be a window into infants' ability to form mental representations because infants must keep an action in mind to reenact it at a later point in time. Imitation is also inherently social, as infants attempt to understand why someone did what they did and determine whether the action is worth mimicking. By observing developmental changes in what infants imitate and at what age, researchers have pieced together a developmental story of infants' growing understanding about other people's actions.

(A) Hands unavailable

(B) Hands available

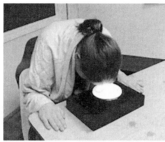

(C) Infants' actions

Percentage of infants

100
80
60
40
20
0

Hands occupied   Hands free

☐ Only manual touch was used
■ Head action was reenacted

FIGURE 5.18 Imitating intended actions. Infants observed an adult pressing a button with her head when (A) her hands were occupied and (B) when her hands were free. (C) Infants imitated pressing a button with their heads after observing an adult do so if the adult's hands were free. Thus, infants appeared to interpret the experimenter's head-bopping as an intentional and acceptable way of doing things. However, if the adult's hands were occupied, making it impossible for her to touch the button with her hands, infants no longer imitated by pressing the button with their heads. They now used their hands. (From G. Gergely et al. 2002. *Nature* 415: 755.)

Although even young infants imitate others' actions, not until the second year do infants selectively imitate actions that other people *intended*, while ignoring actions that were accidental (Carpenter, Akhtar, & Tomasello, 1998; Olineck & Poulin-Dubois, 2005). For example, if a toddler watches someone accidently knock over a tower of blocks, the toddler won't copy the action, whereas the toddler will copy a person who intentionally knocks over the blocks while smiling and saying "There you go! Ah ha!" Similarly, when a person attempts but fails at an action, 15- and 18-month-old toddlers produce the action that the person *meant* to perform rather than the action that was actually performed (Johnson, Booth, & O'Hearn, 2001; Meltzoff, 1995).

Notably, toddlers' tendency to imitate is so strong that they even copy actions that appear to be very odd. For example, when an adult used her forehead to press a button that turns on a light box, 12- and 14- month-old infants imitated the unusual head-pressing action more often when the actor *freely chose* to use her head than when she was *forced* to use her head because her hands were unavailable—such as being tied up with something else— leaving head-bopping as the only option (Gergely, Bekkering, & Király, 2002; Schwier et al., 2006). Infants appeared to interpret the experimenter's freely chosen use of head-bopping as an intentional and acceptable way of doing things, and so even when their own hands were free, infants opted to use their heads (**FIGURE 5.18**).

✓ CHECK YOUR UNDERSTANDING 5.21

1. Describe evidence that infants distinguish between intentional and unintentional behaviors.

Inferring Knowledge and Beliefs

LEARNING OBJECTIVE 5.22 Review evidence that suggests infants understand that other people can have beliefs that differ from one's own.

Infants behave in ways that suggest they infer what others do or do not know. For example, in experimental setups in which an object falls, 12- to 18-month-olds will point to the location where the object has fallen only if the adult has not seen the object fall (Liszkowski, Carpenter, & Tomasello, 2008).

false belief A thought about another person's knowledge that does not match reality, such as believing that someone knows where a toy is located when they were not around to see the toy moved

mental state vocabulary
Vocabulary words that refer to the internal workings of people's minds, such as "think," "know," and "wish"

Infants also may understand that another person has a **false belief**—a belief that does not match reality—as shown in violation-of-expectation experiments (Onishi & Baillargeon, 2005; Song et al., 2008). To illustrate, 15-month-old toddlers viewed a scene in which a female actor played with a toy and then placed it inside a green box that was next to a yellow box and left the room. Toddlers were then presented with a "false-belief condition" in which the toy in the video display "hopped out" from the green box into the yellow box in the woman's absence. When the woman returned, she reached for the toy in the green box (the original location) or the yellow box (new location). Reaching toward the green box would indicate a false belief that the object was still there. Infants looked longer when the woman reached to the new location, suggesting that they expected her to reach where she falsely believed the toy to be hidden. By 2.5 years of age, toddlers help an ignorant adult identify which box to open. If an adult attempts to open the wrong box, toddlers will assist in opening the correct box, seemingly recognizing that the adult wants the toy but does not know its location (Buttelmann, Carpenter, & Tomasello, 2009).

Infants' growing social cognitive understanding of others' knowledge and beliefs eventually manifests in the use of **mental state vocabulary**, words such as "think," "want," "know," "wish," and so on, that refer to the inner workings of people's minds. In fact, infants who performed well on a battery of social cognitive tasks between 7 and 18 months of age had larger mental state vocabularies at 2 and 3 years of age than did infants who scored low on social cognitive understanding (Kristen et al., 2011).

However, the proposition that infants and toddlers understand the knowledge and beliefs of other people has met with controversy, as we will see in Chapter 9. Some classic studies of social cognition indicate that a true understanding of others' minds, including that someone holds a false belief, does not occur until 4 years of age and perhaps even later in development.

✓ CHECK YOUR UNDERSTANDING 5.22

1. How might you test whether a toddler recognizes that another person holds a false belief?

Contexts of Social Cognition

Which contextual factors may explain infants' emerging skills in social cognition? For the most part, infants learn about other people's intentions and beliefs through everyday social interactions, rendering experiences at home and the broader cultural context vital to social cognitive development.

Home Context of Social Cognition

LEARNING OBJECTIVE 5.23 Explain the role of caregiver sensitivity in infant social cognition.

Infants spend a lot of time interacting with people. The quality of infants' engagements with their caregivers feeds into growing social-cognitive skills. Caregiver sensitivity, responsiveness, and emotional availability to infants predicts infants' understanding of others' goal-directed actions (Brink, Lane, & Wellman, 2015; Hofer et al., 2008; Licata et al., 2014).

Why might caregivers' sensitivity facilitate infants' social cognitive development? One possibility is that infants with sensitive and emotionally available caregivers are better able to regulate their emotions. And, when negativity is reduced, infants are more alert and able to learn about their social environments, including the desires, emotions, and intentions of other people's actions. Perhaps as well, infants learn how to be sensitive to other people when their caregivers respond sensitively to them. A parent who reacts to an infant's reach by handing the infant the desired toy may teach the infant that people commonly attend to and respond to one another's actions.

✓ CHECK YOUR UNDERSTANDING 5.23

1. Why might parent sensitivity relate to infants' social-cognitive understanding?

Cultural Context of Social Cognition

LEARNING OBJECTIVE 5.24 Summarize findings from cross-national research on infant social cognition.

Cultural studies of social cognitive development in infancy are rare. Perhaps that's because infants everywhere develop social cognitive skills that allow them to understand, imitate, and learn from other people. However, in the context of such cultural universals, the ways that infants learn about others may differ across cultural contexts.

Developmental researcher Tara Callaghan and colleagues conducted one of the most comprehensive cross-cultural investigations of infants' social cognitive development. They studied infants and toddlers of different ages, ranging from 8 months to over 3 years, from a small, rural town in Canada and from villages in India and Peru. Researchers assessed children on a battery of social cognitive skills, including joint attention, imitation, and the understanding of others' goal-directed actions (Callaghan et al., 2011) (**FIGURE 5.19**). The dramatic differences in the family backgrounds and experiences of infants across the three communities provided a strong test of whether social cognitive developments documented in infants from North-American, middle-class backgrounds, generalize to infants from other cultural backgrounds.

Families from the three communities differed on maternal education, with most mothers being illiterate in India, some literate in Peru, and all literate in Canada. They also differed on maternal work status, with seasonal agriculture being a way of life in India and Peru, compared to professional, service, and trade labor in Canada. Furthermore, infants' physical environments ranged from a scarcity of toys in Peru and India to many toys in Canada. Finally, cultural practices around caregiving differed across communities. Adults in India and Peru included infants in the routines of adult daily life, but adults in Canada segregated infants from adult life, engaging infants in specialized activities such as playtime and bedtime routines.

(A)

(B)

(C)

From T. Callaghan. 2011. Mongr Soc Res Child Dev 76: vii–vii, 1–142

FIGURE 5.19 Universality in the emergence of social-cognitive skills. A cross-cultural investigation of social cognitive development in infants and toddlers from (A) Peru, (B) Canada, and (C) India showed commonalities in children's abilities and ages of acquisition across the three countries, suggesting universality in the emergence of social-cognitive skills.

The more than 5 years of data gathering led Callaghan to conclude that children from the three cultures were highly similar in the course of their social cognitive achievements. For example, infants in the three groups were equally capable of achieving joint attention with an adult, imitating other people's actions, inferring the intentions and goals of others, and helping others to achieve their goals. Furthermore, infants' social cognitive skills emerged at roughly the same ages across the three communities.

Although infants everywhere develop social cognitive skills, they may learn those skills through different types of interaction. For example, adults from U.S., White, non-Hispanic, middle-income families directly teach infants how to use objects, and infants in turn become accustomed to such direct pedagogical interactions: They are highly likely to learn and later imitate the actions that adults teach them (Shneidman, Gaskins, & Woodward, 2016). However, in other cultural communities, direct teaching of infants by adults may be less common, leaving infants to rely on observations to learn and imitate.

To illustrate, researchers directly taught 15- to 18-month-old U.S. infants and Yucatec Mayan infants how to use a novel object (Shneidman et al., 2016). The next day, infants observed a researcher engaging in a novel action with an object, this time in the absence of being directly taught. U.S. children were better able to imitate the action they had been directly taught than the action that they simply observed. However, Mayan children were just as likely to imitate actions that they observed as the actions that they were taught. Thus, infants from the two cultural communities relied on different strategies to learn about how people use specific objects. In some communities, where teaching children is common in everyday life, infants may come to expect others to show them what to do. In other communities, infants may learn about the world by keenly observing what others do.

✓ CHECK YOUR UNDERSTANDING 5.24

1. List similarities in the social-cognitive development of infants from different cultural communities based on Callaghan's research.
2. Describe a study that shows differences in how infants learn from others across cultural communities.

Developmental Cascades

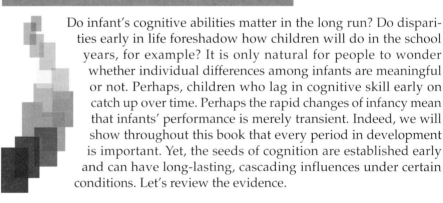

Do infant's cognitive abilities matter in the long run? Do disparities early in life foreshadow how children will do in the school years, for example? It is only natural for people to wonder whether individual differences among infants are meaningful or not. Perhaps, children who lag in cognitive skill early on catch up over time. Perhaps the rapid changes of infancy mean that infants' performance is merely transient. Indeed, we will show throughout this book that every period in development is important. Yet, the seeds of cognition are established early and can have long-lasting, cascading influences under certain conditions. Let's review the evidence.

Cascades from Cognitive Development

If infant habituation taps the efficiency of processing new information, and performance on novelty preference tasks taps memory for information, then infants who show strengths in habituation and novelty preference should likewise show strengths in cognitive skills later in development. Indeed, this is the case.

In an 11-year longitudinal project, developmental researcher Susan Rose and colleagues tested infants repeatedly between 7 and 36 months on a battery of information processing measures like those discussed earlier in the chapter, including attention, processing speed, and memory. They then tested the same children at 11 years of age on a variety of cognitive measures (Rose et al., 2012). Information processing in infancy predicted cognitive performance in later childhood across all tests. And, associations were particularly strong when the researchers related infants' skills in a *specific* area to the same type of skill years later. For example, 7-month-old infants who demonstrated strong memory skills on information processing tests showed strong memory skills on recall and recognition tests at 11 years of age. Moreover, skills in infancy set the stage for complex intermediate skills that then predicted later outcomes. Indeed, Rose found that infants' attention and processing speed related to their language and cognitive skills at 3 years of age, and 3-year-old skill levels then predicted cognitive performance at 13 years of age (Rose et al., 2008; Rose, Feldman, & Jankowski, 2015).

Beyond general skills in information processing, infants' performance on *specific* cognitive tasks, such as their judgments of approximate numbers, shows cascading influences over time. Recall that researchers test infants' early number sense by simultaneously presenting infants with two arrays of dots. In one array, the number of dots remains constant, and in the other array, the number of dots varies. Infants look longer at the numerically changing array, suggesting that they recognize the changing quantities. However, individual infants differ from one another in their number skills, and infants' performance with number arrays predicted their mathematical abilities in early childhood even when researchers statistically controlled for infants' general cognitive ability (Starr, Libertus, & Brannon, 2013). So, rudimentary cognitive abilities in infancy in detecting quantities may set the stage for learning complex mathematical skills in school years later.

Cascades from Social Cognition

Infants' understanding of people's looks, reaches, points, and other actions represent the building blocks for social relationships. Infants who show deficits in early social-cognitive skills may be at risk for later social problems because of persistent, cascading influences. Consider, for example, the social importance of joint attention. When babies engage in joint attention with their primary caregivers, they share and communicate their interests and learn a lot about the give-and-take of social interactions. What might happen if an infant rarely participates in episodes of joint attention? In one study, 12-month-old infants who frequently initiated joint attention and responded to joint attention were more socially competent and less likely to display aggressive, defiant, or impulsive behaviors later in development compared to less skilled infants (Vaughan Van Hecke et al., 2007).

Moreover, early skills in social cognition likewise spill over to affect memory. Recall that infants attend to social interactions between other parties—such as in the study where two actors commented on food—and use this information to reason about the world. Infants' attention to social interactions between two characters has also been found to facilitate memory. For example, infants were only able to remember how four dolls were hidden in boxes if they had first observed dolls "interacting" by facing each other and saying "hello" before being hidden. Infants appeared to have "chunked" the interacting dolls into the two interacting pairs, which reduced the load on their memories from four units to two units—having to remember that two friendly doll pairs were hidden rather than four separate dolls (Stahl & Feigenson, 2014). Thus, observations of social interactions served as the glue that bound units of information together and expanded how much infants remembered.

Language learning represents one of the most central cross-domain cascades in infants' social-cognitive skills. Infants who follow gazes and points of other people are well positioned to interpret the intentions behind the words that people speak. For example, 10- to 11-month-old infants who were better able to follow gaze and points in a lab task showed greater gains in their vocabulary over time than did infants who were less skilled in these areas (Brooks & Melt-zoff, 2008). Similarly, infants who more frequently engaged in joint attention performed better on measures of language acquisition and childhood intelligence than infants who less frequently engaged in joint attention (Mundy et al., 2007; Smith & Ulvund, 2003). Joint attention facilitates language learning because infants learn the words for objects they attend to and show interest in, and adults often teach new words during bouts of joint attention (Konishi et al., 2014; Tomasello & Farrar, 1986).

■ CLOSING THOUGHTS
Looking into the Mind of an Infant

Cognitive development poses a fascinating puzzle to researchers. That's because cognition refers to mental activities—thoughts, beliefs, knowledge, and so on—that occur inside the child's mind and are often unobservable. Indeed, infants' cognitive development differs from many of the things that infancy researchers study. Researchers can study physical development by directly measuring infants' height and weight; language development by analyzing what toddlers say and how they respond to speech; social development by watching how toddlers share and play; and emotional development by observing infants' facial expressions and reactions to emotionally charged events. However, infants' cognition cannot be studied directly. Instead, researchers attempt to infer the process of thinking by observing infants' behaviors or perhaps by studying brain activation patterns. Even when researchers directly question young children about specific problems; probe toddlers on their reasoning and what they know; or calculate with what degree of accuracy young children solve problems and remember lists, they are still left guessing about the mental processes involved in children's thinking.

The challenge of studying cognition is compounded in the case of infants. Tapping into the mind of a baby is not easy. How does a researcher infer what an infant knows and thinks? Do infants look more at a display because they truly "expect" something to happen? Or do infants merely look at things they find to be interesting, perceptually salient, or simply odd (for whatever reason), with no mental expectations required? Are infants armed with core cognitive knowledge that allows them to understand concepts such as number, space, and gravity? Or, might researchers be attributing too much intelligence to infants and imposing adult standards on an infant's simple behaviors?

Straightforward answers to these questions do not exist. There is no clear line that divides the process of perception from that of cognition. And so, the eager news reporter might determine that infants *can* actually count and read minds; the cautious researcher might conclude that infants' looking time alone fails the litmus test for deep cognitive interpretation; and the remaining developmentalists and public will likely waver between skepticism and awe. What do you think?

The Developmentalist's Toolbox

Method	Purpose	Description
Measuring infant learning about the physical world		
The A-not-B task	To test infants' understanding of object permanence	Infants watch an object being hidden in one location (A) and then after successfully retrieving the object several times, the object is hidden in a different location (B). Experimenters vary the number of A and B trials and the experimental conditions to examine how such changes alter infants' reaching to location A or B and success on the task.
Violation-of-expectation studies	To test infants' understanding of object permanence and other characteristics of objects, such as solidity, gravity, and substance	Often used to test infants' attention to a "possible" event that is consistent with an expectation (such as an object falling to a lower surface) compared to infants' attention to an "impossible" event that is inconsistent with an expectation (an object falling and stopping midair). Longer attention to impossible/inconsistent events may indicate that infants' expectations were violated.
Visual search tasks	To test infants' selective attention	A target stimulus is embedded among a background of distractors. Infants' attention to the target stimulus, rather than distractors, indexes selective attention skills.
Conjugate mobile task	To test recognition memory in infants	Infants are placed in a crib, and a ribbon is tied onto a leg and connected to a mobile that jiggles when they kick. Later, infants are again placed in the crib without the ribbon to see if they remember the conditioned action by kicking at the mobile they had seen previously versus a new mobile. The duration of infants' memory can be examined by testing retention periods of hours, days, or weeks.
Deferred imitation task	To test if infants can recall actions they observed in other people (either live or 2D such as video and computer generated)	Infants are shown models who engage in a sequence of actions and are then tested on their ability to imitate what they saw.
The Home Observation for the Measurement of the Environment (HOME)	To evaluate characteristics of children's home environments and experiences at home	An evaluation is made during a 45- to 90-minute home visit of children's home experiences, including the quality and quantity of support and stimulation provided for children, family organization and routines, and the involvement of family members in children's lives. The Infant/Toddler (IT) HOME Inventory is designed for use during infancy (birth to age 3) and consists of 45 questions clustered into six subscales: (1) Parental Responsivity, (2) Acceptance of Child, (3) Organization of the Environment, (4) Learning Materials, (5) Parental Involvement, and (6) Variety in Experience.
Measuring infant learning about the social world		
Goal-directed reaching studies	To assess infants' ability to understand the intentionality of actions	Infants observe actors reaching for a desired object, and then reaching for a different object. Increased attention to reaches to a different object suggests that infants understand other people's intentions to access a goal.
False-belief tasks	To examine whether infants recognize that people can have false or wrong beliefs	Infants observe an actor place an object in location A and leave the room, after which the object's location is switched. When the actor returns, if infants look longer when the actor looks for the object in the *new* location (relative to looking in the original location) it suggests they realize the actor has a false belief of the object's location.

■ Chapter Summary

Piaget's Theory of Cognitive Development

- During the sensorimotor stage of development, infants progress through 6 substages marked by changes in the ways they act on their environments, moving from spontaneous actions involving only the body, to repeating their actions, to intentional actions with objects, to the coordination of actions to achieve a goal, to generating new objects to solve problems, and finally the ability to mentally represent and reason about objects and actions independent of the self.

- During each of the substages, infants advance in their understanding and reasoning about objects in the physical world, until their attainment of object permanence and other forms of mental representation at substage 6.

- Piaget introduced the A-not-B task to show that the infant's failure on object permanence tasks—as signaled by a failure to find an object that is hidden in a new location—can be attributed to a lack of reasoning about the continued existence of objects.

- Infants' achievement of mental representation is seen in object permanence, deferred imitation, language, and pretend play.

Nativist Tests of Infant Core Capacities

- Nativists assert that infants are cognitively capable of much more than Piaget claimed. Using methods primarily based on visual looking time—including violation-of-expectation experiments—infants are thought to have core capacities in their understanding of object permanence, object solidity and substance, gravity and support, and number.

- The nativist tradition has been challenged for over-crediting infants with cognitive understanding; alternative interpretations are based largely on low-level perceptual processes.

Developmental Systems Insights into Cognitive Performance

- Developmental systems theorists show that infant performance on cognitive tasks, such as the A-not-B task, depends on multiple factors, rather than merely the capacity for representation (Piaget) or core knowledge (nativist).

- When researchers modify the A-not-B task, such as modifying the sensory feedback of infants' actions or changing the task itself, infants' performance changes in turn.

Information Processing: Attention in Cognition

- Information processing theorists emphasize infant attention, encoding, and memory for information, and draw analogies between human learning and computers.

- According to information processing accounts of cognitive development, gradual changes occur with age in children's cognitive structures and cognitive processes.

- Infants exhibit four types of attention and are most likely to learn information when they are in a phase of sustained attention.

- Infants have difficulty with selective attention, as shown in visual search tasks. With age, selective attention improves.

- Infants' limited selective attention is best viewed as adaptive, allowing infants to learn a lot about their new worlds during a period of rapid brain growth.

- Habituation tasks test infants' speed of information processing and rebound of attention to novel stimuli.

- Younger infants are slower at processing information on habituation tasks than are older infants. And preterm infants are slower than are term infants.

- Three common methods used to test infant memory are habituation-recovery studies, conjugate mobile experiments, and deferred imitation tasks.

- Between birth and around 2.5 years of age, infants improve in how long they remember information, how flexibly they retrieve information, and the number of details they remember about stimuli or events.

Contexts of Cognitive Development

- Home experiences, including the quantity of support and stimulation provided for infants, aspects of family organization and routines, and the involvement of family members relate to infant cognitive performance.

- Infants from low-income households experience less stimulating home environments, on average, and in turn show delays to cognitive performance on standardized assessments.

- The Carolina Abecedarian Project and Early Head Start are interventions that show positive impacts on the cognitive performance of infants assigned to the treatment group relative to infants in a control group.

- Cultural context influences the types of objects with which infants engage, and the sophistication of infants' actions with those objects.

Understanding Others' Attention

- Social-cognitive development refers to how children process, store, and apply information about people and social situations.

- Developmentalists consider infants' understanding of the psychological states of attention (including interest and joint attention), goals and intentions, and knowledge of self and others to be building blocks to later, mature forms of social cognition.

- Infants follow other people's gaze and points to objects of interest, both of which indicate a desire to share attention with others.

Understanding Others' Actions, Knowledge, and Beliefs

- Infants imitate other people's intentional actions but not accidental actions, suggesting that they understand the intentions (goals) of others.

- Infants' behaviors on false-belief tasks, such as signaling when a person believes an object is in the wrong box, are thought to indicate an early understanding of others' minds, although some researchers challenge the idea that infants understand false belief.

Contexts of Social Cognition

- The quality of caregivers' interactions with infants predicts individual differences in infants' social-cognitive development.
- Cross-cultural investigations indicate that infants from dramatically different rearing environments exhibit similar levels of social-cognitive skills (when considering basic skills such as achieving joint attention with an adult, imitating others' actions, inferring others' intentions and goals, and helping others to achieve their goals). Thus, the early building blocks in social-cognitive skills may be universal, even if acquired in different ways and showing later differences with continued cultural experiences.

Developmental Cascades

- Individual differences among infants in information processing and cognitive tasks (such as approximating numbers) relate to cognitive skills years later, including how children perform on cognitive tasks through early adolescence.
- Infants' social-cognitive skills are associated with their responsiveness to other people, inferences about how others will interact, memory, and language development.

Thinking Like a Developmentalist

1. Nativists showed that infants understand solidity—that objects can't go through other objects. You wonder whether infants also understand that objects can differ in their properties of solidity, with some objects like "sponges" being more malleable than other objects like "bricks." What might you do to test infants' knowledge of these object features?

2. Studies of infants' social cognition suggest that infants understand the intentions and goals of people around them. You wonder whether infants understand which toys their siblings like to play with and if they can then use that knowledge to help their siblings find a lost, favorite toy. In your follow-up study, you wonder whether infants with siblings understand others' intentions at younger ages than infants without siblings. What would you need to do to test both ideas?

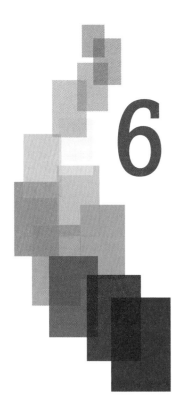

6

Language Development in Infancy and Toddlerhood

Drawing by Minxin Cheng from a photo by Catherine S. Tamis-LeMonda

In 1882, at 18 months of age, Helen Keller was struck by a fever that left her blind and deaf. Over the next several years, she grew increasingly unruly, throwing tantrums and taking out her frustration and rage on the people around her. Rather than institutionalize their daughter, Helen's parents searched for someone who might be able to help. Their search led to Anne Sullivan, a graduate of Perkins Institution for the Blind in Boston, who traveled to Helen's home in Alabama to become Helen's tutor.

At first, Anne's work with Helen appeared to be futile. As Anne struggled to spell words into Helen's hand, her frustrated pupil reacted with defiance: kicking, hitting, biting, and spitting. Then, one day, a breakthrough occurred: Anne held Helen's hand under a water pump and signed the word *water* into Helen's hand, and Helen signed the word back. The insight that 6-year-old Helen gained in that instant—that words could represent objects and events—opened the floodgates to language. Wanting to know the words for everything around her, Helen towed Anne from object to object, place to place. By that evening, Helen had learned 30 words.

Helen Keller's passage into the world of communication is a tribute to the power of language. Language enabled Helen to escape a dark world of silence and frustration and to enter a world of social connection, where she could share her ideas, knowledge, fears, hopes, the past and present with other people (**FIGURE 6.1**). Language gives life to thinking and is the glue that binds social relationships.

In this chapter, you will learn about the complex processes involved in early language development: the many skills that infants must master in their journey towards becoming active participants in their language communities. You will be introduced to theoretical perspectives that differ in the relative emphasis they place on biology versus social context and on top-down versus bottom-up developmental processes, themes that you have become familiar with in previous chapters. You will learn about the many intersecting contexts—ranging from parenting practices to culture—that influence the course of language development and will see how early individual differences can produce cascading effects on learning and development across domains and developmental time.

■ Describing Language Development

Language lays the foundation for the cultural complexity of humanity. Indeed, many scholars consider human language to be the essence of what distinguishes humans from other animals. Unsurprisingly, language learning is one of the most studied topics of developmental psychology, with significant research dedicated to the first years of life as children transition from being babblers to relatively adept conversational partners.

To become competent participants in their language communities, children must integrate information about the physical world, people, and the structure of language itself (Tager-Flusberg & Sullivan, 2000). Children cannot act on the request, "Can you feed Daddy?" unless they understand the reference to food, the familiar guy sitting across the table, and the suggested action of handing over the food.

Over a brief span of two to three years, children learn the sounds (phonology) and words (semantics) of their language and some basic grammatical rules for combining words into sentences (syntax). As receivers of language, children must understand the speech sounds, words, and sentences that others produce. As producers, they must learn how to articulate the sounds and words of their language and how to combine those words into sentences that others can understand. Moreover, children must learn the sociocultural norms and conventions around the use of language (pragmatics)—when to talk, how, and about what.

Phonological Development: Learning Speech Sounds

Infants are drawn to speech sounds and are armed with the biological and perceptual capacities to learn the sounds of their language. **Phonological development** refers to the mastering of the sound system of a language, including how speech sounds combine into words. The smallest distinguishable sound units of a language—its consonant sounds and vowel sounds—are **phonemes**. In any language a phoneme has variants: It sounds somewhat different depending on the sounds around it. For instance, the "p" in the word pun (which is produced with a small puff of air) sounds slightly different than the "p" in the word spun (which is produced without a puff of air). However, most speakers of English hardly notice the subtle variations in phoneme pronunciation. One variant can be substituted for another without changing the meaning of a word. Substituting one phoneme for another, however—such as a "b" for a "p" in the words pun and bun—entirely alters the word's meaning.

Each language has a distinct set of phonemes not only because different languages have different speech sounds but also because sounds that are distinct phonemes in one language might be just variants of the same phoneme in another (**FIGURE 6.2**). And so, infants must learn which sound distinctions are relevant, and which are not. Their task is to perceive, distinguish among, and produce the phonemes of their language.

FIGURE 6.1 Helen Keller.   She is shown here using her fingers to examine President Dwight D. Eisenhower's face during a visit to the White House in 1953.

phonological development
The mastering of a language's sound system (including how speech sounds combine into words) and using speech sounds to communicate effectively

phonemes The smallest distinguishable sound units of a language, such as the /b/ in ball; each language has a distinct set of phonemes, and infants must learn to perceive and produce the phonemes of their language

English word	Faulty German pronunciation
bad	bet
leave	leaf
while	vile

FIGURE 6.2 Phonemic contrasts in two languages.   Each language has a distinct set of phonemes because different languages have different speech sounds, and sounds that are distinct phonemes in one language might be just variants of the same phoneme in another. (After Frankfurt International School. Accessed June 10, 2021. http://esl.fis.edu/grammar/langdiff/phono.htm.)

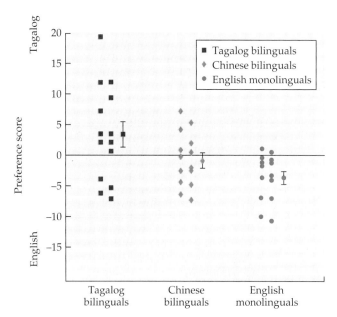

FIGURE 6.3 Newborn preference for the familiar language(s).   Researchers Krista Byers-Heinlein, Tracey Burns, and Janet Werker (2010) tested newborns on their preference for English versus Tagalog (a Philippine language). Newborns whose mothers spoke only English during pregnancy showed a strong preference for English; newborns whose mothers spoke English and Tagalog during pregnancy equally preferred both languages. Newborns of mothers who spoke Chinese and English showed intermediate preference for English and Tagalog. (After K. Byers-Heinlein et al. 2010. *Psych Sci* 21: 343–348.)

Perceiving and Discriminating among the Phonemes of One's Language

LEARNING OBJECTIVE 6.1 Describe how infants perceive and discriminate among the phonemes of their language on the path to identifying words.

Across languages, there are approximately 600 consonants and 200 vowels. Infants enter the world prepared to perceive all these speech sounds and to distinguish among all possible contrasts (Tsao, Liu, & Kuhl, 2004; Werker et al., 1981). With experience, infants zero in on the sounds of the native tongue. As we will see, infants' familiarity with the speech sounds of their native language allows them to recognize and ultimately understand words (e.g., Swingley & Aslin, 2002). Infants display a preference for the sounds of their native language already from birth. In a 2010 study, newborns 0–5 days of age, exposed to English in utero and at birth, preferred to listen to English rather than Tagalog (Byers-Heinlein, Burns, & Werker, 2010). But newborns who had been exposed to both languages showed no preference; both languages were familiar and drew their attention (**FIGURE 6.3**). Over time, infants' experiences with the familiar language(s) leads to enhanced processing of those speech sounds, but a diminished ability to distinguish among the phonemes of languages to which they are not exposed, as revealed by infants' behavioral responses to sounds from foreign languages. Similarly, brain responses to speech in 6- and 12-month-old infants show that automatic and efficient processing of one's native language improves with age (Ortiz-Mantilla et al., 2010; Ortiz-Mantilla et al., 2016).

The channeling of language preference and perception to one's native tongue is an example of perceptual narrowing (see Chapter 4), in which perception is broad at birth but narrows as a function of experience. To illustrate, infants who hear both English and Japanese can distinguish between the speech sounds /r/ and /l/. These two sounds are phonemic in English, as seen for word pairs such as *rag* and *lag*, but not in Japanese, and indeed, Japanese adults have difficulty distinguishing between them. Yet, Japanese 6- to 12-month-old infants have no problem detecting the difference (Tsushima et al., 1994). Similarly, 6- to 8-month-old English-learning infants can distinguish among sounds that are phonemic in Hindi but not in English but lose the ability to do so by the end of their first year, when they show a pattern of phoneme detection more specific to English (Werker & Tees, 1984).

✓ CHECK YOUR UNDERSTANDING 6.1

1. Describe changes over development in infants' ability to discriminate among phonemes in languages other than their own.

Identifying the Phonemes that Comprise Words

LEARNING OBJECTIVE 6.2 Describe how infants learn to build "words" from phonemes.

Languages of the world differ in the phonemes that they contain and in how they combine phonemes into words. **Phonotactics** refers to the permissible sequences of sounds that exist in a language. For example, in English, the word "ball" is composed of the phonemes /b/, /a/, and /l/, a combination of sounds that is

phonotactics The permissible structure of syllables, groups of consonants, and sequences of vowels in a language permissible. And so, before an infant can learn the meaning of the word "ball," or of any word for that matter, the infant must figure out which phonemes belong together as a word, and which are unrelated. For example, in the sentence "The apple is on the table," the infant must figure out that the syllables *ap* and *ple* (which each contain 2 phonemes that form the syllable) belong together to form a single word, whereas the syllables *the* and *ap* do not. Word learning would not proceed if infants were unable to solve this segmenting problem because people tend to run words together without pausing. Thus, the phonemes of a language represent pieces of a puzzle that infants must assemble into a complete picture—a "word." How do infants solve the puzzle of which sounds go together to form specific words? Statistical learning is key.

Infants' ability to perceive and track regularities (patterns) in language—what researchers refer to as **statistical learning**—allows infants to identify candidate "words" in speech streams (Aslin, 2017). In 1996, Jenny Saffran showed that well before infants can talk, they can detect statistical patterns among neighboring speech sounds, the building blocks to learning language (Saffran, Aslin, & Newport, 1996).

To illustrate, Saffran familiarized 8-month-old infants with 2 minutes of a continuous speech stream of syllables—such as *bidakupadotigolabubidaku*—that contained no pauses or other cues to "word" boundaries. Some syllables always occurred next to one another (such as the syllables of "bi-da") and others rarely or never co-occurred (such as "ti-ku") (**FIGURE 6.4**). After two minutes of exposure, infants were presented with familiar "words," such as the co-occurring combination of "bi-da," and novel "nonwords," such as "ti-ku." Infants could influence how long each of the stimuli pairs were presented by attending to a blinking light. Infants fixated on the blinking light longer for novel "nonwords" than for familiar "words." Infants' novelty preference suggested that they were aware of the statistical likelihoods of syllable co-occurrence.

And so, returning to the real-life example of "apple," with continued exposure to the word, infants will come to detect the high likelihood of *ap* being paired with *ple*, just as they will come to learn that "theap" is not a word, because the syllable *the* precedes many other syllables, not just *ap*. Later in the chapter you will see that infants rely on statistical regularities to learn which words refer to which objects and events in the world and the rules around combining words into simple sentences.

✓ CHECK YOUR UNDERSTANDING 6.2

 1. How might a researcher determine when babies have learned to build "words" from phonemes?

tokibu gikoba gopila tipolu tokibu
gopila tipolu tokibu gikoba gopila
gikoba tokibu gopila tipolu gikoba
tipolu gikoba tipolu gopila tipolu
tokibu gopila tipolu tokibu gopila
tipolu tokibu gopila gikoba tipolu
tokibu gopila gikoba tipolu gikoba
tipolu gikoba tipolu tokibu gikoba
gopila tipolu gikoba tokibu gopila

FIGURE 6.4 A statistical learning study. Saffran, Aslin, and Newport (1996) familiarized 8-month-old infants with 2 minutes of a continuous speech stream of syllables that lacked pauses or other cues to "word" boundaries. Some syllables always co-occurred; others rarely co-occurred. Note that combinations of syllables highlighted in the same color always co-occurred (such as "go-pia-la" in green and "to-ki-bu" in red). However, syllables crossing color boundaries, such as "la-ti-po" (as one of several possibilities), did not consistently co-occur. Testing showed that infants detected the statistical likelihood of "words" or syllables that belonged together.

statistical learning The ability of infants to perceive and learn regularities in language such as the speech sounds that comprise a word

Producing Sounds

LEARNING OBJECTIVE 6.3 Describe the changes in infants' vocalizations that lead to their production of first words.

Children produce many sounds over the first years of life, and gradually develop the articulatory and cognitive capabilities to pronounce words intelligibly. Infants move from crying to producing coos, then babbles, and ultimately words that contain a range of consonant and vowel combinations.

Crying

Crying is the sound that announces the newborn's entrance into the world, and it continues to be infants' primary means of communication for many months. Infants cry for a variety of reasons, including hunger and pain, which alerts others to their distress and ensures that their survival needs are met. But, all cries are not equal. Across the first year, crying changes from primarily signaling distress to increasingly being a communicative signal to get caregivers to respond in specific ways, such as when a 10-month-old extends an arm and whine-cries for a bottle that is out of reach (Gustafson & Green, 1989; Lewis, Alessandri, & Sullivan, 1990).

Coos, Babbles, and Words

Cries are not the only sounds of newborns and very young infants. Newborns produce coughs, burps, grunts, wheezes, and sucking sounds—what researchers refer to as vegetative sounds (Oller, 2000). They also produce short, quiet sounds that may be the earliest signs of communication (Oller et al., 2013). Around 2–3 months of age, infants produce vowellike vocalizations—**cooing**—such as "ahhh" and "oooo."

At around 6–7 months, infants begin to make sounds that approximate those of their language, what some people refer to as baby talk. Specifically, infants produce **canonical syllables** or **babbles**—vocalizations in which a consonant precedes or follows a vowel sound (Buder, Warlaumont, & Oller, 2013). Although infants form their first consonants at the back of the mouth (such as /k/ and /g/), babbling sounds typically involve consonants produced at the front of the mouth with the lips or front of the tongue, as in the sounds "ma," "ba," "pa," "da," and "ta." From 6 months onward, infants' range of consonants expands, although they lack consonants that are infrequent in their language (such as /v/ in English) and phonemes that are difficult to pronounce, such as the first sound of *chew* and of *juice*.

Somewhere around their first birthday, infants incorporate the same consonants and vowels they produced in babbling into their first words (Stoel-Gammon, 1998). It takes many more months, however, for them to produce the range of elements found in the adult sound system (Stoel-Gammon & Herrington, 1990). Thus, even 2- and 3-year-old children have difficulties pronouncing certain phonemes or combinations of phonemes, with around 50%–75% of what they say being intelligible to people who don't know the child. For example, young children might say "pasghetti" instead of "spaghetti," or "amblance" instead of "ambulance."

Effects of Hearing Loss

What happens if an infant has limited hearing? When hearing loss is severe, infants' vocal development lags behind hearing infants. Compared to hearing infants, infants with hearing loss display delayed canonical babbling, less frequent canonical babbling, and slower growth in their production of consonant sounds (Ertmer & Nathani Iyer, 2010; Oller & Eilers, 1988).

The lack of auditory feedback after moving the tongue and vocal tract may explain the delay in canonical babbling of infants with hearing loss (Ertmer & Nathani Iyer, 2010). For example, when infants with hearing loss make contact between the tongue and the roof of the mouth in different ways, the distinction between resulting phonemes such as "da" and "ta" is not as salient as for hearing children. However, infants with hearing loss develop a rich language system—sign language. In fact, when infants are exposed to sign language, they engage in manual babbling behaviors that resemble vocal babbling (Petitto & Marentette, 1991). Later in the chapter we return to Deaf children's use of sign language.

✓ CHECK YOUR UNDERSTANDING 6.3

1. Before they produce their first words, what types of vocalizations do infants use to communicate?
2. How do the sounds children produce (including those in their growing vocabularies) change over early development?
3. How do infants with hearing loss differ in sound production from infants without hearing loss?

cooing Vowellike, non-distress vocalizations that infants produce to communicate around two to three months of age

canonical syllables/babbles Vocalizations in which a consonant precedes or follows a vowel sound

Semantic Development: Learning Word Meaning

As infants learn words, their vocabularies grow. And, as they learn different classes of words—nouns and verbs for example—they can combine words to express new meanings. **Semantic development** refers to learning the meanings of words and word combinations.

semantic development The learning of the meanings of words and word combinations

Receptive Language

LEARNING OBJECTIVE 6.4 Define receptive language and infants' developing skills in this area prior to the production of words.

Receptive language refers to words or phrases that an infant understands. Oftentimes, infants understand words they do not yet say, perhaps because they can't yet form the sounds that comprise the word.

receptive language The ability to understand language and the meaning of words and phrases

A first step in language is to be able to identify familiar words in sentences and passages. One of the first words that infants recognize is their own name. When researchers presented 4.5-month-olds with tape recordings of their name (such as *Aaron*) and of other names with the same stress pattern (such as *Corey*) or a different stress pattern (such as *Christine*), infants attended longer to the recording of their own name (Mandel, Jusczyk, & Pisoni, 1995). Six-month-old infants turned their heads toward novel words that followed their own name ("Aaron's blicket"), but not words that followed an unfamiliar name ("Corey's blicket").

After infants can identify certain familiar words, they begin to associate those words with the correct person, object, action, and so forth, which signals a true understanding of a word's meaning. The **intermodal preferential looking paradigm**—an extension of the *preferential looking procedure* (see Chapter 4) is commonly used to test infants' understanding of words (Golinkoff et al., 1987; Golinkoff et al., 2013; Hollich et al., 2000). Researchers present infants with two images side-by-side along with a word or phrase (**FIGURE 6.5**). The word or phrase matches one of the images, and researchers measure whether the infants look to the correct image. For example, infants may see pictures of a boat and a shoe while hearing "Where's the shoe?" If the infant looks at the matching picture, researchers conclude that the infant understands the word *shoe*.

intermodal preferential looking paradigm An extension of the preferential looking procedure used to test infant receptive language, in which researchers present a word and two images side-by-side to assess if the infant looks at the image of the spoken word

Using such an approach, researchers find that infants understand their first nouns, such as some body parts and common objects and people in their everyday lives, by around 6 months of age (Bergelson & Swingley, 2012, 2015; Tincoff & Jusczyk, 1999). It takes several more months—not until between 10 and 13 months—for infants to understand non-nouns such as verbs (Bergeson & Swingley, 2013). We delve into why language learning may involve a noun-over-verb advantage in the next section.

productive vocabulary The words that an infant produces

✓ **CHECK YOUR UNDERSTANDING 6.4**

1. How might a researcher test if an infant understands specific nouns?

Productive Language

LEARNING OBJECTIVE 6.5 Identify and explain the order in which words first appear in an infant's productive vocabulary.

Productive vocabulary—the words an infant says—emerges later and increases more slowly than does receptive vocabulary. Most infants produce their first words around their first birthday, at which point their receptive vocabularies have been growing for several months (Schneider, Yurovsky, & Frank, 2015). Indeed, infants understand many more words and phrases than they

FIGURE 6.5 Intermodal preferential looking paradigm. A baby watches two images presented side-by-side—here a car and dog—and hears "Dog. Where's the dog?" If the baby looks at the dog, the examiner concludes that the infant understands the meaning of the word "dog."

produce (Fenson et al., 1994). The gap in receptive–productive language narrows by the time children are about 3 years of age, at which point they can pronounce the words in their repertoires, although receptive language continues to surpass productive language throughout life. On average, by the time children can produce 10 words, they can understand over 100 words. Note, however, that most research is based on North-American, English-speaking monolinguals.

Early Growth in Productive Vocabulary

Babbling infants sometimes repeat syllables in succession—such as saying *mamama* and *dadada*. Although parents may assume infants are saying mommy and daddy, in reality, infants are simply playing with sounds. There is little evidence that infants attach meaning to their early babbles. By about 9–10 months, infants use sounds more consistently in the presence of certain people or things, the first evidence that infants may be producing conventional words.

Which words do infants learn, and when? Interviews with parents, in which parents report on whether their infants understand and/or produce specific words from various categories (animals, foods, toys), offer insights into the composition of infants' early vocabularies (Fenson et al., 1994; Frank et al., 2017). Parental reports are useful because parents have access to information about infant language across a wider range of settings than can be observed or tested in a single study (Bornstein & Putnick, 2012).

As noted, infants say their first words at the end of the first year on average. Initially, the addition of new words in productive language is slow and effortful. By the time infants have approximately 50 words in their productive vocabularies, typically around 18 months of age, they experience a **vocabulary spurt** (Goldfield & Reznick, 1990): The rate of growth in productive vocabulary accelerates substantially, with the addition of 8–24 new words per week. How this spurt arises, however, is subject to debate. Some researchers attribute the vocabulary spurt to the increased talkativeness of children, rather than infants actually learning new words (Bloom, 2004). Others use computer simulations of learning to show that rapid word acceleration (after a period of slow word learning) occurs because children leverage their knowledge of certain words to more efficiently learn new ones, namely harder ones (McMurray, Horst, & Samuelson, 2012).

During the initial period of vocabulary growth, before children combine words into sentences, they often display **holophrastic language**, in which they use a single word to express an entire thought, such as exclaiming "Allgone!" (which infants actually treat to be one word) to communicate that "Daddy put away the toys and there are no more left!" (Braine, 1963). Then, during the second and third years, and throughout development, children continue to acquire new words at an impressive rate, allowing them to produce increasingly complex sentences.

The Words in Early Vocabularies

What words first appear in children's productive vocabularies? Infants' first words are simple nouns that refer to objects, particularly things that children can manipulate. This is true for U.S. English-speaking children (Mandler, 2006), and also for children who speak Spanish, Dutch, French, Hebrew, Italian, and Korean (Bornstein et al., 2004). The words "hi" and "bye" are also prominent in infants' early vocabularies, being among the first 10 words across hundreds of infants in the United States, Hong Kong, and Beijing (Tardif et al., 2008) **(TABLE 6.1)**. Interestingly, the first 100 words to appear in the vocabularies of infants from Germany, Denmark, Norway, England, and the United States overlap substantially (Mayor & Plunkett, 2014). Moreover, children from different language backgrounds show similar rates of growth in early vocabulary across the first and second year (Frank et al., 2021) **(FIGURE 6.6)**.

As infants expand their vocabularies over the second year, they add verbs, adjectives, adverbs, and **relational words**—words that refer to the state and

vocabulary spurt A naming explosion characterized by an accelerated rate in children's production of new words, typically occurring around 18 months of age

holophrastic language The early period of language development and vocabulary growth in which children use single words to express a complete thought

relational words Words that refer to the state and location of objects that children typically express during the second year of life (e.g., "under")

FIGURE 6.6 Vocabulary growth in the second year. Before their first birthday, children produce a small number of words. Then, during the second year of life, vocabulary growth accelerates significantly, a pattern that generalizes to all languages. (After M. Frank et al. 2019. *Variability and Consistency in Early Language Learning: The Wordbank Project.* MIT Press: Cambridge, MA.)

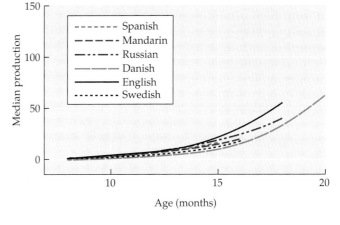

location of objects, such as *under*, *next to*, and *here* (Gopnik & Meltzoff, 1997). Relational words appear relatively later in development because they do not refer to tangible objects. Likewise, verbs are conceptually more difficult to learn than nouns because they refer to abstract relations among objects or people rather than things that share shape and other visible features (Gleitman et al., 2005; Maguire et al., 2008). For example, infants must learn that the verb "bump" can refer to many different types of objects and people who can *bump into* one another across many situations: "Bump" can refer to a dad bumping into a chair, a child bumping into another child, a ball bumping another ball, a foot bumping a bedpost, and so forth. Similarly, children do not

TABLE 6.1 ■ First Words   Twila Tardif and colleagues (2008) found that children learning different languages show similarities in their first learned words. (From T. Tardif et al. 2008. *Dev Psych* 44: 929–938.)

United States (*n* = 264)	Hong Kong (*n* = 367)	Beijing (*n* = 336)
Daddy (54)	Daddy (54)	Mommy (87)
Mommy (50)	*Aah (60)*	**Daddy (85)**
BaaBaa (33)	**Mommy (57)**	*Grandma—paternal (40)*
Bye (25)	*YumYum (36)*	*Grandpa—paternal (17)*
Hi (24)	*Sister—older (21)*	**Hello?/Wei? (14)**
UhOh (20)	**UhOh (Aiyou) (20)**	*Hit (12)*
Grr (16)	*Hit (18)*	Uncle—paternal (11)
Bottle (13)	**Hello?/Wei? (13)**	Grab/Grasp (9)
YumYum (13)	Milk (13)	*Auntie—maternal (8)*
Dog (12)	Naughty (8)	**Bye (8)**
No (12)	*Brother—older (7)*	**UhOh (Aiyou) (7)**
WoofWoof (11)	*Grandma—maternal (6)*	Ya/Wow (7)
Vroom (11)	*Grandma—paternal (6)*	*Sister—older (7)*
Kitty (10)	**Bye (5)**	**WoofWoof (7)**
Ball (10)	Bread (5)	*Brother—older (6)*
Baby (7)	*Auntie—maternal (4)*	Hug/Hold (6)
Duck (6)	*Ball (4)*	Light (4)
Cat (5)	*Grandpa—paternal (4)*	*Grandma—maternal (3)*
Ouch (5)	Car (3)	Egg (3)
Banana (3)	**WoofWoof (2)**	Vroom (3)

Note: All words were translated into English equivalents where possible. **Boldface** indicates the word is common across all three languages. *Italics* indicate commonality between two languages.

use words to refer to internal states and emotions (think, feel, happy, sad) until the second and third years of life, because such words refer to unobservable thoughts and feelings and require a higher level of cognitive understanding than does understanding of tangible objects and actions.

Fast Mapping

fast mapping Children's learning of a new word with only one or two exposures

Word learning accelerates in the second and third years. In fact, children are able to learn a new word with only one or two exposures, a phenomenon called **fast mapping**. This term was introduced in a study in which researchers presented 3-year-old children with two trays, one red and one olive-green, and asked them to "bring the chromium tray, not the red one" (Carey & Bartlett, 1978). Children, who knew what "red" meant, needed just one exposure to the spoken request to infer that the unfamiliar word "chromium" referred to the color of the olive-green tray. Fast mapping is also seen in infants 2 years of age and younger, although young toddlers have difficulties retaining the new words that they learned (Byers-Heinlein & Werker, 2009; Horst & Samuelson, 2008; Markman, Wasow, & Hansen, 2003).

Underextensions and Overextensions

referent mapping The mapping of a word to its referent in the world

underextension The mapping of words to an overly narrow class of referents (e.g., saying "truck" only to a toy truck)

overextensions The overgeneralizing of words to an overly broad class of referents (e.g., saying "dog" for all animals)

Children make mistakes in how they use words. Indeed, it is common for children to make errors in **referent mapping**—the connection of a word to its referent in the world. For example, in early language development, children may map words to an overly narrow class of referents, in what is referred to as an **underextension**. Children underextend words when they first begin to use them—for instance saying "cup" only to a sippy cup or "truck" only to a toy truck. The narrow use of words indicates that infants have not yet generalized the words to all cups or trucks.

Conversely, a bit later in development, when vocabulary expands, children sometimes produce **overextensions** by overgeneralizing words to an overly broad class of referents—such as saying "daddy" to all men or using the word "dog" to refer to animals that share the features of fur, four legs, and a tail. Overextensions are common in the speech of toddlers between the ages of 18 and 30 months, who may label objects that share features such as shape the same way (Clark, 1973; Rescorla, 1980). Children sometimes use overextensions because they forget which word is the correct one or because they don't yet have the word in their vocabulary and therefore fill the gap with a word that they know (Clarke, 1973) (**FIGURE 6.7**).

Overextension

Underextension

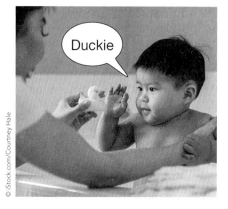

FIGURE 6.7 Overextensions and underextensions. Sometimes in early language development, infants overgeneralize a word to referents that share the same features, such as a child calling an apple "ball" (overextension). Other times, they might use a noun to name only a restricted set of objects, such as duckie to a toy duck but not a real one (underextension).

1. How do infants differ on their receptive vocabulary and productive vocabulary during the early period of word learning?
2. What is the "vocabulary spurt"?
3. What are two common errors toddlers make in the words they use to refer to things? Give one example for each type.

Syntactic Development: Putting Words Together

Human's ability to produce and understand an infinite number of sentences illustrates the remarkable human capacity for language. For instance, the sentence, "The purple dog is sitting on the velvet branch," has likely never been said, yet you understand it, as would other speakers of English. That is because you have learned the **syntax** of your language: Rules that govern the ordering of parts of speech—nouns, verbs, adjectives, adverbs, and prepositions—to form meaningful sentences. In English, word ordering follows the rule of subject–verb–object ("Joey ate pasta"), whereas the ordering of verb–subject–object ("Eat Joey pasta") is unacceptable. Moreover, as in many English sentences with a subject and object, the subject acts on the object.

syntax The set of rules that govern the ordering of parts of speech to form meaningful sentences

Understanding Sentences and Syntactic Bootstrapping

LEARNING OBJECTIVE 6.6 Offer examples of how infants infer the meaning of words from the syntax of a sentence.

Around the middle of the second year, infants are sensitive to word ordering, suggesting that they have acquired some of the regularities that characterize the grammar of their language. For example, 17-month-old English-speaking infants understand the difference between "Cookie Monster is tickling Big Bird" and "Big Bird is tickling Cookie Monster" (characters from the children's television program Sesame Street). They point or look at the picture that matches the sentence word order (Hirsh-Pasek & Golinkoff, 1996).

Infants also use the syntax of a sentence to learn unfamiliar words, what researchers call **syntactic bootstrapping**. To illustrate, researchers present infants with sentences that combine familiar and nonsense words such as, "The duck is gorping the bunny." When this is done, infants attend to pictures that match the syntax. That is, infants can figure out that "gorping" is a verb, the duck is the sentence subject, and the bunny is the recipient of the action. Similarly, 18-month-old infants look at pictures of objects when hearing "This is a gep," but look at pictures of actions when hearing "It geps" (Echols & Marti, 2004). By doing so, infants reveal that they understand how sentence frames specify which words are nouns and which are verbs. And so, infants leverage their rudimentary knowledge of grammar to learn new words from sentence structure (Gertner, Fisher, & Eisengart, 2006; Landau & Gleitman, 1985; Naigles & Swensen, 2007) (**FIGURE 6.8**).

syntactic bootstrapping The use of the syntax of a sentence to infer the meaning of unfamiliar words

✓ **CHECK YOUR UNDERSTANDING 6.6**

1. How might researchers test children's understanding of the grammatical rules in a language?
2. Toddlers are able to use syntactic structure to figure out the meaning of an unfamiliar word. What is the name of this phenomenon? Give an example.

FIGURE 6.8 Syntactic bootstrapping. The syntactic bootstrapping theory holds that children can use the syntax of a sentence to learn unfamiliar words. Thus, in the example "The duck is gorping the bunny," infants can figure out that "gorping" is a verb, that the duck is the sentence subject, and that the bunny is the object.

The Path to Producing Sentences

LEARNING OBJECTIVE 6.7 Describe the features of early-appearing "sentences" as children first begin to combine words.

By around 18–24 months of age, children begin to combine words into simple sentences. Early word combinations look remarkably similar across languages. Children typically first combine two words to make requests ("more milk") and to describe locations ("book table") and actions ("Daddy sit"), possession ("Mama dress"), and so forth (Slobin, 1970). They then combine three or more words into sentences that typically contain only the essential words such as nouns and verbs, such as "Daddy cook pasta" to indicate that "Daddy is cooking the pasta" (Bloom, 1971). Furthermore, a toddler may use the same two-word sentence "Mommy shoe" to convey a variety of meanings—to tell Mother to put on her shoe; to ask Mother to help the toddler put on the toddler's shoes; to indicate that a certain shoe belongs to Mother, and so on (Tamis-LeMonda, Baumwell, & Cristofaro, 2012; Tamis-LeMonda & Bornstein, 1994). Researchers refer to such simplified sentences as **telegraphic speech**, because they resemble the types of messages that were contained in telegrams in the early twentieth century when messages had to first be converted to Morse code (and back), a laborious process. The cost of a telegram was determined by the number of words, which caused people to keep things simple to reduce costs.

Over the course of the next few years, sentence complexity grows as children add prepositions to describe relations among nouns (such as "on," "in," and "behind"); conjunctions to bind words and clauses together (such as "to," "of," "and," and "because"); and articles to modify nouns (such as "a," and "the"). Prepositions, conjunctions, and articles are late-appearing (typically between the ages of 2 and 3) because they require children to have a foundation of nouns and verbs in their vocabularies. Furthermore, these small parts of speech are not as critical as nouns and verbs in communicating the core meaning of sentences.

Sentence complexity also expands as children add prefixes and suffixes to words to mark plurality and tense. These additions modify word meaning, with the smallest unit of meaning being a **morpheme**. For example, the word "dog" consists of the single morpheme *dog*, whereas the word "dogs" consists of two morphemes—*dog* and *s*—where the *s* signifies "more than one." As children acquire rules about morphemes, they can create words such as "eating" and "apples" and eventually generate sentences such as "Mommy likes eating red apples" (Bloom, 1993; Hoff, 2013).

✓ CHECK YOUR UNDERSTANDING 6.7

1. What are some examples of words that contain two morphemes?

Pragmatic Development: Learning Communication Norms

Language development extends well beyond learning the sounds and meaning of words and the grammatical rules of a language. Children must also learn **pragmatics**—the social conventions and norms around language and communication. For example, in many cultural communities, talking while someone else is talking or interrupting another person is considered disrespectful. The seeds of pragmatics are planted in infancy as children learn that effective communication requires turn taking and attention to nonverbal social cues.

---

telegraphic speech A form of communication used commonly by toddlers that is characterized by simple, two-word sentences (e.g., "mommy shoe")

morpheme The smallest unit of meaning in language that cannot be divided further

pragmatics The social conventions and norms around language that children must learn to effectively communicate with others

Turn Taking

LEARNING OBJECTIVE 6.8 Explain how young infants, who do not yet talk, engage in turn taking in their communications.

Infants begin to learn the rules of turn taking well before they talk. In the first weeks of life, infants and caregivers engage in **protoconversations**, a sort of give-and-take dialogue in which the talk and behaviors of parents and the smiles and coos of babies are well timed and responsive to one another (Stern, 2002). Corwyn Trevarthen described the protoconversations of mothers and their 6-week-olds during face-to-face interactions. He noted that the cycle began when the infant focused on the mother's face. The baby then expressed a feeling through movement of the body, a smile, a pleasure sound, or a cry. The mother responded by smiling and whispering back to her cooing baby. Similar to a musical duet, the mother and infant "create together a melody that becomes a coherent and satisfying narrative of feelings" (Trevarthen, 1993, p. 139). With age, infants increasingly respond to their caregivers with well-timed turn taking that paves the way for mature language forms (Beebe, 2014; Gratier et al., 2015; Kuchirko et al., 2018).

protoconversations A sort of give-and-take dialogue, including words, sounds, and gestures, in which the talk and behaviors of caregivers and the smiles and coos of infants are well timed and responsive to one another

✓ CHECK YOUR UNDERSTANDING 6.8

1. What is a "protoconversation"?

Attention to Nonverbal Social Cues

LEARNING OBJECTIVE 6.9 Describe the different types of social cues that infants attend to that help them learn the meaning of words and sentences.

It would be impossible to communicate effectively without attending to nonverbal social cues that signal *attention* (what a person is communicating about) and *intention* (a person's goals in communicating). Gestures and gaze are two social cues that signal a person's attention and intention (see Chapter 5).

Gestures

Gestures are a widespread form of human communication (McNeill, 2005). Most people cannot avoid talking with their hands or attending to the hand motions of other people to interpret social messages. In addition to the pointing and hand motions that people make on the fly, we use gestures to convey specific meanings: We twirl our index finger near our heads to say that someone is crazy, playfully hit our foreheads with our palm to ask "how in the world did I miss that?" use a thumbs-up motion to signal "way to go!" and make other creative uses of our fingers and hands to relay messages that would be inappropriate to describe in a textbook.

Like adults, infants look to others' gestures to figure out what someone is talking about, such as following a pointing finger to learn new words (Rowe, 2013). And infants often use gestures to communicate, especially before they have the words for objects and events (Namy, Campbell, & Tomasello, 2004). Elizabeth Bates and colleagues were the first to describe two main types of infant gestures: protoimperatives and protodeclaratives. (Bates, Camaioni, & Volterra, 1976). **Protoimperatives** are requests for objects or requests for someone to help with an action, as when an infant holds up a cup to ask for more milk. **Protodeclaratives** are attempts to get someone to pay attention to an object or event, as when an infant points to or holds up an object to establish joint attention toward the object (**FIGURE 6.9**).

protoimperatives Gestures used to request something (e.g., holding out a hand to ask for more food)

protodeclaratives Gestures such as pointing that are used to get someone to attend to an object or event

Gaze

Gaze, like pointing, can be a powerful social signal. Imagine that you are faced with three novel objects and must learn their labels from an adult tutor. If the

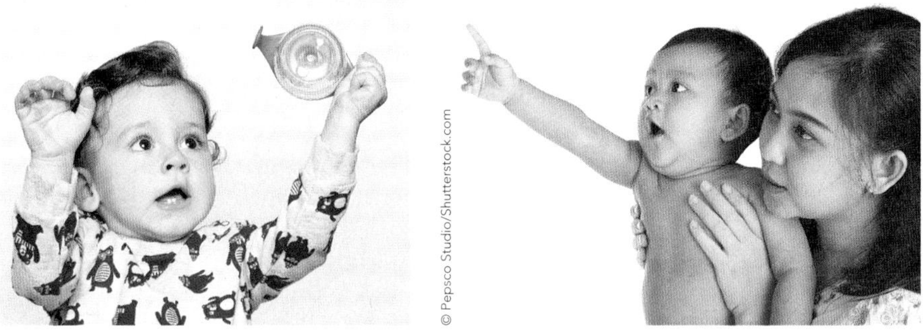

(A)   (B)

FIGURE 6.9 Gesturing in infancy. (A) Protoimperatives are requests for objects or requests for someone to help with an action, as when an infant holds up a cup to ask for a refill of milk or juice. (B) Protodeclaratives are attempts to get someone to pay attention to an object or event, as when an infant points to something to get a parent or other caregiver to look too.

tutor recited the names of the objects—"blix," "komi," "mattly"—without any indication of which name belonged to which object, your learning would be no better than chance. If, instead, the tutor looked to each object as it was labeled, you would quickly learn their names. Infants are able to exploit gaze to figure out the target of people's attention. Dare Baldwin (1993) presented 18-month-olds with two novel objects and then concealed them in separate containers. The experimenter picked up one container, looked inside, and said "There's a modi in here," without the toddler seeing which object was in the container. The adult then removed the two objects from their respective containers and handed them to the toddlers. When the examiner then asked for the modi, the toddlers picked up the object that had been inside the container the experimenter had looked at and labeled, indicating that they had used eye gaze to figure out which object was the modi.

✓ **CHECK YOUR UNDERSTANDING 6.9**

1. How do infants and toddlers use gestures and gaze to understand a person's attention and intention?

FIGURE 6.10 Quine's dilemma. Quine's dilemma illustrates the enormous challenge infants face in figuring out the meaning of words. For example, if someone exclaims "Gavagai!" as a rabbit hops past, the word could refer to anything relating to the rabbit or even its surrounding: the rabbit's color or size, different parts of the rabbit (e.g., the ears or tail), the rabbit's movement, the direction the rabbit is headed, or the ground beneath the rabbit.

■ *Explaining Language Development*

In the book *Word and Object* (1960), philosopher Willard Quine proposed a hypothetical scenario. Suppose you find yourself in a foreign country where you do not speak a word of the language. Suddenly, someone exclaims "Gavagai!" as a rabbit hops past (**FIGURE 6.10**). In trying to figure out the meaning of "gavagai," you might consider several possibilities. "Gavagai" could refer to the rabbit itself, the rabbit's color or size, the rabbit's movement or direction, or the ground beneath the rabbit. Quine's dilemma illustrates the enormous challenge infants face in learning how to figure out what words mean given that words can refer to any one of countless objects and events. Yet, somehow, infants and toddlers figure out which words belong to which things in the world and additionally figure out the many grammatical rules of their language. How do children master the feat of language? The sections that follow review explanations for language development from nativist, connectionist, dynamic systems, and sociocultural perspectives.

Nativist Accounts of Language Development

B.F. Skinner claimed that children learn to associate words with their meanings through imitation, reinforcement, and punishment in his 1957 book *Verbal Behavior*. For example, a parent may say "bottle" while holding out a bottle, which creates an association between the word and the child's visual experience. The child then imitates the word bottle in the future. In contrast, if the child says "spoon" when reaching for a fork, the parent will correct the child by saying "no, that's a fork," reducing the likelihood that the child will use the wrong word in the future. However, nativist theorists (originating with the writings of Noam Chomsky) criticized Skinner's theory as overly simplistic and not backed by evidence on how parents talk to children. According to nativists, parents are unlikely to correct their children's errors in grammar and, even when they do, children are unlikely to pay attention (e.g.,Valian, 1999). Imagine, for example, that a child says "We goed zoo." Parents are more likely to respond to the accuracy of the statement—"Yes we did!"—rather than correct the child's grammar—"We WENT to the zoo, not GOED to the zoo." And so, children learn grammar even in the absence of corrective feedback. Moreover, nativists claim that innate cognitive biases help children learn words by ensuring that children make certain accurate assumptions about what words mean. Furthermore, Deaf children invent language systems even in the absence of exposure to sign language. Such observations reinforced nativist claims that language development is possible because of innately human capacities.

Universal Grammar and the LAD

LEARNING OBJECTIVE 6.10 Describe Chomsky's LAD hypothesis.

Noam Chomsky, a U.S. linguist and cognitive psychologist, was Skinner's fiercest critic. Chomsky wrote a scathing review of Skinner's book (Chomsky, 1959) *Verbal Behavior*, arguing that Skinner's theory failed to account for the complexity of human language acquisition. Chomsky believed that children are innately endowed to learn language and would never be able to acquire language from imitation and feedback alone. Chomsky cited children's creative use of language as evidence for his theory. Children construct sentences that they have never heard, and their abilities to generate an infinite number of sentences must be biologically endowed.

And so, Chomsky argued that humans have an innate component in the brain—a **language acquisition device** (**LAD**)—that explains the rapid acquisition of language. The LAD contains a **universal grammar**, a set of highly abstract grammatical rules shared by all human languages. Chomsky further proposed that rules stipulated by the universal grammar are turned on or off based on a child's native language. For example, one such rule pertains to whether sentence subjects must be expressed. English sentences require a sentence subject, as in "*He* goes to school." In Spanish and Italian, however, the subject can be omitted—the subject is implied in the sentence, "Goes to school." When English-speaking children hear sentences that consistently contain a subject, the LAD turns on the mandatory subject rule.

language acquisition device (LAD) An innate component in the brain claimed to explain the rapid acquisition of language in Noam Chomsky's nativist theory of language

universal grammar An innate set of abstract grammatical rules shared by all human languages in Noam Chomsky's nativist theory of language

✓ CHECK YOUR UNDERSTANDING 6.10

1. Chomsky believed that there exists an innate language acquisition device (LAD), which enables children to rapidly learn language. What evidence supports Chomsky's LAD theory?

Cognitive Biases

LEARNING OBJECTIVE 6.11 Explain two cognitive biases thought to help children figure out which words map to which objects or events in the world.

Beyond Chomsky's LAD, nativist theorists believe that innate cognitive biases help children figure out which words map to which objects or events in the world. That is, human learners are thought to bring specialized knowledge to learning a language, which biases them toward certain hypotheses (Culbertson, 2013). One such bias, **mutual exclusivity,** is the expectation that an entity has only one name (Woodward & Markman, 1998). Mutual exclusivity was first demonstrated in a study of 3-year-olds who were presented with pairs of objects and asked by the examiner to "Show me the blicket" (Markman & Wachtel, 1988). The authors speculated that if children assumed that objects only have one name, they should reliably hand over the unfamiliar object in response to hearing the unfamiliar name. Indeed, this was the case. Children inferred the novel word "blicket" was the name of the object that did not have a label. Even very young word learners use mutual exclusivity to learn words (Byers-Heinlein & Werker, 2009; Woodward, Markman, & Fitzsimmons, 1994).

Relatedly, the **whole object assumption** bias is the expectation that a novel word refers to a whole object, rather than to a part, action, or characteristic of the object (Markman, 1989; Woodward & Markman, 1998). Applying this idea to the Quine's dilemma introduced earlier, if children hear a novel word "gavagai," they would likely infer that it means rabbit, rather than the rabbit's fur or color (see Figure 6.10).

✓ CHECK YOUR UNDERSTANDING 6.11

1. What are two cognitive biases?

Deaf Children and Sign Language

LEARNING OBJECTIVE 6.12 Explain how studies of deaf children support the claim that language is prewired.

Studies of deaf children present a unique test of the claim that children are "prewired" to acquire language. If deaf children with little exposure to sign language manage to learn how to communicate anyway, factors other than environmental inputs must drive their language.

American Sign Language (ASL) is the official language used by the Deaf population in the United States. When children and adults sign, they combine manual gestures according to a set of rules that are as complex as those for spoken language (Anderson & Reilly, 2002; Klima, Bellugi, & Poizner, 1988). However, when a deaf child is born to hearing parents, he or she is unlikely to be exposed to a signed language right away. Unfortunately, the majority of the approximately 500,000 deaf children in the United States have limited access to signed language because over 90% are born to hearing parents who do not know ASL (Anderson & Reilly, 2002; NIDCD, 2016).

Is there evidence that deaf children, despite their limited access to ASL, are prewired to learn language? Support for the innateness of language comes from studies showing that deaf children with no or limited access to sign language acquire language milestones at roughly the same time as hearing children, and spontaneously "invent" a language system of their own.

Language Learning Milestones of Deaf Children

Deaf children learn American Sign Language in a manner similar to how hearing children learn spoken languages. For instance, the sequence and developmental timeline by which deaf toddlers learn emotion words, cognitive verbs,

---

mutual exclusivity A type of cognitive bias that supports word learning in which children expect an entity to have only one name

whole object assumption A type of cognitive bias that supports word learning in which children assume that a novel word refers to a whole object, rather than parts or features of the object

American Sign Language (ASL) A form of sign language used by the Deaf population in the United States and Canada in which people communicate through the hands and face and "WH" questions ("What's that?" "Why?") mirror that of children learning English, and the first 35 signs in ASL are remarkably similar to children's first words in English—referring to foods ("bottle"), greetings ("hi," "bye"), and articles of clothing ("shoe," "hat") (Anderson & Reilly, 2002).

Deaf Children's Spontaneous Signing

Deaf children invent or generate their own language system if they are not taught sign language. Developmental scientist Susan Goldin-Meadow demonstrated children's natural tendencies toward language learning in a set of landmark studies (Goldin-Meadow, 1998; Goldin-Meadow & Singer, 2003; Goldin-Meadow, 2009). Goldin-Meadow pointed out that parents used to be advised to talk rather than sign to their deaf children in an effort to encourage the use of oral language, and that this practice kept children from learning sign language. Although parents believed that talking to their deaf children would prompt spoken language, it did not. But many of these children invented other ways to communicate.

FIGURE 6.11 Homesigning.   A deaf child learns to communicate.

Deaf children with some minimal exposure to signing developed their own unique signing systems, referred to as **homesign** (Goldin-Meadow, 2009) (**FIGURE 6.11**). Homesign languages exhibit a consistent grammatical structure of nouns and verbs and follow consistent rules for combining parts of speech into sentences. Moreover, homesigning arises in different cultural and language backgrounds: Psychologist Ann Senghas and colleagues studied a group of deaf students in Nicaragua who attended school where only Spanish was used, and thus had no exposure to sign language. Nonetheless, students overcame barriers to language learning: Through interactions with other deaf students at the school, they spontaneously created a lexically and grammatically rich Nicaraguan sign language (e.g., Rissman et al., 2020; Senghas, Senghas, & Pyers, 2005). Together, research on homesign and Nicaraguan sign language suggests that deaf children create complex language systems that do not depend on language input.

homesign A unique signing communication system with consistent rules for combining parts of speech into sentences developed by deaf children with minimal exposure to sign language

✓ CHECK YOUR UNDERSTANDING 6.12

1. Describe findings on deaf children's use of "homesign."

Critical Periods and the Case of Genie

LEARNING OBJECTIVE 6.13 Explain how the case of Genie offered intriguing insights into the question of critical periods in language development.

In 1967, psycholinguist Eric Lenneberg (1967) further advanced the nativist idea that language acquisition, and in particular grammar, is biologically endowed. He proposed a "critical period hypothesis" that suggested a critical time window for acquiring language (see Chapter 2). According to Lenneberg, children must acquire language in early childhood, especially before puberty, when the brain's organization is being established. After this critical period, language learning becomes much more difficult. Lenneberg supported his theory with studies of brain lesions, speech lateralization, and interventions with children with Down syndrome, all of which showed that language acquisition or recovery after puberty was unlikely or poor.

Perhaps the most intriguing yet controversial support for a biologically determined critical period in language development comes from cases of children raised in social isolation—that is, without human contact. The argument goes something like this: If language acquisition is innately time bound, then children who are deprived of normal language input for most of their early childhood should be unable to acquire language regardless of the richness of

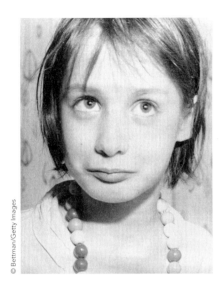

© Bettman/Getty Images

FIGURE 6.12 Nature versus nurture and the case of Genie. In the 1970s, the discovery of Genie, a severely isolated and abused 13-year-old young girl, offered the scientific community the rare opportunity to test the roles of nature and nurture in language learning, including Lenneberg's idea of a critical period in language learning. Genie could barely stand or walk, and couldn't talk. She was also severely malnourished and underdeveloped and had the cognitive capacities of a 1-year-old.

subsequent input. Conversely, if previously isolated children can be taught language skills after the critical period has passed, greater importance can be accorded to "nurture" than to "nature" with respect to language learning.

One case that captured the attention of developmental scientists was that of Genie, a severely isolated and abused young girl whom social workers discovered in 1970 when she was 13 years old (**FIGURE 6.12**). Genie had been locked in a small room for over a decade, where she spent most of her life naked and strapped to a potty-chair. Her mother, older brother, and father rarely spoke to her, and if she made noise her father beat her or barked and growled at her. When Genie was found, she could hardly stand or walk, was severely malnourished and underdeveloped, could not talk, and had the cognitive capacities of a 1-year-old.

Genie offered the scientific community the rare opportunity to test Lenneberg's critical period theory and pit nature against nurture: With enriched language experiences, could Genie overcome her isolation and deprivation of language even though the critical period had passed? A team of psychologists and language experts dedicated several years to the rehabilitation and study of Genie, documenting her progress in detail with funding from the federal government.

With continual language input and training, Genie quickly added new words to her vocabulary and then moved to combining words into two- and then three-word sentences, much like typically developing children learn language. However, she did not advance beyond this relatively immature stage of language development and was unable to construct grammatically complex and meaningful sentences (Goldin-Meadow, 1978). Genie's inability to achieve full command of language, despite intensive environmental support, was interpreted as evidence for Lenneberg's theory of a critical period in language acquisition.

Nonetheless, evidence from Genie's case is shaky and ultimately inconclusive. In addition to being deprived of language, Genie was abused and emotionally neglected for most of her childhood. Additionally, researchers could not determine if she suffered from pre-existing cognitive deficits that interfered with her ability to fully acquire language. Today, debates about critical periods in language development continue, with promising research coming from studies of bilingual children and adults. Studies of dual-language-learning children suggest that a person's ultimate level of language proficiency may depend on the age of exposure to a second language—with advantages seen for exposure at younger versus older ages, likely because of timelines for the establishment of certain networks in the developing brain (Hernandez & Li, 2007: National Academy of Sciences, Engineering, and Medicine, 2017).

✓ CHECK YOUR UNDERSTANDING 6.13

1. Why was the case of Genie limited in its ability to provide scientific evidence for a critical period in learning language?

Connectionist and Dynamic Systems Theory

In contrast with Chomsky's claim that a language acquisition device in the brain orchestrates language development, connectionist and dynamic systems theorists claim that experience with language drives brain development. The two closely related accounts of language claim that children build their knowledge of language from the "bottom up," by extracting meaning out of everyday language inputs. According to dynamic systems theorists, claims of innate cognitive biases fail to explain how children overcome biases such as mutual exclusivity to understand that the same thing can have many names and many descriptors (e.g., understanding that the same object can be called a dog, animal, golden retriever, etc.) (McMurray et al., 2012).

Connectionist Theory

LEARNING OBJECTIVE 6.14 Explain how experience with language leads to a complex neural network of connections among words.

The **connectionist theory** stresses the building of neural networks in the brain that allow children to draw connections/association among various related concepts. Such theories view the brain as a maze of complex neural connections that enable people to recognize and respond to all types of sensory information, language included (Rogers & McClelland, 2004). Experience with language builds and strengthens connections among words and related concepts (Arias-Trejo & Plunkett, 2013) **(FIGURE 6.13)**. As a child plays with "balls" across different contexts and hears the word "ball" repeatedly, the phonological representation or sounds that comprise the word "ball" form connections to other words such as "round," "bounce," "play," "basketball," "baseball," "soccer," and so forth. Furthermore, already in the second year of life, infants establish connections among words within semantic categories, such as animal words, food words, clothing words, and so forth. With age, language connections become increasingly complex and hierarchical (such as knowing that a "poodle" is a "dog" and a "dog" is an "animal"). As one node of the complex network is activated (for instance, the word "dog"), activation spreads to other nodes (for instance, to other "animals" such as "cat"), leading to faster access to related information (Styles & Plunkett, 2009). Words are also connected to one another based on their phonological or sound similarities, as seen when infants

connectionist theory A theory that stresses the building of neural networks in the brain that allow children to draw connections and associations among various related concepts

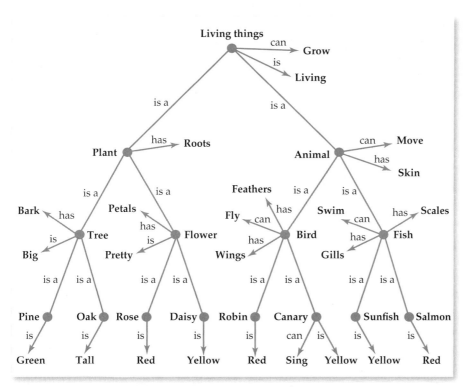

FIGURE 6.13 Connectionist theory. Connectionist theory focuses on neural networks. The complex neural connections that infants build up from experiences enable them to recognize and respond to all types of information in the world, language included. In explaining language development, connectionist theories highlight how experience with language builds and strengthens connections among words and concepts. (From D. E. Rumelhart. 1990. In *An Introduction to Neural and Electronic Networks* [S. F. Zornetzer et al., Eds.], pp. 405–420. Academic Press: San Diego, CA.)

computer simulations Models of neural networks used to test connectionist theories of the brain and language development through feeding a large body of language input into a computer with little preprogrammed knowledge

quickly identify a picture of the word "**b**all" after hearing the word "**b**anana" (Chow, Davies, & Plunkett, 2017).

Researchers often use **computer simulations** to test connectionist theories by building models of neural networks that can modify themselves over the course of learning. In these simulations, a large body of language input, similar to the language that children hear, is fed into a computer that has little preprogrammed grammatical knowledge. Despite the absence of a specific program for language, the computer is able to learn from the language input. Moreover, the computer displays a pattern of learning that is remarkably similar to that of young children (Colunga & Smith, 2005; Rumelhart & McClelland, 1987). For instance, computers can learn to distinguish words for solid objects from words for nonsolid objects based on grammatical regularities in language. To illustrate, English words like "a" and "the" (as in "a cup" or "the book") indicate a solid object, whereas words like "some" and "much" (as in "some milk" or "much sand") indicate nonsolid objects. Young children use these regularities to learn new words, for instance, pointing to a solid object when asked, "Give me the dax," but pointing to a nonsolid object when asked "Give me some dax." When a computer was trained with noun phrases that referred to solid or nonsolid objects, it then used the regularities of the syntax information to learn new solid and nonsolid object names, just like children (Colunga & Smith, 2005).

✓ CHECK YOUR UNDERSTANDING 6.14

1. Give an example of how computer simulations can be used to test connectionist theories of language development.

Dynamic Systems Theory

LEARNING OBJECTIVE 6.15 Demonstrate how children use basic statistical learning processes to learn the sounds, words, and sentences of their language(s).

The dynamic systems theory is a special type of connectionist theory that also emphasizes the building and strengthening of language networks. Two key principles are foundational to dynamic systems theory—the child as active participant in the world and the child as able to detect environmental regularities.

The Active Child

Dynamic systems theorists attend closely to how children's experiences contribute to language development. Children actively participate in their worlds, and their interactions with people, places, and objects result in learning (Hockema & Smith, 2009; Smith & Thelen, 2003). In terms of language learning specifically, children's experiences help them connect words to referents. For instance, the child hears the word "apple" and at the same time sees, tastes, and smells an apple and experiences the smoothness of its surface. The child's actions of touching and eating the apple solidify associations between the experience of an apple and the word "apple."

Detecting Regularities in the Input

Dynamic systems research shows that a child learns language by detecting regularities in spoken language, as documented by developmental scientist Jenny Saffran and colleagues and reviewed earlier in the chapter (see Figure 6.4). By detecting regularities in language inputs, infants can "build" language through a bottom-up, emergent process. For example, speakers use consistent rules to combine syllables into words, such as when the syllables *ap-ple* go together every time an apple is in view. Regularities also occur when spoken words regularly occur in the presence of specific objects and events. For example, the likelihood of hearing the word "apple" in the presence of the fruit apple is greater than the likelihood of hearing "orange" or "banana" in the presence of the fruit apple. Through the process of statistical learning, toddlers come to associate the word "apple" with the fruit apple. Indeed, when researchers paired words with pictures of objects and manipulated how often words were paired with specific objects, 12- and 14-month-old infants reliably figured out that the words for objects were those that co-occurred at high probabilities (Smith & Yu, 2008).

Similarly, words in a sentence are ordered with regularity, such as placing subjects before verbs in English, and even intonation patterns show regularities that offer cues to a speaker's intentions. For example, English speakers use rising intonation or stress patterns to ask a yes-no question by raising pitch toward the end of the sentence. As infants experience such regularities on a daily basis, language develops further.

✓ CHECK YOUR UNDERSTANDING 6.15

1. What do dynamic systems accounts of language mean by the claim that children build their knowledge of language from the "bottom up"? What do they mean when they say language learning is "emergent"?

2. Dynamic system theorists assert that children learn language by detecting language regularities through statistical learning. What is statistical learning? Provide an example study showing how children map words to their associated objects.

Sociocultural Theory

Social interactions provide infants with valuable cues about word meaning. Lev Vygotsky (see Chapter 1), was one of the most prominent theorists to write about social influences on children's learning. Vygotsky asserted that social interactions are the source from which thought and language arise. He claimed that children internalize new information about the world, including language, through interactions with other people. And caregivers support language learning by intuitively adjusting their input to meet the child's level of knowledge (Vygotsky, 1986).

Scaffolding

LEARNING OBJECTIVE 6.16 Describe how scaffolding works in the domain of language learning.

The term **scaffolding** (Bruner, 1977) refers to the rich variety of strategies that adults use to guide and support child learning and raise children to higher levels of thinking. To illustrate the concept of scaffolding, consider a toddler who is looking at a book about vehicles with a parent. The book contains pictures of cars, trucks, airplanes, and buses, with most of the words (with the exception of "car") being unknown to the child. What might the parent do to support the child's learning of an unfamiliar vehicle name? The parent might call the child's name to engage the child's attention, and then say the word "truck" just as the child looks at the picture of a truck. The parent may repeat the word several times while pointing to the truck to ensure the child connects the word to the picture, and perhaps point to the child's toy truck to ensure the child remains attentive to the truck specifically (Zukow-Goldring, 1996)

scaffolding The rich variety of strategies that adults use to guide children to higher levels of thinking than children can achieve on their own

✓ CHECK YOUR UNDERSTANDING 6.16

1. What is scaffolding?

2. What is one way a caregiver can use scaffolding to support a child's language development?

FIGURE 6.14 Learning language from media. Studies show that infants have problems learning language from television and other media. However, when infants remotely interact with family members through videochats, they are able to understand and communicate about the things they or others are doing. This suggests that infants require a responsive social partner for learning to occur.

Can Infants Learn Language from Screens?

LEARNING OBJECTIVE 6.17 Explain why infants may be unable to learn language from screens.

Perhaps the strongest evidence for the importance of social interactions in early language development comes from studies that contrast infant learning from live tutors with learning from television or audio recordings. Parents often place their infants in front of screens or other technology in the belief that their babies can learn from these media. Unfortunately, this belief is misguided—infants learn best from interacting with other people and are unlikely to learn any language from technology.

Developmental scientist Patricia Kuhl demonstrated the limits of technology in infant language learning in a study of 9-month-old English-speaking infants whom she exposed to the phonetic contrasts of Mandarin (Kuhl, Tsao, & Liu, 2003). Kuhl placed infants in one of three conditions: watching a live Mandarin speaker, watching a televised Mandarin speaker, or listening to an audio-recording of a Mandarin speaker. The infants in the live social condition learned the phonetic contrasts of Mandarin, whereas those in the televised and audio conditions did not.

Why do infants have problems learning language from television and other screens? Perhaps they have more difficulty understanding 2D images than 3D real-life images? In a study of verb learning, toddlers aged 24–30 months were exposed to novel verbs through (a) live, in-person interactions, (b) live interactions over videochat, in which infants interacted with a person they saw on a screen, and (c) a prerecorded video of an adult, who could not respond to infants' behaviors. Infants learned the novel verbs from live interactions *and* live videochat, but not from the prerecorded videos (Roseberry, Hirsh-Pasek, & Golinkoff, 2014). Thus, it may not be a "screen" or 2D image that makes learning language difficult for toddlers, but rather the lack of a responsive social partner. Indeed, despite the challenges of communicating through video, when infants remotely interact with grandparents and parents, for the most part, social interactions are rich and infants are able to understand and communicate about the things they and others are doing (McClure et al., 2017) (**FIGURE 6.14**).

✓ CHECK YOUR UNDERSTANDING 6.17

1. Why do infants have problems learning language from television?

Contexts of Language Development

Language learning is universal. All typically developing infants learn language, even though infants from around the globe experience profoundly different language environments. However, children achieve different levels of proficiency in their language skills, with many contextual forces—family, socioeconomic status, childcare, dual-language learning settings, and cultural beliefs and practices—explaining those variations.

Family Context of Language Development

LEARNING OBJECTIVE 6.18 Identify the features of caregiver input that support infant language learning.

As discussed previously in this chapter, sociocultural theorists such as Vygotsky emphasize the role of social partners in infant language learning.

Notably, parents and other primary caregivers are typically infants' first language partners. Several features of caregiver language input support infant language learning, including the use of a special type of speech register (that many people refer to as "baby talk"), the amount and diversity of language directed to infants, responsiveness to infant behaviors, and the use of physical cues to help infants understand language (Tamis-LeMonda & Bornstein, 2015; Tamis-LeMonda, Kuchirko, & Suh, 2018).

Infant-Directed Speech

Imagine how you might talk to a baby compared to an adult. Your manner of speaking likely will be quite different, even if you were unaware of what you were doing. Indeed, adults talk to infants in a way that is special and unique—what is referred to as **infant-directed speech** (Golinkoff et al., 2015). Researchers document the characteristics of infant-directed speech by video recording or audio recording infant-caregiver interactions and later coding features of language input to infants. Several classic studies, with replications over the years, find that infant-directed speech contains:

- High pitch, exaggerated intonation, and slow tempo with frequent pauses.

- Frequent changes in the amplitude (loudness) of speech to highlight specific words. For example, when mothers showed toys to their 1-year-olds, labels were likely to be the loudest word in the sentence (Messer, 1981).

- Short and grammatically simple utterances that contain repetition ("See the bunny? That's a bunny. What a soft bunny!") (Phillips, 1973).

- Talk that is concrete and focused on the here and now rather than past or future (Phillips, 1973; Snow et al., 1976).

Infant-directed speech has been observed in parents from around the globe and is similar across language communities (Grieser & Kuhl, 1988; Kelkar, 1964). Even children as young as 4 years of age talk differently to babies than they do to older children and adults (Weppelman et al., 2003).

But does infant-directed speech help infants learn language? The answer is yes. Several benefits of infant-directed speech help explain why (Golinkoff et al., 2015). As a start, infant-directed speech captures infants' attention: Babies prefer to listen to infant-directed speech than to adult-directed speech (Fernald, 1991). In fact, infant-directed speech, but not adult-directed speech, leads to activation in the prefrontal cortex of infants ages 4 to 13 months (Naoi et al., 2012).

Additionally, the exaggerated intonation and rhythm of infant-directed speech provides cues about the message and helps infants discriminate among speech sounds (Soderstrom et al., 2008). When adults exaggerate vowels in their speech—what scientists refer to as **vowel hyperarticulation**—they facilitate infants' ability to phonologically distinguish new words and recognize repetition of familiar words (Hartman, Ratner, & Newman, 2017). In fact, infants at risk for **dyslexia**—a disorder involving difficulty in learning to read or interpret words, letters, and other symbols—showed poor sensitivity to the sounds of language, which related to their mothers' infrequent use of hyperarticulation when talking to them (Kalashnikova, Goswami, & Burnham, 2018).

Notably, the strong attraction that infants show toward infant-directed speech extends to singing as well, perhaps because infants are drawn to the exaggerated sounds, changes in amplitude and pitch, and predictable rhythms that characterize song. Five-month old infants attended more to songs they had heard their mothers sing compared to unfamiliar songs

infant-directed speech The unique way that adults talk to infants by using exaggerated intonation, frequent changes to the amplitude of speech, short and grammatically simple utterances, and talk that is concrete

vowel hyperarticulation An exaggeration of vowels in speech that facilitates infants' ability to phonologically distinguish new words and understand repetition of familiar words

dyslexia A set of disorders involving challenges in learning to read or interpret words, letters, or other symbols

amount of language The total number or quantity of words

lexical diversity The number of different words in speech

(Mehr, Song, & Spelke, 2016), and 14-month-olds acted positively toward an unfamiliar woman who sang a mother's song compared to an unfamiliar song (Cirelli & Trehub, 2018). During the second year of life, infants begin to sing familiar songs with impressive accuracy in pitch range and contour (Gudmundsdottir & Trehub, 2018).

Amount and Diversity of Speech to Infants

Infants benefit from hearing a lot of language and from hearing a lot of different words. **Amount of language** refers to the number of words and **lexical diversity** refers to the number of *different* words in speech. Language amount and lexical diversity are typically assessed through naturalistic observations (see Chapter 1). Researchers audio- or video-record parent–infant interactions to obtain information on the language directed to infants, sometimes with cameras and other times by placing a small device in infants' pocket called the "Language Environment Analysis" (LENA) device that generates day-long recordings and rough statistics of the language directed to infants (Cristia et al., 2020). Researchers may then transcribe the records and upload them into the Child Language Exchange System (CHILDES) (MacWhinney, 2016; MacWhinney & Snow, 1984), a massive database of language transcripts from scientists in the field. The transcripts can be analyzed with a software program that generates the total number of words (word tokens) and number of different words (word types) spoken by infant and parent. Many researchers have documented the importance of parent word tokens and/or types and child vocabulary size, rate of vocabulary growth, and pragmatic skills (e.g., Hart & Risley, 1995; Hoff, 2006; Huttenlocher et al., 1991; Song, Spier, & Tamis-LeMonda, 2014). And, although most research is based on mothers' language to children, fathers have as much influence on children's language development as do mothers (Pancsofar & Vernon-Feagans, 2006; Rowe, Leech, & Cabrera, 2017; Tamis-LeMonda, et al., 2012).

Contingent Responsiveness

The in-the-moment timing of language inputs to infants matters. Infants are always doing something: They look at people and objects, explore their environments, vocalize, express emotions, gesture, and move about.

contingent responsiveness Caregivers' prompt, attuned responses (typically verbal) to infant behaviors

In what is referred to as **contingent responsiveness**, parents and other caregivers respond to infants' everyday behaviors with prompt and attuned behaviors (Bornstein et al., 2008). For example, a parent may label a giraffe in response to the infant's pointing to a giraffe or imitate the words an infant attempts to say.

Parental contingent responsiveness helps infants connect words to objects and events in the world because infants hear the names for things as they attend to objects and events in their environments (Tamis-LeMonda, Kuchirko, & Tafuro, 2013) (**FIGURE 6.15**). Indeed, parental contingent responsiveness predicts:

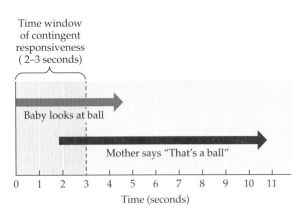

FIGURE 6.15 Contingent responsiveness. Contingent responsiveness is characterized by language input to the infant that occurs promptly within a few seconds of infant behavior (contiguity) and matches in content what the infant is doing (contingency). In this timeline example, the infant looks at a ball and the adult says, "That's a ball" within this brief time window.

- *Quality of babbling in infants*. Infants produce more sophisticated babble sounds, compared to cries and other sounds, when their vocalizations receive a response than when their vocalizations are ignored (Gros-Louis & Miller, 2018; Warlaumont et al., 2014).

- *Sizes of infants' vocabularies*. Infants whose mothers frequently respond to their interests, vocalizations, and play have larger receptive and productive vocabularies in their second year than do infants with mothers who are less responsive (Tamis-LeMonda, Bornstein, & Baumwell, 2001).

- *Timing of language milestones.* Infants who experience high contingent responsiveness attain important language milestones sooner in development than do infants who experience low contingent responsiveness. In a longitudinal study across infants' first two years, infants of high-responsive mothers (90th percentile) achieved language milestones such as first words, vocabulary spurt, and simple grammatical sentences 4–6 months earlier than did those of low-responsive mothers (10th percentile) (Tamis-LeMonda, Bornstein, & Baumwell, 2001).

Of course, most studies on parent contingent responsiveness and infant language development are correlational, leaving open the possibility that the confounding variable of heredity explains parent-child associations. Perhaps, parents' genetic makeup influences their responsiveness, and genetics, not responsiveness, explains infant language skill. Several lines of evidence refute a solely genetic explanation. Parental responsiveness toward adopted children relates to the language skills of the children, who do not share the genetic makeup with parents (Stams, Juffer, & van Ijzendoorn, 2002). Furthermore, experimental manipulations and interventions that increase responsiveness in parents result in enhanced quality of infant babbling and language skills in infants and toddlers (Goldstein, King, & West, 2003; Goldstein & Schwade, 2008; Landry et al., 2008).

Physical Cues to Meaning

Adults often exaggerate their movements when interacting with infants, which scientists refer to as **motionese** or infant-directed action. Mothers were asked to demonstrate how to use novel objects, such as a neon green "twisty," to either their baby or another adult. Mothers' demonstrations to infants were simpler, more interactive, enthusiastic, repetitive, and included a greater range of motion (Brand, Baldwin, & Ashburn, 2002). Similarly, when caregivers sign to deaf infants they display slow, highly repetitive, and exaggerated movements (Masataka, 1992). Exaggerated movements, in turn, capture infant attention and offer cues to a word's meaning (e.g., Koterba & Iverson, 2009).

When adults gesture by pointing or moving things while naming them, they likewise facilitate infant language learning (Namy, Vallas, & Knight-Schwarz, 2008; Rader & Zukow-Goldring, 2010; Rowe & Goldin-Meadow, 2009). Gestures to objects and events foster joint attention and help infants draw connections between words and their referents (Gogate, Bahrick, & Watson, 2000; Tomasello & Farrar, 1986; Yu, Ballard, & Aslin, 2005).

Routines around Literacy

Through the course of a day, infants transition in and out of activities such as grooming, play, and feeding, which affects the language they hear (Hoff, 2010; Soderstrom & Wittebolle, 2013; Tamis-LeMonda et al., 2019). Certain activities, particularly book reading and storytelling, are especially conducive to early language development (**FIGURE 6.16**). Why might this be?

Book reading offers children the opportunity to learn words that they might otherwise not encounter in daily life: animals on farms and zoos, customs and foods of other countries, different types of vehicles, and so on. Mothers of 18- to 29-month-olds used more words, more different words, and grammatically more complex language during book reading than during mealtime, dressing,

motionese Infant-directed action that is characterized by exaggerated and repetitive motions by caregivers (such as sweeping arm movements) as they communicate with infants

FIGURE 6.16 Bedtime stories. Book reading is an activity that supports infant language learning, in part because infants are exposed to novel words and concepts they might not experience in everyday life.

referential language Statements or questions about objects or events that support infants' vocabulary development

regulatory language Directives that regulate infants' attention and actions that often contain many pronouns (e.g., "Put it here")

and toy play (Hoff-Ginsberg, 1991). Relatedly, book sharing expands infants' vocabulary because it frequently contains **referential language**—statements or questions about objects and events in the world ("There are two cookies"). Referential language promotes word learning more than does **regulatory language**—directives that regulate infant attention and action and contain many pronouns ("Look here," "Put it there") (Tamis-LeMonda et al., 2012).

Furthermore, book sharing arms children with pragmatic skills around turn taking. During reading cycles, mothers ask questions, await replies, and provide feedback. As a result, infants quickly learn the turn-taking rules of literacy (Heath, 1982). Over time, children become skilled at their role as listener, wait for adult cues about when to speak, and acknowledge and answer the questions posed to them.

Other literacy activities that promote language development include storytelling, reminiscing about past events, playing rhyming games and singing songs, playing counting games, teaching the ABCs, and visiting libraries and museums (Rodriguez et al., 2008). Such activities provide infants with opportunities to hear a lot of language and talk about past, present, and future events.

✓ CHECK YOUR UNDERSTANDING 6.18

1. In which ways does infant-directed speech differ from adult-directed speech?
2. If you were holding a class for parents, what might you encourage them to do to promote their infants' language development?
3. Why might interactions around book reading support infant language development?

Socioeconomic Context of Language Development

LEARNING OBJECTIVE 6.19 Describe evidence showing how poverty and parent education might affect infants' language exposure and in turn vocabulary development.

Poverty and low parental education may impede infants' language development, largely through the quantity and quality of language that parents direct to children. Children who are reared in poverty hear substantially less language, less varied language, and less grammatically complex language than their peers from families with more resources (Hart & Risely, 1995; Hoff, 2006; Huttenlocher et al., 2010; Golinkoff et al., 2018).

In a seminal longitudinal study of parent-child talk in families in Kansas, Betty Hart and Todd Risley (1995) video recorded interactions between parents and children at home when infants were between 10 and 36 months of age. They compared language inputs to children in low-income families, working-class families, and professional families. Based on their observations, Hart and Risley estimated that children living in poverty heard 30 million fewer words in the first three years of life than children from professional families, a phenomenon that has come to be known as the "30-Million Word Gap" (**FIGURE 6.17**). Moreover, family income differences in language input affected children's vocabulary sizes at age 3 years: Children from professional, working-class, and low-income families averaged about 1,100 words, 750 words, and just above 500 words in their vocabularies, respectively.

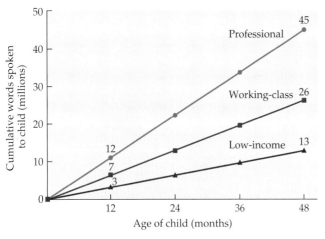

FIGURE 6.17 SES and vocabulary growth, 10 months to 3 years. Hart and Risley estimated that children living in low-income families heard 30 million fewer words in the first three years of life than children from professional families, a phenomenon that has come to be known as the "30-Million Word Gap." The graph shows the cumulative number of words adults direct to infants at home by parents of different income levels. (After B. Hart and T. R. Risley. 1995. *Meaningful Differences in the Everyday Experience of Young American Children.* Paul H. Brookes Publishing: Baltimore, MD.)

Hart and Risley's work has sparked many initiatives and programs at the federal, state, and local levels that aim to support children's language environments and development, such as Too Small to Fail and Race to the Top. However, claims around the 30-million word gap have also ignited intense debate. Some researchers argue that Hart and Risley may have disproportionately underestimated the number of words to which infants from low-income homes are exposed, especially because most definitions of "language input" exclude infants' exposure to bystander talk that is not aimed at them directly (such as talk that occurs among adults or among siblings) (Sperry, Sperry, & Miller, 2019).

✓ CHECK YOUR UNDERSTANDING 6.19
   1. Describe Hart and Risley's study and the impact of their findings.
   2. Critique Hart and Risley's claim of a 30-million word gap.

Childcare Context of Language Development

LEARNING OBJECTIVE 6.20 Explain why quality of childcare might matter for early language development.

With more mothers now in the workforce in the United States than decades ago, more children attend day-care centers from an early age. Many families also rely on friends, relatives, neighbors, and home-based care (where an adult will watch several children at once in the adult's home). During the hours that children are not with their parents, high-quality care, characterized by sensitive and stimulating caregiving, is essential for children's language development (NICHD ECCRN, 2006).

Unfortunately, whereas some children receive high-quality childcare, other children experience poor-quality care that can impede their language development. Day-care centers that serve low-income communities are often characterized by larger child-caregiver ratios and low caregiver warmth, sensitivity, and responsiveness (Barnett, Votruba-Drzal, Dearing, & Carolan, 2017). Thus, although childcare can bolster the language development of children from low-income households, whether it does so depends greatly on the quality of care. Government-funded programs such as Early Head Start (EHS), which serve infants ages 0–3 years from low-income homes, offer high-quality care that promotes children's language development while also aiming to enhance parenting sensitivity and engagement in cognitively stimulating interactions with their infants (Love et al., 2005).

✓ CHECK YOUR UNDERSTANDING 6.20
   1. What are some limitations of early childcare conditions in
      low-income communities?

Multilingual Context of Language Development

LEARNING OBJECTIVE 6.21 Demonstrate how language learning can be both similar and different in children exposed to multiple languages versus one language.

Learning more than one language is a natural human experience (Kroll & McClain, 2013). Roughly two-thirds of the world's population speak two or more languages (Dörnyei & Csizér, 2002). Although people often have the misconception that learning two languages may interfere with overall language development, this is not at all the case. Infants have the capacity to learn two or more languages and to ultimately become proficient in each (National Academy of Sciences, Engineering, and Medicine, 2017).

Moreover, global patterns of heightened immigration mean that a substantial percentage of children throughout the world will be raised in a country

dual-language learners (DLLs)
Children who learn two languages because they are exposed to a native language at home that differs from the language of the community

simultaneous bilinguals Children exposed to two (or more) languages from birth or before 3 years of age

where the host language differs from that of their parents. As one example, in the United States, first- and second-generation immigrant children are the fastest growing sectors of the U.S. child population, with the latest waves of immigrants coming from Central and Latin America and Asia (Radford, 2019). A vast majority are **dual-language learners** (**DLLs**), who are exposed to two languages that differ in their sounds, words, grammar, and pragmatics, and will need to acquire the skills to select and use the appropriate language in the appropriate context. Does the language development of dual-language learning children resemble that of children exposed to a single language? Or, does learning two systems of phonology, vocabulary, and grammar alter the early language trajectories of children?

Similar Language Processes

Children who hear two languages from infancy—referred to as **simultaneous bilinguals**—follow a course of development in each language that mirrors that of monolingual children (De Houwer, 2009). Infants raised in households where two languages are spoken discriminate the sounds of their languages and learn that words refer to things in the world at ages comparable to monolinguals (Sebastian-Galles, 2010). For example, despite the perceptual challenge associated with hearing two languages with different sound systems, dual-language learning infants have the same abilities as infants learning one language to discriminate among phonemes or speech sounds. Infants 4.5 months old in Catalan-Spanish bilingual homes did not differ in their discrimination skills from infants in Catalan or Spanish monolingual homes (Bosch & Sebastian-Galles, 2001). Infants learning two languages also demonstrate similarities to monolingual infants in the words they learn and in the associations between their vocabulary growth and grammatical skill (Conboy & Thal, 2006; Marchman, Martínez-Sussmann, & Dale, 2004; Parra, Hoff, & Core, 2011). When the *total* vocabularies of DLLs are considered—meaning researchers sum the words a child says in both languages—the overall rate of vocabulary growth matches the rate seen in monolingual children (Hoff et al., 2012). But, because DLLs are learning two languages, their vocabulary growth in *each* language is slower than that of children learning one language (Carlo et al., 2004; McCabe et al., 2013).

Of course, the speech that parents direct to their infants facilitates the language development of DLLs, just as is the case for monolinguals (McCabe et al., 2013). The amount and quality of language exposure in each language reliably predicts the language skills of DLLs (De Houwer, 2009; Hoff et al., 2012; Place & Hoff, 2011; Song et al., 2012). In a study of Spanish-English dual-language learning toddlers—the largest subgroup of DLLs in the United States—the proportion of input children received in Spanish related to their vocabulary size in Spanish, and reciprocally, the proportion of input they received in English corresponded to their English vocabulary size (Hoff et al., 2012; Pearson, Fernandez, & Oller, 1993; Place & Hoff, 2011). Additionally, high-quality language inputs in each of the two languages—including diversity of language and responsive language—results in enhanced child language outcomes in each of the languages. Simultaneous bilinguals who were exposed to two languages before age 3 had excellent, monolingual-like reading performance and phonological awareness at school entry in *both* languages, whereas "late bilinguals" who were exposed to a second language between 3 and 6 years of age showed delays in these areas in their new language (Kovelman, Baker, & Petitto, 2008).

What factors heighten the chances that a dual-language learning child will be exposed to high-quality language input? The language proficiency of the speakers who talk to children is key. DLLs' skills in their second language, in this case English, related to the proportion of their input that is provided by *native speakers* of the language—beyond the amount of language exposure alone (Place & Hoff, 2011). As a result, the use of a second language in the home predicts a child's development of that language, but only when caregivers are skilled in the second language (Paradis et al., 2011). When immigrant caregivers attempt to use English, but struggle with the language themselves, they may not be helping their children learn the language, despite their good intentions (Hammer et al., 2009).

Unique Language Processes

Dual-language learning infants display some intriguing differences from monolingual infants in their early language journey. These differences arise because dual-language learning infants must develop strategies to figure out the different sounds, words, and pragmatics of two languages.

In the area of phonological development, DLLs are less sensitive to mispronunciations of words compared to monolinguals, as shown in a study with Spanish and Catalan monolingual toddlers and Catalan-Spanish bilinguals (Sebastián-Gallés & Bosch, 2009). Researchers presented 18-month-olds with side-by-side pictures and a sentence that included a word that was in one of the pictures. The word was either correctly pronounced or mispronounced. Monolinguals looked less to the corresponding picture when it contained a mispronunciation of the word in their native language compared to when the word was correctly pronounced. However, Catalan-Spanish bilinguals tested in Catalan did not respond differently to correctly pronounced versus mispronounced words.

DLLs may fail to detect word mispronunciations because they need a bit more time to learn the phonological properties of their languages compared to monolingual children, who learn a single sound system. Furthermore, DLLs may hear foreign-accented speech if, for example, one of their parents is not a native speaker of one of the two languages (Sebastian-Galles et al., 2009). Exposure to two distinct sound systems and exposure to mispronounced words may expand the range of what DLLs consider to be an acceptable pronunciation of a word. When monolingual English-speaking toddlers were familiarized with a Spanish-speaking adult who spoke English with an accent, they accepted alternative pronunciations of words. In essence, the toddlers expanded the acceptable boundaries of speech sounds to accommodate the speaker's accent (Seidl, Onishi, & Cristia, 2014).

In the area of semantic development, infants exposed to more than one language develop strategies for learning the meaning of words that differ from those observed in monolingual infants. This makes sense because DLLs must learn that objects and events in the world can have at least two names, one in each language. For example, when researchers exposed monolingual and dual-language learning 9-month-old infants to the *same* word repeated twice, infants looked longer to a display that contained two *different* objects than a display that contained two of the same object—as though they found it odd that the same word could refer to different objects. However, when infants heard two *different* words, and were presented with a display of the *same* object, DLLs and monolingual infants responded differently. DLLs did not look longer at the display of the same object, as though they did not find it odd that an object could have two names. Conversely, when monolinguals heard two different words for the same object, they looked longer, as though they were surprised to hear two different words referring to a single object (Byers-Heinlein, 2014) (**FIGURE 6.18**).

In terms of pragmatics, dual-language learning infants quickly learn to attend to social cues that signal the language being spoken (Sebastian et al.,

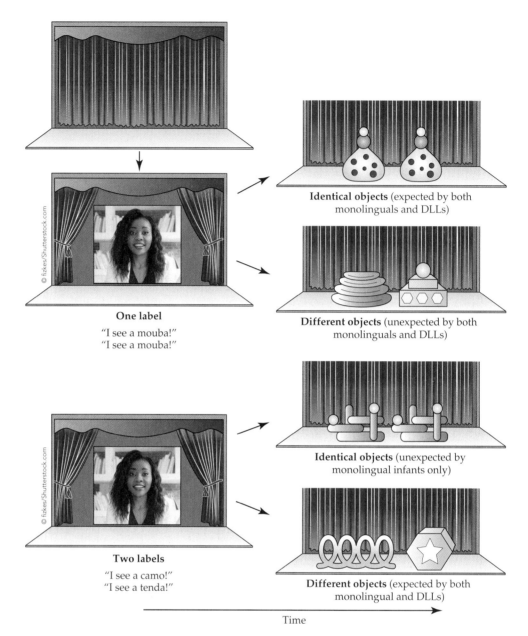

One label

"I see a mouba!"
"I see a mouba!"

Identical objects (expected by both monolinguals and DLLs)

Different objects (unexpected by both monolinguals and DLLs)

Two labels

"I see a camo!"
"I see a tenda!"

Identical objects (unexpected by monolingual infants only)

Different objects (expected by both monolingual and DLLs)

Time

FIGURE 6.18 DLLs versus monolinguals in early language learning. Dual-language learning infants display some intriguing differences from monolingual infants in their early language journey. In one study, infants raised in monolingual versus bilingual contexts showed different patterns of attention when words and objects were presented together. Monolinguals expected a word to be associated with a single object. Thus, they looked more at the unexpected event where a single identical label referred to two different objects, and they looked more at the unexpected event when two different labels referred to the same object. Dual-language learning infants did not show the same expectations in looking based on one-to-one mapping. (After K. Byers-Heinlein. 2014. *Lang Learn* 64: 184–201.)

2012). Spanish-Catalan DLLs and Spanish or Catalan monolingual infants were presented with silent video recordings of French-English bilingual speakers and tested on their ability to detect a language change. That is, the speaker switched from French to English or vice versa, but the sound was turned off. To detect a change then, the infant would have to closely attend to the moving mouth of the speaker. Monolingual infants failed to detect the shift from English to French, whereas dual-language learning infants succeeded, suggesting that the dual-language learning experience heightens babies' attention to mouth movements that signal which language is being spoken.

✓ CHECK YOUR UNDERSTANDING 6.21

1. Why might a dual-language learning infant be less sensitive to the mispronunciation of words than a monolingual infant?
2. How does exposure to more than one language affect infants' attention to people who are talking? Describe a study that shows this effect.

Cultural Context of Language Development

LEARNING OBJECTIVE 6.22 Discuss ways that cultural context shapes how caregivers interact and communicate with their infants.

There is a saying that a fish only knows that it lives in water when it is outside on the riverbank. In the same vein, people often make assumptions about what is normal in the development of children based on their personal experiences. Consider for example infant-directed speech, as reviewed earlier. Notably, the high-pitched, exaggerated speech that caregivers direct to infants in many studied cultural communities is completely nonexistent in others. Indeed, families from different cultural communities embrace unique practices in adapting to the circumstances of their lives (Henrich, Heine, & Norenzayan, 2010). That is, there is no "correct" way to raise infants, but rather parents are the experts on how to meet the needs and expectations of their families and communities. And so, typically developing children everywhere learn language under dramatically different circumstances. Thus, a full understanding of infant language development requires understanding the experiences of children from different cultures.

Communicative Accommodation

In the 1970s and 1980s, cultural anthropologists Bambi Schieffelin and Elinor Ochs observed middle-class, European American families and their infants (under age 2 years); Kaluli families in Papua New Guinea; and Samoan families in the South Pacific (Ochs & Schieffelin, 1984; Schieffelin & Ochs, 1986). Parents of the three cultures differed in their **communicative accommodation**—that is, in how much they adjusted their own behaviors to help young infants communicate their needs and interests.

Middle-class, European American caregivers tended to engage in **child-centered communications**, in which parents interacted with their babies about whatever interested the child (such as toys for play), used child-directed speech, and treated infants like conversational partners. For example, U.S. parents frequently interpreted their infants' coos, babbles, smiles, laughs, and so forth as intentional: If the baby waved an arm and said "bababa," the parent might say "Oh! You want your bottle?" as though the baby was intentionally requesting a bottle. Kaluli and Samoan adults tended toward highly **situation-centered communications**, which placed the burden on infants to figure out what was going on around them (**FIGURE 6.19**). Adults primarily talked with one another and were not concerned with engaging their infants in conversations. For example, Kaluli and Samoan mothers did not attempt to interpret infants' utterances and did not simplify their language to infants. The Kaluli parents rarely addressed their infants directly until the infants said the words corresponding to "mother" and "breast"

communicative accommodation The adjustments that caregivers make to language and behaviors when communicating with young infants

child-centered communications Adult-child interactions in which caregivers interact with infants based on the interest of infants and treat infants like conversational partners, often using infant-directed speech

situation-centered communications Interactions in which adults predominantly interact with one another, leaving infants and young children to figure out what is being talked about

FIGURE 6.19 Child-centered versus situation-centered communications. According to Schieffelin and Ochs, children in cultures that emphasize situation-centered interactions do not experience the high adult involvement in talk and child-centered interactions seen in typically studied U.S. samples.

(Schieffelin, 1979). In the Samoan community, although young infants were addressed through songs or rhythmic vocalizations in soft, high pitch for the first few months, as soon as infants could move, adults dropped their pitch to resemble adult-to-adult interactions and voice quality became loud and sharp.

The striking differences in how parents talk to their infants raises some intriguing questions about how much language support is actually needed for children to learn language. When developmental scientist Alejandria Cristia and colleagues observed Tsimane forager-horticulturalists of lowland Bolivia, they found that adults spoke to infants and children younger than 4 years of age less than 1 minute a day (Cristia, Dupoux, Gurven & Stieglitz, 2019). So how then do infants learn language in such contexts?

Learning language by listening in on other people's conversations may be a fundamental way that children acquire language. In many communities across the globe, children figure out what is being talked about by observing the talk of those around them (e.g., Akhtar, 2005; Rogoff et al., 2003). Indeed, even 2-year-olds can learn new words by listening to the conversations of other people. For example, experimenters talked to one another and labeled a novel object while toddlers were busy at play. The toddlers were then tested on whether they learned the object label even though the adults did not talk directly to them. Even the busy 2-year-olds learned the word from the overheard conversation, which aligns with many common cultural settings in which toddlers learn language by observing third-party interactions (Akhtar, 2005). And, learning language by listening in to conversations of other people is not uncommon. Children everywhere are exposed to the talk of others, and certainly learn a lot through this indirect path (Sperry, Sperry, & Miller, 2019). However, in the period of infancy at least, adult-infant direct interactions facilitate the process of learning language (Golinkoff et al., 2018).

Channels of Communication

Cultural communities differ in the extent to which they rely on language, touch, gaze, and gestures to communicate with babies—what can be referred to as channels of communication.

Anthropologist Robert LeVine and colleagues documented striking cultural differences in the channels of communication of Gusii mothers of Kenya and middle-income, educated mothers from Boston, Massachusetts (LeVine et al., 1994) (**FIGURE 6.20**). Until the 1960s, the Gusii were subsistence farmers, with each household being responsible for growing its own food for survival. Young children were expected to assist with household chores, cultivation, and food-processing so that mothers could spend time in the fields. Family sizes and maternal workloads were large. In this cultural context, adults valued and expected child obedience so that mothers could complete their chores. Consequently, mothers aimed to prevent crying in their infants by feeding, holding, and lulling infants to sleep. Gusii mothers spent nearly all their time in physical contact with their 3- to 10-month-old babies, holding them 93%–100% of the observation time. In contrast, mothers in Boston held their 3–4-month-olds 54% of the observation time; rates of holding decreased to about 25% by the time babies were 9–10 months old. The Gusii mothers' holding of infants effectively calmed babies: Gusii infants cried less than half as often as Bostonian infants.

In contrast, in Boston—a cultural community that places high value on young children's language and literacy skills—mothers spent two

FIGURE 6.20 Channels of communication. Anthropologist Robert LeVine and colleagues found enormous cultural differences in the ways that mothers of the Gusii of Kenya interacted with their infants compared to middle-income, educated mothers from Boston, Massachusetts. Mothers of the Gusii were nearly always holding their 3- to 10-month-old babies, whereas mothers in Boston held their 3- to 4-month-olds 54% of the observation time. Conversely, mothers in Boston talked with their infants much more frequently than did mothers of the Gusii.

to three times as much time talking with their infants than did mothers of the Gusii (LeVine et al., 1994). Bostonian mothers responded to their 9- to 10-month-old infants' vocalizations four times as often as did the Gusii mothers. As a result, Bostonian babies vocalized more often than did Gusii babies, likely due to the high feedback their babbling elicited from their mothers.

Parents also differ in their use of gaze with infants, perhaps because of different views about how babies learn. In the LeVine study, for example, Bostonian mothers spent over 40% of the observation time looking at their infants, whereas Gusii mothers did so a mere 1%–12% of interaction time, leaving their infants to watch other people and events around them. Similarly, Kaluli mothers (in Papua New Guinea; discussed in the previous section) did not look into their infants' eyes but instead faced their babies outward to watch other people and learn from their observations (Ochs & Schieffelin, 1984).

Finally, parents and infants from different cultural communities vary in their use of gestures to communicate. In Italy, a gesture-rich culture, toddlers have a greater repertoire of gestures—particularly gestures that represent objects and actions such as bringing an empty hand to the lips to signal a cup or eating—than do toddlers in the United States (Iverson et al., 2008). Italian infants' large gestural vocabularies may compensate for their relatively fewer spoken words. Similarly, U.S. immigrant Mexican mothers frequently use gestures with their infants, who in turn are skilled at imitating the gestures and actions of others (Tamis-LeMonda et al., 2012). The frequent use of gestures aligns with expectations in some cultural communities that children learn by observing other people's manual actions rather than through direct verbal instruction (Rogoff, 2003).

✓ CHECK YOUR UNDERSTANDING 6.22

1. Contrast child-centered communications with situation-centered communications. Give examples of each.
2. What are key channels of communication, and how might the use of these channels differ across cultural communities?

Developmental Cascades

A cascade model of development highlights how skills in one domain of development can reverberate across many other domains concurrently and over time—a principle that is vividly illustrated in studies of early language development. Early skills in language are building blocks for development in other areas, ranging from cognitive skill to school readiness and success.

Language Development Influences Cognitive Development

Language is integral to how people think. As a result, growth in language goes hand in hand with developments in cognition. Here, we illustrate how language development affects thought, processing speed, and executive control.

Language Development and Thought

As you learned, a fundamental task of learning language is to figure out which words map to which objects or events in the environment. Typically, researchers view the referent-mapping challenge as one in which the infant already has a concept and must learn the name for that concept. For instance, an infant might know what a bottle is based on being fed a bottle daily. Armed with this understanding, the infant then learns to associate the word "bottle" with the concept of bottle.

However, an infant's initial concepts may differ substantially from adult concepts, leading to inaccurate word-to-world connections (Nelson, 2009). For example, as you saw earlier, an infant's concept of "dog" may refer to the child's pet only (an underextension) or to all four-legged animals (an overextension). At some point though, children must learn the adult concept for the word "dog," if they are to use the word correctly. As children learn the word "dog" with all its correct features, their concept of "dog" changes. Children will begin to look at four-legged animals much more closely to determine if the animal is a dog or something else. Language has therefore shaped how the child thinks about the broad category of dogs.

The **principle of linguistic relativity**, or the *Whorfian hypothesis*, after the American linguist Benjamin Whorf, refers to the idea that language can affect thinking. The "weak" version of this hypothesis states that language *influences* thought, and a stronger version says that language *determines* thought. For example, Whorf made the claim—albeit one that has since been challenged—that the large number of words for snow in the Alaskan Inuit language influenced Inuits' ability to perceive fine-grained distinctions in snow that English speakers could not.

Indeed, different words and meanings of a language can shape people's concepts, as illustrated in cross-language analyses. For example, infants who learn English attend to spatial information differently than do infants who learn Korean because of the words in their language (Choi & Bowerman, 1991; Choi et al., 1999). Words in English distinguish between containment ("put *in*") and support ("put *on*") whereas Korean language distinguishes between "tight-fit" relations and "loose-fit" relations, regardless of containment or support. A tight-fit relation, expressed by the word *kkita*, may, for example, characterize a peg in a hole in a pegboard or a ring on a finger since both the peg and ring fit snugly. A loose-fit relation (expressed by various words), may, for example, characterize a block in a large box or coins in a backpack (**FIGURE 6.21**).

principle of linguistic relativity The hypothesis that language can affect thinking, also known as the Whorfian hypothesis

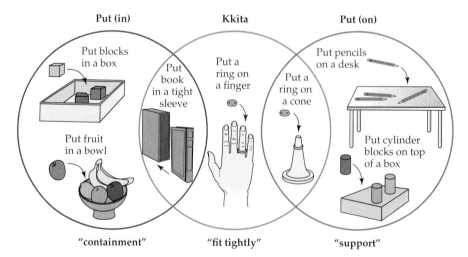

Put (in)	Kkita	Put (on)
Put blocks in a box	Put book in a tight sleeve	Put a ring on a finger	Put a ring on a cone	Put pencils on a desk
Put fruit in a bowl				Put cylinder blocks on top of a box
"containment"	"fit tightly"	"support"

FIGURE 6.21 Tight-fit versus loose-fit Korean language concepts. Words in English distinguish the concepts of containment ("put in") and support ("put on"), without consideration of the fit between objects. In contrast, the Korean language distinguishes between "tight-fit" relations and "loose-fit" relations, without consideration of whether those relations refer to containment or support. (After L. Mcdonough et al. 2003. *Cog Psychol* 46: 229–259.)

Do infants' experiences hearing words that refer to these fit relations make Korean-speaking but not English-speaking infants more attentive to spatial concepts around such fit relations? To test this possibility, researchers presented English and Korean infants 18–23 months of age with two scenes that were accompanied by sentences with and without the target word ("in" for the first group; "kkita" for the second). Sometimes, the matching scene was the same for the two languages, for example, a scene of books being placed in tight box sleeves, which depicted both containment ("in" for English) and tight fit ("kkita" for Korean). Other times, a scene matched only "in" or only "kkita." Infants from the two language groups looked longer at the scenes that matched the spatial concepts of their languages. For example, Korean infants attended to tight or loose fits, whereas English-speaking infants did not. Thus, the language to which infants were exposed shaped their attention to specific details of scenes.

Language Development and Processing Speed

Developmental scientist Anne Fernald and colleagues have shown that vocabulary size can influence how quickly infants process information about words. In their experiments, infants face a monitor that displays pictures to the left and right of center. Researchers assess how quickly infants look at the picture that matches a familiar word they hear, such as looking at a dog rather than a picture of a cup when hearing the word "dog."

Two-year-old English-speaking infants with larger vocabulary sizes showed quicker reaction times to matched pictures than did infants with smaller vocabularies. And, even when infants from both groups knew the word, those with larger vocabularies remained faster at processing known words (Fernald, Perfors, & Marchman, 2006). The connection between processing speed and vocabulary size also holds for bilingual Spanish-English infants, who respond quicker to words in each language when their vocabularies in that language are large (Marchman, Fernald, & Hurtado, 2010). Moreover, infants who hear more talk at home have larger vocabularies and faster processing speeds than do infants exposed to less talk (Weisleder & Fernald, 2013).

Language Development and Executive Control

Recall from Chapter 5 that executive control refers to a child's ability to inhibit a dominant response in favor of an appropriate or newly required response. One way to test executive control in infants is to assess their ability to switch from one rule to another. For example, infants might be taught to feed a small baby doll with a small spoon and a big doll with a large spoon. After a few trials, the experimenter instructs the infants to feed the big doll with the small spoon and the small baby doll with the large spoon. To succeed in the rule switch, an infant must inhibit the dominant response of feeding the dolls with spoons that match their size to feeding them with spoons that don't match. Some infants have a lot of trouble with this; others do a bit better.

Does language affect the types of switching tasks that require executive functioning? Dual-language learning infants—who are exposed to two languages from birth—have been shown to display stronger executive functioning skills than monolingual infants. That's because they have practice switching attention between different languages with different sounds, words, and rules. For example, an eye-tracking study of 7-month-olds assessed infants' control over the direction of their looking. Infants in the study either were raised with two languages from birth or were monolingual. Both groups of infants were trained to respond to a speech or visual cue to anticipate a reward by looking to one side of a screen. The reward was then switched to the opposite side, requiring infants to shift their attention to that side. Only the dual-language learning infants succeeded in redirecting their looks to cues signaling an opposite-side reward (Kovács & Mehler, 2009).

In another study, 2-year-olds were shown pictures of large and small fruits, with the smaller fruit embedded in a different, larger fruit, such as a small banana inside a large apple (Poulin-Dubois et al., 2011). The children were asked to point to each of the small fruits, which required inhibiting a point to the large fruit that dominated the page. Dual-language learning children outperformed monolingual children, again indicating an early dual-language advantage in executive control. Thus, dual-language exposure specifically supported children's ability to inhibit a conflicting cognitive response that was governed by a rule. Notably, however, the connection from DLL status to executive functioning is not that straightforward. Several studies have failed to replicate the connection, perhaps because the relative skills infants show in each language will determine how well they do (National Academy of Sciences, Engineering, and Medicine, 2017).

Language Development Influences Later School Success

Oftentimes, people wonder whether language development early in life matters in the long run. A common assumption is that early delays will diminish over time—that is, children who lag behind their peers will naturally catch up, barring any developmental disabilities.

Such assumptions, as you have learned by now, are largely inaccurate, because they ignore the cascading influences of development. Infants and toddlers who experience rich language input continue to improve in their language skills and have an edge in school readiness and academic performance for years to come, whereas those who experience relatively poor input may learn fewer words and have a tough time catching up throughout the school years (Golinkoff et al., 2018; Huttenlocher et al., 2010; Pan et al., 2005; Rowe, 2012). For example, in the studies of language and processing speed just described, infants' vocabulary and grammatical skills at 2 years of age predicted their scores on standardized tests of language, cognition, and working memory at 8 years of age (Fernald et al., 2008). Furthermore, returning to the work of Hart and Risley (1995), children's productive vocabularies at 3 years of age predicted their academic success at 9 years of age, with disparities in the language skills of 3-year-olds from low-income, working-class, and professional families widening with age.

Notably, positive language experiences and development may help buffer the risks of poverty. Consider a longitudinal study of nearly 2000 children from low-income households across the United States, in which researchers assessed children's home learning experiences—including the sensitivity and cognitive stimulation of mothers' language to children, various routines around learning such as bookreading, and children's access to learning materials such as books and puzzles—when children were approximately 1 year, 2 years, and 3 years of age and right before they entered prekindergarten. At pre-K, researchers assessed children on receptive vocabulary; literacy skills, such as knowing letters; and math skills, such as knowing numbers. Although children were from low-income households, and therefore at risk of language delays, 70% of children who experienced consistently rich learning environments across the first years of life performed at or above national norms, whereas only 7% of children with impoverished learning environments performed in this range (Rodriguez & Tamis-LeMonda, 2011). Even more striking was the finding that early learning experiences cascaded to children's language, reading, and math skills in fifth grade (Tamis-LeMonda et al., 2019).

Why do early language experiences and development matter in the long run? As we have emphasized, cascading influences occur at multiple levels.

Children's language skills in the first years of life feed into a rich network of knowledge that establishes a springboard for later learning. As children's vocabularies grow, so does knowledge and so does the brain, in line with experience dependent processes (see Chapter 2). Indeed, across several studies, infants' brain responses in the first year of life (largely based on event-related potentials or ERPs) predicted language skills between 14 and 30 months, language and preliteracy skills at 5 years, and language and cognitive ability at 8 years (e.g., Deniz, Richards, & Kuhl, 2013; Kuhl, 2009; Kuhl, 2010; Rivera-Gaxiola et al., 2005; Molfese, 2000).

■ CLOSING THOUGHTS

Language Development is Much More than Language

Just as Helen Keller's world was forever changed once she entered the world of language, so too is the world of children forever changed as they come to learn the sounds, words, rules, and norms of their language. Language allows infants to move beyond cries and flailing arms to communicate. Language allows children to share their thoughts and feelings, initiate new relationships, develop a sense of their own identity, and become a full-fledged member of their cultural communities. Reciprocally, language opens the door to understanding what other people know, think, hope, and believe, and thus lies at the nexus of human connection.

In the upcoming chapters, we will see that language expands in its complexity, range, and depth throughout childhood and adolescence, and becomes increasingly vital to healthy cognitive, social, and emotional development. But, we will also see that as children grow in their language skills, they gradually understand that words can be used to deceive, manipulate, hurt, divide, bully, victimize, and reject others. In essence, language is a profoundly powerful tool—it can help build and foster close attachments just as easily as it can chisel away at social bonds.

The Developmentalist's Toolbox

Method	Purpose	Description
Measuring infant language learning		
Statistical learning studies	To test infants' skills in detecting regularities in language input, for example, in the co-occurrence of the speech sounds that comprise words	Infants are familiarized with a continuous stream of syllables with no pauses or cues as to word boundaries. Some syllables have high likelihoods of co-occurrence (e.g., "ba-ga" always being paired in the stream) and others have low likelihoods (e.g., "ti-ga" rarely being paired). After familiarization, infants are presented with high- and low-likelihood pairs. Greater attention to the low-likelihood pairs (novelty preference) than high-likelihood pairs (familiarity) suggests the infants extracted the regularities in speech sound pairings—a first step to identifying "words."
Computer simulations	Used to model how neural networks modify themselves over the course of learning language	Linguistic information that is typical to the experiences of children is fed into a computer that has little pre-programmed language knowledge. Researchers examine whether the computer reproduces the pattern of language learning seen in children.
Intermodal preferential looking paradigm	To assess infants' understanding of words or phrases	Infants are presented with side-by-side images as they hear a word or sentence. If the infant looks to the image that matches the stimulus, it is assumed that the infant understands the word/phrase.
Syntactic bootstrapping studies	To assess infants' understanding of syntax and ability to use that understanding to learn new words	Infants are presented with a grammatical frame that contains novel and familiar words (e.g., "The duck is gorping the bunny"). Attention to pictures that match the syntax (a duck acting on a bunny) versus those that do not indicates their understanding of syntax and ability to learn novel words from grammatical frames.
Digital recording device, such as the LENA	Used to capture extensive audio-recordings of infant and caregiver speech	A small device is placed in the infant's pocket to capture the vocalizations of the baby and the speech that is directed to the child by people in the environment. These audio recordings can be transcribed and then analyzed for various features of infant-directed speech.
The Child Language Exchange System (CHILDES)	A platform for storing and sharing transcripts of infant/toddler and parent language made from video or audio recordings. Software compatible with CHILDES generates information on infants' expressive language and language experiences	The language interactions of infants and parents are transcribed and uploaded into the CHILDES database. Specialized software generates information on the number of total words (word tokens) and number of different words (word types) spoken by infant and parent.

■ Chapter Summary

Phonological Development: Learning Speech Sounds

- The four key components of a language are sounds (phonology), words (semantics), grammatical rules (syntax), and sociocultural norms and conventions around the use of language (pragmatics).
- Very young infants can perceive and discriminate among the phonemes of their language. Over time and with experience, infants become less able to discriminate among sounds that are phonemic in other languages but not their native language, which is known as perceptual narrowing.
- Infants' ability to produce sounds rapidly grows over the first years of life. They move from crying to producing coos, then babbles, and ultimately conventional words that contain a range of consonant and vowel combinations.
- Infants identify words in speech and map words to objects and events in the world through a basic and powerful learning mechanism, statistical learning.

Semantic Development: Learning Word Meaning

- In the area of semantics, infants understand words and phrases well before they produce their first words. Most children produce their first words around their first birthday.
- Initially word learning is effortful and slow. In the second and third years of life, children learn new words with only one or two exposures, known as fast mapping.
- Infants underextend and overextend their use of words.
- The rate of growth in productive vocabulary increases substantially around 18 months of age, which has been referred to as the vocabulary spurt.

Syntactic Development: Putting Words Together

- In the area of syntax, toddlers show sensitivity to grammatical rules as seen in their looking to pictures that map the grammar of a sentence.
- In the second year of life, infants begin to combine words into meaningful sentences.
- Toddlers are able to use the grammatical structure of the sentence to figure out the meaning of the unfamiliar word, a phenomenon referred to as syntactic bootstrapping.

Pragmatic Development: Learning Communication Norms

- Children learn the sociocultural norms and conventions around the use of language, regarding when to talk, how, and about what.
- Infants show rudimentary pragmatic skills in (a) conventions around conversational turn taking, (b) sensitivity to the context of interactions, (c) the use of nonverbal cues in communication, and (d) discerning the attention and intentions of people.

Nativist Accounts of Language Development

- Nativist views of language arose with the Chomskian proposals of a universal grammar and innate language acquisition device (LAD).

- Support for a nativist view of language derives from studies of Deaf children's spontaneous use of sign language, from case studies of children reared in isolation without exposure to language (such as Genie), and from studies of sensitive periods in language development in dual-language learning children.
- Two types of cognitive biases (constraints) have been documented in children's early language learning: the assumption of mutual exclusivity and the whole-object assumption.

Connectionist and Dynamic Systems Theory

- Dynamic systems theory and connectionist theories apply a bottom-up interpretation to language learning in which infants build up knowledge, and neural connections strengthen with experience.
- Computer simulations help researchers identify the ways that children learn language from the bottom up by asking how machines learn from the language inputs that children are likely to experience.

Sociocultural Theory

- Sociocultural accounts emphasize the ways that adults and other people support infant language learning.
- Parents' child-directed speech, language diversity and amount, contingent responsiveness, physical cues (such as gesture), and engagement of children in learning routines such as book reading can support language learning and explain individual differences among toddlers in language skill.

Contexts of Language Development

- Parents and other primary caregivers contribute in major ways to early language development: the use of a special type of speech register (baby talk), the amount and diversity of child-directed speech, responsiveness to infant communicative behaviors, and the use of physical cues to help infants understand language.
- Family poverty and low-quality nonparental childcare experiences are associated with delays in early language development.
- High-quality care, characterized by sensitive and stimulating caregiving, also supports the language development of infants and toddlers.
- Dual-language learning (DLL) children are in many ways similar in the course of their language learning to monolingual children and benefit from high-quality language experiences just as monolingual children do.
- However, DLL children differ from monolingual children in various aspects of language learning, including in their reactions to mispronunciations and their strategies for learning new words.
- Cultural communities vary in their communications to infants, including in the extent to which caregivers alter their speech and behaviors to fit infant needs (accommodation),

whether the communication is verbal or non-verbal, and the social partners who interact with children on a regular basis.

Developmental Cascades

- Language growth goes hand in hand with changes in cognitive skills.
- Different languages have different ways of encoding concepts and events, and children increasingly attend to the concepts and categories particular to their language. The different ways that languages encode concepts and events are thought to have cascading influences on how children and adults think, a concept termed linguistic relativity that draws from the Whorfian hypothesis.

- Vocabulary growth allows children to establish a body of knowledge, which further leads children to perceive and think about the world in new ways.
- Language gains allow children to be faster at processing new information, resulting in snowball effects in learning and better school readiness outcomes.
- Infants who learn more than one language may show heightened skills in areas of executive functioning, although benefits may depend on their strengths.

Thinking Like a Developmentalist

1. You are the director of a childcare center. You wish to implement a new early language and literacy program for parents, to teach them ways to support their toddlers' language development. What would your program highlight? How would you test whether the program leads to improvements in: (a) the amount and quality of language interactions between parents and toddlers and (b) children's skills in phonology, semantics, and syntax?

2. You wish to study whether dual-language learning toddlers' language skills in their home language (which is not English) helps them learn the same words in English—for instance, whether a dual-language learning child who knows the word "gato" in Spanish will learn "cat" in English. Among other questions, you wonder whether a mutual exclusivity bias might interfere with a child learning the word "cat" after learning the word "gato." How might you investigate this question?

3. You are a researcher of infant language development who often gives workshops to parents. A mother and father (both of whom are Deaf) ask your advice about their infant, who has been diagnosed with extreme hearing difficulties. Should they get their infant cochlear implants (electrodes placed in the cochlea of the inner ear to allow some who are severely deaf to perceive sounds)? Should they encourage their infant to speak rather than sign? Why or why not?

Emotional and Social Development in Infancy and Toddlerhood

7

Drawing by Minxin Cheng from a photo by Mikael Stenberg on Unsplash

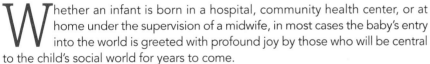

Whether an infant is born in a hospital, community health center, or at home under the supervision of a midwife, in most cases the baby's entry into the world is greeted with profound joy by those who will be central to the child's social world for years to come.

Unfortunately, too many infants are deprived of the healthy social experiences they need to thrive. Historical accounts of infants raised in orphanages present disturbing images of infants lying on their backs in metal cribs with bottles propped up to feed them, and social interactions limited to diaper changes (Spitz, 1945, 1965). Case studies of children reared in isolation—such as that of Genie presented in Chapter 6, who was locked in a small room and deprived of human interaction for the first 13 years of her life—demonstrate that social interaction is crucial to human development (Curtiss, 2014). All too often we hear of newborns who are abandoned, mistreated, or neglected. How do these atypical social-emotional experiences play out in children's development?

In the 1980s, investigations into the horrific environments of infants reared in Romanian institutions led to a landmark study, the Bucharest Early Intervention Project (**FIGURE 7.1**). A group of 136 babies were randomly assigned to either high-quality foster care or "care as usual" in the institutions, and both groups were assessed on a number of outcomes several years later. (Note that babies assigned to the "care as usual" group could be adopted out, so the researchers did not prevent them from moving to a new home). The study design allowed researchers to rigorously test the role of early social and emotional experiences across physical, cognitive, and social domains of

EMOTIONAL DEVELOPMENT
- Evolutionary Theory and the Functions of Emotions
- Expressing Emotions
- Understanding Emotions
- Regulating Emotions
- Temperament
- Social and Cultural Contexts of Emotional Development and Temperament

SOCIAL DEVELOPMENT
- Attachment
- Contexts of Attachment
- Peer Relations and the Origins of Morality
- Self-Identity
- Contexts of Self-Identity

Developmental Cascades

Closing Thoughts: Cultivating Emotional and Social Competence

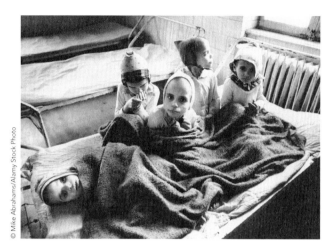

FIGURE 7.1 Romania's abandoned children. Infants reared in Romanian institutions in the 1980s led to the Bucharest Early Intervention Project, which investigated the consequences of severely neglectful rearing conditions on development. Institutionalized children showed impaired mental functioning, abnormal brain development, and social and emotional disorders relative to children who were adopted into foster homes.

development. Relative to children who were adopted into foster homes, institutionalized children were smaller in size, failed to grow properly, were severely impaired in mental functioning, showed abnormal brain development, and displayed social and emotional disorders. Additionally, the severity of negative effects depended on developmental timing: the younger the age of foster care placement, the greater the recovery.

The developmental disturbances that emerge under conditions of extreme deprivation illustrate how much can go wrong when infants do not receive the emotional and social supports that are foundational to development, and conversely, how much typically goes right in the presence of loving caregivers regardless of differences in childrearing practices. In the sections that follow, you will learn about early changes in infant emotional expression, understanding, and regulation; the formation of attachment and social relationships; how a sense of self develops; and the emergence of morality. You will learn about the sources of individual differences in these areas, including biological bases of temperament, variations in early social interactions, and differences in cultural beliefs and practices, and you will come to appreciate the cascading effects of infants' emotional and social development across developmental time and domains.

■ Emotional Development

Infant emotions are in constant flux. Over the course of a day, infants are at times joyful, content, frightened, or distressed. One minute an infant plays with a shape sorter, and the next, throws the shapes across the floor in frustration. A little while later, the infant cries in hunger, and then the cries are subdued by a bottle. When the baby unsuccessfully attempts to pull a book off a shelf, the loud crash of books ushers in a new wave of distress. Fortunately, a caregiver is nearby to offer comfort and a hug.

Infants' emotional experiences in these situations illustrate five fundamental components of emotions (Lewis, Sullivan, & Michalson, 1985; Saarni et al., 2007):

- *Emotion elicitors* (*triggers*). The failed attempt at placing a shape, pangs of hunger, and the crashing of books result in the infant's emotional distress.

- *Physiological changes.* The infant's heart rate and breathing quicken with distress.

- *Cognitive appraisal.* The loud bang is unexpected and signals potential danger. The infant reacts to and evaluates differences between what the infant is currently experiencing and what is familiar or desired.

- *Emotional expression.* The infant cries, scrunches the face, and waves the arms.

- *Communicative function.* The infant's crying gets the attention of someone nearby, who offers a bottle or hug to relieve the distress.

These five features of emotions are universal and adaptive; they characterize the experiences of people everywhere at all periods in life. However, emotional development undergoes a lengthy period of impressive change in the first years of life.

Evolutionary Theory and the Functions of Emotions

Darwin highlighted the role of emotions in human survival in his book *The Expression of Emotions in Man and Animals* (1872). Darwin claimed that both humans and nonhuman animals display a set of basic facial expressions, and he presented photographic evidence of humans' and animals' emotions to support his assertations. His photographs depicted impressive similarities, for example, in the eye muscle contractions and teeth exposure associated with anger in humans and nonhuman primates. He proposed that six **basic emotions** can already be found in infants—anger, fear, surprise, disgust, happiness, and sadness (**FIGURE 7.2**). However, the basis for Darwin's evolutionary perspective of emotions rests on the idea that emotions are universal and adaptive. Let's consider evidence for each claim.

FIGURE 7.2 Darwin claimed that emotions serve critical survival functions in animals and humans.   His observations led him to propose that humans and animals alike experience six basic emotions of anger, fear, surprise, disgust, happiness, and sadness. Here are photos taken from archives of Darwin's work that show similarities among infants in their expression of distress, which offers evidence for the early emerging and universal nature of human basic emotions.

Are Emotions Universal?

LEARNING OBJECTIVE 7.1 Discuss evidence suggesting that humans are hardwired for basic emotions and what indicates that these emotions are universal.

In the late twentieth century, developmental scientists embraced Darwin's theories and set out to investigate the universality of emotions. Paul Ekman (1971) suggested that humans were hardwired for basic emotions of happiness, sadness, fear, disgust, anger, surprise (and possibly contempt). Ekman conducted one of the most-cited studies on the universality of emotions, in which he asked adults from the United States, Japan, Brazil, Argentina, Chile, and a preliterate community in New Guinea to identify emotions of characters in a story by pointing to one of several photos of facial expressions.

Adults across the different cultural communities generally interpreted the facial expressions in the same way, supporting the idea that people everywhere connect specific facial expressions with specific emotions. Similarly, the facial expressions of infants from European American, Chinese, and Japanese backgrounds indicate the early and universal presence of basic emotions. Infants' cries, smiles, and expressions of distaste look the same across the world and are comparable to those of adults (Camras et al., 2007).

basic emotions Universal emotions such as anger, fear, surprise, disgust, happiness, and sadness

✓ CHECK YOUR UNDERSTANDING 7.1

1. List the basic emotions.
2. What evidence supports the proposition that humans are hardwired for basic emotions?

Are Emotions Adaptive?

LEARNING OBJECTIVE 7.2 Describe the two vital functions that emotions serve.

Emotions often get a bad rap, for example when someone is criticized for being overly emotional. However, emotions serve vital roles in everyday functioning: They prepare and motivate individuals for action and underpin social relationships with others (Saarni et al., 2007; Witherington, Campos, & Hertenstein, 2007).

FIGURE 7.3 Disgust. The emotion of disgust leads to a scrunching of the nose and mouth that constricts these openings.

Consider the role of emotions in action. Emotions prepare people to respond to environmental events or threats to survival. As one example, the detection of potentially threatening stimuli may instigate fear and the fight-or-flight response. Fear increases the visual field and speed of eye movements, allowing individuals to spot potentially threatening objects in the periphery (Susskind et al., 2008). Fear also leads to physiological responses that facilitate the ability to escape the threat, such as heavy breathing, the redistribution of blood in preparation for rapid movement, and the organization of attention to promote alertness (Shariff & Tracy, 2011). The emotion of disgust leads to a scrunching of the nose and mouth that constricts these openings (**FIGURE 7.3**) and makes it less likely that the potentially dangerous substance will be inhaled (Chapman et al., 2009). Shame and embarrassment lead to body constrictions—think of a child hovering in the presence of a bully—that reduce and hide vulnerable body areas from potential attackers (Shariff & Tracy, 2011).

Emotions also communicate meaningful social information. The face, voice, and body signal fear, happiness, anger, sadness, disgust, and surprise, communicating to others how a person feels and how others should respond. The squeals of laughter by an infant who delights in her father's tickles elicit further play from him. An infant who is wary of an unfamiliar setting might cling to their mother, who will respond by comforting her baby. Reciprocally, infants can make use of the emotional reactions of others when situations are ambiguous—for example by looking to a sibling to gauge how to respond to a dog. If the sibling smiles and approaches the dog, the infant might also reach out to pet, but if the sibling shies away, the infant might do so as well.

✓ CHECK YOUR UNDERSTANDING 7.2

1. What are some regulatory and social functions of emotions? Give an example of each function.

Expressing Emotions

Emotional expressions, as infants' first communications, may be considered "the language of the baby" (Emde, 1980). Well before infants can talk, they express their emotions through smiles, raised brows, scrunched faces, tightly closed eyes, open and quivering mouths, and distress vocalizations. At the most general level, infants' emotions can be grouped as positive (e.g., joy, love) or negative (e.g., anger, fear). Positive emotional states arise when infants' goals are fulfilled—such as when a baby is pleased by a mother's voice and hug. Negative emotional states arise when infants' goals are blocked—such as when a tired infant does not have a caregiver nearby to comfort or put the infant to sleep (Campos et al., 1983; Izard, 1978).

Infant Positive Emotions

LEARNING OBJECTIVE 7.3 Describe developments in infant smiling across the first year of life.

Smiling is the most eagerly awaited emotional expression by parents. Parents often interpret their newborns' smiles as expressions of joy, even though first smiles do not mean the same thing as the smiles of older infants. Newborn smiles are brief and even occur during sleep (Emde & Harmon, 1972).

Between the third and eighth weeks of life, infants increasingly smile to external stimuli such as high-pitched voices, although they do not yet smile for the purpose of engaging in social interactions (Sroufe, 1996). Between 6 weeks and 3 months of age, **social smiles** emerge—smiles directed to people, particularly primary caregivers (Emde & Harmon, 1972). Social smiles contain cheek raising that is thought to distinguish genuine and nongenuine expressions of happiness (**FIGURE 7.4**) (Messinger, Fogel, & Dickson, 2001).

Smiling continues to change as infants become familiar with people and their environments. By 4 months of age, infants smile in response to the smiles of their caregivers and other familiar people, who continue to respond by smiling back (Ruvolo, Messinger, & Movellan, 2015). By the end of the first year, infants display different smiles across situations and people, such as broad-open smiles and belly laughs during playful interactions but reserved, tentative smiles to a stranger's greeting (Messinger & Fogel, 2007).

✓ **CHECK YOUR UNDERSTANDING 7.3**

1. Approximately when do different types of smiles typically occur in developmental time?

Infant Negative Emotions

LEARNING OBJECTIVE 7.4 Explain alternative interpretations of infant distress around the emotions of anger and fear.

Distress represents the first negative emotion. Newborns express distress across various situations ranging from hunger to getting shots. Over the next several months, infants express negative emotions in situations that arouse anger, fear, wariness, and perhaps frustration.

Anger

Infants as young as 2 months of age react with what some researchers infer to be anger, as seen in "arm restraint" lab tasks in which mothers gently hold down infants' arms for 2 minutes (Stifter & Spinrad, 2002; Moscardino & Axia, 2006). Infants of 4 to 5 months of age express anger when a goal is blocked, as found when infants could no longer play music by pulling on a ribbon after being taught how to do so (Sullivan & Lewis, 2003). Anger increases in intensity and frequency from 4 to 16 months of age (and later into the second year) in line with infants' growing cognitive understanding (Braungart-Rieker, Hill-Soderlund, & Karrass, 2010) (**FIGURE 7.5**). That is, toddlers increase their

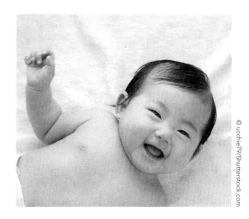

FIGURE 7.4 Social smiles emerge between 6 weeks and 3 months of age. Social smiles are thought to reflect genuine expressions of happiness and are characterized by cheek raising during the smile.

social smiles Smiles directed to people, particularly to caregivers, with the purpose of engaging in social interactions

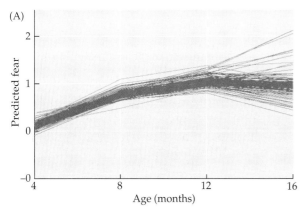

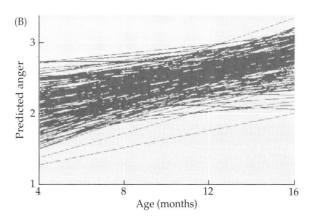

FIGURE 7.5 Infant anger and fear reactions increase from 4 to 16 months of age. The left panel shows increases in infant anger, with each line representing an infant followed over age. The right panel shows increases in infant fear, again with each line representing an infant. (After J. Braungart-Rieker et al. 2010. *Dev Psychol* 46: 791–804. Copyright © 2010 by American Psychological Association. Reproduced with permission.)

FIGURE 7.6 Expressions of anger generalize to a range of situations in toddlerhood. In the second year, infants extend their anger (or distress) to a wide range of situations such as when someone blocks their goals (e.g., being put down for a nap).

FIGURE 7.7 Learning fear. Michael Cook and Susan Mineka (1990) presented rhesus monkeys who had never been in the wild and never seen a snake with edited videos of two other monkeys expressing fear: one monkey expressed fear toward a plastic flower and the other toward a plastic snake. When examiners later presented the rhesus monkeys with the two objects, the monkeys responded with fear to the snake, but did not express fear to the flower. Such findings suggest preparedness toward learning to fear certain types of stimuli. Here is a photo of a frightened juvenile monkey seeking comfort from an adult.

displays of anger because they understand not only that their goals are being blocked, but also that someone is preventing them from getting what they want. That's why they get angry when being put down for a nap.

However, infants cannot tell scientists what they are feeling. And so researchers make their best guesses about infant emotions. Are infants truly *angry* when their arms are restrained? When and whether infants experience specific emotions in ways similar to children and adults has generated much debate (Camras & Shutter, 2010) (**FIGURE 7.6**).

Fear

The emotion of fear has strong roots in infancy. From an evolutionary perspective, an innate, universal, and early fear of snakes, spiders, heights, and other potentially threatening stimuli may benefit survival and thus be adaptive (Poulton & Menzies, 2002). Alternatively, infants may rapidly learn to fear certain threatening stimuli through experience rather than inborn tendencies (Öhman & Mineka, 2001; Seligman, 1971).

How do researchers test whether infants "fear" certain stimuli? One approach is to present infants with pictures or replicas of threatening and nonthreatening stimuli—such as snakes versus frogs—and compare infants' responses to each. Early studies suggested that infants quickly learn to avoid certain stimuli over others. For example, when researchers presented 14-month-old infants with a toy spider, infants avoided the spider when their mothers expressed fear. Even after mothers later expressed joy at seeing the toy spider, infants continued to avoid the spider (Zarbatany & Lamb, 1985). Similar findings have been documented in nonhuman animals. Researchers presented lab-reared rhesus monkeys with videos of wild rhesus monkeys displaying fear in the presence of real and toy snakes and nonfearful behaviors in the presence of wooden blocks or plastic flowers. The rhesus monkeys quickly learned to express fear in the presence of snakes, but not to the blocks or flowers (**FIGURE 7.7**) (Cook & Mineka, 1989, 1990).

However, the interpretation that infants innately experience "fear" in the presence of certain threatening stimuli has been challenged (e.g., LoBue & Adolph, 2019). If infants naturally find spiders, snakes, and the like to be scary, they should show a high startle response and quickened heart rate—physiological markers of fear in adults. But infants *do not* show any such evidence of fear when presented with pictures of snakes versus frogs. They do, however, *look more* at snakes and spiders than at nonthreatening stimuli (Thrasher & LoBue, 2016). Thus, infants may be biased to detect and attend to threatening stimuli, even if they are not naturally afraid. Such perceptual biases may then facilitate learning to fear snakes and other threats after brief exposures, as infants learn through others or their own discoveries that such stimuli are indeed dangerous (LoBue & Adolph, 2019; LoBue & DeLoache, 2010; LoBue & Rakison, 2013) (**FIGURE 7.8**).

Self-Conscious Emotions

Although it may be difficult to infer the meaning of infants' emotional expressions in the first year of life, emotions become more differentiated in the second and third years. Furthermore, toddlers begin to display behaviors that suggest the emergence of the self-conscious emotions. **Self-conscious emotions** relate to a sense of self and other awareness, such as embarrassment, pride, guilt, and shame (Tracy, Robins, & Tangney, 2007). For example, infants avoid eye contact and hide their face when they are the

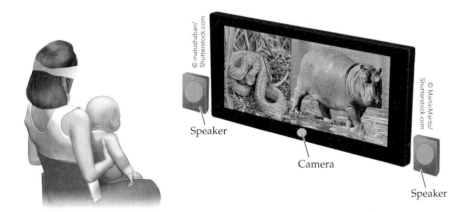

FIGURE 7.8 Infants may be biased to attend to potentially threatening stimuli, without being afraid.   Developmental psychologist Vanessa LoBue and colleagues tested whether infants show evidence of fear to threatening stimuli, or instead are just biased to detecting such stimuli. They assessed infants' propensity to look at snakes relative to other animals such as elephants or rhinoceroses while also monitoring their physiological responses. They found that snakes elicit infant attention, but infants do not necessarily display "fear" based on measures of heart rate and other physiological indices. (After J. S. DeLoache and V. LoBue. 2009. *Dev Sci* 12: 201–207.)

center of attention, suggesting that they are embarrassed (Lewis, 1995). Toddlers also express behaviors that suggest shame and guilt. A 2-year-old may react to accidentally breaking a toy by hiding the toy and avoiding the caregiver (shame) or attempting to repair the toy (guilt) (Barrett, Zahn-Waxler, & Cole, 1993).

self-conscious emotions Emotions that involve a sense of self-awareness and are based on others' perceptions, such as embarrassment, pride, guilt, and shame

✓ CHECK YOUR UNDERSTANDING 7.4

1. How might researchers determine which negative emotion(s) underlie an infant's cry?
2. When do babies begin to show self-conscious emotions? Give an example.

Understanding Emotions

Understanding emotions is critical to social relationships. **Emotion understanding** refers to understanding people's emotional reactions to specific situations, evaluating the circumstances that led to the emotional response, and inferring what people want and might do in specific emotional situations (Camras & Halberstadt, 2017). These are not easy to do. It takes many years of social interactions and cognitive development for children to understand how others feel, and even then, they often make errors.

emotion understanding Infants' ability to discriminate among emotions; connect emotional expressions to meaning; and seek and use emotional information to guide their actions

Infants are so new to the world that their understanding of emotions pales compared to that of children and adults. Still, infants display the precursors of emotion understanding in their abilities to (1) discriminate among different emotions and different intensities of emotions; (2) connect emotional expressions to meaning, such as recognizing that a smile signals joy and a frown signals sadness; and (3) seek and use emotional information to guide their actions.

Discriminating Emotions

LEARNING OBJECTIVE 7.5 Define emotion discrimination and discuss how it is demonstrated by infants.

Emotion discrimination is the ability to distinguish among emotional expressions (Camras & Shuster, 2013). Remarkably, even newborns display rudimentary capacities to discriminate among emotions. They open their eyes more

emotion discrimination The ability to distinguish among emotional expressions such as sad and angry speech or faces when presented with happy speech than when presented with sad, angry, and neutral speech, and they look more at happy than neutral faces (Mastropieri & Turkewitz, 1999; Rigato et al., 2011). And with age, infants' skill at discriminating among emotions improves. A review of studies on infants' emotion understanding showed that 4- and 5-month-olds distinguish happy from negative facial expressions such as anger; and by around 7 months of age, infants recognize similarities among people's emotions, as seen in their categorization of happy faces together and angry faces together (e.g., Ruba & Repacholi, 2019).

Young infants likewise respond to *gradations* in the intensity of emotion expressions, such as by distinguishing between smiles that are subtle versus full-blown. In a clever habituation-novelty preference study (see Chapters 4 and 5) researchers examined 3-month-old infants' perceptions of smiling in relation to their interactions with mothers at home (Kuchuk, Vibbert, & Bornstein, 1986). Infants were shown a series of pictures of a woman smiling, ranging from a subtle upturn of the lips to a full-blown smile with teeth exposed. Infants looked longer to a smile of a different intensity after being habituated to a slightly larger or smaller smile. Moreover, infants' experience with smiles aided their discrimination: Infants with mothers who more frequently encouraged their infants to look at them as they smiled were better able to distinguish among the different smile gradients. Thus, infants' experiences looking at the smiling face of their mothers supported their ability to distinguish among smiles.

Infants are also able to connect emotional information in the face to information in the voice. **Matching studies**, which ask whether infants are able to "match" the emotional content of stimuli presented in different modalities such as face and voice, reveal this ability. In such studies, researchers present infants with side-by-side displays of two facial expressions, such as happy and sad, along with an audio recording of a voice that matches one of the facial expressions. If infants look longer to the facial expression that matches the voice, it suggests that they have connected the emotions across visual and auditory channels. By 5 months of age infants look longer to a positive facial expression when hearing a happy voice than when hearing an angry voice and can even match the emotions in faces to the emotions in vocalizations of other babies (Vaillant-Molina, Bahrick, & Flom, 2013) (**FIGURE 7.9**). Additionally, infants match emotions in facial expressions and voices at even younger ages when

matching studies Studies that assess whether infants are able to match the emotional content of stimuli presented in different modalities, such as face and voice

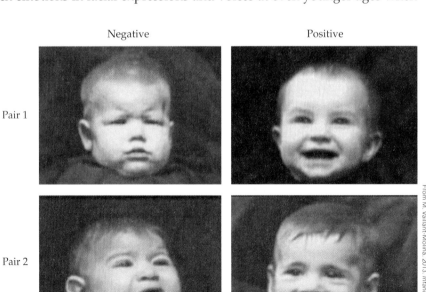

Negative   Positive

Pair 1

Pair 2

FIGURE 7.9 Infants match emotions in the faces of other infants to the emotions expressed by their vocalizations. Researchers presented 5-month-old infants with videos of infants displaying negative and positive expressions. The videos were accompanied by positive or negative infant vocal expressions. Infants "matched" the vocal expressions to their congruent facial expressions by looking more to the face that matched the affect that they heard.

From M. Vaillant-Molina. 2013 *Infancy* 18: E97–E111

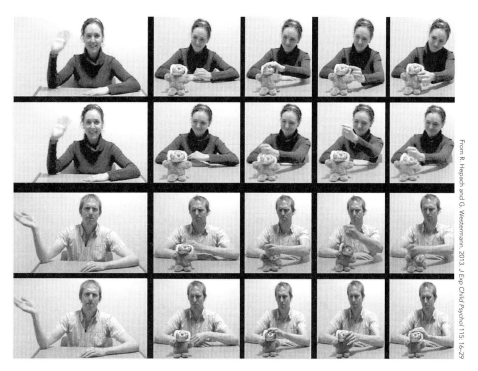

From R. Hepach and G. Westermann. 2013. J Exp Child Psychol 115: 16–29

FIGURE 7.10 Infants match emotions with actions.   Infants were shown clips of actors who displayed happiness or anger, and then either pet or hit a stuffed animal. Infant looking time suggested that they were able to infer that someone who shows a happy face will be more likely to pat a stuffed animal (top row) but unlikely to hit the animal (second row). Conversely, someone who shows an angry face will be more likely to hit an animal (third row) than to pat it (bottom row).

presented with their mothers' faces (Kahana-Kalman & Walker-Andrews, 2001). Late in the first year, infants match positive emotions to positive events (Skerry & Spelke, 2014), and by the second year, infants match negative emotions to negative events (e.g., Reschke et al., 2017; Ruba, Meltzoff, & Repacholi, 2019).

When researchers monitor infants' eye movements with eye trackers, they find that infants attend to the mouth area in particular to figure out how emotions in faces relate to emotions in voices (Palama, Malsert, & Gentaz, 2018). As infants enter their second year, they consider a person's actions when evaluating emotions, such as understanding that a person whose face appears to be angry might hit a toy tiger and a person whose face appears to be happy might pet a toy tiger (Hepach & Westermann, 2013) (**FIGURE 7.10**).

✓ CHECK YOUR UNDERSTANDING 7.5

1. What evidence suggests that newborns and very young infants can distinguish among different types of emotional expressions and gradations of emotional expressions?

Using Emotional Information

LEARNING OBJECTIVE 7.6 Describe evidence suggesting that infants attach meaning to the emotions they observe in other people.

Distinguishing among emotions is only a first step in understanding emotions. Infants must also learn to use emotional information, which requires connecting people's expressions to what people actually feel or intend to communicate. To illustrate, imagine the following situation: A toddler runs across the playground and stumbles over a toy, landing belly down on the ground. She briefly hesitates and looks up to her mother who is seated on a nearby bench. Her mother

social referencing The seeking and use of social information in ambiguous situations, such as when a toddler looks at a mother's face when uncertain about how to react to a strange person

leaps from the bench, scoops up her daughter, and holds her close in panic. The toddler registers her mother's alarm, quickly computes that what happened was scary, and breaks into sobs. The toddler has just demonstrated her skill at seeking and using the emotional information in her mother's face, actions, and voice to guide her own behaviors. **Social referencing** refers to the seeking and use of social information in ambiguous situations.

When do infants exhibit social referencing? During the first year of life, infants remain limited in their social-referencing abilities. They do not yet grasp connections among emotional expressions (such as a fearful voice and face), their causes (the object in front of the child), and behavioral responses (avoidance) (Camras & Shuster, 2013). By around 12 months, however, infants avoid objects of another person's expressed fear. For example, infants cross a visual cliff (see Chapter 4) when their mothers stand at the other side and display joy, but avoid crossing when mothers display fear (Sorce et al., 1985). Similarly, infants approach or avoid toys and strangers based on how other people react (Feinman et al., 1992; Saarni et al., 2007).

Donna Mumme and Anne Fernald (2003) examined 10- and 12-month-old infants' behaviors after an experimenter's different reactions to novel objects. Infants observed the experimenter's neutral, positive, or negative reaction toward one of two unfamiliar objects. When later given the opportunity to play with the objects, 12-month-olds, but not 10-month-olds, avoided the object when the experimenter reacted negatively, but showed no avoidance when the experimenter reacted neutrally or positively (**FIGURE 7.11**).

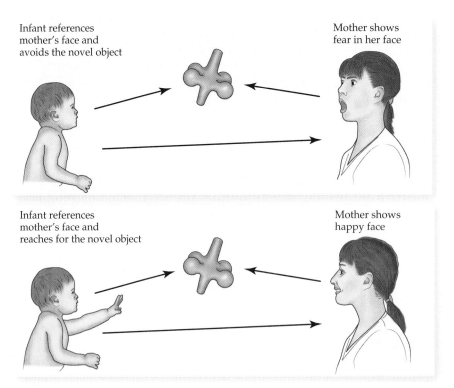

Infant references mother's face and avoids the novel object

Mother shows fear in her face

Infant references mother's face and reaches for the novel object

Mother shows happy face

FIGURE 7.11 Infants approach or avoid stimuli in line with the emotional reactions of other people. Infants use social information offered by others in ambiguous situations (such as when confronting unfamiliar objects or people), a behavior referred to as "social referencing." For example, when the mother or an adult expresses fear to a novel object, the infant avoids playing with the object. In contrast, when the mother or adult expresses happiness to a novel object, the infant reaches and approaches. (After D. Mumme et al. 1996. *Child Dev* 67: 3219–3237.)

✓ CHECK YOUR UNDERSTANDING 7.6

1. What is social referencing and why is it considered adaptive?
2. What methods do developmental researchers use to examine infant social referencing?

Regulating Emotions

Most everyone is familiar with the "terrible twos," the frequent emotional eruptions of toddlers when they don't get what they want. Imagine a common grocery-store scenario: A father and his 2-year-old daughter are in line to pay for their groceries. The toddler pulls a bag of candy off the shelf. The father abruptly removes the candy and places it back on the shelf. His daughter again pulls the candy from the shelf. After several repeats of their tug-of-war, the father warns "No candy!" His daughter arches her back, kicks her legs, and screams. This scene illustrates the immense difficulty that infants and toddlers have in **self-regulation**, the ability to control attention, emotions, thinking, and behavior. In the next section, we examine the emotional component of self-regulation.

self-regulation The ability to control attention, emotions, thinking, and behavior

Development of Infant Emotion Regulation

LEARNING OBJECTIVE 7.7 Describe the development of emotion regulation in the first years of life.

Emotion regulation refers to the monitoring, evaluating, and moderating of emotional responses, particularly under stressful situations (Calkins & Hill, 2007). Across the first two years of life, infants change from initially relying on other people to help them regulate, to independently attempting to calm themselves.

Initially, infants have little control over their emotions. In fact, primary caregivers play a central role in helping young infants regulate their emotions and arousal (Perry, Calkins, & Bell, 2016). Adults may comfort or distract their distressed infants, for example by hugging and rocking them and offering them toys. Such behaviors help teach infants strategies that can reduce emotional arousal.

Toward the end of the first year, infants begin to independently control their emotions. For example, infants may look away from an unpleasant event, or soothe themselves by sucking their thumb (Fox & Calkins, 2003; Stifter & Braungart, 1995). In the second and third years of life, toddlers broaden their regulation strategies to include distractions such as singing and playing finger games to occupy themselves (Grolnick, Bridges, & Connell, 1996; Stansbury & Sigman, 2000).

emotion regulation The monitoring, evaluating, and moderating of emotional responses, especially in stressful situations

effortful control A child's capacity to voluntarily regulate attention and behavior when responding to emotionally challenging situations

✓ CHECK YOUR UNDERSTANDING 7.7

1. What are some strategies that older infants and toddlers might use to regulate their emotions?

Effortful Control

LEARNING OBJECTIVE 7.8 Explain the attentional and behavioral components involved in infants' effortful control.

Effortful control refers to a child's capacity to voluntarily regulate attention and behaviors when responding to emotionally challenging situations (Eisenberg et al., 2010; Rothbart & Bates, 2006). For example, the attentional component of effortful control is seen when a toddler looks away from a frightening scene on television so as not to become distressed (**FIGURE 7.12**). The behavioral component of effortful control might involve refraining from throwing toys across the floor when upset (Grolnick, Cosgrove, & Bridges, 1996). Attentional and

FIGURE 7.12 Effortful control. The attentional component of effortful control might be seen when a toddler looks away from a frightening scene on television or blocks his ears when hearing loud noises as a way to not become distressed.

inhibitory control An executive function that suppresses a dominant or preferred response in favor of an acceptable, more adaptive response

behavioral components of effortful control both require **inhibitory control**—the suppression of a dominant or preferred response in favor of an acceptable one (Diamond, 1991; Eisenberg et al., 2010). In the current examples, looking at the screen and throwing toys would be the dominant response, whereas looking away and refraining from throwing would be the alternative, acceptable response.

Inhibitory control improves throughout toddlerhood, as children learn to manage their impulses and comply with adults. Infants with strong skills in attention and inhibitory control followed requests to clean up toys and not touch forbidden objects months later at 13–15 months of age (Kochanska, Tjebkes, & Fortnan, 1998; Kochanska & Kim, 2014). As we will see in later chapters, the term self-regulation (rather than effortful control) describes older children's management of attention, emotions, thoughts, and behaviors.

✓ CHECK YOUR UNDERSTANDING 7.8

1. What is effortful control?
2. What is the connection between emotion regulation and inhibitory control?

Temperament

temperament Individual differences among infants in intensity of reactivity and regulation of emotions, activity, and attention

Infants differ in how they emotionally respond to different situations, even as newborns. Parents with more than one child can attest to the uniqueness of each baby's disposition. They might describe one infant as easy going, content to play alone, curious, and eager to approach new situations. In contrast, they might describe their other infant as fussy, excitable, unable to be soothed, and easily distracted. What explains early differences among infants? Temperament has received a great deal of attention. **Temperament** refers to a child's intensity of reactivity and regulation of emotions, activity, and attention (Rothbart, Derryberry, & Hershey, 2000). As we will see, a child's temperament is present from birth, stable over time, and thought to offer a window into personality in later life.

The History of Temperament Studies

LEARNING OBJECTIVE 7.9 Discuss how the work of Thomas and Chess advanced an understanding of temperament.

Some of the most influential research on infant temperament can be traced to the work of the husband-wife team of Alexander Thomas and Stella Chess, who launched the New York Longitudinal Study in 1956. Thomas and Chess challenged the assumption (by many behaviorists at the time) that people respond in the same ways to the same stimuli. They noted that the identical situation—such as the approach of a stranger—could yield dramatically different reactions in infants with different temperaments.

To explore differences among infants in temperament, Thomas and Chess (1977) extensively interviewed mothers of 3-month-olds about their infants' reactions to novel people and situations, energy level, positive and negative emotions, adaptability to change, rhythmicity (how regular an infant was in sleeping, eating, etc.), general mood, and distractibility. Based on mothers' responses, they identified three temperament profiles (35% of infants did not fit these profiles):

- *Easy babies*, 40% of the sample, readily adapted to the environment, had regular eating and sleeping patterns, displayed positive emotions, showed low to moderate intensity of reactions, and approached novel stimuli.

- *Difficult babies*, 10% of the sample, took a relatively long time to adjust to new environments, had irregular patterns, cried frequently, displayed high intensity in both positive and negative emotions, and tended to withdraw from new situations.

- *Slow-to-warm-up babies*, 15% of the sample, were slow to adapt to new environments and exhibited low activity and intensity, a moderate level of negative emotions, and a tendency to withdraw from new situations (Thomas, Chess, & Birch, 1970).

✓ CHECK YOUR UNDERSTANDING 7.9

1. Describe "easy babies," "difficult babies," and "slow-to-warm-up babies" as identified by Thomas and Chess.

Contemporary Models of Temperament

LEARNING OBJECTIVE 7.10 Summarize how the research of Rothbart and Bates contributed to the current conceptualization of temperament.

The work of Thomas and Chess sparked much subsequent research, including that of developmentalists Mary Rothbart and Jack Bates (Rothbart & Bates, 2006). Rothbart and Bates measured temperament by asking parents to report on their infants' behaviors across a variety of situations. They asked questions such as, "When being dressed or undressed, how often does your baby cry, sit quietly, watch, etc.?" and "When having a toy taken away, how often does your baby____?" Based on parents' responses, Rothbart identified six dimensions of temperament:

- *Activity*: The infant's level of gross motor activity, including moving the arms, legs, torso, squirming, and so forth
- *Positive affect*: The infant's expressions of happiness through smiling and laughter
- *Fear*: The infant's intensity of reaction to novel stimuli (including distress), time it takes the baby to approach new situations and people, and **inhibition**—withdrawal from unfamiliar situations and people

inhibition A dimension of temperament that reflects an infant's withdrawal from and intense reaction to unfamiliar situations and people

- *Distress to limitations*: The infant's distress in relation to desired goals, such as waiting for food, being confined, being dressed, being prevented from accessing an object
- *Soothability*: The infant's reduction of fussing, crying, or distress when soothed by a caregiver or the self
- *Attention*: The infant's vocalizing, looking at and/or engagement with an object for an extended period of time

When Rothbart and colleagues analyzed these six dimensions together, they identified three components of temperament: surgency, negative reactivity, and orienting regulation (**FIGURE 7.13**) (e.g., Putnam, Gartstein, & Rothbart, 2006). Infants and toddlers ranged from low to high in their scores on these components.

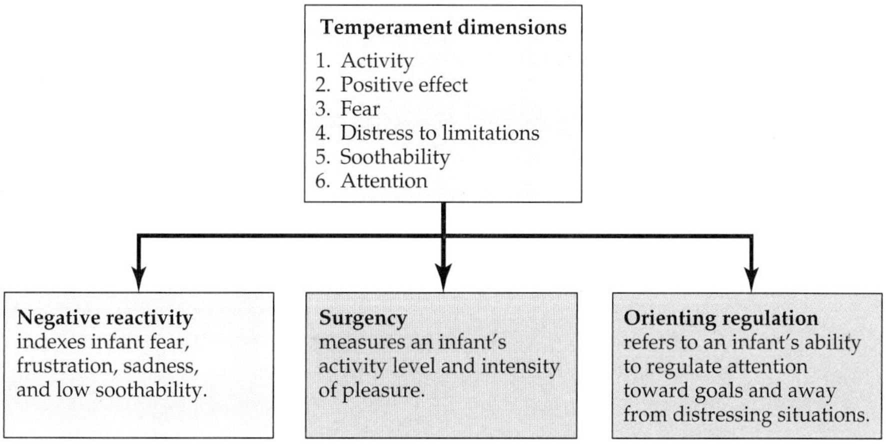

FIGURE 7.13 Rothbart and Bates's temperament dimensions. Temperament refers to a person's intensity of *reactivity* and *regulation* of emotions, activity, and attention. Rothbart and colleagues identified six dimensions of temperament that combined into three overall components of temperament—negative reactivity, surgency, and orienting regulation. Marked differences exist among infants in these components of temperament. (After M. K. Rothbart and J. E. Bates. 2006. In *Handbook of Child Psychology: Social, Emotional, and Personality Development*. N. Eisenberg et al. [Eds.], pp. 99–166. John Wiley & Sons, Inc.: Hoboken, NJ.)

Temperament dimensions
1. Activity
2. Positive effect
3. Fear
4. Distress to limitations
5. Soothability
6. Attention

Negative reactivity indexes infant fear, frustration, sadness, and low soothability.

Surgency measures an infant's activity level and intensity of pleasure.

Orienting regulation refers to an infant's ability to regulate attention toward goals and away from distressing situations.

surgery An infant's activity level and intensity of pleasure; infants with high surgency show a lot of happiness by smiling and laughing

negative reactivity An infant's high arousal in response to sensory stimuli; infants with high negative reactivity display fear, frustration, sadness, and low soothability

orienting regulation An infant's ability to regulate attention toward goals and away from distressing situations

Surgency is a measure of an infant's activity level and intensity of pleasure. Infants who score high in surgency show a lot of happiness through smiling and laughter, energetically approach new situations, and are low on shyness.

Negative reactivity indexes infant fear, frustration, sadness, and low soothability. Infants who are high on negative reactivity are distressed by unfamiliar events or frustrating situations and have difficulties regulating their emotions. For example, 5-month-olds differ in how upset they get at having their arms restrained, a sign of high negative reactivity, and how quickly they recover from distress, a sign of low emotional regulation. Some infants don't cry at all when restrained; others cry but calm down; and others display intense, sustained crying that forces the experiment to end early (Porter et al., 2009).

Orienting regulation refers to an infant's ability to regulate attention toward goals and away from distressing situations. Infants high on orienting are able to regulate their emotions well (Rothbart, Posner, & Boylan, 1990). For example, infants who were more attentive during a block task were less likely to become frustrated during arm restraint and toy removal tasks than were infants with low attention (Calkins et al., 2002). And 9-month-old infants who were better able to attend to a picture without being distracted showed greater positive affect and less social withdrawal from peers than infants who had difficulty maintaining attention (Pérez-Edgar & Fox, 2000).

✓ CHECK YOUR UNDERSTANDING 7.10

1. What are the six dimensions of temperament identified by Mary Rothbart and Jack Bates?
2. How do these six dimensions relate to the temperament components of surgency, negative reactivity, and orienting regulation?

Stability in Temperament

LEARNING OBJECTIVE 7.11 State evidence for the stability of temperament.

Whereas emotions are fleeting, temperament can be stable from infancy through toddlerhood, childhood, and even adulthood (Caspi et al., 2003; Kochanska & Knaack, 2003; Rothbart & Bates, 2006). Thomas and Chess found that "slow-to-warm-up" babies were excessively fearful and cautious in new situations in the preschool and school years (Chess & Thomas, 1984). And infant temperament helps explain sociability, negative reactivity, attention, and effortful control in childhood and adulthood. For example, Mary Rothbart (2007) found similarities between infant and toddler temperaments and adulthood traits of personality as represented in the "Big five of personality":

- *Openness*—the degree of intellectual curiosity and openness to new experiences
- *Conscientiousness*—the tendency to be organized and self-disciplined
- *Extraversion*—energy, surgency, outgoingness, and the tendency to seek stimulation through social interactions
- *Neuroticism*—vulnerability to quickly experiencing unpleasant emotions such as anxiety, anger, and depression
- *Agreeableness*—the tendency to be compassionate and cooperative rather than antagonistic toward others

In particular, the temperament component of negative reactivity predicted adult neuroticism; the temperament component of orienting regulation predicted openness; the temperament component of effortful control predicted conscientiousness; and the temperament component of surgency predicted extraversion (**FIGURE 7.14**).

What accounts for stability from early to later temperament? The answer lies in the interaction between a child's biology and environmental experiences. The term **evocative effects** refers to a type of gene-environment association (see Chapter 2) in which a child's inherited characteristics evoke strong responses from others that strengthen the child's characteristics. For example, an infant may become highly distressed when being changed, meeting new people, hearing loud noises, being put down to sleep, and so forth. The infant's negativity can make it difficult for parents to interact sensitively and calmly. If the infant's parents become irritable and abrupt in their interactions, the infant's negativity may strengthen over time.

✓ CHECK YOUR UNDERSTANDING 7.11

1. What evidence suggests that temperament is stable?
2. Provide an example of how biological factors may interact with experience to influence temperament over time.

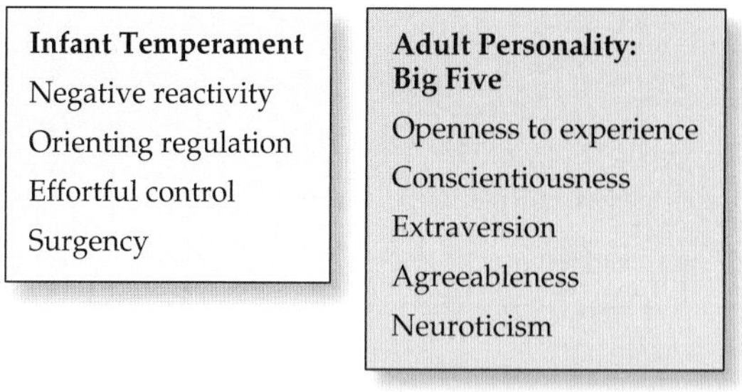

Infant Temperament	Adult Personality: Big Five
Negative reactivity	Openness to experience
Orienting regulation	Conscientiousness
Effortful control	Extraversion
Surgency	Agreeableness
	Neuroticism

FIGURE 7.14 Toddler temperament predicts adulthood traits.   Mary Rothbart and colleagues identified stability from early temperament to later personality. The temperament component of negative reactivity predicted adult neuroticism; the temperament component of orienting/regulation predicted openness; the temperament component of effortful control predicted conscientiousness; and the temperament component of surgency predicted extraversion. (After D. E. Evans and M. K. Rothbart. 2007. *J Res Pers* 41: 868–888.)

Social and Cultural Contexts of Emotional Development and Temperament

All infants grow in their understanding, expression, and regulation of emotions, and show temperamental differences that are stable over time. However, parenting and cultural contexts continually sculpt infants' emotional development and temperament, thus molding the person an infant will one day become.

Contexts of Infant Temperament and Goodness of Fit

LEARNING OBJECTIVE 7.12 Explain the concept of goodness of fit and why an infant's temperament should be studied in the context of social and cultural influences.

We learned that temperament is stable. However, this does not mean that an infant's initial disposition fully determines later personality, or that changes in temperament do not occur. In fact, the strength of associations from early temperament to later outcomes is relatively low (Putnam, Sanson, & Rothbart, 2002). That's because many factors contribute to later personality. An infant who is initially high in negative reactivity can eventually learn how to regulate emotions just as an infant who is frightened by unfamiliar situations may eventually welcome new experiences. Indeed, infants' early experiences and temperament work together to grow a personality (Rothbart, 2007).

Social influences on temperament are best understood under the framework of **goodness of fit**—the extent to which a person's temperament matches the requirements, expectations, and opportunities of the environment (Chess & Thomas, 1991). Specifically, childrearing practices can modify a child's temperament for better or for worse: harsh parenting can lead to escalating negative reactivity in children just as supportive parenting can teach children how to regulate their negative reactions.

Consider how goodness of fit may play out in infants' everyday experiences. Imagine that an infant reacts with high negativity to a new situation, such as a family reunion at an unfamiliar home. If the infant is forced into the arms of strange relatives, the infant's negative reactions may escalate. In contrast, if the infant is allowed some time to adjust to the new environment, the infant will be more likely to positively engage with others. In the latter

evocative effects A type of gene-environment association in which a child's inherited characteristics evoke strong responses from others that strengthen the child's characteristics

goodness of fit The extent to which a person's temperament matches the requirements, expectations, and opportunities of the environment case, parent behaviors show a goodness of fit with the infant's temperament. The infant will learn that it is okay to approach other people, and that nothing bad happened as a result. The importance of goodness of fit for development explains why infants who show high levels of anger or frustration *and* experience negative parenting continue to be angry and frustrated at later ages (Calkins, 2002).

✓ CHECK YOUR UNDERSTANDING 7.12

1. What is goodness of fit?
2. How do social experiences contribute to changes in temperament, in line with the notion of "goodness of fit"?

Parenting Context of Emotional Development

LEARNING OBJECTIVE 7.13 Identify aspects of parenting that influence infants' emotional development.

Parenting is pivotal to emotional development. Parents (and other caregivers) socialize children's emotional development by modeling emotional expressions and responding sensitively or harshly to infants' emotions. Furthermore, parents' psychological functioning shapes how parents interact with their infants.

Parental Emotional Expressivity

Children learn about emotions by observing how caregivers express emotions in different situations. A meta-analysis that aggregated results across several studies found that parents' expressions of happiness, surprise, and interest related to children's positive expressiveness from infancy through adolescence (Halberstadt & Eaton, 2002). Furthermore, infants from families who were high on expressiveness were better able to match happy emotions in faces and voices at 9 months of age than infants from families low on expressiveness (Ogren, Burling, & Johnson, 2018).

Parents' abilities to regulate their emotional experiences also affect their infants' emotional development. Parents with strong **distress tolerance**—the ability to persist when faced with negative emotions and cope with everyday stressors including the demands of parenthood—may be more able to develop positive relationships with children. Indeed, parents low on distress tolerance may increasingly struggle when interacting with infants with difficult temperaments. In turn, parents' abilities to tolerate stress may reduce over time, further heightening the challenges of parenting (Morford, Cookston, & Hagan, 2017).

Parental Depression and Anxiety

Depressed and anxious parents sometimes display low emotional expressions when responding to their infants' emotional expressions. Parents' emotional disconnect to infants then shapes infants' emotional development. The classic **still-face experiment** illustrates how parental depression and anxiety may affect infant emotions. In this experiment, a researcher instructs mothers to interact naturally with their infants for 3 minutes as usual, and to then interact with their infants for another 3 minutes while maintaining a flat, unresponsive still face (**FIGURE 7.15**). After the still-face period, mothers resume natural interactions and soothe their infants if necessary. Typically, infants become upset by their mother's still face, and engage in strategies such as looking away to alleviate their distress (Cohn & Tronick, 1983; Ekas, Lickenbrock, & Braungart-Rieker, 2013). When mothers re-engage their babies, infants typically calm down. Infants who are able to calm down and regulate their emotions after being

distress tolerance The ability to persist when faced with negative emotions and cope with everyday stressors

still-face experiment An experiment in which caregivers interact naturally with their infants for a brief period, followed by maintaining a still, unresponsive face for several minutes; the caregivers' still face elicits distress and negative emotions in infants that can be viewed as a measure of infant and mother emotional connection (among other things) distressed are thought to be securely attached to their caregivers. Infants whose mothers report symptoms of depression, however, have difficulties regulating their emotions during the still-face experiment (Weinberg et al., 2006). Similarly, infants whose mothers report anxiety show heightened physiological reactions during the re-engagement phase of the still-face experiment, indicating their inability to come down from a high level of distress (Ostlund et al., 2017). Why might this be? As we will see, parents' sensitive attunement to infant needs may be crucial for positive infant emotional development.

FIGURE 7.15 The still-face experiment. In the still-face experiment, mothers are asked to interact naturally with their infants for 3 minutes, followed by a 3-minute segment in which they keep their faces unresponsive and still. Typically, infants become upset by their mother's still face, and may engage in strategies such as looking away to soothe their distress.

Parental Sensitivity and Synchrony

Caregiver sensitivity in the domain of emotions, including mirroring behaviors and interaction synchrony, is vital to infant emotional development. Caregivers display **mirroring behaviors** when they reflect back the emotions of their infants, such as by smiling in response to a baby's smile or exaggerating a frown when infants are upset. Imitations help infants form connections between their feelings and those of their caregivers (Holodynski & Friedlmeier, 2006). Infants with mothers who displayed high mirroring during interactions actively attempted to re-engage their mothers during the still-face experiment by vocalizing and bidding for attention (Bigelow et al., 2018). In contrast, infants of mothers who were low in mirroring did not increase their vocalizations or bids.

mirroring behaviors The reflecting back of emotions by caregivers to their infants such as smiling in response to an infant's smile

Interaction synchrony captures the prompt, reciprocal ways that caregivers respond to infant behaviors and emotions, as seen when caregivers alternate their looks, smiles, and vocalizations with those of their infants, especially while expressing emotional warmth. Interaction synchrony and maternal warmth fosters infants' emotion regulation months and even years later (Brady-Smith et al., 2013; Feldman et al., 2011).

interaction synchrony The prompt, reciprocal ways that caregivers respond to infant behaviors and emotions, which support infant emotional regulation

In contrast, parental anger, harshness, and other negative and controlling behaviors impede toddlers' development of emotion regulation, amplify stress in toddlers and young children, and at extremes, can cascade to psychopathology and emotional problems in children (Calkins et al., 1998; Cicchetti & Rogosch, 2012; Gunnar & Vazquez, 2006; Strang, Hanson, & Pollak, 2012). As a key caregiver of infants, fathers influence infant and toddler emotional development through their sensitivity as well. Responsiveness in fathers supports 2-year-olds' emotion regulation skills, with high warmth and responsiveness in fathers relating to low emotional problem behaviors in infants (Cabrera, Shannon, & Tamis-LeMonda, 2007).

Parental Cell Phone Use and Emotional Development

The importance of parental sensitivity in infant emotion development sparks questions about cell phone and technology use. Do distractions from technology divert parents' attention away from their infants and potentially interfere with infants' emotional development (**FIGURE 7.16**)? The answer is an unequivocal yes. Mothers who reported frequent mobile device use had infants who were less positive in their affect during the initial phase of the still-face procedure and who showed less recovery at reunion than were infants of low users (Myruski et al., 2018). Parents may unknowingly

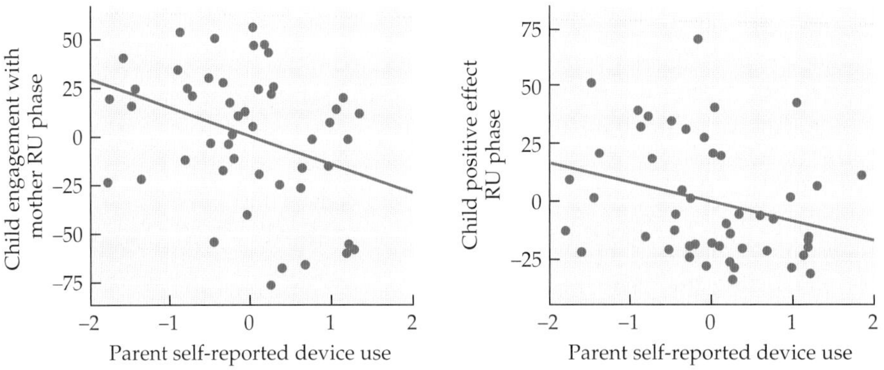

FIGURE 7.16 Technology distractions can affect infants' emotional development. Scatterplots of infants' behaviors (*y* axis) at different levels of parent cell phone use (*x* axis), with each dot representing a mother-infant dyad. Parents who reported using cell phones more had infants who showed less engagement with them during the reunion of the still-face experiment (left panel) and less positive affect (right panel), as shown by the best-fitting line depicting the negative associations. (After S. Myruski et al. 2018. *Dev Sci* 21: e12610. © 2017 John Wiley & Sons Ltd.)

compromise their infants' emotional functioning when they frequently attend to their phones rather than their infants' cues.

✓ CHECK YOUR UNDERSTANDING 7.13

1. List three aspects of parenting related to individual differences in emotional development among infants.
2. Why do you think that cell phone use by parents harms infants' emotional functioning?

Cultural Context of Emotional Development

LEARNING OBJECTIVE 7.14 Discuss aspects of cultural context that might affect infants' emotional development.

Cultural lessons around emotions begin in infancy. Infants gradually learn which emotions are acceptable and expected, when emotions should be expressed, and with what level of intensity. In many U.S. households, parents eagerly await and often attempt to elicit smiles and laughs from their infants. The emphasis on positive emotional expression is not universal, however. As one example, Cameroon Nso caregivers—a small, tightknit agricultural community in Africa—prefer quiet and calm infants, and accordingly discourage infant expressiveness including smiling (Keller & Otto, 2009). As a result, Cameroon adults participate in few face-to-face, smiling interactions with their infants, and their infants display less smiling compared to infants in Westernized cultures, such as Germany (Wörmann et al., 2012).

Culture and Infant Temperament

Cultural expectations further determine the fit between an infant's temperament and social context. Infants whose temperamental characteristics align with cultural values and practices show better adjustment than do infants without such a fit (Ballantine & Klein, 1990; Wachs, 2006). For example, in some cultural settings it may be advantageous for an infant to be difficult in temperament. Fussy infants were more likely to survive in developing countries with high levels of infant mortality and in communities plagued by drought, perhaps because they signaled to their caregivers when they were distressed and in need of attention (DeVries, 1984; Scheper-Hughes, 1987).

Beyond these extreme circumstances, however, views around what makes an infant "difficult" vary across cultures, as revealed in classic studies of the past. In Kenya, where shared caregiving was typical, infants who were unable to adapt to multiple caregivers were considered to be difficult, whereas in communities where a primary caregiver was the norm, the infant's distress at being handed off to multiple caregivers was expected (Super & Harkness, 1986).

Culture and the Perceptions of Emotions

Do cultural differences in infants' experiences affect infants' perceptions of emotions in others? Although researchers have not addressed this question with infants, studies with adults indicate both similarities and differences in adults' perceptions of emotional expressions across cultural communities.

Several decades ago, Paul Ekman (1971) showed that adults from different countries around the world identified facial expressions similarly. People everywhere agree that a broad smile indicates happiness, and similarly discern when a person is angry, sad, and so forth. Yet, researchers have since documented subtle cultural differences in adults' interpretation of emotions in faces. For example, adults from Western nations and adults from East Asia differ in their categorization of the six basic emotions—happiness, surprise, fear, disgust, anger, and sadness. Adults from East Asia have a harder time distinguishing among these emotions in faces than do adults from Western nations, and they primarily base their ratings of emotion intensity on the eyes, whereas adults from Western nations tend to attend to other parts of the face such as the mouth (Jack et al., 2012). Why might this be? One possibility is that East Asians value the ability of individuals to be restrained in their emotional expressions. Emotional restraint might result in fewer visible cues to happiness, for example. And, because the eyes are under less voluntary control than the mouth, even if restraint of emotions occurs in the mouth, the brows continue to reveal what someone is feeling.

Through years of experience interacting with people who maintain generally subdued faces, infants and children may learn to scan subtly different cues in the face to decipher how others are feeling. If so, infants and children from East Asia might come to learn that the eyes hold cues to emotions, whereas infants and children from Western nations might come to learn that the mouth is most telling.

✓ CHECK YOUR UNDERSTANDING 7.14

1. How do cultural values and expectations affect emotional development? Give an example.

■ *Social Development*

Infants are social beings. Except in rare instances of neglect, such as the Romanian orphanage example at the start of the chapter (where infants did not have regular caregivers with whom to form attachments), all infants, regardless of where they live or with whom they interact, form attachments to the people who care for them. In fact, social development begins at birth, if not before. Newborns respond to faces, voices, touch, and smell by orienting their bodies and eyes to those around them, and by moving their bodies in socially responsive ways. Infants' social behaviors in turn elicit attention and nurturance from family members that then foster attachment in infants. In the sections following, you will learn about infants' developing attachments to their primary caregivers, their social relationships with peers, and how the early seeds of morality and prosocial behaviors emerge at this important time in development.

Attachment

Attachment refers to the affectionate bonds that infants develop toward the important people in their lives and their reliance on loved ones for comfort and protection. Infants display their attachment by following caregivers around, visually tracking caregivers' whereabouts, and sometimes clinging

attachment The affectionate bonds that infants develop toward the important people in their lives and their reliance on loved ones for comfort and protection

basic trust versus mistrust The first stage in Erik Erikson's theory of psychosocial development, in which infants learn to trust their caregivers

to caregivers when tired or distressed. The importance of early relationships can be traced to the writings of Erik Erikson (recall from Chapter 1 Erikson's theory of psychosocial development), who asserted over half a century ago that how infants resolve the psychological conflict of **basic trust versus mistrust** depends on their connection to caregivers. Infants who experience loving, positive relationships with their parents later develop trust in people and venture into a world that they view to be rewarding. In contrast, infants who do not experience affection and love may begin to mistrust others, engage in maladaptive behaviors such as withdrawal, and be ill-prepared to face the challenges of toddlerhood.

Evolutionary Views of Attachment

LEARNING OBJECTIVE 7.15 Analyze how the research of Bowlby and Harlow lent support to an evolutionary view of attachment.

Around the same time that Erikson formulated his theory, John Bowlby and Harry Harlow, separately, wrote about the evolutionary roots of infant attachment. They noted that the love infants share with their caregivers extends beyond the need for nourishment and food, to desiring proximity and warmth. Infants' biological desire to be close to people they love functions to ensure survival and protection.

ethological theory of attachment A theory posited by John Bowlby that claims attachment is an evolved response that aids infants' survival

imprinting A phenomenon identified by Konrad Lorenz in which certain animal species are predisposed to follow whatever moving thing they see during a critical period early in life

Bowlby's Ethological Theory of Attachment

The English psychiatrist John Bowlby's interest in attachment grew out of his volunteer work in a residential school for maladjusted children. Bowlby was particularly inspired by his observations of two children. One adolescent had never had a stable relationship with a parent, and the second was anxious and clingy and followed Bowlby everywhere. This anecdotal experience motivated Bowlby's later research at the London Child Guidance Clinic, where he compared juvenile thieves to a matched control group (**FIGURE 7.17**). He found that the juvenile thieves were more likely to have been separated from their mothers for an extended period or to have been deprived of a mother's care than juveniles in the control group (Bowlby, 1944).

A few years later, the World Health Organization commissioned Bowlby to prepare a report on the fate of children without families in Europe. In his report, *Maternal Care and Mental Health* (Bowlby, 1951), Bowlby explained why orphaned infants and children were likely to suffer emotionally:

> …*the infant and young child should experience a warm, intimate, and continuous relationship with his mother (or permanent mother substitute) in which both find satisfaction and enjoyment.*

Bowlby's clinical work with children in orphanages and refugee camps during World War II also influenced his theory of attachment. The initial distress of young children upon separation from their mothers gave way to despair and detachment. Separated children were emotionally disturbed, depressed, or listless, and were unable to develop normal relationships. Even when reunited with their mothers, they remained anxious and defensive (Bowlby, 1953).

Bowlby's observations led to his **ethological theory of attachment** (Bowlby, 1958, 1963): Attachment is an evolved response that aids the baby's survival. Bowlby's evolutionary account aligned with the theories of Konrad Lorenz, who wrote that certain animal species were genetically predisposed to follow whatever moving thing they saw during a specific critical period early in life, a phenomenon referred to as **imprinting** (**FIGURE 7.18**). Imprinting led some species of newborn birds and mammals to follow their mothers everywhere, thereby ensuring proximity to food and protection. Like Lorenz, Bowlby

FIGURE 7.17 John Bowlby's observations at the London Child Guidance Clinic. John Bowlby's clinical work with children deprived of parental care led to his ethological theory of attachment. Bowlby wrote about the emotional suffering of children who failed to experience the consistent, loving care that is core to survival.

FIGURE 7.18 Imprinting.   Konrad Lorenz's work on "imprinting" stated that certain animal species followed the first moving object they saw during a specific critical period early in life. Here, ducklings who had been exposed to Lorenz from birth follow him around. His finding was taken as evidence for an evolutionary view of attachment.

proposed that infants were equipped with a repertoire of behaviors, including crying, sucking, smiling, clinging, and following, which matured over the first months of life and became focused on the primary caregiver. Over the first year of life, infants form attachments with the prominent people in their lives.

Harlow's Monkeys

Around the same time that Bowlby was developing his ethological theory of attachment, the American psychologist Harry Harlow and his colleagues conducted a series of experiments with infant rhesus monkeys that lent further support to the biological importance of infant attachment. Harlow compared infant monkeys reared in isolation from birth to monkeys reared normally. The socially isolated monkeys were fed and kept healthy but kept away from other monkeys for six months. The isolated monkeys displayed socially deviant behaviors, including avoidance of other monkeys, an inability to learn from or communicate with other monkeys, and (for females) a lack of interest in sex. When the isolated females were artificially impregnated, they rejected, ignored, and attacked their babies.

In other experiments, Harlow separated infant monkeys from their mothers and placed them in a cage that contained two "surrogate" mothers: a wire monkey that fed the infants milk and a cloth monkey that provided warmth and contact comfort. The monkeys would spend most of their days clinging to the cloth monkey, and only approached the wire monkey to eat. When exposed to a frightening stimulus, the monkeys fled to the warm, cloth surrogate for comfort, and monkeys whose cloth surrogates were removed displayed high anxiety and fear (**FIGURE 7.19**) (Harlow, 1958).

Harlow's findings supported the conviction that proximity to and close bodily contact with an "attachment figure," rather than the provision of food or oral gratification alone, was responsible for the infant's attachment to its primary caregiver. These findings profoundly challenged Freud's **drive reduction theory** (1927, 1940), which held that a primary motivation of humans is to satisfy biological needs—including the need for nourishment. As Harlow showed, being fed was insufficient to the formation of attachment.

drive reduction theory The idea that a primary motivation of humans is to satisfy biological needs, such as hunger and thirst

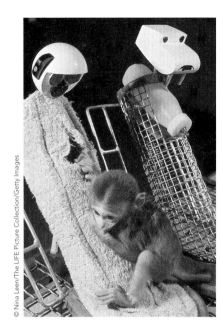

© Nina Leen/The LIFE Picture Collection/Getty Images

FIGURE 7.19 Harry Harlow's studies of attachment in monkeys. Harlow's experiments with monkeys revealed the importance of proximity and close bodily contact with an "attachment figure." Harlow separated infant monkeys from their mothers and placed them in a cage that contained two "surrogate" mothers: a wire monkey that fed the infants milk and a cloth monkey that provided warmth and contact comfort. Monkeys chose to spend their time with the warm, cloth monkey, and only approached the wire monkey to eat. Monkeys whose cloth surrogates were removed displayed high anxiety and fearful responses.

✓ **CHECK YOUR UNDERSTANDING 7.15**
1. What is Bowlby's ethological theory of attachment?
2. How did Harlow's monkey study support Bowlby's theory?

Ainsworth and the Strange Situation

LEARNING OBJECTIVE 7.16 Summarize Mary Ainsworth's contributions to the field of attachment research.

Developmental psychologist Mary Ainsworth sought to test Bowlby's ethological theory by examining attachment formation between infants and mothers. She accompanied her husband to the East African Institute of Social Research in Uganda in 1954, where she conducted an observational study of Ugandan infants and mothers (**FIGURE 7.20**). Ainsworth interviewed mothers about their childcare practices and infants' development and observed infants' interactions with mothers and other family members. Ainsworth observed that infants actively sought contact with their mothers when they were afraid, hurt, hungry, and when their mothers left their vicinity. They treated mothers as a secure base from which to explore and showed distress at separation.

Upon returning to the United States, Ainsworth embarked on a longitudinal study of attachment at Johns Hopkins University. She visited local infant–mother pairs every 3 weeks from 3 to 54 weeks after the infant's birth, recording infants' attachment behaviors and mothers' responses. When infants were around 12 months, she assessed them in an experiment called the **Strange Situation**, which soon became a popular method for studying infant attachment. In this procedure, an infant and mother visited a laboratory playroom, where after being introduced to the unfamiliar room, the infant experienced a series of separations from their caregiver and exposures to a stranger (**TABLE 7.1**).

During these short events, a researcher assessed the infant's exploration of the room, use of the caregiver as a secure base from which to explore, reactions to the caregiver separation, reactions to

Strange Situation An experiment developed by Mary Ainsworth to assess infant attachment to caregivers based on infant behaviors; in a laboratory playroom, infants experience separations from their caregiver, exposure to a stranger, and then reunification with their caregiver

© JHU Sheridan Libraries/Gado/Getty Images

FIGURE 7.20 Mary Ainsworth's research on infant attachment. While doing research at the East African Institute of Social Research in Kampala, Uganda in 1954, Ainsworth recruited 28 babies and their mothers from several villages and visited their homes every two weeks for nine months. She interviewed mothers about their childcare practices and infants' development and observed infants' interactions with mothers and other family members. Ainsworth observed that infants actively sought contact with their mothers when they were afraid, hurt, hungry, and when their mothers left their vicinity. They showed distress at separation, approached mothers when they returned from an absence, and treated mothers as a secure base from which to explore.

TABLE 7.1 ■ The Eight Events of the Strange Situation

(1) Introduction of the infant and caregiver to the unfamiliar room

(2) Infant and caregiver are left alone in the room

(3) Stranger enters the room

(4) Caregiver leaves the infant with the stranger

(5) Caregiver re-enters the room and the stranger departs

(6) Caregiver leaves infant alone in the room

(7) Stranger enters the room

(8) Caregiver enters the room

Source: After M. D. S. Ainsworth et al. 1978. Patterns of Attachment: A Psychological Study of the Strange Situation. Erlbaum: Hillsdale, NJ.

the stranger, the ability to be soothed by the stranger, and reactions to the reunion with the caregiver through attempts for closeness and contact versus avoidance or resistance. Of paramount importance was the infant's behavior upon reunion, such as whether the infant sought comfort from and was comforted by the caregiver, was unable to be comforted, avoided the caregiver, and so forth.

From her observations, which she replicated in larger samples, Ainsworth and colleagues identified three groups of infant attachment (Ainsworth & Bell, 1969; Bretherton & Ainsworth, 1974):

- **Secure attachment**. Securely attached infants (the majority of babies) explored the unfamiliar room and used their caregivers as a secure base for exploration. They protested their mothers' departure and were more likely than insecure infants to greet their mothers positively on reunion.

- **Insecure resistant attachment** (or ambivalent). Ambivalent infants (a small percentage of babies) stayed close to their caregivers upon entering the unfamiliar room and became very upset when the caregivers left the room. They were not easily comforted when the caregivers returned, often alternating between seeking comfort and resisting the caregivers' attempts to console them.

- **Insecure avoidant attachment**. Avoidant infants (a small percentage of babies) explored the room freely and were not distressed by the caregivers' departure. If they became distressed, they were as easily comforted by the strangers as by the parents and were indifferent or avoidant toward the caregivers upon their return.

Years later, researchers Main and Solomon (1990) identified a fourth attachment style that did not fit with Ainsworth's three groups: **disorganized** attachment. Infants with disorganized attachment displayed contradictory behaviors and emotions (such as fear followed by laughter) and disorganized movements, freezing, and apprehension toward the mother. Subsequent research identified associations between infants' disorganized attachment and experiences of abuse or neglect (Baer & Martinez, 2006; Granqvist et al., 2017). Infants' experiences of their caregivers as psychologically unavailable and a source of alarm or fear may explain why some infants develop disorganized attachment (Hesse & Main, 2006; Solomon & George, 2011).

✓ CHECK YOUR UNDERSTANDING 7.16

1. What four attachment styles/categories do researchers identify from the Strange Situation?

secure attachment An attachment status initially identified by Mary Ainsworth in which infants display a strong connection or bond with their caregiver(s) and use their caregivers as a safe base from which to explore their environment; securely attached infants become upset when their caregivers leave the room, are happy when their caregivers return, and seek comfort from their caregivers

insecure resistant An attachment status (also called ambivalent), initially identified by Mary Ainsworth that is characterized by infants who become very upset and anxious when the caregiver leaves the room and are not easily comforted on caregiver return

insecure avoidant An attachment status initially identified by Mary Ainsworth that is characterized by infants who do not become distressed by the caregiver's departure, freely explore the room, are easily comforted by the stranger, and show indifference during reunion with the caregiver

disorganized An infant attachment style characterized by an infant's contradictory emotions and behavior and disorganized movements, freezing, and apprehension toward caregiver

Contexts of Attachment

Ethological theorists such as Bowlby and Harlow underscore the universal adaptiveness of attachment. At the same time, Ainsworth and other researchers found that infants vary considerably in the ways they express attachment. What contextual factors explain differences among infants? Most centrally, infant attachment depends primarily on the sensitivity of caregivers. Furthermore, caregivers from different cultural communities share unique views and practices around childrearing that affect their infants' development and expression of attachment.

Parenting Context of Attachment

LEARNING OBJECTIVE 7.17 Identify the features of high-quality parent-infant interactions that relate to infant attachment.

Ainsworth underscored parents' formative role in infant attachment. Her in-depth observations of infants and mothers in their home environments revealed critical differences between mothers of secure and insecure infants. Mothers of securely attached infants quickly picked up their crying infants, held them longer and with noticeable pleasure, and responded sensitively to the infants' behaviors in general (Ainsworth & Bell, 1969). By contrast, mothers of avoidant and resistant children spent little time holding their babies and were unresponsive to the infants' crying and developmental changes. As a result, when securely attached infants reached a year, they did not cry as much or need as much physical contact as avoidant or resistant infants (Ainsworth, 1979).

Ainsworth's conclusion that caregivers should respond quickly and consistently to infants' cries in the early months flew in the face of contemporary thinking. Many worried that such attention would result in spoiled children or crybabies. However, Ainsworth's revolutionary position has since stood the test of time. Researchers today acknowledge the central role of sensitive parenting for infants' strong and secure attachment, and recognize that contextual factors influence parents' sensitivity (Dagan & Sagi-Schwartz, 2020; Leerkes, Gedaly, & Su, 2016). For example, being a single mother with low education, living in poverty, and having an uninvolved partner heightens the risk of low maternal sensitivity, which can cascade to resistant and avoidant attachment in the infant (Leerkes, Parade, & Gudmundson, 2011; Leerkes, Weaver, & O'Brien, 2012). Furthermore, mothers who fail to remain calm behaviorally and physiologically when their infants cry have infants with disorganized attachments and behavior problems (Leerkes et al., 2017).

✓ CHECK YOUR UNDERSTANDING 7.17
1. How does the quality of parent-infant interaction shape infants' attachment development?
2. What can caregivers do to foster secure attachment in their infants?

Cultural Context of Attachment

LEARNING OBJECTIVE 7.18 Relate the ways that infants' attachment with caregivers is similar and different across cultural communities.

Many features of attachment generalize across cultures, which makes sense given the evolutionary roots of attachment. Infants around the world form attachments and actively attempt to remain close to their caregivers (Dagan & Sagi-Schwartz, 2020; van Ijzendoorn & Sagi, 2010). Children from different cultural communities, including the United States, Israeli Kibbutzim, and hunting and gathering groups in Africa show separation anxiety at similar ages (Kagan, 1976). And, Ainsworth's original attachment patterns—secure, avoidant, and resistant—are found in cultural communities across Africa, East Asia, and Latin America; in affluent and developing economies; and in hunter-gatherer communities where infants are often cared for by nonrelatives (Mesman, van IJzendoorn, & Sagi-Schwartz, 2016). Furthermore, parents from many different countries express similar views on the foundations of secure attachment—that infants should rely on parents in times of need, but be encouraged to explore the world (Posada et al., 1995). Still, differences in parental expectations and practices, the nature of infants' early experiences with caregivers, the structure of infant care, and even the socioeconomic resources of families give rise to cultural differences in attachment (Gojman et al., 2012; Keller & Bard, 2017; Mesman et al., 2016).

Parent Expectations and Practices

Mary Ainsworth pioneered cross-cultural work in attachment (Ainsworth & Marvin, 1995). Ainsworth observed that Ugandan infants displayed more intense protest when separated from their mothers compared to U.S. infants in Baltimore, Maryland, perhaps because Ugandan infants were not accustomed to being separated from their mothers. Additionally, U.S. infants frequently accompanied their caregivers to out-of-home settings, such as the grocery store, post office, sibling's school, and so forth, where they regularly encountered strangers. In Uganda, infants remained in or near their homes and rarely encountered strangers. Ainsworth speculated that such differences in experiences explained the different reactions of infants to the Strange Situation. Indeed, infants from different cultures express their attachment to caregivers in ways that align with the unique views and practices of their cultures.

Consider how parents' views about desirable and appropriate child behaviors affect infants' expressions of attachment. One caregiver might interpret a toddler's reluctance to leave her side as a sign of loving affection; another might interpret the same behavior as immature clinginess. In her book, *Culture and Attachment*, Robin Harwood (1983) described how Anglo-American U.S. mothers and Puerto Rican mothers differed in their views and practices around attachment. Harwood interviewed mothers about the qualities they desired in their infants and the characteristics they felt described securely attached infants. Anglo-American mothers ranked child self-confidence, autonomy, and independence as more important than did Puerto Rican mothers, who placed more emphasis on child obedience, child moods (being happy and calm), and the importance of remaining close to mother. In turn, Anglo-American and Puerto Rican infants fit the attachment profiles their mothers desired.

Child-Care Structure and Arrangements

Cultural differences in child-care arrangements may likewise affect infant attachment. In some cultural communities one or two parents raise infants in a nuclear family; whereas in others multiple caregivers may be involved, including grandparents and other relatives, siblings, and friends. This global reality challenges the matriarchal emphasis that has dominated the study of attachment.

The pioneer of fathering research, Michael Lamb, was the first to ask about infants' attachment to the "other parent." Lamb observed U.S. mother-infant and father-infant interactions at home when infants were at 15, 18, 21, and 24 months and in a laboratory context at 14 months (Lamb, 1977). Infants expressed similar attachment behaviors—smiles, looks, vocalizations, and seeking proximity—toward their mothers and fathers. Perhaps more surprisingly, infants of all ages showed *more* attachment behaviors toward fathers than toward mothers. Infants may have shown a father-preference because fathers engage infants in more play than do mothers, especially in the second to third years of life (Clarke-Stewart, 1978; Paquette, 2004). Moreover, infants raised primarily by fathers seek comfort from their fathers, rather than their mothers, under stressful conditions (Geiger, 1996; Lamb, 1977). Thus, Lamb's work was revolutionary for its time in underscoring the glaring limitations of a mother-only attachment focus.

Beyond fathers, many other people share in the care of infants around the globe, as, for example, in the communal childrearing practices of traditional Israeli Kibbutzim, collective settlements in which members of the community share their material possessions and wealth. In traditional Kibbutz, children spend their time in a house with other children under the watch of multiple professional caregivers, visiting their parents only a few hours per day. When tested in the Strange Situation, infants in Kibbutzim were found to develop attachments with their nonparental, professional caregivers (Sagi et al., 1995) (**FIGURE 7.21**).

Infants' formation of attachments with multiple caregivers has sparked research into how members of such communities distribute responsibility for the care of children among multiple individuals rather than a single person (Keller & Bard, 2017; Morelli et al., 2017; LeVine, 2014). When infants are raised in communities with distributed childcare arrangements, they do not develop a primary attachment relationship with only a single person, and rarely display stranger anxiety (e.g., Keller & Bard, 2017; Otto & Keller, 2014). In fact, a meta-analysis of 40 investigations involving nearly 3,000 children ages birth to 3 years found that children were likely to form secure attachments to nonparental care providers who displayed high sensitivity to them and other children under their care (Ahnert, Pinquart, & Lamb, 2006). (Note that forming attachments to nonparent caregivers does not interfere with infants' development of attachment to their parents!)

Kibbutz Afikim Archive/CC BY-SA 3.0

FIGURE 7.21 Communal childrearing practices. Infants in Kibbutzim develop attachments with their nonparental, professional caregivers.

In some cultural contexts, parents relinquish responsibility for the care of their infants to grandparents for an extended period of years, during which parents are in minimal contact with their children. Some immigrants to North America send their infants back to their country of origin after giving birth, where grandparents and other relatives raise them (Bohr & Tse, 2009). Years later, these "satellite babies" return to their biological parents and attend school in their adopted country. From the perspectives of the parents, economic and social needs drive the decision to send their infants back to the home country. Parents believe they are offering their infants a chance to be reared by loving grandparents while they work to establish an economic foundation before their child returns to the United States, for example, to begin school.

However, according to attachment theory, prolonged infant-parent separation, and the subsequent disruption from relationships with grandparents and relatives, could have long-term, adverse developmental consequences. In fact, children who have been separated from their parents for lengthy periods of time, and then reunited, have been found to suffer depression and mental health problems as adolescents (Suárez-Orozco, Todorova, & Louie, 2002). Thus, there is growing need to better understand how practices around separation and early childrearing affect the trajectories of children's development from cultures around the globe.

✓ CHECK YOUR UNDERSTANDING 7.18

1. How might infants' cultural and social experiences affect their behaviors in the Strange Situation?
2. What conclusions can be drawn about infants' attachments to multiple caregivers beyond the mother? Provide evidence to support your conclusion.

Peer Relations and the Origins of Morality

Primary caregivers are by no means the sole beneficiaries of infant affection. Beyond infants' relationships with primary caregivers, infants display a keen interest in peers and people outside the family and engage in a rich variety of behaviors that may be precursors to mature forms of moral behavior and reasoning.

Prosocial Behaviors

LEARNING OBJECTIVE 7.19 Identify prosocial behaviors exhibited by infants.

When do infants display prosocial behaviors such as helping and sharing? Although such behaviors take months to develop, their origins appear in infants' very early interest in other children. Infants ages 1 to 3 months already respond differently to peers than they do to mothers or their own image in a mirror (Field, 1979; Fogel, 1979). Midway through the first year, infants smile and vocalize toward other infants (Maudry & Nekula, 1939; Vandell, Wilson, & Buchanan, 1980). By the end of the first year and into the second year, infants distinguish between familiar and unfamiliar peers and express more smiling and proximity-seeking toward peers they know and like than toward peers they don't know or dislike (Jacobson, 1981; Howes, 1983). And, toddlers increasingly help, share with, and comfort peers and adults in the second year (Brownell, 2013; Vaish, Carpenter, & Tomasello, 2009).

How do researchers test toddlers' prosocial behaviors? They often place children in situations that elicit behaviors such as sharing and helping. For instance, an examiner may pretend to be distressed or in need of help and observe how children respond. Infants as young as 14 and 18 months helped an experimenter pick up toys that were out of reach (Warneken & Tomasello, 2007), and 18- and 24-month-old toddlers shared their food with an experimenter who had not received any food during "snack time" (Dunfield et al., 2011). Toddlers 30 months of age willingly offered a favorite blanket or toy to comfort a distressed experimenter (Brownell et al., 2009). However, toddlers' propensity to help depends on the friendliness, helpfulness, and trustworthiness of the other person. Toddlers 21 months of age preferred to help people who shared a toy or showed a willingness to share in a previous interaction than to help those who did not (Dunfield & Kuhlmeier, 2010).

Do infants help others for selfish or altruistic reasons? Evolutionary theory suggests that toddlers may be naturally motivated to help others because helping aids species survival (Warneken, 2015). Indeed, toddlers appear to help others because they want to, not because they hope to gain approval or receive something in return. In fact, being rewarded for good behavior may actually deter infants from helping out in the future. For example, an experimenter dropped a pen that 20-month-old infants helped to pick up. Once the infants had helped, the experimenter gave them a material reward (a toy for play), a social reward ("Thank you!"), or no reward. Later, infants who received the material reward were less likely to help the same adult than were infants in the social reward and no reward conditions (Warneken & Tomasello, 2008). Additionally, toddlers may act prosocially out of sympathetic concern. Eighteen- and 25-month-olds were more likely to share their toy with a person who was seemingly "victimized" than with a person who was not (Vaish et al., 2009).

✓ CHECK YOUR UNDERSTANDING 7.19

1. How do researchers assess infants' prosocial behaviors, such as helping and sharing?

Moral Development and Aggression

LEARNING OBJECTIVE 7.20 Evaluate features of morality and early forms of aggression, and the ways they change in infancy and toddlerhood.

The study of moral development originated with Piaget's (1932) and Kohlberg's (1969) investigation of people's reasoning about moral situations, a topic we review in depth in Chapter 10. Piaget and Kohlberg asked children and adults to reason about hypothetical stories that contained moral themes or dilemmas, and developed stage theories of moral development based on their findings. However, neither attended to moral development in the first years of life, leaving unanswered questions around the early origins of morality. Do infants and toddlers have a *moral sense*—that is, a tendency to "see certain actions and individuals as right, good, and deserving of reward, and others as wrong, bad, and deserving of punishment" (Hamlin, 2013, p. 186)? Or, does a moral sense only develop after years of experience?

Nativists (see Chapter 5) suggest that infants have core understandings around being helped or harmed in particular ways and situations (Hamlin, 2010; Hamlin & Stitch, 2020; Mikhail, 2011; Premack & Premack, 1994). If so, the rudimentary building blocks for later advanced forms of morality may be laid down in infancy (Hamlin, 2013). Notably, the notion that infants have even a naïve understanding of right and wrong is heatedly debated (Killen & Rizzo, 2014), and so keep in mind the immense distinction between the early seeds of morality and the sophisticated moral reasoning of children and adults.

Moral Goodness

Moral goodness refers to feelings of concern for others and attempts to help those in need. The empathetic response of infants to others' distress offers evidence of moral goodness. In a historic study, newborns cried when they heard

moral goodness Feelings of concern for others and attempts to help others in need, including empathetic responses to others in distress

moral understanding and evaluation Identifying and liking individuals who are cooperative, empathetic, or helpful, and disliking individuals who are uncooperative, unempathetic, or unhelpful

helper-hinderer studies Studies that assess infants' moral understanding and evaluation by presenting infants with "helping" and "hurting" puppets (for example) and then testing whether infants behave differently toward the "helper" or "hinderer" recordings of another infant crying, but did not respond to the cries of an older infant, a chimpanzee, or their own cries (Martin & Clark, 1982). Early expressions of empathic distress increase in magnitude through 9 months of age (Geangu et al., 2010). Moreover, infants' increasingly help others at home across the second year of life, such as by handing objects to others, cleaning up, putting clothes in the laundry machine, and so on (**FIGURE 7.22**) (Dahl, 2015). Thus, at least by 2 years of age, toddlers display a seemingly natural tendency toward prosocial actions, such as comforting people in distress, helping others achieve goals, and sharing their belongings (Eisenberg, Fabes, & Spinrad, 2006; Warneken & Tomasello, 2008).

Still, prosocial behaviors do not come easily to toddlers, and certain types of situations are especially difficult, particularly those that require self-sacrifice. Eighteen- and 30-month-olds were observed in three "helping" situations that required: (1) an instrumental helping action (giving an adult an object that was dropped or out of reach), (2) an emotion-based response (providing a distressed adult with an object that would alleviate her sadness, cold, or frustration), and (3) altruistic acts that "cost" the toddler (giving an adult an object valued by the child) (Svetlova, Nichols, & Brownell, 2010). Although younger and older toddlers readily assisted in the instrumental tasks, younger toddlers had greater difficulty with the emotion-based condition than with the instrumental helping. And, both age groups had a hard time giving up their own object.

Moral Understanding and Evaluation

Moral understanding and evaluation refers to identifying and liking individuals who are cooperative, empathic, or helpful, and disliking individuals who are uncooperative, unempathic, or unhelpful. **Helper-hinderer studies** are a common way that researchers assess infants' moral understanding and evaluation. In such studies, experimenters present infants with "helping" versus "hurting" puppets and observe infants' responses (Hamlin & Wynn, 2011). For example, infants may be shown a wooden, googly-eyed puppet who attempts (but fails) to achieve a goal, such as trying to reach the top of a hill or trying to open a box that contains a toy. On alternating presentations, infants observe a "helper" who facilitates the goal (for example by bumping the puppet up the hill or opening the box), or a "hinderer" who prevents the goal (for example, by jumping on the box to prevent the opening attempt). By about 4–5 months of age, 75%–100% of infants preferred the helper as indicated by their reaching for the helper object rather than the hinderer object. In essence, infants appear to evaluate prosocial individuals or entities positively and antisocial individuals or entities negatively (Van de Vondervoort & Hamlin, 2016) (**FIGURE 7.23**).

Moral Retribution

Moral retribution is the tendency to punish individuals who misbehave or act immorally toward others. For example, in a helper-hinderer type study, infants observed puppets who helped or hindered another puppet who was attempting to achieve a goal. They were then

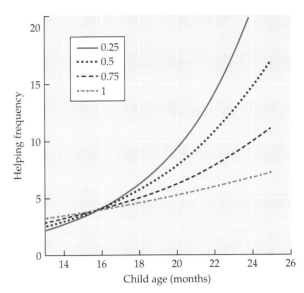

FIGURE 7.22 Infants' natural tendency toward prosocial behaviors.   Home observations of infants' spontaneous helping behaviors show that infants increase their helping behaviors across the second year, such as by giving people objects, offering help with cleaning, putting toys away, and so on. However, at younger ages (e.g., 14 to 16 months), helping is rare, and infants require a high amount of encouragement to assist. But, at older ages, infants spontaneously help in the absence of encouragement (as seen with the solid line showing the highest helping in toddlers under conditions of low encouragement). (After A. Dahl. 2015. *Child Dev* 86: 1080–1093. © 2015 A. Dahl. Child Development © 2015 Society for Research in Child Development, Inc.)

moral retribution The tendency to punish or support individuals who misbehave

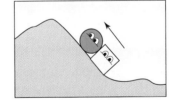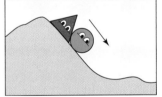

FIGURE 7.23 Helper-hinderer study.   In one of the original studies of moral evaluation, Hamlin, Wynn, and Bloom (2007) presented infants with a 3-dimensional display in which a geometric object with googly eyes, manipulated like puppets, acted out helping/hindering situations. For example, a yellow square would appear to help the circle climb the hill, whereas a red triangle would appear to push the circle down the hill. The experimenter then presented infants with a tray that contained the yellow square (helper) and red triangle (hinderer). Babies ages 6 and 10 months reliably preferred (reached for) the "helpful objects" to the "hindering objects." (After J. K. Hamlin et al. 2007. *Nature* 450: 557–559. https://doi.org/10.1038/nature06288.)

introduced to new characters who either took a dropped ball away from or gave the ball back to the prosocial helper or antisocial hinderer. Both groups of infants preferred the character who gave the ball to the prosocial helper. However, only 8-month-olds preferred the agent who took the ball away from the antisocial hinderer. Thus, as infants approach the end of the first year, they appear to recognize and support the notion of punishing antisocial agents (Hamlin et al., 2011).

In general, however, children do not consistently behave in line with moral retribution until about 2 years of age (Dahl, Schuck, & Campos, 2013), which coincides with the time that they display retribution themselves by taking resources away from someone they had observed hindering a third party (Hamlin et al., 2011). Toddlers aged 19–23 months were taught to give "treats" to different puppets and take treats away from puppets' bowls. They were then shown scenarios with helper and hinderer puppets. Toddlers were more likely to give treats to the prosocial puppet and take treats away from the antisocial puppet, suggesting that they rewarded prosocial behaviors and punished antisocial behaviors.

Aggression

Although infants and toddlers display prosocial behaviors in lab and home studies, researchers question whether infants' behaviors stem from an understanding of right versus wrong (Dahl, 2019). In fact, as infants grow in their "helpfulness" over the second year, they increasingly display **physical aggression** such as hitting, biting, pushing peers, kicking, and so on (Dahl, 2016, 2019). Toddlers engage in physical aggression at around 18 months of age (Coie & Dodge, 1998); and by 3 years of age, they show **relational aggression**, such as withdrawing or threatening to withdraw friendship, ignoring a peer, or excluding a peer from an activity (Ostrov et al., 2004). Although aggression and conflicts among toddlers may appear to be wrong, negative interactions give toddlers insight into the perspectives of others and aid the development of acceptable negotiating skills.

physical aggression Behavior causing physical harm to others, such as hitting, pushing, kicking, and biting

relational aggression A type of nonphysical aggression in which harm is caused by hurting someone's relationships or social status, such as by threatening to withdraw a friendship, withdrawing a friendship, ignoring a peer, or excluding a peer

✓ **CHECK YOUR UNDERSTANDING 7.20**
1. Define (a) moral goodness; (b) moral understanding and evaluation; and (c) moral retribution.
2. What developmental changes are seen in moral retribution across the first three years of life?
3. Define two types of aggression that toddlers display.

Self-Identity

Imagine that someone asks you to describe yourself. You might refer to your physical characteristics and perhaps the things you like to do. You might talk about the internal emotions, traits, values, and beliefs that collectively define you as a unique individual. You might explain how your gender, race, ethnicity, sexual orientation, and religion—key features of identity—define who you are.

Infants, however, do not understand these many aspects of self. Their self-identity remains rudimentary at best. But, it would be a mistake to ignore the early seeds of self-knowledge. Infants' understanding of the self, although basic, sets the stage for understanding and relating to others. And so, researchers and philosophers have long been intrigued with the developmental origins of self-identity: In what ways do infants experience a sense of self? How does infants' understanding of the self change over the first years of life? And how might researchers even begin to address such questions? In the sections following, you will learn about some innovative studies that have shed light on infants' emerging self-identity. Over development, self-identity evolves into a complex, multifaceted portrait that ceaselessly shapes how people think, act, and feel.

Aspects of Self

LEARNING OBJECTIVE 7.21 Distinguish among the different selves in one's identity.

The many characteristics you use to describe yourself illustrate the **conceptual self**, "me," or "objective self"—the organized set of propositions that form a complex web of who you are (**FIGURE 7.24**) (Neisser, 1991, p. 198). But, even when you are not reflecting on who you are, you are aware of yourself as a living, breathing human. In fact, the **subjective self**—the "I" of the self—represents an important but often overlooked aspect of the self. The subjective self is experienced in the moment: It reflects your sense of being alive as you act in and on the environment and differentiate your body from the world around you.

The subjective self further divides into the ecological self and interpersonal self. The **ecological self** refers to the perception of one's body in relation to the physical environment (Neisser, 1991). You rarely look at your limbs as you move through space, yet you are aware of where they are and what they are doing. Right now, for example you might feel yourself seated on a chair or laying across a bed, holding a textbook or tablet and flipping through the pages. The **interpersonal self** refers to the perception of self in relation to other people, including experiences involved in eye contact and the back-and-forth exchanges of social interactions. You do not consciously time the intervals between when you talk relative to others, and vice versa, or gauge where others are looking during conversations, but you would find it disconcerting if another person paused for overly long periods before responding to you or looked at someone else in the room while you were talking. You would be perturbed because a certain degree of responsiveness is anticipated in social exchanges, and people expect and desire others to take interest in what they say. Each of these aspects of the self follows a unique developmental path that is shaped by experiences. As we will see, infancy is the starting point for the development of self.

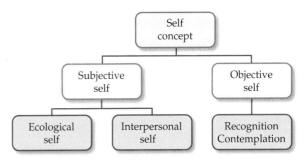

FIGURE 7.24 Self concept. Self concept divides into the subjective self (which comprises an ecological self and interpersonal self) and objective self. Infants show evidence of ecological and interpersonal selves, but it takes time for a conceptual self to develop. (After U. Neisser. 1991. *Dev Rev* 11: 197–209.)

conceptual self The characteristics a person uses to describe oneself, also referred to as the "me" or "objective self"

subjective self The characteristics a person uses to describe oneself, also referred to as the "I" of the self; a person's sense of acting in the environment as a unique entity

ecological self The perception of one's body in relation to the physical environment

interpersonal self The perception of oneself in relation to other people, including experiences with eye-contact and back-and-forth exchanges with others

✓ **CHECK YOUR UNDERSTANDING 7.21**

1. Define and give examples for the (a) conceptual self; (b) subjective self; (c) ecological self; and (d) interpersonal self.

The Ecological and Interpersonal Selves

LEARNING OBJECTIVE 7.22 Describe the methods that researchers use to study infants' ecological and interpersonal selves, and what they reveal.

Margaret Mahler (1897–1985), a Hungarian physician who later became a central figure in psychoanalysis, presented one of the first theories about how infants develop a sense of self as separate from others. Mahler proposed that in the first months of life infants do not yet have a sense of individuality, but rather regard self and other (with other being "mother") as one. Then, at around 5 months, infants differentiate self from mother and enter a world of human connection. But, does it truly take infants until the middle of the first year to become aware of the boundaries between them and other people?

Developmentalists Philippe Rochat and Susan Hespos (1997) designed a clever method—the **single-touch and double-touch experiment**—to investigate whether very young infants can distinguish their own actions from the actions of others. In their experiment, they observed the responses of newborns

single-touch and double-touch experiment An experiment to test infant self-awareness; researchers ask whether very young infants can distinguish between an experimenter touching the infant's cheek (single-touch; other-stimulation) and the infant's own touch of the cheek (double-touch; self-stimulation)

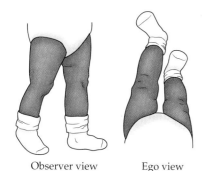

Observer view   Ego view

FIGURE 7.25 The "ego view" and the "observer view" of an infant's moving legs. Infants viewed an image of their legs moving that was taken by a camera above their heads. The image therefore matched their own view. They were also shown an image of their legs moving from a side camera that did not match their view. Infants looked longer at the nonmatching side-camera perspective of their moving legs relative to matching image, as though they found it to be "odd" and unexpected (After P. Rochat and R. Morgan. 1995. *Dev Psychol* 31: 626–636.)

self-stimulation When an infant's hand or finger touches its own cheek (creating a double-touch experience); self-stimulation is part of the single-touch and double-touch experiment

other-stimulation When an experimenter's finger touches the infant's cheek, creating a single-touch experience; other-stimulation is part of the single-touch and double-touch experiment

contingency experiences Environmental effects that arise from infant actions such as a mobile moving in response to a swipe; infants' reactions to contingency are thought to reflect the ecological self

and 4-week-old infants to two types of touch stimulation: (1) **self-stimulation**, when the infant touches their own cheek with a finger and (2) **other stimulation**, when an experimenter's finger touches the infant's cheek. Infants were more likely to turn their heads and open their mouths, as though preparing to breastfeed, when an experimenter touched their cheeks (other stimulation) than when they touched their own cheeks (self-stimulation). Rochat inferred that infants' early ability to differentiate self-touch from other touch is explained by the different sensory experiences associated with the two types of touches. When infants touch themselves, they experience a "double touch," receiving tactile feedback on both finger and cheek as well as feedback from their moving arm. In contrast, touches by other people result in a "single touch" of a finger to cheek—the distinction that inspired the name of the experiment.

Very young infants also recognize that movements such as kicking the legs are self-generated, offering further evidence for their sense of an ecological self. For example, Rochat documented that 3-month-old infants can distinguish between different views of their moving legs (Rochat & Goubet, 1995). To illustrate, he presented infants with an "ego view" from a camera that was located behind the infant's head and thus presented the scene from the infant's viewpoint. The "observer view" was generated by a camera angle different from the infants' perspective. Infants looked longer at the observer view than at the ego view, suggesting that they were intrigued by the novel, unexpected view of their moving legs (**FIGURE 7.25**).

Infants further display their sense of the ecological self through their reactions to **contingency experiences**, environmental effects that arise from one's actions. Infants recognize, for example, when they have caused a mobile to move by kicking their legs (Rovee-Collier, 1989) or brought a picture into view by sucking on a nipple (Siqueland & Delucua, 1969). And, infants' perceptions of contingency extends to social interactions—the interpersonal self—as illustrated in a clever experiment conducted three decades ago.

Infants in a control group communicated visually and vocally with their mothers in real time via a closed-circuit television, such that they experienced the same sort of real-time interactions characteristic of their everyday interactions. Infants in the experimental group, on the other hand, viewed videos of their mothers that had been recorded a few minutes earlier. Although the experimental videos showed mothers expressing positive behaviors toward their infants, mothers' behaviors had no contingent connection to what infants were doing because of the time delay in the video playback. Infants in the experimental group were markedly distressed by the noncontingent videos, whereas infants in the control group enjoyed interacting "live" via the TV monitors. The researchers concluded that infants were sensitive to the contingent timing of their mothers' interactions (Murray & Trevarthen, 1985).

✓ **CHECK YOUR UNDERSTANDING 7.22**

1. Explain the single-touch and double-touch experiment. What does it reveal about infant understanding of self?
2. Explain contingency experiments and what they tell us about infant understanding of the interpersonal self.

The Objective Self

LEARNING OBJECTIVE 7.23 Discuss evidence for infants' understanding of an objective self.

An infant's objective or conceptual self does not emerge until somewhere around the second year. Michael Lewis and Jeanne Brooks-Gunn were the first to study infants' objective self (Lewis & Brooks-Gunn, 1979) by dabbing rouge on the noses of 9-, 12-, and 18-month-old infants who stood in front of a mirror. Nine- and 12-month-olds reached out and touched the mirror to rub off the rouge, seemingly not realizing that they were observing themselves in the reflection. In contrast, the 18-month-old toddlers wiped their noses when they saw their reflection in the mirror. The authors concluded that midway through the second year toddlers begin to think about themselves objectively as they would about other people. Notably, about the time toddlers pass the rouge test, they begin to use personal pronouns ("me", "mine") and refer to themselves by their own names (Lewis & Ramsay, 2004). Electroencephalography (EEG) provides further evidence of infant self-recognition: 18-month-olds show enhanced brain responses when viewing their own faces compared to the faces of unfamiliar infants, their caregivers, or unfamiliar caregivers (Stapel et al., 2017).

Furthermore, toddlers begin to use words such as "boy" or "girl" to label themselves and others. Gender self-labeling indicates that toddlers have formed a basic **gender identity**, which refers to knowing that one is a boy or a girl. Toddlers 24–30 months of age also demonstrate their understanding of gender categories by pointing to boys and girls in photographs or a picture of their own gender when asked (Martin, Ruble, & Szkrybalo, 2002; Stennes et al., 2005).

Notably, the attainment of a gender identity may lead toddlers to engage in stereotyped behaviors, such as playing with toys that are "for boys" or "for girls." Indeed, toddlers who produced gender labels earlier in development increased their sex-typed play over time more so than did children who produced gender labels later in development (Zosuls et al., 2009). And children from different ethnic backgrounds show similar changes in gendered behaviors as they learn about their gender identity (Zosuls et al., 2014). For example, researchers tested whether 2-year-old toddlers from Mexican, Dominican, and African American backgrounds could label their own gender and point to pictures labeled as "girl," "boy," "lady," and "man." They also observed children at 24 and 36 months playing with a set of toys that included a doll and truck. Children who understood gender categories at 24 months increased their gender-stereotyped play between the two ages, with girls gravitating toward the doll and boys toward the truck. Moreover, girls were more likely to engage in nurturing behaviors with the doll, such as cuddling and feeding, whereas boys were more likely to engage in mechanical manipulations of the toys, such as flipping the doll's eyes open and shut or turning the wheels on the truck.

Thus, as children learn about the social categories to which they and others belong, they shift their behaviors to align with their understanding of what members in the category should do. However, knowing one's sex is only the first step in gender identity. With age, children's attitudes and beliefs about gender develop into richly elaborated concepts, as we will discuss in subsequent chapters.

gender identity In infancy, gender identity refers to knowing that one is a boy or a girl

✓ CHECK YOUR UNDERSTANDING 7.23

1. Give an example of how a toddler's understanding of gender affects their behaviors.

Contexts of Self-Identity

Which aspects of context and culture influence infants' knowledge of the self? As is the case for most constructs in developmental psychology, what is known about infant and toddler self-identity is largely based on Anglo-American infants from middle-income households. However, certain early aspects of self-identity are likely universal. As infants act in their worlds, they receive feedback about their movements, location in space, and interactions with others. Thus, contextual influences on infants' awareness of their own actions are typically not studied. In contrast, context and culture may influence development of the conceptual self, in particular gender development. Here, we examine some influences on early gender development in home settings and across cultural communities.

Gender Socialization: Home Context

LEARNING OBJECTIVE 7.24 List the ways that parents socialize gender in infants and toddlers.

Children experience many messages about gender in the home setting. But, what is perhaps most striking about gender socialization is how early in development it occurs. Studies from decades ago revealed that parents of day-old infants described newborn girls as softer, finer featured, less strong, more delicate, and quieter than newborn boys (Karraker, Vogel, & Lake, 1995; Rubin, Provenzano, & Luria, 1974). And, boys received more physical touch, more proximal behaviors such as rocking, and were handled more roughly in the first 6 months of life than girls; girls were talked to more than boys, looked at more, and treated as more fragile (Block, 1983; Stern & Karraker, 1989).

You might speculate that parents treat their infants in gendered ways because of biological differences in the behaviors of boys versus girls. However, parents' differential treatment of boy and girl infants cannot be attributed to infants' behaviors alone, as shown in experimental manipulation of infant gender in what are referred to as **Baby "X" studies**. In the Baby "X" studies, experimenters labeled the *same* infant as a "boy" or "girl" and observed how people talked about and interacted with the baby. Infants labeled as "boys" were rated as bigger, stronger, and louder compared to infants labeled as "girls." Infants labeled as girls received more talk and nurturance from adults than did infants labeled as boys. In a review of 23 Baby "X" studies, adults were more likely to encourage activity and whole-body stimulation with infants labeled as boys. The *actual* sex of the infant in the studies had no effect on how people viewed or treated them (Stern & Karraker, 1989).

Of course, Baby "X" studies and other highly cited studies on parents' socialization of gender date back many years. Clearly, a growing number of parents aim to be gender-neutral in their parenting today. Nonetheless, observations of children's rooms and toys reveal gender differences that mirror findings reported decades ago (MacPhee & Prendergast, 2019). Although blatant differences in parents' behaviors toward girls and boys may be rare, parents implicitly socialize gender in subtle but impactful ways, including through the products they buy and how they respond to their children's behaviors (Mesman & Groeneveld, 2018).

A compelling example of parents' socialization of gender was illustrated in a study of infant motor skill. In a laboratory study, mothers of 11-month-olds were asked to estimate the steepest slope their infants could safely crawl down without falling, by setting the angle on a mechanical sloping walkway. Infants were subsequently tested on their ability to crawl down slopes of different angles on the same walkway (**FIGURE 7.26A**) (Mondschein, Adolph, & Tamis-LeMonda, 2000). Mothers of girls underestimated their infants' crawling ability whereas mothers of boys more accurately estimated their infants' ability. Additionally, mothers of girls underestimated the angle of slope that their infants would *attempt* to crawl down (whether or not infants were successful), whereas mothers of boys overestimated the angle of slope. That is, mothers of boys seemed to expect their infants to be "risk-takers" who would attempt slopes beyond the bounds of their ability. When tested on their actual crawling abilities, boys and girls did not differ on the slopes they could safely crawl down or attempt to crawl down (**FIGURE 7.26B**). Thus, gender differences in crawling skill and risk taking only existed in the eyes of the beholder.

Baby "X" studies Experiments in which researchers label the same infant as a "boy" or a "girl" and then observe how caregivers or adults talk and interact with the infant based on the labeled gender

(A)

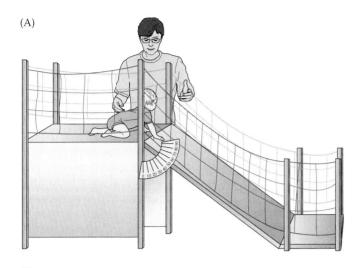

(B)

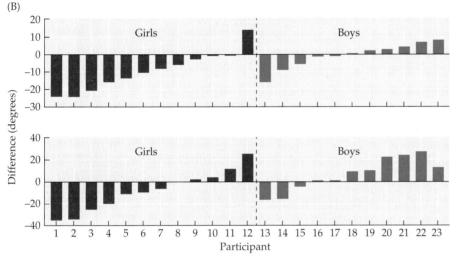

FIGURE 7.26 Parental socialization of gender.   (A) Parents have expectations of their infants' abilities based on infant sex that do not relate to what infants can actually do. Researchers showed mothers an adjustable sloping walkway that could move up and down to different angles. They asked mothers to set the walkway to the steepest slope they believed their infant would crawl down successfully and then the steepest slope their infant would attempt to crawl down, whether successful or not. Infants were later tested on the same walkway to assess their abilities and attempts to crawl down slopes of different angles. (B) Mothers of girls underestimated their infants' crawling ability and also underestimated the angle of slope that their infants would attempt to crawl down. This pattern is indicated by the predominance of red bars (each representing the response of one parent) that fall below the line representing infant actual ability (low expectations) versus above the line (high expectations). In contrast, mothers of boys more accurately estimated their infants' ability, but overestimated the slopes that boys would attempt, suggesting that they viewed their boys to be "risk-takers" who would attempt slopes beyond the bounds of their ability. This pattern is indicated by the tendency of blue lines to fall at or above the line representing infant ability. (After E. R. Mondschein et al. 2000. *J Exp Child Psychol* 77: 304–316.)

Finally, one of the most powerful and consistent ways that parents socialize gender in their infants and toddlers is through the toys they provide. Parents typically buy their girls dolls, tea sets, and play purses and jewelry, and buy their boys balls, cars, trucks, and play tools (Leaper & Friedman, 2007).

Again, the gender divide of toy play continues today. When researchers asked parents of 5- and 12-month-old infants to report the toys they had at home, male children had more trucks than dolls at both ages, and girls had three times more pink toys than did boys at 5 months of age and five times more pink toys by the time they were 12 months old (Boe & Woods, 2018). In turn, the gendered nature of toys fed into infants' toy play by 12 months of age. As reviewed previously, toddlers 1–2 years of age play in gendered ways, with girls spending more time playing with dolls and boys more time with trucks (Boe & Woods, 2018; Zosuls et al., 2014).

Nonetheless, a caution is in order when interpreting the sources of girls' and boys' toy preferences. Although family context is a powerful force in toddler play, biology (including genetics) interacts with environmental experience to affect the course of development (see Chapter 1). In the same way, parenting behaviors may strengthen existing predilections in girl and boy infants. In subsequent chapters, we revisit the influences of biology and family context on identity formation across multiple areas, including gender, race, and ethnicity.

✓ CHECK YOUR UNDERSTANDING 7.24

1. What are some ways that parents socialize gendered behaviors in their infant boys and girls?

Gender Socialization: Cultural Context

LEARNING OBJECTIVE 7.25 Consider ways that cultural context might influence gender socialization.

Although studies on gender socialization in infancy are rare, gender socialization looks quite different across cultural communities. Still, based on existing evidence, differences in the roles of men and women in cultural life influence how boys and girls are raised. In turn, children develop gendered behaviors and attitudes that align with broader cultural messages.

Anthropologist Margaret Mead was a pioneer in the study of gender roles across cultural communities (**FIGURE 7.27**). Mead (1935) extensively observed the behaviors of the two sexes in three societies—the Arapesh, Mundugumor, and Tchambuli. She documented unique patterns of male and female behaviors in each culture, patterns that differed from one another and from the gender role expectations in the United States at the time. In the Arapesh community, both men and women were gentle, responsive, and cooperative. In the Mundugumor community, both genders sought power and position and were violent and aggressive. In the Tchambuli community, women were dominant and managerial and men were emotionally dependent and less responsible than women. Although Mead did not examine the implications for the gender development of infants or young children, her work spotlights how gender roles are socially constructed.

Two decades later, anthropologists Herbert Barry and colleagues examined the socialization of boys and girls across 110 largely nonliterate, geographically distributed cultures (Barry, Bacon, & Child, 1957). They documented how adults trained boys and girls in areas of responsibility and dutifulness, nurturance, obedience, self-reliance, and achievement. In infancy, few gender differences were seen, but over the early childhood years girls were increasingly pressured toward nurturance, obedience, and responsibility and boys toward self-reliance and achievement. Cultural communities with the greatest differences in treatment of boys and girls

FIGURE 7.27 Margaret Mead. Anthropologist Margaret Mead pioneered the study of gender roles by observing patterns of family life and behaviors in communities across the globe. Her work continues to influence theories about how different cultural contexts shape the formation of gender identities and roles. Here she is shown in Bali, Indonesia, in 1957.

were those in which the economy placed a high premium on strength and motor skills, such as the hunting of large animals, keeping of large rather than small domestic animals, and nomadic rather than stable residence. Additionally, cultural communities with large, extended families showed greater differences in the raising of boys versus girls than cultures with small, nuclear families. The authors speculated that in small, nuclear families men must be prepared to take on women's roles, and vice versa, if either member is absent or unable to carry through with their duties. Thus, sex differences in such situations cannot be too great. Larger extended families, in contrast, permit other women (or men) to take over the responsibilities of one another, and so sex-based differences in expectations are large.

Such influential anthropological studies show that cultural differences across a range of areas—from distribution of labor, family structure, beliefs, and practices—influence how children are raised and affect their gender identity. In later chapters we elaborate on cultural influences on children's gender and identity formation.

✓ **CHECK YOUR UNDERSTANDING 7.25**

1. Describe Margaret Mead's observations of cultural differences in gender roles.

Developmental Cascades

Infants differ from one another in all areas of emotional and social development, spanning emotional reactivity, the regulation of emotions, temperament, attachment to caregivers, and prosocial behaviors. Do these early differences foreshadow a child's destiny? Of course not. Infants have a lifetime of experiences ahead of them that will influence what they do and when, how, and why they engage in different behaviors. Still, the principle of developmental cascades suggests that all things being equal, early differences among infants can have rippling effects across domains and time. Here we show that emotional and social development in the first years of life can cascade to language learning, school readiness, academic achievement, and social functioning.

Emotion Regulation and Language Learning

The popular parental refrain "use your words" captures the idea that children must learn to calm themselves down when distressed to be able to effectively communicate their needs. Indeed, emotional development spills over to learning language. Infants who have developed some control over their emotions have more time and attention to devote to learning words, whereas infants who are often highly aroused by emotions take longer to develop language skills (Bloom, 1993; Cole, Armstrong, & Pemberton, 2010).

Developmental researcher Lois Bloom was the first to track how emotional expressions related to the language development of toddlers (Bloom & Capatides, 1987). The more time toddlers spent in neutral affect while playing with their mothers—that is, displaying neither positive nor negative emotions—the younger they were in acquiring first words, experiencing a rapid growth in vocabulary, and combining words into simple sentences. Neutral emotions may facilitate word learning by enabling toddlers to stay focused on what they are hearing and doing so that they can connect words to meaning.

As expected, negative emotions can be especially problematic for language development. Toddlers rated as difficult in temperament by their caregivers, including being high in negativity and low in attention control, had smaller vocabularies and fewer grammar skills than toddlers who were not temperamentally difficult (Salley & Dixon, 2007). Similarly, 12-month-olds who were high in emotional distress in unfamiliar situations had relatively low language skills at 16 months, even if their mothers were highly responsive. In contrast, infants who were low on emotional distress showed high language skills when mothers were responsive (Karrass & Braungart-Rieker, 2003). Infants' negative emotional expressions predict being late versus early talkers, likely because distress makes it difficult to process language information and interferes with the responsiveness of caregivers (Kubicek & Emde, 2012).

Emotion Regulation and Preschool Learning

Consider how important it is for a child to sit still and listen while in school. Emotional outbursts and problems with behavioral control do not fare well in environments that require self-regulation. As a result, poor emotional regulation and reactivity in infancy can interfere with later school performance if those tendencies persist over time, which they often do. Problems in effortful control in the first years of life interfere with children's later task persistence, academic achievement, moral maturity, and positive relationships with peers and adults (Eisenberg, 2010; Posner & Rothbart, 2009; Valiente, Lemery-Chalfant, & Swanson, 2010). As one example, researchers assessed infant emotion regulation using various tasks that we learned about in previous sections (e.g., arm restraint). Infants low on emotion regulation had difficulties as preschoolers in controlling their attention and behaviors (Ursache et al., 2013).

Emotion Regulation and Later Social Functioning

Emotion regulation predicts more than language and academic performance. Problems in emotion regulation during infancy can lead to withdrawing from social situations in childhood at one extreme to engaging in aggressive and delinquent behaviors at the other, what researchers refer to as **externalizing behaviors**.

externalizing behaviors Problem behaviors directed to the external environment, such as physical aggression, disobeying rules, and destroying property

Consider first how negative reactivity in infancy can snowball to later inhibition and social withdrawal. In one study, about half of infants who showed high levels of negative reactivity withdrew from unfamiliar peers at later ages (Fox et al., 2001). For example, behavioral inhibition in infancy and early childhood predicts teenagers' sensitivity to angry faces and social withdrawal at 15 years of age (e.g., Pérez-Edgar et al., 2010). Moreover, early negative reactivity may amplify the bias to attend to potential social threats, such as the anger in a parent's face, which then places children at risk for later anxiety, mood disorders, and withdrawal from social interactions (e.g., Pérez-Edgar et al., 2014; Burris et al., 2019).

At the other extreme, early problems in self-regulation can cascade to behavior problems of acting out. In a longitudinal study, inhibitory control and emotion regulation skills starting at 2 years of age predicted externalizing behaviors through 15 years of age (Perry et al., 2018). But, perhaps the strongest evidence for stability of emotion regulation comes from a longitudinal study that spanned several decades. Three-year-old children who displayed high anger/frustration and poor attention skills reported less satisfaction in social relationships and displayed more antisocial behaviors during adolescence and adulthood than children without this early behavioral profile (Caspi & Silva, 1995).

Attachment and Later Adjustment

Like emotional development, infant attachment is not fleeting. Patterns of interaction between infants and caregivers solidify and extend to other relationships—from peers to teachers to romantic partners. Infants who are neglected, abandoned, or otherwise deprived of a loving relationship with one or more caregivers suffer severe emotional, social, and cognitive problems throughout life.

The Bucharest Intervention Project, described at the start of this chapter, poignantly speaks to the importance of early attachment relationships. The horrific conditions of the Romanian orphanages cascaded to severe developmental delays in the orphaned infants and toddlers across motor, cognitive, social, and emotional development domains (Almas et al., 2012). On nearly every metric, institutionalized infants fared worse than community controls, including being physically smaller and failing to grow along a normal trajectory. Furthermore, brain imaging studies showed structural changes in the brains of children who spent more time in the orphanage compared to children adopted into families at younger ages, and their teachers reported that late-adopted children had more behavior and social problems relative to the early-adopted children. These dire research findings spurred the first foster-care system in Romania as an alternative to government-run orphanages. Orphaned infants placed in the high-quality foster care system surpassed those who remained institutionalized, which led the Romanian government to pass a law forbidding the institutionalization of children younger than age 2.

A question that arises, of course, is whether differences in infant attachment matter in nonextreme situations. Does variation in attachment statuses among non-orphaned, home-reared infants have a cascading influence on their development as well? The answer is yes. Infants who were securely attached at 12 months of age were more curious, played more effectively with peers, and had better relationships with their teachers in nursery and preschool than did children who had been insecurely attached as infants. By 10 years of age, children who were securely attached as infants were more socially skilled, had more friends, had greater self-confidence, and more openly expressed their feelings than did children who had been insecurely attached (Sroufe et al., 2005).

What developmental processes might account for such long-term connections? Early attachment relationships are thought to play out over time because of **internal working models** that people construct about the responsiveness of others and worthiness of the self. For example, infants who experience insensitive caregiving and develop insecure attachments may develop internal working models in which they view others to be untrustworthy and the self as unlovable. These models affect later expectations about others and the quality of social relationships (Dykas & Cassidy, 2011; Fivush & Waters, 2015).

You might wonder how an infant can develop an internal working model, if they do at all. There's some evidence that infants as young as 4–16 months develop internal models of caregivers' responsiveness. In one study, infant attachment was assessed in the Strange Situation, and infants' attention to different attachment-based scenarios was examined. For example, infants were shown a scene of two animated characters, a large ellipse (mother) and a small ellipse (child). During habituation trials, the "mother" and the "child" were together at the foot of a hill. Then the "mother" climbed up the hill and rested halfway on a small plateau. The "child" below started crying (presented in an audio recording of an actual crying infant). During test trials, infants were shown two scenes, one in which the mother responded by descending to help her child, and one in which the mother was unresponsive and kept climbing the hill (**FIGURE 7.28**). Securely attached infants looked longer to the nonresponsive condition than responsive condition whereas insecure infants did not differentiate between the two conditions (Johnson, Dweck, & Chen, 2007). Looking-time patterns suggest that securely attached infants had constructed an internal working model about how caregivers respond to their young and were surprised by the conflicting reactions of the nonresponsive caregiver.

internal working models A mental representation of one's attachment relationship with the primary caregiver, which becomes a model for future social relationships and the quality of these relationships

Habituation event: Separation

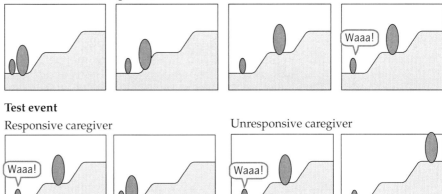

Test event

Responsive caregiver   Unresponsive caregiver

FIGURE 7.28 Internal working models of attachment in infancy. Researchers suggest that infants have "internal working models" of the responsiveness of their attachment figures. Infants were shown a scene of two animated characters, a large ellipse (mother) and a small ellipse (child). During habituation trials, the "mother" and the "child" were together at the foot of a hill. Then the "mother" climbed up the hill and rested halfway on a small plateau. The "child" below started crying (presented in an audio recording of an actual crying infant). During test trials, infants were shown two scenes, one in which the mother responded by descending to help her child, and one in which the mother was unresponsive and kept climbing the hill. Infant attachment status related to their patterns of looking at responsive and unresponsive figures. (After S. C. Johnson et al. 2007. *Psychol Sci* 18: 501–502.)

■ CLOSING THOUGHTS
Cultivating Emotional and Social Competence

Reflect for a moment on the following question. How would you define a socially and emotionally healthy person? Perhaps several vital characteristics spring to mind. Someone who understands other people. Someone who can resolve conflicts, cope with stress, and handle the emotions of self and others. Someone who has developed close and secure relationships with other people. Someone who can make and keep friends. Someone who reaches out to help people in need. Someone who spontaneously displays magnanimity without expecting to receive anything in return.

Now, review your list. Notice that the qualities that characterize this fictitious person align with many of the topics that we reviewed in this chapter. Indeed, the seeds of social and emotional development are planted and cultivated in infancy. When those seeds are placed in toxic soil, they will struggle to grow, just as was the case of orphaned and institutionalized children who failed to thrive under conditions of neglect. The dire circumstances surrounding a lack of love and social connection suffocate infants' social and emotional development and compromise skills across motor, language, and cognitive domains. But, when soil is rich and nourished, the planted seeds will thrive and reach their full genetic potential. The same goes for infants. On Erikson's account, consistent, predictable, and reliable care allows infants to feel secure and trust others even when they face challenges.

But of course, plants can wither without continued watering and care. And so, we will see in later chapters that although the groundwork for social and emotional development is established in infancy, the future of the child depends on continued care and nourishment. Healthy emotional and social development, therefore, is a lifelong goal.

The Developmentalist's Toolbox

Method	Purpose	Description
Measuring infant emotional development		
Emotion matching studies	To assess infants' abilities to detect emotional content communicated in auditory and visual modalities	Infants are presented with visual and auditory stimuli that contain emotional information, such as happy and sad faces or voices. Examiners ask whether infants look longer to visual displays that match the auditory soundtrack (angry voice with angry face).
Social referencing studies	To assess whether infants seek and use information about the emotional meaning of a situation by looking at and behaving in line with another person's emotional cues	Examiners (or sometimes the infants' caregivers) display emotional reactions such as joy or fear to objects in front of the infant. Infants' approach or avoidance of the target objects indicates whether emotional information communicated by others guides infants' behaviors.
Arm restraint studies	To assess differences among infants in their emotional reactions of anger	Examiners hold down infants' arms to assess the intensity of their emotional reactions to a frustrating and anger-provoking situation.
Inhibition tasks	To assess aspects of infants' abilities to regulate their emotions and behaviors	Infants are placed in a situation that requires them to inhibit a dominant response, such as wanting to grab a toy or snack, in favor of a less favorable but required response (waiting). The amount of time infants are able to resist touching the forbidden object indexes inhibitory control.
Still-face experiment	To assess emotion regulation in infants in the context of non-responsive social interactions; also used to examine infant attachment to caregiver	Mothers interact naturally with their infants for a few minutes, followed by a segment during which they keep their face still and unresponsive. Infants' level of distress at their mothers' still face is thought to measure their emotion regulation or attachment to the caregiver.
Measuring infant attachment and prosocial behaviors		
Strange Situation	To assess attachment to a caregiver	Infants and mothers visit a laboratory playroom, where they are introduced to the unfamiliar room. Each infant experiences a series of separations from their mother and exposure to a stranger.
Structured observations to elicit prosocial behaviors	To assess toddlers' prosocial behaviors	Examiners enact situations in which they display distress, the need for help, and so forth. The toddlers' reactions are measured (such as helping behaviors).
Helper-hinderer experiments	To examine foundations to moral understanding, evaluation, and retribution	Infants observe prosocial "helper" entities or antisocial "hurting" entities that are displayed on monitors or enacted by examiners. The infants' looking at and sometimes behaviors toward the two entities are assessed in different situations.
Measuring infant awareness of self		
Single-touch and double-touch experiment	To assess infants' awareness of self	Examiners compare infants' reactions to touches that originate from the infants themselves (such as infants touching their own cheek) to touches that arise from others (examiners touching the infants' cheek).

Chapter Summary

Evolutionary Theory and the Functions of Emotions
- Emotions have adaptive functions of organizing and regulating people's behaviors, including preparing them for action, and communicating relevant social information to other people.
- Three key areas of infant emotional development are: emotion understanding, emotion expression, and emotion regulation.

Expressing Emotions
- Infants develop abilities to discriminate among different emotions, connect emotional expressions to meaning, and seek and use emotional information from other people.
- The spontaneous smiles of newborns do not contain the social meaning seen in later social smiles, which emerge between 6 weeks and 3 months of age, that are socially motivated and increasingly selective in the persons to whom they are directed.
- Generalized distress is infants' first negative emotion, which is expressed across a variety of situations. Over development, generalized distress differentiates into emotions of anger, fear, and sadness in reaction to specific events.

Understanding Emotions
- In the second year, toddlers' emotional expressions become increasingly differentiated, and they begin to display self-conscious emotions, such as embarrassment, pride, guilt, and shame.

Regulating Emotions
- Infants get better at controlling emotions as they grow older. In the first months of life, infants primarily rely on parents to regulate emotion.
- Over time, infants engage in strategies to regulate their emotions, such as self-comforting behaviors and looking away from temptations.

Temperament
- Alexander Thomas and Stella Chess were the first to document individual differences in infant temperament, and classified infants as easy, difficult, and slow-to-warm-up babies.
- Mary Rothbart identified six dimensions of temperament: activity, positive affect, fear, distress, soothability, and attention and three components of temperament: surgency, negative reactivity, and orienting regulation. In toddlers, the component of orienting regulation is referred to as effortful control.
- "Goodness of fit" refers to the fit between a baby's temperament and the demands of the environment, including parenting behaviors.

Social and Cultural Contexts of Emotional Development and Temperament
- Individual differences in infant temperament and emotion regulation can be explained by aspects of family context,

including genetics, infant heart rate changes, and brain activation patterns, as well as family context, including parents' emotional expressions and their responses to and support of children's emotional experiences and expressions.
- Infant temperament, emotion understanding, and expressions differ across cultural communities, which may depend on cultural differences in emotional expressions, values, and practices.

Attachment
- In his ethological theory of attachment John Bowlby asserted that infant proximity-seeking behaviors of crying, sucking, smiling, clinging, and following are biologically based and adaptive to survival. Harry Harlow's studies of rhesus monkeys further supported this idea.
- The Strange Situation developed by Mary Ainsworth assesses infant attachment, and classifies infants as secure, insecure resistant, and insecure avoidant attachment. Main and Solomon added the category of disorganized attachment.

Contexts of Attachment
- The quality of caregiver-infant interactions, including sensitivity, acceptance, attunement to infant needs, and emotional accessibility predict infant attachment statuses.
- The Strange Situation has been criticized as being culturally biased. Most attachment studies focus on infant-mother attachment, leaving out other notable caregivers (such as fathers) or multiple caregivers.
- Longitudinal studies indicate that infant attachment status predicts attachment and social relationships in childhood and even adulthood. These long-term stabilities may be explained by internal working models.

Peer Relations and the Origins of Morality
- Beyond caregivers, toddlers develop positive relationships with peers. They display prosocial behaviors of helping, cooperating, sharing, and comforting.
- Nativists emphasize three main features of infants' "innate moral sense": moral goodness, moral understanding and evaluation, and moral retribution.
- Aggression toward peers emerges in the second year, with most aggressive actions being physical. Conflict between toddlers might offer opportunities for toddlers to learn the perspectives of others and problem resolution.

Self-Identity
- Infants' understanding of the self divides into two broad types: the subjective (or ecological) self and the objective self.
- The ecological self (infants' awareness of their own actions and bodies in relation to the physical world) and the interpersonal self (infants' sensitivity to the reciprocal nature of social interactions) are two aspects of the subjective self—the "I" of the self.
- Infants' understanding of the ecological self is demonstrated in double-touch experiments and studies that test

infants' awareness of the connections between self-action and environmental response.

- Infants' understanding of the interpersonal self is demonstrated in their distress when normally occurring contingencies in social interactions are disrupted, such as an infant not receiving feedback in response to their social behaviors.
- Gender is an early-emerging component of the objective self. In the second year, infants label themselves as boy or girl, and this awareness of one's gender is associated with toddlers' gender-stereotyped play.

Contexts of Self-Identity

- Infants' early gender identity may be influenced by family and cultural context, such as the extent to which parents display gendered expectations and behaviors.

Developmental Cascades

- Infants' ability to regulate their emotions and attention facilitates language development, because infants can learn the words to which they are exposed without negative affect or inattention getting in the way.
- Emotion regulation in infancy relates to later emotion regulation in preschool, which can cascade to academic performance in future years.
- Poor emotion regulation in infancy, especially high negative reactivity, can hinder peer relationships and lead to later anxiety, mood disorders, and withdrawal from social interactions in childhood, adolescence, and even adulthood.
- Lack of social connection, abandonment, and the deprivation of a loving relationship—all associated with problems of attachment, such as seen in orphaned infants—can harm brain structural development and functioning. Even in less extreme cases, insecure attachment with caregivers has the potential to harm later relationships as toddlers and children develop internal working models of themselves as unlovable and others as untrustworthy.

Thinking Like a Developmentalist

1. You wish to examine whether infants' understanding of emotions might explain developmental changes in moral understanding. You reason that babies must be able to first understand others' positive and negative emotions if they are to distinguish helping from hindering behaviors. How might you investigate this question?

2. You wonder if infant attachment is associated with a baby's moral understanding. You hypothesize that securely attached babies might be more likely to display moral understanding and moral goodness compared to insecurely attached babies. How might you test this hypothesis?

3. In many cultural communities, several family members, such as mothers, grandparents, siblings, and other relatives share the responsibility of childrearing. You wish to investigate: (a) Whether infants with multiple caregivers display the same or different attachment statuses across their different caregivers, and (b) Whether a measure of infants' *multiple attachments* would be a stronger predictor of their later prosocial behaviors toward peers than would a measure of infants' attachment to the mother only. What study might be performed to answer these questions?

4. You are an entrepreneur in the toy industry. There are lots of gendered toys for boys and girls on the market. But your company plans to develop some new, gender-neutral toys. However, the owner of the company is concerned that children's gender identity development might negatively influence how much they like the new gender-neutral toys you wish to market, and that gender identity would be associated with a preference for gendered toys. What would you do to test the influence of gender identity on children's toy preferences for gendered versus gender-neutral toys?

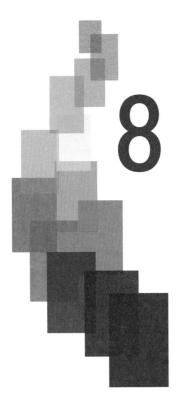

8

Physical Development and Health in Early Childhood

Drawing by Minxin Cheng from a photo by Kiana Bosman on Unsplash

Welcome to the witching hour—a time when demons are at their most powerful and wreak havoc on those around them. I am not referring to the Salem Witch trials, but rather the time of day when young children seem to lose it. Like many parents, I often experienced the witching hour right before dinner, after a long day at work, when our son Michael would cling, whine, scream, jump on the dog, spill his milk, and wrestle with his brother. He was simultaneously tired and hungry. He couldn't reason or control his emotions. After dinner and a bath he would finally exhaust himself and fall asleep. But, hours later, he would wake up from a vivid nightmare and hover over our bed, waiting to be consoled. The sleep disruptions did not help his attitude.

Michael's behavior was similar to how adults feel when tired, hungry, or run down: The physical state of our bodies goes a long way in affecting our thoughts, emotions, and behaviors. For young children, the body's influence on behavior is especially powerful. Children's brains have not yet matured to allow them to control their desires and inhibit behaviors like whining and stomping feet. Children are still learning to manage the small and large movements of their ever-growing bodies. And, they are far from understanding the benefits of nutrition and why they should go to bed at a decent hour.

In this chapter, you will learn about the many changes in brain structures and function, body size and proportions, and indicators of health that characterize early childhood. You will come to understand that physical development and health have far-reaching consequences for young children's everyday life, and appreciate why tired, hungry, impulsive young children often struggle during the witching hour.

■ *Physical Development*

Children can only realize their full potential if the architecture of their brains is sturdy, their bodies are well nourished, and they are rested and free of chronic stress and illness. Here we review changes to young children's brain and body, and the factors that support and impede child health.

Brain, Physical, and Motor Development

Michael was introduced to sports as a preschooler—he joined the local soccer team when he was 4 years old. He and his friends ran around like a swarm of bees, jumping and circling the field with delight. However, it was an enormous challenge to simultaneously maneuver, maintain balance, and handle the ball, and their kicks were lopsided and off target. Michael scored eight goals his first game—because they played without a goalkeeper. He couldn't understand why his sister (who also played soccer) had not scored any goals, despite being 8 years older.

Michael's introduction to sports illustrates the remarkable growth of brain and body during early childhood, while revealing how far children still have to go. Compared to toddlers, young children's bodies are larger and more powerful, due to a higher ratio of muscle to mass. And, changes to the brain allow children to coordinate actions across the two sides of their bodies and exert greater control over their behaviors and thinking. Indeed, each gain in brain and body ushers in new experiences—playing, running, climbing, dressing oneself, and eating—that further contribute to physical prowess and agility and fuel brain development.

cerebral lateralization
The functional dominance of one hemisphere over another hemisphere of the brain; left and right hemispheres control opposite sides of the body and specific body functions

Brain Development

LEARNING OBJECTIVE 8.1 Identify the key ways in which the brain develops in the first 6 years of life.

The brain undergoes enormous change over the first years of life. Neurons in the brain form many new synaptic connections and become increasingly myelinated. Myelination helps nerve impulses travel at faster rates, allowing children to think and act more quickly than before (see Chapter 2). The brain also undergoes increased **cerebral lateralization**—with left and right hemispheres controlling opposite sides of the body (**FIGURE 8.1**). At the same time, changes to the corpus callosum improve communication between the brain's two hemispheres. Collectively, changes in the brain allow young children to think and act in new ways. Children can coordinate eyes and limbs to draw a picture, kick a ball, express their imaginations through play, talk about the past, and reason about what causes things to happen.

Growth in Synaptic Connections

In the first 2 years of postnatal development, neuronal connections dramatically increase, with the brain reaching about 80% of its ultimate adult weight. Between 2 and 6 years of age, the brain reaches 90% of its adult weight. Much of the change in brain weight can be attributed to myelination.

Brain growth during early childhood is especially pronounced in motor and sensory areas involved in language, social understanding, and self-regulation (Kolb & Whishaw, 2009). The brain undergoes so much growth across the first years of life, that the number of synapses in certain parts of

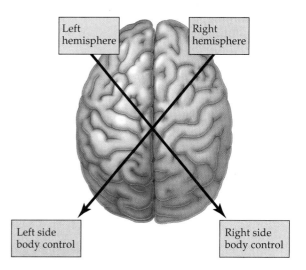

FIGURE 8.1 Brain lateralization. During early childhood, the brain undergoes increased lateralization—with left and right hemispheres controlling opposite sides of the body. (After S. M. Breedlove. 2015. *Principles of Psychology*. Sinauer/Oxford University Press: Sunderland, MA.)

FIGURE 8.2 fMRI imaging of maturing brain. fMRI imaging enables researchers to evaluate which regions of the brain are maturing at different points in development. Portions of the brain depicted in red are least mature, whereas regions in blue are more mature. (After Blausen.com staff. 2014. Medical gallery of Blausen Medical 2014. *Wiki-Journal of Medicine* 1(2). DOI:10.15347/wjm/2014.010. CC BY 3.0 https://creativecommons.org/licenses/by/3.0/.)

the cortex, such as the frontal lobes, surpasses that of the adult brain! In fact, 4-year-old children have nearly double the number of synaptic connections as do adults. Scientists estimate the number of synaptic connections in children's brains, one index of brain maturation, through various magnetic resonance technologies (Casey et al., 2005) (**FIGURE 8.2**). For example, functional magnetic resonance imaging (fMRI) reveals high levels of energy consumption in the cerebral cortex in children, indicating rapid synaptic growth and myelination of neural fibers in that brain region (Huttenlocher, 2002; Johnson, 1998). The proliferation of synaptic connections helps ensure that children will be able to function adaptively in the event of damage to specific areas of the brain. That is, the extremely high numbers of synaptic connections in the brains of young children ensure **neuroplasticity**, the ability of the brain to reorganize itself by rearranging neurons (see Chapter 2). Essentially, other brain regions take over the functions that would otherwise be directed to the damaged regions.

Over the course of early childhood, **synaptic pruning** occurs (see Figure 2.27): Synaptic connections that are rarely used are lost, making room for the more complex and efficient connections that come with learning. The complementary processes of overproduction and then reduction of synapses, a sort of "fine tuning," allow children to flexibly adapt to their unique environments (Tierney & Nelson, 2009). Synaptic pruning extends well beyond early childhood, with some brain regions showing rapid pruning during adolescence, coinciding with pubertal maturation (Campbell et al., 2012).

Brain Lateralization and Handedness

Recall from earlier in this chapter that the human brain is lateralized—meaning the left or right hemisphere controls specific body functions. For example, the left hemisphere of the brain controls the limbs, eyes, and ears of the right side of the body, while the right hemisphere controls the left side. **Handedness** —the tendency to use either the right or the left hand more naturally than the other—illustrates the growing lateralization of everyday functions during

neuroplasticity The ability of the brain to reorganize itself through biological changes and by rearranging neurons

synaptic pruning The process in which synapses are eliminated to increase the efficacy of neural communication

handedness The tendency to use either the right or the left hand more than the other early childhood (Hinojosa, Sheu, & Michel, 2003). Whereas infants and toddlers will switch between their two hands to grasp and manipulate objects from one moment to the next, variability in hand use decreases from 3 to 4 years of age, with children increasingly settling on using one hand over the other (Fagard & Lockman, 2005).

Interestingly, humans tend to settle on primarily using the right hand. In fact, the vast majority of adults, about 90%, are right-handed, which means the left hemisphere guides their dominant manual actions, a proportion that has remained constant for 5,000 years (Coren & Porac, 1977). Right-hand dominance may be a uniquely human trait that is related to the lateralization of language (Annett, 2002), and in fact, consistent right-handedness in infants relates to advanced language skills at 2 years of age (Nelson, Campbell, & Michel, 2014). (Recall from Chapter 6 that language skills are also lateralized in the left hemisphere). However, people vary in the strength of their handedness, with some people using one hand exclusively and others sometimes switching between the two. Switch hitters in baseball, for example, show flexibility in hitting against right- or left-handed pitchers.

How do researchers test the development of handedness? They typically place objects like spoons or toys in different locations or orientations and observe how children pick them up. Researchers then assess whether the child flexibly switches between hands (a sign of low hand preference) or uses the right or left hand to reach across the midline (a strong hand preference). Or researchers present infants with tasks that require certain actions (such as getting to an object that's inside another object), and observe which hand the infant uses to perform the action (**FIGURE 8.3**). Such studies indicate that by 2 years of age, the majority of toddlers are right-handed, with hand preferences sometimes appearing even earlier and persisting over time (Nelson, Campbell, & Michel, 2013). Still, young children show stronger hand preferences than do infants and toddlers (Fagard & Lockman, 2005). But at the same time, younger children ages 4–5 years of age display weaker hand preference and greater flexibility than do older children ages 8–11 years of age (Hill & Khanem, 2009).

Young children's flexibility in hand use, however, diminishes when the task requires high precision, such as picking up a small coin or the handle of a spoon (Fagard & Lockman, 2005; Hill & Khanem, 2009). Under such conditions, children may predominantly use the right or left hand. In fact, improvements in manual dexterity may explain development in the strength of handedness (Hill & Khanem, 2009). Reciprocally, as children increasingly favor one hand over the other, their practice with that hand improves motor precision. Children with **developmental coordination disorder** have difficulties coordinating their movements, which interferes with everyday tasks. Such children show weak hand preference compared to typically developing children (Hill & Bishop, 1998).

Determinants of handedness in children are not completely understood, but two lines of evidence support a genetic basis of handedness. First, the predominant right-handedness of humans is already evident prenatally: As soon as fetuses can move their limbs, they display a motor bias toward the right hand, predominantly sucking the right thumb (Hepper, 2013). Second, monozygotic (MZ) twins, who start out with identical genes, are more similar in their handedness than are dizygotic (DZ) twins or non-twin siblings (Bishop, 2005; Sicotte, Woods, & Mazziotta, 1999).

However, environmental factors also contribute to handedness, although precisely which environmental factors explain why some children are left-handed

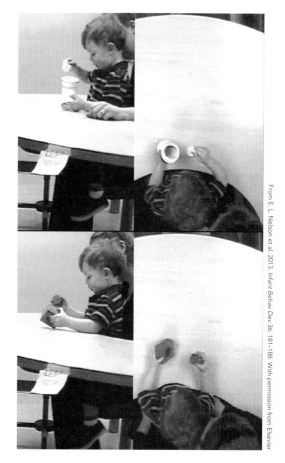

From E. L. Nelson et al. 2013. *Infant Behav Dev* 36: 181–188. With permission from Elsevier

FIGURE 8.3 Examples of tests for infant handedness.   Infants must perform actions with objects to identify which hand they use. (A) *Ball-in-tube test*. Children were presented with a tube and a ball and observed to see which hand they used to hold the tube and which hand they used to manipulate the ball. (B) *Foam-peg-block test*. Children were observed to see which hand they used to manipulate a foam peg and insert it in a block.

developmental coordination disorder A movement condition characterized by difficulty learning fine and gross motor skills and in movement coordination that may interfere with everyday tasks and others right-handed is not fully understood (Michel, 1983; Hepper, 2013). An international study of over 50,000 Australian and Dutch MZ and DZ twins and their siblings found that genetics explained only about 26% of the variance in whether children were right- or left-handed (Medland et al., 2009). Most of the variance in handedness was explained by other factors.

Corpus Callosum

corpus callosum A dense tract of nerve fibers, beneath the cerebral cortex, which facilitates communication between the left and right hemispheres of the brain

Although one hemisphere of the brain governs language and handedness more than the other, both sides of the brain are involved in nearly all skills. The **corpus callosum**—a band of nerve fibers connecting the right and left hemispheres—passes signals between the two hemispheres to ensure that they communicate with one another. Between 3 and 6 years of age, the production of synapses and myelination of the corpus callosum peaks, particularly in the frontal circuits that are responsible for regulating, planning, and organizing new actions (Thompson et al., 2000).

The myelination of the corpus callosum enables faster signaling between the two hemispheres, which facilitates coordination between the two sides of the body. Young children's abilities to jump rope, hop, skip, and walk on ledges and balance beams illustrate how synaptic growth and myelination in the corpus callosum facilitate motor coordination. Development of the corpus callosum is also vital to perception, attention, memory, and language. That is, the two brain hemispheres must efficiently communicate if children are to engage in complex thinking and action.

Prefrontal Cortex

prefrontal cortex The "executive" region of the brain (located at the front part of the outer layer of the frontal lobe) controls functions involved in attention, behavior, working memory, and making decisions

The **prefrontal cortex** is located behind the forehead at the front part of the outer layer of the frontal lobe (see Figure 2.16). This region of the brain is referred to as the "executive" of the brain because it controls functions involved in attention, behavior, and working memory. As we will learn, young children have difficulty in situations that require them to plan and inhibit their behaviors, such as when they are instructed not to touch a tasty marshmallow. The relative immaturity of the prefrontal cortex helps explain young children's difficulties with executive function tasks (Blair, Zelazo, & Greenberg, 2016; Durston et al., 2002) (**FIGURE 8.4**).

Neuroimaging studies reveal that the prefrontal cortex is functional for many tasks by around 4 years of age, and becomes increasingly organized and fine-tuned during later childhood (Tsujimoto, 2008). Similarly, glucose metabolism in the brain reveals information about the brain's use of energy, and consequently, which regions of the brain are most rapidly developing. Positron emission tomography (PET) scans (**FIGURE 8.5**) indicate an extraordinary doubling in the rate of glucose metabolism in frontal regions between 2 and 4 years of age (Thompson et al., 2000).

Cerebellum

cerebellum The brain structure that coordinates movement, such as walking and balancing, and that is involved in memory, cognition, and emotion

The **cerebellum**, a structure at the rear base of the brain, supports balance and control of body movement, thus contributing to young children's growing coordination (see Figure 2.16). From birth through early childhood, myelination of the fibers that connect the cerebellum to the cerebral cortex increases. Myelination leads to faster communications between cerebellum and cortex, which supports the organization of movements necessary for motor skills, and also aids connections important to cognitive skills (Diamond, 2000).

Limbic System

The limbic system, which includes the amygdala, hippocampus, and hypothalamus, is central to young children's emotional expression and regulation

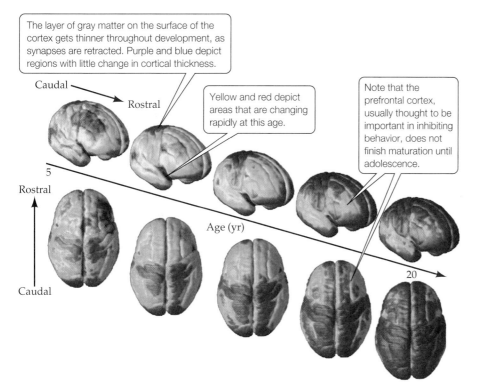

FIGURE 8.4 The developing prefrontal cortex.   The relative immaturity of the prefrontal cortex helps explain young children's difficulties with executive function tasks. (From N. Gogtay et al. 2004. *Proc Natl Acad Sci USA* 101: 8174. © 2004 National Academy of Sciences, U.S.A.; S. M. Breedlove and N. V. Watson. 2020. *The Mind's Machine: Foundations of Brain and Behavior.* Sinauer/Oxford University Press: Sunderland, MA.)

(see Figure 2.17). The **amygdala**—a small structure situated deep in the brain—registers positive and negative emotions, especially fear (Kolb & Whishaw, 2009). High amygdala activity explains children's fear of the dark, thunder, loud noises, and wariness in unfamiliar situations.

amygdala A small structure located deep in the brain that registers positive and negative emotions

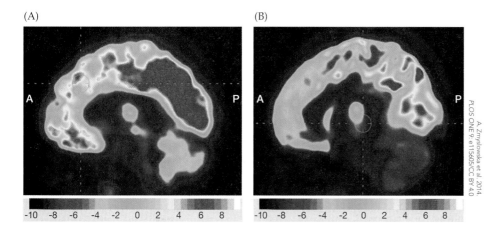

FIGURE 8.5 What PET scans can tell us about the developing brain.   Differences in glucose uptake as seen in PET scans of the brain in (A) a healthy child and (B) a child with Wolfram syndrome, a genetic disorder. The color regions show the magnitude of brain activation patterns (increasing in activation from cooler colors of blue to the warmer colors of red).

hippocampus The part of the brain located in the inner region of the temporal lobe that is involved in regulating emotions and supports children's memory, spatial understanding, and executive functioning

hypothalamus The part of the brain that is involved in experience of emotions such as happiness and sadness; and regulates behaviors such as sleep, eating, and drinking; the hypothalamus responds to signals from the amygdala and hippocampus by producing hormones, such as cortisol, which help control a person's stress response

cortisol A hormone, produced by the hypothalamus, which regulates various processes such as metabolism, the immune response, and the stress response; cortisol also controls blood glucose levels and blood pressure

The **hippocampus**, located next to the amygdala, is a central processor of memory. Across early childhood and childhood, the hippocampus continues to establish connections and transfer information within the limbic system and to the frontal lobes (Nelson, Thomas, and de Haan, 2007). Growth in hippocampal connections supports developments in children's memory, spatial understanding, and executive functioning. The hippocampus's proximity and connection to the amygdala is important in young children's experiences of emotions, because the hippocampus enables children to form and recall memories about the personal past. For example, a young child who has been bullied by a peer in the past will become fearful and anxious in the presence of that peer when past memories surface.

The **hypothalamus** responds to signals from the amygdala and hippocampus by producing hormones, including the hormone **cortisol**, which serves important bodily functions including controlling a person's responses to stress, blood glucose levels, and blood pressure. Researchers commonly assess children's cortisol levels by swiping saliva from inside the mouth with a cotton swab, and then sending samples to a lab to analyze children's response to stress (e.g., Berry, Blair, & Granger, 2016).

✓ CHECK YOUR UNDERSTANDING 8.1

1. Between ages 2 and 6 the brain reaches 90% of its adult weight. To what process is much of this weight attributable?
2. What is synaptic pruning and why is it important?
3. How do researchers study handedness?
4. Describe changes (and limitations where relevant) in early childhood to the corpus callosum, prefrontal cortex, cerebellum, and limbic system. Explain the functions of these brain structures in children's development.

Physical and Motor Development

LEARNING OBJECTIVE 8.2 Identify changes in physical development and fine and gross motor skills in early childhood.

To glimpse the remarkable physical and motor changes of early childhood, all you have to do is visit a preschool or kindergarten classroom. You'll see crayons, pencils, scissors, puzzles, books, blocks, juice boxes, small containers, and so on. The unique design of each object requires highly precise actions—little hands must scribble, twist, flip, latch, unlatch, fit things together, pull things apart, zip, tie, punch straws into tiny holes, and copy onto straight lines (Rachwani et al., 2020). In outside areas you'll see children kicking and hitting balls, climbing, sliding, swinging, and seamlessly shifting from a cross-legged sit to a low squat to a stand to a run. In essence, you'll see how children's changing bodies and growing motor skills usher in opportunities to engage with the environment in fresh, new ways. Still, young children have a long way to go before they display the agility, flexibility, nimbleness in footwork, and eye-hand coordination of older children.

Changing Bodies

Young children look nothing like babies. The pudgy round bodies, large heads, and chubby cheeks of infancy are replaced by a relatively slender body in which limbs and trunks are elongated, fat turns to muscle, and the head is more proportional to body size. On average, children in the United States gain 4.5 pounds and grow 3 inches each year of early childhood, with their muscle mass and body length increasing more quickly than their weight. By 6 years of age, the average U.S. child is 40–50 pounds, at least 3.5 feet tall, and has body proportions that resemble those of adults, with leg length comprising half of total height.

Children's body mass index (BMI), the ratio of height to weight, is lower than the BMI of toddlers and older children, which explains the diminishing body fat or pudginess with age (**FIGURE 8.6**). And, along with changes to torso and limbs, children's head size changes in relative proportion to their body. Whereas the heads of 2-year-old children measure around one-fifth their body length, by 6 years of age, the head reduces to one-sixth of body length, and for adults, head size is one-eighth of body length. Changing head ratios shift the child's appearance away from the top-heavy look of infants and toddlers.

Traditional growth charts (such as those found in a pediatrician's office) imply that growth is continuous—as if bones grow a tiny bit each day. Infants and young children, however, do not grow along smooth trajectories. Instead, their growth is episodic. They go days or weeks on end with no growth in body length at all. And then suddenly over 24 hours, they undergo a dramatic growth spurt (Lampl & Thompson, 2007; Lampl, Veldhuis, & Johnson, 1992). Indeed, so-called growing pains (in which children complain about aches in their legs) are very real. Bones grow in spurts throughout the 24-hour day, mostly at night when the legs do not bear weight (Noonan et al., 2004). Children really do wake up to find themselves noticeably taller, trying to wear pants that are suddenly too short.

Why do traditional growth charts misrepresent growth trajectories? Because of how growth is measured. When children are measured only once or only a few times per year, researchers fit statistical lines through the data and the result is smooth-looking growth curves. But when researchers such as Michelle Lampl measure each child's growth every day, they find growth to be episodic, not continuous. And when they measure growth every few minutes (using instruments in the bones of baby lambs), they see that bone growth occurs sporadically and mostly during sleep.

Hormones produced in the pituitary gland, located at the base of the brain, stimulate changes in body growth, with **growth hormone** being responsible for body tissue development and **thyroid-stimulating hormone** signaling the thyroid gland to release thyroxine, which aids brain development and facilitates the effects of growth hormone. Differences among children in these hormone levels account for differences among children in height and weight, which tend to be stable over time. For example, preschool children who are the tallest remain so as they progress through school, and similarly, children who are overweight remain so over time.

Genetics partly explains variation among children in height and weight. Parents of relatively tall stature are more likely to have relatively tall children than are parents of relatively short stature. The heights of MZ twins show a near perfect association of 0.94, compared to an association of 0.50 for DZ twins and non-twin siblings (Wilson, 1986). Monozygotic twins also show more similar patterns of physical growth than do dizygotic twins, such as in weight and the pace of bone development.

In extreme cases, a child may be unusually short. **Dwarfism**, which is mostly caused by the genetic disorder of achondroplasia, results in extremely short stature (less than 147 centimeters or 4 feet 10 inches) and skeletal immaturity (Horton, Hall, & Hecht, 2007). Sometimes, abnormalities in the secretion of growth hormone cause dwarfism. In rare cases, extreme emotional deprivation,

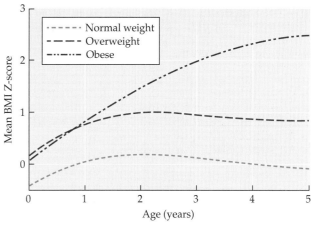

FIGURE 8.6 Changes to BMI across the first years of life. BMI increases from birth to age 2 years, and then declines across early childhood for children of normal weight and those who are overweight. However, BMI continues to increase over this time frame for children who are obese. Note that a value of zero on the Z-score (*y* axis) represents an "average" BMI score for children at a given age (that is, the 50th percentile). Scores between 2 and 3 represent the 97th to 99th percentiles for children's BMI. (After J. M. Braun et al. 2018. *BMC Pediatr* 18: 161. CC BY 4.0, https://creativecommons.org/licenses/by/4.0/.)

growth hormone A hormone produced in the pituitary gland that stimulates the release of hormones involved in growth, including body tissue and bone development

thyroid-stimulating hormone A hormone produced by the anterior pituitary gland that functions to regulate the production of hormones by the thyroid gland; thyroid hormones are essential in regulating such body qualities as weight and energy levels

dwarfism A genetic or medical condition, mostly caused by achondroplasia, in which an individual has an unusually short stature

psychosocial dwarfism
A syndrome characterized by short stature or growth caused by extreme emotional deprivation, neglect, or stress, and potentially resulting in long-term psychological and social adjustment problems

Prader-Willi Syndrome A genetic, neurodevelopmental disorder, with poor regulation of different hormones, associated in infancy with diminished muscle tone, feeding difficulties, and delayed physical development

gross motor skills Body movements that rely on large muscle groups in arms, legs, feet, and torso and include large-scale movements such as locomotion

fine motor skills Small actions or body movements that rely on coordination between small muscles (such as hand and fingers) and are critical to activities of daily living

neglect, or stress can lead to **psychosocial dwarfism**, which can cascade to long term psychological and social adjustment problems (Muños-Hoyos et al., 2011; Tarren-Sweeney; 2006).

Synthetic growth hormone therapy is sometimes used to treat dwarfism and short stature. Children receive daily injections with painless syringes until they begin growing, around adolescence. Children deficient in growth hormone who are treated with synthetic growth hormone experience faster growth and health benefits within months. Growth hormone therapy also improves height, body mass, strength, and agility in children who have **Prader-Willi Syndrome**—a genetic disorder associated with diminished muscle tone, feeding difficulties, and poor weight gain (Bakker et al., 2013).

Changing Motor Skills

As children's bodies change, so do their motor skills. The ratio of muscle to mass allows young children greater control over their bodies and balance relative to toddlers. In turn, children's gains in controlling their body supports their **gross motor skills**—the body movements that rely on large muscle groups in arms, legs, feet, and torso. Gross motor skills take three main forms (Gallahue & Ozmun, 1995):

- *Locomotor movements* propel the body through space, and include walking, running, jumping, hopping, skipping, and climbing a jungle gym.

- *Manipulative movements* relate upper and lower limb movements to other objects, such as throwing, catching, kicking, and dribbling.

- *Stability movements* involve balance of the body, including control of the body relative to gravity, such as standing on one foot, turning, twirling, swinging, bending, rolling, and balancing on a ledge.

Young children improve substantially in their locomotor movements, manipulative movements, stability movements, and abilities to coordinate the complex motor movements involved in riding a bicycle, controlling a skateboard, roller skating, playing on the monkey bars at a park, and so forth. Improvements in gross motor skills, and children's sheer joy at moving their bodies, explain why playgrounds, climbing structures at fast-food restaurants, and jungle gyms are magnets for young children.

Fine motor skills, the small actions that small muscles control, likewise continue to improve in early childhood. Fine motor skills can be classified into two main types:

- *Activities of daily living*, or the actions involved in eating, bathing, dressing, and grooming, such as zipping and buttoning, brushing teeth, opening containers and pouches, using spoons and forks, and so on (**FIGURE 8.7**). The challenge for young children is to discover which actions go with which objects, and then to execute the highly precise biomechanical adjustments of their fingers and hands to successfully implement those actions. And so, something as simple as twisting open the cap of a water bottle takes many months and even years to master (Rachwani et al. 2020). By 4 to 5 years of age, children no longer need assistance from adults for many activities of daily life.

- *Actions involved in literacy and art*, such as using pencils, paintbrushes, and crayons to draw figures and write letters and numbers. Young children's first drawings and attempts at writing are indecipherable scribbles. With experience, young children improve in their drawing and printing (Leyva, Reese, & Wiser, 2012) (**FIGURE 8.8**). Children's

FIGURE 8.7 Fine motor skill activities. Everyday tasks that appear to be relatively simple to adults, such as writing with a pen or inserting shapes into a puzzle, present challenges to young children's fine motor skills. Children must discover which actions go with which objects and make necessary biomechanical adjustments of their fingers and hands to successfully implement the actions.

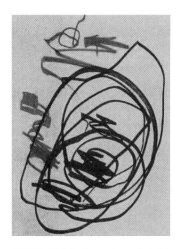  

Courtesy of Nathan Hodges

FIGURE 8.8 Samples of children's drawings between ages 2 and 6.

fine motor skills come in handy in many preschool activities. Young children's abilities to copy figures, draw a person, and create a specific model with blocks relate to children's academic skills in science, math, and reading in later schooling (Grissmer et al., 2010).

✓ **CHECK YOUR UNDERSTANDING 8.2**

1. How does BMI change as children move from toddlerhood to early childhood?
2. Describe improvements to fine and gross motor skills over early childhood.

Home Context of Brain Development

LEARNING OBJECTIVE 8.3 Discuss evidence for the role of home environment in children's brain development.

Animal studies reveal the powerful effects of experience on brain structure and process (see Chapter 2). Rats, monkeys, cats, and other animals reared in enriched environments that contain equipment for play, such as running wheels, mazes, and climbing equipment, show more dendritic spines on their cortical neurons, thicker cortexes, more synapses per neuron, greater overall number of synapses, and more supportive tissues to boost neuronal and synaptic function compared to animals raised in impoverished environments (Juraska, Henderson, & Müller, 1984; Tost, Champagne, & Meyer-Lindenberg, 2015).

Similarly, children who receive enriched experiences such as music lessons and rich language input from parents show changes in brain function and structure. Children who took a year of music lessons between the ages of 4 and 6 showed a higher level of activity in brain regions associated with attention and memory when they listened to music compared to children who did not receive music education (Fujioka, Trainor, & Ross, 2006) (**FIGURE 8.9**).

Conversely, impoverished experiences characterized by low levels of verbal and physical stimulation from parents, particularly in the first 5 years of life, may impede brain development (Walker et al., 2011). In extreme cases, brain development may be especially compromised in children reared in institutions (recall the Bucharest Early Intervention Project from Chapter 7) or in homes where maltreatment, abuse, or neglect occur (Glaser, 2000; Shonkoff et al., 2012; Teicher et al., 2003). In some cases, the stress associated with harsh negative experiences may instigate enduring brain change and psychiatric disorders, such as schizophrenia, later in life (Lieberman et al., 2001).

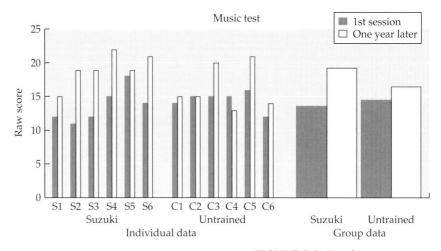

FIGURE 8.9 Enriching experiences foster brain development. This figure shows brain activation in children at a first baseline measurement and 1 year later for music students and nonmusician children. Although the two groups of children did not differ at the baseline assessment, before music lessons began, after a year of lessons, music students showed heightened brain activation in response to piano and violin tones compared to children not exposed to music. (After T. Fujioka et al. 2006. *Brain* 129: 2593-2608. By permission of Oxford University Press.)

✓ **CHECK YOUR UNDERSTANDING 8.3**

1. What do animal studies reveal about environmental influences on brain development?

Cultural and Historical Context of Physical Growth

LEARNING OBJECTIVE 8.4 List examples of cultural differences in height.

Children and adults differ in their average height across cultural communities and regions of the world. As a result, growth norms for one population may not apply to children from a different population. For example, children from different races within the United States diverge in height, with non-Hispanic Black children being taller and Mexican American children being shorter than White children (Dowd, Zajacova, & Aiello, 2009). Similarly, the height of adults varies from country to country. The average height of men in the Netherlands is 6 feet 2 inches and 5 feet 7 inches for women. At the other extreme, Indonesian men average 5 feet 2 inches and women average 4 feet 10 inches.

Inter-country differences in children's height align with those of adults. For example, Efe children in Central Africa taper in their growth between 1 and 6 years much more than do young children from most other communities around the globe. By 5 years of age, the average Efe child is shorter than 97% of 5-year-old children in the United States and Canada, in line with the Efe adult average of around 5 feet. The short stature of the Efe may reflect evolutionary adaptations to food scarcity in the rain forests of Central Africa; their smaller bodies require fewer calories and facilitate movements through dense forest underbrush (Shea & Bailey, 1996).

However, although genetics partly account for cultural differences, nutrition and health play key roles. **Secular changes** in height—nongenetic changes that occur over many generations—offer some of the strongest evidence for environmental influences on physical growth. The height of people around the world has increased historically in line with the population's access to nutrition and health (NCD Risk Factor Collaboration, 2016) (**FIGURE 8.10**). Note that

secular changes Changes in height and weight over the course of history explained by environmental influences on physical development such as access to nutrition and health

1896 birth cohort

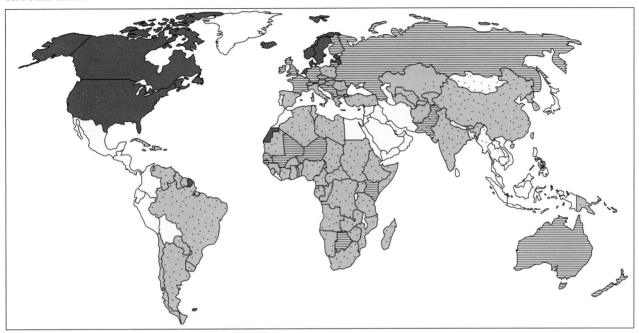

1996 birth cohort

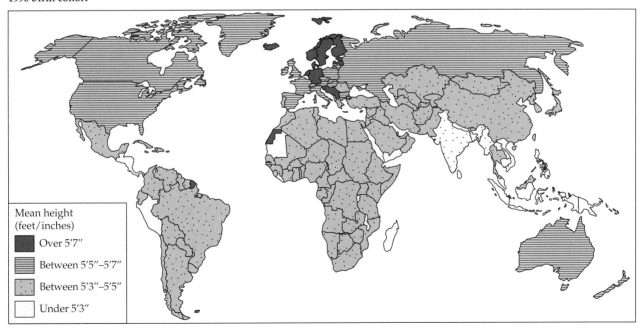

Mean height
(feet/inches)

■ Over 5'7"

▤ Between 5'5"–5'7"

▦ Between 5'3"–5'5"

□ Under 5'3"

FIGURE 8.10 Height differences around the globe.
Final adult height varies in regions around the world, and also has changed across historical time. Blue and green colors represent regions with the tallest adults; orange and yellow the shortest. Although secular changes are seen in adult height overall, the gains differ by region. Height has increased in some countries, but in others, it has plateaued or even decreased over the past century, including in parts of North America. (After NCD Risk Factor Collaboration [NCD-RisC]. 2016. *eLife* 5: e13410. DOI: 10.7554/eLife.13410 CC BY 4.0 https://creativecommons.org/licenses/by/4.0/.)

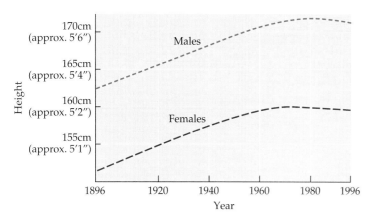

FIGURE 8.11 The average height has changed over the last century. In the 100 years between 1896 and 1996, the height of men and women across the world increased dramatically, in line with societal improvements to nutrition and health. (After M. Roser et al. 2013. Human Height. OurWorldInData.org, updated May 2019. https://ourworldindata.org/human-height. CC BY 4.0, https://creativecommons.org/licenses/by/4.0/deed.en_US. Data from NCD RisC. 2017. Height. http://www.ncdrisc.org/data-downloads-height.html.)

although overall, secular changes are seen in adult height, the gains differ by region. In some countries, height has increased, but in others, it has plateaued or even decreased over the past century, including in parts of North America. People in certain regions of the world, including the United States, Great Britain, Germany, and the Netherlands, have grown taller over the century preceding 2014 (Blaszczak-Boxe, 2014). A British study showed that men are 4 inches taller (averaging 5 feet 10 inches today) than they had been at the start of the twentieth century (when they averaged 5 feet 6 inches) (**FIGURE 8.11**). Similarly, Spain's rapid improvements in health care and sanitary conditions across the latter half of the twentieth century led to an increase in adult height (Spijker, Camara, & Blanes, 2012). Evolution cannot account for such dramatic changes, because 50–100 years is too brief a period to explain growing stature. Rather, improvements in nutrition, medicine, health care, and hygiene practices account for secular changes (Bogin, 2013).

Conversely, under poor nutrition and sanitary conditions, which plague many populations around the world today, height suffers. During World War I, servicemen who had grown up in overcrowded households and heavily industrialized areas were an inch shorter than those who did not endure such circumstances (Hatton, 2017). In countries ridden with disease, extreme poverty, war, and other problems, such as the apartheid experienced by South Africa between the end of the nineteenth century and 1970, height has stayed the same or even decreased (Bogin, 2013). Today, children who receive insufficient nutrients or exposure to toxins and live in unhealthy sanitary conditions in poor regions around the world experience stunted growth (De Onis & Branca, 2016). In the sections that follow, we delve into the importance of health for positive development.

✓ CHECK YOUR UNDERSTANDING 8.4

1. How have historical trends in height shed light on the importance of good nutrition and health?

2. Give examples of national and international differences in population height.

■ *Health*

Ask any parent of a young child their primary concerns and they are likely to mention their child's health. Parents worry about their children eating the right foods, getting enough sleep, catching a cold from friends, contracting a serious illness, or getting hurt while riding a bicycle. Even concerns outside the domain of health—such as whether a young child is paying attention in class, acting out at home and school, or whiny and grumpy—may be traced to health behaviors. Perhaps a child is unfocused because of a lack of sleep; or acting out because of eating too many sugary foods; or in a bad mood because of fending off a cold or recovering from an injury. Indeed, healthy behaviors pave the way to well-being across all domains of development at all ages in the life course. Here, we review several aspects of health in early childhood: Nutrition, sleep, illness, injury, and maltreatment.

Nutrition

Preschoolers can drive their parents crazy with their pickiness around eating foods and the unpredictability of their appetites. Many young children refuse foods that look "weird" on the plate or are "green" or feel strange on the tongue. They may even refuse to eat foods that they had devoured enthusiastically when they were younger. Children may clean their plates one meal but leave food untouched the next; they will be ravenous after returning from preschool but refuse to interrupt what they are doing to join the dinner table, even if it has been hours since they've last eaten.

Still, children gradually grow to accept and enjoy the foods to which they are exposed, and parents should not be overly concerned about their children's fussiness or appetite from meal to meal. Rather, by providing children opportunities to sample a variety of foods, without pressure, parents and other caregivers can expand children's palates and encourage healthy eating. What constitutes healthy eating in early childhood? What are the repercussions of unhealthy eating, and how do family and cultural contexts shape children's behaviors around nutrition? We address these topics in the sections following.

Food Acceptance and Healthy Diets

LEARNING OBJECTIVE 8.5 List nutritional deficiencies that can affect body and brain development.

Unlike infants, whose food intake is completely determined by adults, young children often make independent decisions about what to eat. They freely move around their homes, forage refrigerators and shelves, and spend hours in childcare or preschool where teachers and parents pass out cupcakes to celebrate birthdays and peers indulge in snacks brought from home. Beyond the watch of adults, young children can determine what they will eat, how much, and when—for better or for worse. They may refuse to eat, or avoid an unfamiliar food, or indulge in foods that contain little nutritious value (**FIGURE 8.12**). How can adults get children to accept new foods, and what types of foods do children need?

Avoidance and Acceptance of New Foods

Young children often avoid foods that have unfamiliar tastes and textures. Such avoidance may be evolutionarily adaptive, because a conservative approach to trying new things may prevent children from ingesting dangerous substances (Fisher & Birch, 1995). Still, children must learn to accept new foods if they are to expand their palates to a range of healthy foods.

Research shows that familiarity is key to food acceptance (Menella et al., 2020). The more frequently a child is exposed to a specific food—even if samplings are tiny—the more tolerant the child will be of the food, to the point that eventually, the child may enjoy it. In one study, preschoolers were given tofu (a food that was unfamiliar to them) in a sweet, salty, or plain version. Children readily accepted the tofu after 8–15 exposures, but they only liked the version they had sampled (sweet, savory, or plain) (Sullivan & Birch, 1990). Children presented with sweet or salty versions of tofu did not develop a general liking for tofu, but rather a preference for sweetness or saltiness. Thus, efforts to get children to eat healthy foods—such as milk—by adding sugar (as in chocolate milk) may be futile, because doctoring up plain milk merely intensifies the child's desire for sweets, rather than acceptance of milk generally. Instead, small amounts of plain milk, presented over multiple exposures, will likely lead to acceptance. The rule of familiarity extends to all types of foods. Hispanic children increased their liking of broccoli following exposure, even though broccoli is naturally bitter and often rejected by young children (Anzman-Frasca et al., 2012).

(A)

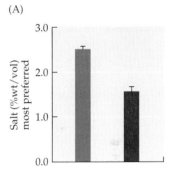

(B)

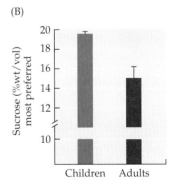

FIGURE 8.12 Promoting a nutritious diet in young children is key to health. Adults should keep in mind that children show greater preferences for (A) salty and (B) sweet foods relative to adults, and so may be drawn to snacks that are unhealthy. (After J. A. Mennella et al. 2014. *PLOS ONE* 9: e92201 © 2014 Mennella et al. CC BY 4.0, https://creativecommons.org/licenses/by/4.0/.)

FIGURE 8.13 Nutrient deficiencies may stunt growth. In particular, deficiencies in protein, vitamins, minerals, iron, calcium, and zinc may affect height. Here, a 13-year-old Malawian boy is shown next to a 12-year-old English boy.

Beyond the importance of frequent exposure, young children may learn to accept foods they dislike when it is creatively prepared. Hispanic preschoolers who would not eat plain broccoli consumed 80% more broccoli when it was served to them with a light dressing as a dip or sauce (Anzman-Frasca et al., 2012). Recipes now abound for ways to incorporate fruits and vegetables into breads and other preparations to entice children to eat.

Healthy and Balanced Diets

Ensuring balanced meals for children is important, and guidelines around nutrition are straightforward. A high-quality diet contains milk products; proteins such as meat, eggs, beans, and peanut butter; fruit and vegetables; breads and cereals; and small amounts of fats, oils, and salt. Children should avoid foods high in sugar and fat content, which contribute to obesity and later health problems including cardiovascular disease and diabetes.

Unfortunately, many young children in the United States and countries around the world experience dietary deficiencies in protein; vitamins; iron, which prevents anemia (low blood count); and minerals, particularly calcium, which supports bone development, and zinc, which supports immune system functioning and cell communication and duplication (Ganji, Hampl, & Betts, 2003) (**FIGURE 8.13**). Children who frequently eat fruits and vegetables and rarely eat fried foods have higher bone mass and lower levels of body fat than do children who rarely consume healthy foods (Wosje et al., 2010). And children who avoid milk, often because they substitute with sweet fruit drinks and soda, are at greater risk for low bone density, bone fractures, and lower strength than are children who drink milk (Black et al., 2002). A major risk of children's unhealthy eating is obesity, which we turn to next.

✓ CHECK YOUR UNDERSTANDING 8.5

1. What may be done to get children to accept a variety of healthy foods?
2. What are some risks of poor nutrition to child health?

Childhood Obesity

LEARNING OBJECTIVE 8.6 Explain factors that contribute to obesity in young children.

obesity The excess storage of fat, typically an outcome of unhealthy eating

Obesity, the excess storage of fat, is one of the most troubling consequences of a poor diet. Children with BMIs at or above the 85th percentile for their age are considered to be overweight; those at or above the 95th percentile are considered to be obese. Unfortunately, obesity in young children has risen sharply, particularly among Black and Hispanic U.S. children relative to White and Asian U.S. children (Skinner et al., 2018). And, young children do not "grow out of their baby fat" when they are obese. Being obese early in life places a child at high risk for obesity years later. Over 90% of obese 3-year-olds continued to be overweight or obese as adolescents. Children who show rapid acceleration in their BMIs between 2 and 6 years of age are nearly 1.5 times as likely to become obese adolescents compared to children whose BMIs remain flat across early childhood (Geserick et al., 2018).

Rates of obesity are high for U.S. children from Hispanic and Black households for several reasons, including high family poverty, parental obesity, maternal diabetes during pregnancy, inadequate physical activity, and children's ingestion of high caloric foods and beverages (Guerrero et al., 2016; Kumanyika, 2008). Additionally, low-income families often live in neighborhoods that have low access to stores that sell healthy foods, higher-than-average access to fast-food restaurants, and little safe, outdoor space for children to exercise and play, characteristics that may lead to an overreliance on high calorie foods and a sedentary lifestyle (e.g., Caprio et al., 2008; Chaparro et al., 2014).

Fortunately, state- and local-level policies to promote healthy diets and physical activity in children may offer some solutions to the obesity epidemic. Early childhood education around physical activity; programs that support children's and families' healthy nutrition and physical activity; screening of child fitness levels and BMI; farm-to-table initiatives; and school programs that encourage proper nutrition and activity have led to declines in childhood obesity in cities in Alaska, North Carolina, New York, and Pennsylvania (Dooyema et al., 2018).

✓ **CHECK YOUR UNDERSTANDING 8.6**

1. What are some factors that contribute to the prevalence of childhood obesity in the United States today?

Family Context of Nutrition

LEARNING OBJECTIVE 8.7 Discuss various ways that parents can promote their children's acceptance of healthy foods.

Children's food preferences and habits develop in the context of their families and cultures. Children learn what and how to eat by observing the people around them, trying different types of foods, and learning family practices around eating. I recall a family visit to the Mayan temples in Mexico. Our tour guide explained that parents in Mexico regularly offer hot peppers to their very young children during family meals. Over time, Mayan Mexican children acquire a love of spicy foods that children from other communities typically reject. It made me think about adults' powerful role in determining children's access to food and the climate around eating.

Access to Foods

Young children can only eat the foods available to them. Shelves lined with sodas, cookies, and chips create unhealthy eating habits and preferences. At mealtime, parents can serve children large portions of healthy, energy dense foods such as vegetables and fruits to increase children's intake of both. When portion sizes of fruit and vegetable side dishes were experimentally doubled in a laboratory study, 4- to 6-year-old children increased their vegetable intake by 37% and their fruit intake by 70%, without increasing their overall consumption of calories (Mathias et al., 2012). Thus, children did not overeat, but rather ate more of the healthy foods. These effects, however, were not seen in children who disliked fruits and vegetables, indicating that parents should engage in strategies to expand children's acceptance of healthy foods before they engage in strategies to increase how much of those healthy foods children eat.

Emotional Climate at Mealtime

Parents can make mealtime unpleasant for children when they are overly concerned about how their young children are eating. Threats ("If you don't eat your green beans you won't be able to go out to play.") and bribes ("If you eat your green beans, you can have ice cream.") are ineffective, because they communicate to children that the food being forced on them is undesirable. In fact, young children's cravings for an unhealthy food increases when the food is labeled as a "forbidden treat" and parents engage in high control tactics. (As the saying goes: People want what they cannot have!) When children's access to a palatable food was restricted, children actually increased in their desire to consume the prohibited food (Fisher & Birch, 1999) (**FIGURE 8.14**). Moreover, parents who exert too much control over children's eating promote overeating in children by limiting children's opportunities to develop self-control (Birch, Fisher, & Davison, 2003).

FIGURE 8.14 Children and forbidden foods. When adults restrict children's access to foods children like a lot but may not be very healthy, they actually increase children's desire to eat the prohibited food.

© rangizzz/Shutterstock.com

Modeling Healthy Eating

Parents and other family members model healthy and unhealthy eating habits themselves, so even when parents encourage their children to drink milk or eat an apple as a snack, children may be disinclined to do so if they see their parents and siblings avoiding those foods. Children often mimic the food choices of people they admire, notably adults and siblings, as illustrated in a study where 5-year old girls' preferences to drink milk or soda mirrored those of their mothers (Fisher et al., 2001).

✓ CHECK YOUR UNDERSTANDING 8.7

1. What strategies work and do not work in encouraging children to eat healthy foods?

Sleep

A good night's rest yields many benefits, just as too little sleep incurs costs. With sleep we are energetic, refreshed, and alert. Without sleep, we are tired, irritable, and lack focus. Young children are no different. In fact, sleep-deprived children can be more ornery than sleep-deprived adults because children do not have the cognitive and emotional resources to understand that it is *not okay* to throw food, toys, and yourself on the floor when things don't go your way. In the sections that follow, you will learn about developmental changes in young children's sleep patterns, how much sleep children need, and family and cultural influences on sleep. (Later in the chapter we will examine the effects of sleep deprivation on academic, behavioral, and physical development.)

Developmental Changes in Sleep Patterns

LEARNING OBJECTIVE 8.8 Describe how sleep patterns change in the transition from infancy to early childhood.

sleep regulation The ability to transition from wakefulness to sleep states and control the quantity and quality of sleep

sleep consolidation The establishment of a single episode of nighttime sleep as children consolidate their sleep into a single nighttime period and eliminate daytime naps

Sleep regulation and consolidation improve from infancy through early childhood (Staples, Bates, & Petersen, 2015). **Sleep regulation** refers to the ability to transition from wakefulness to sleep states. **Sleep consolidation** refers to the establishment of a single episode of nighttime sleep (Staples, Bates, & Petersen, 2015). One of the most noticeable changes to sleep across the early years is the gradual consolidation of sleep and waking bouts. The sleep bouts of human and animal infants are highly fragmented, with rapid transitions between sleep states of short durations (Blumberg et al., 2005; Kleitman & Engelmann, 1953). Then, around 4 to 5 years of age, children consolidate their sleep into a single nighttime period, which coincides with elimination of naps (Iglowstein et al., 2003) (**FIGURE 8.15**).

Young children also differ from infants in the time they spend in different stages of sleep. People experience different stages of sleep that are accompanied by changes to brain waves. During light sleep, a person can be easily awakened. During REM sleep, a person experiences "rapid eye movements" (thus the term REM sleep) and brain waves that are similar to those when awake; however, the body does not move. REM sleep is the stage when dreaming occurs. Finally, the stage of deep sleep features slow brain wave activity, no rapid eye movements, no dreaming, and difficulty in waking up. Deep sleep is the stage when some young children experience bedwetting. Young children reduce their time in REM sleep to 20% of total sleep time from the 50% of REM sleep seen in infants. Developmental change in the amount of REM sleep may be why young children are less likely to wake up in the middle of the night compared to infants.

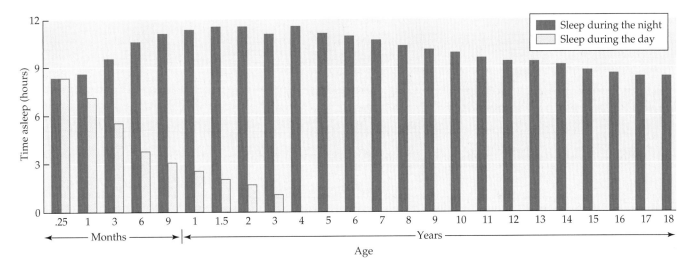

FIGURE 8.15 Sleep requirements of young children. In total, children require more hours of sleep in infancy and early childhood than do older children and adolescents. Furthermore, sleep shifts from time asleep during night and day to sleep only at night. (After E. H. Chudler. Accessed 20 July 2021. https://faculty.washington.edu/chudler/sleep.html. Used with permission of Dr. Eric H. Chudler, University of Washington. Data from B. J. Howard and J. Wong. 2001. *Pediatr Rev* 22: 327–341.)

✓ **CHECK YOUR UNDERSTANDING 8.8**

1. What changes are seen in children's sleep patterns between infancy and early childhood?

How Much Sleep Do Young Children Need?

LEARNING OBJECTIVE 8.9 Contrast the reality of how much sleep children get with how much sleep they need according to pediatric guidelines.

Young children need a lot of sleep! According to pediatric guidelines, children between 1 and 6 years of age should get 10–14 hours of sleep, including naps, in a 24-hour period. Naps are one way that young children get the sleep they need, although children vary in how much they nap during the day and the age at which they abandon naps entirely. Some children take a 1- to 2-hour nap each day, others take two naps, and others don't nap at all. By 4 years of age, naps are rare (Howard & Wong, 2001). However, children who no longer nap get as much sleep as children who continue to nap because non-nappers sleep longer at night (Ward et al., 2007).

All too often, in the midst of typically hectic lives, parents and caregivers underestimate the amount of sleep their children require, and fail to anticipate that sleep deprivation may cause high irritability in children. Furthermore, parents typically *over*-estimate children's actual sleep time, unaware of what goes on behind closed doors after young children head to bed (Sitnick, Goodlin-Jones, & Anders, 2008). Often, parents assume that children are asleep when they are not. In fact, **actigraphs**—lightweight monitors that are generally watch-shaped and worn on the wrist of the nondominant arm—indicate that children often sleep fewer hours than their parents report and fewer hours than needed (Acebo et al., 2005; Staples, Bates, & Petersen, 2015) (**FIGURE 8.16**). In one study, 2- to 5-year-old children slept only 9.5 hours in a 24-hour cycle, well below the recommended 10–14 hours; in another study nearly one-third of children under 5 years showed some type of sleep disruption.

Why do young children not get the sleep they require? One reason is that many young children have difficulty falling asleep, often due to being afraid of the dark and being left alone. Half of children ages 3–6 years wake up at some

actigraphs Lightweight monitors that measure children's wake and sleep patterns

(A)

(B)

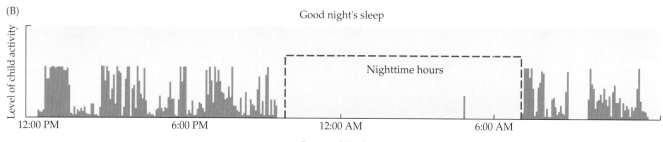

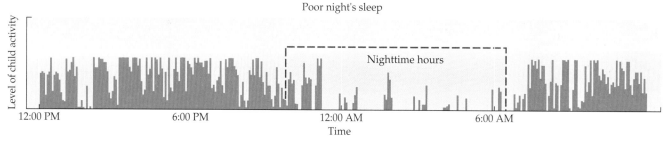

FIGURE 8.16 Sleep monitoring by actigraph.   (A) Toddlers and young children wear small watch-like devices called actigraphs that detect movement and monitor sleep patterns. Researchers typically monitor sleep patterns over a 1-week period. (B) The graph depicts data on changes to movements over a 24-hour period. The top graph shows a day that contains a good night's sleep which is based on higher sleep efficiency (that is a high ratio of hours sleeping to hours in bed), fewer awakenings, and lower average length of time awake per awakening) and the bottom a poor one. The pink highlighted region shows diminished movements (blue lines) during the nighttime hours of the top panel, and short bursts of movement during the nighttime hours in the poorer-sleep pattern represented in the bottom panel. (B after B. Goosby et al. 2018. RSF *The Russell Sage Foundation Journal of the Social Sciences*. pp. 43–61. © 2018 Russell Sage Foundation. https://www.rsfjournal.org/content/4/4/43)

night terrors Arousals or disruptions from deep sleep more dramatic than a nightmare, in which children scream from panic, thrash wildly, and experience raised heart rates and breathing

point during the night, perhaps due to a "bad dream." A small proportion of young children (under 5%) experience **night terrors**, arousals from sleep in which they scream in panic, thrash wildly, experience spikes in heart rate and breathing, and are inconsolable. Stress or extreme fatigue can trigger a night terror, although a genetic component may also exist, as night terrors run in families (Guilleminault et al., 2003; Thorpy & Yager, 2001).

✓ **CHECK YOUR UNDERSTANDING 8.9**

1. What do actigraphs reveal about young children's sleep?
2. How are night terrors different from nightmares?

Family Context of Sleep

LEARNING OBJECTIVE 8.10 Explain why regularity in everyday routines benefits children's sleep.

Families establish daytime and bedtime routines that strongly influence children's sleep patterns. Consider a child who experiences high regularity in her daily life: She wakes up the same time each morning, has breakfast, is dropped off at preschool, picked up by the babysitter, plays before dinner, takes a bath, hears a bedtime story, and then goes to sleep at the same time she went to bed the night before and will go to bed the following day. Such regularity creates a sense of order and predictability and helps establish a consistent circadian rhythm that makes falling asleep and waking up easier. Indeed, regularity in bedtime routines facilitates children's sleep, whereas chaotic, erratic routines interfere with children's sleep (Sadeh et al., 2009).

Consistency in parenting likewise facilitates children's sleep, just as inconsistent parenting hinders children's sleep. A parent who is strict one day and lax the next, who provides a lot of love and attention on certain days but is neglectful and preoccupied on others, and who is firm about sleep one day but flexible the next creates a home environment that lacks the consistency needed for establishing good habits. Children who experienced regular bedtime routines and consistent parenting averaged an hour more of sleep per night than did children who experienced irregular bedtime routines and/or inconsistent parenting (Staples, Bates, & Petersen, 2015).

✓ **CHECK YOUR UNDERSTANDING 8.10**

1. What steps can parents take to ensure their children get a good night's sleep?

Childhood Illness, Injury, and Maltreatment

Protecting young children from illness and injury is a paramount goal of parents, care providers, teachers, and health policies, but doing so is not always feasible. I recall when my son Christopher ran through a glass door at his friend's home while playing tag, shards of glass flying. Another time, he hit his head on our grandfather clock while running, severely splitting open his lip and bleeding profusely as we rushed him to the hospital.

Our children were lucky, however, because their injuries (and illnesses) were relatively minor. Such is not the case for far too many children. Some children are not vaccinated or do not regularly visit a doctor. Some experience chronic health problems that require persistent vigilance and monitoring. Some children suffer injuries with serious consequences, including fatality. Some children are victims of parental negligence or abuse. The cascading influences of illness, injury, and maltreatment cannot be overstated. In the sections that follow, we review research in these areas and investigate the contextual factors that cause and prevent health-related problems.

Notably, the methods used to study child health differ from the typical lab-based, experimental, and naturalistic observational studies of developmental science. In fact, much of what is known about childhood illness and injury comes from **epidemiological studies**, which analyze the prevalence, causes, and consequences of health and illnesses in large samples. Researchers carefully identify a question of importance (for instance, whether the proportion of children who are vaccinated varies by household income), the sample(s) to be studied (for instance, children living below the national poverty line versus those in more resourced homes), and then gather information through community, state, national, or international surveys, health records, and other means. Epidemiological studies tend to be much larger than most research studies, to ensure the generalizability and soundness of health recommendations that may affect thousands or millions of people. Indeed, epidemiological studies shape public health policies, medical care decisions, large-scale interventions, and preventive healthcare by identifying risk factors for disease and avenues for health promotion.

epidemiological studies Large-scale studies that analyze the prevalence, causes, and consequences of health and illness at community, state, national, and international levels

Infectious Diseases

Few, if any, children escape sore throats, ear infections, stomach bugs, rashes, coughs, and so forth, no matter how often they practice good etiquette of washing hands and avoiding the coughing and sneezing of friends or relatives (**TABLE 8.1**). **Infectious diseases** are caused by bacteria, viruses, parasites, or fungi that can be spread among people through personal contact, water, or air. Attendance at childcare centers, nursery school, and preschool increases children's exposure to other sick children and consequently raises the likelihood of being sick. Fortunately, most infectious diseases are acute (short term), typically lasting only a few days. Acute illnesses caused by bacterial infections, such as strep throat, can be treated with antibiotics, and most viral infections will eventually be overcome by a healthy immune system.

infectious diseases Diseases caused by pathogenic micro-organisms such as bacteria, viruses, parasites, or fungi that can be spread among people through personal contact, water, or air

TABLE 8.1 ■ Common childhood illnesses

Illness	Symptoms
Chicken pox	Rash begins as small, red, flat spots that develop into itchy fluid-filled blisters
Common cold	Runny nose, sneezing, sore throat
Conjunctivitis	Teary, red, itchy, painful eye(s)
Flu	Fever, cough, sneezing, runny nose, headache, body aches and pain, exhaustion, sore throat
German measles	Fever, tiredness. Raised, red rash that starts on the face and spreads downward
Glandular fever	High temperature, sore throat, and swollen glands
Hand, foot, and mouth disease	Fever, sore throat, headache, small painful blisters inside the mouth on tongue and gums (may appear on hands and feet)
Impetigo	Clusters of red bumps or blisters surrounded by area of redness
Measles	Fever, cough, runny nose, and watery inflamed eyes. Small red spots with white or bluish white centers in the mouth. Red, blotchy rash
Ringworm	Red, ring-shaped rash. May be itchy. Rash may be dry and scaly or wet and crusty
Scabies	Intense itching, pimple-like rash. Itching and rash may be all over the body but commonly between the fingers, wrists, elbows, arm
Shingles	Pain, itching, or tingling along the affected nerve pathway. Blister-type rash
Sickness bug/diarrhea	Stomach cramps, nausea, vomiting, and diarrhea
Threadworms	Intense itchiness around anus
Tonsilitis	Intense sore throat
Whooping cough	Violent coughing, over and over, until child inhales with "whooping" sound to get air into lungs

Source: Data from NHS Basildon and Brentwood Clinical Commissioning Group. "Advice on Childhood Illnesses Poster."

Some infectious diseases (e.g., diphtheria, meningitis, mumps, measles, rubella, hepatitis, yellow fever, and tuberculosis) are quite serious and highly contagious. For example, the measles virus can spread quickly to people who are not immunized. A cough or sneeze can leave particles from the virus on doorknobs, flat surfaces, toys, hand rails, elevator buttons, and particles can even linger in the air for two hours. Another example is SARS-CoV-2, the contagious virus at the center of the worldwide COVID-19 pandemic. Although initially not thought to be dangerous to children, new variants in 2021 led some schools and daycare centers to close or enforce mask mandates. While such efforts may reduce the likelihood of infection, developmental researchers have begun to study the emotional and social consequences of young children wearing masks and social distancing. As one example, obstructing faces with masks impairs the ability of people to read emotions and is pronounced in young children (Gori, Schiatti, & Amadeo, 2021). Such findings serve as a reminder of cascading influences from one domain (health precautions) to others (social and emotional development).

Fortunately, many infectious diseases can be prevented through vaccines. However, even in the United States, where vaccinations are mandated and available to everyone, national vaccination coverage rates for young children average between approximately 73% and 92%, depending on child age, vaccine type, and study (Hill et al., 2018; Johnson et al., 2014; Phadke et al., 2016). In fact, measles continues to be a leading cause of death in children worldwide. As of publication, there is still no vaccine for SARS-CoV-2 authorized for use in children under 12 years of age. Later in the chapter, we will examine the family, neighborhood, and cultural contexts that influence children's health and likelihood of immunization against infectious diseases.

✓ CHECK YOUR UNDERSTANDING 8.11

1. In what ways can parents protect their children from infectious disease?

Chronic Diseases

LEARNING OBJECTIVE 8.12 Identify prevalent chronic diseases in the United States.

Relative to infectious diseases, which are short lived or prevented through inoculations, chronic diseases pose a much more serious health concern. **Chronic diseases** are noncommunicable, long lasting, and typically can be controlled but not cured (Torpy, Campbell, & Glass, 2010). Examples include:

- *Diseases associated with being overweight.* Many overweight children continue to be overweight as adults, which can lead to diabetes, heart disease, high blood pressure, and high cholesterol.

- *Malnutrition.* Malnutrition occurs when children do not have enough to eat or do not eat enough of the right vitamins and nutrients necessary for their bodies to grow and stay healthy. Children may experience malnutrition for short or long durations in mild or severe forms. Malnutrition can lead to **anemia**, inadequate immune system function, problems in growth, and cognitive deficiencies.

- *Asthma.* Asthma is a respiratory condition that causes difficulty in breathing, and can lead to frequent hospitalizations and death.

- *Cystic fibrosis.* Cystic fibrosis is a genetic disorder that affects the lungs (primarily), pancreas, liver, kidneys, and intestines. Cystic fibrosis leads to several long-term complications including frequent lung infections and difficulty breathing. Although there is no cure, early diagnosis can lead to better treatment for children.

chronic diseases Noncommunicable and long-lasting diseases that typically can be controlled through ongoing medical attention but not cured, such as obesity, malnutrition, diabetes, and developmental disabilities

anemia Low blood count or a condition in which an individual lacks sufficient red blood cells to carry oxygen to the body's tissues, sometimes due to malnutrition

- *Diabetes.* Diabetes is a disease in which the body is unable to produce sufficient insulin, leading to elevated glucose in the blood. Diabetes is associated with an increased risk of heart and blood vessel disease, and stroke.

- *Developmental disabilities.* Developmental disabilities originate at birth or during childhood, continue indefinitely, and affect children's physical and mental functioning. Common developmental disabilities include attention-deficit/hyperactivity disorder (ADHD), cerebral palsy, and autism spectrum disorder.

- *Cholera and malaria.* Cholera and malaria are chronic diseases in some regions outside the United States, including countries in Africa. Cholera is a disease of the small intestine, typically contracted from infected water, and results in severe vomiting and diarrhea. Malaria is caused by a parasite transmitted by mosquitoes that invades red blood cells and causes fever.

Chronic diseases are major causes of death and disability throughout the world, and are responsible for twice the number of deaths as infectious diseases, maternal and perinatal conditions, and nutritional deficiencies combined (World Health Organization, 2010). Children develop chronic illnesses that may last for years or even their whole lives as a result of genetic conditions, environmental factors, or a combination of the two. Children's experiences with chronic disease can have detrimental effects on development across a range of areas if not handled properly.

✓ CHECK YOUR UNDERSTANDING 8.12

1. How does a chronic disease differ from infectious disease? Provide examples of chronic diseases.

Unintentional Childhood Injury

LEARNING OBJECTIVE 8.13 List some common injuries in young children.

Injuries are common in early childhood, ranging from falls to burns to accidental ingestion of toxic substances. Energetic youngsters have the curiosity and know-how to get into everything, and they lack the impulse control to regulate their behaviors. Some injuries are relatively minor and alleviated by stitches or casts, whereas others can be fatal. Falls, firearm-related injuries, burns, chokings, drownings, auto accidents, poisonings, and suffocation are common unintentional childhood injuries (Borse et al., 2009; Cunningham et al., 2018), with children age 5 years and younger being more likely to be hospitalized and more likely to die from such injuries than children of other ages (Grossman, 2000). In the United States, unintentional injuries are the leading cause of childhood death, with about 8,000 children being victims of injury each year (Child Trends, 2016).

Fortunately, fatalities from childhood injury have declined in the United States over the past few decades due to laws and policies aimed at improving the safety of children and campaigns aimed at raising public awareness. These safety precautions include regulations on the use of car seats, safety belts, and bicycle helmets; availability of household safety items such as fire alarms, cabinet locks, and child-proof containers that hold toxic substances; and clear guidelines on packaging, such as marking toys with small parts as potentially hazardous. Still, many parents underestimate their young children's potential for harm and fail to take the proper safety precautions. They allow their children to ride bikes without helmets or to sit in the back seat of the car without an age-appropriate car seat (Mickalide & Carr, 2012).

✓ CHECK YOUR UNDERSTANDING 8.13

1. What are examples of measures adults can implement to help prevent unintentional injuries in young children?

Maltreatment and Exposure to Violence

LEARNING OBJECTIVE 8.14 Classify different types of maltreatment.

It is impossible to escape the reality, prevalence, and horrors of child maltreatment. Not a day goes by without the news reporting on a young child who was severely harmed by the people who cared for the child. Child **maltreatment** refers to the abuse or neglect of children, and is classified into four subtypes (Cicchetti, 2016):

- **Neglect** involves the failure to meet children's basic needs for food, clothing, shelter, and medical treatment. Neglect can include abandonment, a lack of adequate supervision, and disengagement from a child's life and education.
- **Emotional abuse** involves extreme hampering of children's emotional needs, such as by belittling and ridiculing a child, extreme negativity and hostility, and suicidal or homicidal threats.
- **Physical abuse** involves intentionally inflicting physical harm on a child, including bruises, burns, choking, and broken bones.
- **Sexual abuse** involves attempts toward or actual sexual contact with a child or forcing the child into prostitution. Sexual abuse can range from exposure to pornography to fondling and forced intercourse.

Beyond these subtypes, maltreatment is also classified by its severity, frequency, offenders, developmental period (whether it occurs in infancy, early childhood, and so on), and timing (such as whether it occurred only at young ages or continued over time) (Manly, 2005). A child who is chronically abused or neglected is at especially high risk for health and psychological problems.

How prevalent is child maltreatment? Exact statistics are difficult to obtain because many cases occur under the radar and go unreported. Moreover, estimates on the prevalence of maltreatment depend on whether scientists rely on official documentation by the U.S. Child Protective Services (CPS) or ask people to self-report on their experiences of maltreatment in childhood (Wildeman et al., 2014). A 2019 report by the Administration for Children and Families (ACF, 2019) reported that 3.5 million U.S. children were investigated for maltreatment by their caregivers or parents in 2017, which resulted in an estimated 674,000 children being identified as victims. Most children experienced neglect (74.9%), followed by physical abuse (18.3%) or sexual abuse (8.6%).

But identified maltreatment rates are based on one year only, do not reflect the number of children who are maltreated at any point during their childhood, and do not include unidentified cases. In fact, rates on the *cumulative* experiences of self-reported maltreatment rise to between 20% and over 40% if people are asked if they experienced a form of abuse or neglect *at any point* during their childhood (Finkelhor, Saito, & Jones, 2018; Hussey, Chang, & Kotch, 2006; Wildeman et al., 2014). Moreover, the incidence of maltreatment peaks in infancy and early childhood, with three-fourths of children who die from child abuse or neglect being younger than 4 years of age (U.S. Department of Health and Human Services, 2014). An estimated 1,720 children died from abuse and neglect in 2017 alone (ACF, 2019). Fortunately, rates of child sexual and physical abuse have declined over the past few decades, although rates of neglect remain flat or are on the rise (Finkelhor, Saito, & Jones, 2018) (**FIGURE 8.17**).

maltreatment The emotional abuse, physical abuse, sexual abuse, or neglect of children

neglect The failure to meet children's basic needs for food, clothing, shelter, and medical attention and care

emotional abuse Extreme psychological and verbal abuse of children, including hampering of children's emotional needs, such as belittling, ridiculing, extreme negativity and hostility, and making suicidal or homicidal threats

physical abuse The intentional infliction of physical, bodily harm on a child, including choking, bruising, burning, and breaking bones

sexual abuse Attempts toward or actual sexual contact with a child, or forcing a child into prostitution

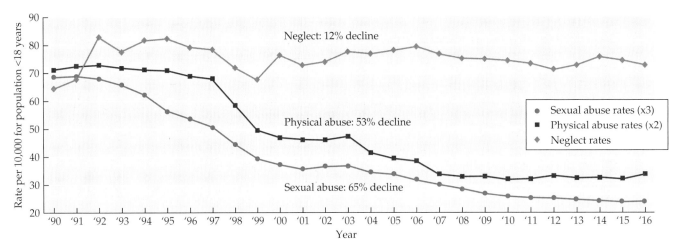

FIGURE 8.17 Rates of types of abuse on the decline. The 2016 data released by the National Child Abuse and Neglect Data System shows declining trends for some forms of abuse over the past several decades, although rates remain alarmingly high. (The annual rates for both physical abuse and sexual abuse have been multiplied by 2 and 3, respectively, for trend comparisons.) (After D. Finkelhor et al. 2018. Updated trends in child maltreatment 2016. Durham, NH: Crimes against Children Research Center.)

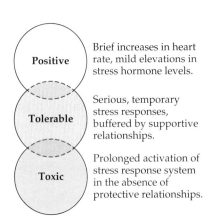

FIGURE 8.18 Types of stress. The National Scientific Council on the Developing Child distinguishes among positive, tolerable, and toxic stress. The three types of stress refer to the intensity and duration of children's response to the stress, not the event itself. (After Center on the Developing Child at Harvard University. 2016. In *From Best Practices to Breakthrough Impacts: A Science-Based Approach to Building A More Promising Future for Young Children and Families.* Key Findings from the Report, pp. 9-20. Center on the Developing Child at Harvard University: Cambridge, MA. http://developing-child.harvard.edu. Republished with permission of Center on the Developing Child at Harvard University; permission conveyed through Copyright Clearance Center.)

✓ CHECK YOUR UNDERSTANDING 8.14

1. What are four types of child maltreatment?
2. What are ways to categorize maltreatment?

Stress

LEARNING OBJECTIVE 8.15 Discuss the positive and negative effects of stress.

Maltreatment, violence, and other negative childhood experiences can harm children's health through the toll that stress takes on the body. When children encounter a harmful event, attack, or threatening situation, the hypothalamus reacts by releasing cortisol to activate the body's stress response, as seen in the fight-or-flight responses of heightened heart rate and dilated pupils.

Notably, however, not all stress is bad. Thus, it's erroneous to assume that protecting children from anything stressful promotes health. In fact, the hypothalamus's production of cortisol may be adaptive for dealing with certain types of everyday challenges. Thus, researchers distinguish among positive, tolerable, and toxic stress based on the intensity and duration of children's response (Shonkoff & Garner, 2012) (**FIGURE 8.18**).

Positive Stress

Positive stress produces brief and mild to moderate changes in children's physiological states, such as the anxiety children experience when visiting the doctor's office or attending the first day of school. When environments are stable and supportive, positive stressors provide children with opportunities to practice healthy and adaptive coping strategies in the face of negative experiences. Production of cortisol during mildly stressful situations causes blood to move from the extremities to large muscles, thereby preparing children for action. For example, moderate levels of cortisol on a young child's first day of school might motivate the child to approach unfamiliar peers and the teacher. Cortisol also yields emotional and cognitive benefits. In one study, 4- to 6-year-old children were assessed in their stress reactions to a fire alarm using brain scans and hormone measurements (Quas, Bauer, & Boycem, 2004). Some children were upset by the alarm and others were not based on measures of cortisol levels. Children with moderately high cortisol reactions to the alarm remembered more details about the event two weeks later than did their peers who experienced less stress, indicating the role of cortisol in memory.

Tolerable Stress

Tolerable stress is associated with exposure to nonnormative experiences such as the death of a family member, a serious illness or injury, or a natural disaster such as a destructive hurricane. Tolerable stressors excessively activate the stress response and cause long-term physiological harm if environmental supports are inadequate. However, supportive adults can buffer the harmful effects of life event stressors on children. Certain forms of stress are regarded as tolerable because children can learn how to engage in adaptive coping and gain a sense of control with the help of a protective adult (Shonkoff & Garner, 2012).

Toxic Stress

Toxic stress occurs when children experience chronic, strong, or prolonged activation of the body's stress response system without the adult support needed to reduce the stress. Examples of toxic stress include enduring exposure to violence, abuse, neglect, and extreme poverty (Gershoff, 2016). Such toxic experiences may trigger a chronic excess of cortisol, placing young children at risk for physical and mental disorders, poor emotional regulation, and learning problems (Walker et al., 2011).

positive stress A type of stress that creates brief and mild or moderate changes in children's psychological states (e.g., anxiety before the first day of school)

tolerable stress A type of stress characterized by exposure to non-normative experiences, such as the death of a family member, a serious illness, or a natural disaster

toxic stress A type of stress that occurs when children experience chronic, persistent, or strong activation of the body's stress response system

✓ CHECK YOUR UNDERSTANDING 8.15

1. Why may stress sometimes be good for a child?
2. What is toxic stress and what evidence indicates its harmful effects?

Family Context of Childhood Illness, Injury, and Maltreatment

LEARNING OBJECTIVE 8.16 Explain how a family's economic resources, access to healthcare, and views and practices around vaccinations may affect children's health.

Family context affects children's health through various pathways, with three key influences being the economic resources of households, access to healthcare, and the views of parents and their efforts to take preventive measures to support their children's health.

Economic Resources

Poverty often robs children of the opportunity to achieve their full potential through harmful effects on children's physical health. Children living in poor families show disproportionately high rates of infectious and chronic disease (**FIGURE 8.19A**) and high rates of accidents and injuries. In fact, poverty compromises children's health across numerous areas, being associated with childhood asthma, hospitalization, emergency room use, missing school, low insurance coverage, and being in poor or fair health (Chaurdry & Wimer, 2016; Flores, Olson, & Tomany-Korman, 2005). Moreover, poverty disproportionately affects children from certain racial and ethnic groups, placing them at risk for negative health outcomes (**FIGURE 8.19B**).

Family poverty is also associated with child maltreatment, neglect, and exposure to violence. Children in low-income households have greater lifetime odds of experiencing physical or sexual abuse and witnessing abuse being carried out on other family members than do children from middle-income households (Turner, Finkelhor, & Ormrod, 2006). Children from poor homes are also likely to witness community violence in the forms of muggings, fights, shootings, or knifings (Finkelhor et al., 2005; Linares et al., 2001).

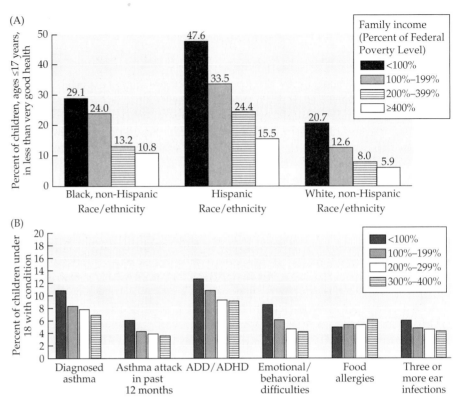

FIGURE 8.19 **Poverty and health.** Children living in poor families (A) are generally in less than very good health and (B) show disproportionately high rates of infectious and chronic disease. (A after S. Egerter et al. 2008. *America's Health Starts with Healthy Children: How Do States Compare?* Washington, DC: Robert Wood Johnson Foundation Commission to Build a Healthier America. Prepared by the Center on Social Disparities in Health [now the Center for Health Equity] at the University of California, San Francisco. Source: 2003 National Survey of Children's Health. B after J. Volberding. 2018. *Compassionate Care for All: Socioeconomic Status and Health Care.* National Athletic Trainers' Association. https://www.nata.org/blog/jordan-grantham/socioeconomic-status-and-its-impact-health-care. Data from CDCP. 2016. Health conditions among children under age 18, by selected characteristics: United States average annual, selected years 1997-1999 through 2013-2015. https://www.cdc.gov/nchs/hus/contents2016.htm#035 2016. Accessed February 1, 2018.)

Access to Healthcare

Parents and other caregivers affect children's development through access to and provision of health care, including regular visits to doctors. Yet too many families, for a variety of reasons, fail to provide their children with necessary preventive care. Families may live far from hospitals or clinics or find health care to be inaccessible due to cost or lack of insurance. However, expansions of Medicaid and other federal health programs have led to gains in U.S. children's health insurance coverage (Perrin, Boat, and Kelleher, 2016). Data released in 2014 from the U.S. Bureau of Labor Statistics & the Census Bureau estimated that 94% of U.S. children have some form of health care insurance coverage, although children from poor households have lower rates of coverage than do those from middle-income households (e.g., Berchick & Mykta, 2019).

Family Views and Practices around Vaccinations

A lack of healthcare is not the only reason that some parents fail to take preventative measures for their children. An alarming number of parents refuse to have their children vaccinated. Even when vaccines are readily available, some parents do not fully immunize their children (for religious reasons or due to misinformation), placing their children and other unvaccinated individuals at serious risk.

The dangers of parents' decisions are illustrated in a case of measles outbreak among visitors to Disneyland in December 2014. A person who had not been immunized for measles visited the park and caused 145 people in the United States and a dozen others in Canada and Mexico to contract the contagious disease. A team of experts analyzed the outbreak data and calculated that only between 50% and 86% of people exposed had been vaccinated (Phadke et al., 2016). After the Disneyland outbreak, California legislators sought to make it difficult for parents to opt out of immunizing their children against measles and other infectious diseases. The scientists concluded that the only explanation for the low rate of immunization was that a substantial proportion of U.S. parents intentionally did not immunize their children from measles, mumps, and rubella. In a similar vein, in 2019, the *New York Times* and other media outlets reported on a measles epidemic in New York City that originated in a small group of communities where parents chose not to vaccinate their children for religious and other reasons (McNeill, 2019). Regulations were implemented to fine parents, mandate vaccinations, and prevent unvaccinated children from attending school.

Unfortunately, a sub-group of parents erroneously believe that vaccinations place children at risk for autism and a weakened immune system, a belief that dates back to a 1998 report in the medical journal *The Lancet*. At that time, a British physician claimed a possible connection between the vaccine for measles, mumps, and rubella (MMR) and autism based on parallel rising trends of childhood vaccinations and autism. Although the common trends were only coincidental, and evidence indicates no association between vaccinations and autism or immune system problems (e.g., Richler et al., 2006; Stehr-Green et al., 2003), the belief has endured and resulted in disease outbreaks in whooping cough, rubella, and measles. The New York City epidemic aptly illustrates the dangers for families when science is misrepresented.

✓ CHECK YOUR UNDERSTANDING 8.16

1. What are the dangers when parents or caregivers fail to vaccinate their children?

Neighborhood Context and Lead Exposure

LEARNING OBJECTIVE 8.17 Discuss how poor neighborhoods can affect children's health through exposure to lead.

Hazards in children's homes pose health problems that affect many young children, especially children living in poor neighborhoods. Children can be exposed to toxins by inhaling them (e.g., from dust particles in the air), ingesting them (e.g., mouthing their hands or an object after touching soil or dust containing toxic particles), or merely through skin contact with the toxin.

Lead, for example, is a toxic substance that tends be found in greater concentrations in poor communities. Several longitudinal studies, conducted in countries around the world, have found lead exposure and concentrations of lead in children's blood to be associated with low child intelligence, deficits in verbal and visual-motor skills, and behavior problems such as distractibility, poor organization, and acting out (Hubbs-Tait et al., 2002). Chronic lead exposure is associated with health problems in children, including headaches, stomach pain, behavioral problems, and decreased cognitive performance.

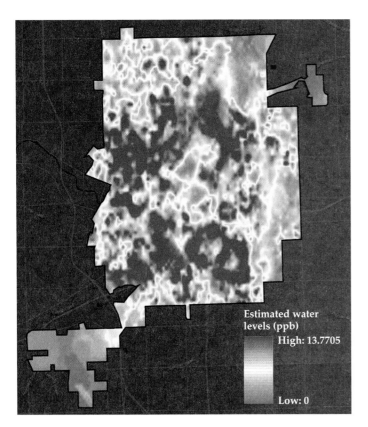

FIGURE 8.20 Poor water quality threatens children. Certain areas of Flint, Michigan showed alarmingly high levels of lead, measured in ppb (parts per billion), in tap water in 2015 (reflected in red sections of the city). Even low levels of lead can be harmful to human health. (From J. Heslin. Azavea's Summer of Maps Fellowship Program. September 15, 2017. https://www.azavea.com/blog/2017/09/15/interpolating-lead-levels-from-tap-water-samples-following-flint-water-crisis/. Data Sources: US Census Bureau, State of Michigan, Esri. Cartographer: J. Heslin.)

Children living in poor neighborhoods may be exposed to lead-based paint and lead-contaminated dust if they live in old buildings, and they may also be exposed to lead through contaminated air, water, or soil (Aelion et al., 2013). The water crisis in Flint, Michigan offers a case in point. In April 2014, Flint, Michigan changed its water source from treated water that originated in Lake Huron and the Detroit River to the Flint River. Corrosive, aging pipes that fed into the new water supply contaminated the water with metals. Thousands of children—an estimated 5% of the 2015 child population in Flint—were exposed to drinking water with alarmingly high levels of lead (**FIGURE 8.20**). In January 2016, the city was declared to be in a state of emergency, and several lawsuits were filed. Given high rates of poverty and unemployment in Flint, as well as other factors, moving to escape contamination was not an option for many families.

Lead has also been found to affect poor neighborhoods in South Carolina. Families with children under 6 years of age who lived in rural and urban areas of South Carolina had high lead levels in their soil, especially in low-income neighborhoods with high concentrations of racial and ethnic minority families (Aelion et al., 2013).

✓ **CHECK YOUR UNDERSTANDING 8.17**

1. Offer an example of a community in which children's exposure to lead became a serious problem.

Cultural Context of Childhood Illness, Injury, and Maltreatment

LEARNING OBJECTIVE 8.18 Describe the different health-related contexts of children living in high-income versus low- and middle-income countries.

The health of young children varies enormously from country to country. The health supports available for children from high-income versus low- and middle-income countries diverge substantially. Poorer countries often lack resources to establish clinics and hospitals, and the facilities that exist are often understaffed and ill-equipped to meet the health care needs of children and families. Consequently, a substantial percentage of the world's children lack adequate access to nutrition; do not receive routine immunizations; and are regularly exposed to environmental hazards such as lead (Stevens et al., 2012; World Health Organization, 2017). Furthermore, unsanitary conditions in poorer countries, such as polluted water and contaminated foods, can cause reduced appetite, persistent diarrhea, malnutrition illness, stunted growth, cognitive delays, and even death in children (e.g., Budge et al., 2019; Niehaus et al., 2002; Thapar & Sanderson, 2004). It is estimated that over 200 million children in poorer countries will not reach their full developmental potential.

However, progress is being made toward establishing family and child health care systems in many countries (**FIGURE 8.21**). For instance, UNICEF is working to address the disproportionate rates of deaths in children under age 5 years in poorer countries by providing children protection through vaccines and other efforts. Programs, such as the GAVI Alliance (formerly the Global Alliance for Vaccines and Immunisation) estimate that nearly 18 million deaths of young children will be averted by vaccinations administered between 2011 and 2020 (Feikin et al., 2006; Lee et al., 2013). Vaccinations are at the forefront of the United Nation's Sustainable Development Goals—a call to action by all countries to promote prosperity and health around the world (**FIGURE 8.22**). In line with the United Nation's goal toward health, UNICEF took action in 2019 to negotiate vaccine prices and help countries identify and serve unreached children. And philanthropists Mark and Chan Zuckerberg donated 3 billion dollars to initiatives to create tools to monitor health and address illness in children globally.

Health care initiatives not only provide children with necessary monitoring and inoculations, but also help create a context for parents in poor countries to learn about the health of their young children. Parents and caregivers generally trust health care providers and have regular contact with them during infancy and early childhood when their children are regularly monitored and vaccinated (Engle et al., 2007). These health care encounters may be the only opportunity that some parents have to learn about child development and ways to support children's health.

✓ **CHECK YOUR UNDERSTANDING 8.18**

  1. List the risks to children's health in poorer countries and efforts being taken to combat those risks.

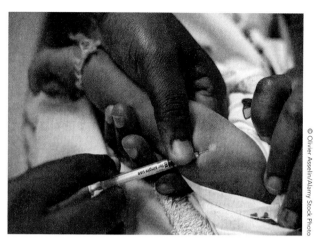

FIGURE 8.21 Health care in poorer countries. UNICEF is working to address the disproportionate rates of deaths in children under age 5 years in poorer countries by providing children protection through vaccines and other efforts.

SUSTAINABLE DEVELOPMENT G☼ALS

FIGURE 8.22 Sustainable Development Goals. The United Nation identified a set of "Sustainable Development Goals" around the key components needed to support world health generally, and children's healthy development more specifically, such as eliminating hunger (Goal #2), access to clean water (Goal #6), and reducing inequalities (Goal #10). UNICEF's efforts around negotiating vaccine prices illustrate an initiative aimed at addressing sustainable goals. (From United Nations. 2019. Sustainable development goals: 17 goals to transform our world. https://www.un.org/sustainabledevelopment/. The content of this publication has not been approved by the United Nations and does not reflect the views of the United Nations or its officials or Member States.)

Developmental Cascades

As conveyed at the beginning of this chapter, developmental science highlights the cascading influences of health on children's functioning across a range of areas. Here, we illustrate the reverberating effects of health on development with select examples from sleep, illness and injury, and maltreatment.

Cascades from Sleep Deprivation

Sleep is vital for children's everyday functioning and overall development. Children better concentrate, learn, and handle the challenges of everyday life when sufficiently rested (El-Sheikh & Sadeh, 2015). Children who do not get sufficient sleep have difficulties focusing attention and getting along socially. Moreover, children's sleep difficulties affect the entire family, because parents' sleep is disrupted when their children do not sleep, which causes stress in the family and may be why parents frequently raise concerns about their children's sleep habits with pediatricians (Meltzer & Mindell, 2007).

Sleep and Academic and Behavioral Outcomes

Disrupted sleep impacts children's functioning concurrently and over the long term. Irregular sleep and insufficient sleep in childhood predict difficulties in preschool, even when statistically controlling for other factors such as family stress and parenting behaviors (Bates et al., 2002). One longitudinal study examined associations between sleep disturbances during kindergarten and children's behavior, cognitive skills, and academic performance in first grade. Data on children's sleep were based on questionnaires and actigraph measures. Actigraph data showed that children who failed the first-grade achievement tests, although they were few in number, took longer to fall asleep, had more arousals from sleep, and less efficient sleep than did children who passed.

Even more striking are developmental cascades connecting sleep problems in early childhood to problem behaviors in adolescence. When researchers tracked the development of boys who were from a high-risk community sample, they found that poor sleep at 3–5 years of age predicted alcohol and drug use in adolescence (Wong et al., 2004). Moreover, the researchers controlled for the alcohol use of the teens' parents to ensure that the associations from sleep to later substance use was not explained by this third, potentially confounding variable.

How can early childhood sleep problems cascade to later problems in cognitive and behavioral domains? As discussed previously, the immediate effects of insufficient or disrupted sleep play out in daytime sleepiness and lower alertness. Moreover, chronic sleep deprivation influences brain functioning by preventing or reducing processes required for brain maturation and restoration, memory consolidation, and learning (El-Sheikh & Sadeh, 2015; Sadeh, 2007). Together, effects of poor sleep may spill over to learning and school performance, and cause children to disengage from school and turn to early and illicit substance use.

Sleep and Obesity

Declines in sleep durations in the United States may contribute to the nation's increase in obesity. Inadequate quality and quantity of sleep places children at risk for being overweight or obese. A representative sample of over 2,000 U.S. children found that children 3–8 years of age who had shorter sleep durations were more likely to be overweight 5 years later at follow-up. But, the association from sleep to overweight status was not seen for older children from 8–13 years of age (Snell, Adam, & Duncan, 2007). Thus, early childhood may be especially critical for developing healthy sleep habits and avoiding the downstream consequences of poor quality sleep.

The connection between sleep and obesity is seen worldwide (Chen, Beydoun, & Wang, 2008), as indicated, for example, in large longitudinal studies conducted in the United Kingdom (Reilly et al., 2005) and Japan (Sekine et al., 2002). A meta-analysis study of 45 studies that included over 30,000 children from around the world revealed a consistent increase in the risk of obesity for children who were short sleepers (Cappuccio et al., 2008). In fact, short sleep durations in childhood doubled the likelihood of being obese!

What might explain the connection between sleep and body weight? One hypothesis posits that sleep deprivation results in fatigue and sleepiness that interferes with activity level and caloric expenditure during awake hours. Sleep also supports hormones related to growth, maturation, and energy homeostasis, which can affect eating habits. For example, sleep deprivation affects the production of the hormones insulin, cortisol, and growth hormone. In turn, hormonal disruption contributes to preference for and selection of calorie-rich foods (Volkow et al., 2013). Additionally, parents who are somewhat lax or permissive around their children's sleep patterns may also be lax or permissive about what their children eat and how much their children exercise.

Cascades from Childhood Illness, Injury, and Maltreatment

Children's experiences with illness, injury, and maltreatment reverberate across developmental domains. Such difficult life experiences can lead to chronic stress and dangerously high levels of cortisol. Children living in poverty are disproportionately likely to experience many of the stressors on health, including exposure to violence, family separation, and poor housing conditions. Moreover, the amount of time children live in poverty predicts mental health problems and disorders in adolescence and adulthood (e.g., Evans & Cassells, 2013).

Exposures to violence and maltreatment in early childhood have been found to trigger long-lasting, devastating developmental consequences across physical, mental, and social domains (e.g., Berens et al., 2019; Cicchetti, 2016; Cicchetti & Doyle, 2016; Margolin & Gordis, 2000). For example, exposure to violence and maltreatment predict the following:

- insecure attachments;
- behavior problems, including a reduced ability to regulate emotions and increased aggression;
- mortality, obesity, viral infections, inflammation, and diabetes;
- mental health problems and suicide;
- criminal behavior, including having a juvenile record;
- psychopathology and psychological disorders, including depression, anxiety disorders, bipolar disorder, schizophrenia, post-traumatic stress disorder, antisocial personality disorder, and internalizing and externalizing symptoms.

Beyond the effects on individuals, child maltreatment exerts a huge economic toll on society. The United States spends over $100 billion each year on the costs associated with maltreatment, including costs associated with child health care, child welfare, criminal justice expenses, special education, and lifetime productivity losses for maltreated children who suffer death or mental health and medical problems into adulthood (Fang et al., 2012; Jud, Fegert, & Finkelhor, 2016; Reading et al., 2009).

So what can be done to prevent maltreatment and help children, families, and society? Recommendations for combatting maltreatment include identifying and tracking children and families at risk; reducing the burden on staff who work with families and carry large caseloads; and implementing ongoing monitoring and supervision of poor and at-risk families, such as the Nurse-Family Partnership and Early Start, which have effectively prevented child maltreatment (Jud, Fegert, & Finkelhor, 2016).

■ CLOSING THOUGHTS
Promotion and Prevention

All too often, people fail to act until things get out of hand and problems escalate. Teachers and educators intervene to help failing children get back on track, perhaps because those children were overly tired in class, insufficiently nourished, or missed days at school due to illnesses and health-related problems. Clinicians and counselors work with adolescents to help them recognize poor health choices and empower them to make smarter ones. And, doctors attempt to convince adults with medical problems to alter their lifestyles by reducing their weight and stress and increasing their sleep and exercise. Of course, being nimble in response to a person's health needs across the lifespan is critical. But, the key lesson revealed by developmental cascades is that promoting positive behaviors early in life goes a long way in preventing problems later. Indeed, the emotional, social, and financial costs involved in intervening *after* problems have solidified swamp the costs involved in fostering positive behaviors before problems firmly take root.

Thus, policies and programs that educate parents and families about ways to instill healthy behaviors in young children—ranging from ensuring that children are properly nourished and getting sufficient sleep to creating a positive family climate—hold promise for reducing the prevalence of disease and health disparities among populations in the United States and globally. Core take-home messages around early promotion and prevention can make a huge difference in the lives of children, families, and communities around the world.

The Developmentalist's Toolbox

Method	Purpose	Description
Measuring children's physical development		
fMRI techniques	To assess the regions of the brain responsible for certain functions (those that are activated) and to index synaptic connections	fMRI images revealing high levels of energy consumption in the cerebral cortex offer a marker of rapid synaptic growth and myelination of neural fibers in that region.
Handedness studies	To determine a child's preference for the right or left hand	A common approach is to present objects in different locations and observe how often the child uses each hand to pick them up.
Neuroimaging techniques and positron emission tomography (PET)	To measure neuroanatomical changes and brain activity associated with learning and development	Scanners generate images of the brain's structure and activity.
Measuring children's health		
Cortisol level measurements	To assess levels of the stress hormone cortisol	A saliva sample is obtained from inside the child's mouth with a cotton swab, which is sent to a lab for analysis. Extremely high levels of cortisol are associated with experiences of toxic stress.
BMI calculations	To assess whether a person is over-weight or obese	For young children, BMI is a calculation of the child's weight relative to height. A BMI above the 85th percentile means overweight, while children above the 95th percentile are considered obese.
Actigraphy	To measure children's actual sleep/wake patterns	Lightweight monitors are used to measure sleep and wake cycles based on activity data.
Epidemiological studies	To document the incidence, patterns, causes, and effects of health and disease conditions in populations	Large-scale survey data or available health information is obtained and analyzed for a sample of individuals from a population of interest.

▇ Chapter Summary

Brain, Physical, and Motor Development

- The brain develops in early childhood in significant ways.
- Myelination in the corpus callosum and fibers that connect the cerebellum to the cerebral cortex speed the rate at which nerve impulses move through neural networks.
- Synaptic density increases in the prefrontal cortex in areas associated with attention, motor skills, cognitive ability, and memory.
- Increased connections transfer information within the limbic system and from the hippocampus to the frontal lobes.
- Synaptic pruning, a reduction of neuron connections, occurs for those connections that are rarely used.
- Growing lateralization of the brain is reflected in children's handedness, the tendency to use the right or left hand predominantly. Young children gradually develop a hand preference, thus moving from the greater flexibility in hand use of toddlers to the strong preferences of older children (although most children settle on use of the right hand).
- Brain changes in early childhood are associated with improved balance and coordination, cognitive and executive functioning skills, information encoding and retrieval, and language development.
- Physical growth in early childhood, resulting from hormonal production directed by the pituitary gland, leads to elongated limbs, high muscle mass (and therefore a relatively low BMI), and a head size that is proportionate to body size.
- Young children show gains in gross motor skills in areas of locomotor movements, manipulative movements, and stability movements, and in fine motor skills used in activities of daily living and art and literacy-related areas.

- Secular trends in greater population height over the past century and inter-country differences in the height of people present strong evidence for environmental influences on physical growth.

Nutrition

- Many young children in the United States and throughout the world experience dietary deficiencies in protein, vitamins, iron, and minerals, especially calcium and zinc, which affect children's prognosis for health and mental functioning.
- Obesity, the excess storage of fat, is a growing epidemic in the United States, and is disproportionately experienced by children living in poverty.
- Frequent exposures to healthy foods, larger portions of healthy foods, and family role models who eat healthy foods leads to greater acceptance and consumption of those foods by children.
- A negative family climate around meals, seen in parental prohibitions, threats, and bribes, is ineffective in getting children to eat healthy foods and avoid unhealthy ones.

Sleep

- Improved sleep regulation (falling and staying asleep) and sleep consolidation (the duration of the longest nighttime sleep episode) is seen from infancy through the early childhood years.
- Actigraphs used to assess children's sleep indicate that parents overestimate the amount of sleep children get, and that many children are not getting the recommended amount of sleep.
- Many children have difficulty falling asleep or wake up during the night due to bad dreams or night terrors.
- Regularity in a family's daytime and bedtime routines is associated with children getting the sleep they need.

Childhood Illness, Injury, and Maltreatment

- Infectious diseases can be spread through personal contact, water, or air, and include acute bacterial and viral infections.

- Chronic diseases are long lasting and typically can be controlled but not cured. Chronic diseases include obesity, asthma, and developmental disabilities.
- Child maltreatment is at its highest for children younger than 5 years of age.
- The early years are also a time when exposure to family violence is high.
- Children who live in poverty are at greater risk for infectious and chronic diseases, maltreatment, and exposure to violence than are children who live in more-resourced homes.
- Children in poorer countries are especially at risk for health problems, due to low levels of immunization, high levels of malnutrition, and exposure to unsanitary living conditions.
- Experiences such as maltreatment can elicit high levels of stress in children.
- Toxic or chronic stress can lead to a chronic excess of cortisol, and can adversely affect brain and physical development.

Developmental Cascades

- Children who do not get the sleep they need have difficulties focusing attention and getting along socially.
- Disruptions in sleep and inadequate sleep have immediate and long-term effects on children's academic performance and behaviors.
- Chronic sleep deprivation influences brain functioning by preventing or reducing processes required for brain maturation and restoration, memory consolidation, and learning.
- Inadequate quality and quantity of sleep place children at risk for being overweight or obese.
- Exposure to violence and maltreatment in early childhood can trigger long-lasting, devastating developmental consequences.
- Numerous studies document the harmful consequences of childhood maltreatment and other related risks such as exposure to violence for physical, mental, and social domains.

Thinking Like a Developmentalist

1. You hypothesize that children's level of stress might cause them to eat unhealthy foods. You speculate that this might be one reason why poverty is associated with obesity in children. How would you go about testing whether stress level relates to unhealthy eating habits? Consider ways you might do this by using a correlational study, and ways you might test this through an experimental design.

2. A national policy organization believes that the heavy pollutants associated with living close to high traffic areas are detrimental to children's health. They raise concerns about the effects of pollutants from trucks and cars on asthma in children. They realize they must first gather evidence to support their claims, and aim to demonstrate this in a large-scale, epidemiologic study. How might they gather evidence for their claim?

3. You wish to advocate for maternity and paternity leave, based on your hypothesis that these early leaves would lead to declines in child maltreatment and injury in early childhood. You receive funding to conduct a longitudinal study to test your hypothesis. What would you do?

Cognitive and Language Development in Early Childhood

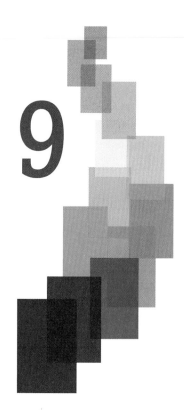

9

Drawing by Minxin Cheng from a photo by Jonathan Borba on Unsplash

E ach year in the United States, over 100,000 people attend the Kentucky Derby, Preakness Stakes, and Belmont Stakes—the Triple Crown horse races. Millions more observe the races on television or online and learn the results from social media and newspapers. At the start of each race, horse and jockey take their position in a numbered stall aligned with the stalls of their competitors (**FIGURE 9.1**). Horses typically enter the rear of the stall and are prevented from exiting by gates at the front. When all horses are in position, the starter presses a button to open the gates and sound a bell. Bets are in, the race is on!

Consider, instead, if horses began the race at different starting points, with some positioned hundreds of meters behind others, and the gates opening for certain horses before others. It is hard to imagine how the hindered horses could ever catch up with their opponents. The race would be on, but the outcomes and winners would be predetermined.

Each year in the United States, millions of children begin school and embark on the academic race—a race in which they will be required to learn new skills, behave in new ways, and navigate unfamiliar spaces, materials, and people. They will wake up early, dress with care, cling to backpacks, and perhaps grip a caregiver's hand, reluctant to let go. They will enter unfamiliar classrooms, find a cubby or place to house their belongings, and sit at desks or on floor mats to greet their teachers. Some children will be ready to go, like Olympic track stars crouching in anticipation of the bell. Others will not yet have the foundation skills or experiences to benefit from the lessons they are expected to learn at school. They may have difficulties paying attention and sitting still, or have limited vocabularies, or

FIGURE 9.1 Horses begin competitive races at equal starting points.   Young children, however, often begin school with dramatically different skills that can significantly impact their learning and development in the long term.

lack basic knowledge about numbers, letters, and other pre-academic skills that many of their peers have mastered—skills that collectively define a child's "school readiness."

Although there are no easy solutions to the persistent problem of early childhood disparities, developmental psychology provides valuable insights into what young children know and do at different ages, how skills change over time, and how biology and environment interact to shape development. In turn, research findings expand the potential of science to inform effective interventions, influence educational practices and social policies, and offer practical advice and support to families from different cultural communities.

This chapter builds on the coverage of cognitive development, language and literacy development, and social-cognitive development introduced in Chapters 5 and 6. For each topic, we consider theoretical foundations and research findings, contextual influences, and the cascading effects of children's cognitive skills for academic and social domains.

■ *Cognitive Development*

Consider a typical scene in a U.S. classroom: Children are seated at a table with a worksheet as their teacher explains the concept and notation system for "more than" (>) and "less than" (<). The children's task is to place the symbol in the correct direction between pictures containing different numbers of objects. As Christopher attends to the teacher and his notebook, his friend Billy taps him on the shoulder to show him a toy. Christopher's attention shifts from the worksheet, to the teacher, to his friend. If Christopher is to learn today's lesson, he must selectively attend to the teacher's instructions, the information on the blackboard, and the pictures on his worksheet while inhibiting the impulse to attend to his friend's toy. He must be able to switch attention from one problem to the next, sequence a set of activities to accomplish the task, and monitor his ongoing performance. If all goes well, Christopher will eventually learn what the strange arrow means, and store that information in memory for future use. As Christopher improves in controlling his attention and behaviors, he will likewise improve his knowledge about math and ability to draw on an ever-expanding store of information in memory. Over time, Christopher will tackle math problems with growing speed and efficiency.

In the following sections, you will learn about key developments in young children's cognitive development, many of which are captured by Christopher's challenges at learning something as seemingly simple as marking which side has more and which has less. We will begin by considering the Swiss psychologist Jean Piaget's pivotal work on young children's cognitive development and critiques of Piaget's claims. We will then consider research on changes in children's information processing skills, and the contextual factors that affect children's cognitive development.

Piaget and the Preoperational Stage

According to Piaget, children between approximately 2 and 7 years of age are in the **preoperational stage** of cognitive development. At this time in development, thinking undergoes a kind of cognitive revolution: Children are now capable of **mental representation** or the internalization of thought, as seen in the growth of language, symbolic play, deferred imitation, and understanding of object permanence (**FIGURE 9.2**). Still, young children's cognitive abilities

preoperational stage The second stage in Jean Piaget's theory of cognitive development in which young children can think symbolically (as seen in pretend play, language, deferred imitation, and object permanence) but still show limitations in areas such as perspective taking, conservation, logical thinking, and causal understanding

mental representation Mental internalization of thought, such as seen in language and symbolic play, that marks the transition from the sensorimotor stage to preoperational thinking according to Jean Piaget

logical mental operations The ability to combine, separate, and transform information logically in the mind without the need to directly perceive or experience the information

symbolic understanding The understanding that things can stand for other things

dual representation The understanding that an object is both an entity in itself and a symbol for something else

© Matthew Stockman/Getty Images

remain limited; they cannot yet perform **logical mental operations**—mental actions that combine, separate, and transform information logically.

Cognitive Achievements in the Preoperational Period

LEARNING OBJECTIVE 9.1 Describe the hallmarks of the preoperational stage of cognitive development, as advanced by Piaget.

Mental representation is the banner of early childhood, representing the transition from the sensorimotor to preoperational stage of thinking (Chapter 5). Young children now understand that words and pictures can stand for objects, events, and ideas and that toys and objects can substitute for other things in pretend play. A child can pretend that a stick is a pirate's sword and that sand molds are cupcakes to serve at a birthday party. Young children's newfound skills at mental representation explain why their imaginations are never at rest and play takes up so much of their days.

Symbolic Understanding

The world is filled with symbols. By definition, a symbol can be anything that someone intends to represent as something other than itself (DeLoache, 2002). Words, numbers, highway signs, flags, pictures, maps, thermometers, television, artwork, and so forth are symbols that we encounter in daily life. According to Piaget, young children in the preoperational stage are capable of **symbolic understanding**, the appreciation that things can stand for or represent other things. However, children do not acquire **dual representation**—the understanding that an object may *simultaneously* be an entity in itself and a symbol for something else—until around 3 years of age (DeLoache, 2002). Dual representation is seen, for example, when a child understands that a toy car is something to play with while also representing a life-size car.

Judy DeLoache (1987) conducted an influential study of children's dual representational skills by asking whether children understand that a 3-dimensional scale model of a room (like a doll-house room) represented its real-life counterpart (**FIGURE 9.3**). Children observed an experimenter hide a miniature doll under a couch pillow in a scale model that was physically identical to the nearby room it was meant to represent. The experimenter then asked children to find a larger version of the toy hidden in the same place in the big room. Three-year-olds were able to use the scale model to locate the large toy in the life-sized, adjacent room, whereas most 2.5-year-olds could not find the

FIGURE 9.2 Preoperational thought According to Piaget, children's thinking during the preoperational stage of development is marked by a kind of cognitive revolution relative to the cognitive development of infants and toddlers in the sensorimotor stage. Children are now capable of mental representation in areas of language, pretend play, deferred imitation, and understanding of object permanence.

FIGURE 9.3 Dual representational skills. Judy DeLoache showed that it was not until 3 years of age that children achieved dual representation, the idea that something can be both an entity itself and a symbol for something else. Children observed an experimenter hide a miniature doll under a couch pillow in a scale model that was physically identical to a nearby room it was meant to represent. The experimenter then asked children to find a larger version of the toy hidden in the same place in the big room. Three-year-olds were able to use the scale model to locate the large toy in the life-sized, adjacent room, whereas most 2.5-year-olds could not find the large toy. (After J. DeLoache. 2000. *Child Dev* 71: 329–338.)

large toy. Memory limitations did not explain children's failure to find the toy, because children remembered where the toy was hidden in the scale room when they were asked to retrieve it there. DeLoache speculated that young children failed the task because the model room was so interesting in its own right that they had trouble recognizing it as a symbol for something else.

About a decade later, DeLoache and her colleagues further tested their dual-representation hypothesis in a clever study that capitalized on the imaginations of young children (DeLoache, Miller, & Rosengren, 1997). DeLoache introduced children to an "incredible shrinking machine," a homemade contraption with dials, lights, and sounds. The experimenter explained that the shrinking machine could make things smaller. The child then watched the experimenter hide a doll in a large, movable room, then the shrinking machine was turned on while the child and experimenter waited in a nearby room. When they returned, a small, scale-model room stood in place of the original room, as though the large room had shrunk. When this was done, 2.5-year-olds were able to find the doll in the scale model room (**FIGURE 9.4**).

Why were children now able to solve the scale model problem? DeLoache concluded that children believed that the magical machine had indeed shrunk

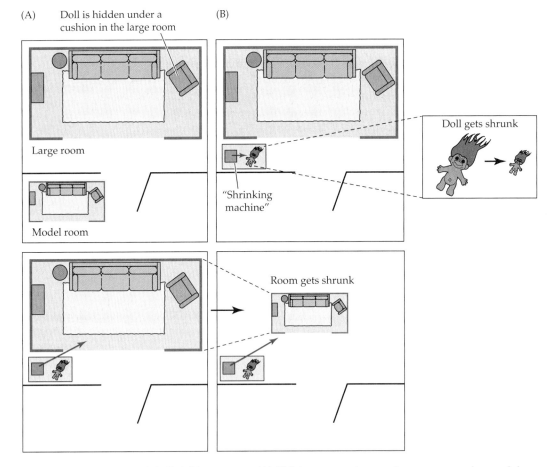

FIGURE 9.4 Shrinking room. (A) Children were shown a large room and a model room and those who were younger than age 3 were unable to locate the hidden toy in a location of the model room that mapped to where it was hidden in the larger room. (B) However, when DeLoache later pretended to "shrink" the large room with a magical machine that children believed could make the room smaller, children younger than 3 years of age could now find the object that had originally been hidden in the larger room in what they believed to now be the "shrunken" room.
(After J. S. DeLoache et al. 1997. *Psych Sci* 8: 308–313.)

FIGURE 9.5 Sociodramatic play.   In early childhood, children engage in pretend play that includes other people (mostly their child playmates) as characters in created play scenarios.

the large room. Thus, the scale model room was actually the original room in their minds. Because the scale model was no longer a symbol for the large room, children no longer had to simultaneously represent the scale model as an interesting object and a symbol for something else. There was no need for dual representation.

Bear in mind, however, that symbolic understanding is not all-or-nothing. Young children attain different forms of symbolic understanding at different ages, depending on their experiences. For example, children understand that pictures represent things in the real world before they understand the connection between written words and their referents (e.g., Allen, Mattock, & Silva, 2014).

Pretend and Fantasy Play

Children's capacity for symbolic understanding comes in quite handy in play. Young children enjoy imagining objects and people as other people or things. Sticks become spoons or swords; flashlights suggest journeys through dark forests. Children can imagine themselves to be someone else—baby, doctor, princess, warrior, waitress—and can assign their play partners complementary pretend roles as daddy, patient, king, foe, or customer. Indeed, early childhood is colorfully marked by **sociodramatic play**, pretend play that includes other people as actors in created play scenarios (**FIGURE 9.5**). In turn, children's engagement in sociodramatic play and other forms of imagination further supports skills in language, perspective taking, causal reasoning, and executive functioning (Kavanaugh, 2006; Pierucci et al., 2014; Thibodeau et al., 2016).

Children's flourishing fantasy skills sometimes lead to the invention of imaginary friends—invisible playmates with whom children spend considerable time talking and playing (Taylor et al., 2004). Although adults may be concerned about their child's relationship with an imaginary friend, a relatively mature cognitive understanding is required to generate the make-believe stories that revolve around imaginary friends. Young children with imaginary friends create and tell more elaborate stories than do children without imaginary friends (Trionfi & Reese, 2009). Moreover, children conceive of imaginary playmates as kind and caring friends who provide the same social-emotional benefits as real friends (Gleason & Hohmann, 2006).

sociodramatic play Pretend play in which children act out imaginary stories related to life experiences and that may involve others in created play scenarios

✓ CHECK YOUR UNDERSTANDING 9.1

1. What is one example of pretend play that illustrates a child's understanding of dual representation?
2. What is an imaginary friend? Should parents be concerned if their children create imaginary friends? Why or why not?

Cognitive Limitations

LEARNING OBJECTIVE 9.2 Describe the tasks Piaget created to examine the limits of children's preoperational thinking.

Although young children exhibit impressive representational skills, they are unable to think logically and have difficulties viewing things from multiple perspectives. These cognitive limitations explain why Piaget used the term preoperational thinking to characterize children's still immature ability to *mentally* operate on actions and objects in their heads—a requisite to logical thought.

Egocentrism

egocentrism The tendency of children to think that other people view the world from their perspective, and thus an inability to consider another person's perspective

If you have ever played hide-and-go seek with young children, you may have been amused by children's assumption that if they can't see you, you can't see them. My son Michael would hide under a table, very much out in the open, and cover his eyes thinking that he would not be found. **Egocentrism** is the tendency of children to believe that other people view the world from their perspective. Indeed, when researchers ask children to cover their eyes, and then ask them "Can I see you?" children respond in the negative (Flavell, Shipstead, & Croft, 1980).

Piaget demonstrated young children's egocentrism in a game called the three mountains task, in which a model of three mountains of different sizes, each with a different landmark at its peak, sat on a table (Piaget & Inhelder, 1956) (**FIGURE 9.6**). Piaget instructed children to walk around the table to view the model, before sitting across from a doll positioned at the other side of the table. The child's task was to identify photographs showing the model from the doll's point of view. Although children were able to remember all the landmarks on the mountains, most children failed Piaget's task. They stated that the doll opposite them saw the same thing that they did. Piaget and Bärbel Inhelder concluded that children are unable to differentiate among alternative perspectives until around 7–10 years of age because of difficulties in manipulating multiple representations in their minds.

However, Piaget may have overstated children's egocentrism by relying on a task that was unfamiliar to children. When researchers played a game with children, asking them to hide a small boy doll from toy police officers who were "looking for the boy," children successfully hid the boy even though the police officer was positioned away from the child (Hughes & Donaldson, 1979). Similarly, when researchers asked children 3–5 years of age to imagine how a familiar room in front of them would look from different positions, children responded correctly to questions such as "Which object would be closest to you?" from different imagined places in the room. Even children who had failed the three mountains task succeeded when things were familiar (Newcombe & Huttenlocher, 1992).

Animistic Thinking

Piaget observed that children in the preoperational stage have a sort of magical thinking, in which they do not fully distinguish between living and nonliving things. He noted that children often attribute life to objects that are not alive, believing that inanimate objects such as

FIGURE 9.6 Piaget's Three Mountains Task. A child walks around a table containing a model of three mountains of different sizes, each with different landmarks positioned on each mountain. The child then sits down across the table from a doll seated in a chair. The child's task is to identify which of several photographs depicts the doll's point of view. (Based on J. Piaget and B. Inhelder. 1967. *A Child's Conception of Space* [F. J. Langdon and J. L. Lunzer, Trans.]. Norton: New York. [Original French work published 1948.])

their teddy bears have thoughts, feelings, and desires (Piaget, 1926). **Animistic thinking** refers to the attribution of human qualities to inanimate entities. Piaget tested children's animistic thinking by asking young children whether various entities were alive, such as dogs, wind, and clouds. Children often responded that wind and clouds were alive, that "the sun is alive because it moves across the sky," and so on, suggesting that they did not understand what distinguishes living from nonliving entities and considered anything that moves to be alive.

But, do children truly fail to understand the difference between animate and inanimate objects? Observations of children's everyday conversations counter Piaget's claims. Children ask questions about inanimate things such as pens, combs, spoons, and hammers that focus on the object's function ("What do you do with it?"), whereas when children ask about animals, they question what the animal *does itself*, not what a person can do with it (Gelman, 2009; Gelman & Koenig, 2003). In fact, young children distinguish between animate and inanimate entities along many dimensions. They understand that nature creates animals, but that humans create objects (e.g., Gelman & Bloom, 2000). They understand that animals have different kinds of insides than do objects (Gottfried & Gelman, 2005). And, they understand that animate things move themselves, whereas cars, balls, mechanical toys, and other inanimate objects move because of human action or because they are propelled by devices that humans built, such as batteries and gears (Gottfried & Gelman, 2005).

Young children also distinguish among *types* of animate objects, such as plants and animals. Preschoolers were shown three pictures labeled as "leaf," "bug," and "bug," respectively (Gelman & Markman, 1986) (**FIGURE 9.7**). Although the leaf insect looked more like a leaf than it did a bug, when children were asked to make inferences about the odd-looking, novel bug, they based their inferences on the object's category label rather than its physical features. That is, when the leaf insect was labeled a bug, they concluded that it would move around by itself.

What allowed children to understand that the leaf-looking bug was actually animate? When hearing the label bug, children drew on their understanding that members of a category share an underlying nature that transcends what things look like. Developmental researchers refer to children's belief that entities have an underlying essence as **essentialism** (Gelman, 2004). In turn, children's assumptions around the underlying essence of things guides their future expectations. For example, children learn that mosquitos and bees are both small insects that fly, but that only bees can be categorized by the unobserved characteristic of stinging. A child who experiences a bee sting or observes someone being stung, will generalize their knowledge of the essence of *all bees*—that all bees sting. (Note that children's essentialist beliefs extend beyond biological characteristics of entities to inferences about people's traits, aptitudes, etc.— such as girls don't do well in math—which can lead to stereotyping and discrimination, as we will learn in later chapters).

FIGURE 9.7 Cards used in the Gelman and Markman study. Preschoolers were shown three pictures labeled as a "leaf," "bug," and "bug," respectively. Although the leaf insect looked more like a leaf than it did a bug, when children were asked to make inferences about the odd-looking, novel bug, they based their inferences on the object's category label rather than its physical features. For example, when the leaf insect was labeled a bug, they concluded that it could move around by itself. (Based on S. Gelman and E. Markman. 1987. *Child Development* 58: 1532–1541.)

animistic thinking A type of reasoning in which children attribute human qualities to inanimate entities

essentialism The understanding that entities in a category have an underlying shared essence that may not be visually apparent (e.g., bees are insects that sting)

Conservation

Piaget wondered if young children understood that superficial changes to objects or materials do not cause objects to change in properties that have to do with quantity. And so, he designed several **conservation tasks** to test whether children recognized that an entity remains the same even if its form changes.

conservation tasks Piagetian tests that assess whether children understand that an entity remains the same in its number, mass, and so on, even if its form changes

To illustrate, imagine that you are serving chocolate chip cookies to a 4-year-old. You present a plate of cookies with several "mini" cookies of one-half inch diameter that you made by cutting a "jumbo" cookie. The other plate holds a jumbo cookie. You present two options to the child: to eat six mini cookies or one jumbo cookie. Although either option would yield the same mass or amount of cookie, young children will invariably choose six cookies over one. They do not realize equivalency in the two situations—that is, they do not yet conserve—because their reasoning is limited to a single dimension (the number of cookies), rather than both dimensions (the number and size of cookies). Older children, in contrast, recognize that six small cookies are not necessarily better than one large cookie.

Piaget tested children's understanding of various types of conservation, including liquid quantity, solid quantity, and number (Piaget & Cook, 1952) (**FIGURE 9.8**). He presented children with two objects or sets of objects of equal mass or number, such as two equal size mounds of clay or two rows of the same number of coins. Young children correctly stated that the two entities were equivalent. Children then watched the examiner transform one of the two entities so that it looked different but did not change in mass or amount. For instance, in a conservation of liquid task, after presenting children with two equal size beakers of liquid, the examiner poured water from one beaker into a tall, narrow beaker. In a conservation of mass task, one of the two clay mounds was rolled into a long, snakelike shape. In a conservation of number task, one row of coins was spread out so that it was longer than the other row. After the transformation, children were asked whether the objects were still equivalent. Piaget found that the majority of 4- to 5-year-old children were unable to conserve. They usually stated that the tall thin beaker had more liquid than the

centration The tendency to focus on a single, perceptually salient feature or characteristic of an entity to the exclusion of other features

reversibility The ability to realize that numbers or objects can be changed or returned to their original state, such as when children recognize that after rolling a ball of clay into a snakelike shape, it is possible to mold it back into its original shape

appearance-reality tasks Tasks that assess children's ability to differentiate between appearance and reality, such as when testing if children understand a cat remains a cat in reality even if wearing a dog mask and appearing to be a dog

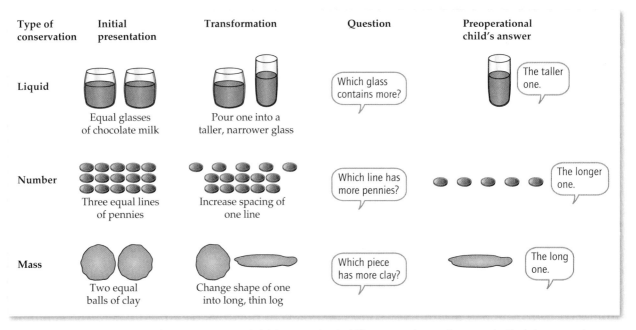

FIGURE 9.8 Conservation tasks. Piaget tested children's skills at conservation using different types of tasks: liquid quantity, number, and mass. In conservations tasks, children are first presented with two objects or sets of objects of equal mass or number, such as two equal size mounds of clay or two rows of the same number of coins. Then, the experimenter transforms the two entities to look different, such as rolling one ball of clay into a long, thin shape. After the transformation, preoperational children did not understand that the amounts remained equivalent and responded that the long, thin shape had more clay. (After K. S. Berger. 2000. *The Developing Person through Childhood*. Worth: New York.)

short, wide beaker; the snakelike clay shape had more clay than the round mass of clay; and the longer row had more coins than a cluster of coins or closely spaced coins that formed a shorter row.

Piaget interpreted children's conservation errors as a problem of **centration**, the tendency to focus on a single, perceptually salient feature of an entity to the exclusion of others. So, a child might attend to the length of a rolled-out piece of clay, without also considering its width. Additionally, Piaget concluded that children have a poor understanding of **reversibility**. They fail to see that rolling out a clay ball or pouring water from one beaker to another could be reversed, returning the material to its original state.

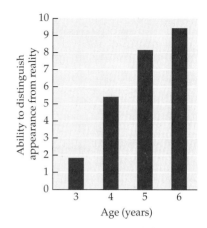

Appearance Reality

Young children's problems with conservation suggest that they are easily misled by how things appear. Indeed, **appearance-reality tasks** reveal that children younger than 5–6 years of age focus on the *appearance* of objects, rather than the *reality* of those objects (Flavell et al., 1986). For example, 3-year-old children were shown milk, and knew that it was white. When researchers gave children special sunglasses that made the milk look green, children stated that the milk was now green.

In a classic study of appearance-reality, an examiner introduced children to Maynard the cat, whose identity was later manipulated with a mask to make him look like a dog (DeVries, 1969) (**FIGURE 9.9**). After playing with Maynard, the examiner hid Maynard's front half behind a screen and attached a mask of a ferocious dog to Maynard's head. When the screen was removed, children were asked what Maynard *looked like* and whether Maynard was really a dog that could bark. The 3-year-olds focused on appearance only, stating that Maynard was a vicious dog who might bite them; 4-year-olds showed a mix of understanding, stating that Maynard was a cat who ate cat food and meowed, but was also a dog now because he looked like a dog. In contrast, 5- and 6-year-olds understood that Maynard was still a cat, even though he looked like a dog. Children's difficulties with appearance-reality tasks might explain why children become so frightened at Halloween when people wear scary masks. They think that people transform into whatever they are wearing.

FIGURE 9.9 DeVries's Appearance-Reality Task featuring Maynard the Cat. In a classic study of appearance-reality, children were introduced to Maynard the cat, whose identity was later manipulated with a mask to make Maynard look like a ferocious dog. After seeing Maynard with the dog mask, children were asked what Maynard looked like and whether Maynard was really a dog that could bark. As seen in the line graph, young children (3–4 years) failed the task, stating Maynard was a dog, whereas with age, children increasingly understood that although Maynard looked like a dog, Maynard was still a cat. (After R. De Vries. 1969. *Monogr Soc Res Child Dev* 34: iii–67.)

Perhaps, however, children fail appearance-reality tasks because their vocabularies are limited and they have difficulties communicating their thoughts. In fact, children younger than 3 years of age understand the appearance-reality distinction when researchers use nonverbal tasks (Cacchione, Schaub, & Rakoczy, 2013; Moll & Tomasello, 2012). For example, researchers showed children an object that looked like a rock but was actually a sponge. The researcher then asked children to identify the object that could wipe up water. Children selected the sponge, even though it resembled a rock (Sapp, Lee, & Muir, 2000) (**FIGURE 9.10**).

Hierarchical Classification

Across early childhood, children learn to categorize things in increasingly sophisticated ways, such as by grouping objects together based on unobservable characteristics rather than physical features alone. So, young children would put planes and trucks and boats together as similar, even though the objects differ in how they look and move.

Still, children continue to have difficulty with **hierarchical classification**, the ability to organize items into superordinate and subordinate categories. To illustrate, Piaget tested children with **class inclusion problems**, in which he asked children to determine which group had more items—a full set of items (superordinate) or a subset of items (subordinate) (**FIGURE 9.11**). For example,

hierarchical classification The ability to organize items into superordinate and subordinate categories

class inclusion problems Tasks that assess children's understanding of hierarchical classification, such as asking children whether there are more "red flowers" or "flowers generally"

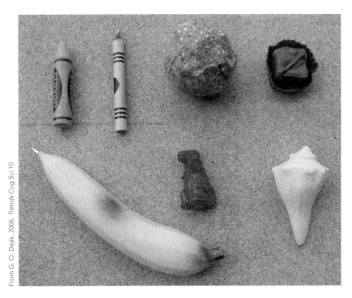

FIGURE 9.10 Distinguishing appearance from reality. Researchers test children's ability to distinguish appearance from reality using many different types of visually deceptive objects, including bananas that are pens and crayons that are erasers. Young children appear to understand what objects really are (reality) rather than basing judgments on appearance alone when researchers word questions in certain ways (such as asking children to choose the object that "wipes up water" or "draws"). Examples of objects used in appearance-reality tasks include: Left to right: crayon eraser, crayon candle, rubber rock, candy magnet. Bottom row: banana pen, crayon dinosaur, seashell soap.

FIGURE 9.11 A class inclusion test. Piaget asked children to determine which was more—the number contained in a subset of objects or the number contained in the full set—to test children's understanding of class inclusion. For example, if Piaget asked children whether there were more chips (the whole set) or more blue chips (a subset), preoperational children erroneously concluded there were more blue chips. They centered on the large number of blue chips, which prevented them from considering the part-whole relation problem before them.

when Piaget presented children with a set of objects (such as colored chips) and asked children whether there were more objects (chips) overall or more of one type of chip (such as a subset of blue chips that were the most prevalent color), preoperational children erroneously concluded there were more "blue chips." Children focused attention on the large number of items in the subset, which prevented them from considering the part-whole relation between blue chips and all chips.

Causal Understanding

According to Piaget, young children also display limited **causal understanding**—the ability to see the relation between a cause and effect. For instance, when Piaget's daughter missed a nap, she commented, "I haven't had a nap, so it isn't afternoon." She reasoned that taking a nap *caused* the afternoon to arrive. **Precausal thinking** refers to errors of logic in cause-effect relations (Piaget, 1930), including circular thinking, in which cause and effect are interchangeable. For example, if you asked a child where snow comes from and the child responded "cold makes snow," and then you asked the child where cold comes from, and the child responded "cold comes from snow," the child's reasoning illustrates such circularity (Piaget, 1929).

However, researchers have since found that young children may be capable of impressive causal reasoning. For example, researchers acted out a scene in which a doll walked across the floor with muddy shoes (Harris, German, & Mills, 1996). They then asked children 3–5 years of age two questions to ensure that they understood the story: "Is the floor dirty now?" and "Was the floor dirty before?" The children understood that muddy shoes would make the floor dirty. But, beyond that, they were able to reason about a hypothetical counter-to-fact situation, such as, "What if Carol had taken her shoes off? Would the floor be dirty?" They correctly answered that the floor would not be dirty, showing that they could reason about altered cause-effect relations. Furthermore, young children can distinguish between probable outcomes of actions, such as a person making onion juice, and improbable outcomes, such as a person turning into an onion (Lane et al., 2016).

✓ CHECK YOUR UNDERSTANDING 9.2

1. How would you test a child's understanding of: (a) conservation; (b) the distinction between appearance and reality; (c) hierarchical classification; and (d) causal understanding?
2. Cite at least three observations suggesting that young children's thinking is not as limited as Piaget described.

Cultural Context of Cognitive Development

LEARNING OBJECTIVE 9.3 Explain how cultural context might affect children's performance on cognitive tasks such as those developed by Piaget.

Children everywhere display striking similarities in cognitive development across the early childhood years. As one example, young children everywhere play and imagine, creating pretend stories using whatever materials are available to them. North American children might rely on toy plates, utensils, and foods to pretend they are running a restaurant. Parakanas children in the Amazon rainforest, however, might play with real objects such as palm leaves to weave pretend baskets (Bjorklund & Blasi, 2011).

Children also diverge in aspects of cognitive development in line with their unique cultural experiences. One of the first cultural studies of cognitive development sought to test conservation in young children from different cultural communities (Price-Williams, Gordon, & Ramirez, 1969). Two groups of Mexican children—children of pottery makers and children whose families did not engage in pottery making—were tested on Piagetian conservation tasks (**FIGURE 9.12**). The children in the two groups were matched on age, years of schooling, and family socioeconomic status. Children in both groups understood conservation of liquid, number, weight, and volume, indicating culture-general developments in these areas. The two groups differed, however, on their conservation of mass. Children of the potters recognized that rolling a clay ball into a long, snakelike shape did not change the amount of clay, whereas children of nonpotters responded that the snakelike shape contained more clay than did the ball of clay. Thus, everyday experience with pottery making—a cultural experience—facilitated children's understanding of conservation of mass.

Cultural studies also find that children from schooled versus unschooled communities differ in how they categorize objects. When young children in the United States were asked to group a set of items, they typically placed objects into superordinate categories, such as "foods," "animals," "vehicles," and so forth, what is referred to as **taxonomic categorization** (Cole, 1990; Rogoff, 2003). In contrast, Michael Cole and colleagues found that adults from the Kpelle tribe in Liberia sorted items on the basis of functional relations—such as by placing a knife with an apple (Cole & Bruner, 1971; Sharp & Cole, 1972). Although Cole carried out his work with adults, it is reasonable to speculate that the preschool experiences of U.S. children already expose them to rules about classifying objects into categories rather than by functional relations (Rogoff & Chavajay, 1995).

✓ CHECK YOUR UNDERSTANDING 9.3

1. How can the cultural context in which a child is raised affect a child's preoperational reasoning skills? Provide an example.

FIGURE 9.12 Conservation. Children of Mexican pottery makers achieved conservation of mass at younger ages than documented by Piaget in his investigations due to their experiences with clay. However, they did not show earlier achievements on other tasks of conservation such as liquid and number.

causal understanding The ability to infer the relation between a cause and its effect

precausal thinking Logical errors that children make in cause-effect relations, including circular thinking, as when a child says "cold makes snow" and "snow makes cold"

taxonomic categorization The classification of entities based on their similar characteristics or functions, such as the category of foods or body parts

Cognitive Development from an Information-Processing Perspective

Researchers from an information-processing tradition focus on the cognitive skills and strategies that allow young children to attend to and learn new

self-regulation The ability to manage and integrate attention, thoughts, and behaviors to attain goals

executive functioning The collection of skills involved in controlling and coordinating attention, memory, and other behaviors involved in goal-directed actions

inhibitory control A component of executive functioning that refers to children's ability to respond appropriately to a stimulus while inhibiting an alternative, dominant response

Stroop tasks Tests that examine inhibitory control through asking children (or adults) to respond to stimuli that are congruent or incongruent with the required response (e.g, saying the color red to red stimuli versus saying red to green stimuli)

go/no-go task An example of a Stroop task in which children (or adults) are presented with pictures, colors, and letters and are asked to touch a computer screen when a target stimulus appears ("go") but not when a non-target stimulus appears ("no-go"); requires inhibition and ability to selectively attend to specific stimuli

day-night Stroop task An example of a Stroop task in which children are required to inhibit their automatic response by saying "day" to a picture of a moon and "night" to a picture of a sun

"Night"   "Day"

FIGURE 9.13 Day-night Stroop task. This task requires children to say "day" when presented with a picture of a moon and "night" when presented with a picture of a sun. Children must focus on the relevant information while inhibiting the more intuitive response of saying "day" to a sun or "night" to a moon. Young children's reaction times are slowed when responding to incongruent stimuli compared to congruent stimuli because of the difficulty in inhibiting dominant responses. (After C. Gerstadt et al. 1994. *Cognition* 53: 129–153.)

information (see Chapter 5). In particular, children's **self-regulation**, the process of controlling thoughts, behaviors, and emotions to achieve goals, is pivotal. Here, we focus on a key component of self-regulation—**executive functioning**, the suite of abilities involved in controlling and coordinating attention and other behaviors involved in goal-directed actions (Willoughby et al., 2012; Zelazo & Carlson, 2012; Zhou, Chen, & Main, 2012).

Executive Functioning

LEARNING OBJECTIVE 9.4 Describe the components of executive functioning.

Executive functioning involves three basic skills—inhibitory control, cognitive flexibility, and working memory—that aid children in the planning and monitoring of performance (e.g., Sulik et al., 2016; Wiebe, Espy, & Charak, 2008; Zelazo & Carlson, 2012). The term executive functioning captures the idea of a central executive who determines which information should be attended to or disregarded and which types of mental activity and strategies should be implemented to achieve a goal. As you will see, children exhibit impressive gains in executive functioning during early childhood, in preparation for the new demands that await them in school and other settings.

Inhibitory Control

Inhibitory control, a first component of executive functioning, refers to children's ability to respond appropriately to a stimulus while inhibiting an alternative, dominant response (Diamond et al., 2007). For example, a child who selectively attends to a worksheet rather than playing with a tempting toy shows inhibitory control.

Most tasks that assess inhibitory control in young children require children to respond in a counterintuitive way to stimuli, such as by saying "cat" to a picture of a dog, and "dog" to a picture of a cat. To succeed, children must attend to which stimulus is presented while suppressing the impulse to say the obvious. Children's reaction times slow down considerably in incongruent situations compared to congruent situations, because it takes a lot of effort to inhibit the response that comes most naturally (Prevor & Diamond, 2005). Many inhibitory control tasks are based on **Stroop tasks**, named after American psychologist John Ridley Stroop, who developed an adult version of the task.

An example Stroop task for children is the **go/no-go task**, in which an examiner presents children with pictures, colors, or letters, and instructs them to push a button or touch a screen (the "go" response) when a target stimulus appears (such as a red object) but not when a nontarget stimulus appears (such as a green object) (e.g., Obradović & Willoughby, 2019). By manipulating the frequency of presentation of the target stimulus, the examiner can control the child's tendency to react with a "go" response. As the number of consecutive "go" stimuli increases, so does the child's likelihood of wrongly responding with a "go" action to a "no-go" stimulus (Casey et al., 1997). The task becomes even more difficult when children are then instructed to give a "go" response (pressing the button) to a "no-go" stimulus, as they must inhibit their earlier tendencies with the new rule. Another example is the **day-night Stroop task**, which requires children to say "day" when presented with a picture of a moon and "night" when presented with a picture of a sun. (Obradovic & Willoughby, 2019) (**FIGURE 9.13**). Across tasks such as these, children between 3 and 5 years of age demonstrate marked improvements in their ability to inhibit the automatic response (Zelazo, 2006).

Cognitive Flexibility

Cognitive flexibility, a second component of executive functioning, refers to children's ability to adapt to changing circumstances, such as switching between rules and tasks (Zelazo, 2015). Children must be able to flexibly tackle a problem from different perspectives, such as being able to sort

Cards to be sorted

Target boxes

FIGURE 9.14 Dimensional card-sorting tasks.   In such tasks, examiners present children with a set of cards containing pictures (e.g. rabbits and flowers). The cards can be sorted in different ways, for example by color or type of object. The examiner asks the children to put all the blue rabbits and blue flowers in one pile and all the red rabbits and red flowers in another. But then, on switch trials, the examiner instructs children to group the cards by placing the rabbits in one pile and the flowers in another, which requires children to flexibly shift from a color-based-rule to an object-based rule. Three-year-olds typically fail this task, but children 4 years of age and older are better able to adjust to the change of rule. (After G. O. Deák and M. Wiseheart. 2015. *J Exp Child Psych* 138: 31–53.)

blocks into bins based on block color and then switching to sorting blocks based on size. **Dimensional card-sorting tasks** are a common way to test cognitive flexibility (**FIGURE 9.14**). In such tasks, examiners present children with a set of cards containing pictures such as rabbits and flowers. The cards can be sorted in different ways, for example by color or type of object. The examiner then tells children it is time to play the "color game." The child's task is to put all the blue rabbits and blue flowers in one pile and all the red rabbits and red flowers in another. (Half the time, the examiner begins with the object game, instructing children to sort cards into piles of rabbits or flowers, for example). Even 3-year-olds have no difficulty with the initial sort. But then, things get harder. On switch trials, the examiner now instructs children to group the cards by object type by placing the rabbits in one pile and the flowers in another. Because children must shift from a color-based-rule to an object-based-rule, 3-year-olds now fail the task. However, children 4-years of age and older can flexibly adjust to the change, although children vary substantially in how well they do. Performance on cognitive flexibility tasks gradually improves over several years. Nonetheless, task difficulty influences how well a child does, and so cognitive flexibility is not an all-or-nothing achievement (Zelazo, 2015).

Working Memory

Working memory, the third component of executive functioning, refers to the ability to maintain and manipulate information in the mind over a short period of time. **Memory span tests**, a popular way to assess children's working memory, typically measure the number of items children can repeat immediately after being presented with a list. In early childhood, 4- to 5-year-olds can recall about four items, whereas adults can recall about seven items (Dempster, 1981). In part, improvements in memory span over age occur because older children and adults can say words at a faster rate when rehearsing, therefore repeating things quickly to keep items in memory (Bjorklund & Causey, 2017; Hulme et al., 1984).

cognitive flexibility A component of executive functioning referring to children's ability to shift between thinking about two different concepts or to think about multiple concepts simultaneously

dimensional card-sorting tasks Tests used to assess cognitive flexibility and executive functioning in which children sort cards one way (e.g., by object color) and then switch their thinking to sort the same cards a different way (e.g., by object type)

working memory A third component of executive functioning referring to the ability to maintain and manipulate information in the mind over a short period of time, thus being important for concentration, focus, and following instructions

memory span tests A test of children's working memory that measures the number of items (e.g., words, letters of the alphabet) children can recall and repeat immediately after being presented with a list

Shape game — "All rabbits go here." — "All flowers go here."

Color game — "All blue things go here." — "All red things go here."

Distractor box

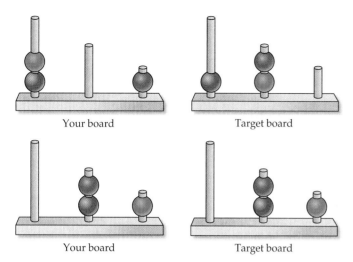

FIGURE 9.15 The Tower of London task.   A common way that researchers test children's planning is with the Tower of London task. The task involves rearranging objects to match a target configuration. Children must move the objects one at a time from an initial configuration to a configuration that matches a display. (After A. Ruocco et al. 2014. *Front Hum Neurosci* 8 [185]: 1–13. CC BY 4.0, https://creativecommons.org/licenses/by/4.0/.)

Tower of London task A test used to assess children's planning abilities that involve rearranging objects (e.g., disks, colored balls) from an initial configuration to a configuration that matches a display

rehearsal A strategy for remembering that relies on repeating information to aid memory

organization A memory strategy marked by imposing a structure on items based on their relations to one another (such as grouping) to aid recall of information

monitoring Keeping track of one's performance on a task and making necessary adjustments

metacognitive skill A person's awareness of what that person knows and how thinking and cognition work; "knowing about knowing"

Planning

Executive functioning is fundamental to planning. To successfully follow a plan, children must select, coordinate, and effectively execute a sequence of actions while inhibiting certain actions and switching among others (Diamond, Kirkham, & Amso, 2002; Kaller et al., 2008).

Researchers sometimes test children's planning with the **Tower of London task** (Berg & Byrd, 2002) (**FIGURE 9.15**). The task involves rearranging objects, such as different color disks that can be placed on rods or colored balls that can be moved on a computer screen to match a target configuration. Children must move the objects one at a time from an initial configuration to a configuration that matches a display. Trials vary in level of difficulty based on the starting position of the disks or balls and the number of moves allowed to complete the task. Throughout early childhood and into middle childhood, children improve in their ability to plan on Tower of London problems, with children who have problems in attention deficit disorder having difficulties relative to their peers (e.g., Unterrainer et al., 2016).

Strategies for Remembering

Although adults and children often rely on strategies to aid memory, young children may not be as successful at using strategies as adults. However, children improve over age in their use of **rehearsal**, repeating information over and over (Flavell, Beach, & Chinsky, 1966; Keeney, Cannizzo, & Flavell, 1967). They also increasingly organize material to aid memory. **Organization** refers to imposing a structure on test items based on their relations to one another, which then helps recall. A common way to test children's organization of information is to show them a large number of objects or read a list of words to them one at a time and then ask them to recall the items. The key to the task is that the items on the list, although randomly presented, can be clustered into categories such as foods, clothes, vehicles, and so forth. Sometimes items on the list rhyme and can be clustered by their sounds. The order in which children report back the information tells researchers how children organized the material when they committed it to memory.

For example, if children recall the words or pictures in order of "hat"-"mat"-"cat," and then recall "coat"-"boat", and then "sock"-"block," they have grouped items by the sounds of words. In contrast, if they report the words "hat"-"coat"-"sock," they have grouped the items into categories, such as clothing. Most young children cluster items at only chance levels (Salatas & Flavell, 1976). Sometimes young children cluster items by sound, recalling rhyming words together. Other times children cluster items by functional associations, recalling that cereal goes with a bowl and spoon. But by around 7–8 years of age, children group items into conceptually related categories, which aids recall (Best & Ornstein, 1986; Schlagmüller & Schneider, 2002) (**FIGURE 9.16**).

Self-Monitoring

Monitoring refers to keeping track of one's performance on a task and making necessary adjustments along the way. Effective monitoring requires **metacognitive skill**, the understanding of how cognition works, or "knowing about knowing." For instance, when memorizing a list of muscle groups for an anatomy course, you might repeatedly test yourself to ensure you know the material. Essentially, you are monitoring your knowledge to determine whether you need additional study time or have sufficiently learned what you need to know.

For the most part, young children exhibit limited meta-cognitive understanding. They are out of touch with what they know. As a result, young children tend to overestimate what they know and underestimate how much effort is required to remember things. In one of the first studies of children's metacognition, experimenters presented 5- and 8-year-old children with ten pictures and asked them if they believed they could remember everything (Flavell, Friedrichs, & Hoyt, 1970). Most 5-year-olds said they could remember all ten pictures, although they could not. That is, 5-year-old children failed to accurately evaluate how much time they needed to memorize the pictures, whereas 8-year-olds were more aware of their memory limitations.

✓ CHECK YOUR UNDERSTANDING 9.4

1. In what situation might a child need to exercise inhibitory control?
2. Which specific aspect of executive functioning can be demonstrated by a Stroop test?
3. What type of test would demonstrate a child's ability to plan?

The Semantic Piece of Long-Term Memory

LEARNING OBJECTIVE 9.5 Discuss developmental changes in semantic memory and the factors that contribute to change.

People hold a lot of information in **long-term memory**, the unlimited and enduring storehouse of knowledge and know-how represented in the brain. **Declarative memory**, a major component of long-term memory, refers to memory for facts and events, including memory of personal experiences from the past. Declarative memory subdivides into two types of memory—semantic and episodic. In this section, we consider children's semantic memory, and in the section following we investigate children's episodic memory (**FIGURE 9.17**).

Words to be remembered:

Shoe
Cat
Doll
Oat
Puzzle
Boat
Sock
Dog
Horse
Block

> Hat, mat, cat... coat, boat... block, sock.

> Hat, sock, coat, shoe... block, doll, puzzle... dog, horse, cat.

FIGURE 9.16 Encoding and retrieval. Researchers study how children organize "to-be-remembered" information by observing the order of items that children recall aloud. For example, when asked to tell a researcher the pictures they saw, children who recall the pictures in order of "hat"-"mat"-"cat," and then recall "coat"-"boat," and so on have grouped items by their sounds. In contrast, if children recall the words "hat"-"coat"-"sock," they have grouped the items into categories, such as clothing. Most of the time, young children cluster items at only chance levels, and sometimes by sound, recalling rhyming words together. By around 7–8 years of age, children group items into conceptually related categories, which aids their memory for items.

long-term memory The unlimited, enduring storehouse of knowledge in the brain that accumulates over time

declarative memory A component of long-term memory that involves memory for facts, events, and personal past experiences; declarative memory subdivides into semantic and episodic memory

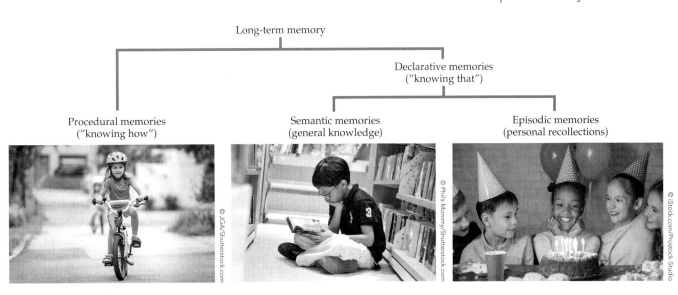

FIGURE 9.17 Types of declarative memory. Long-term memory can be classified as procedural or declarative. Within declarative memory, researchers further distinguish between semantic and episodic memory. (After C. Wade and C. Tavris. 1999. *Invitation to Psychology*, 1st ed. [p. 243]. Addison-Wesley Educational Publishers, Inc.: New York.)

semantic memory The subtype of declarative memory referring to the knowledge a person has acquired around facts, rules, and concepts (including general world knowledge)

scripts A component of semantic memory referring to knowledge about familiar routines, such as the sequence of events and expected behaviors when eating at a restaurant

consolidation A process in which a neural imprint of memories is formed in the brain

Developmental Changes in Semantic Memory

Semantic memory refers to the knowledge a person has acquired around facts, rules, and concepts, such as knowing colors, the meaning of words, facts learned in school, and so on. It also involves knowledge about familiar routines, such as what happens when eating at a restaurant—people sit down, order from a menu, eat, and pay the bill. Such routines are referred to as **scripts** (Hudson & Nelson, 1986).

As information stored in semantic memory grows, children remember increasingly more information than they had before. As a result, declarative memory expands from early childhood through young adulthood (Finn et al., 2016). Improvements in the use of strategies, such as rehearsal and organization, account for much of the age-related differences in children's semantic memory (Ornstein, Naus, & Stone, 1977; Schwenck, Bjorklund, & Schneider, 2007).

Growing complexity in the brain's neural networks also supports developments in children's memory. When individuals form a memory, neuronal connections are modified to create a physical record of the experiences in a process called **consolidation** (McGaugh, 2000). The neural imprint of the memory is widely distributed across the brain. Then, when a memory is retrieved, the pattern of neural activity involves the same circuits that established the initial memory (Winocur & Moscovitch, 2011). For example, experiences with dogs strengthen connections in memory among the words "dog," "animal," "bone," and "tail."

Semantic Memory Aids Working Memory

As information in semantic memory grows in strength and complexity, children can draw on their knowledge base to learn new information, thus placing less burden on working memory (Bjorklund, 1987). The role of a knowledge base in working memory was illustrated in a study of expert chess-playing children who were compared to nonexpert chess-playing adults (Chi, 1978, 2006). The children, chosen from local chess tournaments, and adults who played chess but not well, were given a memory span test for game-possible chess positions and a memory span test for digits. Children outperformed adults on the chess-related memory test, whereas adults outperformed children on the digit memory test. Children's deep understanding of chess moves aided their memory for game-possible moves, whereas adults' greater knowledge of digits aided their memory for digits.

In another classic study, Robbie Case found that a person's knowledge base affects working memory (Case, Kurland, & Golberg, 1982). Case found that 3- to 6-year-old children lag behind adults on working memory span, but when he made things difficult for adults, they did no better than children! Specifically, Case asked adults to remember a list of nonsense words such as "loats," "dast," "thaid," "flim," "brup," "meeth," and "zarch." Now that adults had to memorize material that was unfamiliar, they remembered no more than did children and were no faster than children at repeating the words.

What do findings on children's long-term memory say about developmental changes in children's cognitive development? They highlight the reciprocal connections between long-term memory and improved executive functioning. As children's knowledge grows, they access related information faster, their working memory is freed up to manipulate new information, and learning grows further.

✓ CHECK YOUR UNDERSTANDING 9.5

1. What are some of the strategies children use for remembering?
2. How does expansion in a child's knowledge base affect executive functioning?

Episodic Memory

LEARNING OBJECTIVE 9.6 Describe developmental changes in young children's episodic memory, including research on infantile amnesia.

Episodic memory, the second type of declarative memory, refers to memories about personal experiences, such as what happened during a school trip, last year's vacation, a best friend's party, and so forth. When do episodic memories appear in development? How do they change with age?

episodic memory The subtype of declarative memory referring to everyday memories about personal experiences, situations, and events

Infantile Amnesia

Some scientists claim that children are unable to form episodic memories until early childhood (Tulving, 2005). **Infantile amnesia** refers to the difficulty people have in remembering events from the first years of life. On average, adults report their earliest memory to be from about 3 to 4 years of age (Bauer, 2015; Wang & Peterson, 2014). Perhaps adults don't remember events from the first years of life because they happened so many years ago. However, when developmental scientists tested young children, they found infantile amnesia in children as well (Peterson, Grant, & Boland, 2005). For example, young children could not recall the events surrounding a sibling's birth if it had occurred before their own fourth birthday (Sheingold & Tenney, 1982).

infantile amnesia The difficulty adults have in remembering events from the first years of life

What then might account for infantile amnesia? Researchers offer several possibilities. Perhaps memories prior to 3 years of age are inaccessible because they *never made it to long-term memory* (they never existed in the first place!). Sigmund Freud (1905), in fact, was the first to speculate about infantile amnesia, claiming that children's turmoil over their sexual attraction to their opposite-sex parent led them to repress memories out of consciousness. Today, developmental scientists reject Freud's claim of memory suppression, and also reject the general idea that early episodic memories never existed.

Children's limited language in the early years might also account for why the past seems to have disappeared (Fivush & Hamond, 1990). That is, very young children cannot store memories verbally, making retrieving memories difficult later in development when language is a primary means of representing information. Indeed, when 3- and 4-year-old children participated in a hide-and-seek game, in which they hid toys around a laboratory room, 3-year-olds had problems verbally telling the researcher about the hiding places of the toys relative to 4-year-olds, but showed equivalent performance when they were asked to find the toys they had hidden (Hayne & Imuta, 2011).

An alternative interpretation of infantile amnesia is that children form memories early on (even in infancy and toddlerhood), but the memories do not last very long. In fact, younger children remember experiences from younger ages more than do older children, highlighting clear evidence that children can form memories quite early (Mullally & Maguire, 2014; Peterson, Grant, & Boland, 2005). For example, 5- and 8-year-old children reported memories that happened when they were 2 years of age, and a few children recalled events that occurred before 1 year of age, something not seen in adults (Tustin & Hayne, 2010). If early experiences are indeed encoded as long-term, episodic memories, other factors, including forgetting, may contribute to the absence of early memories.

Forgetting

It is impossible to understand developmental changes in children's memories without considering **forgetting**—the decay or degradation of memories over time. Forgetting may contribute to infantile amnesia and account for age-related improvements in episodic memory (Bauer, 2018; Scarf et al., 2013). For example, young children forget episodic memories at a faster rate

forgetting The loss of memories over time

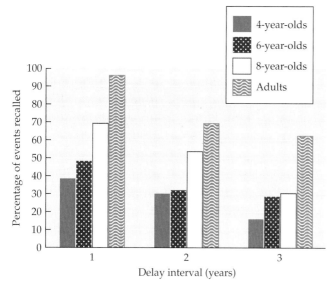

FIGURE 9.18 Developmental changes in semantic memory. Episodic memory improves with age: Young children recall fewer events than 8-year-olds and adults across all types of memory tasks. (After P. J. Bauer and M. Larkina. 2016. *Memory* 24: 1345–1368. Taylor & Francis Ltd, http://www.tandfonline.com.)

than do older children (Bauer, 2015; Bauer & Larkina, 2014; Morris, Baker-Ward, & Bauer, 2010). And, forgetting increases as time passes. When 5.5-year-olds were asked to recall events they had experienced at different points in the past, their forgetting increased as the retention interval increased (Cleveland & Reese, 2008): They only forgot 20% of the events from a month prior, but 60% of events that occurred four years prior.

Why might young children's memories be vulnerable to forgetting? Perhaps as neural structures and networks change and develop in the infant and toddler brain, early memories are displaced. The remodeling of neural networks thus causes degradation of early memories, leading to high rates of forgetting early in life (Josselyn & Frankland, 2012). Perhaps, only memories that have "survived the 'storm and stress' of their infancy and early childhood remain accessible to recollection" (Bauer, 2015).

Developmental Changes in Episodic Memory

Children's episodic memories develop in complexity, detail, and organization across childhood (Bauer, 2015; Waters, Bauer, & Fivush, 2014). With age, children recall an increasing number of past events and greater details about those events (Bauer & Larkina, 2014; Friedman, 2014; Lourenco & Frick, 2013) (**FIGURE 9.18**). For example, 3-year-olds might provide skeletal information about a visit to Disneyland, by simply stating that they saw Mickey Mouse and had fun. Moreover, 3-year-olds and even 4-year-olds require a lot of support to recall events, as when parents ask: "Where did we go yesterday? Do you remember? The zoo? Which animals did you see there?" (e.g., Cristofaro & Tamis-LeMonda, 2012; Nelson & Fivush, 2004; Uccelli et al., 2006). A 5-year-old, in contrast, might offer details about who was there, which characters signed his autograph book, and which exhibits were visited. With age, children increasingly evaluate their experiences, for instance by describing their emotions of being afraid on some rides but excited on others (Bauer, 2015). Impressively, some episodic memories last for months and even years. Children who experienced a trip to Disneyworld when they were 3 or 4 years of age remembered the event 18 months later (Hamond & Fivush, 1991), and the majority of 3-year-olds remembered over 60% of the events three years later (Bauer & Larkina, 2014).

Children's abilities to talk about past experiences also allow them to report on events that they have witnessed—termed **eyewitness testimony**. Eyewitness testimony develops with age, and as long as children are not misled, they can accurately report about events they have observed. But, young children recall fewer details around a witnessed event than do older children and adults (e.g., Ornstein, Gordon, & Larus, 1992; Cassel & Bjorklund, 1995). Furthermore, under certain conditions, children (and adults too!) report inaccuracies.

False Memories

Our memories often fail us. We may have problems recalling someone's name, the information on an exam, or what we ate for dinner two days ago. In other instances, the information we remember is simply *wrong*—which is referred to as a **false memory**.

Cognitive psychologist Elizabeth Loftus conducted groundbreaking studies on the vulnerability of people's memories to suggestion. In fact, Loftus was able to get people to remember things that had never happened to them,

eyewitness testimony A later account of an observed event

false memory The remembering of information that is wrong or different from what actually happened by presenting them with false information (Loftus, 1995). In one of her most cited studies—*Lost in a shopping mall*—participants recalled details about being lost in a mall as children, after an experimenter misled them. Participants were given a brief written description of four events that had supposedly occurred when they were around 4 years of age. Three of the events had happened, based on reports by a relative, but the "lost in a shopping mall" event had not. In different study phases, participants were asked to write about each event in detail, verbally recall events during examiner interviews, and to acknowledge, "I do not remember this" if they could not recall the event. About 25% of the adults "remembered" the false event of being lost in a mall, and provided many details about their experience during interviews. For example, one woman reported remembering crying, and stated that a heavy-set elderly lady helped her find her mom, even though none of it had happened (**FIGURE 9.19**).

Loftus's findings sparked many questions in the developmental community about the memories of young children. Are children especially vulnerable to false memories? And if so, can their word be trusted in legal proceedings, such as custody battles or reports of early abuse? What happens when children must provide eyewitness testimony in forensic cases—the accounting of a witnessed event?

Developmental psychologist Stephen Ceci and his colleagues conducted many studies on children's false memories, showing that children's autobiographical recall can be greatly distorted when interviewers ask questions in a suggestive manner. **Suggestibility**—the inclination to accept false information when recalling an experience—increases in the presence of biased interviewing and leading questions. In particular, preschool age children are likely to report inaccurate information or change their answers when an interviewer (Bruck, Ceci, & Hembrooke, 2002; Ceci & Bruck, 1993):

- asks specific rather than open-ended questions ("Did you see your daddy punch the wall?" vs. "What happened?");
- repeats questions;
- provides information before the child has supplied the information ("Paula told me that your dad hit the wall");
- selectively encourages or reinforces statements that are consistent with the interviewer's position or belief;
- is a person of high status.

In fact, young children provide fantastic details about events they never experienced under experimentally manipulated interviews. Children reported that they had helped a woman find a lost monkey or witnessed a thief steal from a daycare in experimental studies. The false recollections of young children suggest that "it is possible to totally ruin the accuracy of preschoolers' reports about a range of events by exposing them to repeated, potent suggestions" (Bruck, Ceci, & Hembrooke, 2002, p. 545).

But does children's suggestibility affect them in everyday life, outside experimental studies or emotionally charged legal proceedings? It certainly does. When preschool children heard a rumor from adults or classmates, they came to believe they had actually experienced the event themselves! In one study, preschoolers heard adults or classmates talk about an experience at school: A magician was

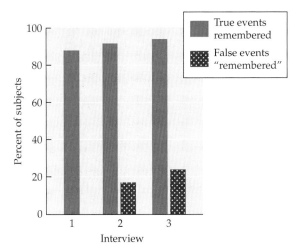

FIGURE 9.19 False memories. Researcher Elizabeth Loftus presented adults with written descriptions of events that had happened to them in the past (based on relative reports) along with an event that participants had not experienced (being lost in a mall). After the adults read the event descriptions, Loftus interviewed participants about their memories. Although Loftus told participants to just say "I don't remember" if they did not remember experiencing an event, over 25% of participants reported remembering being "lost in a mall" even though Loftus had fabricated the event description. (After E. Loftus. 1997. *Sci Am* 22: 70–75. Original graph by Bryan Christie.)

suggestibility The inclination to accept false information when recalling an experience

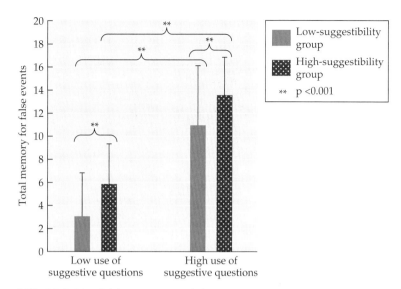

FIGURE 9.20 Children's suggestibility. Examiners tested 4- to 5-year-olds' and 7- to 8-year-olds' memory for events under low-pressure and high-pressure interviewing conditions. Examiners asked children whether a male they had encountered three months prior had behaved inappropriately. Although some children were less suggestible than others, interviews that contained suggestive questions led to a dramatic increase in children's memory of false events. (After K. Finnilä et al. 2003. *J Exp Child Psych* 85: 32–49.)

unable to pull a rabbit out of his hat and the rabbit got loose in the school. Even though the children had not experienced the event first-hand, they were as likely to offer details about the event and to believe that they actually saw the loose rabbit as were children who had been present for the magic show when the rabbit got loose (Principe et al., 2006). And, parents can amplify the effects of false reporting in children. A review of 23 studies found that when parents offer misinformation about an event to children, children's inaccurate reporting to an interviewer increases (Lawson, Rodriguez-Steen, & London, 2018).

Perhaps most disconcerting is the possibility that children will report abuse and other egregious behaviors when questioned in leading ways. Experimental evidence shows that such manipulation is possible. For example, researchers asked young children six misleading questions three months after the children had been read a story and then offered a cookie by a friendly male researcher in a room in their school: "He told you that what you did together was a secret and that you couldn't tell anyone, didn't he?"; "He took a picture of you, didn't he?"; and "Did he touch you anywhere?" Although some children were more susceptible than others, a substantial proportion confirmed the false information under pressured questioning (Finnilä et al., 2003) (**FIGURE 9.20**).

✓ CHECK YOUR UNDERSTANDING 9.6

1. What is infantile amnesia?
2. Why might forgetting occur?
3. Why is young children's rate of forgetting episodic memories disproportionate to that of older children?
4. What are interview techniques that might influence a child to recall events inaccurately?

Family Context of Information Processing

LEARNING OBJECTIVE 9.7 State how a family context of poverty might compromise children's skills in information processing.

Family context can support or harm children's cognitive development, with enduring household poverty being a powerful influence. For example, children from families exposed to chronic poverty across the first years of life performed poorer on executive functioning measures such as inhibitory control and working memory span than did children from families who experienced only transitory poverty (Raver, Blair, & Willoughby, 2013).

Children's stress response may help explain associations between poverty and cognition. That is, chronic poverty alters children's physiological reactions to stress by amplifying levels of the stress hormone cortisol. Cortisol then might compromise children's executive functioning and other forms of self-regulation (Blair et al., 2008, 2011; Evans & Schamberg, 2009). Moreover, poverty instigates cascading effects that can follow children into the school years. Chaos, unpredictability, and inconsistency found in many impoverished households can undermine young children's executive functioning, with downstream effects on academic achievement (Crook & Evans, 2014).

✓ **CHECK YOUR UNDERSTANDING. 9.7**

1. What role does stress play in explaining the connection from poverty to child executive functioning skills?

Preschool Context of Information Processing

LEARNING OBJECTIVE 9.8 Identify ways that preschool curricula might facilitate children's executive functioning.

Preschools provide children with many opportunities to practice cognitive skills. Developmental scientist Adele Diamond designed a preschool **Tools of the Mind curriculum** that aimed to improve preschoolers' executive functioning through a rich range of activities. The curriculum is based on the theoretical position advanced by Soviet psychologist Lev Vygotsky that play is a primary context for the development of self-regulation and higher-level cognitive skills (Vygotsky, 1978).

In Tools of the Mind, children participate in a set of play activities designed to give them practice with attention, inhibitory control, working memory, and cognitive flexibility (**FIGURE 9.21**). For example, in Buddy Reading, pairs of children take turns reading to each other. One child is given a picture of a mouth and the other child a picture of an ear. The child with the mouth gets to read to the child with the ear, who must listen to the story and *wait patiently* until it is their turn to do the reading. In the Freeze game, children dance while music is playing and freeze when it stops. Other activities encourage children to plan out what they want to play with their peers before starting their play.

Has the Tools of the Mind curriculum produced the desired effects? To address this question, Diamond and colleagues set up an experimental study in which teachers and their 3- to 4-year-old students from an urban, low socioeconomic status school district were randomly assigned to either the Tools of the Mind curriculum or a literacy curriculum. Children in the Tools of the Mind program showed gains in executive functioning, and their teachers reported improvements in children's classroom behaviors (Barnett et al., 2008; Diamond et al., 2007), although the effectiveness of the Tools program has not replicated in another large-scale study (Nesbitt and Farran, 2021).

The positive (though inconsistent) impacts of curricula (Nesbitt and Farran, 2021) designed to enhance children's early executive function skills indicate that preschool classrooms are promising contexts for children to learn and practice the behaviors that will be required of them in the later school years (Diamond & Ling, 2016). A meta-analysis of 23 studies showed that the quality of teacher-child interactions related to children's executive functioning, with effects being especially powerful for younger children starting school (Vandenbroucke et al., 2018).

✓ **CHECK YOUR UNDERSTANDING 9.8**

1. Describe the Tools of the Mind curriculum and its impact on children's executive functioning.

© Ariel Skelley/Getty Images

FIGURE 9.21 Tools of the Mind curriculum. Tools of the Mind is an example of a U.S. preschool curriculum that aims to improve preschoolers' executive functioning skills through a rich range of activities that offer children practice with attention, inhibitory control, working memory, and cognitive flexibility in the context of play.

Tools of the Mind curriculum
An early childhood curriculum that focuses on play as a primary vehicle for the development of self-regulation, executive functioning, and higher-level cognitive skills

Cultural Context of Information Processing

LEARNING OBJECTIVE 9.9 Explain how cultural expectations and practices might lead to differences between East Asian and U.S. European American children in areas of executive functioning.

Children from cultural communities around the world differ in their executive functioning skills, in part because of the behavioral expectations of parents and teachers. For instance, compared to North American parents, parents and teachers in East Asian cultures place greater emphasis on socializing self-control in young children (Chen et al., 1998; Tobin, Wu, & Davidson, 1989). In Confucian heritage cultures, including China, impulse control is thought to be a critical skill that children should develop. For example, parents set rules and communicate their expectations about behaviors to their children. However, parents differ in their views and practices around parenting control, child obedience and autonomy, and how much parents should allow children to reason with them (e.g., Chen, Sun, & Yu, 2017; Ng, Pomerantz, & Deng, 2014; Sabbagh, et al., 2006). Asian parents and teachers sometimes rely on "shaming" to instill good behavior in children, for instance, by outwardly disapproving of a child's misconduct and comparing the child to the child's more well-behaved friends or relatives (Liu et al., 2012; Wu, Anderson, & Castiello, 2002).

The value many Asian parents place on self-regulation, and their strategies to promote such behaviors, may help explain the Chinese advantage in executive functioning relative to U.S. preschoolers. Chinese preschoolers in Beijing performed about six months ahead of North American preschoolers on every tested measure of executive functioning (Sabbagh et al., 2006) (**FIGURE 9.22**). Similarly, preschoolers in Mainland China have been found to be more advanced than U.S. preschoolers on tests of inhibitory control and attention control (Lan et al., 2011). Chinese children in the United States, whose parents had immigrated before their birth, likewise displayed higher executive functioning than children from other ethnic minority backgrounds (Ng, Pomerantz, & Deng, 2014).

✓ CHECK YOUR UNDERSTANDING 9.9

1. In which cognitive areas do children from East Asian backgrounds show an advantage over children from U.S. European American backgrounds?

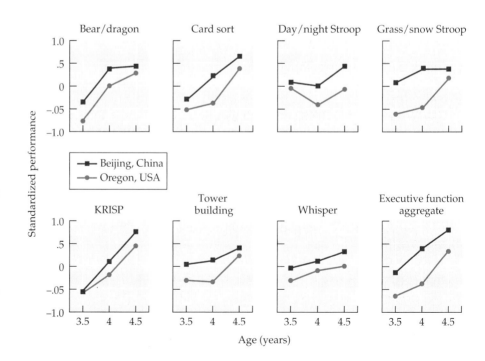

FIGURE 9.22 Cultural differences in executive functioning skills. Cultural beliefs and practices might produce differences in children's executive functioning skills. Chinese preschoolers in Beijing outperformed children from North America on multiple measures of executive functioning, performing approximately six months ahead of North American preschoolers. (After M. A. Sabbagh et al. 2006. *Psych Sci* 17: 74–81.)

■ *Social-Cognitive Development*

Social-cognitive development—the understanding of other people as introduced in Chapter 5—undergoes dramatic transformation in early childhood. Children increasingly understand, for instance, that people differ in their knowledge, areas of expertise, and beliefs. As a result, children express selectivity in whom they turn to for information, whom they trust, and how they reason about the minds of other people.

Evaluating People's Knowledge and Expertise

A key feature of young children's social-cognitive development is their budding understanding that people differ in what they know and can do. Young children do not turn to just anyone for advice or assistance. They consider whether a person is likely to be knowledgeable or have expertise in a specific area; whether a person has provided reliable information in the past; and whether a person is familiar.

Reliability, Trustworthiness, and Familiarity

LEARNING OBJECTIVE 9.10 Explain how children may determine whether an adult is trustworthy.

Children quickly assess what people know and can do, and they use their judgments to determine whom to ask for information or assistance and whom to believe. To illustrate, an examiner asked 3- and 4-year-old children to watch two unfamiliar adults name four familiar objects. One adult named the four objects correctly, for example by saying, "That's a cup" to a cup. The other adult named the four objects incorrectly, for example by labeling the cup a ball. Children judged one adult as more reliable or accurate than the other, and later preferred to ask for information from the adult they viewed to be more trustworthy (Koenig, Clément, & Harris, 2004).

Impressively, young children weigh the specific expertise of different people against one another, for example by recognizing that one person might be more knowledgeable about object names but another might be more capable of fixing things. In one experiment, 4-year-old children observed two unfamiliar people engage with two tools and two broken toys. One person knew the names of the tools but could not fix the toys. The other did not know the names of the tools but used the right tools to fix the toys. When children wanted to know the new labels of things, they directed questions to the person who knew the names of tools. But, when they wanted to fix broken toys, they turned to the person who had fixed the toys in the past. Children also accepted the toy-fixer's explanations about why toys had broken, implying that children were well aware that person held relevant knowledge (Kushnir, Vredenburgh, & Schneider, 2013) (**FIGURE 9.23**).

Children are especially open to information offered by familiar adults (Harris, 2011). For instance, 3-, 4-, and 5-year-old children from two different preschools were shown a film in which the names or functions of novel objects were explained by their familiar caregiver (from their preschool) or an unfamiliar caregiver (from the other preschool) (Corriveau & Harris, 2009). The two teachers presented conflicting information, with caregiver 1 calling an object a "snegg" and caregiver 2 calling it a "hoon." When children were asked which caregiver they wanted to ask about the novel objects and whose account they would believe, children placed more trust in the familiar caregiver.

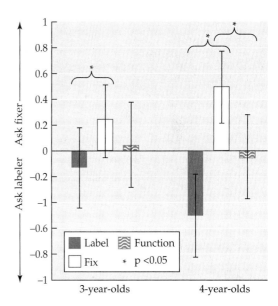

FIGURE 9.23 Reliability and trustworthiness. Young children selectively request information or help from people who are knowledgeable in the relevant areas. Children 3 and 4 years of age were more likely to ask the person they saw fix an object in the past (but who did not know the names of objects: the "fixer") to fix a toy that was broken. In contrast, children were more likely to ask a person who knew the names of objects (but could not fix objects: the "labeler") the label for an object. With age, children improved in their ability to direct requests to the individual with the relevant skills. (After T. Kushnir et al. 2013. *Dev Psychol* 49: 446–453. Copyright © 2013 by American Psychological Association. Reproduced with permission.)

1. Would a child be more likely to ask their parent or a stranger the name of an object? Why?
2. If two adult strangers interacted with toys, and one knew the name of a toy while the other fixed the toy, when would the child turn to each adult for help with a broken toy?

Weighing Familiarity against Reliability

LEARNING OBJECTIVE 9.11 Explain developmental change in children's weighing of familiarity with a person against the person's reliability.

Although it makes sense that children would better trust information from a familiar caregiver, it would be wrong to assume that familiar people are consistently more knowledgeable than are unfamiliar people. Clearly, children encounter many unfamiliar people who know much more about a particular topic than do the people they know. Thus, as children grow in their social-cognitive understanding of other people, a developmental shift occurs in which they begin to take both familiarity and knowledge into account.

Children aged 3, 4, and 5 years old were randomly assigned to one of two conditions. Half of the children saw their familiar caregiver name familiar objects accurately and an unfamiliar person name them inaccurately. The remaining children saw the reverse; the familiar caregiver provided inaccurate information whereas the unfamiliar person provided accurate information. Three-year-olds favored information provided by their familiar caregivers, even when it was inaccurate. Familiarity trumped accuracy. But 4-year-olds, and even more so 5-year-olds, favored information reliability, even if it meant rejecting information from a familiar caregiver (Corriveau & Harris, 2009).

1. Will young children always defer to the advice of a familiar person? Explain your answer.

Theory of Mind

theory of mind The ability to attribute mental states, such as knowledge, beliefs, and desires, to oneself and others, and to understand that other people's knowledge, beliefs, and desires may be different from someone else's

Theory of mind refers to the ability to attribute mental states such as knowledge, beliefs, and desires to oneself and others, and to understand that other people can have knowledge, beliefs, and desires that differ from one's own (**FIGURE 9.24**). Research on children's theory of mind grew rapidly after David Premack and Guy Woodruff (1978) published a paper entitled "Does the chimpanzee have a theory of mind?" The authors claimed that chimpanzees could figure out an actor's goals and identify solutions for the actor to achieve those goals. A few years later, developmental researchers Heinz Wimmer and Josef Perner (1983) published an influential study that revealed the limited skills of young children at understanding the beliefs of other people, a finding that further fueled the debate on what humans (and animals) understand about others' minds.

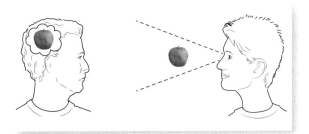

FIGURE 9.24 Theory of mind. Theory of mind refers to the ability to attribute mental states such as knowledge, beliefs, and desires to oneself and others, and to understand that other people can have knowledge, beliefs, and desires that differ from one's own. (After H. M. Wellman et al. 2001. *Child Dev* 72: 655–684. © 2001 by the Society for Research in Child Development, Inc. All rights reserved.)

False-Belief Understanding

LEARNING OBJECTIVE 9.12 Describe a classic study used to test children's understanding of false belief.

Wimmer and Perner (1983) presented children 3–9 years of age with sketches in which a character, Maxi, placed his chocolate into a cupboard. Maxi's mother then moved the chocolate to a different cupboard while Maxi was out of the

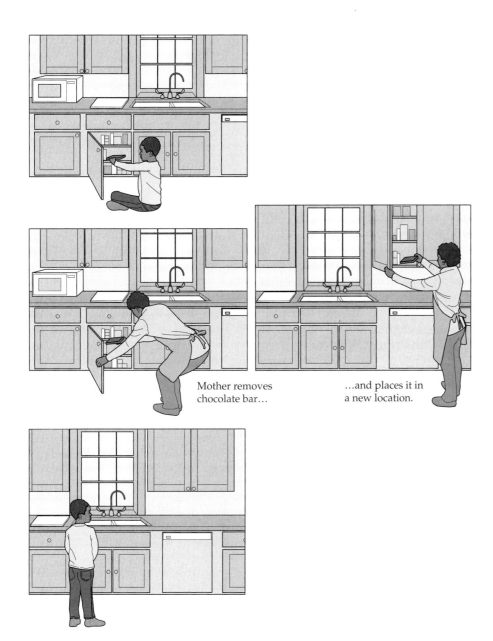

Mother removes
chocolate bar...

...and places it in
a new location.

FIGURE 9.25 False-belief task. Wimmer and Perner presented children between
3 and 9 years of age with sketches in which a character named Maxi placed his chocolate into a cupboard, and his mother then moved it to a different cupboard while Maxi
was out of the room. When asked where Maxi would look for his chocolate when he
re-entered the room, children younger than 4–5 years of age incorrectly stated that
Maxi would look for his chocolate at its new location, whereas children older than
4–5 years of age understood that Maxi would look in the original location. (Based on
experiment in H. Wimmer and J. Perner. 1983. *Cognition* 13: 103–128.)

room (**FIGURE 9.25**). An examiner then asked the children where Maxi would
look for his chocolate when he re-entered the room. Children younger than 4–5
years of age incorrectly stated that Maxi would look for his chocolate at its new
location, whereas children older than 4–5 years of age understood that Maxi
would look in the original location, even though the chocolate was no longer
there. The older children realized that Maxi had a belief about the location
of the chocolate that was wrong. The ability to understand that other people
can hold beliefs that differ from reality is termed **false belief** (see Chapter 5).

false belief The belief that others
can hold beliefs or perspectives that
differ from reality

Wimmer and Perner concluded that children younger than 3–5 years of age do not understand much about the mental states of other people.

Developmental scientists have since examined children's theory of mind using a variety of modifications of the original Maxi false-belief task. One common procedure is to ask children what another person might believe in a deceptive situation, such as when an object appears to be something it is not. For example, an examiner may show young children a familiar-looking box that typically holds candy and ask them what they *think* is inside the box. Children usually respond that candy will be in the box. The examiner then shows the children that the box actually contains something else, such as pencils or crayons. Children are then asked what another person would believe is in the box. Most 3-year-olds state that the other person would believe the container held pencils, indicating they fail to recognize that the other person might hold a false belief about the true contents of the box. By 5 years of age, most children will say the other person will believe candy is in the box, indicating they recognize that the other person has a false belief about the box contents (Gopnik & Astington, 1988).

However, it would be an oversimplification to think that children experience a sudden and momentous change in their false-belief understanding between 3 and 5 years of age. When researchers longitudinally followed individual children over time, they found that some children consistently passed theory-of-mind tasks; some consistently failed; some showed changes in their responses during testing; and many children exhibited variable performance, sometimes passing and sometimes failing (Baker et al., 2016). Still, all children eventually understand false beliefs, a badge of growth in theory of mind.

✓ CHECK YOUR UNDERSTANDING 9.12

1. What classic study was used to test children's understanding of false belief?

Explaining Development in Children's Theory of Mind

LEARNING OBJECTIVE 9.13 Identify three factors that might explain why a young child's theory of mind changes over time.

What might explain developmental changes in children's theory of mind? For some time, researchers speculated that young children's growing language and/or memory skills might explain performance on traditional false-belief tasks. Yet, modifications to the memory and/or language demands of tasks did not improve the performance of 3-year-olds (Wellman et al., 2001). As a result, various other explanations have been proposed.

Theory-Theory

The theory-theory attributes developmental changes in children's performance on false-belief tasks to revisions children make to their theories about the world (Gopnik & Wellman, 2012). According to the theory-theory, children actively seek out the causes and reasons about the behaviors of themselves and others. With age and experience, children modify their earlier-held theories. For example, 3-year-olds tested on the Maxi chocolate task might construct a theory of Maxi's behavior that is based on his desire to get the chocolate. Maxi wants the chocolate and should therefore look to where it was last placed, in this case, where the mother moved the chocolate. But as children learn from everyday experience that objects do not always reside where they were last seen, they realize that people may sometimes hold false beliefs, and that some theories about the world are not reliable. Thus, children's desire-based view of the world becomes obsolete when they realize that people often do not find objects just because they wish to have them.

Executive Functioning

Limited executive functioning may be another reason why children younger than 4 years of age perform poorly on theory-of-mind tasks (Carlson, Mandell, & Williams, 2004). The Maxi task, for example, requires children to (1) identify where the chocolate is *not located*; (2) narrow down possible places where the chocolate truly *is located*; and (3) keep the two conflicting possibilities in mind while figuring out where Maxi will look first (Frye, Zelazo, & Burack, 1998). As children's executive functioning skills improve, performance on theory-of-mind tasks improves (e.g., Sabbagh, Moses, & Shiverick, 2006).

Brain Development

Maturation of the brain may account for improvements in children's social-cognitive skills. Two lines of evidence support this proposition. First, children with autism display limitations on theory-of-mind tasks, suggesting that a specific biological disorder affects their social-cognitive skills. When researchers tested typically developing children, children with autism, and children with Down syndrome on the Wimmer and Perner theory-of-mind task, children with autism were the only group who could not pass the false-belief task even though they had IQ scores that surpassed the two control groups (Baron-Cohen, Leslie, & Frith, 1985).

Second, children's brain maturation based on electroencephalograms (EEGs) relates to social-cognitive skills (Perner & Ruffman, 2005; Richardson et al., 2020; Sabbagh et al., 2009). For example, an examiner placed electrodes over the scalps of children to obtain baseline data on their EEGs. After the EEG recordings, children completed a set of false-belief tasks. Preschoolers' false-belief performance related to their brain maturation based on EEG recordings (Saxe & Powell, 2006). Moreover, preschoolers' EEG responses and theory-of-mind performance predicted theory-of-mind-specific brain responses on fMRIs at 7 years of age, suggesting connections between early brain maturation and later social-cognitive reasoning (Bowman et al., 2019).

✓ CHECK YOUR UNDERSTANDING 9.13

1. What is the theory-theory? Give an example.
2. How might children's executive functioning aid their theory of mind?
3. How would you test whether maturation of the brain accounts for improvements in children's social-cognitive skills?

Lying, Deception, and Persuasion

LEARNING OBJECTIVE 9.14 Explain why theory of mind relates to lying, deception, and persuasion.

Understanding other people's minds can be a double-edged sword. A child who realizes that it is possible to create a false belief in other people may attempt to manipulate people through lies and deception (Chandler, Fritz, & Hala, 1989). To illustrate, an examiner tempted 3- to 8-year-olds to commit a minor transgression—peeking at a toy after being told not to peek. The examiner then assessed whether children would lie or admit to peeking (Talwar & Lee, 2008). Children peeked, as expected, but among the children who lied about peeking, some were better at lying to conceal their transgression and better at sticking to the lie than were others. Children who performed well on false-belief tasks were better liars and sustained liars. Similarly, false-belief reasoning predicted children's success at games such as hide-and-go-seek and their ability to keep secrets, because children must recognize how to keep other people ignorant about what they themselves know (Peskin & Ardino, 2003).

Like lying and deception, persuasion requires children to generate arguments to change another person's thoughts and behaviors. Children's theory-of-mind skills relate to their art of persuasion (Peterson, Slaughter, & Wellman, 2018). For example, a researcher instructed children ages 3–8 years old to try to convince a puppet to do something the puppet did not want to do, such as eat broccoli or brush its teeth. The puppet, which was controlled by an examiner, wavered each time the child offered a suggestion, but then refused to give in to the suggestion. Children were therefore challenged to generate convincing arguments to get the puppet to eat the broccoli or brush its teeth. Children's scores on a battery of false-belief tasks related to the number of persuasive arguments that they generated (Slaughter, Peterson, & Moore, 2013). And so, if you observe young children lying, deceiving, or mustering up arguments to manipulate others, look at the bright side; they are showcasing their talents around understanding others' minds.

✓ CHECK YOUR UNDERSTANDING 9.14

1. Provide research evidence showing that theory of mind helps children with deception and persuasion.

Contexts of Social-Cognitive Development

Young children gradually advance in their understanding of the thoughts, desires, and beliefs of themselves and others. Yet, some children surpass other children in the sophistication of their social-cognitive skills at a given age. Here, we consider how children's interactions with parents and siblings and experiences at school help build their abilities and contribute to individual differences.

Family Context of Social-Cognitive Development

LEARNING OBJECTIVE 9.15 List ways that family context supports social-cognitive development.

Children's interactions with family members help them learn about how other people think and feel. Indeed, parental sensitivity predicts preschoolers' theory-of-mind performance (Cahill et al., 2007; Meins et al., 2002). Additionally, parents and other adults support children's social-cognitive skills by exposing children to **mental state talk**—statements and questions that refer to other people's "minds" using words such as "think," "know," and "want" that encourage children to reflect on people's unobserved thoughts and beliefs. For example, children's theory-of-mind performance at 3 and 4 years of age related to their mothers' use of mental state language while sharing a picture book with them (Ruffman, Slade, & Crowe, 2002).

Parents are not the only ones who promote children's social-cognitive skills. Siblings matter as well. Young children with more siblings perform better than do children with one or no siblings on theory-of-mind tasks, such as false belief (McAlister & Peterson, 2013). Moreover, having siblings is associated with more advanced theory-of-mind performance regardless of whether siblings are older or younger. Sibling interactions provide plentiful opportunities for children to think about others' mental states, thus providing a rich "data base" for building a theory of mind (Perner, Ruffman, & Leekam, 1994). In line with the association between theory of mind and deception, children who peeked at a forbidden toy in an experimental study and had younger siblings were more likely to lie and say they had not

mental state talk Statements and questions that refer to others' minds, such as think, know, and want peeked than were children without younger siblings (O'Connor & Evans, 2018) (**FIGURE 9.26**).

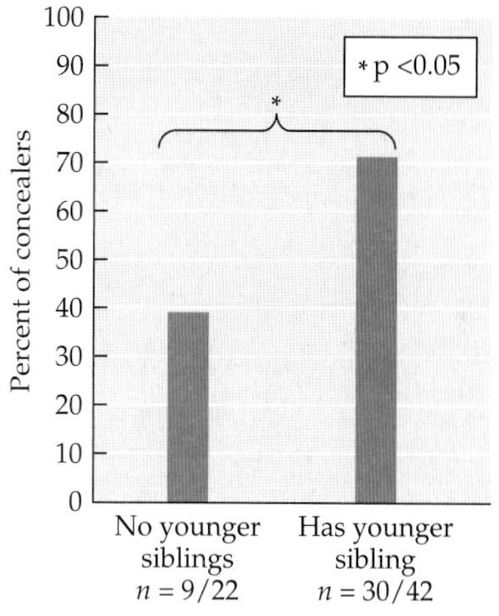

✓ CHECK YOUR UNDERSTANDING 9.15

1. What role does mental state talk play in children's social-cognitive development?

School Context of Social-Cognitive Development

LEARNING OBJECTIVE 9.16 Explain aspects of the school context that support children's social-cognitive development.

Interactions with peers and teachers and engagement with literary materials promote children's social-cognitive skills. Interactions with peers offer children opportunities to learn that other people often have beliefs and desires that differ from their own—such as when a friend says he would rather color than play in the block corner. Teachers expose children to mental state talk, which offers information about the unobserved perspectives and feelings of other people (Frampton, Perlman, & Jenkins, 2009). Finally, literary activities like reading books foster children's reasoning about the motives, beliefs, emotions, and intentions of characters (e.g., Dyer, Shatz, & Wellman, 2000). Reciprocally, children's growing social-cognitive skills allow them to understand the motives of characters and the meaning of stories (Astington & Pelletier, 2005).

✓ CHECK YOUR UNDERSTANDING 9.16

1. Why are literacy experiences important for children's social-cognitive development?

Cultural Context of Social-Cognitive Development

LEARNING OBJECTIVE 9.17 Describe evidence for the universality of early social-cognitive development.

Children everywhere show impressive gains in their understanding of people across the early childhood years. And, as seen for all cognitive phenomena, social-cognitive development follows certain universal processes. For example, developmental transitions observed in U.S. children's skills on theory-of-mind tasks have been found to generalize to children from cultural communities across the globe. A review of 178 false-belief studies, which collectively included over 4,000 children from different societies, indicated highly similar patterns of change in the communities studied. Three- and 4-year-olds uniformly had difficulty with theory-of-mind tasks, but 5-year-olds passed theory-of-mind tasks, indicating their growing understanding of others' minds (Wellman, Cross, & Watson, 2001) (**FIGURE 9.27**).

✓ CHECK YOUR UNDERSTANDING 9.17

1. What evidence supports universal processes in children's social-cognitive development?

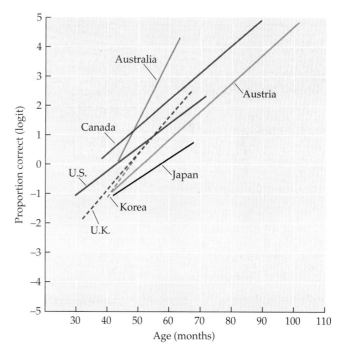

FIGURE 9.26 Siblings and lying. Children are more likely to conceal lies when they have younger siblings than when they do not, suggesting that having siblings feeds into children's theory of mind understanding. (After A. M. O'Connor and A. D. Evans. 2018. *J Exp Child Psych* 168: 49–60.)

FIGURE 9.27 Cultural comparisons of theory of mind. When researchers analyzed data on the theory of mind of over 4,000 children from countries around the world, they saw similar developmental improvements, with most children younger than 5 years of age failing theory-of-mind tasks (represented by negative values on proportion correct), but passing after the age of 5. Children across countries dramatically improved in their performance from 5 years onward. (After H. M. Wellman et al. 2001. *Child Dev* 72: 655–684. © 2001 by the Society for Research in Child Development, Inc. All rights reserved.)

■ Language, Literacy, and Mathematical Understanding

Children's causal understanding, perspective taking, executive functioning, memory, and theory of mind are important to study in their own right. However, basic cognitive skills are also pivotal to learning in formal settings, such as school. The scenario of Christopher's attempts to ignore tempting distractors when learning the concepts of "greater than" and "less than," illustrates the close connection between cognitive skills and academics. In the following sections, we consider young children's developments in language, literacy, and mathematics to underscore the very practical implications of cognitive development for children's school readiness.

Growing Language Skills

Young children can do a lot with language. They use language to pretend, tell stories, joke, explain, evaluate, refuse, whine, and complain. Developments in language support these abilities. Young children hone their phonological skills, expand the breadth and depth of their vocabularies, and learn how to construct grammatically accurate sentences. Additionally, children grow in the pragmatics of language, as they learn the social norms and expectations around communication.

Phonology and Semantics

LEARNING OBJECTIVE 9.18 Discuss improvements in children's phonological and semantic language skills during early childhood.

Infants recognize and produce the sounds of their language(s) and learn the meaning of words as they expand their vocabularies (see Chapter 6). However, infants remain limited in the pronunciation of certain sounds and their knowledge of words. As young children's phonology and semantic skills flourish, they can communicate more effectively and contribute to conversations with other people.

Improvements in Phonology

Children's phonological skills improve rapidly during early childhood. Children transition from being generally difficult to understand to being modestly impressive communicators. In particular, the range and accuracy of children's speech sounds increase and phonological errors decrease, which enables people to understand what children are saying (Stoel-Gammon & Sosa, 2008). By around 4 years of age, children's pronunciation errors no longer interfere much with their intelligibility (Coplan & Gleason, 1988).

What enables children to improve in phonology? Practice talking and greater control and coordination of the muscles involved in speech are key. So is the motivation to communicate. That is, children are driven to improve their language skills because they want to be understood by other people. Consequently, they work hard at making the sound distinctions required by the words in their growing vocabularies.

Improvements in Semantics

Children acquire new words at an astounding rate. By 6 years of age, children have acquired a vocabulary of up to 10,000 words. Vocabulary expansion allows greater specificity and detail in children's sentences. For example, a child can now exclaim "I want to eat *all* the Halloween candy!" rather than being limited to the vague assertion "More!" which is quite frequent in infancy.

Children's semantic development reflects their growing network of information about how the world is structured and how words connect to one another. The hierarchical categorization of words—such as understanding that an apple is a fruit and fruit is a food—captures one aspect of semantic richness. The hierarchical structure of children's language is seen in the ways that children learn words at three levels of increasing specificity: general, basic, and specific (Rosch et al., 1976). The word "plant," for example, is a general word. The word "flower" is a basic, mid-level word. And the word "rose" is a specific word in the hierarchy. Children typically learn words for the basic level of a category before they learn the general and specific categories, partly because of the characteristics of words at each of the three levels. Basic level words, such as "tree," share several characteristics, such as having bark and branches, being tall, and so forth. In contrast, the general category "plant" has fewer shared characteristics, because plants come in a range of shapes, sizes, and colors. Words at the specific level share the same characteristics as those at the basic level, but also have additional ones that children must learn. For example, children must learn that all pine trees, but not all trees, have needle-like leaves. Parents further support children's learning of basic level words: They are more likely to use basic level words such as "dog" than general or specific words such as "animal" or "golden retriever" when talking with their children (e.g., Callanan & Sabbagh, 2004).

✓ CHECK YOUR UNDERSTANDING 9.18

1. Provide an example of how children learn words at three levels of increasing specificity: general, basic, and specific.

Grammar

LEARNING OBJECTIVE 9.19 Identify grammatical skills in morphology and syntax that children acquire in early childhood.

Knowledge of grammar blossoms in early childhood. Children acquire rules about how to form words, **morphology**, by adding prefixes and suffixes to alter a word's meaning. They also learn rules about combining words into sentences, or **syntax**. Developments in morphology and syntax permit longer sentences that contain more meaning than children's initial sentences.

Morphology: Modifying Word Meaning

Young children learn how to make minor changes or additions to words to modify a word's meaning. For example, children express plurality by adding "s" to the end of nouns ("dog" to "dogs") and modify the tense of verbs by adding suffixes such as "ed" or "ing" ("jumped," "jumping"). Modifiers in turn expand the complexity of sentences. For instance, the phrase "dogs jumped" is more complex than "dog jump," because the former indicates that two or more dogs had engaged in the act of jumping sometime in the past.

Jean Berko (1958) used a clever method called the **wug test** to study children's understanding of the English plural "s." Berko showed children a picture of a birdlike animal and labeled the animal with a nonsense word ("This is a wug.") (**FIGURE 9.28**). She then showed children a picture with two birdlike figures,

morphology The study of words and how words are formed

syntax The set of rules that govern the ordering of parts of speech to form meaningful sentences

wug test A method of studying children's understanding of plural formation and other rules in grammar based on children's verbal responses to pictures of invented nouns, verbs, and adjectives (such as whether a child says "wugs" to 2 odd creatures)

FIGURE 9.28 A wug test. Jean Berko (1958) designed the "wug test" to study young children's understanding of grammatical rules, such as English plural "s." She showed children a picture of an animal-like creature named a "wug." She then showed children a picture with two such creatures and said, "There are two of them. There are two _____." Children who correctly answered "wugs" showed that they understood how to construct plurals. (After J. Berko, 1958. *WORD* 14: 150–177. Adapted from The Wug Test © Jean Berko Gleason 2006.)

and said, "Now there is another one. There are two _____." Preschool-age children correctly answered "wugs," indicating that they understood the grammatical rule for constructing plurals. Versions of the wug test have since been used across many studies to test children's understanding of past tense, possessives, and so on (e.g., Bialystok, Peets, & Moreno, 2014; Polite, 2011).

Joining Clauses

Children use conjunctions, words such as "and," "but," and "for," to combine two or more clauses into a single sentence. A **clause** is the smallest grammatical unit that can express a complete thought. For example, the sentence "Mommy opened the door when Daddy was outside" uses the conjunction "when" to combine two ideas: (1) that the mother was opening the door and (2) that the father was outside. As children become familiar with conjunctions, they can construct increasingly complex sentences.

Learning Grammar Takes Time: Rules of Syntax

Learning the grammatical rules of a language takes time. Sometimes, children advance forward but make errors as they attempt new rules. Then, they get the rules just right, and advance once more, this time with grammatical accuracy. Many sentences require children to learn highly complex rules. For example, if you want to transform the sentence: "I can't go outside to play" into a question, you would have to add a question word (such as "Why") and then invert the ordering of the subject ("I") and auxiliary verb ("can't") to ask: "Why can't I go outside to play?" Although proficient speakers do not think twice about such constructions, mastering the formulation of questions extends over early childhood and follows a sequence of developmental changes (Klima, 1966):

1. The earliest questions of toddlers are predominantly of the yes-no variety such as "I ride train?"

2. Next, children include articles, pronouns, and "WH" words into their sentences, leading to questions such as "Where I sleep?"

3. Children then start using the verb "do" in yes-no questions such as "*Does* the kitty stand up?" and intuitively understand the verbs of "being": "*Is* Mommy talking to Grandma?" and "Will Mikey *be* there?" Young children, however, continue to create grammatically incorrect sentences such as, "What he can ride in?" and "Why he doesn't know how to run?"

4. It takes several more months for children to produce questions such as "Why *can't* kitty stand up?" Correct questions generally begin to appear when children are 3 or 4 years of age (Hoff, 2009).

Overregularizations in Grammar

Children's grammatical errors reveal valuable information about children's growing understanding of morphology and syntax. However, errors may baffle parents because their children seem to be going backwards: At younger ages, children correctly said "Mommy went," and then suddenly reverted to the incorrect use of "Mommy goed," only later to return to the correct usage. Yet, these common errors reveal that children are in the process of extracting grammatical rules from their language (Berko, 1958; Xu & Pinker, 1995). That is, children learn the general rules of grammar *before* they learn exceptions to those rules. And, since there are a lot of exceptions to learn, children often apply the regular rule to the irregular form, a situation referred to as **overregularization** (Maratsos, 2000).

clause The smallest grammatical unit (e.g., subject, verb phrase) that expresses a complete thought

overregularization The use of a regular morpheme in a word that is irregular, such as saying "taked" rather than "took" for the past tense or "mouses" rather than "mice" for the plural form

✓ **CHECK YOUR UNDERSTANDING 9.19**

1. What two improvements in children's language skills account for the growing complexity of their grammar?
2. What types of grammatical errors do young children commonly make and why?
3. What is overregularization and why does it occur?

Pragmatics

LEARNING OBJECTIVE 9.20 Identify some conversational skills that emerge in early childhood.

Children's expanding vocabulary and knowledge about grammar usher in a new world of social interactions. Children are now full-fledged participants in the conversations of daily life. At the same time, however, children must learn the norms of language use, such as when to talk, how much to talk, and what to talk about with other people. Such norms are referred to as the **pragmatics** of language. Essentially, language is a social art (Quine, 1960, 2013). Consider, for example, three unspoken expectations around the norms of conversation (Grice, 1975):

pragmatics The norms of language use and the contexts in which language is used, including when to talk, how to talk, and what to talk about

1. *Say no more or no less than is required.* If you pass a casual acquaintance on the street and ask "How're you doing?" you expect her to say something like "Good, you?" You'd be taken aback if she stopped to tell you about her migraine headache and plans to see a doctor.

2. *Be relevant.* If you were with a group of friends who were discussing the lousy season of the town's football team, you would be unlikely to interject with statistics on your favorite basketball team.

3. *Avoid ambiguity and confusion.* If you had gone to a movie that your friend had not seen or heard about, you would be unlikely to analyze the motives of characters without first introducing some information about the storyline.

Oftentimes, children say too much or too little when talking with people around them. Furthermore, their contributions are not always directly relevant to the ongoing conversation. And finally, they frequently fail to consider the perspective of the listener. For instance, a 3-year-old might say, "I told him no, but he took her toy." To an ignorant listener, the child's statements are uninterpretable because they leave out information about who took what toy from whom. Children's incomplete explanations stem from not understanding that a speaker and listener each have different assumptions or knowledge (in line with children's egocentrism and lack of perspective taking described earlier in the chapter) (De Cat, 2013; Schaeffer & Matthewson, 2005). Between 3 and 5 years of age, young children show gains in pragmatic skills as they learn the art of conversing and cognitively advance in perspective taking.

✓ **CHECK YOUR UNDERSTANDING 9.20**

1. What is an example of an error young children might make when communicating with others in the area of pragmatics?

Literacy and Mathematical Understanding

Early childhood ushers in the building blocks to later academic achievement—as seen in early math skills and children's rudimentary reading and writing skills, termed **literacy**. Most U.S. children have shared books with caregivers, understand that words on pages tell a story, and know how to write some letters, including the letters of their names. Young children also acquire basic math

literacy Fundamental reading and writing skills

concepts, ranging from counting to understanding magnitudes to recognizing and naming shapes.

Emergent Literacy: Reading and Writing

LEARNING OBJECTIVE 9.21 Identify emergent literacy skills that are vital for later reading.

emergent literacy The collection of skills, knowledge, and attitudes that are early precursors to reading and writing

code-related skills The formalities of writing, sounding out, and reading letters and words on a page that include skills such as forming letters and connecting letters to sounds

Emergent literacy refers to the suite of skills, knowledge, and attitudes that are precursors to reading and writing (Storch & Whitehurst, 2002). Children's oral language skills, including word knowledge, grammatical knowledge, and narrative abilities set the stage for emergent literacy. But, they are not enough. Children must acquire **code-related skills**—the formalities of writing, sounding out, and reading letters and words on a page (Storch & Whitehurst, 2002). Code-related skills include

- learning the conventions of print, such as knowing that writing moves from the top to the bottom of the page;
- beginning forms of reading and writing, such as naming and writing letters;
- phonological awareness, including connecting letters to sounds, such as the letter "m" having an "mmm" sound and knowing that the word "bat" begins with the /b/ sound and letter.

Oral language and code-related skills are core to recognizing letters and words and understanding text. A child who has code-related skills but insufficient semantic and grammatical skills may be able to read an unfamiliar word by sounding it out, but the word and sentences will remain meaningless. Poor code-related skills also hinder children's reading, because children who have difficulty identifying letters and decoding words won't be able to understand what they are reading, even if they have knowledge about the text. As children advance in their reading skills in Grades 1 and 2, code-related skills become increasingly central to reading success (Evans, Shaw, & Bell, 2000; Sénéchal & LeFevre, 2002).

✓ CHECK YOUR UNDERSTANDING 9.21
   1. Define and give examples of code-related language skills in young children.

Emergent Math

LEARNING OBJECTIVE 9.22 Describe developments in children's early math cognition.

For several decades, developmental researchers and educators placed disproportionate attention on children's early literacy skills relative to children's developments in math. However, attention to young children's math skills continues to grow in response to global trends in the workforce. The majority of current U.S. economic growth revolves around innovations in *science*, *technology*, *engineering*, and *mathematics* (the STEM disciplines). Furthermore, international comparisons placed the United States below many emerging and leading economies such as Taiwan, South Korea, Japan, and Switzerland (OECD, 2018). As a result, math is a growing focus of many U.S. curricula, even those aimed at preschoolers.

But are young children ready for mathematics? The answer is yes. With the proper support, young children learn to count, discriminate quantities, and discern patterns (Berch, 2005; Gersten, Jordan, & Flojo, 2005; Jordan et al., 2009). Consider children's emerging understanding of quantity and number, as one example:

- Number concepts appear in children's vocabularies in the second and third years of life (Gelman, 2006). For example, 2- and 3-year-old children understand and use many words that express magnitudes and compare quantities—such as "big" and "bigger"; "small" and "smaller"; and "more" and "less."

- Many 2- to 3-year-olds can count. However, recall that Piaget correctly noted that counting does not mean that children necessarily connect number words to quantities. Thus, children first memorize the counting sequence: "one," "two," "three," and so forth, without an appreciation for each number's meaning (Fuson, 1988).

- By around 3.5 years of age, children learn (in order) the meaning of "one," then "two," then "three," and sometimes "four" (Wynn, 1990, 1992). They now connect beginning number words to their precise quantities.

- After children understand the meaning of "three" or "four," they rapidly acquire the meanings of higher number words. Children show a conceptual shift in their understanding of the **cardinal principle**, that each number in a sequence represents a specific number of elements in a set (Wynn, 1990, 1992) (**FIGURE 9.29**).

- With age, children's understanding of cardinality improves further, enabling them to solve simple numerical comparisons (Byrnes & Fox, 1998). Four-year-olds can solve problems such as "If Brittany ate five apples, and Lila ate two, who ate more apples?"

- By 5 years of age, most U.S. children can count to 20 and know the relative quantities of the numbers 1–10 (Siegler, 1998). Children can now represent numbers in a set through counting, and not just small numbers.

FIGURE 9.29 The cardinal principle. Once children understand the meaning of "three" or "four," they rapidly acquire the meanings of number words representing greater values. Children have now experienced a conceptual shift in their understanding of the cardinal principle—that each number in a sequence represents a specific number of elements in a set.

cardinal principle The understanding in early math development that each number in a sequence represents a specific number of elements in a set

spatial cognition Abilities to understand and represent shapes, locations, and spatial relations among objects

Young children also display gains in **spatial cognition**—abilities to represent shapes, locations, and spatial relations among objects. When a child realizes that a hexagon shape can't fit into a shapesorter's triangle hole, the child displays spatial understanding. When a child uses language to express spatial concepts such as "on top of," "behind," or words such as "triangle," "square," and "rectangle," the child expresses an understanding of relative spatial positions and the unique spatial features of shapes (Pruden, Levine, & Huttenlocher, 2011).

But why are spatial skills important? Notably, young children's spatial skills relate to math skills concurrently and across development (Gunderson et al., 2012; Verdine et al., 2014b; Zhang et al., 2014). Thus, providing children with opportunities to play with toys that require spatial reasoning, like puzzles and blocks, helps promote math skills in school.

✓ CHECK YOUR UNDERSTANDING 9.22

1. How does growth in vocabulary influence children's understanding of number concepts?
2. What is the cardinal principle, and what types of math problems show that young children understand cardinality?

Contexts: Language, Literacy, and Mathematical Understanding

The horse race metaphor at the start of the chapter spotlighted differences among U.S. children in their readiness for school. Notably, however, school readiness is not just "within the child." Children's readiness for school requires *ready families, ready schools, and ready communities* (Pianta, Cox, & Snow, 2007). Let us consider these various contextual influences on children's developing skills.

Home Context of Language, Literacy, and Mathematical Understanding

LEARNING OBJECTIVE 9.23 Summarize features of the home context that promote children's skills in language, literacy, and math.

During early childhood, caregivers' talk to children and engagement of children in learning activities is important. Activities such as reading books, play, and counting games foster children's growing abilities in language, literacy, and math.

Caregiver Talk to Children

Young children benefit from exposure to the expansive vocabularies and grammatically rich language of their parents and other adults. The number of different words mothers use during interactions with their children relates to many aspects of children's language skills, including vocabulary size, grammatical complexity, and literacy (e.g., Huttenlocher et al., 2007; Quiroz, Snow, & Zhao, 2010).

Parents and other caregivers also provide children with lessons about grammar, often unintentionally. Parents sometimes restructure children's grammatically incorrect sentences into correct forms by using **recasts**. They might elaborate on children's sentences by providing details through **expansions** (Chouinard & Clark, 2003; Taumoepeau, 2016). For example, if a child states, "I runned fast," and a parent remarks, "Yes, you ran very fast at the race yesterday!" the parent has provided both a recast that contains correct grammar and an expansion by offering an extended version of the child's original statement. Of course, children don't have to be directly tutored on their errors in grammar: Mere exposure to grammatically accurate language provides children with the inputs needed to learn because the sentences they hear contain regularities in rules around how to combine words in sentences.

Parents' talk with children supports many skills beyond language. Math talk and spatial talk foster children's number and spatial understanding (Gunderson & Levine, 2011; Levine et al., 2012; Susperreguy & Davis-Kean, 2016). Math talk is defined as parents' counting objects and using number words and math terms such as stating, "There's more in that pile," or "How many coins do you have?" Spatial talk conveys information about the dimensions, features, shapes, orientation, transformation, location, and direction of objects and people in terms such as "more than," "bigger than," or "triangle," "small," "round," and "above." Math and spatial talk can occur during math-related activities such as number games or block play, and can also be used in daily life, such as counting the slices of pizza and figuring out how many pieces each person should get so that everyone has the same pieces.

Book Sharing and Literacy Experiences

Book sharing offers children opportunities to expand their vocabularies and learn about the world. Parents promote literacy and narrative skills in children by reading to them, creating stories when sharing wordless picture books, pointing out letters and words on a page, asking questions, and elaborating on story lines.

Parental elaborations during book reading (sometimes referred to as "elaborativeness") are particularly central to children's narrative skills (Escobar, Melzi, & Tamis-LeMonda, 2017; Melzi, Schick, & Kennedy, 2011). High elaborativeness is seen when mothers, fathers, teachers, and others provide details about stories, ask questions, build on children's responses, and encourage children to participate in creating and telling stories. Low elaborativeness

recasts The restructuring of children's grammatically incorrect sentences into correct forms (often by a caregiver)

expansions The elaboration of children's sentences with additional details or information is seen when caregivers provide skeletal stories, convey facts or knowledge to children without asking any questions, do not follow up on children's responses, and provide children with limited opportunities to contribute to a story (e.g., Haden, Haine, & Fivush, 1997).

Like elaborativeness, **dialogic reading**—a reading style in which adults ask "WH" questions (questions asking what, who, when, why, or where), prompt children to participate, and engage children in discussion while reading to them—promotes children's language, emergent literacy, and early reading skills (e.g., Arnold & Whitehurst, 1994; Flack, Field, & Horst, 2018; Mol et al., 2008) (**FIGURE 9.30**). Dialogic reading encourages children to recall,

dialogic reading A reading style in which adults ask "WH" questions, prompt children to participate, and engage children in discussion during reading time

Guided Reading Bookmark

Predict
- ➤ What do you think will happen in the story?
- ➤ Look at the **book cover**
- ➤ Look at the **pictures**
- ➤ Read the **blurb**

Ask Questions

Who?
Who are the characters?
Where?
Where is the setting?
What?
What are they doing?
When?
When is this story set?
Why?
Why is there a problem?
How?
How can it be solved?

Clarify
- ➤ Find some unfamiliar words. What do they mean?
- ➤ Find a sentence you don't understand. What does it mean?
- ➤ What other things don't you understand in the story?

Personalize
- ➤ Are you like any of the characters?
- ➤ Do the charatcers remind you of anyone?
- ➤ Did any of the events ever happen to you?
- ➤ Does the story seem real or not very real?
- ➤ Did you like this story? Why? Why not?

Summarize
- ➤ What's the main idea?
- ➤ What happened first, next, then, after, finally?
- ➤ What was the main message or problem in the story?

Courtesy of Edward Stones

FIGURE 9.30 Dialogic reading. The use of "WH" questions is a core feature of dialogic reading—a reading style whereby adults prompt children and engage them in discussion while reading to them.

organize, and express specific information in response to queries (Cristofaro & Tamis-LeMonda, 2012; Kang, Kim, & Pan, 2009). In particular, questions that go beyond the story such as, "What will happen next?" and "How do you think he's feeling?" challenge children to reason and draw inferences, in contrast to close-ended questions such as, "What color is that?" (Kuchirko et al., 2016; Luo et al., 2014).

Parent Engagement of Children in Math-Related Activities

Children learn a lot from playing with materials that teach concepts around math. They learn about the sizes of objects, how to count the numbers on a board game, and how to orient shapes to fit into puzzles. Home activities such as playing board games and with puzzles predict children's developing number and spatial skills (e.g., Levine et al., 2012; Skwarchuk, Sowinski, & LeFevre, 2014).

✓ **CHECK YOUR UNDERSTANDING 9.23**

1. Define recast, expansion, and dialogic reading.
2. Give examples of parent elaborativeness during book reading, and explain how elaborativeness supports children's narrative skills.
3. What activities would you engage in as a parent if you wished to promote your child's math and spatial skills?

Family Socioeconomic Context of Language, Literacy, and Mathematical Skills

LEARNING OBJECTIVE 9.24 Identify ways that family socioeconomic status might affect children's language, literacy, and math skills.

A family's socioeconomic status (SES) can affect children's language development, literacy, and math skills through effects on parent talk to children and the opportunities children have to engage in activities such as book reading and block play.

Children in low SES households hear fewer words and less grammatically complex language than do their peers from higher SES households (Leffel & Suskind, 2013; Golinkoff et al., 2019). According to the landmark "30-million word gap" study by Betty Hart and Todd Risley (1995) (discussed in depth in Chapter 6), by preschool entry, children from low SES households had vocabularies half the size of children from high SES homes, and by kindergarten fewer than half of children from low SES backgrounds were at grade level in their school readiness skills (Isaacs, 2012). However, the quality of children's home language experiences is not solely determined by the number of words spoken to them. Therefore, researchers simultaneously recognize the need to expand discussion of poverty's potential detrimental influences beyond a 30-million word-gap narrative to considering the many ways that children learn from people around them, including listening in on the conversations of others (Kuchirko, 2019; Sperry, Sperry, & Miller, 2019).

Family SES relates to young children's learning opportunities around math and spatial concepts as well. On average, children from middle-income families have more opportunities to play with blocks and with games that involve numbers and counting than do children from low-income backgrounds, and such experiences relate to children's math skills (Siegler & Ramani, 2009; Verdine et al., 2014a). Training studies that promoted children's play with counting board games in low-income families led to improvements in preschoolers' counting, sometimes after only four 15- to 20-minute sessions (Siegler & Ramani, 2009; Whyte & Bull, 2008).

A disproportionate percentage of children from low-income households are immigrants or children of immigrants, which means they also confront the challenges of learning more than one language. The combination of poverty and dual-language learning status may lead to language delays (National Academy of Sciences, 2017). For example, young Spanish-speaking children from low SES backgrounds have been shown to have poor oral language abilities, and in particular low levels of vocabulary in *both* English and Spanish, which places them at risk for delays in emergent literacy and other school readiness skills. Gaps between the language skills of dual-language learning children and those documented in monolingual children have been found in 4-year-old children continuing through first grade (e.g., Páez, Tabors, & López, 2007). However, having rich language home experiences in their native language of Spanish facilitated learning English in preschool for dual-language learning children from largely low-SES, Spanish-speaking backgrounds (Marchman et al., 2020). Indeed, children reap great benefits from learning two languages, and with the proper supports, they can ultimately become proficient bilinguals.

✓ CHECK YOUR UNDERSTANDING 9.24

1. Identify several ways that poverty may affect children's language development.

Preschool Context of Language, Literacy, and Mathematical Understanding

LEARNING OBJECTIVE 9.25 Identify features that contribute to quality preschool experiences for children.

Most children in the United States attend preschool, making the early classroom context a rich platform for learning. Quality, early childhood programs support cognitive development across multiple areas, and may help buffer the adverse effects of low-stimulating home environments. Economist Greg Duncan and developmentalist Katherine Magnuson evaluated the impacts of preschool on children's cognitive performance, language development, reading, and mathematics by analyzing data across 84 early education programs, including programs such as Head Start early education (Duncan & Magnuson, 2013). Children across the programs averaged cognitive gains equal to four months of additional learning beyond what they would have achieved in the absence of early childhood education. Furthermore, providing children with targeted, high-quality instructional practices in preschool helps reduce disparities in the language development of dual-language learning children from poor homes (Peisner-Feinberg et al., 2014). Indeed, the benefits of preschool are especially pronounced in the context of high-quality teacher instruction and classroom curricula (Weiland & Yoshikawa, 2013).

Teacher Quality

Teacher quality is one of the most important aspects of school quality. Children show large gains in cognitive skills when teachers provide frequent, warm, and responsive interactions; encourage children to speak; and offer opportunities to elaborate on topics (Burchinal et al., 2008). In fact, the National Association for the Education of Young Children (NAEYC, 2019) has developed a set of standards to guide quality teaching that include

- developing positive relationships with children that involve consistent and predictable care, frequent interactions, acceptance of children's feelings, and acknowledgement of the capabilities of all children;

- developing and maintaining healthy relationships between teachers and families that include regular and reciprocal communications that are responsive to family diversity;
- supporting children's developing friendships by creating opportunities for children to engage with peers, sustain play, and resolve conflict;
- creating classroom environments that present clear limits and expectations, counter bias, and promote prosocial behaviors among children;
- fostering skills in children that protect them from harm and support their developing relationships with peers and adults;
- sharing information and community resources with families to help them advocate for their children and access necessary support;
- identifying positive ways to handle challenging child behaviors and help children regulate their emotions and manage their behaviors.

literacy-focused preschool curriculum A curriculum that targets opportunities for young children to develop literacy skills through the use of activities that include dialogic reading, phonological awareness activities, and play activities that integrate reading and writing

Big Math for Little Kids (BMLK) A comprehensive math program for young children that promotes emergent math skills characterized through activities focused on number, shape, measurement, and space

Curriculum

What and how much children learn depends on the content of curricula. Well-designed preschool curricula show moderate to strong impacts on children's literacy and math skills (Burchinal, 2018).

In one study, the impacts of a **literacy-focused preschool curriculum** on children's emergent literacy skills were examined across 48 preschools with over 700 children, including ethnically diverse children at risk for educational difficulties. Schools were randomly assigned to either a literacy-focused curriculum or a condition in which teachers just continued with the curriculum they typically followed. The literacy-based curriculum included small-group and shared reading episodes with an emphasis on "WH" questions, vocabulary teaching involving word sounds and meanings, picture puzzles, and teaching of print concepts like letter names and sounds using pictures, letters, and writing. Children who received the literacy-focused curriculum showed modest gains in oral language, phonological awareness, and print and knowledge skills, three key ingredients of early literacy (Lonigan et al., 2011).

Preschool curricula have also been designed to promote emergent math skills. One such curriculum, **Big Math for Little Kids (BMLK)** is designed for 4- and 5-year-olds. Activities and stories in the curriculum target children's abilities to solve problems that involve numbers, shapes, patterns, logical reasoning, measurement, operations on numbers, and space. A study of 750 children found that BMLK children showed higher math skills than did controls (Presser et al., 2015). Similarly, a math-based curriculum for young children entitled Building Blocks promoted children's early math skills, and those skills persisted into elementary school (Watts et al., 2018) (**FIGURE 9.31**).

FIGURE 9.31 Big Math for Little Kids and Building Blocks Curriculum. Early childhood curricula such as Big Math for Little Kids (BMLK) and Building Blocks aim to promote children's early math skills. BMLK targets children's thinking and problem solving in mathematics (numbers, shapes, patterns, logical reasoning, measurement, operations on numbers, and space). Building Blocks similarly aims to support children's early math skills and the intervention has been shown to support math skills into elementary school.

✓ CHECK YOUR UNDERSTANDING 9.25

1. List the features associated with high quality teaching.
2. Provide examples of preschool curricula shown to yield demonstrable gains in children's emergent literacy and math.

Cultural Context of Language, Literacy, and Mathematical Understanding

LEARNING OBJECTIVE 9.26 Describe how cultural context might influence children's experiences and development in areas of language, literacy, and mathematics.

The unique practices of cultural communities shape children's language, literacy and math development. Consider the language interactions and conversations typical of many children in the United States. Children talk about their days at school, trips to the zoo, and discuss past and upcoming plans with family and friends. They create elaborate stories during play, count toys and objects, name the colors of things, and talk about what time they have to go to sleep.

U.S. language practices would be completely foreign to Pirahã children of the Amazon in Brazil because language is constrained in ways that make talk about the past and certain concepts implausible. The Pirahã language has few words to express time and does not contain numbers or terms for quantification (Gordon, 2004). Its phonemic inventory is the smallest in the world, being limited to eight consonants and three vowels. Color terms, relative tenses, and any kind of created myth or fiction are absent. Individual or collective stories about the past can be traced back to at most two generations. Characteristics of the Pirahã language are thought to reflect the importance attributed to a person's immediate (rather than past or future) experiences (Everett et al., 2005). As a result, unlike U.S. preschoolers, Pirahã children do not reflect on the past, talk about the future, or ask about time.

Book Reading and Reminiscing across Cultural Communities

Cultural practices around book reading and storytelling differ across communities. As we learned, parents from European American middle-income families in the United States actively involve children in the creation and telling of stories through questioning and encouraging participation (Melzi, 2000; Wahler & Castlebury, 2002). Yet, this style of talk might be culturally specific. Parents from Chinese, Norwegian, and Latinx communities are more likely to control the conversation, expecting children to attend and listen rather than actively contribute (Aukrust, 2004; Melzi & Caspe, 2005; Wang, Leichtman, & Davies, 2000).

Moreover, the *content* of parent-child narratives—namely, which aspects of stories parents highlight and elaborate upon—differs across cultural communities. For example, during book sharing narratives and conversations about the past, Chinese mothers from China and the United States talked about their young children's behaviors and actions, and the consequences of those actions, whereas European American mothers talked about children's thoughts and feelings (Doan & Wang, 2010; Fivush & Wang, 2005). Differences in narrative content may reflect cultural emphases on social norms around behavior (Chinese) versus the personal self (United States). U.S. mothers of European American backgrounds may view language as a tool to express individuality, whereas Chinese mothers might view language as a tool to guide actions and instill norms around the proper ways to behave (Hansen, 1983).

Notably, cultural differences in narrative content relate to how children describe themselves to others. European American and Chinese immigrant mothers and their 3-year-olds were observed as they reminisced about positive and negative past events. European American mothers and their children referred to internal states more frequently than did Chinese mothers and children. In turn, European American children were more likely than were Chinese children to describe their personal traits and characteristics to an examiner during interviews (Wang, Doan, & Song, 2010).

Oral Storytelling across Cultural Communities

Many communities within and outside the United States maintain a rich oral tradition of storytelling as a way to teach children about their culture. Shirley Bryce Heath documented this type of storytelling in certain cultures. She wrote about an African American community in the southeastern United

States where children rarely had books or access to literacy-based materials (Heath & Street, 2008). Adults did not read to their children or expect younger children to sit still and listen when older children tried to read to them. However, adults often shared stories about experiences during conversations with children, and when they did, they asked young children many analytical questions that called for comparisons ("What's that like?"), origin of information ("Where'd you get that from?"), or reasons for actions ("How come you did that?") during conversations. Thus, rather than tutoring children directly, adults engaged in oral exercises that encouraged children to learn various concepts.

The tradition of oral storytelling extends to many communities around the globe, including Australian aboriginal communities, such as the Pitjantjatjara (Klapproth, 2009). Although the British introduced literacy when colonizing the Pitjantjatjara, different forms of oral storytelling, ranging from the telling of stories during everyday activities among small groups of women and children to the messages shared during formal sacred ritual ceremonies, have remained a central vehicle for transmitting cultural knowledge. The storytelling routines of the Australian aboriginal people often take place in particular places that are connected to the story. For example, adults and children of mixed ages may participate in a storytelling event near a waterhole on their homeland. When telling the story, the adults might point at markings in the ground and the rocks to indicate the truth of their stories and the importance of looking after their land to preserve their cultural identity.

Cultural Context of Language Features: Associations to Math and Spatial Cognition

The Pirahã example at the section opening illustrates how languages differ in the concepts they communicate, which in turn influences how people think about their worlds. The ways that numbers are named in a language offers a compelling example of how language influences children's math cognition. Consider, for example, differences between Chinese and English words for numbers. English numbers, such as "eleven" and "twelve," tell a child nothing about what the number means in a base-10 system—that is, that eleven represents 10 + 1 and that twelve represents 10 + 2. In contrast, Chinese number words are transparent and logical, with words above 10 following consistent rules (Ngan Ng & Rao, 2010). For instance, the Chinese translations of the English numbers eleven, twelve, and thirteen, are "ten-one," "ten- two," and "ten-three." Additionally, the Chinese language uses number concepts in words such as days and months, which are referred to as weekday number 1, weekday number 2, month number 1, month number 2, and so forth (Zhang & Zhou, 2003). Because Chinese number words map directly to the numbers they represent, Chinese-speaking children may have an advantage in learning mathematics (Ngan Ng & Rao, 2010). By around 4 years of age, Chinese-speaking children surpass English-speaking children in how high they can count (Miller et al., 1995).

The graphics of Chinese written language may also challenge children to learn an intricate system of notation. Compared with the largely linear, left-to-right writing system of English, Chinese characters are complex, and writing requires strokes in all four directions. The finger and hand movements associated with writing result in brain activation in the visual association cortex of preschoolers (James, 2010), which sparks questions about whether and how writing Chinese might stimulate neural systems in the brain that support math learning (**FIGURE 9.32**).

芸 — Art
鶴 — Crane
働 — Work
禅 — Zen
家族 — Family

福 — Fortune
茶 — Tea
美 — Beauty
富 — Rich
親切 — Kindness

水 — Water
裸 — Nude
力 — Power
健 — Health
楽園 — Paradise

栄 — Prosperity
賢 — Intelligent
心 — Hearth
愛 — Love
平和 — Harmony

神 — God
序 — Beginning
魚 — Fish

© gayekosan/Shutterstock.com

FIGURE 9.32 Cultural differences in learning mathematics. The graphics of Chinese written language challenge children to learn an intricate system of notation that requires strokes in all four directions and may result in different brain activation patterns that support math.

Mathematical Practices across Cultural Communities

Many children in the United States and other technological societies are surrounded by educational television programs, number books, blocks, puzzles, and other learning toys that help prepare them for the math they will encounter in later schooling. Yet, these experiences would be very foreign to children in rural, isolated, or small communities around the globe where advanced education is not commonly available.

Consider children living in the Tsimané community, an indigenous farming-foraging group of the Bolivian rainforest in which many adults have no formal education and little or no knowledge of basic math. Steven Piantadosi and colleagues investigated the development of basic numeracy skills such as early counting and understanding cardinality in the Tsimané (Piantadosi, Jara-Ettinger, & Gibson, 2014). They tested children 3–12 years of age (and adults too) on math problems traditionally used to examine early childhood skills in industrialized communities. For instance, researchers asked children to move a specific number of coins from one-half of a white paper to another, with the number of coins to be moved ranging from one to eight. The Tsimané children's number skills were substantially delayed relative to children from the United States, Russia, and Japan. However, the sequence of children's learning paralleled that of children from technological societies. For example, Tsimané children learned the first three or four number words before they fully understood how counting works, just like U.S. children. Thus, although cultural context might affect the *timing* of skill onsets, the developmental progression around learning numbers may be universal.

Notably, a researcher need not travel across the world to observe cultural differences in parents' practices around math. Ethnic differences are common in U.S. communities. U.S. mothers from low-SES Latinx, African American, and Chinese backgrounds were given a set of blocks that contained numbers and math symbols (+, =) and letters and pictures. An examiner instructed mothers to play with their preschool children, and then observed the concepts they chose to teach their children. Low-SES Chinese immigrant mothers taught symbolic math-related concepts most frequently and Latinx immigrant mothers least, which aligns with cultural disparities in children's math skills in the United States (Tamis-LeMonda et al., 2013).

✓ CHECK YOUR UNDERSTANDING 9.26

1. How might the language a child speaks affect their math skills?
2. How has research on the Tsimané culture illuminated cultural similarities and differences in children's math learning?

Developmental Cascades

It is easy to imagine how young children's cognitive skills can instigate wide-sweeping reverberations across time and developmental domains. In the sections that follow, you will see that young children's cognitive development paves the way for later school performance and social relationships.

Cascades to Academic Domains

Consider what schooling would be like for a child who finds it difficult to sit still and pay attention to the teacher, hold and manipulate information in working memory, and control impulses. Indeed, executive functioning is critical to performance in school, especially in mathematics (Cragg & Gilmore, 2014). Math requires children to hold and manipulate different pieces of information in working memory while executing parts of a problem. Children must inhibit less sophisticated but more familiar strategies in favor of advanced but difficult strategies, for example, by suppressing the urge to count with all their fingers and instead adding the smaller number to the larger number (**FIGURE 9.33**). They must shift attention among parts of a problem and different procedures, such as attending to the numbers they are reciting and the objects they are counting.

Consequently, it is reasonable to expect associations between children's executive function skills and math performance, which is exactly what researchers find. Three- and 4-year-old children who perform well on executive functioning measures such as inhibitory control and working memory show strong early math skills relative to their peers in preschool and kindergarten (Blair & Razza, 2007; Bull et al., 2011; Clark et al., 2014). Moreover, executive functioning skills in early childhood predict *growth* in mathematical skills over time (McClelland et al., 2014).

Similarly, school-related tasks require children to understand what the teacher is talking about and formulate and communicate ideas in oral and written forms. Therefore, children with strong language and narrative skills do well concurrently and over time in many academic areas, including knowledge about print, ability to identify letters, reading and spelling, and math (e.g., Cristofaro & Tamis-LeMonda, 2012; Dickinson et al., 2003).

Children reap long-term benefits when they are equipped with math and reading skills early in development. Researchers integrated data from six longitudinal studies following thousands of children, and found that math and reading skills of young children at school entry predicted their skills in reading and math years later (Duncan et al., 2007). Moreover, long-term associations were seen for boys and girls from high and low SES backgrounds, indicating that prediction from early skills to later academics maintains regardless of a child's sex or family background.

Much developmental research confirms the importance of early math skills for later school performance. Mathematical proficiency at school entry predicts children's math skills years later (Libertus, Feigenson, & Halberda, 2013; Starr, Libertus, & Brannon, 2013), with school math performance being the strongest determinant of whether a person will enter a STEM discipline in adulthood (e.g., Wai, Lubinski, & Benbow, 2009). Similarly, children's early spatial skills predicted children's achievement across several scientific disciplines (Newcombe, 2010).

FIGURE 9.33 Math requires children to hold and efficiently manipulate different pieces of information in working memory while executing parts of a problem.   Children must inhibit less sophisticated but more familiar strategies in favor of advanced but difficult strategies, for example, by suppressing the urge to count with all their fingers.

Cascades to Social Domains

Children's understanding of other people grows tremendously just around the time that their social networks expand to include friends at school and in the neighborhood. In turn, developments in social cognition work together with language skills to shape children's interactions with peers. Reciprocally, social interactions further affect children's social cognition and language development. Here, we illustrate cascading effects of young children's language development and theory of mind on friendships and moral reasoning.

Language and Social Competence

Language skills are essential for social competence. Language enables children to approach and talk with friends, sympathize with a distressed peer, and use emotional language effectively, such as when a child acknowledges that a friend is "angry" or "sad" (Monopoli & Kingston, 2012). And so, much evidence confirms the role of language in young children's social relationships. Kindergarten children with strong receptive and expressive language skills displayed high social competence toward their peers, as rated by their teachers (Longoria et al., 2009). Conversely, children with deficits in language sometimes struggle in social relationships because of difficulties in controlling emotions, initiating conversations, and responding appropriately to other children's requests to play (e.g., Cohen & Mendez, 2009; Fujiki, Brinton, & Clarke, 2002).

Interestingly, children with high language skills sometimes engage in negative social behaviors, such as relational aggression. Relational aggression is seen when children display manipulative and calculated behaviors meant to hurt or control others, such as when children tell friends they will not play unless the friend does what is wanted. Preschool children with advanced language skills are more likely to engage in relational aggression than are children with less advanced skills (Bonica et al., 2003; Estrem, 2005). Why might language skill support relational aggression? One reason is because relational aggression requires verbal sophistication and causal reasoning, as seen in statements such as "You can't come play with us if you don't do what I want."

Theory of Mind and Social Relationships

To maintain friendships, children must recognize that their friends and classmates don't always want to play the same game or like the same thing. Essentially, they must understand that goals and viewpoints differ from person to person. Similarly, prosocial behaviors such as empathy and sympathy require children to understand others' feelings.

Indeed, children who understand others' minds are more capable of positive social interactions than are children without such an understanding (Hughes & Leekam, 2004). For example, 5-year-old children who had more advanced theory of mind when they entered school were more likely to be accepted and less likely to be rejected by their peers two years later than were children with low theory of mind scores (Caputi et al., 2012). Children's prosocial behaviors help explain the connection between theory of mind and peer acceptance and rejection: Young children with strong theory-of-mind skills behave prosocially, which strengthens their acceptance by peers.

Theory of mind also allows children to consider the underlying intentions of others' actions in moral dilemmas. Indeed, connections between children's developing theory of mind and moral judgments are well established (e.g., Killen, Mulvey, & Hitti, 2013). For example, an examiner told 2.5- to 4-year-old children about a transgressor who pushed a child off a swing by accident because the transgressor was trying not to fall. Children were then asked what should be done to the transgressor. Children with relatively more advanced false-belief scores considered the underlying intention of the transgressor's action and therefore were more likely to forgive the transgressor than were children with relatively lower scores (Smetana et al., 2012).

■ CLOSING THOUGHTS

Preventing Inequities at the Starting Gate

Consider the chapter's opening on inequities at the starting gate—what it means to begin a race when contenders have uneven advantages. Consider next, the ending section on how cognitive skills early in life, even before formal schooling begins, can cascade across domains and developmental time. You might begin to wonder: Does how well a young child attends, how fast a child processes information, how well a child understands others' minds, how many words a child knows, or how much a child understands numbers truly bestow an advantage on that child for years to come? Conversely, do early delays in cognitive development truly confer later disadvantage? You might also wonder about what can be done to change things, to perhaps equalize the starting gates. Let's reflect on three points that offer some insight.

First, by definition, development means change. Essentially, a core goal of this book is to describe the engines of change from the prenatal period through adolescence. As you will see, every day, week, month, and year of development welcomes new skills and new opportunities to right what is going wrong, or (unfortunately) derail what is going right. Thus, although the skills that children have developed by the time they start school provide a platform for later developing skills, countless experiences continue to weigh in throughout life.

Second, any longitudinal study of developmental cascades involves many variables that work together to explain long-term associations. A child may show problems in attention or information processing because of insensitive caregiving that fails to create opportunities for the child to participate in activities that scaffold infants' abilities to attend. Or, a child might live in a chaotic household where the child's efforts to attend to tasks are interrupted by loud noises outside the home and an incessant TV blaring from within. If the less-than-adequate social and environmental experiences of the child persist, early problems have the potential to snowball into later cognitive difficulties. But, this also means that altering one or more environmental variables has the potential to change a child's course of development.

This brings us to the final point. The rapid changes and plasticity of infancy and early childhood make early development a time of unsurpassed potential. Programs that educate and support parents, and programs and interventions that identify and help children at cognitive risk early on, can go a long way in establishing a foundation to cognitive success. In fact, interventions in early childhood demonstrate stronger impacts than costlier programs at later points in development, in part because cognitive and academic problems are difficult to remediate once they have solidified.

Thus, if you bear in mind the ideas that change is a lifelong reality, that many variables matter at all points in development, and that early childhood is an opportune time, you can be an engine of positive change. Perhaps you might educate parents or someone you know about the immense value of sensitive, stimulating interactions for children's cognitive growth. Or you might remind a caregiver to shut off the TV to allow a child to focus on building with some blocks. You might encourage a caregiver to count blocks and help the child identify which block goes where. Indeed, by supporting learning in the moment, people can ensure that children are well-positioned to learn over time.

The Developmentalist's Toolbox

Method	Purpose	Description
Measuring children's cognitive development		
Scale model problems	To test children's understanding of dual representation	The experimenter hides a miniature toy in a scale model of a life-size room in front of the child. The child is then asked to find the large version of the toy in the life-size room.
The three mountains task	To test children's skills at taking the perspective of others	Piaget used this task to examine whether young children could take the perspective of other people, by seating them in front of a display, across from a doll, and asking children to describe what the doll saw.
Conservation tasks	To test children's understanding that an entity remains the same in mass or quantity even after superficial changes	Children are asked whether superficial transformations of an object (such as rolling a ball of clay into a snakelike object) change its mass or amount.
Class inclusion problems	To test children's understanding of superordinate-subordinate relations in a group of entities	Examiner asks children to determine which group has more items—a full set of items, such as all beads (superordinate) or a subset of items, such as red beads (subordinate).
Stroop tasks (examples: go/no-go; day-night)	To assess inhibitory control	Children must suppress a dominant response in favor of a correct response. For instance, children are instructed to say "day" when presented with a picture of a moon and "night" when presented with a picture of a sun.

(Continued)

The Developmentalist's Toolbox (continued)

Method	Purpose	Description
Measuring children's cognitive development (continued)		
Tower of London task	To assess a child's ability in planning	A task that requires children to rearrange a set of objects by moving them, one at a time, from their initial configuration to a configuration that matches a display. Researchers vary the number of moves required to complete the task (and thus task difficulty).
Memory span tests	To measure the capacity of short-term memory	Children are read a list of items and asked to immediately repeat them back to see how many they can retain in working memory.
False memory or suggestibility studies	To explore suggestibility and its role in the formation of false memory	Children are presented with false information about an event they witnessed or experienced, such as being told they had been lost in a mall. The extent to which they endorse the false memory reflects their level of suggestibility.
Wug test	To assess a child's understanding of grammatical rules, such as plurals	Originally designed by Berko Gleason to examine children's understanding of plurals, children are asked to respond with the word for a fill-in sentence such as "This is a wug. Now there are two ____." The wug test has since been used to test other aspects of children's grammatical development such as possessives, past tense, and so forth.
Reliability-trustworthiness studies	To examine children's social-cognitive skills in terms of whether they consider another person's knowledge and/or trustworthiness in their interactions with that person	Children watch two people name objects, one correctly and one incorrectly. In test trials, the experimenter assesses which person the child will turn to for information, or whose statements they will accept or trust.
Tools of the Mind curriculum	Activities that encourage the development of executive functioning in preschoolers	This curriculum has been implemented in preschool classes to promote children's executive functioning through various activities including pretend play.
Measuring children's social-cognitive development and language, literacy, and mathematical understanding		
False-belief tasks	To assess a child's theory of mind	In a classic false-belief task, children are shown a character (Maxi) who places chocolate in a cabinet and leaves the room. The chocolate is moved by a second character and then Maxi returns. Children are asked where Maxi will look for his chocolate. Accurately stating Maxi will look in the wrong (original) location indicates false-belief understanding.
Literacy-based curricula	Programs promoting emerging literacy skills	Curricula include small-group and shared reading episodes with an emphasis on "WH" questions, vocabulary teaching (including word sounds and meanings), picture puzzles, and teaching of print concepts (letter names and sounds) through the use of pictures, letters, and writing.
Big Math for Little Kids (BMLK)	A comprehensive program for 4- and 5-year-olds aimed at promoting early math skills	BMLK includes activities and stories in the curriculum, targeting children's thinking and problem solving about number, shape, pattern, logical reasoning, measurement, operations on numbers, and space.

Chapter Summary

Piaget and the Preoperational Stage

- According to Piaget, during the preoperational stage children are capable of mental representation, but are unable to perform logical mental operations.
- By 3 years of age, children are capable of dual representation, understanding that something can both be itself and stand for something else.
- Children's growing representational skills allow them to engage in pretend and fantasy play, and some children create imaginary friends.
- Piaget and followers documented several cognitive limitations of preoperational thinking, including egocentrism, inability to make the appearance-reality distinction, animistic thinking, causal understanding, and lack of conservation of quantities.
- Contemporary research challenges some of Piaget's claims and yields new insights into young children's emerging cognitive skills.
- Children's cultural experiences affect cognitive skills such as conservation and classification.

Cognitive Development from an Information-Processing Perspective

- Young children show improvements in executive functioning skills, in areas of inhibitory control, cognitive flexibility, and working memory. Executive function skills also support children's abilities in planning, strategy use, and monitoring of performance.
- Semantic memory and episodic memory are two forms of declarative memory that grow in complexity and organization over early childhood.
- Development in semantic memory (sometimes referred to as a child's knowledge base) helps account for improvements in working memory and processing speed.
- Infantile amnesia refers to the difficulty people have in remembering events from the first years of life, and has been explained with various accounts, including the impact of forgetting on early memories.
- Episodic memory improves in complexity and detail over early childhood.
- Young children's memories are especially vulnerable to suggestion and misleading information, which has implications for children's accounts in eyewitness testimony.
- Family poverty can impair children's executive functioning through effects on the brain.
- School curricula, such as Tools of the Mind, may strengthen children's executive function skills.
- Chinese children have been shown to outperform U.S. children on measures of executive functioning, which might be explained by cultural values and practices.

Evaluating People's Knowledge and Expertise

- Children show improvement in their social-cognitive skills around understanding of others' knowledge and expertise, and are selective in whom they turn to for information and help.

Theory of Mind

- Children show gains in theory-of-mind skills around 4–5 years of age, as revealed in their understanding that people can hold "false beliefs" or mental states that differ from reality and what children themselves believe and know.
- Developmental changes in children's theory-of-mind skills have been attributed to children's changing theories about the world (the theory-theory), changing executive functioning skills, and brain development.

Contexts of Social-Cognitive Development

- Individual differences among children on theory-of-mind tasks are influenced by factors in the family (mental state talk, the presence of siblings).
- Children's school experiences, including interactions with peers, interactions with teachers, and literacy activities support developments in theory of mind.

Growing Language Skills

- During early childhood, children improve in the range and accuracy of their speech sounds, vocabulary size, grammar, and pragmatics.
- Children's sentence construction grows in complexity as they use parts of speech to modify word meanings and combine separate thoughts (clauses) in sentences.
- Children learn standard grammar rules before they learn exceptions, resulting in the overregularization of grammatical rules.
- Young children grow in the pragmatics of language as they learn norms of conversations.

Literacy and Mathematical Understanding

- Emergent literacy skills rely on oral language and code-related skills, the latter referring to learning the sounds of letters and recognizing letters and words in print.
- Emergent math skills include counting, discriminating quantities, and discerning patterns. In learning number words, children show a clear developmental progression. Spatial skills are likewise pivotal to math learning.

Contexts: Language, Literacy, and Mathematical Understanding

- The amount and diversity of parent talk to children, children's engagement in book reading and shared narratives, and family socioeconomic status relate to young children's language and literacy skills.
- Parents' elaborations in narratives and engagement in dialogic reading support children's language and literacy skills.
- Parent math talk and opportunities provided to children to play with puzzles, blocks, and board games support children's math skills.

- Teacher quality and curriculum are two features of school contexts that support children's language, literacy, and math developments.
- Cultural communities differ in their language and literacy practices, routines around book sharing and oral storytelling, and ways that languages encode concepts in math. These cultural differences shape children's literacy and math skills.

Developmental Cascades

- Young children's language and literacy skills relate to current and future cognitive and language skills and academic performance in areas of reading, writing, attention, and mathematics.
- Early childhood skills in language support social cognition and social relationships.
- Social-cognitive skills in early childhood shape a variety of social behaviors, including making and keeping friends, moral reasoning, persuasion, lying, and deception.

Thinking Like a Developmentalist

1. A group of 5- and 8-year-old children differ on their ability to conserve number. Your task is to figure out what might explain these age-related differences. One hypothesis is that the younger children's lack of conservation of number is explained by a general inability to manipulate multiple representations at the same time (as in Piaget's idea of young children's problems in centration and tendency to focus on one dimension only). A second hypothesis is that younger children have problems with inhibitory control. A third hypothesis is that younger children's problem with conservation is explained by working memory. What tasks would you use to test these three hypotheses and how would you design your study?

2. You wonder whether children's memories about a class trip to a museum can be altered, and which strategies are particularly influential in changing their memories. You also want to see whether you can alter children's feelings to be especially positive about the class mother who joined them on the trip. What would you do to alter their memories and thoughts about the class mother? Which specific strategies would you test?

3. A researcher hypothesizes that individual differences among children in their social-cognitive abilities (in particular, how well they understand others' minds) might relate to the clarity and organization of a story they tell another person about their trip to the zoo. Notably, children are informed that the person listening had never been to a zoo. How would the researcher test this hypothesis, and which aspects of the child's story might the researcher assess?

4. During the COVID-19 pandemic, you learn that parents are feeling stressed because their young children are unable to attend preschool, and, as a result, parents have substantially increased the time they permit children to watch screens to occupy their children's days. However, parents are very worried about their children's early learning during this time and the fact that their children are not getting opportunities to be educated in preschool. They ask what they can do to support their young children. As a developmental expert, you are asked to give a webinar to parents around their role in young children's learning. What points would you make and what suggestions would you offer parents who are clearly stressed but have their children's best interests in mind?

Emotional and Social Development in Early Childhood

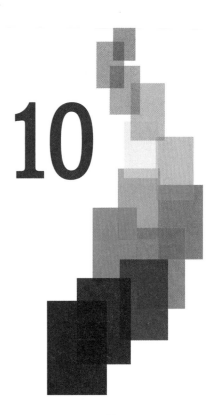

10

Drawing by Minxin Cheng from a photo by Chayene Rafaela on Unsplash

Playgrounds are stages where young children have the opportunity to showcase their talents and limitations in social and emotional areas (**FIGURE 10.1**). Some of my most precious memories are days spent with my children at our local playground. We would dump our toys by the sandbox, and I'd sit on the ledge, wondering whether it was wise to let my children play in the sand that was host to unimagined germs. I would then retreat to a nearby bench to observe the dramas of social-emotional development unfold.

Because I was seated in the "early childhood" wing of the playground, I witnessed firsthand the fast-paced action and excitement that comes from too much energy in the somewhat clumsy bodies of young children who are simultaneously enthralled and intimidated by the presence of peers—a chase through the tunnels of slides, a toy held out to share, a gentle hand encouraging an ignored child to join a game of hide-and-go-seek. These photo-op moments were interspersed with pushes and pulls, name-calling and tattling, screams and wails. When conflicts arose, children would huddle close to their best friends, or run over to their caregivers, seeking reassurance and intervention from the people they trusted and loved.

I also observed the natural segregation of children along gender lines, as boys and girls engaged in highly stereotyped forms of play. Boys leapt from platforms of slides, wielding sticks and pretending to be characters from superhero movies. Girls sat cross-legged in the sandbox, molding cupcakes for a tea party, sometimes wearing frilly dresses and princess crowns. Parents would often groan about their children's fixedness around gender, and how powerless they felt when they

FIGURE 10.1 Children playing in sandbox at playground.   Children's interactions with other children at playgrounds and other peer-group settings reveal their skills and limitations in social and emotional areas.

tried to coax their children to try out new things. When I futilely attempted to get Brittany to *please wear pants to the park*, she crossed her arms across her chest, and refused to budge. When I bought dolls for Christopher and Michael they threw them around like footballs.

This chapter examines young children's growth in emotional and social domains, spanning emotion understanding, emotion expression and regulation, attachment, social relationships, self-identity, and morality. We will see that the playgrounds and places of early childhood are the stages on which children practice the skills they will one day need to integrate into their communities. And, we will delve into cascading influences across domains and time, learning how wrong turns along the route to social competence can lead to rejection and psychological pain, and conversely, how positive growth paves the way to later well-being and school success.

■ *Emotional Development*

Brittany loved the game Candyland® as a young child. It came with cards that would move players along a board of treats, and the winner was the first to arrive at Candyland. The catch was that sometimes you chose a card that sent you back to the start. One day, while playing with her friend, Brittany chose the dreaded card. She threw it down and refused to return to the start, insisting the card was for her friend. The game erupted in name-calling and escalating emotions. Brittany couldn't understand why her friend would not take the card—after all it was Brittany's game and she was in charge. Her friend said she'd never play with Brittany again. I explained to Brittany that she must play fairly, but my words went unheeded. A few minutes later, everyone made up and play continued.

Brittany's behavior illustrates young children's limited abilities to understand and regulate emotions. As we will see, early childhood is when children gradually grow in their emotion understanding and regulation on the way to becoming emotionally competent individuals who are able to recognize, interpret, and respond constructively to the emotions of self and others.

Emotion Understanding

Emotion understanding involves recognizing emotions and their meanings and identifying the causes and consequences of emotions in everyday situations. A child might understand that a peer who is sitting alone in a corner feels sad or that a friend is excited for an upcoming birthday party. The child may figure out how to console her lonely friend or share the joy of the anticipated party with her excited friend. Let's see how children grow in their emotion understanding during early childhood.

Complex and Mixed Emotions

LEARNING OBJECTIVE 10.1 Describe developments in children's abilities to discriminate among complex emotions and understand mixed emotions.

Young children display an impressive understanding of emotions relative to toddlers. They can accurately identify and name emotions. They can group and label emotions in photographs, videos, and stories. They can match emotions on faces to their labels on **emotion matching tasks**. They understand the connection among desires and emotions. However, children's understanding of emotions improves gradually, and it takes some time for children to grasp the nuances of complex and mixed emotions (Farina, Albanese, & Pons, 2007; Zajdel et al., 2013) (**FIGURE 10.2**).

emotion matching tasks A task in which children are asked to label the emotion of a facial expression

One of the first things that children understand is **emotional valence**—whether an emotion is positive or negative. Children typically talk about feeling "good" or "bad" rather than reporting subtle variations in emotions (Fabes et al., 1991; Michalson & Lewis, 1985). When children first begin to distinguish among emotions of the same valence, they do so for emotions that differ in level of arousal (Widen & Russell, 2008). For example, anger is a negative emotion that contains high arousal whereas sadness is a negative emotion that contains low arousal (**FIGURE 10.3**). Children can distinguish between emotions at extremes of arousal, like anger and sadness, before they can distinguish between negative emotions that are similar in arousal, such as sadness and disappointment. In fact, children continue to develop the ability to differentiate among emotions that are similar in valence *and* arousal throughout childhood, with such distinctions being especially challenging for self-conscious emotions such as embarrassment and guilt (e.g., Widen & Russell, 2010).

Young children also improve in their understanding of **mixed emotions**—that a person can feel more than one emotion at a time. For example, researchers showed 3- to 5-year-old children video clips of a robot named Rodney who moved away from his family to pursue his dreams. The video clips portrayed Rodney's excitement about the future, but also his bittersweet goodbye to his parents before departing. Few 3-year-olds reported on Rodney's mixed emotions; however, most 5-year-olds recognized Rodney's conflicted feelings and reported that they also felt mixed emotions after watching the film (Smith, Glass, & Fireman, 2015). Similarly, 5-year-olds who viewed *The Little Mermaid* reported

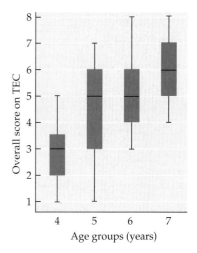

FIGURE 10.2 Emotion matching tasks. When examiners test children of different ages on their understanding of emotions using several tasks, they observe striking developmental improvements throughout early childhood. The figure shows the scores of children of different ages on a measure of total emotion understanding/competence (TEC). Each rectangular box shows the range of scores for children in the 25th–75th quartiles, and the lines represent the lower and upper scores. Horizontal lines in the boxes represent children's median scores. As shown, children's emotion understanding increases with age, with 4-year-olds showing the lowest performance. (After E. Farina et al. 2007. *Psychol Lang Comm* 11: 3–19.)

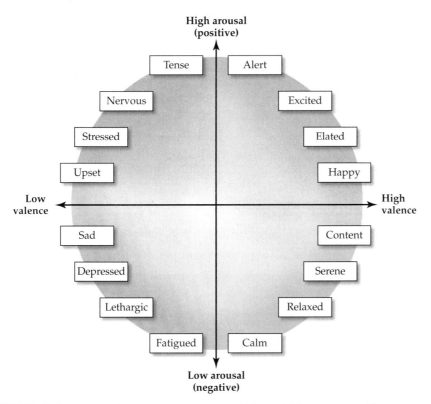

FIGURE 10.3 Distinguishing among emotions. When children learn to differentiate among different emotions of the same valence (i.e., negative versus positive emotions), they first do so for emotions that differ in level of arousal (such as sad versus upset), and only later distinguish between emotions of the same valence and similar arousal levels (such as sad versus depressed). (After J. Russell and L. Barrett. 1999. *J Pers Soc Psychol* 76: 805-819; L. Barrett and J. Russell. 1998. *J Pers Soc Psychol* 74: 967–984. Copyright © 1998 by American Psychological Association. Reproduced with permission.)

emotional valence The affective quality of an emotion as positive ("good") or negative ("bad")

mixed emotions The feeling of two or more emotions at the same time mixed emotions: They understood that the mermaid Ariel achieved her dream of becoming a human at the movie's end, yet also recognized that she had to leave behind her past life and the people she loved (Larsen, To, & Fireman, 2007).

✓ CHECK YOUR UNDERSTANDING 10.1

1. In what ways do children's emotional skills improve on the foundations laid out in infancy?
2. What roles do emotional arousal and valence play in young children's understanding of emotions?

The Causes and Consequences of Emotions

LEARNING OBJECTIVE 10.2 Discuss evidence that children understand the causes and consequences of people's emotions.

With age, children grow to appreciate that emotions occur for a reason. People smile or frown because something made them feel that way, and for the most part, emotions have consequences. And so, the task for children is to figure out what caused an emotion and where the emotion might lead.

emotion vignettes Stories that researchers use to test children's understanding of the causes and consequences of emotions in which children may be asked how a character feels or why a character feels a certain emotion

Emotion vignettes are commonly used to test what children understand about the causes and consequences of emotions. Researchers present children with stories and ask how a story character may feel and why, or alternatively, they might tell children how a character feels or behaves. They might also ask children to reason about the situation that gave rise to the emotion. Based on such work, researchers have determined that by around 5 years of age, children understand how a specific situation might make a character feel—for example, understanding that after receiving a gift, having a fish die, or having a tower of blocks knocked down by a peer, characters will be happy, sad, or angry (Widen & Russell, 2011) (**FIGURE 10.4**).

Young children can also reason about why a person's emotion has changed from one emotion to another. For example, researchers presented children

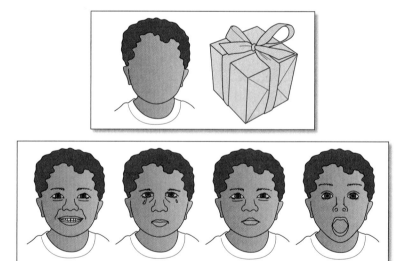

FIGURE 10.4 Understanding the causes of emotions. A common way to test children's understanding of the causes of emotions is to present a picture of a situation, such as receiving a gift (top panel), and then ask children to select which facial expression matches how the person will feel (such as from the bottom panel's four expressions). (After O. Albanese et al. 2006. In *Toward Emotional Competences*, F. Pons et al. [Eds.], pp. 39–53. Aalborg University Press: Aalborg, Denmark. Based on F. Pons and P. L. Harris. 2000. *TEC* [*Test of Emotion Comprehension*]. Oxford University Press: Oxford, United Kingdom.)

with pictures of a character whose face changed from sad to happy or from happy to sad after being given a certain food. Four- and 5-year-olds accurately inferred whether the character wanted a specific food based on changes to the character's facial expressions (Wu & Schultz, 2017). And, when told that someone is angry with another person, 3- to 4-year-old children can predict the consequences of the emotion, for example that an angry child might harm the child who caused the anger (Chalik, Rivera, & Rhodes, 2014).

✓ CHECK YOUR UNDERSTANDING 10.2

1. How might a researcher test whether a child understands the causes of emotions?
2. How might a researcher test whether a child knows what to do to change a person's negative emotion?

Emotion Regulation and Temperament

Emotional development involves much more than understanding emotions. Children must also learn how to regulate their emotions if they are to "keep the lid on" and adapt to expectations at home and in school (Raver et al., 1999). However, young children can be quite intense in their emotional expressions and often struggle with emotional self-regulation (Sulik et al., 2016). It is not uncommon to see preschoolers stomp their feet, exaggerate a frown, and scream "I don't want to go home now!" When young children are upset, they can't simply sit still and calm down (**FIGURE 10.5**). And, when young children want something, they want it *now*. Although all children eventually learn how to cope with emotional challenges, progress is slower for some than for others.

Emotion and Behavior Regulation

LEARNING OBJECTIVE 10.3 Explain how children develop in their ability to delay gratification, and reasons why children show age-related improvement on delay of gratification tasks.

Children begin to learn **display rules**—norms about when, where, and how to express emotions in early childhood. They recognize, for example, that a person should smile even after receiving a disappointing gift (Cole, Zahn-Waxler, & Smith, 1994). However, implementing display rules can be challenging because children's feelings simply take over. Inhibiting behaviors such as yelling at a peer, pulling a toy away, or eating a forbidden treat can be difficult when impulses run strong.

Delay-of-gratification tasks measure whether children can resist an immediate temptation in order to receive a later (often larger) reward and illustrate the difficulties children have in regulating their emotions and behaviors. Over 40 years ago, social psychologist Walter Mischel designed an experiment that has come to be known as the **marshmallow task** (Mischel & Mischel, 1987). An experimenter seated children at a table in front of a tasty marshmallow and instructed them to not touch or eat the marshmallow while the experimenter left the room (**FIGURE 10.6**). If they waited until the experimenter returned, they could have *two* marshmallows. If they couldn't wait, they could ring a bell and the experimenter would return and let them eat the one marshmallow. A camera recorded children's behavior during the experimenter's absence.

So how did children fare on the marshmallow task? Some resisted eating the marshmallow to receive two marshmallows later. Others waited a bit but then caved. And other children popped the marshmallow into

FIGURE 10.5 Problems regulating emotions. Young children struggle with emotional self-regulation. When they are upset, they sometimes have difficulties calming themselves down.

display rules Cultural norms about when, where, and how to express emotions that children learn through social interactions

delay-of-gratification tasks Experiments that measure children's abilities to resist an immediate temptation in order to receive a later (often larger) reward, which shed light on children's emotion regulation

marshmallow task A delay-of-gratification experiment developed by Walter Mischel to test children's ability to not touch or eat a marshmallow as the researcher is out of the room, in order to later receive two marshmallows

FIGURE 10.6 Delay of gratification—the marshmallow task. To measure whether children can resist immediate temptation to receive a later reward, researchers use delay of gratification tasks, such as the marshmallow task developed by Walter Mischel. Examiners instruct children to not touch or eat a treat—Mischel used a marshmallow—while the researcher is in the other room. Then, researchers note the amount of time children are able to wait before touching or eating the treat.

their mouths as soon as the researcher left the room because their desire overwhelmed their ability to delay gratification.

Why do young children find it difficult to delay gratification? Researchers attribute such difficulties to an imbalance between children's motivationally salient "hot" system and primarily cognitive "cool" system in how children react to situations (Metcalfe & Mischel, 1999; Sulik et al., 2016). The hot system is impulsive and emotional and triggered by the temptation to eat the marshmallow. The cool system is rational and based on control and reasoning. Young children presumably fail the delay of gratification task because their hot system overrides their cool system. Older children and adults have a stronger cool system, and so exert more control over their impulses—although, resisting the temptation to eat a chocolate cake is a challenge no matter your age.

With development, children are able to wait somewhat longer for a reward, partly because they learn to implement coping strategies (Grolnick, McMenamy, & Kurowski, 1999; Saarni, 2007). When children ages 18 months to 4 years of age had to wait 8 minutes to receive a gift—a huge amount of time for a young child—toddlers quickly reacted with anger and were unable to shift their attention away from the desired object. By 3 years of age, children engaged in distraction strategies before expressing anger, and their bursts of anger were brief. By 4 years of age, children quickly distracted themselves and did not appear to be angry until later in the session. They used many coping strategies such as looking away from the tempting toy or treat, singing a song (distraction), and telling themselves that by not peeking now they would be more surprised later (reframing) (Cole et al., 2011).

Notably, children's abilities to select effective coping strategies might help them psychologically. Researchers presented preschoolers from Hong Kong with a series of stories about emotionally challenging situations, such as a child who wanted to play but her parents insisted she read and a child who was bullied by her peers. Children were asked to identify the coping strategies that the hypothetical character should deploy. Preschoolers who selected positive coping strategies, such as trying to fix the problem rather than just forgetting about it or getting angry, were less likely to display depressive symptoms as they transitioned to primary school than were children who identified negative coping strategies (Wong & Power, 2019).

✓ CHECK YOUR UNDERSTANDING 10.3

1. What is meant by display rules?
2. What is meant by delay of gratification? How do you test delay of gratification in a preschooler?

Individual Differences in Temperament

LEARNING OBJECTIVE 10.4 Describe the role of temperament in children's ability to regulate their emotions.

Children differ in their abilities to regulate their emotions, whether in a delay task, conflict with friends, or situations that evoke fear and anxiety. Differences among children in emotion regulation can be attributed, at least in part, to temperament (see Chapter 7). Key features of a child's temperament involve their emotional and behavioral reactions to new situations and challenges (Eisenberg et al., 2015; Kagan, Reznick, & Snidman, 1987; Rothbart & Bates, 2006):

- *Highly inhibited or shy children* exhibit a low tolerance for novelty and high levels of fearfulness, which create challenges for regulating emotions—especially fear.

- *Under-controlled children* show difficulties controlling attention, behaviors, and emotions. Some of these children may be exuberant and uninhibited, and thus likely to approach new situations and people. They experience intense pleasure but have difficulties regulating frustration and anger. Under-controlled children may be high in their negative reactions to situations.
- *Well-regulated children* are skilled at controlling emotions, attention, and behaviors. These children are well adjusted and socially competent compared to inhibited and under-controlled children.

Differences among children in temperament are also reflected in their effortful control. The term **effortful control** refers to children's abilities to modulate attention and inhibit behavior, particularly in stressful situations (e.g., Diamond, 2013; Durbin, 2018). Children who are well regulated display strong effortful control: They are able to pursue a goal while inhibiting responses that may interfere with the goal (such as in the marshmallow task described previously). In contrast, children who are under-controlled and have high negative reactions show little effortful control and may display behavior problems when interacting with others (e.g., Delgado et al., 2018). As we will see in the section that follows, contextual influences work together with children's temperament to shape children's responses to everyday stress.

effortful control The ability to modulate attention and inhibit behavior, including in stressful situations

✓ CHECK YOUR UNDERSTANDING 10.4

1. Describe the emotion regulation skills of children classified as (a) highly inhibited, (b) under-controlled, and (c) well regulated.

Contexts of Emotional Development

Although temperament may explain some of the variation among children in emotional development, children learn a lot about emotions from the people around them. Parents, siblings, school, and cultural contexts powerfully shape children's understanding and regulation of emotions.

Parenting Context of Emotional Development

LEARNING OBJECTIVE 10.5 Describe the behaviors of parents that help their children learn about emotions and how to regulate emotions.

Children learn ways to express and regulate their emotions from their caregivers. Parents who sensitively respond to their children's emotions, who show positive emotion regulation themselves, and who encourage children to use language to communicate their feelings help teach children about the meanings of emotions and how to cope with and regulate their reactions to strong feelings (Morris et al., 2017; Perry et al., 2014).

Sensitive Responses to Emotions

Parents' reactions to children's emotions can be supportive or discouraging, with supportive responses promoting children's emotion understanding and regulation and discouraging responses interfering with adjustment (Fabes et al., 2018). **Emotion coaching** refers to the positive socialization of children's emotions, such as when parents accept, empathize with, and validate children's feelings and help children deal with emotionally charged situations (e.g., Fabes et al., 2001; Gottman, Katz, & Hooven, 1997) (**FIGURE 10.7**). When researchers intentionally presented children with a disappointing gift or prize, such as a broken pencil, they found that mothers' emotion

emotion coaching The positive socialization of children's emotions, as when caregivers validate children's feelings and offer coping strategies in emotionally stressful situations

FIGURE 10.7 Emotion coaching. Parents can support children's emotional development by acknowledging the feelings that children have when facing emotionally charged situations and by helping children to learn about and use positive coping strategies.

coaching helped children regulate their reactions. Mothers who refocused their children's attention, for example, by talking about something fun that they might do later, or reframed the situation, for example, by saying, "Although it's broken, we can go home and glue it back together!" reduced children's anger and sadness at receiving the disappointing prize (Morris et al., 2011).

Emotion talk is another way that parents teach children about emotions. The more that parents communicate with young children about feelings and thoughts, the more they support their children's emotion understanding (Brown & Dunn, 1996; Denham, Zoller, & Couchoud, 1994). Conversations about feelings and mental states help children learn about emotional expressions, situations, and causes; provide children with space to reflect on and evaluate their feelings; and teach children ways to express and regulate emotions.

To illustrate the connection between parent emotion talk and children's emotional development, Paul Harris and colleagues examined mothers' talk about emotions and children's understanding of the story *Little Red Riding Hood* (Harris, Rosnay, & Pons, 2005). Recall that Little Red Riding Hood goes to visit her grandma, who lives in the woods, and she is unaware that the hungry wolf is disguised as Grandma and waiting to eat her. Three-year-old children typically fail to realize that Little Red Riding Hood is *unaware* of the wolf's presence and that she expects to be greeted by her grandmother. They mistakenly think she is afraid of the wolf as she knocks on the door. Additionally, many 4-year-olds and even some 5-year-olds say that she must be afraid of the wolf as she knocks on the door. It is not until around 6 years of age that children fully grasp Little Red Riding Hood's ignorance and therefore happy feeling as she knocks on the door. Mothers who frequently talked about emotions had children who understood the emotional content of the story. Conversations about emotions likely helped children grasp the deep, emotional nuances about what was going on.

Emotion talk also helps children to interact with peers in positive ways. Fathers and mothers who talked about and elaborated on emotions with their 2- to 5-year-olds had children who displayed positive behaviors to peers, and emotion talk helped shy children approach even unfamiliar peers. Shy boys especially benefitted from their fathers' emotion talk (Grady & Hastings, 2018).

Similarly, parents who talk about children's mental states, such as by saying "What did you *think* when he did that?" support children's understanding of emotions and relationships with peers. Internationally adopted 3-year-old children— a group at risk for low emotion understanding—who were exposed to high (frequent) mental state talk by their parents showed greater emotion understanding at 5.5 years of age than adopted children not exposed to high mental state talk (**FIGURE 10.8**). In turn, adopted children's emotion understanding at 3 years of age led to fewer internalizing and externalizing problems later in development (Tarullo et al., 2016). **Externalizing problems** are those in which children act out and direct their negative emotions to the external environment, such as by hitting others or throwing objects. **Internalizing problems** are those in which a child internalizes their distress, as seen in anxious and depressive symptoms.

externalizing problems Problem behaviors directed outward in which children act out, such as hitting others or throwing things

Internalizing problems Problem behaviors based on negative emotions that are directed inwards, which may be expressed in anxiety or depression

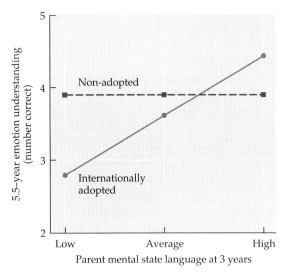

FIGURE 10.8 Adoption and emotion development. Adopted children whose parents directed high mental state talk to them at 3.5 years of age showed higher emotion understanding 2 years later compared to adopted children whose parents did not direct high mental state talk to them (blue line). In fact, only adopted children who were exposed to low mental state talk showed lower scores on emotion understanding when compared to non-adopted children (red line). (After A. R. Tarullo et al. 2016. *Dev Psychopathol* 28: 371–383. Reproduced with permission.)

Insensitive Responses to Emotions

Parents do not always respond sensitively to children's emotions. Sometimes, they punish children for expressing intense emotions or dismiss children's emotions as something to just get over. Disparaging and critical comments, harsh punishment, and ignoring children's emotions hamper children's skills at regulating their emotions, behaviors, and attention (Fabes et al., 2018; Mathis & Bierman, 2015). Parents of boys may harm their children's emotional development by insisting that "Big boys don't cry!" Gendered stereotypes around emotions send messages to young boys that emotions are bad and should be suppressed (Way, 2011).

Finally, parental negativity and overcontrol may incite aggression in preschoolers (Smith et al., 2004). Why might this be? Parents who are overly controlling prevent their children from developing an adequate repertoire of regulation strategies because children come to depend on parents for intervening and making decisions for them rather than learning how to cope on their own (Crockenberg & Litman, 1990; Fox & Calkins, 2003).

✓ CHECK YOUR UNDERSTANDING 10.5

1. Which parental behaviors support children's abilities at regulating emotions?
2. Which parental behaviors harm children's abilities at regulating emotions?

Sibling Context of Emotional Development

LEARNING OBJECTIVE 10.6 Explain how sibling relationships may affect children's emotional development.

The large amount of time children spend interacting with siblings provides many opportunities to share emotions (McHale & Crouter, 1996). Reciprocal, back-and-forth exchanges during play and other activities characterize positive sibling interactions (Howe, Abuhatoum, & Chang-Kredl, 2014). In turn, positive sibling interactions provide an arena for siblings to learn how to help, share, and comfort one another (Hughes, McHarg, & White, 2018). Furthermore, as children interact with their siblings on a daily basis, they learn that others don't always believe or think the way they do, which helps them understand other people's views and feelings. Indeed, children with siblings show better false-belief understanding, an aspect of theory of mind (see Chapter 9), relative to children without siblings (McAlister & Peterson, 2013) (**FIGURE 10.9**).

Sibling interactions are not always positive, and conflicts are frequent. However, sibling conflict allows children to learn how to resolve disagreements and regulate their aggressive behaviors (Dunn & Slomkowski, 1992; Patterson, 1986). Furthermore, sibling conflict may elicit parental intervention, providing another vehicle for children to learn about emotions. When parents attempt to resolve disputes between siblings they often talk about different points of view, which can promote emotion understanding (Dunn & Munn, 1986; Jenkins et al., 2003).

But at an extreme, consistently low-quality sibling interactions marked by conflict, anger, and aggression may be detrimental to young children's emotional development. A meta-analysis—a review that statistically combines findings across many studies—found low-quality sibling relationships to be associated with externalizing and internalizing behavior problems in children (Buist, Deković, & Prinzie, 2013).

✓ CHECK YOUR UNDERSTANDING 10.6

1. How might conflict between siblings help children learn about emotions?

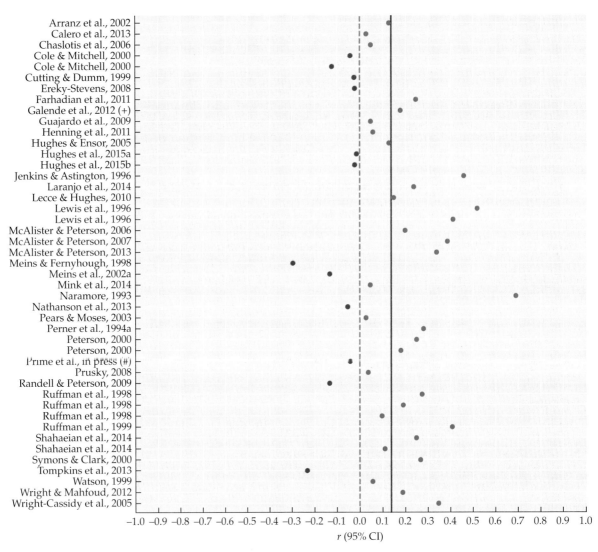

FIGURE 10.9 Siblings and the false belief. A meta-analysis across 93 studies found that the number of siblings related to children's false-belief understanding. Each dot and line represents a separate study, with dots indicating associations between the number of siblings and children's theory of mind. Dots to the right of the dashed green line show average positive associations between having siblings and children's performance, with those at or to the right of the purple line representing high statistical confidence that having siblings relates to children's false-belief understanding. (After R. T. Devine and C. Hughes. 2016. *Child Dev* 89: 971–987. © 2016 The Authors. Child Development © 2016 Society for Research in Child Development, Inc. All rights reserved.)

School Context of Emotional Development

LEARNING OBJECTIVE 10.7 Identify how behaviors of teachers and features of curriculum support children's emotional development.

Young children spend a lot of time in school, where they experience the emotions of self and others. School contexts characterized by positive teacher interactions and high-quality curricula help children understand emotions and learn how to regulate them.

Teachers

Teachers guide children in dealing with emotions in ways similar to parents. Teachers coach children about emotions, respond to children's emotions, and discuss the causes and consequences of emotions (Reimer, 1996). Moreover, teachers tailor their interactions to meet children's developmental level. For example, teachers of toddlers are more likely to respond to children's negative emotions with physical comfort and distraction than are teachers of preschoolers. Conversely, teachers of preschoolers are more likely to offer verbal explanations, help children understand the causes of negative emotions, and teach children strategies for expressing negative emotions (Ahn, 2005).

Positive teacher-child interactions may be especially important for children from poor households. Children who attended Head Start—a federally funded preschool program available to poor families—grew in their emotion understanding across the preschool year when their relationships with teachers and peers were close. In turn, children's growth in emotion knowledge predicted their achievement in kindergarten a year later (Torres, Domitrovich, & Bierman, 2015).

School Quality and Curriculum

Children's emotional development is further enhanced when school quality is high and curricula are designed to support children's emotion regulation. For example, school programs that emphasize social-emotional learning facilitate children's understanding and regulation of emotions and behaviors (Rivers et al., 2013; Schonert-Reichl, Hanson-Peterson, & Hymel, 2015), while also improving children's academic attitudes and performance (Durlak et al., 2011; Jones, McGarrah, & Kahn, 2019). The benefit of social-emotional learning for academic performance suggests a cascading influence in which children who learn how to manage their negative emotions are better able to focus attention on school material (Osher et al., 2016).

Positive school quality and curricula may be particularly important for children from poor households (Weiland & Yoshikawa, 2013). The National Head Start Impact Study found that child problem behaviors, such as hyperactivity in 3-year-olds, were reduced after a year of Head Start (Puma et al., 2005). Similarly, the Tulsa prekindergarten program led to lower child inhibition and higher attentiveness in children compared to children who had not attended prekindergarten or Head Start (Gormley et al., 2011). Notably, quality early childhood education can produce lasting positive effects. For example, the Perry Preschool and Carolina Abecedarian programs were designed to help children and families in poverty, and researchers followed children over decades to evaluate program outcomes. Both programs effectively reduced adult criminal behavior and felony convictions or incarceration when attendees were compared to control groups (Campbell et al., 2002; Heckman et al., 2010) (**FIGURE 10.10**).

The promising impacts of quality preschool on young children's emotional and behavioral development underpin initiatives to integrate social-emotional learning into early school curricula and interventions (Jones, McGarrah, & Kahn, 2019) and to implement universal preschool so that all children have access to supportive, early learning environments (Barnett & Frede, 2017).

✓ CHECK YOUR UNDERSTANDING 10.7

1. Provide evidence that early childhood educational programs positively impact children's development.

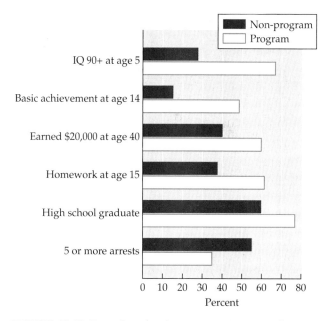

FIGURE 10.10 Perry Preschool program.   In one evaluation of the Perry Preschool study, when children who had been in the program and a control group of children who had not been in the program were followed up at various ages, those who had been in the program showed higher scores on tests of intelligence at age 5, higher all-around achievement at age 14, were more likely to complete homework assignments at age 15, and had higher high school graduation rates, higher earnings, and fewer arrests than those who had not been in the program. (After L. J. Schweinhart et al. 2005. *Lifetime effects: The High/Scope Perry Preschool study through age 40.* Monographs of the High/Scope Educational Research Foundation, 14. High/Scope Press: Ypsilanti, MI. © 2005 by High/Scope® Educational Research Foundation.)

Cultural Context of Emotional Development

LEARNING OBJECTIVE 10.8 Provide examples of how cultural norms around emotions have been shown to affect young children's emotional development.

If children learn about emotions from the people around them, then cultural context should shape young children's emotional development through expectations about which emotions are appropriate to display, when, and with what intensity.

Consider the unique cultural values that characterize many Chinese communities, where open and extreme displays of positive emotions are avoided relative to Western cultures. The tempering of emotional expression reflects the Chinese emphases on modesty, humility, and self-restraint (Luo, Tamis-LeMonda, & Song, 2013; Wu et al., 2002). Moreover, Chinese culture has been characterized as strong on collectivism and intergroup harmony, in contrast with the North American focus on individualism and self-expression (Triandis, 2018). In turn, cultural communities that emphasize collectivism, including China, tend to minimize children's emotional expressiveness (Chan, Bowes, & Wyver, 2009; Friedlmeier, Corapci, & Cole, 2011; Raval & Martini, 2009). Indeed, Chinese mothers are more likely than European American mothers to suggest that their children inhibit their emotions, less likely to explain to children the causes of emotions, and less likely to talk about children's internal states when reminiscing (Chen, 2010; Wang, Doan, & Song, 2010). As a result, young European American children talk more about internal traits, states, and emotions than do Chinese American children (Wang, Doan, & Song, 2010) (**FIGURE 10.11**). When researchers asked mothers to share a storybook with their 4-year-old children, U.S. Chinese immigrant mothers and their children were less likely to talk about the emotions of story characters than were children and mothers from non-Chinese backgrounds (Luo et al., 2014).

Cultural norms around emotions may explain why European American children show better emotion understanding than do Chinese children living in the United States and China. For example, researchers asked U.S. and Chinese children to identify the emotions a story protagonist was feeling from pictures of faces that expressed happiness, sadness, fear, or anger. U.S. children showed greater understanding of the emotional situations than did Chinese children at all ages from 3 to 6 years (Wang, 2003).

However, the socialization of emotional restraint in children may aid children's regulation of emotions and behaviors in certain cultural contexts. Researchers observed children from German middle-class households and young rural Cameroonian Nso children (a group of subsistence farmers in Northwest Cameroon) during the marshmallow delay-of-gratification task described earlier in this chapter (Lamm et al., 2018). Nso 4-year-olds surpassed German children in their ability to delay gratification: Most Nso children did not touch the marshmallow for the entire 10 minutes of the researcher's absence, and they displayed fewer negative emotions while waiting than did German children.

What allowed Nso children to regulate their emotions so well? Cultural practices and expectations

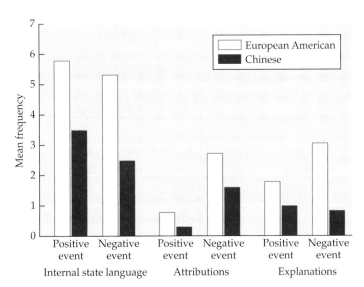

FIGURE 10.11 Culture and emotion talk. European American children talk more about emotions than do Chinese American children when reminiscing about past experiences. They use more internal state language, make more attributions about emotions, and are more likely to explain positive and negative emotional events. (After Q. Wang et al. 2010. *Cog Dev* 25: 380–393.)

likely explain differences between the two groups of children. Specifically, Cameroonian Nso caregivers expect young children to control their emotions and remain calm, and families abide by strict social hierarchies based on age and gender. In contrast, German families support high child autonomy, and display high levels of child-centered parenting and sensitivity to children's wishes. Thus, Nso children patiently followed instructions to wait for the marshmallow, in deference to authority and in line with their socialization experiences.

✓ CHECK YOUR UNDERSTANDING 10.8

1. Why might children of Chinese parents be less likely to express strong emotions than children of European American backgrounds?
2. Offer an example of cultural differences in children's emotion regulation.

■ Social Development

My observations of young children at the playground revealed children's fickle displays of affection towards parents and peers. One minute, a child would climb onto her parent's lap, give a hug, and say, "You're the best daddy in the world," and the next, she would run off to join the antics of a "best friend." Minutes later, she abandoned her best friend in favor of a new arrival. These scenes capture the essence of social relationships in early childhood: Young children continue to grow in their attachment to caregivers, but they also expand the reach of their social relationships to people outside the home, most notably peers. As children interact with other children, they formulate a deeper understanding of who they are. Children's growing sense of self includes beliefs about their social group membership—for instance what it means to be a girl or boy and what girls or boys should do. In the sections that follow we examine changes to young children's attachments with caregivers, social relationships with peers, and understanding of the self.

Attachment and Caregiver-Child Relationship Quality

Compared with research on infant attachment, relatively few studies describe attachment in early childhood. That's because it is difficult to assess attachment using the typical approach designed for infants. Still, when researchers assess attachment in young children using age-appropriate measures, they find much the same story as found for infants: High-quality parenting, including being sensitive to a child's needs, supports secure attachments and well-being in early childhood.

Assessing Attachment in Young Children

LEARNING OBJECTIVE 10.9 Compare different approaches to assessing attachment in young children.

How might a researcher assess young children's attachment to caregivers? Ainsworth's Strange Situation (see Chapter 7) is no longer suitable for young children who are rarely upset if their caregivers leave the room. In the United States and countries around the world, separation from caregivers is common. As a result, researchers have modified methods to validly capture attachment in preschoolers.

The **Preschool Attachment Classification System (PACS)**, developed by Cassidy and Marvin (1992), offers one approach to assessing attachment in 3- to 5-year-olds. The PACS involves four episodes: separation from caregiver,

Preschool Attachment Classification System (PACS)
An assessment of attachment in young children; children experience brief episodes in which they are separated and reunited with their caregivers, and researchers rate children's behaviors to classify children as secure, insecure avoidant, insecure ambivalent/dependent, or insecure disorganized

secure An attachment style characterized by children who are happy and confident to explore their surroundings, using their caregiver as a secure base, and who are positive when reunited with their caregiver

insecure avoidant An attachment style characterized by children who are physically and emotionally avoidant of their caregiver, respond minimally to their caregiver, and generally display neutral affect

insecure ambivalent/dependent An attachment style characterized by children who are simultaneously dependent and resistant toward their caregiver

insecure disorganized An attachment style characterized by children who show disordered, confused, and apprehensive behaviors

Attachment Q-Sort (AQS) An assessment approach to classifying child attachment in which a caregiver or observer sorts cards describing child attachment-related behaviors based on the degree to which the child matches the description

reunion, second separation, and second reunion. The 5-minute episodes of separation are longer than those of the Ainsworth Strange Situation procedure, and children are often left alone, rather than in the presence of a stranger, because being left alone in an unfamiliar place is thought to be stressful and likely to elicit strong attachment behaviors. Examiners code children's use of caregivers as a secure base and children's behaviors upon reunions with caregivers. Such studies yield four categories of attachment:

- **Secure** children use their caregivers as a secure base to explore the room and toys and are generally positive during reunions.
- **Insecure avoidant** children display physical and affective avoidance of their caregivers, are minimally responsive to their caregivers, and neutral in affect.
- **Insecure ambivalent/dependent** children display resistance, aggression, and/or excessive immaturity, such as following their caregiver around or asking to be held.
- **Insecure disorganized** children display odd behaviors such as disordered movements, confusion, and apprehension.

The **Attachment Q-Sort** (**AQS**) offers an alternative, economical approach to measuring young children's attachment (Posada et al., 2018; Waters & Deane, 1985) (**FIGURE 10.12**). The AQS is based on children's proximity-seeking and exploration in the home or other naturalistic settings like a playground. Trained observers or mothers of target children sort 90 cards that contain descriptions of child behaviors, such as "Child readily shares with mother or lets her hold things if she asks." Adults sort the cards based on the degree to which the child fits the description on the card. Once all the cards are sorted, an overall attachment score is calculated that ranges from very secure to very insecure.

✓ **CHECK YOUR UNDERSTANDING 10.9**

1. What are two common approaches for studying attachment in young children?

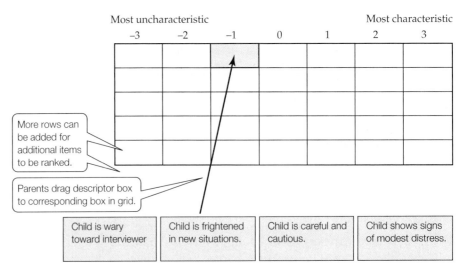

FIGURE 10.12 Attachment Q-Sort. The Attachment Q-Sort is a popular way of assessing children's attachment to a caregiver. A trained observer or parent of the child being assessed sorts cards based on the child's behaviors during the observation. The figure shows a grid of how an observer or parent would enter data for different items that reflect a child's attachment. (After A. Tsiokris. 2015. The child attachment Q-sort: development, training, and validation. Doctoral thesis, UCL [University College London].)

Attachment and Quality of Parenting

LEARNING OBJECTIVE 10.10 Provide evidence for the role of parenting quality in children's attachment.

Just as was seen for infants, the quality of caregiver-child interactions contributes to children's attachment statuses and social and emotional outcomes. High-quality mother-child interactions, typically expressed in mothers' sensitivity to children, relate to secure attachment in 3-year-olds, whereas low-quality mother-child interactions relate to children's disorganized attachment (Moss et al., 2004). Mothers who support their young children's growing need for autonomy by encouraging their preschoolers to solve problems independently and explore new environments and activities have children who display few attention and behavior problems in first grade (Russell et al., 2016). Notably, associations between parental sensitivity and child attachment extend to fathers. Fathers who play with their young children in sensitive ways promote secure attachments in their children and reduce the chances that their children will display conduct problems (Bureau et al., 2017).

✓ CHECK YOUR UNDERSTANDING 10.10

1. The quality of caregiver-child interaction has been found to reliably predict measures of secure attachment. What can parents and teachers do to support secure attachment and positive outcomes in children?

Peers and Friends

Social worlds expand during early childhood. Young children increasingly spend time in out-of-home settings interacting with other children their age. The importance of interacting with someone equal in age and status is not trivial. In fact, tracing developmental science back a bit in history, Piaget asserted that children can be more open and spontaneous with peers than they can be with adults because of equality in power. Children may be more likely to be pushy with their peers than to push their parents, out of fear of the consequences in acting out toward parents. But, children also learn how to compromise, cooperate, and help one another by engaging with peers and friends (Vygotsky, 1978).

Play with Peers and Friends

LEARNING OBJECTIVE 10.11 Explain the strengths and limitations of young children when interacting with peers, as seen in their prosocial and aggressive behaviors.

Young children continually develop skills needed to cooperate during play and establish enduring friendships. But it takes several years for children to play in mutually gratifying ways. That's because children have limited cognitive and language skills, making it difficult for them to sustain play. As a result, much of young children's play occurs side-by-side rather than face-to-face. However, as children's familiarity with peers grows, play expands in complexity and reciprocity. Nearly a century ago, Parten (1932) characterized a shift in children's play from what she referred to as **parallel play**—play where children engage in similar activities, such as building with blocks, but do not interact with one another—to **cooperative play**, which is socially reciprocal (**FIGURE 10.13**).

Prosocial Behaviors

Prosocial behaviors help or benefit another person, and include behaviors of sharing, assisting others, and playing cooperatively. As might be expected, prosocial behaviors come easier to children who are friends and when partners

parallel play A type of play in which children engage in similar activities but do not interact with each other (e.g., building blocks side-by-side)

cooperative play Socially reciprocal play in which children interact with each other as they engage in a shared activity with the same goal (e.g., children working together on a puzzle)

prosocial behaviors Behaviors such as sharing, cooperating, and helping that benefit another person

FIGURE 10.13 Parallel versus cooperative play in preschoolers. With age, children increasingly engage in cooperative play. (A) As toddlers, children largely engage in parallel play, whereas (B) young children are capable of more extended bouts of cooperative play.

reciprocate (Fabes et al., 1996; Moore, 2009; Paulus & Moore, 2014). Children as young as 3.5 years share more toys with cooperative than noncooperative individuals (Warneken & Tomasello, 2013). Furthermore, 5-year-old children are more likely to share, take turns, and cooperate with someone who reciprocates than with someone who does not (e.g., Melis et al., 2016; Sebastián-Enesco & Warneken, 2015).

Conflict and Aggression

Young children do not always cooperate, share, and help one another. Peer relationships are fraught with conflict because children have difficulty considering the perspectives of others and sometimes resort to aggression to get what they want, such as pulling a desired toy out of the hand of a peer or pushing a peer out of line to be first on the slide. However, not all aggression is alike. In fact, researchers classify childhood aggression into three broad categories, each with unique features and developmental timetables:

- **Hostile aggression** involves actions that intentionally injure someone, physically or otherwise. Hostile aggression results from a person's anger toward the victim.

- **Instrumental aggression** is directed at achieving a particular goal, rather than being motivated by anger. For example, a child may threaten another child to obtain a toy.

- **Relational aggression** is intended to harm another child's friendships indirectly, for example through manipulating social situations, stating another child can't join a game, spreading rumors, or gossiping behind the backs of peers (Gower et al., 2014).

As children improve in their ability to inhibit disruptive behaviors and learn social norms about how to act, they change in the three types of aggression. Hostile and instrumental forms of aggression increase in toddlerhood before declining in early childhood (Alink et al., 2006; Cummings, Iannotti, & Zahn-Waxler, 1989). But, as children grow in their language, cognitive, and social skills they increasingly display relational aggression, which continues throughout childhood and adolescence. And, although adults often assume that "little boys are more aggressive than are little girls," the truth is that boys and girls sometimes display different types of aggression. Three- to 5-year-old preschool girls were rated as more relationally aggressive and less physically aggressive than were boys; whereas the reverse pattern was seen for boys (Crick et al., 2006). Furthermore, 4- to 5-year-old girls with many female play partners show higher

hostile aggression A type of reactionary aggression experienced in response to a threat or insult and with the intention to cause pain

instrumental aggression A type of aggression aimed at achieving a specific goal, such as a child threatening another child to get a toy

relational aggression A type of nonphysical aggression in which harm is caused by hurting someone's relationships or social status, such as by threatening to withdraw a friendship, withdrawing a friendship, ignoring a peer, excluding a peer, or spreading rumors relational aggression than do girls with fewer female play partners, and boys with more male play partners show higher physical aggression than those with fewer male play partners (Perry & Ostrov, 2018). Although aggression is harmful, benign conflicts with peers allow children to practice negotiation and learn how to cope with disagreement without resorting to aggression.

✓ **CHECK YOUR UNDERSTANDING 10.11**
1. How do children's relationships with peers change in early childhood?
2. What factors might explain why a child does or does not share with a peer?
3. Describe three types of aggression observed in young children.

Family Context of Social Skills and Aggression

LEARNING OBJECTIVE 10.12 Explain how characteristics of family context, including parenting behaviors, might affect children's developing social skills and aggression.

Children get along well with other children when they share a loving relationship with their parents. And, just as high-quality relationships between parents and children can foster positive behaviors in children, overly harsh discipline may inadvertently have negative repercussions for children's behavior.

Parental Sensitivity

Why might children's positive relationships with parents support strong peer relationships? Positive, responsive parents teach children how to behave in socially competent ways and facilitate children's development of conscience and cooperation (Kochanska et al., 2005). Children who experienced a mutually responsive relationship with their mothers at 2 years of age learned how to understand others' emotions at 3 years of age and displayed strong prosocial skills at 4 years of age (Ensor, Spencer, & Hughes, 2011). Conversely, low-quality mother-child relationships may provoke children's negative interactions with peers and problem behaviors (Ensor et al., 2012). And, although studies of child-father relationships are rare, fathers affect children's social and emotional development just as strongly as do mothers. Fathers' supportive interactions with children foster children's social competence with peers, and fathers' emotional support of children's mothers fosters a positive family climate that is conducive to children's development (Cabrera, Volling, & Barr, 2018).

Corporal Punishment

Corporal punishment refers to the deliberate use of harsh punishment to inflict physical pain or discomfort on a child, such as hitting a child with a belt (Gershoff, 2002; Lee, Altschul, & Gershoff, 2013). Parents sometimes reason that spanking is harmless, which may be why it remains a widely endorsed form of discipline in the United States and many countries around the world (Gershoff, 2013; MacKenzie et al., 2015). In particular, parents with low educational attainment who live in poverty are more likely to resort to corporal punishment than are parents from middle and high socioeconomic status households (Lansford et al., 2009; MacKenzie et al., 2015). However, corporal punishment can lead to serious problems, including antisocial behaviors, alcohol abuse, and mental health problems in adolescence, even if it effectively stops a young child's behavior in the short term (Afifi et al., 2013; Fergusson, Boden, & Horwood, 2008; Werner et al., 2016).

Why does corporal punishment cascade to later behavior problems, rather than help children learn that their actions are wrong and hurtful? Shouldn't

corporal punishment The purposeful use of harmful punishment by a caregiver to inflict physical pain or discomfort on a child the negative feedback of being hit by a caregiver, for example, prevent future problem behaviors? Developmental researcher Elizabeth Gershoff (2013) offers several reasons why corporal punishment is ineffective. One reason is that young children model the behaviors they observe in other people. Children who observe their parents hitting them, their siblings, or even one another are more likely to display aggressive behaviors toward their peers than are children who are not exposed to such aggression. Corporal punishment may also set in motion damaging cycles of coercion, in which a child misbehaves, a parent responds with physical punishment, the child escalates the negative behavior, the parent increases the punishment, and so forth (Baron & Malmberg, 2019; Patterson, 1982). Such findings have led the American Academy of Pediatrics to issue a policy statement against the use of corporal punishment, and to offer parents alternative approaches for disciplining their young children (Sege & Siegel, 2018) (**TABLE 10.1**).

TABLE 10.1 ■ American Academy of Pediatrics guidelines on disciplining young children

Show and tell	Teach children right from wrong with calm words and actions. Model behaviors you would like to see in your children.
Set limits	Have clear and consistent rules your children can follow. Be sure to explain these rules in age-appropriate terms they can understand.
Give consequences	Calmly and firmly explain the consequences if they don't behave. For example, tell children that if they do not pick up their toys, you will put them away for the rest of the day. Be prepared to follow through right away. Don't give in by giving them back after a few minutes. But remember, never take away something your child truly needs, such as a meal.
Hear them out	Listening is important. Let your child finish the story before helping solve the problem. Watch for times when misbehavior has a pattern, such as if your child is feeling jealous. Talk with your child about this rather than just giving consequences.
Give them your attention	The most powerful tool for effective discipline is attention—to reinforce good behaviors and discourage others. Remember, all children want their parent's attention.
Catch them being good	Children need to know when they do something bad—and when they do something good. Notice good behavior and point it out, praising success and good tries. Be specific (for example, "Wow, you did a good job putting that toy away!").
Know when not to respond	As long as your child isn't doing something dangerous and gets plenty of attention for good behavior, ignoring bad behavior can be an effective way of stopping it. Ignoring bad behavior can also teach children natural consequences of their actions. For example, if your child keeps dropping her cookies on purpose, she will soon have no more cookies left to eat. If she throws and breaks her toy, she will not be able to play with it. It will not be long before she learns not to drop her cookies and to play carefully with her toys.
Be prepared for trouble	Plan ahead for situations when your child might have trouble behaving. Prepare them for upcoming activities and how you want them to behave.
Redirect bad behavior	Sometimes children misbehave because they are bored or don't know any better. Find something else for your child to do.
Call a time-out	A time-out can be especially useful when a specific rule is broken. This discipline tool works best by warning children they will get a time-out if they don't stop, reminding them what they did wrong in as few words—and with as little emotion—as possible, and removing them from the situation for a pre-set length of time (1 minute per year of age is a good rule of thumb). With children who are at least 3-years-old, you can try letting the children lead their own time-out instead of setting a timer. You can just say, "Go to time-out and come back when you feel ready and in control." This strategy, which can help the child learn and practice self-management skills, also works well for older children and teens.

Source: From American Academy of Pediatrics. 2018. 10 Healthy Discipline Strategies That Work. healthychildren.org. Last updated 11/5/2018. Reproduced with permission.

Household Chaos and Media Violence

Corporal punishment is not the only characteristic of family context that may cause social problems in children. Chaotic family environments, characterized by high stress, frenetic activity, lack of structure, unpredictability, and high background noise—such as a constantly blaring television—can take a toll on children's social and emotional development and interfere with family relationships (Coldwell, Pike, & Dunn, 2006; Evans et al., 2005; Ferguson, & Evans, 2019).

Furthermore, in many chaotic households, young children are left on their own to entertain themselves with video games and screens, which introduces them to programs containing high aggression and violence. Children's aggression and hostility increase the more time they spend viewing violence on television and other media and playing violent video and computer games (Anderson et al., 2010; Bushman & Huesmann, 2012; Hofferth, 2010).

Nonetheless, critics have questioned whether viewing violence on television or video games actually *causes* child aggression. Perhaps factors associated with children's viewing of violence explain associations to aggression. For example, parents who permit their young children to watch programs and play video games that contain violence may be less likely to be involved with their children in positive ways. Additionally, children who choose to watch violent programming may be prone to aggression from the start. In fact, a review of 101 studies that included young and older children found that playing with video games (violent and nonviolent) had minimal negative influence on children's aggression and prosocial behaviors when other variables were considered (Ferguson, 2015). This does not mean that parents should condone children's viewing of screen violence; however, it calls into question some longstanding assumptions about causal direction. Therefore, developmental researchers continue to ask about the factors that lead children to engage with violent media in the first place.

✓ CHECK YOUR UNDERSTANDING 10.12

1. Why is spanking still a commonly endorsed form of discipline in the United States?
2. Explain how each of the following might lead to problem behaviors in children: (a) corporal punishment, (b) household chaos, and (c) media violence.

Cultural Context of Social Development

LEARNING OBJECTIVE 10.13 Contrast cultural communities on their views around aggression and discipline, and how those differences might affect children.

Family life does not exist in a vacuum. Families are nested within cultural settings that share expectations and norms about children's social behaviors, including who might make a desirable friend. As a result, children are more likely to select a friend who shares their cultural beliefs than one who does not, with cultural influences on friend selection strengthening as children get older (Leman et al., 2013).

Cultural communities likewise share views about valued social behaviors, including what constitutes acceptable levels of aggression. Although you may expect all cultures to reject any form of child aggression, this is not always the case. Cultural differences around aggression are illustrated in anthropologist Douglas Fry's book *The Human Potential for Peace* (2006). Fry presented an intriguing cultural analysis of two Zapotec Indian towns in Central America. In one, people fought at public gatherings, husbands beat wives, and parents disciplined children by hitting them with sticks. The other community was much less violent. Children living in the town where violence was the norm displayed twice as many aggressive acts as did children from the less-violent community. In essence, cultural context can establish a culture of aggression in which children's exposure to aggressive community members guides their interpretations of what are acceptable behaviors.

✓ CHECK YOUR UNDERSTANDING 10.13

1. How might cultural views and practices affect children's aggressive behaviors?

Identity Development

We've seen that children's relationships with caregivers, siblings, and peers feed into their developing emotion understanding, self-regulation, and social competence. Additionally, early childhood is when children begin to figure out what makes them unique. Recall from Chapter 1, developmental psychologist and psychoanalyst Erik Erikson (1902–1994) asserted that a main task of human development is the formation of a unique, personal identity. Erikson claimed that the seeds of identity blossom in early childhood as children begin to internalize messages about their capabilities in relation to what others expect of them. Specifically, young children must learn to strike a balance between **initiative versus guilt** in their quest toward an identity. Young children experience initiative when they establish and work toward goals, such as learning the alphabet or riding a bicycle (**FIGURE 10.14**). In contrast, when children fail to meet their goals, perhaps because parents and other adults discourage children or make them feel ashamed of what they are doing, children experience guilt. As children develop, they gain control over their activities, make choices, and explore opportunities—signs of their growing independence. Gradually, children acquire a multifaceted and relatively complex sense of who they are, including a growing appreciation of their membership in various social groups.

Although Erikson wrote about the development of self-identity decades ago, his work continues to inspire contemporary research. Today, the theme of social group membership cuts across studies of identity development. How do children learn about social groups, and how does a child's social group membership affect their development? In the sections following, we review two salient aspects of social group membership—gender identity and ethnic/racial identity—and consider how societal messages about each shape children's development.

initiative versus guilt The third stage in Erik Erikson's theory of psychosocial development and self-identity in which young children learn to assert themselves by engaging in social interactions, initiating activities, exploring their environment, and exhibiting competence in social interactions; caregivers who discourage or criticize children may create the alternative sense of guilt in their children during this stage

FIGURE 10.14 Initiative versus guilt. According to Erikson, when children establish a goal, such as riding a bicycle, and work toward it they experience initiative. If children fail to meet a goal that they have established, they experience guilt.

Gender Identity

LEARNING OBJECTIVE 10.14 Compare psychodynamic, social learning, and cognitive developmental perspectives on young children's gender development.

Gender identity is an individual's personal identity around being male or female and is a commanding force in the lives of young children. Philosophers, clinicians, educators, and researchers have long recognized that gender shapes children's beliefs, attitudes, activities, and sense of self-worth, and that such influences begin early in development.

Psychodynamic View

Sigmund Freud (see Chapter 1) placed gender identity at the crux of his stage theory of psychosexual development (1933, 1949, 1964). He claimed that in early childhood boys pass through a *phallic stage* during which pleasure is centered on their genitals and they desire to marry their mothers and vanquish their fathers. Freud named this phenomenon the **Oedipus complex** after the Ancient Greek tragedy in which Oedipus the King kills his father and marries his mother. Freud contended that because boys recognize that their feelings are wrong, they experience anguish and fear parental punishment. Boys resolve the unbearable tension between desiring their mothers and fearing punishment by identifying with and becoming closer to their fathers, while differentiating and distancing themselves from their mothers.

According to Freud, girls also pass through a stage of gender identification, in which upon realizing that they do not have a penis, they are "mortified by the comparison with boys' far superior equipment" (Freud, 1933, 1964). Freud believed that girls' "penis envy" leads them to blame their mothers as the source of castration. As a result, girls transfer their love to their fathers. The **Electra complex**—named after the Greek tragedy in which Electra coaxes her brother to kill their mother to avenge the murder of their father—refers to girls' competition with their mothers for the attention of their fathers. Like boys, girls fear being punished for their inappropriate feelings, and therefore protect themselves from their mothers' withdrawal of love by identifying with their mothers and distancing themselves from their fathers.

As you might imagine, Freud's theory of gender development has been criticized on many fronts and stands at odds with current views around gender. Critics allege that Freud harmfully depicted girls as inferior; that his basis of gender development was rooted in conflict, sexual desires, and fear; and that he ignored cognitive and social factors that influence gender identity (Martin & Ruble, 2004). Thus, social learning and cognitive development perspectives have replaced psychodynamic theories on gender development.

Social Learning View

Social learning theory spotlights the roles of modeling and feedback in children's gender development. (See Chapter 1 for a discussion of the principles of social learning theory.) Modeling occurs when children imitate the behaviors of people whom they view to be similar to themselves, such as when girls copy the behaviors of other girls by dressing certain ways and playing with certain toys. Reinforcement takes over when peers and adults praise or encourage gender-appropriate behaviors in children, punish "gender-inappropriate" behavior, or communicate messages about how boys and girls should behave (Ruble, Martin, & Berenbaum, 2007).

Children model the actions that they observe in others in a process called **imitation learning**. Albert Bandura (1962) was the first to document imitation learning in young children (which he also referred to as observational learning). Recall from Chapter 1 that, after watching an adult model punch, kick, and knock down a large, inflated "Bobo doll," children later imitated the behaviors they had witnessed, screaming, "Ka-Pow!" and "Take that!," as they pummeled the doll (**FIGURE 10.15**). Imitation learning is likewise seen in the area of gender development. Young children observe that men and women behave differently, like different things, and so forth. They then act in ways that align with their observations.

Young children also learn from feedback. They quickly catch on that people are more likely to reward certain behaviors than others, and so selectively engage in behaviors they think will gain approval. Parents, siblings, peers, teachers, and other adults reward and punish children's gendered behaviors, in blatant and subtle ways, for example by scolding a boy for "acting like a sissy!" or entertaining a girl with a movie of a vulnerable princess being rescued by a strong prince. Sometimes, they do so unwittingly, just by encouraging gendered forms of play. For example, in preschool classrooms, teachers are more likely to facilitate

Oedipus complex A gender identification phenomenon in Sigmund Freud's stage theory of psychosexual development in which (according to Freud) boys recognize that their strong sexual attraction for their mothers is wrong, experience anguish, and then distance themselves from their mothers and identify with their fathers

Electra complex A gender identification phenomenon in Sigmund Freud' stage theory of psychosexual development, in which (according to Freud) girls compete with their mothers for their fathers' attention, and upon recognition that their feelings are wrong, distance themselves from their fathers and develop a close relationship with their mothers

imitation learning Children's mimicking the actions that they observe in others, a type of social learning first documented by Albert Bandura

Attention

The person must be paying *attention* to the model's behavior.

Retention

Then the person must *retain* the information gained about the observed behavior.

Motivation

I want to be like that lady.

The person must be *motivated* to reproduce the model's behavior.

Reproduction

The person must *reproduce* the behavior, and may get progressively better at imitating the behavior with practice.

FIGURE 10.15 Bandura's Bobo doll study. Children watched as an adult model punched, kicked, and knocked down a large, inflated Bobo doll. When children were later placed in a room with the Bobo doll, they imitated the behaviors they had witnessed. (After S. M. Breedlove. 2015. *Principles of Psychology.* Sinauer/Oxford University Press: Sunderland, MA. Based on A. Bandura et al. 1961. *J Abnorm Soc Psychol* 63: 575–582.)

"masculine activities" such as play with bikes and trucks with boys and "feminine activities" such as play with dolls with girls (Granger et al., 2017).

Cognitive Developmental View

Traditional social learning theories have been criticized for the prominence they assign to modeling and feedback and relative lack of attention to cognitive processes. The cognitive developmental view of gender development, first introduced by Kohlberg (1966), points to children's active role in the formation of a gender identity and the ways that cognitive schema affect how and what children learn (Ruble & Martin, 1998).The cognitive development view contends that once a young boy realizes that he is a boy, will always be a boy, and that boys have certain characteristics, behaviors, and attitudes that distinguish them from girls, he will attempt to look, act, and feel like other boys that he observes, a process referred to as **social identification** (Ruble, Martin, & Berenbaum, 2007; Slaby & Frey, 1975). The cognitive development view describes three stages in children's gender development:

1. **Gender identity** occurs when children can identify themselves and others by gender. Traditionally, gender identity has been thought to emerge at around 3 years of age, although children as young as 18 months to 2 years refer to themselves as a boy or girl (Halim et al., 2018; Zosuls et al., 2011).

2. **Gender stability** is the understanding that one's gender continues over time, for example realizing that boys grow up to be men and girls grow up to be women. At this stage, children understand continuity of gender, yet do not realize the absolute permanency of gender across superficial transformations. As a result, they may believe that if they behave in cross-gender-typed ways (such as if a girl cuts her hair or plays with boy toys) their gender may change (Ruble et al., 2007).

3. **Gender consistency** is the understanding that one's gender remains the same regardless of superficial changes to appearance and behaviors. Even if a girl plays with trucks, wears pants, or cuts her hair, she will remain a girl.

social identification The process in the cognitive developmental view of gender development in which boys and girls create a cognitive schema about their gender as they identify their gender and come to understand that people of their gender have specific characteristics and behaviors

gender identity A stage in gender development described in the cognitive development view in which children identify themselves and others by their sex, traditionally emerging around 3 years of age

gender stability A stage in gender development described in the cognitive development view characterized by children's understanding that one's sex continues over time (e.g., girls grow up to be women)

gender consistency A stage in gender development described in the cognitive development view characterized by children's understanding that one's sex will remain the same regardless of superficial changes to appearance and behaviors

How does gender identity development affect children's behaviors and attitudes? Once children have achieved gender identity and stability they become "gender detectives" who actively seek out gender-related information and apply that information to their own behaviors. Children ages 3–5 years display high rigidity in their behaviors, ranging from the clothes they wear to the activities they pursue (Halim, 2016; Halim et al., 2017).

Young children's insistence on wearing clothes that blatantly mark their genders illustrates their high gender rigidity. Girls swirl around in "pink frilly dresses"—a phenomenon that developmentalist Diane Ruble coined the PFD syndrome—ruffled socks, and sparkly shoes. Boys dress in dark colors, superhero t-shirts, and police and firefighter uniforms (Halim et al., 2012) (**FIGURE 10.16**). Children also play with toys that are designed for their gender. When researchers offered preschoolers the opportunity to play with "masculine," "feminine," or "neutral" toys that were painted white to avoid gendered colors, children exhibited greater interest in the gender-typed toys and neutral toys than the cross-gender-typed toys (Dinella, Weisgram, & Fulcher, 2017).

FIGURE 10.16 Gendered dressing. One example of gender rigidity can be observed in preschool children's insistence on wearing clothes that blatantly mark their genders.

Gender rigidity is also seen in children's gender segregation during play. Preferences for same-gender play partners start around 3 years of age (Martin & Ruble, 2004). Gender-segregated interactions further reinforce gendered behaviors, because when girls play with girls they are likely to play quietly and cooperatively, whereas when boys play with boys they likely to engage in high levels of activity (Halim, 2016; Leaper, 1994).

A bit later in development, when children achieve gender consistency and realize that they will remain girls or boys regardless of superficial transformations, gender rigidity relaxes. Starting around 6 years of age, children begin to be flexible in their attitudes and behaviors around gender, becoming, for example, less concerned about gender appearance than they had been a couple of years earlier (Halim et al., 2012) (**FIGURE 10.17**).

Gender Nonconforming Children

Although most young children display gendered behaviors, some do not. Gender nonconforming children may behave and appear in ways that do not match dominant cultural and social expectations around gender. However, although the preferences of gender nonconforming children diverge from dominant social expectations, in most cases children maintain a gender identity that aligns with their birth sex and present themselves that way to the outside world (Olson, 2016). In rare instances, gender nonconforming children describe themselves as the "other" gender and socially transition to living publicly and expressing themselves as the other gender, even when they have not received

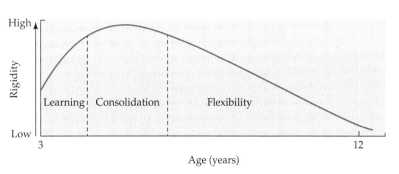

FIGURE 10.17 Rigidity and flexibility in gender attitudes and behaviors. Once young children have learned their gender identity, and are in the process of consolidating information about gender from what they observe around them, they show a peak in rigidity of their attitudes and behaviors around gender. As children then achieve gender consistency, they become more flexible in their gendered attitudes and behavior, and rigidity declines. (After C. Martin and D. Ruble. 2004. *Curr Dir Psychol Sci* 13: 67–70.)

medical interventions to physically transform their bodies into their expressed gender (Fast & Olson, 2018).

Of course, the rarity of young socially transitioned transgender children makes them difficult to study, and information about such children is sparse. Consequently, studies of socially transitioning children draw on extremely small samples. One such study found that socially transitioned children preferred clothing and toys that matched their expressed gender, and believed that they would remain their expressed gender as adults, following a parallel developmental course to gender-typical children. (Fast & Olson, 2018). Similarly, young children who showed strong cross-sex preferences more closely resembled control children of their identified sex than they did children who matched their biological sex. Furthermore, young children with strong cross-sex identification were more likely to socially transition to their identified gender 2 years later than were children with weaker identifications, and they referred to themselves using cross-gendered pronouns (Rae et al., 2019).

✓ CHECK YOUR UNDERSTANDING 10.14

1. According to social learning theory, what are two key ways that children learn about gender roles?
2. Define the stages of gender identity, gender stability, and gender consistency from a cognitive developmental perspective.
3. What does available research say about the gender development of gender nonconforming children?

Family Context of Gender Development

LEARNING OBJECTIVE 10.15 Describe behaviors in parents that shape children's gender development.

Young children spend much time at home, interacting with parents who communicate salient messages about gender through their play and language interactions with children and through the way they allocate household responsibilities (Smith et al., 2012). **Gendered parenting**—parents' messages and practices to children about how boys and girls should behave—is especially strong during early childhood compared to other times in development (Mesman & Groeneveld, 2018).

Play Interactions

Parents prompt different types of play in girls and boys, such as by encouraging girls to hug their dolls and boys to push their trucks (Lytton & Romney, 1991). Little girls who engage with princess-type media and products at home, and whose parents further strengthen those interests, grow in their adherence to gender-stereotypical behavior a year later (Coyne et al. 2016). In playgrounds as well, mothers react differently to their sons and daughters: They are more likely to present sons than daughters with physical challenges, such as encouraging sons to reach a pole without assistance, and more likely to offer daughters help and verbal cautions (e.g., Hagan & Kuebli, 2007).

Of course, many parents actively avoid endorsing gendered play in their children, by offering both boys and girls opportunities to play with trucks and dolls, for example, or keeping toys and child appearance neutral. Such parenting strategies have led to the design and marketing of many gender-neutral toys and growth in industries that sell gender-neutral clothes and other paraphernalia for children.

gendered parenting The messages and practices of parents to children about how boys and girls should behave, which may be conveyed through play interactions, language interactions, and so on

Language Interactions

Parents often talk to children in gendered ways, even though they may be unaware that they do so. For example, mothers used more emotion words with their daughters than with their sons in early childhood (e.g., Fivush et al., 2000). In turn, emotion understanding and talk has been found to develop earlier in girls than in boys, for example, with girls using more emotion labels when telling stories than boys (Tenenbaum, Ford, & Alkhedairy, 2011).

Fathers demonstrate gendered talk as well. For example, both fathers and mothers directed a higher proportion of emotion words to their 4-year-old daughters than sons, with parent emotion talk relating to how much children themselves referred to emotions when reminiscing about the past (Aznar & Tenenbaum, 2014). And gendered talk crosses cultural communities too. U.S. Hispanic fathers of preschool age boys were more likely to talk about memories that contained a lot of action, such as going to an amusement park or riding a bicycle, than were fathers of girls. Conversely, fathers of girls were more likely to talk about quiet or social activities, such as reading books or attending birthday parties (Cristofaro & Tamis-LeMonda, 2008) (**FIGURE 10.18**). Parents who seek gender equality in the attitudes and behaviors of their children should attend closely to the topics they introduce to children and how they talk about children's current and past experiences.

Division of Household Labor and Television Viewing

The ways that families distribute chores among household members and the messages contained in various media can unintentionally communicate female and male roles to children. Homes in which responsibilities are divided along traditional gender lines, such as mothers doing the cooking and cleaning and fathers taking out the trash, shape how young children think about and view their own gender (**FIGURE 10.19**). Disparities in the division of housework between mothers and

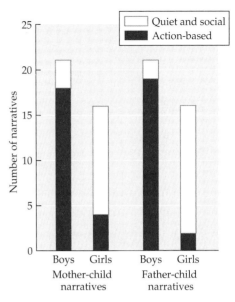

FIGURE 10.18 Gendered talk. When Hispanic mothers and fathers talked to their 4- to 5-year old children about a happy memory, both mothers and fathers were more likely to reminisce about high-action-based events with their boys, such as going on a rollercoaster, and more likely to reminisce about quiet and social activities with their girls, such as reading books and making friends. (After T. N. Cristofaro and C. S. Tamis-LeMonda. 2008. *In Spanish-Language Narration and Literacy: Culture, Cognition, and Emotion*, A. McCabe, A. L. Bailey, & G. Melzi (Eds.), pp. 54–91. Cambridge University Press: New York.)

(A)

(B)

FIGURE 10.19 Gendered division of household labor. When adults divide chores in the home along strict gender lines, children are apt to become stereotyped in their own attitudes and behaviors around gender. Thus, parents and other adults can encourage children to participate in a range of activities that do not adhere to gender stereotypes, such as (A) involving boys in cooking and (B) girls in digging in the yard. Additionally, adults should engage in household chores along non-gendered lines to convey gender flexibility around responsibility and roles to children.

fathers—with women doing more household work than men—related to 4-year-old girls stating that people regard boys to be "better than girls," a measure referred to as public regard (Halim et al., 2012). In the same sample, children's viewing of television at home related to their beliefs about public regard, likely because programming contains pervasive messages about gender roles. Indeed, children who watched more television were more likely to assign higher public regard to boys than to girls. Thus, parents' efforts toward reducing the time their preschoolers watch television and other media may have a positive side effect of reducing young children's gendered attitudes.

✓ CHECK YOUR UNDERSTANDING 10.15

1. What differences have been documented in parents' language and play with girls versus boys?
2. What is division of household labor, and how might it affect children's gender development?

Biological Context of Gender Development

LEARNING OBJECTIVE 10.16 Describe evidence that suggests biological underpinnings to children's gender-based behaviors.

Social learning theory and cognitive development theories commonly emphasize social influences in children's gendered behaviors. Yet, the presence of potent social influences does not refute the role of biology in gender differences. Human and primate research offers compelling evidence that exposure to sex hormones during sensitive developmental periods may shape children's gender-related behaviors (Berenbaum, 2018).

Consider the disorder of congenital adrenal hyperplasia (CAH). CAH results in the fetus being exposed to higher than normal androgen levels (androgens are male sex hormones). As a result, CAH girls have masculinized genitalia, even though they have working ovaries and a uterus. CAH girls display more masculine preferences in play, occupational interests, emotions, and behaviors than do non-CAH girls, even though their parents raise them as girls (e.g., Berenbaum, 1999; Servin et al., 2003). Indeed, exposure to high levels of prenatal androgens exerts large effects on children's interests and engagement in gendered activities, but relatively small or no effects on gender identity and gendered peer involvement (Berenbaum, 2018).

Studies of nonhuman primates lend further support to biological influences. Female rhesus monkeys exposed to high levels of prenatal androgens showed high levels of foot-clasp mounting and rough-and-tumble play as juveniles, behaviors typically seen in male juvenile monkeys (Wallen, 1996). Moreover, female and male rhesus monkeys display marked differences in toy play that mirror gender differences observed in young children. For instance, researchers presented rhesus monkeys with a variety of toys, some plush and some containing wheels. Male monkeys consistently preferred the toys with wheels, whereas female monkeys were flexible in their toy choices, playing with both plush toys and toys with wheels (Hassett, Siebert, & Wallen, 2008) (**FIGURE 10.20**). Toy preferences in monkeys develop without the explicit pressure and socialization from peers and adults that characterize human experiences—that is, for girls to play quietly with dolls and boys to play actively with trucks.

✓ CHECK YOUR UNDERSTANDING 10.16

1. What have researchers learned about gender development from studies of CAH girls and observations of rhesus monkeys?

(A)

(B)

Alexander and Hines, 2002. Evol Hum Behav 23: 467–479

FIGURE 10.20 Biological influences on gender in rhesus monkeys. In one study, (A) male monkeys showed consistent and strong preferences for the toys with wheels, whereas (B) female monkeys were flexible in their toy choices, playing with both plush toys and toys with wheels.

Ethnic and Racial Identities

LEARNING OBJECTIVE 10.17 Document the ways that children's understanding of ethnicity and race changes over the course of early childhood.

Like gender, a child's ethnic and racial identities powerfully influence their attitudes, behaviors, and sense of self. Notably, ethnic and racial identities are especially salient to children from minority and immigrant backgrounds. Ethnic identity is defined as a "subjective sense of belonging to an ethnic group, and the feelings and attitudes that accompany this sense of group membership" (Phinney et al., 2001, p. 136). Despite challenges around the precise definitions of ethnicity and race, the distinction is important (Spencer, 2014). In broad terms, **ethnicity** refers to a group's shared national heritage, in which case, for example, Haitians would be distinguished from Jamaicans because Haitians come from Haiti and Jamaicans from Jamaica. The term **race** refers to a group's shared phenotypical characteristics, such as skin color, in which case, many Haitians and Jamaicans would be grouped within the racial category Black.

ethnicity A social group's national or cultural heritage (e.g., being Russian)

race A group's shared phenotypical, physical characteristics (e.g., being White, Black, or Asian)

Children's Understanding of Ethnic and Racial Identities

What do young children know about race and ethnicity? In early childhood, young children are at the cusp of understanding social categories of ethnicity and race. Over the subsequent years their understanding will grow in depth, breadth, and personal significance. For example, by 3 years of age, White and Black North American children can categorize individuals by race (Aboud, 1988; Katz, 2003). Young U.S. children can also label themselves as African American, Mexican, and so forth, but they have limited understanding of what ethnicity means. For example, young children do not recognize that ethnicity is a lasting feature of the self. When 3- to 6-year-old Mexican American children were asked to label their background ethnicity, about half identified themselves as "Mexican," but only 37% believed that they would remain "Mexican" when they grew up (Bernal et al., 1990).

Several studies confirm that young children have limited understanding of racial and ethnic stability. In fact, young children think that race could change just as readily as emotions! To illustrate, researchers presented 5- to 6-year-olds and 9- to 10-year-olds of different races with images of children who were Black or White and happy or angry, and asked children to indicate which of two adults the child would grow up to be. Children of both age groups did not necessarily conceptualize race to be more stable than emotion, although minority children's judgments were more adultlike than same-aged White children. But, on a different task, children understood that gender was more stable than emotions. In short, children's lack of judgments about racial stability stems from a difficulty in reasoning about race rather than a difficulty in reasoning about stability (Roberts & Gelman, 2017).

Children's Stereotypes and Discrimination around Race

Although young children show limited understanding of the stability of race, they are susceptible to messages about race and discrimination. In particular, when adults make broad-sweeping generalizations about a person's behaviors, for example stating that "people from X group are noisy and rude," rather than *"that specific person* is noisy and rude," young children quickly assume that the behaviors of one person extend to everyone in the group. **Essentialism** refers to statements and beliefs that members of a group share underlying characteristics and behaviors (see Chapter 9), and may be a powerful source of stereotyping and discrimination (e.g., Prentice & Miller, 2007; Rhodes, Leslie, & Tworek, 2012; Rhodes et al., 2018).

To illustrate the harm of essentialist statements, researchers showed children a picture of a character climbing a fence and stated that "Zarpies climb fences!" Children interpreted the statement to mean that *all* Zarpies climb fences. When later shown a picture of a Zarpie stealing a cookie, children then generalized the negative behavior to all Zarpies, and were unlikely to share their resources with Zarpies. However, children who were told that "*This* Zarpie likes to climb fences" did not later assume that all Zarpies are similar, and that if one Zarpie stole a cookie, so would other Zarpies (Rhodes et al., 2018).

Unfortunately, children's exposure to essentialist messages may instigate negative perceptions about specific ethnic or racial groups. For example, researchers presented 5- and 6-year-old children with pictures of men and women of White and Black races, and asked children to choose who was "really, really smart" in each picture. By 6 years of age, children from different races and geographical regions in the United States invariably selected White men as being really, really smart—they were least likely to pick Black men. Also, they were more likely to pick Black women as smart relative to Black men. Thus, very young children are already forming racial (and gender) stereotypes about people's intellectual ability (Jaxon et al., 2019). In subsequent chapters, we will investigate how children's views and attitudes about people from different ethnic and racial backgrounds shape their treatment of others.

essentialism Statements and beliefs that members of a group share underlying characteristics and behaviors

✓ CHECK YOUR UNDERSTANDING 10.17

1. Do young children understand that race is a stable characteristic? Provide evidence to support your answer.
2. How might essentialist language lead to children forming stereotypes?

Family Context and Racial and Ethnic Identity

LEARNING OBJECTIVE 10.18 Explain the ways that parents socialize children around race and ethnicity.

The messages that parents transmit to their children about race and ethnicity fall under the broad umbrella of **racial and ethnic socialization**. The study of *racial* socialization largely focuses on how Black parents prepare their

racial and ethnic socialization Caregivers' socialization practices and messages to children about race and ethnicity children for racial barriers and racial stratification in the United States. The study of *ethnic* socialization largely focuses on the cultural identity of immigrant families and children in the United States as they confront pressures to assimilate into the dominant society.

Types of Racial and Ethnic Socialization Messages

Parents socialize young children about race and ethnicity in various ways. They may convey information *physically*, such as by crossing the street when a person of a different race is hanging out at a storefront. They may convey information *verbally,* by outwardly stating that "Asians excel in math" and making other essentialist comments as just reviewed. They may communicate messages *intentionally*, by purposely talking about racial barriers with a child, and *unintentionally*, for example, through a wary glance directed to a person of a different race or ethnicity. Furthermore, parents' communications may be *unsolicited*, such as when a parent spontaneously talks about the ethnic background of a child's friend, or *solicited,* such as by answering a child's question about why some children speak a different language (Hughes, Bachman, et al., 2006).

Messages about race and ethnicity can further be broken down by content, namely what adults convey to children when they talk about race. Developmental scientist Diane Hughes identified four types of racial socialization messages based on her research with families of color (Hughes, Rodriguez, et al., 2006; Hughes, Watford, & DelToro, 2016):

- **Preparation for bias**: Messages that make children aware of discrimination and arm children with coping mechanisms.

- **Promotion of mistrust**: Messages that foster distrust in interracial interactions through cautions or warnings to children about other racial groups or barriers to success for racial groups.

- **Egalitarianism**: Messages that emphasize similarities among people of all races and ethnicities and encourage children to value individual qualities over racial group membership.

- **Cultural socialization**: Messages that teach children about their racial or ethnic heritage, for example by talking about cultural figures and sharing culturally relevant books and music; promoting cultural traditions, such as by celebrating cultural holidays and eating ethnic foods; and instilling cultural, racial, and ethnic pride, for example by speaking in the family's native language and encouraging children to do so as well.

How Messages Change with Children's Age

How do parents' racial and ethnic socialization messages change with children's age? Parents of young children are less likely to discuss racial or ethnic issues than are parents of older children and adolescents. Often, parents believe their children to be too young to engage in discussions about race, although such beliefs may be misguided and lead to delayed discussions about race with children who would otherwise benefit from such conversations (Sullivan, Wilton, & Apfelbaum, 2020).

Still, Black parents are more likely than White parents to engage in race and ethnicity related discussions with their children, and they do so even with young children (Hughes, Rodriguez, et al., 2006). In particular, Black parents frequently endorse messages of egalitarianism with their preschoolers, perhaps hoping to instill a sense of equality and hope and a feeling of protection in their children (Doucet, Banerjee, & Parade, 2018). Moreover, African American parents of preschoolers who talked about their African heritage, and who provided their children with homes that were rich in African

preparation for bias A type of racial-ethnic socialization message in which adults communicate to children the risk of discrimination toward their group and offer children coping strategies

promotion of mistrust A type of racial-ethnic socialization message identified in which adults communicate to children distrust of people from other groups (e.g., warnings about other racial groups)

egalitarianism A type of racial-ethnic socialization message in which adults highlight similarities and equality among people of all races and ethnicities

cultural socialization A type of racial-ethnic socialization message in which adults educate children about children's racial or ethnic heritage, promote children's cultural heritage, and instill racial and ethnic pride in children

American culture had children with greater knowledge and problem-solving skills compared to children of parents who did not socialize culture in these ways. Additionally, parents who socialized children to be proud of their heritage had children with fewer behavior problems compared to parents who were less likely to express cultural pride (Caughy et al., 2002).

At the other extreme, negative messages about race or ethnicity are clearly harmful, and young children are quick to pick up on such messages. To illustrate, preschool age children from White, middle-class backgrounds were shown films of interactions between a Black actor and a White actor that differed in whether or not the White actor avoided eye contact with the Black actor and maintained physical distance. Children who viewed films in which the White actor acted uneasy in the presence of the Black actor later expressed negative attitudes toward the Black actor. They also extended their negative attitudes to other Black individuals. However, children who had not viewed the White actor's unease did not display negative attitudes toward the Black actor (Castelli, De Dea, & Nesdale, 2008). If a single laboratory session can instill wariness in young children based on a person's race, then it is safe to assume that adults can profoundly influence children's attitudes and behaviors through what they do and say, whether intentionally or unintentionally.

Egalitarianism versus "Color-Blind" Ideologies

Parents frequently communicate the importance of egalitarianism to children. At least two-thirds of parents from African American, White, and Latino families report endorsing egalitarianism (Hughes, Watford, & DelToro, 2016). However, egalitarianism is not the same thing as being "color blind," or avoiding discussion about race altogether. White non-Hispanic U.S. parents are more likely to endorse a color-blind ideology than are parents of color, perhaps out of fear of being viewed as prejudiced (Apfelbaum et al., 2008). Indeed, White parents view categorizing people along racial lines to be objectionable and a contributor to racial inequality (Neville et al., 2000; Ryan et al., 2007).

To illustrate the phenomenon of color-blindness, European American mothers were video recorded while reading race-themed books to their 4- to 5-year-old children. One book, entitled *What If the Zebras Lost Their Stripes?*, was designed to elicit thinking about racial relations through questions such as "Could Black and White friends still hold hands?" Only 11% of the mothers mentioned interracial interactions and nearly all the mothers reported a color-blind approach to racial socialization (Pahlke, Bigler, & Suizzo, 2012).

✓ CHECK YOUR UNDERSTANDING 10.18

1. How might parents intentionally or inadvertently instill racial or ethnic biases in their young children?
2. What are the four types of racial socialization messages parents communicate to children? Provide examples of each.

Moral Development

Research reviewed thus far naturally sparks questions about how children develop a sense of justice and morality and come to learn that certain behaviors are right and others wrong. Even young children make decisions about right and wrong every day. At times, their decisions are fairly straightforward, such as determining whether it is okay to hit someone just because that person made you angry, or whether to assist a child who is injured. At other times, decisions are fraught with uncertainty and require children to consider multiple factors—such as whether it is acceptable to give more cookies to a best friend than to a less-liked peer when handing out school snacks. Because moral judgments vary in complexity, young children sometimes behave in ways that appear to be equitable and at other times in ways that appear to be unfair. What factors contribute to children's moral reasoning and behaviors? How does moral development change over the course of early childhood? Freud, Piaget, and Kohlberg advanced theories on moral development that set the stage for contemporary studies on young children's reasoning about right and wrong.

Psychodynamic View: Freud and the Id

LEARNING OBJECTIVE 10.19 Explain the limitations of Freud's interpretation of why children behave immorally.

If Freud were asked to explain why a child acted immorally, he would attribute the child's behavior to an instinctual, biological drive for pleasure. Freud used the term **id** to describe such drives, noting that the id is especially evident in infants and young children who act with little regard for the consequences of their behaviors. Freud believed that over time children internalize the values of authority figures—parents, teachers, and so forth—and the moral edicts of the larger society. The internalization process involves the superego, which suppresses the urges of the id and begins to dominate so that children behave in socially acceptable ways (Freud, 1923). In essence, Freud claimed that the superego controls a person's development of conscience.

id According to Sigmund Freud, a part of one's personality comprising the primitive, natural biological drives for pleasure and maximum gratification that are present from birth and that explain why a child may act immorally

In Freud's view, moral behavior does not come easily. Children must work against their basic, selfish impulses. He characterized the superego's attempt to suppress selfish desires as an uncomfortable tension between the needs of the individual and the needs of society. Moreover, Freud recognized that children could absorb and reflect the ideologies of authority figures without considering whether those ideologies were right or just, such as when a child internalizes a parent's racist views. So, internalizing parents' and society's values did not necessarily define a moral sense in children.

Although Freud's theory aptly captured the tension that exists between a child's desires and societal norms around right and wrong, his psychodynamic orientation ignored the importance of cognitive factors. Piaget and Kohlberg expanded the study of morality to embrace moral reasoning—how children's thinking guides their judgments and behaviors around moral dilemmas.

✓ CHECK YOUR UNDERSTANDING 10.19

1. Explain how tensions between the id and superego lead children to behave in socially acceptable ways.

Cognitive Developmental View: Piaget and Kohlberg

LEARNING OBJECTIVE 10.20 Compare and contrast Piaget's and Kohlberg's characterization of children's development of moral reasoning.

Piaget and Kohlberg brought cognitive development to the foreground in the study of moral development. Piaget's (1932) observations of children led him to conclude that children younger than 8–10 years of age focus on the outcomes of behaviors and mandates of authority, but they are not yet able to take a person's underlying intentions into account. For example, when Piaget asked children ages 4–7 who should be punished more severely—a boy who accidentally broke twelve cups or a boy who broke a single cup in the process of trying to obtain jam that he was forbidden to eat—most children said that the boy who broke more cups should receive the harsher punishment. By 8–10 years of age, however, children reasoned that the boy who broke one cup should be punished, basing judgment on the boy's intentions.

Lawrence Kohlberg extended Piaget's conceptualization into a theory of six stages of moral development (**FIGURE 10.21**). Kohlberg presented people of different ages with dilemmas and asked them to reason about the situation. In a classic Kohlberg dilemma, a fictitious character, Heinz, had a wife who was dying from a cancer that could only be cured with one drug. The druggist in town was charging ten times the production cost of the drug, and Heinz could only pull together half the money required. Heinz asked the druggist to sell the drug for a lower cost or let him pay later. The druggist refused, so in desperation Heinz broke into the store to steal the drug. Kohlberg then asked whether it was right or wrong for Heinz to have stolen the drug, and why. Kohlberg then categorized participant's responses into one of six stages, which fell under three broad levels of reasoning: pre-conventional, conventional, and post-conventional.

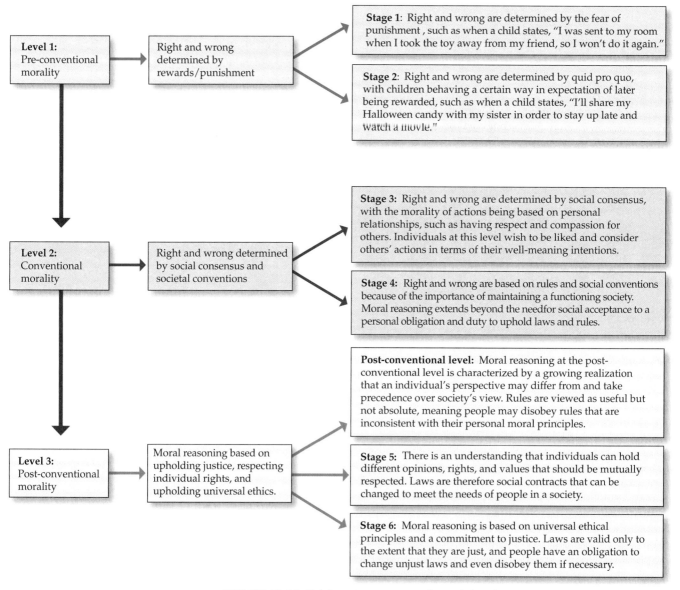

FIGURE 10.21 Kohlberg's six stages of moral development.   Kohlberg's six stages fall under three broad levels of moral reasoning: pre-conventional, conventional, and post-conventional. (After M. W. Eysenck. 2002. *Simply Psychology*, 2nd ed. Psychology Press: New York and London. Copyright 2002. Reproduced by permission of Taylor and Francis Group, LLC, a division of Informa plc.)

- **Pre-conventional**: Moral reasoning is based on the direct consequences of actions—obedience and punishment (stage 1), and self-interest (stage 2); pre-conventional reasoning is seen in early childhood.
- **Conventional**: Moral reasoning is based on social consensus (stage 3) and societal conventions and expectations about right and wrong (stage 4); conventional reasoning typically is not seen until late childhood, adolescence, or adulthood.
- **Post-conventional**: Moral reasoning is characterized by a growing realization that an individual's perspective may differ from and take precedence over society's view (stage 5). Rules are viewed as useful but not absolute (stage 6).

Although Kohlberg primarily tested older children, teens, and adults, his findings pertain to young children, whose moral reasoning fits into the first two stages. Thus, consistent with Piaget's findings, young children's reasoning centered on the outcome of a behavior, such as whether it was rewarded or punished, rather than people's intentions, social conventions, or universal principles.

pre-conventional A broad level of moral reasoning identified by Lawrence Kohlberg based on the direct consequences of actions

conventional A level of moral reasoning identified by Lawrence Kohlberg based on social consensus, societal expectations, and conventional reasoning

post-conventional A level of moral reasoning identified by Lawrence Kohlberg based on abstract principles of human rights, justice, and equality

✓ CHECK YOUR UNDERSTANDING 10.20

1. Describe Kohlberg's theory of moral reasoning and the levels of moral reasoning he identified in children.

Social Domain View

LEARNING OBJECTIVE 10.21 Explain how children's developments in psychological, moral, and social domains relate to their moral judgments.

Social domain theory describes three distinct areas of social knowledge as core to children's judgments about right and wrong—the moral domain, psychological domain, and societal domain (Killen & Smetana, 2015; Smetana, 2013) (**FIGURE 10.22**). Furthermore, social domain theory asserts that children's understanding of psychological and societal domains affects their moral decisions: As children find themselves in situations that range from the straightforward to immensely complex, their moral reasoning and behaviors shift (Smetana, Jambon, & Ball, 2014). Situational influences on moral judgments challenge Piaget's and Kohlberg's assertion that children apply the same moral reasoning across the board because they are in a fixed stage of thinking.

moral domain An area of social knowledge within social domain theory that focuses on reasoning based on moral issues around others' rights, fairness, equal treatment, discrimination, and bias

The Moral Domain

The **moral domain** encompasses reasoning about others' welfare and rights, fairness, justice, and equal treatment. It also includes behaviors at the forefront of current social concerns—prejudice, bias, and discrimination. Social domain theorists observe that even very young children are able to make moral judgments, unlike Piaget and Kohlberg's claim that moral reasoning is only seen in older children. For example, when 3-year-old children witnessed a puppet hurt another puppet in a laboratory study, they objected to the harmful behavior, tattled on the transgressor, and acted prosocially toward the victim (Vaish, Missana, & Tomasello, 2011). And, even when researchers asked children what they would do if a teacher said it was *okay to hit* another child, children continued to view hitting as wrong (Smetana & Braeges, 1990; Smetana, Jambon, & Ball, 2014).

Furthermore, young children stated that it is wrong to exclude other children from activities, even when there was

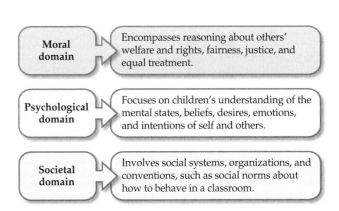

FIGURE 10.22 Moral development from the social domain perspective. According to social domain theory, three distinct areas of social knowledge—the moral domain, psychological domain, and societal domain—are core to children's judgments of right and wrong.

Introduction

Transgression

Punishment

Intentional trial

"If you and Kitty can build a nice big block tower together, you can get some stickers."

Kitty: "Yay!" (Exp 1)
Kitty: "Ha!" (Exp 2)

"Kitty! You knocked the tower over [...] I'm not going to give you any stickers. Here, [child's name], I'm going to put all these stickers right here for you!"

Accidental trial

"If you and Doggie can build a nice big block tower together, you can get some stickers."

Doggie: "Yay! Oops! Oh no!" (Exp 1)
Doggie: "Oops" (Exp 2)

"Doggie! You knocked the tower over [...] I'm not going to give you any stickers. Here, [child's name], I'm going to put all these stickers right here for you!"

FIGURE 10.23 Punishment for intentional and unintentional behavior. When children watched a puppet being punished for accidentally displaying a behavior that resulted in a negative outcome (such as blocks tumbling over), they corrected the punishment. In contrast, they did not correct the punishment on intentional trials. (From N. Chernyak and D. M. Sobel. 2016. *Cog Dev* 39: 13–20.)

psychological domain An area of social knowledge within social domain theory that focuses on children's ability to understand the mental states, beliefs, emotions, and intentions of others

societal domain An area of social knowledge within social domain theory consisting of social systems, organizations, and norms

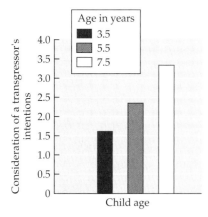

FIGURE 10.24 How children improve in ability to consider a transgressor's intentions. When children are asked to evaluate the wrongness of a transgressor's accidental actions, young children are unlikely to consider the intentions of the transgressor, but with age, children increasingly focus on intention. (After M. Killen et al. 2011. *Cognition* 119: 197–215.)

no apparent punishment for doing so (Mulvey, 2016). And, when a researcher "punished" a protagonist for accidentally doing harm, such as a puppet knocking over blocks unintentionally, children spontaneously corrected the unfair punishment. Yet, they agreed with the punishment when the puppet did so intentionally (Chernyak & Sobel, 2016) (**FIGURE 10.23**). Taken together, children's rejection of hitting, even in the absence of a penalty, and their consideration of a character's intentions rather than simple outcome, challenge Kohlberg's claim that young children's moral reasoning is solely based on punishment and reward.

The Psychological Domain

The **psychological domain** focuses on children's understanding of the mental states, beliefs, desires, emotions, and intentions of self and others. In line with Piaget's emphasis on intentions, as young children develop an understanding of others' beliefs and intentions—aspects of theory of mind (see Chapter 9)—they grow in their moral reasoning around fairness, rights, and equity (e.g., Nobes, Panagiotaki, & Pawson, 2009). To illustrate, developmental scholar Melanie Killen and colleagues tested 3- to 8-year-old children on standard theory of mind tasks and then asked children to judge the transgressions of a story character (Killen et al., 2011). The twist was that children had to make moral judgments about a child who had incomplete knowledge about a situation, and therefore, held a false belief. For example, children were told a story about a character who was cleaning up the lunchroom and threw away a paper bag thinking that it was trash. In reality, the bag contained another child's cupcake. Children who performed well on standard false-belief tasks interpreted the transgressor's actions positively, whereas children who lacked theory of mind had a negative perception and were likely to recommend punishing the child who threw away the cupcake. Consequently, as children grow in false belief understanding over age, they also show increased understanding of a transgressor's intentions (**FIGURE 10.24**). Thus, young children's attainment of false-belief understanding is key to giving the benefit of the doubt to people who act out of ignorance.

The Societal Domain

The **societal domain** involves social systems, organization, and conventions, such as social norms about how to behave in a classroom. It also includes norms around group functioning and group identity, such as the importance of treating peers on a sports team with loyalty. Young children understand and distinguish societal norm violations from moral violations, recognizing that it's okay to "opt out" of societal norms but not okay to treat others in immoral ways (Josephs & Rakoczy, 2016). For example, researchers interviewed children about how they would react to a child wearing pajamas to school, a societal norm violation. The same children were asked how they would react to a child hitting another child, a moral violation. Children judged the moral violation to be less acceptable, more serious, more deserving of punishment, and less dependent on rules or the presence of an authority figure compared to the societal transgression of wearing pajamas to school (Smetana & Braeges, 1990).

Morality and Intergroup Relationships

Up until now, we've seen that young children reject moral violations that harm others; they consider others' intentions (at least partly); and they distinguish between social norm violations and moral violations. However, although young children are able to make moral judgments in relatively straightforward situations, they have difficulty with moral judgments that involve complex situations, especially those involving group identity, an aspect of the societal domain. Young children often have trouble sharing, tend to exclude peers, and may treat peers inequitably when the "in-group" is pitted against the "out-group" (Mulvey et al., 2014a, 2014b). For example, a preschooler who is in charge of handing out treats to classmates might give more treats to friends than to non-friends, or to girls than to boys, because in-group preferences conflict with moral judgments around equity and fairness (Rutland, Killen, & Abrams, 2010). In contrast, the same preschooler might be equitable in her distribution of treats to unfamiliar children.

To study children's moral decisions in the context of intergroup relations, developmental scientists sometimes conduct **resource allocation studies**, in which they ask children to distribute coins, treats, stickers, or other rewards to story characters and other children from different social groups (**FIGURE 10.25**). For example, researchers asked preschoolers to distribute stickers to pictures that were labeled as "drawn by a group of boys" or "drawn by a group of girls." Although the pictures were counterbalanced (that is, the identical pictures were merely labeled differently) children allocated more stickers to pictures they thought were drawn by children of their own gender (Halim et al., 2012). Children's sense of loyalty and obligation to the in-group may therefore result in high favoritism toward others "like me."

resource allocation studies
Studies conducted by developmental researchers to examine children's moral decisions around equitable distribution by asking children to distribute coins, treats, or other rewards to story characters and children from other social groups

FIGURE 10.25 Resource allocation studies. In resource allocation studies, children are asked to distribute stickers or other resources to children of the same or a different social group, such as to boys or girls. Young children typically show an in-group bias, giving more resources or rewards to peers who belong to their group.

Young children not only display preferential treatment toward the in-group, but they are also aware that other people do so as well. Three-year-old children expect people to be more likely to harm members of another social group than to harm members of their own social group (Chalik & Rhodes, 2014). For example, researchers introduced 3- and 4-year-old children to two groups of cartoonlike characters, labeled "Flurps" and "Zazes," asking who would be likely to hurt or harm whom. On over 70% of trials, children predicted that a Flurp would harm a Zaz, but would be unlikely to harm another Flurp (Rhodes, 2012) (**FIGURE 10.26**). Children also offered explanations for *why* a Flurp or

(A)

Sharing   Taking away

(B)

Block setting

Harmful
Who did a Flurp steal a block from?
Who did a Flurp hit while building a block tower?
Who did a Flurp say could not help build a block tower?

Helpful
Who did a Flurp share a block with?
Who did a Flurp hug while building a block tower?
Who did a Flurp say could help build a block tower?

(C)

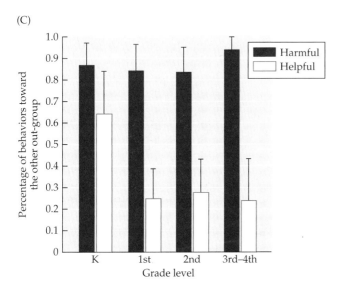

FIGURE 10.26 Children's loyalties to in-group versus out-group peers. (A) Children of different ages were presented with a brief story about two groups defined by their shirt color, the Zazes (red) and the Flurps (blue). (B) A researcher then asked children various questions, such as who was likely to harm or help whom. Even younger children responded that Flurps would hurt Zazes, rather than other Flurps. However, they also expected Flurps to help those of the other group. Older children, however, responded that Flurps would be unlikely to help other Zazes. (C) To illustrate, when plotting children's responses about how likely characters were to help or harm others from the *other* group (the out-group prediction, such as a Flurp toward a Zaz), young children were more likely to still believe that Flurps would help Zazes, but children of older ages believed that Flurps would be unlikely to help Zazes. (B and C after M. Rhodes. 2012. *Child Dev* 83: 1900–1916. © 2012 The Author. Child Development © 2012 Society for Research in Child Development, Inc. All rights reserved.)

Zaz might harm a member of the same category or a different social category (Rhodes, 2014). They stated that category membership explained why a Flurp or Zaz would harm a member of the other group—"He did it because he's a Flurp but the other one's a Zaz." But, when a Flurp or Zaz harmed a member of the *same* group, young children attributed the behavior to the character's emotional state—"He did it because he was angry."

✓ CHECK YOUR UNDERSTANDING 10.21

1. What are some key ways in which social domain theory differs from stage theories in considering how children reason about right and wrong?
2. Why do young children have difficulty making decisions that will affect both in-group and out-group peers?

Family Context of Moral Development

LEARNING OBJECTIVE 10.22 Identify how a child's relationship with parents and siblings might affect children's moral development.

Children learn how to reason and act morally from the people around them. In this regard, children's experiences at home are foundational to the development of a moral sense. Warm and responsive parents are likely to raise children who are motivated to internalize their parents' values and comply with parental discipline and socialization. For example, when a mother is responsive and positive during mother-child interactions, a child comes to value good behavior and wants to please others (Kochanska et al., 2005). In contrast, when parents exert control in aversive and intrusive ways and use punitive discipline in what is referred to as **power assertion**, children show lower moral development, such as being more likely to misbehave and less likely to feel guilty following transgressions than children of parents low in power-assertion (e.g., Volling, Mahoney, & Rauer, 2009).

power assertion Control exerted by caregivers over children that is aversive, intrusive, and punitive

Sibling interactions also provide unique opportunities for young children to learn moral lessons. The arrival of a sibling leads to conversations about moral issues in the family, such as when older siblings misbehave after the birth of a sibling (Dunn & Hughes, 2014). Additionally, parents frequently talk about younger siblings' feelings, needs, and desires with older siblings, which may further support children's moral understanding.

Furthermore, children's positive experiences with their older siblings influence moral reasoning. Kindergarten children who had experienced positive interactions with their older siblings—in the form of nurturance, teaching, affection, and so forth—were more likely to understand how a protagonist from a story would feel after having a toy taken away by a transgressor (Dunn, Brown, & Maguire, 1995).

✓ CHECK YOUR UNDERSTANDING 10.22

1. Which behaviors in parents and siblings relate to children's moral reasoning and behaviors?

Cultural Cosntext of Moral Development

LEARNING OBJECTIVE 10.23 Describe ways that culture might shape children's moral reasoning.

Do children from different communities receive different messages around moral judgments and behaviors? Adults across cultural communities take on different roles in teaching children about moral behaviors. As one example, traditional Chinese Confucian values emphasize parents' role in training and disciplining children around proper behavior. Perhaps for this reason, Chinese parents are more likely to talk about moral standards, children's past transgressions, and negative consequences of misbehaviors than are U.S. European American parents (e.g., Luo et al., 2014; Wang & Fivush, 2005). In turn, Chinese preschool children are also more likely to talk about moral rules and social norms in their conversations with mothers than are U.S. children, suggesting they have internalized those cultural values (Wang & Fivush, 2005).

Preschool children from different cultural communities also differ in their moral behaviors around equitable resource allocation. Researchers compared 3- and 5-year-old children's fairness and equity across seven cultural communities that varied in population density (urban, suburban, rural), socioeconomic status of households (middle-class vs. low-income), and cultural emphases (individualistic vs. collectivist). Children were asked to share desirable items such as candies with an adult experimenter. Children from both middle-class and low-income households from cultures that have been characterized as collectivistic—Peru, Fiji, and China—showed less self-interest and more fairness than did children from middle-class families in cultures characterized as individualistic, such as the United States (Rochat et al., 2009).

✓ CHECK YOUR UNDERSTANDING 10.23

1. List an example of how children's equitable allocation of resources differs by cultural community. Why might this be?

Developmental Cascades

My visits to the playground allowed me to observe how children dealt with their emotions and those of their peers. Conflicts around toys and turns on a swing required children to summon their emotional skills to resolve disputes. But, compromise and solutions did not always come easily. Children had to accurately identify their own and peers' emotions—"I'm frustrated he's hogging the ball!" or "He's angry!" Children had to interpret social information in the context of the current situation—"He's angry because I grabbed the ball from him." Children had to infer the consequences of the emotion—"A fight can break out if we don't fix the situation." And, finally, children had to regulate their own emotions and behaviors—"Instead of yelling, I'll ask if I can play."

This playground scenario illustrates the many steps involved in developmental cascades: Young children who lack understanding of emotions and social norms may use ineffective strategies to control their emotions and behaviors, and thus be rejected by peers. In turn, poor social relationships can lead to poor emotion regulation, social isolation, and compromised well-being. In some instances, young children with persistent emotional and social problems begin to disengage from school and suffer long-term academic consequences.

Cascades from Emotion Understanding

The most direct path from early emotion understanding to later outcomes occurs through children's social interactions. Understanding emotions arms children with the skills to empathize with peers and interact in socially sensitive ways (Denham, 1986). The emotion-to-social path is a robust force in current and later relationships. Consider a study that illustrates this connection:

Researchers acted out scenes with a puppet and tested how well 2-, 3-, and 4-year-olds understood the puppet's emotions. They then observed how the same children behaved in situations with unfamiliar peers. Children who understood the emotions of the puppet played well with the unfamiliar peer, were able to join an ongoing activity, and verbally encouraged the unfamiliar peer to play with them (Ensor & Hughes, 2005). Moreover, 3-year-olds with strong emotion understanding displayed high prosocial behaviors toward peers a year later (Ensor, Spencer, & Hughes, 2011).

Just as strong emotion understanding supports social relationships, low emotion understanding undermines social relationships. Preschoolers with difficulties understanding emotions display poor interactions, including aggression and opposition toward peers (Denham et al., 2003; Hughes & Ensor, 2009). Again, the cascading effects of poor emotion understanding persist over time. Five-year-old children who had difficulties understanding emotions had problems with their peers and withdrew from social situations when they were 9 years of age, with detrimental influences spreading to academic competence as well (Izard et al., 2001).

Why might poor emotion understanding negatively impact peer relationships? One reason is that children low in emotion understanding are prone to hostile attribution bias (Dodge & Somberg, 1987). **Hostile attribution bias** occurs when a child inaccurately interprets another child's accidental behaviors as motivated by hostile intentions. Imagine a child who confronts a peer who has accidently broken his toy. If the child mistakenly perceives the peer broke the toy on purpose, and then retaliates with negative behaviors, the child has set up a situation that can lead to escalating aggression and social rejection in the future (Dodge et al., 2003; van Dijk et al., 2019).

Fortunately, interventions that help children frame others' behaviors in a positive, nonhostile light reduce young children's hostile attribution bias. In an experimental study, researchers presented children with scenarios in which a story character did something wrong (such as ruining a drawing), but the reasons for the provocation were ambiguous. Children were then instructed to tell a peer that the story characters had nonhostile intentions. Children who spoke about the benign intentions of the characters showed reduced hostile attribution bias relative to children in a control group (van Dijk et al., 2019).

Cascades from Emotion Regulation

Children's expression and regulation of emotions likewise exert cascading influences on peer acceptance. Young children who effectively regulate their emotions and behaviors display generally high social competence, peer acceptance, and adaptive behavioral coping in times of stress (e.g., Camras & Halberstadt, 2017). Conversely, children who have difficulty regulating emotions and who frequently express negative emotions are prone to aggression and anxiety (Contreras et al., 2000; Miller et al., 2006). Moreover, aggressive preschoolers tend to gravitate toward aggressive playmates, who further model and reinforce antisocial behaviors, thereby inciting a cycle of escalating problem behaviors that impede social skills down the line (Denham et al., 2001).

Emotion regulation matters for school performance as well. Kindergartners who were able to regulate their emotions and behaviors at school performed better on tests of achievement than those with poor self-regulation skills (Howse et al., 2003). Similarly, young children's effortful control has been shown to predict later math performance, reading and literacy skills, and general adjustment (e.g., Blair & Razza, 2007; Liew et al., 2008; Neuenschwander et al., 2012).

Why might children's ability to regulate emotions play out in cognitive and academic domains? For one, positive emotions and high regulation are conducive to task engagement and persistence, whereas negative emotions and low

hostile attribution bias A child's inaccurate interpretation of another child's accidental behavior as motivated by an antagonistic or hostile intention regulation deplete resources that would otherwise be available for learning. Additionally, children who use ineffective strategies to handle emotions, for instance by withdrawing from the situation or venting their anger, get little practice with cognitive skills of problem solving, distraction, and reframing. Consequently, cognitive abilities involved in effortful control are underused and underdeveloped (Blair, 2002; Denham, 2007).

Perhaps one of the most cited studies of early developmental cascades to academic outcomes is based on Walter Mischel's delay-of-gratification marshmallow task. Preschoolers who were able to wait for the marshmallow had higher high school SAT scores than those who could not wait (Shoda, Mischel, & Peake, 1990). And, when participants in the marshmallow study were followed up as adults, differences in brain activation patterns were seen between those ranked low versus high in their self-control as preschoolers (Casey et al., 2011).

However, researchers debate how to interpret associations between delay of gratification tasks and later outcomes. Perhaps, a family's economic resources accounts for children's ability to hold out longer for a second marshmallow. Young children from poor households might reason that they should take the marshmallow now, rather than wait, because of uncertainty about later receiving a marshmallow. If so, then some of the long-term cascades from delay tasks to outcomes may be due to income differences in children's families. In fact, the long-term effects seen in the marshmallow task diminished somewhat (but not entirely) when controlling for family background and the quality of children's home environment (Watts, Duncan, & Quan, 2018). This serves as a reminder of the multiple influences in child and family that contribute to long-term cascades.

Cascades from Attachment and Peer Relationships

Children's relationships with caregivers and peers reciprocally affect one another and establish patterns of engagement that flourish into mature, future social interactions. Indeed, children who are securely attached to their primary caregiver(s) are more likely to show strong effortful control, be accepted by their peers, engage in reciprocal friendships, and be less likely to experience hostile conflicts with peers than are children who are insecurely attached (e.g., DeMulder et al., 2000; Pallini et al., 2018). Conversely, young children without the benefits of a secure attachment relationship may have few opportunities to witness sensitive, positive role models in their caregivers, which may lead them to view other people as untrustworthy and rejecting. Preschool children with insecure attachment to their caregivers showed higher depression in early adolescence than did those with secure attachments (Priddis & Howieson, 2012). Children with disorganized attachment at 3–4 years scored higher on anxiety and depression and lower on self-esteem at 11–12 years than did children of other attachment groups (Lecompte et al., 2014).

Similarly, poor peer relationships establish conditions that can spiral downward and interfere with later adjustment. Children whose peers rejected them during early childhood were at greater risk for internalizing problems, such as anxiety and depression, and externalizing problems, such as delinquency, hyperactivity, and distraction, through preadolescence (Ladd, 2006). They were also more likely to experience chronic peer maltreatment throughout the school years, which resulted in skipping school, declines in classroom participation, and poor grades years later (Buhs, Ladd, & Herald, 2006).

Cascades from Moral Development

We've seen that early childhood lays the foundation for a moral sense. As young children interact with their peers, teachers, and other people, they have opportunities to reflect on why they or others treated children in kind or unfair ways, and how to remedy those injustices in the future. Notably, differences among young children in their moral reasoning and behaviors persist over time and can affect current and later prosocial and antisocial behaviors (Aksan & Kochanska, 2005; Gummerum et al., 2010). For example, 2- and 4-year-old children's moral conscience, reflected in their respect for the rules established by their caregivers, predicted their prosocial and rule-abiding behaviors at 6–7 years (Kochanska et al., 2010). In turn, the positive, prosocial behaviors associated with moral development enhance children's acceptance by peers. Popular children display better moral understanding than do rejected children, and children's moral understanding correlates with peer popularity even when researchers statistically control for children's theory of mind and language skills (Peterson & Siegal, 2002).

■ CLOSING THOUGHTS
Development Starts Small

Young children understand a lot more about their emotional and social worlds than do infants. Yet, adults often complain about children's limitations and how far children have to go. Children have difficulties regulating emotions; they display an egocentric orientation in their social interactions; they rigidly adhere to gender stereotypes; and their moral reasoning remains narrow when things get complicated. However, the focus on limitations assumes that young children are incomplete because their thinking and behaviors have not yet transitioned to the mature end-state of adults. This view is seriously flawed. Rather than focusing on the unfinished child, developmental scientists recognize that children occupy a unique niche, with demands and challenges that differ significantly from those of adults (e.g., Werchan & Amso, 2017; Bjorklund, 1997; Rovee-Collier & Cuevas, 2009).

And so, as we conclude this chapter, let's take a moment to consider how young children's social and emotional skills are exquisitely adapted to their current needs. As a start, emotions run strong and stand front and center from moment to moment, allowing children to connect their intense feelings to current circumstances. Furthermore, the unfettered emotions of early childhood motivate children to actively pursue their personal interests and learn new things. Thus, emotions are the engines of change. At the same time, young children's relatively small social networks allow them to practice resolving conflicts, tempering aggression, and acting prosocially in familiar, safe environments. Finally, because the rights and wrongs of the world are straightforward, young children learn the basics of morality before they add layers of complexity that are not yet important for them to worry about.

If Erikson was correct in underscoring the importance of young children's initiative and the need for children to internalize social norms, then it is fair to conclude that development is at just the right place at just the right time. Development starts small for a reason. The future will take many years to arrive, making it vitally important that children adapt to the present and learn the fundamentals of reasoning and behavior that will pay off in the long run.

The Developmentalist's Toolbox		
Method	Purpose	Description
Measuring children's emotional development		
Emotion matching tasks	To examine young children's emotion understanding	Children are asked to either sort photographs or drawings of facial expressions into groups based on similarities or select a picture whose facial expression matches a target emotion word (such as pointing to a sad face when asked which face is sad).
Emotion vignettes	To examine young children's emotion understanding	Experimenters tell children brief stories or enact play scenes and then ask children to select a picture or answer questions about how the character feels.
Delay-of-gratification tasks	To assess children's emotion regulation	Experimenters measure children's ability to resist the temptation for an immediate reward with the prospect of a later (often larger) reward.
Measuring children's social development		
Preschool Attachment Classification System (PACS)	To assess attachment in 3- to 5-year-olds	A modification of the Ainsworth Strange Situation involving separation from the mother, reunion, second separation, and second reunion. Examiners code children's behaviors upon reunions with the caregiver as a means of assessing their use of their caregiver as a secure base.
Attachment Q-Sort (AQS)	To assess attachment in 3- to 5-year-olds	Trained observers or mothers sort cards containing behavioral descriptions of proximity-seeking behavior—such as "Child readily shares with mother or lets her hold things if she asks." These cards are then sorted according to how well they fit the behaviors of the target child.
Resource allocation studies	To study children's moral decisions in the context of intergroup relations	Children are asked to distribute coins, treats, stickers, or other rewards to puppets and other children under conditions where group membership is manipulated.
Evaluations of moral transgressions	To evaluate children's moral reasoning	Children are presented with a situation in which a transgression has occurred—such as one child pushing another child off a swing—and are asked to reason about the magnitude of the transgression, the appropriate punishment, and so forth.

■ Chapter Summary

Emotion Understanding

- Parenting sensitivity relates to secure attachment in early childhood.
- Young children are able to understand emotional valence (whether emotions are positive or negative) before they can understand the distinctions among different types of positive or negative emotions.
- Compared to toddlers, children aged 4–7 recognize and name a greater range of emotions; can distinguish among

different types of positive and negative emotions; and are beginning to understand the causes and consequences of emotions.

Emotion Regulation and Temperament

- Young children also show gains in effortful control—skills that help them regulate emotions. As a result, they become less dependent on other people to help them regulate their emotions.

- Researchers often study effortful control using delay-of-gratification tasks.
- Temperament is associated with individual differences in self-regulation.
- Distinctions have been made among children who are highly inhibited, undercontrolled, or well-regulated.

Contexts of Emotional Development

- Emotion coaching—parental sensitivity and talk about emotions—as well as sibling relationships help children regulate and understand their emotions.
- Preschool interventions that specifically target aggression lead to improvements in this area of emotion regulation.
- Cultural norms around emotional displays are associated with children's emotional expressions and understanding, and emotional expressiveness is a risk for children from certain communities but not others.
- Individual differences among children in emotion understanding, emotional expressions, and self-regulation predict children's social competence (including peer status and externalizing and internalizing behaviors) and school performance within and over time.

Attachment and Caregiver-Child Relationship Quality

- Measures of attachment in early childhood can be made using the Preschool Attachment Classification System (a modification of the Strange Situation test) and the Attachment Q-sort, in which cards that describe attachment-related behaviors are sorted based on the target child's behaviors at home.
- Parenting sensitivity relates to secure attachment in early childhood.

Peers and Friends

- Positive parent-child interactions, home climate, and cultural norms and values around social behaviors such as aggression and shyness relate to individual differences among children in their social behaviors.
- The nature and number of children's peer relationships change in early childhood. Children engage in more prosocial behaviors, begin to work through conflicts, and enjoy cooperative play and social pretend play with other children.
- Although conflict and overall aggression decline across early childhood, three types of aggression are seen: hostile aggression, instrumental aggression, and relational aggression.
- Hostile and instrumental types of aggression decline over early childhood, but relational aggression increases from early childhood onward.

Identity Development

- Gender identification is explained by Freud's psychodynamic view as being rooted in children's attraction to their opposite-sex parent—referred to as the Oedipus complex for boys and Electra complex for girls—and guilt over these feelings, which leads to identifying with the same-sex parent.

- Social learning theories emphasize modeling and reinforcement in gender development. Observing others' actions—referred to as imitation learning—powerfully influences children's behaviors.
- Cognitive developmental theories recognize children's active participation in gender identity development, as they construct meaning about what it means to be a boy and girl.
- According to cognitive developmental theorists, children progress through three stages: (1) gender identity, (2) gender stability, and (3) gender consistency.
- Young children are beginning to categorize individuals and self by race and ethnicity, but do not yet fully grasp the idea that race and ethnicity are stable over time.
- Parents are key socializers of children's gender identity development and sense of race and ethnicity.
- Parents engage in gender socialization (whether intentionally or unintentionally) through their play with children, language interactions, and division of household labor.
- Parents' messages about race and ethnicity fall into four broad categories: preparation for bias, promotion of mistrust, egalitarianism, and cultural socialization.

Moral Development

- Freud claimed that the "id" of the personality is responsible for children's impulsive and basic behaviors toward self-fulfillment, and that, over time, the superego develops and represses basic urges, allowing children to internalize the values of authority figures.
- Piaget and Kohlberg stated that stagelike changes in cognition affect children's reasoning about moral situations.
- Piaget believed that young children focus on outcomes of behaviors rather than considering the underlying intentions of people's behavior.
- Kohlberg identified six stages of moral development in three broad categories: pre-conventional, conventional, and post-conventional.
- The social domain view contends that the moral decisions children make fall into three domains that influence one another: the societal domain, the psychological domain, and the moral domain.
- The social domain view of moral development holds that children's moral decisions and behaviors are determined by many factors, including children's understanding of mental states and consideration of intergroup relationships.
- Warm and responsive parenting, parents' talk about moral issues, and experiences with siblings are all positively associated with children's moral development.
- Parents' power assertion and punitive discipline relate negatively to children's moral development.
- Cultural values and emphases around individualism and collectivism are also associated with children's moral development.

Developmental Cascades

- Children's difficulties in understanding emotions can disrupt social relationships, by leading to aggression, hostile attribution bias, and opposition toward peers, which can then cascade to poor academic performance.
- Children who are able to regulate their emotions well display cooperative and positive interactions with peers and strong cognitive and academic achievement.

- Secure attachments with parents and positive relationships with peers in early childhood support children's developing social competence and school achievement, whereas insecure attachments and poor peer relationships can lead to social and mental health problems.
- Children's moral reasoning paves the way to positive social relationships and behaviors, in part because children can reason about the underlying intentions of other people's behaviors and respond appropriately.

Thinking Like a Developmentalist

1. You hypothesize that children's experiences with delay-of-gratification type tasks (that is, opportunities to practice delaying rewards) lead to improvements in their prosocial behaviors with peers. How might you test this question and what kind of findings would lend support to your hypothesis?

2. A researcher hypothesizes that preschool children with siblings of the opposite sex would be more fair or equitable in their treatment of boys and girls in the classroom than would children with only same-sex siblings. The researcher further hypothesizes that preschool children with a secure attachment to their opposite-sex parent/caregiver will also be more fair or equitable in their treatment of boys and girls than will those with an insecure attachment to their opposite-sex parent/caregiver. How might these two hypotheses be tested?

Physical Development and Health in Middle Childhood

Drawing by Minxin Cheng from a photo by Annie Spratt on Unsplash

I often observed children being dropped off at the bus stop as I waited for my children to return home from school. Dozens would tumble out of the bus, deftly jumping off the highest step, vaulting over garbage cans, and chasing one another in games of tag. I marveled at the newfound motor skills and independence of those children, who, just a short time ago, had seemed clumsy and reliant on adults for everything ranging from tying shoelaces to climbing playground slides.

Changes in brain and body support gains in physical prowess, strength, and motor coordination during middle childhood, and enable children to participate in the activities of their cultures in new ways. In the United States, school-age children skillfully use pens, pencils, scissors, smart phones, and computer keyboards, and participate in team sports that require eye-limb coordination. They gain practice with the motor skills expected of them in a society where schooling takes up a major part of middle childhood and technology is widespread. Children in hunter-gatherer communities, in contrast, develop different types of skills under conditions where electricity is sometimes sporadic and survival depends on learning how to obtain food by foraging for wild plants, mollusks, crustaceans, fish, and other animals. In these remote villages, children learn to wield bows, arrows, and spears with impressive accuracy, and deftly navigate rivers, lakes, oceans, and forests (**FIGURE 11.1**).

Notably, children across cultural communities are physically capable of helping their families with everyday survival at similar ages, as their growing body size and strength enable them to climb trees, dig deep for edible roots,

BRAIN AND PHYSICAL DEVELOPMENT
- Brain Development
- Physical Development

HEALTH
- Nutrition
- Sleep
- Disease and Injury

Developmental Cascades

Closing Thoughts: Stability and Change

FIGURE 11.1 Physical changes in middle childhood. Changes in brain and body during middle childhood lead to physical prowess, strength, and motor coordination and enable children to engage in the routine activities of their cultures in new ways. Here, young Xingu Indians hunt in the Amazon, Brazil, displaying the motor skills that they have developed through physical development and their practice with this cultural activity.

and hunt and carry large game for food sustenance (Lew-Levy et al., 2017). For instance, Nayaka children, who live near the southern tip of Africa, begin to independently hunt small game at 6 years of age. They assist adults in butchering large game by holding up torches and aligning the animal's limbs for easy cutting (Hewlett & Lamb, 2017). Around the same age, children of Meriam—a region between Australia's Cape York Peninsula and the southern coast of Papua New Guinea—begin spearing fish and foraging shellfish (Bliege & Bird, 2002). Adults rely on older children who can walk long distances to search for food without tiring and don't require constant warnings to steer clear of dangers (Bliege et al., 2002). Sometimes children forage with other children in "play groups" after school or on weekends. In addition, children of the hunter-gatherer group Hazda in Tanzania hunt small game with bows and arrows by 10 years of age (Jones & Marlowe, 2002).

The physical accomplishments of children in hunting-gathering communities span the ages when children in the United States enter formal schooling and join team sports to work on their physical stamina and precision of their footwork in soccer and aims in football. That's because the universal, physical changes that accompany childhood pave the way to skilled behaviors—ranging from the expert foraging of Nayaka, Meriam, and Hazda children to the adept football throws of U.S. children. In this chapter, we will learn about brain and physical development in middle childhood, the factors that support or impede development, and the long-term cascading influences from physical development and health to domains such as school performance and social relationships.

Brain and Physical Development

Middle childhood, which roughly spans 6–12 years of age, is sandwiched between the seemingly overnight transformations of early childhood and adolescence. Yet, although middle childhood is characterized by slow, gradual growth in brain, body, and motor skills, the end result is a remarkably changed child. Children's brains continue to develop through myelination, synaptogenesis, and pruning (see Chapter 2). Physically, children grow on average over 1 foot (30 cm) in height and 40 pounds (18 kg) in weight, and they acquire the strength, flexibility, balance, and agility needed to control their body. Depending on cultural context, children may learn to ride a bicycle, weave with a loom, kick-flip a skateboard, balance heavy loads on their head, or expertly manipulate pencils, scissors, chopsticks, machetes, spears, or arrows.

Brain Development

The prolonged period of brain development from childhood through adolescence makes possible the extraordinarily complex cognitive, emotional, and social capacities of humans (Giedd & Rapoport, 2010; Menon, 2013). During middle childhood, developments in the brain include changes to white and gray matter volume, growth in the complexity of neural networks, and increased coordination across regions of the brain. Such changes enable children to think and act in new ways. And, in line with the idea that brain and body reciprocally influence one another, as children interact with their environments, their experiences catalyze further brain development.

Changes to White and Gray Matter

LEARNING OBJECTIVE 11.1 Describe what accounts for the distinct patterns of change seen in white and gray matter volumes from middle childhood through adolescence.

The brain continues to form new synapses, myelinate axons, and prune unused synapses throughout middle childhood (Giedd & Rapoport, 2010). **Magnetic resonance imaging (MRI)** scanners use strong magnetic fields to generate images of structures in different brain regions (Keller & Robert, 2009). Such imaging techniques show changes in the brain's gray matter (cell bodies, dendrites, and axon terminals) and white matter (axons that appear white when covered by myelin sheath) across middle childhood and adolescence, reflecting the production, myelination, and pruning of neurons (Mills et al., 2016).

White matter volume increases linearly throughout middle childhood and adolescence, reflecting the myelination of axons (e.g., Giedd et al., 1999; Yap et al., 2013). Recall that myelin is the fatty white sheath that surrounds axons. The growth in myelin helps strengthen brain connections by allowing faster transmission of neural signals. Myelination is pronounced in areas of the prefrontal cortex (Janowsky & Carper, 1996; Sowell et al., 2002) and the corpus callosum, which connects the left and right hemispheres (Lenroot & Giedd, 2006). Improved communication between hemispheres aids motor coordination because the left half of the body is faster than it had been at knowing what the right half is doing, and vice versa.

In contrast to the linear growth of white matter, cortical gray matter increases in childhood and then decreases in adolescence, reflecting the pruning of unused synapses (**FIGURE 11.2**) (Giedd et al., 1999; Mills et al., 2016). However, peaks

magnetic resonance imaging (MRI) A brain imaging technique that uses strong magnetic fields and radio waves to create images of the brain's anatomy, including structures in different brain regions

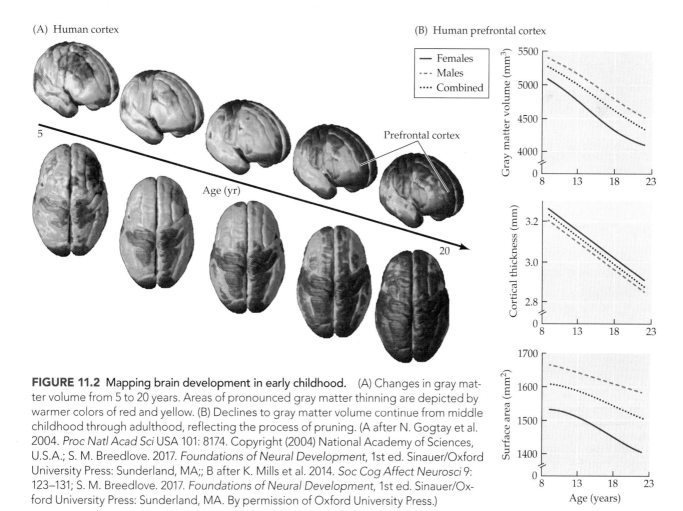

FIGURE 11.2 Mapping brain development in early childhood. (A) Changes in gray matter volume from 5 to 20 years. Areas of pronounced gray matter thinning are depicted by warmer colors of red and yellow. (B) Declines to gray matter volume continue from middle childhood through adulthood, reflecting the process of pruning. (A after N. Gogtay et al. 2004. *Proc Natl Acad Sci* USA 101: 8174. Copyright (2004) National Academy of Sciences, U.S.A.; S. M. Breedlove. 2017. *Foundations of Neural Development*, 1st ed. Sinauer/Oxford University Press: Sunderland, MA;; B after K. Mills et al. 2014. *Soc Cog Affect Neurosci* 9: 123–131; S. M. Breedlove. 2017. *Foundations of Neural Development*, 1st ed. Sinauer/Oxford University Press: Sunderland, MA. By permission of Oxford University Press.)

to gray matter volume occur in different regions of the brain at different times in development (Gogtay et al., 2004). In particular, the basal ganglia—which controls movement and muscle tone—shows the earliest peak in gray matter volume at around 7.5 years in girls and 10.0 years in boys (Lenroot & Giedd, 2006). Maturation of the basal ganglia contributes to children's improved motor skills relative to the clumsy movements of preschoolers.

The parietal lobe—which is involved in spatial orientation, language, and the integration of sensory information from various parts of the body—peaks in gray matter volume a bit later, at around 10.2 years in girls and 11.8 in boys (Gogtay et al., 2004; Lenroot & Giedd, 2006). Finally, the frontal lobes—which are involved in higher cognitive functions such as selective attention, planning, and problem solving—are the last to fully mature, continuing to develop well into adolescence (Giedd et al., 1999; Gogtay et al., 2004).

✓ CHECK YOUR UNDERSTANDING 11.1

1. What are three types of developments seen in the changing brain during middle childhood?

2. What changes in the brain are associated with improved motor coordination in middle childhood?

Changes to Brain Networks

LEARNING OBJECTIVE 11.2 Describe what brain network analyses reveal about the brain's changing functional connections and communication across middle childhood.

The brain is always active. The billions of neurons in the brain must communicate with one another to allow the body to function. Over the course of development, the brain forms increasingly complex networks of connectivity. Changes to the complexity of brain networks enable efficiency of thinking. Developmental neuroscientists use **brain network analyses** to study how brain connections or networks emerge and change from childhood through adulthood (e.g., Menon, 2013). Brain network analyses entail examining functional MRI (fMRI) signals across the whole brain or specific areas. Scientists can then detect connectivity among neurons based on the areas of the brain that are activated during specific tasks (Menon, 2013). Note that fMRI differs from MRI because it tells scientists about brain processes or *functions*, rather than brain *structure*. Brain network analyses indicate three main changes in the restructuring of brain connectivity through middle childhood:

1. Connections become more complex.

2. Connections become more efficient (with unused connections being eliminated).

3. Long-range or distant brain connections increase, while short-range connections weaken.

Brain network analyses also help scientists understand atypical development. Abnormality in the development of brain networks may contribute to the emergence of psychopathology and clinical symptoms in middle childhood. Many major psychopathologies, including attention-deficit/hyperactivity disorder (described later in this chapter) and anxiety disorders have their origins in middle childhood (Cicchetti & Cohen, 2006). By documenting how neurons in the brain communicate with one another in typically developing children, researchers come closer to understanding what goes awry in the brain of children with neurodevelopmental disabilities such as **autism spectrum disorder** (Menon, 2013) (**FIGURE 11.3**).

✓ CHECK YOUR UNDERSTANDING 11.2

1. What are brain network analyses, and what insights have they provided into how neural networks evolve during middle childhood?

brain network analyses The study of brain processes and functions, including how brain connections or networks emerge and change from childhood to adulthood, using functional MRI (fMRI) signals across areas of the brain

autism spectrum disorder A developmental disability that manifests in challenges in social interaction, problems with speech and nonverbal communication, and restricted/repetitive behaviors. The severity of symptoms differs across individuals

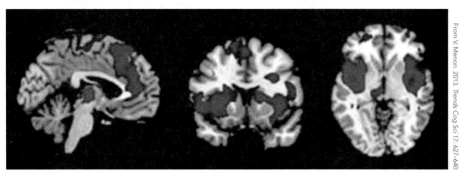

From V. Menon. 2013. *Trends Cog Sci* 17: 627–640

FIGURE 11.3 Brain networks and autism.   The brains of children diagnosed with autism show hyperconnectivity in certain regions of the brain (shown in blue) compared to those of typically developing children, particularly in regions that integrate information about external stimuli, such as sights or sounds, with internal states, such as emotion. (From L. Q. Uddin et al. 2013. *JAMA Psychiatr* 70: 869–879.)

Coordination across Brain Regions

LEARNING OBJECTIVE 11.3 Provide evidence that activities in the brain become increasingly synchronized in middle childhood.

Neurons of the brain communicate by producing electrical signals that generate rhythmic and repetitive activity, or oscillations, known as **brain waves**. Brain waves guide all aspects of human functioning, ranging from moving the eyes to solving abstract math problems.

Researchers can directly measure brain activity using electroencephalography (EEG). EEGs can document whether the brain waves from different cortical networks—for example, the prefrontal and visual cortices—are synchronized. Synchronized brain waves occur when electrical activity of many neurons is coordinated in time (**FIGURE 11.4**).

Coordinated brain wave activity is critical for learning. It's not enough to simply develop complex networks of connection. Neurons across regions of the brain must be synchronized in their firing or activation patterns to allow children to handle the massive connections required for attending to cognitively demanding tasks such as those required in school (e.g., Miller & Buschman, 2013). For example, reading requires children to coordinate areas of the brain responsible for controlling attention, perceiving and recognizing letters and words, perceiving the sounds associated with letters and words, and understanding the meaning of text (Booth et al., 2007). Moreover, synchronized brain waves among regions of the brain help with working memory as children remember and manipulate relevant information (Liebe et al., 2012).

Studies of children's performance on Piagetian conservation tasks (see Chapter 9), conducted nearly 2 decades ago, highlighted the connection between brain activity and cognitive abilities. Between 5 and 7 years of age, children improve in their ability to conserve quantity—they realize, for example, that spreading out a small pile of 10 coins into a long line does not result in more coins than were in the small pile. When children were longitudinally tested on standard Piagetian tasks at 5, 6, and 7 years, their brain activation patterns matched their performance—that is, children who succeeded on the tasks had more coordinated brain activity than those who failed (Stauder, Molenaar, & Van der Molen, 1999). Similarly, brain activity of 9- to 18-year-old children showed higher coordination in older children than younger children in regions involved in attention and spatial working memory. Growing synchronization in brain activity over age, in areas specialized for the demands of this cognitive task, points to its importance in higher-level thinking (Klingberg, Forssberg, & Westerberg, 2002).

brain waves Rhythmic or repetitive patterns of electrical impulses or neural oscillations in the brain that are created when impulses from neurons communicate

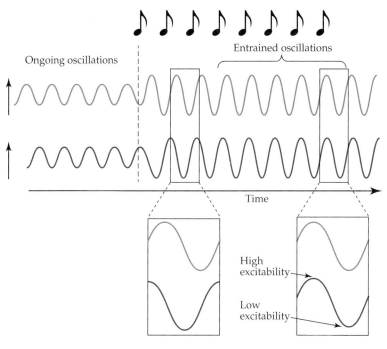

FIGURE 11.4 Synchronized brain waves. Patterns of brain activation measured in two brain regions (lateral prefrontal cortex [LPF] and visual area [V4]) show coordination as seen in the red and blue waves, and how the oscillations of the two areas change in unison when a stimulus such as music is introduced. (After A.-K. R. Bauer et al. 2020. *Trends Cog Sci* 24: 481–495. © 2020 The Authors. Published by Elsevier Ltd. CC BY 4.0, https://creativecommons.org/licenses/by/4.0/.)

✓ **CHECK YOUR UNDERSTANDING 11.3**

1. What can fMRI studies reveal about patterns of brain activation across different regions of the brain?
2. How might these patterns of activation help explain the improved cognitive abilities in middle childhood?

Family Context and Brain Development

LEARNING OBJECTIVE 11.4 Describe features of the family context that influence brain development.

Although the brains of all children undergo many changes, home environmental influences help explain differences from child to child. Brain structure and brain function are chiseled by parenting and stress, with sensitive parenting behaviors supporting brain growth, and negative parenting behaviors (e.g., maltreatment and conflict with children) or stressful life events adversely affecting brain development (Belsky & de Haan, 2011).

In fact, differences exist in the brain sizes of children living in poverty compared to children in more resourced homes, partly because poverty interferes with parenting well-being and sensitivity. For example, poverty exacerbates parent stress and increases parent hostility towards children, which can then cause reduced white and gray matter volumes in children's brains from early childhood through adolescence (Luby et al., 2013) (**FIGURE 11.5**).

✓ **CHECK YOUR UNDERSTANDING 11.4**

1. Describe associations between poverty and children's brain development.

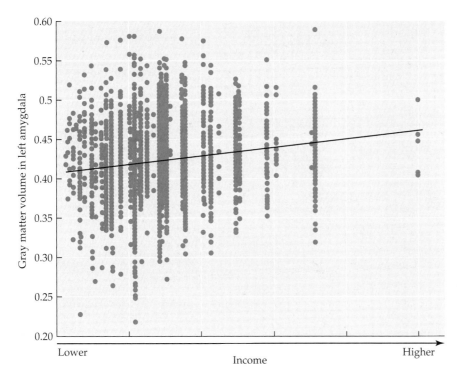

FIGURE 11.5 Poverty and brain development.   Researchers found that poverty was associated with smaller hippocampal volume. The lines show associations from poverty (as represented in family income relative to family needs; Income-to-needs ratio) to parenting and child stress, which in turn relate to lower left hemisphere hippocampal volume. The diagonal black line indicates the "best fitting line" based on statistical analyses and shows the average rate of increase in gray matter volume with household income. (After M. Lotze et al. 2020. *Sci Rep* 10: 18786. CC BY 4.0, https://creativecommons.org/licenses/by/4.0/.)

Physical Development

Children's bodies grow at a fairly steady rate throughout middle childhood. At the start of childhood, the average 6-year-old in the United States weighs around 45 pounds (20 kg) and is 42 inches tall (107 cm). On average, children will grow about 2–3 inches (5–8 cm) and put on 5 to 8 pounds (2–4 kg) each year until, by 12 years of age, girls reach 59 inches (150 cm) and boys 58 inches (147 cm) on average and weigh 93 and 90 pounds (42 and 41 kg), respectively. However, as we learned, averages mask the huge variation that exists among children and by no means define what is normal. At any given age, children differ substantially in their height and weight and other aspects of growth (**FIGURE 11.6**). For example, weight ranges of 44–76 pounds (20–34 kg) are considered normal for 8-year-old U.S. boys and girls. By 12 years of age, when some children have entered puberty and others have not, children can range from below 70 pounds (32 kg) (in the 5th percentile of weight) to 130 pounds (59 kg) (in the 95th percentile).

As children grow, the relatively lean bodies they had as young children disappear. At around 7–8 years of age, children gradually add more fat to their bodies, and as they approach adolescence their fat gain increases even more rapidly, leading to a changing body appearance. The bones in the body continue to grow as the body lengthens and broadens, although the ligaments that connect bones to one another are not yet firmly established. Muscle mass also increases, which causes children to sometimes experience stiffness and aches in the legs—commonly known as "growing pains"—as their muscles attempt to adapt to their changing bones (Evans, 2008; Uziel et al., 2012).

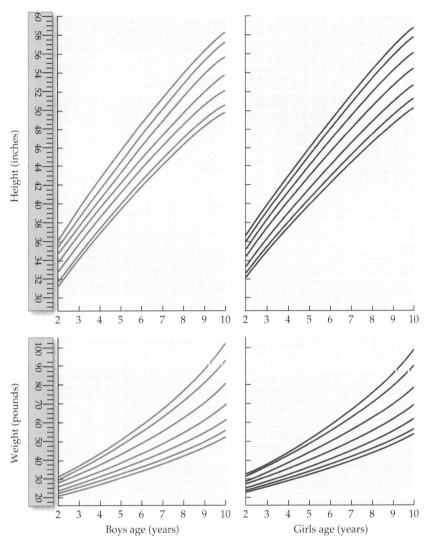

FIGURE 11.6 Growth chart for children. Children grow in height and weight over the course of early childhood, but they differ in their patterns of growth as represented by lines depicting children at different percentiles of growth. (After E. G. Graber. 2021. In *Merck Manual: Consumer Version*. Accessed June 16, 2021. https://www.medicine. com/topic/physical-growth-of-infants-and-children; R. J. Kuczmarski et al. 2002. 2000 CDC *Growth Charts for the United States: Methods and Development. Vital and Health Statistics*, Series 11, no. 246. National Center for Health Statistics: Washington, D.C.)

Gross Motor Skills

LEARNING OBJECTIVE 11.5 Give examples of improvements in gross motor skills typically seen in middle childhood.

Gross motor skills are the large movements that people make with arms, legs, feet, and torsos (see Chapter 8). Growing bones and muscles, coupled with ligaments that are not yet firmly attached to bones, enable children to control their bodies and move in ways that had been quite a challenge just a year or two earlier (Haywood & Getchell, 2005; e.g., Malina et al., 2004). In particular, gross motor skills change in fundamental ways during the childhood years due to improvements in:

- *Strength*, which enables children to run faster, jump higher, kick harder, exercise longer, and throw farther than they had at younger ages.

- *Flexibility*, which makes children's bodies relatively elastic, allowing them to expertly twist and turn their limbs and torsos, as in the body movements required for cartwheels, splits, and jumping over hurdles.
- *Balance*, which is essential for all gross motor skills because children must remain steady and not topple over as they move their limbs and torsos in different directions. Children's growing skills at keeping balance are especially obvious in games such as tag, dodgeball, football, and ice hockey.
- *Agility*, which permits quick and precise movements, as when children skip down steps, dance, jump rope, and dribble balls in soccer.
- *Coordination*, which enables various complex actions to be combined into sequences of movement needed to ride a bicycle, steer a skateboard, roller skate, play tennis, and row a canoe.

Developments in gross motor skills are important for children's participation in team sports that require muscle strength, balance, agility, coordination, and so forth. And, children who remain physically active through formal and informal sports and exercise reap many health benefits. Physical activity promotes muscle and bone growth and heart health, reduces the risk of becoming overweight or obese, and aids the development of gross motor skills. Indeed, practice with a particular motor skill is one of the strongest predictors of expertise with that skill. A child who hopes to master skateboarding must dedicate hundreds of hours of practice to develop and perfect the motor skills needed to control the speed, direction, and angles of the body and skateboard (**FIGURE 11.7**).

Still, the benefits of physical activity and continuous practice can also come at a cost if children engage in extreme activity beyond what their bodies can handle. Because children's bones, muscles, and tendons have not completed their growth, too much force placed on the joints can cause **Osgood-Schlatter disease**—a painful condition in which the area below the knee becomes inflamed where the tendon from the kneecap attaches to the shinbone. Thus, although parents and educators should encourage physical activity in children, overscheduling and pushing a child to do too much too soon can backfire. To avoid injury from overuse, it's critical to ensure that child athletes get the proper sleep and recovery time between training and competition (Luke et al., 2011).

✓ CHECK YOUR UNDERSTANDING 11.5

1. What are ways that gross motor skills change during middle childhood?

Fine Motor Skills

LEARNING OBJECTIVE 11.6 Give examples of improvements in fine motor skills typically seen in middle childhood.

Children must implement many fine motor skills or smaller movements, ranging from buttoning a coat to sticking a straw into a juice box (see Chapter 8). Although young children have difficulties with actions that require precision, by the end of middle childhood children can execute small actions with high proficiency. By around 6 years of age, most children can dress and groom themselves and print letters and numbers somewhat clearly. However, they often use their whole arm to make strokes of letters, rather than controlling the small movements of fingers and wrist. Consequently, their letters and numbers are quite large and lack consistency in size and positioning on the page. By about 8 years of age, children have better control of their fine motor movements (**FIGURE 11.8**). Children's developing fine motor control coupled with their

FIGURE 11.7 Practice makes perfect. Development of the motor skills required for coordinating the many muscles and actions involved in skateboarding (and other sports) takes hours of practice as children learn how to control the body and skateboard.

Osgood-Schlatter disease
A painful condition in which the area below the knee becomes inflamed where the tendon from the kneecap attaches to the shinbone

(A) Kindergartener

(B) Third grader

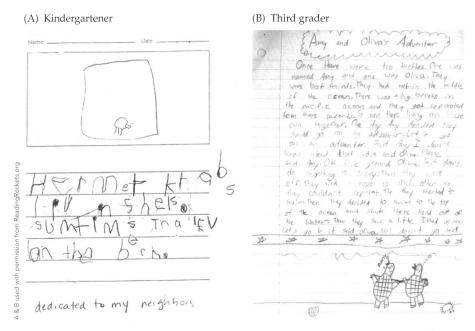

FIGURE 11.8 Progression of fine motor movements. (A) Children in kindergarten have difficult times keeping letters uniform in size and on the lines due to difficulty with fine motor skills. (B) Third graders show neater penmanship due to their improved fine motor control.

growing cognitive skills also lead to improvements in the quality of their artwork. From about third grade onward, children increasingly depict depth cues and relative sizes in their drawings, such as by making distant objects smaller than closer ones (e.g., Liben, 2006).

✓ CHECK YOUR UNDERSTANDING 11.6

1. What are some examples of gains in fine motor skills during middle childhood?

Sex Differences in Physical Growth and Motor Skills

LEARNING OBJECTIVE 11.7 Compare the motor skill development of boys and girls in middle childhood.

Girls and boys differ on their physical growth and motor skill development. In the early years of schooling, from about 6–10 years of age, girls are slightly shorter and weigh less than do boys. Boys have greater muscle mass than do girls at this time. Then, at about 10–11 years of age, this pattern reverses as girls approach the adolescent growth spurt before boys.

Sex differences in motor skills are pronounced in childhood, in line with the different bodies of boys and girls. Boys surpass girls in muscle mass and body size for several years, and thus do better on activities that require strength, such as throwing a football and quick change of body direction. Girls, however, excel on motor skills that require balance and agility, such as balancing on one leg, jumping rope, skipping, and hopping (e.g., Rodríguez-Negro, Huertas-Delgado, & Yanci, 2019).

Of course, sex comparisons are based on group averages. Many girls exceed boys in strength and many boys exceed girls in balance and agility. Moreover, contextual influences account for some of the sex differences in motor skill. For instance, there are many cultural norms and expectations about the types of activities appropriate for boys and girls, and these expectations are communicated to children by families, schools, neighborhoods, and the media. Girls are more likely than are boys to jump rope and engage in extracurricular activities such as dance and gymnastics, all of which aid agility. In contrast, boys are more likely to throw, catch, and hit a ball, and join teams like Little League, community basketball leagues, and the school football team.

✓ **CHECK YOUR UNDERSTANDING 11.7**

1. How do boys and girls differ in physical development, and how might these differences affect their experiences in sports and play?

Contexts of Physical Development

LEARNING OBJECTIVE 11.8 Give examples of how school, neighborhood, and cultural contexts influence children's physical activity.

My children practically lived at the park throughout their school years. When they weren't scheduled for a team sport, they were shooting hoops, climbing jungle gyms, and playing soccer. Sometimes they begged to eat dinner there and, more often than not, would be the last kids to leave as the sun went down. Unfortunately, many children today have little opportunity to spend time outside in safe places, and trends are worsening. In the past, parents could rely on schools to offer free time for children to exercise their bodies during recess, after lunch, or during daily physical education class. However, such opportunities are diminishing in many parts of the United States, leaving little time for children to simply run around and play. Here we examine how contexts of school, neighborhood, and culture affect children's participation in physical activity.

School Context and Physical Activity

Schools offer children occasions to be active during recess, physical education class, and other periods of free time. These precious minutes of physical movement and energy release can be important for children who otherwise might not have the chance to play after school in parks or outdoor areas, perhaps because they live in dangerous neighborhoods or far from open spaces. However, U.S. schools have come under pressure to dedicate increasingly more time to academics, which has come at a cost for physical activity. Recess time in schools has steadily eroded across the United States (Bohn-Gettler & Pelligrini, 2014). Many schools hold physical education classes that meet only once or twice a week, and nearly 10% of U.S. schools have cut out recess entirely for children as young as second grade (e.g., Ramstetter & Murray, 2017). In many counties, cuts to physical activity are greatest in the poorest neighborhoods. For example, Nevada schools in low-income neighborhoods had the fewest classroom activity breaks, fewest bike racks, highest rates of withholding recess or physical education classes for disciplinary reasons, and the fewest recess supervisors trained to promote physical activity (Monnat et al., 2017).

School declines in physical activity have met with backlash from experts who contend that schools should offer *more* not *less* time for physical activity so that children can establish lifelong habits of fitness. Furthermore, physical education classes should appeal to different children by offering a variety of activities, including walking, running, racquet sports, and swimming, so that all children can participate (National Association for Sport Physical Education, 2004).

But does time in physical activity at school actually make a difference? Absolutely. When researchers experimentally manipulate the time schools dedicate to children's physical activity, the effects on motor development are pronounced. A Swedish intervention study showed that daily scheduled lessons around physical activity and motor training at school improved motor development in children and led to lasting effects in children between 7 and 15 years (Ericsson & Karlsson, 2014). After only 1 year, students who had received the school intervention of daily physical activity and motor training surpassed children in a control group on balance and coordination. Differences persisted across the full 9 years of the study. Moreover, sex differences in motor skills were smaller in the intervention than in the control group, suggesting that when schools promote equivalent opportunities for boys and girls to improve their physical skills, sex differences diminish.

Neighborhood Context and Physical Activity

Everyday walking speed offers an interesting case of neighborhood effects on physical activity. Back in the 1970s, developmental scientist Marc Bornstein noticed that people in large cities appeared to walk faster than those in small, rural communities. To determine whether his hypothesis was supported, he stood outside in different communities with a stopwatch in hand and measured how long it took people to walk a certain distance. He (and others) showed that the "pace of life" (the title of one of his papers!) differed among large, urban cities and smaller, rural settings in the United States, Europe, and the Middle East (Bornstein, 1979; Bornstein & Bornstein, 1976; Lowin et al., 1971). As population density increased, so did the speed of everyday activity, including walking.

Researchers have since confirmed these decades-old observations. People walk faster in areas with less greenery and high traffic and noise than they do in places with more greenery and open space and less traffic, for example (Franek, 2013). Moreover, experimental manipulations that exposed people to soundtracks of birdsongs led to slower walking compared to soundtracks of crowded cities (Franek et al., 2019). Although studies on walking speed mainly focus on adolescents and adults, it is reasonable to assume that children raised in large cities will differ in their movements from children raised in small towns, following in the footsteps, so to speak, of their parents.

However, the time a person takes to get from one place to another does not necessarily imply physical fitness. Children need spaces where they can freely move, run around, and play. Indeed, children's access to safe neighborhood parklands and playgrounds relates to their physical activity (An et al., 2017). In an experimental study in Sweden, 5-, 6-, and 7-year-old children improved in their motor fitness, balance, and coordination when given opportunities to play outdoors in a natural environment compared to a control group of children without such an opportunity (Fjørtoft, 2004).

Furthermore, children's time at playgrounds increases with the number of structures that allow for movement and activity. Evaluation of over 162 U.S. parks revealed that each additional play element—slide, ladder, swing, spinning contraption, and so on—increased the number of users by 50%, and the time at play also increased when parks contained available restrooms (Cohen et al., 2019).

Cultural Context and Physical Activity

Cultural influences often go unexamined in the area of physical development because many people assume that all people acquire motor skills similarly at about the same time in development. Yet, nothing could be further from the truth.

Consider the basic motor skills of walking and running. Anthropological accounts of walking in South America and Asia reveal extraordinary capacities of children that fly in the face of what is typical in a U.S. context (Adolph, Karasik, & Tamis-LeMonda, 2010). Children accompanied their caregivers on walking trips of between 35 and 40 miles (56 to 64 km), often in extreme temperatures and while carrying heavy loads (Devine, 1985). Cultural anthropologist Margaret Mead reported that young girls in African and Balinese cultures spent years practicing carrying heavy loads while walking, to transport wares to the market (Mead & Macgregor, 1951) (**FIGURE 11.9**). These childhood experiences resulted in incredible ultimate capacity: By the time they reached adulthood, women in Western Kenya carried up to 70% of their body weight on their heads, exceeding the capabilities of young army recruits (Heglund et al., 1995; Maloiy et al., 1986).

Running long distances is another area of astounding cultural variation. The Tarahumara Indians in the Southwestern United States are known for their running endurance. Historical accounts of this tribe report that they ran kickball races of 93–186 miles (150–300 km) in 24–48 hours (Devine, 1985). They would run down deer for 2 days, until their prey collapsed from exhaustion. To put these running skills in perspective, consider that a typical track race ranges from 1.86 to 6.2 miles (3 to 10 km), cross-country races range from 3 to 7.5 miles (5 to 12 km), and marathons cover 26.2 miles (12.2 km).

Today, Kenyans are known for their running prowess, and are considered to be the fastest runners on earth. Their impressive records in Olympic track events highlight their success (Finn, 2013). What enables Kenyans to attain this remarkable level of running skill? To tackle this question, researchers conducted an extensive study of Kenyan boys and girls 10–17 years of age (Gibson et al., 2013). Kenyan teachers identified children who had not had any formal athletic training but were physically fit. Researchers gathered data on children's performances running outdoor track and gauged their physical activity over 7 consecutive days using GPS-like devices and accelerometers. Researchers also measured the capacity of children's hearts, lungs, and blood to transport oxygen to the working muscles and muscle capacity in using oxygen.

The researchers found that children's physical fitness surpassed that of trained, high-achieving athletic runners of the same age in the United States, which is even more remarkable considering that Kenyan children were tested at their country's geographically, extremely high altitudes (**FIGURE 11.10**). As one example, Kenyan children's **anaerobic threshold** —the point during exercise when lactic acid starts to accumulate in the muscles, leading to cramping—was much higher than that of European American U.S. child athletes.

Where does this physical capacity come from? Is it genetic? At least in part, experience is key. The superior physical fitness and anaerobic thresholds of Kenyan children were matched by their daily high physical activity and energy expenditure. Kenyan children commuted on foot to and from school five days a week, four times a day—once in the morning, home and back for lunch, then home again in the evening—over uneven, hilly terrain. They mixed walking and running on their journeys, averaging 5 miles of travel. Beyond their long school journeys, Kenyan children spent additional time in more vigorous activity than has been reported for populations of American children. The highly active, energy demanding lifestyle of Kenyan children contributed to their high physical fitness, which may help explain the athletic success of record-breaking Kenyan runners.

✓ CHECK YOUR UNDERSTANDING 11.8

1. Should schools be required to offer physical education classes on a regular basis? Provide arguments on both sides of the issue and suggest what policies might be enacted.
2. What initiatives would increase children's access to parks and recreational programs?
3. Describe some cultural differences in gross motor skills and the everyday experiences that contribute to these differences.
4. Offer examples of how cultural practices can shape motor skills.

FIGURE 11.9 Practice with load carrying by children leads to gains in specific skills. Children must develop a specific walking/gait pattern and posture to minimize energy expenditure and ensure loads don't fall to the ground.

anaerobic threshold The lactate inflection point during exercise when lactic acid starts to build up in the muscles and results in cramping

FIGURE 11.10 Kenyan children and physical fitness. Researchers found an enormous capacity for physical activity in Kenyan children. Measures of children's physical fitness surpassed even trained, high-achieving athletic runners of the same age in the United States.

■ *Health*

Healthy habits—particularly around nutrition and sleep—are vital to children's development across domains (see Chapter 8). Yet, many children fail to maintain healthy eating and sleeping habits. Children's growing independence, heightened responsibilities around schoolwork, participation in extracurricular activities, and increased time in the company of friends and away from home mean that they are increasingly masters of their own bodies, for better or for worse. The healthy snacks that parents pack in lunch boxes may be thrown away in favor of salty, fried, and sweet foods. Bedtime warnings may be ignored, as children spend hours playing video games, engaging with social media, and depriving themselves of the quantity and quality of sleep they require.

Diseases and injuries also take a toll on children. Children contract many infectious diseases from their peers, and some children suffer chronic health problems that can interfere with their school engagement and performance and social relationships. Other children sustain injuries caused by motor vehicle accidents, failure to wear a helmet during physical activities like bicycling, or through participation in sports.

Nutrition

Children's growing bodies require nutritious foods to maintain physical health. Well-balanced diets provide children with the energy needed for high levels of physical activity and school learning. School-age children report feeling sluggish after eating junk food, but energetic after eating healthy foods (O'Dea, 2003). If children can be negatively affected by a single meal, as research shows, then consistently poor diets—which can result from not eating enough food or overeating low-quality foods—can play out over time.

Food Insecurity

LEARNING OBJECTIVE 11.9 Define food insecurity and discuss consequences for children's development.

We learned that a healthy diet provides children with the nutrients and energy needed to meet the demands of the day. Yet many children in the United States and globally are victims of malnutrition, which cascades to health and psychological problems (see Chapter 8). Malnutrition is a common problem in young children who live in poverty and can occur when food is insufficient in quantity and quality. **Food insecurity** refers to a family's experience with food insufficiency—that is, families not having access to enough food for all household members. Signs of food insecurity occur when family members:

- worry that food will run out before the family has money to buy more;
- buy food that does not last and do not have enough money to buy more;
- are unable to afford eating balanced meals;
- reduce the size of meals or skip meals because of a lack of money for food; and
- experience hunger or lose weight because of not having enough money for food.

An estimated 10.5% of American households with children were food insecure at least some time during the year (United States Department of Agriculture, 2019). In particular, children who live in households at or below the federal poverty line, single-parent households, and Black and Hispanic headed households experience high rates of food insecurity relative to national averages.

food insecurity A family's experience with insufficient food or not having reliable access to enough affordable and nutritious food for all household members

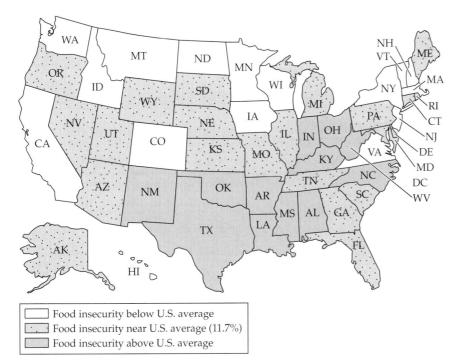

FIGURE 11.11 Food insecurity in the United States.   The USDA monitors food insecurity through the annual U.S. Census Bureau survey. A household designated as food insecure is one that has trouble providing enough food for all of its members at some point during the year. (After USDA Economic Research Service. 2020. https://www.ers.usda.gov/data-products/chart-gallery/gallery/chart-detail/?chartId=98363. Updated May 8, 2020. Data from: Current Population Survey Food Security Supplement, U.S. Dept of Commerce, Bureau of the Census.)

Geographic region is also associated with food insecurity, with comparatively high percentages in rural areas and low percentages in suburban areas. Food insecurity rates also vary from state to state, ranging from a low of 6.6% in New Hampshire to a high of 15.7% in Mississippi (USDA, 2019) (**FIGURE 11.11**).

In more resourced nations, such as the United States, the overwhelming outcome of food insecurity is child obesity, because families in poverty may provide their children with food that is less expensive and has limited nutritional quality (Tanumihardjo et al., 2007). However, federal programs in the United States, such as the Supplemental Nutrition Assistance Program (SNAP), provide families in need with debit cards that they can use to purchase food. Such programs may shield children from disrupted eating and the reduced food intake associated with very low food security (Coleman-Jensen et al., 2015).

✓ CHECK YOUR UNDERSTANDING 11.9

1. What are some signs of food insecurity?

Overweight and Obesity

LEARNING OBJECTIVE 11.10 Discuss evidence suggesting that obesity in middle childhood is increasing in prevalence in the United States and globally.

In Chapter 8 we learned about the growing obesity epidemic in the United States. During middle childhood, the risks of becoming overweight or obese, and of maintaining that status into adolescence and adulthood, intensify. School-age children often make their own food choices, and poor eating habits can snowball into lifetime habits that adversely impact health.

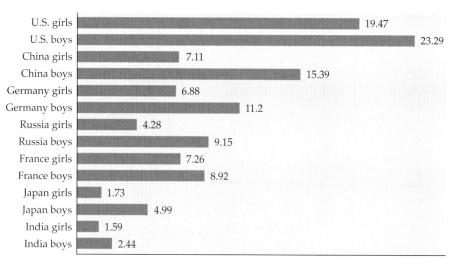

FIGURE 11.12 Obesity around the world. U.S. children have some of the highest rates of obesity when compared with children in other parts of the world. (After "Ranking [% obesity by country]." World Obesity Federation. Accessed July 29, 2021. https://data.worldobesity.org/rankings/. Data from NCD Risk Factor Collaboration [NCD-RisC]. 2017. Lancet 390: 2627–2642.)

Over the past 25–30 years the number of overweight children in the United States doubled, a trend that continues to grow (e.g., Skinner et al., 2018). Similarly, trends in obesity show that 19.8% of children in the United States were obese in 2018, up from 15.8% in 1999 (Ogden et al., 2020). Compounding the medical problems associated with excessive weight, obese children are less physically active than their peers of average weight. When children were tested on motor development and performance on a 6-minute run, overweight and obese children fared poorly compared to normal weight children (Graf et al., 2003).

The U.S. trend of growing childhood obesity extends to countries around the globe (**FIGURE 11.12**), including many less-resourced nations, where children and families are increasingly adopting unhealthy diets and lifestyles (e.g., Freemark, 2018). Analyses of child obesity in 25 countries between 1980 and 2005 reveal that the prevalence of childhood obesity increased in almost all countries for which data were available (Wang & Lobstein, 2006).

Unfortunately, in some communities where poverty is common, excess body fat may be perceived as a sign of prosperity and health, especially by adults who recall famines that resulted in millions of deaths (Wang & Lobstein, 2006). It is not uncommon for parents and grandparents in less-resourced nations and from low-income households in the United States to consider an overweight child to be healthy and well nourished. But, the stigma around being overweight may harm children's health and psychological adjustment.

✓ CHECK YOUR UNDERSTANDING 11.10

1. Is obesity limited to the United States? Explain why or why not.

Contexts of Nutrition

LEARNING OBJECTIVE 11.11 Describe the multiple factors that contribute to children's access to nutritious food and what children eat, and what this means for the future health of children.

Family and environmental factors influence the food to which children have access and what and how much they eat. As a result, these factors also influence which children will experience obesity.

Family Context

Children develop healthy or unhealthy habits around eating first and foremost in their home environments. Family influences introduced in Chapter 8 continue to matter throughout the school years. These include:

- *Modeling eating habits.* Parents of overweight children are likely to be overweight themselves, often due to eating unhealthy foods and engaging in a sedentary lifestyle. By modeling unhealthy eating and lifestyle habits, they cause their children to attach high value to unhealthy types of food (Sherry et al., 2004).

- *Rewarding and punishing children's eating habits.* When parents attempt to fully control their children's food intake, for example by forbidding dessert, their attempts may backfire. Controlling a school-age child's eating can create problems because children increasingly make their own decisions about what to eat at school, after school, at a friend's house, and so on, and must learn how to regulate their food intake independently.

- *Family home-cooked meals.* Cooking meals at home versus eating take-out foods or eating out at restaurants may affect children's weight. Between the ages of 9 and 14, children eat dinner with the family less frequently because of school and extracurricular schedules. This trend is unfortunate because evening meals with caregivers usually involve a higher intake of fruits and vegetables, grains, and milk, and a lower intake of sodas and fast foods (Burgess-Champoux et al., 2009; Fiese & Schwartz, 2008). The benefits of family meals are diminished when the food of choice is fast foods, processed foods, and/or restaurant meals. In the United States, family meals based on fast foods and restaurant food are on the rise, leading to increases in the amount of food that is consumed overall and the consumption of unhealthy foods such as sweetened sodas and snacks (e.g., Janssen et al., 2018; Poti & Popkin, 2011).

- *Family activity and exercise.* Families can help prevent childhood obesity by promoting healthy levels of activity in children. Some parents allow children to engage in extended periods of sedentary behaviors, such as being glued to screens without limits, whereas others closely monitor their children's screen time. Sitting in front of a screen does not burn calories and it is often accompanied by indulging in unhealthy foods such as chips, soda, and cookies. Indeed, the U.S. rise in childhood obesity corresponds with children's growing screen time and accompanying decline in physical activity (Robinson et al., 2017) (**FIGURE 11.13**).

The role of family diet and lifestyle on obesity and health is further illustrated in historical accounts of the Pima Indians of Arizona, who migrated from a mountain location in Mexico. Obesity and diabetes grew to epidemic proportions as the Pimas adopted the unhealthy diets and sedentary lifestyles of the modern-day United States. Scientists compared Pima living in Arizona—who had adopted the U.S. lifestyle—to Pima who continued to live a traditional lifestyle of healthy diet and physical activity in Mexico (Ravussin et al., 1994). The Mexican Pimas were lighter, had lower body mass indexes (BMIs), lower cholesterol, and lower rates of diabetes compared to the Pima living in Arizona. The Pima example mirrors that of many children of U.S. immigrants, who may quickly adopt the unhealthy, fatty, and easily accessible foods of the new country when exposure to their home culture is limited (e.g., Renzaho, McCabe, & Swinburn, 2012; Zhang et al., 2019).

Neighborhood Context

We saw that parks and safe open spaces offer children places to be physically active. In turn, active children lower their risk of being overweight or obese. An 8-year longitudinal study of children living in 12 different communities

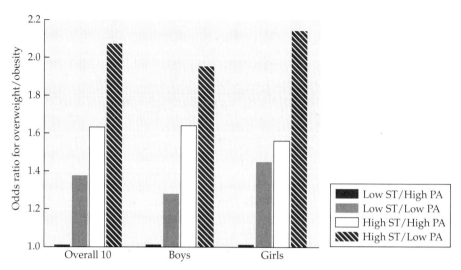

FIGURE 11.13 Obesity and screen time. Screen time (ST) and physical activity (PA) relate to obesity in boys and girls. In particular, children who both spend high amounts of time viewing screens *and* engage in low amounts of physical activity are especially at risk for obesity. (After A. Lane et al. 2013. *J Phys Activ Health* 11: 985–991. http://dx.doi.org/doi:10.1123/jpah.2012-0182. Adapted with permission.)

in Southern California found that children's access to park space and recreational programs predicted their body mass indexes years later (Wolch et al., 2011). Children 9–10 years of age who had parks within 0.3 miles (500 m) of their homes and recreational programs within 6 miles (10 km) of their homes had lower BMIs 8 years later as teens compared to children without nearby parks or programs. Unfortunately, children who live in poor neighborhoods may have few opportunities to spend time in parks or outdoors. Parents are often concerned about neighborhood crime and may insist their children spend their free time at home, leading to heightened sedentary behavior (Caprio et al., 2008). This may be one reason that parents' perceptions of neighborhood safety relate to childhood obesity (Lumeng et al., 2006).

School Context

Children spend a large proportion of their awake hours at school, where they have opportunities to learn about nutrition and put what they learn into practice. Schools can educate children about healthy calories, promote awareness of the risks of obesity, offer children nutritious foods (Lakshman, Elks, & Ong, 2012), and explain the importance of regular exercise. For example, school programs that focus on educating students about the risks of obesity successfully reduced the BMIs of 6- to 12-year-olds. In fact, the effectiveness of school programs surpasses other community initiatives that also aim to reduce obesity, likely because schools reach children on a daily basis where messages about healthy eating are repeated (Waters et al., 2011). A meta-analysis of 12 longitudinal studies revealed associations between several school factors and low rates of obesity, including more recess time, suburban schools, healthy school foods, and parent involvement in school (Gray et al., 2019).

Schools provide snacks, lunch, and sometimes breakfast to children throughout the United States, and the types of foods they offer children may affect children's health. In 2014, federal regulations established standards called Smart Snacks in School that offered guidelines for elementary and high schools to curb sales of unhealthy snacks. The Smart Snack standards recommend that foods sold during school hours should contain whole grains, fruits, vegetables, dairy, or protein (Lott et al., 2018). The Academy of Nutrition and Dietetics endorsed the Smart Snack standards and offered additional suggestions around farm-to-school nutritious offerings and school gardens (Hayes, Contento, & Weekly, 2018). However, whether these recommendations work to reduce obesity depends on whether school districts successfully implement the standards (Lott et al., 2017). Some regions of the country, including rural schools, might need support and guidance to fully incorporate the nutrition standards into their offerings (Mann, Kraak, & Serrano, 2017).

Positive effects have also been shown for student participation in the School Breakfast Program, a federal program that offers breakfast to any student and free breakfast for any low-income student who attends a school that participates in the program (**FIGURE 11.14**). Child participation in the School Breakfast Program was associated with lower child weight after controlling for family and child variables in statistical models, suggesting the program might be effective in the battle against childhood obesity (Millimet, Tchernis, & Husain, 2010). Furthermore, participation in the program predicted children's school achievement, underscoring the importance of children starting off the day with a nutritious meal (Frisvold, 2015). In fact, a review of 36 articles on the effects of breakfast on academic performance in children from different socioeconomic backgrounds revealed a positive effect of consistently eating breakfast—particularly one that contains a variety of food groups and adequate energy—on attention in the classroom and children's academic performance. The clearest effects were documented in mathematics, which requires a great deal of focus (Adolphus, Lawton, & Dye, 2013). Breakfast provides children with about one-fourth of their dietary nutrients and arms them with the energy needed to start their day, which may be why school breakfast programs result in positive outcomes.

Policy and Program Contexts of Nutrition

Policies and programs can promote healthy behaviors and lifestyles in children by tackling the factors that contribute to a sedentary lifestyle and unhealthy eating. Several public awareness campaigns and programs aim to promote physical activity in children. As one example, the National Center for Chronic Disease Prevention and Health Promotion came out with various policy statements about ways to help local communities support physical activity through urban design, land use, and the development of nonmotorized travel options (Centers for Disease Control and Prevention, 2010). Some community-level policies that could benefit children and families include those that improve:

- children's access to parks and outdoor recreational facilities,
- community infrastructures that support bicycling,
- community infrastructures that support walking, and
- personal and traffic safety in areas where children can be physically active.

Another approach to tackling child obesity is through dietary or exercise programs. Dietary programs can involve minor adjustments in diet or major dietary changes; interventions that focus on total calorie intake produce long-term weight loss (Caprio et al., 2008). In contrast, programs that increase activity in obese children only produce small changes in body weight, but show benefits on cardiovascular health (Atlantis, Barnes, & Singh, 2006). Larger treatment effects were seen for childhood obesity when programs focused on comprehensive lifestyle interventions and when family members

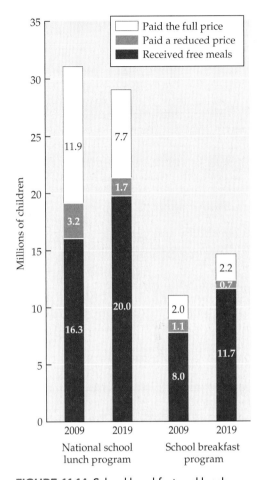

FIGURE 11.14 School breakfast and lunch programs. Participation in national free and reduced-price school breakfast and lunch programs has grown over the years. Between 2009 and 2019, the number of U.S. children receiving reduced or free breakfast and lunch at school increased. (After J. Guthrie. 2020. USDA Economic Research Service. October 05, 2020. https://www.ers.usda.gov/amber-waves/2020/october/free-school-lunch-breakfast-participation-rose-between-2009-and-2019/. Based on data from USDA/FNS, as of December 2019, reported in L. Tiehen. 2020. The Food Assistance Landscape: Fiscal Year 2019 Annual Report, EIB-218. USDA Economic Research Service.)

were included in interventions to help children change behaviors (e.g., Oude Luttikhuis et al., 2009).

Moreover, weight loss programs that tailored messages and practices to the ethnic background and sex of children maximized effectiveness. Examples include Families Improving Together, a program developed for African American children and adolescents and their families (Wilson et al., 2015); the Childhood Health, Education, and Wellness program, a family-centered approach to targeting overweight Latinx children (Gallo et al., 2017); and the incorporation of resistance training into weight-reduction programs for Latino boys (Stovitz, Steffen, & Boostrom, 2008).

✓ **CHECK YOUR UNDERSTANDING 11.11**

1. What can parents do to help prevent obesity in their children?
2. What features of neighborhoods and schools play a role in child overweight status and obesity?

Sleep

A morning did not go by without my children moaning and groaning about waking up for school. Conversely, whenever school was cancelled or delayed because of a snow day, it was cause for celebration and sleeping in. No matter how much we tried to reason that going to bed earlier was a sensible solution to morning sluggishness, our children argued about the lack of time to get everything done and still be well rested for an early wakeup.

Sleep is a major ingredient in children's physical and mental health, rivaling the importance of adequate physical activity and proper nutrition. Children require sufficient sleep to handle their growing responsibilities at home and school and to maintain their physical and mental prowess. And so, parents are rightfully concerned about their children's sleep schedules and ways to ensure that their children get the proper rest. Pediatricians offer guidelines about how much sleep children need at different ages. Educators are quick to spot a child who is groggy and appears to be lacking sleep. And, developmental scientists continue to ask about how much sleep children need versus how much they actually get and the causes and consequences of children's sleep problems.

How Much Sleep do Children Need?

LEARNING OBJECTIVE 11.12 Describe approaches and challenges to measuring children's sleep needs.

Children's time in sleep gradually declines over the childhood years. Children reduce their sleep from an average of around 11.5 hours per night at 5 years, to 9.5 hours between 6 and 8 years, to 8.9 hours by the time they are 12 years of age, as revealed in data from 34 studies across multiple countries (Galland et al., 2012). The decrease in sleep duration occurs for various reasons. Young children (approximately 5 years of age) sleep longest because they no longer nap and easily tire from expending lots of energy over the course of the day. Then, over the course of middle childhood, sleep becomes progressively more consolidated and children wake up less frequently at night (Galland et al., 2012).

Still, these changes do not compensate for children's generally low amounts of sleep, and historical evidence suggests that children today sleep less than they had decades ago. Analysis of children's sleep durations, based on studies of 20 countries and nearly 700,000 children, showed that children's sleep time has decreased each year over the past century (Matricciani, Olds, & Petkov, 2012). Moreover, some children are getting especially low amounts of sleep given that average estimates mask differences from child to child. Some 6-to 8-year-old children average as few as 7.9 hours of sleep per day whereas others average as many as 10.9 hours; this substantial 3-hour spread is seen in children of all ages (Galland et al., 2012).

Do differences in sleep durations mean that some children are severely sleep deprived and/or that others are oversleeping? How much sleep is optimal, and how do scientists determine children's sleep requirements? Answers to these questions are not as straightforward as would appear. First, it is important to define what is meant by "optimal sleep," and second, it is necessary to design a study to assess precisely how many hours of sleep children of different ages require.

Some researchers describe optimal sleep as the amount of sleep that allows a child to feel refreshed in the morning and be fully awake rather than sleepy. Others consider optimal sleep as the amount of sleep needed to sustain normal levels of performance during the day (Engle-Friedman, Palencar, & Riela, 2010; Ferrara & De Gennaro, 2001). Still others aim higher, noting that optimal sleep should maximize desirable outcomes, such as academic performance and mental and physical health (Matricciani et al., 2013).

So, how do researchers determine children's sleep needs? This question has been approached in four basic ways (Matricciani et al., 2013).

- *Ask children if they are sleepy following their natural sleep.* The standard approach simply documents how much children sleep—primarily through parent report—followed by observations of whether children reported wanting more sleep or feeling sleepy.

- *Let children sleep for as long as they want.* Another approach is to place children in an unconstrained sleep situation and assume their sleep behaviors reflect their optimal sleep needs. One such historical study formed the basis for current U.S. sleep guidelines. A small group of 10- to 12-year-olds were monitored at the Stanford University sleep camp for 3 days each year over a 5- or 6-year period. The researchers found that children slept approximately 9 hours per night when permitted to control their amount of sleep (Carskadon et al., 1980; Carskadon & Dement, 1979). However, the study has been critiqued as outdated, based on a very homogenous sample of children, and perhaps being problematic given the unfamiliar (summer camp) setting for obtaining sleep data.

- *Examine associations between time spent in sleep and performance outcomes.* A third approach is correlational. Researchers investigate correlations between sleep time and student performance, and then estimate the hours of sleep that maximize test performance. This approach was taken for a large, national study of children ages 10–19 years, in which researchers assessed sleep durations and test scores (Eide & Showalter, 2012) (**FIGURE 11.15**). Findings revealed that too little or too much sleep

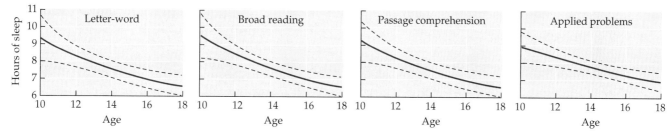

FIGURE 11.15 A large, national sample of children (ages 10–19 years) related sleep duration to academic test scores. Hours of sleep required for high performance in four academic skill areas—letter-word, broad reading, passage comprehension, and math problems—decreases between middle childhood and adolescence. For example, 10-year-olds require over 9 hours of sleep (ranging from 8 to 11) whereas by 18 years of age, children can do well in school with 7 to 8 hours of sleep. (After E. R. Eide and M. H. Showalter. 2012. *East Econ J* 38: 512–524. https://doi.org/10.1057/eej.2011.33.)

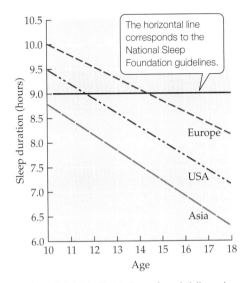

FIGURE 11.16 Guidelines for childhood sleep. Mean sleep durations in Europe, the United States, and Asia indicate that children get less sleep as they get older and far less sleep than suggested by National Sleep Foundation guidelines as they enter late adolescence. (From L. Matricciani et al. 2013. *Sleep* 36: 527–534. By permission of Oxford University Press.)

predicted low test scores. With age, children required fewer hours of sleep, and collapsing across age, optimal hours of sleep was only around 8.25 hours, which fell below the recommended National Sleep Foundation guideline of 9.25 hours (**FIGURE 11.16**).

- *Experimentally manipulate sleep.* A final approach is to manipulate the time children have to sleep, either extending or restricting sleep, and then investigating associations to outcomes. However, studies on sleep restriction are rare and difficult to implement in natural settings. (How many parents would consent to their child being sleep deprived and then tested on their academic performance?)

Despite widespread efforts to pinpoint children's optimal hours of sleep, there appears to be no magic number. Findings vary from study to study, as do the sleep needs of individual children. Critics of sleep guidelines thus argue that current recommendations are based largely on expert opinion rather than strong sources of evidence.

To make matters even more complicated, the duration of sleep varies for children from different parts of the world, raising questions about whether guidelines developed in the United States apply to other cultures. Across all age groups studied, children from countries in Asia sleep 1 to 2 hours less per day than do children from Europe and up to 1 hour less than children from the United States (Galland et al., 2012). When asked, Asian children also report needing less sleep compared to children from other countries. Various explanations for the relatively low sleep durations of Asian children have been advanced, ranging from genetic differences in sleep needs to family practices, including later bedtimes (Galland et al., 2012; Seo et al., 2010).

✓ CHECK YOUR UNDERSTANDING 11.12

1. What sort of changes in sleep occur during middle childhood?
2. How do researchers determine how much sleep children need?

Sleep Problems in Middle Childhood

LEARNING OBJECTIVE 11.13 Enumerate consequences of failing to get a good night's sleep for children.

Of course, the sheer amount of sleep—the basis of sleep guidelines—is not the only thing that matters. Sleep quality is also important to consider (see Chapter 8). A child who wakes up frequently during the night, or has trouble falling asleep, is likely to suffer from low-quality sleep, even if sleep duration is deemed to be sufficient. In addition, having consistent sleep and wake times each day may be even more important than sleep duration (Olds, Maher, & Matricciani, 2011). Children's circadian rhythms may be disrupted when they experience substantial fluctuations in their sleep time.

Irregularities in sleep timing and poor sleep quality may lead to sleep problems, which occur at similar rates in children from around the world (Owens, 2005). Across countries, about 25% of parents report sleep problems in their children, including resisting going to sleep at night, wakening during the night, not getting enough sleep, and experiencing sleepiness during the day. A study of school-age children in Belgium sought to describe the prevalence, odds, and predictors of 36 sleep behaviors. Researchers surveyed over 3,000 parents about the sleep-wake patterns in their 6- to 13-year-old children. Based on parents' reports, six main types of sleep disorders were identified (Spruyt et al., 2005) (**TABLE 11.1**).

nocturnal enuresis Bedwetting or loss of bladder control at nighttime

Nocturnal enuresis, or bedwetting, is a common sleep problem that affects approximately 10% of children. Nocturnal enuresis occurs because of hormonal imbalance, when the muscles that inhibit urination fail to respond to a full bladder, or when children simply do not awaken when their bladder is full (Bascom et al., 2019). Two main treatments are used for nocturnal enuresis. One solution is to administer the synthetic hormone desmopressin, which offers short-term solutions to bedwetting by reducing the amount of urine children produce (Kwak et al., 2010). A second approach is the use of an alarm that is sensitive to any dampness and awakens children before they can wet themselves. Alarm therapy yields success rates of between 50% and 75% (Glazener, Evans, & Peto, 2005). Analysis of 64 studies across 4,071 children showed that drug therapies reduced the number of wet nights children had during the period of treatment but were no longer effective once treatment ended. In contrast, alarm therapy showed better short- and long-term outcomes compared to the drug treatments (Caldwell, Sureshkumar, & Wong, 2016).

✓ CHECK YOUR UNDERSTANDING 11.13
1. What types of sleep problems affect children in middle childhood?

Family Context of Sleep

LEARNING OBJECTIVE 11.14 Describe features of the home environment that can lead to problems in children's sleep.

Why do children differ from one another in how much and how well they sleep? Family context exerts a commanding influence simply because conditions at home can make going to sleep and staying asleep a challenge. Noise, chaos, and erratic schedules interfere with children getting to sleep on time, falling asleep, and staying asleep. Children experience more sleep problems when rooms are noisy and not well darkened (Spruyt et al., 2005). A poor night's sleep, coupled with waking up early for school, results in huge fluctuations between wake-up times on school mornings compared to weekend mornings (Carissimi et al., 2016).

Poor-quality parent-child interactions also contribute to sleep problems. Mothers' negative emotions and low sensitivity to children and mother-child relationships low in closeness and high in conflict predicted sleep problems in over 600 children ages 8 and 11 (Bell & Belsky, 2008). The direction of effects was bidirectional—namely, measures of low interaction quality affected children's sleep over time, and children's problems with sleep led to further disruption to family relationships.

✓ CHECK YOUR UNDERSTANDING 11.14
1. What should parents do to create an environment that supports their children's sleep?

TABLE 11.1 ■ Six Main Types of Sleep Disorders

Disorders of initiating and maintaining sleep	Going to bed reluctantly
	Difficulty falling asleep
	Falling asleep anxiety
	Night awakening
	Difficulty in falling asleep after wakening
	Terminal insomnia
Sleep breathing disorders	Breathing problems
	Sleep apnea
	Loud snoring
	Snorting or gasping
	Wheezing or whistling of the chest
Disorders of arousal	Sleepwalking
	Sleep terrors
	Nightmares
	Awakening before midnight with anxiety and crying
	Awakening after midnight with anxiety and crying
Sleep-wake transition disorders	Hypnic jerks
	Rhythmic movement disorders
	Hypnagogic hallucinations (very realistic, usually visual, hallucinations that occur just as a person is falling asleep)
	Sleep talking
	Bruxism (grinding or clenching of the teeth)
	Hyperkinesias (muscle spasms)
	Repetitive limb movements
Disorders of excessive somnolence	Difficulty waking up
	Tired when waking up
	Sleep paralysis
	Daytime somnolence
	Sleep attacks
	Falling asleep watching TV, studying/reading, playing, etc.
Sleep hyperhydrosis	Falling asleep sweating
	Night sweating

Source: From K. Spruyt et al. 2005. *J Sleep Res* 14: 163–176. © 2005 European Sleep Research Society.

Disease and Injury

One of our three children seemed to always be coming down with a disease. If one child got sick, we waited in trepidation for the next child to follow. Our pediatrician was like a family member, someone we visited regularly. In between diseases, we visited emergency rooms and orthopedic surgeons for sports-related injuries. And, we were never alone in our misery. Waiting rooms were filled with children who had gotten sick from exposure to other sick children at school, were waiting to be seen for a chronic disease, or were injured playing sports at school or on teams. The sections that follow describe some prevalent diseases and injuries of middle childhood, once more distinguishing between infectious and chronic diseases (see Chapter 8).

Infectious Diseases

LEARNING OBJECTIVE 11.15 Describe some common infectious diseases of middle childhood.

Children experience high rates of infectious diseases throughout middle childhood, especially during the first years of school when they are in frequent contact with sniffling and coughing peers and have not yet developed immunity for specific diseases. Common diseases of childhood include chicken pox, conjunctivitis (pink eye), coughs and croup, influenza (the flu), ear infections, sore throats, diarrhea, and vomiting.

Infectious diseases are highly contagious, making the school-attending child especially prone to getting sick. The disease of a single infected child can quickly spread across a classroom or school through various modes of contact. Influenza, pertussis (whooping cough), streptococcal infections, the common cold, and so on, are spread through contact with the respiratory droplets children produce when they cough, sneeze, or talk, and can be transmitted through sharing contaminated items (like pens, pencils, and electronic devices). Conjunctivitis (inflammation and redness in the eye) is transmitted when hands or objects that have been contaminated by food, water, and so on touch the eye.

Although most childhood diseases are short lived and not serious, they may lead to children missing school and harm children's learning under conditions of multiple health problems, untreated conditions, or a lack of access to health care (Allison, Attisha, & Council on School Health, 2019). The unprecedented closing of schools throughout the United States and other parts of the world in the aftermath of COVID-19 is a salient reminder of the close connection between health risks and children's everyday educational experiences. Moreover, some children are at risk of complications if they are exposed to other ill children or adults, such as those who have immune deficiencies, chronic disease, and nutritional deficiencies. Consequently, many school districts put in place policies to protect children from disease, including procedures for informing individuals of the risk of exposure to specific diseases. Guidelines around frequent hand washing are circulated widely to teachers, staff, and students, who are encouraged to do so after playing outside, using the bathroom, and before eating. And school districts train teachers on identifying the common signs of disease, such as loss of appetite, irritability, fever, flushed appearance, rash, nasal discharge, cough, and so on, to guide removal of a child from the classroom to get the needed care (Thronson et al., 2014).

✓ **CHECK YOUR UNDERSTANDING 11.15**

1. What are some common infectious diseases of middle childhood?

Chronic Diseases and Disorders

LEARNING OBJECTIVE 11.16 Differentiate chronic disease from acute disease.

Chronic diseases in U.S. children have risen dramatically over the past few decades (Perrin, Bloom, & Gortmaker, 2007). Altogether, an astounding 20%–25% of U.S. children have chronic diseases and conditions (Compas et al., 2012). Obesity and associated complications of diabetes are prevalent chronic problems of childhood, along with asthma and attention-deficit/hyperactivity disorder (ADHD). Other less prevalent but highly serious chronic diseases include cystic fibrosis, arthritis, and cancer. The dramatic rise seen in the prevalence of childhood chronic diseases over the past several decades may be due to changes in children's home environments—including increased stress on parents, time spent indoors, television viewing and sedentary behaviors, consumption of fast foods, and exposure to pollutants.

Asthma

Asthma is a disease in which the bronchial tubes—which carry air that has passed through the mouth, nasal passages, and windpipe into branches and cells of the lungs—fill with mucus and contract. Asthma is the most common, serious chronic disease of childhood in the United States, affecting over 7% of U.S. children annually (**FIGURE 11.17**). Asthma doubled in prevalence from the 1980s through 1990s, and continues to grow (although slowly) through the present, with children from non-Hispanic Black families most likely to be affected by the disease (Akinbami, Simon, & Rossen, 2016; Akinbami et al., 2017). Children have smaller airways than do adults, which makes asthma especially serious, leading to coughing, wheezing, and breathing difficulties that can result in hospitalization and even death. An asthmatic episode can be triggered by allergies, infection, cold weather, and emotional stress.

Attention-Deficit/Hyperactivity Disorder

Attention-deficit/hyperactivity disorder (ADHD)—marked by persistent inattention, hyperactivity, and sometimes impulsivity—is among the most prevalent chronic developmental disabilities, affecting between 8% and 10% of children (Zablotsky et al., 2019). Children with ADHD have problems concentrating and cannot remain focused on a task for more than a few minutes. Some children also display hyperactivity; they are unable to sit still and their excessive levels of activity wear on parents and teachers alike. In clinically diagnosing ADHD, clinicians rely on guidelines laid out in the fifth edition of the **Diagnostic and Statistical Manual of Mental Disorders (DSM-5)**, a manual that contains indicators of personality disorders to aid assessment, as developed by the American Psychiatric Association. The diagnosis of ADHD includes symptoms that indicate:

- a persistent pattern of inattention;
- hyperactivity and impulsivity;
- a presence of inattentiveness and hyperactivity prior to 12 years of age;
- a presence of symptoms in multiple settings;

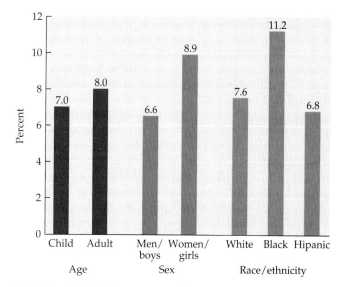

FIGURE 11.17 Asthma rates in the United States. Asthma affects 7.5% of children, a rate that is comparable to that of adults. As shown, the incidence of asthma is higher in females than in males, and asthma rates vary by race, with the highest percentage of affected individuals being Black. (After CDC. Asthma Surveillance Data. Accessed July 30, 2021. https://www.cdc.gov/asthma/asthmadata.htm. National Health Interview Survey, National Center for Health Statistics, Centers for Disease Control and Prevention.)

asthma A respiratory disease in which spasms occur in the bronchi of the lungs due to a buildup of mucus, creating breathing difficulties; asthma is the most common chronic disease of childhood in the United States

attention-deficit/hyperactivity disorder (ADHD) A prevalent and chronic neurobehavioral disorder characterized by persistent inattention and trouble concentrating, hyperactivity, and impulsiveness

Diagnostic and Statistical Manual of Mental Disorders (DSM-5) A manual developed by the American Psychiatric Association that aids with the diagnosis of personality disorders in children and adults

psychosocial treatments
Interventions for problems such
as ADHD, such as counseling and
psychotherapy, which focus on an
individual's psychological growth
and interactions with the social
environment

**psychopharmacalogical
treatments** The use of medications
to treat medical conditions, including
the use of stimulant medicines
to improve symptoms in children
with ADHD

- interference from symptoms in social relationships, schoolwork, and other areas of functioning; and
- symptoms that cannot be attributed to other mental disorders, such as mood disorders, personality disorders, and substance use.

Clinicians use a variety of approaches to treat children with ADHD (DuPaul et al., 2020). **Psychosocial treatments** often train parents and teachers on ways to provide consistent feedback that reinforces children's following of rules and staying on task (e.g., Evans et al., 2018; Fabiano et al., 2009). Such approaches result in reduced ADHD symptoms and behavioral problems (e.g., DuPaul, Eckert, & Vilardo, 2012; Evans et al. 2018). **Psychopharmacological treatments** involve giving children stimulant medication, which improves symptoms and shows high acceptance by children and adolescents (Catala-Lopez et al., 2017). However, a combination of approaches may be especially effective. Children who received a multipronged approach to the treatment of ADHD—namely medications with psychosocial intervention—showed improvement in behavior and quality of life (Velo et al., 2019).

✓ **CHECK YOUR UNDERSTANDING 11.16**
1. Describe two prevalent chronic diseases of middle childhood.

Injuries

LEARNING OBJECTIVE 11.17 Name typical ways in which children sustain injuries in middle childhood.

Middle childhood is injury ridden. Some injuries are minor, others are major, and a small percentage are fatal. As with disease, injuries can interfere with attendance at school and participation in extracurricular activities and take an emotional and social toll on children and families.

Motor Vehicle and Bicycle Injuries

Injury rates are fairly steady through 10 years of age, and then increase dramatically through the end of adolescence, particularly for boys (Centers for Disease Control Prevention, 2013). Two leading causes of childhood injury are motor vehicle injuries and injuries from bicycle accidents (Bailar-Heath & Valley-Gray, 2010). Programs aimed at preventing injuries through educational classes and informational materials may lower rates of motor vehicle and bicycle injuries. For example, encouraging the use of helmets, although not foolproof, reduces head injuries by 9% (Karkhaneh et al., 2013).

Injuries from Team Sports

Children who engage in team sports also risk injury. Injuries of 1,659 children ages 7–13 were examined by sport for rates of injury (calculated as the number of injuries per 100 athletic events, including games and practices) (Radelet et al., 2002). Injury rates averaged 1.7 for baseball; 1.0 for softball; 2.1 for soccer; and 1.5 for football. When the severity of injuries was examined—those that resulted in fracture, dislocation, and concussion—3% of baseball injuries, 1% of soccer injuries, and 14% of football injuries were considered to be serious.

Serious football injuries most often result from contact with other players, rather than equipment failure. Shockingly, rates of **concussion**—temporary unconsciousness brought about by a blow to the head—for 12-year-old boys who played football equaled those seen in high school and even NFL players (Kontos et al., 2013) (**FIGURE 11.18**). The relatively high rate of serious injury for football is why it has received so much negative attention in the United States. A comprehensive review of the consequences of concussions for school performance found that

concussion A brain injury, sometimes marked by temporary unconsciousness, brought about by a blow to the head; symptoms may include headache, dizziness, ringing in the ears, and sleepiness

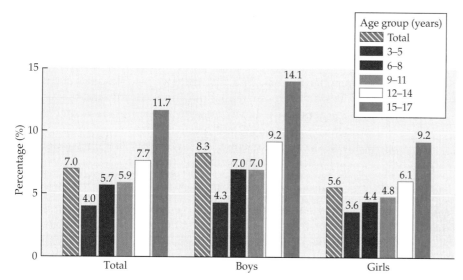

FIGURE 11.18 Concussion injuries are common in childhood. Rates increase over age and are especially high for boys. (After L. I. Black et al. 2018. NCHS Data Brief 302. February 2018. https://www.cdc.gov/nchs/products/databriefs/db302.htm. Source: NCHS, National Health Interview Survey, 2016.)

students who developed headaches and dizziness following a concussion missed more school days than did students with extremity injuries (i.e., injuries to the bones, nerves, vessels, and soft tissues), although concussion had minimal impact on school grades or national exam scores (Rozbacher et al., 2017).

Of course, sport injury rates vary by country and sport popularity. Canadian hospital records of brain injuries in 5- to 19-year-olds between 1990 and 2009 showed that ice hockey accounted for the greatest number of brain injuries (44.3%) when compared to soccer, football, basketball, baseball, and rugby (Cusimano et al., 2013).

Preventing Injury

What can be done to prevent sports-related injuries? Various preventive strategies have been recommended, including improved equipment, training, and educational programs. However, these strategies are not always effective. An evaluation of 14 studies that implemented various prevention strategies, including educational initiatives, showed little to no effects on rates of concussions (Schneider et al., 2016).

In contrast, some measures may be effective in preventing injuries from overuse. These include having children engage in exercises to improve flexibility, balance, control, and core and trunk strength (Pasanen et al., 2015). Additionally, switching among sports from season to season gives children breaks from the stress imposed on specific muscles and joints and gives their bodies time to rest and repair. Finally, avoiding the wear and tear that comes from overdoing sports by adequately resting the body is important. Children experience "overuse" injuries such as stress-related fractures (Frank et al., 2007) and tears to ligaments (Pasanen et al., 2015), even in the absence of injurious contact with equipment or teammates. This is particularly true when children play under highly competitive conditions, with coaches, parents, and peers encouraging high levels of aggression and team rivalry.

✓ CHECK YOUR UNDERSTANDING 11.17

1. What types of preventive measures have been implemented to combat injury in childhood?

Developmental Cascades

Changes in brain and body during middle childhood reverberate across developmental domains and pave the way to adolescence and adulthood. Brain development, malnutrition, obesity, and inadequate physical activity can have cascading influences on mental health, academic performance, and social and emotional development. Children's sleep problems can likewise affect learning and school performance and increase the risk of obesity.

Cascades from Brain Development

Developments in the brain, coupled with experiences that further sculpt the changing brain, spill over to areas of cognitive and emotional development. Indeed, differences among children in patterns and rates of change in brain development during middle childhood affect domains afar, ranging from academic performance, to intelligence, to even fear and anxiety.

Cascades to Cognition and Intelligence

Foundations to complex thinking are situated in changes to the brain's white and gray matter volume, myelination, and composition of network structures. Changes in brain structure and function account for many of the impressive cognitive gains seen during middle childhood. They also help explain why some children may be at risk for academic difficulties. When scientists examine the brain structure and activity of children, they find associations with reading performance and developmental disabilities such as ADHD (e.g., Myers et al., 2014; Nomi et al., 2018; Yeatman et al., 2011).

Consider how slight differences in brain development during middle childhood can cascade to problems such as ADHD. Recall that one of the three key changes to brain networks occurs in the length of path connections: Typical development shows a shift from local to more distant patterns of neural communication. That is, as long-range, or distant, brain connections increase, short-range, or local, connections weaken. However, the brains of children with ADHD contain more local connections, indicating a pattern that diverges from the typical developmental decrease in short-path connections (Marcos-Vidal et al., 2018). Additionally, differences in brain volume exist between diagnosed and non-diagnosed children with ADHD, particularly in the cerebellum (Al-Amin et al., 2018), the part of the brain that regulates motor movements and receives and coordinates information from the sensory systems, the spinal cord, and other brain regions. Because the brain volumes of medicated and unmedicated ADHD children do not differ, researchers discount medication as a source of brain volume differences.

Developmental patterns of brain growth also relate to children's performance on standardized tests of intelligence (Shaw et al., 2006). Specifically, changes in the thickness of the cortex across middle childhood distinguish children with superior intelligence and high intelligence from those with average intelligence. When children were subjected to neuroimaging tests to measure cortical thickness at different ages, children with superior intelligence showed gains in cortical thickness between 7 and 11 years, followed by a rapid decline, a pattern that was also seen, although to a lesser extent, in children of high intelligence. In contrast, children with average intelligence did not show the characteristic peak in cortical thickness. Rather, they showed a steady decline in cortical thickness from age 7 onward (**FIGURE 11.19**). The initial increase in cortical thickening seen in children of superior intelligence may be due to

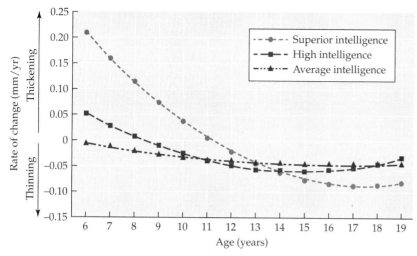

FIGURE 11.19 Cortical thickness. Children who score in the superior range on tests of intelligence (blue line) show a developmental pattern of high cortical thickening (represented by positive values on the y axis) at an earlier age than do children of high and average intelligence. All age groups show a developmental shift from cortical thickening to cortical thinning over age (represented on the x axis). (After P. Shaw et al. 2006. *Nature* 440: 676–679. https://doi.org/10.1038/nature04513.)

myelination and a proliferation of brain cells and synapses, followed by selective pruning of unused synapses.

Cascades to Emotional Development

Most people are unaware of the brain's role in emotional development. Yet, a close connection can be seen between how the brain responds to different situations and how children cope and react in emotionally charged situations. Indeed, brain activation patterns differ among children with different types of emotional problems (Stieben et al., 2007). For example, anxious children show relatively high amygdala activation (based on fMRI) in response to negative stimuli whereas depressed children show relatively low amygdala activation (Thomas et al., 2001). (Recall from Chapter 2 that the amygdala is involved with the experience of emotions.) For example, researchers presented 5- to 11-year-old children with pictures of emotionally expressive faces and then monitored children's brain activation patterns. They found that fearful children showed greater activation in emotion regions than did less fearful children, who showed greater activation in cognitive regions (Perlman & Pelphrey, 2010). Older children also showed activation in cognitive regions. This suggests that older and less fearful children recruit cognitive regions of the brain to process emotional information more than do younger and more fearful children who recruit emotional regions of the brain.

A word of caution is in order, however, regarding associations between brain development and child behavioral functioning. Documented associations are based on correlational studies. As we learned, correlations do not imply causality, and brain-behavior influences are likely bidirectional. As children learn and develop, their experiences drive brain changes, and brain development, in turn, facilitates further learning and comes to be expressed in children's reactions to everyday experiences.

Cascades from Physical Activity

Being active pays off psychologically. Children who participate in organized or informal sports or simply enjoy running around and playing with their friends at a park or during recess show low depression and anxiety and high self-esteem (Biddle & Asare, 2011; Janssen & LeBlanc, 2010). For those who think that time for physical activity interferes with time for schoolwork, research suggests otherwise. A review of 73 studies on children's physical activity showed associations between physical activity and measures of children's cognitive development, academic performance, and even brain functioning (Donnelly et al., 2016). Furthermore, recess is associated with diminished behavior problems in the classroom, with teachers rating declines in classroom disruptions for children who had experienced 15 minutes or more of recess a day (Barros, Silver, & Stein, 2009). When children from six elementary school districts in California were given activity breaks during the day in the forms of recess and physical education, they not only showed gains in activity measured by accelerometers, but also showed gains in attentiveness and effort toward their classwork (Carlson et al., 2015). Thus, providing children with opportunities to be active at school, even if brief, may yield formidable benefits.

Physical activity also supports social development and friendships. As children practice moving their bodies, they become adept and flexible in gross motor skills, which can boost peer acceptance. In a study of 9- to 12-year-old children's motor performance, children who lacked motor skill suffered from low-quality peer relationships and were at risk of withdrawal and low self-worth (Livesey et al., 2011). Additionally, teachers indicated that children with poor motor skills tended to experience high levels of peer rejection in the classroom. The negative effects of low motor performance on peer relationships was stronger for boys than it was for girls, likely because of the importance that society places on boys' motor prowess.

Although team sports carry a risk for injury, children involved in sports at school or clubs display positive self-esteem, a sense of belonging in school, and low levels of depression (e.g., Daniels & Leaper, 2006). Sports participation may be especially important for children who are shy, because it can bolster their self-confidence and provide them with opportunities for group camaraderie (Findlay & Coplan, 2008). Additionally, children who participate in sports and other fitness programs are likely to continue positive habits into adolescence and adulthood, producing cascading effects on later physical and mental health (Marsh et al., 2007; Smith et al., 2014).

developmental coordination disorder (DCD) A condition without known medical or neurological origins in which children show problems in motor coordination such that they are extremely clumsy or awkward

Unfortunately, some children show severe problems in motor skills. Children described as extremely clumsy or awkward by their parents and teachers may be diagnosed with **developmental coordination disorder (DCD)**, a condition that does not have any identifiable medical or neurological origins yet causes about 5%–6% of school-age children to have difficulty organizing the movements involved in everyday actions such as tying shoes and going down stairs. Children with DCD problems at 7 years of age have increased odds of mental health problems (reported by parents) and self-reported depression at 9–10 years of age, with poor self-esteem and experiences of being bullied partly contributing to problems (Lingam et al., 2012). Similarly, 8- to 10-year-old children with and without DCD differed in their perceived competence and social support, self-worth, and anxiety (Skinner & Piek, 2001). Disorders such as DCD are typically treated by physical therapists who work with children on their muscle strength and occupational therapists who help children with motor coordination.

Cascades from Food Insufficiency and Malnutrition

Considering that food nourishes the brain and body, the potential for cascading problems from food insufficiency and malnutrition is evident. Food insufficiency is associated with poor prognoses in children's cognitive, academic, psychological, and social development, with harmful effects even seen in many countries, including the United States, United Kingdom, Canada, and Australia (Alaimo, Olson, & Frongillo, 2001; Shankar, Chung, & Frank, 2017). Additionally, food insufficiency and hunger are often accompanied by other risks that exacerbate the problems associated with low nutrition. Children who faced severe hunger and were living with their homeless, low-income mothers experienced chronic disease, internalizing behaviors, and anxiety or depression (Weinreb et al., 2002).

At the extreme, sustained malnutrition can lead to physical and cognitive problems years later, even when researchers control for risk factors such as poverty and parent education (e.g., Grantham-McGregor, Walker, & Chang, 2007; Liu et al., 2003). In fact, children from middle to high socioeconomic status families who experience insufficient levels of iron and folate showed lower mental test performance than did children with adequate levels (Arija et al., 2006). Moreover, the effects of malnutrition on mental performance can be staggering. Children from different ethnic/racial backgrounds who experienced malnutrition in childhood showed a huge 15.3-point deficit on a standardized measure of intelligence at 11 years of age, a deficit equivalent to being in serious need of intervention (Liu et al., 2003). Malnourishment in childhood also cascaded to high aggression and hyperactivity at 8 and 11 years of age and conduct disorders and excessive motor activity at 17 years of age. The long-term deficits associated with malnourishment occur because a lack of proper nutrients during childhood interferes with children's abilities to concentrate, and even harms cellular growth in the brain (Nichols, 2018).

Cascades from Obesity

Obesity can incur immense physical and psychological costs. The combination of low activity and the toll of excess weight on the body places overweight and obese children at lifetime risk for health problems such as high blood pressure, diabetes, and high cholesterol. Beyond these health problems, children who are overweight may incur enormous psychological toll.

Many children who are overweight or obese experience social stigma because of prevailing social norms around being thin, and the negative attitudes and stereotypes towards people who do not meet societal body ideals (Davison & Birch, 2004; Latner & Stunkard, 2003). Negative attitudes start early and persist for many years. Children between 5 and 8 years of age were more likely to assume that overweight children were less athletic, academic, artistic, and social than average weight children (Penny & Haddock, 2007).

In turn, the stigma around being overweight may affect children's social interactions with peers. Children who are overweight or obese are more likely than their normal-weight peers to be victims of bullying, overt aggression (e.g., name-calling, teasing, hitting, or kicking), and relational aggression, such as when peers spread rumors or lies about a child (Janssen et al., 2004; Harrist et al., 2016). Hurtful peer interactions can then lead to somatic complaints (i.e., excessive focus and distress about physical symptoms, such as pain and shortness of breath), depression, low self-esteem, and at the extreme, suicide attempts (e.g., Harrist et al., 2016; Puhl & Latner, 2007).

However, the negative consequences of being overweight or obese do not occur in a vacuum. Rather, a child's developmental path is the product of many interacting risk and protective factors. Overweight children who do not feel supported at home or by their teachers, or those who live in poverty, are at heightened social and emotional risk relative to children who experience social support and environmental resources. In fact, many children who are overweight have high self-esteem, do not suffer from depression, and achieve well-paid employment and positive social relationships in adulthood (Hill, 2017). Furthermore, timely interventions can make a difference. Children who enter effective weight management programs, and have the support of their parents and peers, achieve weight loss and show accompanying improvements to self-esteem (Hill, 2017; Lowry et al., 2007).

Cascades from Sleep

We learned that sleep is a lot more important than most people think. Sleep allows children's bodies and brains to rest so that they can meet the challenges of the day. Insufficient sleep and poor-quality sleep can disrupt learning, hamper academic achievement, and lead to a heightened risk of being overweight.

Sleep and School Performance

When children do not get enough sleep, they do less well in school (Astill et al., 2012). A lack of sleep might disrupt learning because information is consolidated and integrated with existing knowledge during sleep (Henderson et al., 2012). But beyond that, being tired makes it harder for children to control their behaviors and complete school tasks. In addition, sleep might explain at least some of the association between eating a good breakfast and doing well in school: Children who are extremely tired are less likely to get up early enough to take the time to eat breakfast.

Sleep can also harm academic performance by impacting children's executive processing skills, such as attention and working memory. When researchers manipulated the sleep time of 9- to 12-year-old children, restriction of sleep by only 1 hour for three consecutive nights reduced alertness (Sadeh, Gruber, & Raviv, 2002). Similarly, natural variations in children's sleep durations, night awakenings, types of sleep, and other measures of sleep recorded by actigraphs related to executive functioning skills in second, fourth, and sixth graders (Sadeh, Gruber, & Raviv, 2003). Researchers assessed how quickly children could tap a button when a large square appeared on a screen, their accuracy at solving number problems, and their working memory. Children who had experienced fragmented sleep during the 5-day recording period performed poorly on all measures, with performance worsening as items increased in difficulty. Others find that 7- to 11-year-old children who sleep longer show better performance on reasoning problems, measures of intelligence, and academic performance (Gruber et al., 2010).

Sleep and Overweight Status

Insufficient sleep increases the odds of a child being overweight. Children ages 9–12 who had short sleep durations in third grade were more likely to be overweight in sixth grade compared to children who slept longer. When children also had short sleep durations in sixth grade, their chances of being overweight further increased, even when the researchers statistically controlled for children's weight in third grade (Lumeng et al., 2007). As we have seen, being overweight compromises children's physical activity and participation in team sports. In turn, children's weight status and lack of sports participation might place them at risk of being rejected and victimized by their peers. Thus, sleep can affect body weight, how children engage in school, and ultimately the friendships that children develop—offering yet another example of developmental cascades across distinct domains of child functioning.

Cascades from Chronic Disease

The stressors associated with chronic childhood disease can cause academic, emotional, and social difficulties for many years. Children with a chronic disease might experience painful medical treatments, physical discomfort, change to physical activities, family stress, school absences, and separation from peers (Compas et al., 2012). When conditions of disease worsen, family and child stress levels amplify, exacerbating the negative repercussions of the disease (Marin et al., 2009; Rodriguez et al., 2012). Indeed, childhood chronic disease predicts adolescent depression, low self-esteem, cigarette smoking, and illegal drug use, and even thoughts about and attempts at suicide (Erickson, Gerstle, & Feldstein, 2005). Developmental disabilities, such as ADHD, can compound problems in reading and math, resulting in grade repetition, which can cascade to school dropout, low-skilled labor work and unemployment in adulthood, and mental and physical health problems (Currie et al., 2010). Moreover, children with chronic physical or mental health problems are 10% less likely to be in excellent or very good health as adults (Delaney & Smith, 2012).

Fortunately, many children with chronic diseases show positive adjustment and contribute to their communities in meaningful ways. In particular, positive family relationships help children cope effectively with disease by arming children with the social and emotional skills needed to adapt to stress (Compas et al., 2012; Luecken, Roubinov, & Tanaka, 2013).

■ CLOSING THOUGHTS
Stability and Change

Questions about stability and change lie at the core of developmental science. Do our earlier behaviors persist over time such that when we look at our present self we see a ghost of the past? Or, do we change in so many ways and experience so many different things that our present self hardly resembles the person we once were or one day will be? The answer is a little bit of each. The degree to which childhood shapes the person we become depends on many factors. Changing circumstances continually alter the paths children choose to take, the paths they have the opportunity to take, and the paths they may be forced to take.

Yet, children never entirely escape their past because earlier behaviors shape what happens next, which influences what happens next, and so on. As a result, developmental stability is the norm. Indeed, the children I watched leap off the school bus years ago illustrate the concept of developmental stability. Although they are all now grown, I sometimes see them on the street or at a local café and hear stories about what they're up to from friends and family. Many of those children established healthy habits during the school years that stuck with them. For other children, bumps in the road were difficult to navigate, and unhealthy practices solidified. Seemingly small behaviors, when repeated regularly, cascaded to larger problems in adolescence and beyond.

What distinguishes between children at the extremes of health? The supports and guidance children receive from family members, friends, teachers, schools, and communities hold a lot of the answers. The context-boundedness of child development is why researchers and clinicians take very seriously issues around stability and change in children's physical development and health. By understanding the paths children take and where those paths lead, researchers and clinicians come many steps closer to supporting positive behaviors, intervening when needed, and preventing developmental detours.

The Developmentalist's Toolbox

Method	Purpose	Description
Measuring children's brain development and health		
Magnetic resonance imaging (MRI)	To study the anatomical structure of the brain, to determine brain volume in general and in specific regions of the brain	A neuroimaging technique using strong magnetic fields to generate three-dimensional images of body structures.
Brain network analyses	To characterize connectivity patterns among brain networks based on brain activity	Functional MRI (fMRI) signals are examined across the whole brain or specific regions of the brain and then used to map functional brain connections among neurons, including the degree and length of path connections.
Diagnostic and Statistical Manual of Mental Disorders (DSM-5)	To diagnose various personality disorders in children and adults	A manual developed by the American Psychiatric Association that contains indicators of personality disorders to aid assessment. Psychologists determine the extent to which a participant shows indicators associated with developmental or personality disorders such as ADHD.

■ Chapter Summary

Brain Development

- During middle childhood, brain development includes changes in white and gray matter volume; increased synchronization of brain waves across regions of the brain; and increased coordination in brain activity across regions of the brain.
- Parenting behaviors and contexts of poverty can affect brain volume.

Physical Development

- Physical changes to children's bodies, including growing muscle mass, support gross motor skill developments in areas of strength, flexibility, balance, agility, and coordination.
- Children's gains in fine motor skills help with everyday activities, like getting dressed, and also support writing and artwork.
- On average, boys exceed girls in body size and strength, and girls exceed boys in areas of balance and agility.
- School recess time, physical education classes, and open spaces and parklands in neighborhoods enhance children's physical activity and therefore support motor development. However, cuts to recess time and physical education classes are obstacles to healthy activity.
- Cultural differences in everyday physical activity affect motor development, as illustrated in the extraordinary walking and running stamina of Kenyan children.

Nutrition

- Problems of nutrition in childhood include malnutrition and obesity, which are prevalent in children living in households of poverty, where food insecurity is also high.

- There is a growing epidemic of obesity in the United States and globally because of unhealthy diets and lifestyles.
- Family context affects nutrition and obesity through parents' modeling of eating habits, rewards and punishments of children's eating habits, provision of nutritious home-cooked meals, and encouragement of children's physical activity.
- Neighborhoods can help prevent obesity by offering spaces for physical exercise, and schools can help prevent obesity by educating children about nutrition and offering nutritious foods.
- Public awareness campaigns and weight-loss intervention programs contribute to healthy lifestyles and prevention of obesity.

Sleep

- Sleep duration declines over childhood, and overall sleep duration has declined over the past several decades.
- Various approaches are taken to figuring out how much sleep is optimal for children, including child reports of sleepiness, experimental manipulations of sleep, and correlational studies examining sleep duration and quality in relation to various outcomes.
- A number of sleep problems have been identified in childhood, including disorders in initiating and maintaining sleep and sleep breathing disorders.
- Noisy, chaotic homes and the quality of parent-child interactions affect children's sleep.

Disease and Injury

- Infectious diseases are high in childhood, especially during the first years of school, and can lead to missing school.
- 20%–25% of U.S. children suffer from chronic diseases. Aside from obesity, asthma and ADHD are common chronic diseases and disorders of childhood.
- Motor vehicle and bicycle accidents are leading causes of injuries and fatalities during middle childhood. Participation in team sports can also lead to injury, including concussion and overuse injuries.

Developmental Cascades

- Variations among children in brain development have repercussions for behavior and attention problems such as ADHD, performance on intelligence tests, and emotional functioning such as anxiety and fear.
- Physical activity in middle childhood supports children's engagement in school, peer relationships, and self-esteem.

- Food insecurity and malnutrition show long-term effects on later chronic disease, psychological functioning (including depression and anxiety), and performance on standardized tests of intelligence.
- Being overweight or obese in middle childhood can cascade to health problems years later and being a victim of the social stigma of being overweight.
- Problems with sleep can compromise children's learning and school performance, and lead to risks of being overweight.
- Chronic disease in childhood can exert downstream effects on mental and physical health in adolescence and adulthood, school performance, and even employment in adulthood. However, positive family support can buffer long-term negative effects by providing children with positive coping strategies.

Thinking Like a Developmentalist

1. A developmental scientist is committed to advancing school programs that take a "whole child" approach to development by supporting not only children's academic learning but also their physical health. The scientist wishes to (a) design a school curriculum that would promote physical health across areas covered in this chapter, and (b) test whether the curriculum demonstrated the expected improvements, compared to "business as usual." What are some of the components the scientist might include in the health-based curriculum? How could the effectiveness of the new curriculum be evaluated? Be sure to identify measures in children that would serve as "dependent variables" of health, and present a study design that would enable a rigorous test of whether the new curriculum led to improvements in child health.

2. You wish to address problems in school performance seen in children living in poor households. You wish to design a health-based family intervention that differs from a program developed by your colleagues that simply provides children with extra academic support and tutors. Two areas you will target are nutrition and sleep, and you will work with parents around modifying the family context to support children. Your skeptical colleagues ask you *why* you think nutrition and sleep should have any effect on children's academic performance, and they also ask you *what* factors in the home context you would target. How would you respond? Describe the aspects of home context that you will seek to improve and explain why you chose such an intervention approach.

12 Cognitive Development in Middle Childhood

Drawing by Minxin Cheng from a photo by Ismail Salad Hajji dirir on Unsplash

Nabenchauk is a Mayan village located in the highlands of Chiapas, Mexico. Most children attend only a few years of school, and many families make a living selling flowers and other goods to neighboring villages and distant cities. Nabenchauk children (mostly girls) learn to weave intricate, colorful fabrics as an alternative to school, using tools and practices that have been passed down for thousands of years. Developmental scientist Patricia Greenfield spent years studying life in this remote village, and her observations led to important insights (Greenfield, Maynard, & Childs, 2000, 2003). Greenfield observed that village weaving practices changed over children's development in ways that coincided with the cognitive skills described by Piaget.

Children first learn to weave at 3 years of age, using a simple toy loom that creates a piece of cloth identical in length and design to the threads on the loom. At 8–10 years of age children transition to a more sophisticated weaving tool, a warping frame called a *komen*, which requires them to mentally transform the thread patterns to visualize the final woven cloth because the threads on the frame are folded and their right-left positioning is switched (**FIGURE 12.1**).

The timing of Nabenchauk children's transition from toy loom to komen occurs around the age that children transition to Piaget's concrete operational stage of development, and are capable of mental transformations. In fact, Patricia Greenfield wondered how Nabenchauk children would do on Piagetian tasks of mental transformation that were modified to fit the culture's familiar practice of weaving. She asked 4- to 13-year-old children to match the threads on a komen to the correct fabric pattern in a series of pictures (**FIGURE 12.2**). Nabenchauk children

(A)

(B)

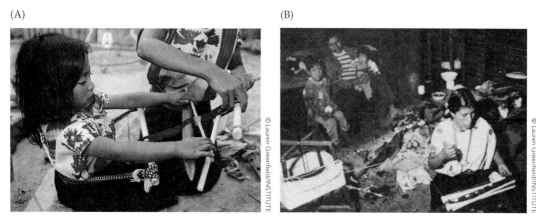

FIGURE 12.1 Weaving on a komen by a native of Nabenchauk, Mexico. The more sophisticated warping frame requires transformative thinking. The weaver must recognize that the threads on the left side of the dowel of the warping frame will end up at one end of a loom, while the threads on the right side of the dowel of the warping frame will wind up at the other end. (A) A child weaves on a toy loom. (B) The child's mother uses a real version.

under 6 years of age could only solve problems that involved direct matches from komen to cloth, suggesting that they were still in the preoperational stage of thinking. Children 6–9 years of age began to solve problems that required mental transformations (e.g., recognizing that the pattern they observed on the komen would be reversed on the cloth), and improved through 13 years of age, suggesting concrete operational thinking. Patricia Greenfield's studies of Nabenchauk children carry an

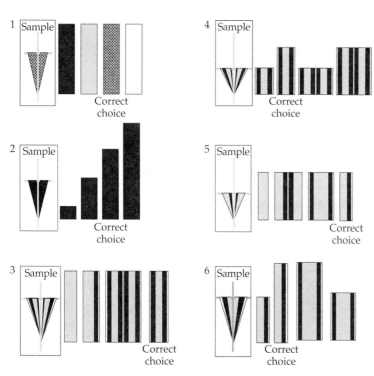

FIGURE 12.2 Weaving practices and Piaget's theory. To test children on Piagetian tasks of mental transformation Patricia Greenfield asked them to match a configuration of threads on a komen to the correct fabric pattern in a series of pictures. The tests involved color-matching (sample 1), size transformation (sample 2), pattern transformation (samples 3 and 5), and both size and pattern transformation (samples 4 and 6). (From A. E. Maynard and P. M. Greenfield. 2003. *Cog Dev* 18: 489–510.)

important message: All children advance in cognitive thinking, yet they express their abilities in unique ways to adapt to the demands of their cultural communities.

In this chapter, we review changes in children's cognitive development during middle childhood, from the perspectives of Piagetian and information processing theories. We then examine children's growing skills in language, reading and writing, and mathematics, and the influence of motivation on school engagement and performance. We consider contextual and cultural influences in these areas, and end with discussion of developmental cascades.

■ *Cognitive Development*

Browse the aisles of any toy store in the United States and you are likely to find games, puzzles, blocks, video games, and tablets organized by age group and grounded in views about what is cognitively suitable for children at different points in development. The same goes for bookstores, where separate sections are dedicated to children of different ages. School curricula have well-defined standards about what should be taught when and in what sequence. In the United States, local and national tests assess whether children have gained specific knowledge by a certain grade. Parents, educators, and policy makers share the goal of stimulating children's thinking in age-appropriate ways.

Yet, in cultural communities around the world, there are no explicit guidelines about what children can and should do by specific ages. In some communities, children do not attend school, and adults do not vigilantly monitor if and when their children are able to read and write, calculate math problems, and reason logically. Nevertheless, children everywhere acquire cognitively sophisticated skills—whether it is the math skills necessary to trade goods and earn a profit, the navigational skills required to steer a fishing boat to remote places and back, the narrative skills to tell elaborate stories, or the weaving skills to create intricate patterns in fabric—that allow them to participate in activities central to community life.

Piagetian Theory

concrete operations A stage in Jean Piaget's theory of cognitive development characterized by children's development of logical, flexible, organized, and rational thinking about concrete things

logical mental operations The ability to manipulate information in the mind and follow rules of logic to solve a problem

According to Piaget, children in the stage of **concrete operations** think logically and flexibly. From approximately 7 to 11 years of age, children can engage in **logical mental operations**—the ability to manipulate information in the mind and follow rules of logic to figure out a problem. For example, a child can now reason in her head that if there is a box of pizza with eight slices, and she ate two slices, six slices would remain. Children can solve this problem without having to actually eat the pizza because they can *mentally calculate* that eight slices reduce to six. Note, however, that children's thinking is limited to "concrete" problems: They can only reason about topics that are familiar to them, as we will see.

Concrete Operational Thought

LEARNING OBJECTIVE 12.1 Identify hallmarks of the concrete operational stage according to Piagetian theory.

As we review children's concrete operational thinking, we will see how children grow in areas of conservation, classification, seriation, perspective taking, and inductive reasoning, thus overcoming many of the cognitive limitations of early childhood (see Chapter 9).

Conservation

Recall Piaget discovered that young children have problems with conservation. They fail to recognize, for example, that the mass of clay does not change when it is rolled into a long, snakelike shape, or that pouring liquid from a short, fat beaker into a tall, thin flask does not change its volume (see Figure 9.8). In middle childhood, children pass conservation tasks because they are capable of **decentration**, which is the ability to focus on multiple parts of a problem, such as beaker width and height in the liquid problem, rather than centering on just one. Children can also think through a series of logical steps that lead from point A to point B, and reverse those steps mentally to arrive back at the starting point A—for example, recognizing that the snakelike string of clay can be molded back into its initial spherical shape. Researchers call this **reversibility**.

Classification

Children in the preoperational stage have difficulties considering relations among sets and subsets. Concrete operational thinkers, in contrast, tackle classification tasks with ease: They can subdivide the superordinate category of "plants" into categories of trees and flowers, and can further subdivide those categories into multiple types, such as oak and pine trees and tulips and roses. Children's interest in different types of collections, such as baseball cards—in which players can be grouped according to league, team, position, batting averages, and so on—reflects their ability to classify things along multiple criteria.

On close inspection, classification tasks require children to group things into **taxonomic categories**—categories based on superordinate and subordinate relations. This method of organizing adheres to what children learn at school. Teachers instruct children to put all the "red objects" together or "triangles" together and often ask children to explain *why* specific items belong together. In fact, taxonomic classification is so ingrained in our thinking that we rarely consider alternative solutions. Yet, children and adults in societies where schooling is rare do not necessarily categorize this way. Rather, they sort objects by their functional relations or purposes. For example, when asked to "put things into groups," unschooled individuals might place a knife with an apple, or a hoe with a potato, because knives cut apples and hoes dig up potatoes (Cole et al., 1971; Luria, 1976).

Seriation

Seriation refers to the systematic ordering of items along dimensions such as length or width. If you asked young children to arrange blocks from shortest to longest, they would have trouble sticking to the rule, sometimes organizing the blocks haphazardly. But, by around 6–8 years of age, children would order the blocks correctly because they can now think logically. Furthermore, if presented with the verbal problem "Christopher is taller than Brittany, and Michael is taller than Brittany, and Michael is taller than Christopher. Who is the tallest?" they'd be able to figure out Michael is the tallest. The term **transitive inference** refers to children's ability to solve verbal problems in their heads (Wright, 2006). Seriation and transitive inference enable children to manipulate information in working memory to solve the types of problems they encounter in school (Desoete et al., 2009).

Perspective Taking

In Chapter 9, we learned that children in the preoperational stage have difficulty taking another person's perspective, such as considering what a scene would look like from another person's vantage point, as tested in Piaget's three mountains task (see Figure 9.6). Children in the concrete operational stage have no problem with this task: They appreciate that people viewing the same display from different positions see different things.

Children's understanding of maps reveals developments in perspective reasoning on spatial tasks. Imagine you ask a child to draw a map of a familiar

decentration The ability to focus on multiple parts of a problem, situation, or object instead of focusing on just one part

reversibility The ability to realize that numbers or objects can be changed or returned to their original state, such as when children recognize that after rolling a ball of clay into a snakelike shape, it is possible to mold it back into its original shape

taxonomic categories Categories or classifications of entities based on their similar characteristics or functions, such as the category of "foods" or "body parts"

seriation The symmetric ordering of items along dimensions, such as length or width

transitive inference A form of deductive reasoning in which an individual is able to infer associations between objects or concepts based on logical reasoning from a set of premises (e.g., if B is related to C and C is related to D, then it is logical that B is related to D)

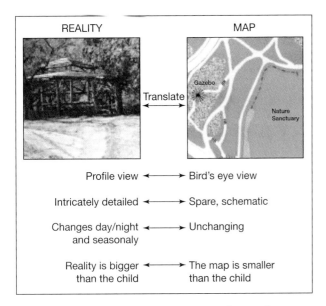

REALITY　　　　　　MAP

Gazebo

Nature
Sanctuary

←Translate→

Profile view ←——→ Bird's eye view

Intricately detailed ←——→ Spare, schematic

Changes day/night ←——→ Unchanging
and seasonaly

Reality is bigger ←——→ The map is smaller
than the child　　　　than the child

FIGURE 12.3 Children's understanding of maps illustrates developmental gains in spatial reasoning. Maps represent spaces, but do so in very abstract ways. They provide challenges to children in translating the features on the map to their real-world referents. The schematics on maps look very different than the actual places they signify, as shown in this example of a map that depicts the location of a gazebo. (From K. Kastens et al. 2001. *J Geosci Educ* 49: 249–266. Taylor & Francis Ltd, http://www.tandfonline.com.)

inductive reasoning Drawing on specific observations, facts, and knowledge to draw logically broader conclusions

space such as a classroom, and then instruct that child to indicate landmarks within that space, such as the teacher's desk, blackboard, cabinets, and sink. The child can easily do so if the map is oriented to match the child's viewpoint. However, the task becomes more challenging when the map is rotated to represent the classroom space from the teacher's viewpoint. Although young children have difficulty with such tasks, older children do not. They can draw and read maps that are oriented in different ways, rotate maps to figure out their current location, trace a route, and instruct other people about how to get from one point to another (e.g., Liben et al., 2013) (**FIGURE 12.3**). By the end of middle childhood, children grasp the concept of scale. They understand that the sizes on a map proportionally represent a larger space—for example, that the length of lines for "streets" relates to the relative length of those streets in the real world (Liben, 2009).

Inductive Reasoning

Perhaps you played the guessing game 20 Questions as a child. The goal is to figure out what someone is thinking by asking a series of questions: "Is it an animal?" "Is it bigger than a breadbox?" "Can you play with it?" and so on. Through **inductive reasoning**—that is, drawing on specific observations or facts to generate broader conclusions—you might guess that an animal with a long tail, four legs, and fur that meows must be a "cat." Piaget noted that children reason inductively once they reach the concrete operational stage.

Piaget's studies of inductive reasoning inspired developmental scientist Deanna Kuhn (1977) to more precisely track developmental changes in this aspect of thought. Kuhn created a game about a faraway city named Tundor in which children 6–14 years of age had to draw conclusions from premises presented in stories about Tundor. For instance: "All of the people in Tundor are happy. Jean lives in Tundor. Is Jean happy?" First graders were able to draw on the specific premises that all people in Tundor are happy and that Jean lives in Tundor to determine that Jean must be happy. However, Kuhn showed that inductive reasoning problems vary in difficulty and that children gradually improve in this form of thinking. Only toward the end of the concrete operational stage were children able to answer questions like: "People living in Tundor are happy. Jean doesn't live in Tundor. Is she happy?" Younger children mistakenly concluded that Jean is not happy because she doesn't live in Tundor. They did not realize the impossibility of determining whether Jean is happy from the premises. Kuhn's studies showed that inductive reasoning develops over time with experience.

✓ CHECK YOUR UNDERSTANDING 12.1

1. How is the capacity for mental operations reflected in conservation tasks undertaken by children in middle childhood?
2. In what cultural contexts might the tendency to classify objects taxonomically be rare, and why?
3. How do children's abilities in classification and seriation tasks improve in middle childhood?
4. What type of tests demonstrate children's capacity for perspective taking on spatial tasks?
5. What is inductive reasoning? What evidence shows that this form of reasoning takes time to develop?

Limitations in Concrete Operational Thought

LEARNING OBJECTIVE 12.2 Describe what Piaget considered to be the limitations of concrete operational thought.

Children in the concrete operational stage boast impressive skills in logical reasoning, and can solve problems flexibly and mentally. However, they show limitations in certain areas of cognitive thinking including abstract thinking and deductive reasoning. In terms of abstract thinking, children in the concrete operational stage remain bound to the here and now, struggling with problems that fall outside the scope of their experiences. For example, a child might have difficulties reasoning about life on Mars, such as whether plant life would be necessary for creatures on Mars who did not breathe oxygen, or whether humans who moved to Mars, and called themselves Martians, would require plant life. Children also show limitations in **deductive reasoning**, the ability to systematically test ideas that are guided by an overarching hypothesis. For example, a child might be unable to figure out what causes a pendulum to swing faster if given the choice of the pendulum's weight, string length, and force of the downward push, because they would get confused by all the possibilities and be unable to formulate a systematic approach to solving the problem.

What allows children to eventually grasp abstract ideas and solve deductive reasoning problems? Beyond maturation of the brain, children's growing knowledge about the world contributes to their reasoning abilities (Goswami, 2015). For example, consider the following problem: "Humans have spleens. Dogs have spleens. Do rabbits have spleens?" (Carey 1985). Younger children have difficulty with this problem because they don't know what spleens are, and so the abstractness of the problem is beyond their grasp. In contrast, even though adolescents may also not know what a spleen is, they are able to answer this problem correctly by building on their world knowledge. They start with the premise that humans, dogs, and rabbits are all mammals, and then use it to reason that if other mammals have spleens, it is likely that rabbits do as well (Goswami, 2015).

deductive reasoning The ability to systematically test ideas that are guided by an overarching hypothesis; the ability to reason from statements to reach a logical conclusion

✓ CHECK YOUR UNDERSTANDING 12.2

1. What are two limitations in children's cognitive skills in the concrete operational stage?

Information Processing

People often take for granted the cognitive demands of what they and others do on a regular basis. Consider the responsibilities of air traffic controllers. They keep track of the arrivals and departures at multiple runways; issue instructions about landings and takeoffs; monitor the movements of aircrafts, baggage vehicles, and airport workers on the ground; integrate information from radar, computers, and their own observations; and apply various strategies to remember and keep on top of things. Clearly, there's a very high cost to error. Now consider the demands on children at school. They must selectively attend to the teacher's words; ignore irrelevant distractors—the sounds of people in the hallway, the creaking radiator, the colorful shirt of a friend; actively manipulate information in working memory to make sense of what they are learning; and apply strategies to help them remember new information and connect it to relevant knowledge. Children are, in essence, young air traffic controllers.

Researchers from an information processing tradition investigate developmental changes in the cognitive processes that underlie children's thinking and action, namely the factors that allow children to handle increasingly complex information with age (Halford & Andrews, 2011). Thus, whereas Piaget described children's developing cognitive abilities, such as the transition from focusing on a single attribute (such as the number of "red things") to simultaneously

cognitive self-regulation
The ability to manage and integrate attention, thoughts, and behaviors to attain goals

considering multiple attributes, information processing researchers quantify the difficulty of specific tasks and then test the factors that explain children's abilities to engage in those tasks. In particular, children grow in several key aspects of **cognitive self-regulation**—the ability to manage thoughts and behaviors to accomplish goals (Blair, 2002; Matthews, Marulis, & Williford, 2014).

In the sections following, we consider how children improve in their capacities of cognitive self-regulation across childhood, particularly executive functioning skills (e.g., attention and working memory) and children's use of strategies. We then consider developments in children's knowledge and memory.

Attention

LEARNING OBJECTIVE 12.3 Identify improvements in executive control processes that are associated with middle childhood.

Although adults expect preschoolers to have difficulties paying attention, they raise the bar when it comes to older children. Teachers expect children to maintain attention, regardless of what else is going on, and to smoothly transition among class activities without being disruptive or distracted. For the most part, children meet those expectations. Across childhood, children improve in their abilities to (1) selectively attend to relevant information while ignoring irrelevant information, (2) flexibly shift attention among competing demands, and (3) plan and be systematic in their approach to goals.

Selective Attention

The environment contains many stimuli vying for attention, and it takes a lot of mental effort to stay focused and attentive to relevant parts of problems. Indeed, skills of selective attention provide a vital foundation for meeting the academic expectations of schooling, with children showing impressive growth in selective attention during middle childhood through adolescence (e.g., Stevens & Bavelier, 2012).

How do researchers test developmental changes in children's selective attention? Sometimes they ask children to identify target stimuli that are embedded in a stream of distractors (see Chapter 9). Children might be asked, for example, to press a button whenever they see a red number 1 as they watch numbers of different colors appear on a screen. Or, children might be instructed to cross out certain digits on a page (such as all the 8s or all the 3s and 5s) as quickly as possible—which is referred to as the **Digit Cancellation Test**. Sometimes, researchers instruct children to draw lines to connect sequences of letters (A-to-B-to-C, etc.), numbers (1-to-2-to-3, etc.), or alternating letters and numbers, which is especially challenging (1-to-A-to-2-to-B, etc.) (e.g., Saarikivi, Huotilainen, Tervaniemi, & Putkinen, 2019) using the **Trail Making Test** (**FIGURE 12.4**). What do these tasks share in common? They all contain a clear goal that can only be achieved by focusing on certain stimuli and inhibiting attention to others.

Children vary enormously in their abilities to stay focused and not get sidetracked. As we will see, children who do well on selective attention tasks do well at school, whereas children with severe attention problems may suffer academically. Genetics may be involved in children's executive functioning skills (e.g., Polderman et al., 2009; Young et al., 2009) and contribute to problems in children's selective attention, such as attention-deficit/hyperactivity disorder (ADHD) (see Chapter 11; e.g., Sun et al., 2018).

Cognitive Flexibility

Learning requires cognitive flexibility—the ability to switch attention and strategies with changing environmental demands. Researchers investigate children's cognitive flexibility by changing the rules and seeing how children

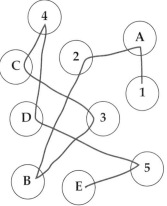

FIGURE 12.4 Trail-Making Test. Children are instructed to draw lines to connect the numbers , or numbers and letters, consecutively. (Based on W. C. Halstead. 1947. *Brain and Intelligence.* University of Chicago Press: Chicago, IL.)

adapt. For example, a researcher might instruct children to press a button any-time a small square appears inside a large shape on a computer screen. Then, the experimenter changes the rule. Children now must respond to large shapes and ignore small ones. Based on such tests, children show age-related gains in cognitive flexibility across middle childhood and continue to improve until 21 years of age (e.g., Huizinga, Dolan, & van de Molen, 2006) (**FIGURE 12.5**).

Planning

Most everyday activities involve multiple, sequenced steps. Planning requires children to efficiently allocate time across tasks—school, dance class, television, homework, video games, etc.—to get things done. One of the first studies of planning involved a pretend grocery store (Gauvain & Rogoff, 1989). Children 5 and 9 years of age had to "buy" foods from a cardboard store that contained shelves stocked with toy groceries. Children received a list of items to buy, and had to start at the store entrance, travel through the aisles to get the items on the list, and return to the door. Nine-year-olds engaged in more advanced scanning of the shelves, which helped them take an efficient route without repeating trips down the aisles, than did 5-year-olds.

Today, developmental scientists test children's planning with tasks such as the Tower of Hanoi and Tower of London (see Chapter 9) that require children to reproduce a pattern by moving colored disks or balls (e.g., Best & Miller, 2010). Planning is involved because children must generate and perform a sequence of

Digit Cancellation Test A test that assesses selective attention. For instance, children are asked to cross out specific digits from a list of numbers on a page as quickly as possible, while disregarding the distractors

Trail Making Test A test that assesses selective attention and mental flexibility; for example, children are asked to draw lines connecting sequences of letters, numbers, or letters and numbers

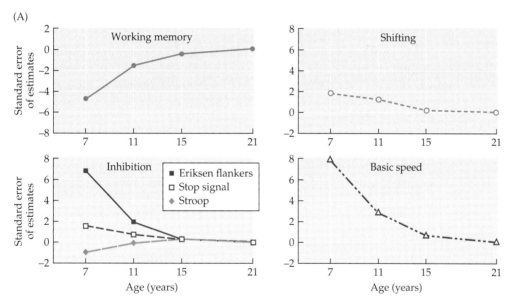

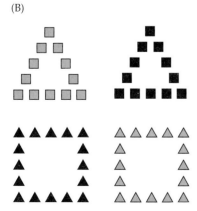

FIGURE 12.5 Developmental changes in cognitive flexibility. (A) Children continue to show improvement in working memory, inhibition, shifting, and speed as they age. These changes have been found in tasks where children must switch their attention and responses as game rules change. Eriksen flankers, stop signal, and Stroop are all inhibition tests in which children have to ignore irrelevant stimuli in a stimulus set. (B) For example, researchers sometimes present children with computerized pictures of large shapes (e.g., rectangles or squares) that are made up from small different shapes (again, rectangles or squares). They then instruct children to respond to a "small shape" by pressing a button (such as when small triangles make up the larger square shape). This requires children to ignore the larger shape. Researchers might then ask children to switch their responding by pressing a button when a triangle represents the larger shape; in this instance, children must now ignore the small square shapes that create the large shape. (A after M. Huizinga et al. 2006. *Neuropsychologia* 44: 2017–2036; B after M. Huizinga et al. 2006. *Neuropsychologia* 44: 2017–2036; based on D. Navon. 1977. *Cog Psychol* 9: 353–383.)

moves and evaluate progress after each move. By requiring more moves or adding more objects (disks or balls), researchers can increase the difficulty of problems.

What do these studies tell us? As you might expect, children improve in planning as they get older: They require fewer moves to copy patterns. However, when tasks call for more steps to be carried out, children struggle. For example, 8-year-olds, but not 4-year-olds, did as well as adults on problems requiring three moves, but 8-year-olds lagged behind adults on problems requiring four and five moves (Luciana & Nelson, 1998). Children reach adult-level performance for number of moves and time to completion by 15 years of age, but planning further improves through 21 years of age (Huizinga et al., 2006).

✓ CHECK YOUR UNDERSTANDING 12.3

1. What is cognitive flexibility? Give an example.

Working Memory and Processing Speed

LEARNING OBJECTIVE 12.4 Explain the roles of children's working memory and processing speed in school performance.

working memory span The number of bits of information that a person can hold in active memory and manipulate at a time

All activities require people to temporarily store and actively manipulate information in working memory. The number of bits of information a person can handle at a time, for example by recalling a set of numbers presented in sequence, is referred to as **working memory span** (see Chapter 9). Throughout childhood and into adolescence, working memory span increases (e.g., Cowan et al., 2011; Cowan et al., 2015). Cognitive researchers attribute such improvements to growth in children's efficiency of processing incoming information (Case, 1985) and ability to maintain information in mind for recall (Gaillard et al., 2011).

Why is working memory so important for learning? Because children must handle and manipulate the massive amount of information that is rapidly fired at them over the course of a school day. Children with limited working memory may have problems following complex instructions, lose track of what teachers are talking about and where they are on problems, and may fail to complete school assignments—problems that can harm reading and math performance without timely intervention (Gathercole, Lamont, & Alloway, 2006; Holmes & Gathercole, 2014). Unfortunately, many teachers are unaware that working memory deficits can hurt children's school performance, and they may misattribute students' difficulties to problems of attention or behavior (Gathercole et al., 2006).

processing speed How quickly a person can process or encode information

In addition to working memory, **processing speed**, how quickly a person can respond to relatively straightforward problems, relates to children's performance on school tasks. When researchers ask children to circle or cross out specific digits or letters on a sheet of paper as quickly (and accurately) as possible, children who are fast at such tasks have an advantage in memory, math performance, and inductive reasoning (e.g., Kail, 2007; Nettelbeck & Burns, 2010). With age, children improve in their processing speed, in part due to myelination and synaptic pruning in the cerebral cortex (e.g., Chevalier et al., 2015; Kail, 2007).

✓ CHECK YOUR UNDERSTANDING 12.4

1. Why might a child with a limited working memory have difficulties in school?
2. How does processing speed change with age, and what helps explain that change?

Metacognition and Memory Strategies

LEARNING OBJECTIVE 12.5 Define metacognition and describe how it helps children develop strategies for remembering material and solving problems.

I used to tell my children that I'd quiz them the night before their tests once they finished studying. More often than not, they'd tell me they were ready and knew everything, and then failed when I quizzed them. Essentially, they were unaware that they were unaware. With age, they improved in their awareness. Developmental scientists refer to the awareness of what one knows and how thinking works as **metacognition**. A related concept, **metamemory**, refers to children's understanding of the memory process. Throughout childhood, children grow in metacognitive and metamemory skills, which allows them to monitor their performance and implement strategies to help them remember material and solve problems.

Monitoring Performance

A major metacognitive accomplishment is children's ability to monitor how they are doing on a task. One way to assess children's monitoring is to ask them to complete a test and indicate how confident they feel about each of their answers. Researchers might also tell children to delete questions that they don't know to receive more credit for the remaining ones, which requires children to monitor their performance as they complete each problem. When this is done, 8-year-old children are fairly accurate in their confidence estimates, but they still struggle with figuring out which questions to delete as they progress on the test. It is not until 11 years of age that children can effectively determine which items to delete as they take the test (Roebers, Schmid, & Roderer, 2009).

Strategies for Remembering

As children develop metacognitive skills, they begin to use strategies to help them remember (Reese, 1962). As children progress through school, they improve in the use of strategies such as rehearsal, chunking, and elaboration (e.g., Best, Miller, & Jones, 2009; Clerc, Miller & Cosnefroy, 2014):

- **Rehearsal** refers to the deliberate repetition of information to aid memory. Children begin to use rehearsal in early grade school, with older children relying on this strategy more than younger children. Developmental improvements in rehearsal help children store and recall information (Lehmann & Hasselhorn, 2010).

- **Chunking** is seen when people group material into meaningful categories, such as by mentally grouping the words "apple," "potato," "cake," and "burger," and then using the superordinate category "foods" to retrieve the items from memory. Older children use chunking strategies more than do younger children and in turn show greater memory for test items (Bjorklund, Ornstein, & Haig, 1977).

- **Elaboration** involves creating a story or detailed image to remember information. A child asked to remember the unrelated words "fishing rod," "donkey," and "dress" might imagine a donkey wearing a dress while fishing. Although elaboration is highly effective for some children, it requires a lot of effort, which may be why it continues to develop into adolescence (Bjorklund et al., 1997).

Strategies like rehearsal help children learn the types of information required at school. But these strategies may have few practical uses in cultural communities with little or no formal schooling. In fact, school-relevant strategies may backfire in everyday situations where common-sense strategies best facilitate memory. This backfiring was seen when 9-year-old U.S. children were compared to Guatemalan Mayan 9-year-olds (who had little or no school experience) on their memory for the locations of 40 familiar objects in a playroom. U.S. children attempted to rehearse the object names to help them remember, whereas Guatemalan children relied on everyday cues in the room, and consequently exceeded U.S. children on their memory for the objects (Rogoff & Waddell, 1982).

metacognition A person's awareness of what that person knows and how thinking works

metamemory An understanding of one's own memory, including content and process

rehearsal A strategy for remembering that relies on repeating information to aid memory

chunking A strategy for remembering in which a person groups material into meaningful categories

elaboration A strategy for remembering in which a person creates a story or detailed image to aid memory

1. What strategies might an 8-year-old use to remember a list of words?
2. What cultural evidence suggests that strategies for remembering may sometimes backfire for children?

Semantic Memory: A Growing Knowledge Base

LEARNING OBJECTIVE 12.6 Explain how children's growing knowledge base helps them learn and remember information.

As children store more and more information in long-term memory, their knowledge base grows, allowing them to better learn and remember new information. (Note that a person's knowledge base reflects the semantic part of memory; see Chapter 9.) Consider how knowledge may facilitate memory. When fourth grade children were asked to remember a list of words about soccer, children who knew a lot about soccer remembered more than children who knew little, even though both groups knew the meaning of all the words on the list. Soccer "experts" remembered the most words because they categorized information as it was presented to them, and then used those categories to cue their memories when tested (Schneider & Bjorklund, 1992).

Knowledge also aids memory by facilitating rehearsal. When third and sixth graders rehearsed a list of words they were asked to remember, sixth graders engaged in more elaborate rehearsals of difficult words such as "astronaut" than did third graders, presumably because they had deeper knowledge about astronauts. Their rich elaborations, in turn, helped them remember more words than younger children. But, age differences disappeared when third graders were asked to remember a list of easy, familiar words and sixth graders were asked to remember a list of difficult, unfamiliar words. In the absence of knowledge to draw upon, sixth graders no longer had the advantage. Their working memories were taxed just as much as those of younger children (Bjorklund, 1987).

✓ CHECK YOUR UNDERSTANDING 12.6

1. Describe a study that shows how children's growing knowledge contributes to age-related changes in memory.

Episodic and Autobiographical Memory

LEARNING OBJECTIVE 12.7 Distinguish between two components of autobiographical memory, and describe how each changes with age.

Think back to your last birthday. You can likely remember details about where you were, who was there, the emotions you experienced, and what you saw, ate, and smelled. In essence, it's as though you can time travel to relive the past. Researchers call this type of memory episodic memory. From around 5 years of age, children talk about their past with some elaboration and detail, moving beyond the skeletal stories of preschoolers (Nelson & Fivush, 2004) (**TABLE 12.1**). Over the childhood years, children steadily improve in episodic memory (e.g., Ghetti & Bunge, 2012).

How do experimenters test children's episodic memory? A common approach is to investigate **autobiographical memory**, the information and memories we accumulate since birth that allow us to construct a unique identity and personal sense of continuity (Piolino et al., 2007). But, before delving into findings, note that autobiographical memory contains episodic *and* semantic components (Willoughby et al., 2012). The episodic part of autobiographical memory involves specific, personally significant events, such as your memory of a childhood camping trip, vacation in Florida, or the events surrounding your tenth birthday party. You have a sense of actually *remembering* the circumstances

autobiographical memory
The memories a person accumulates that allow the person to construct a unique identity and a personal sense of continuity; autobiographical memory contains episodic (specific personal events) and semantic (general knowledge about the past) components

TABLE 12.1 ■ Children's personal narratives over time   Children's episodic memory improves with age, with older children providing more details about a past experience than younger children.

Child's age and speaker	Statement
46 months (3 years, 10 months)	
Interviewer	When you went to (name of beach resort), do you remember doing that?
Child	I saw, um, penguins go to the beach. Sometimes the fin goes in the ice. They got hats.
Interviewer	Oh, really?
Child	Uh huh, when I go to the beach, I got those kinds of hats.
Interviewer	Can you think of the very first thing you did when you got to the beach?
Child	Um, the first thing we did, we had dinner. (unintelligible). Then we went swimming.
Interviewer	You went swimming?
Child	Then we went came down there. We, I, I didn't have my bathing suit on. Mommy took me up to the hotel and we, um, I put on my bathing suit. She didn't want to go when she didn't want to put her bathing suit on. Then I went in. That's it.
70 months (5 years, 10 months)	
Interviewer	Can you tell me when you went to SeaWorld?
Child	Oh, it was fun when we went to SeaWorld. It was real fun. Um, we saw a whale show. And, umm, the whale show, if you saw them dive up, the whales, that you'll get all splashed. And I was wet.
Interviewer	You were wet.
Child	Cause we were like sitting in the second row, and we got wet. But, if you were sitting like very up high, won't get as wet. And we saw Shamu, and um, we, um, what else did we see? We saw a real pretty girl with a white bird. That was (several unintelligible words) like white bird that was (unintelligible word). And I was, then we had lunch there. My mom took a picture of a white bird. A real pretty white bird. That was a long time ago.

Source: After K. Nelson and R. Fivush. 2004. *Psychol Rev* 111: 486–511. Copyright © 2004 by American Psychological Association. Reproduced with permission.

surrounding the event, rather than just knowing that the event occurred (**FIGURE 12.6**). The semantic component, in contrast, contains general knowledge about the past such as the names of relatives and friends, your former address, and general activities, such as the fact you attended church on Sundays as a child. You might know, for example, that you lived in Texas as an infant because your parents told you, but not remember anything about the experience.

So, when developmental scientists study autobiographical memory, they aim to describe changes in both episodic and semantic components. Which component do you think improves most with age? If you said episodic, you would be correct. When children ages 7–8, 9–10, and 11–13 recalled details about events that occurred during the current school year, prior school year, and distant school years—including a school event, a trip or vacation, and a family event—young children *knew* that certain events happened in the past, but the ability to *remember* specific details improved with age (Piolino et al., 2007). With age, children reported more specific and detailed personal events and required fewer prompts from the experimenter to elicit details about the experience. When experimenters then asked children whether they actually remembered the event, knew the

FIGURE 12.6 Episodic memory.   Episodic memory involves a sense of remembering the circumstances surrounding the event, rather than just knowing the event had happened. *Lion* is the true story of a 5-year-old boy from central India who got lost and ended up traveling more than 1,000 km away from home on a train, landing in Calcutta. He wanted to go home but he was too young and illiterate to be able to name his town and last name. More than 20 years later, he used his memory of the landscape of home and episodic memories of the train ride to locate his village using Google Earth.

event had happened without any memory, or were just guessing, 9- to 13-year-old children were more likely to report remembering, whereas 7- to 8-year-old children were more likely to report simply knowing information, particularly events of the distant past. Notably, episodic autobiographical memory continues to develop into adolescence, showing much greater growth than the relatively constant semantic autobiographical memory (e.g., Willough by et al., 2012).

Of course, autobiographical reports are limited in what they can tell us about the accuracy of a memory. Perhaps older children report more details than younger children because they embellish their reports with bits of information that are not central to an event or even accurate. Laboratory studies can test the accuracy of episodic recall by exposing all children to the same event and then testing age-related changes in children's memory. For example, experimenters told 4- to 16-year-old children about a day in the life of a child, and asked them to "act out" the story by moving a character around a "house board" (Picard et al., 2012) (**FIGURE 12.7A**). Children dramatically improved in their memory for

(A)

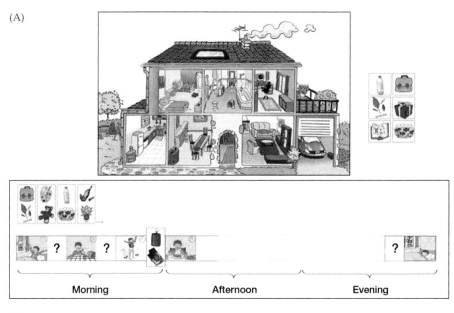

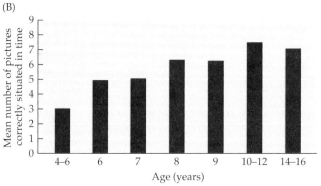

| Morning | Afternoon | Evening |

(B)

FIGURE 12.7 Episodic autobiographical memory continues to develop in its richness and detail throughout late adolescence. (A) Children 4–16 years of age were told about a day in the life of a child and asked to "act out" what they were told by moving a character around a "house board." (B) When later tested on their abilities to remember what happened, when, and where, children's memories showed dramatic improvements from preschool through middle childhood. (From L. Picard et al. 2012. *Child Dev* 83: 1037–1050. © 2012 The Authors. Child Development © 2012 Society for Research in Child Development, Inc. All rights reserved.)

details of the story from preschool through middle childhood, thereby confirming findings from autobiographical studies (**FIGURE 12.7B**).

✓ CHECK YOUR UNDERSTANDING 12.7

1. What is the difference between episodic and semantic components of autobiographical memory?
2. How might you test episodic memory?

■ *Intelligence and Individual Differences*

Not that long ago, you likely took a standardized achievement test (or perhaps several) as you prepared for college. You probably remember the anxiety you felt as you sat through the test and then waited for the outcome. You and your friends may have shared your scores with one another: Some of your peers probably ranked off the charts and others likely fell well below average (**FIGURE 12.8**). Perhaps you wondered why you scored as you did. Are certain individuals just naturally more "intelligent" than others?

Why is the topic of intelligence included in a chapter on cognitive development? The topic of intelligence often takes center stage in childhood, when children are expected to learn and remember vast amounts of material across many subjects over a limited time frame. Nearly all children in the United States and most other industrialized societies will take some form of an intelligence test at some point in their lives. Children who have difficulty reading, solving math problems, tackling complex problems, or memorizing school material may be referred to a psychologist for evaluation to have their "intelligence" assessed. The results of that test may cause them to be tracked to certain classes and guide plans for extra help in subjects. As we will see, debates on the definition of intelligence; the potential bias, validity, and implications of intelligence testing; and the roles of biology and environment in intelligence have a long, contentious history.

Defining Intelligence

What is intelligence? The answer is not straightforward. People are quick to characterize a person as "smart," "bright," or "slow"—in essence drawing conclusions about that person's underlying intelligence. A student who earns an "A" in physics might be presumed to be highly intelligent. A friend who finishes the *NY Times* crossword puzzle in record time might be praised as brilliant. Musicians, artists, writers, and poets are often called geniuses. Yet, despite these commonplace judgments, what makes someone intelligent is fiercely disputed. Most people would agree that Albert Einstein, Steve Jobs, and Ludwig van Beethoven were gifted in their own right, but is it possible to unify these individuals under a broad umbrella of intelligence?

Discussions of intelligence tend to be politically charged and raise moral and social questions about the qualities that we value in other people (Legg & Hutter, 2007). Nonetheless, many scientists agree that intelligence involves abilities to reason, solve problems, think abstractly, comprehend complex ideas, and learn quickly from experience (Gottfredson 1997). However, scientists disagree about whether intelligence should be viewed as a single mental ability or several discrete abilities, and which types of abilities should be folded under the umbrella of intelligence.

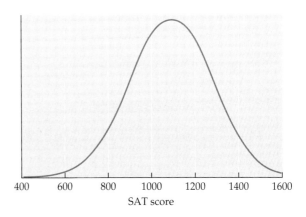

FIGURE 12.8 Making the grade. Standardized testing has become a rite of passage into college. Graphing scores from standardized tests results in a bell-shaped curve. Scores in the 1500–1600 range are well above average, and those in the 400–500 range are well below average. (Data from College Board. 2020. *SAT Suite of Assessments Annual Report*, Total Group. © 2020 College Board. College Board: New York, NY.)

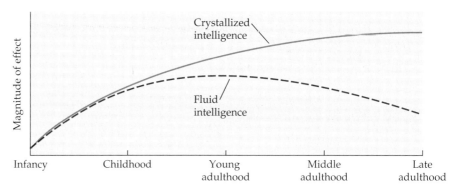

FIGURE 12.9 Crystallized versus fluid intelligence. Crystallized intelligence increases with age, whereas fluid intelligence begins to decline in early adulthood. (After J. L. Horn and G. Donaldson. 1980. In *Constancy and Change in Human Development: A Volume of Review Essays*, O. G. Brim and J. Kagan, [Eds.], pp 445–529. Harvard University Press: Cambridge, MA.)

A Single Mental Ability

LEARNING OBJECTIVE 12.8 List evidence that supports the idea of a single factor in intelligence.

Nearly 100 years ago, Charles Spearman proposed a single factor of general intelligence called the "g-factor" (Spearman 1927). In support of his theory, Spearman found that people who scored low on one type of cognitive problem also scored low on other types of problems, and conversely, those who scored high on one type of problem scored high on other types of problems.

Cattell (1987) slightly modified Spearman's single-factor theory of intelligence to distinguish between fluid and crystalized forms of intelligence. **Fluid intelligence** refers to a person's ability to think abstractly, reason, identify patterns, solve problems, and discern relationships. For example, if you were asked which number is next in the sequence 1, 3, 5, 2, 4, 6, 7, 9, 11, 8, you would have to identify patterns or relationships among the consecutive numbers to figure out that the correct answer is "10." In contrast, **crystallized intelligence** refers to the facts, vocabulary, and knowledge a person accumulates through education and cultural experiences. Knowing that the sun rises in the east taps crystallized intelligence. Crystallized intelligence continues to grow as people amass new knowledge, whereas fluid intelligence peaks in early adulthood and declines thereafter (Schaie, Willis, & Caskie, 2004) (**FIGURE 12.9**).

✓ CHECK YOUR UNDERSTANDING 12.8

1. Explain the difference between fluid intelligence and crystallized intelligence.

fluid intelligence A form of intelligence characterized by a person's ability to think abstractly, reason, identify patterns, solve problems, and determine relationships

crystallized intelligence A form of intelligence characterized by the facts, vocabulary, and knowledge a person accumulates through educational and cultural experiences

Multiple Abilities

LEARNING OBJECTIVE 12.9 Describe at least two theories of multiple intelligences.

Several researchers have proposed alternatives to Spearman's definition of intelligence, dating back to early theorists who argued that a single factor of intelligence failed to capture the range of cognitive abilities that are necessary for survival and advancement in a culture (e.g., Guilford, 1967; Thurstone, 1938). As we will see in the following sections, the idea of multiple types of intelligence is likewise reflected in contemporary views.

Howard Gardner's Theory of Multiple Intelligences

Developmental scientist Howard Gardner believed that conventional tests of intelligence ignored critical skills that fell outside traditional boundaries. He thus advanced a culturally sensitive **theory of multiple intelligences** (1983, 2008) based on his extensive research on children, individuals with brain damage, and **prodigies**—people endowed with exceptional qualities or abilities, such as Mozart, who played the violin at age 4 and wrote his first composition at 5. Gardner referred to these cases as evidence for seven (and later nine) distinct intelligences that could be localized in the human brain (**FIGURE 12.10**):

- *Linguistic intelligence*: The ability to think in words, understand and use language to express and appreciate complex meanings, and reflect on the use of language. Children with this kind of intelligence enjoy writing, reading, telling stories, or doing crossword puzzles.

- *Logical-mathematical intelligence*: The abilities to calculate, quantify, consider propositions and hypotheses, perceive relationships, use symbolic thought, reason deductively and inductively, and carry out mathematical operations. Children with this type of intelligence are interested in mathematical operations, patterns, categories, relationships, games of strategy, and experiments.

- *Spatial intelligence*: Being able to think in three dimensions, engage in mental imagery, use spatial reasoning, manipulate images, and have graphic and artistic skills. Children with this kind of intelligence may enjoy mazes, puzzles, and drawing.

- *Musical intelligence*: The capacity to discern pitch, rhythm, timbre, and tone and to create, reproduce, and reflect on music. Children with this kind of intelligence may sing, listen to music, drum out beats, and be attuned to aspects of sound and music that other people miss.

- *Bodily kinesthetic intelligence*: The capacity to manipulate objects and use a variety of physical skills. This intelligence also involves a sense of timing and the perfection of skills through mind-body union. Children with this kind of intelligence may enjoy athletic training, sports, dancing, and exercising.

- *Interpersonal intelligence*: The ability to understand and interact effectively with others. It includes effective verbal and nonverbal communication, sensitivity to the moods and temperaments of others, and the ability to entertain multiple perspectives. Children with interpersonal intelligence are leaders among their peers, good at communicating, and seem to understand others' feelings and motives.

- *Intrapersonal intelligence*: The capacity to understand oneself and one's thoughts and feelings, and to use such knowledge in planning and directing one's life. It is evident in psychologists, spiritual leaders, and philosophers. These children may be shy but are aware of their own feelings and are self-motivated.

- *Naturalistic intelligence*: The ability to discriminate among living things (plants, animals); sensitivity to features of the natural world (clouds, rock configurations). This ability and sensitivity were of value in our evolutionary past and present as hunters, gatherers, and farmers, and continue to be central in such roles as botanist or chef.

- *Existential intelligence*: The capacity to tackle deep questions about human existence, such as the meaning of life, why do we die, and how did we get here.

theory of multiple intelligences
A theory posited by Howard Gardner claiming the existence of seven (and later nine) distinct intelligences, each of which can be localized in the human brain

prodigies People gifted with outstanding, exceptional abilities or qualities

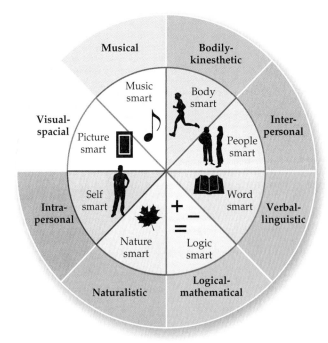

FIGURE 12.10 Gardner's theory of multiple intelligences. Gardner felt that conventional tests of intelligence ignored critical skills. Based on his extensive research, he proposed multiple distinct intelligences. (Based on Howard Gardner's theory, after T. Armstrong. 2000. *Multiple Intelligences in the Classroom*, 2nd ed. Association for Supervision and Curriculum Development: Alexandria, VA. © 2000 by Thomas Armstrong. Adapted with permission. All rights reserved.)

triarchic theory of intelligence
A theory posited by Robert Sternberg claiming that contextual influences affect intelligence and that "successful intelligence" is comprised of analytical, creative, and practical intelligences

Robert Sternberg's Triarchic Theory of Intelligence

Robert Sternberg (1985, 2018) proposed a **triarchic theory of intelligence** that highlighted contextual influences on intelligence (**FIGURE 12.11**). Sternberg defined intelligence as a mental activity directed toward adapting to the real-world, cultural environments relevant to one's life. Sternberg's theory of "successful intelligence" distinguished among analytical, creative, and practical aspects of intelligence:

- *Analytic intelligence*: The ability to analyze problems and generate solutions. Traditional tests of intelligence typically assess analytic skills. Analytic intelligence is seen in problem solving involving academic material, such as word problems in math.

- *Creative intelligence*: The ability to generate unique solutions to new and unusual situations, and to flexibly deal with those situations and problems. Creativity is seen in the designing, creating, and imagining of solutions and ideas.

- *Practical intelligence*: The ability to identify effective solutions or plans in response to environmental demands. This type of intelligence is especially relevant in everyday situations and skills vital to a culture. In the United States, practical intelligence is seen when a child must figure out how long to chat with friends on social media, while leaving time for homework.

The Strengths and Limitations of Theories of Multiple Intelligences

You might wonder which definition of intelligence is correct. As is true for all scientific theories, there is no single gold standard to define intelligence. Rather, different definitions have unique strengths and limitations.

Gardner and Sternberg raised awareness about nontraditional aspects of intelligence that recognized the potential for cultural variations in intelligent behavior. Sternberg's construct of successful intelligence further confirms what many people often observe in their interactions with others—that a person's cognitive skills are not always reflected in their practical skills. Many children excel in academic subjects and/or score well on standardized tests, yet fall short in handling practical matters. Being "book smart" does not automatically translate into being "street smart" or socially skilled. And, some children with low test scores are highly effective in their social interactions at school, home, and in the neighborhood.

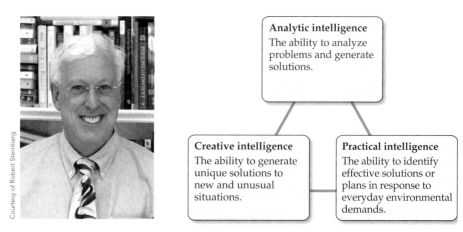

FIGURE 12.11 Robert Sternberg's triarchic theory of intelligence. Sternberg proposed that intelligence has analytic, creative, and practical components. (After S. M. Kassin. 2003. *Psychology*, 4th ed. Pearson/Prentice Hall: Upper Saddle River, NJ.)

Multidimensional views of intelligence also have solid educational implications. Gardner argued that because individual children excel in different areas of intelligence, teachers and schools should aim to promote those intelligences by gearing instructional practice and assessment to the strengths of individual students (Chen & Gardner, 2005).

Despite their strengths, theories of multiple intelligences have come under fire for being too broad and inclusive (Gottfredson, 2003). Expanding intelligence to encompass interpersonal competence, body movement, and so on, makes the definition of intelligence fuzzy and uninterpretable. Critics of Sternberg's theory consider practical intelligence to simply be a set of skills that people learn to cope with their environments. Finally, because goals vary from person to person and across cultural communities, challenges around the measurement of intelligence grow as the number of intelligences increases.

✓ CHECK YOUR UNDERSTANDING 12.9

1. How does Sternberg's triarchic theory of intelligence compare with Gardner's theory of multiple intelligences?
2. What are the strengths and limitations of theories of multiple intelligences?

Measuring Intelligence

Imagine that you must develop a test of intelligence for children. Which abilities would you assess, and which items would you include to measure those abilities? And, whichever decisions you made, how would you know if the test you developed measured what you set out to measure—intelligence? Researchers agree that several features characterize "good tests" (whatever the domain), including tests of intelligence.

The History of Intelligence Testing

LEARNING OBJECTIVE 12.10 Name three criteria a good intelligence test must meet and contrast the approaches taken by Francis Galton, Alfred Binet, and David Wechsler.

The goal of intelligence tests is to accurately measure the underlying trait of a person's intelligence. This is not a simple feat. A test developer can never be sure that the final test actually measures what it aims to measure. However, three attributes can bolster confidence in the efficacy of a test (see Chapter 1):

1. *Reliability*: The test must be reliable such that if the same child were given the same test twice, the child should perform relatively consistently both times.

2. *Validity*: The test must demonstrate various types of validity as described in Chapter 1, including face validity and predictive validity. Face validity means the test measures what it claims to measure, and predictive validity indicates a child's score on the test will tell us something about how that child would do on other similar tests or on external measures of academic success thought to depend on intelligence.

3. *Lack of bias*: The test should be free of bias. That is, it should be equally valid across different populations. It should not favor children of a certain background and disadvantage others.

As you will see, intelligence tests evolved over the years in an effort to increase reliability and validity and reduce bias. Here we review the work of three psychologists who figured prominently in the early history of intelligence testing—Francis Galton, Alfred Binet, and David Wechsler—and then consider current approaches to intelligence testing.

Francis Galton

British psychologist Francis Galton (1822–1911), Charles Darwin's cousin, was convinced that rules of heredity explained how "superior" individuals passed down their capacities to their offspring. To test his theory of inheritance, Galton formulated the first mental tests to evaluate people's basic sensory capacities, including people's speed of reaction to stimuli. Galton reasoned that individuals advanced on basic capacities were more intelligent than those who lagged behind.

When Galton administered his tests to many people, he discovered that their scores fit the profile of a "normal distribution"—the bell-shaped distribution that characterizes the scores of a lot of people on a given measure (Simonton, 2003) (**FIGURE 12.12**). A person's relative standing on the distribution could then be calculated as a percentile score. American Psychologist James McKeen Cattell later adapted Galton's tests for use with U.S. college students and introduced the term "mental test" in the 1890s.

Alfred Binet

France introduced universal public education in the early 1900s, and soon realized that not all children were equipped to handle classroom material. Educators faced a dilemma: What should they do with the many children who were falling behind? The minister of France sought to identify children who were having difficulties in mainstream classrooms. He asked French psychologist Alfred Binet to develop an objective test that could validly pinpoint children who required additional educational support.

In contrast to Galton's focus on sensory and reaction time capacities, Binet used mental tasks comprising short problems: naming parts of the body, comparing lengths and weights, remembering digits, and so on (Binet & Simon

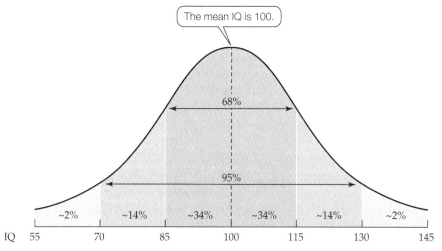

FIGURE 12.12 The distribution of intelligence scores in the general population. When Francis Galton administered his intelligence tests to many people, he discovered that their scores fit the profile of a "normal distribution"—the bell-shaped distribution that characterizes the scores of a lot of people on a given measure. The figure shows the spread of IQ scores in a sample, along with the percentage of people who score within each of the score ranges. (From S. M. Breedlove. 2015. *Principles of Psychology*. Sinauer/Oxford University Press: Sunderland, MA ; based on data in W. C. M. Resing and J. B. Blok. 2002. *Psycholoog* 37: 244–249.)

TABLE 12.2 ■ The Stanford-Binet test measures IQ

IQ range ("deviation IQ")	IQ classification
145–160	Very gifted or highly advanced
130–144	Gifted or very advanced
120–129	Superior
110–119	High average
90–109	Average
80–89	Low average
70–79	Borderline impaired or delayed
55–69	Mildly impaired or delayed
40–54	Moderately impaired or delayed

Source: After G. H Roid. 2003. *Stanford-Binet Intelligence Scales*, 5th ed. PRO-ED, Inc.: Austin, TX.

1905). Children's performance on this new test fell along a normal distribution, which allowed comparison of a specific child's performance to peers of the same age. Although Binet's initial test identified children with learning challenges, he later produced versions to describe variations among children with and without disabilities (Binet, 1911).

In 1916, psychologist Lewis Terman of Stanford University produced a revised English version of Binet's test, the well-known Stanford-Binet test (Terman & Merrill, 1950). A child's score on the Stanford-Binet could be described by an **intelligence quotient** or **IQ**, which indicates how well a person performs relative to individuals of the same age. An IQ score is calculated as the ratio of a child's mental age (MA) (level of performance) to the child's chronological age (CA) multiplied by 100: IQ = MA/CA × 100 (**TABLE 12.2**). Thus, an 8-year-old child (CA) whose performance matched the 8-year-old average (MA) would receive a score of 100 (8/8 × 100 = 100). In contrast, an 8-year-old child with an MA of a 10-year-old would receive an IQ of 125 (10/8 × 100 = 125).

Notably, the original Stanford-Binet test was critiqued for being biased, because items on the test did not reflect the abilities of test takers from diverse backgrounds (Guthrie, 2004). Moreover, some items would be viewed as discriminatory today, such as an item that asked children to determine which of a pair of faces was "prettier." However, the Stanford-Binet has since undergone several modifications to better reflect cultural and linguistic diversity. Thus, educators in the United States continue to rely on revised versions of the test to assess intelligence.

David Wechsler

One of the critiques of the original Stanford-Binet test was its overreliance on verbal skills, potentially disadvantaging Deaf children and children whose first language was not English. Consequently, American psychologist David Wechsler (1896–1981) developed an intelligence test that contained verbal and nonverbal problems (for example, creating patterns from blocks). Today, the Wechsler Intelligence Scale for Children-V (released in 2014) tests 6- to 16-year-olds and yields scores for verbal and nonverbal scales (**FIGURE 12.13**).

intelligence quotient or IQ
A score that describes how well a person performs on a test of intelligence relative to other people of the same age (typically calculated as MA/CA × 100)

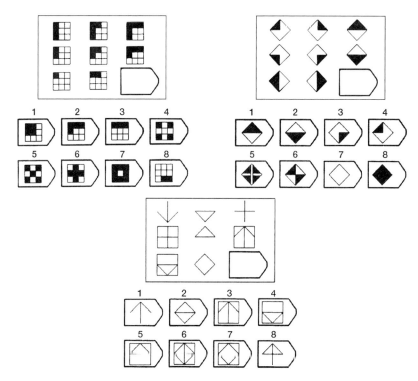

FIGURE 12.13 Wechsler Intelligence Scale for Children-V. Shown are samples of the type of nonverbal questions that are used in standardized tests of intelligence (these items are taken from a test called the Raven Progressive Matrices intelligence test). For each question, test takers must select which of the eight choices correctly completes the series. (After P. A. Carpenter et al. 1990. *Psychol Rev* 97: 404–431. Copyright © 1990 by American Psychological Association. Reproduced with permission.)

✓ CHECK YOUR UNDERSTANDING 12.10

1. What is one of Francis Galton's lasting contributions to the science of intelligence testing?
2. What was the original purpose of the Stanford-Binet test?
3. What criticism of the Stanford-Binet test led to the creation of the Wechsler Intelligence Scale for Children?

Reliability, Validity, and Bias of Intelligence Tests

LEARNING OBJECTIVE 12.11 Explain what makes an intelligence test reliable and valid, what effect bias can have on test results, and what can be done to ensure that tests have similar predictive validity across child sex, ethnicity, and race.

Are scores from intelligence tests reliable and valid? That is, do they yield similar scores for individual children over time (reliability), and do they correspond accurately to a person's intellectual functioning in the real world (validity)? For the most part, the answer is yes. In terms of reliability, children and adolescents' scores on intelligence tests are highly stable over months and years (Plomin & Deary, 2015). And, in terms of validity, intelligence scores represent the strongest, most valid indicators to date of a person's likelihood of success in life across a range of areas, including academic performance, years of education a person will complete, career paths, job performance, and even physical health, illness, and longevity (Converse et al., 2016; Deary, Weiss, & Batty, 2010).

Despite the reliability and validity of intelligence tests, history has spotlighted many challenges to measurement and interpretation of scores. In particular, two types of bias can disadvantage certain groups of children relative to others:

- **Content-validity bias** occurs when a test is comparatively more difficult for one group of children than another, not because of ability but because of relative familiarity. This form of bias can occur when test items or the wording of items are less familiar to certain students because of linguistic or cultural differences. Educators and researchers sometimes interpret the lower average test scores of students of color and students from low-income households as evidence of content-validity bias.

- **Predictive-validity bias** occurs when a test does not accurately predict how well individual children or adolescents will do in the future based on their test performance. An unbiased test is equally predictive of future academic and test performance across different groups of students.

Concerns of test bias are quite serious (Reynolds & Suzuki, 2013). A biased test can harm the future prospects of children, in terms of closing down educational and career opportunities to low performers. And, a paramount concern in intelligence testing is that a certain test might lead to invalid scores. However, even if a specific intelligence test is shown to be reliable and valid, it may be difficult or even impossible to develop a test that is completely free of any bias, because different cultures promote different skills in children, resulting in different levels of familiarity and ease with the material being tested. One way to ensure that bias does not compromise the validity of a test is to carefully examine, using statistical formulas, whether the test predicts outcomes to equivalent degrees across different samples.

Psychometricians—scientists who specialize in the measurement of intelligence and other psychological characteristics—examine whether intelligence tests yield similar predictive validity across different groups. To do so, they administer the test to a large number of individuals and then ask whether specific items on the test differentiate among high- and low-performers in similar ways across different samples, such as boys and girls, Asian Americans and White Americans, and children from different socioeconomic status households. Test items that differ statistically in their predictive power across groups are then dropped or replaced. Rigorous statistical analyses indicate that intelligence tests predict outcomes equally across a range of population characteristics, including sex, ethnicity, race, and socioeconomic background (Gottfredson & Saklofske, 2009).

Nonetheless, experts continue to debate whether they actually measure "intelligence" or something else. In fact, a common criticism of intelligence tests is their static nature: They test a child's knowledge to that point in time, rather than the child's ability to learn new information and adapt over time. A number of psychologists therefore advocate a **dynamic assessment approach** to intelligence, in which the goal is to examine a person's learning potential—how much new material a child can learn with assistance (e.g., Dörfler, Golke, & Artelt, 2009). With the right support, children can rise above their actual level of performance to achieve their ultimate potential.

✓ CHECK YOUR UNDERSTANDING 12.11

1. How is content-validity bias distinguished from predictive-validity bias, and how are these types of bias detected?

2. Can you suggest a way the dynamic assessment approach might be applied to testing at a school?

Nature and Nurture in Intelligence

Historically, the field of intelligence was plagued by intense debates that pitted nature against nurture. Today, scientists recognize that biology and social contexts, ranging from family to school to neighborhood, interact to explain individual differences in children's intelligence.

content-validity bias A type of bias seen when a test is comparatively more difficult for one group of children relative to other groups, perhaps due to familiarity and experiences rather than ability

predictive-validity bias A type of bias seen when a test does not accurately predict how well an individual will do in the future based on their test performance

psychometricians Scientists who specialize in the measurement of intelligence or other psychological characteristics (e.g., aptitude, personality)

dynamic assessment approach An interactive approach to assessing intelligence that focuses on a child's learning potential over time, rather than a static measure of intelligence at one point in time

The Heritability of Intelligence

LEARNING OBJECTIVE 12.12 Identify methods used to assess the heritability of intelligence.

eugenics The now discredited idea put forth by Francis Galton that heritable human characteristics, such as intelligence, should be controlled through breeding to improve the human race

Francis Galton is considered to be the father of **eugenics**, the appalling and now discredited idea that heritable human characteristics should be controlled through breeding to improve the human race. However, Galton was also the first to document the heredity of intelligence. Galton compared intelligence in monozygotic (MZ) and dizygotic (DZ) twins and showed that MZ twins scored much closer on intelligence tests than did DZ twins, although on the very narrow definition of intelligence that he endorsed.

genome-wide complex trait analysis A statistical method that uses mathematical modeling and genetic analysis to estimate genetic influences on intelligence; researchers compare genetic and intelligence similarities across thousands of pairs of individuals to see if genetic closeness informs closeness of intelligence

Today, sophisticated mathematical modeling and genetic analysis support the heritability of intelligence (e.g., Deary, Johnson, & Houlihan, 2009; Plomin & Geary, 2015). For example, **genome-wide complex trait analysis** allows scientists to estimate genetic influences on intelligence through the analysis of DNA, which carries a person's genetic information (Plomin & Geary, 2015). In this approach, the genetic similarity of unrelated individuals can be examined by comparing the DNA of person #1 to persons #2, #3, #4, and so on, until genetic similarities are determined across thousands of pairs of people. Then, genetic similarity between people is related to their observed phenotype similarity for a given trait. For example, people with similar IQ scores (the phenotype) might be compared for genotype similarities based on DNA sequences. If similarities in DNA relate to similarities in intelligence, heritability is supported. This technique reveals that, in addition to intelligence, genetics affects the courses that individuals pursue in college and how well they do in those subjects (Rimfeld et al., 2016) (**FIGURE 12.14**).

✓ CHECK YOUR UNDERSTANDING 12.12

1. Discuss the strengths and weaknesses of Galton's position on the heritability of intelligence.
2. What is a genome-wide complex trait analysis, and how might it be used to examine the inheritability of intelligence?

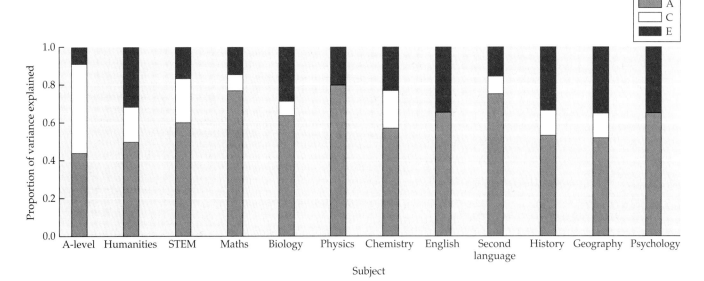

FIGURE 12.14 Genome-wide complex trait analysis. The figure is based on analysis of 6,584 twin pairs. The colors in bars represent the influence of genetics and environmental factors in intelligence based on this type of analysis. A = additive genetic contributions to subjects; C = shared environmental contributions (those experiences that twin pairs share, such as their parents' intelligence); E = non-shared environmental contributions (those experiences that are uniquely experienced by individuals and not shared with their twin pair). (After K. Rimfeld et al. 2016. *Sci Rep* 6: 1–9. doi: 10.1038/srep2637. CC BY 4.0. https://creativecommons.org/licenses/by/4.0/.)

Environmental Influences on Intelligence

LEARNING OBJECTIVE 12.13 Describe four environmental influences on children's performance on intelligence tests.

Recall that genetics interacts with experience to shape development (see Chapter 2). Thus, although a person's genetics contributes to intelligence, environmental experiences exert powerful influences, as indicated by several lines of evidence:

- *Performance on intelligence tests heavily depends on children's home and school experiences.* Countless studies reveal strong associations between the quality of home and school learning environments and children's IQ scores (**FIGURE 12.15**).

- *Intelligence scores are malleable.* IQ scores are highly stable over time, but that does not mean they are unmovable. Fluctuations in IQ can occur with changes in an individual's circumstances. When individuals are followed for many years, their IQ shifts upward and downward with changes to family context, such as economic circumstances (McCall et al., 1977) (**FIGURE 12.16**).

- *IQ test performance has steadily increased over historical time.* IQ scores have improved, globally, over the past 100 years or so, a trend referred to as the **Flynn effect** (Flynn, 2007). Such increases cannot be explained by a changing "gene pool," but instead reflect worldwide changes in quality of life factors such as education, health, and nutrition.

- *Adoption studies show changes to intelligence as children move out of foster homes.* A meta-analysis of nearly 300 adoption studies suggested that adoption is associated with massive catch-up in many developmental domains, including socio-emotional, physical, and cognitive development (van IJzendoorn & Juffer, 2006).

✓ CHECK YOUR UNDERSTANDING 12.13

1. What is the Flynn effect, and what does it tell us about environmental influences on intelligence?

Academic Skills: Language, Literacy, and Math

Intelligence means little if children can't put their thinking to good use. And to do so requires children to flexibly adapt to the cognitive demands of their environments. In Nabenchauk, children express intelligent thinking by mentally imagining how a final cloth will look once weaving is complete (see Figure 12.2). In the United States and other nations where higher education is common, children apply intelligent thinking to a wide range of academic subjects. As children progress through school, they grow in their sophistication and precision of word use; master special forms of discourse found in textbooks; learn to read and write in different genres; and apply sophisticated strategies to compute, estimate, and evaluate mathematical problems.

FIGURE 12.15 Learning environments. Many adolescents face obstacles in their home and school learning environments that interfere with performance on tests.

Flynn effect A trend referring to the improvement of IQ scores globally over the last 100 years

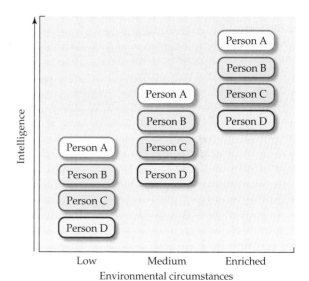

FIGURE 12.16 The malleability of intelligence. When individuals change in their environmental circumstances, their IQ fluctuates in turn. For example, when researchers longitudinally follow individuals for many years, they observe shifts to individuals' IQ scores upward or downward depending on changes to family context, such as economic circumstances. Shown here is a hypothetical example of 4 individuals, ranked in order of their intelligence scores (with A highest and D lowest) as they shift in their experiences from low- to middle- to high-resourced environments (such as moving in family circumstances out of poverty to more enriched opportunities). Although the rank ordering of their intelligence scores remains stable over time (i.e., A always has the highest intelligence score, followed by B, C, and D), their scores increase in line with their experiences of growing environmental enrichment.

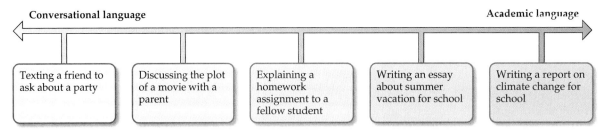

FIGURE 12.17 Conversational and academic language. This continuum shows the differences between conversational language and academic language. During middle childhood, children develop in their use of academic language.

Vocabulary and Grammar

LEARNING OBJECTIVE 12.14 Identify academic milestones of middle childhood in vocabulary and grammar.

The words, concepts, and sentence structures that children acquire in school differ considerably from informal, everyday conversations with friends and relatives (**FIGURE 12.17**). Children's academic success rests on their abilities to read and write texts that introduce many unfamiliar words in complex sentence frames. Vocabulary growth during the school years extends to words that:

- are *longer and more complex* than the words used by younger children, such as "leadership," "desirability," and "derivation" (Carlisle, 2000);
- make use of *synonyms* to refer to the same concept, such as doctor and physician;
- refer to *abstract* ideas such as evil and justice (Olson & Astington, 1986); and
- express subtle but meaningful *variations* on words, such as topple, tumble, and plunge to express how things can fall.

In addition to vocabulary, grammatical skills grow over middle childhood. With age, children construct increasingly complex and lengthy sentences by combining multiple ideas into a single sentence with connectives such as "but," "although," and "however" (Vion & Colas, 2004). And, children become more flexible in sentence constructions as they grasp the rules of grammar and generate different sentence forms. For example, children can apply the passive voice, even for inanimate subjects, as in the sentence "My computer files were destroyed by the fuse that blew out yesterday."

✓ CHECK YOUR UNDERSTANDING 12.14

1. What are some examples of changes to the words in children's vocabularies in middle childhood?

Reading and Writing

LEARNING OBJECTIVE 12.15 Describe the "inside-out" and "outside-in" skills involved in reading and writing.

Over the course of schooling, children shift from a primary reliance on oral language to an increasing reliance on the written word to learn and communicate. This transition is not straightforward. Whereas the spoken word is a symbol system that directly stands for something (the spoken word "dog" refers to the animal, dog), the written word stands for something that stands for something else (the written word "d-o-g" stands for the spoken word "dog," which refers to the animal, dog). And, beyond learning how to read and write isolated words, children must learn the formalities of written language, such as how to use topic sentences and write convincing essays.

Inside-Out and Outside-In Reading Skills

Reading is neither easy nor automatic. It takes several years for children to become competent readers, and some children never achieve a level of reading that allows them to master school material. Indeed, lessons around reading consume much of the day in kindergarten through third grade classrooms. With experience, children eventually transition from "learning to read" to "reading to learn," typically by late elementary school.

Why does proficiency in reading take so long? Because reading draws on many skills, ranging from the nitty-gritty details of decoding letters to the cognitively complex skills involved in understanding complex texts. Researchers often refer to "inside-out" and "outside-in" skills of reading to distinguish specific skills from conceptual skills (Lonigan, Burgess, & Schatschneider, 2018; Whitehurst & Lonigan, 1998).

The inside-out process of reading involves decoding letters into sounds, mapping sounds to words, and discriminating words on a page. The most basic inside-out skill is the mapping of sounds to letters. Children must be familiar with the characters of a language and learn how to associate print units (letters or characters; graphemes) with sound units (phonemes). Next, children must recognize that letters/characters combine to form language units (words). Sometimes, words are relatively easy to decode, particularly when their spelling corresponds to their pronunciation ("tap," "bat," "sit"). However, reading also requires children to learn exceptions, such as "elephant," "knife," and "fight." Typically, children learn how letters combine to form words during first and second grade. This "grunt and groan" stage of early reading is slow and tedious, with young children placing a lot of energy into simply figuring out words (Chall, 1983). Children read one word at a time and take long pauses between words.

The outside-in components of reading require conceptual understanding: figuring out the meanings of words and sentences (that is, semantics), and then applying that understanding to interpreting the meaning of the broader narrative (**FIGURE 12.18**). At the most basic level, children must know the meanings of words—or at least the vast majority of words in a sentence—to understand a text. This knowledge rests on having the necessary vocabulary. For example, a child might be able to read the sentence: *"She told the laborer to coarsely grind the hominy for the grits,"* but still not grasp what the sentence means. Without understanding the words "laborer," "coarsely," "grind," and "hominy," the child will be confused. A child who lacks the knowledge to interpret a text will be at a disadvantage relative to one who is able to connect text to past experiences. For example, a child who has never been to a zoo and has never had the opportunity to read books about zoos might not understand the narrative (or story) about animals who try to escape from a zoo.

Teaching Reading

How can teachers best help children learn how to read? Proponents of a **phonics approach** claim that instruction in decoding is paramount. Educators are encouraged to focus on the inside-out components of reading, such as teaching children how to "sound out" each letter in the word "b-a-l-l" before attempting to understand the whole word. In particular, three phonemic awareness skills distinguish good and poor readers:

phonics approach An approach to reading instruction that teaches children letters of the alphabet and their sounds, with focus on sounding out each letter in a word prior to understanding the whole word

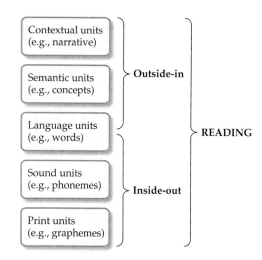

FIGURE 12.18 Learning to read. Researchers distinguish "inside out" from "outside-in" components of reading. Inside-out components refer to deciphering the sound and print units of text to figure out words. Outside-in components refer to the conceptual understanding of the meanings of individual words and sentences (semantics) and understanding the broader meaning of text at the level of the narrative. (After G. J. Whitehurst and C. J. Lonigan. 1998. *Child Dev* 69: 848–872. © by the Society for Research in Child Development, Inc.)

- The ability to categorize words by their initial or ending sounds ("ball" starts with a /b/ sound and ends with an /l/ sound);
- The ability to identify words that rhyme ("bat" and "cat"; "pot" and "cot");
- The ability to figure out the sound that is produced when the first or last letter of a word is dropped, such as dropping "b" from "bat" results in /at/.

whole language approach
An approach to reading instruction that focuses on teaching children to recognize the whole word, rather than sound out each letter

In contrast, proponents of a **whole language approach** argue that children's reading should be kept whole and meaningful, for example by teaching children to identify the word "ball" and the full sentence of "Catch the ball" without sounding out each letter. A whole language approach asserts that children who are surrounded by reading materials that engage their imaginations will naturally learn lower-order decoding skills with experience.

For the most part, however, educators recognize that combining the two approaches helps children succeed at reading. In support of a phonics approach, **phonemic awareness**—the ability to understand that discrete sounds comprise words—relates to reading achievement in childhood (e.g., Casalis & Cole, 2009; Xue & Meisels, 2004). At the same time, an overemphasis on phonics can detract from children's interest in reading, and so educators combine conceptual understanding with a phonics approach. First graders show strong progress in literacy when teachers incorporate strategies that highlight text meaning (Pressley, 2002). Teachers can encourage somewhat older readers to use strategies that facilitate understanding, such as restating passages in their own words and pausing to check that they understand what they have read (McKeown, Beck, & Blake, 2009).

phonemic awareness The ability to identify the discrete sounds that make up words, in line with a phonics approach to reading

Writing

Children's inside-out and outside-in skills apply to writing as well. Children initially focus on the technicalities of writing—how to spell words, the proper notations to end sentences, and how to break up ideas within a sentence with commas, periods, question marks, and so forth. By second or third grade, children understand irregularities in language and strive to use correct conventional spelling and proper punctuation in their writing. However, their writing continues to resemble everyday speech because they do not yet fully appreciate how written discourse differs from everyday conversation (**TABLE 12.3**). By 9–10 years of age, children produce relatively well-structured essays that differ from their everyday talk. But not until adolescence do students achieve skills in **expository writing**—a type of writing that explains, describes, or informs on a thematic topic and requires children to review and modify their essays (e.g., McCutchen, 2006).

expository writing A genre of writing that explains, describes, or informs a specific theme, offering explanations to the reader about the topic

Technology and Literacy

Children today learn a lot about reading and writing through interactions with technology—tablets, computers, smartphones, and the like. Yet, educators and

TABLE 12.3 ■ Everyday speech versus written discourse

Informal language	Academic language
Repetition of words	Variety of words, more sophisticated vocabulary
Sentences start with "and" and "but"	Sentences start with transition words, such as "however," "moreover," and "in addition"
Use of slang: "guy," "cool," and "awesome"	No slang

Source: Webcast: Reading Rockets/ Colorín Colorado. Academic Language for English Language Learners. Featuring Dr. Robin Scarcella, University of California at Irvine. Hosted by Delia Pompa, National Council of La Raza. Colorín Colorado is an educational service of WETA, the flagship public broadcasting station in the nation's capital. © Copyright 2019 WETA Public Broadcasting. Available at https://www.colorincolorado.org/videos/webcasts.

TABLE 12.4 ■ Recommendations for literacy apps
Be age appropriate and linked to the school's early literacy curriculum
Have a high level of interactivity that stimulates all the senses
Build on previous knowledge
Encourage child creativity, problem solving, and critical thinking
Connect children with the printed screen symbols so meaning is constructed
Provide a clear understanding of tasks
Provide opportunities for constructive peer collaboration
Provide regular feedback
Guide the child's performance rather than concluding with a success or failure outcome

Source: After M. M. Neumann and D. L. Neumann. 2014. *Early Child Educ J* 42: 231–239. https://doi.org/10.1007/s10643-013-0608-3.

researchers have a long way to go in understanding the effects of the digital age on children's literacy. Fortunately, findings are promising. Under the right conditions, technology has enormous potential to enhance learning by supplementing ongoing classroom instruction. Interventions that introduce computer programs in classrooms facilitate the reading and writing of young poor readers (Kyle et al., 2013). Similarly, tablets enhance children's learning of letters and their sounds, print concepts, spelling, and writing (Neumann & Neumann, 2014). However, it's not sufficient to just sit a child in front of a screen and expect miracles to happen. The benefits of technology in classroom and home-based teaching practices depend on how teachers, parents, and other adults support children's use of the technology and the quality of the applications (Neumann & Neumann, 2014; **TABLE 12.4**).

✓ CHECK YOUR UNDERSTANDING 12.15

1. What arguments are made concerning the relative value of the phonics approach to reading versus the whole language approach?
2. How do you think the widespread prevalence of computers and other technologies affects children's experiences around reading and writing?

Math

LEARNING OBJECTIVE 12.16 Describe how strategies for solving math problems evolve in middle childhood.

Schooling typically marks the introduction to "formal" mathematics, when children learn addition, subtraction, multiplication, division, and so on. As is true for reading and writing, the early years of math education focus on technical details and mastery of the basics. Then, in late elementary school, children advance to complex arithmetic procedures, such as long division, multiplication of large numbers, and other building blocks to later algebra and geometry.

Basic Math Problems and Changing Strategies

Although most U.S. children can count to 100 at school entry, they are not yet versed in adding or subtracting even small numbers. It takes some time for children to spontaneously answer 8 when asked "How much is 5 + 3?" Quick retrieval of number facts results from a lot of time spent in "drill and practice" exercises, in which children commit basic math facts to memory by solving problems on worksheets and playing math games on computers.

On the path to automaticity, children change in the types of strategies they use to arrive at a math solution (Geary, 2006; Siegler & Braithwaite, 2017). For example, at the cusp of schooling, a 5-year-old child might put up two fingers on one hand and three fingers on the other when asked to solve 2 + 3, and then proceed to count each finger in turn. The same child will soon quickly retrieve the answers to these relatively easy math problems from memory. However, children generate various strategies to solve more difficult problems. To answer the problem 9 + 3, young children may count every single number, 1, 2, 3, 4, 5, 6, 7, 8, 9, 10, 11, 12, before they discover the more expedient strategy of counting forward from the larger addend (here 9: 9… 10, 11, 12) (Resnick, 1989). Sometimes, children solve new problems by drawing on basic facts they have at their disposal (Geary, 2006). For instance, to solve the 9 + 3 problem, a child who knows that 10 + 3 is 13 might subtract 1 from 13 to arrive at the answer 12. Or, a child might use repeated addition to solve multiplication problems, such as by adding 4 + 4 + 4 to solve the problem 3 × 4. Between 7 and 11 years of age, children's gains in knowledge and working memory allow them to solve basic math problems with relative ease (e.g., Holmes & Gathercole, 2014).

Understanding Math Concepts

Knowing the answer to a math problem does not imply that a child has grasped a key mathematical concept. Consider a child who knows the number fact 4 + 5 = 9. The child may still not understand the concept of **mathematical equality**, that the sums on both left and right sides of an "=" equation must balance. At first, children learn to solve problems that contain numbers on the equation's left side and require them to generate a single number on the right side. It takes some time, however, for children to understand that mathematical equality applies to complex problems, such as 1 + 3 + 5 = 2 + ____ (McNeil, 2008). Typically, children younger than 10 years of age assume they should add all the numbers on the left side (coming up with 9), and fail to recognize that this will not balance the equation (Goldin-Meadow & Alibali, 2002).

Children also have difficulty with math concepts that involve **relative magnitudes**, the relative "distances" between numbers, such as knowing that 10 is smaller than 100 but *much* smaller/more distant from the number 1,000. Researchers commonly assess children's understanding of number magnitudes by asking children to estimate where a two-digit number (such as 52) should be placed on a number line that ranges from 0 to 1000, by marking the point on the line (Siegler, 2016) (**FIGURE 12.19**). They find that children improve in their understanding of number magnitudes over the course of childhood. For example, between kindergarten and second grade, children place numbers on a line from 0 to 100 with a fair degree of accuracy, and between second and fourth grade children can approximate where to place numbers in the 0–1,000 range (Siegler, Thompson, & Opfer, 2009).

While you might assume that children primarily learn math at school, in some communities, children learn math through hands-on learning rather than formal training. For instance, street children from Brazil, who do not attend school and cannot read letters or numbers, nevertheless learn how to sell their wares and make change (**FIGURE 12.20**). They rely on their knowledge of colors and pictures to figure out the value of different bills and acquire many sophisticated math skills by participating in trades with street clients and observing other sellers (e.g., Saxe, 2004, 2015). Child vendors learn how to adjust the selling prices

mathematical equality A concept in mathematics that indicates the quantities on both left and right sides of an "=" equation must balance

relative magnitudes A concept in mathematics that indicates the relative "distances" between numbers

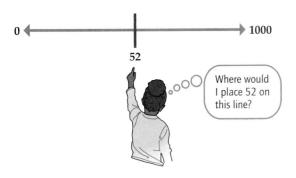

FIGURE 12.19 Learning the concept of magnitude. Children in kindergarten through around second grade have not yet grasped the relative magnitudes of numbers, and do quite poorly when asked to mark the spot on a number line where a two-digit number should be placed, even though many can easily count to 100. It takes several more years for children to understand relative magnitudes, and such determinations are particularly difficult as the final value on a number line increases (such as knowing where 1,000 would be on a number line of 1,000,000). (After R. S. Siegler. 2016. *Dev Sci* 19: 341–361.)

of their wares in response to daily inflation, the cost of goods, and customer demand, and learn relatively advanced computations required for trade, even though they fare poorly on tests of math common in U.S. schools.

✓ CHECK YOUR UNDERSTANDING 12.16

1. What must children understand to appreciate the concepts of mathematical equality and relative magnitude?

Motivation

Sometimes, children who appear to be intellectually capable fall short of reaching their full potential at school: They quit in the face of failure and choose the easy road rather than embrace challenging tasks. At the other extreme are children who seem determined to keep on trying until they master new tasks, no matter the obstacles. **Motivation**—the desire or willingness to accomplish a goal and the maintenance of interest and effort towards that goal—distinguishes children who persist from those who give up.

FIGURE 12.20 Hands-on learning versus formal training.   Unschooled Brazilian children learn math on the street by collaborating in price-setting transactions.

Intrinsic and Extrinsic Motivation

LEARNING OBJECTIVE 12.17 Distinguish between intrinsic and extrinsic motivation.

Many of us are familiar with the child who begins to despise piano lessons after being forced to play week after week, or the child who loses interest in reading once the teacher assigns weekly book reports. We are also familiar with the child who loves to build elaborate constructions, or the child who gets so engrossed in writing that the child won't stop until she gets the story just right. What explains the motivations of these children?

Self-determination theory posits that motivation and engagement in a task is enhanced when a person makes choices without external influence and interference (Ryan & Deci, 2000). **Intrinsic motivation** is seen when people choose to engage in an activity because they find the activity to be interesting and/or enjoyable, like the child who refuses to stop writing her story. Children who are intrinsically motivated expend a lot of energy and persist on tasks, even if they are not rewarded for their performance (e.g., Patall, Cooper, & Robinson, 2008). When researchers combined data from 183 studies on over 200,000 participants, they found that intrinsic motivation predicted children's and adults' performance in school, work, and physical activity (Cerasoli, Nicklin, & Ford, 2014).

Extrinsic motivation, in contrast, occurs when someone engages in an activity because of external pressures, such as rewards, punishments, or to please someone else, like the child who plays the piano because her parents insist (**FIGURE 12.21**). Children who engage in activities for extrinsic reasons often lose interest in the activity (e.g., Cerasoli et al, 2014). This may be why teachers who give children few choices may undermine a child's natural interest in school material, whereas those who support children's autonomy spark motivation and curiosity (Ryan & Deci, 2016).

✓ CHECK YOUR UNDERSTANDING 12.17

1. What would self-determination theory say about a child whose parents force the child to do extra math classes on the weekend?
2. What would self-determination theory say about a child who chooses to do crossword puzzles on the weekend?

motivation The desire and willingness to attain a goal and the continuation of effort and interest towards that goal

self-determination theory A theory of human motivation positing that motivation and engagement in a specific task are heightened when an individual makes choices in the absence of external pressures

intrinsic motivation A form of motivation exhibited when a person chooses to engage in an activity because they find the activity pleasurable and thus persist on the task even without a reward

extrinsic motivation A form of motivation exhibited when a person chooses to engage in an activity because of external pressures, such as rewards or punishments, and thus may lose interest in the particular activity

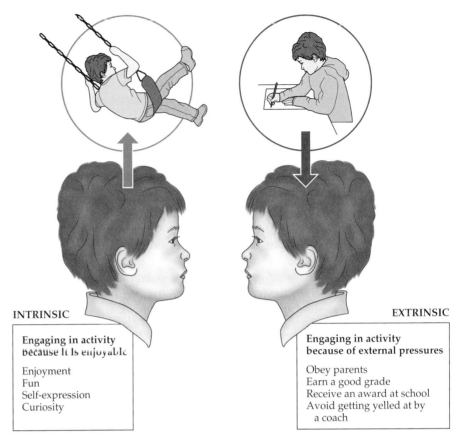

FIGURE 12.21 Intrinsic versus extrinsic motivation. When a person chooses to engage in an activity because it is personally rewarding, interesting, or enjoyable, the person experiences intrinsic motivation. In contrast, extrinsic motivation is seen when someone engages in an activity because of external pressures, such as rewards, punishments, or to please someone else. (Based on concepts in R. M. Ryan and E. L. Deci. 2000. *Am Psychol* 55: 68–78.)

Mindsets

LEARNING OBJECTIVE 12.18 Distinguish between two mindsets identified by Dweck and show how they can affect children's approaches to tasks.

Developmental scientist Carol Dweck pioneered the study of children's motivation. She was inspired by research on animals' "learned helplessness" as a graduate student at Yale. When an animal such as a rat is unable to avoid or escape a repeated aversive stimulus, such as an electric shock, the animal gives up trying to escape, even when escape is later made possible. In essence, they learn to feel helpless. Dweck wondered if learned helplessness could help explain why certain capable children are immobilized by failure whereas others try even harder in the face of challenges.

Dweck's interest inspired a program of research on **mindsets**—children's explanations for their personal failures and successes. According to Dweck, children who explain their failures as due to a lack of *ability* quickly become discouraged, even on tasks within their capabilities. In contrast, children who attribute failure to a lack of *effort* are driven to work harder in the future. Dweck suggested that failure can actually motivate a child to persist and eventually succeed, as long as the child's mindset is in the right place. This idea was at odds with the prevailing belief at the time that the most effective way to motivate children was to offer them opportunities to succeed and receive positive reinforcement.

mindsets Children's explanations for their successes and failures, which they may attribute to either ability or effort

To experimentally test the theory that mindsets influence effort and ultimately performance, Dweck (1975) assigned children who had extreme reactions to math failure (they gave up and avoided the subject) to one of two groups. The "Attribution Retraining Treatment" group of children was given challenging tasks that they failed, but were taught to attribute their failure to insufficient effort and to take responsibility for their performance. The "Success Only Treatment" group was given tasks that always resulted in success, thereby avoiding any failure. The two groups were then tested on several difficult tasks. Dweck's hypothesis was supported: Children in the attribution retraining condition persisted on difficult tasks, and were not discouraged by failure, whereas those in the success-only condition gave up and their performance deteriorated. Thus, failure did not compromise performance, as long as children adopted a mindset focused on effort.

✓ CHECK YOUR UNDERSTANDING 12.18

1. Describe how Carol Dweck investigated the association between children's mindsets and their task motivation.

Views of Intelligence

LEARNING OBJECTIVE 12.19 Describe what is meant by entity and incremental theories of intelligence, and how these affect children's effort or persistence at tasks.

Dweck later showed that children's beliefs about intelligence—as fixed or malleable—affected their motivation to learn (Dweck, 1986, 2006). She distinguished between an entity theory of intelligence and an incremental theory of intelligence. Children who endorse an **entity theory of intelligence** view intelligence to be innate and fixed, placing great weight on nature as the source of a person's performance (**FIGURE 12.22**). Dweck suggested an entity theory of intelligence can be harmful, because children who do not do well on a particular test or subject matter may perceive themselves as incapable or unintelligent. Consider, for example, a child who is doing poorly in math. If the child believes his performance reflects ability rather than effort, the child will be likely to just give up: "There's nothing I can do to change the situation. I'm just not smart in math." The child's lack of effort will further diminish performance, which validates the child's view about not being intelligent, and leads to a downward spiral of effort and performance.

Conversely, children with an **incremental theory of intelligence** (what is also termed a growth mindset) believe that intelligence is malleable and can improve with effort and practice—much like a person's muscles strengthen through exercise (Dweck, 2006). Because children with an incremental view of intelligence aim to gain knowledge and master new material (what can also be referred to as having a "mastery goal orientation"), they demonstrate persistence and high effort, even in the face of failure.

But shouldn't an entity view of intelligence benefit children who do *well* in school? Doesn't success confirm to children that they are "naturally intelligent"? Not necessarily. Believing that intelligence is fixed can make children feel good about themselves as long as they are doing well, but it can backfire when they confront a challenge. When children who endorse an entity view of intelligence

entity theory of intelligence
The view that intelligence is innate, fixed, and unchangeable

incremental theory of intelligence
The view that intelligence is changeable and may improve with practice over time; also commonly referred to as a growth mindset

Growth Mindset
- I can learn anything I want to
- When I'm frustrated, I persevere
- I want to challenge myself
- When I fail, I learn
- Tell me I try hard
- If you succeed, I'm inspired
- My effort and attitude determine everything

Fixed Mindset
- I'm either good at it, or I'm not
- When I'm frustrated, I give up
- I don't like to be challenged
- When I fail, I'm no good
- Tell me I'm smart
- If you succeed, I feel threatened
- My abilities determine everything

© desdemona72/Shutterstock.com

FIGURE 12.22 Growth versus fixed mindset. Children with a growth mindset believe that intelligence is malleable and can improve with effort and practice, whereas children with a fixed mindset view intelligence to be innate and unchangeable.

experience low performance, even if they typically do well, it can have a devastating impact. They may interpret failure as a sign that "I must not be smart!" Children with an entity view of intelligence may then avoid challenging activities to ward off failure and maintain a positive self-image (Dweck, 2006).

Unfortunately, consistently low performance undermines children's motivation, even for those who begin with a mastery goal orientation. German elementary school children who received low grades in second grade declined in their mastery-oriented approach by fourth grade; whereas, children who received strong grades in second grade maintained a primarily mastery-oriented approach through fourth grade (Schwinger, Steinmayr, & Spinath, 2016). Nonetheless, although low grades can reduce children's motivation, associations between grades and motivation are weak (Weidinger, Steinmayr, & Spinath, 2017). Therefore, the idea that grades alone explain children's motivation may be flawed. As we will see next, school context and teachers strongly inspire (or harm) children's motivation.

✓ CHECK YOUR UNDERSTANDING 12.19

1. Why might an entity view of intelligence undermine the academic motivation of a child who is doing well in school?

Contexts of Cognitive Development and Academic Achievement

Why do some children excel in cognitive domains and academic achievement whereas others have difficulties? Three contexts exert powerful impact: family, school, and culture.

Family Context and Cognitive Development

LEARNING OBJECTIVE 12.20 Describe ways that the family environment influences children's motivation, academic achievement, and cognitive development in middle childhood.

A supportive family environment is key to children's cognitive development, investment in school, motivation to learn, and academic achievement. Sensitive, involved parenting boosts children's cognitive development and academic success, whereas insensitive, harsh parenting can harm children's efforts. For example, mothers who are able to regulate their own negative moods and emotions, and provide their children with positive reinforcement and affection, have children who are skilled at planning, problem solving, and cognitive flexibility (Samuelson, Krueger, & Wilson, 2012).

But, sensitivity alone may be insufficient for bolstering children's cognitive and academic learning. Just as children's mindsets matter for motivation, parents' mindsets and the ways they communicate their expectations to their children also impact children's motivation and performance. Mothers of 9- to 12-year-olds who had a fixed mindset of intelligence had children who declined in their academic performance over time, likely because mothers failed to convey the importance of effort and hard work to their children. In contrast, parents with a growth mindset tended to focus on the *process* of learning, rather than merely the end result, thereby instilling in children the belief that intelligence is malleable (Pomerantz & Dong, 2006).

But how do parents communicate their mindsets to children? Notably, whether and how parents praise their children may be key. Parents who praise children's efforts, referred to as **process praise**—"Great job at putting so much effort and time into that assignment!"—spark children's motivation in ways that lead to improved grades over time (Gunderson et al., 2018). On

process praise Praise focused on children's work and efforts (e.g., praising children for completing an assignment) the other hand, **person praise** that focuses on fixed abilities or traits, rather than what a person did—"You are so smart!"—can actually undermine children's motivation and achievement. When researchers tracked mothers' day-to-day praise of their children's successes in school, the more person praise mothers offered their children, the more likely their children were to avoid challenges (Pomerantz & Kempner, 2013).

But what about when children fail? What type of feedback should parents offer? Notably, parents who overreact and blame failure on their children's abilities communicate to children that failure is debilitating. Telling children that they failed a math test because they are simply not good in math may cause them to give up. In contrast, parents who communicate that failure provides an opportunity to grow and learn help their children get back in the saddle and try harder in the future (Haimovitz & Dweck, 2017).

Of course, family context extends beyond what parents say and do. A lack of household resources—as seen in conditions of poverty—can undercut children's academic engagement and performance. Parents from poor households may not have the time to help with homework, or may be unable to provide resources to support children's learning—quiet spaces to study, computers, tutors, etc. Countless studies show that children who live in poor households score lower on measures of cognitive functioning than children in resourced homes (e.g., Farah et al., 2006). And, the harmful effects of poverty accumulate over time. Children who spend several years living in poverty score lower than children from near-poor and middle-income households in academic achievement at the start of schooling in areas such as knowing letters and recognizing shapes (Duncan, Magnuson, & Vortruba-Drzal, 2017) (**FIGURE 12.23**). In addition, children of color are disproportionately impacted by poverty and thus most at risk for academic problems (Garcia Coll & Magnuson, 2019). Furthermore, poverty is associated with elevated blood pressure and high stress hormones such as cortisol. Because the biological consequences of stress interfere with learning, experiences of chronic stress compromise children's working memory capacities in ways that can persist into adulthood (Evans & Shamberg, 2009).

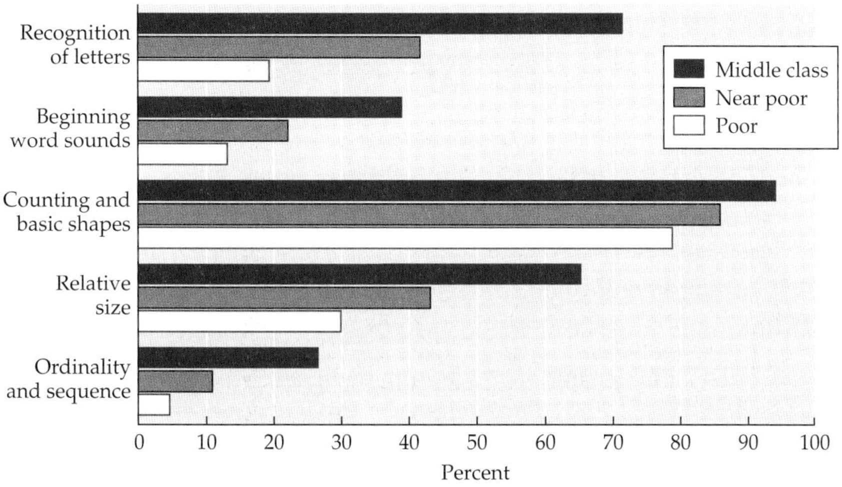

person praise Praise focused on children's fixed abilities or traits (e.g., telling children they are smart)

FIGURE 12.23 Impact of poverty on academic achievement. Children who spend several years living in poor households score lower than children from near-poor and middle-income households (on average) in every academic area at the start of schooling. (After G. J. Duncan et al. 2017. *Annu Rev Psychol* 68: 413–434. Republished with permission of Annual Reviews, Inc.; permission conveyed through Copyright Clearance Center, Inc.)

1. How do parents' praise and reactions to children's failure affect children's motivation and performance in school?
2. How might poverty undermine children's cognitive development?

School Context and Cognitive Development

LEARNING OBJECTIVE 12.21 Describe the various aspects of school context that affect children's school engagement and performance.

In most countries around the world, children spend more time in schools than any other setting outside the home. Therefore, the quality of school experiences affects what children learn, their motivation to learn, and their future life opportunities.

The Curriculum

Children excel in the subject areas that schools prioritize. For instance, an elementary school in Michigan that emphasized literacy produced students who outperformed children in nearby schools on standardized tests of reading (Pressley et al., 2007). The school's success was attributed to the many hours that teachers devoted to teaching reading, the opportunities teachers had to refine their teaching of reading, children's frequent opportunities to read aloud, and shelves stocked with books. The close connection between curriculum content and children's skills extends to all subjects. Lessons that teach children how to reason about maps promote children's abilities to use maps effectively (Kastens & Liben, 2007), just as focus on math promotes math skills, focus on science supports science skills, and so on. Of course, the amount of time spent on a content area is necessary but not sufficient for children's school success. A major task for teachers is to foster children's interest in school subjects, even those that children may view to be unimportant. This is where the quality of teaching comes into play.

Quality of Instruction

Qualified teachers communicate knowledge effectively, spark students' interests, and encourage children to think critically. Teacher quality influences students' academic achievement in all contexts and across wealthy and poor (Hamre & Pianta, 2010; Meece & Eccles, 2010). Several features characterize high quality teaching (Berliner & Glass, 2014; Roeser & Eccles, 2014):

• being knowledgeable in a content area;

• choosing material that challenges children;

• presenting assignments of different types and depicting subject matter in a variety of ways, such as through visual graphics and written text;

• helping children develop strategies that can aid their learning; and

• flexibly adapting instruction to meet the needs of different students.

Of course, it takes time to move from being a novice to an accomplished teacher (Ward et al., 2013). Preparation and experience are critical components of teacher qualification, as shown in an analysis of teacher qualification and student mathematics achievement across 46 countries (Akiba, LeTendre, & Scribner, 2007). Additionally, neighborhood context may affect the quality of instruction that children receive at school. Instructional quality is mediocre in many U.S. public schools, especially those in poor neighborhoods (Hamre & Pianta, 2010). Teachers in high poverty schools engage in less effective teaching strategies than do those in more resourced schools and neighborhoods, perhaps because they feel burdened from teaching students who may struggle with emotional and behavioral problems (e.g., McKown, Gregory, & Weinstein, 2010). Over time, a feeling of burnout can cause teachers to distance themselves from low-achieving students, which may create a downward spiral of student disengagement, teacher withdrawal, and student failure (e.g., Rowley, Helaire, & Banerjee, 2010).

Design of Instruction

Teachers adopt a variety of strategies to deliver material to students. Because it is typically not feasible to spend an entire day teaching in one way, teachers rely on different classroom activities to provide students with unique opportunities to learn and participate.

- **Whole-group instruction** is when a teacher instructs the entire class. Whole group instruction is useful for introducing new material and facilitating classroom discussion around a shared learning experience.

- **Independent practice** is when students work on their own, such as completing math worksheets or writing an essay. Independent practice supports students' information gathering and problem solving and helps boost academic performance (Clements, Sarama, & DiBiase, 2003).

- **Small-group practice** allows students with different strengths to help one another and can foster new friendships and reduce social isolation. Children also benefit from **cooperative learning**—when small groups of students work together and support one another's learning by sharing ideas, asking questions, and offering explanations for problems (**FIGURE 12.24**). When children work with others, they move beyond what they can do on their own to achieve higher, more competent levels of thinking, an idea inspired by Soviet psychologist Lev Vygotsky's writings on the ways that knowledgeable adults guide children's learning (Vygotsky, 1978).

whole-group instruction A form of instruction directed to the entire class at the same time

independent practice A form of instruction in which students are encouraged to work on their own to complete assignments

small-group practice A form of instruction in which children work together in small groups

cooperative learning Learning that occurs when small groups of students work together and learn from one another by sharing ideas and offering explanations

Teacher Expectations

Teacher expectations can support or harm students' school engagement and performance. Over half a century ago, in 1966, Robert Rosenthal and Lenore Jacobson conducted one of the first studies on the influence of teacher expectations on student learning. Rosenthal and Jacobson wondered if they could falsely instill high expectations in teachers about certain students that would then affect student performance. To test this possibility, they gave children from 18 classrooms standard intelligence tests at the start of the school year. Then, without students or teachers knowing, they randomly assigned 20% of students to a "rapid bloomers" group. Rosenthal and Jacobson told the teachers that the randomly chosen students would display unusual intellectual gains during the academic year. Eight months later, the students were tested again. The rapid-bloomer students showed larger gains in IQ than did the 80% of peers in the control group. Rosenthal and Jacobson demonstrated that students "live up" or "live down" to their teachers' initial expectancies (Rosenthal & Jacobson, 1992), a phenomenon called the **Pygmalion effect** based on the Greek myth in which Pygmalion fell in love with a statue that he had carved.

Since this landmark finding, many researchers have shown that negative teacher expectations persist over time and exert large, cumulative effects on students' motivation and achievement (Friedrich, Walter, & Colmenares, 2015). Teacher expectations that begin in kindergarten and first grade may be especially potent because they set in motion a cycle of interactions that affects how teachers

Pygmalion effect A psychological phenomenon in which children "live up" or "live down" to their teachers' initial expectations

FIGURE 12.24 Cooperative learning can be fun. Children can benefit from situations in which small groups of students work together on a common goal and support one another's learning by sharing ideas, asking questions, offering explanations, and working through challenging problems.

treat children (e.g., McKown et al., 2010). Moreover, low teacher expectations may undermine girls' interest and performance in mathematics, science, computers, technology, and sports, and likewise undermine the engagement and performance of minority children and children living in poverty across a range of subject areas (e.g., Jussim, Robustelli, & Cain, 2009).

You might wonder how a teacher's expectations—something that is presumably in the teacher's head—gets transmitted to a student. One way that teachers communicate their expectations is by their reactions to student performance. When teachers hold low expectations for students, they may display pity ("That's too bad you didn't do well"), conveying the message that they expected low performance. However, although teachers may believe that praise helps low-performing students, children may interpret unfounded compliments as a sign of a teacher's pity rather than endorsement of what they have accomplished (e.g., Burnett & Mandel, 2010).

As we've learned, however, correlation does not imply causation. Teachers' expectations typically reflect their appraisals of students' past achievement, and most teachers are highly committed to helping students who are falling behind. Nonetheless, teachers benefit from programs that educate them about effective ways to express high, individualized expectations of students. An intervention that trained teachers to model the practices of "high-expectation" teachers—including being positive toward students, focusing on mastery, monitoring student progress closely, setting clear learning goals, providing feedback on progress, and teaching students how to set their own goals—resulted in impressive mathematics gains in students, including students who started out low in performance (Rubie-Davies et al., 2015).

Classroom Climate and Class Size

classroom climate The intellectual, social, emotional, and physical features of classroom environments that include the tone, attitude, and standards; may be characterized along a continuum of positive to negative

Classroom climate refers to "the intellectual, social, emotional, and physical environments in which students learn" (Ambrose et al., 2010, p. 170). Children who feel safe, respected, and valued by teachers and peers show high commitment to learning (e.g., Burchinal et al., 2008). A sense of belonging may be especially important for children from ethnic and racial minorities, who sometimes feel marginalized by peers and teachers (Battistich, 2010; Garcia-Reid, Reid, & Peterson, 2005). School materials that present images, role models, and historical experiences of underrepresented groups help members of these groups to feel connected and offer their classmates opportunities to learn about the experiences of underrepresented groups throughout history (Burchinal et al., 2008; Roeser & Eccles, 2014).

Small classroom size also promotes children's sense of belonging and connection because teachers can individualize attention. Children in small classes show positive attitudes toward school, strong skills in concentration, high-quality participation in classroom activities, and positive academic outcomes (e.g., Brühwiler & Blatchford, 2011).

Bilingual Education

One in five children in the United States speaks a language other than English at home, and this number continues to grow (Camarota & Ziegler, 2014). Many of those children enter school with limited proficiency in English and may not receive the support needed to achieve in school for a variety of reasons. As many as 50% of teachers feel ill equipped to teach their language-minority students, and teachers serving such students often have fewer years of experience and lower rates of certification than those teaching language-majority students (Samson & Lesaux, 2015).

There continues to be fierce debate about the practices that most effectively promote the learning of English and academic material, and for the most part,

FIGURE 12.25 Various approaches are taken in bilingual education.   Proponents of bilingual classrooms use various strategies to support children's learning of a mainstream language (such as English) while simultaneously supporting the home-based primary language (such as Spanish or Mandarin).

evidence remains inconclusive (Barrow & Markman-Pithers, 2016). Because there are yet no gold standards about what works best (and for whom), individual schools and communities vary enormously in the approaches they take (**FIGURE 12.25**). Some schools advocate immersion in English as a way for children to quickly master the language and school material. They base this endorsement on successful immersion programs where students develop native-like levels of reading, and so forth, in their second language. Others advocate instruction in children's native tongue as a way to ensure that children do not lose their first language, and point to differences in bilingual language development in the U.S. context compared to other countries where the two languages spoken achieve equality in status, such as French and English in Canada, and Dutch and French in Belgium. Language-minority children have been found to be more involved in classwork and quicker to acquire English when both languages are integrated into the curriculum (Guglielmi, 2008).

Sometimes, even children who commonly speak English may be at a disadvantage when their home dialect diverges from standard English, a situation seen in African American children from low socioeconomic status families (Craig & Washington, 2006). Children who have few opportunities to hear standard English outside of school may fall behind in reading and other school subjects because of the mismatch between home and school language forms (Washington & Thomas-Tate, 2009).

✓ CHECK YOUR UNDERSTANDING 12.21

1. What are various types of instruction design used in classrooms?
2. What is the Pygmalion effect?
3. How might teachers promote inclusiveness in the classroom? Discuss ways in which teachers can promote students' sense of belonging in the classroom.
4. Contrast approaches to educating bilingual students. Which approach do you favor and why?

Cultural Context and Cognitive Development

LEARNING OBJECTIVE 12.22 Describe how cultural tools and experience with schooling affect children's cognitive development and learning.

Imagine being dropped off on an uninhabited island with no food or water, and left to fend for yourself. You may consider this absurd and unlikely to be

FIGURE 12.26 Outdoor learning experience in Ketchikan, **Alaska.**   For children in Ketchikan, Alaska, this survival challenge occurs as part of a school program that was initiated in 1972. Children must learn to master the art of survival, because in Alaska, there may be situations that require these practical skills.

seen in the United States, except perhaps in a reality television program. Yet, for children in Ketchikan, Alaska, this survival challenge occurs as part of a school program that was initiated in 1972. Children are dropped off in groups of 20 or so, on a remote island for 3 days, with only a backpack containing some clothes, twine, aluminum foil, compass, basic first-aid supplies, and a fishing line and hooks. They have no food, no water, and no shelter. They must figure out how to survive by boiling ocean water for drinking, building shelter, harvesting food through fishing and foraging, and dealing with encounters with wildlife and the elements (thunderstorms, floods, and forest fires are not uncommon) (**FIGURE 12.26**). Children must learn to master the art of survival, because in Alaska, children may encounter situations that require these practical skills. Alaskan children's participation in a survival challenge reinforces the idea of practical intelligence covered earlier in this chapter—that a key aspect of human intelligence is the ability to adapt to one's real-world cultural environment.

Cultural Tools

Developmental scientists have long viewed cultural tools as fundamental to children's learning and development (Vygotsky, 1978). A cultural tool can be any of the materials or symbols that people interact with on a daily basis—writing instruments and texts, computers, video games, cell phones, tablets, photographs, and other cultural artifacts that offer children practice with symbols and reasoning.

To illustrate how cultural tools shape cognitive development, consider the example of maps. Maps aid people in getting around their environments and can be found just about anywhere in the United States and other countries. Children learn to use maps as a part of their school curriculum and are often exposed to maps outside the school setting (think about following directions with a GPS device or smart phone that visibly tracks a car's movements). In contrast, in many small villages, rural communities, or communities where schooling and technology are scarce, maps are rarely used and are unfamiliar to children. People figure out how to get to their destinations by asking friends, relatives, and people in the neighborhood for directions. How might children's experiences with maps alter their representations of spatial landscapes?

When 12-year-olds in small cities in India and the United States were asked to draw maps of their neighborhoods, U.S. children drew conventional maps that covered a relatively large area and marked directions (north-south-east-west), main streets, and important landmarks. Their maps were similar to the traditional maps they were exposed to in school and daily life. In contrast, Indian children drew vibrant scenes that showed people, vehicles, and landmarks, but covered a small area that surrounded their homes (Parameswaran, 2003). However, once the Indian children were instructed to draw a map that could help other people "find their way," they drew maps that were as organized and broad in area as those drawn by the U.S. children (**FIGURE 12.27**).

Language is another cultural tool that shapes thinking and learning. For example, linguistic features of Chinese and English languages may affect how quickly children learn basic skills in mathematics, because the two languages represent numbers quite differently (Geary et al., 1996a, 1996b).

(A)

(B)

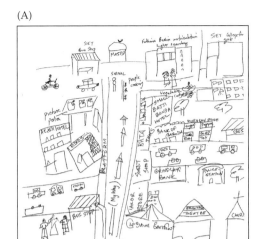

FIGURE 12.27 Maps drawn by children from India and the United States.
Researchers instructed 12-year-olds in small cities in India and the United States to draw maps of their neighborhoods. The two groups of children drew maps that aligned with their experiences. (A) Indian children drew colorful scenes of people, vehicles, and landmarks in small areas surrounding their homes. (B) In contrast, U.S. children drew conventional maps that marked directions, major streets, and significant landmarks over a large area. (From G. Parameswaran. 2003. *J Environ Psychol* 23: 409–417.)

Consider that the English words "eleven," twelve," and "thirteen" do not clearly specify the quantities of 11, 12, and 13, whereas in Chinese, the words for 11, 12, and 13 can be translated to "ten one," "ten two," and "ten three," making apparent that 1, 2, and 3 are added to the base unit of 10. Moreover, English number words take longer to pronounce than their corresponding numbers in Chinese. As a result, English-speaking children take longer than Chinese-speaking children to say digits, which disadvantages them in their memory digit spans and may help explain cultural disparities in math performance across the early school years.

Culture and Schooling

Cultural communities vary in how much adults intentionally and directly teach children versus expect children to learn through participation in daily activities. In the United States and other schooled societies, children learn a lot of information from teachers and adults who tutor them on academic subjects. In other communities, children rarely encounter formal education, and learn many skills by observing the people around them, what researchers refer to as **keen observational learning** (Silva, Shimpi, & Rogoff, 2015). For example, Mayan children from families with little or no experience with schooling closely watch the activities of those around them and rely less on the type of formal instruction experienced by U.S. school children (Correa-Chavez & Rogoff, 2009).

Mayan children and middle-class, European American children visited a laboratory with their siblings and sat nearby as an experimenter taught their siblings how to make an origami figure. Mayan children whose mothers had the least experience with schooling watched what was being taught to their siblings more than did the middle-class U.S. children. A week later, children returned to the lab and were asked to make the origami figure that had been taught to their siblings. Mayan children outperformed U.S. children, and required little assistance. Even after emigrating to California, 5- to 11-year-old Mayan children of mothers with little or no formal schooling were more attentive to the activities that were taught to their siblings and needed

keen observational learning
An individual's learning of skills by watching people, rather than by being directly taught

less help with those same tasks a week later compared to U.S. children and Mayan children of educated mothers (Silva, Correa-Chávez, & Rogoff, 2010).

Culture and Approaches to Teaching

The Mayan example of little formal education is not uncommon. Unesco's 2017–2018 Global Education Monitoring report states that around 17% of the world's children do not complete elementary school, and less than half (45%) complete secondary school. But, even in societies where most children attend school for many years, their experiences in the classroom may differ in line with the different practices, training, and strategies of their teachers.

Psychologist Harold Stevenson spent hundreds of hours observing elementary school classrooms in Japan, Taiwan, China, and the United States with the aim of unpacking the roots of national achievement gaps in mathematics—where U.S. children consistently lag behind students from East Asian countries. In his book entitled *The Learning Gap* (Stevenson & Stigler, 1992), Stevenson wrote about differences across societies in people's reactions to failure and mistakes, which he speculated affected students' tendencies to confront challenges head on versus avoid difficulties out of fear of failure.

To illustrate, Stevenson described a Japanese student who was instructed to work through a problem in front of the class, continually struggling for 45 minutes at the blackboard but showing no signs of embarrassment. When the student finally got the problem correct, the class cheered. Stevenson concluded that making a mistake did not carry the same negative weight as in the United States. Rather, teachers in Japan viewed errors to be a way to gauge what students still needed to learn, and students came to understand that errors are common and key to improvement. Indeed, how else would a person get better at anything without attempting to fix whatever went wrong?

Stevenson viewed similar approaches to learning in the other East Asian cultures he observed, including China. But, more generally, he found that teachers of mathematics in East Asia were highly skilled and fostered a dynamic and interactive learning environment that was met with high student engagement and few disruptive behaviors. In contrast, U.S. teachers feared the public scrutiny that might come with student failure, and their teaching of mathematics was less dynamic and more likely to be met with students acting out in the classroom (Stevenson, 2014).

✓ CHECK YOUR UNDERSTANDING 12.22

1. List some examples of cultural tools.
2. Give an example of keen observational learning.

Developmental Cascades

It is not difficult to imagine how cognitive skills in middle childhood might reverberate across developmental domains and time. Children's abilities to think and solve problems logically, focus attention, manipulate information in working memory, and so on, are vital to school success. In turn, academic achievement paves the way to later jobs, well-being, and social relationships. Children who have difficulties in one or more cognitive areas are at risk of behavior problems, school dropout, substance use, conflict with family, and emotional and psychological problems for years to come. As a result, the challenge for society is to arm children with the skills needed to succeed in school and to ward off the downward spiral caused by cognitive difficulty.

Cascades from Academics to Later School Performance

Just as positive school experiences in childhood provide a springboard for life-long learning, adverse experiences can detract from later adjustment. Indeed, delays in academic skills spill over to functioning across domains and grow over time. Consider falling behind in the basics of reading. Children who experience persistent reading difficulties by second or third grade are at heightened risk of school failure and ultimate drop out. An alarming one in six children who do not read proficiently by third grade fail to graduate from high school on time, and the rate rises to one in four for children facing the additional obstacle of poverty (Hernandez, 2011). In fact, academic disparities between children from low- and middle-socioeconomic status households can be traced to a lack of opportunity and practice with reading that snowballs over time (Chall, 1983; Hernandez, 2011). When 20,000 children from across the United States were assessed on their reading and math skills at school entry, and then followed up in fifth grade, early skills predicted later skills across race and socioeconomic backgrounds (Claessens, Duncan, & Engel, 2009).

Cascades from Academics to Social Relationships

Perhaps you expect stability from child cognitive skills to academic disparities and later school dropout. After all, common sense tells us that cognitive skills support academic achievement, and that early academic achievement cascades to later academic achievement because skills build on skills. However, cross-domain associations—from cognitive to social domains—are likewise striking and remind us to attend to the whole child. Children who do poorly at school often encounter problems in their relationships with peers, because they may be rejected and ostracized as unintelligent or incapable. And, the harmful impacts of low school performance widen when children are placed in remedial classes, because their classmates see them pulled out of classes and treated differently. Children view peers who are assigned to low-performing groups or remedial classes as less desirable as friends compared to their high-performing peers (McKown, Gregory, & Weinstein, 2010).

Cascading Effects in Children with Disabilities

Some of the most powerful cognitive cascades occur in children with intellectual or learning impairments. Children with **intellectual disability** are significantly limited in areas of reasoning, learning, and problem solving, and display problems in everyday adaptive behaviors as basic as following class rules and getting dressed in time for gym class. Children with **learning disabilities** have difficulties acquiring knowledge and skills at levels expected by children of their age. Like low-performing children more generally, children who experience intellectual or learning disabilities may be stigmatized, escalate in behavior problems over time, and they and their family members may experience negative repercussions in relationships and psychological well-being. Collectively, the stigma, behavior problems, stress, and toll on family functioning and friendships created by intellectual and learning disabilities can instigate a downward spiral (e.g., Emerson et al., 2010; Woodman, Mawdsley, & Hauser-Cram, 2015). Over time, learning problems can harm children's belief in their own abilities and place children at risk for later behavior and emotional problems into adulthood (e.g., Chesmore, Ou, & Reynolds, 2016; Lackaye et al., 2006). Such trends are particularly troubling in the case of children of color, who are disproportionately referred to special education (Fish, 2019; Morgan & Farkas, 2016).

Longitudinal studies most effectively reveal the cascading effects of learning disabilities, and likewise show that remedial education services may not always benefit child outcomes. Researchers followed over 1,000 children from low-income minority backgrounds in Chicago across the school years (first grade through high school). About 16% of the children received special

intellectual disability An impairment with significant limitations in intellectual functioning (e.g., learning, reasoning) and/or adaptive behaviors (e.g., getting dressed, following classroom rules)

learning disabilities Disorders that affect a child's ability to acquire knowledge and skills such as math and reading at levels expected for children of the same age education services from first to eighth grade. Children who received special education services had lower rates of high school completion and higher rates of incarceration, substance use (alcohol and drugs), and depression compared to children who had not received special education services (Chesmore et al., 2016). Still, correlational studies do not indicate causality. Perhaps, children would have done even worse without the services they received; and children who received services started out with problems in cognitive areas that may have snowballed over time regardless of the interventions they received.

The negative cascades seen in children with learning and intellectual disabilities raise questions about the best ways to improve their long-term prognosis. Initiatives that compare the effectiveness of different interventions may hold some answers by spotlighting the benefits and limitations of inclusive classroom approaches and family-based approaches. For example, the setting of services is one factor that might make a difference in how children fare. Children in inclusive classrooms are taught alongside their peers, rather than separately, which may reduce stigmatization and enhance participation in academic subjects (Chesmore et al., 2016).

Another approach to helping children with learning and intellectual disabilities focuses intervention on the entire family system, not just the child. Such approaches recognize that parent stress profoundly influences children's well-being and may be a necessary target for intervention. Parents of children with intellectual and learning disabilities generally report higher levels of stress than do parents of typically developing children, which likely spills over to their interactions with children (Hauser-Cram et al., 2013). In turn, parental stress cascades to behavior problems in children (e.g., Woodman et al., 2015).

What can be done to prevent parental stress from spiraling into further child problems? Training studies and mindfulness interventions offer two promising ways to alleviate stress (Crnic et al., 2017). Parent training studies focus on enhancing positive parent-child interactions, reducing negative parent-child interactions, and enhancing parents' positive feelings towards children with intellectual disabilities (McIntyre, 2008). Mindfulness studies help parents handle their emotions and stress through meditation, yoga, and other relaxation techniques. Both approaches recognize the reverberating influences of cognitive delays and learning disabilities across multiple outcomes in children and the people in their social networks, and present new avenues that might avert negative, long-term outcomes (Crnic et al., 2017).

◼ CLOSING THOUGHTS
Thinking about Thinking

Developmental researchers spend a lot of time thinking about thinking. They aim to understand the invisible mental processes involved in cognitive development by observing how children respond to simple tasks like reciting numbers backwards or ignoring distractors while solving problems. But why does it matter? Why should you learn different theoretical and methodological approaches, rather than focus directly on "societally important" topics, such as how to improve school curricula or educate parents and teachers on direct ways to help children learn?

The reason is that any effective intervention requires getting down into the weeds to understand how thinking develops and why. You might firmly *believe* that by arming children with strategies to remember material, for example, their learning will improve. But what are those strategies? Which would work and at what age? You might *believe* that parents should insist that children do their homework (as one option) or give children complete autonomy (as an alternative option). But which side would you advocate and why? You might *believe* that children should be placed in classrooms with peers matched on aptitude. But, how would you determine a child's intellectual aptitude, and would your solution be better than integrating children with different aptitudes within a classroom? You might *believe* that teachers should praise children to motivate them. But should they? In short, every decision that aims to support children's learning has consequences. And so, a first critical step to action is to think about thinking. The second is to study thinking. Only then will the pros and cons of any proposed solution become apparent.

The Developmentalist's Toolbox

Method	Purpose	Description
Measuring children's cognitive development		
Conservation tasks	To test children's understanding of conservation of mass or quantity	Children are asked whether superficial transformations of an object (such as rolling a ball of clay into a snakelike object) will change its mass or amount.
Class-inclusion problems	To test children's understanding of hierarchical classification	Children may be asked to determine which group has more items: the full group of items (superordinate) or a subset of items (subordinate).
Seriation and transitive inference problems	To test children's ability to systematically order items that vary along a continuous dimension such as length or width	When presented with sticks of different lengths and told that Stick A is longer than Stick B and Stick B is longer than Stick C, children in the concrete operation stage can infer that Stick A must be longer than Stick C.
Spatial reasoning problems	To assess a child's ability to comprehend a spatial layout from various vantage points	Children may be asked to draw maps and/or to describe how a person gets from one point on the map to another, even if the map is rotated.
Inductive reasoning problems	To assess how readily a child can deduce an answer given various clues	Children are told a story containing various premises and are asked a question that requires them to draw a conclusion based on story premises.
Deductive reasoning problems	To assess children's ability to systematically test ideas that are guided by an overarching hypothesis, by attempting to manipulate one variable at a time	Piaget asked children to figure out what causes a pendulum to swing faster (its weight, string length, or force of the downward push). Children in the concrete operational stage failed to solve the problem because they did not formulate a systematic approach to solving the problem through testing of single variables at a time.
Selective attention problems: Digit Cancellation Test and Trail Making Test	To measure how readily a child can respond to a target stimulus embedded in a stream of distractors; to measure skill in visual scanning and tracking of information and executive functions such as processing speed and working memory	In the Digit Cancellation Test, children must cross out target digits on a page (such as all the 8s or all the 3s and 5s) as quickly as possible. In the Trail Making Test, children must draw lines to connect sequences of letters (A-to-B-to-C and so forth), numbers (1-to-2-to-3 and so forth), or alternating letters and numbers.
Cognitive flexibility tasks	To assess children's abilities to flexibly switch their attention and responses as the rules of a problem change	Children may be asked to sort cards by color and then switch to sorting the same cards by shape; or they may be asked to press the computer button that corresponds to the large object of a pair, and then later press the button that corresponds to the smaller object. (Continued)

The Developmentalist's Toolbox (continued)		
Method	**Purpose**	**Description**
Measuring children's intelligence and individual differences		
Stanford-Binet Test	To measure intelligence	A standardized measure of intelligence that asks children to answer questions and solve problems and generates a score (intelligence quotient or IQ) on the child's standing relative to same-age peers.
Wechsler Intelligence Scale for Children-V	To measure intelligence	A standardized measure of intelligence that contains both verbal and nonverbal problems (for example, creating patterns from blocks).
Genome-wide complex trait analysis	To estimate genetic influences on intelligence—or on other traits of interest—through the analysis of DNA	DNA samples taken from many individuals are compared so that genotype similarities can be ascertained. The degree of similarity in genotype is then compared to the degree of phenotype similarity in a particular trait, such as intelligence. An association between the genotype and phenotype indicates a genetic basis to the observed trait, or the extent to which genotypic similarity can predict phenotypic similarity.
Understanding of magnitudes tasks	To assess children's abilities to recognize magnitudes of different numbers relative to one another, such as realizing that 100 is much closer to 0 than to 1,000	Children may be asked to indicate where on a number line a specific number belongs. This is repeated for several numbers to assess children's understanding of number magnitudes.

■ Chapter Summary

Piagetian Theory

- According to Piaget, during the concrete operations stage (approximately 7–11 years), children's thinking is logical, flexible, and organized, reflected in their ability in mental operations.
- Children are capable of decentration, reversibility, seriation (including mental seriation or transitive inference), and inductive reasoning. These abilities allow children to solve conservation tasks, logical problems, and understand superordinate-subordinate classifications.
- Children's spatial reasoning improves, allowing them to pass the three mountains task (which requires taking the perspective of others) and to use tools such as maps.

Information Processing

- Children show gains in cognitive self-regulation, as seen in improvements of selective attention, cognitive flexibility, and planning.
- Processing speed and working memory span improve throughout childhood. Children with problems in these areas may fall behind in academics.

- Developments in metacognition allow children to monitor their performance and use strategies such as rehearsal, chunking, and elaboration to remember material and solve problems.
- Children's growing knowledge base (semantic memory) facilitates organization of material, rehearsal strategies, and thus, learning and memory.
- Autobiographical memory contains episodic and semantic components. Children's episodic memories improve over middle childhood, becoming more detailed and elaborate with age.

Defining Intelligence

- Historically, scientists have diverged in their definitions of intelligence as unidimensional or multidimensional. Spearman considered intelligence to be a single factor; Cattell distinguished fluid from crystallized intelligence; Guilfod and Thurstone viewed intelligence as comprised of many abilities.
- Contemporary scientists Howard Gardner and Robert Sternberg propose multidimensional views of intelligence

that highlight contextual influences, rather than a single, underlying capacity of intelligence.

Measuring Intelligence

- A "good" intelligence test should be reliable, valid, and free of bias.

- Galton and Binet are two of the first scientists to develop tests of intelligence. Tests of intelligence assign an "IQ" (intelligent quotient) to individuals, based on the relation between an individual's mental and chronological age.

- Wechsler and Raven designed nonverbal IQ tests to address the potential bias of verbally based instruments.

- Performance on intelligence tests is stable and predicts success across many areas.

- To minimize bias of intelligence tests, a researcher should identify whether the test contains content-validity bias or predictive-validity bias.

- Dynamic assessments of intelligence aim to examine a person's learning potential, rather than static skills at one point in time.

Nature and Nurture in Intelligence

- Intelligence is heritable, as revealed by twin and adoption studies and genome-wide complex trait analysis.

- Environmental influences interact with genetics to explain individual differences in intelligence.

Academic Skills: Language, Literacy, and Math

- Children's vocabularies and grammatical complexity expand during middle childhood.

- Reading and writing require inside-out and outside-in skills, including decoding of letters, sounds, and words, and understanding of word, sentence, and passage meaning.

- Educators recognize the importance of combining a phonics approach and whole language approach in teaching children to read.

- As children acquire knowledge in math, they shift in the strategies they use to solve math problems.

- Children's understanding of math concepts takes time. Examples of challenging concepts include understanding equalities in equations and relative magnitudes.

Motivation

- Intrinsic motivation is associated with persistence and interest in activities, whereas extrinsic motivation undermines persistence and interest.

- Children who attribute failure and success to effort show high motivation, whereas those who attribute failure and success to ability quickly become discouraged.

- These "mindsets" are likewise seen in the distinction between an incremental theory of intelligence and an entity theory of intelligence.

Contexts of Cognitive Development and Academic Achievement

- Family factors, including aspects of sensitive parenting, parents' mindsets, parents' praise, parents' reactions to children's failure, and family socioeconomic status contribute to individual differences among children in cognitive development and academic motivation and achievement.

- Various aspects of the school context influence children's cognitive development, academic achievement, and motivation. School influences include curriculum, quality of instruction, design of instruction, teacher expectations, and classroom climate and size.

- A challenge to the U.S. educational system is how to support children who enter school with limited English proficiency. Two contrasting approaches are immersion in English and bilingual education.

- Schools situated in poor neighborhoods may lack resources to support student learning, and teachers in these settings may experience burnout.

- Two key aspects of cultural communities that influence children's cognitive development are cultural tools and experiences with schooling.

Developmental Cascades

- Children's cognitive development, skills in executive function, and academic performance during middle childhood predict later school performance, likelihood of school dropout, and consequently future job opportunities.

- Individual differences in cognitive development have cascading influences on social relationships, with low-achieving children being at risk of rejection from peers.

- Children with learning or intellectual disabilities are at risk of being stigmatized; having behavior problems; experiencing low self-esteem; and suffering from compromised family and peer relationships.

- Interventions that focus on inclusion and engaging the entire family system may benefit children. Mindfulness training may support parents' and children's handling of stress in cases of student low school performance and learning disabilities.

Thinking Like a Developmentalist

The superintendent of a school district, located in a poor neighborhood, is concerned about the failing grades of her students. After a district-wide competition, she awards grants to three schools to support their proposed evidence-based plans for improving students' performance. All three schools presented solid research evidence around the factors that contribute to student performance, and were determined to implement programmatic interventions to address those factors. However, the three schools differed on where they placed their emphasis.

- School #1 attributed failing grades to problems in student motivation.

- School #2 attributed failing grades to problems in student cognitive self-regulation and failure to use effective strategies.

- School #3 attributed failing grades to school-based factors, including the design and quality of instruction and teacher expectations.

1. What evidence do you think that each school presented to the superintendent to support their explanations for students' low school performance? (By the way, developmental scientists refer to such explanations as "theories of change" because they reflect beliefs about what needs to be changed to fix a situation.)

2. Describe the types of interventions the three schools might design to change the problems they have identified. What specifically might they do? How would they test if their interventions are effective?

3. Can you think of other influential factors on student performance that the three intervention approaches might have overlooked? What are they?

Emotional and Social Development in Middle Childhood

13

Drawing by Minxin Cheng from a photo by Robert Collins on Unsplash

The kids on the school bus taunted him for months, perhaps because they thought he was too chubby or clumsy or socially awkward or too close to his mom, who worried about what to do to help her son fit in. One day, as he walked to the back of the bus, a bunch of kids pulled down his pants, and the busload of children erupted with laughter. He cried in embarrassment, which made it worse, attempted to pull up his pants, and lost his balance. His books tumbled out of his backpack and under the seats of his now hysterical classmates. When I heard about the incident, I asked one of the children who had been on the bus, "What did you do? Why didn't anyone try to stop this?" The child responded with what he believed to be a valid rationale for his inaction, "If I helped him, I'd be the next one they'd make fun of. He's just not cool and some kids are just mean. But, I'm nice to him when we're alone" (**FIGURE 13.1**).

Over my years as a professional, parent, aunt, and friend, I have had ample opportunities to observe children from all walks of life navigate the rough emotional and social waters of middle childhood—humiliation and hurt at being excluded from a party; anger and embarrassment at being bullied; and anxious obsession about what to wear to fit in with the "popular" kids at school. As was the case for the boy on the bus, I've seen children victimize other children through hurtful comments, acts of discrimination, aggressive intimidation, and strategic use of social media to brag, deride, and embarrass. On the other hand, I've observed countless acts of kindness, altruism, and compassion that reflect children's abilities to understand another person's plight and put themselves in another person's shoes. I've watched children support and help one

FIGURE 13.1 To be or not to be. School-age children often struggle about what to do in specific situations and sometimes engage in behaviors for self-protection. A child might comfort a victimized child when alone, but laugh at the victim in the presence of peers.

another, rush to aid a victim, welcome a newcomer into a peer group, and develop close and trusting friendships.

In the sections that follow, you will be introduced to the many sides of middle childhood—the good, the bad, and the ugly. By the end of the chapter, you will more fully appreciate the rich depth of emotional and social development, the role of context and culture in these developments, and the cascading influence of social and emotional skills for domains near and far.

■ Emotional Development

Children's journeys through the emotional world of middle childhood are punctuated by bumps and detours. Yet, for the most part, children make it through with flying colors. Children show gains in their understanding of the nature, causes, and consequences of emotions and in their abilities to regulate their emotions and behaviors. They recognize that it is possible to experience several emotions simultaneously and that the feelings a person shows on the outside are not necessarily what that person feels on the inside. They selectively express and regulate emotions and apply a range of coping strategies to difficult situations.

Understanding Emotions

Consider how difficult it would be to develop close relationships if we did not understand people's emotions. We must be able to put ourselves in other people's shoes if we are to treat our friends, relatives, and even strangers with compassion and empathy. If someone doesn't seem to understand our feelings, we may hesitate to confide in them, or retaliate with aggression and hurtful comments. Emotional disconnection leads to social isolation and emotional pain, and spills over to school and work. It is no wonder that children's growing abilities to understand emotions are so critical to well-being.

Self-Conscious Emotions: Guilt, Shame, and Pride

LEARNING OBJECTIVE 13.1 Define with examples the self-conscious emotions of guilt, shame, and pride.

The self-conscious emotions, such as guilt, shame, and pride, arise from an awareness of how others react to our behaviors. Self-conscious emotions are more complex than emotions such as happiness or sadness, because they require individuals to attribute their emotional experiences to their own behaviors or traits (Tangney & Tracy, 2012) (**TABLE 13.1**). Thus, although some self-conscious emotions arise in early childhood, children sharply improve in their understanding of these emotions in middle childhood (Muris & Meesters, 2014).

Guilt and Shame

Negative self-conscious emotions such as guilt and shame typically result from the violation of a behavioral standard, especially one that affects other people (Muris & Meesters, 2014). For example, a child might feel guilty about choosing to play with friends rather than visiting his grandma, if he realizes his grandma expected him to visit and he let her down. He might internalize the negative feeling toward himself and experience shame. Children's understanding of guilt and shame expands between 5 and 11 years of age in line with their growing ability to reason about self and other (Berti, Garattoni, & Venturini, 2000; Olthof

TABLE 13.1 ■ Guilt, shame, and pride

Emotion	Situation	Cognitive response
Guilt	A boy has used a cheat sheet during an important examination at school. He is the only one of his class who passed. All classmates are really sad, but the teacher gives him a big compliment about his good performance.	"I am relieved that I passed this difficult examination, but I feel really bad because I know I have been cheating and this is not fair to my classmates."
Shame	A women accidentally meets a close friend who she has not seen for a while and then realizes that she has completely forgotten about her birthday.	"I feel really ashamed about myself. How can I forget about her birthday? How could I have been so thoughtless?"
Authentic pride	A girl has played a difficult piece of music on her violin in front of a big audience at school. Afterward, children, parents, and teachers come up to her, praising her because she did so well.	"I am so happy that I did well. I have really practiced a lot on this piece of music and my efforts have been paying off, and I made my parents proud."
Hubristic pride	A child has scored the winning goal for his football team. After the match, his teammates and fans congratulate him on his good performance.	"I am the best. Everything that I do eventually turns out to be a great success."

Source: After P. Muris and C. Meesters. 2013. *Clin Child Fam Psychol Rev* 17: 19–40. https://doi.org/10.1007/s10567-013-0137-z.

et al., 2004). Moreover, children gradually internalize self-conscious emotions, moving from depending on another person's reactions to feel emotions such as guilt (e.g., when a parent points out being upset that a child hasn't done something) to having a personalized consciousness about their behaviors (i.e., feeling guilty for not doing something, even if others don't mention their disappointment). For example, 7- to 9-year-old children focused on how other people reacted when discussing negative self-conscious emotions of guilt and shame, whereas older 10- to 12-year-old children relied on self-evaluations rooted in their personal standards of right and wrong (Ferguson, Stegge, & Damhuis, 1991). Thus, complex self-conscious emotions start to take on a "pure" form during middle childhood (Muris & Meesters, 2014).

Experiencing guilt or shame can be healthy when it prompts children to behave in morally and socially appropriate ways. Maybe next time, the child will visit his grandma rather than going out to play. It can be unhealthy, however, to be frequently and intensely troubled by such feelings or to never experience them at all. Exceedingly high feelings of shame and self-blame can lead to depression and anxiety. Extremely low guilt, on the other hand, may reflect a disregard for social norms and failure to reflect on the consequences of antisocial behaviors (Muris & Meesters, 2014).

Pride

Pride is a self-conscious emotion that is rooted in two sources of happiness—a child's positive feelings about a socially valued accomplishment and the child's happiness at knowing another important person recognized the accomplishment (Harter, 1999; Muris & Meesters, 2014) (**FIGURE 13.2**). For example, children who work hard in school and receive an "A" on a test or as a final grade may be proud of their accomplishments and the fact that they have pleased their teachers and parents. Children rapidly improve in their ability to distinguish pride from mere happiness by around 6–7 years of age (Tracy, Robins, & Lagattuta, 2005). Throughout childhood, children grow in the understanding that pride results from a sense of personal accomplishment and outside acceptance (Lagattuta & Thompson, 2007).

Certain types of pride may be socially adaptive because they reinforce and motivate future positive behaviors, support self-esteem, and elicit

FIGURE 13.2 Pride. Children usually experience pride when they believe they have achieved something that society values.

© iStock.com/PeopleImages

authentic pride A form of pride arising from children's positive evaluation of an achievement

hubristic pride A form of pride arising from children's attribution of an achievement to their overall greatness

respect and acceptance. However, not all types of pride are the same. In fact, researchers distinguish two forms of pride: (1) **authentic pride**, which arises from children's positive evaluation of an accomplishment ("I did that well"), and (2) **hubristic pride**, which arises when children attribute the accomplishment to their overall greatness ("*I* did that well") (Muris & Meesters, 2014). Authentic pride is associated with positive, prosocial behaviors, whereas hubristic pride is associated with antisocial, selfish actions (Tracy & Robins, 2007).

✓ CHECK YOUR UNDERSTANDING 13.1

1. What may be the consequences of extreme low guilt and extreme high shame?
2. Distinguish between two types of pride, and explain which one may be socially adaptive and why.

The Causes and Consequences of Emotions

LEARNING OBJECTIVE 13.2 Give an example of how children display an understanding of causes and consequences of emotions.

Children gradually come to appreciate the causes and consequences of emotions—that many factors determine a person's emotions, and therefore emotions fluctuate across time and situations (Pons & Harris, 2005). By around 8–10 years of age, children grasp that a person's background, characteristics, past experiences, personality, intentions, and beliefs will govern how that person reacts to a situation, and accordingly, that different people may react quite differently to the same event (Lemerise & Arsenio, 2000). One child might ignore an insult from a classmate, whereas another child, receiving the same insult, might aggressively retaliate.

Of course, people often feel more than one emotion at a time, and so children must also learn that situations may produce mixed emotions. A child leaving for sleep-away camp may feel happy, nervous, and sad all at once, and the child's parents might simultaneously experience a sense of freedom and worry. Between 6 and 10 years of age, children increasingly understand that a single event—such as performing in a school play—can simultaneously evoke positive and negative emotions such as happiness and nervousness, and that mixed emotions can differ in their intensity (Larsen, To, & Fireman, 2007; Saarni, 2010).

Children's growing understanding of the causes and consequences of emotions allows them to reason hypothetically about how a person "would have felt" had a situation turned out differently. This type of reasoning is fundamental to the emotions of regret or relief. That is, the same outcome can produce a positive feeling (relief) or a negative feeling (regret) depending on what a person had anticipated. For example, imagine that you receive a 75% on an exam that you expected to fail. In this situation, passing the exam, even with a low score, may cause you to feel relief. If instead you received the same 75% grade on an exam that you expected to ace, maybe because you decided to attend a movie rather than study, you may experience regret. Developmental scientists sometimes use **counterfactual emotion tasks** to test whether children understand that a person's emotions depend on how reality compares to alternatives (e.g., Beck & Riggs, 2014). They ask children to guess how characters who experienced different outcomes will react, such as when receiving a very small prize after expecting a large one (regret) or having money stolen but not that much (relief).

Starting around 7 years of age, children can accurately judge a person's feelings of regret, but they still find situations around feelings of relief difficult to evaluate (Guttentag & Ferrell, 2004). With age, children increasingly understand both regret and relief, and even develop strategies to regulate their emotions around potential future disappointments. For example, 9- to 10-year-old

counterfactual emotion tasks Tasks used by developmental researchers to test whether children understand that an individual's emotions depend on how reality compares to alternative possible outcomes children were found to lower their expectations in advance of an outcome—such as by telling themselves, "I likely will get a low grade on the test"—so that the reality would not catch them by surprise (Guttentag & Ferrell, 2008).

When children understand emotions such as relief and regret, they can console other people who experience a negative event by stating, "It could have been worse." To illustrate, researchers asked 8-, 10-, and 12-year-old children and adults what they would say or do to make characters in a story feel better after the character had some money stolen or won much less money than was possible. With age, counterfactual consoling such as, "You could have been hurt!" or "You could have won nothing!" increased sharply. Yet although 10- and 12-year-old children were more likely to use a counterfactual consoling strategy than were 8-year-olds, 12-year-olds were less likely than adults to generate them (Payir & Guttentag, 2016).

✓ CHECK YOUR UNDERSTANDING 13.2

1. Explain how understanding the causes and consequences of emotions might allow children to forgive a person's behaviors in a specific situation.

2. When might children use counterfactual consoling strategies to make themselves feel better?

Theory of Mind and Moral Reasoning

LEARNING OBJECTIVE 13.3 Distinguish between the false-belief understanding seen in early childhood and the higher-level false belief achieved in middle childhood.

Children's understanding of the causes and consequences of emotions goes hand in hand with their growing social-cognitive skills. Children can now reflect on why people might feel, think, or act in certain ways, and so are better able to reason about moral situations. For example, if your friend accidently spilled a drink on your new shirt, you might get upset for a moment, but you likely would not judge your friend's actions as wrong. That's because you would consider your friend's intentions when judging the situation. Similarly, if your friend lashed out at you in anger because she falsely believed that you had lied to her, you would understand that her anger arose from a misunderstanding. As Piaget and Kohlberg noted (see Chapter 10), children must be able to consider a person's underlying intentions to achieve a level of morality that moves beyond rigid rules around right and wrong.

Developmental researchers test children's moral development with vignettes similar to the spilled-drink scenario. They ask children of different ages to evaluate the actions of story characters and to reason about why they view a character's behaviors as right or wrong (Killen & Smetana, 2014). An example story might involve a child who causes another child to fall off a swing either accidentally or purposefully. With age, children increasingly state that it would be wrong to punish an accidental transgressor. However, some children continue to have difficulties considering others' intentions, and as a result may attribute hostile intentions to people who actually mean no harm. For example, they may perceive someone who bumps them in a hallway at school as being aggressive, when the person was simply in a rush. Such hostile attributions can feed into a cycle of maladaptive interactions that lead children to aggressively retaliate for what they perceive to be threats by other children (Dodge et al., 2015).

Notably, children's growing theory of mind contributes to their abilities to distinguish between intentional versus accidental transgressions. Chinese children 4–7 years of age (Fu et al., 2014) who scored high on a battery of theory-of-mind tasks recognized that the child who accidentally bumped a child off a swing did not have hostile intentions and they rated the child more positively than did children low on theory of mind. In fact, over the course of middle childhood, children's theory-of-mind skills continue to develop in ways that allow them to reason in complex ways about others' emotions, beliefs, and behaviors. For example, children now understand that a person can hold a belief about someone else's belief—that the teacher *thought* that Christopher *thought* that he was an unfair teacher—what researchers call **second-order false belief** (Miller, 2009; Papera et al., 2019).

second-order false belief A type of theory-of-mind understanding that it is possible to have a false belief about someone else's belief

✓ **CHECK YOUR UNDERSTANDING 13.3**

1. What is a second-order false belief? Give an example.

Expressing and Regulating Emotions

People do not always reveal what they feel inside. Consider how often you intentionally mask your true feelings to adapt to what is happening, where you are, and with whom you are interacting. You may feign interest in a professor's lecture to improve your chances for a good grade, compliment a friend's (very unattractive) haircut, or suppress your hurt at a peer's insult. Mismatches between inner and outer selves are a rule of thumb for most people.

Display Rules and Regulating Emotions

LEARNING OBJECTIVE 13.4 Describe the purpose of display rules and how these rules evolve in middle childhood.

display rules Strategies that hide authentic feelings or change emotional expressions to fit a situation, such as when a child shows happiness when receiving an unappealing present

With age, children improve in their use of **display rules**, strategies that mask genuine feelings or alter emotional expressions to fit a situation, such as when a child shows joy upon receiving an unattractive gift (Kromm, Färber, & Holodynski, 2015; Saarni, 1979). Nearly half a century ago, developmental scientists identified four types of emotional display rules that people use to deceive others (Ekman & Friesen, 1969):

1. *Intensification*—magnifying visible emotions beyond what is felt inside. For example, if a child receives a gift that is just okay, the child might exaggerate happiness to please the gift giver.

2. *Minimization*—minimizing visible emotions to keep feelings somewhat hidden. For example, a child who wins a contest might temper excitement because it's inappropriate to express delight at beating a competitor.

3. *Neutralization*—displaying a neutral face in situations where emotional expressions may be inappropriate. For example, a child who is reprimanded by a teacher might display a poker face to maintain neutrality and respect.

4. *Substitution*—substituting one emotion for another when true feelings might be inappropriate or embarrassing. For example, a child might laugh when other children tease a peer to avoid becoming a target of ridicule, even while feeling concern and empathy for the victim.

emotion vignettes Stories presented to children by developmental researchers to examine children's understanding of a character's emotions and facial expressions, their use of display rules, and their reasoning for their responses

Developmental scientists sometimes use **emotion vignettes**—tasks in which researchers present children with stories about a character and ask questions about the character's emotions—to investigate children's understanding of display rules. In one of the first studies on display rules, Carolyn Saarni (1979) presented 7-, 9-, and 11-year-old children with four conflict situations depicted in photographs. Children were shown scenes in which a child:

- boasted about his/her skating ability to another child and then fell down,
- received a disappointing birthday gift,
- was bullied by another child in front of an onlooker who intervened, and
- set off the school fire alarm and was then caught.

For each situation, children were asked to choose the emotion the character felt, the facial expression of the character in the story, and then explain the reasoning behind their answers. For example, in the first situation, a child might conclude that the skateboarder would "laugh" after falling down to mask his embarrassment. Saarni found that older children were more likely than younger children to suggest that characters would hide their true feelings. Older children also reasoned in complex ways about *why* characters' facial expressions differed from what they felt inside, for example by stating that the gift receiver smiled at the disappointing gift to not hurt the feelings of the gift giver.

However, the effective use of display rules depends on how well a child can control emotional reactions in the moment. Some children are quite adept at regulating their emotions, whereas others struggle (Cole & Jacobs, 2018). Children who have difficulties regulating their emotions can respond at two extremes. They may suppress what they feel inside to the point that it becomes unhealthy, referred to as **internalizing behaviors**. Or, they may act out in unacceptable ways, such as by being aggressive to peers, referred to as **externalizing behaviors** (**FIGURE 13.3**). Internalizing behaviors may sometimes develop into symptoms of depression, whereas externalizing behaviors may sometimes develop into aggression and other problem behaviors. Differences among children in emotional regulation also spill over to coping, as we will see next.

FIGURE 13.3 Externalizing behaviors. Children acting out inappropriately or showing aggression toward peers are examples of externalizing behaviors that may develop into aggression or delinquency years later.

internalizing behaviors Problem behaviors based on negative emotions that are directed inwards, such as the development of anxiety or depression, that may stem from emotional regulation challenges

externalizing behaviors Problem behaviors directed to the external environment, such as physical aggression, disobeying rules, and destroying property, that may stem from emotional regulation challenges

✓ CHECK YOUR UNDERSTANDING 13.4

1. What are some common ways that school children disguise their true emotions by using display rules?

Emotional Coping

LEARNING OBJECTIVE 13.5 Define the two main types of coping strategies.

Children often encounter situations that make them angry, worried, nervous, or frightened. How do they cope? Children might manage or modify the problem or situation, referred to as **situation-centered coping**, or regulate their emotional reactions to the problem or situation, referred to as **emotion-centered coping** (Folkman & Lazarus, 2013). For instance, a child who gets upset when made fun of by peers at lunch can choose to sit at a different table (a situation-centered coping strategy) or reframe how she thinks about the situation by telling herself that the rude peers don't know her at all, and are ignorant (an emotion-centered coping strategy). Throughout middle childhood, children improve in their use of the two types of coping strategies (Compas et al., 2014; Denham, 2007).

Furthermore, older children understand when and how to apply specific strategies to cope with situations better than do younger children (Waters & Thompson, 2014). As a result, children shift over age from using coping strategies such as brooding, crying, and aggression to using verbal strategies (for example, "Stop grabbing the ball and wait until it's your turn"). With age, children increasingly implement several coping strategies simultaneously. For example, if an aggressive peer makes fun of a child in the schoolyard, the child may distance himself from the unpleasant situation, redirect attention elsewhere, and problem solve about how to prevent the situation from occurring in the future (e.g., Murphy & Eisenberg, 1996).

As children improve in their regulation of emotions and coping strategies, they acquire a sense of **emotional self-efficacy**—the feeling of being in control

situation-centered coping A coping strategy characterized by the management or modification of a problem or situation

emotion-centered coping A coping strategy characterized by the regulation of emotional reactions to a problem or situation

emotional self-efficacy The feeling of being in control, able to handle emotional challenges, and able to express positive emotions appropriately and able to handle emotional challenges (Thompson & Goodman, 2010). In turn, children with a strong sense of emotional self-efficacy elicit approval from peers and develop positive friendships (Blair et al., 2016).

✓ **CHECK YOUR UNDERSTANDING 13.5**

1. What are some coping strategies children in middle childhood may use to regulate their emotions?

Contexts of Emotional Development

Children show remarkable advances in emotional development across middle childhood. However, children vary substantially in their understanding of emotions and their abilities to express and regulate emotions in socially acceptable ways. Family, peer, and cultural contexts contribute to developments in children's emotions and behaviors, in line with Bronfenbrenner's bioecological model (see Chapter 1; Bronfenbrenner & Morris, 2007).

Family Context of Emotional Development

LEARNING OBJECTIVE 13.6 Describe the ways that parents and siblings influence children's emotional development.

Parents and other family members socialize children's emotional development throughout middle childhood. Parents model emotions and react to children's emotions in ways that support or hinder emotional development. Additionally, the quality of sibling relationships exerts a strong yet relatively understudied influence on children's emotional development.

Parents as Models

In the family context, children learn strategies for coping with their emotions from their parents. The well-known phrase "do as I say, not as I do" captures the hypocrisy that unfortunately characterizes some parents' attempts to teach children how to handle emotions. Parents may warn children not to be aggressive or emotionally over-reactive, but then resort to aggressive tactics and emotional outbursts in their own interactions with one another or their children. In an often-cited study of family conflict, Patterson (1982) found that parents of aggressive children modeled and reinforced aggressive behaviors themselves when they felt provoked. Many researchers have since documented associations between parents' negative behaviors and those of their children in the United States and other countries (e.g., Chang et al., 2003; Kawabata & Crick, 2016).

Parent Responses to Children's Emotions

The ways that parents respond to their children's emotions communicate important messages about which emotions are appropriate and how to cope with negative emotions. Parents support children's emotional competence by reinforcing and accepting their children's emotions, listening, and asking questions. At the other extreme, parents who ridicule or ignore their children's emotions may intensify children's behavior problems (Lunkenheimer, Shields, & Cortina, 2007).

Meta-emotion philosophy, the organized set of thoughts and feelings parents hold about their own emotions and their children's emotions, may help explain differences among parents in their reactions to children's emotions. Parents who display a strong meta-emotion philosophy engage in high **emotion coaching** by being involved in their children's emotional life, respecting their children's emotions, and sharing emotional experiences with

meta-emotion philosophy The organized, structured set of thoughts and feelings caregivers have about their own and children's emotions

emotion coaching The practice of talking with children about emotions, respecting children's emotions, and offering children coping strategies for handling emotionally challenging situations children (Gottman et al., 1996). In contrast, parents who engage in low emotion coaching may have anxious children or children who are vulnerable to emotional problems (Hurrel, Houwing, & Hudson, 2017). Indeed, children who perceive their mothers and fathers as emotionally unsupportive show high levels of anger and depression and have difficulties coping with negative emotions (Sanders et al., 2015).

Parents' emotion coaching is particularly important for children with autism spectrum disorder (ASD), because such children have difficulties understanding emotions (Heerey, Keltner, & Capps, 2003). Parents of children with ASD who recognize their children's limitations in emotional areas and behave in supportive ways can help their children better understand the emotions of self and others (Bougher-Muckian et al, 2016).

Physical Punishment and Maltreatment

Some parents believe that hitting or physically hurting children—what researchers refer to as **corporal punishment**—teaches children how to behave. However, parents who engage in corporal punishment actually communicate to children that it is okay to hit or hurt others. Indeed, children are likely to model their parents' aggressive behaviors when interacting with other people. A meta-analysis of dozens of studies indicated a relationship between parental physical punishment and unfavorable outcomes in children, including heightened aggression (Gershoff & Grogan-Kaylor, 2016).

When physical punishment becomes intense and chronic, it can spill over to **maltreatment**—cruel or violent treatment that causes suffering in children. Children with a history of maltreatment are acutely sensitive to facial expressions of distress because they have learned to attend closely to facial expressions that might signal danger. Maltreated 8- to 15-year-old children show faster reaction times to fearful faces compared to non-maltreated children (Masten et al., 2008) (**FIGURE 13.4**). They also are quicker to detect anger in others' faces or voices, and they detect more subtle forms of negative expressions than do children who have not been maltreated. Perhaps this is because maltreated children have learned to associate angry faces and voices with negative consequences. In fact, imaging studies suggest that child maltreatment can alter brain functioning and make children hypersensitive to social cues of danger (Pollak, 2008). Hypersensitivity to threat can then undermine children's social interactions with peers and teachers (Thompson, 2011). Children who quickly perceive peers to be hostile are likely to respond negatively, leading to further conflict.

corporal punishment The purposeful use of harmful punishment to cause physical pain or discomfort to a child

maltreatment The emotional abuse, physical abuse, sexual abuse, or neglect of children; cruel or violent treatment causing suffering in children

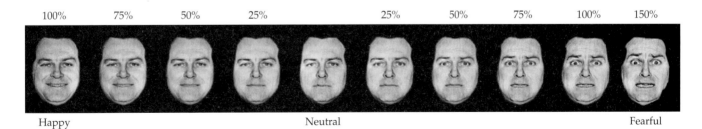

| 100% | 75% | 50% | 25% | | 25% | 50% | 75% | 100% | 150% |

Happy   Neutral   Fearful

FIGURE 13.4 Maltreatment and the detection of fear. When maltreated 8- to 15-year-old children are presented with a set of facial expressions that slowly morph from happy to fearful, they are quicker to detect the subtle signs of fear than children who are not maltreated. Images morphed happy with neutral (left four images) and neutral with fearful (right five images). Percentages are indicative of happy or fearful. (From C. L. Masten et al. 2008. *Child Abuse Neglect* 32: 139–153.)

Sibling Relationships

Siblings spend lots of time with one another, and their interactions vary from highly positive to outwardly negative and hostile. As a result, siblings can support or harm children's emotional development.

For the most part, warm and supportive sibling relationships relate to children's psychological and behavioral adjustment and help children cope with family stressors, such as high conflict between parents (Buist & Vermande, 2014; Dirks et al., 2015; Gass, Jenkins, & Dunn, 2007). But what about sibling conflict? Although conflict between siblings might appear to be harmful, it can actually yield important benefits. Sibling conflict allows children to develop social skills as they figure out how to assert their rights and justify their actions to someone close to them; it also teaches children about effective ways to respond to the emotions of others (Ross & Lazinski, 2014). Of course, problems arise when conflict between siblings escalates. Intense, frequent, and hostile forms of conflict between siblings can signal a dysfunctional relationship and lead to depression, anxiety, and problem behaviors in children (e.g., Dirks et al., 2015; Kim et al., 2007; Ostrov, Crick, & Stauffacher, 2006).

Sometimes, the quality of sibling relationships relates to children's emotional and social development in unlikely ways. That's because sibling age, family income, and level of problem behaviors all play a role. For example, when siblings have a close relationship, younger siblings are more likely to model the behaviors of their older siblings, including negative behaviors such as aggression, perhaps because they look up to their older siblings and want to be accepted by them. Thus, being close to an older sibling who engages in harmful behaviors can place younger children at risk (Dirks et al., 2015). For example, boys living in poverty who are close to their older brothers may engage in antisocial behaviors and associate with problem peers to copy the behaviors of their admired, older siblings (e.g., Criss & Shaw, 2005; Solmeyer, McHale, & Crouter, 2014).

✓ **CHECK YOUR UNDERSTANDING 13.6**

1. What are ways that parent and sibling relationships are found to support children's emotional development?

2. How do maltreated children respond to emotions compared to non-maltreated children?

Peer Context of Emotional Development

LEARNING OBJECTIVE 13.7 Describe the positive influence peers have on children's emotional development.

Peers figure prominently in children's emotional development. Peers provide norms around social behaviors and communicate messages about which emotions are okay to express, when, and to whom—that it's not alright, for example, to show envy over another child's achievement (Rubin, Bukowski, & Bowker, 2015). At the same time, peers allow children to express and validate their emotions in a safe setting. Close friends support each other by offering advice, reframing negative emotional experiences, and distracting their friends from overthinking negative experiences (Denham, 2007; Grotpeter & Crick, 1996). Just as seen for siblings, conflict with peers can promote emotional development by challenging children to regulate emotions such as anger, jealousy, and guilt.

✓ **CHECK YOUR UNDERSTANDING 13.7**

1. What are some of the ways that peers influence emotional development in middle childhood?

Cultural Context of Emotional Development

LEARNING OBJECTIVE 13.8 Provide examples of how cultures differ in the meaning of emotions and norms around emotions.

Through participation in community life, children learn norms and expectations around the meaning, expression, and regulation of emotions. Here, we consider cultural influences on children's emotional development.

Cultures Differ on the Meaning of Specific Emotions

Sometimes, we assume that certain emotions benefit children's development and that others cause harm. However, cultural messages shape views about emotions. Indeed, views around pride and shame are culture specific.

In many European American populations in the United States, pride is thought to signal and reinforce a person's accomplishments and is associated with well-adjusted children (Mesquita & Karasawa, 2004). This may be why many parents in these communities praise their children—to foster a sense of self-esteem in them—but rarely shame them, because shame is considered to damage well-being and might undermine a child's self-confidence (Ng, Pomerantz, & Lam, 2007).

In contrast, in communities that place great emphasis on interdependence, including many Asian communities, pride is viewed as undesirable because it separates the individual from the group, and it works against the valued emotion of humility. Conversely, in these communities, shame is thought to foster social engagement, conformity, and the motivation to improve (e.g., Mesquita & Karasawa, 2004). Children who feel ashamed of their school grades, for example, may work harder to do better. Notably, cultural values around pride and shame result in different outcomes in children in the United States and China. In the United States, feelings of pride and low levels of shame can lead to positive outcomes in children, whereas the reverse has been shown with children in China (Mascolo, Fischer, & Li, 2003).

Cultures Differ in Norms around Emotional Expression

Cultural communities also differ in what they consider to be acceptable ways to express emotions. Many Western cultural communities value the open expression of intense emotions, such as the high arousal that accompanies positive emotions like excitement (Tsai, 2007). In contrast, many non-Western cultures, including Chinese communities, expect children to subdue their emotions. For example, Chinese mothers value emotional restraint to foster the goal of group harmony (Luo, Tamis-LeMonda, & Song, 2013; Wang & Fivush, 2005).

The valuing of emotional restraint in Chinese cultures also extends to expressions of happiness. For example, in many U.S. communities, children are expected to show happiness when they receive a gift from another person, regardless of whether they like the gift, as a way to instill happiness in the gift giver (Wang, 2006). In line with these norms, in one study, U.S. children regulated their feelings of disappointment and displayed happiness when they received a disappointing gift, whereas Chinese children did not show as much happiness when receiving disappointing gifts (Garrett-Peters & Fox, 2007).

Norms around anger likewise illustrate cultural differences. Developmental scientist Pamela Cole studied cultural norms around anger in two ethnic groups in Nepal: Tamang and Brahman. The Brahman culture was more accepting of anger than was the Tamang culture, which believed anger should be suppressed. Tamang elders explained that a hallmark of social competence is never being angry, even when circumstances might provoke it. The Brahman did not share this view. When Cole presented children from the two communities with stories that contained emotional conflicts—such as being slapped for using someone's eraser—and asked them to report on how they would feel and react, children from the two communities responded in different ways. The Tamang children did not support anger as something a child should feel in a difficult social situation, whereas Brahman children did, although they also acknowledged that anger should be controlled (Cole & Tan, 2006; Cole, Bruschi, & Tamang, 2002).

In interpreting cultural views of anger, Cole surmised that spiritual beliefs may affect children's conceptions about what is appropriate to feel in socially charged situations. For instance, the Tamang follow a form of Tibetan Buddhism, which teaches that one's mind should remain calm and void of intense feelings (Cole et al., 2002). In this philosophy, anger is viewed to be a destructive human emotion that can interfere with inner peace and compassion toward others. In contrast, Brahman follow the Hindu caste system, where they hold a high social status that can be traced to a heritage of priestly scholars. This privilege might lead children to believe they are entitled to feel anger, a view shared by the U.S. children that Cole also studied. However, unlike U.S. children, although the Brahman children acknowledged that it was okay to feel anger, their emphasis on group harmony led them to keep their negative emotions inside. U.S. children, in contrast, were likely to endorse the outward expression of negative emotions as an appropriate way to assert their feelings.

✓ CHECK YOUR UNDERSTANDING 13.0

1. How are emotions such as pride and shame viewed in different cultures?
2. Give an example of how cultural context might affect children's emotional feelings or emotional expressions.

■ *Social Development*

The day my children stepped onto the bus to start elementary school, I knew that things would never be the same. As they sized up the children who joined them at the bus stop that first day, I watched the wheels of self-identity and social comparison turning. Over the years that followed, Brittany, Christopher, and Michael formulated and reformulated concepts about who they were and changed in their interactions with me and their friends. Although they boarded the same bus for several years, the consistency in their routine was deceptive. A slightly changed person returned home each day—the dependent kindergarten child who boarded the bus that first day of school had become an independent pre-adolescent by the last.

In the sections that follow, we examine key changes in social development over middle childhood. We will see that children elaborate and extend their self-identities to incorporate multiple psychological characteristics and social categories. As children expand their social identities, their social relationships change as well. Children grow in their independence and intensify their closeness with peers. As a result, family dynamics shift from one in which parents wield most of the power to one in which children increasingly have a say and peers gain in prominence.

Self-Identity Development

In contrast to the relatively immature self-concepts of young children, which tend to be one-dimensional and generally positive, school-age children's conceptions of the self are multifaceted (Harter, 2015). Yet, developmental changes to self-identity can be a double-edged sword. Children now compare themselves to other people, and because they are no longer protected by the egocentric and optimistic view that "I am and will always be the best" they are vulnerable to the opinions of their peers and the extent to which they are accepted (**FIGURE 13.5**). Moreover, children's views and attitudes about their own and others' social-group memberships—whether it be gender, ethnicity/race, or even school clubs and teams—are core features of their evolving self-identity. Children often question the meanings of those memberships in ways that affect how they act and treat others: "Am I a tomboy compared to the girls in my class?" or "I'm Asian, so does that mean I'm good at math?" or "Am I smarter, slower, funnier, moodier, and so forth than my friends?" Together, children's expanding understanding of the self and growing social relationships with friends can lead to different treatment of people in the "in-group" and "out-group," thereby spilling over into moral reasoning and behaviors.

FIGURE 13.5 Fitting in.   Children become increasingly vulnerable to the opinions of their peers and the extent to which they are accepted into social networks at school.

Erik Erikson's Theory

LEARNING OBJECTIVE 13.9 Describe how Erik Erikson's theory contributed to an understanding of identity development in middle childhood.

Erik Erikson (1950) viewed middle childhood as crucial to children's developing conceptions of self. According to Erikson, children must master the psychosocial conflict of **industry versus inferiority**. At this time in development, children have many opportunities to feel a sense of industry or accomplishment through their initiatives at school and in extracurricular activities. In cultures where schooling is not common or extensive, children experience a sense of industry through their contributions to family and village life. For example, in the Baka hunter-gatherer communities in Cameroon, children assist with hunting, fishing, fire making, and tending to siblings (Avis & Harris, 1991) (**FIGURE 13.6**).

Across cultural communities, children who feel supported and encouraged by those around them—including parents, relatives, friends, and teachers—begin to demonstrate industry by persisting at tasks to achieve their goals. Conversely, children who experience ridicule or punishment may develop feelings of inferiority and a resulting lack of motivation. Since the seminal contributions of Erik Erikson, developmental scientists have investigated the many facets and sources of children's developing self-identity.

industry versus inferiority
A psychosocial stage described by Erik Erikson in which children who exhibit industry develop a sense of mastery, such as when they feel a sense of accomplishment as they persist toward goals; alternatively, children may feel inferior and lack motivation when they do not attain their goals or are punished or ridiculed

✓ CHECK YOUR UNDERSTANDING 13.9

1. How might a school child resolve the tension between inferiority and industry, as described by Erikson?

Evaluating Self

LEARNING OBJECTIVE 13.10 Describe ways in which a child's sense of self-identity in middle childhood differs from that held in early childhood.

Recall that Piaget observed that children in the concrete-operational stage of development are able to consider the perspectives of other people. He attributed children's growing ability in perspective taking to decentration: Children

FIGURE 13.6 Industrious children in the Baka community in Cameroon.   In cultures where schooling is not common, such as the Baka hunter-gatherer communities in Cameroon, children experience a sense of industry through their contributions to family and village life, for example, by assisting with hunting, fishing, fire making, and tending to siblings. Here, Baka boys help to make ceremonial fiber crowns.

could now consider more than one dimension at a time to solve problems and reason about social situations (see Chapter 12). Children's decentration and broadening of perspectives likewise apply to how they think about themselves. As children move through middle childhood, their concept of self diverges from that of preschoolers in several key ways (Damon & Hart, 1988):

- *It's not all black-or-white.* Children decline in the use of extreme, all-or-nothing self-descriptions, "I'm the best!" and increase in descriptions that span multiple positive and negative traits and skills, "I'm a great basketball player, but only an average student at math."

- *What's inside matters too.* Children shift from a predominant emphasis on observable characteristics or behaviors, "I have dark hair and watch scary movies," to an emphasis on internal traits and personality dispositions, "I'm shy and anxious."

- *How do I compare?* As children develop, they increasingly compare themselves to peers from multiple social groups. A child might proclaim, "I am a fast runner compared to my close friends," but qualify the observation by noting, "But I'm not as fast as children on the track team." Social comparisons extend to many features of the self—internal and external, physical and psychological (Harter, 2015).

social comparison A child's judgement of their own traits, abilities, and behaviors compared to those of others

Researchers refer to the judgment of one's traits, abilities, and behaviors relative to other people as **social comparison** (Festinger, 1954; Ruble et al., 1980). Social comparisons increase with age and continue throughout life. Young children, around 4–6 years of age, are less likely to make social comparisons than are older children, and when they do, they tend to compare themselves to a single person, making it fairly easy to draw one-sided conclusions (usually very positive) about how good they are in certain areas. In contrast, older children compare themselves across several areas to a large number of people in a far-wider social network, such as children in their class, the school, and neighborhood (e.g., Harter, 2003, 2006). As a result, they are likely to conclude that they outshine their peers in some areas, but fall behind in others. As children's evaluations of their own skills in certain areas decline over the elementary school years, so does self-esteem (Wigfield et al., 1997).

How do children respond to declining self-evaluations? Children cleverly modify their views to protect their sense of self. They might, for instance, minimize the importance of certain areas relative to others, particularly those in which they perceive themselves to be weak. For example, a child who is good at sports, but not doing well in math, might rationalize, "I don't really care about math, so it doesn't matter that I don't do well" (Eccles et al., 2006). This reorganized thinking helps children maintain a positive sense of self. As a result, the dip in self-esteem seen in early elementary school rebounds from about fourth grade onward for most children (e.g., Cole et al., 2001; Impett et al., 2008).

✓ CHECK YOUR UNDERSTANDING 13.10

1. How does the process of social comparison affect self-identity development?

Gender Identity

LEARNING OBJECTIVE 13.11 Describe how children's understanding of gender stereotypes changes in middle childhood and why children grow in flexibility about gender during this period.

By the time children enter school, they have grown in their understanding of gender stereotypes and show declines in the gender-rigid behaviors that characterize early childhood (Halim, Bryant, & Zucker, 2016). As a result, children show flexibility in their beliefs about gender and begin to accept non-gendered

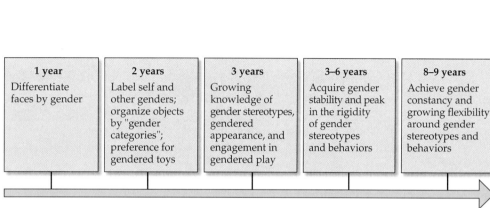

1 year	2 years	3 years	3–6 years	8–9 years
Differentiate faces by gender	Label self and other genders; organize objects by "gender categories"; preference for gendered toys	Growing knowledge of gender stereotypes, gendered appearance, and engagement in gendered play	Acquire gender stability and peak in the rigidity of gender stereotypes and behaviors	Achieve gender constancy and growing flexibility around gender stereotypes and behaviors

FIGURE 13.7 Gender constancy and flexibility.   Children become increasingly flexible in beliefs and behaviors in middle childhood, during the time when they achieve gender constancy.

behaviors in themselves and others (**FIGURE 13.7**). Still, in the context of growing flexibility, stereotypes persist and develop further with age, sometimes taking very subtle, implicit forms, as we will see.

Gender Stereotypes

Stereotypes around gender are beliefs, expectations, and norms held by cultural communities or societies about the characteristics or attributes of men and women, and boys and girls (Halim & Ruble, 2010). School-age children's stereotypes expand beyond the concrete stereotypes understood by preschoolers ("Girls like dolls and boys like trucks") to encompass a range of areas, including sports, school tasks, occupations, and traits (Sinno & Killen, 2009). By around 8 years of age, children connect different stereotypes to one another, enabling them to infer things about a person's traits, behaviors, and preferences based on limited information (Martin & Ruble, 2010). For example, older children (but not younger children) who were told that an unfamiliar child liked trucks, inferred that the child also liked airplanes, even in the absence of information about the unfamiliar child's gender (Martin, Wood, & Little, 1990). They apparently assumed the unlabeled child was a boy (or a girl, depending on the manipulation), and then generalized the child's likes or dislikes to other related things.

Knowledge about gender stereotypes also becomes stronger and more automatic in middle childhood compared to early childhood, as seen in children's reaction times to information that is congruent or incongruent with gender stereotypes. **Implicit association tests (IATs)** measure the strengths of associations people have between concepts. In general, these tests assess whether people's reaction times to certain expected pairings—for instance, an old person and a wheelchair if testing the stereotype of age—are faster than their reactions to other unexpected pairings—a young person and a wheelchair.

In developmental science, IATs can be used to evaluate the strength of children's automatic stereotypes around gender and race. To illustrate, children ages 5, 8, and 11 were instructed to assign stereotyped toys as quickly as possible to boys and girls in a computer task. In the "congruent condition," children were told that, "Sarah likes dolls, doll houses, doll clothes, and other doll items, but Marc prefers cars, trucks, and tools." When a toy appeared on the computer screen, the child had to press the left key to give it to Sarah, or the right key to

implicit association tests (IATs) Experiments that measure the strengths of individuals' unconscious evaluations or stereotypes (e.g., underlying implicit beliefs in boys' and men's and girls' and women's mathematical abilities) based on reaction times to information that is consistent or inconsistent with certain stereotypes (e.g., an elderly person in a wheelchair versus a younger person in a wheelchair)

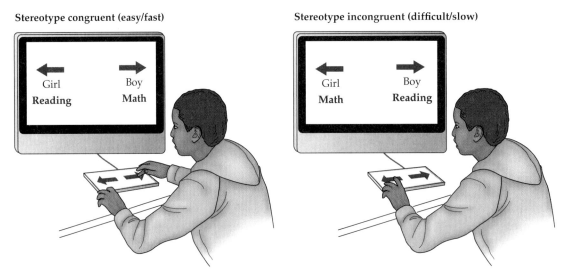

Stereotype congruent (easy/fast) Stereotype incongruent (difficult/slow)

FIGURE 13.8 Implicit association tests for gender stereotypes around math. When children are asked to press a button in response to a pairing that is congruent with stereotypes, such as boys and math, they display faster reaction times than when the word pairs are incongruent with stereotypes, such as boys and reading. (After D. Cvencek et al. 2011. *Child Dev* 82: 766–779. © 2011 The Authors. Child Development © 2011 Society for Research in Child Development, Inc. All rights reserved.)

give it to Marc. On "incongruent trials," children assigned toys to Pierre and Isabella, whose preferences conflicted with gender stereotypes (Pierre liked dolls and Isabella liked trucks). Children's reaction times were slower on the incongruent trials than on the congruent trials indicating an automatic tendency to respond in line with gender stereotypes (Banse et al., 2010).

Implicit association tests have been used to study gender stereotypes about math skills as well (Cvencek, Meltzoff, & Greenwald, 2011). The reaction times of children between 6 and 10 years of age were measured in response to statements reflecting math stereotypes and math self-concepts, such as "boys are better in math than are girls," and "I'm good at math." By second grade, children already had embraced the stereotype that math is for boys, and boys identified with math more strongly than did girls on the implicit and self-report measures (**FIGURE 13.8**).

The power of gender stereotypes in children's math performance becomes evident in studies where gender is made salient to children (Neuville & Croizet, 2007). Half of third graders were assigned to an experimental group where girls were instructed to color a picture of a girl holding a doll and boys were instructed to color a picture of a boy holding a ball. Children in the control group were given a gender-neutral task: to color a landscape. Following the drawing exercise, children in both groups completed math problems. Girls in the experimental group (who had colored gender-stereotyped pictures) solved fewer difficult math problems than did girls in the control group. Interestingly, boys were not affected by coloring gender-stereotyped pictures, perhaps because their gender does not psychologically threaten their feelings about their math performance given stereotypes that boys excel in math relative to girls.

Gender Stereotypes Concerning Status and Occupation

Gender stereotypes can exist at various levels of concreteness or abstractness. For example, the stereotype that "dolls are for girls and trucks are for boys" is more concrete and observable than are stereotypes around abstract concepts such as status, respect, and power. Children acquire abstract stereotypes during middle childhood, such as the views that men are superior to women, have higher status, and elicit more respect from others than do women. Such stereotypes are seen in children's personal views of gender—**private regard**—and perceptions of how other people view gender—**public regard**. For example, children between 7 and 15 years of age increase in the belief that men are granted more power and respect than are women (Neff, Cooper, & Woodruff, 2007).

Children also develop an understanding that occupations of men and women differ in status and power. At around 6 years of age, children begin to believe that male-typical occupations, such as executive and engineer, are higher in status than are female-typical occupations, such as teacher and nurse. By 11 years of age, if not sooner, this understanding extends to fictitious jobs that researchers made up. When researchers told 11-year-old children that a fictitious job was for men, children classified the job as being higher in status than a fictitious job labeled for women (Liben, Bigler, & Krogh, 2001). Moreover, children 6–11 years of age showed greater interest in same-gender fictitious jobs that were described as being for men or for women (Hayes, Bigler, & Weisgram, 2018).

Why are male-dominated jobs considered to be of higher status than female-dominated jobs? School-aged children increasingly understand that discrimination may result in differences in occupational status (**FIGURE 13.9**). When asked why only men had become president of the United States, only 30% of children 5–10 years of age mentioned discrimination. Older children, however, were much more likely than younger children to suggest that the absence of women U.S. presidents might be attributed to discrimination (Bigler et al., 2008).

FIGURE 13.9 Occupation stereotypes. In middle childhood, children increasingly understand that differences in the occupational status of men and women may be due to societal discrimination.

private regard A person's views about their gender

public regard A person's views about how others view gender

Gender-Stereotype Flexibility

Children become increasingly flexible in their behaviors and views around gender stereotypes during middle childhood (Ruble et al., 2007). They accept the idea of a man cooking and a woman taking out the garbage, for example, rather than viewing such behaviors as "only" for men or "only" for women (Halim & Ruble, 2010). However, as seen in the implicit association tests described previously (Banse et al., 2010), stereotypes do not disappear with age. Rather, children continue to be aware of gender stereotypes, and more quickly process stereotypical information than counter-stereotypical information as they get older, even though they may become more open minded.

Children's classification skills, a cognitive ability that grows during childhood, may help explain children's increased flexibility around gender stereotypes. For example, if a child has difficulty understanding that the same person or object can be grouped into more than one category simultaneously (such as a set of blocks can be grouped by size and then by color), the child may be particularly susceptible to rigid stereotypic beliefs around gender. Indeed, 6- to 10-year-old children with advanced classification skills were less influenced by gender stereotypes dealing with occupations than were children with low classification skills (Bigler, 1995). Moreover, training children to classify objects along multiple dimensions helped them to remember information that ran counter to stereotypes and to have more egalitarian beliefs around gender (Bigler & Liben, 1992).

Still, although children increase in their gender-stereotype flexibility with age, they fall short in fully accepting peers who engage in "other-gender behaviors." Children victimize and reject peers who do not behave in typically gendered ways (Zosuls et al., 2016). Rejection by peers may explain why children who engage in other-gender behaviors report low satisfaction with their social relationships and low self-esteem, particularly when they feel high pressure to conform to gender stereotypes (Carver, Yunger, & Perry, 2003; Halim & Ruble, 2010).

The Affective Dimension of Gender Identity

Developmental scientists distinguish between children's knowledge of gender stereotypes—a cognitive component—and their affective evaluations of their own and others' gender—an emotional component. To study affective attitudes around gender, scientists might ask children how positively or negatively they feel toward unfamiliar girls and boys presented in pictures. Such studies indicate strong in-group favoritism, with girls reporting more positive evaluations toward girls and boys reporting more positive evaluations toward boys (Halim & Ruble, 2010; Martin & Ruble, 2010). For example, a female child might refer to other girls as more honest, friendly, and fun than boys.

However, favoritism toward children of the same sex does not necessarily imply that a child feels negativity toward members of the opposite sex (Martin & Ruble, 2010). Researchers asked fifth graders about how much they liked their own- and other-sex peers. Although children favored members of the same sex over those of the opposite sex, they were not more negative toward the out-group relative to the in-group (Zosuls et al., 2011). Therefore, it would be wrong to assume that school-aged children who enjoy hanging out with same-sex peers dislike members of the opposite sex.

✓ CHECK YOUR UNDERSTANDING 13.11

1. What is an implicit association test (IAT)? Give an example of how an IAT can be used to assess the degree to which children hold certain gender stereotypes.

2. How do you suppose children acquire the belief that jobs typically held by men are higher in status than those held by women?

3. What evidence is there for gender-stereotype flexibility in middle childhood, and what factors might explain children's increased gender-stereotype flexibility at this time?

4. How might researchers distinguish between children's knowledge of gender stereotypes and their affective evaluations of their own and others' gender?

Ethnic and Racial Identities

LEARNING OBJECTIVE 13.12 Outline changes in the development of ethnic and racial identity in middle childhood.

Gender is only one aspect of a child's identity. Recall from Chapter 10 that by 3 years of age, children can identify different racial categories and can name their own ethnicity, but they have a limited understanding of what ethnicity means. In middle childhood, children's understanding of race and ethnicity grows. On the positive side, most children develop positive attitudes toward their ethnicity and celebrate their cultural customs through holidays, foods, music, and language. However, in-group pride and loyalty can sometimes lead to out-group hostility. Indeed, news headlines remind us that conflicts among children and adolescents from different ethnic backgrounds plague schools and neighborhoods on a daily basis.

Researchers have long recognized that children are highly susceptible to intergroup divisiveness. In 1954, social psychologist Muzafer Sherif conducted a landmark study that revealed how children's membership in a randomly assigned group can lead to prejudice and discrimination toward out-group members (Sherif, 1988). He took 22 eleven-year-old boys, none of whom knew one another, to a summer camp in Robbers Cave State Park, Oklahoma. He separated the boys into two groups and housed them in separate cabins, where they bonded with their cabin mates. Neither group came in contact with or knew about the others' existence for the first week of camp. A week later, the boys were introduced and quickly engaged in intergroup verbal abuse. The experimenters organized a set of competitive activities between the two groups, which resulted in escalating intergroup conflict and hostility to the point where the boys refused to eat in the same room. Toward the end of the camp session, the experimenters introduced teamwork exercises to encourage the groups to cooperate. Over time, the intergroup conflict diminished and the boys got along.

The Robbers Cave State Park study spotlights how readily children emotionally connect with peers of the same group while rejecting those of a different group, even when the group is based on a superficial separation. It also provides an optimistic glimpse into how social prejudices can be overcome through cooperation and collaboration. Over the past 60 years, researchers have acquired a deeper understanding of why and how social affinities and separations occur within and between ethnic groups, and how ethnic identity and intergroup relationships change over developmental time.

Developing Ethnic and Racial Identities

Ethnic identity refers to an individual's sense of belonging to an ethnic, or cultural, group, and thinking, feelings, and behavior regarding membership in that group (Rotheram & Phinney, 1987; Verkuyten, 2018). Racial identity similarly refers to an individual's sense of group membership, this time in terms of race. A child's ethnic and racial identities and associated attitudes toward members of the in-group and out-group increase in salience during childhood and may be especially important to children who are in the numerical minority.

During middle childhood, children understand that their ethnic and racial identities will remain with them always (Ocampo, Knight, & Bernal, 1997). With this growing understanding, children increasingly reflect on the meaning of ethnicity over the childhood years and into adolescence. For example, what does it mean to be a Dominican in one's community? U.S. children aged 6–12 from Cambodian, Dominican, and Portuguese backgrounds accurately labeled their family's nationality of origin and expressed strong ethnic pride in their heritage (Marks et al., 2007). However, older children were more likely than younger children to explore their ethnic identity, moving beyond merely knowing their ethnicity to thinking deeply about what their ethnicity meant to them.

Notably, most research on children's developing ethnic or racial identity has focused on the experiences of monoracial children, which ignores the growing population of children from mixed racial backgrounds. The biracial population of children under 18 years of age born to parents from different racial groups is the fastest growing youth group in the United States (Nishina & Witkow, 2020). Research on the identity development of biracial children shows that they have a fluid racial identity. They identify with the race of both parents, but shift their identity depending on context (Gaither et al., 2014).

Ethnic and Racial Stereotypes

Stereotypes about members of different ethnicities and races are prevalent in all societies. Consider common racial and ethnic stereotypes in the United States such as "White men can't jump," "African Americans are good athletes," "Asians are good at math and science," "Italians love to cook," and so forth. School-age children are incessantly exposed to stereotypes through social media, television, and conversations in homes, schools, and neighborhoods. To what extent do children endorse those messages?

Developmental scientist Stephanie Rowley and colleagues set out to examine race (and gender) stereotypes in fourth-, sixth- and eighth-grade White

ethnic identity An individual's sense of belonging to an ethnic or cultural group, in addition to thoughts, feelings, and behaviors regarding group membership and Black children. They found that children's endorsement of negative and positive stereotypes about their group depended on group status (Rowley et al., 2007). Children reported on their perceptions of the competence of Black and White female and male children in academic domains, sports, and music. Children in so-called "high-status" groups based on many social structures and stereotypes (White and male children) endorsed the most traditional stereotypes, whether negative or positive, for their social group. In contrast, children in low-status groups (Black children and girls) were likely to endorse stereotypes that favored their social group, and did not endorse those that reflected negatively on their group. Status effects became more pronounced with age, suggesting that children become increasingly aware of and more likely to reject the harmful effects of negative stereotypes. However, the harm of stereotypes is not something that can easily be cast off.

Attitudes toward the In-Group and Out-Group

How do children feel about members of their ethnicity or race relative to outsiders? Much contemporary research aligns with findings of the Robbers Cave State Park study: Children affiliate with members of the in-group and sometimes reject those of the out-group, although the pattern shows some change with development. Children aged 7–8 in both the numerical majority and minority show in-group favoritism, in line with their growing understanding of ethnic identity (Neadale et al., 2005; Ruble et al., 2004), although some minority children demonstrate an out-group preference, perhaps because of status differences in society (Corenblum, 2003). In contrast, out-group attitudes in the form of **prejudice**, a negative, preconceived opinion about someone of a particular group, show an inverted U-shaped pattern: Prejudice peaks around 5–7 years of age, followed by a slight decrease through late childhood (8–10 years) (**FIGURE 13.10**). This U-shaped pattern was shown in a meta-analysis of over 100 studies of children's attitudes around ethnicity and race (Raabe & Beelmann, 2011).

prejudice A negative, preconceived opinion about someone based on that person's membership in a specific group (e.g., such as a group defined by gender, race, ethnicity)

Although all children change in their attitudes toward the ethnic in-group and out-group, individual children vary substantially in those attitudes. And, their attitudes may be influenced by how strongly they identify with their ethnicity. U.S. children ages 6–12 from Cambodian, Dominican, and Portuguese backgrounds who had a strong ethnic identity held positive attitudes toward both the in-group and the out-group (Marks et al., 2007). The researchers concluded that feeling good about one's cultural heritage instills positive feelings toward people from other backgrounds.

Awareness of Bias

Do children from different ethnic and racial backgrounds perceive biased behaviors in others? Perceptions of ethnic bias vary with how much children view their ethnicity as central to their identity. Children from numerical minorities often view ethnicity to be central to their self-identity (Garcia Coll et al., 1996). The centrality of ethnicity may result in high attentiveness toward biases directed toward their group. For example, African American and Hispanic children may be more aware of ethnic bias than White European American children. In contrast, White European American children are more likely to perceive gender bias compared to their peers from ethnic minorities (Brown et al., 2011). Thus, children may be highly attuned to and aware of the categories of identity that are most relevant to them.

Fortunately, racial bias in children diminishes when they are exposed to positive examples of out-group members.

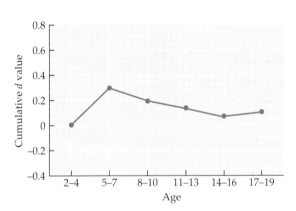

FIGURE 13.10 Patterns of prejudice in middle childhood. A graph of prejudicial attitudes seen in middle childhood has an inverted U-shaped pattern. There is a peak in prejudice around 5–7 years of age followed by a slight decrease through late childhood (8–10 years). The d value is a statistic that depicts the magnitude of the prejudice effect. (After T. Raabe and A. Beelmann. 2011. *Child Dev* 82: 1715–1737. © 2011 The Authors. Child Development © 2011 Society for Research in Child Development, Inc. All rights reserved.)

Researchers presented 10-year-old White children with stories and pictures that depicted positive characteristics of Black individuals, including descriptions of how hard the individuals work to help others. Children's initial pro-White biases diminished relative to a control group of children who were exposed simply to pictures and stories about different types of flowers (Gonzalez, Steele, & Baron, 2017). Moreover, when researchers presented children with puppets who did or did not cooperate with puppets from an "out-group," children later chose to "be friends" with the puppets who acted cooperatively and displayed no out-group bias (Gonzalez-Gadea et al., 2020). Thus, although children may be aware of biases, and sometimes display biases themselves, they favor positive treatment of out-group members over biased and negative behaviors.

✓ CHECK YOUR UNDERSTANDING 13.12

1. Why does in-group pride and loyalty sometimes lead to out-group hostility?
2. Does having a strong ethnic identity lead to prejudice toward other groups? What evidence supports your answer?

Intergroup Relations and Moral Development

LEARNING OBJECTIVE 13.13 Explain how in-group loyalty may lead to moral dilemmas.

Prejudice, discrimination, and preferences for the in-group—whether based on gender, race, ethnicity, or other characteristics—naturally spark questions about morality. Are children more likely to treat children who are like them fairly, but to act less morally toward outsiders, akin to what was seen in the Robbers Cave State Park study? For the most part, the verdict is optimistic: Children reason and behave morally across many situations, and moral judgments often trump in-group favoritism. For example, when researchers present children with stories that contain moral dilemmas, children view excluding a child from an activity because of skin color or because of membership in an out-group to be unfair (Hitti et al., 2014; Killen et al., 2002).

What is perhaps most encouraging is that children use moral principles to judge peoples' behaviors, even in situations where in-group favoritism stands in opposition to moral behaviors. For example, children were assigned to a "diamond team" and asked to judge fictitious peers from the in-group diamond team or an out-group "star team" who acted morally or immorally (Abrams & Rutland, 2008). Moral team members were described as taking turns, not hurting the feelings of players on the other team, and so forth. In contrast, immoral team members were described as pushing, being selfish, hurting others, and not helping children on the other team. Children were then asked how much they liked each of the team members and were instructed to distribute vouchers to members of both teams. Children liked the moral team members more than they did the immoral team members, and allocated more vouchers to out-group members who adhered to moral principles than to in-group members who rejected moral principles. Thus, moral behaviors were viewed to be more important than group membership. Children were also more favorable toward group members who advocated for equal allocation of resources across groups than toward group members who chose to keep more resources for their own group (Killen et al., 2013). In fact, children stated that it would be okay to exclude members who wanted to distribute resources unequally, even though they viewed excluding members from a group to be wrong otherwise (Hitti et al., 2014).

Nonetheless, children sometimes find it challenging to make moral decisions in intergroup contexts. They may forego equitable treatment in favor of supporting members of their group (Killen et al., 2013; Mulvey & Killen, 2015).

It is also presumably easier for children to express high moral principles when asked to reason about or behave toward fictitious characters than it is for them to act morally in real life situations, where the tensions and pressures from in-group peers may be strong.

As a caution, it would be simplistic to view in-group loyalty as wrong. Such loyalties are fundamental to human connection, and arise from the attachments we develop with the people we care about. The problems with in-group loyalty occur when alliances overcome basic dignity and respect of other people, and lead to discrimination and harmful behaviors ranging from the relatively mundane, such as not sharing with members of the out-group, to extreme emotional or physical harm.

✓ **CHECK YOUR UNDERSTANDING 13.13**

1. Offer an example of when children consider moral behaviors more important than group loyalty.

Contexts of Self-Identity Development

Where do stereotypes about gender, race, and so forth come from? How do children learn about their own and outside groups? Family, peer, and media contexts convey influential messages about what boys and girls of different ethnic and racial backgrounds should do, can do, and will do.

Family Context and Gender Self-Identity

LEARNING OBJECTIVE 13.14 Discuss some of the gendered messages that parents convey to children through their attitudes.

Parents and other adults vary in their endorsement of traditional gender boundaries, such as women taking care of housework and men working outside the home, and how much they agree with statements like "sons in a family should be given more help to go to college than daughters." Gendered attitudes in turn influence children's views around gender (Crouter et al., 2007).

Some of the first studies of gendered stereotypes were documented in the area of children's abilities in math. In one investigation, parents of children in kindergarten through third grade believed that math was more important for boys than for girls, and parents with the strongest gender stereotypes also exhibited biased perceptions of their children's math skills (Eccles, Jacobs, & Harold, 1990). By the time the children reached sixth grade, parents believed that their boys had more natural talent in math, anticipated greater future success in math occupations for their boys than their girls, and rated math as more difficult for girls than for boys. Parents from Japan and Germany likewise expressed gendered stereotypes around math (Lummis & Stevenson, 1990; Tiedemann, 2000).

Unfortunately, stereotypes around children's math competencies continue to reflect a gender bias (Gunderson et al., 2012). A longitudinal study of over 300 children, followed from kindergarten through fifth grade, found that third grade girls rated their math competencies lower than did boys, even though they did not differ in their math achievement. Parents of boys also rated their third and fifth graders' math competencies higher than did parents of girls, and parents' ratings predicted children's estimates of their own math skills (Herbert & Stipek, 2005).

Beyond communicating gendered expectations, parents communicate anxiety around math to their children. Parents who experience math anxiety themselves negatively affect their children's math attitudes, sense of math

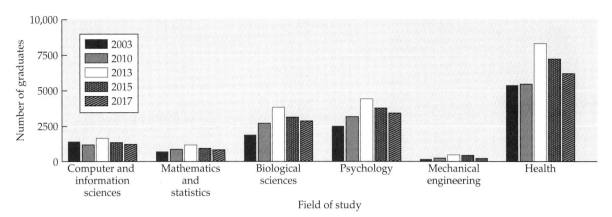

FIGURE 13.11 Women's entry into science-related fields.   There has been little change over the past decades in the type of science majors women pursue. Women dominate in health-related fields and fields such as psychology but are underrepresented in the fields of engineering, math, and biological and computer sciences. Bars represent the number of females graduating with degrees in the respective fields, showing their underrepresentation relative to overall graduates. (Data from NCSES/ NSF. 2019. National Survey of College Graduates. Alexandria, VA: National Center for Science and Engineering Statistics [NCSES]/National Science Foundation [NSF].)

self-efficacy, and math performance, with the strongest associations seen for mothers and their daughters. Thus, mothers who feel anxious about their math abilities are likely to transmit those feelings to their girls, perpetuating a cycle of gender disparities (Casad, Hale, & Wachs, 2015). In turn, gendered attitudes around math may play out in the college majors and ultimate careers pursued by men and women (**FIGURE 13.11**).

✓ **CHECK YOUR UNDERSTANDING 13.14**

1. How does socialization contribute to the belief that boys have more aptitude for math than do girls?

Family and School Contexts and Racial and Ethnic Self-Identity

LEARNING OBJECTIVE 13.15 Describe how parents' messages around race and ethnicity change in middle childhood and how school might affect a child's racial and ethnic identities.

Children learn a lot about race from their families, both directly and indirectly. As children move from early childhood to middle childhood and adolescence, they grow in their cognitive skills, social experiences, and exploration around racial identity. In response to these changes, parents may intensify their messages about race, particularly when their children perceive unfair treatment by peers or teachers (Hughes et al., 2006). Black parents of third, fourth, and fifth graders who perceived that their children were being unfairly treated by an adult because of race prepared their children for bias and discrimination and warned their children about intergroup relationships by promoting mistrust of others.

Children's experiences in school and neighborhoods also affect their ethnic identity and attitudes in powerful ways. In fact, it should come as no surprise that explicit ethnic labeling of peers, teachers, and people can cause children to perceive division among those from different backgrounds. Simply labeling someone as being from a certain group, even if the comment is neutral, can lead to prejudice and divisions among groups (Bigler & Liben,

FIGURE 13.12 Pressures to conform to gender expectations can come from the community, the family, and peers. In the film *Wadjda*, a Saudi girl signs up for her school's Koran recitation competition as a way to raise the funds to buy a forbidden bicycle.

2007). Developmental scientist Becky Bigler revealed the power of labels when she randomly assigned students aged 7–12 to two different groups in a summer school program. One group wore yellow t-shirts, the other blue. Posters of unfamiliar yellow- or blue-group members decorated the walls, depicting yellow-group members as winning more medals, competitions, and so forth, relative to blue-group members. Teachers, however, said nothing about the pictures and did not express different expectations of the two groups. Teachers referred to the groups merely for organizing class activities, as in, "Blue students line up on the left; yellow students line up on the right." Yellow-group children ultimately perceived their group as superior to the blue group (that is, yellow-group kids developed an in-group bias), whereas the blue-group children perceived their group as lower in status (Bigler, Brown, & Markell, 2001). The finding that a relatively simple experimental manipulation can lead to biased attitudes toward members of the out-group underscores the commanding influences of schools and peer groups on children's feelings of self-worth and self-identity.

✓ **CHECK YOUR UNDERSTANDING 13.15**

1. How might a parent implicitly initiate racial distrust and/or bias in their children?
2. Describe a study that shows how labeling children as belonging to social groups can backfire to create biased attitudes.

Peer and Media Contexts and Gender Self-Identity

LEARNING OBJECTIVE 13.16 Describe ways that peers and messages communicated on television and media affect children's gendered behaviors.

TABLE 13.2 ■ Findings from an analysis of 1,200 popular films from 2007 to 2018

- In 2007, only 30% of speaking characters were women, with only 33% of speaking characters being women in 2018.

- In 2018, 29% of female actors wore sexually revealing clothes (as opposed to 7% of men).

- 27% of female actors got partially naked (compared to 7% of men).

- Only 12% of films featured a balanced cast of female-to-male characters

Source: After S. L. Smith et al. 2020. Inequality in 1,300 Popular Films: Examining Portrayals of Gender, Race/Ethnicity, LGBTQ & Disability from 2007 to 2019. USC Annenberg Inclusion Initiative.

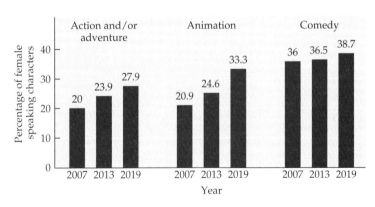

FIGURE 13.13 Influence of media on reinforcing traditional gender roles. When the dialogue for films is broken down by gender, men speak an astounding number of more words than do women across all types of films, reinforcing the importance of men in society relative to women. (After S. L. Smith et al. 2020. Inequality in 1,300 Popular Films: Examining Portrayals of Gender, Race/Ethnicity, LGBTQ & Disability from 2007 to 2019. USC Annenberg Inclusion Initiative.)

Children often feel pressured by friends to accept that boys and girls should act in certain ways. Peers' negative reactions to gender norm violations and segregation into same-sex peer groups send impactful messages about so-called acceptable behaviors. When boys play with boys, they learn how boys "should act" (tough and unemotional in many communities) and are teased when they reject these standards. In this way, peers can perpetuate and reinforce gender biases that home settings put into motion (**FIGURE 13.12**).

However, the effects of peer norms on children's gendered behaviors are complex, and may depend on the gender composition of children's social networks. Researchers investigated negative peer treatment and same-sex and cross-sex friendships in relation to gender conformity of 9-year-old children. They found that peer harassment led to decreases in gender atypical behaviors by boys, but only for boys who had many male friends. The same harassment led to boys increasing behaviors that were gender atypical if they had many female friends and few male friends (Lee & Troop-Gordon, 2011).

Children also spend a lot of time watching television and movies that teach and reinforce traditional gender roles (**TABLE 13.2**; **FIGURE 13.13**). For example, characters on primetime television are more likely to be men than women; young women are often depicted as submissive, sexually provocative, and concerned about their looks; and children's movies are populated with appearance-related messages of women being thin and men being muscular (Gerding & Signoriefli, 2014; Harriger et al., 2018; Sink & Mastro, 2017). Such messages feed into children's perceptions of men as more powerful and of higher status than women, and may feed into the sexual objectification of women (Halim et al., 2014) (**FIGURE 13.14**).

✓ **CHECK YOUR UNDERSTANDING 13.16**

1. How might the gender composition of friendship networks affect children's willingness to display gender atypical behaviors?
2. How is gender bias perpetuated by the media? How might parents and teachers compensate for this?

Women: Men:
28.3%   8%

Percentage of characters in family films wearing sexy attire by gender

FIGURE 13.14 Children's movies often feed into gendered stereotypes.   Children's movies often show girls and women as being thin and boys and men being muscular or girls and women being damsels in distress. These messages feed into school-aged children's perceptions of men as more powerful and of higher status than women, and may feed into the sexual objectification of women. (Data from S. L. Smith et al. 2013. Gender Roles & Occupations: A Look at Character Attributes and Job-Related Aspirations in Film and Television. Geena Davis Institute on Gender in Media.)

Relationships with Parents

Relationships with parents undergo marked change during middle childhood. Parents must learn to strike a balance between setting expectations and appropriate limits and allowing their children to fully express their opinions and emotions (Grusec & Hastings, 2014). So, although the child-parent attachment relationship remains central, it takes a very different form as children grow in autonomy.

Attachment

LEARNING OBJECTIVE 13.17   Provide evidence on the importance of children's attachment to parents in middle childhood.

Child-parent attachment relationships shift in fundamental ways across middle childhood. In one longitudinal study, school-age children reported on their attachment to their parents, including the degree to which their parents were responsive and available and how much they relied on their parents during stressful times. Although children's perceptions of their parents' availability did not change with age, children became less reliant on their parents as attachment figures to help them deal with stressful situations. Thus, children remain close to their parents even as they grow in their independence and seek to figure things out for themselves (Collins, Madsen, & Susman-Stillman, 2005; Kerns, Tomich, & Kim, 2006).

Notably, children with positive emotional relationships with their parents demonstrate positive psychological and behavioral adjustment. In contrast, children with insecure attachments in middle childhood are more likely to develop internalizing problems such as anxiety and depression than are children with secure attachments (Brumariu & Kerns, 2010). A meta-analysis of child-parent attachment relationships across 165 studies, many including fathers, showed that avoidant, ambivalent, and/or disorganized attachments (forms of insecure attachment; see Chapter 7) predicted internalizing and externalizing problems in children (Madigan et al., 2016). Indeed, the child-father relationship, which is too often missing from the literature on parenting, is vitally important to children's emotional and social development (Cabrera, Volling, & Barr 2018). Children who have regular contact and connection with their fathers are better able to regulate their emotions than are children who have little contact and connection with their fathers (Vogel et al., 2006). Additionally, fathers' sensitivity and supportiveness relate to children's social competence and quality of friendships at school (e.g., Cabrera et al., 2011; McDowell & Parke, 2009), perhaps because children model the positive behaviors of their fathers in interactions with other children, and further because children gain a sense of confidence and security from sharing a high-quality relationship with their fathers.

✓ CHECK YOUR UNDERSTANDING 13.17

1. Which type of attachment relationships between children and parents have been found to relate to later internalizing and externalizing behaviors?

Parenting Styles

LEARNING OBJECTIVE 13.18 Describe the four parenting styles identified by Baumrind and their associations to child development.

Parents help guide their children toward expected behaviors, and often do so by monitoring their children's activities and whereabouts. **Monitoring** refers to parents' awareness of their children's activities, friends, and peer groups, including efforts to keep track of what's going on in children's lives (Dishion & McMahon, 1998; Holden, 2010). A lack of parental monitoring places children at risk for problem behaviors, particularly as autonomy increases in late childhood and into adolescence (Smetana, 2008).

The degree to which parents engage in parental monitoring reflects their parenting styles. Developmental scientists sometimes classify parenting styles along a spectrum from "permissive" to "authoritarian" to "neglectful." How do differences in parenting styles ultimately impact children? Over 50 years ago, Diana Baumrind conducted some of the most influential studies on parents' childrearing styles in relation to children's developmental outcomes (Baumrind, 1967, 1991). Through ratings of various aspects of parenting, including warmth and control, Baumrind identified four distinct styles of parenting: (**FIGURE 13.15**).

- *Authoritarian parents are low in warmth/responsiveness and high in control/demandingness.* Authoritarian parents expect children to be obedient and follow instructions. They do not explain to children why rules are implemented or permit children to negotiate. Children of authoritarian parents experience low autonomy, tend to be quiet and obedient, and sometimes suffer from low self-esteem, depression, and low social competence. The aggressive tactics used by authoritarian parents may reinforce aggressive and impulsive behaviors in children.

monitoring Caregiver awareness of children's activities, friends, and peer groups, including efforts to keep track of what's going on in children's lives

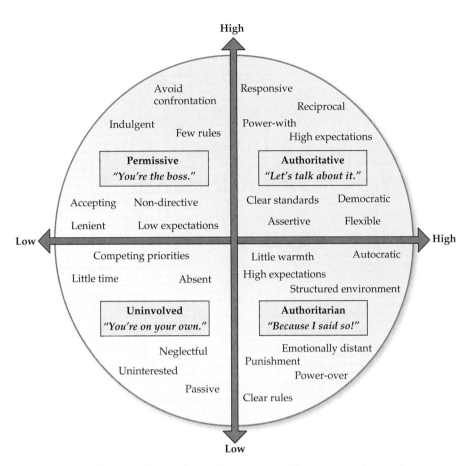

FIGURE 13.15 Baumrind's typology of parenting.   The typology focused on two dimensions—warmth/responsiveness and control, strictness/demandingness. This yields four types of parents, represented in each of the quadrants along with the features of each type. Parental warmth is represented by the vertical line, ranging from low (bottom) to high (top). Parental control is represented by the horizontal line, ranging from low (left) to high (right). (After G. Stuart. Sustaining Community. February 4, 2015. https://sustainingcommunity.wordpress.com/2015/02/04/ what-are-parenting-styles/.)

- *Permissive parents are low in control/demandingness and high in warmth/ responsiveness.* Permissive parents allow children to do whatever they want. These parents often interact with their children as "friends" rather than as parents. They display little discipline, and do not expect their children to follow rules or regulate their behaviors. When children of permissive parents grow up, they tend to demonstrate immature, inappropriate behaviors and have difficulty controlling impulses.

- *Uninvolved parents are low in both control/demandingness and warmth/ responsiveness.* Uninvolved parents are disengaged, uninterested in their children's lives, and rarely respond to children's emotional needs. They do not place demands or expectations on their children, although they do provide children with basic needs, such as food and a place to live. Children of uninvolved parents are at risk of adjustment problems. They may become emotionally withdrawn and unfulfilled in their emotional needs.

- *Authoritative parents are high in both control/demandingness and warmth/ responsiveness.* Authoritative parents are sensitive to their children's needs and allow them some autonomy and say in decisions. Authoritative parents foster their children's independence and balance the use

TABLE 13.3 ■ Effects of parenting styles on children

Parenting style	Description of parent	Child outcome
Authoritative (high warmth/high control)	Parents are sensitive to their children's needs and allow them some autonomy and say in decisions.	Children are more likely to do well academically and socially.
Permissive (high warmth/low control)	Parents allow children to do whatever they want.	Children tend to demonstrate immature, inappropriate behaviors and have difficulty controlling impulses.
Authoritarian (low warmth/high control)	Parents expect children to be obedient and follow instructions.	Children experience low autonomy; tend to be quiet and obedient; and sometimes suffer from low self-esteem, depression, and low social competence.
Uninvolved (low warmth/low control)	Parents are disengaged, uninterested in their children's lives, and rarely respond to children's emotional needs.	Children are at risk of adjustment problems; they may become emotionally withdrawn and unfulfilled in their emotional needs.

of reasoning and discipline. Children of authoritative parents are more likely than those of authoritarian and permissive parents to do well academically and socially.

Although Baumrind's work was conducted several decades ago, it continues to be highly influential. The social and cognitive benefits of authoritative parenting styles and the adverse consequences of authoritarian parenting have been well documented (e.g., Larzelere, Morris, & Harrist, 2013) (**TABLE 13.3**). Some developmentalists focus on specific components of parenting, such as support, warmth, and control, rather than categorizing parents as acting one way or another. Such research likewise shows that parental warmth and support predict children's prosocial behaviors, social competence, and popularity (Eisenberg, Fabes, & Spinrad, 2006). In contrast, controlling, harsh, and punitive parenting, including hitting children, rejection, and criticism, can lead to social withdrawal, anxiety, and aggression (e.g., Barber, 2002; Booth-LaForce et al., 2012; Hastings et al., 2010; Lewis-Morrarty et al., 2012).

Some of Baumrind's findings have generated controversy. Most centrally, her taxonomy of parenting was originally developed with White European American families and may not apply to families from different racial and ethnic backgrounds. A highly cited study found that parent control in the form of physical discipline predicted externalizing problems in European American children from kindergarten through third grade but did not predict problem behaviors in African American children (Deater-Deckard et al., 1996). However, other research finds that harsh parenting may be detrimental to children, regardless of racial background and even country (e.g., Lansford et al., 2014; Tamis-LeMonda et al., 2009).

✓ CHECK YOUR UNDERSTANDING 13.18

1. What is parental monitoring and how is it compatible with giving a child increasing autonomy?
2. What are the four main parenting styles identified by Baumrind, and how do they relate to children's developmental outcomes?

Relationships with Peers

Children spend a lot of time with peers at school, home, neighborhoods, and on social media. The relative equality seen in peer relationships contrasts with the imbalance of power seen in adult-child relationships, making peer relationships especially unique and meaningful. The growing importance of peers, however, makes children especially vulnerable to approval and rejection by their classmates and friends.

Friendships

LEARNING OBJECTIVE 13.19 Identify the benefits of friendships and describe common characteristics of lasting friendships.

Whom did you consider to be a close friend in childhood? How did your relationship with that person differ from your relationships with other children? Children develop special attachments to certain peers, whom they refer to as "friends" or even "best friends." **Friendships** are deeply important relationships that are characterized by mutual affection and liking (Rubin, et al., 2015).

friendships Deeply important relationships or attachments characterized by mutual affection and liking

Mutuality in Friendships

Mutual affection is an important ingredient to friendship. Developmental scientists sometimes ask children to nominate two or three of their "best" or "good" friends in a classroom, grade, or school, and assess whether children reciprocally nominate one another (e.g., Rubin et al., 2006). Using this approach, most children have at least one mutual good friend, although rates vary across studies (Berndt & McCandless, 2009; Wojslawowicz et al., 2006).

However, although most school-age children report having a close friend, the quality of those friendships varies (Rubin et al., 2015). For example, aggressive children may have a mutual best friend who is aggressive as well (Vitaro, Boivin, & Tremblay, 2007). Aggressive children might pair up as friends because their only options are children who have also been rejected by other children (Sijtsema, Lindenberg, & Veenstra, 2010). As a result, friendships between aggressive children often suffer from aggression, exclusivity, negativity, and jealously, and are consequently difficult to maintain (Banny et al., 2011; Ellis & Zarbatany, 2007).

At the other extreme, children who are withdrawn and anxious are likely to form friendships with peers who are similarly withdrawn and possibly victimized by peers (Rubin et al., 2006). In what has been referred to as a "misery loves company" phenomenon, shy and victimized friends depend on other shy and victimized friends, and therefore withdraw further from social interactions, particularly during the transition to middle school (Rubin et al., 2015). Still, having a stable, mutual friendship is better than being isolated, and withdrawn friends may help each other cope with the social challenges of the school years (Oh et al., 2008).

Functions of Friendships

Friendships offer children emotional security and support; enhance self-esteem; validate children's interests, hopes, and fears; and provide opportunities for intimate disclosure and feelings of vulnerability. In middle childhood, friendships attain a special quality of shared intimacy as children move beyond the tangible benefits of friends to valuing unobservable qualities, such as trust and loyalty (Bigelow & LaGaipa, 1980; Bukowski, Motzoi, & Meyer, 2009). Friends are also an important source of assistance, whether instrumental, such as when a friend loans a peer a dress for a party; informational, such as when a friend helps a peer with homework; or emotional, such as when a friend offers advice on how to handle an argument with a parent (Bagwell & Schmidt, 2011; Rubin et al., 2015).

However, friendships may differ somewhat depending on a child's sex. Girls report more intimate exchanges, conflict resolutions, validation, care, and guidance in their friendships than do boys, perhaps because they are more oriented to and emotionally invested in friendships (e.g., Rose & Rudolph, 2006). The gendered nature of friendships might be due to cultural messages about girls' and boys' feelings and intimacy. Girls are expected and encouraged to share their

FIGURE 13.16 School friends tend to be alike. Friends tend to be highly similar, in characteristics such as age and gender, and race and ethnicity.

emotions and develop deep and trusting friendships, whereas boys may experience a "crisis of connection" because of social pressures to be tough and independent (Way, 2013).

Similarities among Friends

What affects children's choice of friends? Perhaps unsurprisingly, friends tend to be highly similar in (**FIGURE 13.16**):

- age and gender (Mehta & Strough, 2009);
- race and ethnicity (McDonald et al., 2013);
- activities, hobbies, and interests (Selfhout et al., 2009);
- engagement in prosocial or delinquent/antisocial behaviors (Hafen et al., 2011);
- personality traits such as being shy or outgoing (Rubin et al., 2015, 2018);
- likelihood of being accepted, rejected, and/or victimized by their peers (Bowker et al., 2011; Logis et al., 2013); and
- academic motivation and performance (Altermatt & Pomerantz, 2003).

Similarities between friends are often the glue that keeps children close. The more similarities friends share, the more they are likely to remain friends over time. Notably, similarities between friends exist *prior to* the formation of many children's friendships, indicating that similarity drives friendship rather than friendship alone driving similarity (de la Haye et al., 2013).

Conflict in Friendships

Perhaps counter to common belief, disagreements and conflict among friends are often higher than they are among non-friends (Rubin et al., 2015, 2018; Simpkins & Parke, 2002). (Think about how often you argue or disagree with someone who is a close friend, compared to how often you argue with someone who is a mere acquaintance.) Of course, because friends spend a lot of time together, they have frequent opportunities to disagree over issues ranging from which movie to see to whether one friend betrayed the other.

Friends differ from non-friends, however, in how they resolve their conflicts. Friends are more likely than are non-friends to resolve conflicts through negotiation and problem solving, and the outcome of their conflicts is more likely to result in fair treatment of one another (de Wied, Branje, & Meeus, 2007). Thus, despite the relatively high conflict that characterizes friendships, friends' relationships tend to persist into the future after the conflict ends (Laursen, Hartup, & Koplas, 1996).

✓ CHECK YOUR UNDERSTANDING 13.19

1. Do children become friends with others who are like them or unlike them? Give examples.
2. Which child traits make it difficult to make and keep friends, and what types of friendships do children with these traits have?
3. Why are childhood friends prone to argue with one another?

Peer Acceptance and Rejection

LEARNING OBJECTIVE 13.20 Explain ways that researchers measure peer acceptance and rejection, and describe the statuses that emerge from these assessments.

School-age children spend a lot of time with peers. Some are friends, but others are not necessarily close friends. **Peer groups** are groups of children (typically

peer groups Groups of at least five or six children who generally share the same age, status, and interests; may be formal (e.g., school club members) or informal (e.g., children hanging out on the playground) five or six members, although there can be more) of generally the same age, status, and interests. Peer groups can be formal, such as the members of a school team or club, or informal, such as the group of children who hang out at a local park. In middle childhood, peer groups are likely to comprise same-gender peers, with mixed-gender peer groups becoming more common later in adolescence (e.g., Berger & Rodkin, 2012; Kindermann, 2007).

Even if children don't feel close to others in their peer groups, they are deeply affected by how their peers act toward them. Peer approval and rejection are powerful forces in a child's emotional and social adjustment. **Peer acceptance** refers to the extent to which a child is liked or accepted by peers, and conversely, **peer rejection** refers to the extent to which a child is disliked and excluded by peers.

Measuring Acceptance and Rejection

Developmental scientists have developed several useful methods to assess peer acceptance and rejection, including behavioral observations, teacher reports, and child reports.

- **Behavioral observations** of peer interactions are based on watching how children interact with one another and rating behaviors such as acceptance, rejection, victimization, and so forth. However, observations consume a lot of time, energy, and money. Moreover, if children are aware that they are being watched, they might be less likely to victimize a peer or behave the way they would in the absence of an adult observer.

- **Teacher reports** offer information on the social interactions, frequencies, and quality of relationships among children in their classrooms. Teachers may be asked to nominate students whom they believe to be "popular" and have many friends or to report on how often different children interact with one another. However, teachers may be biased toward students who perform well in school and be unaware of what goes on outside the classroom (Ladd & Profilet, 1996).

- **Child reports** (also referred to as **peer assessments**) form the basis for the majority of research on peer acceptance and rejection (**FIGURE 13.17**). Children are considered to be accurate and reliable reporters about their peers because they are first-hand witnesses to many of the ongoing interactions among their classmates. As insiders, children are "in the know"

peer acceptance The extent to which a child is liked and accepted by peers

peer rejection The extent to which a child is disliked and excluded by peers

behavioral observations A method to assess peer acceptance and rejection based on observing how children interact with one another

teacher reports A method to assess peer acceptance and rejection based on teachers' reports or ratings of children's interactions with one another

child reports (peer assessments) A method to assess peer acceptance and rejection based on children's reports of the amount or quality of social interactions (e.g., how much time children spend with each other; whether they like one another) among a group of children from inside or outside the classroom

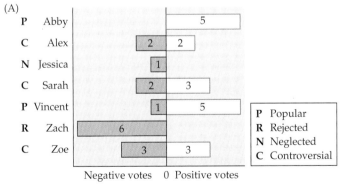

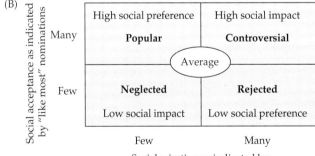

FIGURE 13.17 Popularity as assessed by children. (A) The nomination chart shows how each child in class received a different number of positive or negative nominations on a question about sitting next to a child. (B) The matrix shows how sociometric nominations on items such as "Who do you most like in class?" and "Who do you least like in class?" are used to classify children into different popularity types. Children with many positive nominations (like most) and few negative nominations (like least) are popular; those with many negative nominations are rejected; those with similar numbers of positive and negative nominations are controversial; and children with few of either positive or negative nominations are neglected. (B after K. Košir and S. Pečjak. 2005. *Edu Res* 47: 127–144. Taylor & Francis Ltd, http://www.tandfonline.com)

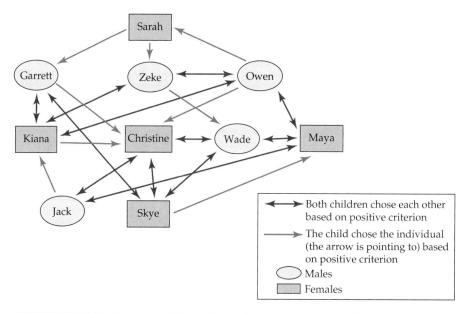

FIGURE 13.18 Sociograms. Researchers often use sociometric data to generate visual depictions like this one of the connection among peers or individuals in a social network. Bidirectional arrows mean that both children nominated one another. Unidirectional arrows mean the nomination was one way and not reciprocated.

sociometric nomination A type of child-report approach or peer rating system in which children nominate peers in their class or grade whom they "like" and "dislike," or report on which students interact with other students; sociometric nominations classify children into popular, rejected, controversial, or neglected

sociograms Visual depictions of the friendships among peers or individuals in a social network

popular children Socially and academically competent children who receive a high number of like nominations and few dislike nominations in sociometric nominations

popular-prosocial Popular children who are considerate and skilled at initiating friendships and prosocial toward other children

perceived popularity Measure of children classified as popular due to their perceived status and power rather than their social competence

popular-antisocial Children who are perceived to be popular and "cool" but who may actually be disliked by peers

rejected children Children who receive many dislikes and few likes in sociometric nominations; rejected-aggressive and rejected-withdrawn represent two types of rejected children

rejected-aggressive children Children who demonstrate problems in how they treat other children and who have goals that undermine social relationships, such as getting even with other children

bullying Seeking to harm, intimidate, or threaten other children, commonly displayed by rejected-aggressive children

rejected-withdrawn children Children who are socially anxious, timid, and withdrawn from the peer group, often watching social interactions from a distance rather than being directly involved

about events that may fall under the radar screen of parents and teachers, such as when a child is punched by another child at the playground (Rubin, Bukowski, & Parker, 2006). In addition, child report methods allow scientists to base assessments of a child's acceptance or popularity on the input of many children—often everyone in the classroom.

Sociometric nomination is a type of child-report approach in which researchers ask children to nominate between 3 and 5 peers in their class or grade whom they "like" and "dislike," or to report on which students interact with which other students (Cillessen, 2009; Van den Berg, Lansu, & Cillessen, 2015). Sociometric nominations provide information about the overall cohesion among members of a group and can be used to generate **sociograms**—visual depictions of the connection among peers or individuals in a social network (Burt, 2017; Cillessen, 2009) (**FIGURE 13.18**).

Sociometric nominations traditionally classify children into groups of: popular, rejected, controversial, and neglected. Children who do not fall into one of these classifications are referred to as average. Notably, children's classifications are not short-lived or fleeting. Over time, popular children tend to remain popular and rejected children remain rejected (Bukowski, Cillessen, & Velásquez, 2012).

Popular Children

Popular children receive a high number of like nominations and few dislike nominations. Most popular children are socially and academically competent. **Popular-prosocial** children are able to achieve their goals while simultaneously being considerate, cooperative, and skilled at initiating friendships and resolving interpersonal dilemmas (Asher & McDonald, 2009; Troop-Gordon & Asher, 2005) (**FIGURE 13.19**). Their peers name them as someone they would enjoy hanging out with or spending time with (**FIGURE 13.20**). As a result, popular children have lots of lines connecting them to their peers on a sociogram, reflecting their dense friendship networks.

However, some children are perceived to be popular among peers due to their status and power rather than their social competence. **Perceived popularity** is

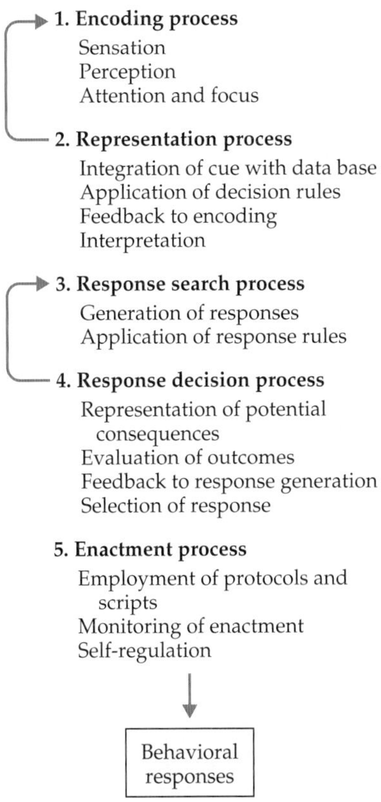

FIGURE 13.19 Getting into the game. Children's skills at resolving interpersonal dilemmas are important for positive relationships with peers. Dodge and colleagues identified multiple steps involved in children's processing, interpretation, and handling of conflicts with peers. For example, if a child is playing a game with a peer who attacks the child by complaining about the rules, the targeted child must (1) attend to and encode relevant information about what is happening, (encoding process); (2) reason about and interpret the situation further (representation process); (3) identify and generate possible responses (response search process); (4) consider the consequences and evaluate what might happen for different responses (response decision process); and (5) implement the appropriate response (enactment process). In some instances, children may resort to negative strategies (such as criticizing the complaining child), which may further incite anger and fuel the conflict. In other instances, children may identify and enact successful strategies (such as by pointing to successful times in the past when they followed the rules and had fun), which may diffuse the situation. Popular children are likely to choose strategies that help to diffuse rather than aggravate the situation, whereas rejected children may choose ineffective strategies. (After K. A. Dodge. 1986. In *Cognitive Perspectives on Children's Social and Behavioral Development: The Minnesota Symposium on Child Psychology* [Vol. 18], M. Perlmutter [Ed.]. Lawrence Erlbaum Associates, Inc.: Hillsdale, NJ. Copyright 1986 by Lawrence Erlbaum Associates, Inc. Copyright 1986. Reproduced by permission of Taylor and Francis Group, LLC, a division of Informa plc.)

1. Encoding process
Sensation
Perception
Attention and focus

2. Representation process
Integration of cue with data base
Application of decision rules
Feedback to encoding
Interpretation

3. Response search process
Generation of responses
Application of response rules

4. Response decision process
Representation of potential consequences
Evaluation of outcomes
Feedback to response generation
Selection of response

5. Enactment process
Employment of protocols and scripts
Monitoring of enactment
Self-regulation

Behavioral responses

measured by asking children to nominate peers they *believe to be* the most popular and least popular, rather than by asking children to nominate peers they like or prefer (Bukowski, 2011). Peers may perceive certain children to be popular and others to be unpopular, but this does not mean that the child who is perceived to be popular is well liked by many children. Conversely, the child who is perceived to be unpopular is not necessarily rejected in any way.

A small subgroup of children who are perceived to be popular can be classified as **popular-antisocial**. Peers often consider these children to be "cool" even though they may actually dislike them. Popular-antisocial children are likely to engage in both physical and relational aggression by spreading rumors about or ignoring other children, acting tough and aggressive to enhance their social status, and defying authority (Cillessen & Mayeux, 2004; Rodkin et al., 2006; Vaillancourt & Hymel, 2006).

Rejected Children

Rejected children receive many dislikes and few likes in sociometric nominations. Children who are rejected by their peers fall into two distinct types: rejected-aggressive children and rejected-withdrawn children.

Rejected-aggressive children demonstrate problems in how they treat other children and tend to have goals that undermine their social relationships, such as aiming to "get even" with or "defeat" their peers. Rejected-aggressive children engage in various forms of **bullying** by harming or threatening other children (Salmivalli & Peets, 2009). Bullying can take the form of physical aggression, such as hitting or physically harming another child for various reasons, or relational aggression, such as when a child manipulates or disrupts relationships through covert strategies like whispering rumors (Crick et al., 2009).

Rejected-withdrawn children, in contrast, are often socially anxious, timid, and withdrawn from the peer group (Ladd et al., 2011; Oh et al., 2008). They may watch other children from a distance, rather than becoming socially involved. Rejected-withdrawn children are also likely to solve interpersonal dilemmas by asking adults to intervene or by withdrawing from the situation rather than being direct about their feelings, opinions, and wishes (Burgess et al., 2006).

FIGURE 13.20 Popularity. The majority of popular children are socially competent and academically capable. They are frequently named as someone their peers would enjoy spending time with. However, some children are perceived to be popular among peers due to their status and power rather than their social competence.

Notably, the consequences of social withdrawal for peer rejection may differ by child gender. Boys who are withdrawn are more likely to be rejected by their peers than are girls who are withdrawn (e.g., Doey, Coplan, & Kingsbury, 2014; Gazelle, 2008). This is likely because social withdrawal violates male gender norms around assertiveness and power, whereas social withdrawal in girls is viewed as being shy and quiet, which is more acceptable (Doey, Coplan, & Kingsbury, 2014).

Controversial Children

controversial children Children who show a mixture of positive and negative social behaviors toward peers and who receive a mixture of positive and negative sociometric nominations from peers

Controversial children display a mix of positive and negative social behaviors toward peers, and receive a mix of positive and negative nominations by their peers. Although they may be disliked by some peers, they have a substantial number of friends and are pleased with their relationships (de Bruyn & Cillessen, 2006). Sometimes, they behave in ways similar to aggressive-rejected peers by bullying and using relational aggression (DeRosier & Thomas, 2003; Putallaz et al., 2007). Controversial children can transition to popular or rejected groups over time, based on how they treat their peers in different social situations.

Neglected Children

neglected children Children who receive few likes and few dislikes in sociometric nominations

Neglected children receive few likes and few dislikes on sociometric nominations, meaning they are rarely mentioned. Neglected children are often considered to be shy by their classmates, but are not withdrawn to the extent of rejected-withdrawn children. Consequently, they do not report dissatisfaction with their social life and are able to form positive, stable friendships (Ladd et al., 2011). Over time, however, some neglected children may be rejected if they engage in socially anxious behaviors and further withdraw from their peers.

✓ CHECK YOUR UNDERSTANDING 13.20

1. What are sociometric nominations, and what purpose do they serve?
2. What five social status groups are identified by sociometric methods?
3. How and why might a child's perceived popularity differ from their actual popularity, and how would you obtain information on each type to show this difference?

The Pain of Exclusion

LEARNING OBJECTIVE 13.21 Understand how studies of the brain can reveal the "pain" of social exclusion.

Being rejected by peers is emotionally hurtful, and the brain reveals just how children respond to the pain of exclusion (Masten et al., 2010). To test the brain's response to peer rejection, researchers use **virtual social exclusion experiments**, in which children are made to think that they are being excluded from a game or situation by unknown children. For example, during a game of "Cyberball" (Williams, Cheung, & Choi, 2000) participants played "catch" with the two other virtual players whose avatars were displayed on a computer monitor. Children were told that two peers in another room controlled the avatars. After a baseline period of equal passing of the ball, the two virtual players threw the ball to one another and excluded the child (**FIGURE 13.21A**). The child's psychological experience of exclusion in the game led to extremely high activation in the region of the brain associated with mood and anxiety that connects to the amygdala.

virtual social exclusion experiments Studies that assess the brain's response to peer rejection by making children think that they are being excluded from a game or activity by unknown children or by using peer-chat room simulations

Other virtual exclusion studies have used peer chat room simulations, in which children are told that unfamiliar peers in another room saw their photographs and chose not to interact with them (Guyer et al., 2009, 2012). When

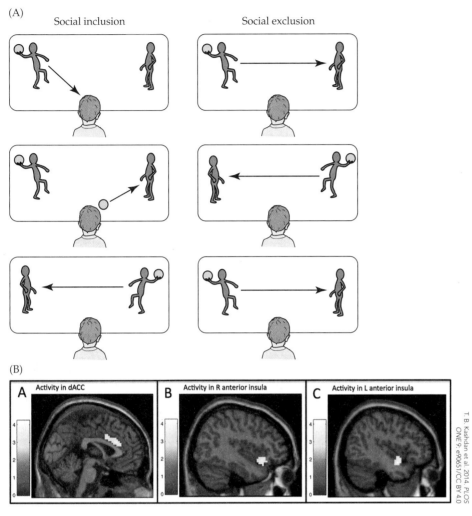

FIGURE 13.21 Virtual exclusion experiments. Such experiments monitor how a child's brain responds to being excluded by others. (A) In the inclusion condition (left side panels), a child plays a computer game with two avatars. The avatar on the left throws the ball to the child playing the computer game. The child then throws the ball to the other avatar, who then throws the ball to the other avatar. Thus, the child is included in the game. In the exclusion condition (right side panels), the two avatars only throw to one another and entirely exclude the child playing the game. (B) fMRI images show the regions of the brain that show greater activation (yellow) under conditions of exclusion compared to inclusion. Note that both the dACC and the anterior insula, areas activated by simulated exclusion, are the same ones that respond to physical pain. (A after K. Williams and B. Jarvis. 2006. *Behav Res Methods* 38: 174–180. Based on K. D. Williams et al. 2000. *J Pers Social Psychol* 79: 748–762.)

researchers track children's brain activation during such simulated situations, they show that the regions of the brain that respond to exclusion are precisely those that are involved in the experience of physical pain (e.g., Eisenberger & Lieberman, 2004; Guyer et al., 2009; Howarth, Guyer, & Pérez-Edgar, 2013) (**FIGURE 13.21B**). The evolutionary human need for social attachment and connectedness to others may explain why brain responses to physical pain are so highly similar to the "social pains" of exclusion.

✓ **CHECK YOUR UNDERSTANDING 13.21**
1. How does the brain respond to social exclusion?

Contexts of Social Development

Family, school, social media, and cultural contexts shape children's social relationships with friends and peers. Let us consider these central influences.

Family and School Contexts of Social Development

LEARNING OBJECTIVE 13.22 Describe the effects of parents and school climate on middle childhood peer relationships.

Parents and school climate contribute to children's development of social competence and peer relationships in various ways. Parents provide children with opportunities to have contact with peers, monitor children's friendships, coach children on ways to handle interpersonal relationships, teach children positive social skills, and discipline unacceptable behaviors (e.g., Healy, Sanders, & Iyer, 2015; Parke & Ladd, 2016). Additionally, the quality of parent-child relationships can be a model for peer relationships. Children who have secure attachment relationships with their parents are more likely to be socially competent and accepted by their peers and to have high-quality friendships than are children with insecure attachment relationships (Rubin et al., 2004). Conversely, children with parents who are punitive, neglectful, or fail to provide emotional support may exhibit aggressiveness toward peers and be bullied themselves (Healy et al., 2015; Pinquart, 2017).

School climate is also a major force in children's peer relationships. School climate involves the physical features of schools (such as safety, health, cleanliness, space, and resources) and social features of schools (such as the extent to which teachers, students, and parents experience mutual respect, open collaboration, trust, and a sense of connection). Children who attend schools with a positive climate are less likely to have social and emotional problems or experience problems with victimization and bullying than those who experience a negative school climate (e.g., Klein, Cornell, & Konold, 2012; Khoury-Kassabri, 2011; Leadbeater et al., 2015; Richard, Schneider, & Mallet, 2012; Wang & Dishion, 2012).

✓ CHECK YOUR UNDERSTANDING 13.22

1. Which types of behaviors can parents engage in to support their children's relationships with peers? Which behaviors might cause problems in children's peer relationships?
2. What features of schools establish the type of school climate needed to support positive student relationships?

Social Media Context of Social Development

LEARNING OBJECTIVE 13.23 Understand the potential risks of social media misuse and overuse, including the harm of cyberbullying.

Technology and social media platforms offer children opportunities to socialize and share details of their lives with friends and acquaintances. Such interactions can help friends stay emotionally connected with one another. However, there is also a clear downside, including misuse and overuse of social media. Policies exist that prohibit children under 13 years of age from using social media for these reasons. Despite these conditions, in a European study 42% of children ages 9–12 were found to have a social media profile (Barbovschi, Macháčková, & Ólafsson, 2015).

Concerns about children's misuse and overuse of social media continue to grow (Christakis & Moreno, 2009; Hoge, Bickman, & Cantor, 2017). Misuse takes many forms, including exploiting the internet to victimize or bully other children. **Cyberbullying** refers to the intentional and repeated use of technology and social media platforms to harm another person or group of

---

school climate A school's physical (e.g., safety, resources) and social (e.g., teacher-child respect, open collaboration) characteristics

cyberbullying The exploitation of technology and social media platforms to victimize or bully others; the repeated intentional use of technology (e.g., emails, text messaging, social media, online gaming) to harm another person or a group of people through hostile, aggressive acts

TABLE 13.4 ■ Bullying versus Cyberbullying	
Traditional bullying	Cyberbullying
The victim can avoid the bully by going home or escaping to a safe place, thereby preventing the bully from engaging in continued aggressive behavior.	The victim cannot escape the bully because the bully can continue to harass the victim by posting offensive and belittling comments on the internet that follow the victim everywhere.
The victim knows who the bully is, can avoid being around the bully, and can confide in others (e.g., teachers, coaches) who may intervene and punish the bully.	The bully can avoid punishment by assuming a false identity and thus engage in victimization without any consequences.
Few people are present or involved during threats and aggression between bully and victim. The victim is therefore protected from the humiliation of peers observing the bullying experience.	Cyberbullying reaches a very wide audience, with many peers witnessing the threats and aggression from bully to victim through posts on social media. This may lead to others also bullying the victim.
Bullying is confined to discrete events that end when the victim separates from the bully or someone intervenes.	Bullying continues over time, with people being able to download and widely distribute content created by the bully to other users.

people through hostile or aggressive acts (e.g., DePaolis & Williford, 2015). Cyberbullying can occur through emails, text messages, postings on social media sites, and online gaming (**TABLE 13.4**).

Although most research on cyberbullying focuses on teenagers, elementary school children also fall prey to this harmful social practice. One study indicated that about 18% of children in third through fifth grade experienced cyberbullying; the majority (62%) did not know the identity of the bully; and only about half of the victimized students reported their victimization to someone, usually a friend or parent (DePaolis & Williford, 2015). Many children were bullied through online games, with boys being especially likely to be victimized through this platform.

Moreover, cyberbullying increases across the school years. The more time children in grades three through eight spent on social media, the more they were involved in cyberbullying (Meter & Bauman, 2015). In addition, victims of cyberbullying were more likely to exhibit bullying behaviors themselves and less likely to defend other victims, compared to children who were not cyberbullying victims. Perhaps, victims of cyberbullying seek ways to retaliate against other children, and become numb to the emotional damage that bullying inflicts on others.

✓ CHECK YOUR UNDERSTANDING 13.23

1. What strategies can you suggest to curb and/or combat cyberbullying of school children?

Cultural Context of Social Development

LEARNING OBJECTIVE 13.24 Provide examples of how cultural goals and behavioral standards influence children's peer relationships.

Cultural norms and values strongly influence children's peer relationships, ranging from views about the purpose of friendships to the characteristics associated with peer approval and rejection.

Cultural communities emphasize the goals of independence and interdependence to different degrees, which in turn can affect views about the purpose of friendships. In many Western cultures, independence and autonomy are important goals; whereas, in many Asian and Latinx cultures, social connectedness, interdependence, and conformity are valued (Greenfield, Suzuki, & Rothstein-Fisch, 2006). Different cultural emphases help define the characteristics of what makes a good friend. In Western cultures, including the United

States, friends play an important role in enhancing a child's sense of self-worth. In contrast, people in Chinese, Indonesian, Arab, and Caribbean cultures place high value on social connectedness and interdependence (Chen, 2012; French, Pidada, & Victor, 2005). Additionally, individuals in some Asian and Latinx cultures view instrumental support, such as assisting a friend who is short of money or needs help with chores, as important to friendship (e.g., Way & Greene, 2006).

Cultural communities also differ in the standards they hold about peer interactions, such as the social behaviors they view to be acceptable. In turn, cultural norms and expectations around social relationships can shape the degree to which peers accept or reject a child who acts in a particular way. For example, Chinese adults and children view disruptive and aggressive behaviors as highly deviant from cultural norms, and often publicly criticize children who display such behaviors. As a result, aggressiveness in children is more likely to lead to rejection, loneliness, and depression in China than it is in Canada where aggression is more often tolerated (Chen et al., 2004).

Behaviors associated with shyness likewise vary by culture. In European American populations in North America and in other Western communities, children who display socially withdrawn, restrained behaviors are perceived as anxious, fearful, socially incompetent, immature, and/or at risk for poor outcomes such as anxiety and fearfulness (Rubin, Coplan, & Bowker, 2009). By contrast, in China, shy children with inhibited behaviors are considered to be accomplished, mature, and well behaved and to have high social understanding (Chen, 2010). Similarly, Chinese children who are highly sensitive in social situations are perceived to show positive adjustment, whereas being a highly sensitive child in Canada can lead to perceptions that a child is overly emotional, weak, and vulnerable (Chen et al., 2018).

✓ CHECK YOUR UNDERSTANDING 13.24

1. How do varying cultural emphases of the value of autonomy affect the functions of friendship?
2. How might cultural context affect the degree to which a child with specific traits is liked or disliked by peers?

Developmental Cascades

Most of us can recall critical turning points in our childhoods that left indelible impressions and sometimes difficult-to-erase scars. Children's emotional competence, self-identity, and friendships are foundational to later relationships, school engagement, and even career success. Positive social experiences go a long way in helping children navigate the rough waters of childhood, whereas peer rejection can compromise psychological adjustment for years to come. The boy described at the chapter opening, who was taunted on the school bus, became a victim of repeated teasing. What other children viewed to be harmless fun carried the mark of humiliation into high school. Over time, he withdrew from school and fell into trouble with the law. As brain activation patterns show, the pain of rejection is real and physical, and its psychological toll can endure for years.

Cascades from Emotional Development

Problems in emotion understanding and regulation place children at risk for mental health problems, social isolation, and disengagement from school. For example, children who had problems regulating their emotions at ages 5 and 7 experienced low friendship quality and low peer acceptance at 10 years of age

(Blair et al., 2016). Moreover, harmful cascading influences are magnified when combined with other risks, including household poverty or stressful relationships with parents. Children from low-income households with difficulties understanding emotions in first grade reported symptoms of anxiety and depression later in fifth grade (Fine et al., 2003).

On the positive side, strong emotional and social skills provide a springboard for academic achievement (e.g., Agnoli et al., 2012; Elias & Haynes, 2008). These long-term impacts exist partly because self-regulation allows children to discipline their time around studying, attend to school subjects, and modulate their arousal and anxiety during exams. Moreover, children who understand others' emotions are more civically engaged and more likely to volunteer for worthy causes than are children who have difficulty understanding emotions (Schonert-Reichl et al., 2012). Emotional insight allows children to sympathize with less advantaged individuals (**FIGURE 13.22**).

FIGURE 13.22 Emotion understanding allows children to understand the plight of other people, which can lead to initiative in helping others. This boy helps the Salvation Army serve Thanksgiving dinner to the neediest people in New York.

Cascades from Self-Identity

Erik Erikson was among the first to write about the importance of a positive self-identity for life-long well-being. Years later, we see that Erikson's writings were spot on. Children with strong self-esteem view school to be important and are willing to put effort toward doing well, which then heightens college options and ultimately occupational choices (e.g., Denissen, Zarrett, & Eccles, 2007; Whitesell, Mitchell, & Spicer, 2009).

Self-esteem also affects social relationships. Children are more likely to reject peers with low self-esteem, which can instill anxiety and depression in rejected children (e.g., Marsh, Parada, & Ayotte, 2004; Rudolph, Caldwell, & Conley, 2005). Children who are overly concerned about what their peers think about them and need constant approval ride a roller coaster of self-esteem, in which their feelings about themselves increase and decrease as other children's opinions of them fluctuate (Harter & Whitesell, 2003).

Cascades from Gender Self-Identity

The world is highly gendered, making gender self-identity one of the strongest influences in development. Think about the ways that gender has shaped the choices and behaviors you have made in your life—ranging from the people you hung out with to how you dressed and the activities you pursued. Indeed, gender stereotypes, attitudes, and behaviors infiltrate all domains, including school performance, career paths, social relationships, and marriage and parenthood.

A primary way that gender stereotyping affects children is through pressures on girls and boys to behave in certain ways. Children who adhere to gender norms typically receive high approval from peers, and those who fail to do so may experience negative social consequences (Carver, Yunger, & Perry, 2003; Yu & Xie, 2010). However, overly rigid adherence to same-gender stereotypic activities can undermine adjustment. Children who hold a positive view of the self as a typical member of their gender but are open to cross-gender options— that is, those who are gender-stereotype flexible—may be better adjusted than children who are rigid in their gender views and behaviors (Halim & Ruble, 2010; Martin, Cook, & Andrews, 2017).

Cascades from Peer Acceptance and Rejection

Friends help children negotiate the social and cognitive demands of middle childhood, just as a lack of friends and peer rejection can interfere with adjustment. Indeed, children who are chronically friendless are at risk for negative adjustment, depressive symptoms, and peer victimization during childhood and early adolescence (e.g., Bukowsk, Motzoi, & Meyer, 2009; Wojslawowicz et al., 2006). Chronically friendless children may lack social skills or try to befriend peers who are unlikely to reciprocate their affection (Bowker et al., 2010; Parker & Seal, 1996). Similarly, children who are rejected by their peers are at risk for aggression, conduct disorder, attention difficulties, and even substance abuse (e.g., Dodge et al., 2003; Ladd & Burgess, 2001; Parker et al., 2006).

Being victimized by peers likewise harms psychological well-being and perceptions of school climate. Children who report being victimized may either join aggressive groups or withdraw from social interactions to protect themselves from bullying (Leadbeater & Hoglund, 2009; Troop-Gordon & Ladd, 2005). Furthermore, third and fourth grade children who reported being victimized early on showed declines in their views of school climate and grew in their emotional detachment from school (Leadbeater et al., 2015).

Of course, rejected children may have engaged in antisocial behaviors that elicited their negative peers' reactions in the first place. Thus, the combination of early behavior problems *and* later peer rejection or victimization may be especially detrimental to long-term outcomes. Such cascading influences were found in children whom researchers followed from kindergarten through seventh grade (Bierman, Kalvin, & Heinrichs, 2015). In kindergarten and first grade, researchers assessed children's aggression, inability to regulate emotions, and internalizing problems, and in grades two, three, and four, they assessed children's rejection and victimization by peers. In seventh grade, adolescents reported on their social problems, depressed mood, school adjustment difficulties, and problem behaviors. As the researchers hypothesized, children who had problems with aggression and regulating emotions at the start of schooling were then rejected or victimized by peers a few years later, and this rejection and victimization led to long-term problems in adolescence.

Notably, childhood aggression or withdrawal alone, in the absence of peer rejection, does not portend negative cascading influences. For example, girls who were aggressive in childhood engaged in more substance use and sexual risk behaviors in junior high school, but only if they had also been disliked or rejected (Prinstein & LaGreca, 2004). Similarly, children who were shy and anxious as kindergartners *and* were socially excluded by peers continued to feel anxious and lonely in fourth grade, whereas shy children who had not been rejected by their peers became less anxious and lonely over time (Gazelle & Ladd, 2003). Conversely, children who believed that they were rejected by peers showed increases in internalizing and externalizing behaviors over time, even if they were not actually rejected based on peer reports (Sandstrom, Cillessen, & Eisenhower, 2003).

Cascades as Illustrated through a 20-Year Study

Perhaps the most powerful evidence for the long-term reverberations of early peer relationships comes from the work of developmental scientist Ann Masten. In a landmark 20-year longitudinal study, Masten examined cascading influences of children's social competence and peer relationships on work competence in early adulthood (Masten et al., 2005, 2010). She followed over 200 people from elementary school, initially seeing children who were 8 to 12 years of age (third to sixth grade), with follow-up observations 7, 10, and 20 years later (in adolescence and through adulthood ~30 years of age; **FIGURE 13.23**). In elementary school and adolescence, researchers assessed three categories of children's competence:

- *Social competence*, which included children's acceptance by their peers, social skills, and their formation and maintenance of friendships.

- *Internalizing and externalizing behaviors*, based on reports of children's anxiety and depression, loneliness, problem behaviors, and aggression, such as stealing and bullying other children.

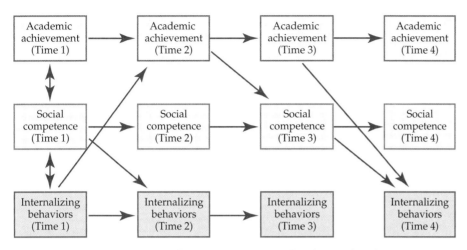

FIGURE 13.23 Developmental cascades associated with social and academic competence in school children.   A 20-year longitudinal study underscores the importance of social and emotional adaptations in middle childhood for success in later life. The authors followed individuals across four periods from childhood through adulthood, and showed cascading effects among areas of social competence, internalizing behaviors, and academic competence over time. For example, as shown by connecting red arrows, social competence at Time 1 cascaded to internalizing behaviors at Time 2, which related to internalizing behaviors at Time 3. Similarly, social competence at Time 1 spilled over to social competence at Times 2 and 3, which then affected internalizing behaviors at Time 4 (representing a 20-year path of influence). (After J. Obradovic et al. 2010. *J Clin Child Adolesc Psychol* 39: 90–102. Taylor & Francis Ltd, http://www.tandfonline.com.)

- *Academic achievement*, which included children's grades, test scores, and teacher evaluations of academic performance.

In support of a cascade model of development, children's functioning across the three domains at age 10 years predicted adolescent functioning at the midpoint of the study, which then predicted work competence 20 years later in adulthood. For example, children's earlier social competence predicted how well they later carried out job responsibilities as adults, how successful they were at work, and whether they were able to hold down a job for long periods of time. Specifically, children with low social competence, behavior problems, and low academics in grade school continued to suffer in these areas throughout adolescence, which harmed their work performance later in life. Such findings —across two decades of life—spotlight the importance of social and emotional adaptations in childhood for life success, and underscore the importance of intervening early, before problems spiral out of control with children who exhibit low social and emotional skills.

■ CLOSING THOUGHTS
Vulnerabilities and Strengths

The trials and tribulations, joys, and accomplishments of middle childhood are universal and integrally intertwined with context and culture. Children learn a lot about emotions, they grow in their self-identity, and they change in their social relationships. At the same time, children struggle with what to do in specific situations, and they sometimes act in ways that may appear to be inappropriate or even harmful. The good news is that difficulties in emotional and social domains are normative and educational. Social interactions of all types provide children with opportunities to learn about the complexity of emotions, how to regulate their emotions and behaviors, and how to reason morally and act competently in social situations. There is no better teacher than experience.

Of course, striking individual differences accompany the universal changes of middle childhood. Some children better adapt to emotional challenges than do others because of biology, past experiences, cognitive skills, and the types and levels of support they receive from peers, family, teachers, and community. Although individual differences can cascade to long-term outcomes, they are not deterministic. As we will see in the closing chapters on adolescence, children require supportive environments throughout development if they are to flourish and become competent, well-adjusted adults. And, for children whose personalities and social contexts create vulnerabilities, developmental science continues to identify evidence-based ways for parents, teachers, peers, and society to intervene to make the journey a bit smoother.

The Developmentalist's Toolbox

Method	Purpose	Description
Measuring children's emotional development		
Counterfactual emotion tasks	To test whether children understand that a person's emotions can depend on how reality compares to an alternative	Children are told a story in which a character experiences an outcome that is better or worse than expected (such as winning $10 after expecting to win nothing or after expecting to win $100; or receiving a low grade when expecting a high one or expecting an even lower grade). The experimenter might assess whether the children judge the character's emotions accurately (considering that there would be a sense of relief or regret/disappointment), or whether children spontaneously generate consoling strategies that assert the situation could have been worse.
Emotion vignettes	To investigate children's understanding of the emotions of characters in a story, including understanding of emotion display rules	Children may be asked to identify emotions felt by characters presented in various short scenarios, and how characters might try to disguise those emotions in different situations.
Measuring children's social development		
Implicit association tests (IATs)	To assess children's stereotypes around gender and race	Children may be asked to assign gender stereotyped gifts to either a boy or a girl.
Affective evaluation studies	To study affective dimensions of gender attitudes	Researchers might ask children how positively or negatively they feel toward unfamiliar girls and boys presented in pictures.
Sociometric nominations	To assess the extent to which a child is liked or disliked and accepted or rejected by peers	In sociometric nominations, all the children of a class or group are asked to nominate between three and five peers whom they "like" and "dislike." Based on the group responses, each child in the classroom can be classified as popular, rejected, neglected, controversial, or average.
Perceived popularity ratings	To assess who in the group or classroom children perceive to be most and least popular, rather than nominating who they like	Similar to sociometric nominations, the responses of all children are used to quantify how popular or unpopular each child in the group or class is perceived to be. Perceived popularity can differ from actual popularity as measured by sociometric nominations.
Virtual social exclusion experiments	To investigate changes to children's brain activation responses to the experience of social rejection	A child is led to believe that he/she is playing a video game with a peer(s) in the other room (which is not the case), who excludes and rejects the child. Brain activation patterns are recorded in response to the virtual exclusion by the peer.

Chapter Summary

Understanding Emotions

- During middle childhood, children increasingly understand the self-conscious emotions (such as guilt, pride, and shame), the causes and consequences of emotions (including how emotions might have been different had there been a different outcome), and recognize that multiple emotions can be experienced simultaneously.

Expressing and Regulating Emotions

- Children's understanding and use of display rules for emotions changes significantly in the school years.
- Children learn to amplify, minimize, neutralize, and substitute outward emotions in response to their growing understanding of social expectations.
- Children improve in their problem-centered and emotion-centered coping strategies in middle childhood, which helps them regulate their emotions and cope with negative situations.

Contexts of Emotional Development

- How parents model emotions and respond to children's emotions strongly influence their children's emotional development.
- Warm and supportive sibling relationships relate to positive psychological and behavioral adjustment, whereas high sibling conflict may lead to mental health problems such as anxiety and depression.
- Peers communicate norms about the expressions of emotions. Children learn to mask their emotions as they become aware of display rules.
- Cultures vary in the norms of emotional expression, and these differences are reflected in cross-cultural differences in children's emotional expressions and behaviors.

Self-Identity Development

- Erik Erikson stated that the psychosocial conflict of industry versus inferiority characterizes the process of identity development during middle childhood.
- Children's sense of self expands in middle childhood to embrace multiple traits, internal traits and personality dispositions, and comparisons to peers from different groups.
- Self-esteem drops in the early elementary school years as children recognize they may not be as good as their peers in certain areas. Children may respond to these social comparisons by devaluing or minimizing the importance of certain skills, which can lead to declines in motivation and performance in those areas.
- Children become increasingly aware of gender stereotypes, including inequities in status and respect.
- At the same time that knowledge of stereotypes grows, children become more gender-stereotype flexible, although they may still reject others who are extreme in gender norm violations.
- Children show strong in-group favoritism for their own gender, but do not show negativity toward the out-group.

- By middle childhood, children understand that ethnic and racial identity are stable, increasingly reflect on the meaning of ethnicity and race for self and others, and grow in awareness of ethnic and racial biases.
- Children's endorsement of ethnic group stereotypes and the extent to which they perceive ethnic and racial bias depend on their group status.
- Most children show in-group favoritism in their attitudes. Prejudice to the ethnic or racial out-group peaks and then declines over the childhood years.
- Children strongly adhere to moral judgments of fairness and equity and recognize it is unfair to engage in differential treatment based on ethnicity or race. However, they sometimes find it challenging to make moral decisions in intergroup contexts, showing favoritism to the in-group to maintain group loyalty.

Contexts of Self-Identity Development

- Many contexts, including family, peers, and media, convey powerful messages about gender and ethnicity and race and influence children's identity, attitudes, and behaviors in childhood and beyond.
- Gender stereotypes around math illustrate the powerful influence of stereotypes on the self-identity of boys and girls.

Relationships with Parents

- The parent-child attachment relationship continues to be important in the middle-childhood years.
- Children with positive relationships with their parents in middle childhood demonstrate positive psychological and behavioral adjustment.
- Baumrind's taxonomy of parenting styles characterized parents as authoritarian, permissive, uninvolved, or authoritative.
- Parental monitoring and authoritative parenting styles (in contrast to authoritarian, permissive, and neglectful styles) are associated with positive outcomes in children.

Relationships with Peers

- Friendships in middle childhood serve many critical functions, including offering children emotional security and support; enhancing self-esteem; and validating children's interests, hopes, and fears.
- Children spend time with friends and peer groups who are similar to them.
- The number and quality of children's friendships, and the extent to which children are accepted or rejected by their peers, vary from child to child. Aggressive and shy children are at risk for having few friends and lower quality friendships.
- Observations, teacher reports, and peer nominations and ratings (notably, sociometric nominations and nominations of perceived peer popularity) are used to assess child acceptance or rejection and popularity.

- Peer nominations and ratings yield five types of children: popular, rejected, neglected, controversial, and average.
- Rejected children fall into two subtypes: rejected-aggressive and rejected-withdrawn.
- Some children are popular because of social competence and skills in social problem-solving. A subgroup of children is perceived to be popular because of status and power.
- Rejection by peers is painful, as can be seen in how the brain responds to simulated experiences of peer rejection.

Contexts of Social Development

- Family context (including the quality of parent-child relationships) and school context (including school climate) affect children's relationships with peers.
- The misuse and overuse of technology and social media are a growing context of potential problems, including victimization and cyberbullying.
- Cultural context can affect children's relationships with peers through differences in cultural views about the purpose of friendships and the personality characteristics associated with approval and rejection in different communities.

Developmental Cascades

- Problems in understanding and regulating emotions place children at risk for mental health problems, social isolation, and disengagement from school.
- Various aspects of emotional development support academic achievement and social relationships.
- Poor self-esteem can interfere with positive peer relationships, cascading to rejection and depression.
- Children who are gender-stereotype flexible may be better adjusted than children who are rigid in their gender views and behaviors.
- Peer rejection shows negative cascading influences to a range of problems, including poor psychological well-being, aggression, detachment from school, and substance use.
- Children who have problems with aggression, coupled with peer rejection, are especially at risk for later psychological problems.
- Ann Masten's 20-year longitudinal study on developmental cascades showed that children's low social competence, externalizing behavior problems, and low academic achievement in grade school predicted problems in these areas in adolescence, which harmed their work outcomes later in life.

Thinking Like a Developmentalist

1. You are studying the social interactions of children in an elementary school and wonder why some children are aggressive toward other children and rejected by their peers whereas others are prosocial and popular. You hypothesize that rejected-aggressive children have problems understanding and experiencing the self-conscious emotions compared to popular prosocial children. How would you design a study to test your hypothesis? What would you do? Be sure to address how you would identify children who are rejected-aggressive and prosocial popular, the self-conscious emotions you would examine (and why); and the methods you would use to test whether differences among children in the understanding of self-conscious emotions are associated with peer rejection/acceptance statuses.

2. You are a teacher at an all-girls school, and are concerned about women's low labor-force participation in STEM (science, technology, engineering, and mathematics) disciplines. You wish to design a school-wide intervention that can promote girls' interests in math and self-efficacy around their math abilities, starting with one in your own classroom. Because this is a new project, you have limited resources to implement your intervention, and thus decide to focus on girls who maintain the stereo-

type that math and science are for boys. To your surprise, when you hand out a questionnaire to girls in your classroom asking them how much they believe math is for boys, you find that NO ONE seems to hold this stereotype! What alternative approach might you take to investigate stereotypes around math and science? And what would you then do to intervene on these stereotypes?

3. A clinical developmental researcher works with children who attend a therapeutic program after school to deal with experiences of neglect and/or maltreatment by their parents. The researcher has designed an intervention to improve the child-parent relationship and has been successful at getting parents and children to agree to participate in the program. To demonstrate the efficacy of the intervention, the researcher wants to show (a) improvements in parenting behaviors and (b) that children suffer from less "emotional pain" when interacting with their parents at the end of the program compared to the start of the program. What behaviors in parents might the researcher examine to test program effects on parenting? How might the researcher draw upon virtual exclusion studies to address reductions to child emotional pain?

Physical Development and Health in Adolescence

Drawing by Minxin Cheng from a photo by Jonathan Borba on Unsplash

There is a gym two blocks away from our local high school. It is inexpensive to join—which appeals to teens who wish to do "a little toning or bulking." The 13- to 18-year-olds who visit the gym enjoy the challenge, dedication, and hard work that it takes to run for miles on treadmills, lift weights, and attend kickboxing and barre classes. And their membership represents much more than just machines and classes. It symbolizes their passage from childhood to adulthood—an outward expression of their changing bodies and commitment to health. Many other teens who are not gym members spend hours jogging around town, lifting weights in their rooms, and making smoothies and other healthy concoctions (**FIGURE 14.1**).

Still, not all adolescents pursue health-conscious behaviors. Many do not have the time, inclination, or finances to exercise and eat healthy foods. Some teens feel self-conscious about their bodies, wear baggy clothes to hide how they look, and isolate themselves in a corner at lunch to quickly down a sandwich. And even teens following a fitness regime can become obsessed with their changing bodies. As the saying goes, "too much of a good thing is not good for you." Some adolescents have difficulty adjusting to the body and hormonal changes of puberty. In their eyes, their bodies consistently fall short of societal ideals. They fail to see themselves as thin enough, fit enough, strong enough, or beautiful enough.

This chapter describes the profound changes in brain and body that usher in adolescence and pave the way to adulthood. We will consider how asymmetrical brain development and hormonal changes motivate adolescents to embark on new social challenges but may also leave them vulnerable to risky behaviors that can jeopardize physical and psychological health.

PHYSICAL AND BRAIN DEVELOPMENT
- Brain Development
- Puberty
- Emergence of Sexual Behavior

HEALTH
- Sexually Transmitted Infections and Pregnancy
- Nutrition
- Sleep

Developmental Cascades

Closing Thoughts: Primed to Learn

FIGURE 14.1 Transition from childhood to adolescence. Many teens have a healthy attitude toward diet and exercise.

■ *Physical and Brain Development*

Adolescence is deceiving. Changes to physical appearance transform children into "adults" seemingly overnight. Yet, adolescents are far from ready to assume adult responsibilities. Their brains have not fully matured. They have not yet acquired the skills for financial independence, and they will undergo formative cognitive, emotional, and social changes over the forthcoming years. A glaring disconnect exists between the outer and inner selves of adolescents: Teens look like adults, are able to be sexually active and reproduce, and yet they are not yet sufficiently competent in their judgments or emotional maturity to handle adult obligations. In essence, "puberty arrives too early" (Lancy & Grove, 2011, p. 296).

Brain Development

Scientists used to consider brain development largely complete by early childhood. After all, with 95% of the brain's structure formed by 5 or 6 years of age, what else is left to develop? We now know differently. Advances in neuroimaging allow scientists to study brain functioning with greater precision than was possible decades earlier—for example, by monitoring which brain regions use energy and light up when adolescents perform certain tasks. While the adolescent brain maintains its basic structures, it prunes unused neural connections and strengthens others.

Synaptogenesis, Pruning, and Myelination

LEARNING OBJECTIVE 14.1 Describe changes to gray matter and white matter in the adolescent brain.

Processes in brain development, such as the overproduction of synapses, synaptic pruning, and myelination, continue throughout adolescence (see Chapter 2). As we will see, neural imaging reveals changes to the brain's gray and white matter that affect how adolescents think and act.

Changes to Gray Matter

synaptogenesis The rapid formation of synapses between neurons in the brain

pruning The process in which synapses are eliminated to increase the efficacy of neural communication

gray matter The nerve tissue of the central nervous system that comprises the cell bodies of neurons and forms the majority of the brain's structure

Young adolescents, around 11–12 years old, experience rapid **synaptogenesis**, the explosion of connections among neurons in the brain. This overproduction of synapses is concentrated in the frontal lobes, particularly the prefrontal cortex—the region of the brain that sits behind the forehead and is responsible for executive functions such as selective attention, planning, and strategy use.

Synaptogenesis is followed by synaptic **pruning** between 12 and 20 years of age (see Figure 2.27). Synaptic pruning retains synapses that are useful and eliminates those that are not used, thereby reducing the overabundance of connections. Just like the muscles of a body, which build up when exercised and atrophy when not used, neurons operate under this "use it or lose it" principle, strengthening connections among practiced areas. As a result, each person's brain wiring is different and responsive to what that person does on a daily basis: Playing video games will build up different connections than will composing music or doing math equations.

The pattern of synaptogenesis followed by pruning applies to **gray matter**, which comprises the cell bodies of neurons, the nonmyelinated axons and dendrites that project from them, and supporting cells. Gray matter forms the majority of the brain's structure and processing capacity. When scientists graph developmental changes in gray matter brain volume, they see an inverted U-shaped pattern reflecting an increase in early adolescence followed by a decline into adulthood (Blakemore, 2008; Goddings & Giedd, 2014) (**FIGURE 14.2A**). Like synaptogenesis, most pruning occurs in the frontal lobes, particularly the **prefrontal cortex**. Consequently, the brain's frontal regions become more specialized and work more efficiently than they had in childhood, approaching adult levels by mid-adolescence. In fact, rapid synaptic pruning during adolescence correlates with measures of intelligence (Shaw et al., 2006).

The peak in gray matter density occurs 1–2 years earlier in girls than in boys—on average, around 11.2 versus 12.6 years (Giedd et al., 1999; Lenroot and Giedd, 2006). Overall, however, boys show greater reductions to gray matter than do girls (Blanton et al., 2004; De Bellis et al., 2001). Sex differences in gray matter development correspond to differences in puberty onset, which also occurs earlier in girls than in boys (Peper & Dahl, 2013).

Changes to White Matter

Unlike gray matter pruning during adolescence, **white matter** increases steadily into adulthood, and then stabilizes in the late 20s (**FIGURE 14.2B**). White matter refers to the neurons that connect and communicate with one another through nerve impulses and consists primarily of myelinated axons and the glia cells that create myelin. **Myelin** is the fatty sheath that surrounds axons and makes them appear white in images.

The myelination of axons expands efficiency in communication between the two hemispheres and between the prefrontal cortex and other brain regions (Giedd et al., 1999; 2009; Tamnes et al., 2009). Improved efficiency occurs because myelinated axons conduct electrical impulses up to 100 times faster than unmyelinated axons, and they recover quickly after firing. Just as is seen for gray matter, changes to white matter projections are most pronounced in the prefrontal cortex (Blakemore & Choudhury, 2006; Paus, 2005; Toga, Thompson, & Sowell, 2006). Again, white matter changes help account for adolescent gains in abstract thinking, moral reasoning, decision-making, planning, inhibitory control, language, and problem solving (Blakemore & Choudhury, 2006; Paus, 2005; Toga et al., 2006).

✓ CHECK YOUR UNDERSTANDING 14.1

1. Why does synaptic pruning occur?
2. What aspects of brain functioning are most affected by the synaptic pruning that occurs during adolescence?
3. In what part of the brain is ongoing myelination most pronounced during adolescence?

Asymmetry in Brain Development

LEARNING OBJECTIVE 14.2 Explain the asymmetry of brain development in adolescence and the implications for adolescents' sensitivity to rewards.

You might assume that changes in white and gray matter mean that the brains of teens have caught up with adults. However, this is only partly true. When scientists scan the brains of hundreds of children, they find that different regions of the brain take different amounts of time to develop. Pruning and myelination generally progress from the back to the front of the brain. Thus, although massive reorganization takes place in the prefrontal cortex during adolescence, it is the last region of the brain to complete pruning and myelination (Smith, Xiao, & Bechara, 2012). Because the prefrontal cortex is the control region of the

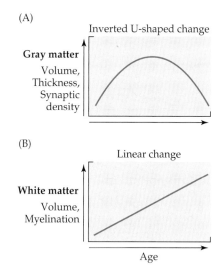

FIGURE 14.2 Gray and white matter change during adolescence. (A) The density, volume, and thickness of gray matter change during childhood and adolescence in an inverted U-shaped pattern, reflecting synaptogenesis followed by synaptic pruning: Gray matter increases during childhood, peaks in adolescence around 12–14 years, and declines across the late adolescent years and into adulthood. (B) White matter continues to increase across childhood and adolescence. (After T. Morita et al. 2016. *Front Hum Neurosci* 10: 464. © 2016 Morita, Asada and Naito. CC BY 4.0, https://creativecommons.org/licenses/by/4.0/.)

prefrontal cortex The part of the brain located behind the forehead that controls executive functioning

white matter The neurons of the central nervous system that connect and communicate with one another through nerve impulses; white matter comprises mainly myelinated axons and glial cells

myelin The fatty sheath that surrounds axons and increases the speed at which information travels on neurons brain, its prolonged maturation means that adolescents struggle with inhibition, impulse control, and planning, especially when they need to regulate behaviors in emotion-laden situations (e.g., Steinberg et al., 2008). Teens might drink and drive while blasting music at deafening levels when with peers, even though they understand the risks involved in these behaviors.

Limbic System

limbic system Subcortical regions of the brain (including the hippocampus, amygdala, and cingulate gyrus) that are involved in emotions, memory, motivation, and learning

To fully appreciate adolescent thinking and decision making, it's helpful to consider the asymmetrical maturity of different brain regions across development. Notably, by adolescence, the prefrontal cortex is relatively immature in its development compared to the more complete maturation of the **limbic system**, the subcortical regions of the brain referred to as the emotional (and sometimes social) brain. The highly active adolescent limbic system—which includes the hippocampus, amygdala, and cingulate gyrus, among other structures (Chapter 2)—is packed with neurons that are involved in motivation and emotions. When emotions are high, the limbic system is galvanized to seek out pleasure and reward. Indeed, when researchers offer rewards and incentives in laboratory tasks—such as in mock gambling games—the limbic system lights up a lot more in the teen brain than it does in adults' or children's brains (Barkley-Levenson & Galvan, 2014; Geier et al., 2010; Padmanabhan et al., 2011; Van Leijenhorst et al., 2010). Furthermore, the size of the reward matters. Relative to adults and children, reward regions of the adolescent brain fire at a frenzied pace when rewards are large, but fire at subdued rates when rewards are small (Galvan et al., 2006). And, compounding this tendency toward large rewards, the adolescent brain is less sensitive to the unpleasant properties of stimuli, which may explain propensities to substance use and other risk-taking behaviors (Doremus-Fitzwater, Varlinskaya, & Spear, 2011).

sensation seeking A personality trait characterized by a desire for pursuing varied, novel, and intense experiences and feelings

serotonin A neurotransmitter produced in the brain that regulates mood and appetite

What does limbic activation mean for adolescent behavior? The highly excitable limbic system primes adolescents to seek out exciting and pleasurable social situations. At the same time, adolescents are somewhat immune to the potential negative consequences of their behaviors. As such, they engage in more risk-taking behaviors such as drug and alcohol use than their younger and older counterparts, largely in the presence of peers and exciting social situations (Doremus-Fitzwater et al., 2011) (**FIGURE 14.3**).

Neurotransmitters

What explains the high limbic system activation of the teen brain? The answer lies in neurotransmitters. The physical and behavioral changes of puberty cause heightened release of neurotransmitters such as dopamine. Dopamine is involved in reward-motivated behavior and **sensation seeking**, the quest for varied, novel, and intense experiences and feelings (Schulz & Sisk, 2016). In turn, high concentrations of dopamine in the brain prompt a proliferation of receptors in the amygdala and other subcortical areas of the limbic system, making adolescents acutely sensitive to social situations (Suraev et al., 2014). **Serotonin**, a neurotransmitter that regulates mood and appetite, is likewise important for healthy adolescent functioning. Low serotonin levels in adolescence may lead to loneliness, eating disorders, depression, and self-harming behaviors like cutting, especially in girls (Bethea et al., 2002).

FIGURE 14.3 Limbic activation. Sensation taking by adolescents may be explained by asynchronous maturation of the prefrontal and limbic systems of the adolescent brain.

Autonomic Nervous System

Our bodies have systems in place that allow us to adjust to changes in the environment by controlling our heart rate, breathing, and other bodily functions. The hypothalamus controls many of these functions by communicating with the parasympathetic and sympathetic branches of the **autonomic nervous system**. These two systems switch on and off in response to what's going on around us. When we are at rest and calm, the parasympathetic branch allows our hearts to beat slow and steadily. If we confront a stressor—a friend's insult, a teacher's angry remark, the outbreak of a fight—the brain signals the sympathetic branch, which kicks into gear by pumping up our heart rate, thus preparing us for fight or flight to protect us from danger or threat. Once the stressor subsides, we physiologically recover and return to baseline. Adolescents, like all people, differ from one another in their autonomic nervous system reactivity for various reasons, including temperament and variations in the quality of their relationships with parents. In turn, adolescents with highly regulated autonomic system reactivity show correspondingly good skills at regulating emotions and coping with stress (e.g., Diamond & Cribbet, 2013; Yang et al., 2019).

autonomic nervous system
The part of the peripheral nervous system that regulates involuntary bodily functions, such as heartbeat, breathing, and digestion

✓ CHECK YOUR UNDERSTANDING 14.2

1. How does asymmetry in brain development lead to risky adolescent behaviors?
2. What role does the autonomic nervous system play in regulating bodily functions?

Puberty

The beginning of adolescence roughly coincides with the onset of **puberty**—the biological process that starts in the brain, involves pronounced hormonal changes, and results in remarkable physical and physiological transformations that enable reproduction—namely, the ability of girls to menstruate, gestate, and lactate, and of boys to impregnate (Peper & Dahl, 2010; Sisk, 2016). Over the course of puberty, which can take from 2 to 6 years, adolescents transition from the physical immaturity of children to inhabiting an adult-size body: They become taller and stronger, and their body shapes, voices, and facial features increasingly resemble adults. Perhaps most centrally, hormones that trigger pubertal changes also instigate adolescents' motivation to engage in romantic relationships and heightened feelings of desire, love, and social connection (Crone & Dahl, 2012; Suleiman et al., 2016). It is no wonder that so many books, movies, and plays portray the exhilaration and anguish of teenage love, and the great lengths adolescents will go for someone to whom they are sexually attracted.

puberty The biological process that begins in the brain and involves hormonal changes and physical and psychological transformations that enable reproduction

Primary and Secondary Sex Characteristics

LEARNING OBJECTIVE 14.3 Differentiate between primary and secondary sex characteristics.

Puberty produces both unobservable and observable changes, referred to as primary and secondary sex characteristics. **Primary sex characteristics** are associated with the reproductive organs—ovaries, uterus, and vagina in girls, and penis, scrotum, and testes in boys. Primary sex changes result in the production of ova in girls and sperm in boys, which enable reproduction. **Secondary sex characteristics** include observable body changes such as a growth spurt, pubic hair, breasts in girls, and facial hair and changes to voice in boys.

Breast development represents perhaps the most notable secondary sex characteristic in girls. On average, a girl's breasts begin to develop between 8 and 13, but take over 4 years to fully develop (Brooks-Gunn & Reiter, 1990). The process begins with breast budding around 8 or 9 years of age on average, and continues until the breasts reach their full size several years later. Pubic hair typically appears shortly after breast budding, and generally follows the same time

primary sex characteristics
Changes during puberty in the reproductive organs—ovaries, uterus, and vagina in girls and penis, scrotum, and testes in boys—that make reproduction possible

secondary sex characteristics
Observable body changes during puberty such as a growth spurt, pubic hair, breasts in girls, and facial hair and changes to voice in boys

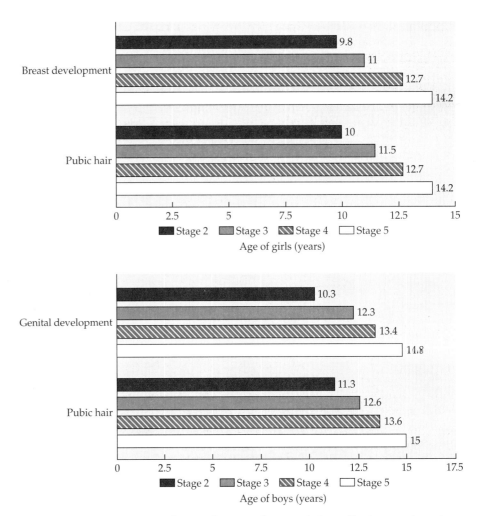

FIGURE 14.4 Appearance of secondary sex characteristics. For boys, pubertal onset occurs slightly later than for girls. (After E. J. Susman et al. 2010. *Arch Pediatr Adolesc Med* 164: 166–173.)

menarche The first occurrence of menstruation in girls during puberty

spermarche The beginning of boys' development of sperm in the testicles during puberty and capacity for ejaculation

course from 8 to 13 years. However, about 20% of girls experience pubic hair growth before breast budding. Girls in the United States experience **menarche**, the first occurrence of menstruation, at 12–13 years of age on average. Of course, this average age does not determine what will happen in any given girl, and girls from different races vary enormously in ages of pubertal changes.

For boys, pubertal onset occurs slightly later than it does for girls (**FIGURE 14.4**). Changes to the size of testicles and genitals occur at 11–11.5 years on average in the United States, and it takes about 3 years before boys' genitals reach adultlike size and shape (Brooks-Gunn & Reiter, 1990). Boys' pubic hair begins to appear shortly after age 12 and is followed by **spermarche**—the beginning of development of sperm in the testicles and capacity for ejaculation—1 to 2 years later, at about 13–14 years of age. The deepening of the voice marks another change in boys, which results from enlargement of the larynx and lengthening of vocal cords. Voice changes take time, beginning around the peak of boys' growth spurt and lasting until the end of puberty (Archibald, Graber, & Brooks-Gunn, 2006).

✓ **CHECK YOUR UNDERSTANDING 14.3**

1. What is the difference between primary and secondary sex characteristics?
2. Define menarche and spermarche.

The Growth Spurt

LEARNING OBJECTIVE 14.4 Identify changes in the body that are associated with the growth spurt experienced in adolescence.

One of the most noticeable outcomes of puberty is the **growth spurt**—acceleration of growth in hands, legs, and feet followed by torso length (**FIGURE 14.5**). Boys and girls differ, however, on what those changes look like. Boys' shoulders broaden relative to their hips, but girls' hips broaden relative to their shoulders. Girls also add fat to their limbs and torso, whereas boys reduce fat and add more muscle mass to their bodies than do girls (Rogol, Roemmich, & Clark, 2002). The greater muscle mass of boys means they exceed girls in strength, speed, and endurance by mid-adolescence (Haywood & Getchell, 2005). Moreover, the growth spurt occurs at a later age and lasts longer in boys than in girls. Thus, during middle school and the first year or two of high school, it is common to see girls towering over boys, with this pattern reversing a couple of years later.

Many adolescents (and boys in particular) in the United States respond to their changing bodies with the aim of being even stronger, wishing to bulk up to impress their peers. Some high school students augment physical exercise with performance-enhancing substances to improve muscle mass and physical strength (Castillo & Comstock, 2007; LaBotz & Griesemer, 2016). The majority of these substances, such as protein supplements, are harmless, but illegally obtained steroids can adversely affect health (Johnston et al., 2012). Around 1.5% of U.S. high school students report using steroids, based on data released by the National Institute of Drug Abuse (Witmer, 2019). Because steroids produce increased muscle mass, teenagers are likely to ignore or trivialize the side effects of mood swings, aggression, and damage to the liver, brain, and heart (Casavant et al., 2007).

growth spurt Rapid increase in height and weight during puberty and an acceleration of growth in hands, legs, feet, and torso length

✓ CHECK YOUR UNDERSTANDING 14.4

1. Describe sex differences in the timing of the growth spurt.

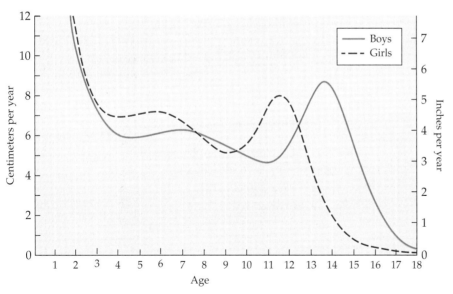

FIGURE 14.5 Growth spurts. Puberty brings the acceleration of growth in hands, legs, and feet followed by torso length. Girls show a spurt in growth about 2–3 years prior to boys. (After R. D. Bock and D. Thissen. 1980. In *Human Physical Growth and Maturation: Methodologies and Factors.* F. E. Johnston et al. [Eds.]. Published in cooperation with NATO Scientific Affairs Division. Plenum Press: New York. https://link.springer.com/chapter/10.1007/978-1-4684-6994-3_16.)

TABLE 14.1 ■ Factors that may lead to injury in adolescence

Factor	Comments
Height and weight	The stress and load on skeletal structures increase; momentum and force during collisions increase.
Muscle growth	Muscle sizes increase, leading to increased strength.
Bone structure	The weakness of growing bones can lead to tendon or ligamentous injuries.
Growth in cartilage near the ends of bones	Stress injuries can occur due to the immature growth plate.
Flexibility	Flexibility may decrease during the adolescent growth spurt, although the decrease in flexibility is more pronounced in boys than in girls.
Psychological maturity	Adolescents may have difficulty in coping with injuries or following treatment recommendations.

Source: D. R. Patel et al. 2017. *Transl Pediatr* 6: 160–166.

Injuries

LEARNING OBJECTIVE 14.5 Describe some injuries that adolescents are at particular risk for due to their changing bodies.

Many adolescents participate in sports at school or in their communities, which can support positive self-esteem and psychological well-being (e.g., Lubans et al., 2016). However, sports participation also raises the risk for injury, particularly because the intensity of sports training and specialization has grown in the United States over the past decades (Patel, Yamasaki, & Brown, 2017). Additionally, factors specific to adolescence may lead to injury, including decreased flexibility during the growth spurt and immaturity of the growth plates (**TABLE 14.1**). As a result, adolescent athletes may sustain musculoskeletal injuries to soft tissue caused by sudden impact and force (Patel et al., 2017).

Concussions are another form of injury that have received heightened attention over the past years, with rates of concussion being the highest for football players. Fortunately, recurrence rates of concussions and other injuries have declined for all sports over the past decade, largely due to improvements in preventive measures, diagnosis, and treatment (Kerr et al., 2019).

In general, injuries can be reduced with warm-ups, stretching, and exercises that are tailored to each sport; by educating adolescents on the need for proper hydration and nutrition; by wearing protective equipment; and by monitoring athletes who may be most at risk for injury.

✓ CHECK YOUR UNDERSTANDING 14.5

1. Why are adolescent athletes at heightened risk for musculoskeletal injuries?

Hormones

LEARNING OBJECTIVE 14.6 Describe how the hypothalamus and the pituitary gland interact in stimulating the onset of puberty.

What triggers puberty? Adolescents experience complex hormonal changes that result from communication between the body and brain: The body tells the brain when it is time to release pubertal hormones—such as estrogen and testosterone—and then the brain releases those hormones to produce further changes to the body.

How does the brain know when to release hormones? By monitoring an individual's body fat. Specifically, the brain's hypothalamus registers the proportion of a child's body fat, and moves into action once body fat reaches a particular threshold. In girls, fat cells release a protein called leptin, which signals to the brain that the body's energy stores are sufficient for puberty to begin (Rubin et al., 2009). The hypothalamus then communicates with the pituitary gland—a tiny, pea-sized gland—causing a series of chemical changes that trigger the physical transformations of puberty (**FIGURE 14.6**). The pituitary gland secretes gonadotropin hormones that stimulate the activity of the **gonads**, the reproductive organs—ovaries in girls and testes in boys (Fechner, 2003). In response to gonadotropins, the gonads increase production of the sex hormones—estrogens (particularly estradiol) and androgens (particularly testosterone).

Although estrogens are commonly thought of as female hormones and androgens as male hormones, both types are found in boys and girls, and their levels do not differ in the two sexes during childhood. However, once puberty begins, the hormones shift in their relative amounts. In girls, estradiol levels increase and work together with other hormones to trigger ovulation and menstruation. Estradiol remains elevated for girls during each menstrual cycle, in

gonads The reproductive organs—ovaries in girls and testes in boys

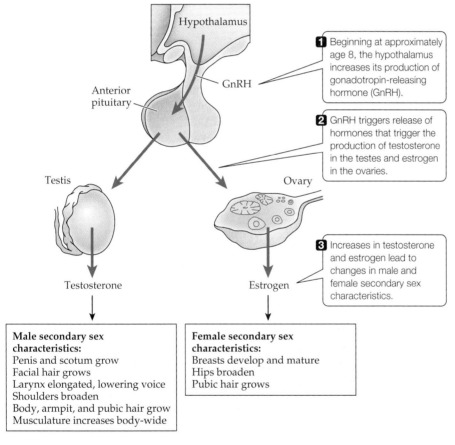

FIGURE 14.6 The role of the pituitary gland in puberty. The hypothalamus increases production of gonadotropin-releasing hormone, which stimulates the pituitary gland to release gonadotropin hormones, which trigger the production of testosterone and estrogen. The release of testosterone and estrogen from the pituitary gland causes a series of chemical changes that trigger the physical transformations of puberty. (After J. G. Betts et al. *Anatomy and Physiology*. Accessed 21 June 2021. https://openstax.org/details/books/anatomy-and-physiology CC BY 4.0. https://creativecommons.org/licenses/by/4.0/; S. M. Breedlove and N. V. Watson. 2019. *Behavioral Neuroscience*, 9th ed. Sinauer/Oxford University Press: Sunderland, MA.)

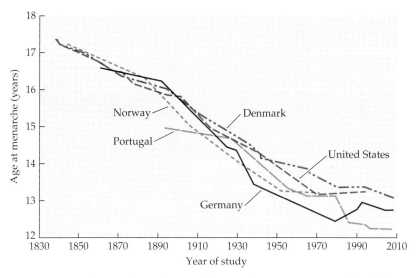

FIGURE 14.7 Secular trends in the age of menarche. Nutrition and health have improved over the centuries, leading to earlier puberty onset in girls in countries across the world. (After K. Sørensen et al. 2012. *Horm Res Paediatr* 77: 137–145.)

contrast to testosterone, which only slightly rises. For boys, in contrast, estradiol begins to decrease by mid-puberty as testosterone increases. Sex differences in the relative balance of estradiol and testosterone result in further changes to physical appearance. For both sexes, however, estrogens and androgens contribute to gains in bone density through the end of adolescence and into early adulthood (Cooper, Sayer, & Dennison, 2006).

Notably, the connection between body fat and puberty helps explain why diet and exercise contribute to pubertal timing. Puberty begins earlier for heavier girls (especially girls who are obese), and conversely, girls who engage in rigorous athletic training at an early age or who eat very little may experience delayed puberty (Kaplowitz, 2008; Rubin et al., 2009). **Secular trends**—nongenetic changes in human development that occur over extended time frames—further illustrate diet's effect on pubertal timing. Worldwide improvements in nutrition and health over centuries have led to earlier and earlier onsets of puberty (e.g., Belachew et al., 2011; Nabi et al., 2014) (**FIGURE 14.7**). However, even today, menarche occurs as late as 14–16 years of age in poor regions of the world, such as many areas in Africa, where malnutrition and infectious disease are common. Within poor countries, girls from economically disadvantaged homes reach menarche 6–18 months later than do girls from more resourced homes (Parent et al., 2003).

secular trends Changes in human development that take place over extended time frames; the average age of puberty has historically decreased

✓ CHECK YOUR UNDERSTANDING 14.6

1. What event(s) cause the pituitary to begin releasing sex hormones that initiate puberty?
2. How does the balance of the hormones estradiol and testosterone change in adolescent girls and boys, respectively, and what are the effects of this change?

Stages of Puberty

LEARNING OBJECTIVE 14.7 Describe a way that pubertal timing is measured and explain why early or late pubertal timing, relative to peers, can affect adolescent adjustment.

The physical changes of puberty can be catalogued as a set of stages, with some teenagers progressing through the stages at earlier ages than others. The

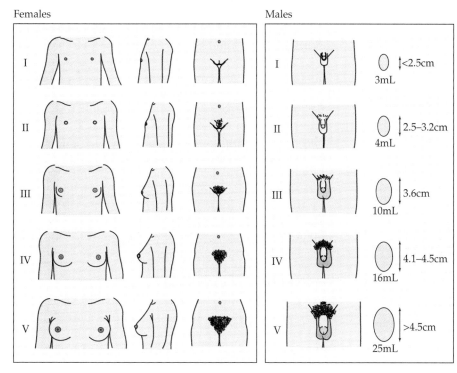

Females   Males

FIGURE 14.8 Tanner scale. The British pediatrician James Tanner developed the Tanner scale to assess adolescents' pubertal development. Adolescents' physical pubertal status is rated on a 5-point scale based on characteristics of pubic hair and breast development in females and pubic hair and genital development in males. (After M. Komorniczak. 2009. Tanner Scale Male, http://goo.gl/7cxTLM; Tanner Scale Female, http://goo.gl/haB9Cb. Accessed July 28, 2021. CC BY-SA 3.0, https://creative-commons.org/licenses/by-sa/3.0/deed.en.)

Tanner scale—named after the British pediatrician James Tanner—is commonly used to assess adolescents' pubertal development (Tanner & White-house, 1976) (**FIGURE 14.8**). Adolescents are classified on a scale from 1 to 5 based on certain secondary sexual characteristics—pubic hair and breast development in girls and pubic hair and genital development in boys. Typically, trained physicians classify teens based on a physical exam. For example, a girl who has no glandular breast tissue and no pubic hair would be classified at Tanner Stage 1; a girl with fully developed breasts and extended pubic hair would be classified at Tanner Stage 5. Although developed over 40 years ago, the Tanner scale continues to be a gold standard of pubertal development; self-report is another common approach when physical exams are impractical (Blakemore, Burnett, & Dahl, 2010; Dorn, 2006).

Tanner scale A standard assessment of pubertal development that describe the stage of physical development in children and adolescents based on primary and secondary sex characteristics

Pubertal Timing and Adolescent Adjustment

Adolescents are keenly aware of how their bodies compare to those of their peers—that is, whether they are ahead of their peers (early pubertal onset), in synchrony with them (on-time pubertal onset), or lagging behind (late pubertal onset). Perceptions around timing differences may in turn affect adolescent well-being.

In general, early pubertal timing relative to peers may render adolescents susceptible to depression and behavior problems, although such negative effects have been most consistently documented for female adolescents (Celio, Karink, & Steiner, 2006; Mendle, Turkheimer, & Emery, 2007; Negriff & Susman, 2011). Although the preponderance of evidence indicates that

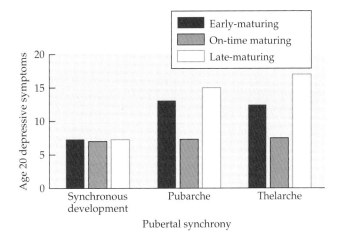

FIGURE 14.9 Pubertal synchrony. Female adolescents who show asynchronous development in the physical changes associated with puberty are at greater risk of depressive symptoms at age 20, with early-maturing and late-maturing adolescents being especially at risk. (After S. M. Thompson et al. 2016. *J Youth Adolesc* 45: 494–504. https://doi.org/10.1007/s10964-015-0402-1.)

early maturation is more detrimental than on-time or late maturation, late maturation can also lead to depression and behavior problems (Dorn et al., 2003; Graber et al., 2004; Negriff & Susman, 2011). Moreover, adolescents who show asynchronous development in the physical changes associated with puberty, such as developing breasts very late or very early relative to pubic hair (thelarche and pubarche, respectively), are at greater risk of depressive symptoms at age 20 than are adolescents who show synchronous, on-time puberty development in different physical markers of puberty (Thompson, Hannon & Brennan, 2016) (**FIGURE 14.9**). In short, adolescents are emotionally vulnerable when they are maturing too early or too late, and the psychological ramifications of timing may cascade to mental health and behavior problems, as reviewed later in the chapter.

Mechanisms of Influence

Why does the timing of puberty relative to one's peers matter? Scientists propose four hypotheses to explain why pubertal timing may cause behavioral problems and psychological distress in adolescents:

peer-influence hypothesis
A theory in which older peers are thought to affect the behaviors of younger adolescents who experience early puberty in ways that may lead to earlier-than-usual exposure to risky behaviors in younger adolescents

- **Peer-influence hypothesis**: Early puberty may instigate problem behaviors because of the influence of older peers. Early maturing adolescents are likely to hang out with older teens who look like them physically. They are thus prone to earlier-than-usual exposure to risky behaviors, such as alcohol use and sexual activity, at a time when they are insufficiently mature to handle peer influences (e.g., Caspi et al., 1993).

maturational deviance hypothesis
A theory positing that an adolescent's physical deviation from his or her peer group may place the adolescent at risk for mood and behavioral problems, regardless of early or late maturation

- **Maturational deviance hypothesis**: The adolescent's physical deviation from his or her peer group, whether due to early or late maturation, is stressful and may increase vulnerability for mood and behavior problems. Early maturing girls are the most physically "deviant" because they enter puberty before most other girls their age and before nearly all boys their age. In contrast, late-maturing boys are the most physically "deviant" because they are the last to develop relative to boys and girls of their age (Negrif & Susman, 2011).

readiness hypothesis A theory positing that early maturing adolescents may experience asynchrony among physical, cognitive, social, and emotional maturity and thus be at risk for adjustment problems

- **Readiness hypothesis**: Early maturation may be problematic because of the asynchrony it creates between physical, cognitive, social, and emotional maturity (Negriff & Susman, 2011). Early-maturing adolescents look like adults but are far from being adults, which may amplify the risk of adjustment problems (Ge et al., 2002).

contextual amplification hypothesis A theory positing that an adolescent's adjustment to early puberty depends on sociocultural context

- **Contextual amplification hypothesis**: Adolescent adjustment to early pubertal timing, especially in girls, depends on social and cultural context. Social messages about sexuality and body image interact with a teen's experience of puberty to determine whether and to what degree early timing cascades to problem behaviors (Ge et al., 2011).

✓ CHECK YOUR UNDERSTANDING 14.7

1. List four hypotheses that explain how the timing of puberty may lead to behavior problems and stress in adolescents.

Home Context of Puberty

LEARNING OBJECTIVE 14.8 Provide examples of how stressful home environments and diet influence the onset of puberty.

People often think that the onset of **puberty** is predetermined, much like an alarm clock that is set to go off at a certain time. Although there is a genetic component to pubertal timing, environmental forces, such as social interactions in the family and foods available at home, also contribute.

Adolescents who experience prolonged, unpleasant conditions at home, including conflict and stress among family members, parental divorce, poor attachment relationships, child maltreatment, and low parental involvement, are prone to early pubertal onset (e.g., Belsky, Houts, & Feron, 2010; Nabi Amin, Sultan, & Kamil, 2014). Tense, inconsistent, and/or intimidating family environments may affect pubertal onset by chronically elevating adolescent stress levels (e.g., Boynton-Jarrett et al., 2013; Braithwaite et al., 2009). Adolescents with absent or uninvolved fathers are also likely to show early signs of puberty, effects that may be further compounded by genetics (Schlomer & Cho, 2017) (**FIGURE 14.10**). Moreover, adolescents from poor households are more likely to experience father absence than adolescents from more affluent households, with father absence accelerating the effect of socioeconomic status on pubertal onset (Deardroff et al., 2011; Ryan, 2015) (**FIGURE 14.11**).

Beyond the social stressors of poverty, adolescents from poor U.S. households may consume diets that are relatively high in fat and protein content, leading to a high percentage of body fat, which triggers the release of pubertal hormones (Reagan et al., 2012). Children with a high intake of animal proteins experienced puberty 7 months earlier on average than did children with a high intake of vegetables (Cheng et al., 2012).

✓ CHECK YOUR UNDERSTANDING 14.8

1. How can the family environment affect the onset of puberty?

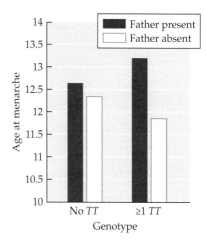

FIGURE 14.10 Presence of fathers and age at menarche. Girls with absent fathers experience earlier menarche than those with present fathers, and this effect is even stronger for females who have a specific genotype (*TT*). (After G. L. Schlomer and H.-J. Cho. 2017. *Evol Hum Behav* 38: 761–769.)

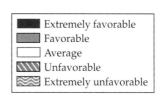
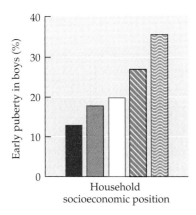
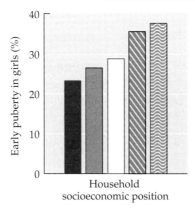

FIGURE 14.11 Socioeconomic status and the age at puberty onset. A greater percentage of adolescents from poor households show early puberty onset. As the economic circumstances of families become increasingly unfavorable, the percentage of adolescents experiencing early onset of puberty grows, with similar patterns in boys and girls. (After Y. Sun et al. 2017. *Pediatrics* 139: e20164099. Reproduced with permission. Copyright © 2017 by the AAP.)

Cultural Context of Puberty

LEARNING OBJECTIVE 14.9 Identify ways in which attitudes toward puberty vary by culture.

We opened the chapter by suggesting that "puberty arrives too early." In the United States, for example, although adolescents inhabit adult bodies, they are rarely treated as adults at home or by society. Different laws and penal codes exist for teens and adults. Parents monitor, discipline, and guide adolescents toward "good judgment" and "good choices." Schools educate adolescents about health and risk, through classes on sex education and the dangers of substance use, inadequate sleep, and poor nutrition. Do these views and practices generalize across cultures? Do all societies perceive a disconnect between adolescents' physical and psychological maturity? How do adolescents from different parts of the world react to puberty, and how do community members help prepare adolescents for entry into the adult world?

Cultural Reactions to Puberty

It is not uncommon for adolescents in the United States to feel self-conscious about puberty, even when they are informed and psychologically prepared for the event. Most girls would be embarrassed if their parents or other adults announced their first menstruation to relatives or friends, and boys would similarly be embarrassed to have the details of their changing bodies disclosed to others. At the same time, adolescents are proud of their changing bodies, eager to transition to greater independence and responsibility, and excited about the romantic interests triggered by puberty. Are these reactions to puberty common in other parts of the world? The answer is yes. Adolescents from cultures spanning Nigeria, Kenya, Mexico, Iran, and Tanzania express mixed emotions as they enter puberty—including anxiety, embarrassment, and pride (Ahmadi et al., 2009; Bello et al., 2017; Marván et al., 2007; Sommer, Likindikoki, & Kaaya, 2014). And, their parents worry, just as do parents in the United States, that the physical changes of their adolescents might lead to romantic and sexual relations and unwanted pregnancy (Bello et al., 2017).

puberty rites Ritual activities and teachings that prepare adolescents for new roles in a type of "rite of passage" into adulthood

Cultural Traditions around Puberty

Cultures everywhere have historically engaged in special traditions to mark the adolescent's transition to puberty. These traditions include ceremonies where girls and boys wear special clothes, display fancy hairstyles, and participate in events that involve feasts, dances, music, speeches, and even fire displays (Ottenberg, 1994; Schlegal & Barry, 2017) (**FIGURE 14.12**). Sometimes, ceremonies take on special themes such as "taking responsibilities of one's adult status" for boys and "reproduction, fertility, sexual capacity, and attractiveness for girls" (Weisfeld, 1997).

Some cultures engage in **puberty rites**—ritual activities and teachings that prepare adolescents for their new roles (Schlegel & Barry, 1980, 2017). Puberty rites sometimes appear to be harsh, and may include lengthy initiations, extended periods of training, and even seclusion from families and members of the opposite sex (Lancy & Grove, 2011). In the past, for example:

- The !Kung Bushmen boys of the Kalahari received a painful scar at their puberty ceremony as a way to subdue them and teach them responsibility (Eibl-Eibesfeldt, 1989).

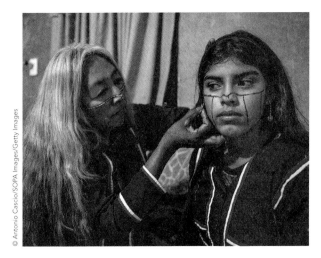

FIGURE 14.12 Many cultures celebrate the transition to adolescence. Here, a 12-year-old girl in the Comcáac community gets her face painted by her godmother with ancestral patterns in preparation for a four-day ceremony of puberty.

© Antonio Cascio/SOPA Images/Getty Images

- The South American Guajiro farmers confined adolescent girls for up to 5 years to indoctrinate them into childbearing and women's work and to protect their virtue (Schlegel and Barry 1980, 2017; Whiting, Burbank, & Ratner, 1986).

- The !Xoo of Zutschwa in Botswana secluded females at their first menstruation, keeping them in a hut under the watch of a caretaker who would offer instructions on how to be a good wife and mother, sometimes through songs and dance that symbolized the path to successful maturity (Nhlekisana, 2017).

- Puberty rites for boys in remote villages around the globe, such as the MButi in Africa, included teaching them economic skills and masculine tasks, such as working with heavy materials, defending the family, hunting large game, and so forth. If they failed at these tasks, they might be denied acceptance into adulthood and would be unlikely to marry (Lancy & Grove, 2011; Weisfeld, 1977).

Of course, many of the practices observed decades ago have changed with globalization and modernization. Today, !Xoo girls attend school, and teachers warn caretakers against secluding girls, arguing that it causes girls to miss their education. Yet, many families find a way to merge their old traditions with new ones, for example by isolating !Xoo girls only during menstruation, rather than extended periods of time, and continuing the songs and dances that initiate girls into the joys of womanhood (Nhlekisana, 2017).

Although these practices may be unfamiliar to many people, other familiar traditions symbolize a passage from childhood to adulthood around the time of puberty—bar mitzvahs and bat mitzvahs (religious initiations in Jewish communities), confirmations (a religious rite in Christian communities), and quinceañeras (a celebration to mark a girl's coming of age in Hispanic communities). Furthermore, many traditions today contain symbolic rites of passage. As one example, circumcision of boys is a rite of passage and hallmark of adolescence in Nigeria and Kenya, where adolescent boys express pride at being circumcised and take on responsibilities associated with the so-called end of childhood (Bello et al., 2017).

Preparing Adolescents for Adulthood

Once puberty begins, and is perhaps celebrated in a special way, do cultures around the world regard the adolescent's physical transformation as a sign of adulthood? It is fascinating to consider how societies might have viewed adolescents in the distant past, when marriage and childbearing occurred at much younger ages than they do today and when life expectancies were much shorter (**FIGURE 14.13**). It is equally intriguing to consider how cultures with different schooling practices, levels of industrialization, and expectations about the responsibilities of youth respond to adolescence and its associated physical changes. Is an extended period of transition common everywhere, or only in cultures where extensive schooling is typical?

Surprisingly perhaps, not much has changed over time. Throughout history, adolescence has been characterized as a time of psychological turmoil and lack of judgment. Plato, the Greek philosopher, cautioned against permitting adolescents to drink until they were 18 years of age, and further stated that even then, adolescents and young

FIGURE 14.13 American adolescents were once expected to take on adult responsibilities. Shown here are child coal mine workers in 1911.

FIGURE 14.14 In some Inuit cultures, children married right after puberty and were considered adults ready to bear children and run their own households. Shown here are a young Inuit mother and her baby girl in Itilleq, a village of 80 Inuit people on the southwest coast of Greenland.

adults should only indulge in moderation until they turned 30 years of age, "lest they become highly excitable" (Plato, 360 BCE).

Moreover, the vast majority of communities, urban or rural, industrialized or less resourced, consider adolescence to be distinct from adulthood, and parents express concerns about keeping their adolescents safe (Bello et al., 2017; Schlegel & Barry, 1991). Only a handful of exceptions exist, from accounts decades old. For example, the Berber and Inuit Arctic foragers, whose children married right after puberty, were considered adults ready to bear children and run their own households (Condon, 1987) (**FIGURE 14.14**).

As a result, most cultures have implemented strategies and formal institutions to protect adolescents and indoctrinate them with skills needed to join the adult world. In the United States, high school and college function to delay entry into adulthood by occupying adolescents for years as they acquire skills for entering the job market. Many adolescents intern at professional training sites, where they gain expertise working with people and being exposed to the skills required for different occupations.

✓ **CHECK YOUR UNDERSTANDING 14.9**

1. What secular trends have been observed with respect to the onset of puberty?
2. Describe cultural variations around perceptions of puberty and practices around puberty.

Emergence of Sexual Behavior

Adolescents' heightened desire to engage in romantic relationships signifies one of the most important consequences of puberty (Dahl, 2016). Hormonal changes lead to erotic feelings that can propel sexual behavior (Best & Fortenberry, 2013). Adolescents must effectively manage their increased sex drive, which includes facing pivotal decisions about whether to engage in sex, and if so, when, with whom, and under what circumstances.

Learning about Sexuality and Engaging in Sex

LEARNING OBJECTIVE 14.10 Describe how U.S. adolescents learn about and engage in sexual activity.

Over the past 50 years, societal acceptance of sex before marriage has grown along with fewer taboos around teenage pregnancy (e.g., Elisas, Fullerton, & Simpson, 2015). Societal acceptance has occurred at the same time as major changes in how adolescents acquire information about sexuality. Although adolescents learn about sexuality from schools and parents, they are also likely to seek information from friends, the internet, and social media (Bleakley et al., 2018; Sprecher, Harris, & Myers, 2008; Negriff & Subrahmanyam, 2020).

Furthermore, the variety of programs, platforms, and streaming content has shifted dramatically since the mid-twentieth century, with sexual content (i.e., scenes that reference or explicitly portray sexual interactions between characters) appearing in 80%–85% of programming (Ward et al., 2016; Wright, Malamuth, & Donnerstein, 2012). Some adolescents view sexually explicit material online, which relates to engagement in sexual activity and being victims of sexual harassment (O'Hara et al., 2013; Wright et al., 2012). There is also a strong feedback loop in these associations: Teens who are sexually active are more likely to consume sexual media than those who are not active (Steinberg & Monahan, 2011; Vandenbosch & Eggermont, 2013).

Adolescents differ in whether or not they choose to engage in sexual behaviors and the age at which they engage in specific forms of sexual activity. However, in the context of wide variations among adolescents, the number of adolescents who report being sexually active increases with age (Mulinax, Mathur, & Santelli, 2017) (**FIGURE 14.15**). For example, in the United States, around 10% of teens report engaging in sex prior to 14 years of age, whereas the majority (over 60%) report having had sexual intercourse by the time they graduate from high school (Kahn et al., 2014). The rate of sexual intercourse rises to 74% by 20 years of age (Kaplan et al., 2013; Finer & Philbin, 2013).

Given that sexuality is central to human development, many educational programs aim to instill principles of positive sexual health in teens. A sexual health approach to education recognizes that adolescents have sexual rights and should be provided with information and services to help them understand their sexuality and develop a healthy and respectful approach to sexual relationships, including how to say no to unwanted sex and how to use birth control if sex is desired (Mulinax et al., 2017) (**FIGURE 14.16**). The goal of such programs is to ensure that sexual activity is safe, free of coercion, and a source of pleasure. Indeed, adolescents who engage in sex in the context of a stable and caring relationship can find the experience to be rewarding, whereas casual sex and sex that results from lowered inhibitions from drinking and drugs can lead to depression and guilt (Harden, 2014).

Notably, a substantial percentage of U.S. teens have *not* had sex by the time they reach 20 years of age. Some adolescents favor abstinence for religious reasons or to avoid contracting sexually transmitted infections (STIs). Clearly, decisions around sexuality are highly personal, and many factors contribute to an adolescent's ultimate decision around whether to refrain from sexual

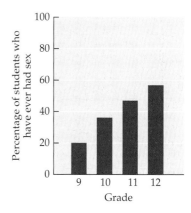

FIGURE 14.15 The number of teens who report being sexually active increases with age. By the time they reach twelfth grade, a majority of U.S. high school students have had sexual intercourse. (After E. Witwer et al. 2018. *Sexual Behavior and Contraceptive and Condom Use among U.S.High School Students*, 2013–2017. Guttmacher Institute: New York. [adapted]. https://doi.org/10.1363/2018.29941.

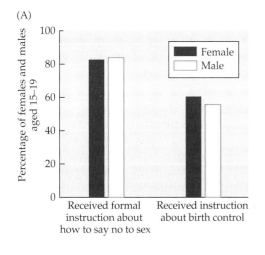

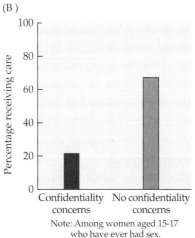

FIGURE 14.16 Sex education. (A) The majority of adolescents receive formal education about abstinence and contraception. (B) When adolescents have concerns about the confidentiality of their use of contraception, they are unlikely to obtain it. (A after Guttmacher Institute. Adolescent Sexual and Reproductive Health in the United States. September 2019. https://www.guttmacher.org/fact-sheet/american-teens-sexual-and-reproductive-health. [adapted] Source: V. Guilamo-Ramos et al. 2015. *Prev Sci* 16: 53–60. doi:10.1007/s11121-014-0469-z; B after K. Hasstedt. Guttmacher Policy Review 21. November 15, 2018. https://www.guttmacher.org/gpr/2018/11/ensuring-adolescents-ability-obtain-confidential-family-planning-services-title-x. [adapted] Source: Guttmacher Institute.)

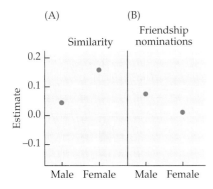

FIGURE 14.17 The effects of sexual intercourse on male and female adolescents' experience of friendships.   (A) Female adolescents show greater similarity in friends than do male adolescents after having engaged in sexual intercourse. (B) Male adolescents show a greater increase than female adolescents in the number of friendship nominations they receive from their peers (suggesting increased popularity after having had sex). (After S. L. Trinh et al. 2018. *Child Dev* 90: e132–e147. © 2018 Society for Research in Child Development, Inc. All rights reserved.)

sexual homophily The adolescent's tendency to form strong bonds and connections with others who are similar in their sexual activities

relationships, including their own attitudes toward abstinence and the attitudes of their peers and families (Akers et al., 2011).

✓ **CHECK YOUR UNDERSTANDING 14.10**
  1. How has technology affected the ways that teens learn about sexuality?
  2. What is meant by a "sexual health approach" in adolescent health education?

Peer Context of Sexuality

LEARNING OBJECTIVE 14.11 Explain the concept of sexual homophily and its role in the friendships of adolescent boys and girls.

Peers powerfully influence adolescents' views and behaviors around sexuality. A longitudinal study of over 2,500 14- to 18-year-old adolescents revealed high **sexual homophily** among friends—the tendency to form strong social connections with people who are similar in sexual activities. Specifically, an adolescent's likelihood of engaging in sex related to whether their friends had also engaged in sex: Adolescents who engage in sex influence their friends to engage in sex, and adolescents choose friends who have similar sexual statuses (Trinh et al., 2019).

However, adolescent girls may be more inclined toward sexual homophily than adolescent boys. Whereas adolescent girls narrowed their network of friends once they had engaged in sex, adolescent boys were more likely to be friends with individuals who had different sexual statuses than they did. Additionally, adolescent boys, but not girls, gained in popularity after their sexual activities (Kraeger et al., 2016; Trinh et al., 2019). Diverging patterns in popularity may reflect enduring double standards of greater acceptance of sexuality in adolescent boys than girls (**FIGURE 14.17**).

✓ **CHECK YOUR UNDERSTANDING 14.11**
  1. How do adolescent boys and girls differ in sexual homophily?

Cultural Context of Sexuality

LEARNING OBJECTIVE 14.12 Identify how a culture's views around sexuality may affect adolescents' sexual behaviors and adjustment to sexuality.

Cultural norms and attitudes strongly shape adolescents' feelings around sexuality and their decisions to become sexually active. Adolescents in cultures with a high tolerance for sexual involvement are more inclined to engage in sex as teens than those living in less tolerant, highly conservative communities. For example, many countries in the Middle East view premarital sexual activity as inappropriate and against the Islamic faith, resulting in few comprehensive sex education programs for adolescents (Zaabi et al., 2019).

Notably, a culture's permissiveness around adolescent sexuality may affect how teenagers adjust to their own developing sexuality. For example, adolescents who experience early puberty may be more prone to engaging in sexual intercourse at a young age if they live in a community where adolescent sexual activity is tolerated. Because these early maturing adolescents may not be emotionally mature enough to handle their sexual relationships, they may be at risk for problem behaviors, such as high conflict with their parents and staying out late, lying, and using alcohol or other drugs.

To explore a possible connection between cultural acceptance of adolescent sexuality and the onset of problem behaviors, researchers asked whether early onset of puberty in girls led to differences in problem behaviors in Slovakia and Sweden, countries where permissiveness for adolescent sexuality differs substantially—Slovakia has a history of conservatism around sexuality and Sweden has high acceptance of adolescent intercourse (Skoog et al., 2013).

As predicted, early maturing girls in Sweden are more likely to become active sexually than are early maturing girls in Slovakia. Early experimentation with sexual relationships in Sweden, in turn, relates to problem behaviors, such as ignoring parents' prohibitions, staying out late without permission, smoking pot, and getting drunk. The researchers concluded that Sweden's open, accepting attitudes toward sex amplified pressures to engage in sexual intercourse before adolescent girls were psychologically ready (Skoog et al., 2013). This is not to say that cultural tolerance of adolescent sexuality is always problematic. Cultures that openly provide information and resources to teens about safe ways to engage in sexual intercourse may support adolescents who are psychologically ready and mature enough to enter romantic relationships, and help reduce the likelihood of pregnancy and STIs. However, sex education varies enormously across communities, even within a country, as seen in the enormous state-to-state variations in sex education coverage in the United States (Schmidt, Wandersman, & Hills, 2015).

✓ CHECK YOUR UNDERSTANDING 14.12

1. Provide an example of a cultural difference in attitudes and behaviors around adolescent sexuality.

■ *Health*

Adolescents are stronger and more resistant to disease than they will ever be in their lifetimes. Still, many teenagers engage in behaviors that jeopardize their health. Adolescents who are sexually active may contract STIs or become pregnant without proper protection. Beyond the risks involved in unprotected sex, poor eating habits and eating disorders can lead to obesity at one extreme and anorexia or bulimia at the other. Moreover, many adolescents get insufficient sleep, which makes it tough to cope with stress and may lead to mental and physical exhaustion.

Sexually Transmitted Infections and Pregnancy

My 15-year-old neighbor Joey and his girlfriend got pregnant when I was a teen myself. His girlfriend's parents told her to pack her bags and never come back, and she eventually moved into Joey's house, where his parents provided some financial support and help with the baby. Neither Joey nor his girlfriend completed high school, and Joey cobbled together odd jobs to support his baby and girlfriend. Despite their immense love for their baby, they often fought, eventually split up, and suffered financially, emotionally, and psychologically for many years. Their son repeated the pattern, becoming a dad himself 17 years later.

Unfortunately, adolescents often fail to reason about the potential consequences of unprotected sex or have limited knowledge and access to contraceptives. Some adolescents, especially teens who cannot talk openly with their parents, don't know where to go for counseling and assistance around birth control and worry that their parents might find out about their visits to a clinic or doctor (Lehrer et al., 2007; Widman et al., 2014). Moreover, the brain's asymmetrical development interferes with self-regulation precisely at a time in development when romantic attraction is strongest. As a result, sexually active teens may be at risk for contracting an STI or becoming pregnant.

Sexually Transmitted Infections

LEARNING OBJECTIVE 14.13 Name the most prevalent STIs and their causes.

Sexually transmitted infections can lead to sterility, health problems, and even death if not treated properly, and can be psychologically traumatic if the infected adolescent feels betrayed by a partner. Many adolescents believe that they are immune to STIs as long as their partners remain faithful. Others believe that oral sex avoids infection. Both beliefs are misguided. Furthermore, escalations in adolescent sexting and the use of "hookup apps" have been associated with an increase in sexual behaviors and STIs in recent years (Macapagal et al., 2018; Romo et al., 2017). Whether an adolescent engages in sex with a longstanding partner or through a brief hookup, failure to use protection raises the chances of various STIs, including herpes and gonorrhea (Vasilenko, Lefkowitz, & Welsh, 2014) (**TABLE 14.2**).

Notably, adolescents in the United States have higher rates of STIs than do adults, which in part can be traced to a lack of appropriate contraceptive use. According to the Centers for Disease Control (CDC), in 2017, over 46% of high school students reported not using a condom the last time they had sex, and over half of STIs occurred in individuals 15–24 years of age. Moreover, the likelihood of being infected with an STI differs for men and women: It is easier for a man to infect a woman with an STI than it is for a woman to infect a man.

Acquired immunodeficiency syndrome (AIDS) arises from infection by human immunodeficiency virus (HIV), the most serious of sexually transmitted infections. AIDS leads to progressive failure of the immune system and can result in life-threatening infections and cancers. A 2019 report from the CDC found that 21% of U.S. individuals diagnosed with HIV were 13–24 years of age. Although most male adolescents and young adults diagnosed with HIV (93%) were infected through male-to-male sexual contact, transmission among female adolescents and young adults was largely through heterosexual contact (86%). Several factors contribute to the high incidence of HIV in adolescents

TABLE 14.2 ■ STIs in adolescence: Description and prevalence

Infection	Description	Prevalence
Chlamydia	Most common sexually transmitted infection that can result in painful urination, discharge from the vagina or penis, painful sexual intercourse in adolescent girls, and testicular pain in adolescent boys.	Approximately 2.5% of adolescents in the United States between 14 and 39 years of age experience chlamydia, with rates higher among adolescent girls than adolescent boys (Datta et al., 2012).
Human papillomavirus (HPV)	In most cases, HPV goes away on its own. When it does not, it can cause genital warts—a small bump or group of bumps in the genital area—and in extreme cases, cancer.	A highly prevalent STI among sexually active youth in the United States. In 2003/2004, nearly 25% of adolescent girls 15–19 years had an HPV infection.
Trichomoniasis	A sexually transmitted infection that in 70% of cases does not have any signs or symptoms. When symptoms occur, they can range from mild burning and itching in the genital area to severe inflammation.	Trichomoniasis affects 2.1% of females aged 14–59 and 0.5% of males (CDC STD Surveillance Report).
Gonorrhea	Infects men and women and can cause inflammation and discharge in the urethra and rectum and inflammation of the pelvis in women, although only a fraction of women show symptoms. Gonorrhea is a leading cause of female infertility.	The prevalence of gonorrhea in women aged 15–24 is double that of men the same age, about 0.62% and 0.32%, respectively (Satterwhite et al., 2013).
HIV	A disease of the immune system caused by a retrovirus and transmitted chiefly through blood or blood products that enter the body's bloodstream, especially by sexual contact or contaminated hypodermic needles.	In 2016, 610,000 young people worldwide between the ages of 15 and 25 were newly infected with HIV, of whom 260,000 were adolescents between the ages of 15 and 19 (UNICEF, 2017).

Source: Sources: Miscellaneous, including, but not limited to CDC STD Surveillance Report; C. L. Satterwhite et al. 2013. *Sex Transm Dis* 40: 187–193; S. D. Datta et al. 2012. *Sex Transm Dis* 39: 92–96; UNICEF. 2017. The State of the World's Children 2017. © United Nations Children's Fund (UNICEF) December 2017. New York: UNICEF.

TABLE 14.3 ■ Factors that contribute to the high incidence of HIV in adolescents

Factors	Statistics
Low rates of testing	Only 9% of high school students have been tested for HIV. Low rates of testing mean more young people have undiagnosed HIV.
Substance use	Nationwide, 19% of all students who are currently sexually active used alcohol or drugs before their most recent sexual intercourse. Young people may engage in high-risk behaviors when under the influence of alcohol or drugs.
Low rates of condom use	Nationwide, 46% of all sexually active high school students did not use a condom the last time they had sexual intercourse.
Number of partners	Nearly 25% of male students who had sexual contact with male partners reported sexual intercourse with four or more persons during their life, compared to 10% of all students.

Source: CDC. HIV and Youth. Accessed July 28, 2021. https://www.cdc.gov/hiv/group/age/youth/index.html

and young adults, spotlighting the continued need to monitor and encourage healthy behaviors at these ages (**TABLE 14.3**).

✓ **CHECK YOUR UNDERSTANDING 14.13**

1. List some common STIs.
2. What are the most effective ways to prevent STIs?

Pregnancy and Parenthood in Adolescence

LEARNING OBJECTIVE 14.14 Describe factors associated with teen pregnancy.

Most adolescents are ill-equipped to have a baby. The majority who become pregnant—nearly 80% based on a national survey—had not intended to have a baby (Martin et al., 2017). The phrase "children raising children" captures the challenges of adolescent childbearing.

Adolescent Pregnancy Rates

Relative to the past, adolescents today are more likely to take the necessary precautions to prevent pregnancy through abstinence and contraceptive use (Kost & Henshaw, 2014; Lindberg, Santelli, & Desai, 2016) (**FIGURE 14.18**). These precautions have resulted in declining rates of adolescent pregnancy in the United

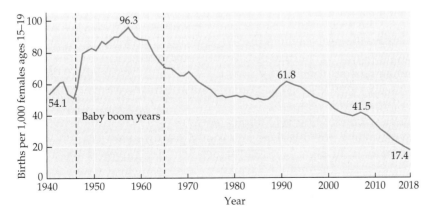

FIGURE 14.18 Pregnancy rates. Adolescent pregnancy rates are falling in the United States. (After G. Livingston and D. Thomas. Why is the teen birth rate falling? Pew Research Center, Washington, D.C. August 2, 2019. https://www.pewresearch.org/fact-tank/2019/08/02/why-is-the-teen-birth-rate-falling/ Source: National Center for Health Statistics published data.)

States over the past two decades, from 61.8 births for every 1,000 adolescent females (between 15 and 19 years of age) in 1991 to 18.8 births per 1,000 in 2017 (Centers for Disease Control, 2019).

Consequences of Adolescent Parenthood for the Infant

Pregnant adolescents, especially those who don't have the support of their parents or lack health care coverage, may receive inadequate prenatal care that places the unborn baby at risk. Moreover, adolescent mothers' high rate of poverty increases the odds of medical complications during the pregnancy or birth. Infants born to adolescent mothers are more likely to be born prematurely and to have a low birth weight. In turn, the earlier an infant is born, the greater the risk of respiratory, digestive, vision, cognitive, and other problems. Over the longterm, children born to adolescents have poorer health, educational outcomes, and behavioral outcomes throughout their lives than do those born to adult parents (Hamilton et al., 2015).

Consequences of Adolescent Parenthood for Girls

Adolescent parents face a cascade of negative social and economic circumstances. Adolescent mothers are at high risk of enduring mental and physical health problems into adulthood (Patel & Sen, 2012). Additionally, adolescent childbearing affects marriage patterns, education, and income. Women who give birth to children as adolescents are less likely to get married in the future, and those who do marry are more likely to divorce compared to women who delay childbearing (Maynard, 2018; Moore & Brooks-Gunn, 2002).

School prospects of adolescent parents are also limited. Many adolescent girls who become pregnant drop out of school to take care of their infants, making it difficult to land future employment. Indeed, only about 50% of adolescent mothers earn a high school diploma by 22 years of age, compared to 90% of women who had not given birth during adolescence (Centers for Disease Control, 2019; Perper, Peterson, & Manlove, 2010).

Consequences of Adolescent Parenthood for Boys

Fathers of children born to adolescent mothers are often only teens themselves or slightly older. Although some of these fathers may express a strong desire to be involved with their children, they often perceive barriers to their involvement, including a lack of money, lack of knowledge about children and parenting, struggles in their relationship with the infant's mother and family, and high stress and anxiety (Beers & Hollo, 2009). As a result, becoming a father at a relatively young age exerts a financial and emotional toll on young men's well-being and social relationships. Many fathers to the children of adolescent mothers find themselves unemployed, working at unskilled jobs, and struggling to support their children because of their limited education and employment prospects (Bunting & McAuley, 2004; Hoffman & Maynard, 2008). The low resources of adolescent and young-adult fathers place further stress on the mother-father relationship.

Fathers of children born to adolescent mothers vary in their adjustment to fatherhood and how involved and committed they are to their infants and mothers of their children. Generally, fathers who are employed maintain good relationships with the mothers of their children and show involvement during the prenatal period by attending doctor visits, participating in parenting classes, and buying things for the future baby. They are also more likely to be involved with their children financially and through spending time with them (e.g., Fagan, 2014; Ryan, Kalil, & Ziol-Guest, 2008; Shannon et al., 2009).

✓ CHECK YOUR UNDERSTANDING 14.14

1. What factors may explain recent declines to U.S. adolescent pregnancy rates?

Contexts of Adolescent Pregnancy

LEARNING OBJECTIVE 14.15 List factors that increase the probability of adolescent pregnancy.

Adolescent pregnancy does not occur in a vacuum. Contextual factors relate to the risk of adolescent pregnancy and how well an adolescent adjusts to pregnancy and parenthood.

For example, women who get pregnant as teenagers are more likely to have a history of poverty, to come from homes with low education of their parents, and to live in neighborhoods with few resources (Furstenberg, 2016). Adolescents who had been raised by a single parent or whose mothers gave birth as teens or earned only a high school degree are the most vulnerable to adolescent pregnancy (Martinez, Copen, & Abma, 2011). Such contextual disadvantages, when combined with the added challenge of parenthood at such a young age, may magnify the poor prognosis for adolescent mothers and their children (Hoffman & Maynard, 2008).

Many adolescents who live in harsh family conditions seek to run away from their past and see a romantic relationship as a promising solution to their painful home circumstances. Some get pregnant to gain the love they seek from an infant who will need them, as expressed in one adolescent's statement to a researcher that "You need somebody to love and somebody to love you back" (Tanner et al., 2015, p. 257). Reciprocally, adolescents who have warm relationships with their parents and live in supportive homes see promise in future opportunities for relationships and employment. Such positive life experiences reduce the likelihood that adolescents will become pregnant (Kirby, Lepore, & Ryan, 2007).

✓ CHECK YOUR UNDERSTANDING 14.15

1. What factors influence the likelihood of adolescent pregnancy?

Nutrition

My niece had a friend who began to obsess about weight when she hit puberty. She worked out for hours each day and skipped family meals that she described as "gross and fattening." Her peers complimented her on how skinny she was—"How do you do it?"—and complained about how "fat and flabby" they felt next to her. Her obsession with her body intensified, and her parents had less and less influence on her choices, despite their best intentions. At the start of senior year, she was rushed to the hospital and warned that her now-emaciated body was shutting down and that she was at risk of dying. Fortunately, after lengthy, intensive counseling for her and her family, she was able to adopt a healthy nutritional program and leave home a year after graduating high school to attend college.

The search for bodily perfection is not uncommon and may interfere with proper nutrition and healthy habits. Some adolescents have eating disorders, with the two most prevalent being anorexia nervosa and bulimia nervosa. Others suffer from poor eating habits at the other extreme, overindulging in fattening or sugary foods that have limited nutritional benefit, resulting in being overweight or obese.

Eating Disorders

LEARNING OBJECTIVE 14.16 Define anorexia nervosa and bulimia nervosa and list factors associated with the development of each eating disorder.

Far too many teens have an eating disorder, and prevalence rates continue to grow (Rosen, 2010). Adolescent girls are most at risk for eating disorders,

FIGURE 14.19 Cultural triggers for body image dissatisfaction. Eating disorders are more prevalent in adolescent girls than boys, perhaps because societal role models such as models and actresses are often exceptionally thin.

anorexia nervosa A serious disorder marked by a pathological fear of gaining weight, resulting in severe dieting, malnutrition, excessive weight loss, and a distorted body image

behavior modification A therapeutic approach in which desired behaviors are rewarded and undesirable behaviors changed

family-based therapy A therapeutic approach in which all members of a family attend therapy sessions with a therapist who helps them recognize how their behaviors and interaction patterns may affect a child's behaviors, such as an adolescent's eating disorder

perhaps because of pressures to be thin that arise from cultural standards of beauty and attractiveness (**FIGURE 14.19**). The risk of developing an eating disorder is further magnified in adolescents who participate in sports and activities—such as gymnastics, track, dance, modeling, and acting—where lean bodies are valued and rewarded (Joy, Kussman, & Nattiv, 2016; Nichols et al., 2006). Often, what starts out as innocent dieting balloons into a full-blown eating disorder. Dieters are at significant risk of disordered eating behaviors—including intentional vomiting, ingesting of diet pills, and overuse of laxatives—when compared to non-dieters, as found in a 5-year longitudinal study of over 2,500 adolescents (Neumark-Sztainer et al., 2006).

Anorexia Nervosa

Anorexia nervosa is a serious eating disorder with a lifetime prevalence of 0.6%. Anorexia is characterized by a pathological fear of gaining weight that leads to severe dieting and malnutrition and excessive weight loss. Individuals with anorexia have a distorted body image: They view themselves as fat, even after becoming severely underweight. To achieve their desired weight, they exercise strenuously, consume minimal calories, and criticize themselves if they succumb even slightly to their extreme hunger pangs. Adolescent girls are more likely to display anorexia nervosa than are adolescent boys, with gender differences applying to eating disorders more generally (Merikangas et al., 2010).

On average, individuals with anorexia lose between 25%–50% of their body weight, which may interfere with the onset of menarche, or monthly menstruation. Additional physical symptoms include brittle discolored nails, pale skin, fine dark hair covering the body, and extreme sensitivity to cold. If left untreated, anorexia nervosa can lead to heart problems, kidney failure, loss of bone mass, brain damage, and even death due to physical complications or suicide (Katzman, 2005).

Anorexia nervosa is an extremely harmful psychological disorder that can take years and extensive treatment to overcome. Because adolescents with anorexia nervosa deny they have a problem and go to great lengths to hide the disorder and minimize its seriousness, treatment is very difficult and hospitalization is often necessary to interrupt the dive into severe malnutrition (Couturier & Lock, 2006). Medications may be used to reduce anxiety and chemical imbalances, coupled with **behavior modification**—a therapeutic approach in which desired behaviors are rewarded. **Family-based therapy** is also used to treat adolescents with anorexia nervosa (Stiles-Shields et al., 2012). In this type of therapeutic approach, all members of the family attend sessions with a therapist who helps them recognize how their behaviors and patterns of interaction may contribute to the adolescent's eating disorder (**FIGURE 14.20**). The father of my niece's friend, for example, did not realize until a family-based therapy session

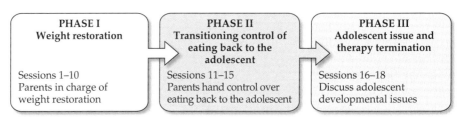

FIGURE 14.20 Family-based therapy approach to adolescent eating disorders. Family-based therapy approaches take a phased approach to treatment, beginning with parents being in charge of what the adolescent eats (Phase I), followed by gradually handing over decisions to the adolescent (Phase II). Once the adolescent achieves a normal body weight and eating behavior, discussion focuses on developmental issues that may have caused problems in the first place, including working on the adolescent-parent relationship (Phase III). (After R. Dalle Grave et al. 2019. *J Eating Disord* 7: 42. CC BY 4.0. https://creativecommons.org/licenses/by/4.0/.)

TABLE 14.4 ■ Relapse rates for anorexia nervosa

Illness status	BMI criteria	Symptoms	Behaviors	Scales	Duration
Full recovery	BMI ≥ 20 or ≥ 90% ideal body weight	No significant fear of gaining weight or disturbance in body image	No restricting, bingeing, or purging	EDE within 1 SD of normal	12 months
Partial recovery	BMI ≥ 19 or ≥ 85% ideal body weight	No significant fear of gaining weight or disturbance in body image	No restricting, bingeing, or purging	EDE within 1.5 SD of normal	6 months
Full remission	BMI ≥ 19 or ≥ 85% ideal body weight	Fear of gaining weight or disturbance in body image present	No restricting, bingeing, or purging	EDE within 2 SD of normal	3 months
Partial remission	BMI ≥ 18.5 or ≥ 85% ideal body weight	Fear of gaining weight or disturbance in body image	No restricting, bingeing, or purging	EDE within 2 SD of normal	1 month
Partial relapse	BMI ≤ 18.5 or ≤ 85% ideal body weight	Significant fear of gaining weight or disturbance in body image	Restricting, bingeing, or purging present	EDE ≥ 2 SD of normal	1 month
Full relapse	BMI ≤ 18.5 or ≤ 85% ideal body weight	Significant fear of gaining weight or disturbance in body image	Significant restricting, bingeing, or purging	EDE ≥ 2 SD of normal	3 months

Source: After S. Khalsa et al. 2017. *J Eating Disord* 5. CC BY 4.0. https://creativecommons.org/licenses/by/4.0/.

that what he thought were innocuous comments to his daughter at the precipice of puberty—"Getting a little chubby, aren't you?"—had a serious impact on her body image. Still, relapse rates for anorexia nervosa can be high, ranging from 9% to 52% across studies, depending on factors such as an individual's body weight, time of follow-up, and so on (Khalsa et al., 2017) (**TABLE 14.4**).

Bulimia Nervosa

Bulimia nervosa is a disorder in which bouts of extreme overeating are followed by self-induced vomiting, purging, or fasting because of an obsessive desire to lose weight. Approximately 1%–2% of teens meet diagnostic criteria for bulimia nervosa, although even higher rates have been documented, with as many as 2.6% of about 500 adolescents in a large city reporting having had bulimia nervosa by the time they were 20 years of age, and an additional 4.4% having had milder forms of the disorder (Stice, Marti, & Rohde, 2013).

Some teens with bulimia nervosa misuse laxatives, diuretics, and enemas to further reduce their weight. Most adolescents with bulimia experience guilt around their eating habits and want to be helped. Fortunately, although bulimia is more common than anorexia nervosa, it is easier to treat. Treatments for bulimia nervosa include education around nutrition and healthy eating, support groups, cognitive-based therapies to modify adolescent perceptions about weight and behaviors, and family-based therapies (Le Grange et al. 2016). Such treatments lead to abstinence from binging and purging, although success rates are modest with typically less than half of adolescents showing improvements and substantial numbers showing remission (Le Grange et al., 2016).

Prevalence Rates for Eating Disorders

Most statistics on anorexia nervosa and bulimia nervosa are based on strict diagnostic criteria that fail to capture the larger percentage of teenagers afflicted with an eating disorder. Individuals who do not meet the criteria for anorexia nervosa or bulimia nervosa may be diagnosed as having "partial syndromes" or "eating disorders not otherwise specified" (Rosen, 2010). Taking this group into consideration, a systematic review of the lifetime prevalence of eating disorders across 94 studies

bulimia nervosa A serious eating disorder in which bouts of extreme overeating are followed by self-induced vomiting, purging, or fasting because of an obsessive desire to lose weight spanning several countries indicated average rates of 8.4% for women and 2.2% for men, with women in the United States having higher likelihoods of an eating disorder than women in Europe and Asia (Galmiche et al., 2019). Moreover, rates may be even higher considering that many individuals engage in unhealthy and unsupervised dieting, yet go undetected and never seek treatment.

Although White U.S. adolescent girls have traditionally been most at risk for eating disorders, the prevalence of eating disorders has increased in adolescent boys ages 16–19, minority populations in the United States, and in countries where eating disorders had not been common in the past (Rosen, 2010). Eating disorders are likewise high in lesbian, gay, bisexual, and other sexual minority individuals, with disparities especially high when comparing nonheterosexual men to heterosexual men (Calzo et al., 2017).

The prevalence of eating disorders peaks during adolescence and young adulthood, with 95% of people with eating disorders falling between the ages of 12 and 26. However, an alarming trend is the increasing prevalence of disorders at progressively younger ages. From 1999 to 2006, hospitalizations for eating disorders increased most sharply—119%—for children who were younger than 12 years of age (Zhao & Encinosa, 2009). Pre-teens are keen observers of the trends around them and may be vulnerable to the dieting behaviors of older siblings and older students at school.

✓ CHECK YOUR UNDERSTANDING 14.16

1. What are some of the physical effects of anorexia nervosa?
2. What are the most common eating disorders, and who is most at risk for them?

Overweight or Obese

LEARNING OBJECTIVE 14.17 Differentiate between overweight and obese.

The stigma and discrimination of being overweight can take a psychological toll on adolescents, especially when society encourages a rail thin, false ideal. The term **overweight** is used for a person who falls between the 85th and 94th percentiles for their body mass index, or BMI (the ratio of weight to height). The term **obese** applies to someone who falls at or above the 95th percentile for BMI compared to peers of the same age and sex.

Prevalence Rates of Obesity

Rates of obesity and overweight status in children and adolescents are concerning. Nearly one-third of children and adolescents were classified as overweight or obese in a nationally representative sample (Ogden et al., 2014). Moreover, childhood overweight status or obesity places a person at heightened risk for obesity in adolescence and adulthood (Spruigt-Metz, 2011; Sinha & Kling, 2009). The high stability of overweight and obesity status over age is not restricted to the United States. A review of 25 longitudinal studies from around the world indicated that rates of overweight status and obesity are high, and that adolescents with weight problems are consistently prone to becoming overweight or obese adults (Singh et al., 2008).

Why is weight status so stable? Although people often attribute being overweight or obese to heredity and bad eating habits, the social stigma surrounding weight and the lack of acceptance of different body sizes and types may contribute to the stability of weight problems from adolescence to adulthood. Indeed, individuals who internalized negative social stigmas around their weight showed no improvements to their eating habits after participating in weight-management programs, whereas individuals with low internalized stigma improved (Mensinger, Calogero, & Tylka, 2016). Furthermore, "weight-neutral" programs

overweight Body weight of an individual who falls between the 85th and 94th percentiles for body mass index compared to peers of the same age and sex

obese A term referring to an individual who falls at or above the 95th percentile for body mass index compared to peers of the same age and sex that focused on healthy living and avoided stigmatized messages about weight status led individuals to maintain positive habits two years later. In contrast, individuals who participated in conventional weight-reduction programs showed no long-term improvements in their lifestyle and weight. Such findings point to the potential benefits of weight-inclusive approaches that emphasize diversity of bodies and positive self-care, rather than negative attitudes toward overweight individuals (Calogero et al., 2019).

Still, global rates of overweight and obesity status suggest that human genetics may confer advantages for a tendency toward being overweight. Indeed, at one time in human evolution, the storage of fat protected against the possibility of food scarcity. For example, early hunter-gatherers had to rely on hunting animals to feed family members, and it may have been advantageous to eat a lot and store fat in case the hunt was unsuccessful. In poor countries, where hunger is rampant, this may still be the case. Indeed, in poor countries around the globe, children and adolescents from wealthier families are more likely to be overweight than are those from poor families.

However, in resourced countries, the human tendency toward overeating no longer confers a health advantage (Wang & Lobstein, 2006). In fact, a review of 45 studies conducted in the United States between 1989 and 2008 showed that as income and education increased, weight decreased or did not change in 72% of cases. In essence, being overweight was not associated with "having plenty," and so a genetic inclination to overeat does not aid survival in resourced societies (Shrewsbury & Wardle, 2008).

Nutrition and Exercise

Healthy lifestyle habits around exercise and nutrition, together with the ability to avoid internalizing societal stigma around weight, contribute to physical wellness (Calogero et al., 2019). In contrast, excessive sedentary behavior increases the risk for obesity in adolescents, particularly during puberty (Berkey et al., 2000; McMurray et al., 2000). Unfortunately, fewer than 25% of adolescents meet the recommended health guidelines of getting an hour per day of moderate to vigorous activity (U.S. Department of Health and Human Services, 2018). Moreover, teens spend substantial time engaged with screens of one form or another. Screen time affects BMI because of the sedentary nature of the activity and also because advertisers promote unhealthy foods that are high in sugar and fat content that may trigger snacking regardless of hunger (Powell & Nyugen, 2013; Sinha & Kling, 2009).

Unfortunately, U.S. adolescents consume a high percentage of their daily calories from fast foods (Powell & Nyugen, 2013). Many adolescents regularly visit fast-food restaurants or rely on take-out for meals, which explains the dramatic rise in daily fast-food consumption in recent decades (Janssen et al., 2018; Vikraman, Fryar, & Ogden, 2015). Once adolescents develop such habits, they continue into adulthood. The harmful implications for health are obvious. Fast-food consumption increases sugar, fat, saturated fat, and sodium intake while reducing intake of fish, whole grains, fruits, and vegetables (Janssen et al., 2018).

You might assume the fast-food frenzy is limited to the United States and other highly industrialized societies. However, this is not the case. Fast-food companies have proliferated across the globe, and ready-to-eat processed foods have replaced traditional home-cooked meals in many cultures, resulting in a decline of nutritious meals. As one example, when 15- to 16-year-olds from India were asked about their diets, 30% reported no daily intake of vegetables, 45% reported no intake of fruits, and 70% reported consuming at least three low-nutrition snacks a day (Rathi, Riddell, & Worsley, 2017). Moreover, adolescents who consume fast food also tend to be more sedentary than those who consume healthier foods, further exacerbating risks to health. A cross-national study of over 100,000 adolescents from 44 low- and middle-income countries

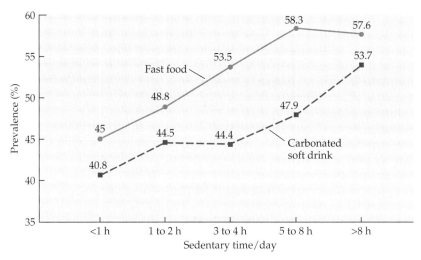

FIGURE 14.21 Relationship between sedentary behavior and fast-food consumption. A study of 133,555 adolescents aged 12–15 across 44 low- and middle-income countries found that hours spent in sedentary behavior during the day (*x* axis) increased in parallel with fast-food consumption. Here, fast-food consumption (*y* axis) refers to the percentage of teens who had eaten food from a fast-food restaurant at least once in the prior week, and soft-drink consumption refers to daily consumption of soft drinks in the past 30 days. (After G. Ashdown-Franks et al. 2019. *Int J Behav Nutr Phys Act* 16: 35. CC BY 4.0. https://creativecommons.org/licenses/by/4.0/.)

found that fast-food intake increased in parallel with sedentary behavior (Ashdown-Franks et al., 2019) (**FIGURE 14.21**).

✓ CHECK YOUR UNDERSTANDING 14.17

1. What factors contribute to the growing prevalence rates of obesity in adolescence?

Contexts of Eating Disorders and Obesity

LEARNING OBJECTIVE 14.18 List family and racial factors that promote and deter healthy eating habits.

Why are some adolescents prone to depriving their bodies of food, others prone to eating unhealthy foods, and yet others (fortunately, the remaining majority) prone to generally eating healthy foods? As you might expect, beyond the contributions of genetics, eating habits arise from environmental triggers and individual characteristics (Rosen, 2010; Sinha & Kling, 2009).

Family Context

The parent-adolescent relationship may lead to eating disorders and obesity in teens. Parents who are controlling and who impose high expectations on their adolescents are more likely to have teens with eating disorders than are more laid-back parents (Grolnick & Pomerantz, 2009). For example, mothers who are overly concerned about their daughters' physical appearance, achievement, and social acceptance and/or who are overprotective may unintentionally push their daughters to seek control of their body through binging, purging, and excessive dieting (Depestele et al., 2017; Goddard & Treasure, 2013).

Emotional involvement, or lack thereof, by parents may also play a role. For example, fathers who are emotionally distant are more likely to have girls with eating disorders than are fathers who are emotionally involved. These parental attitudes and behaviors may contribute to the persistent anxiety and fierce pursuit of perfection for achievement and thinness that characterize anorexia nervosa (Kaye, 2008).

Finally, harsh parenting increases the odds that an adolescent will be overweight or obese, whereas high-quality mother-adolescent and father-adolescent relationships reduce the likelihood that a teen will consume fast foods and become overweight or obese (Haines et al., 2016). The negative effects of harsh parenting are compounded when adolescents also experience food insecurity or regularly lack access to nutritious foods (Lohman, Gillettte, & Neppl, 2016) (**FIGURE 14.22**).

Ethnicity and Racial Context

Rates of adolescent obesity and eating disorders differ across ethnic and racial lines. A greater proportion of U.S. non-Hispanic Black and Hispanic adolescent girls are overweight or obese compared to non-Hispanic White adolescent girls: 23.6% of non-Hispanic Black adolescent girls and 23.4% of Mexican American adolescent girls are obese, nearly double the rate of obesity among non-Hispanic White adolescent girls (12.7%). Such statistics may in part be driven by the high rates of poverty in U.S. Black and Hispanic communities. Indeed, the risk of adolescent obesity heightens in individuals from low SES households (Ogden, et al., 2010).

In contrast, eating disorders are less common among U.S. Black adolescent girls than among Asian, White, and Hispanic adolescent girls, perhaps because of racial differences in body image. Black adolescent girls tend to be more satisfied with their body size and shape than girls from other racial backgrounds and they are less prone to anorexia or bulimia than are non-Hispanic White adolescent girls (Granillo, Jones-Rodriguez, & Carvajal, 2005; Ozer & Irwin, 2009).

Black adolescent girls may also be less inclined to worry about reducing their weight than White adolescent girls, even when overweight (Cameron, Muldrow, & Stefani, 2018). In part, racial disparities around body image may exist because Black women consider labeling of overweight status and obesity to be based on White norms of health and an inappropriate societal ideal around being thin (Cameron et al., 2018).

Neighborhood Context

If fast-food consumption magnifies the risk of obesity, then adolescents who live in neighborhoods with available and plentiful unhealthy food may be at special risk. Fast-food restaurants are prevalent in low-income neighborhoods, with many outlets strategically positioned near high schools (Simon et al., 2008; Zenck & Powell, 2008). At the same time, affordable healthy foods are often lacking in many low-income neighborhoods, making fast-food meals the main option (Ver Ploeg et al., 2009). Furthermore, low-income urban neighborhoods tend to lack parks and safe places to run around and hang out, which may dispose adolescents toward sedentary behaviors like playing computer games rather than obtaining adequate exercise (Gordon-Larsen, Adair, & Popkin, 2003).

✓ CHECK YOUR UNDERSTANDING 14.18

1. What are some contextual factors that may lead to eating disorders and obesity?

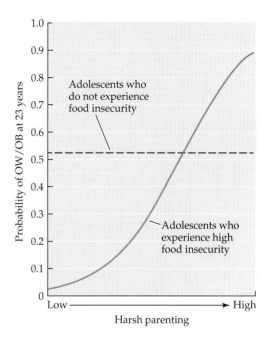

FIGURE 14.22 Harsh parenting and food insecurity. Adolescent girls who experience high food insecurity (solid blue line) *and* harsh parenting have greater odds of being overweight (OW) or obese (OB) in early adulthood (23 years of age) compared to adolescent girls who experience high food insecurity but not harsh parenting. However, harsh parenting does not change the likelihood of being overweight or obese for adolescents who do not experience food insecurity (dashed red line). (After B. J. Lohman et al. 2016. *J Adolesc Health* 59: 123–127.)

Sleep

Most adolescents groan about their early morning classes and would spend the period with their heads on their desks if they could get away with it. When adolescents don't get enough sleep, or their nights are filled with fits and starts, they tend to be sleepy, and often quite moody, during the day. In college, the first courses to fill up start after 11 a.m., and 8 a.m. classes remain available until adolescents have taken advantage of all other options. Unsurprisingly, adolescents who feel sleep deprived tend not to do as well in school as those who are rested. Here, we consider two important indices of adolescent sleep health—sleep duration, or how much a person sleeps, and sleep quality, or how well a person sleeps (Colrain & Baker, 2011). We examine how adolescents' changing circadian rhythms and intensifying academic and social activities affect each.

Circadian Rhythm

LEARNING OBJECTIVE 14.19 Describe how circadian rhythm changes during adolescence.

circadian rhythm The patterns of sleeping, waking, and eating that are controlled by an internal "body clock" that guides physical, mental, and behavioral changes over a daily cycle

melatonin A hormone/naturally occurring compound released by the brain in response to darkness that regulates circadian rhythm and supports the immune system

Relative to children, adolescents tend to stay up longer and sleep later, deviating from the 24-hour **circadian rhythm**—the pattern of sleeping, waking, and eating governed by our internal "body clock" (Hagenauer et al., 2009). Changes to adolescents' circadian rhythm were first discovered in experiments on melatonin's role in sleep. **Melatonin** is a hormone that regulates circadian rhythm and is released by the brain in response to darkness.

Scientists studied adolescents under highly controlled conditions in which all participants followed the same routine: They lived in the laboratory for several days, under dimly lit conditions, and received small meals and fluids every 2 hours. The goal was to see when melatonin was naturally released in individuals of different ages (Carskadon et al., 1997). The researchers found that melatonin was released later in the evening in older adolescents than in younger teens, indicating a shift in the circadian rhythm with age. Because sleep conditions were experimentally controlled, these differences could not be attributed to the confounding effects of daylight exposure, food metabolism, physical activity, and so on, that might otherwise distinguish older and younger adolescents.

For most of human history, the adolescent circadian shift toward later hours did not significantly disturb sleep patterns, because people generally went to sleep when it got too dark to do much else. Sunlight and nightfall basically determined wake-up and bedtime. But the advent of artificial light and other technologies have thrown off natural circadian rhythms and may amplify the adolescent's propensity to stay up late (Peper & Dahl, 2013). We now know that light signals from TVs, computers, phones, and other screens alter circadian rhythm (**FIGURE 14.23**). On top of this, school assignments and social pressures compel adolescents to stay up late into the night. As a result, many adolescents have problems with the quantity and quality of sleep, which interferes with their physical and psychological health.

FIGURE 14.23 Modern technology interferes with our circadian rhythm. Use of the internet has been related to delayed bedtimes, delayed weekend wake-up times, more out-of-bed time, shorter total sleep durations, shorter time in bed on weekdays, higher levels of tiredness, and higher levels of insomnia.

© TORWAISTUDIO/Shutterstock.com

✓ CHECK YOUR UNDERSTANDING 14.19

1. How do we know that circadian rhythm changes during adolescence?

Too Little Sleep

LEARNING OBJECTIVE 14.20 Indicate how much sleep an adolescent needs and define the concept of "sleep debt."

Scientists have long been interested in adolescent declines in amount of sleep. In 1913, psychologist Lewis Terman and colleague Adeline Hocking tracked changing sleep patterns from childhood through adolescence in over 2,500 children 6–20 years of age (Terman & Hocking, 1913). They documented a decrease in the time spent in bed and an increase in the need for a parent to wake the child up in the morning—from 21% of 6-year-olds needing their parents to wake them up to 58% of 18-year-olds needing a push from their parents.

So, how much sleep does an adolescent need? You may be surprised to learn that adolescents require an average of 9 hours of sleep per night, much more than what most adolescents or even their parents believe. In fact, as children progress through puberty they actually require *more* sleep rather than less (Carskadon, 1997). Yet, an alarming proportion of U.S. teens sleep fewer than 7 hours per night. In fact, teens' low sleep tendencies have worsened over the past three decades, as seen when researchers compare yearly national surveys of around 300,000 teenagers (Keyes et al., 2015) (**FIGURE 14.24**). Furthermore, older teenagers go to bed later, spend more time in evening activities, and consequently sleep less than do younger teenagers.

(A)

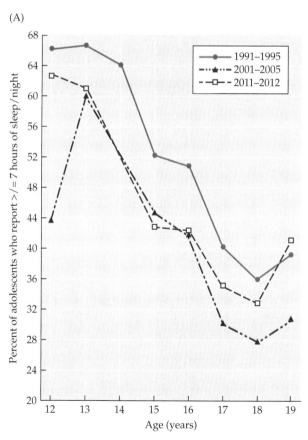

(B)

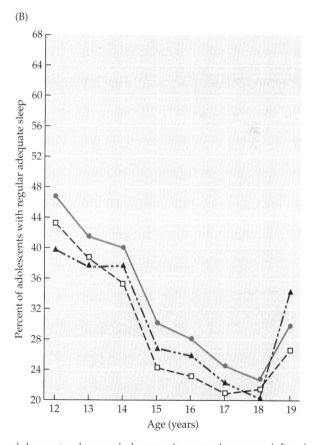

FIGURE 14.24 **Insufficient adolescent sleep.** (A) The proportion of adolescents who regularly got 7 hours or more of sleep was defined as those who responded about the frequency with which they obtain 7 hours or more of sleep (with options being every day or almost every day versus sometimes, rarely, or never). (B) The proportion of adolescents who regularly get adequate sleep was defined as those who reported that they get less sleep than they should (with options being never or seldom versus sometimes, every day, or almost every day). (After K. M. Keyes et al. 2015. *Pediatrics* 135: 460–468. Reproduced with permission. Copyright © 2015 by the AAP.)

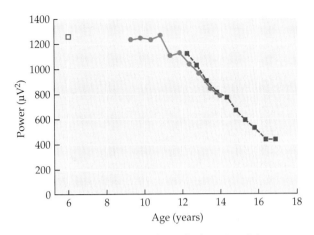

FIGURE 14.25 Slow-wave sleep declines in adolescence. The two lines shown here represent two cohorts of children followed longitudinally. The first sample was followed from 9 to 14 years of age and the second from 12 to 17 years of age. The value of power on the *y* axis represents the power of slow waves as monitored by EEG recorders while children/teens slept. (After I. G. Campbell and I. Feinberg. 2009. *Proc Natl Acad Sci USA* 106. 5177–5180.)

sleep debt Sleep deficit that is the cumulative effect of not getting enough sleep night after night

Going to sleep late, coupled with the requirements of waking up early for school, invariably results in weekday sleep durations as low as 5 hours (Gradisar, Gardner, & Dohnt, 2011). By the time U.S. teens are seniors in high school, they go to sleep on average after 11:30 p.m. and wake up around 6:15 a.m. (Peper & Dahl, 2013). Sleep deprivation most noticeably affects adolescents who get the least sleep. They exhibit dramatic declines in slow-wave sleep—the type of deep sleep that does not contain rapid eye movements (Colrain & Baker, 2011; Feinberg & Campbell, 2010) (**FIGURE 14.25**). As a result, an estimated 30% of high-school students in the United States are chronically sleep deprived (Peper & Dahl, 2013).

As adolescents repeat their weekday pattern of insufficient sleep night after night, they experience a **sleep debt** (Van Dongen, Rogers, & Dinges, 2003): They owe their bodies the missed hours of sleep. Typically, teens repay the debt by sleeping longer on weekends (typically, 9–12 hours) (Gradisar et al., 2011). However, more sleep on weekends does not solve the sleep deprivation problem. Highly variable sleep patterns may indicate delayed sleep phase disorder (DSPD) (American Academy of Sleep Medicine, 2005), in which later sleep times during certain parts of the week interfere with weekly responsibilities at other times (Gradisar et al., 2011). The average difference between adolescents' bedtime and wake-up times during weekdays and weekends is a substantial 2 hours across many societies.

✓ CHECK YOUR UNDERSTANDING 14.20

1. How much sleep do adolescents need and how much does the typical adolescent actually get?
2. How do adolescents typically compensate for sleep debt and is this an effective strategy?

Poor-Quality Sleep

insomnia Sleeplessness or the habitual inability to sleep; a disorder characterized by difficulties with falling or staying asleep

bruxism The excessive grinding of teeth or jaw clenching at night

LEARNING OBJECTIVE 14.21 List signs of poor-quality sleep.

Beyond quantity, the quality of sleep falls short of what adolescents require. Adolescents often have difficulty initiating and maintaining sleep, which can lead to **insomnia**—the habitual inability to sleep (e.g., Thorleifsdottir et al., 2002). Sleep quality can also be hampered by **bruxism**, the grinding of teeth at night, which increases between 15 and 23 years of age (Strausz et al. 2010).

Insufficient sleep interferes with the overnight brain activity that is necessary for neurocognitive functioning, consolidation of information, and health (Dewald et al., 2010). Problems in sleep quality can disrupt school performance and motivation, memory, executive functioning, attitudes toward teachers, and control of aggression (Carskadon & Rechtschaffen, 2011; Carskadon et al., 1998; Colrain & Baker, 2011; Dewald et al., 2010; Meijer et al., 2008). And over the long term, insufficient sleep harms much more than school performance. Persistent sleep problems can produce mood-related disturbances, psychological stress, obesity, traffic accidents, alcohol and drug abuse, relationship problems, and even suicidal thoughts (Colrain & Baker, 2011; Gangwisch et al. 2010; Noland et al., 2009).

Of course, correlational studies do not directly test causation, and psychological vulnerability may lead to sleep problems rather than the reverse. However, experimental manipulations of sleep durations confirm that restricted sleep predicts negative feelings such as worry, particularly in young adolescents (Talbot et al., 2010). After being intentionally deprived of sleep in experimental studies, adolescents perceive their problems to be significantly more threatening than when they are well rested. Everyday troubles that appear to be insurmountable when an adolescent is tired may be viewed as manageable after getting the needed sleep.

✓ CHECK YOUR UNDERSTANDING 14.21

   1. What are some potential consequences of poor-quality sleep?

Contexts of Sleep

LEARNING OBJECTIVE 14.22 Describe factors that conspire to interfere with sleep duration and quality.

Knowing that adolescents fall short of the sleep they need is only half the story. A key question is *why* are adolescents so sleep deprived? As we will see, technology use and the pressures adolescents experience in academics, social relationships, and extracurricular activities may interfere with sleep (Colrain & Baker, 2011).

Technology Context

Technology is evolving at an astounding rate, with new applications and gadgets hitting the market each day. Adolescents are consumed with streaming, social media exchanges, electronic gaming, and texting. A poll conducted by the National Sleep Foundation found that 89% of U.S. adolescents between 15 and 17 have at least one electronic device in their room (National Sleep Foundation, 2014). Twenty percent of U.S. adolescents ages 12–15 reported "almost always" checking their social media or text messages on their phones throughout the night (Power et al., 2017). Furthermore, technology use contributes to the crisis of adolescent sleep deprivation globally (Zhang, Tillman, & Song, 2017). A national study of nearly 10,000 adolescents in Norway showed that between 30% and 95% of teens 16–19 years old used computers, cell phones, game consoles, iPads, TVs, or streaming before sleep (Hysing et al., 2015) (**FIGURE 14.26**).

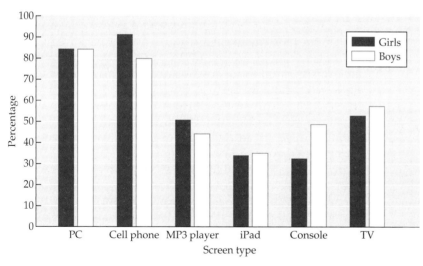

FIGURE 14.26 Screentime use before sleep by adolescents in Norway. The majority of adolescents spend time with a wide variety of screens late at night, which can delay sleep and interfere with sufficient sleep. Teens today are especially likely to engage with computers and cell phones. This pattern is seen in countries around the globe, as shown in this figure, which depicts the percentage of teens in Norway who engage with different types of screens before bedtime. (After M. Hysing et al. 2015. *BMJ Open* 5: e006748. © 2015. Reproduced with permission from BMJ Publishing Group Ltd. https://doi.org/10.1136/bmjopen-2014-006748. Source: youth@ hordaland study [n=9846].)

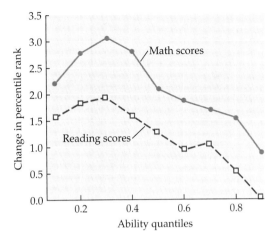

FIGURE 14.27 Sleep and academics.
The boost from extra sleep is especially pronounced for children who show lower academic abilities. A study of students in North Carolina showed that percentiles of scores for reading and math improve with each extra hour of sleep (*y* axis), but improvement was higher for students at lower ends of the ability continuum (*x* axis). (After F. Edwards. 2012. *Econ Edu Rev* 31: 970–983.)

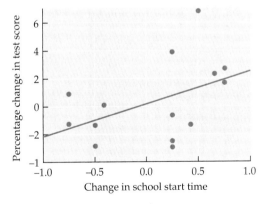

FIGURE 14.28 Delays and test scores.
A one-hour delay in school start times is associated with a 2.32 percentage point increase in test scores. (After F. Edwards. 2012. *Econ Edu Rev* 31: 970–983.)

Electronic devices undoubtedly interfere with adolescents' sleep patterns. The use of electronic devices delays bedtime and leads to shorter sleep durations in adolescents based on a review of 36 papers (Cain & Gradisar, 2010). Indeed, the use of electronic devices predicts delayed bedtimes, delayed weekend wake-up times, more out-of-bed times, shorter total sleep durations, shorter time in bed on weekdays, higher levels of tiredness, and higher levels of insomnia. Children and adolescents who leave two or more electronic devices on during their sleeping hours are nearly three times as likely to experience poor sleep than those who never leave electronic devices on (National Sleep Foundation, 2014).

Screen time interferes with getting in bed and shutting out the lights, but additionally, exposure to the bright lights emitted by screens may suppress melatonin release and delay circadian rhythms (Higuchi et al., 2005; LeBourgeois et al., 2017; Loughran et al., 2005). The sleep disturbances caused by electronic media use can cascade to depressive symptoms (Lemola et al., 2015), low physical activity, and high intake of calories (Kenney & Gortmaker, 2017).

School Context

Despite adolescents' need for sleep, disruptions to circadian rhythms, and ever-later bedtimes, schools typically begin early in the morning and require early rise times. The "developmental mismatch" between school hours and adolescent sleep needs may result in daytime sleepiness that undermines the ability to learn (Colrain & Baker, 2011). Although middle school and high school starting times tend to be earlier than primary school start times, most adolescents simply resign themselves to sleeping less rather than going to bed earlier. In fact, when adolescents transitioned to earlier school start times (typically from 8:25 a.m. to 7:20 a.m.), none adjusted bedtimes to the new schedule (Carskadon et al., 1998). Rather, students reduced their sleep by about 20 minutes to an average of 6 hours 50 minutes, and they gave themselves less time in the morning to get ready.

Concerns about adolescent sleep deficits have led to considerable debate about whether schools should synchronize their start times with students' body clocks. Later school start times effectively counter chronic sleep loss in adolescents and benefit students' physical and mental health, safety, and academic achievement. The American Academy of Pediatrics released a policy statement recommending that high schools and middle schools implement start times that allow students to get 8.5–9.5 hours of sleep as a way to reduce risks such as obesity, depression, anxiety, car accidents, and poor academic performance (American Academy of Pediatrics, 2014). Indeed, student test scores improve across all subjects for each hour of extra sleep that students get (**FIGURE 14.27**) Consequently, delaying middle and high school start times reduces sleepiness during the day, promotes student health outcomes, and leads to gains in school performance and test scores (Edwards 2012; Owens et al., 2017; Watson et al., 2017) (**FIGURE 14.28**). In fact, as students move from class to class over the course of the day—and presumably overcome their initial early morning grogginess—their grades improve relative to their first period. However, changing school schedules is not easy: Delaying start times impacts extracurricular and athletic activities, transportation, family work schedules, and adolescent chores and responsibilities, including time for homework and school assignments (Malone, Ziporyn, & Buttenheim, 2017).

Cultural Context

If you think sleep deprivation is confined to U.S. teenagers, you would be wrong. A meta-analysis based on 41 surveys worldwide confirmed that sleep problems increase in adolescence across the globe, with only half of adolescents obtaining the recommended 9 hours of sleep per night (Gradisar et al., 2011).

However, the problem of adolescent sleep intensifies in certain cultural contexts (Gradisar et al., 2011). Adolescents from Asia have even later bedtimes and earlier wake times than do teens from North America and Europe. For example, most Korean adolescents have late bedtimes that lead to insufficient sleep on school nights, and many adolescents from China wake up at 6:15 in the morning to participate in exercises prior to school. In contrast, most Icelandic youth consistently go to bed and wake up later than adolescents in other Western countries. The sleep patterns in Iceland may be explained by extreme fluctuations in hours of daylight in Iceland across the year, from the sun never setting in June to a lack of sunlight in December (Gradisar et al., 2011).

✓ CHECK YOUR UNDERSTANDING 14.22

1. How has technology interfered with the ability to get a good night's sleep?
2. What measures might parents take to reduce the impact of technology on adolescents' sleep-wake cycles?
3. What changes in school schedules might ensure that students arrive at school rested and ready to learn?

Developmental Cascades

If I had to summarize the essence of adolescence in a single word, I would choose the word "intense." Adolescence is a time of intense changes to body and brain. It's a time of intense energy, thoughts, and emotions. It's a time when passion, romance, and sexual attraction intensify. Adolescents are aware of the temptations of the moment and opportunities of the future. And, adolescents' sense of daring, courage, and adventure makes many adults longingly recall the free-spirited boldness of their own past.

Yet, the unprecedented changes of adolescence can lead to confusion. Some adolescents struggle with the social expectations that come with a fully mature body but still unfinished brain. Growing up can be painful and spark sadness or dejection when teens encounter bumps along the road to adulthood. In this final section, we illustrate the cascading influences of adolescent physical development and health by revisiting topics of brain development, pubertal timing, and obesity.

Cascades from Brain Development

Changes in the adolescent brain—including the pruning of gray matter, myelination of white matter, and asymmetrical maturation of prefrontal and limbic regions—dramatically alter the cognitive, social, and emotional worlds of adolescents.

Brain Cascades to Cognitive Development

Adolescents are capable of impressive abstract thought and scientific reasoning made possible by their relatively sophisticated brain architecture. Advances in neuroimaging have shed light on the ways that brain development supports cognitive functioning. Scientists now consider pruning and myelination of the prefrontal cortex to underpin improvements in adolescent working memory, inhibition, and planning (e.g., Bjork et al., 2004; Blakemore, 2008; Crone & Dahl, 2012). Structural and functional changes in the brain may likewise be involved in adolescents' growing skills at perspective taking, social cognition, and moral reasoning (Blakemore, 2008; Rilling & Sanfey, 2011).

A word of caution is in order, however, when interpreting the brain bases of cognitive development. Brain development affects cognitive development, just as practice with reasoning and thinking reciprocally affects brain development. That is, adolescents have amassed many more experiences than have children, and these experiences contribute to their superior abstract thinking, attention control, and perspective taking, which further prompt changes in the brain (Choudhury, Charman, & Blakemore 2008). Still, the brain's causal role in cognition becomes apparent when things go awry. Individuals who experience brain injury to the prefrontal cortex, for example, show compromised performance in moral reasoning in adolescence and adulthood (Anderson et al., 1999; Couper, Jacobs, & Anderson, 2002).

Brain Cascades to Risk Taking

Maturity of the limbic system allows teens to achieve new depths in their feelings and connection with peers. But, asynchronous brain development means that the intense emotions and behaviors of the reward-sensitive limbic system sometimes overwhelm the rational system of the prefrontal cortex. And so, adolescents and young adults are more likely than adults over 25 years of age to binge drink, use drugs, have casual sex partners, and be involved in serious car accidents (Steinberg, 2008). A survey of over 40,000 teenagers in grades 8, 10, and 12 found that 49% of American youth had tried an illicit drug by the time they left high school (Meich et al., 2014). Today opioid addiction in the United States has reached staggering levels and continues to threaten the lives of thousands of teens, many of whom move from prescribed opiates to heroin (McCabe et al., 2017) (**FIGURE 14.29**).

For some time, scientists attributed adolescent risk taking to adolescent ignorance: Adolescents were either unaware of the dangers involved in drug use, unsafe sex, and so on, or at minimum, they underestimated those risks. However, such attributions were found to be blatantly wrong. Adolescents are aware of the dangers of risky behaviors and do not differ from adults in their judgments about their own vulnerability to risks (Beyth-Marom et al., 1993; Millstein & Halpern-Felsher, 2002). Now, much research on adolescent risk taking focuses on brain mechanisms. Specifically, the limbic "emotional core" of the brain may be responsible for adolescents' frequent urges to pursue novel, exciting, and sometimes dangerous activities at a time when the prefrontal cortex is insufficiently developed to keep impulses in check (e.g., Blakemore & Robbins, 2012; Casey, Jones, & Somerville, 2011; Duell et al., 2016; Somerville, 2013).

Brain Bases of Depression and Anxiety

Rates of depression and anxiety peak during adolescence. Rapid changes in brain development may heighten adolescents' vulnerability to depression (Romeo, 2013). In fact, some scientists consider adolescent depression to be a serious recurrent brain-based disorder. Moreover, environmental stressors, including a history of maltreatment, conflict with family, difficulties at school, and family poverty may alter adolescent brain development and place adolescents at risk for depression and other forms of psychopathology (e.g., Teicher et al., 2016).

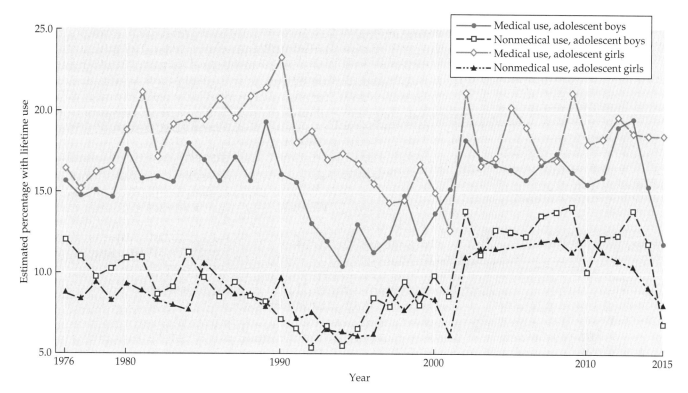

FIGURE 14.29 Adolescent opioid use. An alarming percentage of U.S. high school students reports using opioids in their lifetime, a trend that has continued for many decades. Although the most prevalent form of use is due to medical reasons (green and blue lines), nonmedical usage is also high (purple and red lines). (From S. E. McCabe et al. 2017. *Pediatrics* 139: e20162387. Reproduced with permission. Copyright © 2017 by the AAP.)

Adolescent anxiety and fear likewise can be traced to amygdala activity. The maturation of this brain region makes adolescents susceptible to experiencing fear and anxiety under stressful conditions at a time when they are not fully capable of reasoning calmly (Pagliaccio et al., 2015; Tottenham & Galvan, 2016). When adolescents view pictures of people with fearful expressions, fMRI scans show higher levels of activation in their amygdala than seen in adults who view the same faces, which may account for adolescents' heightened vulnerability to affective disorders (Guyer et al., 2008). Adolescents may therefore be more emotionally reactive and less rational in situations that involve strong feelings and other people.

Cascades from Pubertal Timing

It is easy to understand how difficult it can be for teens to adjust to their new bodies and changing hormones, and how comparing one's body to the bodies of peers can become a daily preoccupation. At the same time, people often dismiss adolescents' preoccupation as something teens will get over in due course or something that will wash away once the adolescent physically catches up and everyone has finally transitioned to puberty. But such assumptions ignore the potential cascading effects of early or late pubertal onset relative to peers.

We have seen that early puberty can spur a host of problem behaviors. Adolescent girls who experience early puberty, for example, may spend time with older peers, particularly older male peers, and consequently devote less time to classwork. These behaviors, in turn, can increase the likelihood of sexual activity, drinking, drug use, pregnancy, school dropout, delinquency, depression, and conflict with parents (e.g., DeRose & Brooks-Gunn, 2006; Ge, Conger, & Elder, 1996).

Over time, the stress of entering social situations before being emotionally ready may cause problems that spill over into adulthood. In fact, early pubertal onset predicts higher incidence of later obesity, reproductive cancers, and cardiovascular disease (DeRose & Brooks-Gunn, 2006). The influence of early puberty on weight gain may be due to the development of insulin resistance in certain early maturing adolescents, reflecting bidirectional associations between body fat and puberty. Stressors associated with early puberty may cascade into chemical-related disruptions in the body and exacerbate vulnerability to negative psychological functioning and health (Walvoord, 2010).

Cascades from Overweight and Obesity

Being overweight or obese can lead to harmful health cascades. Obesity places teens at risk for high cholesterol, hypertension, insulin resistance, type 2 diabetes, liver disease, and various cancers (e.g., Calle & Kaaks, 2004; Cruz et al., 2005; Shaibi & Goran, 2008).

The health-related reverberations of obesity are only a part of the story. The social stigma surrounding obesity is pronounced and difficult to reverse. Discrimination against overweight and obese adolescents can be brutal, particularly in Western cultures where thin is the societal ideal (Spruijt-Metz, 2011; Tiggemann & Anesbury, 2000). The poor body image and low self-esteem associated with being overweight may produce anxiety, hopelessness, depression, and low quality of life (e.g., Griffiths, Parson & Hill, 2010; Luppino et al., 2010). Negative feelings and persistent negative attitudes toward overweight individuals in turn can have life-long economic consequences. Obese adolescents have lower education, income, and likelihood of getting married as adults than do their thinner peers (e.g., Glass, Haas, Reither, 2010).

Negative outcomes of being overweight are not inevitable. When adolescents hold positive perceptions of their bodies, they can avoid some of the harmful effects. In fact, the effects of body weight on later psychological problems depend strongly on body image. A study of over 5,000 Dutch adolescents investigated associations between BMI, self-perception of body weight, and psychological problems such as mental distress, social problems, attention, and thought problems. Body weight image was the stronger predictor of adolescent psychological problems, regardless of adolescents' actual BMI (ter Bogt et al., 2006). Specifically, adolescents who were either underweight *or* overweight relative to their peers, but considered themselves to be in good shape, did not have any more problems than their peers with normal BMIs. In contrast, adolescent girls and boys who perceived themselves as "too heavy," or to a lesser extent, "too thin," were prone to psychological problems. In essence, feeling good about oneself is a good thing.

In short, positive self-perception can support adolescent psychological adjustment, regardless of when or how the body changes. As noted throughout this chapter, perception often trumps reality, for good or for bad. Anorexia nervosa offers a case in point. No matter how thin their bodies, anorexic adolescents continue to view themselves as overweight, and consequently diet to extremes that place their physical and mental health in severe jeopardy for years to come. Helping adolescents view their changing bodies in a positive light can go far in fostering positive developmental cascades.

■ CLOSING THOUGHTS
Primed to Learn

The vulnerabilities of adolescence have the potential to set in motion harmful developmental cascades that are hard to ignore. Yet, the same conditions that establish vulnerabilities—including asynchronous brain development and heightened release of hormones and neurotransmitters—may be nature's way of priming adolescents for learning (Giedd, 2009).

Indeed, development is best viewed as adaptive, priming individuals to maximally learn through their everyday experiences. As such, the changes of adolescence spur positive developments in cognitive, social, and emotional domains. The revved-up, dramatically altered adolescent brain and body arm adolescents with the desire and courage to venture into the world, learn new things, seek out new relationships, and forge new ground.

The Developmentalist's Toolbox		
Method	Purpose	Description
Measuring adolescents' physical development and health		
Tanner scale	To classify the stage of an adolescent's pubertal development	Adolescents are classified on a scale from 1 to 5 based on secondary sexual characteristics of pubic hair and breast development in girls and pubic hair and genital development in boys.
Body mass index (BMI) calculator	To assess whether a person falls within the average range for his or her weight relative to height, is underweight, or is overweight	A ratio is calculated by dividing a person's weight in kilograms by the square of the person's height in meters. In general, people with BMIs of less than 18.5 are underweight; those with BMIs between 18.5 and 25 are average; those with BMIs between 25 and 30 are classified as overweight; and those with BMIs over 30 are obese.

Chapter Summary

Brain Development

- The adolescent brain undergoes a period of synaptogenesis followed by pruning of gray matter volume. White matter volume shows a linear increase due to myelination of axons.
- Asymmetry is seen in adolescent brain development, with limbic subcortical regions maturing before prefrontal cortex regions.
- These brain changes and asymmetry enable high-order cognitive thinking, but also explain the adolescent propensity toward risk-taking behaviors.
- The neurotransmitter dopamine is involved in reward-motivated behaviors and sensation seeking; serotonin aids the regulation of mood and appetite.
- The hypothalamus controls the parasympathetic and sympathetic branches of the autonomic nervous system, with the sympathetic branch reacting to stressful or emotionally arousing situations with a fight-or-flight response.

Puberty

- Hormonal changes during adolescence trigger primary (internal) and secondary (external) sex characteristics, including menarche (in girls) and spermarche (in boys).
- A growth spurt is one of the most noticeable outcomes of puberty. Boys and girls differ in terms of timing and what those changes look like.
- Adolescents experience a series of complex hormonal changes that result from bidirectional communication between the body and brain.
- Puberty occurs over a prolonged period of time and follows a sequence that is often assessed using the Tanner scale.

- Adolescents who diverge from their peers in the timing of puberty are at risk for psychological, social, and physical health concerns. Peer influence, maturational deviance, readiness, and contextual amplification hypotheses have been put forth to explain these negative effects. The consequences of early or late puberty onset (relative to one's peers) are magnified for teens with a poor body image.
- Pubertal timing is affected by genetics, exercise and diet, home context, and a country's economics and poverty.
- Cultural communities around the world differ in their traditions around puberty, preparation of adolescents for adulthood, and messages about sexuality.

Emergence of Sexual Behavior

- Adolescents seek information about sexuality from highly accessible sexual content on media and from their friends.
- Teens who consume relatively high amounts of sexual content from media are likely to be sexually active and increase their likelihood of sexual harassment.
- The majority of adolescents in the United States have engaged in intercourse by the time they graduate high school, although abstinence is practiced by many teens.

Sexually Transmitted Infections and Pregnancy

- Nearly half of U.S. adolescents report having had sexual intercourse, with a substantial percentage of those teens stating they had not used a condom.
- Unsafe sexual practices place adolescents at high risk for pregnancy and sexually transmitted infections such as chlamydia, human papillomavirus (HPV), trichinosis, gonorrhea, and the most serious STI, human immunodeficiency virus (HIV) that leads to acquired immunodeficiency syndrome (AIDS).

- Adolescent pregnancy rates in the United States are high and associated with a range of negative consequences for baby, mother, and father, including increased likelihood of premature birth, low educational and employment attainment, and conflict in the mother-father relationship.
- Adolescents who have low self-regulation, are disengaged from school, and live in impoverished and conflict-ridden homes and communities are at heightened risk for teenage pregnancy.

Nutrition

- An alarming percentage of adolescents have an eating disorder or are obese or overweight.
- Eating disorders such as anorexia nervosa and bulimia nervosa are a major risk during adolescence, particularly among girls.
- Treatments for anorexia and bulimia include medications, behavior modification, family-based therapy, education around nutrition and healthy eating, support groups, and cognitive-based therapies to modify adolescent perceptions about weight.
- Adolescent obesity or overweight status places youth at risk for health-related diseases, discrimination and stigmatization, and psychological problems. However, the psychological effects of weight status differ across racial groups in the United States, perhaps due to differences in body image.
- Adolescent obesity and eating disorders result from a combination of genetic, behavioral, family, and neighborhood factors.
- The prevalence of obesity and eating disorders varies across racial groups.

Sleep

- Circadian rhythm shifts in adolescence toward later bedtime hours.
- Problems of sleep duration and low quality of sleep plague adolescents around the world, affecting academic engagement and performance, health (including obesity), and psychological functioning.
- Sleep problems negatively impact attention and learning, academic achievement, and mental health.
- Sleep problems may be affected by school start times, technology use, and culture.

Developmental Cascades

- Changes in the adolescent brain support cognitive development. Asynchronous brain changes (between prefrontal and limbic regions) increase adolescents' risk-taking behaviors. Anxiety, fear, and depression in adolescence may be rooted in brain changes at this time in development.
- Early pubertal timing can cascade to sexual activity, drinking, pregnancy, school dropout, delinquency, depression, and conflict with parents.
- Obesity and overweight status have harmful effects on physical and mental health, and can have lifelong consequences for an individual's education level, employment, and relationships.
- Adolescents who hold a positive body image are buffered from risks associated with being overweight.

Thinking Like a Developmentalist

1. You are hired by a school district to implement an intervention to promote positive eating habits in adolescents. You are expected to design a comprehensive intervention that will target family, school, and adolescent factors that contribute to two main problems: (a) adolescent eating disorders, and (b) adolescent overweight status and obesity. What would you do in these interventions for each of these problems and why? Would you only target teens with eating disorders or problems of obesity, or would you offer the program to all teens, regardless of their BMI? Why?

2. You are asked to develop a curriculum for an all-day, 8-hour workshop aimed at reducing teen pregnancy. All adolescents in a school district are mandated to attend the workshop. Prepare the agenda for the full-day workshop, with the topics and main points you would cover, the order in which you would cover them, and the length of time each topic would take. Include some "exercises" or "break-out groups" that might actively engage adolescents in the workshop and keep their interest.

3. You are a researcher who studies the effects of poverty on development. You wish to investigate how experiences of neighborhood and family poverty affect physical development and health of teens. You believe that poverty adversely affects family and neighborhood factors, and in turn, harms teen outcomes (see figure). You have funding to conduct your study in 10 communities and to gather data on 500 adolescents and their parents in each community. What would you do to test poverty's effect on family and neighborhood and, ultimately, teen physical and health outcomes? Which measures in family and neighborhood would you target as most influential in adolescent physical development and health? Which physical development, health, and other outcomes would you examine in teens?

Cognitive Development in Adolescence

15

Drawing by Minxin Cheng from a photo by Brad Neathery on Unsplash

I n the early 1960s, developmental psychologist Michael Cole visited a small college in Liberia, West Africa where he sought to understand why Liberian teens had difficulty learning certain school material. Cole conducted a set of landmark studies on the cognitive development of children and adults from the Kpelle tribe—a group of people who lived in small huts in an agricultural community devoted to growing rice (**FIGURE 15.1**). In one study, he compared the logical reasoning of Kpelle farmers to U.S. and Canadian college students using problems such as the following:

- "Spider and black deer always eat together."
- "Spider is eating."
- "Is black deer eating?"

For U.S. and Canadian students, such questions were straightforward. Of course, black deer is eating! In contrast, the Kpelle farmers remarked, "But I was not there. How can I answer such a question?" (Cole et al., 1971, p. 187). For Kpelle farmers, reasoning about something they had not directly experienced was a foreign concept, a view also expressed by members of other cultural communities where schooling is largely absent (Luria, 1976).

In another study, Cole and his colleagues presented U.S. and Canadian college students and Kpelle farmers with classification problems (Cole et al., 1971). But this time, the testing materials were indigenous to the region, which advantaged the Kpelle farmers. The goal was to determine whether certain leaves belonged to trees or vines. The Kpelle farmers correctly classified the 14 leaves from the

FIGURE 15.1 Kpelle in Liberia. Michael Cole's studies of children and adults from the Kpelle tribe offered important insights into the roles of schooling and culture-specific experiences in aspects of cognitive development including logical thinking.

outset, whereas the Canadian and U.S. students required 9 presentations to correctly classify all the leaves. However, when Kpelle famers were then tricked into thinking that the leaves belonged to two fictitious groups, in which the researchers made up novel names of leaves, they struggled with the problem. The farmers got stuck on the unfamiliar category, which prevented them from drawing on their knowledge to solve the problem.

What does Michael Cole's work tell us about cognitive development? First, it underscores a prominent theme of this book: The study of cognitive development requires a deep appreciation for the diverse cultural materials and activities that infuse people's everyday lives. Second, it inspires questions about how experiences with school—a place where children learn to think abstractly, logically, and hypothetically—contribute to certain cognitive skills in adolescents from the United States and other high-resourced societies. Finally, it highlights how practice, familiarity, and background knowledge affect what people attend to and how quickly they learn new material.

In the sections following, we will see how these lessons apply in Piagetian and information processing accounts of adolescent cognitive development. We will examine how motivation, schooling, neighborhood, and cultural contexts affect adolescent cognitive development and academic performance. And we will see how new ways of thinking in adolescence reverberate across developmental domains near and far.

■ *Cognitive Development*

Do you remember the types of cognitive problems teachers expected you to master during adolescence? Probably you were asked to reason about different political orientations and historical events, to apply mathematical principles to abstract problems, to be systematic and scientific in your approach to problems, and to write essays defined by a clear, logical argument that was backed by evidence. You were likely challenged to move beyond your own experiences to generate new solutions to unique types of problems. You had to avoid distractions and remain focused on the material in order to learn lots of new information. You were expected to put aside your own biases to consider viewpoints that differed from your own.

What cognitive skills allowed you to tackle these challenges? Three theoretical approaches provide insight. Piaget attributed adolescents' impressive gains in cognitive abilities to scientific reasoning. Information processing theorists attribute cognitive development to improvements in adolescent attention, working memory, strategies, knowledge, and understanding of the memory process. Social-cognitive theorists spotlight adolescents' growing ability to reason about people's minds and social situations.

Piagetian Theory

According to Piaget, cognitive development reaches its full potential during the **formal operational stage**, which starts around 11 years of age and continues throughout adolescence. During the formal operational stage, thinking moves beyond the "here and now" to consider the abstract and hypothetical.

Abstract and Propositional Thinking

LEARNING OBJECTIVE 15.1 Give examples of abstract and propositional thinking.

Consider the following questions: "What would happen if men could give birth?" or "What would happen if ice did not float?" If you asked children these

formal operational stage The final stage in Piaget's theory of cognitive development characterized by the development of advanced abstract thinking and the ability to manipulate information mentally, use logical thought, and engage in hypothetical, deductive reasoning questions, they might look confused and even challenge you: "But only women can have babies!" and "Ice always floats!" But if you asked adolescents the same questions, they would conjure up many intriguing possibilities. **Abstract thinking** allows adolescents to mentally manipulate ideas and reflect on situations that are not real or tangible (Brain & Mukherji, 2005).

Imagine, for example, what you would do if you had a "third eye" and could place that eye anywhere on your body. When researchers asked 6- and 9-year-old children this question, children stated they would place the third eye in the middle of their foreheads between their two existing eyes (e.g., Low & Hollis, 2003). They appeared to lack the cognitive ability to think beyond the reality of where their eyes belong (Mushoriwa, Sibanda, & Nkambule, 2010). In contrast, 12-year-olds and adults reasoned that it might be possible to place eyes in unique locations. They placed the hypothetical third eye at the top of the head, on arms, legs, palm of their hands, backs, and other locations throughout the body—aiming to gain a new vantage on the world. Such imaginative responses reveal the cognitive flexibility that accompanies abstract thinking. In turn, being freed from the concrete world empowers adolescents to reason logically about statements that may not reflect reality. Adolescents thus surpass children in deductive reasoning skills (see Chapter 12) because they are capable of **propositional thought**—the ability to determine whether a set of propositions (statements) is logical based on the wording of the statement, without having to experience the situation firsthand (Pillow, 2002). To illustrate, consider the following propositions:

- If you hit a loaf of bread in its center with an ax, you will have two pieces.
- Brittany hit a loaf of bread in its center with an ax.
- How many pieces does she have?

Children and adolescents alike will deduce the correct answer "two," following the logic, "If A, then B. A occurs. Therefore, B must be the outcome." However, consider a modified version of the same problem:

- If you hit a loaf of bread in its center with a rose petal, you will have two pieces.
- Brittany hit a loaf of bread in its center with a rose petal.
- How many pieces does she have?

Children in the concrete operational stage will have difficulty with this problem because in reality rose petals cannot cut through bread. Perhaps children are unable to inhibit knowledge about the real world when solving such problems (Klaczynski, Shuneman, & Daniel, 2004). Adolescents, in contrast, can reason on an entirely verbal, logical plane by considering whether the scientific evidence supports the conclusion. As we will see, scientific thinking lies at the crux of formal operations.

abstract thinking The ability to understand concepts by mentally manipulating ideas that are not tangible

propositional thought The ability to determine whether a set of verbal propositions (statements) is logical based on the wording of the statement, even if the person has not directly experienced the situation

✓ CHECK YOUR UNDERSTANDING 15.1

1. What is propositional thinking? Give an example.
2. How might you test whether an individual is capable of abstract thought?

Hypothetical-Deductive Reasoning

LEARNING OBJECTIVE 15.2 Discuss why hypothetical-deductive reasoning is also called scientific reasoning.

Imagine that you have developed a rash because of something you ate. Yet, you are unsure about what prompted the rash. How would you go about figuring out which foods to avoid? You might try changing one food in your diet at a time, and observe the outcome, because making too many changes at once would fail to pinpoint the problem. Your strategy entails generating

hypothetical-deductive reasoning
A systematic, scientific approach to problem solving, referred to as scientific thinking, in which individuals test hypotheses about variables that may influence an outcome to reach a conclusion

combination of liquids problem
An experiment in which children and adolescents must use the scientific method to determine which liquids from four bottles combine with a mysterious liquid "g" to create a chemical reaction that results in a yellow liquid

hypotheses and methodically testing each. Adolescents regularly engage in such **hypothetical-deductive reasoning**—a systematic, scientific approach to problem solving in which they test hypotheses about variables that might influence an outcome to arrive at (deduce) a conclusion. Researchers commonly refer to this type of reasoning as scientific thinking, because a person must generate and test alternative hypotheses. To investigate developmental changes in hypothetical-deductive reasoning, Piaget designed several problems that require systematic hypothesis testing, including the combination of liquids problem and pendulum problem (Inhelder & Piaget, 1958).

Combination of Liquids Problem

The **combination of liquids problem** entails determining which liquid or combination of liquids causes a chemical reaction that produces a vibrant yellow liquid. In this task, Piaget presented children and adolescents with four large bottles filled with liquid (labeled 1–4) and test beakers that contained clear-colored liquid (**FIGURE 15.2**). Piaget then demonstrated that a drop of liquid "g" produces a bright yellow liquid in the beaker. But where does the mysterious liquid "g" come from? The goal is to figure out which liquids from the four bottles, either alone or in combination, combine with liquid "g" to produce a color change. The solution is to combine liquids 1 and 3 together, with or without liquid 2 being present. But, a twist is that the liquid in bottle 4 acts as a neutralizer, keeping the color clear across any liquid combinations. Thus, combining liquids from bottles 1 and 3 or 1, 2, and 3 will produce the yellow color; any other combinations will not.

As you might expect, the combination of liquids problem can only be solved through the scientific method. To succeed, you have to first add the "g" liquid to each of the four liquids separately (1, 2, 3, and 4), then test all two-way combinations (liquids 1 and 2, 1 and 3, etc.), and then all three-way combinations. Adolescents in the formal operational stage approached the problem systematically and arrived at the correct solution, whereas children in the concrete operational stage were haphazard in their approach, randomly testing different combinations and failing to solve the problem.

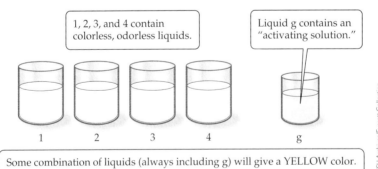

1, 2, 3, and 4 contain colorless, odorless liquids.

Liquid g contains an "activating solution."

1   2   3   4   g

Some combination of liquids (always including g) will give a YELLOW color. How can you find the combination that makes YELLOW?

© CSU Archives/Everett Collection
Historical/Alamy Stock Photo

Jean Piaget

FIGURE 15.2 The combination of liquids problem. This problem entails determining which liquid or combinations of liquids causes a chemical reaction that produces a vibrant yellow liquid. (Note that g in the real task is also a clear liquid and only turns yellow when combined with one or more other liquids.) The problem can only be solved through the scientific method. In essence, individuals must solve the equation of $g + x = y$, with x being one or more liquids and y = the production of a yellow liquid. (After B. Inhelder and J. Piaget. 1958. *The Growth of Logical Thinking from Childhood to Adolescence; An Essay on the Construction of Formal Operational Structures*, A. Parsons and S. Milgram [Trans.]. Basic Books: New York.)

Pendulum Problem

In the **pendulum problem**, Piaget gave children and adolescents a set of weights varying in heaviness and strings of different lengths (**FIGURE 15.3**). The challenge was to figure out which variable(s) affect the rate of the pendulum's swing: the length of the string, heaviness of the weight, height of the release, or force of the push. Adolescents, but not children, considered each variable and their possible combinations in their testing of alternative hypotheses, which allowed them to solve the problem.

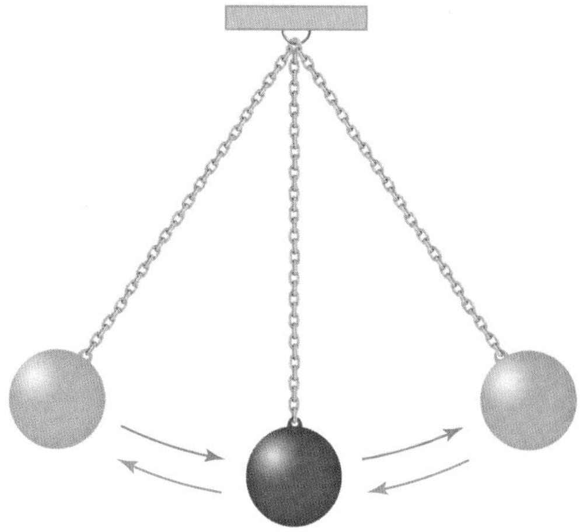

✓ CHECK YOUR UNDERSTANDING 15.2

1. Provide two examples of Piagetian tasks that capture hypothetical-deductive reasoning. Why do these tasks require this type of reasoning?

Rethinking the Formal Operational Stage

LEARNING OBJECTIVE 15.3 Describe objections to Piaget's description of formal operational thought.

Not everyone engages in the sort of scientific reasoning that Piaget described. Sometimes people rely on intuitive reasoning and personal experiences to solve problems, rather than systematic hypothesis testing. In fact, Piaget acknowledged that not everyone achieves the formal operational stage, and even adults continue to adapt and reorganize their thinking as they encounter and learn from new experiences. Today, researchers recognize that formal operational thinking takes many years—from childhood through adolescence and even adulthood—and depends on opportunities such as schooling (Artman, Cahan, & Avni-Babad, 2006).

✓ CHECK YOUR UNDERSTANDING 15.3

1. What observations suggest that formal operational thinking is not universally acquired in adolescence?

Information Processing

Adolescence is a juggling act. Teens keep lots of balls in the air, and for the most part, do so with impressive skill. They manage to stay on top of assignments with different due dates; commit to extracurricular activities, clubs, sports, family obligations, and friends; and still find time to update social media and respond to posts on a daily, largely hourly, basis. Information processing theorists focus on the ways that people attend to, manipulate, store, and retrieve information, and the various strategies that people apply in their thinking. Cognitive factors such as skills in executive functioning allow adolescents to navigate complex school material and challenging problems (see Chapters 9 and 12).

Selective Attention and Flexibility

LEARNING OBJECTIVE 15.4 Understand the roles of attention focus, inhibition, and flexibility in attention and cognitive performance.

What would you do to solve the equation: $90 - (3^2 + 4^2) \times 3 - 2$? Even before you drew on your knowledge of number facts (e.g., that $3^2 = 9$), you would have to figure out which parts of the equation to tackle first, and then determine how to order the steps of the equation. As you did so, the parts of your brain that control attention would be hard at work. To arrive at the correct answer (which is 13, by the way), you would have to focus attention on subcomponents of the

FIGURE 15.3 Pendulum problem. Piaget used several tasks to test children's and adolescents' abilities to engage in hypothetical thinking. The pendulum problem, one such task, required children to figure out which variable or combination of variables affects the rate of the pendulum's swing: the length of the string, heaviness of the weight, height of the release, or force of the push. To solve the problem, each variable must be tested systematically one at a time. (After R. S. Siegler et al. 2003. *How Children Develop*, 1st ed. Worth Publishers: New York.)

pendulum problem A task in which children and adolescents must figure out which variable(s) affect the speed of an object swinging on a string (e.g., length of the string, heaviness of a set of weights) problem and work through those pieces; inhibit attention to distractors, such as your strong tendency to solve problems from left to right; and flexibly shift attention among the various operations and numbers.

Adolescents are fairly good at focusing attention and flexibly shifting attention to relevant information, based on their performance on tasks such as those introduced in Chapters 9 and 12 (Huizinga, Dolan, & van der Molen, 2006; Lee, Bull, & Ho, 2013). Two common tasks are flanker tasks and switching tasks:

- **Flanker tasks** require focusing on a relevant stimulus while inhibiting attention to distractors. An adolescent might be instructed to signal the direction an arrow is facing by pressing on a right or left button. The task becomes increasingly difficult when the arrow is surrounded (flanked) by many distractor arrows facing the opposite direction (**FIGURE 15.4**).

- **Switching tasks** assess the ability to shift attention to different target stimuli. For example, the adolescent might be instructed to press buttons or touch computer screens in response to pictures and their locations. They might be told that when a picture appears in the top half of a computer's window, they should determine whether it is an animal, but when the picture appears in the bottom half they should determine whether it is a number. This requires adolescents to simultaneously attend to the location and pictures, and quickly shift between different responses.

Adolescent performance on executive functioning tasks relates to academic achievement, likely because high school tests require adolescents to allocate attention to different parts of problems and weed out central bits of information from texts and other sources. Mathematics provides a useful illustration of

flanker tasks Response inhibition tasks used to test selective attention and flexibility to a specific stimulus while inhibiting attention to distractors, such as when an adolescent is asked to identify the direction a target arrow faces when surrounded by many distractor arrows

switching tasks Executive functioning tasks used to test the ability to shift attention between one task and another, such as when adolescents are asked to attend to different pictures simultaneously and to quickly shift between responses

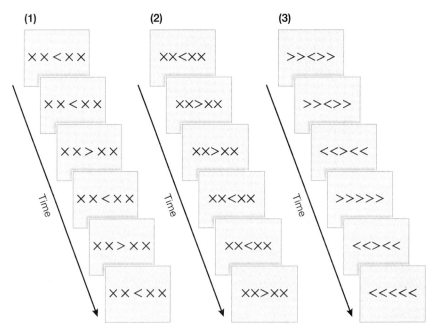

FIGURE 15.4 Flanker task. In flanker tasks, participants are instructed to press a left or right button to indicate the direction of a center arrow. (Note: The line pointing downward indicates the order of stimuli presentation.) Researchers can vary the difficulty of problems in several ways. For example, the second set of pictures is more difficult than the first because the distractors (Xs) are more closely spaced together, making it hard to perceive the center arrow. The third set of pictures is harder still, as the distractors are closely spaced and also the same visually as the target stimulus (i.e., all are arrows). (After M. Chun and S. Most. 2021. *Cognition*, 1st ed. Sinauer/Oxford University Press: Sunderland, MA.)

why selective attention supports multi-step problem solving (Bull & Lee, 2014; Cragg & Gilmore, 2014):

- Adolescents must inhibit or suppress incorrect strategies—such as the strong tendency to work through problems from left to right in the math problem introduced earlier.

- Adolescents must inhibit or suppress salient, familiar number representations that do not apply under certain conditions. For example, large numbers typically express large magnitudes (8 is greater than 4). But, this rule does not apply to large numbers that appear in the denominator of a fraction (1/8 is smaller than 1/4). Adolescents must therefore inhibit conclusions about larger numbers that appear in a denominator.

- Adolescents must shift attention among operations, strategies, notation types (such as words and numbers) and the multiple steps of complex problems, and then focus attention on the target component of the problem.

✓ CHECK YOUR UNDERSTANDING 15.4

1. Describe a flanker task and its purpose.
2. Why are executive functioning skills crucial in mathematical problem solving? Give examples.

Working Memory and Processing Speed

LEARNING OBJECTIVE 15.5 Describe how working memory and processing speed improve in adolescence, and discuss the factors that help account for improvements.

Working memory is always at work. As you tackle problems ranging from a complicated calculus equation to something as straightforward as following a recipe, you must keep lots of information in mind and continually update that information as you work through the steps, for example, monitoring that you've already added sugar to the mixing bowl but have not yet added the cinnamon. **Working memory** refers to the manipulation and temporary storing of information in active memory, and working memory span refers to how many items or chunks of information an individual can actively hold in mind (see Chapters 9 and 12). As a rule, you might be able to keep in mind seven (plus or minus two) ingredients and measurements to prepare a dish, but beyond that you may be in trouble if you don't refer to a recipe.

Working memory span gradually improves between childhood and adolescence as critical brain systems continue to mature (Simmons, Hallquist, & Luna, 2017). Furthermore, many of the things that people do on a daily basis—such as reading words and sentences, and calculating simple number facts—become automatic with practice, which helps free up working memory for other purposes. **Automatic processes** are cognitive activities that require no effort and therefore do not drain the limited cognitive resources available in working memory (Rubinstein, Meyer, & Evans, 2001). Returning to the math equation discussed previously, adolescents automatically process 3^2 as 3×3, and know that 3×3 is 9 without mentally calculating. In contrast, children with less knowledge have to calculate the smaller steps of math problems, which taxes their working memory capacity. When individuals expend a lot of mental effort or resources on a problem—what researchers refer to as **cognitive load**—working memory becomes depleted and performance declines (Chen et al., 2018).

Developments in adolescent working memory aid **processing speed** as well—how quickly and efficiently a person encodes information or solves a problem, as typically measured by reaction time. When individuals name pictures, match colors or numbers, solve simple math problems, and so forth,

working memory The manipulation and temporary storing of information in active memory

automatic processes Mental cognitive activities that are fast, efficient, and require no effort and so do not draw on the limited cognitive resources available in working memory

cognitive load The required amount of working memory resources needed for a task

processing speed How quickly and efficiently a person conducts a mental task, such as encoding information or solving a problem they show consistent age-related gains in the quickness of their responses from early childhood throughout the adolescent years (e.g., Kail, 1991; Kail, Lervag, & Hulme, 2016).

In turn, improvements in processing speed help explain age-related gains in children's cognitive skills. Researchers gave a battery of cognitive and processing speed tests to nearly 7,000 13- to 17-year-olds and timed adolescents on how fast they could match numbers and words and solve single-digit math problems such as 2 + 3 (Coyle et al., 2011). Although adolescents improved in their cognitive performance over age, when *both* age and processing speed were pitted against one another in statistical analyses, processing speed surfaced as a stronger predictor of success than age.

✓ CHECK YOUR UNDERSTANDING 15.5

1. What task might you present to adolescents to assess working memory?
2. How might a researcher test processing speed?
3. How does processing speed change over the course of development?

Memory Strategies and Metacognition

LEARNING OBJECTIVE 15.6 Identify developmental changes in memory strategies and metacognition during adolescence.

Sometimes, strategies aid in solving problems. But, strategies can only be useful if people recognize when and how to use them. To illustrate, let's revisit the opening math problem: $90 - (3^2 + 4^2) \times 3 - 2$. To solve this problem, perhaps you remembered the useful hint PEMDAS ("*Please excuse my dear Aunt Sally*"). This simple phrase serves as a reminder that certain operations precede others: *p*arentheses, *e*xponents, *m*ultiplication, *d*ivision, *a*ddition, then *s*ubtraction. But, to make use of the PEMDAS rule requires metacognition and implementation of the strategy. First, you have to recognize that the problem is not as straightforward as merely moving from left to right, and some mental work is needed. This type of understanding is called **metacognition**—the awareness and understanding of one's thought processes. Second, you have to select and execute the strategy (here, the PEMDAS rule) to solve the problem. **Strategies** refer to the set of techniques that help us to encode and remember information. Memory strategies and metacognition go hand in hand, and both improve over the course of adolescence.

Changes in Memory Strategies

Which strategies improve during adolescence and how do they change? Strategies of rehearsal, chunking, and organization (see Chapters 9 and 12) become faster, more accurate, and easier over the adolescent years (Bjorklund, 2012). Moreover, the complexity of strategies also changes across development. Adolescents are more likely than children to rely on deep versus shallow memory strategies when asked to remember a random list of words (Craik & Tulving, 1975). Deep strategies include things like creating a sentence or story, imagining a scene, and relating information to a personal experience, whereas shallow strategies include repeating words and focusing on the information in one's mind (Daugherty & Ofen, 2015).

For example, if you wanted to remember the cognitive skills we've reviewed so far (selective attention, processing speed, working memory, metacognition, and strategies), you might create a mental image of a race-car driver. The driver is very fast (speed), focuses attention on the current lane, and is not distracted by competing drivers to the left and right (selective attention). The driver continually monitors the dashboard to update current speed and car functioning (working memory) and is aware of the different tactics required to maintain an

metacognition A person's awareness of what that person knows and how thinking works

strategies The set of techniques that help a person encode and remember information edge in the race (metacognition and strategies). This deep-strategy scene would more effectively aid your memory than would a shallow strategy of listing off the cognitive skills in your head—"selective attention, processing speed, working memory, metacognition, and strategies."

Researchers find developmental changes in strategy use when they ask children and adolescents to evaluate which strategies help in remembering a list of word pairs—saying the word pair once, repetition, focusing on the word pair in one's mind, creating a sentence, imagining a scene, assigning personal significance, or rhyming. Adolescents are more likely than younger children to evaluate deep encoding strategies as effective. In contrast, children underrate the usefulness of deep strategies, and prefer simple repetition, perhaps because repetition is easy to implement and demands fewer cognitive resources than do deep strategies (Best et al., 2009; Craik & Tulving, 1975). In fact, the race-car driver "deep" mnemonic requires a lot more initial effort to generate than simply repeating the list. However, in the long run, deep memory strategies win out. Adolescents remember more than children do because they effectively implement deep memory strategies (Daugherty & Ofen, 2015) (**FIGURE 15.5**).

Metacognition

Of course, implementing a strategy requires metacognition, or understanding how the mind works. Adolescents surpass children in metacognition: They understand the limitations to their thinking and memory, recognize that they might benefit from using strategies to remember and solve problems, and revise strategies as needed. Metacognitive awareness helps adolescents

(A)

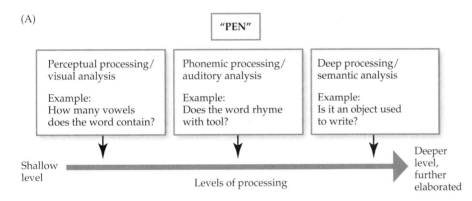

(B)

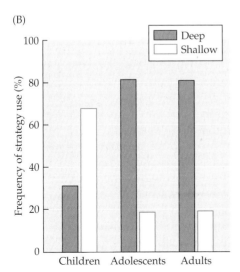

FIGURE 15.5 Deeper levels of analysis are associated with more elaborate, longer lasting and stronger memories. (A) A common procedure for assessing level of processing is to present words to participants (e.g., "pen") and ask a variety of questions designed to influence depth of processing. (B) Adolescents and adults are more likely to use deep strategies for remembering material; whereas, children ages 8–12 are more likely to use shallow strategies. Such differences may contribute to changing memory skill. (A after R. Ekuni et al. 2011. *Psychol Neurosci* 4: 333–339. Copyright © 2011 by American Psychological Association. Reproduced with permission. B after A. M. Daugherty and N. Ofen. 2015. *J Exp Child Psychol* 136: 17–29.)

tackle all sorts of problems, ranging from the formal operational tasks that Piaget developed to academic skills that involve critical thinking, including reasoning, constructing arguments with supportive evidence, and evaluating counterarguments (Kuhn, 2018).

✓ CHECK YOUR UNDERSTANDING 15.6

1. Describe a deep processing memory strategy and indicate why it supports better long-term memory than a shallow one.

Social Cognition

It's intriguing to study the social cognition of adolescents because of the cognitive and social changes that occur at this time in the life course. Adolescents are able to think flexibly, abstractly, and hypothetically, which sparks questions about whether and how their growing cognitive skills play out in their understanding of other people. Additionally, relationships with peers, close friends, romantic partners, teachers, employers, and so forth, take on unprecedented importance, as you will learn in Chapter 16. And so, adolescents must consider which thoughts and emotions are reasonable, appropriate, and expected in specific situations if they are to successfully navigate their expanding social worlds (Brizio et al., 2015).

Still, adolescents are far from perfect in their reasoning about others. Despite their relatively sophisticated social-cognitive understanding, adolescents are intensely immersed in exploring their identities, which amplifies their self-focus and a new form of egocentrism. And, although adolescents display relatively advanced moral reasoning, sometimes they treat others in ways that contradict their moral judgments.

Perspective Taking

LEARNING OBJECTIVE 15.7 Describe the ways that adolescent perspective taking improves on children's abilities but falls short of adults' abilities.

Compared with children, adolescents are remarkably adept at seeing the world from another person's perspective. From childhood through the end of adolescence, individuals improve in their abilities to monitor, understand, explain, and predict the beliefs, desires, thoughts, and behaviors of others. For example, adolescents surpass children on first- and second-order theory-of-mind tasks when asked to interpret positive and negative emotions of fictitious characters, with older adolescents being especially skilled at understanding others' negative emotions, perhaps because they think deeply about their own negative emotions at this time in development (Bosco, Gabbatore, & Tirassa, 2014).

Adolescents are also more competent than children in their ability to take the perspective of another person relative to considering their own perspective. Let's consider what this means. Imagine that you are asked to guess what your friend would do if her mother wouldn't let her go to a party, and to then report on what you would do if your mother did the same. Which question would be easier for you to answer? Why? When developmental researchers compare children's and adolescents' responses to the two types of questions, they see age-related changes in reaction times. **Point-of-view tasks**—a common approach to studying perspective taking—compare individuals' reaction times to first-person questions ("Imagine how *you* would feel if…" "What would *you* do if…") with their reaction times to third-person questions ("Imagine how *Brittany* would feel if…" "What would *Brittany* do if…") (**FIGURE 15.6**). From a developmental perspective, because it is presumably easier to take your own perspective than that of another person, we might hypothesize that adolescents

point-of-view tasks Tasks used to study perspective taking that compare individuals' reaction times to first-person questions (e.g., "What would *you* do if…?") with their reaction times to third-person questions (e.g., "What would *person X* do if…?")

surpass children in their abilities to consider the perspectives of others. Thus, we might predict that the difference in reaction times between first- and third-person questions will decrease with age as adolescents' perspective-taking abilities improve.

Evidence supports this hypothesis. When individuals 8–36 years of age answered questions on a computer about their own perspective or that of another person, differences in reaction times between first- and third-person perspectives decreased with age (Choudhury, Blakemore, & Charman, 2006). Adolescents were quicker at assessing the emotional experiences of other people than were children, although they were not as good as adults. Impressively, adults answered third-person perspective questions just as quickly as first-person questions, whereas adolescents were faster at first- than third-person questions. Thus, although adolescents outperform children on perspective taking, they do not do as well as adults on certain types of tasks (Dumontheil et al., 2010; Vetter et al., 2013).

But, how can adolescents be limited in perspective taking, when even young children are able to consider other people's beliefs on theory-of-mind tasks? The seeming contradiction between the social-cognitive understanding of young children but continued social-cognitive limitations of teens relative to adults has led researchers to distinguish between two types of theory of mind. **Cognitive theory of mind** refers to understanding the mental states, beliefs, thoughts, and intentions of others, as in the Maxi task introduced in Chapter 9. In contrast, **affective theory of mind** refers to understanding the emotions of others. Although children are competent at cognitive theory of mind tasks, they attain affective theory of mind later in development because it requires them to integrate cognitive inferences about others' knowledge and beliefs with empathy for other people (Sebastian et al., 2012, 2015; Shamay-Tsoory et al., 2010). In fact, adolescents lag behind adults in their capacity to draw inferences about a character's response to an emotional situation, such as what a person would do if a companion got hurt, perhaps because distinct brain regions involved in affective theory of mind are still developing (Sebastian et al., 2012).

You are not allowed to go to your best friend's party.

How do you feel?

A girl is not allowed to go to her best friend's party.

How does she feel?

FIGURE 15.6 Point-of-view tasks. These tasks assess the adolescent's ability to take the perspective of others. Researchers measure differences in an adolescent's response times to first- and third-person questions to assess the difficulty the adolescent has in taking another person's perspective. (Note, responses might include being sad or angry.) (After S. Choudhury et al. 2006. *Soc Cog Affect Neurosci* 1: 165–174. By permission of Oxford University Press.)

cognitive theory of mind
The ability to understand the mental states, beliefs, thoughts, and intentions of others

affective theory of mind
The ability to understand the emotions of others

✓ CHECK YOUR UNDERSTANDING 15.7

1. Can you come up with a point-of-view task that might be used to test cognitive theory of mind? Affective theory of mind?

Adolescent Egocentrism

LEARNING OBJECTIVE 15.8 Define adolescent egocentrism, and discuss how it might be adaptive.

We learned that adolescents are not as good as adults at certain perspective-taking tasks. Why? Piaget observed that self-focus intensifies in adolescence, giving rise to a unique form of egocentrism that makes it difficult for teens to understand the perspectives of others (Inhelder & Piaget, 1958). Adolescents are sometimes so preoccupied with their own experiences that they may appear to have blinders on when it comes to understanding where other people are coming from, particularly those who don't agree with them.

American psychologist David Elkind (1967) expanded on Piaget's theory of adolescent egocentrism by suggesting that adolescents experience distorted self-importance that takes the form of a **personal fable**. Adolescents believe that their feelings are vastly unique from those of other people, that others have not been through what they have, and as a result they exaggerate differences between their own experiences and those of their peers and other adults. It's

personal fable The adolescent's belief that their own experiences hold high, special importance relative to others' experiences and that their uniqueness will prevent life's difficulties from affecting them negatively

FIGURE 15.7 Imaginary audience. According to Elkind, adolescents' absorption in their unique life stories leads to intense preoccupation about what others think about them. These ruminations reflect the exaggerated perception that other people are attending to everything the adolescent says and does (the imaginary audience).

imaginary audience An exaggerated perception that other people are attending to everything an individual says or does

as though adolescents forget that throughout human history, people have experienced the universal emotions of love, lust, greed, envy, anger, revenge, and so on.

According to Elkind, adolescents' absorption in their unique life stories leads to intense preoccupation about what others think about them: "How will my friends react to the zit on my nose, what I'm wearing, and my embarrassing parents?" These ruminations reflect what Elkind referred to as an **imaginary audience** —the adolescent's exaggerated perception that other people are attending to everything the teen says and does (**FIGURE 15.7**).

Are there benefits to adolescent self-focus? We will see in Chapter 16 that the adolescent's intense introspection and persistent self-exploration are critical to developing a unique identity. In fact, adolescent egocentrism, the personal fable, and the imaginary audience may be adaptive and indicate a growth in cognitive maturity that enables teens to adjust to new environmental situations and consider the potential consequences of their behaviors for their social relationships (Schwartz, Maynard, & Uzelac, 2008; Vartanian, 2001). Adolescents who perceive and understand peer norms around dressing, for example, may be appropriately concerned about what they wear to maintain connection to the group.

✓ CHECK YOUR UNDERSTANDING 15.8

1. What is meant by a personal fable and imaginary audience? Connect these ideas to Piaget's observation of adolescent egocentrism.

Moral Reasoning

LEARNING OBJECTIVE 15.9 Describe how researchers assess adolescent moral reasoning, and how their approach builds on the work of Kohlberg.

What would you do if you found a wallet at school that contained money? Would you keep the money, but return the wallet to its owner? Would you return it with the money intact? Most centrally—*Why* would you make that choice? Because you fear getting caught? Because you respect the rights and property of others? People confront moral dilemmas all the time, some of which are straightforward and others more nuanced—few people would keep a wallet or its contents, but many might not think twice about inviting only certain people to a party.

Lawrence Kohlberg inspired developmental scientists to consider the cognitive underpinnings to moral reasoning (see Chapter 10). Recall that Kohlberg formulated a cognitive theory of moral development that emphasized people's reasoning about moral dilemmas, such as whether Heinz should steal a drug to save his wife's life. From interviews with many individuals, Kohlberg and followers found convincing support for a stage sequence in reasoning: Children and adolescents progress through Kohlberg's pre-conventional and conventional stages in a relatively consistent order, increasingly reasoning at higher stages as reasoning at lower stages tapers (Boom, Wouters, & Keller, 2007; Dawson, Gilovich, & Regan, 2002). However, people rarely respond to dilemmas at Kohlberg's post-conventional level, which has led researchers to question Kohlberg's ordering of stages and assumption that post-conventional thinking reflects a more sophisticated, complex moral orientation than does reasoning at other levels (Gibbs, 2013; Gilligan, 1982).

Despite limitations to Kohlberg's stage theory, his approach to studying moral reasoning continues to inspire contemporary science. Today, researchers

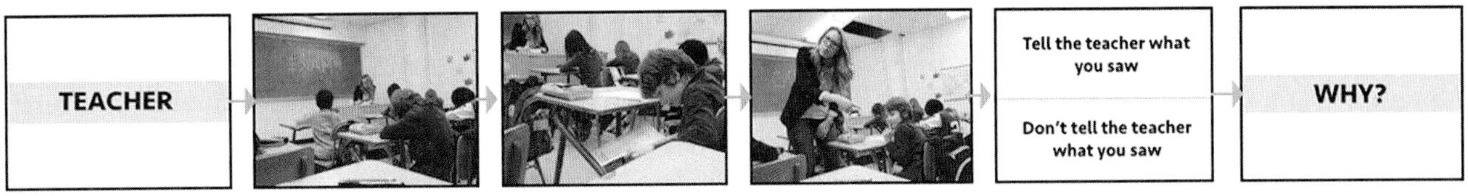

From E Vera-Estay et al.
2016. Front Psychol 7:
227. doi: 10.3389/fpsyg
2016.00227/CC BY 4.0

FIGURE 15.8 The So-Moral task presents an adolescent with moral dilemmas. Mature moral reasoning correlates with four executive functions (cognitive flexibility, feedback utilization, conceptual reasoning, and verbal fluency) and is predicted by four variables: age, intelligence, nonverbal flexibility, and verbal fluency. For example, researchers might present pictures such as the ones shown here, depicting a student cheating on a test by looking down at notes. The question is whether another student should inform the teacher of the cheating and, most centrally, why the student would choose that course of action (i.e., the moral reasoning behind decisions).

can exploit modern technology by presenting stories and tracking participants' moral reasoning on computers. One such approach is the **So-Moral task** (**FIGURE 15.8**). Researchers present adolescents with scenes of moral dilemmas acted out by other teens and ask them to make yes or no decisions for each dilemma—whether to return a lost wallet, steal from a shop, cheat at a game, and so on (Beauchamp, Dooley, & Anderson, 2013; Vera-Estay, Dooley, & Beauchamp, 2015). Again, like Kohlberg, researchers classify adolescents' answers along a scale of increasing moral reasoning. For example, an adolescent who reasons about stealing from the perspective of personal consequences (e.g., "I shouldn't steal because I would get caught") would be classified at a low level of morality, whereas an adolescent who reasoned about stealing from the perspective of fairness and respect (e.g., "I shouldn't steal because I should respect others' belongings and the hard work that went into obtaining them") would be classified at a high level of morality.

So, what do findings reveal about adolescent moral development? They confirm that moral reasoning between 13 and 20 years of age relates closely to gains in general cognitive development (Vera-Estay, Dooley, & Beauchamp, 2015). Specifically, as adolescents grow in their conceptual reasoning, cognitive flexibility, speed of accessing vocabulary, and social cognition, they show parallel and related improvements in moral development (e.g., Labelle-Chiasson et al., 2012; Vera-Estay, Dooley, & Beauchamp, 2015).

So-Moral task An approach to studying moral reasoning in which individuals are presented with scenes of moral dilemmas and are asked to make decisions about each dilemma

✓ CHECK YOUR UNDERSTANDING 15.9

1. Describe the So-Moral task.

Moral Behavior

LEARNING OBJECTIVE 15.10 Explain why adolescent behavior does not always rise to the level of adolescent moral reasoning.

Does moral reasoning translate to moral behavior? In many ways, yes. Adolescents' sense of moral obligation and their ability to think about what it might be like to walk in another person's shoes give rise to acts of compassion, care, and altruism (e.g., Lerner & Lerner, 2006). And yet, adolescent behaviors frequently fail the moral litmus test. Sometimes, teens lie and deceive. Other times they discriminate or display preferential treatment toward certain people. Why would someone who can reason in morally sophisticated ways treat others unfairly?

For one, adolescents' sophisticated social-cognitive capacities allow them to craft clever ways to deceive or manipulate others to serve their self-interests. Adolescents may lie to their parents about their grades or avoid discussing what happened at a college party because they know how to make their parents believe something other than the truth. Adolescents might reason about those "necessary lies" in fairly complex ways that ultimately provide them with a rationale for their behaviors: "I should be able to make my own decisions. If my parents don't know about the party, everyone wins—they won't be stressed, and I'll have fun."

Another reason that adolescents' behaviors don't always match up with their moral reasoning is because social situations are very complicated, and many factors influence what people do at any point in time. Adolescents must constantly juggle moral obligations, personal goals, societal norms, and their relationships with people who share similar and different interests or social memberships (Killen & Smetana, 2015).

To illustrate, consider an adolescent who must decide whether to invite certain peers to a party. Although the adolescent recognizes that it may be insensitive to exclude some peers from a party, she may be inclined to only invite friend athletes, reasoning that she is an athlete and it's her party. In this case, her in-group favoritism may trump her inclination toward inclusion because she is able to generate a rationale that is based on multiple factors. Yet, the excluded nonathletes may feel differently. Research on in- and out-group social interactions confirms that individuals use complex justifications in their moral judgments, and believe that certain forms of exclusion are more acceptable than others. For example, Swiss adolescents (12 and 15 years of age) believed that exclusion based on nationality was more acceptable than exclusion based on gender or personality. In contrast, their non-Swiss peers, who were recent immigrants, viewed exclusion based on nationality to be wrong, likely because they had personally experienced exclusion and suffered its consequences (Malti, Killen, & Gasser, 2012).

✓ CHECK YOUR UNDERSTANDING 15.10

1. List two reasons why adolescents' behaviors in a moral situation might not live up to their moral reasoning.

Cultural Context of Adolescent Cognitive Development

Does cognitive development differ in cultural communities where valued skills and practices diverge from what people are accustomed to in WEIRD (Western, educated, industrialized, rich, and democratic) societies? Perhaps abstract, hypothetical-deductive thinking is a hallmark of cognitive development in cultures where schooling is mandatory and a path to career opportunities. But what about adolescents in hunter-gatherer and fishing communities, for example, where schooling is not available or where children attend school for only a few years? What benefits would abstract, hypothetical-deductive reasoning offer them? Here, we examine how culture shapes adolescent cognition through cultural tools and experiences around schooling, topics introduced in Chapter 12.

Cultural Tools and Activities

LEARNING OBJECTIVE 15.11 Provide examples of how cultural tools and activities can affect cognitive development.

The tools and materials of a culture can affect how people think. The domain of mathematics offers an intriguing example. Recall that Michael Cole compared logical reasoning on verbal problems in Kpelle and U.S. college students, as described at the start of the chapter. Cole also compared the two communities on various math tasks, and found fascinating differences that could be attributed to the cultural tools of each community. For instance, the Kpelle were better than were U.S. college students at estimating the number

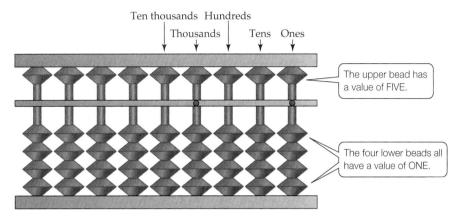

Ten thousands Hundreds
Thousands   Tens Ones

The upper bead has a value of FIVE.

The four lower beads all have a value of ONE.

FIGURE 15.9 How to count on the soroban, the Japanese abacus. In Japan, primary school students use the soroban to help with mental calculation. Once they have learned how to use the tool, students are able to visualize it to answer mathematical questions in the same amount of time, or sometimes even faster, than they could with the actual soroban.

of stones in a pile, whereas U.S. college students were better at estimating length using hand span (Gay & Cole, 1967). The Kpelle's skill at estimating the number of stones could be explained by the importance of stones in their everyday life. Stones were commonly used to approximate the number of cups in a container of rice—the main staple of their community. The U.S. students had experiences with rulers and other tools that measure length and width and knowledge of formulas that converted one measurement to another (for instance, understanding that 1 foot = 12 inches). The U.S. cultural emphasis on length and width, and everyday practice with rulers, allowed them to estimate how many inches were in a hand span and in turn, to use hand span to estimate the overall length of objects or spaces.

The abacus is another cultural tool that influences mathematical cognition. In Japan, expertise with the abacus was found to facilitate memory for numbers, even when the abacus was absent, because expert users visually imagined digits on the abacus to help them remember (Hatano, 1982) (**FIGURE 15.9**). This visualization strategy allowed them to recall a series of 15 digits forward or backward. Their impressive memory, however, was specific to numbers. Memory for letters or fruit names, for instance, did not exceed the standard memory span of seven, plus or minus two units, found in other countries.

✓ CHECK YOUR UNDERSTANDING 15.11

1. Give an example of a cultural tool that influences how individuals solve math problems.

Culture and Schooling

LEARNING OBJECTIVE 15.12 Describe how cognitive skills may differ in communities where adolescents attend school versus communities where they do not.

Cultural communities differ in how much schooling they require of children. Adolescents and adults from cultures where schooling is nonexistent or limited to only a few years do not gain practice with the abstract, hypothetical, and deductive reasoning that is commonly taught to adolescents in the United States and other technological societies (Rogoff & Chavajay, 1995). As emphasized at the start of this chapter, schooled individuals learn how to engage in logical, deductive forms of reasoning based on abstract premises, whereas individuals from communities in which schooling is not common tend to draw conclusions on the basis of practical experience. The reasoning styles of Liberian adults, as described at the chapter's opening, can also be found in other communities.

Developmental psychologist Alexander Luria (1976) used a classic test of hypothetical-deductive reasoning to document Central Asian villagers' reliance on concrete experience: "In the North, where there is snow, all bears are white. Novaya Zemlya is in the Far North, and it always has snow. What colors are the bears there?" The villagers refused to respond to this question, even when Luria pushed them to answer and even just guess if they had to. The villagers stated that they would have to experience the event firsthand to give an answer. One villager then supported his answer by saying that if a man had seen a white bear and told him about it, then he might believe that white bears exist. So, if we think about this response, we see that villagers did engage in hypothetical thinking when Luria pushed. However, Luria's observations illustrate that cultural experiences related to schooling affect familiarity with the types of problems posed by Piaget and the tendency to use specific modes of thought.

✓ **CHECK YOUR UNDERSTANDING 15.12**

1. How might schooling affect how people reason about problems?

◼ *Language, Literacy, and Academic Skills*
....

My son's friend Marc struggled in school for most of his childhood years. With support at school and home, Marc was able to keep up with his peers and found time to play sports and volunteer at charities during elementary school. He worked harder than any of his friends to maintain decent grades, and often shared his goal of one day going to college. High school, however, posed a huge challenge, and life quickly unraveled. Academic material increased in difficulty, and Marc found himself falling further and further behind in his schoolwork. He began to disengage from his teachers and classes. He lost his motivation to do well and began to cut classes. His poor grades and low attendance got him kicked off the baseball team—the one thing that had kept him connected to school and friends. Now, with time on his hands and nowhere to go after school, it did not take long for Marc to get into trouble, drop out of school, and eventually get arrested. Years later, Marc completed a high school general equivalency degree (GED) and started classes at a community college. The last I heard, his struggle is not over.

Marc's story is one of thousands in the United States. All too many children who had kept up in the past become adolescents who disengage from school in the future. Why? Notably, meeting the demands of high school takes a lot of effort. Adolescents must learn new words and specialized forms of reading and writing that diverge from the language of everyday conversations. They must apply their skills in abstract thinking to scientific hypotheses and complex math problems that require them to manipulate unknown values and variables. They must establish goals and apply strategies to achieve them. Moreover, adolescents are expected make their own schedules and carve out time for studying and homework, school clubs and sports teams, chores and sibling care, and maybe work to help pay bills. Many adolescents succeed at meeting responsibilities, while others, like Marc, struggle and do not.

Language and Literacy Development

Language and literacy skills flourish in adolescence. Armed with foundational tools in language and literacy, adolescents are ready to assemble all the bits and pieces that they've learned into masterful pieces of artwork. They can capitalize on the rich language and literacy opportunities offered in school, peer, family, and neighborhood contexts in unprecedented ways—by participating in classroom discussions and debates; arguing political and social viewpoints; and reaping the benefits of reading material that exposes them to new words, concepts, and subject matter.

Vocabulary and Grammar

LEARNING OBJECTIVE 15.13 Identify improvements in vocabulary and grammar typically seen in adolescence.

Think about the things you talk about with family and friends. Maybe you discuss the latest movies, gossip about friends, or grumble about the injuries on your favorite sports team. Now consider the topics you were introduced to in high school. You were likely exposed to words, concepts, and sentence constructions outside of your casual, everyday conversations. It's safe to say that much of your growth in vocabulary and grammar occurred within the walls of your high school.

How much vocabulary do adolescents actually learn? Adolescents add words to their vocabularies at an astounding rate and, unsurprisingly, much of that growth can be credited to their experiences at school. Over the late elementary and high school years U.S. teens are estimated to add between 3,000 and 5,400 words per year, a whopping 10–15 words per day (Landauer & Dumais, 1997)! Much of that vocabulary comes from the words adolescents encounter in subjects such as literature, social studies, and science—what researchers refer to as **academic vocabulary**. And, academic vocabulary is embedded in books and scholarly articles that contain abstract, specialized, and conceptually dense language—what researchers refer to as **academic language** (Kieffer & Lesaux, 2010; Uccelli et al., 2018). As a result of schooling, adolescents' vocabularies enlarge to include words such as "revolutionized," "counterintuitive," and "hypothesize" (e.g., Sun & Nippold, 2012). Proficiency with academic vocabulary facilitates school success, because adolescents must understand the words contained in reading materials and produce them in their own writing (Snow & Uccelli, 2009).

In the same vein, adolescents increasingly use advanced grammatical forms contained in school books, such as **embedded clauses**—that is, statements that are nested within other statements (Blum-Kulka, 2008). For example, a child might write an essay stating, "My cousin Ashleigh is a vegetarian and told the waiter. But he didn't listen and served her red meat. So, she got angry at him." But, an adolescent is able to formulate a single sentence to capture the same idea, "My cousin Ashleigh told the waiter she's a vegetarian and got angry when he didn't listen and served her red meat."

Unfortunately, a substantial number of struggling readers have a tough time digesting school material because they are unfamiliar with the sophisticated words and grammar of academic language (e.g., Lesaux et al., 2010). As a result, high-level readers surpass mid-level readers who surpass low-level readers on vocabulary across the entirety of adolescence (Duff, Tomblin, & Catts, 2015) (**FIGURE 15.10**). And, adolescents who struggle with complex grammatical constructions may not grasp the meaning of words, because they are unable to unpack sentence grammar to decipher what's going on (Lesaux et al., 2010). Many low-proficient readers are English-language learners (ELLs), who have limited English vocabularies and limited understanding of English and therefore have difficulty deciphering the meaning of written texts (Kieffer & Lesaux, 2010).

academic vocabulary Words that a person encounters in academic subjects such as literature, science, and social studies

academic language Specialized, conceptually dense, and abstract language that is used in classrooms and academic programs

embedded clauses Statements nested within other statements that provide elaborated information

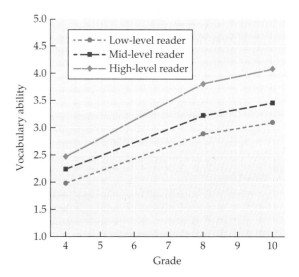

FIGURE 15.10 Growth in vocabulary relates to reading skill.   Adolescents' skills in reading relate closely to their vocabulary: High-level readers exceed mid-level and low-level readers, at a time when academic vocabulary grows substantially. (After D. Duff et al. 2015. *J Speech Lang Hear Res* 58: 853–864. Republished with permission of American Speech-Language-Hearing Association; permission conveyed through Copyright Clearance Center, Inc.)

✓ CHECK YOUR UNDERSTANDING 15.13
1. What is meant by academic vocabulary? Give examples.
2. How might textbooks be improved to accommodate ELLs who have a limited understanding of English?

Reading and Writing

LEARNING OBJECTIVE 15.14 Explain why academic success depends on more than a robust academic vocabulary.

Because academic texts contain an entirely different writing style than is typical of everyday conversations, adolescents must achieve a wide set of core academic language skills (Uccelli et al., 2015). To succeed in school, students must be able to:

- *Unpack complex words.* The ability to break up unfamiliar, complex words into their morphemes, or smaller units of meaning (see Chapters 6 and 8).

- *Understand complex sentences.* Academic texts are often filled with densely packed information contained in complex sentences such as: "Because humans are not rats or monkeys, we must be careful about generalizing from animal studies to human behavior."

- *Connect ideas.* Many words and phrases serve to connect ideas within and across sentences (e.g., "although," "because," "however," and so forth). An understanding of the connectives in academic texts aids adolescents' understanding of and memory for reading material.

- *Track themes.* Readers must keep track of the themes in academic texts to make sense of what they are reading. For example, consider the following two sentences: "The evaporation of water occurs due to rising temperatures. This process...." The reader must realize that the phrase "This process" refers to "water evaporation" in the prior sentence.

- *Appreciate the organizational logic of texts.* Academic texts generally are structured around a logically organized framework. For example, a history chapter might be organized chronologically around a series of battles, presenting the events leading up to and following each battle. Knowledge of the overall structure of academic texts develops gradually through the high school years.

Writing essays that include these features is even more difficult than reading such material. Beyond composing essays that contain sophisticated words and grammar, adolescents must present their ideas thematically and logically while writing to a specific audience in different voices and with different levels of depth and persuasion. Older adolescents are more capable of writing persuasive essays that include evidence for, and rebuttals against, their positions than are younger adolescents (Midgette, Haria, & MacArthur, 2008). Indeed, time and practice go a long way toward improving the quality of adolescents' writing, with most teens achieving at least a modest level of proficiency (Uccelli et al., 2015).

✓ CHECK YOUR UNDERSTANDING 15.14
1. What skills will adolescents need in order to read and write academic material?

Gender Differences in Academic Proficiencies

LEARNING OBJECTIVE 15.15 Discuss social and cultural explanations for differences in verbal and mathematical proficiencies observed in adolescent boys and girls.

In the United States and many other technological countries, adolescent boys and girls diverge in the academic subjects they excel at and pursue. Data across 65 nations revealed that boys outperformed girls in mathematics,

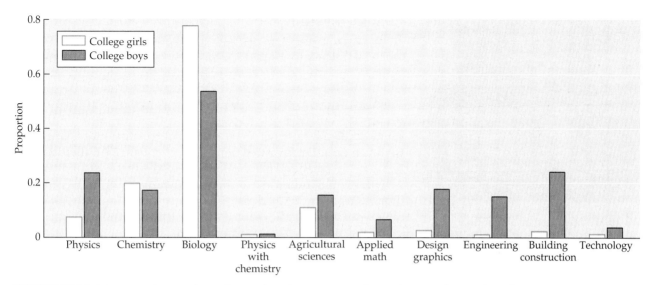

FIGURE 15.11 Disparities by gender in STEM disciplines. By early adolescence, boys tend to outperform girls on advanced problems in science and mathematics. These differences, in combination with other factors, such as stereotypes and attitudes around gender, contribute to the greater likelihood of teen boys pursuing STEM-related coursework in college and entering STEM careers in adulthood than teen girls. As shown in the graph, college-aged boys are three times more likely to study physics and applied mathematics; whereas, college-aged girls are more likely to study chemistry and biology. Furthermore, less than 5% of college-aged girls pursue subjects such as engineering and technology. (After J. Delaney and P. Devereux. 2019. VoxEU. April 19, 2019. https://voxeu.org/article/understanding-gender-differences-stem.)

whereas girls outperformed boys in reading and literacy (Reilly, 2012). The girls' advantage in reading and literacy may in part explain current disparities in college enrollment by teen girls (60%) and teen boys (40%). However, by early adolescence, boys tend to outperform girls on advanced problems in science and mathematics (Gibbs, 2010; Lindberg, 2010). In fact, twice as many teen boys as girls score above 700 on the quantitative section of the Scholastic Aptitude Test (SAT) (Wai et al., 2010). And, scores released by the College Board in 2016 reveal that the teen boys' advantage in math continues a persistent, 50-year trend. Such statistics contribute to teen boys' greater likelihood to pursue STEM (science, technology, engineering, and math) related coursework in college and enter STEM careers in adulthood than teen girls (**FIGURE 15.11**).

Gendered Socialization

Of course, gendered socialization practices feed into the academic inclinations of boys and girls. For example, both mothers and fathers read more to their girls than they do to their boys during early childhood (Leavell Smith et al., 2012), which may be why girls devote more time to reading as a pastime than do boys through the adolescent years. And, conversely, from an early age, boys spend more time playing with blocks and puzzles, toys that promote the spatial and math skills core to careers in technology and math (LeVine et al., 2016).

Boys also spend a lot more time than do girls playing video games. The fast-action movements and demands of digital gaming provide boys with opportunities to practice spatial-attention skills that can yield cognitive benefits in STEM disciplines (Bavelier et al., 2016). In fact, contrary to conventional beliefs that video games lead to laziness and low academic performance, gaming may support executive functioning because of the high demands on attention and practice with fast reaction times. Indeed, executive functioning skills relate to achievements in STEM subjects (Granic, Lobel, & Engels, 2014) (**FIGURE 15.12**).

FIGURE 15.12 Video games and STEM achievements.   Contrary to conventional beliefs that video games lead to laziness and low academic performance, video games support skills in executive functioning associated with achievements in important STEM disciplines.

Cultural Messages

Finally, cultural messages contribute to gender differences in academic skills and ultimate career paths. Consider the popular claim that men are better at "analyzing systems" and women better at "understanding emotions," a position Baron-Cohen advanced in the 2004 book *The Essential Difference*, which asserted major differences in the brains of men and women. If people believe and accept the view that men and women think in fundamentally different ways, then social pressures may help explain why men enter fields that require analytic thought (STEM disciplines) and women enter fields that call for people skills (health, education, and psychology). Of course, a single book is not responsible for the gendered distribution of careers, and many factors contribute to gender divides in career choices. However, this example illustrates how cultural messages shape and are shaped by real-world circumstances.

Developmental scientists Sara-Jane Leslie and Andrei Cimpian wondered whether cultural stereotypes about professions that require "brilliance" and "genius" might explain the underrepresentation of women in certain fields. To test their hypothesis, they compared the views of academics (perhaps some of your professors!) about fields with a high representation of female PhDs or high representation of male PhDs in a nationwide survey. They found that academics perceived professions with an underrepresentation of women as requiring "raw, innate talent" for success, as though women did not have the intellectual capacities to succeed in such male-dominated fields (Leslie et al., 2015) (**FIGURE 15.13**).

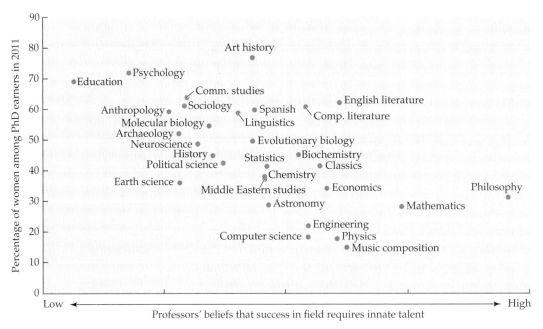

FIGURE 15.13 Academic judgment of professions.   Developmental scientists Sara-Jane Leslie and Andrei Cimpian compared the views of academics about fields with high representations of women PhDs to their views of fields with high representations of men PhDs in a nationwide survey. They found that academics perceived "raw, innate talent" to be necessary for success in fields characterized by an underrepresentation of women. Such perceptions suggest that they did not view women as having the intellectual talents to make it in male-dominated fields. (For example, note that education and psychology, fields with high representations of women, are viewed to require little innate talent compared to male-dominated fields like computer science and mathematics). (From D. Miller. The Conversation. June 9, 2015. https://theconversation.com/beliefs-about-innate-talent-may-dissuade-students-from-stem-42967. After S.-J. Leslie et al. 2015. Science 347: 262–265. Reprinted with permission from AAAS. https://doi.org/10.1126/science.1261375.)

Leslie and Cimpian analyzed students' reviews of their professors and counted how many times students used the words "brilliant" and "genius" in over 14 million reviews on RateMyProfessors.com. In line with the responses of their professors, the more students described their professors in a field as "brilliant" and "genius," the fewer women PhDs were in the field. Furthermore, the gender difference in evaluations was not due to generally positive reviews of certain professions. Gender differences were *not* seen for words that don't suggest raw intellectual ability, such as "amazing" or "excellent." As you might expect, the pipeline to "brilliant" careers begins in adolescence, if not sooner. Fewer women than men seek degrees in "brilliance-focused" fields, which suggests that cultural messages around ability contribute to high school students' choices about what to study in college (Storage et al., 2016).

Cross-cultural research offers further evidence of socialization effects on the gender divide in adolescent academic achievement. As nations increase the value they place on gender equality, and where science and math are *not* viewed as predominantly male subject material, gender differences in math and/or science achievement decline and the proportion of women in research disciplines increases (Else-Quest, Hyde & Linn, 2010; Guiso et al., 2008; Reilly, 2012) (**FIGURE 15.14**).

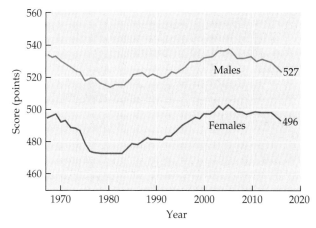

FIGURE 15.14 Gender differences in SAT math scores. On average, boys score higher than girls on the math SAT. The pattern of scores is consistent across years and does not appear to be diminishing, contrary to other lines of evidence that show gender differences in mathematics are small. (After M. J. Perry. Carpe Diem, AEI blog. September 27, 2016. https://www.aei.org/carpe-diem/2016-sat-test-results-confirm-pattern-thats-persisted-for-45-years-high-school-boys-are-better-at-math-than-girls/. © 2021 American Enterprise Institute. Source: College Board.)

✓ **CHECK YOUR UNDERSTANDING 15.15**

1. What changes might be made in a school curriculum to engage girls in STEM disciplines?
2. Why do you suppose boys tend to be less interested in reading than girls? Do you think this has always been true?
3. Give an example of how cultural messages around brilliance relate to gendered career paths.

School Engagement and Motivation

What does it take to do well in school? Of course, the cognitive skills discussed to this point are fundamental to school success. However, school performance requires much more than an ability to think abstractly and flexibly, focus attention, manipulate information in working memory, and so on. It requires fierce dedication to schoolwork and a willingness to resist tempting opportunities in the short term to benefit academically in the long term. In short, doing well in school requires engagement and motivation.

Components of School Engagement

LEARNING OBJECTIVE 15.16 Describe different types of school engagement.

Think of someone who you consider to be really into school. In what ways is that person engaged? Like many constructs in developmental psychology, academic engagement is multidimensional and involves several components (e.g., Fredricks, Blumenfeld, & Paris, 2004; Wang et al., 2019):

- **Behavioral engagement** refers to participation in learning activities, including attentiveness, positive conduct in classes, and school attendance.
- **Emotional engagement** refers to affective attitudes toward school, including feeling positively toward school and experiencing a sense of school belonging.

behavioral engagement A type of school engagement characterized by participation in learning activities (e.g., attending to class lessons)

emotional engagement A type of school engagement describing affective attitudes toward school (e.g., feeling positively toward school)

cognitive engagement A type of school engagement referring to a self-regulated approach to learning (e.g., using strategies to support learning)

- **Cognitive engagement** refers to a self-regulated approach to learning that includes being invested in the process of learning and using effective strategies to support learning of school material.

Engagement is especially important during high school, when the difficulty of subject matter intensifies and adolescents take responsibility for their own learning. Students who abide by school rules, avoid problem behaviors, and remain open to teachers and peers are likely to earn solid grades and set a goal to attend college (e.g., Wentzel et al., 2010). Conversely, a lack of engagement in one or more areas interferes with school success. Adolescents who displayed declines in their behavioral and cognitive engagement between seventh and eleventh grade had lower grade point averages (GPAs) and lower ambitions to pursue college than did those without declines (Wang & Eccles, 2011).

✓ **CHECK YOUR UNDERSTANDING 15.16**

1. How are the different types of engagement associated with school performance?

Academic Motivation and Performance

LEARNING OBJECTIVE 15.17 Discuss grit and choice and how they affect an adolescent's performance in academics and other areas.

What enables an adolescent to remain behaviorally, emotionally, and cognitively engaged in school? Motivation is key. Let's use an analogy of driving a car to clarify the distinction between engagement and motivation. If engagement is viewed as driving the car, then motivation can be seen as the gasoline. A traditional car won't move without gas, just as an adolescent low on motivation is at risk of disengaging from school.

Lack of Motivation Undermines Engagement and Performance

Unfortunately, many teens are bored and unexcited about school (e.g., Roeser & Eccles, 2014) (**FIGURE 15.15**). In fact, academic motivation declines substantially in adolescence, particularly around school transitions. Grades tend to drop at the transition to middle school and drop again from middle school to high school (e.g., Benner, 2011; Ryan, Shim, & Makara, 2013). And declines in grades are accompanied by declines in school attendance and achievement test scores (Benner & Wang, 2014; Schwerdt & West, 2013). As students lose interest, their performance drops further, with interest diminishing to new lows, a downward cycle that may snowball.

grit The steadfast perseverance and passion for long-term goals, even when a person encounters challenges

© wavebreakmedia/Shutterstock.com

FIGURE 15.15 Many teens are bored or unexcited by school. Academic motivation declines substantially in adolescence, particularly as teens transition from one school to another.

Motivation also determines how well students do on intelligence and standardized tests (see Chapter 12). Adolescents who do well on such tests are not only smart: They are motivated to do well. That is, scoring in upper percentiles requires intelligence *and* motivation. The story is different for adolescents who show poor performance on IQ and standardized tests. Low aptitude, a lack of motivation, or both may explain their low scores. Does this mean that some low-scoring adolescents may be a lot smarter than their scores would suggest? Absolutely. When researchers gave adolescents material rewards to incentivize them to score well on an intelligence test, low-performing adolescents substantially improved in their scores, suggesting they initially had not worked to their maximum potential and needed a motivational boost to try harder. In contrast, incentives did not improve the scores of high-scoring adolescents, who may have already exerted maximum effort to reach their potential (Duckworth et al., 2011)

Psychologist Angela Duckworth claims that the characteristic of **grit**—the tenacious perseverance and passion for long-term goals,

TABLE 15.1 ■ Grit

Take a quiz on grit. Mark down the number that corresponds to your level of agreement with the statements, and then sum your score. Higher scores reflect higher grit.

	Not like me at all	Not much like me	Somewhat like me	Mostly like me	Very much like me
New ideas and projects sometimes distract me from previous ones.	5	4	3	2	1
Setbacks don't discourage me. I don't give up easily.	1	2	3	4	5
I often set a goal but later choose to pursue a different one.	5	4	3	2	1
I am a hard worker.	1	2	3	4	5
I have difficulty maintaining my focus on projects that take more than a few months to complete.	5	4	3	2	1
I finish whatever I begin.	1	2	3	4	5
My interests change from year to year.	5	4	3	2	1
I am diligent. I never give up.	1	2	3	4	5
I have been obsessed with a certain idea or project for a short time but later lost interest.	5	4	3	2	1
I have overcome setbacks to conquer an important challenge.	1	2	3	4	5

Source: After A. L. Duckworth et al. 2007. *J Pers Soc Psychol* 9: 1087–1101. Copyright © 2007 by American Psychological Association. Reproduced with permission; A. Duckworth. 2016. *Grit: The Power of Passion and Perseverance.* Scribner: New York.

even in the face of setbacks—distinguishes high performers from low performers on standardized tests (Duckworth, 2016) (**TABLE 15.1**). Gritty adolescents and young adults are more likely to graduate from high school, earn high GPAs in college, keep their jobs, and even stay married than are individuals low on grit (e.g., Duckworth & Gross, 2014; Park et al., 2018).

Choice Matters

On first glance, you might assume that as long as an adolescent has grit and is doing well in school, the adolescent must be excited by learning. However, success is distinct from enjoyment. When academically successful students—adolescents from gifted programs who excelled academically—were interviewed about their feelings about school, surprisingly, *none* of them spoke passionately about what they were learning. Their desire for good grades and desire to maintain their image as a good student, rather than an interest in school material, drove their high performance (Fredricks, Alfeld, & Eccles, 2010). In essence, they had grit, but were unenthused. In contrast, students who were talented in nonacademic areas such as sports or music expressed a lot of passion about their nonacademic activities. Such findings suggest that schools may undermine rather than stimulate adolescents' passion for academic materials. Even students who do well in school do not necessarily enjoy being there.

Why might an adolescent be more passionate about nonacademic subjects than academic ones? Perceptions about choice explain some of the difference. Adolescents who participate in activities of their own choosing express more enjoyment than do those pressured to do something by parents or teachers. In fact, some adolescents become deeply absorbed in subjects or activities of their choice and want to do them all the time and into the future (Fredricks et al., 2010; Hidi & Renninger, 2006). Unfortunately, parents and teachers may exert high control and push adolescents to achieve high grades to a degree that their good intentions backfire.

✓ CHECK YOUR UNDERSTANDING 15.17

1. How do grit and choice affect academic achievement?

Explaining Motivation

LEARNING OBJECTIVE 15.18 Describe key sources of influence on adolescent motivation and school engagement.

So, what can be done to ameliorate declines in adolescent academic motivation? A first step is to identify the factors that help or harm an adolescent's motivation and engagement in school subjects. We saw that choice is one critical factor. Let's turn to four other influences on motivation: mindsets and goal orientations, expectations for success, task value, and test anxiety.

Mindsets and Goal Orientations

In Chapter 12 we learned that children's mindsets—their attributions for success and failure—can affect their engagement in tasks. Recall that children who hold an entity view of intelligence believe that intelligence is fixed and attribute success or failure to a person's innate intellect. In contrast, children who hold an incremental view of intelligence believe that effort and practice can improve intelligence, and thus attribute success or failure to their efforts. Over time, an entity view of intelligence can lead to declines in motivation and engagement, whereas an incremental view of intelligence ignites motivation and effort. Why might this be?

One way that mindsets affect motivation and engagement is by influencing **goal orientations**—the reasons people give for *why* they invest time in a subject or activity. Children and adolescents with an entity view of intelligence often take a **performance goal orientation**; they focus on demonstrating their superior ability (Dweck & Leggett, 1988). They tend to choose safe, easy tasks where they can "show off" how smart they are to others (Dweck, 2002). When tasks become challenging, presenting a threat that children and adolescents may appear to be less intelligent or talented than their peers, performance-oriented individuals give up to save face. In contrast, children and adolescents who view intelligence to be malleable adopt a **mastery goal orientation**; they exert much effort to master new skills and learn. They persist on challenging tasks because their goal is to improve, rather than boast about their skills (**FIGURE 15.16**).

Expectations for Success

As the saying goes: The best predictor of future behavior is past behavior. If you think you are capable of succeeding at something, then you will exert more effort, persist, and likely do well. For example, adolescents who believe they are competent in math likely expect to be successful in math, and will work harder at studying for an upcoming math exam than will teens with low perceptions of competence and success expectations. In turn, expectations for success predict grades and test performance (Eccles et al., 2004).

Task Value

How many times during high school did you ask yourself, "Why do I have to learn this? What good will geometric proofs do me in the future?" Such attitudes likely interfered with your motivation to study and learn the subject material. Indeed, one way to improve adolescents' motivation is to change their perceptions about the importance and usefulness of academic material.

goal orientations The reasons individuals give for why they invest time in an activity or their motivation for achieving an objective for a specific activity

performance goal orientation Motivation that is focused on the outcome rather than process, such as studying to get a specific grade rather than learning

mastery goal orientation Motivation that is focused on learning and mastering a specific task

Theory of intelligence	Goal orientation	Behavior pattern
Entity theory (intelligence is fixed) →	Performance goal	Avoids challenge Low persistence
Incremental theory (intelligence is malleable) →	Learning goal	Seeks challenge High persistence

FIGURE 15.16 Entity versus incremental theories of intelligence. Children and adolescents who view intelligence to be fixed are said to hold an "entity view of intelligence"; they tend to have goals consistent with simply wanting to show high performance, and attribute success or failure to a person's inborn intellect. In contrast, children and adolescents who believe that it is possible to improve intelligence through effort and practice are said to hold an "incremental view of intelligence"; they tend to have goals to learn, and attribute success or failure to an individual's behaviors. (After C. Dweck and E. L. Leggett. 1988. *Psychol Rev* 95: 256–273. Copyright © 1988 by American Psychological Association. Reproduced with permission.)

Developmental scientist Jacquelynne Eccles and her colleagues have devoted much attention to **task value**, the subjective value a person attaches to a particular task. According to Eccles, four factors influence the value a child or adolescent attaches to a particular academic outcome (Eccles, Vida, & Barber, 2004):

- *Interest in the material*: An adolescent who finds material to be enjoyable and rewarding is likely to work harder in that area.

- *Attainment value of the material*: Whether an adolescent views material to be central to one's identity affects task value. A teen may work hard at math, even if math is not interesting, because she views it to define her identity as a "math whiz."

- *Utility value*: How relevant the adolescent perceives the task to be to future goals feeds into task value. A teen who wants to major in finance may invest time in calculus, whereas a teen who aims to become a dancer may shun such "useless" classes.

- *Cost*: The adolescent's perception of a task's emotional cost (boredom, stress) and demands on time and effort will affect task value. A teen may avoid studying for history because she finds the material to be boring and difficult, and it interferes with her time for friends.

task value The subjective value (e.g., interest, usefulness) a person attaches to a specific task

Test Anxiety

Recall your junior or senior year in high school, when you took the SAT or ACT to determine your eligibility for various colleges. How anxious did you feel on test day? Many of you might have been so anxious that your performance suffered relative to what you otherwise might have achieved. **Test anxiety** is the fear of failing that occurs before or during an important exam, and the negative symptoms that accompany those fears.

Two major components of test anxiety are worry and negative emotionality (Wigfield & Meece, 1988; Zeidner, 2007). Worry includes the negative thoughts that precede and/or accompany an exam—"I'm not going to do well on this," and "What happens if I fail?" Unsurprisingly, fears about upcoming performance consistently predict low test scores. The negative emotionality component of test anxiety refers to the negative feelings and somatic symptoms that result from heightened arousal around the test or exam. As you might imagine, when anxiety around achievement is too high, performance declines (Owens et al., 2012; Putwain et al., 2016).

test anxiety The fear of failing that may involve negative physiological, cognitive, or behavioral symptoms before or after an exam

Students who believe that a test will be difficult and feel that they are not very good in a subject may be susceptible to high test anxiety. This makes sense in light of evidence that past success produces high expectations for continued success (e.g., Cassady, 2004; Hancock, 2001). What is interesting is how task value enters this equation. Teens who *care* about how they do (that is, they assign high value to a task) but fear they won't do well are actually more anxious than those who *don't care* about their performance. In short, if you value something—such as viewing your performance in math to be important for college applications—but don't expect to do well, your test anxiety may soar (Selkirk, Bouchey, & Eccles, 2012). In contrast, if you value a task and feel confident about your success, your anxiety remains manageable, and you are likely to do well.

✓ CHECK YOUR UNDERSTANDING 15.18

1. What is the difference between a performance goal orientation and a mastery goal orientation? Provide an example typically seen in adolescence.

2. Describe how mindsets, expectations, task value, and test anxiety affect motivation and achievement.

3. What factors influence the task value an adolescent associates with an assigned activity?

Contexts of Academic Achievement

In an ideal world, all adolescents would receive the resources, emotional support, and academic guidance to spark their motivation and help them to achieve their full potential. For some adolescents, this is the case. For others, family members, peers, schools, and experiences of discrimination exert harmful effects.

Family and Peer Context of Academic Achievement

LEARNING OBJECTIVE 15.19 Describe some ways family and peers affect academic motivation and achievement.

Consider the factors that motivate adolescents to do well in school. Recall that choice is one significant influence. In fact, adolescents greatly value autonomy and self-direction, and reject being overcontrolled by adults. Still, adolescents want their parents to be there for them and seek emotional support and guidance as they carve their own path in the world. And so, parents who strike a balance between structure and warmth are likely to have adolescents who do well in school (e.g., Steinberg, 2001). A review of over 300 studies showed that parental warmth, support for autonomy, and authoritative parenting styles predicted adolescents' grade point average and achievement scores (Pinquart, 2015). Moreover, although most studies focus on adolescents' relationships with mothers, supportive and involved fathers support academic achievement based on a meta-analysis of 66 studies across a range of ethnic and racial communities (Jeynes, 2012).

Parents are also significant sources of information about education and careers, and can help their adolescents plan for the future. Parents who encourage educational pursuits and offer academic advice help their adolescents cement their academic goals and make sound educational decisions (Lee & Oyserman, 2007; Wang & Sheikh-Khalil, 2014). Of course, parents' abilities to help adolescents navigate the educational process may depend on their own educational history and knowledge about the education system—such as knowing how to register for standardized tests and prepare a college application. Parents with limited education and financial resources may be at a disadvantage in guiding their children toward academic and career choices (Kalil, Levine, & Ziol-Guest, 2005). In such instances, adolescents can turn to counselors, teachers, and even peers who may be familiar with the educational system.

In particular, peers often function to assist one another in learning activities, clarifying tasks, and offering a sounding board for venting about the burdens of schoolwork and teachers. Of course, peer influences are bidirectional. Adolescents choose friends who are similar to them in motivation, school performance, and activity preferences, and then are further influenced by their friends' motivation, performance, and preferences (Shin & Ryan, 2014). So, for example, low achievers may become involved with other low-achieving peers, and then find themselves even less motivated to spend time on schoolwork and academic activities (Hamm & Zhang, 2010; Shin & Ryan, 2014). The opposite occurs when high-achieving peers spend time with one another.

✓ CHECK YOUR UNDERSTANDING 15.19

1. What are some of the best ways a family can encourage an adolescent's cognitive growth?
2. Should high-achieving adolescents avoid low-achieving adolescents? Discuss bidirectional effects of peer interactions.

School Context of Academic Achievement

LEARNING OBJECTIVE 15.20 Explain how student relationships with teachers and peers—including experiences of discrimination—may lead to declines in academic motivation and engagement.

School context powerfully impacts adolescent academic motivation and engagement. In particular, relationships with teachers may help adolescents maintain their investment in school. And, because adolescents are actively exploring their identities—a topic we review in Chapter 16—they are acutely aware of stereotypes and discrimination from teachers and peers. In the sections that follow, we examine the effects of the student-teacher relationship, stereotypes, and discrimination on adolescent engagement and performance. Remember that **stereotypes** are widely held, fixed and oversimplified views about a group of people on the grounds of their race, ethnicity, language, gender, and so on. **Discrimination** refers to the unjust or prejudicial treatment of people often based on their race, ethnicity, gender, age, sexual orientation, religion, or national origin.

Quality of the Teacher-Student Relationship

Students who hold positive perceptions of their teachers and positive attitudes about school report a sense of belonging and commitment (Roeser & Eccles, 2014). Unfortunately, the quality of teacher-student relationships declines in middle school and high school relative to relationships in elementary school (**FIGURE 15.17**). Whereas elementary school children spend most of their day with a single teacher, middle school and high school students move from class to class, often spending fewer than 45 minutes with a given teacher on a given day. Reciprocally, middle school and high school teachers may teach hundreds of students, leaving them little time to get to know students as individuals. As a result, teachers may implement rigid rules to maintain control and keep on top of the assignments of their students. Perhaps, they take off points when an assignment is late, with no exceptions. An adolescent who tries to explain that his computer broke down the night before, but gets penalized anyway, may feel unsupported. Or, there are only certain books accepted for a report, limiting flexibility for adolescents to make their own choices at a time when they seek autonomy and independence. As a result, teachers may fail to learn what makes each student tick, and students may fail to grasp the teacher's vision for the course. Adolescents who perceive low teacher support may eventually lose interest in class content, just as those who feel strongly supported by their teachers do well academically (e.g., Dotterer, McHale, & Crouter, 2009; Wentzel, Russell, & Baker, 2016).

Stereotype Threat

People sometimes hold negative stereotypes about the academic abilities of members of ethnic, racial, gender, or other groups, and those stereotypes can undermine the performance of adolescents. For example, Black adolescents display anxiety, declines in academic confidence, disengagement from school, and declines in performance when they believe that teachers and adults hold negative stereotypes about their abilities (e.g., Rowley, Kurtz-Costes, & Cooper, 2010). Victims of a stereotype may fear that they will confirm a widespread, negative belief about their social group, and experience anxiety

stereotypes Widely held, fixed, and overgeneralized views about a group of people based on their race, ethnicity, gender, language, and so forth

discrimination The unjust or prejudicial treatment of people often based on their race, ethnicity, gender, age, sexual orientation, religion, or national origin

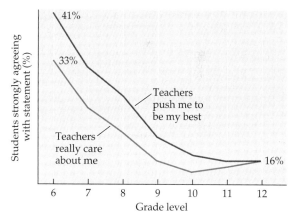

FIGURE 15.17 Quality of teacher-student relationships. The quality of teacher-student relationships declines over the school years, with students reporting higher quality relationships with teachers in elementary school compared to in middle school and high school. Declines can be seen in students' perceptions about how much teachers care about them and whether they believe that teachers push them to be the best that they could be, among other perceptions. (After Search Institute. What We're Learning about Developmental Relationships. Accessed 23 June 2021. https://www.search-institute.org/developmental-relationships/learning-developmental-relationships/. Source: Search Institute surveys from 2012-2015 of 122,269 U.S. youth in grades 6 to 12.)

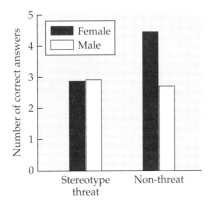

FIGURE 15.18 Stereotype threat.
Stereotype threat has been shown to reduce the performance of female college students on math tests (but not the scores of male college students), as found in a classic study by Good, Aronson, and Harder (2008). In fact, female college students *outperformed men on math when they* experienced no stereotype threat. (After C. Good et al. 2008. *J Appl Dev Psychol* 29: 17–28.)

stereotype threat A situation in which people feel that they are at risk of conforming to stereotypes about their social group and, therefore, experience anxiety and lowered performance

stereotype threat experiments Experiments in which researchers manipulate information presented to individuals before a test to study how stereotype threat may affect academic performance or other outcomes

and lowered performance as a result. Researchers call this **stereotype threat** (Aronson & Steele, 2005).

How do researchers demonstrate the effects of stereotype threat on academic performance? They typically conduct **stereotype threat experiments**, in which they manipulate the information that is presented to individuals right before a test and then assess how performance is altered. For example, they may tell adolescent girls that they are being tested on math to examine "whether boys do better than girls." A control group is given neutral instructions. In such studies, teen girls exposed to the threat perform worse than those who were not (e.g., Good, Aronson, & Harder, 2008) (**FIGURE 15.18**). Similarly, Black college students who were subjected to negative stereotypes about their groups' intellectual ability did less well on standardized tests compared to Black students who were not subjected to stereotype threat (Steele & Aronson, 1995).

What is particularly striking is that stereotype threat can even harm the performance of students who otherwise do well, as long as students are led to believe that their group generally underperforms compared to another group. Consider an early illustration of this phenomenon. Social psychologist Joshua Aaronson randomly assigned White Stanford University college students who scored between 600 and 800 on their math SATs (great scores!) to either a stereotype threat or control condition. Students in the threat condition were asked to skim articles about the outstanding math achievement of Asian Americans, and were told that there seemed to be a growing discrepancy in the superior academic performance of Asian Americans over White students in math. They were then tested with items from a standardized math test. As hypothesized, students in the threat condition performed worse than those in the control condition (Aronson et al., 1999).

Stereotype threat can also *positively* affect academic performance. Asian American girls performed better on math tests when their Asian American identity was made salient, for example, if they were told that the purpose of a test was to examine the superiority of Asian American performance in math. In contrast, they did worse on the same tests when researchers made female identity salient (Ambady et al., 2001; Shih, Pittinsky, & Ambady, 1999). However, the size of effects in stereotype studies can be large, small, or nonexistent. Thus, it is important to understand the conditions that exacerbate the effects of stereotype threat and the characteristics that make certain individuals most vulnerable (Galdi, Cadinu, & Tomasetto, 2014).

Experiences of Discrimination

Like stereotypes, perceptions of discrimination or anticipation of discrimination toward one's ethnic group can lead to declines in academic performance and the undermining of education benefits (e.g., Banerjee, Byrd, & Rowley, 2018; Brody, et al., 2006; Chavous et al., 2008; Fordham & Ogbu, 1986). For example, Black adolescents who perceived or witnessed acts of racial discrimination from teachers, school staff, and classmates between seventh and ninth grade declined in their grades and perceptions of their academic abilities and increased in psychological distress over the two-year period (Wong, Eccles, & Sameroff, 2003). Similarly, adolescents from ethnic minority backgrounds who reported discrimination from their teachers displayed low school engagement and a feeling of disconnect from their schools (Benner & Wang, 2017).

Notably, the negative effects of stereotypes and discrimination diminish when adolescents feel strongly connected to their ethnic/racial group and have a positive ethnic/racial identity. For example, Black adolescents with positive identities were less affected by discrimination than were their peers with lower feelings of self-worth (Harris-Britt et al., 2007). In the same vein, positive cross-ethnic friendships reduce the negative effects of discrimination on school belonging and engagement (Benner & Wang, 2017) (**FIGURE 15.19**).

✓ **CHECK YOUR UNDERSTANDING 15.20**

1. Why does the quality of teacher/student relationships tend to decline in middle school and high school?

2. What are the ways that discrimination by teachers affects adolescents?

Neighborhood Context of Academic Achievement

LEARNING OBJECTIVE 15.21 Summarize the influence of neighborhoods on adolescent academic achievement.

Throughout this book, we have seen that neighborhoods affect development in a variety of ways. Neighborhood effects become even more pronounced as adolescents gain independence to choose where to go and how to spend their time. Poor neighborhoods place adolescents at risk for low school performance, school dropout, and delinquent behavior, and it is not difficult to imagine why. Schools in low-income neighborhoods may have few resources and teachers with little training (Owens & Candipan, 2019). Between 50% and 70% of young adolescents from poor, ethnic minority families had math teachers who were not college trained in a math-related field (Peske & Haycock, 2006). Schools in low-income neighborhoods are also plagued by high teacher turnover and high rates of substitute teachers, with rates of turnover negatively affecting student achievement (Ronfeldt, Loeb, & Wyckoff, 2013; Whipp & Geronime, 2017).

Skeptics may argue that individual or family influences account for the low academic performance of adolescents living in poor neighborhoods, rather than neighborhoods per se. Indeed, the harmful effects of low-quality schools and neighborhoods intensify when low-income parents—who may feel depleted from the stressors of poverty—are uninvolved in their adolescents' school experiences (Bunting et al., 2013). Family blame, however, is shortsighted. As Uri Bronfenbrenner pointed out in his ecological systems theory (see Chapter 1), the contexts of development are interrelated. Poverty has cascading effects on biology, the home environment, the school environment, and the neighborhood, all of which influence development (**FIGURE 15.20**).

Some of the strongest evidence for neighborhood effects on adolescent school performance comes from experimental studies that randomly assign families to live in more or less resourced neighborhoods and then examine the effects of community placement on adolescent development. One of the first experimental studies to evaluate the effects of housing placement took place in Chicago following a 1976 Chicago Housing Authority mandate that required low-income families to be offered the opportunity to move to better housing. The mandate was instituted in recognition of widespread, negative effects of discrimination on children and families. Families were randomly assigned to housing in a more-resourced inner-city neighborhood or a middle-class neighborhood on the outskirts of Chicago. Adolescents who moved into middle-class neighborhoods were much more likely to graduate from high school, complete advanced high school courses, and attend college than were those who ended up living in the more-resourced inner-city neighborhoods (Rosenbaum, 1991; Rosenbaum, Kulieke, & Rubinowitz, 1988). Other neighborhood-intervention experiments yield similar positive effects on adolescent school engagement and

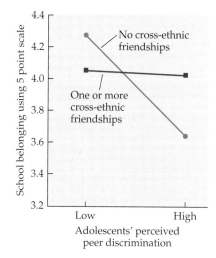

FIGURE 15.19 Influence of cross-ethnic friendships. Adolescents who perceive high discrimination but have strong cross-ethnic friendships show a higher sense of school belonging than do adolescents who experience high discrimination without having cross-ethnic friendships. (After A. D. Benner and Y. Wang. 2017. *Child Dev* 88: 493–504. © 2016 The Authors. Child Development © 2016 Society for Research in Child Development, Inc. All rights reserved.)

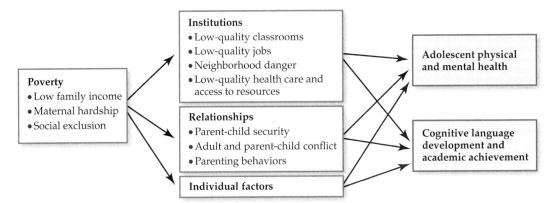

FIGURE 15.20 The combined effects of neighborhood, family, and individual factors on adolescent well-being. As Uri Bronfenbrenner pointed out in his ecological systems theory, many interrelated contexts shape an individual's development over time. Poverty is a powerful context of development that has rippling effects for other contexts. For example, as shown in the figure, poverty has cascading effects on (1) institutions such as school, jobs, neighborhoods, and healthcare; (2) parent-child relationships; and (3) individual factors, such as a teen's personality. In turn, these influences play out over time on adolescent physical and mental health, cognitive and language development, and academic achievement. (After H. Yoshikawa et al. 2012. *Am Psychol* 67: 272–284; U. Bronfenbrenner. 1979. *The Ecology of Human Development: Experiments by Nature and Design*. Harvard University Press: Cambridge, MA.)

college completion, and even reduce single parenthood (e.g., Chetty, Hendren, & Katz 2016) (**FIGURE 15.21**).

How and why do neighborhoods influence adolescent development, even after considering family-level influences? Various explanations have been offered:

• As described, under-resourced schools in low-income neighborhoods tend to have fewer qualified teachers than those in middle-income neighborhoods.

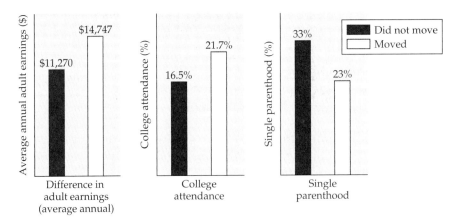

FIGURE 15.21 Adolescents who attend schools in wealthier neighborhoods have better success rates. The children of families that used housing vouchers to move to wealthier neighborhoods were more likely to attend college and earn more as adults than similar children who remained in extremely poor neighborhoods. Children in the wealthier neighborhoods were also less likely to grow up in single-parent households. (After Center on Budget and Policy Priorities. CBPP.org. Accessed 23 June 2021. https://www.cbpp.org/moving-with-voucher-to-lower-poverty-neighborhoods-while-young-children-improves-key-adult-8. Data from R. Chetty et al. 2015. National Bureau of Economic Research, Working Paper #21156.)

- Adolescents pick up and model good and bad behaviors of other adolescents in the neighborhood, spanning drug and alcohol use, violence, and early sexual activity.

- Residents of a community share values and expectations for their adolescents and a set of strategies to accomplish their goals (Fagan, Wright, & Pinchevsky, 2014).

- The institutional resources available to adolescents and their families vary by neighborhood. Some communities offer opportunities for adolescents to get involved in volunteering, sports teams, and other community activities (**FIGURE 15.22**). Adolescents who engage in community activities have high motivation and positive attitudes toward school and learning, and consequently are likely to do well academically (Lerner et al., 2015).

- Neighborhoods provide adolescents with opportunities for employment, which teach adolescents responsibility and organization. Adolescents who averaged 20 hours of work per week had high self-confidence, time management skills, and likelihood of attending and finishing college compared to those who did not work or worked too many hours (Staff & Mortimer, 2007).

FIGURE 15.22 Volunteering. Participating in community-based activities has a positive effect on adolescent development.

✓ **CHECK YOUR UNDERSTANDING 15.21**

1. Describe the ways that neighborhoods influence adolescent academic performance.

Developmental Cascades

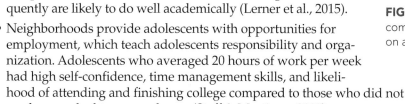

Every four years in January, thousands of supporters line the streets of the National Mall in Washington, DC, to welcome the new president of the United States. It is not uncommon for demonstrators to line the same streets days later to protest the platform of the new commander in chief. Adolescents are typically strong in number. Teens spend hours traveling and standing in crowds to express their intense loyalties and opinions around issues that are core to them. The passionate political engagement of adolescents illustrates the cascading influences that cognitive development has for domains of functioning far afield.

Adolescents' capacity to reason about multiple positions and perspectives explains their interest in complex social topics such as universal healthcare, affirmative action, personal responsibility, social justice, and the minimum wage. Moreover, because adolescent thought is no longer limited to concrete experience, adolescents are able to ponder alternative experiences: "What would it be like to live in a world lacking poverty, hunger, abuse, sexism, discrimination, social injustices, and war?" It is no wonder that John Lennon's song *Imagine* continues to resonate with adolescents decades after it was written. And adolescents' cognitive development and academic experiences reverberate well beyond civic engagement to shape individual life paths for years to come.

Cascading Effects of Cognitive Development on Civic Engagement

Developments in cognitive and social-cognitive reasoning—including a deep moral understanding of fairness, justice, and the circumstances of other people—inspire adolescents to help people in need, locally and globally. Many adolescents avidly consume news media, discuss social issues with friends, and

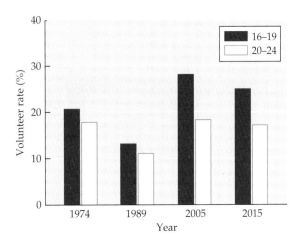

FIGURE 15.23 Volunteering by youth demonstrates a strong sense of altruism. Over the past two decades, teenagers have volunteered at higher rates than they did from the mid-1970s through the late 1980s. Moreover, a record number of entering college students become community leaders and believe that it is very important to help others in need. (After R. T. Grimm, Jr. and N. Dietz. 2018. Good Intentions, Gap in Action: The Challenge of Translating Youth's High Interest in Doing Good into Civic Engagement. Research Brief: Do Good Institute, University of Maryland.)

display their citizenship through volunteering at clubs, food banks, community and youth organizations, homeless shelters, and faith-based institutions (Flanagan & Levine, 2010). The numbers behind these observations are impressive. Surveys across 200 colleges and universities found that one-third of first-year students stated that there was a good chance they would get involved in volunteering (Eagan et al., 2013) (**FIGURE 15.23**).

Civic-minded activities in turn cascade into stable patterns of involvement in young adulthood and beyond. Adolescents who work with people from different social, ethnic, and economic backgrounds chart a course for long-lasting community and global involvement (Arnett, 2013; Flanagan & Levine, 2010). Still, despite adolescents' sophisticated cognitive skills and commitment to civic activities, many feel marginalized, remain disenchanted with the political system, and may be disinclined to vote, especially racial and ethnic minority teens from poor and working-class backgrounds (Diemer & Rapa, 2015).

Cascading Effects of Academic Motivation on Life Trajectories

When adolescents fail to invest in school they find themselves falling further behind in their grades, which places them at heightened risk for problem behaviors such as delinquency and substance use. These behaviors can result in dropping out of school, which severely undercuts adolescents' future life opportunities. When researchers followed over 1,000 ethnically and racially diverse adolescents from seventh through eleventh grade, they documented a recurring pattern of cascading influences: Disengagement from school led to problem behaviors; problem behaviors led to further disengagement from school; and disengagement from school increased the likelihood of school dropout (Wang & Fredricks, 2014).

Sadly, this domino effect continues beyond adolescence. Indeed, high school GPA is one of the strongest predictors of earnings in adulthood (French et al., 2015). A national study of thousands of individuals found that cognitive performance in adolescence predicted long-term happiness, self-esteem, and delinquent behavior. Adolescents with low cognitive scores reported low self-worth and high delinquency, and these psychological and behavioral outcomes led to low graduation rates and low college attendance. Adolescents with high cognitive ability, on the other hand, pursued higher education and found their way to complex, skilled jobs that offered solid incomes and high job satisfaction (Converse et al., 2016).

Cascading Effects of School Dropout

Dropout rates have declined over the past several decades. However, a report by the U.S. Department of Education indicates that about 16% of adolescents in the United States fail to complete high school within 4 years, and 4.8% of adolescents drop out of school entirely (McFarland et al., 2018). Furthermore, dropout rates are especially high for adolescents from low-income, minority households, including African Americans, Latinos, American Indians, and Indigenous Alaskans, with rates climbing over 17% for American Indians and Indigenous Alaskans (McFarland et al., 2018).

Circumstances almost never improve for the adolescent who drops out of school. Adverse downstream consequences include poverty, unemployment, delinquency, and teenage pregnancy. Students who fail to complete high school show lower rates of labor force participation than their better educated peers, with employment gaps being especially wide for men with low education

(Binder & Bound, 2019). School dropout increases the likelihood of incarceration for young men of all ethnic groups. Indeed, young men who had dropped out of high school were 47 times more likely to be incarcerated than their peers with a 4-year college degree (Sum et al., 2009). Beyond economic consequences, school dropout negatively impacts health. School dropout predicts heavy drinking and smoking, inadequate physical activity, high stress, and a sense of lack of control at work years later, which together can contribute to reduced mortality (e.g., Lee et al., 2016).

Preventing School Dropout

The vital importance of a high school degree is undeniable. However, designing and implementing effective programs to curb the risks of dropout pose challenges. Still, three core ingredients define successful interventions around school dropout.

First, interventions should *be proactive*, targeting children who are at risk before problems get out of hand, ideally starting in elementary school and continuing through the adolescent years (Lee St-John et al., 2018). When adolescents reach high school, people in the school system should work together to identify vulnerable individuals. Effective interventions include counseling students to deter them from dropping out and offering adolescents options in high school education, such as the choice to attend schools with vocational emphases and to take classes that cultivate individual talents.

Second, interventions should *target multiple components*—academic skills, behavior, attendance, study skills, and school organization. Multicomponent interventions achieve high success, although in reality, most existing programs target a single component (Freeman & Simonsen, 2015). Moreover, interventions that are most successful in preventing dropout combine academic assistance and resources with emotional support to counter the negative psychological effects of academic failure (e.g., Christenson & Thurlow, 2004).

Finally, effective interventions should *engage students as active participants*. Recall that choice matters for adolescent engagement, and control often backfires despite good intentions. Rather than telling students what to do, counselors and educators should invite students to articulate their career goals, and then tailor academic programs to fit adolescents' needs. For example, a student who wishes to pursue construction may be convinced that math classes are worth taking if those classes help develop skills relevant to the desired vocation. Academic coursework that combines with vocational training may be more gratifying to some adolescents than coursework alone. Moreover, vocational training opportunities may be especially important for teens who have already disengaged from school and may benefit from job placement training and remedial education (Shore & Massimo, 2014; Levin, 2012).

◼ CLOSING THOUGHTS

The Blurred Boundary between Ability and Performance

Sometimes, we assume that people are born with a fixed amount of cognitive ability—that students who do well in school are more capable than those who do not. But, throughout this book, you have been reminded of the simplicity of assumptions around innate ability. There is no clear line connecting an adolescent's potential to an adolescent's performance. Rather, many individual and contextual factors co-determine whether and how adolescents realize their cognitive capabilities.

And so, the question is *not* how to grow cognitive ability, but rather, how to nurture and sustain an adolescent's passion for learning. How can parents, educators, clinicians, communities, and society ensure that adolescents—who sit at the precipice of adulthood—succeed? What ingredients support a teen's excitement for and engagement in school; ensure a teen's persistence when subjects intensify in difficulty; and foster a teen's resilience in the face of stereotypes that may label a teen's abilities and limit a teen's choices? Developmental science does not hold all the answers. However, it provides a treasure trove of knowledge about the cascading influences of families, peers, schools, and communities on adolescent cognitive development. And so, the most promising way to support adolescents' engagement and performance in school may rest on application of scientific findings to the design of effective programs and curricula for teens. If given the chance, what would you do to ensure the successful translation of science to practice?

The Developmentalist's Toolbox

Method	Purpose	Description
Measuring adolescents' cognitive ability		
The combination of liquids problem	To assess whether adolescents demonstrate hypothetical-deductive reasoning	The problem involves determining which liquid or combinations of liquids would cause a visible chemical reaction.
The pendulum problem	To assess whether adolescents demonstrate hypothetical-deductive reasoning	Given a set of weights of different heaviness and strings of different lengths, children are asked to determine which variable(s) affect the rate of the pendulum's swing.
Flanker tasks	To assess development of selective attention, specifically the ability to focus on relevant stimuli and inhibit attention to distractors	An individual might be instructed to change the direction of an arrow by pressing on a right or left button. The task becomes increasingly difficult when the target arrow is surrounded (flanked) by many distractor arrows facing the opposite direction.
Switching tasks	To assess development of selective attention, specifically the ability to shift attention to different relevant stimuli	Individuals might be instructed to press buttons in response to two different categories of questions, requiring that they attend simultaneously to more than one type of information.
So-Moral tasks	To assess developmental changes in moral reasoning	Adolescents are asked to resolve moral dilemmas and provide the rationale underlying the proposed solution.
Point-of-view tasks	To assess developmental changes in perspective taking	Researchers compare teens' reaction times to first-person questions ("Imagine how you would feel if…") with their reaction times to third-person questions ("Imagine how Brittany would feel if…").
Measuring contexts affecting adolescents' academic achievement		
Stereotype threat experiments	To assess the extent to which an individual's performance is affected by a feeling of being at risk of conforming to a stereotype about the person's identity (e.g., race, gender)	Researchers present individuals with information intended to induce a stereotype threat (e.g., by informing teen girls that a test is meant to determine whether teen boys do better than teen girls in math) followed by a test of performance. A control group is not exposed to the stereotype threat. Differences between experimental and control group participants on the test are taken as an index of stereotype threat.

■ Chapter Summary

Piagetian Theory

- According to Piaget, adolescents' achievement of formal operational thinking is characterized by capacities for abstract thinking, propositional thought, and hypothetical-deductive reasoning.
- Piaget's combination of liquids and pendulum problems test whether children and adolescents are capable of the type of scientific thinking that characterizes the formal operational stage.
- Formal operational thinking is not universal, and its expression depends on schooling and people's experiences.

Information Processing

- Selective attention requires adolescents to focus attention, inhibit attention to distractors, and flexibly shift attention among relevant stimuli. These skills may be especially important to mathematics.
- Working memory span improves in adolescence, in part because adolescents' greater knowledge frees up working memory.
- Processing speed improves with age and is associated with skills in reading and math.
- Adolescents show gains in strategy use relative to children, especially in their use of deep versus superficial memory strategies. Metacognitive awareness contributes to changes in strategy use in adolescence.

Social Cognition

- Adolescents exceed children in their performance on theory-of-mind tasks and abilities to consider other people's perspectives relative to their own, as seen in point-of-view tasks. Still, their perspective-taking skills do not reach adult levels, particularly when considering affective theory-of-mind tasks compared to cognitive theory-of-mind tasks.
- Adolescents show a unique form of egocentrism, marked by the personal fable and imaginary audience. Adolescent egocentrism may be adaptive.
- Kohlberg's theory proposed a stagelike progression in moral reasoning. Today, So-Moral tasks confirm developments in moral reasoning that are explained by cognitive developments in reasoning, flexibility, social cognition, and so forth.
- Adolescents' moral behavior sometimes diverges from moral reasoning because many factors influence what an adolescent does, including personal and societal considerations.

Cultural Context of Adolescent Cognitive Development

- Cultural tools, everyday activities, and experiences around schooling explain differences among adolescents in their cognitive development.

Language and Literacy Development

- Much language development in adolescence is seen in academic vocabulary and grammatical complexity—skills that are fundamental to reading and writing academic texts.
- Core academic language skills involve unpacking complex words, understanding complex sentences, connecting ideas, tracking themes, and appreciating the organizational logic of texts.
- Girls tend to exceed boys in reading and boys tend to exceed girls in advanced science and math. These differences may be traced to early differences in parenting and the types of toys boys and girls play with at home.
- Video gaming is more prevalent in boys, and supports executive function skills that help with STEM subjects.
- Cultural stereotypes around professions suggest that fields dominated by men are perceived to require "brilliance" and "genius."

School Engagement and Motivation

- Three components of school engagement that support academic achievement are behavioral engagement, emotional engagement, and cognitive engagement.
- Academic motivation declines in adolescence, which may harm school performance and lead to low scores on standardized tests.
- Grit distinguishes high and low scorers on standardized tests.
- Some students do well in school, even though they don't enjoy what they are doing. The lack of choice may explain why many students lose interest in school subjects.
- Factors that affect adolescent engagement include mindsets (attributions for success and failure) and goal orientations (performance orientation versus mastery orientation), expectations for success, task value, and test anxiety.
- Factors that affect how an adolescent views the value of a task include interest in the material, attainment value of the material, utility value, and cost.
- Worry and negative emotionality are two components of test anxiety. Adolescents who place high value on a task, yet don't expect to do well, are likely to experience high test anxiety.

Contexts of Academic Achievement

- Parental warmth, autonomy support, and authoritative parenting relate to high adolescent academic performance, whereas physical/punitive control, psychological control, permissiveness, and neglect relate to low academic performance.
- Adolescents gravitate toward peers who display similar academic engagement and performance, which can cause further disengagement by adolescents who are not motivated to do well in school.
- The adolescent's perception of teacher support is important to academic achievement. Overall, however, perceptions of teacher support decline in adolescence.
- Adolescents experience stereotype threat when they fear that they will confirm a widespread, negative stereotype about their ethnicity, race, gender, or other aspect of their

identity. Stereotype threat typically reduces the performance of adolescents when the threat is manipulated in experimental studies.

- Discrimination harms academic performance, although the negative effects of discrimination decrease when adolescents regard their ethnic group positively.

- Neighborhoods affect academic performance through the quality of schools, the behaviors modeled by other adolescents, the shared values and expectations, and opportunities for learning and employment. Experimental studies that randomly assign families to neighborhoods provide strong evidence for neighborhood effects.

- Cognitive developments in adolescence explain the political and social interests of adolescents and the reasons they participate in community activities at high rates.

Developmental Cascades

- Low motivation and school dropout have cascading negative effects into adulthood, including low self-esteem, poor health, low labor market participation, depression, and incarceration.

- Effective interventions to address school dropout should be proactive, contain multiple components, and engage adolescents as active participants in their plans for the future.

Thinking Like a Developmentalist

1. You are a test developer who is familiar with Piaget's studies of cognitive development. You want to examine whether adolescents' performance on standard IQ tests are associated with their performance on Piagetian tasks. Which tasks would you give adolescents from Piaget's studies and why, and which IQ test would you choose to examine in relation to those skills, and why?

2. A school district is concerned about the high dropout rates of high school students. They call in a developmental scientist to advise on the factors that are affecting students' school dropout and ways to remedy the problem. Which factors might the developmental scientist pinpoint as important, and what type of interventions might be implemented?

3. The students of a very large school district live in communities that vary substantially on their socioeconomic status (SES). The principal worries that the low cognitive performance of some adolescents might be explained by their vulnerability to stereotype threat around where they live. She asks a researcher to test if this might be the case. Design an experiment(s) that tests whether student performance is susceptible to stereotype threat such that individuals from low SES neighborhoods do worse and those from high SES neighborhoods do better on tests when exposed to stereotype threat about their home communities. Hint: Remember to include control groups!

Emotional and Social Development in Adolescence

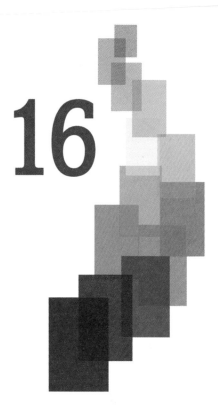

16

Drawing by Minxin Cheng from a photo © dmbaker/123RF

How often as a teen did you hear your parents or teachers express concern about what you or your friends were (or were not) doing? How many times have you read a headline or watched a program about the problems of "today's youth"? It is not uncommon for adults and media to portray teenagers as emotionally volatile, critical of authority, and prone to unsafe sex, smoking, reckless driving, alcohol consumption, and illegal drug use. Newspapers, movies, social media, educators, and parents alike consider adolescents to be emotionally and socially vulnerable. Are these claims valid? Or are they exaggerated?

It would be ignorant to dismiss these warnings as entirely false. As described in Chapter 14, adolescents are more likely than children or adults to make risky decisions that can compromise their health and well-being. Depression and anxiety peak during adolescence. Victimization and bullying are common. And as adolescents strive for autonomy and are forming a sense of identity, they may experience confusion and isolation and create wedges in their relationships with family, peers, and community.

Yet, when I presented this picture of adolescence to my son Michael, who had recently been a teen himself, he rejected it as naive. He pointed out that adolescents are profoundly attuned to their feelings, acutely aware of their complicated social situations, and do not need to be judged by adults who think they understand teens more than teens understand themselves. He ended his lecture with a quote from David Bowie's 1971 song "Changes":

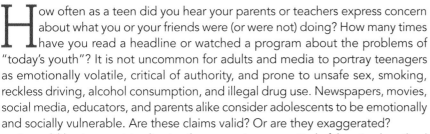

And these children that you spit on
As they try to change their worlds
Are immune to your consultations
They're quite aware of what they're going through

Michael's reaction speaks to the importance of a balanced narrative about adolescent emotional and social development at a time when teens want to direct their own lives and figure things out for themselves. As we will see, social and emotional skills blossom during adolescence and deserve to be celebrated.

Yet, if adolescents boast such impressive emotional and social skills, why do they sometimes struggle in these areas? Why do some adolescents succumb to pressures to engage in risky behaviors, whereas others do not? And how do adolescents' decisions and behaviors shape their futures? In the sections that follow, we will learn about the sometimes tumultuous but largely inspiring emotional and social lives of adolescents.

■ *Emotional Development*

Adolescents experience many developmental transitions in a relatively brief window of time. Hormonal and physical changes radically transform their bodies and spark unfamiliar feelings and sexual attraction toward peers. Most adolescents transition at least once to new schools that may uproot familiar relationships and require adjustment to new ones. As they leave childhood behind, adolescents sense an urgency to understand who they are, what they like, and what they should do in the future. In many ways, adolescence is an emotional rollercoaster without any brakes.

emotional reactivity The predisposition to experience frequent, intense, and volatile emotions

experience sampling A research method that requires participants to record their emotions, behaviors, etc., on a daily or regular basis when prompted by a pager or smart phone

2/06/21   2/11/21

FIGURE 16.1 Mood swings. These texts that a cousin received from her teenage daughter reflect the volatile mood swings of many adolescents.

Emotional Experiences

My cousin received a text from her daughter who called her uncaring and unsupportive. Four days later, she received another text from her daughter—this one filled with thanks for her love and thoughtfulness (**FIGURE 16.1**). Both texts brought tears to my cousin's eyes—and utter confusion. How could such extreme emotions be possible? The answer is because adolescent emotions are extreme: Adolescents experience frequent, intense, and volatile emotions—what researchers refer to as **emotional reactivity**.

Emotional Reactivity

LEARNING OBJECTIVE 16.1 Describe two methods researchers use to track adolescents' everyday emotions and what those methods reveal.

Adolescents react with high emotional intensity to many things that adults take for granted. They are profoundly moved, for better or for worse, by music, movies, social issues, and relationships with peers and parents. As a result, adolescents frequently transition between strong positive and negative emotions over the course of a day. What scientific evidence backs the personal anecdote of the texts my cousin received from her daughter?

Researchers track adolescents' feelings using experience sampling and daily diaries, and both confirm adolescents' high emotional volatility. Over three decades ago, researchers sought to "sample" teens' everyday emotional experiences. Using **experience sampling**, they asked adolescents to carry electronic pagers that beeped at random intervals, and to report on how they were feeling when the pager went off (Czikszentmihalyi & Larson, 1987). Smart phones and other devices later made it easier for researchers to monitor

FIGURE 16.2 Experience sampling.   Shown here are examples of emotional experiences that might be tracked in an experience sampling experiment.

adolescent emotions, and to analyze data in relation to variables such as gender and psychological adjustment (Csikszentmihalyi & Larson, 2014). (**FIGURE 16.2**). The **daily diary method**—in which teens rate emotions such as happiness, anger, sadness, and anxiety over several days or weeks—is another common way to assess adolescents' emotional experiences from day to day and across longer time frames.

So, what do experience sampling and diary studies show? They indicate that adolescents experience frequent day-to-day (and hour-to-hour) changes to emotions, and they reach emotional highs and lows relatively often, in line with what they are doing. Adolescents are happy when they are at parties, on the phone, using social media, hanging out watching screens, listening to music, playing games, and generally spending time with other people. They are not very happy when doing schoolwork (not surprising), and they don't like being alone (Weinstein & Mermelstein, 2007).

Yet, *choice* is key to adolescent emotions. Adolescents report positive emotions when doing things that they choose to do, which may be why they are unhappy while doing schoolwork, which they view as imposed on them. In fact, the perception of choice matters so much that teens who perceive choosing most of their activities show high stability of emotions over the course of a week, whereas teens who perceive low choice show high emotional volatility (Weinstein & Mermelstein, 2007).

Of course, adolescents differ in their emotional reactions to situations and how well they control their emotions. Adolescents who have problems controlling their negative emotions are at risk for aggressive behaviors, which can jeopardize their relationships with parents and peers (Rabinowitz et al., 2016). However, emotional volatility declines with age as adolescents improve in self-regulation (Steinberg, 2005), a topic we delve into later in the chapter.

daily diary method A research methodology requiring participants to rate their emotions on a daily basis and for an extended number of days or weeks to assess emotional experiences over time

✓ CHECK YOUR UNDERSTANDING 16.1

1. What do experience sampling and daily diaries tell us about fluctuations in adolescents' emotions?
2. What type of activities are associated with adolescent "happiness" and why might this be?

Emotional Valence

LEARNING OBJECTIVE 16.2 Describe how emotions such as happiness, anxiety, anger, and sadness change across adolescence.

We've seen that adolescents' emotions are in constant flux. Let's now consider how often adolescents experience positive and negative emotions, and how their emotions change with age. Longitudinal studies (see Chapter 1) are useful, because they

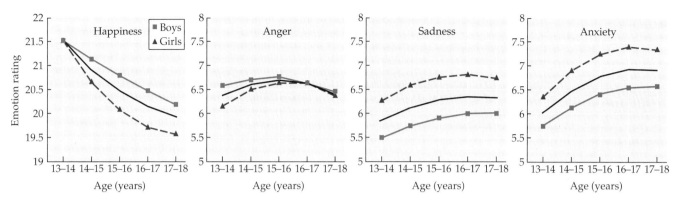

FIGURE 16.3 Daily diary studies.   In a daily diary study, adolescents rated their emotions during each day of a normal school week (Monday to Friday) for three weeks per year for five years. Happiness decreased from early to middle adolescence, whereas anger, sadness, and anxiety increased. (After D. F. Maciejewski et al. 2017. *Psychol Assess* 29: 35–49. © 2017 by American Psychological Association. Reproduced with permission.)

allow researchers to track emotions in the same adolescents across several years. The take-home messages from these investigations are both good and bad. On the one hand, adolescents experience positive emotions more than 70% of the time. On the other hand, adolescents' positive emotions decline from early to middle adolescence (approximately tenth grade), with positive emotions remaining relatively low throughout adolescence, compared to where they started (Larson et al., 2002).

If happiness declines over the adolescent years, then which emotions take its place? In an incredibly ambitious diary study, researchers followed nearly 400 adolescents from 13 to 18 years of age. Adolescents rated their emotions from Monday to Friday for three weeks every year over a five-year period, allowing the researchers to track developmental changes. Confirming prior studies, teens' reports of happiness decreased from early to middle adolescence and never rebounded (Maciejewski et al., 2017). And, as positive emotions declined, negative emotions of anger, sadness, and anxiety increased (**FIGURE 16.3**).

Adolescents' frequent negative emotions spark questions about adolescent coping. Fortunately, most teens do a fairly good job of coping with their emotions over the long run. However, other adolescents respond with **internalizing problems**, by directing their negative thoughts and feelings inward, which may lead to depression and low self-worth. Still others exhibit **externalizing problems**, by directing their negative feelings outwards, in the form of aggression.

internalizing problems Problem behaviors based on negative emotions that are directed inwards and may be expressed in anxiety or depression

externalizing problems Problem behaviors directed outward, such as physical aggression, disobeying rules, and destroying property

✓ CHECK YOUR UNDERSTANDING 16.2

1. How do emotions change across adolescence?
2. Distinguish between internalizing and externalizing problems in adolescents; how might these problems be expressed?

Adolescent Depression

LEARNING OBJECTIVE 16.3 Describe what we know about the prevalence of depression in adolescence overall, in adolescent girls and adolescent boys, and the type of therapies that are helpful in treating depression.

depression A mood disorder characterized by negative symptoms that are experienced nearly every day, such as constant sadness, diminished interest and pleasure in activities, social withdrawal, significant weight loss or gain, and feelings of worthlessness

No teen or adult is immune to periodic bouts of emotional pain. But, extreme and prolonged emotional pain can be debilitating. Adolescents are vulnerable to **depression**—negative symptoms that are experienced nearly every day, including depressed mood, diminished interest and pleasure in activities, social withdrawal, significant weight loss or gain, insomnia or excessive sleep, fatigue or loss of energy, diminished concentration, recurrent thoughts of death, and feelings of worthlessness (**TABLE 16.1**). Notably, depression is a mental illness

TABLE 16.1 ■ DSM-5 criteria for major depressive disorder and persistent depressive disorder

Major depressive disorder

Diagnostic criteria

A. Five (or more) of the following symptoms have been present during the same 2-week period and represent a change from previous functioning: at least one of the symptoms is either (1) depressed mood or (2) loss of interest or pleasure.
   Note: Do not include symptoms that are clearly attributable to another medical condition.

   1. Depressed mood most of the day, nearly every day, as indicated by either subjective report (e.g., feels sad, empty, hopeless) or observation made by others (e.g., appears tearful). (Note: In children and adolescents, can be irritable mood.)

   2. Markedly diminished interest or pleasure in all, or almost all, activities most of the day, nearly every day (as indicated by either subjective account or observation).

   3. Significant weight loss when not dieting or weight gain (e.g., a change of more than 5% of body weight in a month), or decrease or increase in appetite nearly every day. (Note: In children, consider failure to make expected weight gain.)

   4. Insomnia or hypersomnia nearly every day.

   5. Psychomotor agitation or retardation nearly every day (observable by others, not merely subjective feelings of restlessness or being slowed down).

   6. Fatigue or loss of energy nearly every day.

   7. Feelings of worthlessness or excessive or inappropriate guilt (which may be delusional) nearly every day (not merely self-reproach or guilt about being sick).

   8. Diminished ability to think or concentrate, or indecisiveness, nearly every day (either by subjective account or as observed by others).

   9. Recurrent thoughts of death (not just fear of dying), recurrent suicidal ideation without a specific plan, or a suicide attempt or a specific plan for committing suicide.

B. The symptoms cause clinically significant distress or impairment in social, occupational, or other important areas of functioning.

C. The episode is not attributable to the physiological effects of a substance or to another medical condition.

Persistent depressive disorder (Dysthymia)

Diagnostic criteria

This disorder represents a consolidation of DSM-IV-defined chronic major depressive disorder and dysthymic disorder.

A. Depressed mood for most of the day, for more days than not, as indicated by either subjective account or observation by others, for at least 2 years.
   Note: In children and adolescents, mood can be irritable and duration must be at least 1 year.

B. Presence, while depressed, of two (or more) of the following:

   1. Poor appetite or overeating.

   2. Insomnia or hypersomnia.

   3. Low energy or fatigue.

   4. Low self-esteem.

   5. Poor concentration or difficulty making decisions.

   6. Feelings of hopelessness.

C. During the 2-year period (1 year for children or adolescents) of the disturbance, the individual has never been without the symptoms in Criteria A and B for more than 2 months at a time.

D. Criteria for a major depressive disorder may be continuously present for 2 years.

E. There has never been a manic episode or a hypomanic episode, and criteria have never been met for cyclothymic disorder.

F. The disturbance is not better explained by a persistent schizoaffective disorder, schizophrenia, delusional disorder, or other specified or unspecified schizophrenia spectrum and other psychotic disorder.

G. The symptoms are not attributable to the physiological effects of a substance (e.g., a drug of abuse, a medication) or another medical condition (e.g. hypothyroidism).

H. The symptoms cause clinically significant distress or impairment in social, occupational, or other important areas of functioning.

Source: DSM-5. 2013. Diagnostic and Statistical Manual of Mental Disorders (5th ed.). American Psychiatric Association, Washington, DC.

that differs from sadness (a normal reaction to disappointment, loss, and life problems) in its duration, intensity, impact on life, and accompanying sense of hopelessness. Academic pressures, changing bodies, sexual feelings, new school contexts, pressures from social media use, and so forth, may contribute to the intensifying of depressive symptoms during adolescence.

Adolescents who display depressive symptoms frequently and intensely may be experiencing **clinical depression**—severe bouts of depression in need of treatment. Oftentimes, depression is accompanied by other psychological problems that magnify its negative effects. For instance, anxiety and fearfulness surge during adolescence due to exaggerated amygdala activity (the region of the brain involved in emotions as described in Chapter 14) (e.g., Ahmed, Bittencourt-Hewitt, Sebastian, 2015; Hare et al., 2008).

Sex Differences in Depression

Does depression differ by an adolescent's biological sex? The short answer is yes. Female adolescents display higher prevalence rates of depression than do male adolescents. A meta-analysis that combined findings across 150 articles and 90 different nations showed that sex differences emerge as early as 12 years of age, peak in adolescence, and then remain stable into adulthood (Salk, Hyde, Abramson, 2017). Moreover, sex differences in depression can be traced back several decades (Twenge, 2017) (**FIGURE 16.4**).

But sex chromosomes do not carry genetic blueprints that make female adolescents more prone to "depression," so why do such sex differences exist? One possibility is that male adolescents are less inclined than female adolescents to seek treatment for psychological problems, leading to lower rates of diagnosis. However, that is not the entire story. Female adolescents experience higher rates of cyberbullying and use mobile phones more than do male adolescents, which can produce symptoms of depression (Salk et al., 2017). Additionally, how adolescents experience and cope with stress may shed light on the higher prevalence of depressive symptoms in female adolescents. From 13 to 18 years of age, female adolescents are more likely to report daily stress than are male adolescents, and female adolescents react more strongly to interpersonal problems than do male adolescents (Hankin, Mermelstein, & Roesch, 2007). Adolescents who identify with "feminine" traits, regardless of their biological sex, tend to **ruminate** by thinking intensely and repeatedly about their problems, which

clinical depression A mental health disorder marked by severe bouts of depression necessitating treatment, including therapy, medication, or a combination of both

ruminate To continuously and deeply reflect on the same things, such as problems, which may result in depressive symptoms

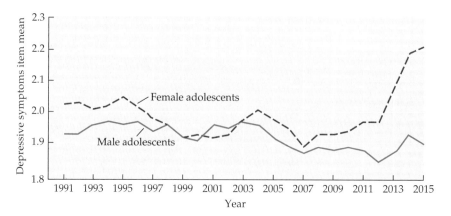

FIGURE 16.4 Sex differences in depression. Female adolescents show higher scores on depressive symptoms than do male adolescents, with sex differences maintaining and even increasing over the past three decades. (From Twenge, 2017 iGen: Why Today's Super-Connected Kids Are Growing Up Less Rebellious, More Tolerant, Less Happy—and Completely Unprepared for Adulthood—and What That Means for the Rest of Us.)

can magnify the perception of difficulties and lead to depressive symptoms (Lopez, Driscoll, & Kistner, 2009).

Nonetheless, male adolescents surpass female adolescents in rates of suicide, which, on the face of it, appears to contradict their lower depression rates (**FIGURE 16.5**). One reason for a sex disparity in suicide rates is because male adolescents may resort to methods that result in instant death, such as hanging or gunfire, whereas female adolescents use methods that have the possibility of reversal, such as drug overdose (e.g., Bachmann, 2018). Perhaps, as well, the predominant way that depression is defined—as symptoms that are turned *inward*, such as extreme sadness—leads to missing signs of risk in male adolescents. Anger, irritability, and antisocial behaviors may signal psychological pain and depression in male adolescents that may be ignored or punished, rather than met with help (Sigurdsson et al., 2015). This is a problem of diagnosing depression, rather than a problem specific to male adolescents. Sadly, however, suicide trends in the United States are on the rise in both male and female adolescents, and so the tragic outcomes of depression are far from only an adolescent male problem (Curtin, Warner, & Hedegaard, 2016).

Diagnosing Depression

There is no magic formula for figuring out whether an adolescent's moody retreat to a room signals a deep psychological problem or a normal reaction to the hormonal and social changes of adolescence. And so, despite the high prevalence of depression in adolescence, the mental health needs of adolescents may go unnoticed or misdiagnosed (Kieling et al., 2011). Although the criteria for adolescent depression do not differ from those of adults, some adolescents have difficulty identifying and describing their feelings (Bhatia & Bhatia, 2007). In other instances, people close to the adolescent may interpret the teen's low mood as "just a phase" that will soon pass. Moreover, as we just learned, irritability and anger may be overlooked as symptoms of depression. And, depression may be neglected in adolescents who are depressed but have other physical health problems, because medical practitioners may focus on the "main" problem at the expense of attention to mental health issues. For example, about 40% of adolescents with epilepsy show clinically significant rates of internalizing behaviors associated with depression, yet many remain undiagnosed or are not treated in a timely manner (e.g., Schraegle & Titus, 2017).

Treating Depression

Several evidence-based therapies have been found to effectively reduce adolescent symptoms of depression (Brown et al., 2018). **Cognitive behavior therapy**— an approach that focuses on a person's thoughts, feelings, and behaviors—is effective for treating mild to moderate depression. Adolescents may be encouraged to reexamine and modify counter-productive thoughts ("I'm too boring and no one likes me") as a way to change their feelings and behaviors. Sometimes clinicians take a **family-systems approach**, working with the adolescent, parents, and other family members to facilitate change (e.g., Connell & Dishion, 2008). Other times, antidepressants are used in conjunction with therapy, particularly for severe depression. However, very rare but significant side effects, including a risk of suicidal behavior, should be monitored when adolescents use antidepressants (Nischal et al., 2012).

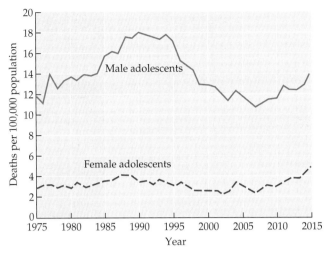

FIGURE 16.5 Suicide rates. Suicide rates for adolescents ages 15 to 19 years, as reported by the Centers for Disease Control in 2017. Male adolescents greatly surpass female adolescents in rates of suicide, a trend that has persisted over the past several decades, despite statistics showing higher prevalence of depression in female adolescents than in male adolescents. (After CDC. 2017. QuickStats: Suicide Rates for Teens Aged 15–19 Years, by Sex — United States, 1975–2015. MMWR Morb Mortal Wkly Rep 66: 816. DOI: http://dx.doi.org/10.15585/mmwr.mm6630a6. Source: CDC. National Vital Statistics System, mortality data. https://www.cdc.gov/nchs/nvss/deaths.htm.)

cognitive behavior therapy
An evidence-based psychological approach to treating depression (and other mental health disorders) that focuses on a person's thoughts, feelings, and behaviors and offers individuals coping strategies to manage challenges

family-systems approach
An evidence-based psychological approach to treating mental health disorders such as depression that focuses on working with the person, caregivers, and other family members to facilitate change

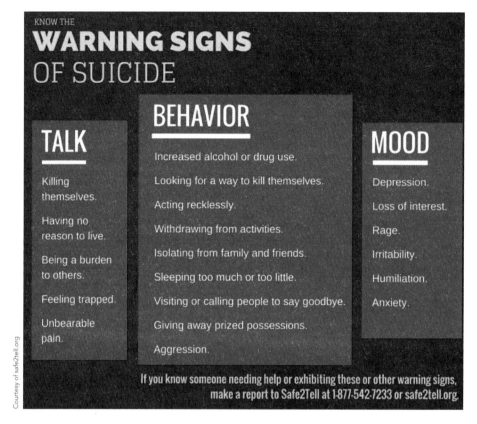

Courtesy of safe2tell.org

FIGURE 16.6 Warning signs of suicide. A critical step in the prevention of suicide is for parents, teachers, school guidance counselors, and so on to be aware of warning signs to ensure timely and caring intervention.

A vital piece to suicide prevention is the detection of risk for depression in adolescents, particularly at extremes that may lead to self-harm. Parents, teachers, and school guidance counselors should be aware of the warning signs of suicide, and intervene in a prompt and caring way (**FIGURE 16.6**). Moreover, when an adolescent suicide occurs, counseling for peers should be offered to help them cope with feelings of grief, anger, or guilt. A peer's death can increase the likelihood that a depressed peer will commit suicide, making timely interventions critical (Feigelman & Gorman, 2008).

✓ **CHECK YOUR UNDERSTANDING 16.3**

1. What psychological problems often accompany depression? What is the greatest risk of depression in adolescence?
2. What sex differences exist in rates of depression and suicide? What might explain the differences?
3. What are two types of therapeutic approaches for treating depression?

Self-Regulation

When my son Christopher was a junior in high school, he and his friends went away with their mothers for a weekend. They had just learned to drive, and asked if they could go out and buy ice cream around 10 p.m. We agreed, with the typical warnings: "Drive safely," "buckle up," and "don't stay out late." They returned without a hitch. However, at 1 a.m., we were awoken by the sound of deafening explosions outside. The boys had bought firecrackers on their ice-cream expedition and decided to set them off in the woods for excitement (it was February, not July 4th, and setting off fireworks in the community was illegal). A few minutes later, several police cars, sirens blasting, arrived to investigate. The boys fled into the woods, and we ran outside to track them down with the police tailing closely behind. Christopher and his friends were thrilled by the excitement, while the moms were furious. How could they think of doing such a thing? You will learn that adolescents—despite being advanced in cognitive reasoning—often lack self-regulation. This is especially true when they are having fun with friends and desires for adventure overwhelm their better judgment. Let's review the science that backs these observations.

Development of Adolescent Self-Regulation

LEARNING OBJECTIVE 16.4 Describe the difficulties adolescents have in self-regulation and impulse control, and one way researchers study adolescent self-regulation.

The exhilarating freedom and growing independence of adolescence calls for new types of self-regulation. **Self-regulation** refers to the purposeful control of thoughts, emotions, and behaviors. Here we focus on the emotional and behavioral aspects of self-regulation, which take on special significance during adolescence. New freedoms, including unsupervised time with friends, a driver's license, exposure to older teens, and so forth, present challenges to self-regulation. Sometimes, adolescents appear to act without thinking and may pay a steep price for a momentary lapse. **Impulsiveness**—acting on the spur of the moment without foresight or thought—is a sign of low self-regulation, and conversely, a decline in impulsiveness over age is a hallmark of growing self-regulation.

How do developmental scientists measure self-regulation without putting adolescents in dangerous situations? Sometimes, they simply ask teens to rate themselves on impulsivity (such as, "I act on the spur of the moment"), inability to delay gratification (such as, "I spend more money than I should"), and lack of perseverance (such as, "It's hard for me to think about two different things at the same time"), and then analyze developmental changes in adolescents' responses. Such self-report measures reveal improvements to self-regulation from adolescence through 30 years of age (Steinberg et al., 2009).

Delay discounting tasks are another way to measure self-regulation (Odum, 2011). The term comes from the idea that the psychological value of a reward declines with a time delay. In a classic delay discounting task, an immediate and small monetary reward is pitted against a delayed, larger monetary reward, much like the delay-of-gratification marshmallow task introduced in Chapter 10 (**FIGURE 16.7**). For example, you might be more likely to choose to receive $10 now than $20 a month from now, even though the later reward is twice as large. Lottery winners often prefer to collect a smaller bulk sum at once rather than a larger amount distributed over many years.

When adolescents are placed in such dilemmas, they find it harder to wait for a delayed reward than do adults (Steinberg et al., 2009). Putting this in context, an adult might work a few extra hours before attending a party, but an adolescent would want to attend the party as soon as possible. Unsurprisingly, adolescents who choose to receive a delayed reward are less likely to use alcohol and other drugs than are those who choose to receive an immediate reward (Romer et al., 2010).

✓ CHECK YOUR UNDERSTANDING 16.4

1. Why are adolescents more impulsive than adults? Give an example.

self-regulation The ability to manage and integrate attention, thoughts, emotions, and behaviors to attain goals

impulsiveness Acting on the spur of the moment without foresight or thought, thus reflecting challenges with emotional or behavioral self-control

delay discounting tasks Experiments that measure self-regulation in which participants are presented with a choice between a small, immediate reward and a larger, delayed reward

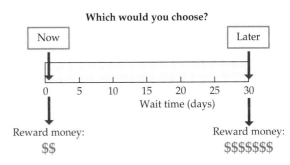

FIGURE 16.7 Delay discounting tasks. A delay discounting task pits a small but immediate reward against a larger but later reward. (After K. S. Rosch and S. H. Mostofsky. 2015. *J Int Neuropsychol Soc* 22: 12–23.)

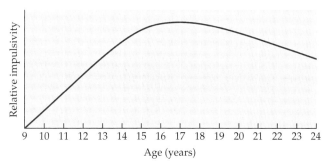

FIGURE 16.8 Risk taking. Risk taking increases in adolescence and then declines in early adulthood. (After L. Steinberg. 2013. *Nat Rev Neurosci* 14: 513–518. https://doi.org/10.1038/nrn3509.)

risk taking Decision making with potentially harmful consequences

sensation seeking The quest for novel, intense, and varied experiences and taking risks to pursue such experiences

Are you a Sensation Seeker?

Rate each of the following as 0, 1, or 2
(0 = Not at all true of me; 1 = True of me;
2 = Very true of me). High scores represent
high sensation seeking.

☐ I like to try activities that are physically thrilling like skydiving and bungee jumping.

☐ I thrive on the thrill of trying new things.

☐ I would take a dare for the fun and excitement of it.

☐ I love traveling to new places.

☐ I get bored very easily.

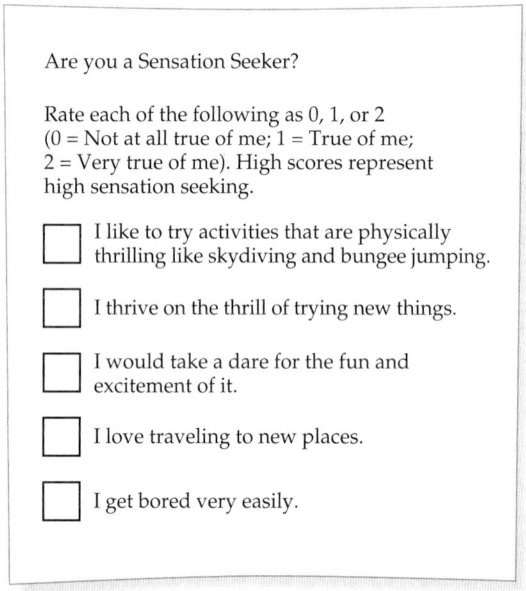

FIGURE 16.9 Sensation-seeking quiz. Based on their responses to questions such as, "I like doing things just for the thrill of it" on a sensation-seeking quiz, adolescents show higher sensation seeking than do children and adults.

Development of Risk Taking

LEARNING OBJECTIVE 16.5 Describe patterns of change in risk taking and sensation seeking in adolescence and the potential harm and benefits of these tendencies.

In contrast to the steady improvements of self-regulation from adolescence through young adulthood, **risk taking**—decision making that has potentially harmful consequences—follows an inverted U-shaped pattern: It increases during early adolescence, peaks in middle and late adolescence, and then declines in adulthood (Duell, Icenogle, & Steinberg, 2016) (**FIGURE 16.8**). The inverted U-shaped pattern of risk taking has been documented across cultures and historical time (Hirschi & Gottfredson, 1983; Piquero, Farrington, & Blumenstein, 2003). Some refer to it as the "age-crime curve" because teens sometimes engage in illegal activities that may result in arrest (Shulman, Steinberg, & Piquero, 2013). And it is no coincidence that development of grey matter follows the same inverted U-shaped pattern seen for risk taking (see Chapter 14).

Adolescent risk taking goes hand in hand with **sensation seeking**, the pursuit of novel, intense, and varied experiences (Smith, Chein, & Steinberg, 2013). People who seek thrills by gambling large amounts of money, driving fast, and participating in adventurous activities, such as riding mega-rollercoasters, parachuting, and ice climbing glaciers, rank high on sensation seeking. Adolescents show higher sensation seeking than do children and adults, based on their responses to questions such as, "I like doing things just for the thrill of it" (Steinberg, 2008) (**FIGURE 16.9**).

So, let's return for a minute to the delay discounting tasks to put together what we've learned. Perhaps adolescents' sensation seeking helps explain why they find it difficult to wait for a reward and ultimately take risks? Maybe adolescents are so caught up in the excitement of the moment, they find it difficult to pass on getting something now rather than waiting until later?

Developmental researcher Lawrence Steinberg and colleagues sought to understand connections among sensation seeking, risk taking, and reward. They placed adolescents in a simulated driving task, where they had to decide between running a yellow traffic signal and risking a crash versus playing it safe and driving slowly. Adolescents were told that if they completed the course quickly, they would receive a tangible reward: money. However, they would not get paid anything if they had an accident. In this example, Steinberg and colleagues interpreted fast driving as risk taking and sensation seeking and the money as "the reward" (Chein et al., 2011). Adolescents were more likely to run the light and crash than were adults, seemingly unable to control their behaviors in the presence of a possible high, immediate reward. Furthermore, adolescents' tendency to drive fast to receive a reward was magnified when teens were led to believe that a friend was watching from another room (**TABLE 16.2**). Adults, on the other hand, were not affected by the supposed presence of a friend and were willing to drive safely to obtain a later reward.

Notably, male adolescents are the most prone to drive faster in simulated conditions, especially when they are simultaneously in a happy mood and next to a friend passenger (Rhodes, Pivik, & Sutton, 2015). And, real-world statistics on car accidents fit research patterns. Male adolescents and young adults incur the highest rate of accidents in the United States, and accidents in this population rise each year until beginning a slow descent by age 25 years (**FIGURE 16.10**).

And so, putting the pieces together, adolescents who score high on *both* reward sensitivity—typically measured by brain activation (in areas associated with emotion and pleasure) in the presence of rewards—and sensation seeking are prone to substance use, delinquent behaviors, casual and unprotected sexual encounters, and gambling (e.g., Derefinko et al., 2014; Leeman et al., 2014; Peach & Gaultney, 2013).

Before you conclude that adolescents should avoid sensation seeking and risk taking at all costs, consider the evolutionary benefits of these tendencies. The desire for excitement propels adolescents toward activities with new people, including those to whom they are sexually attracted (Suleiman et al., 2016). Furthermore, as adolescents actively search to understand their unique identities, they are open to trying new things and venturing into new experiences. Adolescents who navigate new adventures and relationships responsibly will reap social and emotional benefits, as we will see in later sections.

✓ CHECK YOUR UNDERSTANDING 16.5

1. What connections can you draw between sensation-seeking behaviors and delay discounting in adolescence?

2. Describe a study that examines the association between adolescent risk taking and delay discounting. How do adolescent responses differ from those of adults?

3. How does the presence of peers affect adolescent behavior in risk-taking studies?

TABLE 16.2 ■ Sensation seeking and peers	
Number of teen passengers	Driving risk
0	Normal
1 or more	2.5 times more likely to take risks
2 or more	3 times more likely to take risks

Source: After Scholastic and the National Institute on Drug Abuse, National Institutes of Health, U.S. Department of Health and Human Services. Heads Up Compilation 2015-16, Student Edition. Accessed 23 June 2021. https://www.drugabuse.gov/publications/heads-up-real-news-about-drugs-your-body-year-15-16-compilations.

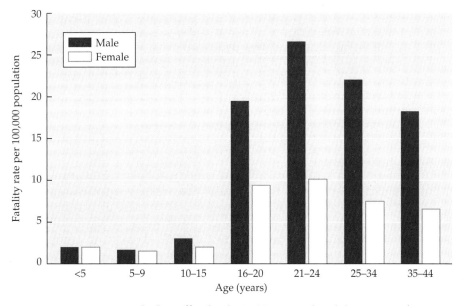

FIGURE 16.10 Motor vehicle traffic deaths in 2016. Male adolescents and young adults are the population with the highest rates of accidents in the United States, and accidents in this population rise each year until beginning a slow descent from 23 to 25 years that then continues into later years (not shown). (After National Highway Traffic Safety Administration [NHTSA]. 2019. Traffic Safety Facts 2017: A Compilation of Motor Vehicle Crash Data. U.S. Department of Transportation, National Center for Statistics and Analysis, NHTSA: Washington, DC.)

Contexts of Emotional Development

By this final chapter, you are undoubtedly familiar with the many factors that contribute to development. Think about what you learned in prior chapters about contextual influences on emotional development. Which contexts do you think affect adolescent emotional development? Why do you think those contexts matter? If you guessed that family, peer, school, and neighborhood contexts contribute significantly to the emotional development of adolescents, you would be correct.

Family and Peer Contexts of Emotional Development

LEARNING OBJECTIVE 16.6 Describe the types of parenting behaviors that have been shown to support and undermine adolescents' emotional development, and the effect of peers on depression and risk taking.

Imagine how difficult it would be to be in the throes of hormonal, bodily, and social changes while simultaneously arguing with parents, witnessing violence in the family, or being a victim of harsh discipline. It is no wonder that teens who live in toxic family environments and have poor relationships with their parents are prone toward emotional problems. Parents who offer low support of their children or adolescents, or display aggression and harsh punishment toward their adolescents, place their teens at risk of depression and antisocial behavior (e.g., Deane et al., 2020; Sousa, Herrenkohl et al., 2011; Yap, Allen, & Ladouceur, 2008). Reciprocally, emotionally supportive parents who set reasonable limits on their children arm adolescents with strategies to deal with the hassles and emotional burdens of everyday life. In fact, an adolescent has a decent chance of bouncing back from negative experiences in the presence of supportive family members.

Sometimes, maladaptive interactions in the family arise when parents experience high stress and depleted emotional resources themselves, including the stressors associated with poverty. Indeed, adolescents who live in poverty exhibit higher rates of emotional and behavior problems, including depression, than do teens without such risks (Coley et al., 2013; Reiss, 2013). And, teens whose parents show difficulties remaining calm during conflicts show similar difficulties in controlling their own reactions, sometimes to the point of losing control (Cui et al., 2015).

Adolescents also spend lots of time with friends and peers who can affect their mental health. Adolescents who perceive their peers to be caring and trustworthy are less likely to be depressed than are adolescents without positive friendships (Millings, Buck, Montgomery, Spears, Stallard, & 2012). But, peers can also urge their friends to take risks. Peers reward actions they approve of and reject those they view to be unpleasant. Peer feedback affects how an adolescent will behave the next time he or she encounters a situation (Bechara, 2005; Seymour & Dolan, 2008). For example, an adolescent may decide to try marijuana when coaxed by peers out of a desire to fit in, rather than a desire to experience the drug per se.

✓ CHECK YOUR UNDERSTANDING 16.6

1. Give an example of how a parent's own experiences of stress and depression might affect an adolescent's depression.
2. Under what circumstances might a peer be better positioned to offer emotional support than a parent or teacher?

School and Neighborhood Contexts of Emotional Development

LEARNING OBJECTIVE 16.7 Identify features of a school and neighborhood that can encourage—or conversely, discourage—adolescent self-regulation.

Adolescents spend most of their non-sleep hours at school and in their neighborhoods, where experiences can be positive or negative. On the positive side, schools and neighborhoods provide adolescents with opportunities to participate in extracurricular activities, such as clubs and faith-based gatherings. School- and community-based activities foster a sense of belonging and allow adolescents to share interests, experiences, and goals with friends. Adolescents who affiliate with faith-based organizations show low rates of emotional distress and antisocial behavior and relatively low contact with deviant peers (e.g., King, Ramos, & Clardy, 2013). Similarly, adolescents who participate in structured after-school activities, including sports and employment, show positive self-identity and low involvement in substance use, delinquent activity, and sexual activity (e.g., Barber, Stone, & Eccles, 2010; Lee et al., 2018; Mahoney, Vandell, & Simpkins, 2009).

Still, the association between extracurricular activities and peer relationships is not straightforward. The close camaraderie among members of a sports team may undermine self-regulation by encouraging excessive partying after games as a way to bond. High levels of alcohol consumption and risky hazing rituals are often associated with team sports and social groups such as sororities and fraternities (e.g., Chin & Johnson, 2011) (**FIGURE 16.11**).

Furthermore, although neighborhoods can be a source of positive social interactions, neighborhoods in areas of extreme poverty may harm adolescent emotional well-being by raising the likelihood that an adolescent will be exposed to various life stressors including violence and racial discrimination. In fact, because a higher percentage of Black adolescents live in impoverished neighborhoods, are exposed to neighborhood violence, and experience discrimination, they may be at disproportionate risk of depression (Deo, & Prelow, 2018; Patil et al., 2018). And, although neighborhood poverty most strongly relates to adolescent engagement in violence in teen boys, the gap between violence rates for teen boys versus teen girls shrinks in the context of extremely impoverished neighborhoods (Zimmerman & Messner, 2010) (**FIGURE 16.12**).

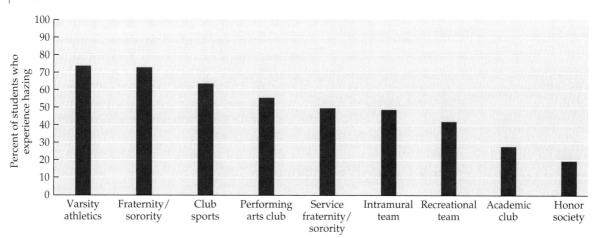

FIGURE 16.11 **Hazing.** Hazing in college is a dangerous behavior, and its prevalence reaches astounding rates in varsity athletics and fraternities and sororities. (After E. J. Allan and M. Madden. 2008. Hazing in View: College Students at Risk. Initial Findings from the National Study of Student Hazing. http://www.stophazing.org/wp-content/uploads/2014/06/hazing_in_view_web1.pdf.)

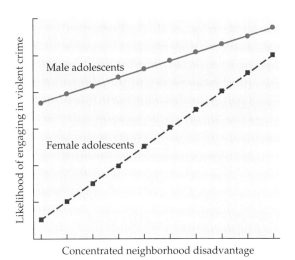

FIGURE 16.12 Violent crime rates. The connection between neighborhood poverty and adolescent exposure to and engagement in violence is seen for both teen boys and teen girls, with boys being involved in more violence than girls. However, the gap between teen boys and teen girls shrinks in the context of extremely impoverished neighborhoods. That is, rates of violent crime increase rapidly for teen girls from disadvantaged neighborhoods. (After G. M. Zimmerman and S. F. Messner. 2010. *Am Sociol Rev* 75: 958–980.)

It is simplistic, however, to assume that only adolescents from low-income neighborhoods are at risk for negative behaviors. Adolescents in affluent neighborhoods display many problems that are often neglected because people typically assume that their neighborhood and family resources buffer them from risk. Developmental scientist Suniya Luthar has conducted several eye-opening studies on the behaviors of adolescents from affluent neighborhoods. When Luthar compared adolescents from predominantly White, suburban families with minority adolescents living in inner cities, she found that adolescents from the suburbs scored high on several measures of maladjustment—including alcohol and substance use, anxiety, and depression—and the prevalence of their problems often exceeded that of youth from inner cities (**FIGURE 16.13**). Luthar interpreted suburban adolescents' negative outcomes as the "cost of privilege," noting that adolescents in affluent settings felt intense pressure to do well, had unrealistic goals of perfectionism, and sometimes perceived isolation from their parents who worked long hours to financially support their lifestyles (Luthar, Small, & Ciciolla, 2018; Lyman & Luthar, 2014).

✓ CHECK YOUR UNDERSTANDING 16.7

1. How does participation in extracurricular activities positively enhance emotional development in adolescence? When might extracurricular activities backfire?

2. Distinguish between the characteristics of neighborhoods that support positive development in adolescents versus those that place adolescents at risk for problem behaviors.

■ *Self-Identity Development*

For adolescents, the question "Who am I?" is profoundly important. But, figuring out the answer takes time. As adolescents explore their identities, they frequently consider the meaning of their many social roles: They are friends to peers, students to teachers, children to parents, and members of groups defined by ethnicity, race, sexual identity, and so on. How do adolescents integrate all these facets of self into a coherent identity? Sometimes, adolescents reject the views of other people—a sort of reinvention of the self. As my good colleague often reminds our students, figuring out who you *are not* is just as important as figuring out who you *are*. Although exploring one's identity involves many ups and downs, the outcome can be very rewarding: Adolescents who formulate a clear sense of their unique identity display confidence and an ability to focus on their goals and make positive decisions.

Erik Erikson's Theory

Individuals continually make choices, revisit those choices, and then make new ones—about the courses they aim to study, the political views they endorse, the relationships they wish to nurture, and the careers they aim to pursue. **Identity development** refers to the lifelong quest to figure out these aspects of the self. For Erik Erikson (1950, 1963), the quest for an identity peaks in adolescence, with a positive self-identity being crucial for an adolescent's psychological adjustment (see Chapter 1). Erikson (1963) once stated: "In the social jungle of human existence there is no feeling of being alive without a sense

identity development The lifelong process in which individuals actively work on understanding who they are and what makes them unique within a sociocultural context

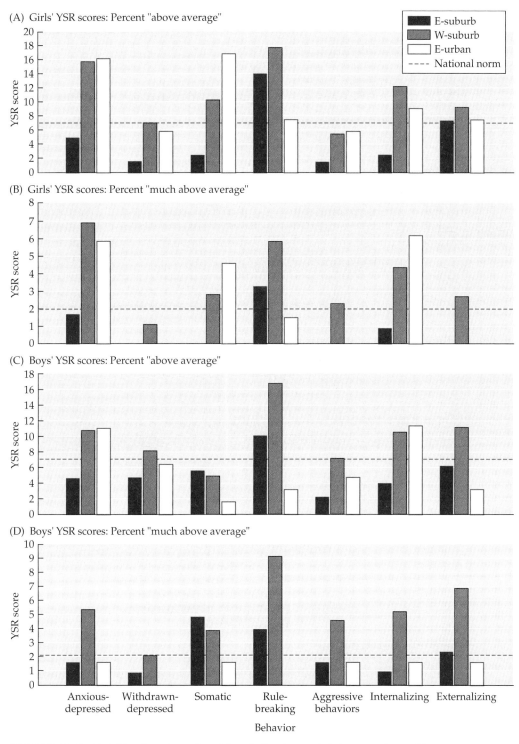

(A) Girls' YSR scores: Percent "above average"

(B) Girls' YSR scores: Percent "much above average"

(C) Boys' YSR scores: Percent "above average"

(D) Boys' YSR scores: Percent "much above average"

E-suburb
W-suburb
E-urban
- - - - National norm

Behavior: Anxious-depressed, Withdrawn-depressed, Somatic, Rule-breaking, Aggressive behaviors, Internalizing, Externalizing

FIGURE 16.13 **Neighborhoods and problem behaviors.** Adolescents from affluent suburban neighborhoods show higher rates of problem behaviors than national norms (based on their responses to the Youth Self Report Measure on problems such as internalizing and externalizing symptoms and rule breaking in underage drinking and smoking). In some cases, rates exceed those of inner-city youth. The higher rates of problems in teen girls and boys from affluent neighborhoods was seen in samples from different parts of the country. "E-suburb" denotes an East Coast suburb and "W-suburb" denotes a Northwestern suburb relative to national rates and to adolescents from an East Coast urban center, "E-urban." (After S. Luthar and S. Barkin. 2012. *Dev Psychopathol* 24: 429–449. Reproduced with permission.)

of identity." As we will see, although most adolescents successfully achieve a unified, mature identity, others struggle for various reasons. (Keep in mind, however, that identity is fluid and always changing; and so adolescence by no means represents the "endpoint" of identity formation).

Identity Achievement versus Role Confusion

LEARNING OBJECTIVE 16.8 Identify the conflict at the heart of what Erikson called the crisis of identity achievement.

identity achievement versus role confusion A stage in Erik Erikson's theory of psychosocial development when adolescents search for a sense of who they are by intensely exploring their personal values and beliefs, accepting some from their caregivers and rejecting others

According to Erikson, adolescents' major task is to negotiate the psychosocial crisis of **identity achievement versus role confusion**. Adolescents go through a period of "crisis" as they question the values and goals set by parents and society and accept some of those goals and values but reject others. Adolescents who successfully resolve this psychosocial crisis are able to integrate multiple aspects of the self into a stable and coherent whole. In contrast, adolescents with an incoherent sense of self may feel lost and isolated. Today, developmental scientists agree that the quest for identity is a principal task of adolescence, but they reject the notion of a crisis (Moshman, 2011). Instead, the process of identity development entails a period of exploration, in which adolescents gather and analyze many bits of information, much like the pieces to a puzzle, and fit them together into a meaningful picture.

✓ CHECK YOUR UNDERSTANDING 16.8

1. According to Erikson, what is an "identity crisis"?

The Psychosocial Moratorium

LEARNING OBJECTIVE 16.9 Define the concept of psychosocial moratorium.

psychosocial moratorium A time during adolescent identity development when the individual explores different identities and roles prior to committing to a unified identity

Adolescents do not achieve a unique self-identity overnight. All adolescents experience some confusion as they explore who they are, and their confusion can endure for several years. During a period of exploration, or **psychosocial moratorium**, adolescents take the time they need to freely experiment with and search for a unique niche (Erikson, 1956). In fact, college may be thought of as a time of psychosocial moratorium and identity fluctuation: Students test various subjects, lifestyles, and possible career paths as they progress toward attaining a unique self-identity (Klimstra et al., 2010).

Some adolescents, however, prematurely commit to a self-identity without having the luxury of experiencing a psychosocial moratorium. They may take on family obligations and adult responsibilities at the expense of self-exploration, such as when a teenager must work to help pay the bills. In other situations, adolescents might adopt a self-identity that others have determined, such as when an adolescent feels pressured to enter a parent's business without considering other options. Some individuals never quite settle on what they want to do in life. Over the long haul, the failure to achieve an integrated, coherent self-identity can cause deep, psychological problems.

✓ CHECK YOUR UNDERSTANDING 16.9

1. What is a psychosocial moratorium, and why did Erikson feel it is important for adolescents to experience this?
2. Why might some adolescents not experience a psychosocial moratorium?

James Marcia and Identity Statuses

James Marcia (1966, 1980) modified and extended Erikson's work on adolescent self-identity formation by describing the steps involved in the journey toward a coherent self. According to Marcia, the adolescent's search for self-identity involves two processes: exploration and commitment. **Exploration** is a time when the adolescent actively reexamines the past and explores alternative beliefs, interests, and values across various areas, including intimate relationships, friendships, gender roles, politics, religion, and occupation, much like Erikson's notion of the psychosocial moratorium. The period of exploration is followed by a **commitment** to alternative possibilities, such as relationships and a future occupation. Adolescents who successfully explore their options and make meaningful commitments are likely to feel good about who they are and optimistic about their futures.

exploration The process during identity formation when adolescents actively explore alternative beliefs, interests, occupations, and values across different areas

commitment The dedication of an individual to a particular relationship, cause, goal, and so on

Marcia's Identity Statuses

LEARNING OBJECTIVE 16.10 Identify the four identity statuses associated with James Marcia's theory of adolescent development.

Marcia (1966, 2002) interviewed college students about their choices of occupation, and beliefs about politics and religion. Based on these semi-structured interviews, Marcia distinguished four **identity statuses** reflecting combinations of exploration and commitment (**FIGURE 16.14**):

1. *Foreclosure.* Adolescents who make a life course commitment without exploring alternatives fall into this identity status. Foreclosure may occur when economic circumstances, or pressure from parents or other adults, prevents an adolescent from exploring life alternatives.

2. *Identity diffusion.* Identity diffusion occurs when an adolescent avoids exploring options and making commitments across different areas of life. Some adolescents experience identity diffusion because of a lack of interest, and others because of continued indecision. Most identity-diffused adolescents later move to a moratorium status.

3. *Moratorium.* Adolescents who are actively exploring alternatives but have not yet made firm commitments are in a state of moratorium, similar to the psychosocial moratorium described by Erikson. They may experience anxiety as they struggle to figure out who they are and which life path to pursue.

4. *Identity achievement.* Adolescents who have gone through a period of exploration and made commitments have achieved an internally driven identity rather than one that is imposed by others.

identity statuses The four categories in the search for an identity that represent combinations of exploration and commitment: foreclosure, identity diffusion, moratorium, and identity achievement

Marcia's theoretical framework has inspired much research. Overall, the majority of adolescents are in statuses of identity diffusion or foreclosure, and between 17 and 19 years of age the status of moratorium peaks (Nurmi, 2004). As adolescents move into early adulthood, most who had been in identity-diffused and moratorium statuses achieve an identity (Kroger, 2012). Some adolescents, however, remain in a diffused state for years. They avoid dealing directly with personal decisions and problems (Berzonsky et al., 2011; Crocetti et al., 2013). Surprisingly, many long-term diffused individuals experience little anxiety because they are apathetic rather than invested in life areas. Identity-diffused adolescents tend to lack close relationships, often simply go along with the crowd, and may display impulsiveness, academic difficulties, substance use, depression, and even suicidal thoughts (Berzonsky et al., 2011).

Finally, adolescents of a foreclosed status rarely attain the status of identity achievement, because they typically depend on other people to make life decisions for them. Adolescents who remain in a foreclosed status may adopt the values and beliefs of parents and other adults without exploring other options, perhaps because they fear being rejected by the people who support them (Berzonsky et al., 2011).

		Commitment	
		YES	NO
Exploration	YES	Identity achievement	Moratorium
	NO	Foreclosure	Identity diffusion

FIGURE 16.14 Marcia's identity statuses. This figure shows the combination of commitment and exploration and how those lead to different types of identity statuses. (After E. Marcia. 1966. *J Pers Soc Psychol* 3: 551–558.)

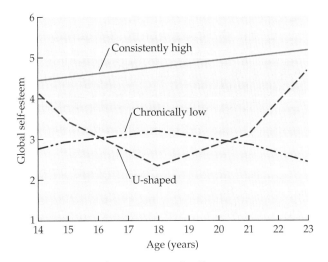

FIGURE 16.15 Three groups of self-esteem. When adolescents were followed to young adulthood (from adolescence through 23 years of age), researchers identified three patterns of change to self-esteem: consistently high, chronically low, and U-shaped. After M. S. Birkeland et al. 2012. *J Adolesc* 35: 43–54.)

self-esteem The positive or negative attitudes and beliefs a person has toward the self that are essential to self-identity

ethnic identity An individual's sense of belonging to an ethnic group, and perceptions and feelings about group membership

Multigroup Ethnic Identity Measure A measure/scale of adolescents' subjective sense of pride and belongingness to their ethnic group

Ethnic Identity Scale An instrument based on the Multigroup Ethnic Identity Measure that assesses three aspects of ethnicity: ethnic identity exploration, ethnic identity resolution, and affirmation

✓ **CHECK YOUR UNDERSTANDING 16.10**

1. What are the four identity statuses identified by Marcia? Can you think of people you know (yourself included) who fit within each of them?

Adolescent Self-Esteem

LEARNING OBJECTIVE 16.11 Define self-esteem and discuss changes to self-esteem over the period of adolescence.

The attainment of a unique self-identity yields psychological benefits. Adolescents who have achieved a unique identity tend to be curious, open-minded, and persistent; feel in control of their lives and futures; and have a positive sense of self-worth (Berzonsky et al., 2011; Schwartz et al., 2013). **Self-esteem**—the positive or negative attitudes and evaluations a person has toward the self—is integral to an individual's self-identity. Individuals with high self-esteem have successfully navigated the physical, psychological, and social transitions of adolescence, and achieve fulfilling social relationships with family and peers (Birkeland, Breivik, & Wold, 2014). At the other extreme, teens with low self-esteem perceive themselves as unworthy and inferior to their peers.

However, self-esteem is constantly in flux and may change over the course of development. Researchers sought to describe developmental changes in adolescent self-esteem by following a group of over 1,000 adolescents from 13 to 20 years of age (Birkeland et al., 2012). Although at any point in time, some adolescents scored higher on self-esteem than did other adolescents, the researchers identified three distinct groups (**FIGURE 16.15**):

- The majority of adolescents had consistently high self-esteem.
- A second group of adolescents (from 6% to 16%) showed a pattern of chronically low self-esteem.
- A third group (about 7%) exhibited a U-shaped pattern of change in which their self-esteem was high in early adolescence, dropped during middle to late adolescence, and then gradually rebounded in adulthood.

✓ **CHECK YOUR UNDERSTANDING: 16.11**

1. With what identity status would high self-esteem be associated? Offer an example.
2. Describe three patterns of change in adolescent self-esteem.

Ethnic and Racial Identity

If someone asked you to describe who you are, would your ethnicity and race bubble up in your self-description? Or would you avoid talking about ethnicity and race? The topics of ethnicity and race can be challenging to discuss. But, for adolescents—particularly those who are ethnic or racial minorities or immigrants—ethnicity and race are salient features of their self-identity (Umaña-Taylor et al., 2014). In earlier chapters we defined ethnicity as a shared cultural heritage and race as a shared biological ancestry. For simplicity, in this chapter we use the term **ethnic identity** to refer to an individual's sense of belonging to an ethnic (or racial) group, and perceptions, feelings, and behaviors regarding the individual's ethnic (or racial) group membership (Phinney, 1996). And, because all adolescents consider their relationships to others as they explore their self-identities, ethnicity and race are likely to be integral to the exploration process, regardless of heritage (**FIGURE 16.16**).

Development of Ethnic Identity

LEARNING OBJECTIVE 16.12 What are three core aspects of ethnic identity, and how do they change over adolescence?

Like Erikson and Marcia, developmental scientist Jean Phinney (2008) views ethnic identity as involving processes of exploration and commitment. During a prolonged period of exploration, adolescents come to understand the values, beliefs, and practices of their ethnic group and how those may differ from other groups. Sometimes, one or several experiences trigger an intense period of exploration, such as when an adolescent views newscasts about hate crimes against minority groups or is the target of ethnic slurs.

Phinney's deep interest in the psychological processes involved in ethnic identity led her to develop the **Multigroup Ethnic Identity Measure** (**MEIM**) to measure adolescents' subjective sense of pride and belonging to their ethnic group (Phinney, 1992) (**FIGURE 16.17**). Developmental scientist Adriana Umaña-Taylor built on the MEIM with an instrument called the **Ethnic Identity Scale**, which distinguishes three core aspects of ethnic identity (Umaña-Taylor et al., 2004):

- *Ethnic identity exploration*: an individual's active exploration of and learning about their ethnic background
- *Ethnic identity resolution*: an individual's sense of commitment to and clarity about the meaning of their ethnicity
- *Affirmation*: the degree to which an individual has positive or negative feelings about membership in their ethnic group

Developmental scientists have tracked changes in these aspects of ethnic identity in different ethnic groups in the United States. They find that ethnic exploration and resolution generally increase during middle to late adolescence, as teens search for meaning around their ethnic identity (exploration) and then come to terms with what their identity means to them (resolution). As they come to a resolution, adolescents may view their ethnicity positively or negatively (affirmation). For example, two Chinese-American teens may explore their ethnic identity by attending cultural events, cooking and eating certain foods, reading about the history of China, and talking to parents and friends about their culture. Both adolescents may come to a confident resolution about what their identity means to them personally, although one may have a negative view of being Chinese American and the other a positive one (Umaña-Taylor & Guimond, 2010). Diverging affirmations toward one's ethnic identity, in turn, relate to psychological adjustment. When results from 46 studies on ethnic identity and youth adjustment were combined, adolescents who felt positively about their ethnic identities were psychologically well-adjusted and had few health problems and low rates of depression (Rivas-Drake et al., 2014).

✓ CHECK YOUR UNDERSTANDING 16.12

1. What three core aspects of ethnic identity does the Ethnic Identity Scale measure?

FIGURE 16.16 Capturing every skin tone on the planet. For her ongoing project, Humanae, Brazilian photographer Angélica Dass is attempting to capture every single skin tone on the planet. And when Angélica says she plans to capture every single possible skin tone, she really means it. Having started the project back in 2012, Angélica has now photographed an astonishing 2,500 people, and says "The only limit would be reached by completing all of the world's population."

Use the numbers below to indicate how much you agree or disagree with each statement.

(4) Strongly agree
(3) Agree
(2) Disagree
(1) Strongly disagree

☐ I have spent time trying to find out more about my ethnic group, such as its history, traditions, and customs.

☐ I am active in organizations or social groups that include mostly members of my own ethnic group.

☐ I have a clear sense of my ethnic background and what it means for me.

☐ I think a lot about how my life will be affected by my ethnic group membership.

☐ I am happy that I am a member of the group I belong to.

☐ I have a strong sense of belonging to my own ethnic group.

FIGURE 16.17 Phinney's Multigroup Ethnic Identity Measure (MEIM). Jean Phinney developed a measure to evaluate adolescents' subjective sense of pride and belonging to their ethnic group. (After J. S. Phinney. 1992. *J Adolesc Res* 7: 156–176.)

Navigating Two Identities

LEARNING OBJECTIVE 16.13 Describe internal conflicts about cultural values that an adolescent member of a minority ethnic group may experience as they attempt to navigate their different identities, and list some possible outcomes of the process.

Being an ethnic minority often means living in two different worlds and figuring out how to be a part of each. Because the cultural values and expectations of one's ethnic group may differ from those of the majority population, adolescents must reconcile these two cultures, or "hyphenated selves," as expressed by a 17-year-old Syrian who observed, "I guess you could say I live on the hyphen" (Fine & Sirin, 2008). This is not easy. Immigrant and minority adolescents may struggle with achieving an integrated sense of self.

Sometimes, teens feel conflicted about which beliefs to follow (Greene, Way, & Pahl, 2006; Qin, 2009). For example, East Asian families place great importance on family obligation, expecting adolescent children to help care for their siblings or elders and to fulfill other family responsibilities. For East Asian adolescents living in the United States, the expectation that family obligations come first is sometimes at odds with the prevailing European American emphases on autonomy and independence in which an adolescent's primary goal is to pursue personal interests. As East Asian adolescents attempt to handle competing values, parents may view their children as pulling away, rejecting family, and avoiding responsibilities (Fuligni, 2007). In rare instances, adolescents may respond to the tensions of two cultural worlds with defiance, such as when they reject the behaviors and attitudes of other groups that they perceive to be perpetrators of discrimination—a reaction termed **oppositional identity formation**.

For the most part, however, exploration of one's ethnic identity results in a sense of commitment, pride, and belonging (Juang & Cookston, 2009). Most minority and immigrant adolescents benefit from learning about different beliefs and practices and flexibly adapt their behaviors to accommodate a multicultural world. They comfortably identify with home and majority cultures and easily switch between different languages, views, and lifestyles, thereby achieving a **bicultural identity** (Cross et al., 2017; Kiang, Yip, & Fuligni, 2008) (**FIGURE 16.18**).

oppositional identity formation Adolescents' response to tensions of two cultural worlds with rebelliousness and defiance

bicultural identity The formation of an identity that reflects a combination of two cultures (often "home" and "mainstream" cultures)

✓ CHECK YOUR UNDERSTANDING 16.13

1. What is meant by a bicultural identity? Can you think of an example?

FIGURE 16.18 Bicultural identity. Adolescents from immigrant households often feel a pull between their obligations to the family and helping out at home versus going out with friends and doing things for themselves.

Gender Identity and Sexual Orientation

Gender identity and sexual orientation are core aspects of a person's identity. Often, a person's sex assigned at birth and physical body align with their gender identity and sexual orientation—such as when a child with female genitalia perceives herself to be a girl and is sexually attracted to boys. At other times, traditional views around sex assigned at birth may misalign with an adolescent's gender identity and/or sexual orientation. This can cause emotional and social difficulties at a vulnerable time in development, especially if parents, adults, or peers reject a teen's gender identity or sexual orientation. In the sections that follow, we consider the process of gender identity development, sexual orientation, and romantic relationships in adolescence. We also delve into the experiences of adolescents whose gender identity, sexual orientation, or practices differ from the majority.

Gender Identity

LEARNING OBJECTIVE 16.14 Differentiate between a cisgender and transgender identity.

By adolescence, the physical transformations of puberty lead to deep reflection around one's **gender identity**—the internal self-perceptions about being a girl/woman, a boy/man, or nonbinary (neither a woman nor a man). Because sex and gender are not interchangeable, an adolescent's gender identity may or may not align with the teen's sex assigned at birth. **Cisgender** adolescents have a gender identity that matches their sex assigned at birth. **Transgender** adolescents identify with a gender that is different than their sex assigned at birth. Transgender adolescents may feel disconnected from their bodies, as though they are living as a gender that differs from their true self. Some transgender adolescents have had histories of cross-gender behavior that emerged in early childhood (Drummond et al., 2008). Note that an adolescent's gender identity is distinct from their sexual orientation. Thus, transgender teens can be attracted to people of the same or another sex.

gender identity A person's internal self-perceptions about being a boy/man or girl/woman or non-binary

cisgender A term describing individuals whose gender identity matches their biological sex at birth

transgender A term describing individuals who identify with a gender that is different from their birth sex

✓ CHECK YOUR UNDERSTANDING 16.14

1. Define cisgender and transgender.

Sexual Orientation

LEARNING OBJECTIVE 16.15 Identify four main types of sexual orientation and describe the factors that may affect the timing and outcome of coming out.

Adolescents' feelings of sexual attraction are a highly salient and meaningful part of a developing identity. But feelings of sexual attraction are sometimes tough to navigate. Adolescents must come to terms with their sexual orientation and the societal and family expectations around sexual activity. **Sexual orientation** refers to a person's erotic feelings and attraction toward another individual of a particular sex.

The main types of sexual orientation have been identified:

sexual orientation A person's attraction toward a particular sex or gender, which is often classified as heterosexual, homosexual, bisexual, or asexual

- *Heterosexual orientation* is when a person is attracted to individuals of another sex.
- *Gay or lesbian orientation* is when a person is attracted to individuals of the same sex.
- *Bisexual orientation* is when a person is attracted to individuals of two or more sexes.
- *Asexual orientation* is when a person is not attracted to any sex.

sexual fluidity One or more changes in sexual identity

The majority (88.2%) of individuals in the United States between 12 and 23 years of age identify as completely heterosexual, 9.5% as mostly heterosexual, and the remaining 2.4% as lesbian, gay, or bisexual, based on a national survey of nearly 14,000 youth (Calzo et al., 2017).

Notably, individuals who view themselves to be heterosexual also sometimes find themselves attracted to peers of the same sex. For example, it is not uncommon for women to identify as mostly straight but to be somewhat attracted to other women (Thompson & Morgan, 2008). And, adolescents' descriptions of their sexual orientation may change with personal experiences, internal reflection, and the extent to which family and community support non-heterosexual attractions (Calzo et al., 2017; Diamond, 2012; Ott et al., 2011). The majority (about two-thirds) of women who identified as lesbian, bisexual, and questioning changed their stated sexual preference over a 10-year period (Diamond, 2008). **Sexual fluidity**, defined as one or more changes to sexual identity, suggests that sexual orientation is a dynamic process rather than one marked by a static "milestone" or onset time (Saewyc, 2011). It is not until adolescence, and sometimes later, that a sexual orientation is considered to be a stable part of a person's identity.

LGBTQ+ adolescents may find it emotionally and socially difficult to adjust to and inform others about their sexuality, which helps explain why coming out is a gradual process that involves multiple developmental milestones (Savin-Williams, 1996, 2019):

1. *Self-recognition.* In what is sometimes called "coming out to oneself," a person realizes the self is different from many and acknowledges an LGBTQ+ attraction. At this early stage, however, the individual does not reveal the attraction to other people.

2. *Identity tolerance.* The individual has mixed feelings about their attraction, but feels increasingly alienated from heterosexuality. The individual begins to make contact with the LGBTQ+ community.

3. *Identity acceptance.* The individual fully accepts their identity and discloses it to family and friends. At this point, the individual shows a clear preference for interacting with other members of the LGBTQ+ community.

4. *Identity integration.* The individual feels pride in self and the sexual community with which the person identifies and publicly comes out to many people. There is finally a feeling of congruence between the public and private self.

Each of these components to coming out varies from person to person in terms of timing, intensity, and content (Savin-Williams & Ritch, 2019). Moreover, the ages when people pass though the phases of coming out vary and may last several years. For example, although individuals on average personally accept attraction to members of the same sex by about 15 years of age, some recall first noticing same-sex attraction at an early age, whereas others do not recall having such feelings until young adulthood. Most individuals do not disclose their same-sex preference to a best friend, peer, or sibling until a year or more after they have accepted their sexual orientation—between 16.5 and 19 years of age. Then, they typically wait another year or more to tell their parents, and typically confide in their mothers before their fathers (Savin-Williams & Cohen, 2004) (**FIGURE 16.19**).

Unfortunately, the process of coming out can disrupt the status quo of relationships with friends and families. LGBTQ+ youth reported widespread discrimination and victimization relative to heterosexual youth in a survey of over 55,000 individuals, with sexual minority boys being the most victimized (Russell et al., 2014). Parents too may respond to their adolescent's identity disclosures with anger, disappointment, and denial, with some parents viewing same-sex attractions as violating religious beliefs and family values (Puckett et al., 2015; Samarova, Shilo, & Diamond, 2013). Parents' negative reactions fall along a continuum from subtle **microaggressions**—intentional or unintentional insults—to outright violence (Garnter & Sterzing, 2018).

Fortunately, few parents respond to their adolescents' coming out with outright rejection. Most attempt to be accepting, some are slightly rejecting, and others are at first disbelieving but eventually accept their child's identity. LGBTQ+ adolescents who feel accepted by their families and people close to them show greater self-esteem, psychological well-being, and general health status, and less depression, substance abuse, anxiety, and suicidal ideation compared to adolescents who feel rejected or victimized (van Beusekom et al., 2015; Legate, Ryan, & Rogge, 2017; Ryan et al., 2010).

✓ CHECK YOUR UNDERSTANDING 16.15

1. What are four main types of sexual orientation?
2. Can a person's sexual identity change over time? Explain.
3. Why do LGBTQ+ teens find it especially difficult to talk to others about their sexual orientation?
4. Describe the multiple milestones involved in the process of coming out.

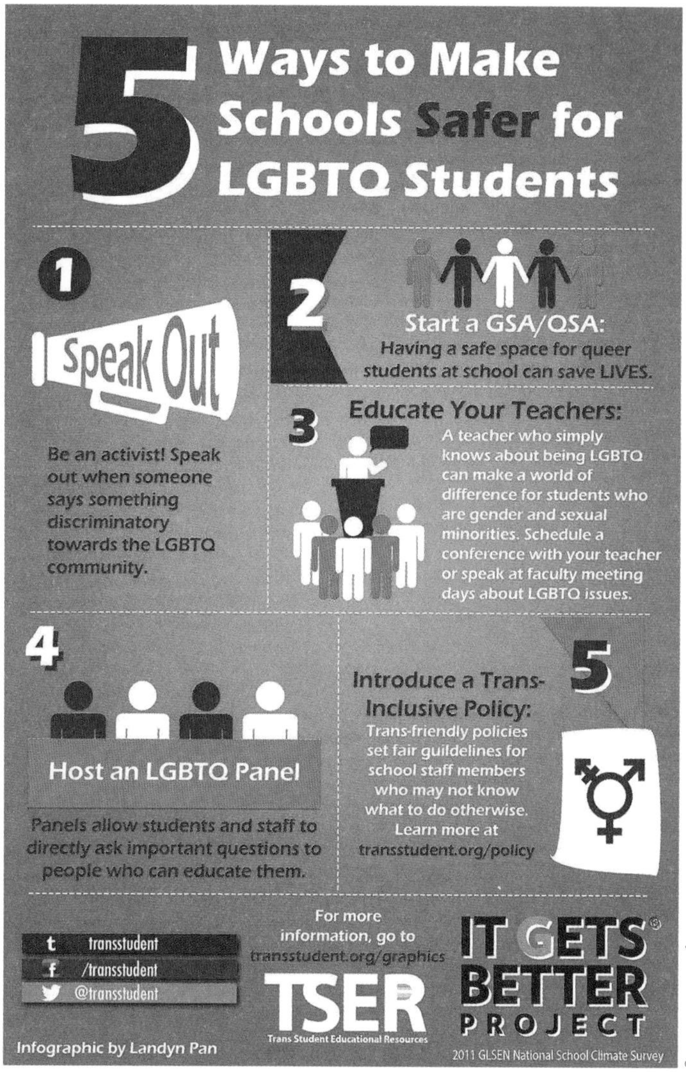

Romantic Relationships

LEARNING OBJECTIVE 16.16 Distinguish among different types of romantic relationships in terms of level of sexual activity and depth of commitment, and describe how romantic relationships change over adolescent development.

The sexual feelings of puberty pave the way for romantic relationships. When do adolescents enter romantic relationships, what meaning do those relationships have for teens, and how do romantic relationships change over time?

Dating and Sexual Activity

Adolescents differ in the onset and extent of their romantic experiences, with cultural norms and expectations shaping teens' relationship and sexual behaviors (see Chapter 14). Indeed, definitions around romantic relationships have changed dramatically over the past decades. Your grandparents might have shared symbols of romantic commitment, such as wearing a class ring to indicate their dating status, and they might have mutually agreed on "going steady" and being exclusive in a fairly formal way. In contrast, formalities around dating may be rare today. In fact, the percentage of U.S. high school adolescents who reported "never dating" has increased over the past several decades (Child Trends, 2018; Rowley & Hertzog, 2016) (**FIGURE 16.20**).

FIGURE 16.19 Coming out. Coming out is easier in a tolerant society. Various organizations and educational platforms seek to support the experiences of trans and gender non-conforming adolescents. One such organization is Trans Student Educational Resources (TSER), a youth-led organization with a mission to transform the educational environment for trans and gender non-conforming students.

microaggressions Intentional or unintentional insults

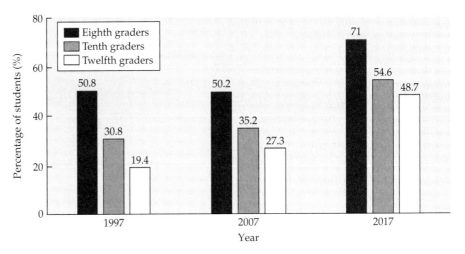

FIGURE 16.20 Adolescent reports of never dating. Compared to past decades, a greater percentage of U.S. adolescents today report never having dated someone romantically. (Data from Child Trends' original analysis of data from Monitoring the Future: A Continuing Study of American Youth, 1976-2017, Appendix 1. Accessed 8/18/21. https://www.childtrends.org/indicators/dating.)

As you might expect, sexual activity increases with age and follows a general sequence in the United States from light to heavy activities (Furman, Schaffer, & Florsheim, 2003; Connolly et al., 2004). A majority of young adolescents (ages 13–15) report engaging in light heterosexual activities, such as attending mixed-gender events and organized outings and sometimes hugging, kissing, and holding hands. Fewer young adolescents report heavy dating activities, such as going out alone with a boy or girl at night and engaging in petting and/or genital contact. By middle adolescence, U.S. teens begin to establish one-on-one relationships, and by late adolescence and young adulthood, relationships become increasingly intimate sexually (Owen et al., 2010). Notably, trends in sexual activity mirror trends for dating, with the percentage of sexually active adolescents decreasing over the past several decades. Unfortunately, however, fewer sexually active youth report having used a condom during their last intercourse experience when compared with previous years (CDC Youth Risk Behavior Survey, 2017) (**FIGURE 16.21**).

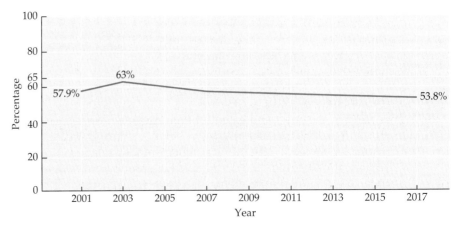

FIGURE 16.21 Unprotected sexual activity. Although over 50% of adolescents reported using a condom during their last sexual intercourse, the number has been on a downward trend since 2003. (After CDC. 2018. 2017 National Youth Risk Behavior Survey (YRBS), Trends in Sexual Risk Behaviors Among Youth: 2001-2017. Accessed August 2, 2021. https://www.cdc.gov/nchhstp/newsroom/2018/2017-YRBS.html.)

The Blurred Boundaries of Romantic Relationships

Compared to the past, relationships today are characterized by greater ambiguity in their boundaries and commitments. That is not to say that monogamous and committed relationships are uncommon, but rather that many adolescents and young adults understand and accept that relationships may involve sexual activity (light or heavy) without an exclusive commitment. For the most part, when adolescents today talk about their romantic or dating relationships, they refer to many possibilities, including "having a thing," "hooking up," and for some, dating (Rowley & Hertzog, 2016). Hooking up illustrates the ambiguity of some relationships. The type of physical contact involved in hooking up ranges from kissing to petting to oral sex or intercourse, even though there is no commitment between partners and no anticipated future (Bisson & Levine, 2009; Rowley & Hertzog, 2016).

Like "hooking up," college students are also familiar with the term "friends with benefits (FWBs)." In this type of relationship, sex is a part of a comfortable relationship that does not come with any demands (Armstrong, Hamilton, & England, 2010; Fortunato et al., 2010). Of course, nothing is ever easy, and the uncomplicated convenience of hooking up or having friends with benefits can be emotionally stressful. Teen girls are less likely than teen boys to feel positively about such relationships (Rowley & Hertzog, 2016). Indeed, teen girls experience sexual double standards that leave them vulnerable around their feelings of sexual desire and fears of being sexually objectified (Tolman & Chmielewski, 2019; Chmielewski, Tolman, & Kincaid, 2017).

Developmental Changes in Romantic Relationships

How do romantic relationships change across development? Most centrally, they last longer and grow in mutual support and intimacy as adolescents mature and draw on the lessons they have learned from the past (Lantagne & Furman, 2017; Meier & Allen, 2009).

A longitudinal study spanning adolescence through young adulthood shed light on how age and relationship length jointly influence relationship quality (Lantagne & Furman, 2017). Long-term relationships and perceptions of partner support increased with age. However, longer relationships also involved more negative interactions and greater feelings of jealousy than did shorter ones, especially for young teens, who may not have been ready to handle the intense emotions that accompany long relationships (**FIGURE 16.22**). In contrast, although older teens and young adults also experienced jealousy and negative interactions in long relationships, they did so less often than did younger teens. What do these observations tell us? They underscore the importance of experience and maturity. Older adolescents and young adults are (relatively) psychologically equipped to manage their emotions and deal with conflicts in relationships. But, young teens, although capable of intense feelings and sexuality, may not yet be able to curb negative emotions such as jealousy.

✓ CHECK YOUR UNDERSTANDING 16.16

1. How do romantic relationships today differ from those in the past?
2. What factors affect an adolescent's feelings of jealousy?

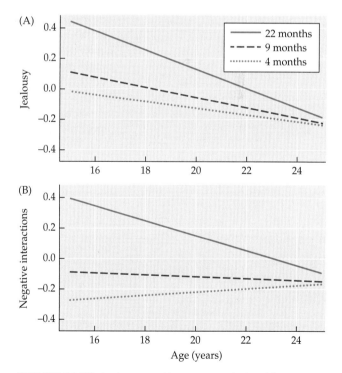

FIGURE 16.22 Jealousy and long-term relationships. Long-term relationships are characterized by more jealousy and negative interactions, particularly for young adolescents who may not have the psychological maturity to handle conflicts in committed relationships. (After A. Lantagne and W. Furman. 2017. *Dev Psychol* 53: 1738–1749. © 2017 by American Psychological Association. Reproduced with permission.)

looking-glass self An individual's self-identity based on others' perceptions and treatment

Contexts of Self-Identity

In 1902, sociologist Charles Horton Cooley proposed the notion of a **looking-glass self**: Our sense of self-identity is shaped by our perceptions of how others view and treat us. Indeed, we may be more powerfully influenced by what other people *think* about us than by the person we are inside. And so, the people who interact with an adolescent on a daily basis are pivotal to an adolescent's self-identity.

Family Context of Self-Identity

LEARNING OBJECTIVE 16.17 Identify ways in which parents and other family members influence adolescents' self-identity development.

Parents and other family members can obstruct or support an adolescent's achievement of a coherent self-identity. Parents who are overly protective and controlling increase chances their adolescents will have a foreclosed identity status (Berzonsky & Adams, 1999). Perhaps they force their adolescents to pursue certain majors or determine their adolescents' friends, outings, curfews, and future plans, which leave little room for the adolescent to take responsibility for their own decisions. Conversely, adolescents who are granted autonomy and feel that their family members have their backs are better able to handle developmental challenges and achieve a sense of efficacy in the face of difficulty (Huang, 2010; Laible, Carlo, & Roesch, 2004).

Family members also influence adolescent ethnic identity. Parents convey important messages that can influence an adolescent's exploration, resolution, and affirmation of ethnic identity (Umaña-Taylor, O'Donnell, et al., 2014). For example, a parent may talk about family heritage, fill the home with artifacts of the culture, speak the native language, cook ethnic meals, plan family gatherings where relatives share stories of their cultural histories, and encourage the adolescent to embrace where they came from. Such behaviors foster adolescents' pride in their culture and help establish a positive ethnic identity (Umaña-Taylor, Bhanot, & Shin, 2006).

When adolescents from minority and immigrant backgrounds experience self-doubt in the face of discrimination, parents can reduce or amplify adolescent stress by the environments they provide. For example, Black adolescents in the rural South who experienced high discrimination and low emotional support from their parents showed premature biological aging of their cells and health problems (e.g., Brody et al., 2014; Brody, Miller, & Yu, 2016). In contrast, adolescents who experienced discrimination, but had the support of their parents, were buffered from health problems.

✓ CHECK YOUR UNDERSTANDING 16.17

1. How might an adolescent benefit by strongly identifying with his or her family's values? Offer an example.

School Context of Self-Identity

LEARNING OBJECTIVE 16.18 Describe ways in which an adolescent's sense of self-identity can be both challenged and fostered in the school environment.

School transitions are turning points. School experiences can foster positive growth or instigate temporary setbacks in adolescent self-esteem and self-identity. Most adolescents experience one or more school transitions: the transition to middle school around early adolescence and transition to high school a few years later. School transitions require adolescents to adjust to unfamiliar people, new spaces and classrooms, challenging academic requirements, and perhaps changes to their relative peer status—from being among the "oldest" in one school to the "youngest" in the next. How adolescents adjust to changing school settings depends on a school's resources and ethnic composition.

Impoverished school settings can take a toll on adolescent self-esteem. Adolescents who attended low-quality schools showed long-lasting declines to self-esteem, in part because they were unable to establish the friendships needed to feel good about themselves (Seidman et al., 1994; Wigfield, Byrnes, & Eccles, 2006).

A school's ethnic composition likewise shapes adolescent ethnic identity development. Adolescents who attend high schools in which their ethnic group is a numerical minority show heightened exploration of their ethnicity (Umaña-Taylor et al., 2009). Perhaps, ethnicity prompts adolescents to reflect about their heritage in unique ways relative to contexts where ethnic differences are not as pronounced (Pahl & Way, 2006). When students of an ethnic minority are surrounded by peers from the same ethnicity, they may be buffered from discrimination, victimization, exclusion, and feelings of alienation (Benner & Crosnoe, 2011; Fleischmann et al., 2012). Similarly, immigrant students of ethnic minorities in England, Germany, the Netherlands, and Sweden who were surrounded by a high proportion of co-ethnic peers showed high adjustment (Geven, Kalmijn, & Tubergen, 2016).

✓ **CHECK YOUR UNDERSTANDING 16.18**

1. In what ways might the school context affect the development of self-esteem? Provide an example.
2. In what ways might the school context affect ethnic identity? Provide an example.

Cultural Context of Self-Identity

LEARNING OBJECTIVE 16.19 Discuss cultural differences in the importance of self-esteem and self-enhancement goals.

Most people agree that self-esteem is central to mental health. And research backs this up. For the most part, self-esteem is strongly endorsed in cultural communities that value "individualism"—as expressed in personal achievement, independence, and autonomy—including European American, middle-income communities in the United States and communities in Western Europe. In such contexts, adults often use praise to bolster their children's sense of self-worth (Hadley, Hair, & Moore, 2008). In turn, many U.S. teenagers seek positive feedback and reject negative statements about the self (Farruggia et al., 2004). Essentially, **self-enhancement goals**—the motivation to make people feel good about themselves and to maintain self-esteem—are a top priority in many communities (Markus & Kitayama, 2010).

However, not all cultural communities are motivated by self-enhancement goals and seeking high self-esteem. Some cultural communities may even consider high self-esteem to be harmful because it risks producing self-absorbed children (Miller et al., 2002). Communities that promote principles of "collectivism" (more so than individualism) value group harmony, humility, and interdependence (Triandis, 1995; Hofstede, 2011), and are not as concerned about adolescents' pursuit of self-identity and self-esteem (**FIGURE 16.23**). In fact, East Asians, who emphasize collectivism, or the group, over the individual, display lower scores on self-enhancement goals and self-evaluations than do Westerners (Falk & Heine, 2015).

self-enhancement goals Goals or motivations that focus on feeling good about the self and achieving high self-esteem

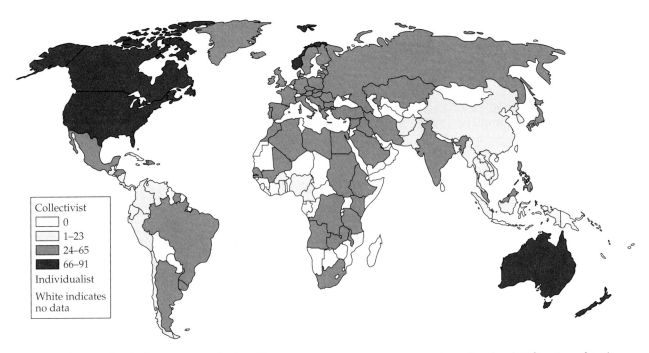

FIGURE 16.23 Individualism versus collectivism.
Cultures that emphasize collectivist goals place greater emphasis on group harmony than do cultures that emphasize individualism, where personal choice and autonomy are more strongly valued. (After G. Hofstede. The 6-D model of national culture. Accessed August 3, 2021. https://geerthofstede.com/culture-geert-hofstede-gert-jan-hofstede/6d-model-of-national-culture/.).

✓ **CHECK YOUR UNDERSTANDING 16.19**

1. How might the concept of self-identity develop differently in a collectivist culture as opposed to one founded on principles of individualism?

2. Why are some cultural communities not motivated by self-enhancement goals?

■ *Social Relationships*

Social relationships with parents and peers undergo major transformation during adolescence. As adolescents search for a unique self-identity, their interactions with peers become an important staging area for trying out different selves: ways to act, dress, talk, laugh, think, eat, and feel. Time with friends increases as time with parents and family members declines. Sometimes, family time becomes a hassle to adolescents—half eaten meals are interrupted by texts from friends with a dash out the door and plea to parents: "Don't wait up for me!" And, even when adolescents spend time at home, they may be preoccupied with social media as a way to maintain connection with friends, which sometimes backfires.

For many parents, the realization that they are no longer at the center of their children's lives can be difficult. Yet, the adolescent's desire for independence and gravitation toward peers is normal and essential to their quest for a unique self-identity. And, although adolescents may seek emotional independence and engage in behaviors that bring stress to family relationships, most continue to rely on their parents or other caregivers for emotional support, guidance, and financial assistance. In essence, adolescence marks the blurred boundary between the dependence of childhood and the independence of adulthood. It is a time, metaphorically speaking, when parents are expected to bring home the bacon but to leave the kitchen so the adolescent can take charge of the cooking.

Relationships with Parents and Siblings

Take a few minutes to reflect on your childhood and adolescent years. Who influenced you the most? Do those individuals continue to influence you today? Sometimes, it may feel as though you are in a time warp, with the voices of your past injecting into your interactions with friends and romantic partners. For some, that's a good thing. For others, relationships with parents and siblings may stir up self-doubt or anger.

Closeness and Attachment to Parents

LEARNING OBJECTIVE 16.20 Discuss evidence suggesting that close relationships with parents support adolescents' successful transition to adulthood.

For most of the twentieth century, adolescence was considered to be a period of emotional turbulence and conflict with parents (Coleman, 1961; Freud, 1958). Fortunately, little evidence points to doom and gloom in the adolescent-parent relationship. Most adolescents feel emotionally close to their parents, and the vast majority turn to their parents for advice and support. And parents reciprocate these feelings of closeness. When interviewed about their relationships with one another, parents and adolescents describe one another as friends (Solomon et al., 2002). And positive feelings toward parents yield benefits: Adolescents who view their parents as warm and loving are less likely than peers who view their parents as harsh or cold to engage in externalizing behaviors, such as acting out at school and fighting with peers and adults (Padilla-Walker & Christensen, 2011).

Unsurprisingly then, attachment quality is an important feature of the adolescent-parent relationship, just as it was for infants and children (see Chapters 7, 10, and 13). And researchers have developed unique ways to study adolescents' attachment to parents, such as asking teens to talk about their childhood memories and how those affect their current relationships. The **Adult Attachment Interview**, developed by Mary Main, classifies adolescents' and young adults' attachment relationships through a series of open-ended questions (Fisher, 2017; George, Kaplan, & Main, 1985; Main & Goldwyn, 1994). This interview generates three attachment categories:

- *Autonomous.* Autonomous adolescents value their parents, view them to be influential and supportive, and describe their relationship as balanced (neither overly idealizing nor criticizing).

- *Dismissive.* Dismissive adolescents minimize negative aspects of their relationships with parents and deny that their parents have an impact on their development. They may selectively "forget" negative interactions with their parents, report contradictory information, and be defensive in their descriptions.

- *Preoccupied.* Preoccupied adolescents are obsessively concerned about their relationships with parents. They have angry or ambivalent representations of their past, provide incoherent descriptions of their relationships with parents, and are unable to move beyond their negative experiences.

Adult Attachment Interview (AAI) A method for assessing attachment status in adolescents and young adults through open-ended questions about early childhood experiences; the AAI classifies an individual's attachment status as autonomous, dismissive, or preoccupied

✓ CHECK YOUR UNDERSTANDING 16.20

1. What does the Adult Attachment Interview measure?

Conflict with Parents

LEARNING OBJECTIVE 16.21 Discuss the types of conflicts adolescents have with their parents.

Being close to one's parents does not imply the absence of conflict. In fact, adolescents may argue with their parents in the process of negotiating power and authority around who will decide what (Weymouth et al., 2016). However, counter to the idea that conflict involves extreme turmoil, the majority of disagreements between adolescents and their parents revolve around everyday issues, such as chores, what teens wear, messy rooms, hygiene, curfew, and appropriate behaviors (Collins & Laursen, 2004; Smetana, 2011). Such everyday conflicts are both normative and a healthy part of the adolescent's quest for autonomy. Thus, although teens may accept their parents' authority, they may oppose parents making rules without their input. By contrast, parents believe that making rules comes with the turf of being a parent. Herein lies the conflict.

In the end, what matters most is how adolescents and parents resolve their disputes, not whether they disagree (they will!). Dysfunctional adolescent-parent conflicts that are highly negative, intense, and (in rare instances) involve violence can cascade to adolescent psychological maladjustment and behavior problems (Moed et al., 2015; Weymouth et al., 2016).

✓ CHECK YOUR UNDERSTANDING 16.21

1. What does parent-adolescent conflict look like, and how might it relate to adolescent adjustment?

Parental Monitoring and Adolescent Disclosure

LEARNING OBJECTIVE 16.22 Compare and contrast the kind of information a parent gets from an adolescent through solicitation versus disclosure.

As a parent, I wanted to know where my adolescent children were going, what they were doing, and with whom they were spending time. I would ask lots of questions, but to my dismay, only received answers some of the time. Developmental researchers refer to parents' attempts to gather information about their children's everyday activities as **monitoring** (Dishion & McMahon, 1998) (see Chapter 13). **Parent solicitation** refers to the monitoring strategy of asking questions to obtain information.

Although adolescents often gripe about the nosiness of their parents, monitoring in moderation is effective. Monitoring communicates a parent's love and concern, keeps parents informed, and can prevent adolescents from engaging in dangerous behaviors. Indeed, parental monitoring predicts low levels of adolescent antisocial behaviors, low substance use, and high academic achievement, just as low parental monitoring relates to adolescent susceptibility toward substance use and peer pressure (Fairlie, Wood, & Laird, 2012; Kiesner, Poulin, & Dishion, 2010; Padilla-Walker et al., 2011). Moreover, parental monitoring may help adolescents to regulate their internet use. Parents who establish rules around adolescents' internet use and attempt to keep track of how much time adolescents spend online reduce the likelihood that their teens will spend excessive time online or experience online harassment (Khurana et al., 2015; Vaala & Bleakley, 2015).

But being aware of what is going on in an adolescent's life is not just a matter of monitoring. Adolescent **disclosure**, the willingness to divulge information to parents, strongly determines parental knowledge (Criss et al., 2015; Smetana et al., 2010). Teenagers sometimes intentionally hide information from parents or avoid parents' questions. Consequently, a parent may be ignorant about their

monitoring Caregiver awareness of children's activities, friends, and peer groups, including efforts to keep track of what is going on in children's lives

parent solicitation A monitoring strategy of asking questions to gather information

disclosure The willingness to reveal information to caregivers adolescent's activities because the teen decides to keep certain things secret—a failure of disclosure—rather than because the parent did not ask the right questions—a failure of solicitation.

Adolescents are masters at selective disclosure. As the popular saying goes, "What you don't know can't hurt you." Teens quickly become strategic about what to tell or not tell their parents (Moilanen et al., 2009; Spaeth, Weichold, & Silbereisen, 2015). They can formulate hypotheses about how their parents will react, consider the various possibilities, and then modify their behaviors accordingly. For example, a teen might reason that "If I tell my dad that no adults will be at the party, he won't let me go; so I simply won't tell him the party is unsupervised."

Of course, disclosure varies from person to person. Boys are more likely than girls to hide information from parents. Adolescents with difficult personalities, poor family relationships, problems with peers, and those who often get into trouble are unlikely to be forthcoming about what is going on in their lives (Padilla-Walker et al., 2011; Spaeth Weichold, & Silbereisen et al., 2015).

✓ CHECK YOUR UNDERSTANDING 16.22

1. Where would you draw the line with respect to parental monitoring?
2. What are the two key factors involved in what a parent knows about an adolescent's life?

Siblings

LEARNING OBJECTIVE 16.23 How is the sibling relationship unique to other relationships, and how does it change in adolescence?

Most research on family relationships spotlights parents. Yet, this leaves out immensely influential members of the family—siblings. Those of you who have siblings might agree that there are certain things that no one else can understand as much as your brother or sister. At the same time, perhaps no one else knows how to press your buttons more than a sibling who knows what bothers you. Let's consider what makes sibling relationships special, how they change over adolescence, and how they affect adolescent development.

A Special Relationship

Sibling relationships are different from all others. Siblings are typically present in one another's lives longer than anyone else (**FIGURE 16.24**). They commonly grow up together, likely outlive parents, and endure beyond many marriages and friendships (McHale & Crouter, 1996). Their common history—years of frequent contact, companionship, and shared experiences—creates a special bond and shared identity that involves both intense conflict and deep intimacy (Dunn, 1983; Stocker, Burwell, & Briggs, 2002). Sibling relationships are also unique because they are obligatory, not optional. A friend is a friend as long as you both work at the relationship. In contrast, regardless of life changes, and even if siblings grow distant physically or emotionally, they will always remain siblings because of the biological and legal bonds that connect them.

Adolescent Sibling Relationships

How might sibling relationships in adolescence differ from those of childhood? Although older siblings typically hold a more powerful position than do their younger siblings in childhood, they relinquish much of that power in adolescence. Sibling pairs who were followed longitudinally from 12 to 18 years of age reported declines in the relative power of older siblings as younger siblings grew in their competence and teenage siblings prepared for adulthood (Lindell & Campione-Barr, 2017).

FIGURE 16.24 Images of the author's three children at young and older ages.   Siblings share a special relationship, different than all others. They largely grow up together and have a history of shared experiences that creates a special bond that involves both intense conflict and deep intimacy. In the photos here, Michael (youngest), Christopher (middle child), and Brittany (oldest) pet their dog Comet at their neighborhood park. As teenagers and young adults, Brittany, Christopher (middle) and Michael (right) share a visit to Disney World.

Notably, the quality of sibling relationships affects how adolescents interact with their peers and romantic partners. Close sibling relationships enhance interpersonal skills and social confidence in adolescents' romantic relationships, and adolescents who feel in control of their sibling relationships also feel empowered and close in their relationships with romantic partners. Conversely, adolescents who report high sibling conflict report low romantic intimacy, which is especially true for teen girls (Doughty, McHale, & Feinberg, 2015; McHale, Udegraff, & Whiteman, 2012).

However, sibling relationships are nested within a family system, and adolescents who view their parents as treating siblings differently (perhaps by favoring one sibling over the other) may experience depressive symptoms and feelings of low self-worth and engage in risky behaviors such as substance use (Loeser, Whiteman, & McHale, 2016).

✓ CHECK YOUR UNDERSTANDING 16.23

1. Why is the sibling relationship unique?
2. How can sibling relationships affect romantic relationships?

Immigrant Context of the Adolescent-Parent Relationship

LEARNING OBJECTIVE 16.24 Identify challenges to the adolescent-parental relationship when adolescents are the children of first-generation immigrants.

We saw that some adolescents and parents experience minor bumps in the road, whereas others experience major hurdles and declining relationships. Navigating the sometimes tumultuous parent-adolescent relationship may be especially challenging for teens from immigrant U.S. families, where cultural expectations at home may differ from those outside the home, and where teens may perceive their parents to be unfairly strict compared to parents of their peers.

As one example, many adolescents from first-generation Asian American families report high conflict and alienation in their relationships with parents because they perceive the expectations of their family to differ from those of their peers' families (Qin, Way, & Mukherjee, 2008). Developmental scientist Desiree Qin explored Asian American immigrant adolescents' perceptions of alienation through qualitative interviews in which she asked adolescents to talk in depth about their family relationships (Qin, 2008; Qin et al., 2012). Many U.S. Chinese adolescents observed that their parents' belief systems stood in opposition to their U.S. experiences. One teen noted: "It's like they lived in different times and have different expectations of life. It doesn't matter where they are in the world, their expectations of certain things wouldn't be different. They expect you to behave in ways that they are used to."

Several adolescents talked about how child-rearing practices in China and the United States differ, and how those differences created a wedge in their relationships with parents.

- "The way of teaching a child is different in China. In America, you teach them. You don't force them and stuff. So it just don't match . . . . I grew up in China but I really grew up mentally in here. So we got like different ways and stuff so it don't match. So we just like don't like each other."

- "Main conflicts around . . . the way she gets really angry like at a failing grade . . . I don't know what I'm afraid of, but whenever I get a bad grade, I just feel so bad about it. And I wouldn't tell my mom sometimes. And like if she finds out, she just like yells at me, and asks me why I did that."

- "Parents from China, they tend to yell at the kids for hours and hours . . . and Chinese parents often lack communications with their kids. In contrast, American parents sometimes do have more communication. They talk more to each other."

- "American parents are nicer. They treat their children as if they were their friends. They can talk about anything. Chinese parents are very strict. They yell at or lecture their kids all the time. Chinese parents do not allow their children to reason with them. When you reason with them, they then say you are talking back at them."

These poignant quotes capture the struggle that U.S. Chinese adolescents may experience in navigating the mismatch between Chinese and U.S. culture. Despite their parents' best intentions and high expectations for their children, adolescents may respond with feelings of disconnect and emotional distancing. However, although gaps in communication may be more magnified for adolescents who confront differences in cultural expectations both within and outside the home, such communication gaps are also typical of adolescent-parent relationships more generally.

✓ **CHECK YOUR UNDERSTANDING 16.24**

1. How can cultural background affect the parental-adolescent relationship?

Relationships with Peers

You may be familiar with the classic 2004 film *Mean Girls* (which became a Broadway show in 2019), a comedy about the harmful social consequences of high school cliques. The film depicts Cady, a 16-year-old girl, who attends a public school for the first time after being home schooled for 12 years in Africa by her zoologist parents. She is warned to steer clear of "The Plastics," an exclusive clique led by Regina, a wealthy, beautiful girl. To Cady's delight, Regina befriends her, offering Cady the alluring chance to join the cool crowd. Cady quickly abandons her old friends, becomes superficial, and reinvents herself in Regina's image. From there on, acts of revenge and mischief unravel on all sides—tricks to get Regina to put on weight, attempts to steal boyfriends, a wild party in the absence of parents, drinking, lies, rumors, duplicity, riots, deception, betrayal, and a severe accident that results in a broken spine—all in the name of fitting in, being a part of the popular crowd, and garnering the approval of peers.

Despite the predictability of its plot, *Mean Girls* fittingly reveals the power of peers and adolescents' acute sensitivity to status and popularity differences among their schoolmates (**FIGURE 16.25**). Most of us recall experiences in which our peers engaged in reproachable behaviors, such as following the crowd by bullying, shoplifting when dared, or driving recklessly, merely to gain approval and/or avoid rejection. For the most part, however, peers do more good than harm, especially those who are close friends.

FIGURE 16.25 Mean Girls.   As evidenced in *Mean Girls*, peer groups often exhibit conformity in dress and actions.

Friendships

LEARNING OBJECTIVE 16.25 Discuss how friendships mature in adolescence and yet still reveal certain limitations in maturity.

Friendships are central to adolescent well-being, reaching depths well beyond those of children. Friends can be counted on to listen to dreams, applaud efforts, forgive sins, and wipe away tears—to share in the joys and commiserate in the falls. Perhaps this is why adolescents without close friends suffer psychologically and are

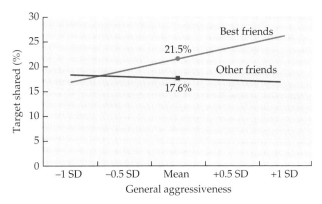

FIGURE 16.26 Compatibility. Adolescent friends tend to be highly similar across many behaviors, including aggression. As seen in the figure, best friends who were high on aggression relative to their peers (represented on the x axis) tended to display aggression toward the same people as one another (% of shared targets), more so than did other friends. Note that values to the right of the x-axis "mean" represent scores of higher-than-average levels of aggression (After N. A. Card and E. V. Hodges. 2006. *Dev Psychol* 42: 1327–1338. Copyright © 2006 by American Psychological Association. Reproduced with permission.)

at risk for negative outcomes for years to come (Erath et al., 2010). When researchers compare the friendships of teens to those of children, they observe several significant developments in compatibility, stability, reciprocity, and individuality.

- *Compatibility.* As discussed in Chapter 13, friends tend to be similar to one another. By adolescence, similarities extend to attitudes about school, sports, leisure time activities, and academic goals; they also extend to negative behaviors such as aggression, bullying, and risk-taking behaviors (Card & Hodges, 2006; Ellis & Zarbatany, 2007; Hafen et al., 2011) (**FIGURE 16.26**).

- *Stability.* Adolescents recognize that friendships endure over time and space, which contrasts with the relatively fragile and transient friendships of childhood (Bukowski, Laursen, & Rubin, 2019). Adolescents go to great lengths to maintain contact and intimacy with their friends, whereas children have not yet developed a full appreciation of stability in friendship.

- *Reciprocity.* Adolescent friendship depends on reciprocated trust and intimacy. However, the value adolescents place on mutual trust makes them vulnerable to perceived and actual betrayal by their peers (Way, 2006).

- *Respect for individuality.* Erikson (1963) noted that in mature relationships, people are simultaneously able to express their own views and respect the views of others. However, it is not until the end of adolescence that teenagers recognize that they can embrace others' individuality without losing their own uniqueness (Selman, 2017).

Because adolescent friendships take time to mature, adolescents often feel possessive and jealous of their friends (Parker et al., 2005). Adolescents get caught up in competing loyalties and must often decide whether to hang out with one friend or another. At the same time, they become distressed when their friends decide to hang out with someone else and sometimes perceive their friends' choices as betrayal. Online contexts spark even greater jealousy than face-to-face interactions, with 90% of adolescents reporting feelings of jealousy over the course of two weekends (Lennarz et al., 2017). And as the sparks of jealousy ignite, teens may experience tension and difficulties with friends, followed by further rejection and loneliness. However, older adolescents understand that no single relationship can fulfill all of one's needs, and so possessiveness and jealousy decline (Parker et al., 2005). Moreover, older adolescents are better able to evaluate online postings by friends than are younger adolescents: They recognize that their friends' attempts to portray themselves online in a positively skewed light may not reflect reality. Thus, experiences of jealousy during online interactions decline with adolescent age (Lennarz et al., 2017).

✓ CHECK YOUR UNDERSTANDING 16.25

1. In what ways do adolescent friendships differ from those of children and adults?

Cliques and Crowds

LEARNING OBJECTIVE 16.26 Describe the advantages and disadvantages of being part of a stable peer group.

Although we often spend time with a few close friends, much of our lives are spent in small or large groups that share common characteristics with us—whether it is the students in our classes, people at work, or co-members at a volunteer organization. Adolescents similarly organize their lives around groups, with cliques and crowds being two common forms (Brown & Dietz, 2009; Crabbe et al., 2019).

Cliques are relatively small friendship-based groups that contain intensive interactions and emotional involvement among group members. These small groups of about half a dozen members often are of the same gender and resemble one another in attitudes, interests, and family backgrounds.

Crowds are loosely connected groups of individuals who are not as close as the friends within a clique, but share reputation-based stereotypes (e.g., brains, jocks, emo/goths, druggies, loners, etc.) because of their shared attitudes or activities, and sometimes shared ethnic identity.

Crowds are less intimate than cliques, and many members may not even know or interact with one another. However, membership in a crowd gives adolescents an identity within a large, organized social structure (Rubin, Bukowski, & Bowker, 2015). That identity can be associated with a positive reputation, such as the reputation of debate team members, or negative one, such as the reputation of a college male athlete in a setting where harassment is high, regardless of a person's behaviors. In fact, most crowds carry stigmas that influence how peers judge and relate to one another. And, when situations are ambiguous, adolescents may resort to stereotypes to figure out who did what. For example, when a teen sees two peers fighting but has no information about who started the fight, the teen might conclude that the "druggie" started the fight with the "brain." Such social stigmas perpetuate stereotypes and channel adolescents to relationships with peers who share a crowd label with them, which can discourage adolescents from exploring new identities and expanding their social networks (Rubin et al., 2015).

cliques Relatively small friendship-based groups characterized by intensive interactions and emotional involvement among group members

crowds Loosely connected groups of individuals who are not as close as friends in a clique but share activities and interests and sometimes ethnicity

✓ CHECK YOUR UNDERSTANDING 16.26

1. What were some of the peer groups at your high school? Describe two to three of these groups and the degree to which they were exclusive, and why.
2. Is conformity in high school harmful or helpful? Why?

Bullying

LEARNING OBJECTIVE 16.27 Define various types of bullying.

The ugly face of adolescent peer relationships surfaces in the alarming prevalence of bullying at this time in development (Holt et al., 2017). A report on national rates of bullying revealed that 71% of middle school and high school students reported being bullied at school (U.S. Department of Education, 2019). Bullying peaks at 37% of students in middle school and levels off to about 22% of students by twelfth grade, with 8% of students reporting daily experiences of bullying (Robers et al., 2015; U.S. Department of Education, 2015). And, perpetrators of bullying find many ways to torment their victims, with some tactics being overt and others subtle (Wang, Iannotti, & Nansel, 2009):

- *physical aggression*, such as punching a peer;
- *verbal aggression*, such as threatening or insulting a peer;
- *relational aggression*, such as excluding peers from activities or spreading rumors about them; and
- *cyberbullying*, such as engaging in aggressive acts through texts or social media posts.

Over the course of adolescence, physical and verbal aggression—the "direct" forms of bullying—decrease, at the same time that relational aggression—the "indirect" forms of bullying—increases (Yeager et al., 2015) **(FIGURE 16.27)**. Cyberbullying is likewise on the rise, corresponding to increased use of social media by adolescents. How often adolescents are cyberbullied is difficult to estimate, because studies vary in how questions are asked, the type of cyberbullying

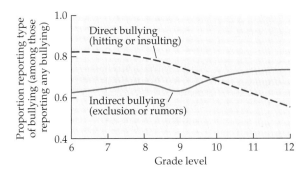

FIGURE 16.27 The form of bullying changes across development. Over the course of adolescence, direct bullying decreases at the same time that indirect bullying increases. (After D. S. Yeager et al. 2015. *J Appl Dev Psychol* 37: 36–51.)

being investigated, populations studied, and the time frame of questions (such as, were you bullied in the past week, month, etc.). Thus, prevalence rates differ enormously across studies—ranging from 1% to 72%, but with overall rates likely in the range of 10%–40% of adolescents (Kowalski et al., 2014; Selkie, Fales, & Moreno, 2016; Ybarra et al., 2012). Nonetheless, a substantial percentage of adolescents are perpetrators or victims of cyberbullying. Cyberbullying is especially painful because rumors may spread through social networks instantaneously (see Table 13.4). Perhaps this is why cyberbullying leads to more negative outcomes than does physical bullying (Litwiller & Brausch, 2013).

Most people find bullying appalling, particularly when carried out by adolescents who should know better. Why would anyone be so aggressive toward another person? What possible benefits does bullying yield? Unfortunately, aggression benefits perpetrators by enhancing power in relationships, elevating status among peers, and providing access to resources (Volk, Dane, & Marini, 2014).

So what can be done to prevent adolescents from victimizing one another? To reach adolescents, programs must be developmentally appropriate and psychologically wise (Swearer et al., 2017; Yeager et al., 2015). One promising intervention aims to teach adolescents that personality is malleable such that people can change how they act. These types of messages may reduce adolescents' responses to conflict and help victims and perpetrators alike (Yeager, 2017).

✓ CHECK YOUR UNDERSTANDING 16.27

1. Why do aggressive behaviors tend to emerge in adolescence? Categorize various kinds of aggression.
2. What policies might a school consider implementing to ensure inclusiveness in group activities?

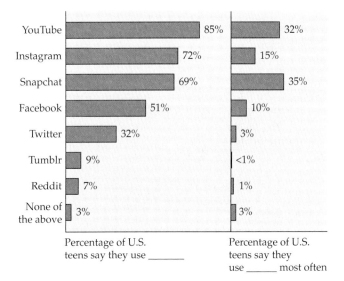

FIGURE 16.28 Social media use by teens. Use of social media is common and increasing among teens. (After Pew Research Center. 2018. Teens, Social Media and Technology 2018. Pew Research Center, Washington, D.C. May 31, 2018. https://www.pewresearch.org/internet/2018/05/31/teens-social-media-technology-2018/.)

Social Media

Social media and networking sites have surged in popularity around the globe as a way to share feelings and experiences (**FIGURE 16.28**). The majority of middle school students in the United States have their own profile page on a social networking site; 95% of U.S. adolescents have access to a smart phone; and nearly half of U.S. adolescents report using the internet "almost constantly" (Anderson & Jiang, 2018; Espinoza & Juvonen, 2011; Twenge, Spitzberg, & Campbell, 2019). Social media allows for social connection and a sense of autonomy, but adolescents may have problems in overuse, disclosure of inappropriate information, exposure to harmful content, and bullying and victimization (Bleakley et al., 2014; Madden et al., 2012).

Benefits of Social Media Use

LEARNING OBJECTIVE 16.28 Describe some positive aspects of social media use in adolescents.

Online social networking provides adolescents with emotional connection and fosters prosocial behavior, positive self-esteem, and opportunities for self-disclosure (Best, Manktelow, & Taylor, 2014; Cao & Lin, 2015). The online environment may be especially important during adolescence, a time in development when individuals seek to establish unique identities, goals for the future, and relationships with peers (Uhls, Ellison, & Subramahnyam, 2017).

Furthermore, the use of social media may be a protective factor for individuals who otherwise experience geographic isolation or feel socially isolated, including those who identify as LGBTQ+ (Escobar-Viera et al., 2018). Indeed, LGBTQ+ individuals engage with social media more often than do heterosexual individuals (Pew Research Center, 2018), perhaps because social media allows them to more easily disclose their sexual orientation and gain support from others (Escobar-Viera et al., 2018; Haimson et al., 2015; Primack & Escobar-Viera, 2017).

✓ CHECK YOUR UNDERSTANDING 16.28

1. In what ways can social media use benefit adolescents?

Overuse of Social Media

LEARNING OBJECTIVE 16.29 Provide evidence of the drawbacks of overuse of social media.

Parents, teachers, educators, developmental scientists, and even adolescents often wonder when social media use crosses the fine line to overuse. Teenagers may depend on social media to the point that it can be labeled a behavioral addiction (Kuss & Griffiths, 2011) (**FIGURE 16.29**). Researchers have developed various surveys to study overuse, with problems suggested when teenagers respond in the affirmative to statements such as:

- I use social media as a way of making me feel good.
- I get into arguments with other people about the amount of time I spend on social media.
- I prefer to spend time on social media rather than attend social activities/events.
- If I can't access social media, I feel moody and irritable.

Overuse can be problematic because it detracts from time for hobbies, sports, clubs, family, chores, schoolwork, and face-to-face interactions with peers, and can snowball into mental health problems. Indeed, overuse of digital media displaces adolescent face-to-face interactions, leading to low socializing and high feelings of isolation and loneliness (Boyd, 2014; Twenge et al., 2019).

Consider, for example, the negative impacts of overuse of social media by Canadian adolescents. About 20% of teens reported infrequent or no use of social media; a little more than 50% reported using social media for 2 hours or less per day; and a little more than 25% of teens reported using social media for more than 2 hours per day. Adolescents who spent more than 2 hours per day on social media were more likely than those in the other two groups to report mental health problems ranging from psychological distress to suicidal thoughts (Sampasa-Kanyinga & Lewis, 2015). Indeed, overuse of social media and the internet is associated with various psychological problems (e.g., Giota & Kleftaras, 2013; Vernon, Barber, & Modecki, 2015; Tsitsika et al., 2014), including the following:

- depression,
- low self-esteem,
- low social empathic skills and low life satisfaction,
- sleep disturbances and low school satisfaction, and
- generally high dysfunctional internet behaviors, including online gambling.

FIGURE 16.29 Social media can be addicting and dangerous.   Some teenagers may devote so much time and effort to social networking it can be labeled a behavioral addiction.

Additionally, consider the types of body images that adolescents are likely to encounter when they surf the internet and browse social media. Preoccupation with social media goes hand-in-hand with poor body image concerns in teenage girls. Studies have shown that middle school and high school girls who spent a lot of time online had internalized a thin ideal of body image, were unhappy with their weight, and dieted to achieve the ideal body (Meier & Gray, 2014; Tiggemann & Slater, 2014).

This is not to say that media use *causes* psychological problems in adolescents. Teenagers who are socially rejected, feel isolated, have problems in academics, suffer from low self-esteem, and/or have a poor body image may turn to social media for virtual companionship and as an escape from their problems, and they may use social media inappropriately. As we have seen before, many influences on development are bidirectional and can spiral into growing problems over time.

✓ CHECK YOUR UNDERSTANDING 16.29

1. What sort of problems are associated with the overuse of social media?

Disclosing Too Much Information

LEARNING OBJECTIVE 16.30 Describe why some adolescents may divulge too much information on social media and some of the dangers in doing so.

Teenagers mostly disclose relatively innocuous information on social media. However, a sizeable percentage of adolescents talk about or post photos or videos of drinking, substance use, and/or sexual activities (e.g., Egan & Moreno, 2011; Morgan, Snelson, & Elison-Bowers, 2010). Such inappropriate disclosures can place adolescents at risk with regard to later education or career advancement (Swzedo, Mikami, & Allen, 2012; Wilson, Gosling, & Graham, 2012). Most managers (93%) involved in job placement and recruitment stated that they review applicants' social profiles before making hiring decisions, and they hold posts of substance use and sexual activity against candidates (Davidson, 2014).

Why Do Some Teens Divulge Too Much?

Why would an adolescent jeopardize his or her future by posting too much information? Peers powerfully influence what adolescents disclose. Dutch adolescents who perceived their peers as approving of sex and as being sexually active were more likely to display romantic and sexual content in their profiles than were adolescents who did not perceive their peers as approving (Doornwaard et al., 2014).

A teenager's personality likewise relates to disclosing excessive and/or inappropriate information about sexuality, drinking, or substance use, as indicated by the online profiles of 13- to 18-year-olds (Liu, Ang, & Lwin, 2013). Adolescents with high **social anxiety**—a fear of interaction with other people and of being negatively judged that can lead to self-consciousness and social avoidance—had *low* online disclosure, largely because socially anxious teens were concerned about their privacy. In contrast, adolescents with high **narcissism**—a personality trait characterized by an inflated sense of importance, self-centeredness, and a strong need for admiration—disclosed excessive amounts of information. Perhaps, narcissistic adolescents' desire for social validation led them to high self-promotion to get attention (Carpenter, 2012).

Other adolescents may use social media to appear interesting, exciting, and popular as a way to cope with a fear of losing social power (Panek, Nardis, & Konrath, 2013). In fact, adolescents who fear losing power and have a narcissistic personality are likely to display excessive and inappropriate disclosure on social media to protect their self-image (Hawk et al., 2015).

social anxiety A mental health condition characterized by a fear of interaction with other people, feelings of embarrassment, and fear of being negatively judged, which may lead to social avoidance

narcissism A personality disorder marked by an exaggerated sense of importance, self-centeredness, and a strong need for admiration

Adolescents often present less authentic and nonrepresentative sides of themselves online to retain their social status (Lenhart et al., 2015). Notably, adolescents are aware of the social pressures and problems associated with social media use. They report that social media paints an unrealistic view of others' lives, is used to spread rumors, and harms social relationships because of the lack of in-person contact (Pew Research Center, 2018) (**FIGURE 16.30**).

Dangerous Encounters

Chat rooms, instant messaging, and social media can be a breeding ground for harassment by strangers, especially when teens divulge private information and encourage contact with people they do not know (Sengupta & Chaudhuri, 2011). Incidents of abuse on the internet are growing at an alarming rate, causing concern among parents and prompting legislation to regulate internet use among teenagers. A meta-analysis of several studies and over 37,000 adolescents found that 20% of adolescents experienced unwanted exposure to sexually explicit material and 11% experienced unwanted sexual solicitation during online activities (Madigan et al., 2018).

✓ CHECK YOUR UNDERSTANDING 16.30

1. Why are narcissistic individuals prone to divulging too much information online?
2. What are some of the dangers of divulging too much information online?

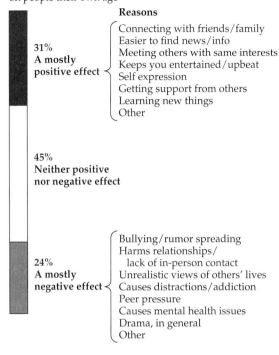

FIGURE 16.30 Teen views on social media use. Adolescents have mixed views on social media's effects on people their age. (After Pew Research Center. 2018. *Teens, Social Media and Technology 2018*. Pew Research Center, Washington, D.C. May 31, 2018. https://www.pewresearch.org/internet/2018/05/31/teens-social-media-technology-2018/.)

Developmental Cascades

I am an artist. Driven by passion, seized by obsession, delighted by creation, enthralled by expression, entranced by vision, diverted by daydreams, filled with emotion, fueled by compulsion, consumed with beauty, and blindsided by inspiration. Welcome to my mind.

(Anonymous)

I recently came across this quote and was struck by the parallels between the unknown author of the passage and the deeply feeling, sometimes confused, often inspired, and always passionate adolescent whom we learned about in this final chapter. Adolescence is a pivotal point in the life course, full of emotional and social excitement, temptations, and challenges at a time when hormones are running wild and the body and brain are rapidly changing. The daily experiences of adolescence—both good and bad—pave the way to adulthood, and hopefully to an individual who has established a solid sense of self and is capable of enduring, honest, and supportive friendships.

For most adolescents, navigating emotional and social hurdles provides a springboard for learning how to negotiate later relationships. For others, however, social and emotional difficulties may lead to a rocky future journey. Adolescents who experience depression without support; who encounter obstacles to their self-identity, sense of self-worth, and emerging sexuality; who reject their families or are rejected by them; and who are victimized or isolated by peers, or who bully and victimize others, are at risk for years to come. Let us consider how adolescents' emotional and social development can affect physical and psychological outcomes into adulthood, with examples from areas of depression and social relationships with parents and peers.

Cascades from Adolescent Depression and Self-Esteem

"All I want is for him to be happy," "I just want her to be okay, nothing more…" I have heard these pleas one too many times from family members and friends experiencing the pain of their teenager's depression and oftentimes, the low self-esteem that accompanies psychological distress. Such concerns serve as a constant reminder that the statistics on adolescent psychological health include our friends, relatives, children, and perhaps even ourselves. With timely intervention, adolescents can overcome their distress, but left unheeded, adolescent depression and low self-esteem can derail school performance, compromise psychological adjustment, and leave permanent scars on family and peer relationships.

Adolescents who experience depressive symptoms often have poor social relationships with peers and are at risk for behavioral problems such as stealing, delinquency, substance misuse, and aggression (e.g., Rudolph, Ladd, & Dinella, 2007; Wiesner & Kim, 2006). Some adolescents may come to rely on harmful behaviors to manage their symptoms, rather than addressing the underlying issues (Auerbach et al., 2015). Also troubling are the long-term consequences of adolescent depression. Adolescent depression predicts mental disorders, education and economic circumstances, and work impairment due to physical health, family circumstances, and partner relationships up to 20 years later (McLeod, Horwood, & Fergusson, 2016; Keenan-Miller, Hammen, & Brennan, 2007). Low self-esteem shows similar cascading influences to aggression, social withdrawal, depression, poor relationships with friends and romantic partners, substance misuse, weak employment prospects, and even bodily complaints and insomnia (e.g., Boden, Fergusson, & Horwood, 2008; Orth, Robins, & Roberts, 2008).

Moreover, longitudinal studies reveal reciprocal and snowballing effects between self-esteem and depression over time. A study of over 1,500 individuals followed from age 12 through age 35 found that low self-esteem between 15 and 18 years of age predicted depression at 21 years of age (Orth, Robins, & Roberts, 2008). Even more concerning: Low self-esteem between 12 and 16 years of age, and declining self-esteem across the adolescent years, predicted symptoms of depression two decades later when individuals were 35 years old (Steiger et al., 2014).

Cascades from Relationships with Parents

Although adolescents' relationships with parents change across development, the quality of those relationships can spill over to how adolescents interact with their peers. For example, adolescents with secure attachments to their parents are rated by their peers as high on prosocial behaviors and low on aggression relative to adolescents with dismissive or preoccupied attachments (Dykas, Ziv, & Cassidy, 2008).

Attachment to parents also shapes later adult romantic relationships. Jude Cassidy (2000) proposed a theoretical model to explain these potential connections. According to Cassidy, adolescents and adults who have a history of insecure attachment relationships with parents will selectively attend to, expect, and remember negative behaviors in their romantic partners, and will attribute those behaviors to negative intentions. For instance, if a romantic partner is late because of traffic, the insecurely attached adolescent or adult might attend selectively to the lateness (ignoring the dozens of times the romantic partner was on time), attribute the lateness to negative intentions (my partner doesn't care and wanted to be late), remember the event for months to come, and come to expect such behaviors in the future. These expectations of romantic partners then serve as a self-fulfilling prophecy: Romantic partners will eventually behave in ways that confirm the expectations of their partners. In contrast, adolescents and adults who have a history of secure attachments and view others as trustworthy selectively attend to, expect, and remember positive behaviors in their partners. Notably, research evidence supports the theorized connection from attachment with parents to romantic relationships. The quality of relationships 12- to 19-year-olds shared with their mothers and fathers predicted the quality of their romantic relationships when they were 25–32 years of age (Johnson & Galambos, 2014).

Cascades from Relationships with Peers

A sense of connectedness with peers goes a long way in supporting adolescent positive psychological functioning. By contrast, social isolation, victimization, or rejection by peers can cause a teen to turn to alcohol and other substances to escape psychological loneliness.

Social Isolation and Substance Use

In the 1970s Canadian psychologist Bruce Alexander conducted what became a seminal study on the role of social isolation on drug use in rats. Alexander theorized that drug use reflects a form of social helplessness, which challenged prevalent views that substance use was solely rooted in addiction. To test his hypothesis, Alexander built Rat Park, a spacious rat housing colony that contained food, play toys, and space, and rats of both sexes (**FIGURE 16.31**).

Rats living in Rat Park chose to drink plain tap water rather than water laced with morphine. In contrast, a control group of socially isolated rats chose to consume morphine. When a group of rats who had been forced to consume drugs daily for two months was moved out of social isolation to the socially stimulating Rat Park, they chose to drink tap water rather than water laced with morphine. Alexander concluded that the rats in Rat Park wanted morphine -laced water only if it did not disrupt their normal social behavior. Although the Rat Park study has been critiqued as being oversimplified based on its animal focus, it illuminates how relationships with peers can have cascading effects on an adolescent's susceptibility to harmful behaviors.

(A)   (B)

Courtesy of Bruce Alexander

FIGURE 16.31 Rat Park. (A) Caged and isolated male rats drank 19 times more morphine than did (B) socially content Rat Park male rats.

Victimization

Victimization from peers—in the forms of physical or verbal aggression, relational aggression, or cyberbullying—predicts a range of disturbing psychological and behavioral problems. The psychological consequences of bullying extend to low self-esteem, feelings of powerlessness, social anxiety, depression, suicidal attempts, sleep problems, somatic symptoms, and fear and anger toward the bully (e.g., Chang et al., 2017; Hager & Leadbeater, 2016; Litwiller & Brausch, 2013; Patchin & Hinduja, 2010; Raskauskas & Stoltz, 2007). Moreover, drops in grades, lateness to school, and school absences are pronounced in victims of bullying (Katzer et al., 2009; Ybarra et al., 2007).

Some adolescents try to numb the psychological pain of bullying through maladaptive coping strategies, turning to substances like alcohol and drugs and engaging in unsafe, casual sex (Mitchell, Ybarra, & Finkelohor, 2007; Zweig, Phillips, & Lindbergh, 2002). However, rather than making the adolescent feel better, such behaviors may exacerbate the harmful effects of being bullied by increasing the odds that an adolescent will later be suicidal (e.g., Bolognini et al., 2003; Spirito et al., 2003). Moreover, victimized teens may become perpetrators themselves. Adolescents who experience physically violent victimization are more likely to display violence toward others (Cleary, 2000; Nickerson & Slater, 2009).

■ CLOSING THOUGHTS
Positive Cascades

The chapter's opening stated the importance of a balanced narrative about adolescence—one that applauds the developmental achievements of adolescents' emotional and social lives. Sometimes, when we learn about the potential downward spiral of developmental cascades, we lose sight of adolescents' assets, and the fact that, for most teens, the journey is optimistic, even though bumpy. So, let me end with a few lessons to shift attention to the many things that typically go right in development.

Reflecting on Chapter 1, it's important to distinguish developmental achievement of the "group" from developmental trajectories of the "individual." All children and adolescents, regardless of the course of their individual paths, show inspiring achievements across multiple domains. The deeply thinking, feeling, and socially engaged adolescent we learned about in this chapter was once an infant who was limited to discriminating among facial expressions and expressing attachment to a small set of familiar people. Maturity and experience bring about remarkable developmental accomplishments and expansion in emotional and social domains.

Furthermore, when we consider the sources of individual differences, just about every statistical association can be interpreted as a glass half empty or a glass half full. When researchers observe, for example, that adolescents with low-quality peer relationships are prone to substance misuse, unsafe sex, or what have you, the flip side is that adolescents with high-quality peer relationships are unlikely to engage in those same behaviors. When we say that conflict with parents may spill over to emotional and behavioral problems in the adolescent, we likewise say that low conflict and high parent support facilitates adolescent self-regulation.

Finally, when we learn about the risk factors that threaten to derail adolescent well-being, we sometimes lose sight of the many protective factors that buffer teens from risk and help reorient them when they veer off course. Because multiple interacting contexts (ranging from biology to culture) shape development, for every push there are several pulls. And so, even if poor attachment with parents interferes with the quality of a romantic relationship, it is only a single piece of the equation and by no means deterministic. Positive life experiences and personal achievements that bolster self-confidence and/or effective counseling and therapy are likely to lead to healthy and happy adult romantic relationships, regardless of childhood attachments. The mountain stream of development (see Chapter 3) continues throughout life to slowly carve new future paths and possibilities.

And so, as we conclude our examination of child development, let us remember to recognize the massive developmental accomplishments that pave the path from infancy to adulthood; flexibly consider alternative interpretations of developmental findings; and acknowledge the complex, multiple interacting forces that work together to shape the course of human development.

The Developmentalist's Toolbox

Method	Purpose	Description
Measuring adolescents' emotional development		
Experience sampling	To obtain information on adolescents' in-the-moment emotional experiences	Participants might be prompted by electronic pagers or smart phones at random intervals to report on their current feelings.
Daily diaries	To track changes in emotional experiences over time and in relationship to specific events	Teens record feelings of happiness, anger, sadness, and anxiety over several days or weeks.
Delay discounting tasks	To measure the degree to which impulsiveness toward immediate gratification is curbed by self-regulation	An immediate and small monetary reward is typically pitted against a delayed, larger monetary reward to assess whether an individual is willing to wait to receive the larger reward.
Multigroup Ethnic Identity Measure (MEIM)	A measure for assessing ethnic identity	The MEIM measures feelings of commitment, pride, and belonging to an ethnic group using the Ethnic Identity Scale to assess (1) ethnic identity exploration, (2) ethnic identity resolution, and (3) affirmation.
Measuring adolescents' social development		
Adult Attachment Interview	A method for assessing attachment status in adolescents/adults through open-ended questions about early childhood experiences	Researchers ask adolescents or adults about their childhood experiences around acceptance and rejection by their parents, and from responses code the adult's attachment status.

■ Chapter Summary

Emotional Experiences

- Adolescence is a time of high emotional reactivity and volatility, as indicated by experience sampling and diary studies.
- Happiness decreases and anger, sadness, and anxiety increase across adolescence, which may lead to internalizing or externalizing behaviors in some teens.
- Depression peaks in prevalence in adolescence. Rates of depression are higher in adolescent girls than adolescent boys. Gender differences may be attributed to differences in reactions to stress, rumination, and the ways that depression is expressed.
- Cognitive behavior therapy, a family-systems approach, and prescriptions of antidepressants are common approaches to treatment of depression. Many treatments combine approaches (e.g., antidepressants with therapy).

Self-Regulation

- Adolescents show difficulties in aspects of self-regulation, as seen in their high impulsiveness, problems delaying gratification, and risk-taking behaviors.
- Sensation seeking is high in adolescents and is seen in the high activation in regions of the brain associated with emotions and pleasure.
- However, sensation seeking may be adaptive by allowing adolescents to seek out new activities and social encounters, including romantic relationships.

Contexts of Emotional Development

- Low-quality parent-adolescent relationships, peer relationships, and impoverished neighborhoods and schools are associated with adolescent depression and risk taking.
- Extracurricular school activities and community involvement reduce the likelihood of teen substance use, delinquency, and other problem behaviors.

Erik Erikson's Theory

- Erik Erikson proposed a theory of identity development that distinguished identity achievement and role confusion.
- On the path to achieving a self-identity, adolescents experience a psychosocial moratorium, which is when they explore opportunities.

James Marcia and Identity Statuses

- Marcia elaborated on Erikson's theory, and identified four identity statuses that resulted from the processes of identity exploration and commitment: foreclosure, identity diffusion, moratorium, and identity achievement.
- Most adolescents in moratorium or diffused statuses ultimately achieve an identity, whereas, those in foreclosed status may never achieve a coherent self-determined identity.
- Adolescents who achieve a unique identity often have high self-esteem. Most adolescents maintain high self-esteem over the period of adolescence; some show a dip in self-esteem that later rebounds; and others remain chronically low in self-esteem.

Ethnic and Racial Identity

- Ethnic identity is central to adolescent identity, especially for adolescents from immigrant and minority backgrounds.
- Three aspects of ethnic identity are exploration, resolution, and affirmation.
- During adolescence, ethnic exploration is high and is typically resolved, with teenagers varying on how positive versus negative they feel about their identity (the aspect called affirmation).
- Adolescents from minority ethnic groups may experience conflict between their family's heritage and that of the majority culture. Some ways they may resolve these tensions are by rejecting their home culture, opposing mainstream culture, or achieving a bicultural identity.

Gender Identity and Sexual Orientation

- A person's gender identity can match their sex assigned at birth (cisgender), differ from their sex assigned at birth (transgender), or be non-binary.
- Gender identity differs from sexual orientation.
- Four main types of sexual orientation are heterosexual orientation, bisexual orientation, gay or lesbian orientation, and asexual orientation.
- Sexual orientation may change over the course of adolescence and only become a stable part of one's identity in late adolescence or later.
- The process of coming out occurs in four phases: self-recognition, identity tolerance, identity acceptance, and identity integration.
- LGBTQ+ adolescents may take time to come out because they fear peers and family members may be unaccepting.
- Adolescents distinguish among different romantic and dating relationships, with definitions today differing substantially from those of the past.
- Rates of romantic relationships and the characteristics of those relationships—including levels of sexual activity, length of time, and commitment—change over adolescence.
- Young adolescents may experience high jealousy in long-term romantic relationships, perhaps not yet being psychologically ready to manage their emotions.

Contexts of Self-Identity

- Over-controlling parents may interfere with an adolescent's process of self-identity exploration and achievement.
- Parents who are loving, supportive, and engage in behaviors that instill cultural pride in their children help their adolescents achieve a positive ethnic identity and combat the negative consequences of discrimination.
- School composition affects the self-identity exploration and achievement of adolescents of minority backgrounds by making ethnicity salient and providing adolescents with opportunities to interact with co-ethnic peers.

- Cultures that emphasize individuality and self-enhancement goals are likely to view self-esteem as a central asset, whereas cultures that emphasize collectivism are less likely to endorse the merits of high self-esteem.

Relationships with Parents and Siblings

- Attachment and closeness to parents maintains importance throughout adolescence. The Adult Attachment Interview measures adolescent attachment to parents, and generates three attachment statuses: autonomous, dismissive, and preoccupied.
- Conflict with parents in adolescence is typically not high (as stereotypes would lead people to believe) and focuses on everyday issues rather than major problems.
- Parental monitoring is associated with positive adolescent outcomes. However, what parents know about their adolescents' lives depends on adolescent disclosure as well. Adolescents engage in selective disclosure, and teens with difficult personalities and other problems are less likely to keep their parents informed.
- Sibling relationships are unique, and the quality of these relationships is associated with adolescent friendships, romantic relationships, and risk-taking behavior.
- Conflict and alienation between parents and adolescents may be high in immigrant and minority families as adolescents come to terms with differences in parent and peer values and behaviors.

Relationships with Peers

- Friendships in adolescence differ from those in childhood on compatibility, stability, reciprocity, and respect for individuality. However, respect for individuality takes years to achieve, and adolescents may be very possessive and jealous in their friendships compared to children and adults.
- Adolescents' peer relationships are structured into cliques and crowds.
- Bullying takes many forms: physical aggression and verbal aggression (direct bullying), relational aggression (indirect bullying), and cyberbullying.

Social Media

- Social media use can provide benefits to adolescents by fostering a sense of autonomy, enhancing social connections, providing opportunities for self-disclosure, and offering a platform for social exchanges in individuals who may feel socially and geographically isolated, including LGBTQ+ youth.
- Adolescent use of social media is high and can become problematic when teens display overuse, disclose too much information, interact with strangers, experience cyberbullying, or are bystanders to cyberbullying.
- Personality factors including social anxiety and narcissism relate to how much teens use social media.

Developmental Cascades

- Adolescent depression and low self-esteem can cascade to poor social relationships, delinquency, substance use, mental and physical health problems, and suicide.
- Relationships with parents can cascade to other social relationships, including with romantic partners.
- Isolation, rejection, and victimization from peers place adolescents at risk for substance use, suicide, and health problems in adulthood.
- Positive life experiences and personal achievements in adolescence, and proactively reaching out for support and help when needed, go far in allowing adolescents to achieve healthy and happy adult romantic relationships and psychological well-being.

Thinking Like a Developmentalist

1. You are a developmental scientist who aims to better understand the specific in-the-moment situations that might "trigger" adolescent problems in self-regulation and risk taking on a daily basis, including who is around when teens engage in certain risky behaviors, where teens are, their moods, and so forth. What methods might you use to tackle these questions and why?

2. You are concerned that excessive use of social media might feed into an adolescents' unhealthy identity development, and you wonder if those influences might differ by adolescent race and gender. As a first step to an intervention, you want to examine associations between social media use and different aspects of identity development in different samples of adolescents. Which aspects of identity development would you consider and why? How would you evaluate those? How would you study teen social media use? What information would you wish to gather? Which specific hypotheses would you test around the different influences of social media on identity by adolescent gender and adolescent race or ethnicity?

3. COVID-19 led to a dramatic increase in adolescent social media use as a way to connect with friends and "meet" new potential romantic partners. As a researcher who studies adolescent social media use, you are concerned about this trend. What precise concerns might you have and why? What would you do to communicate potential risks to teens?

Glossary

Chapter 1

accommodation Children's modification of a schema to fit reality that is the result of disequilibrium

adoption study A study that tests whether adopted children are more similar to their biological parents and siblings (who have a similar genetic makeup) or to their adoptive parents and siblings (who share their home environment but are dissimilar genetically)

applied developmental science An approach in developmental psychology that focuses on the application of scientific principles and knowledge to real-life problems

assimilation Incorporation of new experiences or information into an existing schema that move children from one stage to the next according to Piaget

attrition The dropping out of participants from a research study

basic developmental science An approach in developmental psychology that focuses on description and explanation of basic learning and developmental processes

behavioral genetic study Studies that address questions about genetic influences on development by measuring the degree of behavioral similarity among people who vary in genetic relatedness

behaviorism A scientific approach that emerged in the early twentieth century that explained people's behaviors as learned through conditioning (experiences)

bioecological perspective Theory, proposed by Uri Bronfenbrenner, that focuses on how the environment affects human development; this approach highlights development as the product of different nested environmental "systems" (microsystem, mesosystem, exosystem, macrosystem, and chronosystem) and biology

classical conditioning A learning process that occurs when a neutral stimulus takes on new significance after being paired with another meaningful stimulus

cohort sequential design A study that follows two or more groups of children of different ages over time, creating a mixture of longitudinal and cross-sectional designs

concurrent validity The degree to which scores on a test correspond to those on another test of the same construct at the same point in time

confederate An actor who pretends to be a participant in a research study but actually works for the researcher

confounding variable A "third variable" that relates to both the independent and dependent variables and can thus affect the outcome of a study

constructivist theory A theory of development proposed by Jean Piaget that spotlights children's active role in learning and development

construct validity The extent to which a test measures what it purports to measure

control group The participants who do not receive the "treatment" in an experimental manipulation

convenience sampling The recruitment of participants into a study based on ease of access to them, such as the students in a researcher's class or children in the local community

correlational study A study that tests associations between two or more variables without manipulating any variables

cross-sectional study A study that compares children of different ages at roughly the same point in time to enable researchers to explore age-related differences in a certain phenomenon

cultural learning environment A concept introduced by Beatrice and John Whiting that encompasses the consistent elements of daily living, including a "physically defined space, a characteristic group of people, and norms of behavior"

culture The shared physical, behavioral, and symbolic features of a community

dependent variable A variable whose value depends on another (independent) variable(s)

developmental cascades The idea that changes of one kind can have cascading effects, setting other kinds of changes in motion, both immediately and at later ages; developmental cascades may be positive or negative and typically exert spillover effects across different areas of development

developmental domain Area of child development such as motor development (related to physical growth, movement, and action), perceptual development (related to the senses), cognitive development (related to thought processes), language development (related to communication), social development (related to interaction with others), or emotional development (related to understanding and expressing feelings)

developmental niche A concept introduced by Charles Super and Sara Harkness that encompasses the physical and social settings of children's lives, the customs of childcare and child-rearing, and the beliefs and views of caregivers

developmental onset Approximate age when specific skills emerge, such as first words, first steps, and first signs of puberty

developmental systems theorists Theorists who posit that human behavior is the product of a complex, ever-changing system, in which multiple factors affect developmental change; this approach highlights the shared contributions of genes and environment on development and rejects the nativist approach of innate core capacities

direct assessment A specific task or test that researchers administer to children

discovery-based science Research that seeks to discover principles of children's learning and development without presuppositions about what might be found

disequilibrium When new experiences do not fit a schema, creating an imbalance between the schema and reality; Jean Piaget posited that disequilibrium moves children from one stage to the next through the process of accommodation

DNA   The carrier of genetic information on chromosomes

ego   According to Sigmund Freud, the rational component of personality that helps keep inappropriate thoughts, impulses, and desires from rising to consciousness and being acted upon

equilibration   A cognitive balance or alignment between existing knowledge and new information

experiment   A research method that tests a hypothesis about a cause-and-effect relation between two (sometimes more) variables, an independent variable, and a dependent variable

experimental group   The participants who receive the "treatment" in an experimental manipulation

external, or ecological, validity   The degree to which a test can be applied across different settings or groups of people

face validity   The degree to which the purpose of a test is clear to people who look it over

generalizability   The degree to which research findings and conclusions based on a specific study and sample extend to the population at large

genome-wide association tests   Tests that analyze massive amounts of DNA information across thousands of participants and then relate people's DNA composition to specific outcomes

hypothesis   An assumption or proposed explanation that is based on limited or even no evidence

hypothesis-driven research   Research that seeks to examine a specific and measurable question along with specified hypotheses

id   According to Sigmund Freud, a part of one's personality comprised of the primitive biological drives that are present from birth

independent variable   A variable that is manipulated to see whether changes follow in the dependent variable, or in non-experimental studies, a variable that is thought to explain another variable

individual differences   The spread or variability among children in various aspects of development, including age onsets, rates of change, and the forms that skills take

information processing theories   Theories that focus on the flow of information (in the forms of sounds, sights, and smells) through the mind; information is perceived, manipulated, stored, retrieved, and acted on, much like a computer manipulates and stores information

interobserver reliability   The degree to which different observers using a test arrive at the same results

interview   Questions asked of participants face-to-face or via phone

longitudinal study   A study that follows the same participants over time, typically across months or years

mediator   An intervening, explanatory variable that explains the association between the dependent and independent variable

microgenetic study   A study that involves frequent, closely spaced observations of children, for instance, daily or weekly tracking of child learning and/or detailed observations of learning in real time

nativist approach   An approach to development that asserts people are born with innate, or core, capacities that are essential for human adaptation

naturalistic observations   Observations of participants in everyday settings, such as at home, school, or on playgrounds

natural selection   Individuals with physical and behavioral traits that are well suited to their environments have an increased chance of surviving and reproducing, thereby passing these adaptive traits on to subsequent generations, an observation first advanced by Charles Darwin

nature   Influences on learning and development arising from a child's genetic inheritance and other biological factors

negative reinforcement   The presentation of an aversive stimulus that involves some type of discomfort (e.g., car alarm) to strengthen a target behavior (e.g., fastening a seat belt)

nurture   Influences on learning and development that arise from life experiences and environmental contexts

observation   Watching what participants do in a controlled laboratory setting or in natural settings such as home or school

observational learning   A form of learning in which children figure out how to act by watching and modeling other people; Albert Bandura first demonstrated the importance of children's observational learning

open science   A movement that encourages researchers to fully document and share information on a study's procedures, recruitment methods, participant characteristics, measures, raw data, analyses, and funding sources

operant conditioning   A learning process that leads to an increase or decrease in behaviors depending on whether the behaviors are rewarded or punished

physiological assessments   Measures of the functioning of different parts of the body including brain activation, heart rate, blood pressure, eye movements, and even the hormones people produce in response to stress

plasticity   The capacity to adapt and change in response to changing environments and experiences

population   The target sample to which a researcher aims to generalize findings based on a specific study sample

positive reinforcement   The introduction of a desirable or pleasant stimulus to reward and encourage a particular behavior

predictive validity   The degree to which scores on a test at one point in time predict scores on a similar or related test or criterion (often over time)

psychodynamic theories   A set of theories that consider personality to be a product of conscious and unconscious forces; Sigmund Freud and Erik Erikson were two prominent theorists of this tradition

psychosexual stage theory   A theory developed by Sigmund Freud that emphasized the central role of children's biological drives, particularly the sex drive, in behavior

psychosocial stage theory   A theory, developed by Erik Erikson, positing that people's search for an identity presents developmental challenges throughout the life course; at each of eight psychosocial stages, people experience a unique internal conflict about their identity that they must resolve to move on to the next stage in a healthy way

qualitative change   Progression through a sequence of distinct stages in children's thinking and acting

qualitative research   An approach in which researchers explore in depth a phenomenon without a set of specific hypotheses; qualitative research may include unstructured interviews

quantitative change   Gradual changes over time in the amount, frequency, or degree of children's behaviors

random assignment   The use of chance procedures, such as flipping a coin or using a random-number table, to assign participants to treatment or control; these procedures ensure that every person in the study has the same opportunity to be assigned to one or the other group

rate of change   Course of change over time, including how fast children progress in their skills

reliability   The consistency of scores for participants across different observers or over time; two common types of reliability are interobserver reliability and test-retest reliability

replicability   The degree to which the findings of a study are confirmed when repeated using the identical procedures applied in the original study with a new sample

replication   The ability of other scientists to obtain similar findings if they were to use the same methods and measures on a similar population as in the original study

research method   How data are gathered to test predictions and interpret results

sample size   The number of people who participate in a study

schemas   Basic units of information, as posited by Jean Piaget, that are cognitive representations of the world; Piaget believed that schemas determine how children of different ages organize and understand information

scientific method   Steps that scientists use to test hypotheses: identifying a question; formulating a hypothesis that answers the question; testing the hypothesis with a research study; and analyzing study results and drawing conclusions

scientific review board   A university board that reviews research study plans to ensure they are ethical and well designed; the board is usually comprised of scientists from multiple disciplines and also might include legal representatives, university staff, and community members with no affiliation to the university

Skinner box   An operant conditioning chamber, originally used by B.F. Skinner, in which animals learn to increase or decrease specific behaviors to obtain food, water, or other types of reinforcement

social desirability bias   When participants answer questions in a way they believe is desired or "correct," rather than truthfully

social learning theory   An approach to development that echoes some of the principles of behaviorism regarding learning through reinforcement, yet advances on those principles in key ways; social learning theory also emphasizes how children learn new behaviors by imitating others

sociocultural theories   Theories that build on the foundational work of Lev Vygotsky that focus on the contexts of child development, placing much weight on the nurture end of the nature-nurture seesaw and assigning a very central role to culture

stability   Consistency in the rank-ordering of children on a specific behavior or skill, such as when children who are relatively high or low on a particular behavior or characteristic at a certain point in time are also relatively high or low on the same behavior or characteristic at later times

structured interview   Interview in which researchers ask specific, close-ended questions; for example, a structured interview may ask an adolescent about specific risk behaviors

structured observations   Observations in which researchers observe participants performing a specific activity—for example, interacting with peers during a game—typically in a laboratory setting

study design   A specific plan for conducting a study that allows the researcher to test a study's hypotheses

superego   According to Sigmund Freud, a part of one's late-developing personality that functions as a conscience to ensure that children behave in morally acceptable ways and uphold family and community standards and expectations

survey   Questions asked of participants through written format

test-retest reliability   The degree to which an individual receives the same score (or at least a close score) when tested at different times under similar conditions

the form of skills   The form that a specific behavior takes in children from different communities, such as learning to use chopsticks or forks as implements for eating

theory   A set of interconnected statements or general principles that explain a set of observable events

twin study   A study that tests whether genetic similarity relates to behavioral similarity

unstructured interview   Interview in which researchers ask open-ended questions to elicit more information from participants than would be possible with close-ended questions; unstructured interviews are a part of qualitative research

validity   The degree to which a test (which can be an actual test, questionnaire, and so forth) measures what it is supposed to measure; there exist different forms of validity

variables   Factors of interest in a study (such as a child's sex); a characteristic or something that can be examined in relation to something else (i.e., another variable), such as whether a child's sex relates to the type of play children display

vicarious reinforcement   A form of observational learning in which children learn how to behave by watching others get rewarded or punished

zone of proximal development   The distance between what a child can achieve independently versus with the guidance of a more knowledgeable or skilled social partner. Vygotsky proposed that children learn best when caregivers adjust their input to be slightly above the child's current or "actual" level of understanding

Chapter 2

alleles   Different versions or forms of a gene; the various forms are on a particular location on a chromosome

amygdala   A region of the brain that is a part of the limbic system and involved in emotion processes, particularly fear and the fight-or-flight response.

apoptosis   The death of neurons as part of development; about 40% of excess connections are eliminated by apoptosis

arborization   The growth and branching of dendrite "trees" and the creation of spines on the branches; arborization enables extensive synaptogenesis

association areas   Parts of the cerebral cortex that receive input from different areas and which form connections between sensory and motor areas of the brain; association areas process information from the lobes to create meaningful experiences

axon   A long threadlike fiber that extends out from the cell body; electrical impulses travel down the axon from the cell body to axon terminals

axon terminals   The parts of the nerve cell that create synaptic connections with other cells; axon terminals release neurotransmitters to send signals to other neurons

basal ganglia   A cluster of nerve cells that surrounds the hypothalamus and is involved in movement/motor control and the coordination of automatic behaviors

bases   Long sequences of chemical subunits that make up each DNA molecule

brain plasticity   The ability of the brain to change and adapt due to experience; two main forms of brain plasticity are experience-expectant plasticity and experience-dependent plasticity

brainstem   The part of the brain consisting of the midbrain, the pons, and the medulla oblongata; the brainstem controls the messages between the brain and the rest of the body

canalization   The ability of a genotype to produce the same phenotype regardless of environmental variability

cell body   The spherical portion of a neuron that contains the nucleus and connects to dendrites; the cell body controls all of the cell functions

cerebellum   The brain structure that coordinates movement, such as walking and balancing, and that is involved in memory, cognition, and emotion

cerebral cortex   The layer of gray matter that covers the left and right hemispheres, consisting of folds of axons and neurons; the cerebral cortex is involved in higher functions of the nervous system, including language and memory; the cortex has four lobes in each hemisphere

cerebral lateralization   A phenomenon referring to the specialized functions of regions in the right and left hemispheres; the left hemisphere is largely involved in language and the right hemisphere is largely involved in processing social and emotional information, although both hemispheres are involved in mostly all processes

chromosomes   Threadlike structures found in living cells that carry genetic information; human cells have 23 pairs of chromosomes

cingulate cortex   A region of the brain that is a part of the limbic system that communicates with different regions of the brain and is involved in emotion processes.

contralateral organization   The physical body control of the brain; the right brain controls the left side of the body and the left brain controls the right side of the body

corpus callosum   A dense tract of nerve fibers, beneath the cerebral cortex, which facilitates communication between the left and right hemispheres of the brain as it stretches across the midline of the brain

critical periods   Times when specific experiences result in permanent changes in a child's brain that cannot be altered

dandelion children   "Resilient" children who are able to cope with stress and flourish despite adverse environmental conditions; drawn from a metaphor used by Dr. Thomas Boyce on the resilience of children

dendrites   Fibers or branched extensions of a nerve cell that receive signals from other neurons and transmit signals to the cell body and down the axon

DNA (deoxyribonucleic acid)   A nucleic acid that is the main constituent of chromosomes; DNA contains the genetic information for the development of living organisms

dominant allele   A variation of a gene that will create a phenotype even while other alleles are present

epigenetics   The complex, dynamic process through which environments shape the expression of the genetic code; the term was originally used to illustrate gene-environment interactions

evocative effects   The effects of a person's traits or characteristics on the environment, which may heighten those traits and characteristics.

experience-dependent plasticity   A form of brain plasticity in which changes in brain wiring occur in response to an individual's unique personal experiences and life circumstances

experience-expectant plasticity   A form of brain plasticity in which the brain adapts in response to sensory information; much research demonstrates how everyday, common, universal, and "expected" experiences affect brain development

fertilization   The process in which gametes join together to form a zygote

forebrain   The largest part of the human brain that consists of the cerebral cortex and subcortical structures; the forebrain controls such functions as body temperature, reproductive functions, eating, and emotions

frontal lobe   One of the four lobes of the brain located at the front of the cerebral hemispheres that contains the primary motor cortex; the frontal lobe, or the "executive" area of the brain, is involved in reasoning, planning, impulse control, attention, and goal-directed behaviors

gametes   Sex cells or an organism's reproductive cells; female gametes are called ova or egg cells and male gametes are called sperm; gametes have only 23 chromosomes each

gene   A small segment of DNA that codes for the production of a particular protein and specifies the sequence of base pairs in the DNA segment; a unit of heredity that is passed on from parent to offspring; hundreds to thousands of genes exist in each human chromosome

gene therapy   An experimental technique using genes to prevent or treat diseases

genetic code   A set of rules by which particular sequences of bases create the proteins that govern the workings of living cells

genetic mutation   A gene mutation that occurs in a germ cell or gamete and is a permanent alteration in the DNA sequence making up a gene; the hereditary mutations are inherited from a parent

genetics   The study of genes and heredity and how genes affect an individual's characteristics, such as personality and physical appearance

genotype   The gene or set of genes that determines an individual's traits; the genotype may be considered an individual's genetic makeup

glial cells   Nonneuronal cells that surround and protect neurons and are involved in a number of important functions, including the strengthening of synapses

hindbrain   The central core of the brain that includes the rest of the brainstem, the cerebellum, the pons, and the medulla oblongata; the hindbrain controls automatic functions such as breathing and digestion

hippocampus   The part of the brain located in the inner region of the temporal lobe that is involved in regulating emotions and supports children's memory, spatial understanding, and executive functioning

Human Genome Project   An international research program (1990–2003) to map and understand all the genes of humans in an effort to explore the genetic foundations of human physical and behavioral characteristics and to create new strategies for identifying and treating disorders

hypothalamus   The part of the brain located below the thalamus and involved in the experience of emotions such as happiness and sadness; the hypothalamus is also involved in such behaviors as eating and drinking

Klinefelter syndrome   A random negative mutation or chromosomal abnormality resulting in an extra copy of the X chromosome in males (XXY, not XY); males with Klinefelter syndrome have small testes and produce low amounts of testosterone, leading to infertility

limbic system   The collection of brain structures involved in emotions and memory; the limbic system consists of the hippocampus, amygdala, and cingulate cortex

medulla oblongata   The brain structure that is responsible for vital functions such as blood pressure, breathing, and heart rate

meiosis   The process in which a single human cell divides twice to create four cells that contain half the amount of the original genetic information

microbiome   Genetic material or microbes that have many times the number of genes as identified in the human genome; in utero, mothers pass on microbes to the fetus and, by the end of their first year, infants have a distinct microbiome that continues to develop until about age 3

midbrain   The uppermost region of the brainstem that controls reflex actions and is involved in vision, hearing, movements, and sleep-wake cycles

migration   The movement of new neurons to locations within the brain where they will serve their ultimate, final functions; during the process of migration, some cells become nerve cells and others become different types of cells, such as muscle cells and skin cells

mitosis   The process in which the zygote's chromosome replicates, resulting in two identical cells with 23 chromosome pairs, which replicate and divide to create four cells containing the identical 46 chromosomes in 23 pairs; this process repeats and every cell keeps the identical genetic information

mixed mutations   Mutations with either positive or negative effects under various conditions

mutation   An alteration in the structure of an individual's DNA that arises from an error in chromosomal replication or from exposure to environmental factors such as radiation, toxic chemicals, or other toxins; mutations vary in size, from a single DNA building block to a large part of a chromosome with multiple genes

myelination   The formation of an insulating myelin sheath around the axons of neurons that allows signals to travel down the axon more quickly

negative mutations   Harmful mutations in DNA that have a negative effect on the individual, leading to adverse, even lethal, consequences; negative mutations may be inherited or occur randomly during the formation of reproductive cells

neurogenesis   The process in which new neurons are formed in the brain through cell division or mitosis; neurogenesis begins during the third or fourth week of prenatal life

neurons   Specialized cells that transmit chemical and electrical signals in the brain; neurons are structured in three main parts: cell body, axon, and dendrites

neurotransmitters   Chemical substances that are involved in communication between neurons

neutral mutations   Silent mutations in DNA that have no effect on an individual's phenotype

norm of reaction   The range of possible phenotypes for a given genotype; the norm of reaction may be viewed as a curve that relates variation in the environment to phenotypic variation

occipital lobe   One of the four lobes of the brain in the rearmost area of the brain; the occipital lobe is involved in processing visual information

orchid children   Children characterized by "low resilience," who seem to wilt in the face of environmental challenges, drawing from a metaphor used by Dr. Thomas Boyce on the resilience of children

parietal lobe   One of the four lobes of the brain located in the back of the brain, divided into two hemispheres; the parietal lobe is involved in processing spatial information, integrating information from other modalities, connecting information with memory, and interpreting visual information and processing such as for language and mathematics

phenotype   A set of outward, observable characteristics of an individual; these characteristics result from the interaction between the individual's genotype and the environment

phenotypic plasticity   The degree to which environmental factors affect a given trait; the ability of one genotype to create more than one phenotype in different environments, or the ability of an organism to change in response to stimuli from the environment

polygenetic inheritance   An occurrence when one characteristic is controlled by two or more genes; height, weight, skin color, and eye color are examples of polygenetic inheritance

pons   The brain structure located above the medulla that regulates sleep, arousal, consciousness, and sensory processes; the pons has nerve fibers that connect the cerebrum and cerebellum

positive mutations   Beneficial mutations in DNA that have a positive effect on the individual, leading to new versions of proteins that enable organisms to better adapt to changes in their environment

recessive allele   A variation of a gene that needs to be homozygous when inherited to create a phenotype

resilience   Differences among children in their responses to adversity or the process of adapting to challenges, stress, or trauma; it is important to view resilience along a continuum, with most children falling somewhere in the middle of the continuum

sensitive periods   Times in development when the brain is most susceptible to experiences, but changes are still reversible

sex chromosomes   A type of chromosome that is involved in sex determination; one of the 23 pairs of chromosomes in the zygote is made up of the sex chromosomes; sex chromosomes have two forms: X or male and Y or female

sex-linked traits   Traits in which a gene is located on a sex chromosome; the majority of sex-linked traits are located on the X chromosome

synapses   Microscopic separations between axon terminals and dendrites; neurons send signals to each other through a flow of neurotransmitters across synapses

synaptic pruning   The process in which synapses are eliminated to increase the efficacy of neural communication

synaptogenesis   The process by which neurons form synapses with each other; one neuron may form multiple synapses with thousands of other neurons; synaptogenesis begins prenatally and is quite rapid before and after birth

temporal lobe   One of the four lobes of the brain that is located closest to the ear; the temporal lobe is involved in processing emotional and auditory information, memory, and visual recognition

thalamus   The part of the brain located above the brainstem and between the cerebral cortex and midbrain; the thalamus relays information to and from the spinal cord and between the two hemispheres

Turner syndrome   A random negative mutation or chromosomal abnormality resulting in a missing or partially missing X chromosome in females (X, not XX); females with Turner syndrome may have different medical and developmental challenges (e.g., failure of the ovaries)

X chromosome   One of two sex chromosomes; females have two X chromosomes in their cells

Y chromosome   One of two sex chromosomes; males have one X chromosome and one Y chromosome in their cells

zygote   The cell that is created when gamete cells (ovum and sperm) are joined; the zygote has 46 chromosomes in 23 pairs

Chapter 3

active labor The second phase in the first stage of labor during which contractions increase in intensity, frequency, and length and cause dilation of the cervix

amniotic sac A membrane developing out of the trophoblast that has a clear, watery fluid in which the fetus floats; the amniotic fluid protects the fetus

androgens Male sex hormones such as testosterone that are involved in male sex and reproductive function

anencephaly A neural tube defect resulting in the absence of a major portion of the brain, skull, and scalp during embryonic development, usually between days 23 and 26 after conception; a mother's folic acid deficiencies may be a factor

anoxia A situation in which infants experience an inadequate supply of oxygen during labor or after birth; prolonged minutes without breathing may result in brain damage

Apgar scale The most common assessment of newborn health typically conducted by a nurse or doctor at 1 minute and then at 5 minutes after the infant's birth; the Apgar scale is based on ratings of neonate appearance, pulse, grimace, activity, and respiration

assisted reproduction The use of various medical techniques to aid with pregnancy, from conception to the birth of a child

blastocyst A ball of 100 cells that becomes firmly embedded in the lining of the uterus one week after conception; forms a structure with two layers

breech A bottom-first or feet-first position of the baby right before birth

Broca's area A region in the frontal lobe of the left hemisphere that is involved in such activities as speech and language production

caesarean birth (C-section) A surgical procedure used to deliver a baby through incisions in the abdomen and uterus, in contrast to a vaginal delivery; C-sections may be advised if there are complications during labor (such as breech position)

cell specialization Cell differentiation or changes in cell shape, structure, and composition to enable cells to carry out specific bodily functions

cephalocaudal development The growth pattern of organisms in which areas near the head develop earlier than areas farther down (i.e., head before body, arms before legs)

circadian rhythms The biological 24-hour cycle ("internal clock") regulating physiological functioning, such as when individuals sleep, wake, and eat

contingent reinforcement paradigm The delivery of positive reinforcement in response to specific behaviors, such as by presenting a recording of the mother's voice in response to infant sucking

contractions A tightening and relaxing of the muscles of the uterus at intervals before and during childbirth; contractions help push the baby out

cortisol A hormone produced by the adrenal cortex that regulates body processes such as metabolism and the immune response and helps the body respond to stress

co-sleeping Caregivers' sharing of a bed with an infant or child; cultural practices and cultural goals often inform parents' views and practices around co-sleeping

dizygotic twins Two separate fertilized eggs, also referred to as fraternal twins, which typically develop two separate amniotic sacs and placentas; dizygotic twins have genetically unique material

Down syndrome A genetic disorder coming from a defect in chromosome 21, usually an extra copy (trisomy-21), resulting in intellectual impairment and physical abnormalities, such as short stature and flat facial features

ectoderm The outer layer of the embryo that develops into the nervous system, sensory organs, nails, teeth, and the outer surface of the skin

embryonic disk The inner layer or flattened inner cell mass at the end of the blastocyst stage that becomes the embryo

embryonic period The period between the third and eighth week of pregnancy during which cells of the embryo start to differentiate into specialized cells and brain regions; three layers make up the mass of inner cells: ectoderm, mesoderm, and endoderm

endoderm The inner layer of the embryo that develops into the digestive and reproductive systems

fetal alcohol syndrome (FAS) A set of fetal problems caused by a mother's alcohol consumption during pregnancy; FAS is associated with unique physical features (e.g., small eye openings, thin upper lip), sleep and feeding difficulties, brain and heart damage, and failure to thrive

fetus An unborn offspring; from the end of the eighth week after conception until birth in humans

first stage of labor The first and longest stage of vaginal delivery during which the mother feels regular contractions, causing the cervix to open/dilate, soften, shorten, and thin

germinal/zygotic period A 2-week prenatal period from conception until the zygote implants in the uterine wall; the organism starts cell division and growth during this time

gestational age The time that passes from conception to the infant's birth; term newborns are born between 37 and 41 weeks of pregnancy

implantation The attachment of the blastocyst to the wall of the uterus; by the end of the second week, the blastocyst is embedded in the uterine wall completely

infant mortality rate The number of infant deaths out of live births that occur before age one year

intrauterine insemination (IUI) An assisted reproductive technique/fertility treatment involving placing sperm inside a woman's uterus to enable fertilization

in vitro fertilization (IVF) An assisted reproductive technique/fertility treatment involving incubating eggs and sperm outside a woman's body (such as in a laboratory dish) to create an embryo

macrosomic infants Infants who are born much larger than average

mesoderm The middle layer of the embryo between the ectoderm and endoderm that develops into muscles, bones, the circulatory system, inner layers of the skin, and other internal organs

microcephaly A condition in which the head is smaller than normal; microcephaly may be caused by genetic abnormalities or fetal exposure to toxins, drugs, alcohol, or infectious disease

monozygotic twins Identical twins resulting from the fertilization of a single egg that splits in two; monozygotic twins share all their genes and are of the same sex

neonates Infants who are less than four weeks of age; neonates typically spend over 16 hours a day sleeping

perinatal period The time that precedes and follows an infant's birth, specifically, the period between 22 weeks of gestation and seven days after birth

placenta An organ developing out of the trophoblast that enables the exchange of substances between the fetus and mother through the bloodstream

postnatal period The time right after birth typically defined by the first six weeks after childbirth

premature birth A birth that occurs more than three weeks before the infant's estimated due date (before week 37 of pregnancy), which may lead to medical challenges at and after birth

prenatal care   The various forms of medical attention and health care of pregnant women (including regular doctor visits during pregnancy and blood, urine, and ultrasound tests) to support healthy pregnancy and birth

prenatal period   The period from conception to birth that divides into three key periods or stages: germinal, embryonic, and fetal

proximodistal development   The growth pattern of organisms in which areas near the center of the body develop before areas near the periphery (i.e., forearms before fingers)

REM (rapid eye movement)   A type or stage of active sleep that involves dreaming and is characterized by quick, erratic eye movements under closed lids, frequent body movements, a distinct pattern of brain activity, and irregularity in breathing and heart rate

respiratory distress syndrome (RDS)   A breathing disorder in newborns that occurs when fluid collects in the air sacs of lungs, depriving newborns of oxygen and resulting in breathing challenges

second stage of labor   The pushing stage of labor that begins when the cervix is fully dilated and ends with the birth of the baby; contractions propel the fetus down the birth canal

skeletal ossification   The process of bone formation or laying of new bone material by cells

small-for-date infants   Infants who weigh less than expected at birth based on the time they spent in the womb; they may have experienced inadequate nutrition in the womb

spina bifida   A birth defect of the spine causing paralysis and mental disability when the spine and spinal cord do not form correctly; a mother's folic acid deficiencies may be a factor

stem cells   Embryonic cells from the undifferentiated mass of cells of a human embryo; cells from which cells with specialized functions grow

sudden infant death syndrome (SIDS)   A situation in which a seemingly healthy infant under age 1 dies while sleeping due to an apparent stop to breathing

Tay-Sachs disease   An inherited metabolic disorder passed from parent to child that destroys nerve cells in the brain and spinal cord; leads to death in childhood

teratogens   External agents that can produce physical malformation and negative psychological and behavioral effects on the developing embryo and fetus

thalidomide   A drug that pregnant mothers took to treat morning sickness that was marketed as harmless but led to malformed limbs in children

third-party assisted reproduction   The use of eggs, sperm, or embryos that have been donated by a third person to enable an infertile individual or couple to become parents

third stage of labor   The shortest stage of labor occurring right after the birth of the infant and ending with the delivery of the placenta

trophoblast   The outer layer of the blastocyst that becomes the environment holding and protecting the developing fetus; the trophoblast forms the main part of the placenta and comprises three structures: amniotic sac, placenta, and umbilical cord

ultrasonography   An imaging technique using echoes of ultra- sound pulses to visualize the body structure and movements of the developing fetus

umbilical cord   A flexible cordlike structure developing out of the trophoblast that connects the placenta and embryo and contains blood vessels running between the two

vernix   A slimy, white substance that covers the skin of a fetus as a form of protection from the amniotic fluid

Wernicke's area   A region to the rear of Broca's area, in the temporal lobe in the left hemisphere of the brain, which is involved in understanding spoken and written language

zygote   A cell that results from a sperm fertilizing an egg; a zygote contains all the genetic information needed for development

Chapter 4

absolute threshold   The minimum sound level of a stimulus required to detect a sound; absolute threshold is one way to define perception of loudness and pitch

anticipatory eye movements   Eye movements that occur before something occurs in anticipation of a stimulus's movement direction

attractiveness effect   The phenomenon that infants look longer at attractive faces than unattractive ones, perhaps because attractive faces map to the "average" facial prototype or contain symmetry

binocular cues   Depth perception cues develop from two eyes that signal depth and distance; binocular cues develop because the two eyes send different signals to the brain

contingent reinforcement studies   Techniques used by researchers to test whether infants increase a specific behavior in response to certain stimuli; for example, researchers may test infants' sucking behaviors in response to hearing their mothers' voice

contrast sensitivity   The minimum difference in brightness between an image and its background that infants can perceive; infants' contrast sensitivity improves as their eyes mature

depth perception   The ability to perceive vertical distance from a top surface or space to a bottom one

ecological theory of perception   A theory of development posited by Eleanor Gibson and James Gibson that highlights the evolutionary foundations of human perceptual abilities and the connections between perception and action

eye-trackers   Devices that researchers use to assess infant eye movements and patterns of visual fixation; eye-trackers are built into computer monitors or worn on a participant's head

fovea   The central portion of the retina where the field of vision is focused; the fovea contains a high density of cones (cells that respond to color wavelengths), thus allowing for sharp central vision

gait-mat procedure   A technique used by researchers to examine infants' walking proficiency; infants are encouraged to walk across a portable, flexible mat or walkway with pressure sensors that record the length of footsteps and how long it takes

gauging affordances for action   An individual's interpretation of which actions are possible and which are not possible based on their perceptions, as in when infants determine they can walk on a flat surface

Gestalt theory of perception   Principles or laws of human perception that describe humans' spontaneous and natural organization of visual stimuli into meaningful patterns, such as perceiving objects as whole

good continuation   A Gestalt principle of organization claiming an innate tendency for individuals to view objects or stimuli as continuous, as when an infant perceives a rod to be whole even when part of the rod is hidden by another object

habituation-recovery test   A research method that involves presenting infants with a stimulus until infants habituate; researchers then present a new stimulus to which infants typically recover or rebound attention

intermodal perception The process in which an individual perceives and connects information that is available to multiple senses simultaneously

maturation A genetically determined process that controls and preserves the order of behaviors and skills as children develop

monocular cues Depth perception cues from one eye that signal depth and distance to figure out an object's distance; monocular cues provide information about visual angles

motion parallax A monocular depth perception cue that results from the relative velocities of objects at different distances as they move across the retina

newborn stepping A phenomenon in which newborns demonstrate spontaneous and coordinated "stepping" movements by lifting one leg and then the other leg when held over a surface

novelty preference Seen when an infant looks longer at a novel stimulus relative to a familiar stimulus, suggesting that the infant discriminates between the two and remembers having experienced the familiar stimulus

other-race effect A type of perceptual narrowing in which infants have a reduced ability to distinguish among faces of other races due to their experiences with faces of generally the same race

perception The psychological process of organizing and interpreting sensory information

perception-action feedback loop The continuous cycle that connects perception and action as individuals perceive, act, and adjust their actions in response to an environment that changes

perceptual narrowing A developmental process characterized by a diminished ability to distinguish among stimuli because of a lack of experience with them; infants display perceptual narrowing for faces as they attend to familiar faces, such as faces of a specific sex or race

pincer grasp The coordination of an infant's index finger and thumb to grasp small objects, usually developed toward the end of the first year of life

posture The position in which a person holds their head and body

preferential-looking test A research method to study infant perceptual development introduced by Robert Fantz to determine whether young infants discriminate between two stimuli by looking more to one image than the other

prehension The action of reaching and grasping an object

prospective control The ability to act adaptively in an anticipatory manner, such as when an infant opens the hands to match an object's size before grasping the object

relative threshold The minimum difference in loudness or pitch needed to distinguish between two sounds; relative threshold is one way to define perception of loudness and pitch

sensation The process of sensing the environment, beginning with a stimulus activating receptors in the sensory organs (i.e., eyes, ears, nose, mouth, and skin); receptor neurons convert the stimulus into signals that are sent to the brain

shape constancy The perception of an object having a constant shape despite changes to the retinal image

size constancy The perception of an object having a constant size despite changes in the size of the retinal image

speech perception The interpretation of sounds of language; infants show speech perception by discriminating speech from nonspeech sounds

temporal synchrony When different types of perceptual information occur at the same time, creating a unitary perceptual experience

visual accommodation A physical process in which the lens of the eyes changes shape to focus on objects of different distances

visual acuity The ability to see fine detail including the clearness and sharpness of a visual image; physical maturation of the eye facilitates visual acuity

visual cliff A test developed by Eleanor Gibson and Richard Walk, which involves an apparatus with an apparent drop-off or cliff, to determine if infants perceive depth; the famous visual cliff experiment showed that infants crawled across the shallow side of the cliff but not the deep side, indicating perception of depth

Chapter 5

A-not-B error Infants' repeated and unsuccessful searches for hidden objects at location A, not B; Jean Piaget suggested that infants' repeated errors indicate limited reasoning about objects and a lack of object permanence

A-not-B task A test used to study infants' understanding of object permanence in which a researcher hides an object at location A while the infant watches; the infant retrieves the toy from location A; and then the researcher hides the object at location B after one or several trials

approximate number sense (ANS) Infants' ability to estimate the approximate magnitude of items in a set without relying on counting (e.g., an infant choosing a pile of 18 cheerios versus a pile of 6 cheerios)

attention termination The fourth phase of attention when an individual no longer processes the stimulus information

automatic response The first phase of attention, characterized by the detection of a stimulus before orienting to it

Carolina Abecedarian Project One of the most widely cited intervention programs for children growing up in poverty; children between infancy and five years attended full-time day care with activities focused on cognitive stimulation, language development, and social growth, and showed sustained academic and cognitive achievements years later compared to individuals who did not receive the intervention

cognitive processes Mental processes, such as attention and perception, involved in cognition

cognitive structures Regions and neural connections in the brain involved in cognitive processes such as memory and comprehension

conjugate mobile experiment A test used to study infant memory in which the infant's leg is tied to a mobile, with kicking causing the mobile to move; when the tie is removed, infants later kick in response to the familiar mobile, indicating they remembered that their kicking elicited a response

core capacities Innate, mental capacities that are building blocks to cognitive development and allow infants to make sense of the environment; nativists claim that infants are born with core capacities, including object permanence

deferred imitation Copying another person's actions hours or days later

displaced reference A major symbolic accomplishment in which children understand and use words to refer to things that are not present

false belief A thought about another person's knowledge that does not match reality, such as believing that someone knows where a toy is located when they were not around to see the toy moved

habituation rate The time it takes for a decrease in infants' response to a stimulus after repeated exposures to the stimulus, which is thought to measure how long infants require to process the stimulus information

Home Observation for the Measurement of the Environment (HOME)
A widely used assessment of children's home environments based on observations of the quantity and quality of caregiver support and stimulation; family organization and routines; and family involvement in children's lives

imitation The act of copying another person's actions

intersensory redundancy hypothesis
A hypothesis that attention is recruited and learning is enhanced in the presence of multi-modal stimuli (such as sight and sound)

joint attention The shared attention of two individuals on the same object or event; shifts in gaze, head turning, and pointing are ways that infants engage in joint attention

means-end analysis The ability to identify and execute the necessary actions or means to attain a specific goal or end; by the fourth substage of the sensorimotor stage (coordination of secondary circular reactions), infants engage in goal-directed behaviors to solve problems, such as how to get a desired toy

memory recall Memory for a past experience in the absence of the stimulus; deferred imitation requires memory recall

mental representation The ability to hold and manipulate objects and events in the mind; according to Jean Piaget, toddlers achieve this ability during the sixth substage of the sensorimotor stage (mental representation)

mental state vocabulary Vocabulary words that refer to the internal workings of people's minds, such as "think," "know," and "wish"

motor habits Movements individuals make with their bodies without having to think about them; during the second substage of the sensorimotor stage (primary circular reactions), infants will display simple motor habits as they extend their behaviors in new ways

novelty preference The rebounding of infant attention to a novel stimulus relative to a familiar stimulus experienced previously

object permanence The understanding that objects continue to exist independent of one's immediate perceptual experiences

orientation The second phase of attention, characterized by turning head and eyes to a picture, object, or person

principle of persistence As claimed by nativists, an innate understanding that objects retain their physical properties, such as height

recognition memory Recognition that a specific stimulus had been experienced in the past; it is thought to be seen when infants rebound attention to a new stimulus relative to a familiar stimulus following experience with the familiar stimulus

selective attention The process of directing attention to relevant information in the environment while ignoring irrelevant information

sensorimotor stage The earliest stage in Piaget's cognitive theory of development that spans between birth to about 18 months of age when schemas are limited to sensory experiences and motor actions; the sensorimotor stage is divided into six substages

social cognition The processing, storing, and application of information about people and social situations

stimulus salience The features (e.g., brightness, different sounds) of an object that characterize how attractive, prominent, and noticeable it is

sustained attention The third phase of attention when an individual begins to process a stimulus, during which learning occurs

violation-of-expectation paradigm
A looking technique, based on a habituation and dishabituation procedure that compares infant looking at certain events (such as "impossible" events or "unexpected outcomes") compared to other events (such as "possible" events or "expected outcomes")

visual search tasks Perceptual tasks in which a target stimulus is embedded in a background of distractors and infants' attention to the target is measured as they look at the target

Chapter 6

American Sign Language (ASL)
A form of sign language used by the Deaf population in the United States and Canada in which people communicate through the hands and face

amount of language The total number or quantity of words

canonical syllables/babbles Vocalizations in which a consonant precedes or follows a vowel sound

child-centered communications Adult-child interactions in which caregivers interact with infants based on the interest of infants and treat infants like conversational partners, often using infant-directed speech

communicative accommodation
The adjustments that caregivers make to language and behaviors when communicating with young infants

computer simulations Models of neural networks used to test connectionist theories of the brain and language development through feeding a large body of language input into a computer with little preprogrammed knowledge

connectionist theory A theory that stresses the building of neural networks in the brain that allow children to draw connections and associations among various related concepts

contingent responsiveness Caregivers' prompt, attuned responses (typically verbal) to infant behaviors

cooing Vowellike, non-distress vocalizations that infants produce to communicate around two to three months of age

dual-language learners (DLLs)
Children who learn two languages because they are exposed to a native language at home that differs from the language of the community

dyslexia A set of disorders involving challenges in learning to read or interpret words, letters, or other symbols

fast mapping Children's learning of a new word with only one or two exposures

holophrastic language The early period of language development and vocabulary growth in which children use single words to express a complete thought

homesign A unique signing communication system with consistent rules for combining parts of speech into sentences developed by deaf children with minimal exposure to sign language

infant-directed speech The unique way that adults talk to infants by using exaggerated intonation, frequent changes to the amplitude of speech, short and grammatically simple utterances, and talk that is concrete

intermodal preferential looking paradigm An extension of the preferential looking procedure used to test infant receptive language, in which researchers present a word and two images side-by-side to assess if the infant looks at the image of the spoken word

language acquisition device (LAD)
An innate component in the brain claimed to explain the rapid acquisition of language in Noam Chomsky's nativist theory of language

lexical diversity The number of different words in speech

morpheme The smallest unit of meaning in language that cannot be divided further

motionese Infant-directed action that is characterized by exaggerated and repetitive motions by caregivers (such as sweeping arm movements) as they communicate with infants

mutual exclusivity A type of cognitive bias that supports word learning in which children expect an entity to have only one name

overextensions The overgeneralizing of words to an overly broad class of referents (e.g., saying "dog" for all animals)

phonemes The smallest distinguishable sound units of a language, such as the /b/ in ball; each language has a distinct set of phonemes, and infants must learn to perceive and produce the phonemes of their language

phonological development The mastering of a language's sound system (including how speech sounds combine into words) and using speech sounds to communicate effectively

phonotactics The permissible structure of syllables, groups of consonants, and sequences of vowels in a language

pragmatics The social conventions and norms around language that children must learn to effectively communicate with others

principle of linguistic relativity The hypothesis that language can affect thinking, also known as the Whorfian hypothesis

productive vocabulary The words that an infant produces

protoconversations A sort of give-and-take dialogue, including words, sounds, and gestures, in which the talk and behaviors of caregivers and the smiles and coos of infants are well timed and responsive to one another

protodeclaratives Gestures such as pointing that are used to get someone to attend to an object or event

protoimperatives Gestures used to request something (e.g., holding out a hand to ask for more food)

receptive language The ability to understand language and the meaning of words and phrases

referential language Statements or questions about objects or events that support infants' vocabulary development

referent mapping The mapping of a word to its referent in the world

regulatory language Directives that regulate infants' attention and actions

that often contain many pronouns (e.g., "Put it here")

relational words Words that refer to the state and location of objects that children typically express during the second year of life (e.g., "under")

scaffolding The rich variety of strategies that adults use to guide children to higher levels of thinking than children can achieve on their own

semantic development The learning of the meanings of words and word combinations

simultaneous bilinguals Children exposed to two (or more) languages from birth or before 3 years of age

situation-centered communications Interactions in which adults predominantly interact with one another, leaving infants and young children to figure out what is being talked about

statistical learning The ability of infants to perceive and learn regularities in language such as the speech sounds that comprise a word

syntactic bootstrapping The use of the syntax of a sentence to infer the meaning of unfamiliar words

syntax The set of rules that govern the ordering of parts of speech to form meaningful sentences

telegraphic speech A form of communication used commonly by toddlers that is characterized by simple, two-word sentences (e.g., "mommy shoe")

underextension The mapping of words to an overly narrow class of referents (e.g., saying "truck" only to a toy truck)

universal grammar An innate set of abstract grammatical rules shared by all human languages in Noam Chomsky's nativist theory of language

vocabulary spurt A naming explosion characterized by an accelerated rate in children's production of new words, typically occurring around 18 months of age

vowel hyperarticulation An exaggeration of vowels in speech that facilitates infants' ability to phonologically distinguish new words and understand repetition of familiar words

whole object assumption A type of cognitive bias that supports word learning in which children assume that a novel word refers to a whole object, rather than parts or features of the object

Chapter 7

attachment The affectionate bonds that infants develop toward the important people in their lives and their

reliance on loved ones for comfort and protection

Baby "X" studies Experiments in which researchers label the same infant as a "boy" or a "girl" and then observe how caregivers or adults talk and interact with the infant based on the labeled gender

basic emotions Universal emotions such as anger, fear, surprise, disgust, happiness, and sadness

basic trust versus mistrust The first stage in Erik Erikson's theory of psychosocial development, in which infants learn to trust their caregivers

conceptual self The characteristics a person uses to describe oneself, also referred to as the "me" or "objective self"

contingency experiences Environmental effects that arise from infant actions such as a mobile moving in response to a swipe; infants' reactions to contingency are thought to reflect the ecological self

disorganized An infant attachment style characterized by an infant's contradictory emotions and behavior and disorganized movements, freezing, and apprehension toward caregiver

distress tolerance The ability to persist when faced with negative emotions and cope with everyday stressors

drive reduction theory The idea that a primary motivation of humans is to satisfy biological needs, such as hunger and thirst

ecological self The perception of one's body in relation to the physical environment

effortful control A child's capacity to voluntarily regulate attention and behavior when responding to emotionally challenging situations

emotion discrimination The ability to distinguish among emotional expressions such as sad and angry speech or faces

emotion regulation The monitoring, evaluating, and moderating of emotional responses, especially in stressful situations

emotion understanding Infants' ability to discriminate among emotions; connect emotional expressions to meaning; and seek and use emotional information to guide their actions

ethological theory of attachment A theory posited by John Bowlby that claims attachment is an evolved response that aids infants' survival

evocative effects A type of gene-environment association in which a child's inherited characteristics evoke strong responses from others that strengthen the child's characteristics

externalizing behaviors   Problem behaviors directed to the external environment, such as physical aggression, disobeying rules, and destroying property

gender identity   In infancy, gender identity refers to knowing that one is a boy or a girl

goodness of fit   The extent to which a person's temperament matches the requirements, expectations, and opportunities of the environment

helper-hinderer studies   Studies that assess infants' moral understanding and evaluation by presenting infants with "helping" and "hurting" puppets (for example) and then testing whether infants behave differently toward the "helper" or "hinderer"

imprinting   A phenomenon identified by Konrad Lorenz in which certain animal species are predisposed to follow whatever moving thing they see during a critical period early in life

inhibition   A dimension of temperament that reflects an infant's withdrawal from and intense reaction to unfamiliar situations and people

inhibitory control   An executive function that suppresses a dominant or preferred response in favor of an acceptable, more adaptive response

insecure avoidant   An attachment status initially identified by Mary Ainsworth that is characterized by infants who do not become distressed by the caregiver's departure, freely explore the room, are easily comforted by the stranger, and show indifference during reunion with the caregiver

insecure resistant   An attachment status (also called ambivalent), initially identified by Mary Ainsworth that is characterized by infants who become very upset and anxious when the caregiver leaves the room and are not easily comforted on caregiver return

interaction synchrony   The prompt, reciprocal ways that caregivers respond to infant behaviors and emotions, which support infant emotional regulation

internal working models   A mental representation of one's attachment relationship with the primary care-giver, which becomes a model for future social relationships and the quality of these relationships

interpersonal self   The perception of oneself in relation to other people, including experiences with eye- contact and back-and-forth exchanges with others

matching studies   Studies that assess whether infants are able to match the emotional content of stimuli presented in different modalities, such as face and voice

mirroring behaviors   The reflecting back of emotions by caregivers to their infants such as smiling in response to an infant's smile

moral goodness   Feelings of concern for others and attempts to help others in need, including empathetic responses to others in distress

moral retribution   The tendency to punish or support individuals who misbehave

moral understanding and evaluation   Identifying and liking individuals who are cooperative, empathetic, or helpful, and disliking individuals who are uncooperative, unempathetic, or unhelpful

negative reactivity   An infant's high arousal in response to sensory stimuli; infants with high negative reactivity display fear, frustration, sadness, and low soothability

orienting regulation   An infant's ability to regulate attention toward goals and away from distressing situations

other-stimulation   When an experimenter's finger touches the infant's cheek, creating a single-touch experience; other-stimulation is part of the single-touch and double-touch experiment

physical aggression   Behavior causing physical harm to others, such as hitting, pushing, kicking, and biting

relational aggression   A type of nonphysical aggression in which harm is caused by hurting someone's relationships or social status, such as by threatening to withdraw a friendship, withdrawing a friendship, ignoring a peer, or excluding a peer

secure attachment   An attachment status initially identified by Mary Ainsworth in which infants display a strong connection or bond with their caregiver(s) and use their caregivers as a safe base from which to explore their environment; securely attached infants become upset when their caregivers leave the room, are happy when their caregivers return, and seek comfort from their caregivers

self-conscious emotions   Emotions that involve a sense of self-awareness and are based on others' perceptions, such as embarrassment, pride, guilt, and shame

self-regulation   The ability to control attention, emotions, thinking, and behavior

self-stimulation   When an infant's hand or finger touches its own cheek (creating a double-touch experience); self-stimulation is part of the single-touch and double-touch experiment

single-touch and double-touch experiment   An experiment to test infant self-awareness; researchers ask whether very young infants can distinguish between an experimenter touching the infant's cheek (single-touch; other-stimulation) and the infant's own touch of the cheek (double-touch; self-stimulation)

social referencing   The seeking and use of social information in ambiguous situations, such as when a toddler looks at a mother's face when uncertain about how to react to a strange person

social smiles   Smiles directed to people, particularly to caregivers, with the purpose of engaging in social interactions

still-face experiment   An experiment in which caregivers interact naturally with their infants for a brief period, followed by maintaining a still, unresponsive face for several minutes; the caregivers' still face elicits distress and negative emotions in infants that can be viewed as a measure of infant and mother emotional connection (among other things)

Strange Situation   An experiment developed by Mary Ainsworth to assess infant attachment to caregivers based on infant behaviors; in a laboratory playroom, infants experience separations from their caregiver, exposure to a stranger, and then reunification with their caregiver

subjective self   The characteristics a person uses to describe oneself, also referred to as the "I" of the self; a person's sense of acting in the environment as a unique entity

surgency   An infant's activity level and intensity of pleasure; infants with high surgency show a lot of happiness by smiling and laughing

temperament   Individual differences among infants in intensity of reactivity and regulation of emotions, activity, and attention

Chapter 8

actigraphs   Lightweight monitors that measure children's wake and sleep patterns

amygdala   A small structure located deep in the brain that registers positive and negative emotions

anemia   Low blood count or a condition in which an individual lacks sufficient red blood cells to carry oxygen to the body's tissues, sometimes due to malnutrition

cerebellum   The brain structure that coordinates movement, such as walking and balancing, and that is involved in memory, cognition, and emotion

cerebral lateralization   The functional dominance of one hemisphere over another hemisphere of the brain; left and right hemispheres control opposite sides of the body and specific body functions

chronic diseases   Noncommunicable and long-lasting diseases that typically can be controlled through ongoing medical attention but not cured, such as obesity, malnutrition, diabetes, and developmental disabilities

corpus callosum   A dense tract of nerve fibers, beneath the cerebral cortex, which facilitates communication between the left and right hemispheres of the brain

cortisol   A hormone, produced by the hypothalamus, which regulates various processes such as metabolism, the immune response, and the stress response; cortisol also controls blood glucose levels and blood pressure

developmental coordination disorder   A movement condition characterized by difficulty learning fine and gross motor skills and in movement coordination that may interfere with everyday tasks

dwarfism   A genetic or medical condition, mostly caused by achondroplasia, in which an individual has an unusually short stature

emotional abuse   Extreme psychological and verbal abuse of children, including hampering of children's emotional needs, such as belittling, ridiculing, extreme negativity and hostility, and making suicidal or homicidal threats

epidemiological studies   Large-scale studies that analyze the prevalence, causes, and consequences of health and illness at community, state, national, and international levels

fine motor skills   Small actions or body movements that rely on coordination between small muscles (such as hand and fingers) and are critical to activities of daily living

gross motor skills   Body movements that rely on large muscle groups in arms, legs, feet, and torso and include large-scale movements such as locomotion

growth hormone   A hormone produced in the pituitary gland that stimulates the release of hormones involved in growth, including body tissue and bone development

handedness   The tendency to use either the right or the left hand more than the other

hippocampus   The part of the brain located in the inner region of the temporal lobe that is involved in regulating emotions and supports children's memory, spatial understanding, and executive functioning

hypothalamus   The part of the brain that is involved in experience of emotions such as happiness and sadness; and regulates behaviors such as sleep, eating, and drinking; the hypothalamus responds to signals from the amygdala and hippocampus by producing hormones, such as cortisol, which help control a person's stress response

infectious diseases   Diseases caused by pathogenic micro-organisms such as bacteria, viruses, parasites, or fungi that can be spread among people through personal contact, water, or air

maltreatment   The emotional abuse, physical abuse, sexual abuse, or neglect of children

neglect   The failure to meet children's basic needs for food, clothing, shelter, and medical attention and care

neuroplasticity   The ability of the brain to reorganize itself through biological changes and by rearranging neurons

night terrors   Arousals or disruptions from deep sleep more dramatic than a nightmare, in which children scream from panic, thrash wildly, and experience raised heart rates and breathing

obesity   The excess storage of fat, typically an outcome of unhealthy eating

physical abuse   The intentional infliction of physical, bodily harm on a child, including choking, bruising, burning, and breaking bones

positive stress   A type of stress that creates brief and mild or moderate changes in children's psychological states (e.g., anxiety before the first day of school)

Prader-Willi Syndrome   A genetic, neurodevelopmental disorder, with poor regulation of different hormones, associated in infancy with diminished muscle tone, feeding difficulties, and delayed physical development

prefrontal cortex   The "executive" region of the brain (located at the front part of the outer layer of the frontal lobe) controls functions involved in attention, behavior, working memory, and making decisions

psychosocial dwarfism   A syndrome characterized by short stature or growth caused by extreme emotional deprivation, neglect, or stress, and potentially resulting in long-term psychological and social adjustment problems

sexual abuse   Attempts toward or actual sexual contact with a child, or forcing a child into prostitution

sleep consolidation   The establishment of a single episode of nighttime sleep as children consolidate their sleep into a single nighttime period and eliminate daytime naps

sleep regulation   The ability to transition from wakefulness to sleep states and control the quantity and quality of sleep

synaptic pruning   The process in which synapses are eliminated to increase the efficacy of neural communication

thyroid-stimulating hormone   A hormone produced by the anterior pituitary gland that functions to regulate the production of hormones by the thyroid gland; thyroid hormones are essential in regulating such body qualities as weight and energy levels

tolerable stress   A type of stress characterized by exposure to nonnormative experiences, such as the death of a family member, a serious illness, or a natural disaster

toxic stress   A type of stress that occurs when children experience chronic, persistent, or strong activation of the body's stress response system

Chapter 9

animistic thinking   A type of reasoning in which children attribute human qualities to inanimate entities

appearance-reality tasks   Tasks that assess children's ability to differentiate between appearance and reality, such as when testing if children understand a cat remains a cat in reality even if wearing a dog mask and appearing to be a dog

Big Math for Little Kids (BMLK)   A comprehensive math program for young children that promotes emergent math skills characterized through activities focused on number, shape, measurement, and space

cardinal principle   The understanding in early math development that each number in a sequence represents a specific number of elements in a set

causal understanding   The ability to infer the relation between a cause and its effect

centration   The tendency to focus on a single, perceptually salient feature or characteristic of an entity to the exclusion of other features

class inclusion problems   Tasks that assess children's understanding of hierarchical classification, such as asking children whether there are more "red flowers" or "flowers generally"

clause   The smallest grammatical unit (e.g., subject, verb phrase) that expresses a complete thought

code-related skills   The formalities of writing, sounding out, and reading letters and words on a page that include skills such as forming letters and connecting letters to sounds

cognitive flexibility   A component of executive functioning referring to children's ability to shift between thinking about two different concepts or to think about multiple concepts simultaneously

conservation tasks   Piagetian tests that assess whether children understand that an entity remains the same in its number, mass, and so on, even if its form changes

consolidation   A process in which a neural imprint of memories is formed in the brain.

day-night Stroop task   An example of a Stroop task in which children are required to inhibit their automatic response by saying "day" to a picture of a moon and "night" to a picture of a sun

declarative memory   A component of long-term memory that involves memory for facts, events, and personal past experiences; declarative memory subdivides into semantic and episodic memory

dialogic reading   A reading style in which adults ask "WH" questions, prompt children to participate, and engage children in discussion during reading time

dimensional card-sorting tasks   Tests used to assess cognitive flexibility and executive functioning in which children sort cards one way (e.g., by object color) and then switch their thinking to sort the same cards a different way (e.g., by object type)

dual representation   The understanding that an object is both an entity in itself and a symbol for something else

egocentrism   The tendency of children to think that other people view the world from their perspective, and thus an inability to consider another person's perspective

emergent literacy   The collection of skills, knowledge, and attitudes that are early precursors to reading and writing

episodic memory   The subtype of declarative memory referring to everyday memories about personal experiences, situations, and events

essentialism   The understanding that entities in a category have an underlying shared essence that may not be visually apparent (e.g., bees are insects that sting)

executive functioning   The collection of skills involved in controlling and coordinating attention, memory, and other behaviors involved in goal-directed actions

expansions   The elaboration of children's sentences with additional details or information

eyewitness testimony   A later account of an observed event

false memory   The remembering of information that is wrong or different from what actually happened

forgetting   The loss of memories over time

go/no-go task   An example of a Stroop task in which children (or adults) are presented with pictures, colors, and letters and are asked to touch a computer screen when a target stimulus appears ("go") but not when a non-target stimulus appears ("no-go"); requires inhibition and ability to selectively attend to specific stimuli

hierarchical classification   The ability to organize items into superordinate and subordinate categories

infantile amnesia   The difficulty adults have in remembering events from the first years of life

inhibitory control   A component of executive functioning that refers to children's ability to respond appropriately to a stimulus while inhibiting an alternative, dominant response

literacy   Fundamental reading and writing skills

literacy-focused preschool curriculum   A curriculum that targets opportunities for young children to develop literacy skills through the use of activities that include dialogic reading, phonological awareness activities, and play activities that integrate reading and writing

logical mental operations   The ability to combine, separate, and transform information logically in the mind without the need to directly perceive or experience the information

long-term memory   The unlimited, enduring storehouse of knowledge in the brain that accumulates over time

mental representation   Mental internalization of thought, such as seen in

language and symbolic play, that marks the transition from the sensorimotor stage to preoperational thinking according to Jean Piaget

memory span tests   A test of children's working memory that measures the number of items (e.g., words, letters of the alphabet) children can recall and repeat immediately after being presented with a list

mental state talk   Statements and questions that refer to others' minds, such as think, know, and want

metacognitive skill   A person's awareness of what that person knows and how thinking and cognition work; "knowing about knowing"

monitoring   Keeping track of one's performance on a task and making necessary adjustments

morphology   The study of words and how words are formed

organization   A memory strategy marked by imposing a structure on items based on their relations to one another (such as grouping) to aid recall of information

overregularization   The use of a regular morpheme in a word that is irregular, such as saying "taked" rather than "took" for the past tense or "mouses" rather than "mice" for the plural form

pragmatics   The norms of language use and the contexts in which language is used, including when to talk, how to talk, and what to talk about

precausal thinking   Logical errors that children make in cause-effect relations, including circular thinking, as when a child says "cold makes snow" and "snow makes cold"

preoperational stage   The second stage in Jean Piaget's theory of cognitive development in which young children can think symbolically (as seen in pretend play, language, deferred imitation, and object permanence) but still show limitations in areas such as perspective taking, conservation, logical thinking, and causal understanding

recasts   The restructuring of children's grammatically incorrect sentences into correct forms (often by a caregiver)

rehearsal   A strategy for remembering that relies on repeating information to aid memory

reversibility   The ability to realize that numbers or objects can be changed or returned to their original state, such as when children recognize that after rolling a ball of clay into a snakelike shape, it is possible to mold it back into its original shape

scripts A component of semantic memory referring to knowledge about familiar routines, such as the sequence of events and expected behaviors when eating at a restaurant

self-regulation The ability to manage and integrate attention, thoughts, and behaviors to attain goals

semantic memory The subtype of declarative memory referring to the knowledge a person has acquired around facts, rules, and concepts (including general world knowledge)

sociodramatic play Pretend play in which children act out imaginary stories related to life experiences and that may involve others in created play scenarios

spatial cognition Abilities to understand and represent shapes, locations, and spatial relations among objects

Stroop tasks Tests that examine inhibitory control through asking children (or adults) to respond to stimuli that are congruent or incongruent with the required response (e.g, saying the color red to red stimuli versus saying red to green stimuli)

suggestibility The inclination to accept false information when recalling an experience

symbolic understanding The understanding that things can stand for other things

syntax The set of rules that govern the ordering of parts of speech to form meaningful sentences

taxonomic categorization The classification of entities based on their similar characteristics or functions, such as the category of foods or body parts

theory of mind The ability to attribute mental states, such as knowledge, beliefs, and desires, to oneself and to others, and to understand that other people's knowledge, beliefs, and desires may be different from someone else's

Tools of the Mind curriculum An early childhood curriculum that focuses on play as a primary vehicle for the development of self- regulation, executive functioning, and higher-level cognitive skills

Tower of London task A test used to assess children's planning abilities that involve rearranging objects (e.g., disks, colored balls) from an initial configuration to a configuration that matches a display

working memory A third component of executive functioning referring to the ability to maintain and manipulate information in the mind over a short period of time, thus being important for concentration, focus, and following instructions

wug test A method of studying children's understanding of plural formation and other rules in grammar based on children's verbal responses to pictures of invented nouns, verbs, and adjectives (such as whether a child says "wugs" to 2 odd creatures)

Chapter 10

Attachment Q-Sort (AQS) An assessment approach to classifying child attachment in which a caregiver or observer sorts sort cards describing child attachment-related behaviors based on the degree to which the child matches the description

conventional A level of moral reasoning identified by Lawrence Kohlberg based on social consensus, societal expectations, and conventional reasoning

cooperative play Socially reciprocal play in which children interact with each other as they engage in a shared activity with the same goal (e.g., children working together on a puzzle)

corporal punishment The purposeful use of harmful punishment by a caregiver to inflict physical pain or discomfort on a child

cultural socialization A type of racial-ethnic socialization message in which adults educate children about children's racial or ethnic heritage, promote children's cultural heritage, and instill racial and ethnic pride in children

delay-of-gratification tasks Experiments that measure children's abilities to resist an immediate temptation in order to receive a later (often larger) reward, which shed light on children's emotion regulation

display rules Cultural norms about when, where, and how to express emotions that children learn through social interactions

effortful control The ability to modulate attention and inhibit behavior, including in stressful situations

egalitarianism A type of racial-ethnic socialization message in which adults highlight similarities and equality among people of all races and ethnicities

Electra complex A gender identification phenomenon in Sigmund Freud' stage theory of psychosexual development, in which (according to Freud) girls compete with their mothers for their fathers' attention, and upon recognition that their feelings are wrong, distance themselves from their fathers and develop a close relationship with their mothers

emotion coaching The positive socialization of children's emotions, as when caregivers validate children's feelings and offer coping strategies in emotionally stressful situations

emotion matching tasks A task in which children are asked to label the emotion of a facial expression

emotional valence The affective quality of an emotion as positive ("good") or negative ("bad")

emotion vignettes Stories that researchers use to test children's understanding of the causes and consequences of emotions in which children may be asked how a character feels or why a character feels a certain emotion

essentialism Statements and beliefs that members of a group share underlying characteristics and behaviors

ethnicity A social group's national or cultural heritage (e.g., being Russian)

externalizing problems Problem behaviors directed outward in which children act out, such as hitting others or throwing things

gender consistency A stage in gender development described in the cognitive development view characterized by children's understanding that one's sex will remain the same regardless of superficial changes to appearance and behaviors

gendered parenting The messages and practices of parents to children about how boys and girls should behave, which may be conveyed through play interactions, language interactions, and so on

gender identity A stage in gender development described in the cognitive development view in which children identify themselves and others by their sex, traditionally emerging around 3 years of age

gender stability A stage in gender development described in the cognitive development view characterized by children's understanding that one's sex continues over time (e.g., girls grow up to be women)

hostile aggression A type of reactionary aggression experienced in response to a threat or insult and with the intention to cause pain

hostile attribution bias A child's inaccurate interpretation of another child's accidental behavior as motivated by an antagonistic or hostile intention

id According to Sigmund Freud, a part of one's personality comprising the primitive, natural biological drives for pleasure and maximum gratification that are present from birth and that explain why a child may act immorally

imitation learning Children's mimicking the actions that they observe in others, a type of social learning first documented by Albert Bandura

initiative versus guilt   The third stage in Erik Erikson's theory of psychosocial development and self-identity in which young children learn to assert themselves by engaging in social interactions, initiating activities, exploring their environment, and exhibiting competence in social interactions; caregivers who discourage or criticize children may create the alternative sense of guilt in their children during this stage

insecure ambivalent/dependent   An attachment style characterized by children who are simultaneously dependent and resistant toward their caregiver

insecure avoidant   An attachment style characterized by children who are physically and emotionally avoidant of their caregiver, respond minimally to their caregiver, and generally display neutral affect

insecure disorganized   An attachment style characterized by children who show disordered, confused, and apprehensive behaviors

instrumental aggression   A type of aggression aimed at achieving a specific goal, such as a child threatening another child to get a toy

internalizing problems   Problem behaviors based on negative emotions that are directed inwards, which may be expressed in anxiety or depression

marshmallow task   A delay-of-gratification experiment developed by Walter Mischel to test children's ability to not touch or eat a marshmallow as the researcher is out of the room, in order to later receive two marshmallows

mixed emotions   The feeling of two or more emotions at the same time

moral domain   An area of social knowledge within social domain theory that focuses on reasoning based on moral issues around others' rights, fairness, equal treatment, discrimination, and bias

Oedipus complex   A gender identification phenomenon in Sigmund Freud's stage theory of psychosexual development in which (according to Freud) boys recognize that their strong sexual attraction for their mothers is wrong, experience anguish, and then distance themselves from their mothers and identify with their fathers

parallel play   A type of play in which children engage in similar activities but do not interact with each other (e.g., building blocks side-by-side)

post-conventional   A level of moral reasoning identified by Lawrence Kohlberg based on abstract principles of human rights, justice, and equality

power assertion   Control exerted by caregivers over children that is aversive, intrusive, and punitive

pre-conventional   A broad level of moral reasoning identified by Lawrence Kohlberg based on the direct consequences of actions

preparation for bias   A type of racial-ethnic socialization message in which adults communicate to children the risk of discrimination toward their group and offer children coping strategies

Preschool Attachment Classification System (PACS)   An assessment of attachment in young children; children experience brief episodes in which they are separated and reunited with their caregivers, and researchers rate children's behaviors to classify children as secure, insecure avoidant, insecure ambivalent/dependent, or insecure disorganized

promotion of mistrust   A type of racial-ethnic socialization message identified in which adults communicate to children distrust of people from other groups (e.g., warnings about other racial groups)

prosocial behaviors   Behaviors such as sharing, cooperating, and helping that benefit another person

psychological domain   An area of social knowledge within social domain theory that focuses on children's ability to understand the mental states, beliefs, emotions, and intentions of others

race   A group's shared phenotypical, physical characteristics (e.g., being White, Black, or Asian)

racial and ethnic socialization   Caregivers' socialization practices and messages to children about race and ethnicity

relational aggression   A type of nonphysical aggression in which harm is caused by hurting someone's relationships or social status, such as by threatening to withdraw a friendship, withdrawing a friendship, ignoring a peer, excluding a peer, or spreading rumors

resource allocation studies   Studies conducted by developmental researchers to examine children's moral decisions around equitable distribution by asking children to distribute coins, treats, or other rewards to story characters and children from other social groups

secure   An attachment style characterized by children who are happy and confident to explore their surroundings, using their caregiver as a secure base, and who are positive when reunited with their caregiver

social identification   The process in the cognitive developmental view of gender development in which boys and girls create a cognitive schema about their

gender as they identify their gender and come to understand that people of their gender have specific characteristics and behaviors

societal domain   An area of social knowledge within social domain theory consisting of social systems, organizations, and norms

Chapter 11

anaerobic threshold   The lactate inflection point during exercise when lactic acid starts to build up in the muscles and results in cramping

asthma   A respiratory disease in which spasms occur in the bronchi of the lungs due to a buildup of mucus, creating breathing difficulties; asthma is the most common chronic disease of childhood in the United States

attention-deficit/hyperactivity disorder (ADHD)   A prevalent and chronic neurobehavioral disorder characterized by persistent inattention and trouble concentrating, hyperactivity, and impulsiveness

autism spectrum disorder   A developmental disability that manifests in challenges in social interaction, problems with speech and nonverbal communication, and restricted/repetitive behaviors. The severity of symptoms differs across individuals

brain network analyses   The study of brain processes and functions, including how brain connections or networks emerge and change from childhood to adulthood, using functional MRI (fMRI) signals across areas of the brain

brain waves   Rhythmic or repetitive patterns of electrical impulses or neural oscillations in the brain that are created when impulses from neurons communicate

concussion   A brain injury, sometimes marked by temporary unconsciousness, brought about by a blow to the head; symptoms may include headache, dizziness, ringing in the ears, and sleepiness

developmental coordination disorder (DCD)   A condition without known medical or neurological origins in which children show problems in motor coordination such that they are extremely clumsy or awkward

Diagnostic and Statistical Manual of Mental Disorders (DSM-5)   A manual developed by the American Psychiatric Association that aids with the diagnosis of personality disorders in children and adults

food insecurity   A family's experience with insufficient food or not having reliable access to enough affordable and nutritious food for all household members

magnetic resonance imaging (MRI) A brain imaging technique that uses strong magnetic fields and radio waves to create images of the brain's anatomy, including structures in different brain regions

nocturnal enuresis Bedwetting or loss of bladder control at nighttime

Osgood-Schlatter disease A painful condition in which the area below the knee becomes inflamed where the tendon from the kneecap attaches to the shinbone

psychopharmacalogical treatments The use of medications to treat medical conditions, including the use of stimulant medicines to improve symptoms in children with ADHD

psychosocial treatments Interventions for problems such as ADHD, such as counseling and psychotherapy, which focus on an individual's psychological growth and interactions with the social environment

Chapter 12

autobiographical memory The memories a person accumulates that allow the person to construct a unique identity and a personal sense of continuity; autobiographical memory contains episodic (specific personal events) and semantic (general knowledge about the past) components

chunking A strategy for remembering in which a person groups material into meaningful categories

classroom climate The intellectual, social, emotional, and physical features of classroom environments that include the tone, attitude, and standards; may be characterized along a continuum of positive to negative

cognitive self-regulation The ability to manage and integrate attention, thoughts, and behaviors to attain goals

concrete operations A stage in Jean Piaget's theory of cognitive development characterized by children's development of logical, flexible, organized, and rational thinking about concrete things

content-validity bias A type of bias seen when a test is comparatively more difficult for one group of children relative to other groups, perhaps due to familiarity and experiences rather than ability

cooperative learning Learning that occurs when small groups of students work together and learn from one another by sharing ideas and offering explanations

crystallized intelligence A form of intelligence characterized by the facts, vocabulary, and knowledge a person accumulates through educational and cultural experiences

decentration The ability to focus on multiple parts of a problem, situation, or object instead of focusing on just one part

deductive reasoning The ability to systematically test ideas that are guided by an overarching hypothesis; the ability to reason from statements to reach a logical conclusion

Digit Cancellation Test A test that assesses selective attention. For instance, children are asked to cross out specific digits from a list of numbers on a page as quickly as possible, while disregarding the distractors

dynamic assessment approach An interactive approach to assessing intelligence that focuses on a child's learning potential over time, rather than a static measure of intelligence at one point in time

elaboration A strategy for remembering in which a person creates a story or detailed image to aid memory

entity theory of intelligence The view that intelligence is innate, fixed, and unchangeable

eugenics The now discredited idea put forth by Francis Galton that heritable human characteristics, such as intelligence, should be controlled through breeding to improve the human race

expository writing A genre of writing that explains, describes, or informs a specific theme, offering explanations to the reader about the topic

extrinsic motivation A form of motivation exhibited when a person chooses to engage in an activity because of external pressures, such as rewards or punishments, and thus may lose interest in the particular activity

fluid intelligence A form of intelligence characterized by a person's ability to think abstractly, reason, identify patterns, solve problems, and determine relationships

Flynn effect A trend referring to the improvement of IQ scores globally over the last 100 years

genome-wide complex trait analysis A statistical method that uses mathematical modeling and genetic analysis to estimate genetic influences on intelligence; researchers compare genetic and intelligence similarities across thousands of pairs of individuals to see if genetic closeness informs closeness of intelligence

incremental theory of intelligence The view that intelligence is changeable and may improve with practice over time; also commonly referred to as a growth mindset

independent practice A form of instruction in which students are encouraged to work on their own to complete assignments

inductive reasoning Drawing on specific observations, facts, and knowledge to draw logically broader conclusions

intellectual disability An impairment with significant limitations in intellectual functioning (e.g., learning, reasoning) and/or adaptive behaviors (e.g., getting dressed, following classroom rules)

intelligence quotient or IQ A score that describes how well a person performs on a test of intelligence relative to other people of the same age (typically calculated as MA/CA x 100)

intrinsic motivation A form of motivation exhibited when a person chooses to engage in an activity because they find the activity pleasurable and thus persist on the task even without a reward

keen observational learning An individual's learning of skills by watching people, rather than by being directly taught

learning disabilities Disorders that affect a child's ability to acquire knowledge and skills such as math and reading at levels expected for children of the same age

logical mental operations The ability to manipulate information in the mind and follow rules of logic to solve a problem

mathematical equality A concept in mathematics that indicates the quantities on both left and right sides of an "=" equation must balance

metacognition A person's awareness of what that person knows and how thinking works

metamemory An understanding of one's own memory, including content and process

mindsets Children's explanations for their successes and failures, which they may attribute to either ability or effort

motivation The desire and willingness to attain a goal and the continuation of effort and interest towards that goal

person praise Praise focused on children's fixed abilities or traits (e.g., telling children they are smart)

phonemic awareness The ability to identify the discrete sounds that make up words, in line with a phonics approach to reading

phonics approach An approach to reading instruction that teaches children letters of the alphabet and their sounds, with focus on sounding out each letter in a word prior to understanding the whole word

predictive-validity bias A type of bias seen when a test does not accurately predict how well an individual will do in the future based on their test performance

processing speed How quickly a person can process or encode information

process praise Praise focused on children's work and efforts (e.g., praising children for completing an assignment)

prodigies People gifted with outstanding, exceptional abilities or qualities

psychometricians Scientists who specialize in the measurement of intelligence or other psychological characteristics (e.g., aptitude, personality)

Pygmalion effect A psychological phenomenon in which children "live up" or "live down" to their teachers' initial expectations

rehearsal A strategy for remembering that relies on repeating information to aid memory

relative magnitudes A concept in mathematics that indicates the relative "distances" between numbers

reversibility The ability to realize that numbers or objects can be changed or returned to their original state, such as when children recognize that after rolling a ball of clay into a snakelike shape, it is possible to mold it back into its original shape

self-determination theory A theory of human motivation positing that motivation and engagement in a specific task are heightened when an individual makes choices in the absence of external pressures

seriation The symmetric ordering of items along dimensions, such as length or width

small-group practice A form of instruction in which children work together in small groups

taxonomic categories Categories or classifications of entities based on their similar characteristics or functions, such as the category of "foods" or "body parts"

theory of multiple intelligences A theory posited by Howard Gardner claiming the existence of seven (and later nine) distinct intelligences, each of which can be localized in the human brain

Trail Making Test A test that assesses selective attention and mental flexibility; for example, children are asked to draw lines connecting sequences of letters, numbers, or letters and numbers

transitive inference A form of deductive reasoning in which an individual is able to infer associations between objects or concepts based on logical reasoning from a set of premises (e.g., if B is related to C and C is related to D, then it is logical that B is related to D)

triarchic theory of intelligence A theory posited by Robert Sternberg claiming that contextual influences affect intelligence and that "successful intelligence" is comprised of analytical, creative, and practical intelligences

whole-group instruction A form of instruction directed to the entire class at the same time

whole language approach An approach to reading instruction that focuses on teaching children to recognize the whole word, rather than sound out each letter

working memory span The number of bits of information that a person can hold in active memory and manipulate at a time

Chapter 13

authentic pride A form of pride arising from children's positive evaluation of an achievement

behavioral observations A method to assess peer acceptance and rejection based on observing how children interact with one another

bullying Seeking to harm, intimidate, or threaten other children, commonly displayed by rejected-aggressive children

child reports (peer assessments) A method to assess peer acceptance and rejection based on children's reports of the amount or quality of social interactions (e.g., how much time children spend with each other; whether they like one another) among a group of children from inside or outside the classroom

controversial children Children who show a mixture of positive and negative social behaviors toward peers and who receive a mixture of positive and negative sociometric nominations from peers

corporal punishment The purposeful use of harmful punishment to cause physical pain or discomfort to a child

counterfactual emotion tasks Tasks used by developmental researchers to test whether children understand that an individual's emotions depend on how

reality compares to alternative possible outcomes

cyberbullying The exploitation of technology and social media platforms to victimize or bully others; the repeated intentional use of technology (e.g., emails, text messaging, social media, online gaming) to harm another person or a group of people through hostile, aggressive acts

display rules Strategies that hide authentic feelings or change emotional expressions to fit a situation, such as when a child shows happiness when receiving an unappealing present

emotional self-efficacy The feeling of being in control, able to handle emotional challenges, and able to express positive emotions appropriately

emotion-centered coping A coping strategy characterized by the regulation of emotional reactions to a problem or situation

emotion coaching The practice of talking with children about emotions, respecting children's emotions, and offering children coping strategies for handling emotionally challenging situations

emotion vignettes Stories presented to children by developmental researchers to examine children's understanding of a character's emotions and facial expressions, their use of display rules, and their reasoning for their responses

ethnic identity An individual's sense of belonging to an ethnic or cultural group, in addition to thoughts, feelings, and behaviors regarding group membership

externalizing behaviors Problem behaviors directed to the external environment, such as physical aggression, disobeying rules, and destroying property, that may stem from emotional regulation challenges

friendships Deeply important relationships or attachments characterized by mutual affection and liking

hubristic pride A form of pride arising from children's attribution of an achievement to their overall greatness

implicit association tests (IATs) Experiments that measure the strengths of individuals' unconscious evaluations or stereotypes (e.g., underlying implicit beliefs in boys' and men's and girls' and women's mathematical abilities) based on reaction times to information that is consistent or inconsistent with certain stereotypes (e.g., an elderly person in a wheelchair versus a younger person in a wheelchair)

industry versus inferiority A psychosocial stage described by Erik Erikson in which children who exhibit industry develop a sense of mastery, such as when they feel a sense of accomplishment as they persist toward goals; alternatively, children may feel inferior and lack motivation when they do not attain their goals or are punished or ridiculed

internalizing behaviors   Problem behaviors based on negative emotions that are directed inwards, such as the development of anxiety or depression, that may stem from emotional regulation challenges

maltreatment   The emotional abuse, physical abuse, sexual abuse, or neglect of children; cruel or violent treatment causing suffering in children

meta-emotion philosophy   The organized, structured set of thoughts and feelings caregivers have about their own and children's emotions

monitoring   Caregiver awareness of children's activities, friends, and peer groups, including efforts to keep track of what's going on in children's lives

neglected children   Children who receive few likes and few dislikes in sociometric nominations

peer acceptance   The extent to which a child is liked and accepted by peers

peer groups   Groups of at least five or six children who generally share the same age, status, and interests; may be formal (e.g., school club members) or informal (e.g., children hanging out on the playground)

peer rejection   The extent to which a child is disliked and excluded by peers

perceived popularity   Measure of children classified as popular due to their perceived status and power rather than their social competence

popular-antisocial   Children who are perceived to be popular and "cool" but who may actually be disliked by peers

popular children   Socially and academically competent children who receive a high number of like nominations and few dislike nominations in sociometric nominations

popular-prosocial   Popular children who are considerate and skilled at initiating friendships and prosocial toward other children

prejudice   A negative, preconceived opinion about someone based on that person's membership in a specific group (e.g., such as a group defined by gender, race, ethnicity)

private regard   A person's views about their gender

public regard   A person's views about how others view gender

rejected-aggressive children   Children who demonstrate problems in how they treat other children and who have goals that undermine social relationships, such as getting even with other children

rejected children   Children who receive many dislikes and few likes in sociometric nominations; rejected-aggressive and rejected-withdrawn represent two types of rejected children

rejected-withdrawn children   Children who are socially anxious, timid, and withdrawn from the peer group, often watching social interactions from a distance rather than being directly involved

school climate   A school's physical (e.g., safety, resources) and social (e.g., teacher-child respect, open collaboration) characteristics

second-order false belief   A type of theory-of-mind understanding that it is possible to have a false belief about someone else's belief

situation-centered coping   A coping strategy characterized by the management or modification of a problem or situation

social comparison   A child's judgement of their own traits, abilities, and behaviors compared to those of others

sociograms   Visual depictions of the friendships among peers or individuals in a social network

sociometric nomination   A type of child-report approach or peer rating system in which children nominate peers in their class or grade whom they "like" and "dislike," or report on which students interact with other students; sociometric nominations classify children into popular, rejected, controversial, or neglected

teacher reports   A method to assess peer acceptance and rejection based on teachers' reports or ratings of children's interactions with one another

virtual social exclusion experiments Studies that assess the brain's response to peer rejection by making children think that they are being excluded from a game or activity by unknown children or by using peer-chat room simulations

Chapter 14

anorexia nervosa   A serious eating disorder marked by a pathological fear of gaining weight, resulting in severe dieting, malnutrition, excessive weight loss, and a distorted body image

autonomic nervous system   The part of the peripheral nervous system that regulates involuntary bodily functions, such as heartbeat, breathing, and digestion

behavior modification   A therapeutic approach in which desired behaviors are rewarded and undesirable behaviors changed

bruxism   The excessive grinding of teeth or jaw clenching at night

bulimia nervosa   A serious eating disorder in which bouts of extreme overeating are followed by self-induced vomiting, purging, or fasting because of an obsessive desire to lose weight

circadian rhythm   The patterns of sleeping, waking, and eating that are controlled by an internal "body clock" that guides physical, mental, and behavioral changes over a daily cycle

contextual amplification hypothesis   A theory positing that an adolescent's adjustment to early puberty depends on sociocultural context

family-based therapy   A therapeutic approach in which all members of a family attend therapy sessions with a therapist who helps them recognize how their behaviors and interaction patterns may affect a child's behaviors, such as an adolescent's eating disorder

gonads   The reproductive organs—ovaries in girls and testes in boys

gray matter   The nerve tissue of the central nervous system that comprises the cell bodies of neurons and forms the majority of the brain's structure

growth spurt   Rapid increase in height and weight during puberty and an acceleration of growth in hands, legs, feet, and torso length

insomnia   Sleeplessness or the habitual inability to sleep; a disorder characterized by difficulties with falling or staying asleep

limbic system   Subcortical regions of the brain (including the hippocampus, amygdala, and cingulate gyrus) that are involved in emotions, memory, motivation, and learning

maturational deviance hypothesis A theory positing that an adolescent's physical deviation from his or her peer group may place the adolescent at risk for mood and behavioral problems, regardless of early or late maturation

melatonin   A hormone/naturally occurring compound released by the brain in response to darkness that regulates circadian rhythm and supports the immune system

menarche   The first occurrence of menstruation in girls during puberty

myelin   The fatty sheath that surrounds axons and increases the speed at which information travels on neurons

obese   A term referring to an individual who falls at or above the 95th percentile for body mass index compared to peers of the same age and sex

overweight   Body weight of an individual who falls between the 85th and 94th percentiles for body mass index compared to peers of the same age and sex

peer-influence hypothesis   A theory in which older peers are thought to affect the behaviors of younger adolescents who experience early puberty in ways that may lead to earlier-than-usual exposure to risky behaviors in younger adolescents

prefrontal cortex   The part of the brain located behind the forehead that controls executive functioning

primary sex characteristics   Changes during puberty in the reproductive organs—ovaries, uterus, and vagina in girls and penis, scrotum, and testes in boys—that make reproduction possible

pruning   The process in which synapses are eliminated to increase the efficacy of neural communication

puberty   The biological process that begins in the brain and involves hormonal changes and physical and psychological transformations that enable reproduction

puberty rites   Ritual activities and teachings that prepare adolescents for new roles in a type of "rite of passage" into adulthood

readiness hypothesis   A theory positing that early maturing adolescents may experience asynchrony among physical, cognitive, social, and emotional maturity and thus be at risk for adjustment problems

secondary sex characteristics   Observable body changes during puberty such as a growth spurt, pubic hair, breasts in girls, and facial hair and changes to voice in boys

secular trends   Changes in human development that take place over extended time frames; the average age of puberty has historically decreased

sensation seeking   A personality trait characterized by a desire for pursuing varied, novel, and intense experiences and feelings

serotonin   A neurotransmitter produced in the brain that regulates mood and appetite

sexual homophily   The adolescent's tendency to form strong bonds and connections with others who are similar in their sexual activities

sleep debt   Sleep deficit that is the cumulative effect of not getting enough sleep night after night

spermarche   The beginning of boys' development of sperm in the testicles during puberty and capacity for ejaculation

synaptogenesis   The rapid formation of synapses between neurons in the brain

Tanner scale   A standard assessment of pubertal development that describe the stage of physical development in children and adolescents based on primary and secondary sex characteristics

white matter   The neurons of the central nervous system that connect and communicate with one another through nerve impulses; white matter comprises mainly myelinated axons and glial cells

Chapter 15

abstract thinking   The ability to understand concepts by mentally manipulating ideas that are not tangible

academic language   Specialized, conceptually dense, and abstract language that is used in classrooms and academic programs

academic vocabulary   Words that a person encounters in academic subjects such as literature, science, and social studies

affective theory of mind   The ability to understand the emotions of others

automatic processes   Mental cognitive activities that are fast, efficient, and require no effort and so do not draw on the limited cognitive resources available in working memory

behavioral engagement   A type of school engagement characterized by participation in learning activities (e.g., attending to class lessons)

cognitive engagement   A type of school engagement referring to a self-regulated approach to learning (e.g., using strategies to support learning)

cognitive load   The required amount of working memory resources needed for a task

cognitive theory of mind   The ability to understand the mental states, beliefs, thoughts, and intentions of others

combination of liquids problem   An experiment in which children and adolescents must use the scientific method to determine which liquids from four bottles combine with a mysterious liquid "g" to create a chemical reaction that results in a yellow liquid

discrimination   The unjust or prejudicial treatment of people often based on their race, ethnicity, gender, age, sexual orientation, religion, or national origin

embedded clauses   Statements nested within other statements that provide elaborated information

emotional engagement   A type of school engagement describing affective attitudes toward school (e.g., feeling positively toward school)

flanker tasks   Response inhibition tasks used to test selective attention and flexibility to a specific stimulus while inhibiting attention to distractors, such as when an adolescent is asked to identify the direction a target arrow faces when surrounded by many distractor arrows

formal operational stage   The final stage in Piaget's theory of cognitive development characterized by the development of advanced abstract thinking and the ability to manipulate information mentally, use logical thought, and engage in hypothetical, deductive reasoning

goal orientations   The reasons individuals give for why they invest time in an activity or their motivation for achieving an objective for a specific activity

grit   The steadfast perseverance and passion for long-term goals, even when a person encounters challenges

hypothetical-deductive reasoning   A systematic, scientific approach to problem solving, referred to as scientific thinking, in which individuals test hypotheses about variables that may influence an outcome to reach a conclusion

imaginary audience   An exaggerated perception that other people are attending to everything an individual says or does

mastery goal orientation   Motivation that is focused on learning and mastering a specific task

metacognition   A person's awareness of what that person knows and how thinking works

pendulum problem   A task in which children and adolescents must figure out which variable(s) affect the speed of an object swinging on a string (e.g., length of the string, heaviness of a set of weights)

performance goal orientation   Motivation that is focused on the outcome rather than process, such as studying to get a specific grade rather than learning

personal fable   The adolescent's belief that their own experiences hold high, special importance relative to others' experiences and that their uniqueness will prevent life's difficulties from affecting them negatively

point-of-view tasks   Tasks used to study perspective taking that compare individuals' reaction times to first-person questions (e.g., "What would *you* do if…?") with their reaction times to third-person questions (e.g., "What would *person X* do if…?")

processing speed   How quickly and efficiently a person conducts a mental task, such as encoding information or solving a problem

propositional thought   The ability to determine whether a set of verbal propositions (statements) is logical based on the wording of the statement, even if the person has not directly experienced the situation

So-Moral task   An approach to studying moral reasoning in which individuals are presented with scenes of moral dilemmas and are asked to make decisions about each dilemma

stereotypes   Widely held, fixed, and over generalized views about a group of people based on their race, ethnicity, gender, language, and so forth

stereotype threat   A situation in which people feel that they are at risk of conforming to stereotypes about their social group and, therefore, experience anxiety and lowered performance

stereotype threat experiments   Experiments in which researchers manipulate information presented to individuals before a test to study how stereotype threat may affect academic performance or other outcomes

strategies   The set of techniques that help a person encode and remember information

switching tasks   Executive functioning tasks used to test the ability to shift attention between one task and another, such as when adolescents are asked to attend to different pictures simultaneously and to quickly shift between responses

task value   The subjective value (e.g., interest, usefulness) a person attaches to a specific task

test anxiety   The fear of failing that may involve negative physiological, cognitive, or behavioral symptoms before or after an exam

working memory   The manipulation and temporary storing of information in active memory

Chapter 16

Adult Attachment Interview (AAI)   A method for assessing attachment status in adolescents and young adults through open-ended questions about early childhood experiences; the AAI classifies an individual's attachment status as autonomous, dismissive, or preoccupied

bicultural identity   The formation of an identity that reflects a combination of two cultures (often "home" and "mainstream" cultures)

cisgender   A term describing individuals whose gender identity matches their biological sex at birth

clinical depression   A mental health disorder marked by severe bouts of depression necessitating treatment, including therapy, medication, or a combination of both

cliques   Relatively small friendship-based groups characterized by intensive interactions and emotional involvement among group members

cognitive behavior therapy   An evidence-based psychological approach to treating depression (and other mental health disorders) that focuses on a person's thoughts, feelings, and behaviors and offers individuals coping strategies to manage challenges

commitment   The dedication of an individual to a particular relationship, cause, goal, and so on

crowds   Loosely connected groups of individuals who are not as close as friends in a clique but share activities and interests and sometimes ethnicity

daily diary method   A research methodology requiring participants to rate their emotions on a daily basis and for an extended number of days or weeks to assess emotional experiences over time

delay discounting tasks   Experiments that measure self-regulation in which participants are presented with a choice between a small, immediate reward and a larger, delayed reward

depression   A mood disorder characterized by negative symptoms that are experienced nearly every day, such as constant sadness, diminished interest and pleasure in activities, social withdrawal, significant weight loss or gain, and feelings of worthlessness

disclosure   The willingness to reveal information to caregivers

emotional reactivity   The predisposition to experience frequent, intense, and volatile emotions

ethnic identity   An individual's sense of belonging to an ethnic group, and perceptions and feelings about group membership

Ethnic Identity Scale   An instrument based on the Multigroup Ethnic Identity Measure that assesses three aspects of ethnicity: ethnic identity exploration, ethnic identity resolution, and affirmation

experience sampling   A research method that requires participants to record their emotions, behaviors, etc., on a daily or regular basis when prompted by a pager or smart phone

exploration   The process during identity formation when adolescents actively explore alternative beliefs, interests, occupations, and values across different areas

externalizing problems   Problem behaviors directed outward, such as physical aggression, disobeying rules, and destroying property

family-systems approach   An evidence-based psychological approach to treating mental health disorders such as depression that focuses on working with the person, caregivers, and other family members to facilitate change

gender identity   A person's internal self-perceptions about being a boy/man or girl/woman or non-binary.

identity achievement versus role confusion   A stage in Erik Erikson's theory of psychosocial development when adolescents search for a sense of who they are by intensely exploring their personal values and beliefs, accepting some from their caregivers and rejecting others

identity development   The lifelong process in which individuals actively work on understanding who they are and what makes them unique within a sociocultural context

identity statuses   The four categories in the search for an identity that represent combinations of exploration and commitment: foreclosure, identity diffusion, moratorium, and identity achievement

impulsiveness   Acting on the spur of the moment without foresight or thought, thus reflecting challenges with emotional or behavioral self-control

internalizing problems   Problem behaviors based on negative emotions that are directed inwards and may be expressed in anxiety or depression

looking-glass self   An individual's self-identity based on others' perceptions and treatment

microaggressions Intentional or unintentional insults

monitoring Caregiver awareness of children's activities, friends and peer groups, including efforts to keep track of what is going on in children's lives

Multigroup Ethnic Identity Measure A measure/scale of adolescents' subjective sense of pride and belongingness to their ethnic group

narcissism A personality disorder marked by an exaggerated sense of importance, self-centeredness, and a strong need for admiration

oppositional identity formation Adolescents' response to tensions of two cultural worlds with rebelliousness and defiance

parent solicitation A monitoring strategy of asking questions to gather information

psychosocial moratorium A time during adolescent identity development when the individual explores different identities and roles prior to committing to a unified identity

risk taking Decision making with potentially harmful consequences

ruminate To continuously and deeply reflect on the same things, such as problems, which may result in depressive symptoms

self-enhancement goals Goals or motivations that focus on feeling good about the self and achieving high self-esteem

self-esteem The positive or negative attitudes and beliefs a person has toward the self that are essential to self-identity

self-regulation The ability to manage and integrate attention, thoughts, emotions, and behaviors to attain goals

sensation seeking The quest for novel, intense, and varied experiences and taking risks to pursue such experiences

sexual fluidity One or more changes in sexual identity

sexual orientation A person's attraction toward a particular sex or gender, which is often classified as heterosexual, homosexual, bisexual, or asexual

social anxiety A mental health condition characterized by a fear of interaction with other people, feelings of embarrassment, and fear of being negatively judged, which may lead to social avoidance

transgender A term describing individuals who identify with a gender that is different from their birth sex

References

Chapter 1

Adolph, K. E., Robinson, S. R., Young, J. W., & Gill-Alvarez, F. (2008). What is the shape of developmental change? *Psychol Rev* 115, 527–543.

Adolph, K. E., Karasik, L. B., & Tamis-LeMonda, C. S. (2010). Motor skill. In M. H. Bornstein (Ed.), *Handbook of Cultural Developmental Science* (pp. 61–88). Psychology Press.

Adolph, K. E., & Robinson, S. R. (2011). Sampling development. *Journal of Cognition and Development* 12, 411–423.

Adolph, K. E., & Robinson, S. R. (2015). *Handbook of Child Psychology and Developmental Science: Vol. 2: Cognitive Processes* (pp. 114–157).

Adolph, K. E., & Tamis-LeMonda, C. S. (2014). The costs and benefits of development: The transition from crawling to walking. *Child Development Perspectives* 8, 187–192.

Asbury, K., & Plomin, R. (2014). *G is for Genes: The Impact of Genetics on Education and Achievement*. John Wiley & Sons: Malden, MA.

Bandura, A., & Walters, R. H. (1963). *Social Learning and Personality Development*. Holt Rinehart and Winston: New York.

Baumrind, D. (1980). New directions in socialization research. *American Psychologist* 35, 639.

Bjorklund, D. F., & Causey, K. B. (2017). *Children's Thinking: Cognitive Development and Individual Differences*. Sage Publications.

Bornstein, M. H., Hahn, C. S., & Suwalsky, J. T. (2013). Developmental pathways among adaptive functioning and externalizing and internalizing behavioral problems: Cascades from childhood into adolescence. *Applied Developmental Science* 17, 76–87.

Bronfenbrenner, U. (2000). Ecological theory. *Encyclopedia of Psychology* 3, 129–133.

Bronfenbrenner, U. (2004). *The Ecology of Human Development*. Harvard University Press: Cambridge, MA.

Bronfenbrenner, U., & Morris, P. A. (1998). The ecology of developmental processes. In W. Damon & R. M. Lerner (Eds.), *Handbook of Child Psychology: Theoretical Models of Human Development* (pp. 993–1028). John Wiley & Sons Inc.

Brooks-Gunn, J., Markman-Pithers, L., & Rouse, C. E. (2016). Starting early: Introducing the issue. *The Future of Children* 26, 3–19.

Buss, D. M. (2012). The evolutionary psychology of crime. *Journal of Theoretical and Philosophical Criminology* 1, 90–98.

Campos, J. J., Anderson, D. I., Barbu-Roth, M. A., et al. (2000). Travel broadens the mind. *Infancy* 1, 149–219.

Chisholm, J. S. (1996). The evolutionary ecology of attachment organization. *Human Nature* 7, 1–37.

Chomsky, N. (1965). *Aspects of the Theory of Syntax*. MIT Press: Cambridge, MA.

Cicchetti, D., & Gunnar, M. R. (2008). Integrating biological measures into the design and evaluation of preventive interventions. *Development and Psychopathology* 20, 737–743.

Cole, M., Cole, S. R., & Lightfoot, C. (2005). *The Development of Children*. Macmillan: New York.

Dodge, K. A., Greenberg, M. T., Malone, P. S., & Conduct Problems Prevention Research Group. (2008). Testing an idealized dynamic cascade model of the development of serious violence in adolescence. *Child Development* 79, 1907–1927.

Erikson, E. H. (1963). *Childhood and Society. Revised and Enlarged*. New York.

Erikson, E. H. (1968). *Identity: Youth and Crisis* (No. 7). W.W. Norton & Company: New York.

Fausto-Sterling, A. (2014). Letting go of normal. *Boston Review*.

Feigenson, L., Dehaene, S., & Spelke, E. (2004). Core systems of number. *Trends in Cognitive Sciences* 8, 307–314.

Fenson, L., Dale, P. S., Reznick, J. S., et al. (1994). Variability in early communicative development. *Monographs of the Society for Research in Child Development*, i–185.

Frank, M. C., Braginsky, M., Yurovsky, D., & Marchman, V. A. (2017). Wordbank: An open repository for developmental vocabulary data. *Journal of Child Language* 44, 677.

Gauvain, M., & Nicolaides, C. (2015). Cognition in childhood across cultures. In *The Oxford Handbook of Human Development and Culture*. Oxford University Press: Oxford, United Kingdom.

Gennetian, L.A., Tamis-LeMonda, C. S., & Frank, M. (2020). Advancing transparency and openness in developmental research: Opportunities. *Child Development Perspectives* 14, 3–8.

Gilmore, R. O., & Adolph, K. E. (2017). Video can make behavioural science more reproducible. *Nature Human Behavior* 1, 128.

Gilmore, R. O., Diaz, M. T., Wyble, B. A., & Yarkoni, T. (2017). Progress toward openness, transparency, and reproducibility in cognitive neuroscience. *Annals of the New York Academy of Sciences* 1396, 5.

Gordon, P. (2004). Numerical cognition without words: Evidence from Amazonia. *Science* 306, 496–499.

Heckman, J. J. (2006). Skill formation and the economics of investing in disadvantaged children. *Science* 312, 1900–1902.

Ioannidis, J. P. (2005). Why most published research findings are false. *PLoS Medicine* 2, e124.

Inhelder, B., & Piaget, J. (1969). *The Psychology of the Child*. Basic Books: New York.

Kail, R. V. (2003). Information processing and memory. In M. H. Bornstein, L. Davidson, C. L. M. Keyes, & K. A. Moore (Eds.), *Crosscurrents in Contemporary Psychology. Well-Being: Positive Development across the Life Course* (pp. 269–279). Lawrence Erlbaum Associates Publishers: Hillsdale, NJ.

Karasik, L. B., Tamis-LeMonda, C. S., & Adolph, K. E. (2011). Transition from crawling to walking and infants' actions with objects and people. *Child Development* 82, 1199–1209.

Keller, H., & Kärtner, J. (2013). Development: The cultural solution of universal developmental tasks. In M. J. Gelfand, C.-Y. Chiu, & Y.-Y. Hong (Eds.), *Advances in Culture and Psychology* (pp. 63–116). Oxford University Press: New York.

Kuhl, P. K. (2010). Brain mechanisms in early language acquisition. *Neuron* 67, 713–727.

Lampl, M., Veldhuis, J. D., & Johnson, M. L. (1992). Saltation and statis: A model of human growth. *Science* 258, 801–803.

Lerner, R. M. (Ed.). (2019). *Developmental Psychology: Historical and Philosophical Perspectives*. Routledge: New York.

LoBue, V., Kim, E., & Delgado, M. (2019). Fear in development. In *Handbook of Emotional Development* (pp. 257–282). Springer: Cham, Switzerland.

Magnuson, K., & Duncan, G. J. (2016). Can early childhood interventions decrease inequality of economic opportunity? *RSF: The Russell Sage Foundation Journal of the Social Sciences* 2, 123–141.

Martin, C. L., & Ruble, D. N. (2010). Patterns of gender development. *Annual Review of Psychology* 61, 353–381.

Masten, A. S., Desjardins, C. D., McCormick, C. M., et al. (2010). The significance of childhood competence and problems for adult success in work: A developmental cascade analysis. *Development and Psychopathology* 22, 679–694.

McCall, R. B., Groark, C. J., Hawk, B. N., et al. (2019). Early caregiver–child interaction and children's development: Lessons from the St. Petersburg-USA Orphanage Intervention Research Project. *Clin Child Fam Psychol Rev* 22, 208–224.

Miller, P. H. (2002). *Theories of Developmental Psychology*. Macmillan: New York.

Munakata, Y. (2007). Information processing approaches to development. In R. Lerner (Ed.), *Handbook of Child Psychology*, 6th ed. Volume II. Cognition, Perception, and Language (pp. 426–462). Wiley: Hoboken, NJ.

Nevo, B. (1985). Face validity revisited. *Journal of Educational Measurement* 22, 287–293.

Nosek, B. A. (2017). Opening science. In R. S. Jhangiani & R. Biswas-Diener (Eds.), *Open: The Philosophy and Practices That Are Revolutionizing Education and Science* (pp. 89–99).

Perry, N. B., Calkins, S. D., Dollar, J. M., Keane, S. P., & Shanahan, L. (2018). Self-regulation as a predictor of patterns of change in externalizing behaviors from infancy to adolescence. *Development and Psychopathology* 30, 497–510.

Plomin, R., & von Stumm, S. (2018). The new genetics of intelligence. *Nature Reviews Genetics* 19, 148.

Pope Edwards, C., and Bloch, M. (2010). The Whitings' concepts of culture and how they have faced in contemporary psychology and anthropology. *Journal of Cross-Cultural Psychology* 41, 485–498.

Reynolds, A. J., Ou, S. R., Mondi, C. F., & Giovanelli, A. (2019). Reducing poverty and inequality through preschool-to-third-grade prevention services. *American Psychologist* 74, 653.

Rogoff, B., Moore, L., Najafi, B., et al. (2007). Children's Development of Cultural Repertoires through Participation in Everyday Routines and Practices. In J. E. Grusec & P. D. Hastings (Eds.), *Handbook of Socialization: Theory and Research* (pp. 490–515). Guilford Press.

Rothbart, M. K., and Bates, J. E. Temperament. In Damon, W., and Eisenberg, N., (Eds.) *Handbook of Child Psychology*, 6th ed., Vol. 3 (pp. 99–166). John Wiley & Sons: Hoboken, NJ.

Sameroff, A. J., & Chandler, M. J. (1975). Reproductive risk and the continuum of caretaking casualty. *Review of Child Development Research* 4, 187–244.

Shrout, P. E., & Rodgers, J. L. (2018). Psychology, science, and knowledge construction: Broadening perspectives from the replication crisis. *Annual Review of Psychology* 69, 487–510.

Siegler, R. S. (1987). The perils of averaging data over strategies: An example from children's addition. *Journal of Experimental Psychology: General* 116, 250.

Siegler, R. S. (1995). How does change occur: A microgenetic study of number conservation. *Cognitive Psychology* 28, 225–273.

Siegler, R. S., Jenkins, E. (1989). *How Children Discover Strategies*. Erlbaum: Hillsdale, NJ.

Spelke, E. S. (2016). Core knowledge and conceptual change. *Core Knowledge and Conceptual Change* 279, 279–300.

Starr, A., Libertus, M. E., & Brannon, E. M. (2013). Number sense in infancy predicts mathematical abilities in childhood. *Proceedings of the National Academy of Sciences* 110, 18116–18120.

Super, C. M., & Harkness, S. (1986). The developmental niche: A conceptualization at the interface of child and culture. *International Journal of Behavioral Development* 9, 545–569.

Super, C. M., & Harkness, S. (1999). The environment as culture in developmental research. In *Measuring Environment across the Life Span: Emerging Methods and Concepts* (pp. 279–323). American Psychological Association.

Thelen, E. (1984). Learning to walk: Ecological demands and phylogenetic constraints. *Advances in Infancy Research*.

Ullsperger, J. M., & Nikolas, M. A. (2017). A meta-analytic review of the association between pubertal timing and psychopathology in adolescence: Are there sex differences in risk? *Psychological Bulletin* 143, 903.

Ursache, A., Blair, C., & Raver, C. C. (2012). The promotion of self-regulation as a means of enhancing school readiness and early achievement in children at risk for school failure. *Child Development Perspectives* 6, 122–128.

van Izendoorn, M. H., & Juffer, F. (2006). The Emanuel Miller Memorial Lecture 2006: Adoption as intervention. Meta-analytic evidence for massive catch-up and plasticity in physical, socio-emotional, and cognitive development. *Journal of Child Psychology and Psychiatry* 47, 1228–1245.

van Rijn, S., Urbanus, E., & Swaab, H. (2019). Eyetracking measures of social attention in young children: How gaze patterns translate to real-life social behaviors. *Social Development* 28, 564–580.

Watson, J. B., & Rayner, R. (1920). Conditioned emotional reactions. *Journal of Experimental Psychology* 3, 313.

Watson, J. B. (1926). *What the nursery has to say about instincts.* In C. Murchison (Ed.), *International University Series in Psychology. Psychologies of 1925* (pp. 1–35). Clark University Press: Worcester, MA.

Weisner, T. S., Matheson, C., Coots, J., & Bernheimer, L. P. (2005). Sustainability of daily routines as a family outcome. In *Learning in Cultural Context* (pp. 41–73). Springer: Boston, MA.

Whiting, B. B. (1963). Six cultures: Studies of child rearing.

Whiting, B. B. (1980). Culture and social behavior: A model for the development of social behavior. *Ethos* 8, 97.

Whiting, B. B., & Whiting, J. W. (1975). Children of six cultures: A psycho-cultural analysis.

Chapter 2

Aslin, R. N., Shukla, M., & Emberson, L. L. (2015). Hemodynamic correlates of cognition in human infants. *Annual Review of Psychology* 66, 349–379.

Atallah, H. E., Frank, M. J., & O'Reilly, R. C. (2004). Hippocampus, cortex, and basal ganglia: Insights from computational models of complementary learning systems. *Neurobiology of Learning and Memory* 82, 253–267.

Auerbach, J. G., Faroy, M., Ebstein, R., et al. (2001). The association of the dopamine D4 receptor gene (DRD4) and the serotonin transporter promoter gene (5-HTTLPR) with temperament in 12-month-old infants. *The Journal of Child Psychology and Psychiatry and Allied Disciplines* 42, 777–783.

Bates, E. (2014). Plasticity, localization, and language development. In *Biology and Knowledge Revisited* (pp. 223–272). Routledge: New York.

Blakemore, C., & Cooper, G. F. (1970). Development of the brain depends on the visual environment. *Nature* 228, 477–478.

Boyce, W. T., & Ellis, B. J. (2005). Biological sensitivity to context: I. An evolutionary–developmental theory of the origins and functions of stress reactivity. *Development and Psychopathology* 17, 271–301.

Bolhuis, J. J. (1991). Mechanisms of avian imprinting: a review. *Biological Reviews* 66, 303–345.

Brodwin, E. (2018). NASA sent Scott Kelly to space for a year, and now 7% of his genes are expressed differently than his identical twin Mark. *Business Insider*, March 15, 2018.

Can, D. D., Richards, T., & Kuhl, P. (2013). Early gray-matter and white-matter concentration in infancy predict later language skills: A whole brain voxel-based morphometry study. *Brain and Language* 124, 34–44.

Caspi, A., McClay, J., Moffitt, T.E., et al. (2002). Role of genotype in the cycle of violence in maltreated children. *Science* 297, 851–854.

Caspi, A., & Moffitt, T. E. (2006). Gene–environment interactions in psychiatry: joining forces with neuroscience. *Nature Reviews Neuroscience* 7, 583–590.

Caspi, A., Williams, B., Kim-Cohen, J., et al. (2007). Moderation of breastfeeding effects on the IQ by genetic variation in fatty acid metabolism. *Proceedings of the National Academy of Sciences* 104, 18860–18865.

Cecil, C. A. M., Walton, E., Smith, R. G., et al. (2016). DNA methylation and substance-use risk: a prospective, genome-wide study spanning gestation to adolescence. *Translational Psychiatry* 6, e976.

Champagne, F. A., & Mashoodh, R. (2009). Genes in context: Gene–environment interplay and the origins of individual differences in behavior. *Current Directions in Psychological Science* 18, 128.

Champagne, F. A., & Meaney, M. J. (2006). Stress during gestation alters postpartum maternal care and the development of the offspring in a rodent model. *Biological Psychiatry* 59, 1227–1235.

Champagne, F. A., & Meaney, M. J. (2007). Transgenerational effects of social environment on variations in maternal care and behavioral response to novelty. *Behavioral Neuroscience* 121, 1353.

Champagne, F. (2020). Dynamic epigenetic impact of the environment on the developing brain. In J. J. Lockman & C. S. Tamis-LeMonda (Eds.), *Cambridge Handbook of Infant Development*. Cambridge University Press: New York.

Cicchetti, D., Hetzel, S., Rogosch, F. A., Handley, E. D., & Toth, S. L. (2016). Genome-wide DNA methylation in 1-year-old infants of mothers with major depressive disorder. *Development and Psychopathology* 28, 1413–1419.

Cicchetti, D., Rogosch, F. A., & Sturge-Apple, M. L. (2007). Interactions of child maltreatment and serotonin transporter and monoamine oxidase A polymorphisms: depressive symptomatology among adolescents from low socioeconomic status backgrounds. *Development and Psychopathology* 19, 1161–1180.

Cooper, R. M., & Zubek, J. P. (1958). Effects of enriched and restricted early environments on the learning ability of bright and dull rats. *Canadian Journal of Psychology/Revue Canadienne de Psychologie* 12, 159.

Coulam CB, Jeyendran RS, Fishel LA, Roussev R. (2006) Multiple thrombophilic gene mutations rather than specific gene mutations are risk factors for recurrent miscarriage. *American Journal of Reproductive Immunology* 55, 360–368.

Crabbe, J. C. (2008). Neurogenetic studies of alcohol addiction. *Philosophical Transactions of the Royal Society: Biological Sciences* 363, 3201–3211.

Crabbe, J. C., & Harris, R. A. (Eds.). (2013). *The Genetic Basis of Alcohol and Drug Actions.* Springer Science + Business Media.

Curry, A. (2013). Archaeology: the milk revolution. *Nature News* 50, 20.

Deater-Deckard, K., & O'Connor, T. G. (2000). Parent–child mutuality in early childhood: Two behavioral genetic studies. *Developmental Psychology* 36, 561.

Edelman, G. M. (1987). *Neural Darwinism: The Theory of Neuronal Group Selection.* Basic Books: New York.

Fedorenko, E., Hsieh, P. J., Nieto-Castañón, A., et al. (2010). New method for fMRI investigations of language: defining ROIs functionally in individual subjects. *Journal of Neurophysiology* 104, 1177–1194.

Ganesan, A. K., Ho, H., Bodemann, B., et al. (2008). Genome-wide siRNA-based functional genomics of pigmentation identifies novel genes and pathways that impact melanogenesis in human cells. *PLoS Genetics* 4.

Gerbault, P., Liebert, A., Itan, Y., et al. (2011). Evolution of lactase persistence: an example of human niche construction. *Philosophical Transactions of the Royal Society B: Biological Sciences* 366, 863–877.

Greenough, W. T., Black, J. E., & Wallace, C. S. (1987). Experience and brain development. *Child Development* 539–559.

Greenough, W. T., & Volkmar, F. R. (1973). Pattern of dendritic branching in occipital cortex of rats reared in complex environments. *Experimental Neurology* 40, 491–504.

Hackman, D. A., & Farah, M. J. (2009). Socioeconomic status and the developing brain. *Trends in Cognitive Sciences* 13, 65–73.

Hanson, J. L., Hair, N., Shen, D. G., et al. (2013). Family poverty affects the rate of human infant brain growth. *PLoS ONE* 8.

Hickok, G., & Poeppel, D. (2007). The cortical organization of speech processing. *Nature Reviews Neuroscience* 8, 393–402.

Hubel, D. H., & Wiesel, T. N. (1963). Shape and arrangement of columns in cat's striate cortex. *The Journal of Physiology* 165, 559–568.

Hubel, D. H., & Wiesel, T. N. (1965). Binocular interaction in striate cortex of kittens reared with artificial squint. *Journal of Neurophysiology* 28, 1041–1059.

Hubel, D. H., & Wiesel, T. N. (1979). Brain mechanisms of vision. *Scientific American* 241, 150–163.

Huttenlocher, P. R. (1994). Synaptogenesis in human cerebral cortex. In G. Dawson & K. W. Fischer (Eds.), *Human Behavior and the Developing Brain* (pp. 137–152). Guilford Press.

Jensen, S. K., Berens, A. E., & Nelson 3rd, C. A. (2017). Effects of poverty on interacting biological systems underlying child development. *The Lancet Child & Adolescent Health* 1, 225–239.

Johnson, M. H. (1999). Cortical plasticity in normal and abnormal cognitive development: Evidence and working hypotheses. *Development and Psychopathology* 11, 419–437.

Johnson, M. H. (2005). Sensitive periods in functional brain development: Problems and prospects. *Developmental Psychobiology: The Journal of the International Society for Developmental Psychobiology* 46, 287–292.

Juraska, J. M., Henderson, C., & Müller, J. (1984). Differential rearing experience, gender, and radial maze performance. *Developmental Psychobiology: The Journal of the International Society for Developmental Psychobiology* 17, 209–215.

Kaufman, J., Yang, B. Z., Douglas-Palumberi, H., et al. (2006). Brain-derived neurotrophic factor–5-HTTLPR gene interactions and environmental modifiers of depression in children. *Biological Psychiatry* 59, 673–680.

Kertes, D. A., Bhatt, S. S., Kamin, H. S., et al. (2017). BNDF methylation in mothers and newborns is associated with maternal exposure to war trauma. *Clinical Epigenetics* 9, 68.

Kim-Cohen, J., & Gold, A. L. (2009). Measured gene–environment interactions and mechanisms promoting resilient development. *Current Directions in Psychological Science* 18, 138–142.

Kolb, B., & Whishaw, I. Q. (1998). Brain plasticity and behavior. *Annual Review of Psychology* 49, 43–64.

Labella, M. H., Narayan, A. J., McCormick, C. M., et al. (2019). Risk and adversity, parenting quality, and children's social-emotional adjustment in families experiencing homelessness. *Child Development* 90, 227–244.

LaFreniere, P., & MacDonald, K. (2013). A postgenomic view of behavioral development and adaptation to the environment. *Developmental Review* 33, 89–109.

Lewis, T. L., & Maurer, D. (2005). Multiple sensitive periods in human visual development: evidence from visually deprived children. *Developmental Psychobiology: The Journal of the International Society for Developmental Psychobiology* 46, 163–183.

Luck, S. J. (2014). *An Introduction to the Event-Related Potential Technique.* MIT Press: Cambridge, MA.

Luthar, S. S., Doernberger, C. H., & Zigler, E. (1993). Resilience is not a unidimensional construct: Insights from a prospective study of inner-city adolescents. *Development and Psychopathology* 5, 703–717.

Lyall, A. E., Savadjiev, P., Shenton, M. E., & Kubicki, M. (2016). Insights into the brain: Neuroimaging of brain development and maturation. *Journal of Neuroimaging, Psychiatry, and Neurology* 1, 10–19.

Maurer, D. (2020). Visual Development. In J. J. Lockman & C. S. Tamis-LeMonda (Eds.), *Cambridge Handbook of Infant Development.* Cambridge University Press: New York.

McClearn G.E., & Rodgers, D.A. (1959). Differences in alcohol preference among inbred strains of mice. *Quarterly Journal of Studies on Alcohol* 20, 691–695.

Melchior, M., Hersi, R., van der Waerden, J., et al. (2015). Maternal tobacco smoking in pregnancy and children's socio-emotional development at age 5: The EDEN mother-childbirth cohort study. *European Psychiatry: The Journal of the Association of European Psychiatrists* 30, 562–568.

Merz, E. C., Desai, P. M., Maskus, E. A., et al. (2019). Socioeconomic disparities in chronic physiologic stress are associated with brain structure in children. *Biological Psychiatry* 86, 921–929.

Michel, G. F., & Tyler, A. N. (2005). Critical period: A history of the transition from questions of when, to what, to how. *Developmental Psychobiology: The Journal of the International Society for Developmental Psychobiology* 46, 156–162.

Moore, R. E., & Townsend, S. D. (2019). Temporal development of the infant gut microbiome. *Open Biology* 9, 190128.

Mortensen, E. L., Michaelsen, K. F., Sanders, S. A., & Reinisch, J. M. (2002). The association between duration of breastfeeding and adult intelligence. *JAMA* 287, 2365–2371.

Nestler, E. J., & Landsman, D. (2001). Learning about addiction from the genome. *Nature* 409, 834–835.

Neville, H. J. (1995). Developmental specificity in neurocognitive development in humans. In M. S. Gazzaniga (Ed.), *The Cognitive Neurosciences* (pp. 219–231). MIT Press: Cambridge, MA.

Noble, D. (2015). Conrad Waddington and the origin of epigenetics. *Journal of Experimental Biology* 218, 816–818.

Noble, K. G., Houston, S. M., Brito, N. H., et al. (2015). Family income, parental education and brain structure in children and adolescents. *Nature Neuroscience* 18, 773–778.

Pasqualotto, A., & Proulx, M. J. (2012). The role of visual experience for the neural basis of spatial cognition. *Neuroscience & Biobehavioral Reviews* 36, 1179–1187.

Pigliucci, M. (2001). *Phenotypic Plasticity: Beyond Nature and Nurture.* Johns Hopkins University Press: Baltimore, MD.

Polderman, T. J., Benyamin, B., De Leeuw, C. A., et al. (2015). Meta-analysis of the heritability of human traits based on fifty years of twin studies. *Nature Genetics* 47, 702.

Rakic, P. (1995). A small step for the cell, a giant leap for mankind: a hypothesis of neocortical expansion during evolution. *Trends in Neurosciences* 18, 383–388.

Richards, J. E. & Conte, S. (2020). Brain development in infants: Structure and experience. In J. J. Lockman & C. S. Tamis-LeMonda (Eds.), *Cambridge Handbook of Infant Development.* Cambridge University Press: New York.

Rodríguez, J.M., Murphy, K., Stanton, C., et al. (2015) The composition of the gut microbiota throughout life, with an emphasis on early life. *Microbial Ecology in Health and Disease* 26: 26050.

Rosenzweig, M. R., Bennett, E. L., & Diamond, M. C. (1972). Cerebral effects of differential experience in hypophysectomized rats. *Journal of Comparative and Physiological Psychology* 79, 56.

Saudino, K. J. (2005). Behavioral genetics and child temperament. *Journal of developmental and behavioral pediatrics: JDBP* 26, 214.

Scarr, S., & McCartney, K. (1983). How people make their own environments: A theory of genotype→environment effects. *Child Development* 424–435.

Scott, G. B. I. (2016). NASA and NSBRI's Kelly Twins Study: Progress Implementing the First Integrated Omics Pilot Demonstration Study in Space American Society for Gravitational and Space Research (ASGSR) Annual Meeting: Cleveland, OH.

Sharp, G. C., Salas, L. A., Monnereau, C., et al. (2017). Maternal BMI at the start of pregnancy and offspring epigenome-wide DNA methylation: findings from the pregnancy and childhood epigenetics (PACE) consortium. *Human Molecular Genetics* 26, 4067–4085.

Shorey-Kendrick, L. E., McEvoy, C. T., Ferguson, B., et al. (2017). Vitamin C Prevents Offspring DNA Methylation Changes Associated with Maternal Smoking in Pregnancy. *American Journal of Respiratory and Critical Care Medicine*, 196, 745–755.

Sowell, E. R., Thompson, P. M., Leonard, C. M., et al. (2004). Longitudinal mapping of cortical thickness and brain growth in normal children. *Journal of Neuroscience* 24, 8223–8231.

Stiles, J. (2017). Principles of brain development. *Wiley Interdisciplinary Reviews: Cognitive Science* 8, e1402.

Stiles, J. (2000). Neural plasticity and cognitive development. *Developmental Neuropsychology* 18, 237–272.

Talati, A., Wickramaratne, P. J., Wesselhoeft, R., & Weissman, M. M. (2017). Prenatal tobacco exposure, birthweight, and offspring psychopathology. *Psychiatry Research* 252, 346–352.

Tanaka, M., & Nakayama, J. (2017) Development of the gut microbiota in infancy and its impact on health in later life. *Allergol Int.* 66, 515–522.

Thomas, M. S. C., & Johnson, M. H. (2008). New Advances in Understanding Sensitive Periods in Brain Development. *Current Directions in Psychological Science* 17, 1–5.

Trauner, D. A., Eshagh, K., Ballantyne, A. O., & Bates, E. (2013). Early language development after peri-natal stroke. *Brain and Language* 127, 399–403.

van Dongen, J., Slagboom, P., Draisma, H. et al. (2012). The continuing value of twin studies in the omics era. *Nature Review of Genetics* 13, 640–653.

Vicari, S., Albertoni, A., Chilosi, A. M., et al. (2000). Plasticity and reorganization during language development in children with early brain injury. *Cortex* 36, 31–46.

Waddington, C. (1942). Canalization of development and the inheritance of acquired characters. *Nature* 150, 563–565.

Weaver, I. C., Cervoni, N., Champagne, F. A., et al. (2004). Epigenetic programming by maternal behavior. *Nature Neuroscience* 7, 847–854.

Werker, J. F., & Tees, R. C. (2005). Speech perception as a window for understanding plasticity and commitment in language systems of the brain. *Developmental Psychobiology: The Journal of the International Society for Developmental Psychobiology* 46, 233–251.

Werker, J. F. and Hensch, T. K. (2015). Critical periods in speech perception: New directions. *Annual Review of Psychology* 66: 173–196.

Chapter 3

Aarnoudse-Moens, C. S. H., Weisglas-Kuperus, N., van Goudoever, J. B., & Oosterlaan, J. (2009). Meta-analysis of neurobehavioral outcomes in very preterm and/or very low birth weight children. *Pediatrics* 124, 717–728.

Abrams, R., Gerhardt, K., & Antonelli, P. (1998). Fetal hearing. *Developmental Psychobiology* 33, 1.

Adolph, K. E., & Robinson, S. R. (2015). Motor development. In R. M. Lerner, L. Liben, & U. Muller (Eds.), *Handbook of Child Psychology and Developmental Science: Vol. 2: Cognitive Processes* (pp. 114–157).

Allister, L., Lester, B. M., Carr, S., & Liu, J. (2001). The effects of maternal depression on fetal heart rate response to vibroacoustic stimulation. *Developmental Neuropsychology* 20, 639–651.

Apgar, V. (1952). A proposal for a new method of evaluation of the newborn. *Classic Papers in Critical Care* 32, 97.

Barker, D. J., & Thornburg, K. L. (2013). Placental programming of chronic diseases, cancer and lifespan: a review. *Placenta* 34, 841–845.

Barratt, M. S., Roach, M. A., & Leavitt, L. A. (1996). The impact of low-risk prematurity on maternal behaviour and toddler outcomes. *International Journal of Behavioral Development* 19, 581–602.

Bateson, P., Barker, D., Clutton-Brock, T., et al. (2004). Developmental plasticity and human health. *Nature* 430, 419–421.

Bauerfeld, S. L., & Lachenmeyer, J. R. (1992). Prenatal nutritional status and intellectual development. In *Advances in Clinical Child Psychology* (pp. 191–222). Springer, Boston, MA.

Benson, D. F., & Ardila, A. (1996). *Aphasia: A Clinical Perspective*. Oxford University Press: New York.

Birnholz, J. C. (1984). Ultrasonic visualization of endometrial movements. *Fertility and Sterility* 41, 157–158.

Blumberg, M. S., Marques, H. G., & Iida, F. (2013). Twitching in sensorimotor development from sleeping rats to robots. *Current Biology* 23, R532–R537.

Boemio, A., Fromm, S., Braun, A., & Poeppel, D. (2005). Hierarchical and asymmetric temporal sensitivity in human auditory cortices. *Nature Neuroscience* 8, 389–395.

Bornstein, M. H. (2002). Parenting infants. *Handbook of Parenting*, 1.

Boulet, S. L., Schieve, L. A., & Boyle, C. A. (2011). Birth weight and health and developmental outcomes in US children, 1997–2005. *Maternal and Child Health Journal* 15, 836–844.

Buss, C., Davis, E. P., Muftuler, L. T., et al. (2010). High pregnancy anxiety during mid-gestation is associated with decreased gray matter density in 6–9-year-old children. *Psychoneuroendocrinology* 35, 141–153.

Butte, N., Cobb, K., Dwyer, J., et al. (2004). The start healthy feeding guidelines for infants and toddlers. *Journal of the American Dietetic Association* 104, 442–454.

Byers-Heinlein, K., Burns, T. C., & Werker, J. F. (2010). The roots of bilingualism in newborns. *Psychological Science* 21, 343–348.

Castro, L. C., & Avina, R. L. (2002). Maternal obesity and pregnancy outcomes. *Current Opinion in Obstetrics and Gynecology* 14, 601–606.

CDC (Centers for Disease Control and Prevention). (2010). Racial and ethnic differences in breastfeeding initiation and duration, by state-National Immunization Survey, United States, 2004–2008. *MMWR. Morbidity and Mortality Weekly Report* 59, 327–334.

Chen, A., Oster, E., & Williams, H. (2014). Why is infant mortality in the US higher than in Europe? University of Chicago: Chicago, IL.

Cheour, M., Martynova, O., Näätänen, R., et al. (2002). Speech sounds learned by sleeping newborns. *Nature* 415, 599–600.

Colen, C. G., & Ramey, D. M. (2014). Is breast truly best? Estimating the effects of breast-feeding on long-term child health and wellbeing in the United States using sibling comparisons. *Social Science & Medicine* 109, 55–65.

Colombo, J., Kannass, K. N., Jill Shaddy, D., et al. (2004). Maternal DHA and the development of attention in infancy and toddlerhood. *Child Development* 75, 1254–1267.

Creasy, R. K., & Resnik, R. (1999). Intrauterine growth restriction. *Maternal-Fetal Medicine* 4, 569–584.

Cuevas, K., Swingler, M. M., Bell, M. A., et al. (2012). Measures of frontal functioning and the emergence of inhibitory control processes at 10 months of age. *Developmental Cognitive Neuroscience* 2, 235–243.

Cunningham, C., Taylor, H. G., Minich, N. M., & Hack, M. (2001). Constipation in very-low-birth-weight children at 10 to 14 years of age. *Journal of Pediatric Gastroenterology and Nutrition* 33, 23–27.

Cutler, D., & Miller, G. (2005). The role of public health improvements in health advances: The twentieth-century United States. *Demography* 42, 1–22.

Davis, E. P., & Sandman, C. A. (2010). The timing of prenatal exposure to maternal cortisol and psychosocial stress is associated with human infant cognitive development. *Child Development* 81, 131–148.

DeCasper, A. J., & Spence, M. J. (1986). Newborns prefer a familiar story over an unfamiliar one. *Infant Behavior and Development* 9, 20–36.

DeCasper, A. J., & Fifer, W. P. (1980). Of human bonding: Newborns prefer their mothers' voices. *Science* 208, 1174–1176.

Dehaene-Lambertz, G., Montavont, A., Jobert, A., et al. (2010). Language or music, mother or Mozart? Structural and environmental influences on infants' language networks. *Brain and Language* 114, 53–65.

de Kloet, E. R., Sibug, R. M., Helmerhorst, F. M., & Schmidt, M. (2005). Stress, genes and the mechanism of programming the brain for later life. *Neuroscience & Biobehavioral Reviews* 29, 271–281.

Démonet, J. F., Chollet, F., Ramsay, S., et al. (1992). The anatomy of phonological and semantic processing in normal subjects. *Brain* 115, 1753–1768.

de Paula Freitas, B., de Oliveira Dias, J. R., Prazeres, J., et al. (2016). Ocular Findings in Infants with Microcephaly Associated with Presumed Zika Virus Congenital Infection in Salvador, Brazil. *JAMA Ophthalmology* 134, 529–535.

Der, G., Batty, G. D., & Deary, I. J. (2006). Effect of breast feeding on intelligence in children: prospective study, sibling pairs analysis, and meta-analysis. *BMJ* 333, 945.

DeSilva, J. M., & Lesnik, J. J. (2008). Brain size at birth throughout human evolution: a new method for estimating neonatal brain size in hominins. *Journal of Human Evolution* 55, 1064–1074.

De Snoo, K. (1937). The drinking child in the uterus. *Journal of Obstetric Gynecology* 105, 88–97.

De Vries, J. I., Visser, G. H., & Prechtl, H. F. (1982). The emergence of fetal behaviour. I. Qualitative aspects. *Early Human Development* 7, 301–322.

DiPietro, J. A. (2010). Maternal influences on the developing fetus. In *Maternal Influences on Fetal Neurodevelopment* (pp. 19–32). Springer: New York.

DiPietro, J. A., Costigan, K. A., & Pressman, E. K. (2002). Fetal state concordance predicts infant state regulation. *Early Human Development* 68, 1–13.

Draganova, R., Eswaran, H., Murphy, P., et al. (2007). Serial magnetoencephalographic study of fetal and newborn auditory discriminative evoked responses. *Early Human Development* 83, 199–207.

Duzinski, S. V., Yuma-Guerrero, P. J., Fung, A., et al. (2013). Sleep behaviors of infants and young children: associated demographic and acculturation characteristics among Hispanic teen mothers. *Journal of Trauma Nursing* 20, 189–198.

Edwards, J., Berube, M., Erlandson, K., et al. (2011) Developmental coordination disorder in school-aged children born very preterm and/or at very low birth weight: A systematic review. *Journal of Developmental & Behavioral Pediatrics* 32, 678–687.

Evenhouse, E., & Reilly, S. (2005). Improved estimates of the benefits of breastfeeding using sibling comparisons to reduce selection bias. *Health Services Research* 40, 1781–1802.

Fazzi, C., Saunders, D.H., Linton, K. et al. (2017). Sedentary behaviours during pregnancy: A systematic review. *International Journal of Behavioral Nutrition and Physical Activity* 14, 32.

Feldman, R. (2007). Parent–infant synchrony and the construction of shared timing; physiological precursors, developmental outcomes, and risk conditions. *Journal of Child Psychology and Psychiatry* 48, 329–354.

Field, T. (2010). Postpartum depression effects on early interactions, parenting, and safety practices: a review. *Infant Behavior and Development* 33, 1–6.

Field, T., Diego, M., Dieter, J., et al. (2004). Prenatal depression effects on the fetus and the newborn. *Infant Behavior and Development* 27, 216–229.

Fifer, W. P., Byrd, D. L., Kaku, M., et al. (2010). Newborn infants learn during sleep. *Proceedings of the National Academy of Sciences* 107, 10320–10323.

Fried, P. A. (2002). The consequences of marijuana use during pregnancy: A review of the human literature. *Journal of Cannabis Therapeutics* 2, 85–104.

Friedrich, M., Wilhelm, I., Mölle, M., et al. (2017). The sleeping infant brain anticipates development. *Current Biology* 27, 2374–2380.

Fronczak, C. M., Kim, E. D., & Barqawi, A. B. (2013) The insults of illicit drug use on male fertility. *Journal of Andrology* 33, 515–528.

Galler, J. R., Harrison, R. H., & Ramsey, F. (2006). Bed-sharing, breastfeeding, and maternal moods in Barbados. *Infant Behavior and Development*, 29, 526–534.

Glover, V. (2011). Annual research review: prenatal stress and the origins of psychopathology: an evolutionary perspective. *Journal of Child Psychology and Psychiatry* 52, 356–367.

Glynn, L. M., & Sandman, C. A. (2006). The influence of prenatal stress and adverse birth outcome on human cognitive and neurological development. *International Review of Research in Mental Retardation* 32, 109–129.

Glynn, L. M., & Sandman, C. A. (2011). Prenatal origins of neurological development: A critical period for fetus and mother. *Current Directions in Psychological Science* 20, 384–389.

Goodman, S. H., & Brand, S. R. (2009). Infants of depressed mothers. *Handbook of Infant Mental Health* 153–170.

Groothuis, T. G., Müller, W., von Engelhardt, N., et al. (2005). Maternal hormones as a tool to adjust offspring phenotype in avian species. *Neuroscience & Biobehavioral Reviews* 29, 329–352.

Grove, G., Ziauddeen, N., Harris, S., & Alwan, N. A. (2019). Maternal interpregnancy weight change and premature birth: Findings from an English population-based cohort study. *PLoS ONE* 14.

Han, Z., Mulla, S., Beyene, J., et al. (2011). Maternal underweight and the risk of preterm birth and low birth weight: a systematic review and meta-analyses. *International Journal of Epidemiology* 40, 65–101.

Harkness, S., & Super, C. M. (1995). Culture and parenting. In M. H. Bornstein (Ed.), *Handbook of Parenting, Vol. 2. Biology and Ecology of Parenting* (pp. 211–234). Lawrence Erlbaum Associates, Inc.: Hillsdale, NJ.

Harley, K., Stamm, N. L., & Eskenazi, B. (2007). The effect of time in the US on the duration of breastfeeding in women of Mexican descent. *Maternal and Child Health Journal*, 11, 119–125.

Harpaz, Y., Levkovitz, Y., & Lavidor, M. (2009). Lexical ambiguity resolution in Wernicke's area and its right homologue. *Cortex* 45, 1097–1103.

Hauck, F. R., Thompson, J. M., Tanabe, K. O., et al. (2011). Breastfeeding and reduced risk of sudden infant death syndrome: a meta-analysis. *Pediatrics* 128, 103–110.

Heck, K. E., Braveman, P., Cubbin, C., et al. (2006). Socioeconomic status and breastfeeding initiation among California mothers. *Public Health Reports* 121, 51–59.

Hepper, P. G. (2003). Prenatal psychological and behavioural development. *Handbook of Developmental Psychology*, 91–113.

Hopkins-Golightly, T., Raz, S., & Sander, C. J. (2003). Influence of slight to moderate risk for birth hypoxia on acquisition of cognitive and language function in the preterm infant: A cross-sectional comparison with preterm-birth controls. *Neuropsychology* 17, 3.

Horta, B. L., & Victora, C. G. (2013). Long-term effects of breastfeeding. *Geneva: World Health Organization* 1–74.

Hoyert, D. L., Kochanek, K. D., & Murphy, S. L. (1999). Deaths: final data for 1997. *National Vital Statistics Report* 47, 1–104.

Hulubaş, A. (2011). Romanian beliefs and rites of pregnancy with special reference to Moldova. *Folklore* 122, 264–282.

James, D. K., Spencer, C. J., & Stepsis, B. W. (2002). Fetal learning: a prospective randomized controlled study. *Ultrasound in Obstetrics and Gynecology: The Official Journal of the International Society of Ultrasound in Obstetrics and Gynecology* 20, 431–438.

Jenni, O. G., Deboer, T., & Achermann, P. (2006). Development of the 24-h rest-activity pattern in human infants. *Infant Behavior and Development* 29, 143–152.

Johnson, M. H. (2008). Human ES cells and a blastocyst from one embryo: exciting science but conflicting ethics? *Cell Stem Cell* 2, 103–104.

Jones, R. L. (2006). Reproduction and nesting of the endangered ringed map turtle, *Graptemys oculifera*, in Mississippi. *Chelonian Conservation and Biology* 5, 195–209.

Kaiser, S., & Sachser, N. (2009). Effects of prenatal social stress on offspring development: pathology or adaptation? *Current Directions in Psychological Science* 18, 118–121.

Kelly, Y. J., Watt, R. G., & Nazroo, J. Y. (2006). Racial/ethnic differences in breastfeeding initiation and continuation in the United Kingdom and comparison with findings in the United States. *Pediatrics* 118, e1428–e1435.

Kendall, G., & Peebles, D. (2005). Acute fetal hypoxia: The modulating effect of infection. *Early Human Development* 81, 27–34.

Knickmeyer, R. C., Gouttard, S., Kang, et al. (2008). A structural MRI study of human brain development from birth to 2 years. *Journal of Neuroscience* 28, 12176–12182.

Kramer, M. S., Aboud, F., Mironova, E., et al. (2008). Breastfeeding and child cognitive development: new evidence from a large randomized trial. *Archives of General Psychiatry* 65, 578–584.

Kurth, S., Olini, N., Huber, R., & LeBourgeois, M. (2015). Sleep and early cortical development. *Current Sleep Medicine Reports*, 1, 64–73.

Kurth, S., Ringli, M., Geiger, A., et al. (2010). Mapping of cortical activity in the first two decades of life: A high-density sleep electroencephalogram study. *Journal of Neuroscience* 30, 13211–13219.

Larsson, G., Bohlin, A. B., & Tunell, R. (1985). Prospective study of children exposed to variable amounts of alcohol in utero. *Archives of Disease in Childhood* 60, 316–321.

Lorenz, J. M., Ananth, C. V., Polin, R. A., & D'alton, M. E. (2016). Infant mortality in the United States. *Journal of Perinatology* 36, 797–801.

Lovely, C., Rampersad, M., Fernandes, Y., & Eberhart, J. (2017). Gene–environment interactions in development and disease. *WIREs Developmental Biology* 6, e247.

Loudon I. (1992). *Death in Childbirth: An International Study of Maternal Care and Maternal Mortality, 1800–1950.* Oxford University Press: New York.

Luijk, M. P., Mileva-Seitz, V. R., Jansen, P. W., et al. (2013). Ethnic differences in prevalence and determinants of mother–child bed-sharing in early childhood. *Sleep Medicine* 14, 1092–1099.

Lyall, A. E., Savadjiev, P., Shenton, M. E., & Kubicki, M. (2016). Insights into the brain: Neuroimaging of brain development and maturation. *Journal of Neuroimaging, Psychiatry, and Neurology* 1, 10–19.

MacDorman, M. F., & Mathews, T. J. (2011). Understanding racial and ethnic disparities in US infant mortality rates. *NCHS Data Brief* 74, 1–8.

Mark, P. J., Crew, R. C., Wharfe, M. D., & Waddell, B. J. (2017). Rhythmic three-part harmony: the complex interaction of maternal, placental and fetal circadian systems. *Journal of Biological Rhythms* 32, 534–549.

Marseglia, L., D'Angelo, G., Granese, R., et al. (2019). Role of oxidative stress in neonatal respiratory distress syndrome. *Free Radical Biology and Medicine* 142, 132–137.

Mathews, T. J., MacDorman, M. F., & Thoma, M. E. (2015). Infant mortality statistics from the 2013 period linked birth/infant death data set. *National Vital Statistics Reports* 64. National Center for Health Statistics: Hyattsville, MD.

Matoba, N., & Collins Jr, J. W. (2017). Racial disparity in infant mortality. *Seminars in Perinatology* 41, 354–359.

Maurer, D., & Maurer, C. (1988). *The World of the Newborn.* Basic Books: New York.

Mayes, L. C., & Fahy, T. (2001). Prenatal drug exposure and cognitive development. *Environmental Effects on Cognitive Abilities*, 189–219.

McCoy, R. C., Hunt, C. E., Lesko, S. M., et al. (2004). Frequency of bed sharing and its relationship to breastfeeding. *Journal of Developmental & Behavioral Pediatrics* 25, 141–149.

McDonald, S. D., Han, Z., Mulla, S., et al. (2011). High gestational weight gain and the risk of preterm birth and low birth weight: A systematic review and meta-analysis. *Journal of Obstetrics and Gynaecology Canada* 33, 1223–1233.

McDowell, M. A., Wang, C. Y., & Kennedy-Stephenson, J. (2008). *Breastfeeding in the United States: findings from the national health and nutrition examination surveys*, 1999–2006 (No. 5). US Department of Health and Human Services, Centers for Disease Control and Prevention, National Center for Health Statistics.

McLean, M., Bisits, A., Davies, J., et al. (1995). A placental clock controlling the length of human pregnancy. *Nature Medicine* 1, 460–463.

Meckel, R.A. (1998). *Save the Babies: American Public Health Reform and the Prevention of Infant Mortality, 1850–1929.* Michigan University Press.

Ment, L. R., Vohr, B., Allan, W., et al. (2003). Change in cognitive function over time in very low-birth-weight infants. *JAMA* 289, 705–711.

Mercier, C. E., Dunn, M. S., Ferrelli, K. R., et al. & Vermont Oxford Network ELBW Infant Follow-Up Study Group. (2010). Neurodevelopmental outcome of extremely low birth weight infants from the Vermont Oxford network: 1998–2003. *Neonatology* 97, 329–338.

Miller, P. M., & Commons, M. L. (2010). The benefits of attachment parenting for infants and children: A behavioral developmental view. *Behavioral Development Bulletin* 16, 1–14.

Mindell, J. A., Sadeh, A., Kohyama, J., & How, T. H. (2010). Parental behaviors and sleep outcomes in infants and toddlers: a cross-cultural comparison. *Sleep Medicine* 11, 393–399.

Moessinger, A. C. (1983). Fetal akinesia deformation sequence: an animal model. *Pediatrics* 72, 857–863.

Monk, C., Sloan, R. P., Myers, M. M., et al. (2004). Fetal heart rate reactivity differs by women's psychiatric status: an early marker for developmental risk? *Journal of the American Academy of Child & Adolescent Psychiatry* 43, 283–290.

Moore, K. L., & Persaud, T. V. N. (2003). The cardiovascular system. In *The Developing Human: Clinically Oriented Embryology*, 7th ed. Saunders: Philadelphia, PA.

Morelli, G. A., Rogoff, B., Oppenheim, D., & Goldsmith, D. (1992). Cultural variation in infants' sleeping arrangements: Questions of independence. *Developmental Psychology* 28, 604–613.

Morgane, P. J., Austin-LaFrance, R., Bronzino, J., et al. (1993). Prenatal malnutrition and development of the brain. *Neuroscience & Biobehavioral Reviews* 17, 91–128.

Morokuma, S., Doria, V., Ierullo, A., et al. (2008). Developmental change in fetal response to repeated low-intensity sound. *Developmental Science* 11, 47–52.

Myowa-Yamakoshi, M., & Takeshita, H. (2006). Do human fetuses anticipate self-oriented actions? A study by four-dimensional (4D) ultrasonography. *Infancy* 10, 289–301.

Nie, C., Bailey, A. M., Istre, G. R., & Anderson, R. (2010). Population-based survey of infant bed sharing. *Injury Prevention* 16, A69.

Owens, J. A. (2004). Sleep in children: Cross-cultural perspectives. *Sleep and Biological Rhythms* 2, 165–173.

Poehlmann, J., Schwichtenberg, A. J. M., Shlafer, R. J., et al. (2011). Emerging self-regulation in toddlers born preterm or low birth weight: Differential susceptibility to parenting? *Development and Psychopathology* 23, 177–193.

Pressman, A., Hernandez, A., & Sikka, S. C. (2018). Lifestyle stress and its impact on male reproductive health. In *Bioenvironmental Issues Affecting Men's Reproductive and Sexual Health* (pp. 73–83). Academic Press.

Querleu, D., Renard, X., & Crépin, G. (1981). Bruit intra-utérin et perceptions auditives du foetus.[Intra-uterine sound and fetal auditory perception]. *Bulletin de l'Académie Nationale de Médecine* (165), 5.

Rayburn, W. F. (1982). Antepartum fetal assessment: Monitoring fetal activity. *Clinics in Perinatology* 9, 231–252.

Reissland, N., Francis, B., Aydin, E., et al. (2014). The development of anticipation in the fetus: A longitudinal account of human fetal mouth movements in reaction to and anticipation of touch. *Developmental Psychobiology* 56, 955–963.

Reiter, R. J., Tan, D. X., Korkmaz, A., & Rosales-Corral, S. A. (2014). Melatonin and stable circadian rhythms optimize maternal, placental and fetal physiology. *Human Reproduction Update* 20, 293–307.

Ricci, E., Al Beitawi, S., Cipriani, S., et al. (2017). Semen quality and alcohol intake: a systematic review and meta-analysis. *Reprod Biomed Online* 34, 38–47.

Robinson, S., & Fall, C. (2012). Infant nutrition and later health: a review of current evidence. *Nutrients* 4, 859–874.

Robinson S. R. (2016) Yoke motor learning in the fetal rat: A model system for prenatal behavioral development. In N. Reissland & B. Kisilevsky (Eds.), *Fetal Development*. Springer: Cham, Switzerland.

Roffwarg, H. P., Muzio, J. N., and Dement, W. C. (1966). Ontogenetic development of the human sleep-dream cycle. *Science* 152, 604–619.

Rojas, M. A., Kaplan, M., Quevedo, M., et al. (2003). Somatic growth of preterm infants during skin-to-skin care versus traditional holding: a randomized, controlled trial. *Journal of Developmental & Behavioral Pediatrics* 24, 163–168.

Romeo, R. R., Segaran, J., Leonard, J. A., et al. (2018). Language exposure relates to structural neural connectivity in childhood. *Journal of Neuroscience* 38, 7870–7877.

Roseboom, T., de Rooij, S., & Painter, R. (2006). The Dutch famine and its long-term consequences for adult health. *Early Human Development* 82, 485–491.

Sachser, N., Hennessy, M. B., & Kaiser, S. (2011). Adaptive modulation of behavioural profiles by social stress during early phases of life and adolescence. *Neuroscience & Biobehavioral Reviews* 35, 1518–1533.

Sambeth, A., Ruohio, K., Alku, P., et al. (2008). Sleeping newborns extract prosody from continuous speech. *Clinical Neurophysiology* 119, 332–341.

Shimizu, M., & Teti, D. M. (2018). Infant sleeping arrangements, social criticism, and maternal distress in the first year. *Infant and Child Development* 27, e2080–e2096.

Singh, G. K., & Stella, M. Y. (2019). Infant mortality in the United States, 1915–2017: large social inequalities have persisted for over a century. *International Journal of MCH and AIDS* 8, 19.

Smith, L. A., Geller, N. L., Kellams, A. L., et al. (2016). Infant sleep location and breastfeeding practices in the United States, 2011–2014. *Academic Pediatrics* 16, 540–549.

Smotherman, W. P., & Robinson, S. R. (1996). The development of behavior before birth. *Developmental Psychology* 32, 425.

Stoodley, C. J., & Limperopoulos, C. (2016). Structure-function relationships in the developing cerebellum: Evidence from early-life cerebellar injury and neurodevelopmental disorders. *Seminars in Fetal and Neonatal Medicine* 21, 356–364.

Streissguth, A. P., & Connor, P. D. (2001). Fetal alcohol syndrome and other effects of prenatal alcohol: Developmental cognitive neuroscience implications. *Handbook of Developmental Cognitive Neuroscience*, 505–518.

Sunderam, S., Kissin, D. M., Zhang, Y., et al. (2019). Assisted reproductive technology surveillance-United States, 2016. *Morbidity and Mortality Weekly Report. Surveillance Summaries (Washington, DC: 2002)* 68, 1–23.

Super, C. M., & Harkness, S. (1986). The developmental niche: A conceptualization at the interface of child and culture. *International Journal of Behavioral Development* 9, 545–569.

Super, C. M., & Harkness, S. (2013). Culture and children's sleep. In A. R. Wolfson & H. E. Montgomery-Downs (Eds.), *Oxford Library of Psychology. The Oxford Handbook of Infant, Child, and Adolescent Sleep and Behavior* (pp. 81–98). Oxford University Press: New York.

Talge, N. M., Neal, C., & Glover, V. (2007). Early stress, translational research and prevention science network: fetal and neonatal experience on child and adolescent mental health. Antenatal maternal stress and long-term effects on child neurodevelopment: how and why. *Journal of Child Psychology and Psychiatry* 48, 245–261.

Thelen, E., & Smith, L. B. (1998). Dynamic systems theories. In W. Damon & R. M. Lerner (Eds.), *Handbook of Child Psychology: Theoretical Models of Human Development* (pp. 563–634). John Wiley & Sons Inc: Hoboken, NJ.

Thelen, E. (2005). Dynamic systems theory and the complexity of change. *Psychoanalytic Dialogues* 15, 255–283.

Thoman, E. B., & Whitney, M. P. (1989). Sleep states of infants monitored in the home: Individual differences, developmental trends, and origins of diurnal cyclicity. *Infant Behavior and Development* 12, 59–75.

Tiemann-Boege, I., Navidi, W., Grewal, R., et al. (2002). The observed human sperm mutation frequency cannot explain the achondroplasia paternal age effect. *Proceedings of the National Academy of Sciences* 99, 14952–14957.

Tononi, G., & Cirelli, C. (2006). Sleep function and synaptic homeostasis. *Sleep Medicine Reviews* 10, 49–62.

Von Stumm, S., & Plomin, R. (2015). Socioeconomic status and the growth of intelligence from infancy through adolescence. *Intelligence* 48, 30–36.

Werchan, D. M., Collins, A. G., Frank, M. J., & Amso, D. (2016). Role of prefrontal cortex in learning and generalizing hierarchical rules in 8-month-old infants. *Journal of Neuroscience* 36, 10314–10322.

Whitney, M. P., & Thoman, E. B. (1994). Sleep in premature and full-term infants from 24-hour home recordings. *Infant Behavior and Development* 17, 223–234.

Wilhelm, I., Diekelmann, S., & Born, J. (2008). Sleep in children improves memory performance on declarative but not procedural tasks. *Learning & Memory* 15, 373–377.

Wilhelm, I., Kurth, S., Ringli, M., et al. (2014). Sleep slow-wave activity reveals developmental changes in experience-dependent plasticity. *Journal of Neuroscience* 34, 12568–12575.

Willinger, M., Ko, C. W., Hoffman, H. J., et al. (2003). Trends in infant bed sharing in the United States, 1993–2000: The National Infant Sleep Position study. *Archives of Pediatrics & Adolescent Medicine* 157, 43–49.

Wolf, J. B. (2013). The politics of dissent. *Journal of Women, Politics & Policy* 34, 306–316.

Wolpert, L. (2011). Positional information and patterning revisited. *Journal of Theoretical Biology* 269, 359–365.

Xie, L., Kang, H., Xu, Q., et al. (2013). Sleep drives metabolite clearance from the adult brain. *Science* 342, 373–377.

Zeskind, P. S., & Ramey, C. T. (1981). Preventing intellectual and interactional sequelae of fetal malnutrition: A longitudinal, transactional, and synergistic approach to development. *Child Development* 213–218.

Chapter 4

Adolph, K. E. (2000). Specificity of learning: Why infants fall over a veritable cliff. *Psychological Science* 11, 290–295.

Adolph, K. E., & Berger, S. E. (2006). Motor development. In D. Kuhn, R. S. Siegler, W. Damon, & R. M. Lerner (Eds.), *Handbook of*

Child Psychology: Cognition, Perception, and Language (pp. 161–213). John Wiley & Sons Inc: Hoboken, NJ.

Adolph, K. E., & Franchak, J. M. (2017). The development of motor behavior. *Wiley Interdisciplinary Reviews: Cognitive Science* 8, e1430.

Adolph, K. E., Karasik, L. B., & Tamis-LeMonda, C. S. (2010). Using social information to guide action: Infants' locomotion over slippery slopes. *Neural Networks* 23, 1033–1042.

Adolph, K. E., Kretch, K. S., & LoBue, V. (2014). Fear of heights in infants? *Current Directions in Psychological Science* 23, 60–66.

Adolph, K. E., Berger, S. E., & Leo, A. J. (2011). Developmental continuity? Crawling, cruising, and walking. *Developmental Science* 14, 306–318.

Adolph, K. E., Cole, W. G., Komati, M., et al. (2012). How do you learn to walk? Thousands of steps and dozens of falls per day. *Psychological Science* 23, 1387–1394.

Adolph, K. E. & Robinson, S. R. (2015). Motor development. In R. M. Lerner (Series Ed.) & L. Liben & U. Muller (Vol. Eds), *Handbook of Child Psychology and Developmental Science: Vol. 2: Cognitive Processes*, 7th ed. (pp. 114–157). Wiley: Hoboken, NJ.

Adolph, K. E., Vereijken, B., & Shrout, P. E. (2003). What changes in infant walking and why. *Child Development* 74, 475–497.

Adolph, K. E., Vereijken, B., & Denny, M. A. (1998). Learning to crawl. *Child Development* 69, 1299–1312.

Adolph, K. E., & Tamis-LeMonda, C. S. (2014). The costs and benefits of development: The transition from crawling to walking. *Child Development Perspectives* 8, 187–192.

Adolph, K. E., & Franchak, J. M. (2017). The development of motor behavior. *Wiley Interdisciplinary Reviews: Cognitive Science* 8, e1430.

Ainsworth, M. D. S. (1967). Patterns of attachment behavior. MDS Ainsworth.

American Academy of Pediatrics (2016). SIDS and other sleep-related infant deaths: Updated 2016. Recommendations for a safe infant sleeping environment. *Pediatrics* 138, e20162938.

Anzures, G., Wheeler, A., Quinn, P. C., et al. (2012). Brief daily exposures to Asian females reverses perceptual narrowing for Asian faces in Caucasian infants. *Journal of Experimental Child Psychology* 112, 484–495.

Aslin, R. N. (1981). Development of smooth pursuit in human infants. In D. F. Fisher, R. A. Monty, & J. W. Senders (Eds.), *Eye Movements: Cognition and Visual Perception* (pp. 31–51). Erlbaum: Hillsdale, NJ.

Bahrick, L. E., & Lickliter, R. (2014). Learning to attend selectively: The dual role of intersensory redundancy. *Current Directions in Psychological Science* 23, 414–420.

Beauchamp, G. K., Cowart, B. J., & Moran, M. (1986). Developmental changes in salt acceptability in human infants. *Developmental Psychobiology: The Journal of the International Society for Developmental Psychobiology* 19, 17–25.

Beauchamp, G. K., & Mennella, J. A. (2009). Early flavor learning and its impact on later feeding behavior. *Journal of Pediatric Gastroenterology and Nutrition* 48, S25–S30.

Berger, S. E., Theuring, C., and Adolph, K. E. (2007). How and when infants learn to climb stairs. *Infant Behavior and Development* 30, 36–49.

Bertenthal, B. I., Campos, J. J., & Barrett, K. C. (1984). Self-produced locomotion. In *Continuities and Discontinuities in Development* (pp. 175–210). Springer: Boston, MA.

Bornstein, M. H., Hahn, C. S., & Suwalsky, J. T. (2013). Physically developed and exploratory young infants contribute to their own long-term academic achievement. *Psychological Science* 24, 1906–1917.

Bornstein, M. H., Kessen, W., & Weiskopf, S. (1976). Color vision and hue categorization in young human infants. *Journal of Experimental Psychology: Human Perception and Performance* 2, 115–129.

Bly, L. (1994). *Motor Skills Acquisition in the First Year: An Illustrated Guide to Normal Development*. Psychological Corp.

Braddick, O., & Atkinson, J. (2011). Development of human visual function. *Vision Research* 51, 1588–1609.

Brazelton, T. B., Koslowski, B., & Tronick, E. (1976). Neonatal behavior among urban Zambians and Americans. *Journal of the American Academy of Child Psychiatry* 15, 97–107.

Brown, A. M., & Lindsey, D. T. (2009). Contrast insensitivity: the critical immaturity in infant visual performance. *Optometry and Vision Science* 86, 572.

Byford, A. (2013). Parent diaries and the child study movement in late imperial and early Soviet Russia. *The Russian Review* 72, 212–241.

Campos, J. J., Hiatt, S., Ramsay, D., et al. (1978). The emergence of fear on the visual cliff. In: M. Lewis & L. A. Rosenblum (Eds.), *The Development of Affect. Genesis of Behavior, Vol 1*. Springer: Boston, MA.

Campos, J. J., Anderson, D. I., Barbu-Roth, M.A., et al. (2000). Travel broadens the mind. *Infancy* 1, 149–219.

Cannon, E. N., Woodward, A. L., Gredebäck, G., et al. (2012). Action production influences 12-month-old infants' attention to others' actions. *Developmental Science* 15, 35–42.

Cirelli, L. K., & Trehub, S. E. (2020). Infants' perception of auditory patterns. In J. J. Lockman & C. S. Tamis-LeMonda (Eds.), *Cambridge Handbook of Infant Development*. Cambridge University Press: New York.

Clearfield, M. W. (2004). The role of crawling and walking experience in infant spatial memory. *Journal of Experimental Child Psychology* 89, 214–241.

Clifton, R. K., Muir, D. W., Ashmead, D. H., & Clarkson, M. G. (1993). Is visually guided reaching in early infancy a myth? *Child Development* 64, 1099–1110.

Colombo, J. (1993). *Infant Cognition: Predicting Later Intellectual Functioning*. Sage Publications: London, United Kingdom.

Cone, B., & Whitaker, R. (2013). Dynamics of infant cortical auditory evoked potentials (CAEPs) for tone and speech tokens. *International Journal of Pediatric Otorhinolaryngology* 77, 1162–1173.

Curtindale, L. M., Bahrick, L. E., Lickliter, R., & Colombo, J. (2019). Effects of multimodal synchrony on infant attention and heart rate during events with social and nonsocial stimuli. *Journal of Experimental Child Psychology* 178, 283–294.

de Haan, M., Johnson, M. H., & Halit, H. (2003). Development of face-sensitive event-related potentials during infancy: a review. *International Journal of Psychophysiology* 51, 45–58.

de Onis, M., Onyango, A. W., Borghi, E., et al. (2006). Comparison of the World Health Organization (WHO) Child Growth Standards and the National Center for Health Statistics/WHO international growth reference: Implications for child health programmes. *Public Health and Nutrition*, 942–947.

Ellis, A. E., Xiao, N. G., Lee, K., & Oakes, L. M. (2017). Scanning of own-versus other-race faces in infants from racially diverse or homogenous communities. *Developmental Psychobiology* 59, 613–627.

Fair, J., Flom, R., Jones, J., & Martin, J. (2012). Perceptual learning: 12-month-olds' discrimination of monkey faces. *Child Development* 83, 1996–2006.

Fantz, R. (1961). The origin of form perception. *Scientific American* 204, 66–73.

Fantz, R. L. (1963). Pattern vision in newborn infants. *Science* 140, 296–297.

Falck-Ytter, T., Nyström, P., Gredebäck, G., et al. (2018). Reduced orienting to audiovisual synchrony in infancy predicts autism diagnosis at 3 years of age. *Journal of Child Psychology and Psychiatry* 59, 872–880.

Fernandez, M., Blass, E. M., Hernandez-Reif, M., et al. (2003). Sucrose attenuates a negative electroencephalographic response to an aversive stimulus for newborns. *Journal of Developmental & Behavioral Pediatrics* 24, 261–266.

Franklin, A., Pilling, M., & Davies, I. (2005). The nature of infant color categorization: Evidence from eye movements on a target detection task. *Journal of Experimental Child Psychology* 91, 227–248.

Frick, A., & Möhring, W. (2013). Mental object rotation and motor development in 8-and 10-month-old infants. *Journal of Experimental Child Psychology* 115, 708–720.

Gaither, S. E., Pauker, K., & Johnson, S. P. (2012). Biracial and monoracial infant own-race face perception: An eye tracking study. *Developmental Science* 15, 775–782.

Geber, M. (1958). The psycho-motor development of African children in the first year, and the influence of maternal behavior. *The Journal of Social Psychology* 47, 185–195.

Geber, M. (1962). Longitudinal study and psycho-motor development among Baganda children. *Proceedings of the XIV International Congress of Applied Psychology* 3, 50–60.

Geber, M., & Dean, R. F. A. (1957). The state of development of newborn African children. *Lancet*, 1216–1219.

Gesell, A. (1925). *The Mental Growth of the Preschool Child: A Psychological Outline of Normal Development from Birth to the Sixth Year, Including a System of Developmental Diagnosis*. Macmillan: New York.

Gesell, A., & Thompson, H. (1929). Learning and growth in identical infant twins. *Genetic Psychology Monographs*.

Gesell, A., Thompson, H., & Amatruda, C. S. (Collaborator). (1934). *Infant Behavior: Its Genesis and Growth*. McGraw-Hill Book Company: New York.

Gesell, A., & Ilg, F. L. (1937). Feeding behavior of infants.

Gibson, E., & Walk, R. (1960). The "visual cliff." *Scientific American* 202, 64–71.

Gibson, J. J. (1979). *The Ecological Approach to Visual Perception*. Psychology Press: New York.

Gibson, E. J. (2000). Where is the information for affordances? *Ecological Psychology* 12, 53–56.

Gibson, E. J., & Pick, A. D. (2000). *An Ecological Approach to Perceptual Learning and Development*. Oxford University Press: New York.

Gill, S. V., Adolph, K. E., & Vereijken, B. (2009). Change in action: How infants learn to walk down slopes. *Developmental Science* 12, 888–902.

Goren, C. C., Sarty, M., & Wu, P. Y. (1975). Visual following and pattern discrimination of face-like stimuli by newborn infants. *Pediatrics* 56, 544–549.

Gottwald, J. M., De Bortoli Vizioli, A., Lindskog, M., et al. (2017). Infants prospectively control reaching based on the difficulty of future actions: To what extent can infants' multiple-step actions be explained by Fitts' law? *Developmental Psychology* 53, 4.

Gredebäck, G., & Falck-Ytter, T. (2015). Eye movements during action observation. *Perspectives on Psychological Science* 10, 591–598.

Gudmundsdottir, H., & Trehub, S. (2018). Adults recognize toddlers' song renditions. *Psychology of Music* 46, 281–291.

Háden, G. P., Honing, H., Török, M., & Winkler, I. (2015). Detecting the temporal structure of sound sequences in newborn infants. *International Journal of Psychophysiology* 96, 23–28.

Hainline, L., & Abramov, I. (1985). Saccades and small-field optokinetic nystagmus in infants. *Journal of the American Optometric Association.*

Hainline, L. (1993). Conjugate eye movements of infants. *Early Visual Development: Normal and Abnormal*, 47–79.

Hainline, L., Riddell, P., Grose-Fifer, J., & Abramov, I. (1992). Development of accommodation and convergence in infancy. *Behavioural Brain Research* 49, 33–50.

Hannon, E. E., & Trehub, S. E. (2005). Tuning in to musical rhythms: Infants learn more readily than adults. *Proceedings of the National Academy of Sciences* 102, 12639–12643.

Hannon, E. E., Schachner, A., & Nave-Blodgett, J. E. (2017). Babies know bad dancing when they see it: Older but not younger infants discriminate between synchronous and asynchronous audiovisual musical displays. *Journal of Experimental Child Psychology* 159, 159–174.

Hauck, F. R., & Tanabe, K. O. (2017). Beyond "back to sleep": Ways to further reduce the risk of sudden infant death syndrome. *Pediatric Annals* 46, e284–e290.

Hebb, D. O. (1968). Concerning imagery. *Psychological Review* 75, 466.

Heron-Delaney, M., Anzures, G., Herbert, J. S., et al. (2011). Perceptual training prevents the emergence of the other race effect during infancy. *PLoS ONE* 6.

Hewitt, L., Kerr, E., Stanley, R. M., & Okely, A. D. (2020). Tummy time and infant health outcomes: A systematic review. *Pediatrics* 145, e20192168.

Hopkins, B. (1976). Culturally determined patterns of handling the human infant. *Journal of Human Movement Studies* 2, 1–27.

Hopkins, B., & Westra, T. (1988). Maternal handling and motor development: an intracultural study. *Genetic, Social, and General Psychology Monographs.*

Hopkins, B., & Westra, T. (1989). Maternal expectations of their infants' development: some cultural differences. *Developmental Medicine & Child Neurology* 31, 384–390.

Hopkins, B., & Westra, T. (1990). Motor development, maternal expectations, and the role of handling. *Infant Behavior and Development* 13, 117–122.

Hopkins, B., & Rönnqvist, L. (2002). Facilitating postural control: Effects on the reaching behavior of 6-month-old infants. *Developmental Psychobiology* 40, 168–182.

Jayaraman, S., Fausey, C. M., & Smith, L. B. (2015). The faces in infant-perspective scenes change over the first year of life. *PLoS ONE* 10, e0123780.

Jensen, J. K., & Neff, D. L. (1993). Development of basic auditory discrimination in preschool children. *Psychological Science* 4, 104–107.

Johnson, S. P., Amso, D., & Slemmer, J. A. (2003). Development of object concepts in infancy: Evidence for early learning in an eye-tracking paradigm. *Proceedings of the National Academy of Sciences* 100, 10568–10573.

Kahrs, B. A., Jung, W. P., & Lockman, J. J. (2012). What is the role of infant banging in the development of tool use? *Experimental Brain Research* 218, 315–320.

Kaplan, H., & Dove, H. (1987). Infant development among the Ache of eastern Paraguay. *Developmental Psychology* 23, 190.

Karasik, L. B., Tamis-LeMonda, C. S., & Adolph, K. E. (2011). Transition from crawling to walking and infants' actions with objects and people. *Child Development* 82, 1199–1209.

Karasik, L. B., Tamis-LeMonda, C. S., & Adolph, K. E. (2014). Crawling and walking infants elicit different verbal responses from mothers. *Developmental Science* 17, 388–395.

Karasik, L. B., Tamis-LeMonda, C. S., Adolph, K. E., & Bornstein, M. H. (2015). Places and postures: A cross-cultural comparison of sitting in 5-month-olds. *Journal of Cross-Cultural Psychology* 46, 1023–1038.

Karasik, L. B., Tamis-LeMonda, C. S., Össmy, O., & Adolph, K. E. (2018). The ties that bind: Cradling in Tajikistan. *PLoS ONE* 13.

Kattwinkel, J., Hauck, F. R., Keenan, M. E., et al., & Task Force Infant Death Syndrome. (2005). The changing concept of sudden infant death syndrome: Diagnostic coding shifts, controversies regarding the sleeping environment, and new variables to consider in reducing risk. *Pediatrics* 116, 1245–1255.

Keen, R., Lee, M. H., & Adolph, K. (2014). Planning an action: A developmental progression in tool use. *Ecological Psychology* 26, 98–108.

Keefer, C. H., Tronick, E., Dixon, S., & Brazelton, T. B. (1982). Specific differences in motor performance between Gusii and American newborns and a modification of the Neonatal Behavioral Assessment Scale. *Child Development* 53, 754–759.

Kellman, P. J., & Spelke, E. S. (1983). Perception of partly occluded objects in infancy. *Cognitive Psychology* 15, 483–524.

Kelly, D. J., Quinn, P. C., Slater, A. M., et al. (2007). The other-race effect develops during infancy: Evidence of perceptual narrowing. *Psychological Science* 18, 1084–1089.

Kilbride, J. E., Robbins, M. C., & Kilbride, P. L. (1970). The comparative motor development of Baganda, American White, and American Black infants. *American Anthropologist* 72, 1422–1428.

Kilbride, J. E., & Kilbride, P. L. (1975). Sitting and smiling behavior of Baganda infants: The influence of culturally constituted experience. *Journal of Cross-Cultural Psychology* 6, 88–107.

Konner, M. J. (1977). Infancy among the Kalahari Desert San. In P. H. Leiderman, S. R. Tulkin, and A. Rosenfield (Eds.), *Culture and Infancy: Variations in the Human Experience* (pp. 287–328). Academic Press: New York.

Krumhansl, C. L., & Jusczyk, P. W. (1990). Infants' perception of phrase structure in music. *Psychological Science* 1, 70–73.

Kretch, K. S., & Adolph, K. E. (2013). Cliff or step? Posture-specific learning at the edge of a drop-off. *Child Development* 84, 226–240.

Kretch, K. S., Franchak, J. M., & Adolph, K. E. (2014). Crawling and walking infants see the world differently. *Child Development* 85, 1503–1518.

Langlois, J. H., & Roggman, L. A. (1990). Attractive faces are only average. *Psychological Science* 1, 115–121.

Ledebt, A., van Wieringen, P. C., & Savelsbergh, G. J. (2004). Functional significance of foot rotation asymmetry in early walking. *Infant Behavior and Development* 27, 163–172.

Lee, D. K., Cole, W. G., Golenia, L., & Adolph, K. E. (2018). The cost of simplifying complex developmental phenomena: a new perspective on learning to walk. *Developmental Science* 21, e12615.

Lewkowicz, D. J. (1996). Perception of auditory–visual temporal synchrony in human infants. *Journal of Experimental Psychology: Human Perception and Performance* 22, 1094–1106.

Libertus, K., & Needham, A. (2010). Teach to reach: The effects of active vs. passive reaching experiences on action and perception. *Vision Research* 50, 2750–2757.

Libertus, K., Gibson, J., Hidayatallah, N. Z., et al. (2013). Size matters: how age and reaching experiences shape infants' preferences for different sized objects. *Infant Behavior and Development* 36, 189–198.

Lisboa, I. C., Queirós, S., Miguel, H., et al. (2020). Infants' cortical processing of biological motion configuration–A fNIRS study. *Infant Behavior and Development* 60, 101450.

Lockman, J. J. (2000). A perception–action perspective on tool use development. *Child Development* 71, 137–144.

Lockman, J. J., & Kahrs, B. A. (2017). New insights into the development of human tool use. *Current Directions in Psychological Science* 26, 330–334.

Lockman, J., & Tamis-LeMonda, C. S. (2021). Young children's interactions with objects: Play as practice and practice as play. *Annual Review of Developmental Psychology.*

Macchi, V. C., Turati, C., & Simion, F. (2004). Can a nonspecific bias toward top-heavy patterns explain newborns' face preference? *Psychological Science* 15, 379–383.

Mandler, J. M., & McDonough, L. (1993). Concept formation in infancy. *Cognitive Development* 8, 291–318.

Mandler, J. M. (2000) Perceptual and conceptual processes in infancy. *Journal of Cognition and Development* 1, 3–36.

Mandler, J. M. (2004). Thought before language. *Trends in Cognitive Science* 8, 508–513.

Markant, J., Oakes, L. M., & Amso, D. (2015). An attentional but not racial bias underlies the other-race effect in infancy. *Developmental Psychobiology* 57, S22.

Markant, J., & Scott, L. S. (2018). Attention and perceptual learning interact in the development of the other-race effect. *Current Directions in Psychological Science* 27, 163–169.

Maurer, D., and Lewis, T. L. (2001). Visual acuity: The role of visual input in inducing postnatal change. *Clinical Neuroscience Research* 1, 239–247.

McCarty, M. E., Clifton, R.K., & Collard, R. R. (2001) The beginnings of tool use by infants and toddlers. *Infancy* 2, 233–256.

McGraw, M. B. (1935). *Growth: A Study of Johnny and Jimmy.* Appleton-Century.

Mead, M., & Macgregor, F. C. (1951). *Growth and Culture: A Photographic Study of Balinese Childhood.*

Mennella, J. A., Jagnow, C. P., & Beauchamp, G. K. (2001). Prenatal and postnatal flavor learning by human infants. *Pediatrics* 107, e88.

Mennella, J. A., & Beauchamp, G. K. (2002). Flavor experiences during formula feeding are related to preferences during childhood. *Early Human Development* 68, 71–82.

Mennella, J. A., Forestell, C.A., Ventura, A. K., & Fisher, J. O. (2020). Development of infant feeding. In J. J. Lockman & C. S. Tamis-LeMonda (Eds.), *Cambridge Handbook of Infant Development*. Cambridge University Press: New York.

Morton, J., & Johnson, M. H. (1991). CONSPEC and CONLERN: A two-process theory of infant face recognition. *Psychological Review* 98, 164.

Needham, A., Barrett, T., & Peterman, K. (2002). A pick-me-up for infants' exploratory skills: Early simulated experiences reaching for objects using 'sticky mittens' enhances young infants' object exploration skills. *Infant Behavior and Development* 25, 279–295.

Newcombe, N. S. (2002). The nativist-empiricist controversy in the context of recent research on spatial and quantitative development. *Psychological Science* 13, 395–401.

Newell, K. M., Scully, D. M., McDonald, P. V., and Baillargeon, R. (1989). Task constraints and infant grip configurations. *Developmental Psychobiology* 22, 817–831.

Oakes, L. M. (2020). Infant categorization. In J. J. Lockman & C. S. Tamis-LeMonda (Eds.), *Cambridge Handbook of Infant Development*. Cambridge University Press: New York.

Oakes, L. M., & Kovack-Lesh, K. A. (2013). Infants' visual recognition memory for a series of categorically related items. *Journal of Cognitive Development* 4, 63–86.

Olsho, L. W., Koch, E. G., Carter, E. A., et al. (1988). Pure-tone sensitivity of human infants. *Journal of the Acoustical Society of America* 84, 1316–1324.

Oudgenoeg-Paz, O., Volman, M. C. J., & Leseman, P. P. (2012). Attainment of sitting and walking predicts development of productive vocabulary between ages 16 and 28 months. *Infant Behavior and Development* 35, 733–736.

Peeles, D. R., & Teller, D. Y. (1975). Color vision and brightness discrimination in two-month-old human infants. *Science* 189, 1102–1103.

Peiper, A. (1963). *Cerebral Function in Infancy and Childhood*. Plenum Pub Corp.

Peterzell, D. H., & Teller, D. Y. (1996). Individual differences in contrast sensitivity functions: The lowest spatial frequency channels. *Vision Research* 36, 3077–3085.

Piaget, J. (1969). *The Mechanisms of Perception*. Rutledge & Kegan Paul: London, United Kingdom.

Pons, F., & Lewkowicz, D. J. (2014). Infant perception of audio-visual speech synchrony in familiar and unfamiliar fluent speech. *Acta Psychologica* 149, 142–147.

Porter, R., & Winberg, J. (1999). Unique salience of maternal breast odors for newborn infants. *Neuroscience & Biobehavioral Reviews* 23, 439–449.

Quinn, P. C. (2016). Establishing cognitive organization in infancy: From perceptual grouping of objects to social classification of faces. In L. Balter & C. S. Tamis-LeMonda (Eds.), *Child Psychology: A Handbook of Contemporary Issues*, 3rd ed. Psychology Press: Philadelphia, PA.

Quinn, P. C., Yahr, J., Kuhn, A., et al. (2002). Representation of the gender of human faces by infants: A preference for female. *Perception* 31, 1109–1121.

Quinn, P. C., Brown, C. R., & Streppa, M. L. (1997). Perceptual organization of complex visual configurations by young infants. *Infant Behavior and Development* 20, 35–46.

Quinn, P. C., & Slater, A. (2003). Face perception at birth and beyond. In O. Pascalis & A. Slater (Eds.), *The Development of Face Processing in Infancy and Early Childhood: Current Perspectives* (pp. 3–11). Nova Science Publishers.

Quinn, P. C., Kelly, D. J., Lee, K., et al. (2008). Preference for attractive faces in human infants extends beyond conspecifics. *Developmental Science* 11, 76–83.

Rachwani, J., Tamis-LeMonda, C. S., Lockman, J. J., et al. (2020). Learning the designed actions of everyday objects. *Journal of Experimental Psychology: General* 149, 67–78.

Rakison, D. H., & Oakes, L. M. (Eds.). (2003). *Early Category and Concept Development: Making Sense of the Blooming, Buzzing Confusion*. Oxford University Press: New York.

Rennels, J. L., Juvrud, J., Kayl, A. J., et al. (2017). Caregiving experience and its relation to perceptual narrowing of face gender. *Developmental Psychology* 53, 1437–1446.

Rochat, P., & Goubet, N. (1995). Development of sitting and reaching in 5-to 6-month-old infants. *Infant Behavior and Development* 18, 53–68.

Rosenstein, D., & Oster, H. (1988). Differential facial responses to four basic tastes in newborns. *Child Development* 59, 1555–1568.

Schwartz, C., Issanchou, S., & Nicklaus, S. (2009). Developmental changes in the acceptance of the five basic tastes in the first year of life. *British Journal of Nutrition* 102, 1375–1385.

Schum, N., Jovanovic, B., & Schwarzer, G. (2011). Ten-and twelve-month-olds' visual anticipation of orientation and size during grasping. *Journal of Experimental Child Psychology* 109, 218–231.

Sheya, A., & Smith, L. B. (2010) Changing priority maps in 12- to 18-month-olds: an emerging role for object properties. *Psychological Bulletin Review* 17, 22–28.

Skelton, A. E., Catchpole, G., Abbott, J. T., et al. (2017). Biological origins of color categorization. *Proceedings of the National Academy of Sciences* 114, 5545–5550.

Slater, A., & Morison, V. (1985). Shape constancy and slant perception at birth. *Perception* 14, 337–344.

Slater, A., Mattock, A., & Brown, E. (1990). Size constancy at birth: Newborn infants' responses to retinal and real size. *Journal of Experimental Child Psychology* 49, 314–322.

Slater, A., Bremner, G., Johnson, S. P., et al. (2000). Newborn infants' preference for attractive faces: The role of internal and external facial features. *Infancy* 1, 265–274.

Slater, A., Riddell, P., Quinn, P. C., et al. (2010). Visual perception. In J. G. Bremner & T. D. Waches (Eds.), *Handbook of Infant Development*. Wiley-Blackwell: Hoboken, NJ.

Smith, L. B. (2005). Action alters shape categories. *Cognitive Science* 29, 665–679.

Soley, G., & Hannon, E. E. (2010). Infants prefer the musical meter of their own culture: a cross-cultural comparison. *Developmental Psychology* 46, 286.

Soska, K. C., Adolph, K. E., & Johnson, S. P. (2010). Systems in development: Motor skill acquisition facilitates three-dimensional object completion. *Developmental Psychology* 46, 129–138.

Soska, K. C., & Adolph, K. E. (2014). Postural position constrains multimodal object exploration in infants. *Infancy* 19, 138–161.

Soderquist, D. R., & Moore, M. J. (1970). Effect of training on frequency discrimination in primary school children. *Journal of Auditory Research*.

Spangler, S. M., Schwarzer, G., Freitag, C., et al. (2013). The other-race effect in a longitudinal sample of 3-, 6-and 9-month-old infants: Evidence of a training effect. *Infancy* 18, 516–533.

Super, C. M. (1976). Environmental effects on motor development: The case of "African infant precocity." *Developmental Medicine and Child Neurology* 18, 561–567.

Stein, L. J., Cowart, B. J., & Beauchamp, G. K. (2012). The development of salty taste acceptance is related to dietary experience in human infants: a prospective study. *The American Journal of Clinical Nutrition* 95, 123–129.

Tamis-LeMonda, C. S., Kuchirko, Y., & Song, L. (2014). Why is infant language learning facilitated by parental responsiveness? *Current Directions in Psychological Science* 23, 121–126.

Tamis-LeMonda, C. S., & Lockman, J. J. (2020). Infant exploration and play. In J. J. Lockman & C. S. Tamis-LeMonda (Eds.), *Cambridge Handbook of Infant Development*. Cambridge University Press: New York.

Tamis-LeMonda, C. S., Adolph, K. E., Lobo, S. A., et al. (2008) When infants take mothers' advice: 18-month-olds integrate perceptual and social information to guide motor action. *Developmental Psychology* 44, 734–746.

Teller, D. Y. (1997). First glances: The vision of infants. *Investigative Opthmalogy & Visual Science* 38, 2183–2203.

Thelen, E., Fisher, D. M., Fisher, D. M., et al. (1982). Effects of body build and arousal on newborn-infant stepping. *Developmental Psychobiology* 15, 447–453.

Thelen, E., Fisher, D. M., & Ridley-Johnson, R. (1984). The relationship between physical growth and a newborn reflex. *Infant Behavior and Development* 7, 479–493.

Trehub, S. E., & Gudmundsdottir, H. R. (2015). *Mothers as Singing Mentors for Infants*. Oxford University Press: New York.

van der Meer A. L., van der Weel, F. R., & Lee, D. N. (1994). Prospective control in catching by infants. *Perception* 23, 287–302.

van Hof, P., van der Kamp, J., Caljouw, S. R., & Savelsbergh, G. J. (2005). The confluence of intrinsic and extrinsic constraints on 3-to 9-month-old infants' catching behavior. *Infant Behavior and Development* 28, 179–193.

van Wermeskerken, M., van der Kamp, J., Te Velde, A. F., et al. (2011). Anticipatory reaching of seven- to eleven-month-old infants in occlusion situations. *Infant Behavior and Development* 34, 45–54.

Vouloumanos, A., & Werker, J. F. (2004). Tuned to the signal: the privileged status of speech for young infants. *Developmental Science* 7, 270–276.

von Hofsten, C., & Rönnqvist, L. (1988). Preparation for grasping an object: A developmental study. *Journal of Experimental Psychology: Human Perception and Performance* 14, 610–621.

von Hofsten, C. (1991). Structuring of early reaching movements: a longitudinal study. *Journal of Motor Behavior* 23, 280–292.

Vouloumanos, A., & Werker, J. F. (2007). Listening to language at birth: Evidence for a bias for speech in neonates. *Developmental Science* 10, 159–164.

Vouloumanos, A., Hauser, M. D., Werker, J. F., & Martin, A. (2010). The tuning of human neonates' preference for speech. *Child Development* 81, 517–527.

Warren, N., & Parkin, J. M. (1974). A neurological and behavioral comparison of African and European newborns in Uganda. *Child Development* 966–971.

West, K., Leezenbaum, N., Northrup, J. B., & Iverson, J. (2019). The relation between walking and language in infant siblings of children with autism spectrum disorder. *Child Development* 90, 356–372.

Winkler, I., Háden, G. P., Ladinig, O., et al. (2009). Newborn infants detect the beat in music. *Proceedings of the National Academy of Sciences* 106, 2468–2471.

Woods, R. J., & Wilcox, T. (2013). Posture support improves object individuation in infants. *Developmental Psychology* 49, 1413–1424.

Yonas, A., Granrud, C. E., & Pettersen, L. (1985). Infants' sensitivity to relative size information for distance. *Developmental Psychology* 21, 161–167.

Yonas, A., & Hartman, B. (1993). Perceiving the affordance of contact in four and five-month-old infants. *Child Development* 64, 298–308.

Zentner, M., & Eerola, T. (2010). Rhythmic engagement with music in infancy. *Proceedings of the National Academy of Sciences* 107, 5768–5773.

Chapter 5

Adamson, L. B., & Bakeman, R. (1984). Mothers' communicative acts: Changes during infancy. *Infant Behavior and Development* 7, 467–478.

Amso, D., & Johnson, S. P. (2006). Learning by selection: Visual search and object perception in young infants. *Developmental Psychology* 42, 1236–1245.

Anderson, E., Hespos, S. J., & Rips, L. (2018). Five-month-old infants have expectations for the accumulation of nonsolid substances. *Cognition* 175, 1–10.

Atkinson, J., Hood, B., Wattam-Bell, J., & Braddick, O. (1992). Changes in infants' ability to switch visual attention in the first three months of life. *Perception* 21, 643–653.

Bahrick, L. E., Flom, R., & Lickliter, R. (2002). Intersensory redundancy facilitates discrimination of tempo in 3-month-old infants. *Developmental Psychobiology* 41, 352–363.

Bahrick, L. E., Lickliter, R., & Flom, R. (2004). Intersensory redundancy guides the development of selective attention, perception, and cognition in infancy. *Current Directions in Psychological Science* 13, 99–102.

Bahrick, L. E., McNew, M. E., Pruden, S. M., & Castellanos, I. (2019). Intersensory redundancy promotes infant detection of prosody in infant-directed speech. *Journal of Experimental Child Psychology* 183, 295–309.

Baillargeon, R. (1986). Representing the existence and the location of hidden objects: Object permanence in 6- and 8-month-old infants. *Cognition* 23, 21–41.

Baillargeon, R. (1987). Object permanence in 3½- and 4½-month-old infants. *Developmental Psychology* 23, 655–664.

Baillargeon, R. (2008). Innate ideas revisited: For a principle of persistence in infants' physical reasoning. *Perspectives on Psychological Science* 3, 2–13.

Baillargeon, R., & DeJong, G.F. (2017). Explanation-based learning in infancy. *Psychonomic Bulletin and Review* 24, 1511–1526.

Baillargeon, R., & DeVos, J. (1991). Object permanence in young infants: Further evidence. *Child Development* 62, 1227–1246.

Baillargeon, R., Spelke, E. S., & Wasserman, S. (1985). Object permanence in five-month-old infants. *Cognition* 20, 191–208.

Baillargeon, R., Li, J., Gertner, Y., & Wu, D. (2011). How do infants reason about physical events? In *The Wiley-Blackwell Handbook of Childhood Cognitive Development,* 2nd ed. (pp. 11–48). Wiley-Blackwell: Hoboken, NJ.

Baldwin, D. A., & Moses, L. J. (1996). The ontogeny of social information gathering. *Child Development* 67, 1915–1939.

Barr, R., Marrott, H., & Rovee-Collier, C. (2003). The role of sensory preconditioning in memory retrieval by preverbal infants. *Animal Learning & Behavior* 31, 111–123.

Barr, R. (2010). Transfer of learning between 2D and 3D sources during infancy: Informing theory and practice. *Developmental Review* 30, 128–154.

Barr, R. (2013). Memory constraints on infant learning from picture books, television, and touchscreens. *Child Development Perspectives* 7, 205–210.

Bates, E., Benigni, L., Bretherton, I., et al. (1979). *The Emergence of Symbols: Communication and Cognition in Infancy.* Academic Press: New York.

Bauer, P. J. (2020). Long-term recall memory: Behavioral and neuro-developmental changes in the first 2 years of life. *Current Directions in Psychological Science* 11, 137–141.

Bauer, P. J. (2007). Recall in infancy: A neurodevelopmental account. *Current Directions in Psychological Science* 16, 142–146.

Behne, T., Carpenter, M., Call, J., & Tomasello, M. (2005). Unwilling versus unable: Infants' understanding of intentional action. *Developmental Psychology* 41, 328–337.

Blair, C., & Raver, C. C. (2016). Poverty, stress, and brain development: New directions for prevention and intervention. *Academic Pediatrics* 16, S30–S36.

Blumberg, M. S. (2005). *Basic Instinct: The Genesis of Behavior.* Basic Books: New York.

Bogartz, R. S., Shinskey, J. L., & Speaker, C. J. (1997). Interpreting infant looking: The event set × event set design. *Developmental Psychology* 33, 408–422.

Bower, T. G. R. (1971). The object in the world of the infant. *Scientific American* 225, 30–39.

Bradley, R., & Corwyn, R. (2005). Caring for children around the world: A view from HOME. *International Journal of Behavioral Development* 29, 468–478.

Bradley, R. H., & Corwyn, R. F. (2016) Home life and the development of competence in mathematics: Implications of research with the HOME inventory. In B. Blevins-Knabe & A. Austin (Eds.), *Early Childhood Mathematics Skill Development in the Home Environment.* Springer: Cham, Switzerland.

Bradley, R. H., & Caldwell, B. M. (1979). Home observation for measurement of the environment: A revision of the preschool scale. *American Journal of Mental Deficiency* 84, 235–244.

Brink, K. A., Lane, J. D., & Wellman, H. M. (2015). Developmental pathways for social understanding: Linking social cognition to social contexts. *Frontiers in Psychology* 6, 719.

Brooks, R., & Meltzoff, A. N. (2005). The development of gaze following and its relation to language. *Developmental Science* 8, 535–543.

Brooks, R., & Meltzoff, A. N. (2008). Infant gaze following and pointing predict accelerated vocabulary growth through two years of age: a longitudinal, growth curve modeling study. *Journal of Child Language* 35, 207–220.

Buttelmann, D., Carpenter, M., & Tomasello, M. (2009). Eighteen-month-old infants show false belief understanding in an active helping paradigm. *Cognition* 112, 337–342.

Butterworth, G. (2003). Pointing is the royal road to language for babies. *Pointing: Where Language, Culture, and Cognition Meet*, 9–33.

Callaghan, T., Moll, H., Rakoczy, H., et al. (2011). Early social cognition in three cultural contexts. *Monographs of the Society for Research in Child Development* 76, i–142.

Campbell, F. A., Pungello, E. P., Miller-Johnson, S., et al. (2001). The development of cognitive and academic abilities: Growth curves from an early childhood educational experiment. *Developmental Psychology* 37, 231–242.

Carpenter, M., Akhtar, N., & Tomasello, M. (1998). Fourteen- through 18-month-old infants differentially imitate intentional and accidental actions. *Infant Behavior and Development* 21, 315–330.

Chaudry, A., & Wimer, C. (2016). Poverty is not just an indicator: The relationship between income, poverty, and child well-being. *Academic Pediatrics* 16, S23–S29.

Chazan-Cohen, R., Green, B. L., Ayoub, C., et al. (2015). To-practice brief: Promising evidence that early head start can prevent child maltreatment.

Colombo, J., Mitchell, D. W., O'Brien, M., & Horowitz, F. D. (1987). The stability of visual habituation during the first year of life. *Child Development* 58, 474–487.

Courage, M. L., Reynolds, G. D., & Richards, J. E. (2006). Infants' attention to patterned stimuli: Developmental change from 3 to 12 months of age. *Child Development* 77, 680–695.

Craik, F. I. M., Govoni, R., Naveh-Benjamin, M., & Anderson, N. D. (1996). The effects of divided attention on encoding and retrieval processes in human memory. *Journal of Experimental Psychology: General* 125, 159–180.

D'Entremont, B., Hains, S. M. J., & Muir, D. W. (1997). A demonstration of gaze following in 3- to 6-month-olds. *Infant Behavior and Development* 20, 569–572.

Dannemiller, J. L. (2000). Competition in early exogenous orienting between 7 and 21 weeks. *Journal of Experimental Child Psychology* 76, 253–274.

Dasen, P. R., Ngini, L., & Lavallée, M. (1979). Cross-cultural training studies of concrete operations. In L. Eckensberger, Y. Poortinga, & W. Lonner (Eds.), *Cross-Cultural Contributions to Psychology* (pp. 94–104). Swets & Zeitlinger: Amsterdam.

Dasen, P. R. (1984). The cross-cultural study of intelligence: Piaget and the Baoule. *International Journal of Psychology* 19, 407–434.

Downes, M., Kelly, D., Day, K., et al. (2018). Visual attention control differences in 12-month-old preterm infants. *Infant Behavior and Development* 50, 180–188.

Feigenson, L., Dehaene, S., & Spelke, E. (2004). Core systems of number. *Trends in Cognitive Sciences* 8, 307–314.

Field, T. M., Dempsey, J. R., Hatch, J., et al. (1979). Cardiac and behavioral responses to repeated tactile and auditory stimulation by preterm and term neonates. *Developmental Psychology* 15, 406–416.

Gergely, G., Bekkering, H., & Király, I. (2002). Rational imitation in preverbal infants. *Nature* 415, 755.

Godden, D. R., & Baddeley, A. D. (1975). Context-dependent memory in two natural environments: On land and underwater. *British Journal of Psychology* 66, 325–331.

Haith, M. M. (1998). Who put the cog in infant cognition? Is rich interpretation too costly? *Infant Behavior and Development* 21, 167–179.

Henrich, J., Heine, S., & Norenzayan, A. (2010). Most people are not WEIRD. *Nature* 466, 29.

Herzberg, O., Fletcher, K., Schatz, J., et al. (in press). Infant exuberant object play at home: Immense amounts of time-distributed, variable practice. *Child Development*

Hespos, S. J., & Anderson, E. M. (2020). Infant physical knowledge. In J. J. Lockman & C. S. Tamis-LeMonda (Eds.) *Cambridge Handbook of Infant Development*. Cambridge University Press: New York.

Hespos, S. J., Ferry, A., Anderson, E., et al. (2016). Five-month-old infants have expectations about how substances behave and interact. *Psychological Science* 27, 244–256.

Hofer, T., Hohenberger, A., Hauf, P., & Ascher-sleben, G. (2008). The link between maternal interaction style and infant action understanding. *Infant Behavior and Development* 31, 115–126.

Johnson, S. C., Booth, A., & O'Hearn, K. (2001). Inferring the goals of a nonhuman agent. *Cognitive Development* 16, 637–656.

Jones, S. S. (2007). Imitation in infancy: The development of mimicry. *Psychological Science* 18, 593–599.

Kagan, J. (2008). In defense of qualitative changes in development. *Child Development* 79, 1606–1624.

Klahr, D. (1978). Goal formation, planning, and learning by preschool problem solvers or: "my socks are in the dryer." *Children's Thinking: What Develops*, pp. 181–212.

Konishi, H., Kanero, J., Freeman, M. R., et al. (2014). Six principles of language development: Implications for second language learners. *Developmental Neuropsychology* 39, 404–420.

Kristen, S., Sodian, B., Thoermer, C., & Perst, H. (2011). Infants' joint attention skills predict toddlers' emerging mental state language. *Developmental Psychology* 47, 1207–1219.

Liberman, Z., Kinzler, K. D., & Woodward, A. L. (2014). Friends or foes: Infants use shared evaluations to infer others' social relationships. *Journal of Experimental Psychology: General* 143, 966–971.

Licata, M., Paulus, M., Thoermer, C., et al. (2014). Mother–infant interaction quality and infants' ability to encode actions as goal-directed. *Social Development* 23, 340–356.

Linver, M. R., Martin, A., & Brooks-Gunn, J. (2004). Measuring infants' home environment: The IT-HOME for infants between birth and 12 months in four national data sets. *Parenting* 4, 115–137.

Liszkowski, U., Carpenter, M., Henning, A., et al. (2004). Twelve-month-olds point to share attention and interest. *Developmental Science* 7, 297–307.

Liszkowski, U., Carpenter, M., & Tomasello, M. (2008). Twelve-month-olds communicate helpfully and appropriately for knowledgeable and ignorant partners. *Cognition* 108, 732–739.

Love, J. M., Kisker, E. E., Ross, C., et al. (2005). The effectiveness of early head start for 3-year-old children and their parents: Lessons for policy and programs. *Developmental Psychology* 41, 885–901.

Lukowski, A. F., & Bauer, P. J. (2014). Long-term memory in infancy and early childhood. In P. J. Bauer & R. Fivush (Eds.), *The Wiley Handbook on the Development of Children's Memory* (pp. 230–254). Wiley Blackwell: Hoboken, NJ.

McCune, L. (1995). A normative study of representational play in the transition to language. *Developmental Psychology* 31, 198–206.

Meltzoff, A. N. (1995). Understanding the intentions of others: Re-enactment of intended acts by 18-month-old children. *Developmental Psychology* 31, 838–850.

Meltzoff, A. N., & Moore, M. K. (1977). Imitation of facial and manual gestures by human neonates. *Science* 198, 75–78.

Meltzoff, A. N. (2017). Re-examination of Oostenbroek et al. (2016): evidence for neonatal imitation of tongue protrusion. *Developmental Science* 21.

Milgram, S., Bickman, L., & Berkowitz, L. (1969). Note on the drawing power of crowds of different size. *Journal of Personality and Social Psychology* 13, 79–82.

Moll, H., & Tomasello, M. (2007). How 14- and 18-month-olds know what others have experienced. *Developmental Psychology* 43, 309–317.

Moore, C., & Corkum, V. (1994). Social understanding at the end of the first year of life. *Developmental Review* 14, 349–372.

Mullally, S. L., & Maguire, E. A. (2014). Learning to remember: the early ontogeny of episodic memory. *Developmental Cognitive Neuroscience* 9,12–29.

Mundy, P., Block, J., Delgado, C., et al. (2007). Individual differences and the development of joint attention in infancy. *Child Development* 78, 938–954.

Needham, A., & Baillargeon, R. (1993). Intuitions about support in 4.5-month-old infants. *Cognition* 47, 121–148.

Niklas, F., Nguyen, C., Cloney, D.S. et al. (2016). Self-report measures of the home learning environment in large scale research: Measurement properties and associations with key developmental outcomes. *Learning Environments Research* 19, 181–202.

Olineck, K. M., & Poulin-Dubois, D. (2005). Infants' ability to distinguish between intentional and accidental actions and its relation to internal state language. *Infancy* 8, 91–100.

Onishi, K. H., & Baillargeon, R. (2005). Do 15-month-old infants understand false beliefs? *Science* 308, 255–258.

Oostenbroek, J., Suddendorf, T., Nielsen, M., et al. (2016). Comprehensive longitudinal study challenges the existence of neonatal imitation in humans. *Current Biology* 26, 1334–1338.

Piaget, J., & Inhelder, B. (1969). *The Psychology of the Child*, translated from the French by Helen Weaver. Basic Books: New York.

Quinn, S., Donnelly, S., & Kidd, E. (2018). The relationship between symbolic play and language acquisition: A meta-analytic review. *Developmental Review* 49, 121–135.

Ramey, C. T., & Ramey, S. L. (2004). Early learning and school readiness: Can early intervention make a difference? *Merrill-Palmer Quarterly* 50, 471–491.

Richards, J. (1997). Effects of attention on infants' preference for briefly exposed visual stimuli in the paired-comparison recognition-memory paradigm. *Developmental Psychology* 33, 22–31

Robson, S. J., & Kuhlmeier, V. A. (2016). Infants' understanding of object-directed action: An interdisciplinary synthesis. *Frontiers in Psychology* 7, 111.

Rodriguez, E. T., & Tamis-LeMonda, C. S. (2011). Trajectories of the home learning environment across the first 5 years: Associations with children's vocabulary and literacy skills at prekindergarten. *Child Development* 82, 1058–1075.

Rose, S. (1983). Differential rates of visual information processing in full-term and preterm infants. *Child Development* 54, 1189–1198.

Rose, S. A., Feldman, J. F., & Jankowski, J. J. (2002). Processing speed in the 1st year of life: A longitudinal study of preterm and full-term infants. *Developmental Psychology* 38, 895–902.

Rose, S. A., Feldman, J. F., Jankowski, J. J., & Van Rossem, R. (2008). A cognitive cascade in infancy: Pathways from prematurity to later mental development. *Intelligence* 36, 367–378.

Rose, S. A., Feldman, J. F., & Jankowski, J. J. (2015). Pathways from toddler information processing to adolescent lexical proficiency. *Child Development* 86, 1935–1947.

Rose, S. A., Feldman, J. F., Jankowski, J. J., & Van Rossem, R. (2012). Information processing from infancy to 11years: Continuities and prediction of IQ. *Intelligence* 40, 445–457.

Rovee-Collier, C., & Barr, R. (2001). Infant learning and memory. In *Blackwell Handbook of Infant Development* (pp. 139–168). Blackwell Publishing: Malden, MA.

Rovee-Collier, C., & Giles, A. (2010). Why a neuromaturational model of memory fails: Exuberant learning in early infancy. *Behavioural Processes* 83, 197–206.

Scaife, M., & Bruner, J. S. (1975). The capacity for joint visual attention in the infant. *Nature* 253, 265.

Schwier, C., van Maanen, C., Carpenter, M., & Tomasello, M. (2006). Rational imitation in 12-month-old infants. *Infancy* 10, 303–311.

Shneidman, L., & Woodward, A. L. (2016). Are child-directed interactions the cradle of social learning? *Psychological Bulletin* 142, 1–17.

Slater, A., & Morison, V. (1985). Selective adaptation cannot account for early infant habituation: A response to Dannemiller and Banks. *Merrill-Palmer Quarterly* 31, 99–103.

Smith, L., & Ulvund, S. E. (2003). The role of joint attention in later development among preterm children: Linkages between early and middle childhood. *Social Development* 12, 222–234.

Smith, L. B. (2005). Action alters shape categories. *Cognitive Science* 29, 665–679.

Smith, L. B., Thelen, E., Titzer, R., & McLin, D. (1999). Knowing in the context of acting: The task dynamics of the A-not-B error. *Psychological Review* 106, 235–260.

Sokolov, E. N. (1963). *Perception and the Conditioned Reflex*. Macmillan: New York.

Song, H.-j., Onishi, K. H., Baillargeon, R., & Fisher, C. (2008). Can an agent's false belief be corrected by an appropriate communication? Psychological reasoning in 18-month-old infants. *Cognition* 109, 295–315.

Spelke, E. S. (2013). Where perceiving ends and thinking begins: The apprehension of objects in infancy. In *Perceptual Development in Infancy* (pp. 209–246). Psychology Press: Philadelphia, PA.

Spelke, E. S., & Kinzler, K. D. (2006). Core knowledge. *Developmental Science*.

Spencer, J. P., Smith, L. B., & Thelen, E. (2001). Tests of a dynamic systems account of the A-not-B error: The influence of prior experience on the spatial memory abilities of two-year-olds. *Child Development* 72, 1327–1346.

Stahl, A. E., & Feigenson, L. (2014). Social knowledge facilitates chunking in infancy. *Child Development* 85, 1477–1490.

Starr, A., Libertus, M. E., & Brannon, E. M. (2013). Infants show ratio-dependent number discrimination regardless of set size. *Infancy* 18, 927–941.

Sullivan, M. W., Rovee-Collier, C. K., & Tynes, D. M. (1979). A conditioning analysis of infant long-term memory. *Child Development* 50, 152–162.

Tomasello, M., & Farrar, M. J. (1986). Joint attention and early language. *Child Development* 57, 1454–1463.

Vaughan Van Hecke, A., Mundy, P. C., Acra, C. F., et al. (2007). Infant joint attention, temperament, and social competence in preschool children. *Child Development* 78, 53–69.

Vygotsky, L. (1978). Interaction between learning and development. *Readings on the Development of Children* 23, 34–41.

Wang, J., Libertus, M. E., & Feigenson, L. (2018). Hysteresis-induced changes in preverbal infants' approximate number precision. *Cognitive Development* 47, 107–116.

White-Traut, R. C., Schwertz, D., McFarlin, B., & Kogan, J. (2009). Salivary cortisol and behavioral state responses of healthy newborn infants to tactile-only and multisensory interventions. *Journal of Obstetric, Gynecologic, & Neonatal Nursing* 38, 22–34.

Wood, J. N., & Spelke, E. S. (2005). Infants' enumeration of actions: numerical discrimination and its signature limits. *Developmental Science* 8, 173–181.

Woodward, A. L. (1998). Infants selectively encode the goal object of an actor's reach. *Cognition* 69, 1–34.

Woodward, A. L. (2009). Infants' grasp of others' intentions. *Current Directions in Psychological Science* 18, 53–57.

Xie, W., Mallin, B. M., & Richards, J. E. (2017). Development of infant sustained attention and its relation to EEG oscillations: an EEG and cortical source analysis study. *Developmental Science* 21, e12562.

Yu, C., Suanda, S. H., & Smith, L. B. (2019). Infant sustained attention but not joint attention to objects at 9 months predicts vocabulary at 12 and 15 months. *Dev Sci* 22, e12735.

Zack, E., & Barr, R. (2016). The role of interactional quality in learning from touch screens during infancy: Context matters. *Frontiers in Psychology* 7, 1264.

Chapter 6

Akhtar, N. (2005). The robustness of learning through overhearing. *Developmental Science* 8, 199–209.

Anderson, D., & Reilly, J. (2002). The MacArthur communicative development inventory: Normative data for American Sign Language. *The Journal of Deaf Studies and Deaf Education* 7, 83–106.

Arias-Trejo, N., & Plunkett, K. (2013). What's in a link: Associative and taxonomic priming effects in the infant lexicon. *Cognition* 128, 214–227.

Aslin, R. N. (2017). Statistical learning: A powerful mechanism that operates by mere exposure. *Wiley Interdisciplinary Reviews: Cognitive Science* 8, e1373.

Baldwin, D. A. (1993). Infants' ability to consult the speaker for clues to word reference. *Journal of Child Language* 20, 395–418.

Barnett, W. S., Votruba-Drzal, E., Dearing, E., & Carolan, M. E. (2017). Publicly supported early care and education programs. In E. Votruba-Drzal & E. Dearing (Eds.), *The Wiley Handbook of Early Childhood Development Programs, Practices, and Policies* (pp. 161–186). John Wiley and Sons: Hoboken, NJ.

Bates, E., Camaioni, L., & Volterra, V. (1976). Sensorimotor performatives. *Language and Context*.

Beebe, B. (2014). My journey in infant research and psychoanalysis: Microanalysis, a social microscope. *Psychoanalytic Psychology* 31, 4–25.

Bergelson, E., & Swingley, D. (2012). At 6–9 months, human infants know the meanings of many common nouns. *Proceedings of the National Academy of Sciences* 109, 3253–3258.

Bergelson, E., & Swingley, D. (2015). Early word comprehension in infants: Replication and extension. *Language Learning and Development* 11, 369–380.

Bloom, L. (1971). Why not pivot grammar? *Journal of Speech and Hearing Disorders* 36, 40–50.

Bloom, L. (1993). *Language Development from Two to Three*. Cambridge University Press: New York.

Bloom, P. (2004). Myths of word learning. *Weaving a Lexicon*, 205–224.

Bornstein, M. H., Cote, L. R., Maital, S., et al. (2004). Cross-linguistic analysis of vocabulary in young children: Spanish, Dutch, French, Hebrew, Italian, Korean, and American English. *Child Development* 75, 1115–1139.

Bornstein, M. H., & Putnick, D. L. (2012). Cognitive and socioemotional caregiving in developing countries. *Child Development* 83, 46–61.

Bornstein, M. H., Tamis-LeMonda, C. S., Hahn, C.-S., & Haynes, O. M. (2008). Maternal responsiveness to young children at three ages: Longitudinal analysis of a multidimensional, modular, and specific parenting construct. *Developmental Psychology* 44, 867–874.

Bosch, L., & Sebastian-Galles, N. (2001). Evidence of early language discrimination abilities in infants from bilingual environments. *Infancy* 2, 29–49.

Braine, M. D. S. (1963). The ontogeny of English phrase structure: The first phase. *Language* 39, 1–13.

Brand, R. J., Baldwin, D. A., & Ashburn, L. A. (2002). Evidence for 'motionese': Modifications in mothers' infant-directed action. *Developmental Science* 5, 72–83.

Brand, R. J., Shallcross, W. L., Sabatos, M. G., & Massie, K. P. (2007). Fine-grained analysis of motionese: Eye gaze, object exchanges, and action units in infant-versus adult-directed action. *Infancy* 11, 203–214.

Bruner, J. (1977). Early social interaction and language development. *Studies in Mother-Child Interaction*, 271–289.

Buder, E. H., Warlaumont, A. S., & Oller, D. K. (2013). An acoustic phonetic catalog of prespeech infant vocalizations in a developmental perspective. In B. Peter & A. N. MacLeod (Eds.), *Comprehensive Perspectives on Child Speech Development and Disorders: Pathways from Linguistic Theory to Clinical Practice*. Nova Science Publishers.

Byers-Heinlein, K. (2014). Languages as categories: Reframing the "one language or two" question in early bilingual development. *Language Learning* 64, 184–201.

Byers-Heinlein, K., Burns, T. C., & Werker, J. F. (2010). The roots of bilingualism in newborns. *Psychological Science* 21, 343–348.

Byers-Heinlein, K., & Werker, J. F. (2009). Monolingual, bilingual, trilingual: infants' language experience influences the development of a word-learning heuristic. *Developmental Science* 12, 815–823.

Carey, S., & Bartlett, E. (1978). Acquiring a single new word. *Papers and Reports on Child Language Development* 15, 17–29.

Carlo, M. S., August, D., Mclaughlin, B., et al. (2004). Closing the gap: Addressing the vocabulary needs of English-language learners in bilingual and mainstream classrooms. *Reading Research Quarterly* 39, 188–215.

Choi, S., & Bowerman, M. (1991). Learning to express motion events in English and Korean: The influence of language-specific lexicalization patterns. *Cognition* 41, 83–121.

Choi, S., McDonough, L., Bowerman, M., & Mandler, J. M. (1999). Early sensitivity to language-specific spatial categories in English and Korean. *Cognitive Development* 14, 241–268.

Chomsky, N. (1959). A review of B. F. Skinner's verbal behavior. *Language* 35, 26–58.

Chow, J., Davies, A. A., & Plunkett, K. (2017). Spoken-word recognition in 2-year-olds: The tug of war between phonological and semantic activation. *Journal of Memory and Language* 93, 104–134.

Cirelli, L. K., & Trehub, S. E. (2018). Infants help singers of familiar songs. *Music & Science* 1, 2059204318761622.

Clark, E. V. (1973). What's in a word? On the child's acquisition of semantics in his first language. In T. E. Moore (Ed.), *Cognitive Development and Acquisition of Language* (pp. 65–110). Academic Press: San Diego, CA.

Colunga, E., & Smith, L. B. (2005). From the lexicon to expectations about kinds: A role for associative learning. *Psychological Review* 112, 347–382.

Conboy, B. T., & Thal, D. J. (2006). Ties between the lexicon and grammar: Cross-sectional and longitudinal studies of bilingual toddlers. *Child Development* 77, 712–735.

Cristia, A., Dupoux, E., Gurven, M., & Stieglitz, J. (2019). Child-directed speech is infrequent in a forager-farmer population: A time allocation study. *Child Development* 90, 759–773.

Cristia, A., Lavechin, M., Scaff, C. et al. (2020). A thorough evaluation of the Language Environment Analysis (LENA) system. *Behavioral Research*.

Culbertson, J., Smolensky, P., & Wilson, C. (2013). Cognitive biases, linguistic universals, and constraint-based grammar learning. *Topics in Cognitive Science* 5, 392–424.

De Houwer, A. (2009). *An Introduction to Bilingual Development: Multilingual Matters.*

Deniz Can, D., Richards, T., & Kuhl, P. K. (2013). Early gray-matter and white-matter concentration in infancy predict later language skills: A whole brain voxel-based morphometry study. *Brain and Language* 124, 34–44.

Dörnyei, Z., & Csizér, K. (2002). Some dynamics of language attitudes and motivation: Results of a longitudinal nationwide survey. *Applied Linguistics* 23, 421–462.

Echols, C. H., & Marti, C. N. (2004). The identification of words and their meanings: From perceptual biases to language-specific. *Weaving a Lexicon*, 41.

Ertmer, D. J., & Nathani Iyer, S. (2010). Prelinguistic vocalizations in infants and toddlers with hearing loss: Identifying and stimulating auditory-guided speech development. In M. Marschark & P. E. Spencer (Eds.), *The Oxford Handbook of Deaf Studies, Language, and Education.* Oxford University Press: Oxford, United Kingdom.

Fenson, L., Dale, P. S., Reznick, J. S., et al. (1994). Variability in early communicative development. *Monographs of the Society for Research in Child Development* 59, i–185.

Fernald, A. (1991). Prosody in speech to children: Prelinguistic and linguistic functions. *Annals of Child Development* 8, 43–80.

Fernald, A., Perfors, A., & Marchman, V. A. (2006). Picking up speed in understanding: Speech processing efficiency and vocabulary growth across the 2nd year. *Developmental Psychology* 42, 98–116.

Fernald, A., Zangl, R., Portillo, A. L., & Marchman, V. A. (2008). Looking while listening: Using eye movements to monitor spoken language. *Developmental Psycholinguistics: Online Methods in Children's Language Processing* 44, 97.

Frank, M., Braginsky, M., Yurovsky, D., & Marchman, V. (2017). Wordbank: An open repository for developmental vocabulary data. *Journal of Child Language* 44, 677–694.

Frank, M., Braginsky, M., Marchman, V., & Yurovsky, D. (2021). *Variability and Consistency in Early Language Learning: The Wordbank Project*. MIT Press: Cambridge, MA.

Gertner, Y., Fisher, Y., & Eisengart, J. (2006). Learning words and rules: Abstract knowledge of word order in early sentence comprehension. *Psychological Science* 17, 684–691.

Gleitman, L. R., Cassidy, K., Nappa, R., et al. (2005). Hard words. *Language Learning and Development* 1, 23–64.

Gogate, L. J., Bahrick, L. E., & Watson, J. D. (2000). A study of multimodal motherese: The role of temporal synchrony between verbal labels and gestures. *Child Development* 71, 878–894.

Goldfield, B. A., & Reznick, J. S. (1990). Early lexical acquisition: rate, content, and the vocabulary spurt. *Journal of Child Language* 17, 171–183.

Goldin-Meadow, S. (1978). A study in human capacities [Genie. A Psycholinguistic Study of a Modern-Day "Wild Child", Susan Curtiss]. *Science* 200, 649–651.

Goldin-Meadow, S., & Mylander, C. (1998). Spontaneous sign systems created by deaf children in two cultures. *Nature* 391, 279.

Goldin-Meadow, S., & Singer, M. A. (2003). From children's hands to adults' ears: Gesture's role in the learning process. *Developmental Psychology* 39, 509–520.

Goldin-Meadow, S. (2009). How gesture promotes learning throughout childhood. *Child Development Perspectives* 3, 106–111.

Goldstein, M. H., King, A. P., & West, M. J. (2003). Social interaction shapes babbling: Testing parallels between birdsong and speech. *Proceedings of the National Academy of Sciences* 100, 8030–8035.

Goldstein, M. H., & Schwade, J. A. (2008). Social feedback to infants' babbling facilitates rapid phonological learning. *Psychological Science* 19, 515–523.

Golinkoff, R. M., Hirsh-Pasek, K., Cauley, K. M., & Gordon, L. (1987). The eyes have it: Lexical and syntactic comprehension in a new paradigm. *Journal of Child Language* 14, 23–45.

Golinkoff, R. M., Ma, W., Song, L., & Hirsh-Pasek, K. (2013). Twenty-five years using the intermodal preferential looking paradigm to study language acquisition: What have we learned? *Perspectives on Psychological Science* 8, 316–339.

Golinkoff, R. M., Can, D. D., Soderstrom, M., & Hirsh-Pasek, K. (2015). (Baby)talk to me: The social context of infant-directed speech and its effects on early language acquisition.

Current Directions in Psychological Science 24, 339–344.

Golinkoff, R. M., Hoff, E., Rowe, M. L., et al. (2018). Language matters: Denying the existence of the 30-million-word gap has serious consequences [Commentary on "Reexamining the verbal environments of children from different socioeconomic backgrounds" by D. E. Sperry, L. L. Sperry, & P. J. Miller (2018)]. *Child Development*.

Gopnik, A., & Meltzoff, A. N. (1997). Words, thoughts, and theories. *Trends in Cognitive Sciences* 1.

Gratier, M., Devouche, E., Guellai, B., et al. (2015). Early development of turn-taking in vocal interaction between mothers and infants. *Frontiers in Psychology* 6, 103389.

Grieser, D. L., & Kuhl, P. K. (1988). Maternal speech to infants in a tonal language: Support for universal prosodic features in motherese. *Developmental Psychology* 24, 14–20.

Gros-Louis, J., & Miller, J. L. (2018). From 'ah' to 'bah': Social feedback loops for speech sounds at key points of developmental transition. *Journal of Child Language* 45, 807–825.

Gudmundsdottir, H., & Trehub, S. (2018). Adults recognize toddlers' song renditions. *Psychology of Music* 46, 281–291.

Gustafson, G. E., & Green, J. A. (1989). On the importance of fundamental frequency and other acoustic features in cry perception and infant development. *Child Development* 60, 772–780.

Hammer, C. S., Davison, M. D., Lawrence, F. R., & Miccio, A. W. (2009). The effect of maternal language on bilingual children's vocabulary and emergent literacy development during head start and kindergarten. *Scientific Studies of Reading* 13, 99–121.

Hart, B., & Risley, T. R. (1995). *Meaningful Differences in the Everyday Experience of Young American Children*. Paul H Brookes Publishing: Baltimore, MD.

Hartman, K. M., Ratner, N. B., & Newman, R. S. (2017). Infant-directed speech (IDS) vowel clarity and child language outcomes. *Journal of Child Language* 44, 1140–1162.

Heath, S. B. (1982). What no bedtime story means: Narrative skills at home and school. *Language in Society* 11, 49–76.

Henrich, J., Heine, S. J., & Norenzayan, A. (2010). Most people are not WEIRD. *Nature* 466, 29.

Hernandez, A. E., & Li, P. (2007). Age of acquisition: Its neural and computational mechanisms. *Psychological Bulletin* 133, 638.

Hirsh-Pasek, K., & Golinkoff, R. M. (1996). The intermodal preferential looking paradigm: A window onto emerging language comprehension. In *Methods for Assessing Children's Syntax* (pp. 105–124). MIT Press: Cambridge, MA.

Hockema, S., A., & Smith, L., B. (2009). Learning your language, outside-in and inside-out. *Linguistics* 47, 453.

Hoff-Ginsberg, E. (1991). Mother-child conversation in different social classes and communicative settings. *Child Development* 62, 782–796.

Hoff, E. (2006). How social contexts support and shape language development. *Developmental Review* 26, 55–88.

Hoff, E. (2010). Context effects on young children's language use: The influence of conversational setting and partner. *First Language* 30, 461–472.

Hoff, E. (2013). *Language Development*. Cengage Learning: Boston, MA.

Hoff, E., Core, C., Place, S., et al. (2012). Dual language exposure and early bilingual development. *Journal of Child Language* 39, 1–27.

Hollich, G. J., Hirsh-Pasek, K., Golinkoff, R. M., et al. (2000). Breaking the language barrier: An emergentist coalition model for the origins of word learning. *Monographs of the Society for Research in Child Development* 65, i–135.

Horst, J. S., & Samuelson, L. K. (2008). Fast mapping but poor retention by 24-month-old infants. *Infancy* 13, 128–157.

Huttenlocher, J., Haight, W., Bryk, A., et al. (1991). Early vocabulary growth: Relation to language input and gender. *Developmental Psychology* 27, 236–248.

Huttenlocher, J., Waterfall, H., Vasilyeva, M., et al. (2010). Sources of variability in children's language growth. *Cognitive Psychology* 61, 343–365.

Iverson, J. M., Capirci, O., Volterra, V., & Goldin-Meadow, S. (2008). Learning to talk in a gesture-rich world: Early communication in Italian vs. American children. *First Language* 28, 164–181.

Kalashnikova, M., Goswami, U., & Burnham, D. (2018). Mothers speak differently to infants at-risk for dyslexia. *Developmental Science* 21, e12487.

Kelkar, A. R. (1964). Marathi baby talk. *Word* 20, 40–54.

Klima, E. S., Bellugi, U., & Poizner, H. (1988). Grammar and space in sign aphasiology. *Aphasiology* 2, 319–327.

Koterba, E. A., & Iverson, J. M. (2009). Investigating motionese: The effect of infant-directed action on infants' attention and object exploration. *Infant Behavior and Development* 32, 437–444.

Kovács, Á. M., & Mehler, J. (2009). Cognitive gains in 7-month-old bilingual infants. *Proceedings of the National Academy of Sciences* 106, 6556–6560.

Kovelman, I., Baker, S. A., & Petitto, L.-A. (2008). Age of first bilingual language exposure as a new window into bilingual reading development. *Bilingualism: Language and Cognition* 11, 203–223.

Kroll, J. F., & McClain, R. (2013). What bilinguals tell us about culture, cognition, and language. *Proceedings of the National Academy of Sciences* 110, 11219–11220.

Kuchirko, Y., Tafuro, L., & Tamis-LeMonda, C. S. (2017). Becoming a communicative partner: Infant contingent responsiveness to maternal language and gestures. *Infancy* 23, 558–576.

Kuhl, P. K. (2010). Brain mechanisms in early language acquisition. *Neuron* 67, 713–727.

Kuhl, P. K. (2010). Early language acquisition: Phonetic and word learning, neural substrates, and a theoretical model. In B. Moore, L. Tyler, & W. Marslen-Wislon (Eds.), *The Perception of Speech: From Sound to Meaning*. Oxford University Press: New York.

Kuhl, P. K., Tsao, F.-M., & Liu, H.-M. (2003). Foreign-language experience in infancy: Effects of short-term exposure and social interaction on phonetic learning. *Proceedings of the National Academy of Sciences* 100, 9096–9101.

Landau, B., & Gleitman, L. R. (1985). *Language and Experience: Evidence from the Blind Child* (Vol. 8). Harvard University Press: Cambridge, MA.

Landry, S. H., Smith, K. E., Swank, P. R., & Guttentag, C. (2008). A responsive parenting intervention: The optimal timing across early childhood for impacting maternal behaviors and child outcomes. *Developmental Psychology* 44, 1335–1353.

Lenneberg, E. H. (1967). The biological foundations of language. *Hospital Practice* 2, 59–67.

LeVine, R., Dixon, S., LeVine, R., et al. (1994). *Child Care and Culture: Lessons from Africa*.

Lewis, M., Alessandri, S. M., & Sullivan, M. W. (1990). Violation of expectancy, loss of control, and anger expressions in young infants. *Developmental Psychology* 26, 745.

Love, J. M., Kisker, E. E., Ross, C., et al. (2005). The effectiveness of early head start for 3-year-old children and their parents: Lessons for policy and programs. *Developmental Psychology* 41, 885–901.

MacWhinney, B. (2016). Your laptop to the rescue: Using the CHILDES archive and CLAN utilities to improve child language sample analysis. Paper presented at the Seminars in Speech and Language.

MacWhinney, B., & Snow, C. (1984). *CHILDES (CHIld Language Data Exchange System)*. Carnegie Mellon University: Pittsburgh, PA.

Maguire, M. J., Hirsh-Pasek, K., Golinkoff, R. M., & Brandone, A. C. (2008). Focusing on the relation: fewer exemplars facilitate children's initial verb learning and extension. *Developmental Science* 11, 628–634.

Mandel, D. R., Jusczyk, P. W., & Pisoni, D. B. (1995). Infants' recognition of the sound patterns of their own names. *Psychological Science* 6, 314–317.

Mandler, J. M. (2006). Actions organize the infant's world. *Action Meets Word: How Children Learn Verbs* 2010, 111.

Marchman, V. A., Fernald, A., & Hurtado, N. (2010). How vocabulary size in two languages relates to efficiency in spoken word recognition by young Spanish–English bilinguals. *Journal of Child Language* 37, 817–840.

Marchman, V. A., Martínez-Sussmann, C., & Dale, P. S. (2004). The language-specific nature of grammatical development: evidence from bilingual language learners. *Developmental Science* 7, 212–224.

Markman, E. M. (1989). *Categorization and Naming in Children: Problems of Induction*. MIT Press: Cambridge, MA.

Markman, E. M., & Wachtel, G. F. (1988). Children's use of mutual exclusivity to constrain the meanings of words. *Cognitive Psychology* 20, 121–157.

Markman, E. M., Wasow, J. L., & Hansen, M. B. (2003). Use of the mutual exclusivity assumption by young word learners. *Cognitive Psychology* 47, 241–275.

Masataka, N. (1992). Motherese in a signed language. *Infant Behavior and Development* 15, 453–460.

Mayor, J., & Plunkett, K. (2014). Shared understanding and idiosyncratic expression in early vocabularies. *Developmental Science* 17, 412–423.

McCabe, A., Tamis-LeMonda, C. S., Bornstein, M. H., et al. (2013). Multilingual children. *Social Policy Report* 27, 2014–2451.

McClure, E. R., Chentsova-Dutton, Y. E., Holochwost, S. J., et al. (2017). Look at that! Video chat and joint visual attention development among babies and toddlers. *Child Development* Special Section.

McMurray, B., Horst, J. S., & Samuelson, L. K. (2012). Word learning emerges from the interaction of online referent selection and slow associative learning. *Psychological Review* 119, 831–877.

McNeill, D. (1966). The creation of language by children. *Psycholinguistic Papers*, 99–115.

McNeill, D. (2005). *Gesture and Thought* (Vol. 18). University of Chicago Press: Chicago, IL.

Mehr, S. A., Song, L. A., & Spelke, E. S. (2016). For 5-month-old infants, melodies are social. *Psychological Science* 27, 486–501.

Messer, D. J. (1981). The identification of names in maternal speech to infants. *Journal of Psycholinguistic Research* 10, 69–77.

Molfese, D. L. (2000). Predicting dyslexia at 8 years of age using neonatal brain responses. *Brain and Language* 72, 238–245.

Naigles, L. R., & Swensen, L. D. (2007). Syntactic supports for word learning. In *Blackwell Handbook of Language Development*.

Namy, L. L., Campbell, A. L., & Tomasello, M. (2004). The changing role of iconicity in nonverbal symbol learning: A U-shaped trajectory in the acquisition of arbitrary gestures. *Journal of Cognition and Development* 5, 37–57.

Namy, L. L., Vallas, R., & Knight-Schwarz, J. (2008). Linking parent input and child receptivity to symbolic gestures. *Gesture* 8, 302–324.

Naoi, N., Minagawa-Kawai, Y., Kobayashi, A., et al. (2012). Cerebral responses to infant-directed speech and the effect of talker familiarity. *NeuroImage* 59, 1735–1744.

National Academies of Sciences, Engineering, and Medicine. (2017). *Promoting the Educational Success of Children and Youth Learning English: Promising Futures*. National Academies Press: Washington, DC.

Nelson, K. (2009). *Young Minds in Social Worlds: Experience, Meaning, and Memory*: Harvard University Press: Cambridge, MA.

NICHD ECCRN (2006). *Child Care and Child Development: Results from the NICHD Study of Early Child Care and Youth Development*. Guilford Press.

Ochs, E., & Schieffelin, B. (1984). Language acquisition and socialization: Three developmental stories and their implications. *Linguistic Anthropology: A Reader* 2001, 263–301.

Oller, D. K. (2000). *The Emergence of the Speech Capacity*. Lawrence Erlbaum Associates: Hillsdale, NJ.

Oller, D. K., Buder, E. H., Ramsdell, H. L., et al. (2013). Functional flexibility of infant vocalization and the emergence of language. *Proceedings of the National Academy of Sciences of the United States of America* 110, 6318–6323.

Oller, D. K., & Eilers, R. E. (1988). The role of audition in infant babbling. *Child Development* 59, 441–449.

Ortiz-Mantilla, S., Choe, M.-s., Flax, J., et al. (2010). Associations between the size of the amygdala in infancy and language abilities during the preschool years in normally developing children. *NeuroImage* 49, 2791–2799.

Ortiz-Mantilla, S., Hämäläinen, J. A., Realpe-Bonilla, T., & Benasich, A. A. (2016). Oscillatory dynamics underlying perceptual narrowing of native phoneme mapping from 6 to 12 months of age. *Journal of Neuroscience* 36, 12095–12105.

Pan, B. A., Rowe, M. L., Singer, J. D., & Snow, C. E. (2005). Maternal correlates of growth in toddler vocabulary production in low-income families. *Child Development* 76, 763–782.

Pancsofar, N., & Vernon-Feagans, L. (2006). Mother and father language input to young children: Contributions to later language development. *Journal of Applied Developmental Psychology* 27, 571–587.

Paradis, J., Nicoladis, E., Crago, M., & Genesee, F. (2011). Bilingual children's acquisition of the past tense: A usage-based approach. *Journal of Child Language* 38, 554–578.

Parra, M., Hoff, E., & Core, C. (2011). Relations among language exposure, phonological memory, and language development in Spanish–English bilingually developing 2-year-olds. *Journal of Experimental Child Psychology* 108, 113–125.

Pearson, B. Z., Fernandez, S. C., & Oller, D. K. (1993). Lexical development in bilingual infants and toddlers: Comparison to monolingual norms. *Language Learning* 43, 93–120.

Petitto, L. A., & Marentette, P. F. (1991). Babbling in the manual mode: Evidence for the ontogeny of language. *Science* 251, 1493–1496.

Phillips, J. R. (1973). Syntax and vocabulary of mothers' speech to young children: Age and sex comparisons. *Child Development* 44, 182–185.

Place, S., & Hoff, E. (2011). Properties of dual language exposure that influence 2-year-olds' bilingual proficiency. *Child Development* 82, 1834–1849.

Poulin-Dubois, D., Blaye, A., Coutya, J., & Bialystok, E. (2011). The effects of bilingualism on toddlers' executive functioning. *Journal of Experimental Child Psychology* 108, 567–579.

Quine, W. V. O. (1960). *Word and Object: An Inquiry into the Linguistic Mechanisms of Objective Reference*. John Wiley: Hoboken, NJ.

Rader, N. d. V., & Zukow-Goldring, P. (2010). How the hands control attention during early word learning. *Gesture* 10, 202–221.

Radford, J. (2019). *Key Findings about U.S. Immigrants*. Pew Research Center: Washington D.C.

Rescorla, L. A. (1980). Overextension in early language development. *Journal of Child Language* 7, 321–335.

Rissman, L., Horton, L., Flaherty, M., et al. (2020). The communicative importance of agent-backgrounding: Evidence from home-sign and Nicaraguan sign language. *Cognition* 203.

Rivera-Gaxiola, M., Klarman, L., Garcia-Sierra, A., & Kuhl, P. K. (2005). Neural patterns to speech and vocabulary growth in American infants. *Neuroreport* 16, 495–498.

Rodriguez, E. T., & Tamis-LeMonda, C. S. (2011). Trajectories of the home learning environment across the first 5 years: Associations with children's vocabulary and literacy skills at prekindergarten. *Child Development* 82, 1058–1075.

Rodriguez, E. T., Tamis-LeMonda, C. S., Spellmann, M. E., et al. (2008). The formative role of home literacy experiences across the first three years of life in children from low-income families. *Journal of Applied Developmental Psychology* 30, 677–694.

Rogers, T. T., & McClelland, J. L. (2004). *Semantic Cognition: A Parallel Distributed Processing Approach*. MIT Press: Cambridge, MA.

Rogoff, B. (2003). *The Cultural Nature of Human Development*. Oxford University Press: New York.

Rogoff, B., Paradise, R., Arauz, R. M., et al. (2003). Firsthand learning through intent participation. *Annual Review of Psychology* 54, 175–203.

Roseberry, S., Hirsh-Pasek, K., & Golinkoff, R. M. (2014). Skype me! Socially contingent interactions help toddlers learn language. *Child Development* 85, 956–970.

Rowe, M. L. (2012). A longitudinal investigation of the role of quantity and quality of child-directed speech in vocabulary development. *Child Development* 83, 1762–1774.

Rowe, M. L. (2013). Decontextualized language input and preschoolers' vocabulary development. Paper presented at the Seminars in speech and language.

Rowe, M. L., & Goldin-Meadow, S. (2009). Early gesture selectively predicts later language learning. *Developmental Science* 12, 182–187.

Rowe, M. L., Leech, K. A., & Cabrera, N. (2017). Going beyond input quantity: Wh- questions matter for toddlers' language and cognitive development. *Cognitive Science* 41, 162–179.

Rumelhart, D. E., & McClelland, J. L. (1987). Learning the past tenses of English verbs: Implicit rules or parallel distributed processing. *Mechanisms of Language Acquisition*, 195–248.

Saffran, J. R., Aslin, R. N., & Newport, E. L. (1996). Statistical learning by 8-month-old infants. *Science* 274, 1926–1928.

Schieffelin, B. B. (1979). How Kaluli children learn what to say, what to do, and how to feel. Unpublished Ph. D. dissertation. Columbia University: New York.

Schieffelin, B. B., & Ochs, E. (1986). Language socialization. *Annual Review of Anthropology* 15, 163–191.

Schneider, R. M., Yurovsky, D., & Frank, M. C. (2015). Large-scale investigations of variability in children's first words. In D. C. Noelle, R. Dale, A. S. Warlaumont, et al. (Eds.), *Proceedings of the 37th Annual Meeting of the Cognitive Science Society*. Cognitive Science Society.

Sebastian-Galles, N. (2010). Bilingual language acquisition: Where does the difference lie? *Human Development* 53, 245–255.

Sebastián-Gallés, N., Albareda-Castellot, B., Weikum, W. M., & Werker, J. F. (2012). A bilingual advantage in visual language discrimination in infancy. *Psychological Science* 23, 994–999.

Sebastian-Galles, N., Vera-Constan, F., Larsson, J. P., et al. (2009). Lexical plasticity in early bilinguals does not alter phoneme categories: II. Experimental evidence. *Journal of Cognitive Neuroscience* 21, 2343–2357.

Sebastián-Gallés, N., & Bosch, L. (2009). Developmental shift in the discrimination of vowel contrasts in bilingual infants: is the distributional account all there is to it? *Developmental Science* 12, 874–887.

Seidl, A., Onishi, K. H., & Cristia, A. (2014). Talker variation aids young infants' phonotactic learning. *Language Learning and Development* 10, 297–307.

Senghas, R.J., Senghas, A., & Pyers, J. E. (2005). The emergence of Nicaraguan Sign Language: Questions of development, acquisition, and evolution. In S. Parker, J. Langer, & C. Milbrath (Eds.), *Biology and Knowledge Revisited: From Neurogenesis to Psychogenesis*. Lawrence Erlbaum: Hillsdale, NJ.

Shatz, M. (1978). On the development of communicative understandings: An early strategy for interpreting and responding to messages. *Cognitive Psychology* 10, 271–301.

Skinner, B. F. (1957). *Verbal Behavior*. Appleton Century-Crofts: New York.

Slobin, D. I. (1970). *Suggested Universals in the Ontogenesis of Grammar*, 20.

Smith, L., & Yu, C. (2008). Infants rapidly learn word-referent mappings via cross-situational statistics. *Cognition* 106, 1558–1568.

Smith, L. B., & Thelen, E. (2003). Development as a dynamic system. *Trends in Cognitive Sciences* 7, 343–348.

Snow, C. E., Arlman-Rupp, A., Hassing, Y., et al. (1976). Mothers' speech in three social classes. *Journal of Psycholinguistic Research* 5, 1–20.

Soderstrom, M., Blossom, M., Foygel, R., & Morgan, J. L. (2008). Acoustical cues and grammatical units in speech to two preverbal infants. *Journal of Child Language* 35, 869–902.

Soderstrom, M., & Wittebolle, K. (2013). When do caregivers talk? The influences of activity and time of day on caregiver speech and child vocalizations in two childcare environments. *PLoS ONE* 8.

Song, L., Tamis-LeMonda, C. S., Yoshikawa, H., et al. (2012). Language experiences and vocabulary development in Dominican and Mexican infants across the first 2 years. *Developmental Psychology* 48, 1106–1123.

Song, L., Spier, E. T., & Tamis-Lemonda, C. S. (2014). Reciprocal influences between maternal language and children's language and cognitive development in low-income families. *Journal of Child Language* 41, 305–326.

Sperry, D. E., Sperry, L. L., & Miller, P. J. (2019). Reexamining the verbal environments of children from different socioeconomic backgrounds. *Child Development* 90, 1303–1318.

Stams, G.-J. J. M., Juffer, F., & van Ijzendoorn, M. H. (2002). Maternal sensitivity, infant attachment, and temperament in early childhood predict adjustment in middle childhood: The case of adopted children and their biologically unrelated parents. *Developmental Psychology* 38, 806–821.

Stern, D. N. (2002). *The First Relationship*. Harvard University Press: Cambridge, MA.

Stiles, J. (2000). Neural plasticity and cognitive development. *Developmental Neuropsychology* 18, 237–272.

Stoel-Gammon, C. (1998). Sounds and words in early language acquisition: The relationship between lexical and phonological development. *Exploring the Speech-Language Connection* 8, 25–52.

Stoel-gammon, C., & Herrington, P. B. (1990). Vowel systems of normally developing and phonologically disordered children. *Clinical Linguistics & Phonetics* 4, 145–160.

Styles, S. J., & Plunkett, K. (2009). How do infants build a semantic system? *Language and Cognition* 1, 1–24.

Tager-Flusberg, H., & Sullivan, K. (2000). A componential view of theory of mind: evidence from Williams syndrome. *Cognition* 76, 59–90.

Tamis-LeMonda, C. S., Song, L., Leavell, A. S., et al. (2012). Ethnic differences in mother–infant language and gestural communications are associated with specific skills in infants. *Developmental Science* 15, 384–397.

Tamis-LeMonda, C. S., Baumwell, L., & Cristofaro, T. (2012). Parent–child conversations during play. *First Language* 32, 413–438.

Tamis-LeMonda, C. S., & Bornstein, M. H. (1994). Specificity in mother-toddler language-play relations across the second year. *Developmental Psychology* 30, 283–292.

Tamis-LeMonda, C. S., & Bornstein, M. H. (2015). Infant word learning in biopsychosocial perspective. In S. D. Calkins (Ed.), *Handbook of Infant Biopsychosocial Development* (pp. 152–185). The Guilford Press.

Tamis-LeMonda, C. S., Bornstein, M. H., & Baumwell, L. (2001). Maternal responsiveness and children's achievement of language milestones. *Child Development* 72, 748–767.

Tamis-Lemonda, C. S., Bornstein, M. H., Kahana-Kalman, R., et al. (1998). Predicting varia-

tion in the timing of language milestones in the second year: an events history approach. *Journal of Child Language* 25, 675–700.

Tamis-LeMonda, C. S., Shannon, J. D., Cabrera, N. J., & Lamb, M. E. (2004). Fathers and mothers at play with their 2-and 3-year-olds: contributions to language and cognitive development. *Child Development* 75, 1806–1820.

Tamis-LeMonda, C. S., Luo, R., McFadden, K. E., et al. (2019) Early home learning environment predicts children's 5th grade academic skills. *Applied Developmental Science* 23, 153–169.

Tamis-LeMonda, C. S., Kuchirko, Y., & Suh, D. D. (2018). Taking center stage: infants' active role in language learning. In *Active Learning from Infancy to Childhood* (pp. 39–53). Springer: Cham, Switzerland.

Tamis-LeMonda, C. S., Kuchirko, Y., & Tafuro, L. (2013). From action to interaction: Infant object exploration and mothers' contingent responsiveness. *IEEE Transactions on Autonomous Mental Development* 5, 202–209.

Tamis-LeMonda, C. S., Custode, S., Kuchirko, Y., et al. (2018). Routine language: Speech directed to infants during home activities. *Child Development* 90, 2135–2152.

Tardif, T., Fletcher, P., Liang, W., et al. (2008). Baby's first 10 words. *Developmental Psychology* 44, 929–938.

Tincoff, R., & Jusczyk, P. W. (1999). Some beginnings of word comprehension in 6-month-olds. *Psychological Science* 10, 172–175.

Tomasello, M., & Farrar, M. J. (1986). Joint attention and early language. *Child Development* 57, 1454–1463.

Trevarthen, C. (1993). The self born in intersubjectivity: The psychology of an infant communicating. In *The Perceived Self: Ecological and Interpersonal Sources of Self-Knowledge* (pp. 121–173). Cambridge University Press: New York.

Tsao, F. M., Liu, H. M., & Kuhl, P. K. (2004). Speech perception in infancy predicts language development in the second year of life: A longitudinal study. *Child Development* 75, 1067–1084.

Tsushima, T., Takizawa, O., Sasaki, M., et al. (1994). Discrimination of English /r-l/ and /w-y/ by Japanese infants at 6–12 months: Language-specific developmental changes in speech perception abilities. *ICSLP* 1695–1698.

Valian, V. (1999). Input and language acquisition. In *Handbook of Child Language Acquisition* (pp. 497–530). Academic Press: San Diego, CA.

Vicari, S., Albertoni, A., Chilosi, A. M., et al. (2000). Plasticity and reorganization during language development in children with early brain injury. *Cortex* 36, 31–46.

Vygotsky, L. (1986). *Thought and Language - Revised Edition*. MIT Press: Cambridge, MA.

Warlaumont, A. S., Richards, J. A., Gilkerson, J., & Oller, D. K. (2014). A social feedback loop for speech development and its reduction in autism. *Psychological Science* 25, 1314–1324.

Weisleder, A., & Fernald, A. (2013). Talking to children matters: Early language experience strengthens processing and builds vocabulary. *Psychological Science* 24, 2143–2152.

Weppelman, T. L., Bostow, A., Schiffer, R., et al. (2003). Children's use of the prosodic characteristics of infant-directed speech. *Language & Communication* 23, 63–80.

Werker, J. F., Gilbert, J. H. V., Humphrey, K., & Tees, R. C. (1981). Developmental aspects of cross-language speech perception. *Child Development* 52, 349–355.

Werker, J. F., & Tees, R. C. (1984). Cross-language speech perception: Evidence for perceptual reorganization during the first year of life. *Infant Behavior and Development* 7, 49–63.

Woodward, A. L., & Markman, E. M. (1998). Early word learning. In *Handbook of Child Psychology: Volume 2: Cognition, Perception, and Language* (pp. 371–420). John Wiley & Sons Inc: Hoboken, NJ.

Woodward, A. L., Markman, E. M., & Fitzsimmons, C. M. (1994). Rapid word learning in 13- and 18-month-olds. *Developmental Psychology* 30, 553–566.

Yu, C., Ballard, C., & Aslin, C. (2005). The role of embodied intention in early lexical acquisition. *Cognitive Science* 29, 961–1005.

Zukow-Goldring, P. (1996). Sensitive caregiving fosters the comprehension of speech: When gestures speak louder than words. *Early Development and Parenting* 5, 195–211.

Chapter 7

Ahnert, L., Pinquart, M., & Lamb, M. E. (2006). Security of children's relationships with nonparental care providers: A meta-analysis. *Child Development* 77, 664–679.

Ainsworth, M. S. (1979). Infant–mother attachment. *American Psychologist* 34, 932–937.

Ainsworth, M. D., & Bell, S. M. (1969). Some contemporary patterns of mother-infant interaction in the feeding situation. *Stimulation in Early Infancy*, 133–170.

Ainsworth, M. D. S., & Marvin, R. S. (1995). On the shaping of attachment theory and research: An interview with Mary D. S. Ainsworth (Fall 1994). *Monographs of the Society for Research in Child Development* 60, 3–21.

Almas, A. N., Degnan, K. A., Radulescu, A., et al. (2012). Effects of early intervention and the moderating effects of brain activity on institutionalized children's social skills at age 8. *Proceedings of the National Academy of Sciences* 109, 17228–17231.

Baer, J. C., & Martinez, C. D. (2006). Child maltreatment and insecure attachment: A meta-analysis. *Journal of Reproductive and Infant Psychology* 24, 187–197.

Ballantine, J. H., & Klein, H. A. (1990). The relationship of temperament and adjustment in Japanese schools. *The Journal of Psychology* 124, 299–309.

Barrett, K. C., Zahn-Waxler, C., & Cole, P. M. (1993). Avoiders vs. amenders: Implications for the investigation of guilt and shame during toddlerhood? *Cognition and Emotion* 7, 481–505.

Barry, H., Bacon, M. K., & Child, I. L. (1957). A cross-cultural survey of some sex differences in socialization. *The Journal of Abnormal and Social Psychology* 55, 327–332.

Bigelow, A. E., Power, M., Bulmer, M., & Gerrior, K. (2018). The effect of maternal mirroring behavior on infants' early social bidding during the still-face task. *Infancy* 23, 367–385.

Block, J. H. (1983). Differential premises arising from differential socialization of the sexes: Some conjectures. *Child Development* 54, 1335–1354.

Bloom, L. (1993). *Language Development from Two to Three*. Cambridge University Press: New York.

Bloom, L., & Capatides, J. B. (1987). Expression of affect and the emergence of language. *Child Development* 58, 1513–1522.

Boe, J. L., & Woods, R. J. (2018). Parents' influence on infants' gender-typed toy preferences. *Sex Roles* 79, 358–373.

Bohr, Y., & Tse, C. (2009). Satellite babies in transnational families: A study of parents' decision to separate from their infants. *Infant Mental Health Journal* 30, 265–286.

Bowlby, J. (1944). Forty-four juvenile thieves: Their characters and home-life. *The International Journal of Psycho-Analysis* 25, 19.

Bowlby, J. (1951). *Maternal Care and Mental Health* (Vol. 2). World Health Organization: Geneva, Switzerland.

Bowlby, J. (1953). Some pathological processes set in train by early mother-child separation. *The British Journal of Psychiatry* 99, 265–272.

Bowlby, J. (1958). The nature of the child's tie to his mother. *The International Journal of Psycho-Analysis* 39, 350.

Bowlby, J. (1963). Pathological mourning and childhood mourning. *Journal of the American Psychoanalytic Association* 11, 500–541.

Brady-Smith, C., Brooks-Gunn, J., Tamis-LeMonda, C. S., et al. (2013). Mother–infant interactions in early head start: A person-oriented within-ethnic group approach. *Parenting* 13, 27–43.

Braungart-Rieker, J. M., Hill-Soderlund, A. L., & Karrass, J. (2010). Fear and anger reactivity trajectories from 4 to 16 months: The roles of temperament, regulation, and maternal sensitivity. *Developmental Psychology* 46, 791–804.

Bretherton, I., & Ainsworth, M. D. S. (1974). Responses of one-year-olds to a stranger in a strange situation. In *The Origins of Fear* (pp. 131–164). Wiley: New York.

Brownell, C. A. (2013). Early development of prosocial behavior: Current perspectives. *Infancy* 18, 1–9.

Brownell, C. A., Svetlova, M., & Nichols, S. (2009). To share or not to share: When do toddlers respond to another's needs? *Infancy* 14, 117–130.

Burris, J. L., Buss, K., LoBue, V., et al. (2019). Biased attention to threat and anxiety: On taking a developmental approach. *Journal of Experimental Psychopathology*.

Cabrera, N. J., Shannon, J. D., & Tamis-LeMonda, C. (2007). Fathers' influence on their children's cognitive and emotional development: From toddlers to pre-K. *Applied Developmental Science* 11, 208–213.

Calkins, S. D., & Hill, A. (2007). Caregiver influences on emerging emotion regulation. In J. Gross (Ed.), *Handbook of Emotion Regulation* (pp. 229–248). Guilford Press: New York.

Calkins, S. D. (2002). Does aversive behavior during toddlerhood matter? The effects of difficult temperament on maternal perceptions and behavior. *Infant Mental Health Journal* 23, 381–402.

Calkins, S. D., Dedmon, S. E., Gill, K. L., et al. (2002). Frustration in infancy: Implications for emotion regulation, physiological processes, and temperament. *Infancy* 3, 175–197.

Calkins, S. D., Smith, C. L., Gill, K. L., & Johnson, M. C. (1998). Maternal interactive style across contexts: Relations to emotional, behavioral, and physiological regulation during toddlerhood. *Social Development* 7, 350–369.

Campos, J., Barrett, K., Lamb, M., & Goldsmith, H. (1983). *Socioemotional Development* (Vol. 2).

Camras, L. A., & Halberstadt, A. G. (2017). Emotional development through the lens of affective social competence. *Current Opinion in Psychology* 17, 113–117.

Camras, L. A., Oster, H., Bakeman, R., et al. (2007). Do infants show distinct negative facial expressions for fear and anger? Emotional expression in 11-month-old European American, Chinese, and Japanese infants. *Infancy* 11, 131–155.

Camras, L. A., & Shutter, J. M. (2010). Emotional facial expressions in infancy. *Emotion Review* 2, 120–129.

Camras, L. A., & Shuster, M. M. (2013). Current emotion research in developmental psychology. *Emotion Review* 5, 321–329.

Caspi, A., Harrington, H., Milne, B., et al. (2003). Children's behavioral styles at age 3 are linked to their adult personality traits at age 26. *Journal of Personality* 71, 495–514.

Caspi, A., & Silva, P. A. (1995). Temperamental qualities at age three predict personality traits in young adulthood: Longitudinal evidence from a birth cohort. *Child Development* 66, 486–498.

Chapman, H. A., Kim, D. A., Susskind, J. M., & Anderson, A. K. (2009). In bad taste: Evidence for the oral origins of moral disgust. *Science* 323, 1222–1226.

Chess, S., & Thomas, A. (1984). *Origins and Evolution of Behavior Disorders: From Infancy to Early Adult Life*. Harvard University Press: Cambridge, MA.

Chess, S., & Thomas, A. (1991). Temperament and the concept of goodness of fit. In J. Strelau & A. Angleitner (Eds.), *Explorations in Temperament. International Perspectives on Theory and Measurement* (pp. 15–28). Springer: Boston, MA.

Cicchetti, D., & Rogosch, F. A. (2012). Gene × environment interaction and resilience: Effects of child maltreatment and serotonin, corticotropin releasing hormone, dopamine, and oxytocin genes. *Development and Psychopathology* 24, 411–427.

Clarke-Stewart, K. A. (1978). And Daddy makes three: The father's impact on mother and young child. *Child Development* 49, 466–478.

Cohn, J. F., & Tronick, E. Z. (1983). Three-month-old infants' reaction to simulated maternal depression. *Child Development* 54, 185–193.

Coie, J. D., & Dodge, K. A. (1998). Aggression and antisocial behavior. In *Handbook of Child Psychology: Social, Emotional, and Personality Development*. Vol. 3, 5th ed. (pp. 779–862). John Wiley & Sons Inc.: Hoboken, NJ.

Cole, P. M., Armstrong, L. M., & Pemberton, C. K. (2010). The role of language in the development of emotion regulation. *Child Development at the Intersection of Emotion and Cognition* (pp. 59–77). American Psychological Association: Washington, DC.

Cook, M., & Mineka, S. (1989). Observational conditioning of fear to fear-relevant versus fear-irrelevant stimuli in rhesus monkeys. *Journal of Abnormal Psychology* 98, 448–459.

Cook, M., & Mineka, S. (1990). Selective associations in the observational conditioning of fear in rhesus monkeys. *Journal of Experimental Psychology: Animal Behavior Processes* 16, 372–389.

Curtiss, S. (2014). *Genie: A Psycholinguistic Study of a Modern-Day Wild Child*. Academic Press: Boston, MA.

Dagan, O., & Sagi-Schwartz, A. (2020). Infant attachment (to mother and father) and its place in human development: Five decades of promising research (and an unsettled issue). In J. J. Lockman & C. S. Tamis-LeMonda (Eds.), *Cambridge Handbook of Infant Development: Brain, Behavior, and Cultural Context*. Cambridge University Press: New York.

Dahl, A. (2015). The developing social context of infant helping in two U.S. samples. *Child Development* 86, 1080–1093.

Dahl, A. (2016). Infants' unprovoked acts of force toward others. *Developmental Science* 19, 1049–1057.

Dahl, A. (2019). Chapter one- the science of early moral development: on defining, constructing, and studying morality from birth. *Advances in Child Development and Behavior* 56, 1–35.

Dahl, A., Schuck, R. K., & Campos, J. J. (2013). Do young toddlers act on their social preferences? *Developmental Psychology* 49, 1964–1970.

Darwin, C. (1872). *The Expression of Emotion in Animals and Man.* Murray: London, United Kingdom.

DeVries, M. W. (1984). Temperament and infant mortality among the Masai of East Africa. *The American Journal of Psychiatry* 141, 1189–1194.

Diamond, A. (1991). Neuropsychological insights into the meaning of object concept development. *The Epigenesis of Mind: Essays on Biology and Cognition* (pp. 67–110). Lawrence Erlbaum Associates, Inc.: Hillsdale, NJ.

Dunfield, K., Kuhlmeier, V. A., O'Connell, L., & Kelley, E. (2011). Examining the diversity of prosocial behavior: Helping, sharing, and comforting in infancy. *Infancy* 16, 227–247.

Dunfield, K. A., & Kuhlmeier, V. A. (2010). Intention-mediated selective helping in infancy. *Psychological Science* 21, 523–527.

Dykas, M. J., & Cassidy, J. (2011). Attachment and the processing of social information across the life span: Theory and evidence. *Psychological Bulletin* 137, 19–46.

Eisenberg, N. (2010). Early social cognition: Comments on Astington and Edward, Miller, Moore and Sommerville. In R. E. Tremblay, R. G. Barr, R. DeV. Peters, & M. Boivin (Eds.), *Encyclopedia on Early Childhood Development* (pp. 1–5). Centre of Excellence for Early Childhood Development: Montreal, Canada.

Eisenberg, N., Spinrad, T. L., Eggum, N. D., et al. (2010). Relations among maternal socialization, effortful control, and maladjustment in early childhood. *Development and Psychopathology* 22, 507–525.

Eisenberg, N., Fabes, R. A., & Spinrad, T. L. (2006). Prosocial development. In N. Eisenberg, W. Damon, & R. M. Lerner (Eds.), *Handbook of Child Psychology: Social, Emotional, and Personality Development*, Vol. 3, 6th ed (pp. 646–718). John Wiley & Sons Inc.: Hoboken, NJ.

Ekas, N. V., Lickenbrock, D. M., & Braungart-Rieker, J. M. (2013). Developmental trajectories of emotion regulation across infancy: Do age and the social partner influence temporal patterns. *Infancy* 18, 729–754.

Ekman, P. (1971). Universals and cultural differences in facial expressions of emotion. *Nebraska Symposium on Motivation* 19, 207–283.

Emde, R. N. (1980). Emotional availability: A reciprocal reward system for infants and parents with implications for prevention of psychosocial disorders. *Parent-Infant Relationships*, 87–115.

Emde, R. N., & Harmon, R. J. (1972). Endogenous and exogenous smiling systems in early infancy. *Journal of the American Academy of Child & Adolescent Psychiatry* 11, 177–200.

Feinman, S., Roberts, D., Hsieh, K.-F., et al. (1992). A critical review of social referencing in infancy. In S. Feinman (Ed.), *Social Referencing and the Social Construction of Reality in Infancy* (pp. 15–54). Springer: Boston, MA.

Feldman, R., Magori-Cohen, R., Galili, G., et al. (2011). Mother and infant coordinate heart rhythms through episodes of interaction synchrony. *Infant Behavior and Development* 34, 569–577.

Field, T. (1979). Differential behavioral and cardiac responses of 3-month-old infants to a mirror and peer. *Infant Behavior and Development* 2, 179–184.

Fivush, R., & Waters, T. E. (2015). Patterns of attachments across the lifespan. In R. A. Scott & S. M. Kosslyn (Eds.), *Emerging Trends in the Social and Behavioral Sciences.*

Fogel, A. (1979). Peer vs. mother directed behavior in 1- to 3-month-old infants. *Infant Behavior and Development* 2, 215–226.

Fox, N. A., & Calkins, S. D. (2003). The development of self-control of emotion: Intrinsic and extrinsic influences. *Motivation and Emotion* 27, 7–26.

Fox, N. A., Henderson, H. A., Rubin, K. H., et al. (2001). Continuity and discontinuity of behavioral inhibition and exuberance: Psychophysiological and behavioral influences across the first four years of life. *Child Development* 72, 1–21.

Freud, S. (1927). *The Ego and the Id.* Hogarth Press: London, United Kingdom.

Freud, S. (1940). Constructions in analysis. *The Psychoanalytic Review (1913–1957)* 27, 374.

Geangu, E., Benga, O., Stahl, D., & Striano, T. (2010). Contagious crying beyond the first days of life. *Infant Behavior and Development* 33, 279–288.

Geiger, B. (1996). *Fathers as Primary Caregivers.* Greenwood Publishing Group.

Gojman, S., Millán, S., Carlson, E., et al. (2012). Intergenerational relations of attachment: A research synthesis of urban/rural Mexican samples. *Attachment & Human Development* 14, 553–566.

Otto, H., & Keller, H. (Eds.). (2014). *Different Faces of Attachment: Cultural Variations on a Universal Human Need.* Cambridge University Press: Cambridge, United Kingdom.

Granqvist, P., Sroufe, L. A., Dozier, M., et al. (2017). Disorganized attachment in infancy: a review of the phenomenon and its implications for clinicians and policy-makers. *Attachment & Human Development* 19, 534–558.

Grolnick, W. S., Bridges, L. J., & Connell, J. P. (1996). Emotion regulation in two-year-olds: Strategies and emotional expression in four contexts. *Child Development* 67, 928–941.

Grolnick, W. S., Cosgrove, T. J., & Bridges, L. J. (1996). Age-graded change in the initiation of positive affect. *Infant Behavior and Development* 19, 153–157.

Gunnar, M. R., & Vazquez, D. (2006). Stress neurobiology and developmental psychopathology. *Developmental Psychopathology* 2, 533–577.

Halberstadt, A. G., & Eaton, K. L. (2002). A meta-analysis of family expressiveness and children's emotion expressiveness and understanding. *Marriage & Family Review* 34, 35–62.

Hamlin, J. K. (2010). Social evaluation by preverbal infants. *Nature* 450, 557.

Hamlin, J. K. (2013). Moral judgment and action in preverbal infants and toddlers: Evidence for an innate moral core. *Current Directions in Psychological Science* 22, 186–193.

Hamlin, J.K., & Stitch, M. (2020). Understanding and evaluating the moral world in infancy. In J. J. Lockman & C.S. Tamis-LeMonda (Eds.), *The Cambridge Handbook of Infant Development* (pp. 777–804). Cambridge University Press: New York.

Hamlin, J. K., & Wynn, K. (2011). Young infants prefer prosocial to antisocial others. *Cognitive Development* 26, 30–39.

Hamlin, J., Wynn, K. & Bloom, P. (2007). Social evaluation by preverbal infants. *Nature* 450, 557–559.

Hamlin, J. K., Wynn, K., & Bloom, P. (2010). Three-month-olds show a negativity bias in their social evaluations. *Developmental Science* 13, 923–929.

Hamlin, J. K., Wynn, K., Bloom, P., & Mahajan, N. (2011). How infants and toddlers react to antisocial others. *Proceedings of the National Academy of Sciences* 108, 19931–19936.

Harlow, H. F. (1958). The nature of love. *American Psychologist* 13, 673–685.

Harwood, R. L. (1983). *Culture and Attachment: Perceptions of the Child in Context.* Guilford Press.

Hepach, R., & Westermann, G. (2013). Infants' sensitivity to the congruence of others' emotions and actions. *Journal of Experimental Child Psychology* 115, 16–29.

Hesse, E., & Main, M. (2006). Frightened, threatening, and dissociative parental behavior in low-risk samples: Description, discussion, and interpretations. *Development and Psychopathology* 18, 309–343.

Holodynski, M., & Friedlmeier, W. (2006). *Development of Emotions and Emotion Regulation* (Vol. 8). Springer Science & Business Media: New York.

Howes, C. (1983). Patterns of friendship. *Child Development* 54, 1041–1053.

Izard, C. E. (1978). On the ontogenesis of emotions and emotion-cognition relationships in infancy. In M. Lewis & L. A. Rosenblum (Eds.), *The Development of Affect* (pp. 389–413). Springer: Boston, MA.

Jack, R. E., Garrod, O. G. B., Yu, H., et al. (2012). Facial expressions of emotion are not culturally universal. *Proceedings of the National Academy of Sciences* 109, 7241–7244.

Jacobson, J. L. (1981). The role of inanimate objects in early peer interaction. *Child Development* 52, 618–626.

Johnson, S. C., Dweck, C. S., & Chen, F. S. (2007). Evidence for infants' internal working models of attachment. *Psychological Science* 18, 501–502.

Kagan, J. (1976). Emergent themes in human development: Some basic assumptions about the development of cognitive and affective structures and their stability from infancy to later childhood are reexamined in light of new evidence from a variety of sources. *American Scientist* 64, 186–196.

Kahana-Kalman, R., & Walker-Andrews, A. S. (2001). The role of person familiarity in young infants' perception of emotional expressions. *Child Development* 72, 352–369.

Karraker, K. H., Vogel, D. A., & Lake, M. A. (1995). Parents' gender-stereotyped perceptions of newborns: The eye of the beholder revisited. *Sex Roles* 33, 687–701.

Karrass, J., & Braungart-Rieker, J. M. (2003). Parenting and temperament as interacting agents in early language development. *Parenting* 3, 235–259.

Keller, H., & Bard, K. A. (Eds.) (2017). *The Cultural Nature of Attachment.* MIT Press: Cambridge, MA.

Keller, H., & Otto, H. (2009). The cultural socialization of emotion regulation during infancy. *Journal of Cross-Cultural Psychology* 40, 996–1011.

Killen, M., & Rizzo, M. T. (2014). Morality, intentionality and intergroup attitudes. *Behaviour* 151, 337–359.

Kochanska, G., & Knaack, A. (2003). Effortful control as a personality characteristic of young children: Antecedents, correlates, and consequences. *Journal of Personality* 71, 1087–1112.

Kochanska, G., Tjebkes, J. L., & Fortnan, D. R. (1998). Children's emerging regulation of conduct: Restraint, compliance, and internalization from infancy to the second year. *Child Development* 69, 1378–1389.

Kochanska, G., & Kim, S. (2014). A complex interplay among the parent–child relationship, effortful control, and internalized, rule-compatible conduct in young children: Evidence from two studies. *Developmental Psychology* 50, 8–21.

Kohlberg, L. (1969). *Stages in the Development of Moral Thought and Action*. Holt, Rinehart & Winston: New York.

Kubicek, L. F., & Emde, R. N. (2012). Emotional expression and language: A longitudinal study of typically developing earlier and later talkers from 15 to 30 months. *Infant Mental Health Journal* 33, 553–584.

Kuchuk, A., Vibbert, M., & Bornstein, M. H. (1986). The perception of smiling and its experiential correlates in three-month-old infants. *Child Development* 57, 1054–1061.

Lamb, M. E. (1977). Father-infant and mother-infant interaction in the first year of life. *Child Development* 48, 167–181.

Leaper, C., & Friedman, C. K. (2007). The socialization of gender. In *Handbook of Socialization: Theory and Research* (pp. 561–587). Guilford Press: New York.

Leerkes, E. M., Gedaly, L., & Su, J. (2016). Parental sensitivity and infant attachment. In *Child Psychology: A Handbook of Contemporary Issues* (pp. 21–42). Routledge: New York.

Leerkes, E. M., Parade, S. H., & Gudmundson, J. A. (2011). Mothers' emotional reactions to crying pose risk for subsequent attachment insecurity. *Journal of Family Psychology* 25, 635–643.

Leerkes, E., Su, J., Calkins, S., et al. (2017). Maternal physiological dysregulation while parenting poses risk for infant attachment disorganization and behavior problems. *Development and Psychopathology* 29, 245–257.

Leerkes, E. M., Weaver, J. M., & O'Brien, M. (2012). Differentiating maternal sensitivity to infant distress and non-distress. *Parenting* 12, 175–184.

LeVine, R. A. (2014). Attachment theory as cultural ideology. In H. Otto & H. Keller (Eds.), *Different Faces of Attachment: Cultural Variations on a Universal Human Need* (pp. 50–65). Cambridge University Press: New York..

Lewis, M. (1995). Self-conscious emotions. *American Scientist* 83, 68–78.

Lewis, M., & Brooks-Gunn, J. (1979). *The Origins of Self. In: Social Cognition and the Acquisition of Self*. Springer: Boston, MA.

Lewis, M., & Ramsay, D. (2004). Development of self-recognition, personal pronoun use, and pretend play during the 2nd year. *Child Development* 75, 1821–1831.

Lewis, M., Sullivan, M. W., & Michalson, L. (1985). The cognitive-emotional fugue. In C. E. Izard, J. Kagan, & R. B. Zajonc (Eds.), *Emotions, Cognition, and Behavior* (pp. 264–288). Cambridge University Press: New York.

LoBue, V., & Adolph, K. E. (2019). Fear in infancy: Lessons from snakes, spiders, heights, and strangers. *Developmental Psychology* 55, 1889–1907.

LoBue, V., & DeLoache, J. S. (2010). Superior detection of threat-relevant stimuli in infancy. *Developmental Science* 13, 221–228.

LoBue, V., & Rakison, D. H. (2013). What we fear most: A developmental advantage for threat-relevant stimuli. *Developmental Review* 33, 285–303.

MacPhee, D &, Prendergast, S. (2019). Room for improvement: Girls' and boys' home environments are still gendered. *Sex Roles* 80, 332–346.

Main, M., & Solomon, J. (1990). Procedures for identifying infants as disorganized/disoriented during the ainsworth strange situation. In M. T. Greenberg, D. Cicchetti, & E. M. Cummings (Eds.), *Attachment in the Preschool Years: Theory, Research and Intervention* (pp. 121–160). University of Chicago Press: Chicago, IL.

Martin, C. L., Ruble, D. N., & Szkrybalo, J. (2002). Cognitive theories of early gender development. *Psychological Bulletin* 128, 903–933.

Martin, G. B., & Clark, R. D. (1982). Distress crying in neonates: Species and peer specificity. *Developmental Psychology* 18, 3–9.

Mastropieri, D., & Turkewitz, G. (1999). Prenatal experience and neonatal responsiveness to vocal expressions of emotion. *Developmental Psychobiology* 35, 204–214.

Maudry, M., & Nekula, M. (1939). Social relations between children of the same age during the first two years of life. *The Pedagogical Seminary and Journal of Genetic Psychology* 54, 193–215.

Mead, M. (1935). *Sex and Temperament in Three Primitive Societies*. William Morrow: Oxford, United Kingdom.

Mesman, J., & Groeneveld, M. G. (2018). Gendered parenting in early childhood: Subtle but unmistakable if you know where to look. *Child Development Perspectives* 12, 22–27.

Mesman, J., van IJzendoorn, M. H., & Sagi-Schwartz, A. (2016). Cross-cultural patterns of attachment: Universal and contextual dimensions. In J. Cassidy & P. R. Shaver (Eds.), *Handbook of Attachment: Theory, Research and Clinical Applications* (pp. 790–815). Guilford Press: New York.

Messinger, D., & Fogel, A. (2007). The interactive development of social smiling. *Advances in Child Development and Behaviour* 35, 328–366.

Messinger, D. S., Fogel, A., & Dickson, K. L. (2001). All smiles are positive, but some smiles are more positive than others. *Developmental Psychology* 37, 642–653.

Mikhail, J. (2011). *Elements of Moral Cognition: Rawls' Linguistic Analogy and the Cognitive Science of Moral and Legal Judgment*. Cambridge University Press: New York.

Mondschein, E. R., Adolph, K. E., & Tamis-Le-Monda, C. S. (2000). Gender bias in mothers' expectations about infant crawling. *Journal of Experimental Child Psychology* 77, 304–316.

Moscardino, U., & Axia, G. (2006). Infants' responses to arm restraint at 2 and 6 months: A longitudinal study. *Infant Behavior and Development* 29, 59–69.

Morford, A. E., Cookston, J. T., & Hagan, M. J. (2017). Parental distress tolerance in three periods of child development: The moderating role of child temperament. *Journal of Child and Family Studies* 26, 3401–3411.

Morelli, G. A., Chaudhary, N., Gottlieb, A., et al. (2017). A pluralistic approach to attachment. In H. Keller & K. A. Bard (Eds.) *The Cultural Nature of Attachment: Contextualizing Relationships and Development* (pp. 139–170). MIT Press: Cambridge, MA.

Mumme, D. L., & Fernald, A. (2003). The infant as onlooker: Learning from emotional reactions observed in a television scenario. *Child Development* 74, 221–237.

Murray, L., & Trevarthen, C. (1985). Emotional regulation of interactions between two-month-olds and their mothers. In T. Field & N. Fox (Eds.), *Social Perception in Infants* (pp. 177–197). Ablex Publisher: Norwood, NJ.

Myruski, S., Gulyayeva, O., Birk, S., et al. (2018). Digital disruption? Maternal mobile device use is related to infant social-emotional functioning. *Developmental Science* 21, e12610.

Neisser, U. (1991). Two perceptually given aspects of the self and their development. *Developmental Review* 11, 197–209.

Ogren, M., Burling, J. M., & Johnson, S. P. (2018). Family expressiveness relates to happy emotion matching among 9-month-old infants. *Journal of Experimental Child Psychology* 174, 29–40.

Öhman, A., & Mineka, S. (2001). Fears, phobias, and preparedness: Toward an evolved module of fear and fear learning. *Psychological Review* 108, 483–522.

Ostlund, B. D., Measelle, J. R., Laurent, H. K., et al. (2017). Shaping emotion regulation: Attunement, symptomatology, and stress recovery within mother–infant dyads. *Developmental Psychobiology* 59, 15–25.

Ostrov, J. M., Woods, K. E., Jansen, E. A., et al. (2004). An observational study of delivered and received aggression, gender, and social-psychological adjustment in preschool: "This white crayon doesn't work." *Early Childhood Research Quarterly* 19, 355–371.

Palama, A., Malsert, J., & Gentaz, E. (2018). Are 6-month-old human infants able to transfer emotional information (happy or angry) from voices to faces? An eye-tracking study. *PLoS ONE* 13.

Paquette, D. (2004). Theorizing the father-child relationship: Mechanisms and developmental outcomes. *Human Development* 47, 193–219.

Pérez-Edgar, K., & Fox, N. (2000). The impact of frontal asymmetry and attentional control on social reticence. Paper presented at the Poster presented at the International Conference on Infant Studies: Brighton, England.

Pérez-Edgar, K., Bar-Haim, Y., McDermott, J. M., et al. (2010). Attention biases to threat and behavioral inhibition in early childhood shape adolescent social withdrawal. *Emotion* 10, 349–357.

Pérez-Edgar, K., Taber-Thomas, B., Auday, E., & Morales, S. (2014). Temperament and attention as core mechanisms in the early emergence of anxiety. In *Children and Emotion* (Vol. 26, pp. 42–56). Karger Publishers.

Perry, N. B., Calkins, S. D., & Bell, M. A. (2016). Indirect effects of maternal sensitivity on infant emotion regulation behaviors: The role of vagal withdrawal. *Infancy* 21, 128–153.

Perry, N., Calkins, S., Dollar, J., et al. (2018). Self-regulation as a predictor of patterns of change in externalizing behaviors from infancy to adolescence. *Development and Psychopathology* 30, 497–510.

Piaget, J. (1932). *The Language and Thought of the Child, 1926; Judgment and Reasoning in the Child, 1928; The Child's Conception of the World,*

1929; The Child's Conception of Physical Causality, 1930; The Moral Judgment of the Child, 1932. Harcourt, Brace: Oxford, United Kingdom.

Porter, C. L., Jones, B. L., Evans, C. A., & Robinson, C. C. (2009). A comparative study of arm-restraint methodology: Differential effects of mother and stranger restrainers on infants' distress reactivity at 6 and 9 months of age. *Infancy* 14, 306–324.

Posada, G., Gao, Y., Wu, F., et al. (1995). The secure-base phenomenon across cultures: Children's behavior, mothers' preferences, and experts' concepts. *Monographs of the Society for Research in Child Development* 60, 27–48.

Posner, M. I., & Rothbart, M. K. (2009). Toward a physical basis of attention and self-regulation. *Physics of Life Reviews* 6, 103–120.

Poulton, R., & Menzies, R. G. (2002). Non-associative fear acquisition: A review of the evidence from retrospective and longitudinal research. *Behaviour Research and Therapy* 40, 127–149.

Premack, D., & Premack, A. J. (1994). Levels of causal understanding in chimpanzees and children. *Cognition* 50, 347–362.

Putnam, S. P., Gartstein, M. A., & Rothbart, M. K. (2006). Measurement of fine-grained aspects of toddler temperament: The early childhood behavior questionnaire. *Infant Behavior and Development* 29, 386–401.

Putnam, S. P., Sanson, A. V., & Rothbart, M. K. (2002). Child temperament and parenting. *Handbook of Parenting* 1, 255–277.

Reschke, P., Walle, E., Flom, R., & Guenther, D. (2017). Twelve-month-old infants' sensitivity to others' emotions following positive and negative events. *Infancy* 22, 874–881.

Rigato, S., Menon, E., Johnson, M. H., & Farroni, T. (2011) The interaction between gaze direction and facial expressions in newborns. *European Journal of Developmental Psychology* 8, 624–636.

Rochat, P., & Goubet, N. (1995). Development of sitting and reaching in 5- to 6-month-old infants. *Infant Behavior and Development* 18, 53–68.

Rochat, P., & Hespos, S. J. (1997). Differential rooting response by neonates: Evidence for an early sense of self. *Early Development & Parenting* 6, 105–112.

Rothbart, M. K. (2007). Temperament, development, and personality. *Current Directions in Psychological Science* 16, 207–212.

Rothbart, M. K., & Bates, J. E. (2006). Temperament. In N. Eisenberg, W. Damon, & R. M. Lerner (Eds.), *Handbook of Child Psychology: Vol. 3: Social, Emotional, and Personality Development* (pp. 99–166). John Wiley & Sons Inc.: Hoboken, NJ.

Rothbart, M. K., Derryberry, D., & Hershey, K. (2000). Stability of temperament in childhood: Laboratory infant assessment to parent report at seven years. In *Temperament and Personality Development across the Life Span* (pp. 85–119). Lawrence Erlbaum Associates Publishers: Hillsdale, NJ.

Rothbart, M. K., Posner, M. I., & Boylan, A. (1990). Regulatory mechanisms in infant development. In J. T. Enns (Ed.), *Advances in Psychology* (Vol. 69, pp. 47–66): North-Holland.

Rovee-Collier, C. (1989). The joy of kicking: Memories, motives, and mobiles. In P. R. Solomon, G. R. Goethals, C. M. Kelley, & B. R. Stephens (Eds.), *Memory: Interdisciplinary Approaches* (pp. 151–180). Springer: New York.

Ruba, A. L., & Repacholi, B. M. (2019). Do preverbal infants understand discrete facial expressions of emotion? *Emotion Review*.

Ruba, A. L., Meltzoff, A. N., & Repacholi, B. M. (2019). How do you feel? Preverbal infants match negative emotions to events. *Developmental Psychology* 55, 1138–1149.

Rubin, J. Z., Provenzano, F. J., & Luria, Z. (1974). The eye of the beholder: Parents' views on sex of newborns. *American Journal of Orthopsychiatry* 44, 512–519.

Ruvolo, P., Messinger, D., & Movellan, J. (2015). Infants time their smiles to make their moms smile. *PLoS ONE* 10.

Saarni, C., Campos, J. J., Camras, L. A., & Witherington, D. (2007). Emotional development: Action, communication, and understanding. *Handbook of Child Psychology*, 3.

Sagi, A., IJzendoorn, M. H., Aviezer, O., et al. (1995). Attachments in a multiple-caregiver and multiple-infant environment: The case of the Israeli Kibbutzim. *Monographs of the Society for Research in Child Development* 60, 71–91.

Salley, B. J., & Dixon, W. E. (2007). Temperamental and joint attentional predictors of language development. *Merrill-Palmer Quarterly* 53, 131–154.

Scheper-Hughes, N. (1987). *Child Survival: Anthropological Perspectives on the Treatment and Maltreatment of Children* (Vol. 11). Springer Science & Business Media: New York.

Seligman, M. E. (1971). Phobias and preparedness. *Behavior Therapy* 2, 307–320.

Shariff, A. F., & Tracy, J. L. (2011). What are emotion expressions for? *Current Directions in Psychological Science* 20, 395–399.

Siqueland, E. R., & Delucua, C. A. (1969). Visual reinforcement of nonnutritive sucking in human infants. *Science* 165, 1144–1146.

Skerry, A., & Spelke, E. (2014). Preverbal infants identify emotional reactions that are incongruent with goal outcomes. *Cognition* 130, 204–216.

Solomon, J., & George, C. (Eds.). (2011). *Disorganized Attachment and Caregiving.* Guilford Press: New York.

Sorce, J. F., Emde, R. N., Campos, J. J., & Klinert, M. D. (1985). Maternal emotional signaling: Its effect on the visual cliff behavior of 1-year-olds. *Developmental Psychology* 21, 195–200.

Spitz, R. A. (1945). Hospitalism; An inquiry into the genesis of psychiatric conditions in early childhood. *The Psychoanalytic Study of the Child* 1, 53–74.

Spitz, R. A. (1965). *The First Year of Life: A Psychoanalytic Study of Normal and Deviant Development of Object Relations.* International Universities Press: Oxford, United Kingdom.

Sroufe, L. A. (1996). *Emotional Development: The Organization of Emotional Life in the Early Years* (Cambridge Studies in Social and Emotional Development). Cambridge University Press: New York.

Sroufe, L. A., Egeland, B., Carlson, E., & Collins, W. A. (2005). Placing early attachment experiences in developmental context. In *Attachment from Infancy to Adulthood: The Major Longitudinal Studies* (pp. 48–70).

Stansbury, K., & Sigman, M. (2000). Responses of preschoolers in two frustrating episodes: Emergence of complex strategies for emotion regulation. *The Journal of Genetic Psychology* 161, 182–202.

Stapel, J. C., Wijk, I., Bekkering, H., & Hunnius, S. (2017). Eighteen-month-old infants show

distinct electrophysiological responses to their own faces. *Developmental Science* 20, e12437.

Stennes, L. M., Burch, M. M., Sen, M. G., & Bauer, P. J. (2005). A longitudinal study of gendered vocabulary and communicative action in young children. *Developmental Psychology* 41, 75–88.

Stern, M., & Karraker, K. H. (1989). Sex stereotyping of infants: A review of gender labeling studies. *Sex Roles* 20, 501–522.

Stifter, C. A., & Braungart, J. M. (1995). The regulation of negative reactivity in infancy: Function and development. *Developmental Psychology* 31, 448–455.

Stifter, C. A., & Spinrad, T. L. (2002). The effect of excessive crying on the development of emotion regulation. *Infancy* 3, 133–152.

Strang, N. M., Hanson, J. L., & Pollak, S. D. (2012). The importance of biological methods in linking social experince with social and emotional development. *Monographs of the Society for Research in Child Development* 77, 61–66.

Suárez-Orozco, C., Todorova, I. L. G., & Louie, J. (2002). Making up for lost time: The experience of separation and reunification among immigrant families. *Family Process* 41, 625–643.

Sullivan, M. W., & Lewis, M. (2003). Contextual determinants of anger and other negative expressions in young infants. *Developmental Psychology* 39, 693–705.

Super, C. M., & Harkness, S. (1986). The developmental niche: A conceptualization at the interface of child and culture. *International Journal of Behavioral Development* 9, 545–569.

Susskind, J. M., Lee, D. H., Cusi, A., et al. (2008). Expressing fear enhances sensory acquisition. *Nature Neuroscience* 11, 843.

Svetlova, M., Nichols, S. R., & Brownell, C. A. (2010). Toddlers' prosocial behavior: From instrumental to empathic to altruistic helping. *Child Development* 81, 1814–1827.

Thrasher, C., & LoBue, V. (2016). Do infants find snakes aversive? Infants' physiological responses to "fear-relevant" stimuli. *Journal of Experimental Child Psychology* 142, 382–390.

Thomas, A., & Chess, S. (1977). *Temperament and Development.* Brunner/Mazel: Oxford, United Kingdom.

Thomas, A., Chess, S., & Birch, H. G. (1970). The origin of personality. *Scientific American* 223, 102–109.

Tracy, Jessica L., Robins, R. W., & Tangney, J. P. (Eds.). (2013) *The Self-Conscious Emotions: Theory and Research.* Guilford Press: New York.

Ursache, A., Blair, C., Stifter, C., & Voegtline, K. (2013). Emotional reactivity and regulation in infancy interact to predict executive functioning in early childhood. *Developmental Psychology* 49, 127–137.

Vaillant-Molina, M., Bahrick, L. E., & Flom, R. (2013). Young infants match facial and vocal emotional expressions of other infants. *Infancy* 18, E97–E111.

Vaish, A., Carpenter, M., & Tomasello, M. (2009). Sympathy through affective perspective taking and its relation to prosocial behavior in toddlers. *Developmental Psychology* 45, 534–543.

Valiente, C., Lemery-Chalfant, K., & Swanson, J. (2010). Prediction of kindergartners' academic achievement from their effortful control and emotionality: Evidence for direct and moderated relations. *Journal of Educational Psychology* 102, 550–560.

Van de Vondervoort, J. W., & Hamlin, J. K. (2016). Evidence for intuitive morality: Preverbal infants make sociomoral evaluations. *Child Development Perspectives* 10, 143–148.

van Ijzendoorn, M. H., & Sagi, A. (2010). Cross-cultural patterns of attachment: Universal and contextual dimensions. In *Handbook of Attachment: Theory, Research, and Clinical Applications* (pp. 713–734). Guilford Press: New York.

Vandell, D. L., Wilson, K. S., & Buchanan, N. R. (1980). Peer interaction in the first year of life: An examination of its structure, content, and sensitivity to toys. *Child Development* 51, 481–488.

Wachs, T. D. (2006). The nature, etiology, and consequences of individual differences in temperament. In *Child Psychology: A Handbook of Contemporary Issues* (pp. 27–52). Psychology Press: New York.

Warneken, F. (2015). Precocious prosociality: Why do young children help? *Child Development Perspectives* 9, 1–6.

Warneken, F., & Tomasello, M. (2007). Helping and cooperation at 14 months of age. *Infancy* 11, 271–294.

Warneken, F., & Tomasello, M. (2008). Extrinsic rewards undermine altruistic tendencies in 20-month-olds. *Developmental Psychology* 44, 1785–1788.

Weinberg, M. K., Olson, K. L., Beeghly, M., & Tronick, E. Z. (2006). Making up is hard to do, especially for mothers with high levels of depressive symptoms and their infant sons. *Journal of Child Psychology and Psychiatry* 47, 670–683.

Witherington, D., Campos, J. J., & Hertenstein, M. J. (2007). Principles of emotion and its development in infancy. *Blackwell Handbook of Infant Development*.

Wörmann, V., Holodynski, M., Kärtner, J., & Keller, H. (2012). A cross-cultural comparison of the development of the social smile: A longitudinal study of maternal and infant imitation in 6- and 12-week-old infants. *Infant Behavior and Development* 35, 335–347.

Zarbatany, L., & Lamb, M. E. (1985). Social referencing as a function of information source: Mothers versus strangers. *Infant Behavior and Development* 8, 25–33.

Zosuls, K. M., Field, R. D., Martin, C. L., et al. (2014). Gender-based relationship efficacy: Children's self-perceptions in intergroup contexts. *Child Development* 85, 1663–1676.

Zosuls, K. M., Ruble, D. N., Tamis-LeMonda, C. S., et al. (2009). The acquisition of gender labels in infancy: Implications for gender-typed play. *Developmental Psychology* 45, 688–701.

Chapter 8

Acebo, C., Sadeh, A., Seifer, R., et al. (2005). Sleep/wake patterns derived from activity monitoring and maternal report for healthy 1- to 5-year-old children. *Sleep* 28, 1568–1577.

Administration for Children and Families (2019). *Child abuse, neglect data released. Child Maltreatment Report, 28th ed.* United States Department of Health and Human Services.

Aelion, C. M., Davis, H. T., Lawson, A. B., et al. (2013). Associations between soil lead concentrations and populations by race/ethnicity and income-to-poverty ratio in urban and rural areas. *Environmental Geochemistry and Health* 35, 1–12.

Annett, J. (2002). Subjective rating scales: science or art? *Ergonomics* 45, 966–987.

Anzman-Frasca, S., Savage, J. S., Marini, M. E., et al. (2012). Repeated exposure and associative conditioning promote preschool children's liking of vegetables. *Appetite* 58, 543–553.

Attwell, D., & Gibb, A. (2005). Neuroenergetics and the kinetic design of excitatory synapses. *Nature Reviews Neuroscience* 6, 841.

Bakker, N. E., Kuppens, R. J., Siemensma, E. P. C., et al. (2013). Eight years of growth hormone treatment in children with Prader-Willi syndrome: Maintaining the positive effects. *The Journal of Clinical Endocrinology & Metabolism* 98, 4013–4022.

Bates, J. E., Viken, R. J., Alexander, D. B., et al. (2002). Sleep and adjustment in preschool children: Sleep diary reports by mothers relate to behavior reports by teachers. *Child Development* 73, 62–75.

Berchick, E. R., & Mykta, L. (2019). Children's public health insurance coverage lower than in 2017. *Health*, United States Census Bureau.

Berens, A.E., Kumar, S., Tofail, F. et al. (2019). Cumulative psychosocial risk and early child development: validation and use of the Childhood Psychosocial Adversity Scale in global health research. *Pediatric Research* 86, 766–775.

Berry, D., Blair, C., & Granger, D. A. (2016). Child care and cortisol across infancy and toddlerhood: Poverty, peers, and developmental timing. *Family Relations* 65, 51–72.

Birch, L. L., Fisher, J. O., & Davison, K. K. (2003). Learning to overeat: Maternal use of restrictive feeding practices promotes girls' eating in the absence of hunger. *American Journal of Clinical Nutrition* 78, 215–220.

Birch, L. L., Zimmerman, S. I., & Hind, H. (1980). The influence of social-affective context on the formation of children's food preferences. *Child Development* 51, 856–861.

Bishop, D. V. M. (2005). Handedness and specific language impairment: A study of 6-year-old twins. *Developmental Psychobiology* 46, 362–369.

Black, R. E., Williams, S. M., Jones, I. E., & Goulding, A. (2002). Children who avoid drinking cow milk have low dietary calcium intakes and poor bone health. *American Journal of Clinical Nutrition* 76, 675–680.

Blair, C., Zelazo, P. D., & Greenberg, M. T. (2016). The measurement of executive function in early childhood. *Developmental Neuropsychology* 28, 561–571.

Blaszczak-Boxe, A. (2014). Taller, fatter, older: How humans have changed in 100 years. *Live Science*.

Blumberg, M. S., Seelke, A. M. H., Lowen, S. B., & Karlsson, K. Æ. (2005). Dynamics of sleep-wake cyclicity in developing rats. *Proceedings of the National Academy of Sciences USA* 102, 14860–14864.

Bogin, B. (2013). The evolution of human growth. In N. Cameron & B. Bogin (Eds.), *Human Growth and Development*, 2nd ed. (pp. 287–324). Academic Press: Boston, MA.

Borse, N. N., Gilchrist, J., Dellinger, A. M., et al. (2009). Unintentional childhood injuries in the United States: Key findings from the CDC childhood injury report. *Journal of Safety Research* 40, 71–74.

Brenzel, L., Wolfson, L. J., Fox-Rushby, J., et al. (2006). *Vaccine-Preventable Diseases* (2nd ed.). World Bank: Washington DC.

Brewer, J. M. (2002). State of the world's vaccines and immunization. WHO, UNICEF and the World Bank. Geneva: World Health Organization. *Transactions of The Royal Society of Tropical Medicine and Hygiene* 97, 181.

Budge, S., Parker, A. H., Hutchings, P. T., & Garbutt, C. (2019). Environmental enteric dysfunction and child stunting. *Nutrition Reviews* 77, 240–253.

Butchart, A., Phinney Harvey, A., Mian, M., et al. (2006). Preventing child maltreatment: A guide to taking action and generating evidence.

Canadian Department of Justice. (2016). *Risk Factors for Children in Situations of Family Violence in the Context of Separation and Divorce.*

Cappuccio, F. P., Taggart, F. M., Kandala, N.-B., et al. (2008). Meta-analysis of short sleep duration and obesity in children and adults. *Sleep* 31, 619–626.

Caprio, S., Daniels, S. R., Drewnowski, A., et al. (2008). Influence of race, ethnicity, and culture on childhood obesity: Implications for prevention and treatment. *Obesity* 16, 2566–2577.

Carlier, M., Doyen, A. L., & Lamard, C. (2006). Midline crossing: Developmental trend from 3 to 10 years of age in a preferential card-reaching task. *Brain and Cognition* 61, 255–261.

Case, A., & Paxson, C. (2006). Children's health and social mobility, *The Future of Children* 16, 151–173.

Casey, B. J., Tottenham, N., Listen, C., & Durston, S. (2005). Imaging the developing brain: What have we learned about cognitive development? *Trends in Cognitive Sciences* 9, 104–110.

Chaparro, M. P., Whaley, S. E., Crespi, C. M., et al. (2014). Influences of the neighbourhood food environment on adiposity of low-income preschool-aged children in Los Angeles County: a longitudinal study. *Journal of Epidemiology and Community Health* 68, 1027–1033.

Chaudry, A., & Wimer, C. (2016). Poverty is not just an indicator: The relationship between income, poverty, and child well-being. *Academic Pediatrics* 16, S23–S29.

Chen, X., Beydoun, M. A., & Wang, Y. (2008). Is sleep duration associated with childhood obesity? a systematic review and Meta-analysis. *Obesity* 16, 265–274.

Child Trends. (2014). Unintentional Injury. Retrieved from https://www.childtrends.org/indicators/unintentional-injuries/

Cicchetti, D. (2016). Socioemotional, personality, and biological development: illustrations from a multilevel developmental psychopathology perspective on child maltreatment. *Annual Review of Psychology* 67, 187–211.

Cicchetti, D., & Doyle, C. (2016). Child maltreatment, attachment and psychopathology: mediating relations. *World Psychiatry* 15, 89–90.

Coren, S., & Porac, C. (1977). Fifty centuries of right-handedness: The historical record. *Science* 198, 631–632.

Dales, L., Hammer, S., & Smith, N. J. (2001). Time trends in autism and in MMR immunization coverage in California. *JAMA* 285, 1183–1185.

Diamond, A. (2000). Close interrelation of motor development and cognitive development and of the cerebellum and prefrontal cortex. *Child Development* 71, 44–56.

Dietrich, K. N., Ris, M. D., Succop, P. A., et al. (2001). Early exposure to lead and juvenile delinquency. *Neurotoxicology and Teratology* 23, 511–518.

Dooyema, C., Jernigan, J., Warnock, et al. (2018). *Childhood Obesity* 14, S22–S31.

Durston, S., Thomas, K. M., Yang, Y., et al. (2002). A neural basis for the development of inhibitory control. *Developmental Science* 5, F9–F16.

El-Sheikh, M., & Sadeh, A. (2015). I. Sleep and development: Introduction to the monograph. *Monographs of the Society for Research in Child Development* 80, 1–14.

Engle, P. L., Black, M. M., Behrman, J. R., et al. (2007). Strategies to avoid the loss of developmental potential in more than 200 million children in the developing world. *The Lancet* 369, 229–242.

Fagard, J., & Lockman, J. J. (2005). The effect of task constraints on infants' (bi)manual strategy for grasping and exploring objects. *Infant Behavior and Development* 28, 305–315.

Fang, X., Brown, D. S., Florence, C. S., & Mercy, J. A. (2012). The economic burden of child maltreatment in the United States and implications for prevention. *Child Abuse & Neglect* 36, 156–165.

Feikin, D. R., Flannery, B., Hamel, M. J., et al. (2006). Vaccines for children in low-and middle-income countries. *Reproductive, Maternal, Newborn, and Child Health*, 187.

Campbell, I. G., Grimm, K. J., Bie, E. D., & Feinberg, I. (2012). Sex, puberty and the adolescent delta EEG decline. *Proceedings of the National Academy of Sciences* 109, 5740–5743.

Dowd, J. B., Zajacova, A., & Aiello, A. (2009). Early origins of health disparities: Burden of infection, health, and socioeconomic status in U.S. children. *Social Sciences and Medicine* 68, 699–707.

Evans, G. W., & Cassells, R. C. (2014). Childhood poverty, cumulative risk exposure, and mental health in emerging adults. *Clinical Psychological Science* 2, 287–296.

Finkelhor, D., Ormrod, R., Turner, H., & Hamby, S. L. (2005). The victimization of children and youth: A comprehensive, national survey. *Child Maltreatment* 10, 5–25.

Finkelhor, D., Turner, H. A., Shattuck, A., & Hamby, S. L. (2013). Violence, crime, and abuse exposure in a national sample of children and youth: An update. *JAMA Pediatrics* 167, 614–621.

Finkelhor, D., Saito, K., & Jones, L. (2018). Updated trends in child maltreatment 2016. Crimes against Children Research Center.

Fischman, M. G., Moore, J. B., & Steele, K. H. (1992). Children's one-hand catching as a function of age, gender, and ball location. *Research Quarterly for Exercise and Sport* 63, 349–355.

Fisher, J. O., & Birch, L. L. (1995). Fat preferences and fat consumption of 3- to 5-year-old children are related to parental adiposity. *Journal of the Academy of Nutrition and Dietetics* 95, 759–764.

Fisher, J. O., & Birch, L. L. (1999). Restricting access to foods and children's eating. *Appetite* 32, 405–419.

Fisher, J. O., Mitchell, D. C., Smiciklas-Wright, H., & Birch, L. L. (2001). Maternal milk consumption predicts the tradeoff between milk and soft drinks in young girls' diets. *The Journal of Nutrition* 131, 246–250.

Flores, G., Olson, L., & Tomany-Korman, S. C. (2005). Racial and ethnic disparities in early childhood health and health care. *Pediatrics* 115, e183–e193.

Foundation, N. S. (2004). *2004 Sleep in America Poll*. NW: National Sleep Foundation Retrieved from https://sleepfoundation.org/sleep-polls-data/sleep-in-america-poll/2004-children-and-sleep.

Frank, M. G., Issa, N. P., & Stryker, M. P. (2001). Sleep enhances plasticity in the developing visual cortex. *Neuron* 30, 275–287.

Franken, P., & Dijk, D. J. (2009). Circadian clock genes and sleep homeostasis. *European Journal of Neuroscience* 29, 1820–1829.

Fujioka, T., Trainor, L. J., & Ross, B. (2008). Simultaneous pitches are encoded separately in auditory cortex: an MMNm study. *Neuroreport* 19, 361–366.

Gallahue, D., & Ozmun, J. (1995). Motor development. *Adapted Physical Education and Sport* 12, 253–269.

Ganji, V., Hampl, J. S., & Betts, N. M. (2003). Race-, gender- and age-specific differences in dietary micronutrient intakes of US children. *International Journal of Food Sciences and Nutrition* 54, 485–490.

Garn, S. M., & LaVelle, M. (1985). Two-decade follow-up of fatness in early childhood. *Chance* 48, 27.

Gershoff, E. T. (2016). Should parents' physical punishment of children be considered a source of toxic stress that affects brain development? *Family Relations* 65, 151–162.

Geserick, M., Vogel, M., Gausche, R., et al. (2018). Acceleration of BMI in early childhood and risk of sustained obesity. *New England Journal of Medicine* 379, 1303–1312.

Glaser, D. (2000). Child abuse and neglect and the brain—A review. *The Journal of Child Psychology and Psychiatry and Allied Disciplines* 41, 97–116.

Grantham-McGregor, S., Cheung, Y. B., Cueto, et al. (2007). Developmental potential in the first 5 years for children in developing countries. *The Lancet* 369, 60–70.

Grissmer, D., Grimm, K. J., Aiyer, S. M., et al. (2010). Fine motor skills and early comprehension of the world: Two new school readiness indicators. *Developmental Psychology* 46, 1008–1017.

Grossman, D. C. (2000). The history of injury control and the epidemiology of child and adolescent injuries. *The Future of Children* 10, 23–52.

Guerrero, A.D., Mao, C., Fuller, B., et al. (2016). Racial and ethnic disparities in early childhood obesity: Growth trajectories in body mass index. *Journal of Racial and Ethnic Health Disparities* 3, 129–137.

Guilleminault, C., Palombini, L., Pelayo, R., & Chervin, R. D. (2003). Sleepwalking and sleep terrors in prepubertal children: What triggers them? *Pediatrics* 111, e17–e25.

Hatton, T. J. (2017). Stature and sibship: historical evidence. *The History of the Family* 22, 175–195.

Hepper, P. G. (2013). The developmental origins of laterality: Fetal handedness. *Developmental Psychology* 55, 588–595.

Hill, H. A., Elam-Evans, L. D., Yankey, D., et al. (2018). Vaccination coverage among children aged 19–35 Months - United States, 2017. *MMWR* 67, 1123–1128.

Hill, E. L., & Bishop, D. V. M. (1998). A reaching test reveals weak hand preference in specific language impairment and developmental coordination disorder. *Laterality: Asymmetries of Body, Brain and Cognition* 3, 295–310.

Hill, E. L., & Khanem, F. (2009). The development of hand preference in children: The effect of task demands and links with manual dexterity. *Brain and Cognition* 71, 99–107.

Hinojosa, T., Sheu, C. F., & Michel, G. F. (2003). Infant hand-use preferences for grasping objects contributes to the development of a hand-use preference for manipulating objects. *Developmental Psychobiology: The Journal of the International Society for Developmental Psychobiology* 43, 328–334.

Horton, W. A., Hall, J. G., & Hecht, J. T. (2007). Achondroplasia. *The Lancet* 370, 163–172.

Howard, B. J., & Wong, J. (2001). Sleep disorders. *Pediatrics in Review* 22, 327–342.

Howard, T., & William, P. D. (2005). Obesity and student performance at school. *Journal of School Health* 75, 291–295.

Hubbs-Tait, L., Culp, A. M., Huey, E., et al. (2002). Relation of head start attendance to children's cognitive and social outcomes: Moderation by family risk. *Early Childhood Research Quarterly* 17, 539–558.

Hursti, U.-K. K. (1999). Factors influencing children's food choice. *Annals of Medicine* 31, 26–32.

Hussey, J. M., Chang, J. J., & Kotch, J. B. (2006). Child maltreatment in the united states: Prevalence, risk factors, and adolescent health consequences. *Pediatrics* 118, 933–942.

Huttenlocher, P. R. (2002). *Neural Plasticity: The Effects of Environment on the Development of the Cerebral Cortex.* Harvard University Press: Cambridge, MA.

Iglowstein, I., Jenni, O. G., Molinari, L., & Largo, R. H. (2003). Sleep duration from infancy to adolescence: Reference values and generational trends. *Pediatrics* 111, 302–307.

Jha, S. K., Jones, B. E., Coleman, T., et al. (2005). Sleep-dependent plasticity requires cortical activity. *The Journal of Neuroscience* 25, 9266–9274.

Johnson, M. H. (1998). The neural basis of cognitive development. In *Handbook of Child Psychology: Volume 2: Cognition, Perception, and Language* (pp. 1–49). John Wiley & Sons Inc.: Hoboken, NJ.

Johnson, N. B., Hayes, L. D., Brown, K., et al. (2014). CDC National Health Report: leading causes of morbidity and mortality and associated behavioral risk and protective factors—United States, 2005–2013.

Jud, A., Fegert, J. M., & Finkelhor, D. (2016). On the incidence and prevalence of child maltreatment: a research agenda. *Child and Adolescent Psychiatry and Mental Health* 10, 17.

Juraska, J. M., Henderson, C., & Müller, J. (1984). Differential rearing experience, gender, and radial maze performance. *Developmental Psychobiology* 17, 209–215.

Kleitman, N., & Engelmann, T. G. (1953). Sleep characteristics of infants. *Journal of Applied Physiology* 6, 269–282.

Kolb, B., & Whishaw, I. Q. (2009). *Fundamentals of Human Neuropsychology.* Macmillan: New York.

Kumanyika, S. K. (2008). Environmental influences on childhood obesity: Ethnic and cultural influences in context. *Physiology & Behavior* 94, 61–70.

Kurth, S., Olini, N., Huber, R., & LeBourgeois, M. (2015). Sleep and early cortical development. *Current Sleep Medicine Reports* 1, 64–73.

Kurth, S., Ringli, M., Geiger, A., et al. (2010). Mapping of cortical activity in the first two decades of life: A high-density sleep electroencephalogram study. *The Journal of Neuroscience* 30, 13211–13219.

Lampl, M., & Thompson, A. L. (2007). Growth chart curves do not describe individual growth biology. *American Journal of Human Biology* 19, 643–653.

Lampl, M., Veldhuis, J. D., & Johnson, M. L. (1992). Saltation and stasis: A model of human growth. *Science* 258, 801–803.

Latz, S., Wolf, A. W., & Lozoff, B. (1999). Co-sleeping in context: Sleep practices and problems in young children in japan and the united states. *Archives of Pediatrics & Adolescent Medicine* 153, 339–346.

Lee, L. A., Franzel, L., Atwell, J., et al. (2013). The estimated mortality impact of vaccinations forecast to be administered during 2011–2020 in 73 countries supported by the GAVI Alliance. *Vaccine* 31, B61–B72.

Leyva, D., Reese, E., & Wiser, M. (2012). Early understanding of the functions of print: Parent–child interaction and preschoolers' notating skills. *First Language* 32, 301–323.

Lieberman, J., Chakos, M., Wu, H., et al. (2001). Longitudinal study of brain morphology in first episode schizophrenia. *Biological Psychiatry* 49, 487–499.

Linares, L. O., Heeren, T., Bronfman, E., et al. (2001). A mediational model for the impact of exposure to community violence on early child behavior problems. *Child Development* 72, 639–652.

Liu, J., Raine, A., Venables, P. H., Dalais, C., & Mednick, S. A. (2003). Malnutrition at age 3 years and lower cognitive ability at age 11 years: Independence from psychosocial adversity. *Archives of Pediatrics & Adolescent Medicine* 157, 593–600.

Lynch, M., Manly, J. T., & Cicchetti, D. (2015). A multilevel prediction of physiological response to challenge: Interactions among child maltreatment, neighborhood crime, endothelial nitric oxide synthase gene (eNOS), and GABA(A) receptor subunit alpha-6 gene (GABRA6). *Development and Psychopathology* 27, 1471–1487.

Lynn, R. (1990). The role of nutrition in secular increases in intelligence. *Personality and Individual Differences* 11, 273–285.

Manly, J. T. (2005). Advances in research definitions of child maltreatment. *Child Abuse & Neglect* 29, 425–439.

Margolin, G., & Gordis, E. B. (2000). The effects of family and community violence on children. *Annual Review of Psychology* 51, 445–479.

Mathias, K. C., Rolls, B. J., Birch, L. L., et al. (2012). Serving larger portions of fruits and vegetables together at dinner promotes intake of both foods among young children. *Journal of the Academy of Nutrition and Dietetics* 112, 266–270.

McNeill, D. G. (2019). New York City is requiring vaccinations against measles. Can officials do that? *New York Times*, April 9.

Medland, S. E., Duffy, D. L., Wright, M. J., et al. (2009). Genetic influences on handedness: Data from 25,732 Australian and Dutch twin families. *Neuropsychologia* 47, 330–337.

Meltzer, L. J., & Mindell, J. A. (2007). Relationship between child sleep disturbances and maternal sleep, mood, and parenting stress: A pilot study. *Journal of Family Psychology* 21, 67–73.

Michel, G. F. (1983). *Development of Hand-Use Preference*. Academic Press: New York.

Mickalide, A., & Carr, K. (2012). Safe kids worldwide. *Pediatric Clinics* 59, 1367–1380.

Miller, J. E. (2000). The effects of race/ethnicity and income on early childhood asthma prevalence and health care use. *American Journal of Public Health* 90, 428–430.

Morelli, G. A., Rogoff, B., Oppenheim, D., & Goldsmith, D. (1992). Cultural variation in infants' sleeping arrangements: Questions of independence. *Developmental Psychology* 28, 604–613.

Nafstad, P., Hagen, J. A., Øie, L., et al. (1999). Day care centers and respiratory health. *Pediatrics* 103, 753–758.

NCD Risk Factor Collaboration (2016). A century of trends in adult human height. *eLife*.

Needleman, H. L., Schell, A., Bellinger, D., et al. (1990). The long-term effects of exposure to low doses of lead in childhood. *New England Journal of Medicine* 322, 83–88.

Nelson, C. A. I., Thomas, K.M., & de Haan, Michelle. (2007). Neural bases of cognitive development. In *Handbook of Child Psychology*.

Nelson, E. L., Campbell, J. M., & Michel, G. F. (2014). Early handedness in infancy predicts language ability in toddlers. *Developmental Psychology* 50, 809–814.

New, R. S., & Richman, A. L. (1996). Maternal beliefs and infant care practices in Italy and the United States. In *Parents' Cultural Belief Systems: Their Origins, Expressions, and Consequences* (pp. 385–404).

Niehaus, M. D., Moore, S. R., Patrick, P. D., et al. (2002). Early childhood diarrhea is associated with diminished cognitive function 4 to 7 years later in children in a northeast Brazilian shantytown. *The American Journal of Tropical Medicine and Hygiene* 66, 590–593.

Noonan, K. J., Farnum, C. E., Leiferman, E. M., et al. (2004). Growing pains: Are they due to increased growth during recumbency as documented in a lamb model? *Journal of Pediatric Orthopedics* 24, 726–731.

Ogden, C. L., Carroll, M. D., Curtin, L. R., et al. (2010). Prevalence of high body mass index in us children and adolescents, 2007–2008. *JAMA* 303, 242–249.

Onis, M., & Branca, F. (2016). Childhood stunting: a global perspective. *Maternal & Child Nutrition* 12, 12–26.

Ottaviano, S., Giannotti, F., Cortesi, F., et al. (1996). Sleep characteristics in healthy children from birth to 6 years of age in the urban area of Rome. *Sleep* 19, 1–3.

Pahlevanian, A. A., & Ahmadizadeh, Z. (2014). Relationship between gender and motor skills in preschoolers. *Middle East Journal of Rehabilitation and Health* 1.

Perrin, J. M., Boat, T. F., & Kelleher, K. J. (2016). The influence of health care policies on children's health and development. *Social Policy Report* 29, 3–17.

Phadke, V. K., Bednarczyk, R. A., Salmon, D. A., & Omer, S. B. (2016). Association between vaccine refusal and vaccine-preventable diseases in the united states: A review of measles and pertussis. *JAMA* 315, 1149–1158.

Previc, F. H. (1991). A general theory concerning the prenatal origins of cerebral lateralization in humans. *Psychological Review* 98, 299–334.

Quas, J. A., Bauer, A., & Boycem, W. T. (2004). Physiological reactivity, social support, and memory in early childhood. *Child Development* 75, 797–814.

Rachwani, J., Tamis-LeMonda, C. S., Lockman, J. J., et al. (2020). Learning the designed actions of everyday objects. *Journal of Experimental Psychology: General* 149, 67–78.

Reading, R., Bissell, S., Goldhagen, J., et al. (2009). Promotion of children's rights and prevention of child maltreatment. *Lancet* 373, 332–343.

Reilly, J. J., Armstrong, J., Dorosty, A. R., et al. (2005). Early life risk factors for obesity in childhood: cohort study. *BMJ* 330, 1357.

Richler, J., Luyster, R., Risi, S., et al. (2006). Is there a 'regressive phenotype' of autism spectrum disorder associated with the measles-mumps-rubella vaccine? A CPEA study. *Journal of Autism and Developmental Disorders* 36, 299–316.

Riva, D., & Giorgi, C. (2000). The cerebellum contributes to higher functions during development: Evidence from a series of children surgically treated for posterior fossa tumours. *Brain* 123, 1051–1061.

Rosenbaum, S., & Blum, R. (2015). How healthy are our children? *The Future of Children* 25.

Sadeh, A. (2007). Consequences of sleep loss or sleep disruption in children. *Sleep Medicine Clinics* 2, 513–520.

Sadeh, A., Mindell, J. A., Luedtke, K., & Wiegand, B. (2009). Sleep and sleep ecology in the first 3years: A web-based study. *Journal of Sleep Research* 18, 60–73.

Sekine, M., Yamagami, T., Handa, K., et al. (2002). A dose–response relationship between short sleeping hours and childhood obesity: results of the Toyama Birth Cohort Study. *Child: Care, Health and Development* 28, 163–170.

Serdula, M. K., Ivery, D., Coates, R. J., et al. (1993). Do obese children become obese adults? A review of the literature. *Preventive Medicine* 22, 167–177.

Shahinfar, A., Fox, N. A., & Leavitt, L. A. (2000). Preschool children's exposure to violence: Relation of behavior problems to parent and child reports. *American Journal of Orthopsychiatry* 70, 115–125.

Shan, Z. Y., Leiker, A. J., Onar-Thomas, A., et al. (2014). Cerebral glucose metabolism on positron emission tomography of children. *Human Brain Mapping* 35, 2297–2309.

Shea, B. T., & Bailey, R. C. (1996). Allometry and adaptation of body proportions and stature in African pygmies. *American Journal of Physical Anthropology* 100, 311–340.

Shonkoff, J. P., & Garner, A. S. (2012). The lifelong effects of early childhood adversity and toxic stress. *Pediatrics* 129, e232–e246.

Shonkoff, J. P., Garner, A. S., Siegel, B. S., et al. (2012). The lifelong effects of early childhood adversity and toxic stress. *Pediatrics* 129, e232–e246.

Sicotte, N. L., Woods, R. P., & Mazziotta, J. C. (1999). Handedness in twins: A meta-analysis. *Laterality: Asymmetries of Body, Brain and Cognition* 4, 265–286.

Sitnick, S. L., Goodlin-Jones, B. L., & Anders, T. F. (2008). The use of actigraphy to study sleep disorders in preschoolers: Some concerns about detection of nighttime awakenings. *Sleep* 31, 395–401.

Skinner, A. C., Ravanbakht, S. N., Skelton, J. A., et al. (2018). Prevalence of obesity and severe obesity in US children, 1999–2016. *Pediatrics* 141, e20173459.

Snell, E. K., Adam, E. K., & Duncan, G. J. (2007). Sleep and the body mass index and overweight status of children and adolescents. *Child Development* 78, 309–323.

Spijker, J. J. A., Camara, A. D., & Blanes, A. (2012). The health transition and biological living standards: Adult height and mortality in 20th-century Spain. *Economics & Human Biology* 10, 276–288.

Staples, A. D., Bates, J. E., & Petersen, I. T. (2015). Bedtime routines in early childhood: Prevalence consistency and associations with nighttime sleep. *Monographs of the Society for Research in Child Development* 80, 141–159.

Stehr-Green, P., Tull, P., Stellfeld, M., et al. (2003). Autism and thimerosal-containing vaccines. *American Journal of Preventive Medicine* 25, 101–106.

Steuerle, C. E. (2014). Dead men ruling: How to restore fiscal freedom and rescue our future. *Century Foundation Press.*

Stevens, G. A., Finuncane, M. M., et al. (2012). Trends in mild, moderate, and severe stunting and underweight, and progress towards MDG 1 in 141 developing countries: A systematic analysis of population representative data. *The Lancet* 380, 824–834.

Stretesky, P. B., & Lynch, M. J. (2001). The relationship between lead exposure and homicide. *Archives of Pediatrics & Adolescent Medicine* 155, 579–582.

Sullivan, S. A., & Birch, L. L. (1990). Pass the sugar, pass the salt: Experience dictates preference. *Developmental Psychology* 26, 546–551.

Tarren-Sweeney, M. (2006). Patterns of aberrant eating among preadolescent children in foster care. *J Abnorm Child Psychology* 34, 621–632.

Teicher, M. H., Andersen, S. L., Polcari, A., et al. (2003). The neurobiological consequences of early stress and childhood maltreatment. *Neuroscience & Biobehavioral Reviews* 27, 33–44.

Thapar, N., & Sanderson, I. R. (2004). Diarrhoea in children: an interface between developing and developed countries. *The Lancet* 363, 641–653.

Thomas, J. R., & French, K. E. (1985). Gender differences across age in motor performance: A meta-analysis. *Psychological Bulletin* 98, 260–282.

Thompson, P. M., Giedd, J. N., Woods, R. P., et al. (2000). Growth patterns in the developing brain detected by using continuum mechanical tensor maps. *Nature* 404, 190.

Thorpy, M. J., & Yager, J. (2001). *The Encyclopedia of Sleep and Sleep Disorders.* Infobase Publishing.

Tierney, A. L., & Nelson, C. A. (2009). Brain development and the role of experience in the early years. *Zero to Three* 30, 9–13.

Tononi, G., & Cirelli, C. (2003). Sleep and synaptic homeostasis: a hypothesis. *Brain Research Bulletin* 62, 143–150.

Tononi, G., & Cirelli, C. (2006). Sleep function and synaptic homeostasis. *Sleep Medicine Reviews* 10, 49–62.

Torpy, J. M., Campbell, A., & Glass, R. M. (2010). Chronic diseases of children. *JAMA* 303, 682.

Tost, H., Champagne, F. A., & Meyer-Lindenberg, A. (2015). Environmental influence in the brain, human welfare and mental health. *Nature Neuroscience* 18, 1421.

Trisha, H., Ching-Fan, S., & F., M. G. (2003). Infant hand-use preferences for grasping objects contributes to the development of a hand-use preference for manipulating objects. *Developmental Psychobiology* 43, 328–334.

Tsujimoto, S. (2008). The prefrontal cortex: Functional neural development during early childhood. *The Neuroscientist* 14, 345–358.

Turner, H. A., Finkelhor, D., & Ormrod, R. (2006). The effect of lifetime victimization on the mental health of children and adolescents. *Social Science & Medicine* 62, 13–27.

Tuyen, J. M., & Bisgard, K. (2000). Community setting: Centers for Disease Control and Prevention.

U.S. Department of Health and Human Services. (2014). *Child Maltreatment* 2014. Children's Bureau: Washington, DC. Retrieved from https://www.acf.hhs.gov/sites/default/files/cb/cm2014.pdf.

UNICEF. (2007). The State of the World's Children 2008: Child Survival (Vol. 8): UNICEF.

Volkow, N. D., Wang, G. J., Tomasi, D., & Baler, R. D. (2013). Obesity and addiction: Neurobiological overlaps. *Obesity Reviews* 14, 2–18.

Walker, S. P., Wachs, T. D., Grantham-McGregor, S., et al. (2011). Inequality in early childhood: Risk and protective factors for early child development. *The Lancet* 378, 1325–1338.

Ward, T. M., Gay, C., Anders, T. F., et al. (2007). Sleep and napping patterns in 3-to-5-year old children attending full-day childcare centers. *Journal of Pediatric Psychology* 33, 666–672.

Wilhelm, I., Diekelmann, S., & Born, J. (2008). Sleep in children improves memory performance on declarative but not procedural tasks. *Learning & Memory* 15, 373–377.

Wilhelm, I., Kurth, S., Ringli, M., et al. (2014). Sleep slow-wave activity reveals developmental changes in experience-dependent plasticity. *The Journal of Neuroscience* 34, 12568–12575.

Wilson, R. (1986). Twins: Genetic influence on growth. *Sport and Human Genetics*, 1–21.

Wong, M. M., Brower, K. J., Fitzgerald, H. E., & Zucker, R. A. (2004). Sleep problems in early childhood and early onset of alcohol and other drug use in adolescence. *Alcoholism: Clinical and Experimental Research* 28, 578–587.

World Health Organization. (2010). *World Health Statistics* 2010. World Health Organization.

World Health Organization. (2017). International Agency for Research on Cancer 2016. Available at: http://gco.iarc.fr/today/data/pdf/factsheets/cancers/cancer-fact-sheets-15. pdf. Accessed Jun 9, 2020.

Wosje, K. S., Khoury, P. R., Claytor, R. P., et al. (2010). Dietary patterns associated with fat and bone mass in young children. *American Journal of Clinical Nutrition* 92, 294–303.

Xie, L., Kang, H., Xu, Q., et al. (2013). Sleep drives metabolite clearance from the adult brain. *Science* 342, 373–377.

Yu, Z. B., Han, S. P., Cao, X. G., & Guo, X. R. (2010). Intelligence in relation to obesity: a systematic review and meta-analysis. *Obesity Reviews* 11, 656–670.

Chapter 9

Allen, M. L., Mattock, K., & Silva, M. (2014). Symbolic understanding of pictures and written words share a common source. *Journal of Cognition and Culture* 14, 187–198.

Arnold, D. S., & Whitehurst, G. J. (1994). Accelerating language development through picture book reading: A summary of dialogic reading and its effect. In D. K. Dickinson (Ed.), *Bridges to Literacy: Children, Families, and Schools* (pp. 103–128). Blackwell Publishing.

Astington, J. W., & Pelletier, J. (2005). Theory of mind, language, and learning in the early years: Developmental origins of school readiness. *The Development of Social Cognition and Communication*, 205–230.

Aukrust, V. G. (2004). Talk about talk with young children: pragmatic socialization in two communities in Norway and the US. *Journal of Child Language* 31, 177.

Baker, S. T., Leslie, A. M., Gallistel, C. R., & Hood, B. M. (2016). Bayesian change-point analysis reveals developmental change in a classic theory of mind task. *Cognitive Psychology* 91, 124–149.

Baron-Cohen, S., Leslie, A. M., & Frith, U. (1985). Does the autistic child have a "theory of mind." *Cognition* 21, 37–46.

Bauer, P. J. (2007). Event memory. *Handbook of Child Psychology*, 2.

Bauer, P. J. (2008). Toward a neuro-developmental account of the development of declarative memory. *Developmental Psychobiology: The Journal of the International Society for Developmental Psychobiology* 50, 19–31.

Bauer, P. J. (2015). Development of episodic and autobiographical memory: The importance of remembering forgetting. *Developmental Review* 38, 146–166.

Bauer, P. J., & Larkina, M. (2014). Childhood amnesia in the making: Different distributions of autobiographical memories in children and adults. *Journal of Experimental Psychology: General* 143, 597.

Bauer, P. J., & Larkina, M (2019) Predictors of age-related and individual variability in autobiographical memory in childhood, *Memory* 27, 63–78.

Berch, D. B. (2005). Making sense of number sense: Implications for children with mathematical disabilities. *Journal of Learning Disabilities* 38, 333–339.

Berg, W. K., & Byrd, D. L. (2002). The Tower of London spatial problem-solving task: Enhancing clinical and research implementation. *Journal of Clinical and Experimental Neuropsychology* 24, 586–604.

Berko, J. (1958). The child's learning of English morphology. *Word* 14, 150–177.

Best, D. L., & Ornstein, P. A. (1986). Children's generation and communication of mnemonic organizational strategies. *Developmental Psychology* 22, 845.

Bialystok, E., Peets, K. F., & Moreno, S. (2014). Producing bilinguals through immersion education: Development of metalinguistic awareness. *Applied Psycholinguistics* 35, 177.

Bjorklund, D. F. (1987). How age changes in knowledge base contribute to the development of children's memory: An interpretive review. *Developmental Review* 7, 93–130.

Bjorklund, D. F., & Blasi, C. H. (2011). *Child and Adolescent Development: An Integrated Approach.* Wadsworth.

Bjorklund, D. F., & Causey, K. B. (2017). *Children's Thinking: Cognitive Development and Individual Differences.* Sage Publications.

Blair, C., Granger, D. A., Kivlighan, K. T., et al. (2008). Maternal and child contributions to cortisol response to emotional arousal in young children from low-income, rural communities. *Developmental Psychology* 44, 1095–1109.

Blair, C., & Razza, R. P. (2007). Relating effortful control, executive function, and false belief understanding to emerging math and literacy ability in kindergarten. *Child Development* 78, 647–663.

Blair, C., Granger, D. A., Willoughby, M., et al. (2011). Salivary cortisol mediates effects of poverty and parenting on executive functions in early childhood. *Child Development* 82, 1970–1984.

Bonica, C., Arnold, D. H., Fisher, P. H., et al. (2003). Relational aggression, relational victimization, and language development in preschoolers. *Social Development* 12, 551–562.

Bowman, L. C., Dodell-Feder, D., Saxe, R., & Sabbagh, M. A. (2019). Continuity in the neural system supporting children's theory of mind development: Longitudinal links between task-independent EEG and task-dependent fMRI. *Developmental Cognitive Neuroscience* 40, 100705.

Bruck, M., Ceci, S. J., & Hembrooke, H. (2002). The nature of children's true and false narratives. *Developmental Review* 22, 520–554.

Bull, R., Espy, K. A., Wiebe, S. A., et al. (2011). Using confirmatory factor analysis to understand executive control in preschool children: Sources of variation in emergent mathematic achievement. *Developmental Science* 14, 679–692.

Burchinal, M. (2018). Measuring early care and education quality. *Child Development Perspectives* 12, 3–9.

Burchinal, M., Howes, C., Pianta, R., et al. (2008). Predicting child outcomes at the end of kindergarten from the quality of pre-kindergarten teacher–child interactions and instruction. *Applied Development Science* 12, 140–153.

Byrnes, J. P., & Fox, N. A. (1998). The educational relevance of research in cognitive neuroscience. *Educational Psychology Review* 10, 297–342.

Cacchione, T., Schaub, S., & Rakoczy, H. (2013). Fourteen-month-old infants infer the continuous identity of objects on the basis of nonvisible causal properties. *Developmental Psychology* 49, 1325.

Cahill, K. R., Deater-Deckard, K., Pike, A., & Hughes, C. (2007). Theory of mind, self-worth and the mother–child relationship. *Social Development* 16, 45–56.

Callanan, M. A., & Sabbagh, M. A. (2004). Multiple labels for objects in conversations with young children: Parents' language and children's developing expectations about word meanings. *Developmental Psychology* 40, 746.

Caputi, M., Lecce, S., Pagnin, A., & Banerjee, R. (2012). Longitudinal effects of theory of mind on later peer relations: the role of prosocial behavior. *Developmental Psychology* 48, 257.

Carlson, S. M., Mandell, D. J., & Williams, L. (2004). Executive function and theory of mind: Stability and prediction from ages 2 to 3. *Developmental Psychology* 40, 1105–1122.

Case, R., Kurland, D. M., & Goldberg, J. (1982). Operational efficiency and the growth of short-term memory span. *Journal of Experimental Child Psychology* 33, 386–404.

Casey, B. J., Trainor, R. J., Orendi, J. L., et al. (1997). A developmental functional MRI study of prefrontal activation during performance of a go-nogo task. *Journal of Cognitive Neuroscience* 9, 835–847.

Cassel, W. S., & Bjorklund, D. F. (1995). Developmental patterns of eyewitness memory and suggestibility. *Law and Human Behavior* 19, 507–532.

Ceci, S. J., & Bruck, M. (1993). Suggestibility of the child witness: A historical review and synthesis. *Psychological Bulletin* 113, 403.

Chandler, M., Fritz, A. S., & Hala, S. (1989). Small-scale deceit: Deception as a marker of two-, three-, and four-year-olds' early theories of mind. *Child Development,* 1263–1277.

Chen, X., Hastings, P. D., Rubin, K. H., et al. (1998). Child-rearing attitudes and behavioral inhibition in Chinese and Canadian toddlers: A cross-cultural study. *Developmental Psychology* 34, 677.

Chen, J. J., Sun, P., & Yu, Z. (2017). A comparative study on parenting of preschool children between the Chinese in China and Chinese immigrants in the United States. *Journal of Family Issues* 38, 1262–1287.

Chi, M.T.H. (1978). Knowledge structure and memory development. In R. Siegler (Ed.), *Children's Thinking: What Develops?* (pp. 73–96). Erlbaum: Hillsdale, NJ.

Chi, M.T.H. (2006). Laboratory methods for assessing experts' and novices' knowledge. In K. A. Ericsson, R. R. Hoffman, A. Kozbelt, & A. M. Williams (Eds.), *The Cambridge Handbook of Expertise and Expert Performance*. Cambridge University Press: New York.

Chouinard, M. M., & Clark, E. V. (2003). Adult reformulations of child errors as negative evidence. *Journal of Child Language* 30, 637–670.

Cleveland, E. S., & Reese, E. (2008). Children remember early childhood: Long-term recall across the offset of childhood amnesia. *Applied Cognitive Psychology: The Official Journal of the Society for Applied Research in Memory and Cognition* 22, 127–142.

Cohen, J. S., & Mendez, J. L. (2009). Emotion regulation, language ability, and the stability of preschool children's peer play behavior. *Early Education and Development* 20, 1016–1037.

Cole, N. S. (1990). Conceptions of educational achievement. *Educational Researcher* 19, 2–7.

Cole, M., & Bruner, J. S. (1971). Cultural differences and inferences about psychological processes. *American Psychologist* 26, 867.

Coplan, J., & Gleason, J. R. (1988). Unclear speech: Recognition and significance of unintelligible speech in preschool children. *Pediatrics* 82, 447–452.

Corriveau, K., & Harris, P. L. (2009). Choosing your informant: Weighing familiarity and recent accuracy. *Developmental Science* 12, 426–437.

Cristofaro, T. N., & Tamis-LeMonda, C. S. (2012). Mother-child conversations at 36 months and at pre-kindergarten: Relations to children's school readiness. *Journal of Early Childhood Literacy* 12, 68–97.

Crook, S. R., & Evans, G. W. (2014). The role of planning skills in the income–achievement gap. *Child Development* 85, 405–411.

De Cat, C. (2013). Egocentric definiteness errors and perspective evaluation in preschool children. *Journal of Pragmatics* 56, 58–69.

DeLoache, J. S. (2002). The symbol-mindedness of young children. In W. Hartup & R. A. Weinberg (Eds.), *The Minnesota symposia on child psychology, Vol. 32. Child psychology in retrospect and prospect: In celebration of the 75th anniversary of the Institute of Child Development* (p. 73–101). Lawrence Erlbaum Associates Publishers: Hillsdale, NJ.

DeLoache, J. S., Miller, K. F., & Rosengren, K. S. (1997). The credible shrinking room: Very young children's performance with symbolic and nonsymbolic relations. *Psychological Science* 8, 308–313.

DeLoache, J. S. Rapid change in the symbolic functioning of very young children (1987). *Science* 238, 1556–1557.

Dempster, F. N. (1981). Memory span: Sources of individual and developmental differences. *Psychological Bulletin* 89, 63–100.

DeVries, R. (1969). Constancy of generic identity in the years three to six. *Monographs of the Society for Research in Child Development* 34, iii–67.

Diamond, A., Barnett, W. S., Thomas, J., & Munro, S. (2007). Preschool program improves cognitive control. *Science* 318, 1387.

Diamond, A., Kirkham, N., & Amso, D. (2002). Conditions under which young children can hold two rules in mind and inhibit a prepotent response. *Developmental Psychology* 38, 352.

Diamond, A., & Ling, D. S. (2016). Conclusions about interventions, programs, and approaches for improving executive functions that appear justified and those that, despite much hype, do not. *Developmental Cognitive Neuroscience* 18, 34–48.

Dickinson, D. K., McCabe, A., Anastasopoulos, L., et al. (2003). The comprehensive language approach to early literacy: The interrelationships among vocabulary, phonological sensitivity, and print knowledge among preschool-aged children. *Journal of Educational Psychology* 95, 465.

Doan, S. N., & Wang, Q. (2010). Maternal discussions of mental states and behaviors: Relations to emotion situation knowledge in European American and immigrant Chinese children. *Child Development* 81, 1490–1503.

Duncan, G. J., Dowsett, C. J., Claessens, A., et al. (2007). School readiness and later achievement. *Developmental Psychology* 43, 1428.

Duncan, G. J., & Magnuson, K. (2013). Investing in preschool programs. *Journal of Economic Perspectives* 27, 109–132.

Dyer, J. R., Shatz, M., & Wellman, H. M. (2000). Young children's storybooks as a source of mental state information. *Cognitive Development* 15, 17–37.

Escobar, K., Melzi, G., & Tamis-LeMonda, C. S. (2017). Mother and child narrative elaborations during booksharing in low-income Mexican-American dyads. *Infant and Child Development* 26, e2029.

Estrem, T. L. (2005). Relational and physical aggression among preschoolers: The effect of language skills and gender. *Early Education & Development* 16, 207–232.

Evans, G. W., & Schamberg, M. A. (2009). Childhood poverty, chronic stress, and adult working memory. *Proceedings of the National Academy of Sciences* 106, 6545–6549.

Evans, M. A., Shaw, D., & Bell, M. (2000). Home literacy activities and their influence on early literacy skills. *Canadian Journal of Experimental Psychology/Revue canadienne de psychologie expérimentale* 54, 65.

Everett, D., Berlin, B., Gonalves, M., et al. (2005). Cultural constraints on grammar and cognition in Pirahã: Another look at the design features of human language. *Current Anthropology* 46, 621–646.

Finn, A. S., Kalra, P. B., Goetz, C., et al. (2016). Developmental dissociation between the maturation of procedural memory and declarative memory. *Journal of Experimental Child Psychology* 142, 212–220.

Finnilä, K., Mahlberg, N., Santtila, P., et al. (2003). Validity of a test of children's suggestibility for predicting responses to two interview situations differing in their degree of suggestiveness. *Journal of Experimental Child Psychology* 85, 32–49.

Fivush, R., & Hamond, N. R. (1990). Autobiographical memory across the preschool years: Toward reconceptualizing childhood amnesia. In R. Fivush & J. A. Hudson (Eds.), *Emory Symposia in Cognition, Vol. 3. Knowing and Remembering in Young Children* (pp. 223–248). Cambridge University Press: New York.

Fivush, R., & Wang, Q. (2005). Emotion talk in mother-child conversations of the shared past: The effects of culture, gender, and event valence. *Journal of Cognition and Development* 6, 489–506.

Flack, Z. M., Field, A. P., & Horst, J. S. (2018). The effects of shared storybook reading on word learning: A meta-analysis. *Developmental Psychology* 54, 1334.

Flavell, J. H., Beach, D. R., & Chinsky, J. M. (1966). Spontaneous verbal rehearsal in a memory task as a function of age. *Child Development*, 283–299.

Flavell, J. H., Friedrichs, A. G., & Hoyt, J. D. (1970). Developmental changes in memorization processes. *Cognitive Psychology* 1, 324–340.

Flavell, J. H., Green, F. L., Flavell, E. R., et al. (1986). Development of knowledge about the appearance-reality distinction. *Monographs of the Society for Research in Child Development*, i–87.

Frampton, K. L., Perlman, M., & Jenkins, J. M. (2009). Caregivers' use of metacognitive language in child care centers: Prevalence and predictors. *Early Childhood Research Quarterly* 24, 248–262.

Freud, S. (1905). Three essays on the theory of sexuality (1905). In *The Standard Edition of the Complete Psychological Works of Sigmund Freud, Volume VII (1901–1905): A Case of Hysteria, Three Essays on Sexuality and Other Works* (pp. 123–246).

Flavell, J. H., Shipstead, S. G., & Croft, K. (1980). What young children think you see when their eyes are closed. *Cognition*, 369–387.

Friedman, W. J. (2014). The development of memory for the times of past events. In P. J. Bauer & R. Fivush (Eds.), *The Wiley Handbook on the Development of Children's Memory* (pp. 394–407). Wiley Blackwell: Hoboken, NJ.

Frye, D., Zelazo, P. D., & Burack, J. A. (1998). Cognitive complexity and control: I. Theory of mind in typical and atypical development. *Current Directions in Psychological Science* 7, 116–121.

Fujiki, M., Brinton, B., & Clarke, D. (2002). Emotion regulation in children with specific language impairment. *Language, Speech, and Hearing Services in Schools*.

Fuson K.C. (1988) Early relationships among sequence number words, counting correspondence, and cardinality. In *Children's Counting and Concepts of Number*. Springer Series in Cognitive Development. Springer: New York.

Gelman, S. A. (2004). Psychological essentialism in children. *Trends in Cognitive Sciences* 8, 404–409.

Gelman, S. A. (2006). Naive theories, development of. *Encyclopedia of Cognitive Science*.

Gelman, S. A. (2009). Learning from others: Children's construction of concepts. *Annual Review of Psychology* 60, 115–140.

Gelman, S. A., & Bloom, P. (2000). Young children are sensitive to how an object was created when deciding what to name it. *Cognition* 76, 91–103.

Gelman, S. A., & Koenig, M. A. (2003). Theory-based categorization in early childhood. In D. H. Rakison & L. M. Oakes (Eds.), *Early Category and Concept Development: Making Sense of the Blooming, Buzzing Confusion* (pp. 330–359). Oxford University Press: New York.

Gelman, S. A., & Markman, E. M. (1986). Categories and induction in young children.

Gersten, R., Jordan, N. C., & Flojo, J. R. (2005). Early identification and interventions for stu-

dents with mathematics difficulties. *Journal of Learning Disabilities* 38, 293–304.

Golinkoff, R. M., Hoff, E., Rowe, M. L., et al. (2019). Language matters: Denying the existence of the 30-million-word gap has serious consequences. *Child Development* 90, 985–992.

Gopnik, A., & Astington, J. W. (1988). Children's understanding of representational change and its relation to the understanding of false belief and the appearance-reality distinction. *Child Development*, 26–37.

Gopnik, A., & Wellman, H. M. (2012). Reconstructing constructivism: Causal models, Bayesian learning mechanisms, and the theory theory. *Psychological Bulletin* 138, 1085–1108.

Gordon, P. (2004). Numerical cognition without words: Evidence from Amazonia. *Science* 306, 496–499.

Gottfried, G. M., & Gelman, S. A. (2005). Developing domain-specific causal-explanatory frameworks: The role of insides and immanence. *Cognitive Development* 20, 137–158.

Gleason, T. R., & Hohmann, L. M. (2006). Concepts of real and imaginary friendships in early childhood. *Social Development* 15, 128–144.

Harris, P. L., German, T., & Mills, P. (1996). Children's use of counterfactual thinking in causal reasoning. *Cognition* 61, 233–259.

Grice, H. P. (1975). Logic and conversation. In *Speech Acts* (pp. 41–58). Brill.

Gunderson, E. A., & Levine, S. C. (2011). Some types of parent number talk count more than others: relations between parents' input and children's cardinal-number knowledge. *Developmental Science* 14, 1021–1032.

Gunderson, E. A., Ramirez, G., Beilock, S. L., & Levine, S. C. (2012). "The relation between spatial skill and early number knowledge: The role of the linear number line": Correction to Gunderson et al. (2012).

Haden, C. A., Haine, R. A., & Fivush, R. (1997). Developing narrative structure in parent–child reminiscing across the preschool years. *Developmental Psychology* 33, 295.

Hamond, N. R., & Fivush, R. (1991). Memories of Mickey Mouse: Young children recount their trip to Disneyworld. *Cognitive Development* 6, 433–448.

Hansen, C. (1983). *Language and Logic in Ancient China* (p. 35). University of Michigan Press: Ann Arbor, MI.

Hart, B., & Risley, T. R. (1995). *Meaningful Differences in the Everyday Experience of Young American Children*. Paul H Brookes Publishing.

Hayne, H., & Imuta, K. (2011). Episodic memory in 3-and 4-year-old children. *Developmental Psychobiology* 53, 317–322.

Heath, S. B., & Street, B. V. (2008). *On Ethnography: Approaches to Language and Literacy Research. Language & Literacy (NCRLL)*. Teachers College Press. New York.

Hoff, E. (2009). Language development at an early age: Learning mechanisms and outcomes from birth to five years. In *Encyclopedia on Early Childhood Development* (pp. 1–5).

Hudson, J., & Nelson, K. (1986). Repeated encounters of a similar kind: Effects of familiarity on children's autobiographic memory. *Cognitive Development* 1, 253–271.

Hughes, M. & Donaldson, M. (1979) The use of hiding games for studying the coordination of viewpoints. *Educational Review* 31, 133–140.

Hughes, C., & Leekam, S. (2004). What are the links between theory of mind and social relations? Review, reflections and new directions

for studies of typical and atypical development. *Social Development* 13, 590–619.

Hulme, C., Thompson, N., Muir, C., & Lawrence, A. (1984). Speech rate and the development of spoken words: The role of rehearsal and item identification processes. *Journal of Experimental Child Psychology* 38, 241–253.

Huttenlocher, J., Vasilyeva, M., Waterfall, H. R., et al. (2007). The varieties of speech to young children. *Developmental Psychology* 43, 1062–1083.

Isaacs, T. (2012). Disentangling accent from comprehensibility. *Bilingualism: Language and Cognition* 15, 905–916.

James K. H. (2010). Sensori-motor experience leads to changes in visual processing in the developing brain. *Dev. Sci.* 13, 279–288.

Jordan, N. C., Kaplan, D., Ramineni, C., & Locuniak, M. N. (2009). Early math matters: kindergarten number competence and later mathematics outcomes. *Developmental Psychology* 45, 850.

Josselyn, S. A., & Frankland, P. W. (2012). Infantile amnesia: A neurogenic hypothesis. *Learning & Memory* 19, 423–433.

Kaller, C. P., Rahm, B., Spreer, J., et al. (2008). Thinking around the corner: The development of planning abilities. *Brain and Cognition* 67, 360–370.

Kang, J. Y., Kim, Y. S., & Pan, B. A. (2009). Five-year-olds' book talk and story retelling: Contributions of mother—child joint bookreading. *First Language* 29, 243–265.

Kavanaugh, R. D. (2006). Pretend play and theory of mind. In L. Balter & C. S. Tamis-LeMonda (Eds.), *Child Psychology: A Handbook of Contemporary Issues* (pp. 153–166). Psychology Press: New York.

Keeny, T. J., Cannizzo, S. R., & Flavell, J. H. (1967). Spontaneous and induced verbal rehearsal in a recall task. *Child Development* 38, 953–966.

Killen, M., Mulvey, K. L., & Hitti, A. (2013). Social exclusion in childhood: A developmental intergroup perspective. *Child Development* 84, 772–790.

Klima, E. S. (1966). Syntactic regularities in the speech of children. *Psycholinguistics Papers*, 183–207.

Koenig, M. A., Clément, F., & Harris, P. L. (2004). Trust in testimony: Children's use of true and false statements. *Psychological Science* 15, 694–698.

Kuchirko, Y. (2019). On differences and deficits: A critique of the theoretical and methodological underpinnings of the word gap. *Journal of Early Childhood Literacy* 19, 533–562.

Kuchirko, Y., Tamis-LeMonda, C. S., Luo, R., & Liang, E. (2016). 'What happened next?': Developmental changes in mothers' questions to children. *Journal of Early Childhood Literacy* 16, 498–521.

Kushnir, T., Vredenburgh, C., & Schneider, L. A. (2013). "Who can help me fix this toy?" The distinction between causal knowledge and word knowledge guides preschoolers' selective requests for information. *Developmental Psychology* 49, 446.

Lan, X., Legare, C. H., Ponitz, C. C., et al. (2011). Investigating the links between the subcomponents of executive function and academic achievement: A cross-cultural analysis of Chinese and American preschoolers. *Journal of Experimental Child Psychology* 108, 677–692.

Lane, J. D., Ronfard, S., Francioli, S. P., & Harris, P. L. (2016). Children's imagination and belief:

Prone to flights of fancy or grounded in reality? *Cognition* 152, 127–140.

Lawson, M., Rodriguez-Steen, L., & London, K. (2018). A systematic review of the reliability of children's event reports after discussing experiences with a naïve, knowledgeable, or misled parent. *Developmental Review* 49, 62–79.

Leffel, K., & Suskind, D. (2013). Parent-directed approaches to enrich the early language environments of children living in poverty. In *Seminars in Speech and Language* 34, 267–278

Levine, S. C., Ratliff, K. R., Mollocher, J., & Cannon, J. (2012). Early puzzle play: a predictor of preschoolers' spatial transformation skill. *Developmental Psychology* 48, 530.

Libertus, M. E., Feigenson, L., & Halberda, J. (2013). Is approximate number precision a stable predictor of math ability? *Learning and Individual Differences* 25, 126–133.

Liu, L. L., Wang, S. W., Fung, J., et al. (2012). Psychology of Asian American children: Contributions of cultural heritage and the minority experience. In *Handbook of Race and Development in Mental Health* (pp. 147–167). Springer: New York.

Loftus, E. (1995). Remembering dangerously; Recovered memory. *Skeptical Inquirer* 19, 20.

Longoria, A. Q., Page, M. C., Hubbs-Taja, J., & Kennison, S. M. (2009). Relationship between kindergarten children's language ability and social competence. *Early Child Development and Care* 179, 919–929.

Lonigan, C. J., Farver, J. M., Phillips, B. M., et al. (2011). Promoting the development of preschool children's emergent literacy skills: A randomized evaluation of a literacy-focused curriculum and two professional development models. *Read Write* 24, 305–337.

Lourenco, S. F., & Frick, A. (2013). Remembering where: the origins and early development of spatial memory. *The Wiley Handbook on the Development of Children's Memory*, 361–393.

Luo, R., Tamis-LeMonda, C. S., Kuchirko, Y., et al. (2014). Mother–child book-sharing and children's storytelling skills in ethnically diverse, low-income families. *Infant and Child Development* 23, 402–425.

Maratsos, M. (2000). More overregularizations after all: new data and discussion on Marcus, Pinker, Ullman, Hollander, Rosen & Xu. *Journal of Child Language* 27, 183–212.

Marchman, V. A., Bermúdez, V. N., Bang, J. Y., & Fernald, A. (2020). Off to a good start: Early Spanish-language processing efficiency supports Spanish-and English-language outcomes at 4½ years in sequential bilinguals. *Developmental Science*, e12973.

McAlister, A. R., & Peterson, C. C. (2013). Siblings, theory of mind, and executive functioning in children aged 3–6 years: New longitudinal evidence. *Child Development* 84, 1442–1458.

McClelland, M. M., Cameron, C. E., Duncan, R., et al. (2014). Predictors of early growth in academic achievement: The head-toes-knees-shoulders task. *Frontiers in Psychology* 5, 599.

McGaugh, J. L. (2000). Memory—A century of consolidation. *Science* 287, 248–251.

Meins, E., Fernyhough, C., Wainwright, R., et al. (2002). Maternal mind–mindedness and attachment security as predictors of theory of mind understanding. *Child Development* 73, 1715–1726.

Melzi, G. (2000). Cultural variations in the construction of personal narratives: Central American and European American mothers' elicitation styles. *Discourse Processes* 30, 153–177.

Melzi, G., & Caspe, M. (2005). Variations in maternal narrative styles during book reading interactions. *Narrative Inquiry* 15, 101–125.

Melzi, G., Schick, A. R., & Kennedy, J. L. (2011). Narrative elaboration and participation: Two dimensions of maternal elicitation style. *Child Development* 82, 1282–1296.

Miller, K. F., Smith, C. M., Zhu, J., & Zhang, H. (1995). Preschool origins of cross-national differences in mathematical competence: The role of number-naming systems. *Psychological Science* 6, 56–60.

Mol, S. E., Bus, A. G., De Jong, M. T., & Smeets, D. J. (2008). Added value of dialogic parent–child book readings: A meta-analysis. *Early Education and Development* 19, 7–26.

Moll, H., & Tomasello, M. (2012). Three-year-olds understand appearance and reality—just not about the same object at the same time. *Developmental Psychology* 48, 1124.

Monopoli, W. J., & Kingston, S. (2012). The relationships among language ability, emotion regulation and social competence in second-grade students. *International Journal of Behavioral Development* 36, 398–405.

Morris, G., Baker-Ward, L., & Bauer, P. J. (2010). What remains of that day: The survival of children's autobiographical memories across time. *Applied Cognitive Psychology: The Official Journal of the Society for Applied Research in Memory and Cognition* 24, 527–544.

Mullally, S. L., & Maguire, E. A. (2014). Memory, imagination, and predicting the future: a common brain mechanism? *The Neuroscientist* 20, 220–234.

NAEYC (2019). *NAEYC Early Learning Program Accreditation Standards and Assessment Items*. National Association for the Education of Young Children.

Nelson, K., & Fivush, R. (2004). The emergence of autobiographical memory: a social cultural developmental theory. *Psychological Review* 111, 486.

Newcombe, N. S. (2010). Picture this: Increasing math and science learning by improving spatial thinking. *American Educator* 34, 29.

Newcombe, N., & Huttenlocher, J. (1992). Children's early ability to solve perspective-taking problems. *Developmental Psychology* 28, 635.

Ngan Ng, S. S., & Rao, N. (2010). Chinese number words, culture, and mathematics learning. *Review of Educational Research* 80, 180–206.

Ng, F. F. Y., Pomerantz, E. M., & Deng, C. (2014). Why are Chinese mothers more controlling than American mothers? "My child is my report card." *Child Development* 85, 355–369.

Obradović, J., & Willoughby, M. T. (2019). Studying executive function skills in young children in low- and middle-income countries: Progress and directions. *Child Development Perspectives* 13, 227–234.

O'Connor, A. M., & Evans, A. D. (2018). The relation between having siblings and children's cheating and lie-telling behaviors. *Journal of Experimental Child Psychology* 168, 49–60.

OECD (2018). PISA 2018: Insights and Interpretations.

Ornstein, P. A., Gordon, B. N., & Larus, D. M. (1992). Children's memory for a personally experienced event: Implications for testimony. *Applied Cognitive Psychology* 6, 49–60.

Ornstein, P. A., Naus, M. J., & Stone, B. P. (1977). Rehearsal training and developmental differences in memory. *Developmental Psychology* 13, 15.

Páez, M. M., Tabors, P. O., & López, L. M. (2007). Dual language and literacy development of Spanish-speaking preschool children. *Journal of Applied Developmental Psychology* 28, 85–102.

Peisner-Feinberg, E., Buysse, V., Fuligni, A., et al. (2014). Using early care and education quality measures with dual language learners: A review of the research. *Early Childhood Research Quarterly* 29, 786–803.

Perner, J., Ruffman, T., & Leekam, S. R. (1994). Theory of mind is contagious: You catch it from your sibs. *Child Development* 65, 1228–1238.

Perner, J., & Ruffman, T. (2005). Infants' insight into the mind: How deep? *Science* 308, 214–216.

Peskin, J., & Ardino, V. (2003). Representing the mental world in children's social behavior: Playing hide-and-seek and keeping a secret. *Social Development* 12, 496–512.

Peterson, C. C., Slaughter, V., & Wellman, H. M. (2018). Nimble negotiators: How theory of mind (ToM) interconnects with persuasion skills in children with and without ToM delay. *Developmental Psychology* 54, 494.

Peterson, C., Grant, V., & Boland, L. (2005). Childhood amnesia in children and adolescents: Their earliest memories. *Memory* 13, 622–637.

Piaget, J. (1926). Psychology. *The Monist* 36, 430–455.

Piaget, J. (1929). *The Child's Concept of the World*. Routledge: London, United Kingdom.

Piaget, J. (1930). *The Child's Conception of Causality*. Routledge: London, United Kingdom.

Piaget, J., & Cook, M. (1952). *The Origins of Intelligence in Children* (Vol. 8, No. 5, p. 18). International Universities Press: New York.

Piaget, J., & Inhelder, B. (1956). *The Child's Conception of Space*. Routledge: London, United Kingdom.

Pianta, R. C., Cox, M. J., & Snow, K. L. (Eds.). (2007). *School Readiness and the Transition to Kindergarten in the Era of Accountability*. Paul H. Brookes Publishing: Baltimore, MD.

Piantadosi, S. T., Jara-Ettinger, J., & Gibson, E. (2014). Children's learning of number words in an indigenous farming-foraging group. *Developmental Science* 17, 553–563.

Pierucci, J. M., O'Brien, C. T., McInnis, M. A., et al. (2014). Fantasy orientation constructs and related executive function development in preschool: Developmental benefits to executive functions by being a fantasy-oriented child. *International Journal of Behavioral Development* 38, 62–69.

Polite, E. J. (2011). The contribution of part-word phonological factors to the production of regular noun plural–s by children with and without specific language impairment. *First Language* 31, 425–441.

Premack, D., & Woodruff, G. (1978). Does the chimpanzee have a theory of mind? *Behavioral and Brain Sciences* 1, 515–526.

Presser, A., Clements, M., Ginsburg, H., & Ertle, B. (2015). Big math for little kids: The effectiveness of a preschool and kindergarten mathematics curriculum. *Early Education and Development* 26, 399–426.

Prevor, M. B., & Diamond, A. (2005). Color–object interference in young children: A Stroop effect in children 3½–6½ years old. *Cognitive Development* 20, 256–278.

Price-Williams, D., Gordon, W., & Ramirez, M. (1969). Skill and conservation: A study of pottery-making children. *Developmental Psychology* 1, 769.

Principe, G. F., Kanaya, T., Ceci, S. J., & Singh, M. (2006). Believing is seeing: How rumors can engender false memories in preschoolers. *Psychological Science* 17, 243–248.

Pruden, S. M., Levine, S. C., & Huttenlocher, J. (2011). Children's spatial thinking: Does talk about the spatial world matter? *Developmental Science* 14, 1417–1430.

Quine, W. V. O. (1960, 2013). *Word and Object*. MIT Press: Cambridge, MA.

Quiroz, B. G., Snow, C. E., & Zhao, J. (2010). Vocabulary skills of Spanish—English bilinguals: impact of mother—child language interactions and home language and literacy support. *International Journal of Bilingualism* 14, 379–399.

Raver, C. C., Blair, C., & Willoughby, M. (2013). Poverty as a predictor of 4-year-olds' executive function: New perspectives on models of differential susceptibility. *Developmental Psychology* 49, 292.

Richardson, H., Koster-Hale, J., Caselli, N. et al. (2020). Reduced neural selectivity for mental states in deaf children with delayed exposure to sign language. *Nature Communications* 11, 3246.

Rogoff, B. (2003). *The Cultural Nature of Human Development*. Oxford University Press: New York.

Rogoff, B., & Chavajay, P. (1995). What's become of research on the cultural basis of cognitive development? *American Psychologist* 50, 859.

Rosch, E., Mervis, C. B., Gray, W. D., et al. (1976). Basic objects in natural categories. *Cognitive Psychology* 8, 382–439.

Ruffman, T., Slade, L., & Crowe, E. (2002). The relation between children's and mothers' mental state language and theory-of-mind understanding. *Child Development* 73, 734–751.

Sabbagh, M. A., Bowman, L. C., Evraire, L. E., & Ito, J. M. (2009). Neurodevelopmental correlates of theory of mind in preschool children. *Child Development* 80, 1147–1162.

Sabbagh, M. A., Moses, L. J., & Shiverick, S. (2006). Executive functioning and preschoolers' understanding of false beliefs, false photographs, and false signs. *Child Development* 77, 1034–1049.

Sabbagh, M. A., Xu, F., Carlson, S. M., et al. (2006). The development of executive functioning and theory of mind: A comparison of Chinese and US preschoolers. *Psychological Science* 17, 74–81.

Salatas, H., & Flavell, J. H. (1976). Behavioral and metamnemonic indicators of strategic behaviors under "remember" instructions in first grade. *Child Development*, 81–89.

Sapp, F., Lee, K., & Muir, D. (2000). Three-year-olds' difficulty with the appearance–reality distinction: Is it real or is it apparent? *Developmental Psychology* 36, 547.

Saxe, R., & Powell, L. J. (2006). It's the thought that counts: Specific brain regions for one component of theory of mind. *Psychological Science* 17, 692–699.

Scarf, D., Gross, J., Colombo, M., & Hayne, H. (2013). To have and to hold: Episodic memory in 3-and 4-year-old children. *Developmental Psychobiology* 55, 125–132.

Schaeffer, J., & Matthewson, L. (2005). Grammar and pragmatics in the acquisition of article systems. *Natural Language & Linguistic Theory* 23, 53–101.

Schlagmüller, M., & Schneider, W. (2002). The development of organizational strategies in children: Evidence from a microgenetic longitudinal study. *Journal of Experimental Child Psychology* 81, 298–319.

Schneider, W., & Sodian, B. (1997). Memory strategy development: Lessons from longitudinal research. *Developmental Review* 17, 442–461.

Schwenck, C., Bjorklund, D. F., & Schneider, W. (2007). Factors influencing the incidence of utilization deficiencies and other patterns of recall/strategy-use relations in a strategic memory task. *Child Development* 78, 1771–1787.

Sénéchal, M., & LeFevre, J. A. (2002). Parental involvement in the development of children's reading skill: A five-year longitudinal study. *Child Development* 73, 445–460.

Sharp, D., & Cole, M. (1972). Patterns of responding in the word associations of West African children. *Child Development*, 55–65.

Sheingold & Tenney, Y. J. (1982). Memory for a salient childhood event. In U. Neisser (Ed.), *Memory Observed: Remembering in Natural Contexts* (pp. 201–212) Freeman: New York.

Siegler, R. S. (1998). *Emerging Minds: The Process of Change in Children's Thinking*. Oxford University Press: New York.

Siegler, R. S., & Ramani, G. B. (2009). Playing linear number board games—but not circular ones—improves low-income preschoolers' numerical understanding. *Journal of Educational Psychology* 101, 545.

Skwarchuk, S. L., Sowinski, C., & LeFevre, J. A. (2014). Formal and informal home learning activities in relation to children's early numeracy and literacy skills: The development of a home numeracy model. *Journal of Experimental Child Psychology* 121, 63–84.

Slaughter, V., Peterson, C. C., & Moore, C. (2013). I can talk you into it: Theory of mind and persuasion behavior in young children. *Developmental Psychology* 49, 227.

Smetana, J. G., Rote, W. M., Jambon, M., et al. (2012). Developmental changes and individual differences in young children's moral judgments. *Child Development* 83, 683–696.

Sperry, D. E., Sperry, L. L., & Miller, P. J. (2019). Language does matter: But there is more to language than vocabulary and directed speech. *Child Development* 90, 993–997.

Starr, A., Libertus, M. E., & Brannon, E. M. (2013). Number sense in infancy predicts mathematical abilities in childhood. *Proceedings of the National Academy of Sciences* 110, 18116–18120.

Stoel-Gammon, C., & Sosa, A. V. (2008). Phonological development. In *Blackwell Handbook of Language Development* (pp. 238–256). Blackwell Publishing Ltd.

Storch, S. A., & Whitehurst, G. J. (2002). Oral language and code-related precursors to reading: evidence from a longitudinal structural model. *Developmental Psychology* 38, 934.

Sulik, M. J., Daneri, P. M., Pintar-Breen, A., & Blair, C. (2016). Self-regulation in early childhood: Theory and measurement. In L. Balter & C. S. Tamis-LeMonda (Eds.), *Child Psychology: A Handbook of Contemporary Issues*, 3rd ed. Psychology Press: New York.

Susperreguy, M. I., & Davis-Kean, P. E. (2016). Maternal math talk in the home and math skills in preschool children. *Early Education and Development* 27, 841–857.

Talwar, V., & Lee, K. (2008). Social and cognitive correlates of children's lying behavior. *Child Development* 79, 866–881.

Tamis-LeMonda, C. S., Sze, I. N. L., Ng, F. F. Y., et al. (2013). Maternal teaching during play with four-year-olds: Variation by ethnicity and family resources. *Merrill-Palmer Quarterly* 59, 361–398.

Taumoepeau, M. (2016). Maternal expansions of child language relate to growth in children's vocabulary. *Language Learning and Development* 12, 429–446.

Taylor, M., Carlson, S. M., Maring, B. L., et al. (2004). The characteristics and correlates of fantasy in school-age children: Imaginary companions, impersonation, and social understanding. *Developmental Psychology* 40, 1173.

Thibodeau, R. B., Gilpin, A. T., Brown, M. M., & Meyer, B. A. (2016). The effects of fantastical pretend-play on the development of executive functions: An intervention study. *Journal of Experimental Child Psychology* 145, 120–138.

Tobin, J. J., Wu, D. Y., & Davidson, D. H. (1989). *Preschool in Three Cultures: Japan, China, and the United States*. Yale University Press: New Haven, CT.

Trionfi, G., & Reese, E. (2009). A good story: Children with imaginary companions create richer narratives. *Child Development* 80, 1301–1313.

Tulving, E. (2005). Episodic memory and autonoesis: Uniquely human?

Tustin, K., & Hayne, H. (2010). Defining the boundary: Age-related changes in childhood amnesia. *Developmental Psychology* 46, 1049.

Uccelli, P., Hemphill, L., Pan, B. A., & Snow, C. (2006). Conversing with toddlers about the nonpresent: Precursors to narrative development in two genres. In L. Balter & C. S. Tamis-LeMonda (Eds.), *Child Psychology: A Handbook of Contemporary Issues* (pp. 215–237). Psychology Press: New York.

Unterrainer, J. M., Rauh, R., Rahm, B., et al. (2016). Development of planning in children with high-functioning autism spectrum disorders and/or attention deficit/hyperactivity disorder. *Autism Research* 9, 739–751.

Verdine, B. N., Irwin, C. M., Golinkoff, R. M., & Hirsh-Pasek, K. (2014). Contributions of executive function and spatial skills to preschool mathematics achievement. *Journal of Experimental Child Psychology* 126, 37–51.

Vygotsky, L. S. (1978). *Mind in Society: The Development of Higher Psychological Processes*. Harvard University Press: Cambridge, MA.

Wahler, R. G., & Castlebury, F. D. (2002). Personal narratives as maps of the social ecosystem. *Clinical Psychology Review* 22, 297–314.

Wai, J., Lubinski, D., & Benbow, C. P. (2009). Spatial ability for STEM domains: Aligning over 50 years of cumulative psychological knowledge solidifies its importance. *Journal of Educational Psychology* 101, 817.

Wang, Q., Doan, S. N., & Song, Q. (2010). Talking about internal states in mother–child reminiscing influences children's self-representations: A cross-cultural study. *Cognitive Development* 25, 380–393.

Wang, Q., Leichtman, M. D., & Davies, K. I. (2000). Sharing memories and telling stories: American and Chinese mothers and their 3-year-olds. *Memory* 8, 159–177.

Wang, Q., & Peterson, C. (2014). Your earliest memory may be earlier than you think: Prospective studies of children's dating of earliest childhood memories. *Developmental Psychology* 50, 1680.

Waters, T. E., Bauer, P. J., & Fivush, R. (2014). Autobiographical memory functions served by multiple event types. *Applied Cognitive Psychology* 28, 185–195.

Watts, T. W., Duncan, G. J., Clements, D. H., & Sarama, J. (2018). What is the long-run impact of learning mathematics during preschool? *Child Development* 89, 539–555.

Weiland, C., & Yoshikawa, H. (2013). Impacts of a prekindergarten program on children's mathematics, language, literacy, executive function, and emotional skills. *Child Development* 84, 2112–2130.

Wellman, H. M., Cross, D., & Watson, J. (2001). Meta-analysis of theory-of-mind development: The truth about false belief. *Child Development* 72, 655–684.

Whyte, J. C., & Bull, R. (2008). Number games, magnitude representation, and basic number skills in preschoolers. *Developmental Psychology* 44, 588.

Wiebe, S. A., Espy, K. A., & Charak, D. (2008). Using confirmatory factor analysis to understand executive control in preschool children: I. Latent structure. *Developmental Psychology* 44, 575.

Willoughby, M. T., Wirth, R. J., & Blair, C. B. (2012). Executive function in early childhood: Longitudinal measurement invariance and developmental change. *Psychological Assessment* 24, 418.

Wimmer, H., & Perner, J. (1983). Beliefs about beliefs: Representation and constraining function of wrong beliefs in young children's understanding of deception. *Cognition* 13, 103–128.

Winocur, G., & Moscovitch, M. (2011). Memory transformation and systems consolidation. *Journal of the International Neuropsychological Society* 17, 766.

Wu, K. K., Anderson, V., & Castiello, U. (2002). Neuropsychological evaluation of deficits in executive functioning for ADHD children with or without learning disabilities. *Developmental Neuropsychology* 22, 501–531.

Wynn, K. (1990). Children's understanding of counting. *Cognition* 36, 155–193.

Wynn, K. (1992). Addition and subtraction by human infants. *Nature* 358, 749–750.

Xu, F., & Pinker, S. (1995). Weird past tense forms. *Journal of Child Language* 22, 531–556.

Zelazo, P. D. (2006). The Dimensional Change Card Sort (DCCS): A method of assessing executive function in children. *Nature Protocols* 1, 297–301.

Zelazo, P. D. (2015). Executive function: Reflection, iterative reprocessing, complexity, and the developing brain. *Developmental Review* 38, 55–68.

Zelazo, P. D., & Carlson, S. M. (2012). Hot and cool executive function in childhood and adolescence: Development and plasticity. *Child Development Perspectives* 6, 354–360.

Zhang, H., & Zhou, Y. (2003). The teaching of mathematics in Chinese elementary schools. *International Journal of Psychology* 38, 286–298.

Zhang, X., Koponen, T., Räsänen, P., et al. (2014). Linguistic and spatial skills predict early arithmetic development via counting sequence knowledge. *Child Development* 85, 1091–1107.

Zhou, Q., Chen, S. H., & Main, A. (2012). Commonalities and differences in the research on children's effortful control and executive function: A call for an integrated model of self-regulation. *Child Development Perspectives* 6, 112–121.

Chapter 10

Aboud, F. E. (1988). *Children and Prejudice*. Blackwell: New York.

Afifi, T. O., Mota, N., MacMillan, H. L., & Sareen, J. (2013). Harsh physical punishment in childhood and adult physical health. *Pediatrics* 132, e333–340.

Ahn, H. J. (2005). Childcare teachers' strategies in children's socialization of emotion. *Early Child Development and Care* 175 49–61.

Aksan, N., & Kochanska, G. (2005). Conscience in childhood: Old questions, new answers. *Developmental Psychology* 41, 506–516.

Alink, L. R., Mesman, J., Van Zeijl, J., et al. (2006). The early childhood aggression curve: Development of physical aggression in 10-to 50-month-old children. *Child Development* 77, 954–966.

Anderson, C. A., Shibuya, A., Ihori, N., et al. (2010). Violent video game effects on aggression, empathy, and prosocial behavior in Eastern and Western countries: A meta-analytic review. *Psychological Bulletin* 136, 151–173.

Apfelbaum, E. P., Pauker, K., Ambady, N., et al. (2008). Learning (not) to talk about race: When older children underperform in social categorization. *Developmental Psychology* 44, 1513–1518.

Arsenio, W. F., Cooperman, S., & Lover, A. (2000). Affective predictors of preschoolers' aggression and peer acceptance: Direct and indirect effects. *Developmental Psychology* 36, 438–448.

Arthur, A. E., Bigler, R. S., Liben, L. S., et al. (2008). Gender stereotyping and prejudice in young children: A developmental intergroup perspective. In K. M. Levy S (Ed.), *Intergroup Relations: An Integrative Developmental and Social Psychological Perspective* (pp. 66–86). Psychology Press: Philadelphia, PA.

Aznar, A., & Tenenbaum, H. R. (2015). Gender and age differences in parent–child emotion talk. *British Journal of Developmental Psychology* 33, 148–155.

Baird, J. A., & Astington, J. W. (2004). The role of mental state understanding in the development of moral cognition and moral action. *New Directions for Child and Adolescent Development* 2004, 37–49.

Bandura, A. (1962). Social learning through imitation.

Bandura, A. (1965). Influence of models' reinforcement contingencies on the acquisition of imitative responses. *Journal of Personality and Social Psychology* 1, 589–595.

Barnett, W. S., & Frede, E. C. (2017). Long-term effects of a system of high-quality universal preschool education in the United States. In *Childcare, Early Education and Social Inequality*. Edward Elgar Publishing.

Baron, A., & Malmberg, L. E. (2019). A vicious or auspicious cycle: The reciprocal relation between harsh parental discipline and children's self-regulation. *European Journal of Developmental Psychology* 16, 302–317.

Barrett, K. (1995). A functionalist approach to shame and guilt. In K. F. r. J. Tangney (Ed.), *Self-Conscious Emotions. The Psychology of Shame, Guilt, Embarrassment and Pride* (pp. 25–63). The Guilford Press: New York.

Barth, J. M., & Bastiani, A. (1997). A longitudinal study of emotion recognition and preschool children's social behavior. *Merrill-Palmer Quarterly* 43, 107–128.

Benjet, C., & Kazdin, A. E. (2003). Spanking children: The controversies, findings, and new directions. *Clinical Psychology Review* 23, 197–224.

Berenbaum, S. A. (1999). Effects of early androgens on sex-typed activities and interests in adolescents with congenital adrenal hyperplasia. *Hormones and Behavior* 35, 102–110.

Berenbaum, S. A. (2018). Beyond pink and blue: The complexity of early androgen effects on gender development. *Child Development Perspectives* 12, 58–64.

Bernal, M. E., Knight, G. P., Garza, C. A., et al. (1990). The development of ethnic identity in Mexican-American children. *Hispanic Journal of Behavioral Sciences* 12, 3–24.

Beuf, A. H. (1977). *Red Children in White America*. University of Pennsylvania Press: Philadelphia, PA.

Bigelow, B. J. (1977). Children's friendship expectations: A cognitive-developmental study. *Child Development* 48, 246–253.

Bigler, R. S. (1995). The role of classification skill in moderating environmental influences on children's gender stereotyping: A study of the functional use of gender in the classroom. *Child Development* 66, 1072–1087.

Bigler, R. S., & Liben, L. S. (2006). A developmental intergroup theory of social stereotypes and prejudice. In *Advances in Child Development and Behavior* (Vol 34) (pp. 39–89). Elsevier Academic Press: San Diego, CA.

Bjorklund, D. F. (1997). The role of immaturity in human development. *Psychological Bulletin* 122, 153–169.

Blair, C. (2002). School readiness: Integrating cognition and emotion in a neurobiological conceptualization of children's functioning at school entry. *American Psychologist* 57, 111–127.

Blair, C., & Razza, R. P. (2007). Relating effortful control, executive function, and false belief understanding to emerging math and literacy ability in kindergarten. *Child Development* 78, 647–663.

Boykin, A. W., & Toms, F. D. (1985). Black child socialization: A conceptual framework. In *Black Children: Social, Educational, and Parental Environments* (pp. 33–51). Sage Publications, Inc.: Thousand Oaks, CA.

Bretherton, I., Fritz, J., Zahn-Waxler, C., & Ridgeway, D. (1986). Learning to talk about emotions: A functionalist perspective. *Child Development* 57, 529–548.

Brooks-Gunn, J., & Lewis, M. (1984). The development of early visual self-recognition. *Developmental Review* 4, 215–239.

Brown, J. R., Donelan-McCall, N., & Dunn, J. (1996). Why talk about mental states? The significance of children's conversations with friends, siblings, and mothers. *Child Development* 67, 836–849.

Brown, J. R., & Dunn, J. (1996). Continuities in emotion understanding from 3–6 yrs. *Child Development* 67, 789–802.

Brownell, C. A., Zerwas, S., & Ramani, G. B. (2007). "So big": The development of body self-awareness in toddlers. *Child Development* 78, 1426–1440.

Buhs, E. S., Ladd, G. W., & Herald, S. L. (2006). Peer exclusion and victimization: Processes that mediate the relation between peer group rejection and children's classroom engagement and achievement? *Journal of Educational Psychology* 98, 1–13.

Buist, K. L., Deković M., & Prinzie, P. (2013). Sibling relationship quality and psychopathology of children and adolescents: A meta-analysis. *Clinical Psychology Review* 33, 97–106.

Bureau, J. F., Martin, J., Yurkowski, K., et al. (2017). Correlates of child–father and child–mother attachment in the preschool years. *Attachment & Human Development* 19, 130–150.

Bushman, B. J., & Huesmann, L. (2012). Effects of violent media on aggression. *Handbook of Children and the Media*, 231–248.

Cabrera, N. J., Volling, B. L., & Barr, R. (2018). Fathers are parents, too! Widening the lens on parenting for children's development. *Child Development Perspectives* 12, 152–157.

Calkins, S. D. (1994). Origins and outcomes of individual differences in emotion regulation. *Monographs of the Society for Research in Child Development* 59, 53–283.

Calkins, S. D., Dedmon, S. E., Gill, K. L., et al. (2002). Frustration in infancy: Implications for emotion regulation, physiological processes, and temperament. *Infancy* 3, 175–197.

Calkins, S. D., & Johnson, M. C. (1998). Toddler regulation of distress to frustrating events: Temperamental and maternal correlates. *Infant Behavior & Development* 21, 379–395.

Calkins, S. D., & Keane, S. P. (2004). Cardiac vagal regulation across the preschool period: Stability, continuity, and implications for childhood adjustment. *Developmental Psychobiology* 45, 101–112.

Campbell, F. A., Ramey, C. T., Pungello, E., et al. (2002). Early childhood education: Young adult outcomes from the Abecedarian project. *Applied Developmental Science* 6, 42–57.

Camras, L. A., & Allison, K. (1985). Children's understanding of emotional facial expressions and verbal labels. *Journal of Nonverbal Behavior* 9, 84–94.

Camras, L. A., & Halberstadt, A. G. (2017). Emotional development through the lens of affective social competence. *Current Opinion in Psychology* 17, 113–117.

Casey, B. J., Somerville, L. H., Gotlib, I. H., et al. (2011). Behavioral and neural correlates of delay of gratification 40 years later. *Proceedings of the National Academy of Sciences of the United States of America* 108, 14998–15003.

Cassidy, J., & Marvin, R. (1992). Attachment organization in preschool children: Procedures and coding manual. Pennsylvania State University and University of Virginia; 1992. Unpublished manuscript.

Castelli, L., De Dea, C., & Nesdale, D. (2008). Learning social attitudes: Children's sensitivity to the nonverbal behaviors of adult models during interracial interactions. *Personality and Social Psychology Bulletin* 34, 1504–1513.

Castelli, L., Zogmaister, C., & Tomelleri, S. (2009). The transmission of racial attitudes within the family. *Developmental Psychology* 45, 586–591.

Caughy, M. O. B., O'Campo, P. J., Randolph, S. M., & Nickerson, K. (2002). The influence of racial socialization practices on the cognitive and behavioral competence of African American preschoolers. *Child Development* 73, 1611–1625.

Chalik, L., & Rhodes, M. (2014). Preschoolers use social allegiances to predict behavior. *Journal of Cognition and Development* 15, 136–160.

Chalik, L., Rivera, C., & Rhodes, M. (2014). Children's use of categories and mental states to predict social behavior. *Developmental Psychology* 50, 2360–2367.

Chan, S. M., Bowes, J., & Wyver, S. (2009). Parenting style as a context for emotion socialization. *Early Education and Development* 20, 631–656.

Chen, X. (2000). Growing up in a collectivist culture: Socialization and socioemotional development in Chinese children. In *International Perspectives on Human Development* (pp. 331–353). Pabst Science Publishers: Lengerich, Germany.

Chen, X. (2010). Socioemotional development in Chinese children. *Handbook of Chinese Psychology* (pp. 37–52).

Chernyak, N., & Sobel, D. M. (2016). "But he didn't mean to do it": Preschoolers correct punishments imposed on accidental transgressors. *Cognitive Development* 39, 13–20.

Clark, K. B., & Clark, M. K. (1939). The development of consciousness of self and the emergence of racial identification in Negro preschool children. *The Journal of Social Psychology* 10, 591–599.

Clark, K. B., & Clark, M. P. (1950). Emotional factors in racial identification and preference in Negro children. *Journal of Negro Education* 19, 341–350.

Coldwell, J., Pike, A., & Dunn, J. (2006). Household chaos—links with parenting and child behaviour. *Journal of Child Psychology and Psychiatry* 47, 1116–1122.

Cole, P. M., Tan, P. Z., Hall, S. E., et al. (2011). Developmental changes in anger expression and attention focus: Learning to wait. *Developmental Psychology* 47, 1078–1089.

Cole, P. M., Zahn-Waxler, C., & Smith, K. D. (1994). Expressive control during a disappointment: Variations related to preschoolers' behavior problems. *Developmental Psychology* 30, 835–846.

Contreras, J. M., Kerns, K. A., Weimer, B. L., et al. (2000). Emotion regulation as a mediator of associations between mother–child attachment and peer relationships in middle childhood. *Journal of Family Psychology* 14, 111–124.

Coyne, S. M., Linder, J. R., Rasmussen, E. E., et al. (2016). Pretty as a princess: Longitudinal effects of engagement with Disney princesses on gender stereotypes, body esteem, and prosocial behavior in children. *Child Development* 87, 1909–1925.

Crick, N. R., Casas, J. F., & Mosher, M. (1997). Relational and overt aggression in preschool. *Developmental Psychology* 33, 579–588.

Crick, N. R., Ostrov, J. M., Burr, J. E., et al. (2006). A longitudinal study of relational and physical aggression in preschool. *Journal of Applied Developmental Psychology* 27, 254–268.

Crick, N. R., Werner, N. E., Casas, J. F., et al. (1999). Childhood aggression and gender: A new look at an old problem. In *Gender and Motivation* (pp. 75–141). University of Nebraska Press: Lincoln, NE.

Cristofaro, T. N., & Tamis-LeMonda, C. S. (2008). Lessons in mother-child and father-child personal narratives in Latino families. In A. McCabe, A. L. Bailey, & G. Melzi (Eds.), *Spanish-Language Narration and Literacy: Culture, Cognition, and Emotion* (pp. 54–91). Cambridge University Press: New York.

Crockenberg, S., & Litman, C. (1990). Autonomy as competence in 2-year-olds: Maternal correlates of child defiance, compliance, and self-assertion. *Developmental Psychology* 26, 961–971.

Crouter, A. C., Helms-Erickson, H., Updegraff, K., & McHale, S. M. (1999). Conditions underlying parents' knowledge about children's daily lives in middle childhood: Between-and within-family comparisons. *Child Development* 70, 246–259.

Cummings, E. M., Iannotti, R. J., & Zahn-Waxler, C. (1989). Aggression between peers in early childhood: Individual continuity and developmental change. *Child Development* 60, 887–895.

de Rosnay, M., Pons, F., Harris, P. L., & Morrell, J. M. B. (2004). A lag between understanding false belief and emotion attribution in young children: Relationships with linguistic ability and mothers' mental-state language. *British Journal of Developmental Psychology* 22, 197–218.

DeConti, K. A., & Dickerson, D. J. (1994). Preschool children's understanding of the situational determinants of others' emotions. *Cognition and Emotion* 8, 453–472.

Delgado, B., Carrasco, M.A., González-Peña, P., et al. (2018). Temperament and behavioral problems in young children: The protective role of extraversion and effortful control. *Journal of Child and Family Studies* 27, 3232–3240.

DeMulder, E. K., Denham, S., Schmidt, M., & Mitchell, J. (2000). Q-sort assessment of attachment security during the preschool years: Links from home to school. *Developmental Psychology* 36, 274–282.

Denham, S., & Kochanoff, A. T. (2002). Parental contributions to preschoolers' understanding of emotion. *Marriage & Family Review* 34, 311–343.

Denham, S., Mason, T., Caverly, S., et al. (2001). Preschoolers at play: Co-socialisers of emotional and social competence. *International Journal of Behavioral Development* 25, 290–301.

Denham, S., Mason, T., Kochanoff, A., et al. (2003). Emotional development. In *International Encyclopedia of Marriage and Family Relationships* (pp. 419–426).

Denham, S. A. (1986). Social cognition, prosocial behavior, and emotion in preschoolers: Contextual validation. *Child Development* 57, 194–201.

Denham, S. A. (1997). "When I have a bad dream mommy holds me": Preschoolers' conceptions of emotions, parental socialisation, and emotional competence. *International Journal of Behavioral Development* 20, 301–319.

Denham, S. A. (1998). *Emotional Development in Young Children*. Guilford Press: New York.

Denham, S. A. (2007). Dealing with feelings: How children negotiate the worlds of emotions and social relationships. *Cogniţie Creier Comportament* 11, 1–48.

Denham, S. A., & Grout, L. (1992). Mothers' emotional expressiveness and coping: Relations with preschoolers' social-emotional competence. *Genetic, Social, and General Psychology Monographs* 118, 73–101.

Denham, S. A., McKinley, M., Couchoud, E. A., & Holt, R. (1990). Emotional and behavioral predictors of preschool peer ratings. *Child Development* 61, 1145–1152.

Denham, S. A., Renwick-DeBardi, S., & Hewes, S. (1994). Emotional communication between mothers and preschoolers: Relations with emotional competence. *Merrill-Palmer Quarterly* 40, 488–508.

Denham, S. A., Zoller, D., & Couchoud, E. A. (1994). Socialization of preschoolers' emotion understanding. *Developmental Psychology* 30, 928–936.

Derryberry, D., & Rothbart, M. K. (1997). Reactive and effortful processes in the organization of temperament. *Development and Psychopathology* 9, 633–652.

Diamond, A. (2013). Executive functions. *Annual Review of Psychology* 64, 135–168.

Dinella, L. M., Weisgram, E. S., & Fulcher, M. (2017). Children's gender-typed toy interests: Does propulsion matter? *Archives of Sexual Behavior* 46, 1295–1305.

Dix, T., Ruble, D. N., & Zambarano, R. J. (1989). Mothers' implicit theories of discipline: Child effects, parent effects, and the attribution process. *Child Development* 60, 1373–1391.

Dodge, K. A., Lansford, J. E., Burks, V. S., et al. (2003). Peer rejection and social information-processing factors in the development of aggressive behavior problems in children. *Child Development* 74, 374–393.

Dodge, K. A., & Somberg, D. R. (1987). Hostile attributional biases among aggressive boys are exacerbated under conditions of threats to the self. *Child Development* 58, 213–224.

Doucet, F., Banerjee, M., & Parade, S. (2018). What should young Black children know about race? Parents of preschoolers, preparation for bias, and promoting egalitarianism. *Journal of Early Childhood Research* 16, 65–79.

Dunn, J. (1983). Sibling relationships in early childhood. *Child Development*, 787–811.

Dunn, J., Brown, J. R., & Maguire, M. (1995). The development of children's moral sensibility: Individual differences and emotion understanding. *Developmental Psychology* 31, 649–659.

Dunn, J., & Hughes, C. (1998). Young children's understanding of emotions within close relationships. *Cognition and Emotion* 12, 171–190.

Dunn, J., & Hughes, C. (2014). Family talk about moral issues: The toddler and preschool years. In *Talking about Right and Wrong: Parent-Child Conversations as Contexts for Moral Development* (pp. 21–43).

Dunn, J., & Munn, P. (1986). Sibling quarrels and maternal intervention: Individual differences in understanding and aggression. *Child Psychology & Psychiatry & Allied Disciplines* 27, 583–595.

Dunn, J., & Slomkowski, C. (1992). Conflict and the development of social understanding In *Conflict in Child and Adolescent Development* (pp. 70–92). Cambridge University Press: New York.

Durbin, C. E. (2018). Applied implications of understanding the natural development of effortful control. *Current Directions in Psychological Science* 27, 386–390.

Durlak, J. A., Weissberg, R. P., Dymnicki, A. B., et al. (2011). The impact of enhancing students' social and emotional learning: A meta-analysis of school-based universal interventions. *Child Development* 82, 405–432.

Eisenberg, N., Cumberland, A., Spinrad, T. L., et al. (2001). The relations of regulation and emotionality to children's externalizing and internalizing problem behavior. *Child Development* 72, 1112–1134.

Eisenberg, N., Fabes, R. A., Shepard, S. A., et al. (1999). Parental reactions to children's negative emotions: Longitudinal relations to quality of children's social functioning. *Child Development* 70, 513–534.

Eisenberg, N., Fabes, R. A., Shepard, S. A., et al. (1997). Contemporaneous and longitudinal prediction of children's social functioning from regulation and emotionality. *Child Development* 68, 642–664.

Eisenberg, N., Taylor, Z. E., Widaman, K. F., & Spinrad, T. L. (2015). Externalizing symptoms, effortful control, and intrusive parenting: A test of bidirectional longitudinal relations during early childhood. *Development and Psychopathology* 27, 953–968.

Eisenberg, N., Valiente, C., Fabes, R. A., et al. (2003). The relations of effortful control and ego control to children's resiliency and social functioning. *Developmental Psychology* 39, 761–776.

Ensor, R., & Hughes, C. (2005). More than talk: Relations between emotion understanding and positive behaviour in toddlers. *British Journal of Developmental Psychology* 23, 343–363.

Ensor, R., Roman, G., Hart, M. J., & Hughes, C. (2012). Mothers' depressive symptoms and low mother–toddler mutuality both predict children's maladjustment. *Infant and Child Development* 21, 52–66.

Ensor, R., Spencer, D., & Hughes, C. (2011). 'You feel sad?' emotion understanding mediates effects of verbal ability and mother–child mutuality on prosocial behaviors: Findings from 2 years to 4 years. *Social Development* 20, 93–110.

Evans, G. W., Gonnella, C., Marcynyszyn, L. A., et al. (2005). The role of chaos in poverty and children's socioemotional adjustment. *Psychological Science* 16, 560–565.

Fabes, R. A., Eisenberg, N., Nyman, M., & Michealieu, Q. (1991). Young children's appraisals of others' spontaneous emotional reactions. *Developmental Psychology* 27, 858–866.

Fabes, R. A., Eisenberg, N., Smith, M. C., & Murphy, B. C. (1996). Getting angry at peers: Associations with liking of the provocateur. *Child Development* 67, 942–956.

Fabes, R. A., Leonard, S. A., Kupanoff, K., & Martin, C. L. (2001). Parental coping with children's negative emotions: Relations with children's emotional and social responding. *Child Development* 72, 907–920.

Fabes, R. A., Poulin, R. E., Eisenberg, N., & Madden-Derdich, D. A. (2018). The Coping with Children's Negative Emotions Scale (CCNES): Psychometric properties and relations to children's emotional competence. In R. Fabes, G. W. Peterson, & S. Steinmetz (Eds.), *Emotions and the Family*. Routledge Taylor and Francis: New York.

Fagot, B. I., & Leinbach, M. D. (1995). Gender knowledge in egalitarian and traditional families. *Sex Roles* 32 8), 513–526.

Farina, E., Albanese, O., & Pons, F. (2007). Making inferences and individual differences in emotion understanding. *Psychology of Language and Communication* 11, 3–19.

Fast, A. A., & Olson, K. R. (2018). Gender development in transgender preschool children. *Child Development* 89, 620–637.

Ferguson, C. J. (2015). Clinicians' attitudes toward video games vary as a function of age, gender and negative beliefs about youth: A sociology of media research approach. *Computers in Human Behavior* 52, 379–386.

Ferguson, K. T., & Evans, G. W. (2019). Social ecological theory: Family systems and family psychology in bioecological and bioecocultural perspective. In B. H. Fiese, M. Celano, K. Deater-Deckard, et al. (Eds.), *APA Handbook of Contemporary Family Psychology: Foundations, Methods, and Contemporary Issues across the Lifespan* (pp. 143–161). American Psychological Association.

Fergusson, D. M., Boden, J. M., & Horwood, L. J. (2008). Exposure to childhood sexual and physical abuse and adjustment in early adulthood. *Child Abuse and Neglect* 32, 607–619.

Fivush, R., Brotman, M. A., Buckner, J. P., & Goodman, S. H. (2000). Gender differences in parent–child emotion narratives. *Sex Roles* 42 4), 233–253.

Fox, N. A., & Calkins, S. D. (2003). The development of self-control of emotion: Intrinsic and extrinsic influences. *Motivation and Emotion* 27, 7–26.

Freeman, N. K. (2007). Preschoolers' perceptions of gender appropriate toys and their parents' beliefs about genderized behaviors: Miscommunication, mixed messages, or hidden truths? *Early Childhood Education Journal* 34, 357–366.

Freud, S. (1921). Psicologia das massas e análise do eu. Edição standard brasileira das obras psicológicas completas de Sigmund Freud, 7.

Freud, S. (1923). Certain neurotic mechanisms in jealousy, paranoia and homosexuality. *The International Journal of Psychoanalysis* 4, 1–10.

Freud, S. (1933). *Introductory Lectures on Psychoanalysis*. WW Norton & Company: New York.

Freud, S. (1949). An outline of psycho-analysis (J. Strachey, Ed. & Trans.). *The Standard Edition of the Complete Psychological Works of Sigmund Freud,* 23.

Freud, S. (1964). *Leonardo da Vinci and a Memory of His Childhood*. WW Norton & Company: New York.

Friedlmeier, W., Corapci, F., & Cole, P. M. (2011). Emotion socialization in cross cultural perspective. *Social and Personality Psychology Compass* 5, 410–427.

Frosch, C. A., Mangelsdorf, S. C., & McHale, J. L. (2000). Marital behavior and the security of preschooler–parent attachment relationships. *Journal of Family Psychology* 14, 144–161.

Fry, D. P. (2006). *The Human Potential for Peace: An Anthropological Challenge to Assumptions about War and Violence*. Oxford University Press: New York.

Gaffrey, M. S., Barch, D. M., Singer, J., et al. (2013). Disrupted amygdala reactivity in depressed 4- to 6-year-old children. *Journal of the American Academy of Child & Adolescent Psychiatry* 52, 737–746.

Garner, P. W., Jones, D. C., Gaddy, G., & Rennie, K. M. (1997). Low-income mothers' conversations about emotions and their children's emotional competence. *Social Development* 6, 37–52.

Gerardi, G., Rothbart, M., Posner, M., & Kepler, S. (1996). The development of attentional control: Performance on a spatial stroop-like task at 24, 30 and 36–38 months of age. *Infant Behavior and Development* 19, 470.

Gershoff, E. T. (2002). Corporal punishment by parents and associated child behaviors and experiences: A meta-analytic and theoretical review. *Psychological Bulletin* 128, 539–579.

Gershoff, E. T. (2013). Spanking and child development: We know enough now to stop hitting our children. *Child Development Perspectives* 7, 133–137.

Gershoff, E. T., Lansford, J. E., Sexton, H. R., et al. (2012). Longitudinal links between spanking and children's externalizing behaviors in a national sample of White, Black, Hispanic, and Asian American families. *Child Development* 83, 838–843.

Gilliom, M., Shaw, D. S., Beck, J. E., et al. (2002). Anger regulation in disadvantaged preschool boys: Strategies, antecedents, and the development of self-control. *Developmental Psychology* 38, 222–235.

Gormley Jr, W. T., Phillips, D. A., Newmark, K., et al. (2011). Social-emotional effects of early childhood education programs in Tulsa. *Child Development* 82, 2095–2109.

Gottman, J. M., Katz, L. F., & Hooven, C. (1997). *Meta-Emotion: How Families Communicate Emotionally.* Lawrence Erlbaum Associates, Inc.: Hillsdale, NJ.

Gower, A. L., Lingras, K. A., Mathieson, L. C., et al. (2014). The role of preschool relational and physical aggression in the transition to kindergarten: Links with social-psychological adjustment. *Early Education and Development* 25, 619–640.

Granger, K. L., Hanish, L. D., Kornienko, O., & Bradley, R. H. (2017). Preschool teachers' facilitation of gender-typed and gender-neutral activities during free play. *Sex Roles* 76, 498–510.

Grolnick, W. S., McMenamy, J. M., & Kurowski, C. O. (1999). Emotional self-regulation in infancy and toddlerhood. In C. S. Tamis-LeMonda (Ed.), *Child Psychology: A Handbook of Contemporary Issues* (pp. 3–22). Psychology Press: New York.

Gross, A. L., & Ballif, B. (1991). Children's understanding of emotion from facial expressions and situations: A review. *Developmental Review* 11, 368–398.

Gross, J. J., & Thompson, R. A. (2007). Emotion regulation: Conceptual foundations. In J. J. Gross (Ed.), *Handbook of Emotion Regulation* (pp. 3–24). Guilford Press: New York.

Gummerum, M., Hanoch, Y., Keller, M., et al. (2010). Preschoolers' allocations in the dictator game: The role of moral emotions. *Journal of Economic Psychology* 31, 25–34.

Gunnar, M. R., & Nelson, C. A. (2013). *Developmental Behavioral Neuroscience: The Minnesota Symposia on Child Psychology* (Vol. 24): Psychology Press: New York.

Hagan, L. K., & Kuebli, J. (2007). Mothers' and fathers' socialization of preschoolers' physical risk taking. *Journal of Applied Developmental Psychology* 28, 2–14.

Halim, M. L. D. (2016). Princesses and superheroes: Social-cognitive influences on early gender rigidity. *Child Development Perspectives* 10, 155–160.

Halim, M. L. D., Gutierrez, B. C., Bryant, D. N., et al. (2018). Gender is what you look like: Emerging gender identities in young children and preoccupation with appearance. *Self and Identity* 17, 455–466.

Halim, M., Ruble, D., Lurye, L., et al. (2012). The case of the pink frilly dress and the avoidance of all things "girly": Girls' and boys' appearance rigidity and cognitive theories of gender development. *Developmental Psychology.*

Halim, M. L. D., Ruble, D. N., Tamis-LeMonda, C. S., et al. (2017). Gender attitudes in early childhood: Behavioral consequences and cognitive antecedents. *Child Development* 88, 882–899.

Harris, P. (1995). Children's awareness and lack of awareness of mind and emotion. Paper presented at the Rochester Symposium on Developmental Psychopathology.

Harris, P. L. (1989). *Children and Emotion: The Development of Psychological Understanding.* Basil Blackwell: Cambridge, MA.

Harris, P. L., & Kavanaugh, R. D. (1993). Young children's understanding of pretense. *Monographs of the Society for Research in Child Development* 58, v–92.

Harris, P. L., Rosnay, M. d., & Pons, F. (2005). Language and children's understanding of mental states. *Current Directions in Psychological Science* 14, 69–73.

Hartup, W. W., Laursen, B., Stewart, M. I., & Eastenson, A. (1988). Conflict and the friendship relations of young children. *Child Development* 59, 1590–1600.

Hassett, J. M., Siebert, E. R., & Wallen, K. (2008). Sex differences in rhesus monkey toy preferences parallel those of children. *Hormones and Behavior* 54, 359–364.

Hastings, P. D., Nuselovici, J. N., Utendale, W. T., et al. (2008). Applying the polyvagal theory to children's emotion regulation: Social context, socialization, and adjustment. *Biological Psychology* 79, 299–306.

Heckman, J. J., Moon, S. H., Pinto, R., et al. (2010). The rate of return to the HighScope Perry Preschool Program. *Journal of Public Economics* 94, 114–128.

Hofferth, S. L. (2010). Home media and children's achievement and behavior. *Child Development* 81, 1598–1619.

Holden, G. W., Thompson, E. E., Zambarano, R. J., & Marshall, L. A. (1997). Child effects as a source of change in maternal attitudes toward corporal punishment. *Journal of Social and Personal Relationships* 14, 481–490.

Howe, N., Abuhatoum, S., & Chang-Kredl, S. (2014). "Everything's upside down. We'll call it Upside Down Valley!": Siblings' creative play themes, object use, and language during pretend play. *Early Education and Development* 25, 381–398.

Howes, C. (1983). Patterns of friendship. *Child Development* 54, 1041–1053.

Howes, C., & Matheson, C. C. (1992). Sequences in the development of competent play with peers: Social and social pretend play. *Developmental Psychology* 28, 961–974.

Howes, C., & Phillipsen, L. (1992). Gender and friendship: Relationships within peer groups of young children. *Social Development* 1, 230–242.

Howes, C., & Smith, E. W. (1995). Children and their child care caregivers: Profiles of relationships. *Social Development* 4, 44–61.

Howse, R. B., Calkins, S. D., Anastopoulos, A. D., et al. (2003). Regulatory contributors to children's kindergarten achievement. *Early Education and Development* 14, 101–120.

Hughes, C., & Ensor, R. (2009). Independence and interplay between maternal and child risk factors for preschool problem behaviors? *International Journal of Behavioral Development* 33, 312–322.

Hughes, D., Bachman, M. A., Ruble, D. N., & Fuligni, A. (2006). Tuned in or tuned out: Parents' and children's interpretation of parental racial/ethnic socialization practices. In *Child Psychology: A Handbook of Contemporary Issues,* 2nd ed. (pp. 591–610). Psychology Press: New York.

Hughes, D., & Chen, L. (1997). When and what parents tell children about race: An examination of race-related socialization among African American families. *Applied Developmental Science* 1, 200–214.

Hughes, D., & Chen, L. (1999). The nature of parents' race-related communications to children: A developmental perspective. In *Child Psychology: A Handbook of Contemporary Issues* (pp. 467–490). Psychology Press: New York.

Hughes, D., & Johnson, D. (2001). Correlates in children's experiences of parents' racial socialization behaviors. *Journal of Marriage and Family* 63, 981–995.

Hughes, C., McHarg, G., & White, N. (2018). Sibling influences on prosocial behavior. *Current Opinion in Psychology* 20, 96–101.

Hughes, D., Rodriguez, J., Smith, E. P., et al. (2006). Parents' ethnic-racial socialization practices: A review of research and directions for future study. *Developmental Psychology* 42, 747–770.

Izard, C., Fine, S., Schultz, D., et al. (2001). Emotion knowledge as a predictor of social behavior and academic competence in children at risk. *Psychological Science* 12, 18–23.

Jaxon, J., Lei, R. F., Shachnai, R., et al. (2019). The acquisition of gender stereotypes about intellectual ability: Intersections with race. *Journal of Social Issues* 75, 1192–1215.

Jenkins, J. M., Turrell, S. L., Kogushi, Y., et al. (2003). A longitudinal investigation of the dynamics of mental state talk in families. *Child Development* 74, 905–920.

Jones, S. M., McGarrah, M. W., & Kahn, J. (2019). Social and emotional learning: A principled science of human development in context. *Educational Psychologist* 54, 129–143.

Justice, E. M., Lindsey, L. L., & Morrow, S. F. (1999). The relationship of self-perceptions to achievement among African American preschoolers. *Journal of Black Psychology* 25, 48–60.

Kagan, J., Reznick, J. S., & Snidman, N. (1987). The physiology and psychology of behavioral inhibition in children. *Child Development* 58, 1459–1473.

Kahana-Kalman, R. (1995). *Children's Understanding of States and Emotions in Pretend Play.* Rutgers University: New Brunswick, NJ.

Katz, P. A. (2003). Racists or tolerant multiculturalists? How do they begin? *American Psychologist* 58, 897–909.

Kazdin, A. E., & Benjet, C. (2003). Spanking children: Evidence and issues. *Current Directions in Psychological Science* 12, 99–103.

Killen, M., Mulvey, K. L., Richardson, C., et al. (2011). The accidental transgressor: Morally-relevant theory of mind. *Cognition* 119, 197–215.

Killen, M., & Smetana, J. G. (2015). Origins and development of morality. In *Handbook of Child Psychology and Developmental Science,* Vol. 3: *Socioemotional Processes* (pp. 701–749). John Wiley & Sons Inc.: Hoboken, NJ.

Kochanska, G., Clark, L. A., & Goldman, M. S. (1997). Implications of mothers' personality for their parenting and their young children's development outcomes. *Journal of Personality* 65, 387–420.

Kochanska, G., Forman, D. R., Aksan, N., & Dunbar, S. B. (2005). Pathways to conscience: early mother-child mutually responsive orientation and children's moral emotion, conduct, and cognition. *Journal of Child Psychology and Psychiatry* 46, 19–34.

Kochanska, G., Gross, J. N., Lin, M.-H., & Nichols, K. E. (2002). Guilt in young children: Development, determinants, and relations with a broader system of standards. *Child Development* 73, 461–482.

Kochanska, G., Koenig, J. L., Barry, R. A., et al. (2010). Children's conscience during toddler and preschool years, moral self, and a competent, adaptive developmental trajectory. *Developmental Psychology* 46, 1320–1332.

Kohlberg, L. (1966). A cognitive-developmental analysis of children's sex-role concepts and attitudes. In E. E. Maccoby (Ed.), *The Development of Sex Differences* (pp. 82–173). Stanford University Press: Stanford, CA.

Kohlberg, L., & Kramer, R. (1969). Continuities and discontinuities in childhood and adult moral development. *Human Development* 12, 3–120.

Kruger, A. C., & Tomasello, M. (1986). Transactive discussions with peers and adults. *Developmental Psychology* 22, 681–685.

Kurtz-Costes, B., DeFreitas, S. C., Halle, T. G., & Kinlaw, C. R. (2011). Gender and racial favouritism in Black and White preschool girls. *British Journal of Developmental Psychology* 29, 270–287.

Ladd, G. W. (2006). Peer rejection, Aggressive or withdrawn behavior, and psychological maladjustment from ages 5 to 12: An examination of four predictive models. *Child Development* 77, 822–846.

Laible, D. J. (2004). Mother-child discourse surrounding a child's past behavior at 30 months: Links to emotional understanding and early conscience development at 36 months. *Merrill-Palmer Quarterly* 50, 159–180.

Laible, D. J., & Thompson, R. A. (1998). Attachment and emotional understanding in preschool children. *Developmental Psychology* 34, 1038–1045.

Laible, D. J., & Thompson, R. A. (2000). Mother–child discourse, attachment security, shared positive affect, and early conscience development. *Child Development* 71, 1424–1440.

Lamm, B., Keller, H., Teiser, J., et al. (2018). Waiting for the second treat: Developing culture-specific modes of self-regulation. *Child Development* 89, e261–e277.

Lansford, J. E., Criss, M. M., Dodge, K. A., et al. (2009). Trajectories of physical discipline: Early childhood antecedents and developmental outcomes. *Child Development* 80, 1385–1402.

Larsen, J. T., To, Y. M., & Fireman, G. (2007). Children's understanding and experience of mixed emotions. *Psychological Science* 18, 186–191.

Leaper, C. (1994). Exploring the consequences of gender segregation on social relationships. In *Childhood Gender Segregation: Causes and Consequences* (pp. 67–86). Jossey-Bass: San Francisco, CA.

Lecompte, V., Moss, E., Cyr, C., & Pascuzzo, K. (2014). Preschool attachment, self-esteem and the development of preadolescent anxiety and depressive symptoms. *Attachment & Human Development* 16, 242–260.

Lee, S. J., Altschul, I., & Gershoff, E. T. (2013). Does warmth moderate longitudinal associations between maternal spanking and child aggression in early childhood? *Developmental Psychology* 49, 2017–2028.

Lehrman, D. S. (1953). A critique of Konrad Lorenz's theory of instinctive behavior. *The Quarterly Review of Biology* 28, 337–363.

Leman, P. J., Ben-Hmeda, M., Cox, J., et al. (2013). Normativity and friendship choices among ethnic majority- and minority-group children. *International Journal of Behavioral Development* 37, 202–210.

Lewis, M., Takai-Kawakami, K., Kawakami, K., & Sullivan, M. W. (2010). Cultural differences in emotional responses to success and failure. *International Journal of Behavioral Development* 34, 53–61.

Liew, J., McTigue, E. M., Barrois, L., & Hughes, J. N. (2008). Adaptive and effortful control and academic self-efficacy beliefs on achievement: A longitudinal study of 1st through 3rd graders. *Early Childhood Research Quarterly* 23, 515–526.

Linares, L. O., Heeren, T., Bronfman, E., et al. (2001). A mediational model for the impact of exposure to community violence on early child behavior problems. *Child Development* 72, 639–652.

Lindsey, E. W., & Mize, J. (2001). Contextual differences in parent–child play: Implications for children's gender role development. *Sex Roles* 44, 155–176.

Luo, R., Tamis-LeMonda, C. S., & Song, L. (2013). Chinese parents' goals and practices in early childhood. *Early Childhood Research Quarterly* 28, 843–857.

Luo, R., Tamis-LeMonda, C. S., Kuchirko, Y., et al. (2014). Mother–child book-sharing and children's storytelling skills in ethnically diverse, low-income families. *Infant and Child Development* 23, 402–425.

Lytton, H., & Romney, D. M. (1991). Parents' differential socialization of boys and girls: A meta-analysis. *Psychological Bulletin* 109, 267–296.

MacKenzie, M. J., Nicklas, E., Brooks-Gunn, J., & Waldfogel, J. (2015). Spanking and children's externalizing behavior across the first decade of life: Evidence for transactional processes. *Journal of Youth and Adolescence* 44, 658–669.

Martin, C. L., & Fabes, R. A. (2001). The stability and consequences of young children's same-sex peer interactions. *Developmental Psychology* 37, 431–446.

Martin, C. L., & Ruble, D. (2004). Children's search for gender cues: Cognitive perspectives on gender development. *Current Directions in Psychological Science* 13, 67–70.

Martin, R. P., Drew, K. D., Gaddis, L. R., & Moseley, M. (1988). Prediction of elementary school achievement from preschool temperament: Three studies. *School Psychology Review* 17, 125–137.

Marvin, R. S., & Britner, P. A. (1999). Normative development: The ontogeny of attachment. In *Handbook of Attachment: Theory, Research, and Clinical Applications* (pp. 44–67). Guilford Press: New York.

Mathis, E. T. B., & Bierman, K. L. (2015). Dimensions of parenting associated with child prekindergarten emotion regulation and attention control in low-income families. *Social Development* 24, 601–620.

McAlister, A. R., & Peterson, C. C. (2012). Siblings, theory of mind, and executive functioning in children aged 3–6 years: New longitudinal evidence. *Child Development* 84, 1442–1458.

McHale, S. M., & Crouter, A. C. (1996). The family contexts of children's sibling relationships. In *Sibling Relationships: Their Causes and Consequences* (pp. 173–195). Ablex Publishing: Westport, CT.

Melis, A. P., Grocke, P., Kalbitz, J., & Tomasello, M. (2016). One for you, one for me: Humans' unique turn-taking skills. *Psychological Science* 27, 987–996.

Mesman, J., & Groeneveld, M. G. (2018). Gendered parenting in early childhood: Subtle but unmistakable if you know where to look. *Child Development Perspectives* 12, 22–27.

Metcalfe, J., & Mischel, W. (1999). A hot/cool-system analysis of delay of gratification: Dynamics of willpower. *Psychological Review* 106, 3–19.

Michalson, L., & Lewis, M. (1985). What do children know about emotions and when do they know it? In M. Lewis & C. Saarni (Eds.), *The Socialization of Emotions* (pp. 117–139). Springer: Boston, MA.

Miller, A. L., Fine, S. E., Gouley, K. K., et al. (2006). Showing and telling about emotions: Interrelations between facets of emotional competence and associations with classroom adjustment in Head Start preschoolers. *Cognition and Emotion* 20, 1170–1192.

Mischel, H. N., & Mischel, W. (1987). *The Development of Children's Knowledge of Self-Control Strategies*. Springer: Berlin.

Moore, C. (2009). Fairness in children's resource allocation depends on the recipient. *Psychological Science* 20, 944–948.

Morris, A. S., Criss, M. M., Silk, J. S., & Houltberg, B. J. (2017). The impact of parenting on emotion regulation during childhood and adolescence. *Child Development Perspectives* 11, 233–238.

Morris, A. S., Silk, J. S., Morris, M. D. S., et al. (2011). The influence of mother–child emotion regulation strategies on children's expression of anger and sadness. *Developmental Psychology* 47, 213–225.

Morris, A. S., Silk, J. S., Steinberg, L., et al. (2007). The role of the family context in the development of emotion regulation. *Social Development* 16, 361–388.

Morrison, E. F., Rimm-Kauffman, S., & Pianta, R. C. (2003). A longitudinal study of mother-child interactions at school entry and social and academic outcomes in middle school. *Journal of School Psychology* 41, 185–200.

Moss, E., Bureau, J.-F., Cyr, C., et al. (2004). Correlates of attachment at age 3: Construct validity of the preschool attachment classification system. *Developmental Psychology* 40, 323–334.

Moss, E., Smolla, N., Cyr, C., et al. (2006). Attachment and behavior problems in middle childhood as reported by adult and child informants. *Development and Psychopathology* 18, 425–444.

Mulvey, K. L., Hitti, A., Rutland, A., et al. (2014a). Context differences in children's ingroup preferences. *Developmental Psychology* 50, 1507–1519.

Mulvey, K. L., Hitti, A., Rutland, A., et al. (2014b). When do children dislike ingroup members? Resource allocation from individual and group perspectives. *Journal of Social Issues* 70, 29–46.

Mulvey, K. L., Palmer, S. B., & Abrams, D. (2016). Race-based humor and peer group dynamics in adolescence: Bystander intervention and social exclusion. *Child Development* 87, 1379–1391.

Murphy, B. C., Eisenberg, N., Fabes, R. A., et al. (1999). Consistency and change in children's emotionality and regulation: A longitudinal study. *Merrill-Palmer Quarterly* 45, 413–444.

Nelson, D. A., Nelson, L. J., Hart, C. H., et al. (2006). Parenting and peer-group behavior in cultural context. In X. Chen, D. C. French, & B. H. Schneider (Eds.), *Peer Relationships in Cultural Context* (pp. 213–246). Cambridge University Press: New York.

Network, N. E. C. (2001). Nonmaternal care and family factors in early development: An overview of the NICHD Study of Early Child Care. *Journal of Applied Developmental Psychology* 22, 457–492.

Neuenschwander, R., Rothlisberger, M., Cimeli, P., & Roebers, C. M. (2012). How do different aspects of self-regulation predict successful adaptation to school? *Journal of Experimental Child Psychology*.

Neville, H. A., Lilly, R. L., Duran, G., et al. (2000). Construction and initial validation of the Color-Blind Racial Attitudes Scale (CoBRAS). *Journal of Counseling Psychology* 47, 59–70.

Nielsen, M., Dissanayake, C., & Kashima, Y. (2003). A longitudinal investigation of self–other discrimination and the emergence of mirror self-recognition. *Infant Behavior and Development* 26, 213–226.

Nobes, G., Panagiotaki, G., & Pawson, C. (2009). The influence of negligence, intention, and outcome on children's moral judgments. *Journal of Experimental Child Psychology* 104, 382–397.

Olson, K. R. (2016). Prepubescent transgender children: what we do and do not know. *Journal of the American Academy of Child & Adolescent Psychiatry* 55, 155–156.

O'Neil, R., Welsh, M., Parke, R. D., et al. (1997). A longitudinal assessment of the academic correlates of early peer acceptance and rejection. *Journal of Clinical Child Psychology* 26, 290–303.

Osher, D., Kidron, Y., Brackett, M., et al. (2016). Advancing the science and practice of social and emotional learning: Looking back and moving forward. *Review of Research in Education* 40, 644–681.

Ostrov, J. M., & Crick, N. R. (2006). How recent developments in the study of relational aggression and close relationships in early childhood advance the field. *Journal of Applied Developmental Psychology* 27, 189–192.

Ostrov, J. M., & Keating, C. F. (2004). Gender differences in preschool Aggression during free play and structured interactions: An observational study. *Social Development* 13, 255–277.

Ostrov, J. M., Woods, K. E., Jansen, E. A., et al. (2004). An observational study of delivered and received aggression, gender, and social-psychological adjustment in preschool: "This white crayon doesn't work." *Early Childhood Research Quarterly* 19, 355–371.

Pahlke, E., Bigler, R. S., & Suizzo, M. A. (2012). Relations between colorblind socialization and children's racial bias: Evidence from European American mothers and their preschool children. *Child Development* 83, 1164–1179.

Palisin, H. (1986). Preschool temperament and performance on achievement tests. *Developmental Psychology* 22, 766–770.

Pallini, S., Chirumbolo, A., Morelli, M., et al. (2018). The relation of attachment security status to effortful self-regulation: A meta-analysis. *Psychological Bulletin* 144, 501–531.

Park, K. A., Lay, K.-l., & Ramsay, L. (1993). Individual differences and developmental changes in preschoolers' friendships. *Developmental Psychology* 29, 264–270.

Parten, M. B. (1932). Social participation among pre-school children. *The Journal of Abnormal and Social Psychology* 27, 243–269.

Patterson, G. (1986). The contribution of siblings to training for fighting: A microsocial analysis. In *Development of Antisocial and Prosocial Behavior* (pp. 235–261).

Patterson, G. R. (1967). Prediction of victimization from an instrumental conditioning procedure. *Journal of Consulting Psychology* 31, 147–152.

Patterson, G. R. (1982). *Coercive Family Process* (Vol. 3): Castalia Publishing Company.

Paulus, M., & Moore, C. (2014). The development of recipient-dependent sharing behavior and sharing expectations in preschool children. *Developmental Psychology* 50, 914–921.

Perlman, S. B., Luna, B., Hein, T. C., & Huppert, T. J. (2014). fNIRS evidence of prefrontal regulation of frustration in early childhood. *NeuroImage* 85, 326–334.

Perry, N. B., Mackler, J. S., Calkins, S. D., & Keane, S. P. (2014). A transactional analysis of the relation between maternal sensitivity and child vagal regulation. *Developmental Psychology* 50, 784–793.

Perry, K. J., & Ostrov, J. M. (2018). Testing a bi-factor model of relational and physical aggression in early childhood. *Journal of Psychopathology and Behavioral Assessment* 40, 93–106.

Peterson, C. C., & Siegal, M. (2002). Mindreading and moral awareness in popular and rejected preschoolers. *British Journal of Developmental Psychology* 20, 205–224.

Phinney, J. S., Romero, I., Nava, M., & Huang, D. (2001). The role of language, parents, and peers in ethnic identity among adolescents in immigrant families. *Journal of Youth and Adolescence* 30, 135–153.

Piaget, J. (1932). *The Language and Thought of the Child, 1926; Judgment and Reasoning in the Child, 1928; The Child's Conception of the World, 1929; The Child's Conception of Physical Causality, 1930; The Moral Judgment of the Child, 1932.* Harcourt, Brace: Oxford, United Kingdom.

Posada, G. E., Trumbell, J. M., Lu, T., & Kaloustian, G. (2018). The mother-child attachment partnership in early childhood: Secure base behavioral and representational processes: III. The organization of attachment behavior in early childhood: Links with maternal sensitivity and child attachment representations. *Monographs of the Society for Research in Child Development* 83, 35–59.

Porges, S. W. (1995). Cardiac vagal tone: A physiological index of stress. *Neuroscience and Biobehavioral Reviews* 19, 225–233.

Porges, S. W. (2007). The polyvagal perspective. *Biological Psychology* 74, 116–143.

Prentice, D. A., & Miller, D. T. (2007). Psychological essentialism of human categories. *Current Directions in Psychological Science* 16, 202–206.

Priddis, L., & Howieson, N. (2012). Insecure attachment patterns at five years. What do they tell us? *Early Child Development and Care* 182, 45–58.

Puma, M., Bell, S., Cook, R., et al. (2005). Head start impact study: First year findings. In *Administration for Children & Families*.

Rae, J. R., Gülgöz, S., Durwood, L., et al. (2019). Predicting early-childhood gender transitions. *Psychological Science* 30, 669–681.

Raval, V. V., & Martini, T. S. (2009). Maternal socialization of children's anger, sadness, and physical pain in two communities in Gujarat, India. *International Journal of Behavioral Development* 33, 215–229.

Raver, C. C., Blackburn, E. K., Bancroft, M., & Torp, N. (1999). Relations between effective emotional self-regulation, attentional control, and low-income preschoolers' social competence with peers. *Early Education and Development* 10, 333–350.

Reese, E., Haden, C. A., & Fivush, R. (1996). Mothers, fathers, daughters, sons: Gender differences in autobiographical reminiscing. *Research on Language and Social Interaction* 29, 27–56.

Reichenbach, L., & Masters, J. C. (1983). Children's use of expressive and contextual cues in judgments of emotion. *Child Development* 54, 993–1004.

Reimer, M. S. (1996). "Sinking into the ground": The development and consequences of shame in adolescence. *Developmental Review* 16, 321–363.

Rhodes, M., Leslie, S.-J., Saunders, K., et al. (2017). How does social essentialism affect the development of inter-group relations? *Developmental Science* 21, e12509.

Rhodes, M. (2012). Naïve theories of social groups. *Child Development* 83, 1900–1916.

Rhodes, M. (2014). Children's explanations as a window into their intuitive theories of the social world. *Cognitive Science* 38, 1687–1697.

Rhodes, M., & Chalik, L. (2013). Social categories as markers of intrinsic interpersonal obligations. *Psychological Science* 24, 999–1006.

Rhodes, M., Leslie, S.-J., & Tworek, C. M. (2012). Cultural transmission of social essentialism. *Proceedings of the National Academy of Sciences of the United States of America* 109, 13526–13531.

Rivers, S. E., Brackett, M. A., Reyes, M. R., Elbertson, N. A., & Salovey, P. (2013). Improving the social and emotional climate of classrooms: A clustered randomized controlled trial testing the RULER approach. *Prevention Science* 14, 77–87.

Roberts, S. O., & Gelman, S. A. (2017). Now you see race, now you don't: Verbal cues influence children's racial stability judgments. *Cognitive Development* 43, 129–141.

Roberts, C. W., Green, R., Williams, K., & Goodman, M. (1987). Boyhood gender identity development: A statistical contrast of two family groups. *Developmental Psychology* 23, 544–557.

Roberts, W., & Strayer, J. (1996). Empathy, emotional expressiveness, and prosocial behavior. *Child Development* 67, 449–470.

Rochat, P., Dias, M. D. G., Guo, L., et al. (2009). Fairness in distributive justice by 3- and 5-year-olds across seven cultures. *Journal of Cross-Cultural Psychology* 40, 416–442.

Rothbart, M. K., & Bates, J. E. (2006). Temperament. In N. Eisenberg, W. Damon, & R. M. Lerner (Eds.), *Handbook of Child Psychology: Vol. 3, Social, Emotional, and Personality Development* (6th ed.) (pp. 99–166). John Wiley & Sons Inc.: Hoboken, NJ.

Rovee-Collier, C., & Cuevas, K. (2009). Multiple memory systems are unnecessary to account for infant memory development: an ecological model. *Developmental Psychology* 45, 160–174.

Rubin, K. H., Bukowski, W. M., & Parker, J. G. (2006). Peer interactions, relationships, and groups. In N. Eisenberg, W. Damon, & R. M. Lerner (Eds.), *Handbook of Child Psychology: Vol. 3, Social, Emotional, and Personality Development* (6th ed.) (pp. 571–645). John Wiley & Sons Inc.: Hoboken, NJ.

Ruble, D. N., & Martin, C. L. (1998). Gender development. In *Handbook of Child Psychology*, 5th ed. *Vol 3. Social, Emotional, and Personality Development* (pp. 933–1016). John Wiley & Sons Inc.: Hoboken, NJ.

Ruble, D. N., Martin, C. L., & Berenbaum, S. A. (2007). Gender development. In N. Eisenberg, W. Damon, & R. M. Lerner (Eds.), *Handbook of Child Psychology: Vol. 3, Social, Emotional, and Personality Development* (6th ed.) (pp. 858–932). John Wiley & Sons Inc.: Hoboken, NJ.

Ruffman, T., Slade, L., Devitt, K., & Crowe, E. (2006). What mothers say and what they do: The relation between parenting, theory of mind, language and conflict/cooperation. *British Journal of Developmental Psychology* 24, 105–124.

Russell, C. D., & Ellis, J. B. (1991). Sex-role development in single parent households. *Social Behavior and Personality* 19, 5–9.

Russell, B. S., Lee, J. O., Spieker, S., & Oxford, M. L. (2016). Parenting and preschool self-regulation as predictors of social emotional competence in 1st grade. *Journal of Research in Childhood Education* 30, 153–169.

Russell, J. A., & Yik, M. S. M. (1996). Emotion among the Chinese. In *The Handbook of Chinese Psychology* (pp. 166–188). Oxford University Press: New York.

Rust, J., Golombok, S., Hines, M., et al. (2000). The role of brothers and sisters in the gender development of preschool children. *Journal of Experimental Child Psychology* 77, 292–303.

Rutland, A., Killen, M., & Abrams, D. (2010). A new social-cognitive developmental perspective on prejudice: The interplay between morality and group identity. *Perspectives on Psychological Science* 5, 279–291.

Ryan, C. S., Hunt, J. S., Weible, J. A., et al. (2007). Multicultural and colorblind ideology, stereotypes, and ethnocentrism among Black and White Americans. *Group Processes & Intergroup Relations* 10, 617–637.

Rydell, A.-M., Berlin, L., & Bohlin, G. (2003). Emotionality, emotion regulation, and adaptation among 5- to 8-year-old children. *Emotion* 3, 30–47.

Saarni, C. (1999). *The Development of Emotional Competence*. Guilford Press: New York.

Saarni, C. (2001). The continuity dilemma in emotional competence. *Psychological Inquiry* 12, 94–96.

Saarni, C. (2007). The development of emotional competence: Pathways for helping children to become emotionally intelligent. In R. Bar-On, J. G. Maree, & M. J. Elias (Eds.), *Educating People to be Emotionally Intelligent* (pp. 15–35). Praeger Publishers/Greenwood Publishing Group: Westport, CT.

Schonert-Reichl, K. A., Hanson-Peterson, J. L., & Hymel, S. (2015). SEL and preservice teacher education. In J. A. Durlack, C. E. Domitrovich, R. P. Weissberg, & T. P. Gullotta (Eds.), *Handbook of Social and Emotional Learning: Research and Practice* (pp. 406–421). Guilford Press: New York.

Sebastián-Enesco, C., & Warneken, F. (2015). The shadow of the future: 5-year-olds, but not 3-year-olds, adjust their sharing in anticipation of reciprocation. *Journal of Experimental Child Psychology* 129, 40–54.

Sege, R. D., Siegel, B. S., & Committee on Psychosocial Aspects of Child and Family Health. (2018). Effective discipline to raise healthy children. *Pediatrics* 142, e20183112.

Selman, R. L. (1981). The development of interpersonal competence: The role of understanding in conduct. *Developmental Review* 1, 401–422.

Servin, A., Nordenström, A., Larsson, A., & Bohlin, G. (2003). Prenatal androgens and gender-typed behavior: A study of girls with mild and severe forms of congenital adrenal hyperplasia. *Developmental Psychology* 39, 440–450.

Shantz, C. U. (1987). Conflicts between children. *Child Development*, 283–305.

Shields, A., Dickstein, S., Seifer, R., et al. (2001). Emotional competence and early school adjustment: A study of preschoolers at risk. *Early Education and Development* 12, 73–96.

Shoda, Y., Mischel, W., & Peake, P. K. (1990). Predicting adolescent cognitive and self-regulatory competencies from preschool delay of gratification: Identifying diagnostic conditions. *Developmental Psychology* 26, 978–986.

Slaby, R. G., & Frey, K. S. (1975). Development of gender constancy and selective attention to same-sex models. *Child Development* 46, 849–856.

Slaughter, V., & Brownell, C. A. (2011). *Early Development of Body Representations* (Vol. 13): Cambridge University Press: New York.

Smetana, J. G. (1984). Toddlers' social interactions regarding moral and conventional transgressions. *Child Development* 55, 1767–1776.

Smetana, J. G. (2013). Moral development: The social domain theory view. In *The Oxford Handbook of Developmental Psychology (Vol 1): Body and Mind* (pp. 832–863). Oxford University Press: New York.

Smetana, J. G., & Braeges, J. L. (1990). The development of toddler's moral and conventional judgments. *Merrill-Palmer Quarterly* 36, 329–346.

Smetana, J. G., Jambon, M., & Ball, C. (2014). The social domain approach to children's moral and social judgments. In *Handbook of Moral Development*, 2nd ed. (pp. 23–45). Psychology Press: New York.

Smetana, J. G., Jambon, M., Conry-Murray, C., & Sturge-Apple, M. L. (2012). Reciprocal associations between young children's developing moral judgments and theory of mind. *Developmental Psychology* 48, 1144–1155.

Smetana, J. G., & Letourneau, K. J. (1984). Development of gender constancy and children's sex-typed free play behavior. *Developmental Psychology* 20, 691–696.

Smith, C. L., Calkins, S. D., Keane, S. P., et al. (2004). Predicting stability and change in toddler behavior problems: Contributions of maternal behavior and child gender. *Developmental Psychology* 40, 29–42.

Smith, J. P., Glass, D. J., & Fireman, G. (2015). The understanding and experience of mixed emotions in 3–5-year-old children. *Journal of Genetic Psychology* 176, 65–81.

Smith, H. J., Sheikh, H. I., Dyson, M. W., et al. (2012). Parenting and child DRD4 genotype interact to predict children's early emerging effortful control. *Child Development*.

Spencer, M. B. (1983). Children's cultural values and parental child rearing strategies. *Developmental Review* 3, 351–370.

Spencer, S. (2014). *Race and Ethnicity: Culture, Identity and Representation*. Routledge: London, United Kingdom.

Sroufe, L. A., Schork, E., Motti, F., et al. (1984). The role of affect in social competence. *Emotions, Cognition, and Behavior*, 289.

Stifter, C. A., Dollar, J. M., & Cipriano, E. A. (2011). Temperament and emotion regulation: The role of autonomic nervous system reactivity. *Developmental Psychobiology* 53, 266–279.

Stoneman, Z., Brody, G. H., & MacKinnon, C. E. (1986). Same-sex and cross-sex siblings: Activity choices, roles, behavior, and gender stereotypes. *Sex Roles* 15, 495–511.

Strayer, J. (1980). A naturalistic study of empathic behaviors and their relation to affective states and perspective-taking skills in preschool children. *Child Development* 51, 815–822.

Sulik, M. J., Daneri, M. P., Pintar-Breen, A. I., & Blair, C. (2016). Self-regulation in early childhood: Theory and measurement. In L. Balter, Tamis-LeMonda, C. S. (Eds.), *Child Psychology: A Handbook of Contemporary Issues* (3rd ed., pp. 123–140). Routledge: New York.

Sullivan, J., Wilton, L., & Apfelbaum, E. P. (2020). Adults delay conversations about race because they underestimate children's processing of race. *Journal of Experimental Psychology: General*.

Tarullo, A. R., Youssef, A., Frenn, K. A., et al. (2016). Emotion understanding, parent mental state language, and behavior problems in internationally adopted children. *Development and Psychopathology* 28, 371–383.

Tenenbaum, H. R., Ford, S., & Alkhedairy, B. (2011). Telling stories: Gender differences in peers' emotion talk and communication style. *British Journal of Developmental Psychology* 29, 707–721.

Teti, D. M., Nakagawa, M., Das, R., & Wirth, O. (1991). Security of attachment between preschoolers and their mothers: Relations among social interaction, parenting stress, and mother's sorts of the Attachment Q-Set. *Developmental Psychology* 27, 440–447.

Teti, D. M., Sakin, J. W., Kucera, E., et al. (1996). And baby makes four: Predictors of attachment security among preschool-age firstborns during the transition to siblinghood. *Child Development* 67, 579–596.

Thornton, M. C., Chatters, L. M., Taylor, R. J., & Allen, W. R. (1990). Sociodemographic and environmental correlates of racial socialization by Black parents. *Child Development* 61, 401–409.

Torres, M. M., Domitrovich, C. E., & Bierman, K. L. (2015). Preschool interpersonal relationships predict kindergarten achievement: Mediated by gains in emotion knowledge. *Journal of Applied Developmental Psychology* 39, 44–52.

Triandis, H. C. (2018). *Individualism and Collectivism*. Routledge: New York.

Umaña-Taylor, A. J., & Fine, M. A. (2004). Examining ethnic identity among Mexican-origin adolescents living in the United States. *Hispanic Journal of Behavioral Sciences* 26, 36–59.

Vaish, A., Missana, M., & Tomasello, M. (2011). Three-year-old children intervene in third-party moral transgressions. *British Journal of Developmental Psychology* 29, 124–130.

van Dijk, A., Thomaes, S., Poorthuis, A. M. G., et al. (2019). Can self-persuasion reduce hostile attribution bias in young children? *Journal of Abnormal Child Psychology* 47, 989–1000.

Vaughn, B. E. (2001). A hierarchical model of social competence for preschool-age children: Cross-sectional and longitudinal analyses. *Revue Internationale de Psychologie Sociale* 14, 13–40.

Vaughn, B. E., Kopp, C. B., & Krakow, J. B. (1984). The emergence and consolidation of self-control from eighteen to thirty months of age: Normative trends and individual differences. *Child Development* 55, 990–1004.

Vaughn, B. E., Vollenweider, M., Bost, K. K., et al. (2003). Negative interactions and social competence for preschool children in two samples: Reconsidering the interpretation of aggressive behavior for young children. *Merrill-Palmer Quarterly* 49, 245–278.

Verschueren, K., & Marcoen, A. (1999). Representation of self and socioemotional competence in kindergartners: Differential and combined effects of attachment to mother and father. *Child Development* 70, 183–201.

Volling, B. L., Mahoney, A., & Rauer, A. J. (2009). Sanctification of parenting, moral socialization, and young children's conscience development. *Psychology of Religion and Spirituality* 1, 53–68.

Vygotsky, L. S. (1978). *Mind in Society: The Development of Higher Mental Process*. Harvard University Press: Cambridge, MA.

Walden, T., Lemerise, E., & Smith, M. C. (1999). Friendship and popularity in preschool classrooms. *Early Education and Development* 10, 351–371.

Wallen, K. (1996). Nature needs nurture: The interaction of hormonal and social influences on the development of behavioral sex differences in rhesus monkeys. *Hormones and Behavior* 30, 364–378.

Wang, Q. (2003). Emotion situation knowledge in American and Chinese preschool children and adults. *Cognition and Emotion* 17, 725–746.

Wang, Q., Doan, S. N., & Song, Q. (2010). Talking about internal states in mother–child reminiscing influences children's self-representations: A cross-cultural study. *Cognitive Development* 25, 380–393.

Wang, Q., & Fivush, R. (2005). Mother-child conversations of emotionally salient events: Exploring the functions of emotional reminiscing in European-American and Chinese families. *Social Development* 14, 473–495.

Warneken, F., & Tomasello, M. (2013). The emergence of contingent reciprocity in young children. *Journal of Experimental Child Psychology* 116, 338–350.

Waters, E. (1995). Appendix A: The attachment Q-set (Version 3.0). *Monographs of the Society for Research in Child Development* 60, 234–246.

Waters, E., & Deane, K. E. (1985). Defining and assessing individual differences in attachment relationships: Q-methodology and the organization of behavior in infancy and early childhood. *Monographs of the Society for Research in Child Development* 50, 41–65.

Way, N. (2011). *Deep Secrets.* Harvard University Press: Cambridge, MA.

Weiland, C., & Yoshikawa, H. (2013). Impacts of a prekindergarten program on children's mathematics, language, literacy, executive function, and emotional skills. *Child Development* 84, 2112–2130.

Weiss, B., Dodge, K. A., Bates, J. E., & Pettit, G. S. (1992). Some consequences of early harsh discipline: Child aggression and a maladaptive social information processing style. *Child Development* 63, 1321–1335.

Wellman, H. M. (1988). First steps in the child's theorizing about the mind. *Developing Theories of Mind*, 64–92.

Werner, K. B., Grant, J. D., McCutcheon, V. V., et al. (2016). Differences in childhood physical abuse reporting and the association between CPA and alcohol use disorder in European American and African American women. *Psychology of Addictive Behaviors* 30, 423–433.

Widen, S. C., & Russell, J. A. (2008a). Children's and adults' understanding of the "disgust face." *Cognition and Emotion* 22, 1513–1541.

Widen, S. C., & Russell, J. A. (2008b). Children acquire emotion categories gradually. *Cognitive Development* 23, 291–312.

Widen, S. C., & Russell, J. A. (2010). Differentiation in preschooler's categories of emotion. *Emotion* 10, 651–661.

Widen, S. C., & Russell, J. A. (2011). In building a script for an emotion, do preschoolers add its cause before its behavior consequence? *Social Development* 20, 471–485.

Wong, M., & Power, T. G. (2019). Links between coping strategies and depressive symptoms among girls and boys during the transition to primary school. *Early Education and Development* 30, 178–195.

Wu, Y. & Schulz, L. E. (2017). What do you really think? Children's ability to infer others' desires when emotional expressions change between social and nonsocial contexts. In *Proceedings of the 39th Annual Conference of the Cognitive Science Society* (pp. 1363–1368).

Wu, P., Robinson, C. C., Yang, C., et al. (2002). Similarities and differences in mothers' parenting of preschoolers in China and the United States. *International Journal of Behavioral Development* 26, 481–491.

Youniss, J. (1980). *Parents and Peers in Social Development: A Sullivan-Piaget Perspective.* University of Chicago Press: Chicago, IL.

Zajdel, R. J., Bloom, J. M., Fireman, G., & Larsen, J. T. (2013) Children's understanding and experience of mixed emotions: The roles of age, gender, and empathy, *The Journal of Genetic Psychology* 174, 582–603.

Zhou, Q., Lengua, L. J., & Wang, Y. (2009). The relations of temperament reactivity and effortful control to children's adjustment problems in China and the United States. *Developmental Psychology* 45, 724–739.

Zosuls, K. M., Miller, C. F., Ruble, D. N., et al. (2011). Gender development research in sex roles: Historical trends and future directions. *Sex Roles*, 64, 826–842.

Chapter 11

Adolph, K. E., Karasik, L. B., & Tamis-LeMonda, C. S. (2010). Motor skill. In M. H. Bornstein (Ed.), *Handbook of Cultural Developmental Science* (pp. 61–88). Psychology Press: New York.

Adolphus, K., Lawton, C. L., & Dye, L. (2013). The effects of breakfast on behavior and academic performance in children and adolescents. *Frontiers in Human Neuroscience* 7, 425.

Alaimo, K., Olson, C. M., & Frongillo, E. A. (2001). Food insufficiency and American school-aged children's cognitive, academic, and psychosocial development. *Pediatrics* 108, 44–53.

Akinbami, L. J., Rossen, L. M., Fakhouri, T. H., et al. (2017). Contribution of weight status to asthma prevalence racial disparities, 2–19 year olds, 1988–2014. *Annals of Epidemiology* 27, 472–478.

Akinbami, L. J., Simon, A. E., & Rossen, L. M. (2016). Changing trends in asthma prevalence among children. *Pediatrics* 137, e20152354.

Al-Amin, M., Zinchenko, A., & Geyer, T. (2018). Hippocampal subfield volume changes in subtypes of attention deficit hyperactivity disorder. *Brain Research* 1685, 1–8.

Al-Amin, M., Allison, M. A., & Attisha, E., and Council on School Health (2019). The link between school attendance and good health. *Pediatrics* 143.

An, R., Yang, Y., Hoschke, A., et al. (2017). Influence of neighbourhood safety on childhood obesity: a systematic review and meta-analysis of longitudinal studies. *Obesity Reviews* 18, 1289–1309.

Arija, V., Esparó, G., Fernández-Ballart, J., et al. (2006). Nutritional status and performance in test of verbal and non-verbal intelligence in 6 year old children. *Intelligence* 34, 141–149.

Astill, R. G., Van der Heijden, K. B., Van Ijzendoorn, M. H., & Van Someren, E. J. W. (2012). Sleep, cognition, and behavioral problems in school-age children: A century of research meta-analyzed. *Psychological Bulletin* 138, 1109–1138.

Atlantis, E., Barnes, E. H., & Singh, M. A. F. (2006). Efficacy of exercise for treating overweight in children and adolescents: a systematic review. *International Journal of Obesity* 30, 1027.

Bailar-Heath, M., & Valley-Gray, S. (2010). *Pediatric Disorders: Current Topics and Interventions for Educators.* Corwin Press: Thousand Oaks, CA.

Barros, R. M., Silver, E. J., & Stein, R. E. K. (2009). School recess and group classroom behavior. *Pediatrics* 123, 431–436.

Bascom, A., McMaster, M. A., Alexander, R. T., & MacLean, J. E. (2019). Nocturnal enuresis in children is associated with differences in autonomic control. *Sleep* 42, zsy239.

Bell, B. G., & Belsky, J. (2008). Parents, parenting, and children's sleep problems: Exploring reciprocal effects. *British Journal of Developmental Psychology* 26, 579–593.

Belsky, J., & de Haan, M. (2011). Annual research review: Parenting and children's brain development: the end of the beginning. *Journal of Child Psychology and Psychiatry* 52, 409–428.

Biddle, S. J. H., & Asare, M. (2011). Physical activity and mental health in children and adolescents: a review of reviews. *British Journal of Sports Medicine.*

Bliege Bird, R., & Bird, D. W. (2002). Constraints of knowing or constraints of growing? Fishing and collecting by the children of Mer. *Human Nature* 13, 239–267.

Bohn-Gettler, C. M., & Pellegrini, A. D. (2014). Recess in primary school: The disjuncture between educational policy and scientific research. In *Justice, Conflict and Wellbeing* (pp. 313–336). Springer: New York.

Booth, J. R., Bebko, G., Burman, D. D., & Bitan, T. (2007). Children with reading disorder show modality independent brain abnormalities during semantic tasks. *Neuropsychologia* 45, 775–783.

Bornstein, M. H. (1979). The pace of life: Revisited. *International Journal of Psychology* 14, 83–90.

Bornstein, M. H., & Bornstein, H. G. (1976). The pace of life. *Nature* 259, 557.

Burgess-Champoux, T. L., Larson, N., Neumark-Sztainer, D., et al. (2009). Are family meal patterns associated with overall diet quality during the transition from early to middle adolescence? *Journal of Nutrition Education and Behavior* 41, 79–86.

Caldwell, P. H. Y., Sureshkumar, P., & Wong, W. C. F. (2016). Tricyclic and related drugs for nocturnal enuresis in children. *Cochrane Database of Systematic Reviews.*

Caprio, S., Daniels, S. R., Drewnowski, A., et al. (2008). Influence of race, ethnicity, and culture on childhood obesity: Implications for prevention and treatment. *Obesity* 16, 2566–2577.

Carissimi, A., Martins, A. C., Dresch, F., et al. (2016). School start time influences melatonin and cortisol levels in children and adolescents – A community-based study. *Chronobiology International* 33, 1400–1409.

Carlson, J. A., Engelberg, J. K., Cain, K. L., et al. (2015). Implementing classroom physical activity breaks: Associations with student physical activity and classroom behavior. *Preventive Medicine* 81, 67–72.

Carskadon, M., A., Harvey, K., Duke, P., et al. (1980). Pubertal changes in daytime sleepiness. *Sleep* 2, 453–460.

Carskadon, M. A., & Dement, W. C. (1979). Effects of total sleep loss on sleep tendency. *Perceptual and Motor Skills* 48, 495–506.

Catalá-López, F., Hutton, B., Núñez-Beltrán, A., et al. (2017). The pharmacological and non-pharmacological treatment of attention deficit hyperactivity disorder in children and adolescents: a systematic review with network meta-analyses of randomised trials. *PLoS ONE* 12, e0180355.

Centers for Disease Control Prevention. (2010). *The association between school based physical activity, including physical education, and academic performance.* US Department of Health and Human Services: Atlanta, GA.

Centers for Disease Control Prevention. (2013). National center for injury prevention and control. Web-based injury statistics query and reporting system (WISQARS).

Cicchetti, D., & Cohen, D. (2006). *Developmental Psychopathology.* Wiley: Hoboken, NJ.

Cohen, D. A., Han, B., Park, S., et al. (2019). Park use and park-based physical activity in low-income neighborhoods. *Journal of Aging and Physical Activity* 27, 334–342.

Coleman-Jensen, A., Rabbitt, M., Gregory, C., & Singh, A. (2015). Statistical supplement to household food security in the United States in 2014. In *AP-069, USDA. Economic Research Service.*

Compas, B. E., Jaser, S. S., Dunn, M. J., & Rodriguez, E. M. (2012). Coping with chronic illness in childhood and adolescence. *Annual Review of Clinical Psychology* 8, 455–480.

Currie, J., Stabile, M., Manivong, P., & Roos, L. L. (2010). Child health and young adult outcomes. *Journal of Human Resources* 45, 517–548.

Cusimano, M. D., Cho, N., Amin, K., et al. (2013). Mechanisms of team-sport-related brain injuries in children 5 to 19 years old: Opportunities for prevention. *PLoS ONE* 8, e58868.

Daniels, E., & Leaper, C. (2006). A longitudinal investigation of sport participation, peer acceptance, and self-esteem among adolescent girls and boys. *Sex Roles* 55, 875–880.

Davison, K. K., & Birch, L. L. (2004). Predictors of fat stereotypes among 9-year-old girls and their parents. *Obesity Research* 12, 86–94.

Delaney, L., & Smith, J. P. (2012). Childhood health: Trends and consequences over the life-course. *The Future of Children/Center for the Future of Children, the David and Lucile Packard Foundation* 22, 43–63.

Devine, J. (1985). The versatility of human locomotion. *American Anthropologist* 87, 550–570.

Donnelly, J. E., Hillman, C. H., Castelli, D., et al. (2016). Physical activity, fitness, cognitive function, and academic achievement in children: a systematic review. *Medicine and Science in Sports and Exercise* 48, 1197.

DuPaul, G. J., Eckert, T. L., & Vilardo, B. (2012). The effects of school-based interventions for attention deficit hyperactivity disorder: A meta-analysis 1996–2010. *School Psychology Review* 41, 387–412.

DuPaul, G. J., Evans, S. W., Mautone, J. A., et al. (2020). Future directions for psychosocial interventions for children and adolescents with ADHD. *Journal of Clinical Child & Adolescent Psychology* 49, 134–145.

Eide, E. R., & Showalter, M. H. (2012). Sleep and student achievement. *Eastern Economic Journal* 38, 512–524.

Engle-Friedman, M., Palencar, V., & Riela, S. (2010). Sleep and effort in adolescent athletes. *Journal of Child Health Care* 14, 131–141.

Erickson, S. J., Gerstle, M., & Feldstein, S. W. (2005). Brief interventions and motivational interviewing with children, adolescents, and their parents in pediatric health care settings: A review. *Archives of Pediatrics & Adolescent Medicine* 159, 1173–1180.

Ericsson I, Karlsson MK. (2014). Motor skills and school performance in children with daily physical education in school--a 9-year intervention study. *Scand J Med Sci Sports* 24, 273–278.

Evans, A. M. (2008). Growing pains: Contemporary knowledge and recommended practice.

Evans, S. W., Owens, J. S., Wymbs, B. T., & Ray, A. R. (2018). Evidence-based psychosocial treatments for children and adolescents with attention deficit/hyperactivity disorder. *Journal of Clinical Child & Adolescent Psychology* 47, 157–198.

Fabiano, G. A., Chacko, A., Pelham Jr, W. E., et al. (2009). A comparison of behavioral parent training programs for fathers of children with attention-deficit/hyperactivity disorder. *Behavior Therapy* 40, 190–204.

Ferrara, M., & De Gennaro, L. (2001). How much sleep do we need? *Sleep Medicine Reviews* 5, 155–179.

Fiese, B. H., & Schwartz, M. (2008). Reclaiming the family table: Mealtimes and child health and wellbeing. Social Policy Report 22(4). Society for Research in Child Development.

Findlay, L. C., & Coplan, R. J. (2008). Come out and play: Shyness in childhood and the benefits of organized sports participation. *Canadian Journal of Behavioural Science* 40, 153–161.

Finn, A. (2013). *Running with the Kenyans: Passion, Adventure, and the Secrets of the Fastest People on Earth.* Ballantine Books.

Fjørtoft, I. (2004). Landscape as playscape: The effects of natural environments on children's play and motor development. *Children, Youth and Environments* 14, 21–44.

Frank, J. B., Jarit, G. J., Bravman, J. T., & Rosen, J. E. (2007). Lower extremity injuries in the skeletally immature athlete. *Journal of the American Academy of Orthopaedic Surgeons* 15, 356–366.

Franěk, M. (2013). Environmental factors influencing pedestrian walking speed. *Perceptual and Motor Skills* 116, 992–1019.

Franěk, M., Režný, L., Šefara, D., & Cabal, J. (2019). Effect of birdsongs and traffic noise on pedestrian walking speed during different seasons. *Peer J* 7, e7711.

Freemark, M. (2018). Childhood obesity in the modern age: Global trends, determinants, complications, and costs. In *Pediatric Obesity* (pp. 3–24). Humana Press: Cham, Switzerland.

Frisvold, D. E. (2015). Nutrition and cognitive achievement: An evaluation of the School Breakfast Program. *Journal of Public Economics* 124, 91–104.

Galland, B. C., Taylor, B. J., Elder, D. E., & Herbison, P. (2012). Normal sleep patterns in infants and children: A systematic review of observational studies. *Sleep Medicine Reviews* 16, 213–222.

Gallo, S., Rhoades, S. K., de Jonge, L., et al. (2017). Childhood Health, Education, & Wellness (CHEW): A pilot trial for an individualized, family-centered and culturally adapted program targeting childhood obesity among Latino children. *Journal of the Academy of Nutrition and Dietetics* 117, A19.

Gibson, A. R., Ojiambo, R., Konstabel, K., et al. (2013). Aerobic capacity, activity levels and daily energy expenditure in male and female adolescents of the Kenyan Nandi sub-group. *PLoS ONE* 8, e66552.

Giedd, J. N., Blumenthal, J., Jeffries, N. O., et al. (1999). Brain development during childhood and adolescence: A longitudinal MRI study. *Nature Neuroscience* 2, 861–863.

Giedd, J. N., & Rapoport, J. L. (2010). Structural MRI of pediatric brain development: What have we learned and where are we going? *Neuron* 67, 728–734.

Glazener, C. M. A., Evans, J. H. C., & Peto, R. E. (2005). Alarm interventions for nocturnal enuresis in children. *Cochrane Database of Systematic Reviews.*

Gogtay, N., Giedd, J. N., Lusk, L., et al. (2004). Dynamic mapping of human cortical development during childhood through early adulthood. *Proceedings of the National academy of Sciences of the United States of America* 101, 8174–8179.

Graf, C., Koch, B., Kretschmann-Kandel, E., et al. (2003). Correlation between BMI, leisure habits and motor abilities in childhood (CHILT-Project). *International Journal of Obesity* 28, 22.

Grantham-McGregor, S. M., Walker, S. P., & Chang, S. (2007). Nutritional deficiencies and later behavioural development. *Proceedings of the Nutrition Society* 59, 47–54.

Gray, H. L., Buro, A. W., Barrera Ikan, et al. (2019). School-level factors associated with obesity: A systematic review of longitudinal studies. *Obesity Reviews* 20, 1016–1032.

Gruber, R., Laviolette, R., Deluca, P., et al. (2010). Short sleep duration is associated with poor performance on IQ measures in healthy school-age children. *Sleep Medicine* 11, 289–294.

Harrist, A. W., Swindle, T. M., Hubbs-Tait, L., et al. (2016). The social and emotional lives of overweight, obese, and severely obese children. *Child Dev* 87, 1564–1580.

Hayes, D., Contento, I. R., & Weekly, C. (2018). Position of the Academy of Nutrition and Dietetics, Society for Nutrition Education and Behavior, and School Nutrition Association: Comprehensive nutrition programs and services in schools. *Journal of the Academy of Nutrition and Dietetics* 118, 913–919.

Haywood, K. M., & Getchell, N. (2005). *Life Span Motor Development,* 4th ed. Human Kinetics: Champaign, IL.

Heglund, N. C., Willems, P. A., Penta, M., & Cavagna, G. A. (1995). Energy-saving gait mechanics with head-supported loads. *Nature* 375, 52–54.

Henderson, L. M., Weighall, A. R., Brown, H., & Gareth Gaskell, M. (2012). Consolidation of vocabulary is associated with sleep in children. *Developmental Science* 15, 674–687.

Hewlett, B. S., & Lamb, M. E. (2017). Emerging issues in the study of hunter-gatherer children. In *Hunter-Gatherer Childhoods* (pp. 3–18). Routledge: London, United Kingdom.

Hill, A. J. (2017). Obesity in children and the 'Myth of Psychological Maladjustment': Self-esteem in the spotlight. *Current Obesity Reports* 6, 63–70.

Janowsky, J. S., & Carper, R. (1996). Is there a neural basis for cognitive transitions in school-age children? In *The Five to Seven Year Shift: The Age of Reason and Responsibility* (pp. 33–60). University of Chicago Press: Chicago, IL.

Janssen, H. G., Davies, I. G., Richardson, L. D., & Stevenson, L. (2018). Determinants of takeaway and fast food consumption: A narrative review. *Nutrition Research Reviews* 31, 16–34.

Janssen, I., Craig, W. M., Boyce, W. F., & Pickett, W. (2004). Associations between overweight and obesity with bullying behaviors in school-aged children. *Pediatrics* 113, 1187–1194.

Janssen, I., & LeBlanc, A. G. (2010). Systematic review of the health benefits of physical activity and fitness in school-aged children and youth. *International Journal of Behavioral Nutrition and Physical Activity* 7, 40.

Jones, N. B., & Marlowe, F. W. (2002). Selection for delayed maturity. *Human Nature* 13, 199–238.

Karkhaneh, M., Rowe, B. H., Saunders, L. D., et al. (2013). Trends in head injuries associated with mandatory bicycle helmet legislation targeting children and adolescents. *Accident Analysis & Prevention* 59, 206–212.

Keller, S. S., & Robert, S. N. (2009). Measurement of brain volume using MRI. *Journal of Anthropological Sciences* 87, 251.

Klingberg, T., Forssberg, H., & Westerberg, H. (2002). Increased brain activity in frontal and parietal cortex underlies the development of visuospatial working memory capacity during childhood. *Journal of Cognitive Neuroscience* 14, 1–10.

Kontos, A. P., Elbin, R. J., Fazio-Sumrock, V. C., et al. (2013). Incidence of sports-related concussion among youth football players aged 8–12 years. *The Journal of Pediatrics* 163, 717–720.

Kwak, K. W., Lee, Y.-S., Park, K. H., & Baek, M. (2010). Efficacy of desmopressin and enuresis alarm as first and second line treatment for primary monosymptomatic nocturnal enuresis: Prospective randomized crossover study. *The Journal of Urology* 184, 2521–2526.

Lakshman, R., Elks, C. E., & Ong, K. K. (2012). Childhood obesity. *Circulation* 126, 1770–1779.

Latner, J. D., & Stunkard, A. J. (2003). Getting worse: The stigmatization of obese children. *Obesity Research* 11, 452–456.

Lenroot, R. K., & Giedd, J. N. (2006). Brain development in children and adolescents: Insights from anatomical magnetic resonance imaging. *Neuroscience and Biobehavioral Reviews* 30, 718–729.

Lew-Levy, S., Reckin, R., Lavi, N., et al. (2017). How do hunter-gatherer children learn subsistence skills? *Human Nature* 28, 367–394.

Liben, L. S. (2006). Education for spatial thinking. In *Handbook of Child Psychology.* John Wiley & Sons, Inc.: Hoboken, NJ.

Liebe, S., Hoerzer, G. M., Logothetis, N. K., & Rainer, G. (2012). Theta coupling between V4 and prefrontal cortex predicts visual short-term memory performance. *Nature Neuroscience* 15, 456–462.

Lingam, R., Jongmans, M. J., Ellis, M., et al. (2012). Mental health difficulties in children with developmental coordination disorder. *Pediatrics* 129, e882–e891.

Liu, J., Raine, A., Venables, P. H., Dalais, C., & Mednick, S. A. (2003). Malnutrition at age 3 years and lower cognitive ability at age 11 years: Independence from psychosocial adversity. *Archives of Pediatrics & Adolescent Medicine* 157, 593–600.

Livesey, D., Lum Mow, M., Toshack, T., & Zheng, Y. (2011). The relationship between motor performance and peer relations in 9- to 12-year-old children. *Child: Care, Health and Development* 37, 581–588.

Lott, M., Schwartz, M., Story, M., & Brownell, K. D. (2018). Why we need local, state, and national policy-based approaches to improve children's nutrition in the United States. In *Pediatric Obesity* (pp. 731–755). Humana Press, Cham: Switzerland.

Lowin, A., Hottes, J. H., Sandler, B. E., & Bornstein, M. (1971). The pace of life and sensitivity to time in urban and rural settings: A preliminary study. *The Journal of Social Psychology* 83, 247–253.

Lowry, K. W., Sallinen, B. J., & Janicke, D. M. (2007). The effects of weight management programs on self-esteem in pediatric overweight populations. *Journal of Pediatric Psychology* 32, 1179–1195.

Luby, J., Belden, A., Botteron, K., et al. (2013). The effects of poverty on childhood brain development: The mediating effect of caregiving and stressful life events. *JAMA Pediatrics* 167, 1135–1142.

Luecken, L. J., Roubinov, D. S., & Tanaka, R. (2013). Childhood family environment, social competence, and health across the lifespan. *Journal of Social and Personal Relationships* 30, 171–178.

Luke, A., Lazaro, R. M., Bergeron, M. F., et al. (2011). Sports-related injuries in youth athletes: is overscheduling a risk factor? *Clinical Journal of Sport Medicine* 21, 307–314.

Lumeng, J. C., Appugliese, D., Cabral, H. J., et al. (2006). Neighborhood safety and overweight status in children. *Archives of Pediatrics & Adolescent Medicine* 160, 25–31.

Lumeng, J. C., Somashekar, D., Appugliese, D., et al. (2007). Shorter sleep duration is associated with increased risk for being overweight at ages 9 to 12 years. *Pediatrics* 120, 1020–1029.

Malina, R. M., Eisenmann, J. C., Cumming, S. P., et al. (2004). Maturity-associated variation in the growth and functional capacities of youth football (soccer) players 13–15 years. *European Journal of Applied Physiology* 91, 555–562.

Maloiy, G. M. O., Heglund, N. C., Prager, L. M., et al. (1986). Energetic cost of carrying loads: have African women discovered an economic way? *Nature* 319, 668.

Mann, G., Kraak, V., & Serrano, E. (2017). Smart snacks in school standards in Appalachian Virginia middle schools. *Health Behavior and Policy Review* 4, 245–255.

Marcos-Vidal, L., Martínez-García, M., Pretus, C., et al. (2018). Local functional connectivity suggests functional immaturity in children with attention-deficit/hyperactivity disorder. *Human Brain Mapping* 39, 2442–2454.

Marin, T. J., Chen, E., Munch, J. A., & Miller, G. E. (2009). Double-exposure to acute stress and chronic family stress is associated with immune changes in children with asthma. *Psychosomatic Medicine* 71, 378–384.

Marsh, H. W., Gerlach, E., Trautwein, U., et al. (2007). Longitudinal study of preadolescent sport self-concept and performance: Reciprocal effects and causal ordering. *Child Development* 78, 1640–1656.

Matricciani, L., Blunden, S., Rigney, G., et al. (2013). Children's sleep needs: Is there sufficient evidence to recommend optimal sleep for children? *Sleep* 36, 527–534.

Matricciani, L., Olds, T., & Petkov, J. (2012). In search of lost sleep: Secular trends in the sleep time of school-aged children and adolescents. *Sleep Medicine Reviews* 16, 203–211.

Mead, M., & Macgregor, F. C. (1951). *Growth and Culture: A Photographic Study of Balinese Childhood.* Putnam: Oxford, United Kingdom.

Menon, V. (2013). Developmental pathways to functional brain networks: emerging principles. *Trends in Cognitive Sciences* 17, 627–640.

Miller, E. K., & Buschman, T. J. (2013). Cortical circuits for the control of attention. *Current Opinion in Neurobiology* 23, 216–222.

Millimet, D. L., Tchernis, R., & Husain, M. (2010). School nutrition programs and the incidence of childhood obesity. *Journal of Human Resources* 45, 640–654.

Mills, K. L., Goddings, A.-L., Herting, M. M., et al. (2016). Structural brain development between childhood and adulthood: Convergence across four longitudinal samples. *NeuroImage* 141, 273–281.

Monnat, S. M., Lounsbery, M. A., McKenzie, T. L., & Chandler, R. F. (2017). Associations between demographic characteristics and physical activity practices in Nevada schools. *Preventive Medicine* 95, S4–S9.

Myers, C. A., Vandermosten, C. A., Farris, E. A., et al. (2014). White matter morphometric changes uniquely predict children's reading acquisition. *Psychological Science* 25, 1870–1883.

National Association for Sport Physical Education. (2004). *National Standards for Physical Education.* McGraw-Hill Humanities/Social Sciences/Languages: New York.

Nichols, B. L. (2018). 90th anniversary commentary: Malnutrition affects cellular growth and competency; Propositions by Myron Winick, *The Journal of Nutrition* 148, 1650–1651.

Nomi, J. S., Schettini, E., Voorhies, W., et al. (2018). Resting-state brain signal variability in prefrontal cortex is associated with ADHD symptom severity in children. *Frontiers in Human Neuroscience* 12, 90.

O'Dea, J. A. (2003). Why do kids eat healthful food? Perceived benefits of and barriers to healthful eating and physical activity among children and adolescents. *Journal of the American Dietetic Association* 103, 497–501.

Ogden, C. L., Fryar, C. D., Martin, C. B., et al. (2020). Trends in obesity prevalence by race and Hispanic origin—1999–2000 to 2017–2018. *JAMA* 324, 1208–1210.

Olds, T. S., Maher, C. A., & Matricciani, L. (2011). Sleep duration or bedtime? Exploring the relationship between sleep habits and weight status and activity patterns. *Sleep* 34, 1299–1307.

Oude Luttikhuis, H., Baur, L., Jansen, H., et al. (2009). Cochrane review: Interventions for treating obesity in children. *Evidence-Based Child Health: A Cochrane Review Journal* 4, 1571–1729.

Owens, J. A. (2005). Introduction: Culture and sleep in children. *Pediatrics* 115, 201–203.

Pasanen, K., Rossi, M. T., Parkkari, J., et al. (2015). Predictors of lower extremity injuries in team sports (PROFITS-study): A study protocol. *BMJ Open Sport & Exercise Medicine* 1.

Penny, H., & Haddock, G. (2007). Children's stereotypes of overweight children. *British Journal of Developmental Psychology* 25, 409–418.

Perlman, S. B., & Pelphrey, K. A. (2010). Regulatory brain development: balancing emotion and cognition. *Social Neuroscience* 5, 533–542.

Perrin, J. M., Bloom, S. R., & Gortmaker, S. L. (2007). The increase of childhood chronic conditions in the United States. *JAMA* 297, 2755–2759.

Poti, J. M., & Popkin, B. M. (2011). Trends in energy intake among US children by eating location and food source, 1977–2006. *Journal of the American Dietetic Association* 111, 1156–1164.

Puhl, R. M., & Latner, J. D. (2007). Stigma, obesity, and the health of the nation's children. *Psychological Bulletin* 133, 557–580.

Radelet, M. A., Lephart, S. M., Rubinstein, E. N., & Myers, J. B. (2002). Survey of the injury rate for children in community sports. *Pediatrics* 110, e28.

Ramstetter, C., & Murray, R. (2017). Time to play: Recognizing the benefits of recess. *American Educator* 41, 17.

Ravussin, E., Valencia, M. E., Esparza, J., et al. (1994). Effects of a traditional lifestyle on obesity in Pima Indians. *Diabetes Care* 17, 1067–1074.

Renzaho, A. M., McCabe, M., & Swinburn, B. (2012). Intergenerational differences in food, physical activity, and body size perceptions among African migrants. *Qualitative Health Research* 22, 740–754.

Robinson, T. N., Banda, J. A., Hale, L., et al. (2017). Screen media exposure and obesity in children and adolescents. *Pediatrics* 140, S97–S101.

Rodriguez, E. M., Dunn, M. J., Zuckerman, T., et al. (2012). Cancer-related sources of stress for children with cancer and their parents. *Journal of Pediatric Psychology* 37, 185–197.

Rodríguez-Negro, J., Huertas-Delgado, F. J., & Yanci, J. (2019) Motor skills differences by gender in early elementary education students, *Early Child Development and Care*.

Rozbacher, A., Selci, E., Leiter, J., et al. (2017). The effect of concussion or mild traumatic brain injury on school grades, national examination scores, and school attendance. a systematic review. *Journal of Neurotrauma* 34, 2195–2203.

Sadeh, A., Gruber, R., & Raviv, A. (2002). Sleep, neurobehavioral functioning, and behavior problems in school-age children. *Child Development* 73, 405–417.

Sadeh, A., Gruber, R., & Raviv, A. (2003). The effects of sleep restriction and extension on school-age children: What a difference an hour makes. *Child Development* 74, 444–455.

Schneider, D. K., Grandhi, R. K., Bansal, P., et al. (2016). Current state of concussion prevention strategies: a systematic review and meta-analysis of prospective, controlled studies. *British Journal of Sports Medicine*.

Seo, W. S., Sung, H.-M., Lee, J. H., et al. (2010). Sleep patterns and their age-related changes in elementary-school children. *Sleep Medicine* 11, 569–575.

Shankar, P., Chung, R., & Frank, D. A. (2017). Association of food insecurity with children's behavioral, emotional, and academic outcomes: a systematic review. *Journal of Developmental & Behavioral Pediatrics* 38, 135–150.

Shaw, P., Greenstein, D., Lerch, J., et al. (2006). Intellectual ability and cortical development in children and adolescents. *Nature* 440, 676–679.

Sherry, B., McDivitt, J., Birch, L. L., et al. (2004). Attitudes, practices, and concerns about child feeding and child weight status among socioeconomically diverse white, Hispanic, and African-American mothers. *Journal of the American Dietetic Association* 104, 215–221.

Skinner, A. C., Ravanbakht, S. N., Skelton, J. A., et al. (2018). Prevalence of obesity and severe obesity in US children, 1999–2016. *Pediatrics* 141.

Skinner, R. A., & Piek, J. P. (2001). Psychosocial implications of poor motor coordination in children and adolescents. *Human Movement Science* 20, 73–94.

Smith, J. J., Eather, N., Morgan, P. J., et al. (2014). The health benefits of muscular fitness for children and adolescents: A systematic review and meta-analysis. *Sports Medicine* 44, 1209–1223.

Sowell, E. R., Trauner, D. A., Gamst, A., & Jernigan, T. L. (2002). Development of cortical and subcortical brain structures in childhood and adolescence: A structural MRI study. *Developmental Medicine & Child Neurology* 44, 4–16.

Spruyt, K., O'Brien, L. M., Cluydts, R., et al. (2005). Odds, prevalence and predictors of sleep problems in school-age normal children. *Journal of Sleep Research* 14, 163–176.

Stauder, J. E. A., Molenaar, P. C. M., & Van der Molen, M. W. (1999). Brain activity and cognitive transition during childhood: A longitudinal event-related brain potential study. *Child Neuropsychology* 5, 41–59.

Stieben, J., Lewis, M. D., Granic, I., et al. (2007). Neurophysiological mechanisms of emotion regulation for subtypes of externalizing children. *Development and Psychopathology* 19, 455–480.

Stovitz, S. D., Steffen, L. M., & Boostrom, A. (2008). Participation in physical activity Among normal- and overweight Hispanic and non-Hispanic White adolescents. *Journal of School Health* 78, 19–25.

Tanumihardjo, S. A., Anderson, C., Kaufer-Horwitz, M., et al. (2007). Poverty, obesity, and malnutrition: An international perspective recognizing the paradox. *Journal of the American Dietetic Association* 107, 1966–1972.

Thomas, K. M., Drevets, W. C., Dahl, R. E., et al. (2001). Amygdala response to fearful faces in anxious and depressed children. *Archives of General Psychiatry* 58, 1057–1063.

Thronson, G., Park Fast, G., & Gray, L. (2014). *Infectious Disease Control Guide for School Staff*. Office of Superintendent of Public Instruction: Olympia, WA.

Uziel, Y., Chapnick, G., Oren-Ziv, A., et al. (2012). Bone strength in children with growing pains: long-term follow-up. *Clinical and Experimental Rheumatology* 30, 137–140.

Velő, S., Keresztény, Á., Ferenczi-Dallos, G., & Balázs, J. (2019). Long-term effects of multimodal treatment on psychopathology and health-related quality of life of children with attention deficit hyperactivity disorder. *Frontiers in Psychology* 10, 2037.

Wang, Y., & Lobstein, T. I. M. (2006). Worldwide trends in childhood overweight and obesity. *International Journal of Pediatric Obesity* 1, 11–25.

Waters, E., de Silva-Sanigorski, A., Burford, B. J., et al. (2011). Interventions for preventing obesity in children. *Cochrane Database of Systematic Reviews* 12.

Weinreb, L., Wehler, C., Perloff, J., et al. (2002). Hunger: Its impact on children's health and mental health. *Pediatrics* 110, e41.

Wilson, D. K., Kitzman-Ulrich, H., Resnicow, K., et al. (2015). An overview of the Families Improving Together (FIT) for weight loss randomized controlled trial in African American families. *Contemporary Clinical Trials* 42, 145–157.

Wolch, J., Jerrett, M., Reynolds, K., et al. (2011). Childhood obesity and proximity to urban parks and recreational resources: A longitudinal cohort study. *Health & Place* 17, 207–214.

World Health Organization (2013). Obesity and overweight. Fact Sheet No 311. Updated March 2013. World Health Organization. http://www.who.int/mediacentre/factsheets/fs311/en/index.html.

Yap, Q. J., Teh, I., Fusar-Poli, P., et al. (2013). Tracking cerebral white matter changes across the lifespan: insights from diffusion tensor imaging studies. *Journal of Neural Transmission* 120, 1369–1395.

Yeatman, J. D., Dougherty, R. F. R., Sherbondy, A. J., et al. (2011). Anatomical properties of the arcuate fasciculus predict phonological and reading skills in children. *Journal of Cognitive Neuroscience* 23, 3304–3317.

Zablotsky, B., Black, L. I., Maenner, M. J., et al. (2019). Prevalence and trends of developmental disabilities among children in the United States: 2009–2017. *Pediatrics* 144, e20190811.

Zhang, Q., Liu, R., Diggs, L. A., et al. (2019). Does acculturation affect the dietary intakes and body weight status of children of immigrants in the US and other developed countries? A systematic review. *Ethnicity & Health* 24, 73–93.

Chapter 12

Ambrose, S. A., Bridges, M. W., DiPietro, M., et al. (2010). *How Learning Works: Seven Research-Based Principles for Smart Teaching*. John Wiley & Sons: Hoboken, NJ.

Akiba, M., LeTendre, G. K., & Scribner, J. P. (2007). Teacher quality, opportunity gap, and national achievement in 46 countries. *Educational Researcher* 36, 369–387.

Barrow, L., & Markman-Pithers, L. (2016). Supporting young English learners in the United States. *The Future of Children* 26, 159 183.

Battistich, V. (2010). School contexts that promote students' positive development. In J. L. Meece & J. S. Eccles, *Handbook of Research on Schools, Schooling and Human Development* (pp. 111–127). Routledge: London, United Kingdom.

Berliner, D. C. & Glass, G. V. (Eds.). (2014). *50 Myths and Lies That Threaten America's Public Schools: The Real Crisis in Education*. Teachers College Press: New York.

Best, J. R., & Miller, P. H. (2010). A developmental perspective on executive function. *Child Development* 81, 1641–1660.

Best, J. R., Miller, P. H., & Jones, L. L. (2009). Executive functions after age 5: Changes and correlates. *Developmental Review* 29, 180–200.

Binet, A. (1911). The development of intelligence in children (The Binet-Simon scale) translated from articles in *L'Année psychologique from 1905, 1908* by E. S. Kite. Publications of the Training School at Vineland, New Jersey.

Binet, A., & Simon, T. (1905). Upon the necessity of establishing a scientific diagnosis of inferior states of intelligence. *The History of Mental Retardation: Collected Papers* 1, 329–354.

Blair, C. (2002). School readiness: Integrating cognition and emotion in a neurobiological conceptualization of children's functioning at school entry. *American Psychologist* 57, 111.

Bjorklund, D. F. (1987). How age changes in knowledge base contribute to the development of children's memory: An interpretive review. *Developmental Review* 7, 93–130.

Bjorklund, D. F., Miller, P. H., Coyle, T. R., & Slawinski, J. L. (1997). Instructing children to use memory strategies: Evidence of utilization deficiencies in memory training studies. *Developmental Review* 17, 411–441.

Bjorklund, D. F., Ornstein, P. A., & Haig, J. R. (1977). Developmental differences in organization and recall: Training in the use of organizational techniques. *Developmental Psychology* 13, 175–183.

Brühwiler, C., & Blatchford, P. (2011). Effects of class size and adaptive teaching competency on classroom processes and academic outcome. *Learning and Instruction* 21, 95–108.

Burchinal, M., Howes, C., Pianta, R., et al. (2008). Predicting child outcomes at the end of kindergarten from the quality of pre-kindergarten teacher–child interactions and instruction. *Applied Development Science* 12, 140–153.

Burnett, P. C., & Mandel, V. (2010). Praise and feedback in the primary classroom: Teachers' and students' perspectives. *Australian Journal of Educational & Developmental Psychology* 10, 145–154.

Camarota, S. A., & Ziegler, K. (2014). One in five U.S. residents speaks foreign language at home, record 61.9 million. Center for immigration studies.

Carey, S. (1985). *Conceptual Change in Childhood.* MIT Press: Cambridge, MA.

Carlisle, J. F. (2000). Awareness of the structure and meaning of morphologically complex words: Impact on reading. *Reading and Writing* 12, 169–190.

Casalis, S., & Colé, P. (2009). On the relationship between morphological and phonological awareness: Effects of training in kindergarten and in first-grade reading. *First Language* 29, 113–142.

Case, R. (1985). *Intellectual Development: Birth to Adulthood.* Academic Press: New York.

Cattell, R. B. (1987). *Intelligence: Its Structure, Growth and Action.* Elsevier: Boston, MA.

Cerasoli, C. P., Nicklin, J. M., & Ford, M. T. (2014). Intrinsic motivation and extrinsic incentives jointly predict performance: A 40-year meta-analysis. *Psychological Bulletin* 140, 980–1008.

Chall, J. S. (1983). *Stages of Reading Development.* McGraw Hill: New York.

Chen, J., & Gardner, H. (2005). Assessment based on multiple-intelligences theory. In D.P. Flanagan & P. L. Harrison (Eds.), *Contemporary Intellectual Assessment: Theories, Tests, and Issues,* 2nd ed. (pp. 77–102). Guilford Press: New York.

Chesmore, A. A., Ou, S. R., & Reynolds, A. J. (2016). Childhood placement in special education and adult well-being. *The Journal of Special Education* 50, 109–120.

Chevalier, N., Kurth, S., Doucette, M. R., et al. (2015). Myelination is associated with processing speed in early childhood: Preliminary insights. *PLoS ONE* 10, e0139897.

Clerc, J., Miller, P. H., & Cosnefroy, L. (2014). Young children's transfer of strategies: Utilization deficiencies, executive function, and metacognition. *Developmental Review* 34, 378–393.

Claessens, A., Duncan, G., & Engel, M. (2009). Kindergarten skills and fifth-grade achievement: Evidence from the ECLS-K. *Economics of Education Review* 28, 415–427.

Clements, D. H., Sarama, J., & DiBiase, A. M. (2003). *Engaging Young Children in Mathematics: Standards for Early Childhood Mathematics Education.* Routledge: London, United Kingdom.

Cole, M., Gay, J., Glick, J. A., & Sharp, D. W. (1971). *The Cultural Context of Thinking and Learning.* Basis: New York.

Converse, P. D., Thackray, M., Piccone, K., et al. (2016). Integrating self-control with physical attractiveness and cognitive ability to examine pathways to career success. *Journal of Occupational and Organizational Psychology* 89, 73–91.

Correa-Chávez, M., & Rogoff, B. (2009). Children's attention to interactions directed to others: Guatemalan Mayan and European American patterns. *Developmental Psychology* 45, 630–641.

Cowan, N., AuBuchon, A. M., Gilchrist, A. L., et al. (2011). Age differences in visual working memory capacity: Not based on encoding limitations. *Developmental Science* 14, 1066–1074.

Cowan, N., Ricker, T. J., Clark, K. M., et al. (2015). Knowledge cannot explain the developmental growth of working memory capacity. *Developmental Science* 18, 132–145.

Craig, H. K., & Washington, J. A. (2006). Recent research on the language and literacy skills of African American students in the early years. In D. K. Dickinson & S. B. Neuman (Eds.), *Handbook of Early Literacy Research,* 2, 163–172. The Guilford Press: New York.

Crnic, K. A., Neece, C. L., McIntyre, L. L., et al. (2017). Intellectual disability and developmental risk: Promoting intervention to improve child and family well-being. *Child Development* 88, 436–445.

Deary, I. J., Johnson, W., & Houlihan, L. M. (2009). Genetic foundations of human intelligence. *Human Genetics* 126, 215–232.

Deary, I. J., Weiss, A., & Batty, G. D. (2010). Intelligence and personality as predictors of illness and death: How researchers in differential psychology and chronic disease epidemiology are collaborating to understand and address health inequalities. *Psychological Science in the Public Interest* 11, 53–79.

Desoete, A., Stock, P., Schepens, A., et al. (2009). Classification, seriation, and counting in grades 1, 2, and 3 as two-year longitudinal predictors for low achieving in numerical facility and arithmetical achievement? *Journal of Psychoeducational Assessment* 27, 252–264.

Dörfler, T., Golke, S., & Artelt, C. (2009). Dynamic assessment and its potential for the assessment of reading competence. *Studies in Educational Evaluation* 35, 77–82.

Duncan, G. J., Magnuson, K., & Votruba-Drzal, E. (2017). Moving beyond correlations in assessing the consequences of poverty. *Annual Review of Psychology* 68, 413–434.

Dweck, C. S. (1975). The role of expectations and attributions in the alleviation of learned helplessness. *Journal of Personality and Social Psychology* 31, 674.

Dweck, C. S. (2006). *Mindset: How We Can Learn to Fulfill Our Potential.* Robinson Publishing: New York.

Dweck, C. S. (1986). Motivational processes affecting learning. *American Psychologist* 41, 1040–1048.

Emerson, E., McCulloch, A., Graham, H., et al. (2010). Socioeconomic circumstances and risk of psychiatric disorders among parents of children with early cognitive delay. *American Journal on Intellectual and Developmental Disabilities* 115, 30–42.

Evans, G. W., & Schamberg, M. A. (2009). Childhood poverty, chronic stress, and adult working memory. *Proceedings of the National Academy of Sciences* 106, 6545–6549.

Farah, M. J., Shera, D. M., Savage, J. H., et al. (2006). Childhood poverty: Specific associations with neurocognitive development. *Brain Research* 1110, 166–174.

Fish, R. E. (2019). Standing out and sorting in: Exploring the role of racial composition in racial disparities in special education. *American Educational Research Journal* 56, 2573–2608.

Flynn, J. R. (2007). *What is Intelligence? Beyond the Flynn Effect.* Cambridge University Press: New York.

Friedrich, D., Walter, M., & Colmenares, E. (2015). Making all children count: Teach for all and the universalizing appeal of data. *Education Policy Analysis Archives* 23, n48.

Gaillard, V., Barrouillet, P., Jarrold, C., & Camos, V. (2011). Developmental differences in working memory: Where do they come from? *Journal of Experimental Child Psychology* 110, 469–479.

Garcia-Coll, C., & Magnuson, K. (2019). Theory and research with children of color: Implications for social policy. In *Children of Color* (pp. 219–255). Routledge: London, United Kingdom.

Garcia-Reid, P., Reid, R. J., & Peterson, N. A. (2005). School engagement among Latino youth in an urban middle school context: Valuing the role of social support. *Education and Urban Society* 37, 257–275.

Gardner, H. (1983). *The Theory of Multiple Intelligences.* Heinemann.

Gardner, H. (2008). *Multiple Intelligences: New Horizons in Theory and Practice.* Basic Books: New York.

Gathercole, S. E., Lamont, E., & Alloway, T. P. (2006). Working memory in the classroom. In *Working Memory and Education* (pp. 219–240). Academic Press.

Gauvain, M., & Rogoff, B. (1989). Collaborative problem solving and children's planning skills. *Developmental Psychology* 25, 139–151.

Geary, D. C. (2006). Dyscalculia at an early age: Characteristics and potential influence on socio-emotional development. *Encyclopedia on Early Childhood Development* 15, 1–4.

Geary, D. C., Bow-Thomas, C. C., Liu, F., & Siegler, R. S. (1996). Development of arithmetical competencies in Chinese and American children: Influence of age, language, and schooling. *Child Development* 67, 2022–2044.

Geary, D. C., Salthouse, T. A., Chen, G. P., & Fan, L. (1996). Are East Asian versus American differences in arithmetical ability a recent phenomenon? *Developmental Psychology* 32, 254–262.

Ghetti, S., & Bunge, S. A. (2012). Neural changes underlying the development of episodic memory during middle childhood. *Developmental Cognitive Neuroscience* 2, 381–395.

Goldin-Meadow, S., & Alibali, M. W. (2002). Looking at the hands through time: A microgenetic perspective on learning and instruction. In N. Granott & J. Parziale (Eds.), *Cambridge Studies in Cognitive Perceptual Development. Microdevelopment: Transition Processes in Development and Learning* (pp. 80–105). Cambridge University Press: New York.

Goswami, U. (2015). Sensory theories of developmental dyslexia: three challenges for research. *Nature Reviews Neuroscience* 16, 43–54.

Gottfredson, L. S. (2003). Dissecting practical intelligence theory: Its claims and evidence. *Intelligence* 31, 343–397.

Gottfredson, L. S. (1997). Mainstream science on intelligence: An editorial with 52 signatories, history, and bibliography. *Intelligence* 24, 13–23.

Gottfredson, L., & Saklofske, D. H. (2009). Intelligence: Foundations and issues in assessment. *Canadian Psychology/Psychologie Canadienne* 50, 183–195.

Greenfield, P. M., Maynard, A. E., & Childs, C. P. (2000). History, culture, learning, and development. *Cross-Cultural Research* 34, 351–374.

Greenfield, P. M., Maynard, A. E., & Childs, C. P. (2003). Historical change, cultural learning, and cognitive representation in Zinacantec Maya children. *Cognitive Development* 18, 455–487.

Guglielmi, R. S. (2008). Native language proficiency, English literacy, academic achievement, and occupational attainment in limited-English-proficient students: A latent growth modeling perspective. *Journal of Educational Psychology* 100, 322–342.

Guilford, J. P. (1967). *The Nature of Human Intelligence*. McGraw Hill: New York.

Gunderson, E. A., Park, D., Maloney, E. A., et al. (2018). Reciprocal relations among motivational frameworks, math anxiety, and math achievement in early elementary school. *Journal of Cognition and Development* 19, 21–46.

Guthrie, R. V. (2004). *Even the Rat Was White: A Historical View of Psychology*. Pearson Education: Boston, MA.

Haimovitz, K., & Dweck, C. S. (2017). The origins of children's growth and fixed mindsets: New research and a new proposal. *Child Development* 88, 1849–1859.

Halford, G. S., & Andrews, G. (2011). Information-processing models of cognitive development. In U. Goswami (Ed.), *The Wiley-Blackwell Handbook of Childhood Cognitive Development* (pp. 697–721). Wiley-Blackwell.

Hamre, B. K., & Pianta, R. C. (2010). Classroom environments and developmental processes: Conceptualization and measurement. In J. L. Meece & J. S. Eccles (Eds.), *Handbook of Research on Schools, Schooling and Human Development* (pp. 43–59). Routledge: New York.

Hauser-Cram, P., Cannarella, A., Tillinger, M. & Woodman, A. (2013). Disabilities and development. In R.M. Lerner, A. Easterbrooks, & J. Mistry (Vol. Eds.), *Handbook of Psychology, Vol. 6, Developmental Psychology*, 2nd ed. (pp. 547–569). Wiley: Hoboken, NJ.

Hernandez, D. J. (2011). *Double Jeopardy: How Third-Grade Reading Skills and Poverty Influence High School Graduation.* Annie E. Casey Foundation.

Holmes, J., & Gathercole, S. E. (2014). Taking working memory training from the laboratory into schools, *Educational Psychology* 34, 440–450.

Huizinga, M., Dolan, C. V., & van der Molen, M. W. (2006). Age-related change in executive function: Developmental trends and a latent variable analysis. *Neuropsychologia* 44, 2017–2036.

Jussim, L., Robustelli, S. L., & Cain, T. R. (2009). Teacher expectations and self-fulfilling prophecies. In K. R. Wenzel & A. Wigfield (Eds.), *Educational Psychology Handbook series. Handbook of Motivation at School* (pp. 349–380). Routledge/Taylor & Francis Group: New York.

Kail, R. V. (2007). Longitudinal evidence that increases in processing speed and working memory enhance children's reasoning. *Psychological Science* 18, 312–313.

Kastens, K. A., & Liben, L. S. (2007). Eliciting self-explanations improves children's performance on a field-based map skills task. *Cognition and Instruction* 25, 45–74.

Kuhn, D. (1977). Conditional reasoning in children. *Developmental Psychology* 13, 342–353.

Kyle, F., Kujala, J., Richardson, U., et al. (2013). Assessing the effectiveness of two theoretically motivated computer-assisted reading interventions in the United Kingdom: G. G. Rime and G. G. Phoneme. *Reading Research Quarterly* 48, 61–76.

Lackaye, T., Margalit, M., Ziv, O., & Ziman, T. (2006). Comparisons of self-efficacy, mood, effort, and hope between students with learning disabilities and their non-LD-matched peers. *Learning Disabilities Research & Practice* 21, 111–121.

Legg, S., & Hutter, M. (2007). Universal intelligence: A definition of machine intelligence. *Minds and Machines* 17, 391–444.

Lehmann, M., & Hasselhorn, M. (2010). The dynamics of free recall and their relation to rehearsal between 8 and 10 years of age. *Child Development* 81, 1006–1020.

Liben, L. S. (2009). The road to understanding maps. *Current Directions in Psychological Science* 18, 310–315.

Liben, L. S., Myers, L. J., Christensen, A. E., & Bower, C. A. (2013). Environmental-scale map use in middle childhood: Links to spatial skills, strategies, and gender. *Child Development* 84, 2047–2063.

Lonigan, C. J., Burgess, S. R., & Schatschneider, C. (2018). Examining the simple view of reading with elementary school children; Still simple after all these years. *Remedial and Special Education* 39, 260–273.

Luciana, M., & Nelson, C. A. (1998). The functional emergence of prefrontally-guided working memory systems in four-to eight-year-old children.

Luria, A. R. (1976). *Cognitive Development: Its Cultural and Social Foundations*. Harvard University Press: Cambridge, MA.

Matthews, J. S., Marulis, L. M., & Williford, A. P. (2014). Gender processes in school functioning and the mediating role of cognitive self-regulation. *Journal of Applied Developmental Psychology* 35, 128–137.

McCall, R. B., Eichorn, D. H., Hogarty, P. S., et al. (1977). Transitions in early mental development. *Monographs of the Society for Research in Child Development*, 1–108.

McCutchen, D. (2006). Cognitive factors in the development of children's writing. *Handbook of Writing Research* 8, 115–130.

McIntyre, L. L. (2008). Parent training for young children with developmental disabilities: Randomized controlled trial. *American Journal on Mental Retardation* 113, 356–368.

McKeown, M. G., Beck, I. L., & Blake, R. G. (2009). Rethinking reading comprehension instruction: A comparison of instruction for strategies and content approaches. *Reading Research Quarterly* 44, 218–253.

McKown, C., Gregory, A., & Weinstein, R. S. (2010). Expectations, stereotypes, and self-fulfilling prophecies in classroom and school life. In J. L. Meece & J. S. Eccles (Eds.), *Handbook of Research on Schools, Schooling, and Human Development* (pp. 256–274). Routledge: New York.

McNeil, N. M. (2008). Limitations to teaching children 2+ 2= 4: Typical arithmetic problems can hinder learning of mathematical equivalence. *Child Development* 79, 1524–1537.

Meece, J. L., & Eccles, J. S. (2010). Learner-centered practices: Providing the context for positive learner development, motivation, and achievement. In J. L. Meece & J. S. Eccles (Eds.), *Handbook of Research on Schools, Schooling, and Human Development* (pp. 78–92). Routledge: New York.

Morgan, P. L., & Farkas, G. (2016). Evidence and implications of racial and ethnic disparities in emotional and behavioral disorders identification and treatment. *Behavioral Disorders* 41, 122–131.

Nelson, K., & Fivush, R. (2004). The emergence of autobiographical memory: a social cultural developmental theory. *Psychological Review* 111, 486–511.

Nettelbeck, T., & Burns, N. R. (2010). Processing speed, working memory and reasoning ability from childhood to old age. *Personality and Individual Differences* 48, 379–384.

Neumann, M. M., & Neumann, D. L. (2014). Touch screen tablets and emergent literacy. *Early Childhood Education Journal* 42, 231–239.

Olson, D. R., & Astington, J. W. (1986). Children's acquisition of metalinguistic and metacognitive verbs. In William Demopoulos (ed.), *Language Learning and Concept Acquisition* (pp. 184–199). Ablex.

Parameswaran, G. (2003). Experimenter instructions as a mediator in the effects of culture on mapping one's neighborhood. *Journal of Environmental Psychology* 23, 409–417.

Patall, E. A., Cooper, H., & Robinson, J. C. (2008). The effects of choice on intrinsic motivation and related outcomes: a meta-analysis of research findings. *Psychological Bulletin* 134, 270–300.

Picard, L., Cousin, S., Guillery-Girard, B., et al. (2012). How do the different components of episodic memory develop? Role of executive functions and short-term feature-binding abilities. *Child Development* 83, 1037–1050.

Piolino, P., Hisland, M., Ruffeveille, I., et al. (2007). Do school-age children remember or know the personal past? *Consciousness and Cognition* 16, 84–101.

Plomin, R., & Geary, I. J. (2015). Genetics and intelligence differences: five special findings. *Molecular Psychiatry* 20, 98–108.

Polderman, T. J., de Geus, E. J., Hoekstra, R. A., et al. (2009). Attention problems, inhibitory control, and intelligence index overlapping genetic factors: A study in 9-, 12-, and 18-year-old twins. *Neuropsychology* 23, 381–391.

Pomerantz, E. M., & Dong, W. (2006). Effects of mothers' perceptions of children's competence: The moderating role of mothers' theories of competence. *Developmental Psychology* 42, 950–961.

Pomerantz, E. M., & Kempner, S. G. (2013). Mothers' daily person and process praise: Implications for children's theory of intelligence and motivation. *Developmental Psychology* 49, 2040–2046.

Pressley, M. (2002). *Reading Instruction That Works: The Case for Balanced Teaching.* Guilford Press: New York.

Pressley, M., Mohan, L., Raphael, L. M., & Fingeret, L. (2007). How does Bennett Woods Elementary School produce such high reading and writing achievement? *Journal of Educational Psychology* 99, 221–240.

Reese, H. W. (1962). Verbal mediation as a function of age level. *Psychological Bulletin* 59, 502–509.

Resnick, L. B. (1989). Developing mathematical knowledge. *American Psychologist* 44, 162.

Reynolds, C. R., & Suzuki, L. A. (2013). Bias in psychological assessment: An empirical review and recommendations. In I. B. Weiner (Ed.), *Handbook of Psychology*, 2nd ed. (pp. 82–113). Wiley: Hoboken, NJ.

Rimfeld, K., Ayorech, Z., Dale, P. S., et al. (2016). Genetics affects choice of academic subjects as well as achievement. *Scientific Reports* 6, 1–9.

Roebers, C., M., Schmid, C., & Roderer, T. (2009). Metacognitive monitoring and control processes involved in primary school children's test performance. *British Journal of Educational Psychology* 79, 749–767.

Roeser, R. W., & Eccles, J. S. (2014). Schooling and the mental health of children and adolescents in the United States. In *Handbook of Developmental Psychopathology* (pp. 163–184). Springer: Boston, MA.

Rogoff, B., & Waddell, K. J. (1982). Memory for information organized in a scene by children from two cultures. *Child Development,* 1224–1228.

Rosenthal, R., & Jacobson, L. (1992) *Pygmalion in the Classroom: Teacher Expectation and Pupils' Intellectual Development* (newly expanded ed.). Crown House Pub: Bancyfelin, Carmarthen, Wales.

Rowley, S. J., Helaire, L. J., & Banerjee, M. (2010). Reflecting on racism: School involvement and perceived teacher discrimination in African American mothers. *Journal of Applied Developmental Psychology* 31, 83–92.

Rubie-Davies, C. M., Peterson, E. R., Sibley, C. G., & Rosenthal, R. (2015). A teacher expectation intervention: Modelling the practices of high expectation teachers. *Contemporary Educational Psychology* 40, 72–85.

Ryan, R. M., & Deci, E. L. (2000). Self-determination theory and the facilitation of intrinsic motivation, social development, and well-being. *American Psychologist* 55, 68–78.

Ryan, R. M., Deci, E. L., & Vansteenkiste, M. (2016). Autonomy and autonomy disturbances in self-development and psychopathology: Research on motivation, attachment, and clinical process. *Developmental Psychopathology, 1–54.*

Saarikivi, K. A., Huotilainen, M., Tervaniemi, M., & Putkinen, V. (2019). Selectively enhanced development of working memory in musically trained children and adolescents. *Frontiers in Integrative Neuroscience* 13, 62.

Samson, J. F., & Lesaux, N. (2015). Disadvantaged language minority students and their teachers: A national picture. *Teachers College Record* 117, 1–26.

Samuelson, K. W., Krueger, C. E., & Wilson, C. (2012). Relationships between maternal emotion regulation, parenting, and children's executive functioning in families exposed to intimate partner violence. *Journal of Interpersonal Violence* 27, 3532–3550.

Saxe, G.B. (2004). Practices of quantification from a sociocultural perspective. In A. Demetriou & A. Raftopoulos (Eds.), *Cognitive Developmental Change: Theories, Models and Measurement* (pp. 241–263). Cambridge University Press: New York.

Saxe, G. B. (2015). *Culture and Cognitive Development: Studies in Mathematical Understanding.* Psychology Press: New York.

Schaie, K. W., Willis, S. L., & Caskie, G. I. (2004). The Seattle longitudinal study: Relationship between personality and cognition. *Aging Neuropsychology and Cognition* 11, 304–324.

Schneider, W., & Bjorklund, D. F. (1992). Expertise, aptitude, and strategic remembering. *Child Development* 63, 461–473.

Schwinger, M., Steinmayr, R., & Spinath, B. (2016). Achievement goal profiles in elementary school: Antecedents, consequences, and longitudinal trajectories. *Contemporary Educational Psychology* 46, 164–179.

Siegler, R. S. (2016). Magnitude knowledge: The common core of numerical development. *Developmental Science* 19.

Siegler, R. S., & Braithwaite, D. W. (2017). Numerical development. *Annual Review of Psychology* 68, 187–213.

Siegler, R. S., Thompson, C. A., & Opfer, J. E. (2009). The logarithmic-to-linear shift: One learning sequence, many tasks, many time scales. *Mind, Brain, and Education* 3, 143–150.

Silva, K. G., Correa-Chávez, M., & Rogoff, B. (2010). Mexican-heritage children's attention and learning from interactions directed to others. *Child Development* 81, 898–912.

Silva, K. G., Shimpi, P. M., & Rogoff, B. (2015). Young children's attention to what's going on: Cultural differences. *Advances in Child Development and Behavior* 4, 207–227.

Simonton, D. K. (2003). *Francis Galton's Hereditary Genius: Its place in the history and psychology of science.* American Psychological Association.

Spearman, C. (1927). The abilities of man: Their nature and measurement. *Nature* 120, 181–183.

Sternberg, R.J. (1985). Implicit theories of intelligence, creativity, and wisdom. *Journal of Personality and Social Psychology* 49, 607–627.

Sternberg, R. J. (2018). The triarchic theory of successful intelligence. In D. P. Flanagan & E. M. McDonough (Eds.), *Contemporary Intellectual Assessment: Theories, Tests, and Issues* (pp. 174–194). The Guilford Press: New York.

Stevens, C., & Bavelier, D. (2012). The role of selective attention on academic foundations: A cognitive neuroscience perspective. *Developmental Cognitive Neuroscience* 2, 530–548.

Stevenson, H. J. (2014). Myths and motives behind STEM (science, technology, engineering, and mathematics) education and the STEM-worker shortage narrative. *Issues in Teacher Education* 23, 133–146.

Stevenson, H., & Stigler, J. (1992). *Why Our Schools Are Failing and What We Can Learn from Japanese and Chinese Education.* Summit: New York.

Sun, X., Wu, Z., Cao, Q., et al. (2018). Genetic variant for behavioral regulation factor of executive function and its possible brain mechanism in attention deficit hyperactivity disorder. *Scientific Reports* 8, 7620.

Terman, L. M., & Merrill, M. A. (1950). Medida de la inteligencia: Método para el empleo de las pruebas de Stanford-Binet nuevamente revisadas. *Revista Española de Pedagogía* 3, 145–148.

Thurstone, L. L. (1938). *Primary Mental Abilities* (Vol. 119). University of Chicago Press: Chicago, IL.

Van IJzendoorn, M. H., & Juffer, F. (2006). The Emanuel Miller Memorial Lecture 2006: Adoption as intervention. Meta-analytic evidence for massive catch-up and plasticity in physical, socio-emotional, and cognitive development. *Journal of Child Psychology and Psychiatry* 47, 1228–1245.

Vion, M., & Colas, A. (2005). Using connectives in oral French narratives: Cognitive constraints and development of narrative skills. *First Language* 25, 39–66.

Vygotsky, L.S. (1978). *Mind in Society.* Harvard University Press: Cambridge, MA. (Collection of edited essays from Vygotsky).

Ward, L., Grudnoff, L., Brooker, B., & Simpson, M. (2013). Teacher preparation to proficiency and beyond: Exploring the landscape. *Asia Pacific Journal of Education* 33, 68–80.

Washington, J.A., & Thomas-Tate, S. (2009). How research informs cultural-linguistic differences in the classroom. In S. Rosenfield & V. Berninger (Eds.), *Implementing Evidence-Based Academic Interventions in School Settings* (pp. 147–163). Oxford University Press: New York.

Weidinger, A. F., Steinmayr, R., & Spinath, B. (2017). Math grades and intrinsic motivation in elementary school: A longitudinal investigation of their association. *British Journal of Educational Psychology* 87, 187–204.

Whitehurst, G. J., & Lonigan, C. J. (1998). Child development and emergent literacy. *Child Development* 69, 848–872.

Willoughby, K. A., Desrocher, M., Levine, B., & Rovet, J. F. (2012). Episodic and semantic autobiographical memory and everyday memory during late childhood and early adolescence. *Frontiers in Psychology.*

Woodman, A. C., Mawdsley, H. P., & Hauser-Cram, P. (2015). Parenting stress and child behavior problems within families of children with developmental disabilities: Transactional relations across 15 years. *Research in Developmental Disabilities* 36, 264–276.

Wright, B. C. (2006). On the emergence of the discriminative mode for transitive-inference. *European Journal of Cognitive Psychology* 18, 776–800.

Xue, Y., & Meisels, S. J. (2004). Early literacy instruction and learning in kindergarten: Evidence from the early childhood longitudinal study—kindergarten class of 1998–1999. *American Educational Research Journal* 41, 191–229.

Young, S. E., Friedman, N. P., Miyake, A., et al. (2009). Behavioral disinhibition: Liability for externalizing spectrum disorders and its genetic and environmental relation to response inhibition across adolescence. *Journal of Abnormal Psychology* 118, 117–130.

Chapter 13

Abrams, D., & Rutland, A. (2008). The development of subjective group dynamics. In S. R. Levy & M. Killen (Eds.), *Intergroup Attitudes and Relations in Childhood through Adulthood* (pp. 47–65). Oxford University Press: New York.

Agnoli, S., Mancini, G., Pozzoli, T., et al. (2012). The interaction between emotional intelligence and cognitive ability in predicting scholastic performance in school-aged children. *Personality and Individual Differences* 53, 660–665.

Altermatt, E. R., & Pomerantz, E. M. (2003). The development of competence-related and motivational beliefs: An investigation of similarity and influence among friends. *Journal of Educational Psychology* 95, 111–123.

Asher, S. R., & McDonald, K. L. (2009). The behavioral basis of acceptance, rejection, and perceived popularity. In K. H. Rubin, W. M. Bukowski, & B. Laursen (Eds.), *Handbook of Peer Interactions, Relationships, and Groups* (pp. 232–248). Guilford Press: New York.

Avis, J., & Harris, P. L. (1991). Belief-desire reasoning among Baka children: Evidence for a universal conception of mind. *Child Development* 62, 460–467.

Bagwell, C. L., & Schmidt, M. E. (2011). *Friendships in Childhood and Adolescence.* Guilford Press: New York.

Banny, A. M., Heilbron, N., Ames, A., & Prinstein, M. J. (2011). Relational benefits of relational aggression: Adaptive and maladaptive associations with adolescent friendship quality. *Developmental Psychology* 47, 1153–1166.

Banse, R., Gawronski, B., Rebetez, C., et al. (2010). The development of spontaneous gender stereotyping in childhood: Relations to stereotype knowledge and stereotype flexibility. *Developmental Science* 13, 298–306.

Barber, B. K. (2002). *Intrusive Parenting: How Psychological Control Affects Children and Adolescents.* American Psychological Association: Washington, DC.

Barbovschi, M., Macháčková, H., & Ólafsson, K. (2015). Underage use of social network sites: It's about friends. *Cyberpsychology, Behavior, and Social Networking* 18, 328–332.

Baumrind, D. (1991). The influence of parenting style on adolescent competence and substance use. *The Journal of Early Adolescence* 11, 56–95.

Baumrind, D., & Black, A. E. (1967). Socialization practices associated with dimensions of competence in preschool boys and girls. *Child Development* 38, 291–327.

Beck, S. R., & Riggs, K. J. (2014). Developing thoughts about what might have been. *Child Development Perspectives* 8, 175–179.

Berger, C., & Rodkin, P. C. (2012). Group influences on individual aggression and prosociality: Early adolescents who change peer affiliations. *Social Development* 21, 396–413.

Berndt, T. J., & McCandless, M. A. (2009). Methods for investigating children's relationships with friends. In K. H. Rubin, W. M. Bukowski, & B. Laursen (Eds.), *Handbook of Peer Interactions, Relationships, and Groups* (pp. 63–81). Guilford Press: New York.

Berti, A. E., Garattoni, C., & Venturini, B. (2000). The understanding of sadness, guilt, and shame in 5-, 7-, and 9-year-old children. *Genetic, Social, and General Psychology Monographs* 126, 293–318.

Bierman, K. L., Kalvin, C. B., & Heinrichs, B. S. (2015). Early childhood precursors and adolescent sequelae of grade school peer rejection and victimization. *Journal of Clinical Child & Adolescent Psychology* 44, 367–379.

Bigelow, B. J., & LaGaipa, J. J. (1980). The development of friendship values and choice. In H. C. Foot, A. J. Chapman, & J. R. Smith (Eds.), *Friendship and Social Relations in Children* (pp. 15–44). Transaction Publishers: Piscataway, NJ.

Bigler, R. S. (1995). The role of classification skill in moderating environmental influences on children's gender stereotyping: A study of the functional use of gender in the classroom. *Child Development* 66, 1072–1087.

Bigler, R. S., Arthur, A. E., Hughes, J. M., & Patterson, M. M. (2008). The politics of race and gender: Children's perceptions of discrimination and the U.S. presidency. *Analyses of Social Issues and Public Policy (ASAP)* 8, 83–112.

Bigler, R. S., Brown, C. S., & Markell, M. (2001). When groups are not created equal: Effects of group status on the formation of intergroup attitudes in children. *Child Development* 72, 1151–1162.

Bigler, R. S., & Liben, L. S. (1992). Cognitive mechanisms in children's gender stereotyping: Theoretical and educational implications of a cognitive-based intervention. *Child Development* 63, 1351–1363.

Bigler, R. S., & Liben, L. S. (2007). Developmental intergroup theory: Explaining and reducing children's social stereotyping and prejudice. *Current Directions in Psychological Science* 16, 162–166.

Blair, B. L., Gangel, M. J., Perry, N. B., et al. (2016). Indirect effects of emotion regulation on peer acceptance and rejection: The roles of positive and negative social behaviors. *Merrill-Palmer Quarterly* 62, 415–439.

Booth-LaForce, C., Oh, W., Kennedy, A. E., et al. (2012). Parent and peer links to trajectories of anxious withdrawal from grades 5 to 8. *Journal of Clinical Child and Adolescent Psychology* 41, 138–149.

Bougher-Muckian, H. R., Root, A. E., Coogle, C. G., & Floyd, K. K. (2016). The importance of emotions: the socialisation of emotion in parents of children with autism spectrum disorder. *Early Child Development and Care* 186, 1584–1593.

Bowker, J. C., Fredstrom, B. K., Rubin, K. H., et al. (2010). Distinguishing children who form new best-friendships from those who do not. *Journal of Social and Personal Relationships* 27, 707–725.

Bowker, J. C., Thomas, K. K., Norman, K. E., & Spencer, S. V. (2011). Mutual best friendship involvement, best friends' rejection sensitivity, and psychological maladaptation. *Journal of Youth and Adolescence* 40, 545–555.

Bronfenbrenner, U., & Morris, P. A. (2007). The bioecological model of human development. *Handbook of Child Psychology*, 1.

Brown, C. S., Alabi, B. O., Huynh, V. W., & Masten, C. L. (2011). Ethnicity and gender in late childhood and early adolescence: Group identity and awareness of bias. *Developmental Psychology* 47, 463–471.

Brumariu, L. E., & Kerns, K. A. (2010). Parent-child attachment and internalizing symptoms in childhood and adolescence: A review of empirical findings and future directions. *Development and Psychopathology* 22, 177–203.

Buist, K. L., & Vermande, M. (2014). Sibling relationship patterns and their associations with child competence and problem behavior. *Journal of Family Psychology* 28, 529.

Bukowski, W. M. (2011). Popularity as a social concept: Meanings and significance. In A. H. N. Cillessen, D. Schwartz, & L. Mayeux (Eds.), *Popularity in the Peer System* (pp. 3–24). Guilford Press: New York.

Bukowski, W. M., Cillessen, A. H. N., & Velásquez, A. M. (2012). Peer ratings. In B. Laursen, T. D. Little, & N. A. Card (Eds.), *Handbook of Developmental Research Methods* (pp. 211–228). Guilford Press: New York.

Bukowski, W. M., Motzoi, C., & Meyer, F. (2009). Friendship as process, function, and outcome. In K. H. Rubin, W. M. Bukowski, & B. Laursen (Eds.), *Handbook of Peer Interactions, Relationships, and Groups* (pp. 217–231). Guilford Press: New York.

Burgess, K. B., Wojslawowicz, J. C., Rubin, K. H., et al. (2006). Social information processing and coping strategies of shy/withdrawn and aggressive children: Does friendship matter? *Child Development* 77, 371–383.

Burt, R. S., & Soda, G. (2017). Social origins of great strategies. *Strategy Science* 2, 226–233.

Cabrera, N. J., Cook, G. A., McFadden, K. E., & Bradley, R. H. (2011). Father residence and father-child relationship quality: Peer relationships and externalizing behavioral problems. *Family Science* 2, 109–119.

Cabrera, N. J., Volling, B. L., & Barr, R. (2018). Fathers are parents, too! Widening the lens on parenting for children's development. *Child Development Perspectives* 12, 152–157.

Carver, P. R., Yunger, J. L., & Perry, D. G. (2003). Gender identity and adjustment in middle childhood. *Sex Roles* 49, 95–109.

Casad, B. J., Hale, P., & Wachs, F. L. (2015). Parent-child math anxiety and math-gender stereotypes predict adolescents' math education outcomes. *Frontiers in Psychology* 6, 1597.

Chang, L., Schwartz, D., Dodge, K. A., & McBride-Chang, C. (2003). Harsh parenting in relation to child emotion regulation and aggression. *Journal of Family Psychology* 17, 598–606.

Chen, X. (2010). Socio-emotional development in Chinese children. In M. H. Bond (Ed.), *The Oxford Handbook of Chinese Psychology* (pp. 37–52). Oxford University Press: New York.

Chen, X. (2012). Culture, peer interaction, and socioemotional development. *Child Development Perspectives* 6, 27–34.

Chen, X., Fu, R., Liu, J., et al. (2018). Social sensitivity and social, school, and psychological adjustment among children across contexts. *Developmental Psychology* 54, 1124.

Chen, X., He, Y., De Oliveira, A. M., et al. (2004). Loneliness and social adaptation in Brazilian, Canadian, Chinese and Italian children: A multi-national comparative study. *Journal of Child Psychology and Psychiatry* 45, 1373–1384.

Christakis, D. A., & Moreno, M. A. (2009). Trapped in the net: Will internet addiction become a 21st-century epidemic? *Archives of Pediatrics & Adolescent Medicine* 163, 959–960.

Cillessen, A. H. N. (2009). Sociometric methods. In K. H. Rubin, W. M. Bukowski, & B. Laursen (Eds.), *Handbook of Peer Interactions, Relationships, and Groups* (pp. 82–99). Guilford Press: New York.

Cillessen, A. H. N., & Mayeux, L. (2004). Sociometric status and peer group behavior: Previous findings and current directions. In *Children's Peer Relations: From Development to Intervention* (pp. 3–20). American Psychological Association: Washington, DC.

Cole, P. M., & Jacobs, A. E. (2018). From children's expressive control to emotion regulation: Looking back, looking ahead. *European Journal of Developmental Psychology* 15, 658–677.

Cole, D. A., Maxwell, S. E., Martin, J. M., et al. (2001). The development of multiple domains of child and adolescent self-concept: A cohort sequential longitudinal design. *Child Development* 72, 1723–1746.

Cole, P., & Tan, P. (2006). Capturing the culture in the cultural socialization of emotion. *ISSBD Newsletter* 49, 5–7.

Cole, P. M., Bruschi, C. J., & Tamang, B. L. (2002). Cultural differences in children's emotional reactions to difficult situations. *Child Development* 73, 983–996.

Collins, W. A., Madsen, S. D., & Susman-Stillman, A. (2005). Parenting during middle childhood. In *Handbook of Parenting* (Vol. 1, pp. 73–101). Lawrence Erlbaum Associates Inc.: Mahwah, NJ.

Compas, B. E., Jaser, S. S., Dunbar, J. P., et al.. (2014). Coping and emotion regulation from childhood to early adulthood: Points of convergence and divergence. *Australian Journal of Psychology* 66, 71–81.

Corenblum, B. (2003). What children remember about ingroup and outgroup peers: Effects of stereotypes on children's processing of information about group members. *Journal of Experimental Child Psychology* 86, 32–66.

Crick, N. R., Murray-Close, D., Marks, P. E. L., & Mohajeri-Nelson, D. (2009). Aggression and peer relationships in school-age children: Relational and physical aggression in group and dyadic contexts. In K. H. Rubin, W. M. Bukowski, & B. Laursen (Eds.), *Handbook of Peer Interactions, Relationships, and Groups* (pp. 287–302). Guilford Press: New York.

Criss, M. M., & Shaw, D. S. (2005). Sibling relationships as contexts for delinquency training in low-income families. *Journal of Family Psychology* 19, 592.

Crouter, A. C., Whiteman, S. D., McHale, S. M., & Osgood, D. W. (2007). Development of gender attitude traditionality across middle childhood and adolescence. *Child Development* 78, 911–926.

Cvencek, D., Meltzoff, A. N., & Greenwald, A. G. (2011). Math–gender stereotypes in elementary school children. *Child Development* 82, 766–779.

Damon, W., & Hart, D. (1988). *Self-Understanding in Childhood and Adolescence*. Cambridge University Press: New York.

de Bruyn, E. H., & Cillessen, A. H. N. (2006). Popularity in early adolescence: Prosocial and antisocial subtypes. *Journal of Adolescent Research* 21, 607–627.

de la Haye, K., Robins, G., Mohr, P., & Wilson, C. (2013). Adolescents' intake of junk food: Processes and mechanisms driving consumption similarities among friends. *Journal of Research on Adolescence* 23, 524–536.

de Wied, M., Branje, S. J. T., & Meeus, W. H. J. (2007). Empathy and conflict resolution in friendship relations among adolescents. *Aggressive Behavior* 33, 48–55.

Deater-Deckard, K., Dodge, K. A., Bates, J. E., & Pettit, G. S. (1996). Physical discipline among African American and European American mothers: Links to children's externalizing behaviors. *Developmental Psychology* 32, 1065–1072.

Denham, S. A. (2007). Dealing with feelings: How children negotiate the worlds of emotions and social relationships. *Cogniţie Creier Comportament* 11, 1–48.

Denissen, J. J. A., Zarrett, N. R., & Eccles, J. S. (2007). I like to do it, I'm able, and I know I am: Longitudinal couplings between domain-specific achievement, self-concept, and interest. *Child Development* 78, 430–447.

DePaolis, K., & Williford, A. (2015). The nature and prevalence of cyber victimization among elementary school children. *Child & Youth Care Forum* 44, 377–393.

DeRosier, M. E., & Thomas, J. M. (2003). Strengthening sociometric prediction: Scientific advances in the assessment of children's peer relations. *Child Development* 74, 1379–1392.

Dirks, M. A., Persram, R., Recchia, H. E., & Howe, N. (2015). Sibling relationships as sources of risk and resilience in the development and maintenance of internalizing and externalizing problems during childhood and adolescence. *Clinical Psychology Review* 42, 145–155.

Dishion, T. J., & McMahon, R. J. (1998). Parental monitoring and the prevention of child and adolescent problem behavior: A conceptual and empirical formulation. *Clinical Child and Family Psychology Review* 1, 61–75.

Dodge, K. A., Lansford, J. E., Burks, V. S., et al. (2003). Peer rejection and social information-processing factors in the development of aggressive behavior problems in children. *Child Development* 74, 374–393.

Dodge, K. A., Malone, P. S., Lansford, J.E., et al. (2015). Attributions and aggression in global context. *Proceedings of the National Academy of Sciences* 112 (30) 9310–9315.

Doey, L., Coplan, R. J., & Kingsbury, M. (2014). Bashful boys and coy girls: A review of gender differences in childhood shyness. *Sex Roles* 70, 255–266.

Eccles, J. S., Jacobs, J. E., & Harold, R. D. (1990). Gender role stereotypes, expectancy effects, and parents' socialization of gender differences. *Journal of Social Issues* 46, 183–201.

Eccles, J. S., Roeser, R., Vida, M., et al. (2006). Motivational and achievement pathways through middle childhood. In *Child Psychology: A Handbook of Contemporary Issues*, 2nd ed. (pp. 325–355). Psychology Press: New York.

Eisenberg, N., Cumberland, A., & Spinrad, T. L. (1998). Parental socialization of emotion. *Psychological Inquiry* 9, 241–273.

Eisenberg, N., Fabes, R. A., & Spinrad, T. L. (2006). Prosocial development. In N. Eisenberg, W. Damon, & R. M. Lerner (Eds.), *Handbook of Child Psychology: Social, Emotional, and Personality Development*, Vol. 3, 6th ed (pp. 646–718). John Wiley & Sons Inc.: Hoboken, NJ.

Eisenberger, N. I., & Lieberman, M. D. (2004). Why rejection hurts: A common neural alarm system for physical and social pain. *Trends in Cognitive Sciences* 8, 294–300.

Ekman, P., & Friesen, W. V. (1969). Nonverbal leakage and clues to deception. *Psychiatry: Journal for the Study of Interpersonal Processes* 32, 88–106.

Elias, M. J., & Haynes, N. M. (2008). Social competence, social support, and academic achievement in minority, low-income, urban elementary school children. *School Psychology Quarterly* 23, 474–495.

Ellis, W. E., & Zarbatany, L. (2007). Explaining friendship formation and friendship stability: The role of children's and friends' aggression and victimization. *Merrill-Palmer Quarterly* 53, 79–104.

Ferguson, T. J., Stegge, H., & Damhuis, I. (1991). Children's understanding of guilt and shame. *Child Development* 62, 827–839.

Festinger, L. (1954). Motivations leading to social behavior. In M. R. Jones (Ed.), *Nebraska Symposium on Motivation 1954* (pp. 191–219). University of Nebraska Press.

Fine, S. E., Izard, C. E., Mostow, A. J., et al. (2003). First grade emotion knowledge as a predictor of fifth grade self-reported internalizing behaviors in children from economically disadvantaged families. *Development and Psychopathology* 15, 331–342.

Folkman, S., & Lazarus, R. (2013). Coping and emotion. *Psychological and Biological Approaches to Emotion*, 313.

French, D. C., Pidada, S., & Victor, A. (2005). Friendships of Indonesian and United States youth. *International Journal of Behavioral Development* 29, 304–313.

Fu, G., Xiao, W. S., Killen, M., & Lee, K. (2014). Moral judgment and its relation to second-order theory of mind. *Developmental Psychology* 50, 2085–2092.

Gaither, S. E., Chen, E. E., Corriveau, K. H., et al. (2014). Monoracial and biracial children: Effects of racial identity saliency on social learning and social preferences. *Child Development* 85, 2299–2316.

Garcia Coll, C., Lamberty, G., Jenkins, R., et al. (1996). An integrative model for the study of developmental competencies in minority children. *Child Development* 67, 1891–1914.

Garrett-Peters, P. T., & Fox, N. A. (2007). Cross-cultural differences in children's emotional reactions to a disappointing situation. *International Journal of Behavioral Development* 31, 161–169.

Gass, K., Jenkins, J., & Dunn, J. (2007). Are sibling relationships protective? A longitudinal study. *Journal of Child Psychology and Psychiatry* 48, 167–175.

Gazelle, H. (2008). Behavioral profiles of anxious solitary children and heterogeneity in peer relations. *Developmental Psychology* 44, 1604–1624.

Gazelle, H., & Ladd, G. W. (2003). Anxious solitude and peer exclusion: A diathesis–stress model of internalizing trajectories in childhood. *Child Development* 74, 257–278.

Gerding, A., & Signorielli, N. (2014). Gender roles in tween television programming: A content analysis of two genres. *Sex Roles* 70, 43–56.

Gershoff, E. T., & Grogan-Kaylor, A. (2016). Spanking and child outcomes: old controversies and new meta-analyses. *Journal of Family Psychology* 30, 453.

Gonzalez, A. M., Steele, J. R., & Baron, A. S. (2017). Reducing children's implicit racial bias through exposure to positive out-group exemplars. *Child Development* 88, 123–130.

Gonzalez-Gedea, M. L., Santamaria-Garcia, H., Aragon, I., et al. (2020). Transgression of cooperative helping norms outweighs children's intergroup bias. *Cognitive Development* 54.

Gottman, J. M., Katz, L. F., & Hooven, C. (1996). Parental meta-emotion philosophy and the emotional life of families: Theoretical models and preliminary data. *Journal of Family Psychology* 10, 243–268.

Greenfield, P. M., Suzuki, L. K., & Rothstein-Fisch, C. (2006). Cultural pathways through human development. In K. A. Renninger et al. (Eds.), *Handbook of Child Psychology: Child Psychology in Practice*, Vol. 4, 6th ed (pp. 655–699). John Wiley & Sons Inc.: Hoboken, NJ.

Grotpeter, J. K., & Crick, N. R. (1996). Relational aggression, overt aggression, and friendship. *Child Development* 67, 2328–2338.

Grusec, J. E., & Hastings, P. D. (Eds.) (2014). *Handbook of Socialization: Theory and Research*: Guilford Publications: New York.

Gunderson, E. A., Ramirez, G., Levine, S. C., & Beilock, S. L. (2012). The role of parents and teachers in the development of gender-related math attitudes. *Sex Roles* 66, 153–166.

Guttentag, R., & Ferrell, J. (2004). Reality compared with its alternatives: Age differences in judgments of regret and relief. *Developmental Psychology* 40, 764–775.

Guttentag, R., & Ferrell, J. (2008). Children's understanding of anticipatory regret and disappointment. *Cognition and Emotion* 22, 815–832.

Guyer, A. E., Choate, V. R., Pine, D. S., & Nelson, E. E. (2012). Neural circuitry underlying affective response to peer feedback in adolescence. *Social Cognitive and Affective Neuroscience* 7, 81–92.

Guyer, A. E., McClure-Tone, E. B., Shiffrin, N. D., et al. (2009). Probing the neural correlates of anticipated peer evaluation in adolescence. *Child Development* 80, 1000–1015.

Hafen, C. A., Laursen, B., Burk, W. J., et al. (2011). Homophily in stable and unstable adolescent friendships: Similarity breeds constancy. *Personality and Individual Differences* 51, 607–612.

Halim, M. L. D., Bryant, D., & Zucker, K. J. (2016). Early gender development in children and links with mental and physical health. In *Health Promotion for Children and Adolescents* (pp. 191–213). Springer, Boston, MA.

Halim, M. L., & Ruble, D. (2010). Gender identity and stereotyping in early and middle childhood. In J. C. Christie & D. R. McCreary (Eds.), *Handbook of Gender Research in Psychology, Vol 1: Gender Research in General and Experimental Psychology* (pp. 495–525). Springer: New York.

Halim, M. L., Ruble, D. N., Tamis-LeMonda, C. S., et al. (2014). Pink frilly dresses and the avoidance of all things "girly": Children's appearance rigidity and cognitive theories of gender development. *Developmental Psychology* 50, 1091–1101.

Harriger, J. A., Serier, K. N., Luedke, M., et al. (2018). Appearance-related themes in children's animated movies released between 2004 and 2016: A content analysis. *Body Image* 26, 78–82.

Harter, S. (1999). The authenticity of the self. In *The Construction of the Self: A Developmental Perspective* (pp. 228–262). Guilford Press: New York.

Harter, S. (2003). The development of self-representations during childhood and adolescence. In *Handbook of Self and Identity* (pp. 610–642). Guilford Press: New York.

Harter, S. (2006). The development of self-esteem. In *Self-Esteem Issues and Answers: A Sourcebook of Current Perspectives* (pp. 144–150). Psychology Press: New York.

Harter, S. (2015). *The Construction of the Self: Developmental and Sociocultural Foundations.* Guilford Publications: New York.

Harter, S., & Whitesell, N. R. (2003). Beyond the debate: Why some adolescents report stable self-worth over time and situation, whereas others report changes in self-worth. *Journal of Personality* 71, 1027–1058.

Hastings, P. D., Nuselovici, J. N., Rubin, K. H., & Cheah, C. S. L. (2010). Shyness, parenting, and parent-child relationships. In *The Development of Shyness and Social Withdrawal* (pp. 107–130). Guilford Press: New York.

Hayes, A. R., Bigler, R. S., & Weisgram, E. S. (2018). Of men and money: characteristics of occupations that affect the gender differentiation of children's occupational interests. *Sex Roles* 78, 775–788.

Healy, K. L., Sanders, M. R., & Iyer, A. (2015). Parenting practices, children's peer relationships and being bullied at school. *Journal of Child and Family Studies* 24, 127–140.

Heerey, E. A., Keltner, D., & Capps, L. M. (2003). Making sense of self-conscious emotion: Linking theory of mind and emotion in children with autism. *Emotion* 3, 394–400.

Herbert, J., & Stipek, D. (2005). The emergence of gender differences in children's perceptions of their academic competence. *Journal of Applied Developmental Psychology* 26, 276–295.

Hitti, A., Mulvey, K. L., Rutland, A., et al. (2014). When is it okay to exclude a member of the ingroup? Children's and adolescents' social reasoning. *Social Development* 23, 451–469.

Hoge, E., Bickham, D., & Cantor, J. (2017). Digital media, anxiety, and depression in children. *Pediatrics* 140(S2), S76–S80.

Holden, G. W. (2010). Childrearing and developmental trajectories: Positive pathways, off-ramps, and dynamic processes. *Child Development Perspectives* 4, 197–204.

Howarth, G. Z., Guyer, A. E., & Pérez-Edgar, K. (2013). Young children's affective responses to acceptance and rejection from peers: A computer-based task sensitive to variation in temperamental shyness and gender. *Social Development* 22, 146–162.

Hughes, D., Bachman, M. A., Ruble, D. N., & Fuligni, A. (2006). Tuned in or tuned out: Parents' and children's interpretation of parental racial/ethnic socialization practices. In *Child Psychology: A Handbook of Contemporary Issues*, 2nd ed. (pp. 591–610). Psychology Press: New York.

Hurrell, K. E., Houwing, F. L., & Hudson, J. L. (2017). Parental meta-emotion philosophy and emotion coaching in families of children and adolescents with an anxiety disorder. *Journal of Abnormal Child Psychology* 45, 569–582.

Impett, E. A., Sorsoli, L., Schooler, D., et al. (2008). Girls' relationship authenticity and self-esteem across adolescence. *Developmental Psychology* 44, 722–733.

Kawabata, Y., & Crick, N. R. (2016). Differential associations between maternal and paternal parenting and physical and relational aggression. *Asian Journal of Social Psychology* 19, 254–263.

Kerns, K. A., Tomich, P. L., & Kim, P. (2006). Normative trends in children's perceptions of availability and utilization of attachment figures in middle childhood. *Social Development* 15, 1–22.

Khoury-Kassabri, M. (2011). Student victimization by peers in elementary schools: Individual, teacher-class, and school-level predictors. *Child Abuse & Neglect* 35, 273–282.

Killen, M., Lee-Kim, J., McGlothlin, H., & Stangor, C. (2002). How children and adolescents evaluate gender and racial exclusion. *Monographs of the Society for Research in Child Development* 67, vii.

Killen, M., Rutland, A., Abrams, D., et al. (2013). Development of intra- and intergroup judgments in the context of moral and social-conventional norms. *Child Development* 84, 1063–1080.

Killen, M. & Smetana, J. G. (Eds.) (2014). *Handbook of Moral Development,* 2nd ed. Psychology Press: New York.

Kim, J.Y., McHale, S. M., Crouter, A. C., & Osgood, D. W. (2007). Longitudinal linkages between sibling relationships and adjustment from middle childhood through adolescence. *Developmental Psychology* 43, 960–973.

Kindermann, T. A. (2007). Effects of naturally existing peer groups on changes in academic engagement in a cohort of sixth graders. *Child Development* 78, 1186–1203.

Klein, J., Cornell, D., & Konold, T. (2012). Relationships between bullying, school climate, and student risk behaviors. *School Psychology Quarterly* 27, 154–169.

Kromm, H., Färber, M., & Holodynski, M. (2015). Felt or false smiles? Volitional regulation of emotional expression in 4-, 6-, and 8-year-old children. *Child Development* 86, 579–597.

Ladd, G. W., & Burgess, K. B. (2001). Do relational risks and protective factors moderate the linkages between childhood aggression and early psychological and school adjustment? *Child Development* 72, 1579–1601.

Ladd, G. W., Kochenderfer-Ladd, B., Eggum, N. D., et al. (2011). Characterizing and comparing the friendships of anxious-solitary and unsociable preadolescents. *Child Development* 82, 1434–1453.

Ladd, G. W., & Profilet, S. M. (1996). The Child Behavior Scale: A teacher-report measure of young children's aggressive, withdrawn, and prosocial behaviors. *Developmental Psychology* 32, 1008–1024.

Lagattuta, K. H., & Thompson, R. A. (2007). The development of self-conscious emotions: Cognitive processes and social influences. In *The Self-Conscious Emotions: Theory and Research* (pp. 91–113). Guilford Press: New York.

Lansford, J. E., Woodlief, D., Malone, P. S., et al. (2014). A longitudinal examination of mothers' and fathers' social information processing biases and harsh discipline in nine countries. *Development and Psychopathology* 26, 561–573.

Larsen, J. T., To, Y. M., & Fireman, G. (2007). Children's understanding and experience of mixed emotions. *Psychological Science* 18, 186–191.

Larzelere, R. E., Morris, A. S., & Harrist, A. W. (2013). *Authoritative Parenting: Synthesizing Nurturance and Discipline for Optimal Child Development.* American Psychological Association: Washington, DC.

Laursen, B., Hartup, W. W., & Koplas, A. L. (1996). Towards understanding peer conflict. *Merrill-Palmer Quarterly* 42, 76–102.

Leadbeater, B. J., & Hoglund, W. L. (2009). The effects of peer victimization and physical aggression on changes in internalizing from first to third grade. *Child Development* 80, 843–859.

Leadbeater, B., Sukhawathanakul, P., Smith, D., & Bowen, F. (2015). Reciprocal associations between interpersonal and values dimensions of school climate and peer victimization in elementary school children. *Journal of Clinical Child and Adolescent Psychology* 44, 480–493.

Lee, E. A. E., & Troop-Gordon, W. (2011). Peer processes and gender role development: Changes in gender atypicality related to negative peer treatment and children's friendships. *Sex Roles* 64, 90–102.

Lemerise, E. A., & Arsenio, W. F. (2000). An integrated model of emotion processes and cognition in social information processing. *Child Development* 71, 107–118.

Lewis-Morrarty, E., Degnan, K. A., Chronis-Tuscano, A., et al. (2012). Maternal over-control moderates the association between early childhood behavioral inhibition and adolescent social anxiety symptoms. *Journal of Abnormal Child Psychology* 40, 1363–1373.

Liben, L. S., Bigler, R. S., & Krogh, H. R. (2001). Pink and blue collar jobs: Children's judgments of job status and job aspirations in relation to sex of worker. *Journal of Experimental Child Psychology* 79, 346–363.

Logis, H. A., Rodkin, P. C., Gest, S. D., & Ahn, H. J. (2013). Popularity as an organizing factor of preadolescent friendship networks: Beyond prosocial and aggressive behavior. *Journal of Research on Adolescence* 23, 413–423.

Lummis, M., & Stevenson, H. W. (1990). Gender differences in beliefs and achievement: A cross-cultural study. *Developmental Psychology* 26, 254–263.

Lunkenheimer, E. S., Shields, A. M., & Cortina, K. S. (2007). Parental emotion coaching and dismissing in family interaction. *Social Development* 16, 232–248.

Luo, R., Tamis-LeMonda, C. S., & Song, L. (2013). Chinese parents' goals and practices in early childhood. *Early Childhood Research Quarterly* 28, 843–857.

Madigan, S., Brumariu, L. E., Villani, V., et al. (2016). Representational and questionnaire measures of attachment: A meta-analysis of relations to child internalizing and externalizing problems. *Psychological Bulletin* 142, 367.

Marks, A. K., Szalacha, L. A., Lamarre, M., et al. (2007). Emerging ethnic identity and interethnic group social preferences in middle childhood: Findings from the Children of Immigrants Development in Context (CIDC) study. *International Journal of Behavioral Development* 31, 501–513.

Marsh, H. W., Parada, R. H., & Ayotte, V. (2004). A multidimensional perspective of relations between self-concept (self description questionnaire II) and adolescent mental health (youth self-report). *Psychological Assessment* 16, 27–41.

Martin, C. L., Cook, R. E., & Andrews, N. C. (2017). Reviving androgyny: A modern day perspective on flexibility of gender identity and behavior. *Sex Roles* 76, 592–603.

Martin, C. L., & Ruble, D. N. (2010). Patterns of gender development. *Annual Review of Psychology* 61, 353–381.

Martin, C. L., Wood, C. H., & Little, J. K. (1990). The development of gender stereotype components. *Child Development* 61, 1891–1904.

Mascolo, M. F., Fischer, K. W., & Li, J. (2003). Dynamic development of component systems of emotions: Pride, shame and guilt in China and the United States. In R. J. Davidson, K. R. Scherer, & H. H. Goldsmith (Eds.), *Handbook of Affective Sciences* (pp. 375–408). Oxford University Press: New York.

Masten, C. L., Eisenberger, N. I., Pfeifer, J. H., & Dapretto, M. (2010). Witnessing peer rejection during early adolescence: Neural correlates of empathy for experiences of social exclusion. *Social Neuroscience* 5, 496–507.

Masten, A. S., Desjardins, C. D., McCormick, C. M., et al. (2010). The significance of childhood competence and problems for adult success in work: A developmental cascade analysis. *Development and Psychopathology* 22, 679–694.

Masten, C. L., Guyer, A. E., Hodgdon, H. B., et al. (2008). Recognition of facial emotions among maltreated children with high rates of post-traumatic stress disorder. *Child Abuse & Neglect* 32, 139–153.

Masten, A. S., Roisman, G. I., Long, J. D., et al. (2005). Developmental cascades: Linking academic achievement and externalizing and internalizing symptoms over 20 years. *Developmental Psychology* 41:733–746.

McDonald, K. L., Dashiell-Aje, E., Menzer, M. M., et al. (2013). Contributions of racial and sociobehavioral homophily to friendship stability and quality among same-race and cross-race friends. *The Journal of Early Adolescence* 33, 897–919.

McDowell, D. J., & Parke, R. D. (2009). Parental correlates of children's peer relations: An empirical test of a tripartite model. *Developmental Psychology* 45, 224.

Mehta, C. M., & Strough, J. (2009). Sex segregation in friendships and normative contexts across the life span. *Developmental Review* 29, 201–220.

Mesquita, B., & Karasawa, M. (2004). Self-conscious emotions as dynamic cultural processes. *Psychological Inquiry* 15, 161–166.

Meter, D. J., & Bauman, S. (2015). When sharing is a bad idea: The effects of online social network engagement and sharing passwords with friends on cyberbullying involvement. *Cyberpsychology, Behavior, and Social Networking* 18, 437–442.

Miller, S. A. (2009). Children's understanding of second-order mental states. *Psychological Bulletin* 135, 749–773.

Mulvey, K. L., & Killen, M. (2015). Challenging gender stereotypes: Resistance and exclusion. *Child Development* 86, 681–694.

Muris, P., & Meesters, C. (2014). Small or big in the eyes of the other: On the developmental psychopathology of self-conscious emotions as shame, guilt, and pride. *Clinical Child and Family Psychology Review* 17, 19–40.

Murphy, B. C., & Eisenberg, N. (1996). Provoked by a peer: Children's anger-related responses and their relations to social functioning. *Merrill-Palmer Quarterly* 42, 103–124.

Neff, K. D., Cooper, C. E., & Woodruff, A. L. (2007). Children's and adolescents' developing perceptions of gender inequality. *Social Development* 16, 682–699.

Nesdale, D., Griffith, J., Durkin, K., & Maass, A. (2005). Empathy, group norms and children's ethnic attitudes. *Journal of Applied Developmental Psychology* 26, 623–637.

Neuville, E., & Croizet, J.-C. (2007). Can salience of gender identity impair math performance among 7–8 year old girls? The moderating role of task difficulty. *European Journal of Psychology of Education* 22, 307–316.

Ng, F. F.-Y., Pomerantz, E. M., & Lam, S.-f. (2007). European American and Chinese parents' responses to children's success and failure: Implications for children's responses. *Developmental Psychology* 43, 1239–1255.

Nishina, A., & Witkow, M. R. (2020). Why developmental researchers should care about biracial, multiracial, and multiethnic youth. *Child Development Perspectives*.

Ocampo, K. A., Knight, G. P., & Bernal, M. E. (1997). The development of cognitive abilities and social identities in children: The case of ethnic identity. *International Journal of Behavioral Development* 21, 479–500.

Oh, W., Rubin, K. H., Bowker, J. C., et al. (2008). Trajectories of social withdrawal from middle childhood to early adolescence. *Journal of Abnormal Child Psychology* 36, 553–566.

Olthof, T., Ferguson, T., Bloemers, E., & Deij, M. (2004). Morality- and identity-related antecedents of children's guilt and shame attributions in events involving physical illness. *Cognition and Emotion* 18, 383–404.

Ostrov, J. M., Crick, N. R., & Stauffacher, K. (2006). Relational aggression in sibling and peer relationships during early childhood. *Journal of Applied Developmental Psychology* 27, 241–253.

Papera, M., Richards, A., van Geert, C. V., & Valenti, C. (2019). Development of second-order theory of mind: Assessment of environmental influences using a dynamic system approach. *International Journal of Behavioral Development* 43, 245–254.

Parke, R. D., & Ladd, G. W. (Eds.). (2016). *Family-Peer Relationships: Modes of Linkage*. Routledge: New York.

Parker, J. G., Rubin, K. H., Erath, S. A., et al. (2006). Peer relationships, child development, and adjustment: A developmental psychopathology perspective. In D. Cicchetti & D. J. Cohen (Eds.), *Developmental Psychopathology: Theory and Method* (p. 419–493). John Wiley & Sons Inc.: Hoboken, NJ.

Parker, J. G., & Seal, J. (1996). Forming, losing, renewing, and replacing friendships: Applying temporal parameters to the assessment of children's friendship experiences. *Child Development* 67, 2248–2268.

Patterson, G. R. (1982). *Coercive Family Process* (Vol. 3). Castalia Publishing Company.

Payir, A., & Guttentag, R. (2016). "It could have been worse": Developmental change in the use of a counterfactual consoling strategy. *Journal of Experimental Child Psychology* 148, 119–130.

Pinquart, M. (2017). Associations of parenting dimensions and styles with externalizing problems of children and adolescents: An updated meta-analysis. *Developmental Psychology* 53, 873.

Pollak, S. D. (2008). Mechanisms linking early experience and the emergence of emotions: Illustrations from the study of maltreated children. *Current Directions in Psychological Science* 17, 370–375.

Pons, F., & Harris, P. L. (2005). Longitudinal change and longitudinal stability of individual differences in children's emotion understanding. *Cognition and Emotion* 19, 1158–1174.

Prinstein, M. J., & La Greca, A. M. (2004). Childhood peer rejection and aggression as predictors of adolescent girls' externalizing and health risk behaviors: a 6-year longitudinal study. *Journal of Consulting and Clinical Psychology* 72, 103.

Putallaz, M., Grimes, C. L., Foster, K. J., et al. (2007). Overt and relational aggression and victimization: Multiple perspectives within the school setting. *Journal of School Psychology* 45, 523–547.

Raabe, T., & Beelmann, A. (2011). Development of ethnic, racial, and national prejudice in childhood and adolescence: A multinational meta-analysis of age differences. *Child Development* 82, 1715–1737.

Richard, J. F., Schneider, B. H., & Mallet, P. (2012). Revisiting the whole-school approach to bullying: Really looking at the whole school. *School Psychology International* 33, 263–284.

Rodkin, P. C., Farmer, T. W., Pearl, R., & Van Acker, R. (2006). They're cool: Social status and peer group supports for aggressive boys and girls. *Social Development* 15, 175–204.

Rose, A. J., & Rudolph, K. D. (2006). A review of sex differences in peer relationship processes: Potential trade-offs for the emotional and behavioral development of girls and boys. *Psychological Bulletin* 132, 98–131.

Ross, H. S., & Lazinski, M. J. (2014). Parent mediation empowers sibling conflict resolution. *Early Education and Development* 25, 259–275.

Rotheram, M. J., & Phinney, J. S. (1987). Introduction: Definitions and perspectives in the study of children's ethnic socialization. *Children's Ethnic Socialization: Pluralism and Development* 10, 293–328.

Rowley, S. J., Kurtz-Costes, B., Mistry, R., & Feagans, L. (2007). Social status as a predictor of race and gender stereotypes in late childhood and early adolescence. *Social Development* 16, 150–168.

Rubin, K. H., Bowker, J. C., & Kennedy, A. E. (2009). Avoiding and withdrawing from the peer group. In K. H. Rubin, W. M. Bukowski, & B. Laursen (Eds.), *Handbook of Peer Interactions, Relationships, and Groups* (pp. 303–321). Guilford Press: New York.

Rubin, K. H., Bukowski, W. M., & Bowker, J. C. (2015). Children in peer groups. In M. H. Bornstein, T. Leventhal, & R. M. Lerner (Eds.), *Handbook of Child Psychology and Developmental Science: Ecological Settings and Processes*, Vol. 4, 7th ed (pp. 175–222). John Wiley & Sons Inc.: Hoboken, NJ.

Rubin, K. H., Bukowski, W. M., & Parker, J. G. (2006). Peer interactions, relationships, and groups. In N. Eisenberg, W. Damon, & R. M. Lerner (Eds.), *Handbook of Child Psychology: Vol. 3, Social, Emotional, and Personality Development*, 6th ed. (pp. 571–645). John Wiley & Sons Inc.: Hoboken, NJ.

Rubin, K. H., Coplan, R. J., & Bowker, J. C. (2009). Social withdrawal in childhood. *Annual Review of Psychology* 60, 141–171.

Rubin, K. H., Dwyer, K. M., Booth-LaForce, C., et al. (2004). Attachment, friendship, and psychosocial functioning in early adolescence. *The Journal of Early Adolescence* 24, 326–356.

Rubin, K. H., Wojslawowicz, J. C., Rose-Krasnor, L., et al. (2006). The best friendships of shy/withdrawn children: Prevalence, stability, and relationship quality. *Journal of Abnormal Child Psychology* 34, 143–157.

Rubin, K. H., Bowker, J. C., Barstead, M. G., & Coplan, R. J. (2018). Avoiding and withdrawing from the peer group. In W. M. Bukowski, B. Laursen, & K. H. Rubin (Eds.), *Handbook of Peer Interactions, Relationships, and Groups* (pp. 322–346). The Guilford Press: New York.

Ruble, D. N., Boggiano, A. K., Feldman, N. S., & Loebl, J. H. (1980). Developmental analysis of the role of social comparison in self-evaluation. *Developmental Psychology* 16, 105–115.

Ruble, D. N., Alvarez, J., Bachman, M., et al. (2004). The development of a sense of "we": The emergence and implications of children's collective identity. *The Development of the Social Self*, 29–76.

Ruble, D. N., Taylor, L. J., Cyphers, L., et al. (2007). The role of gender constancy in early gender development. *Child Development* 78, 1121–1136.

Rudolph, K. D., Caldwell, M. S., & Conley, C. S. (2005). Need for approval and children's well-being. *Child Development* 76, 309–323.

Saarni, C. (1979). Children's understanding of display rules for expressive behavior. *Developmental Psychology* 15, 424–429.

Saarni, C. (2010). The plasticity of emotional development. *Emotion Review* 2, 300–303.

Salmivalli, C., & Peets, K. (2009). Bullies, victims, and bully-victim relationships in middle childhood and early adolescence. In K. H. Rubin, W. M. Bukowski, & B. Laursen (Eds.), *Handbook of Peer Interactions, Relationships, and Groups* (pp. 322–340). Guilford Press: New York.

Sanders, W., Zeman, J., Poon, J., & Miller, R. (2015). Child regulation of negative emotions and depressive symptoms: The moderating role of parental emotion socialization. *Journal of Child and Family Studies* 24, 402–415.

Sandstrom, M. J., Cillessen, A. H., & Eisenhower, A. (2003). Children's appraisal of peer rejection experiences: Impact on social and emotional adjustment. *Social Development* 12, 530–550.

Schonert-Reichl, K. A., Smith, V., Zaidman-Zait, A., & Hertzman, C. (2012). Promoting children's prosocial behaviors in school: Impact of the "Roots of Empathy" program on the social and emotional competence of school-aged children. *School Mental Health* 4, 1–21.

Selfhout, M. H. W., Branje, S. J. T., ter Bogt, T. F. M., & Meeus, W. H. J. (2009). The role of music preferences in early adolescents' friendship formation and stability. *Journal of Adolescence* 32, 95–107.

Sherif, M. (1988). *The Robbers Cave Experiment: Intergroup Conflict and Cooperation*. [Orig. pub. as Intergroup conflict and group relations]. Wesleyan University Press: Middletown, CT.

Sijtsema, J. J., Lindenberg, S. M., & Veenstra, R. (2010). Do they get what they want or are they stuck with what they can get? Testing homophily against default selection for friendships of highly aggressive boys. The TRAILS study. *Journal of Abnormal Child Psychology* 38, 803–813.

Simpkins, S. D., & Parke, R. D. (2002). Do friends and nonfriends behave differently? A social relations analysis of children's behavior. *Merrill-Palmer Quarterly* 48, 263–283.

Sink, A., & Mastro, D. (2017). Depictions of gender on primetime television: A quantitative content analysis. *Mass Communication and Society* 20, 3–22.

Sinno, S. M., & Killen, M. (2009). Moms at work and dads at home: Children's evaluations of parental roles. *Applied Developmental Science* 13, 16–29.

Smetana, J. G. (2008). "It's 10 o'clock: Do you know where your children are?" Recent advances in understanding parental monitoring and adolescents' information management. *Child Development Perspectives* 2, 19–25.

Solmeyer, A. R., McHale, S. M., & Crouter, A. C. (2014). Longitudinal associations between sibling relationship qualities and risky behavior across adolescence. *Developmental Psychology* 50, 600.

Tamis-LeMonda, C. S., Briggs, R. D., McClowry, S. G., & Snow, D. L. (2009). Maternal control and sensitivity, child gender, and maternal education in relation to children's behavioral outcomes in African American families. *Journal of Applied Developmental Psychology* 30, 321–331.

Tangney, J. P., & Tracy, J. L. (2012). The self-conscious emotions: Shame, guilt, embarrassment and pride. In C. Mohiyeddini, M. Eysenck, & S. Bauer (Eds.), *Handbook of Cognition and Emotion* (pp. 541–568). John Wiley & Sons, Ltd.: Hoboken, NJ.

Thompson, R. A. (2011). Emotion and emotion regulation: Two sides of the developing coin. *Emotion Review* 3, 53–61.

Thompson, R. A., & Goodman, M. (2010). Development of emotion regulation: More than meets the eye. In A. M. Kring & D. M. Sloan (Eds.), *Emotion Regulation and Psychopathology: A Transdiagnostic Approach to Etiology and Treatment* (pp. 38–58). The Guilford Press: New York.

Tiedemann, J. (2000). Parents' gender stereotypes and teachers' beliefs as predictors of children's concept of their mathematical ability in elementary school. *Journal of Educational Psychology* 92, 144–151.

Tracy, J. L., & Robins, R. W. (2007). Emerging insights into the nature and function of pride. *Current Directions in Psychological Science* 16 147–150.

Tracy, J. L., Robins, R. W., & Lagattuta, K. H. (2005). Can children recognize pride? *Emotion* 5, 251–257.

Troop-Gordon, W., & Asher, S. R. (2005). Modifications in children's goals when encountering obstacles to conflict resolution. *Child Development* 76, 568–582.

Tsai, J. (2007). Ideal affect: Cultural causes and behavioral consequences. *Perspectives in Psychological Science* 2, 242–254.

Vaillancourt, T., & Hymel, S. (2006). Aggression and social status: The moderating roles of sex and peer-valued characteristics. *Aggressive Behavior* 32, 396–408.

Van den Berg, Y. H., Lansu, T. A., & Cillessen, A. H. (2015). Measuring social status and social behavior with peer and teacher nomination methods. *Social Development* 24, 815–832.

Verkuyten, M. (2018). The benefits of studying immigration for social psychology. *European Journal of Social Psychology* 48, 225–239.

Vitaro, F., Boivin, M., & Tremblay, R. E. (2007). Peers and violence: A two-sided developmental perspective. In D. J. Flannery, A. T. Vazsonyi, & I. D. Waldman (Eds.), *The Cambridge Handbook of Violent Behavior and Aggression* (pp. 361–387). Cambridge University Press: New York.

Vogel, C. A., Bradley, R. H., Raikes, H. H., et al. (2006). Relation between father connectedness and child outcomes. *Parenting* 6, 189–209.

Wang, M.-T., & Dishion, T. J. (2012). The trajectories of adolescents' perceptions of school climate, deviant peer affiliation, and behavioral problems during the middle school years. *Journal of Research on Adolescence* 22, 40–53.

Wang, Q. (2006). Relations of maternal style and child self-concept to autobiographical memories in Chinese, Chinese immigrant, and European American 3-year-olds. *Child Development* 77, 1794–1809.

Wang, Q., & Fivush, R. (2005). Mother-child conversations of emotionally salient events: Exploring the functions of emotional reminiscing in European-American and Chinese families. *Social Development* 14, 473–495.

Waters, S. F., & Thompson, R. A. (2014). Children's perceptions of the effectiveness of strategies for regulating anger and sadness. *International Journal of Behavioral Development* 38, 174–181.

Way, N. (2013). *Boys' Friendships and the Crisis of Connection*. Harvard University Press: Cambridge, MA.

Way, N., & Greene, M. L. (2006). Trajectories of perceived friendship quality during adolescence: The patterns and contextual predictors. *Journal of Research on Adolescence* 16, 293–320.

Whitesell, N. R., Mitchell, C. M., & Spicer, P. (2009). A longitudinal study of self-esteem, cultural identity, and academic success among American Indian adolescents. *Cultural Diversity and Ethnic Minority Psychology* 15, 38–50.

Wigfield, A., Eccles, J. S., Yoon, K. S., et al. (1997). Change in children's competence beliefs and subjective task values across the elementary school years: A 3-year study. *Journal of Educational Psychology* 89, 451–469.

Williams, K. D., Cheung, C. K. T., & Choi, W. (2000). Cyber-racism: Effects of being ignored over the Internet. *Journal of Personality and Social Psychology* 79, 748–762.

Wojslawowicz Bowker, J. C., Rubin, K. H., Burgess, K. B., et al. (2006). Behavioral characteristics associated with stable and fluid best friendship patterns in middle childhood. *Merrill-Palmer Quarterly* 52, 671–693.

Yu, L., & Xie, D. (2010). Multidimensional gender identity and psychological adjustment in middle childhood: A study in China. *Sex Roles* 62, 100–113.

Zosuls, K. M., Andrews, N. C., Martin, C. L., et al. (2016). Developmental changes in the link between gender typicality and peer victimization and exclusion. *Sex Roles* 75, 243–256.

Zosuls, K. M., Martin, C. L., Ruble, D. N., et al. (2011). "It's not that we hate you": Understanding children's gender attitudes and expectancies about peer relationships. *British Journal of Developmental Psychology* 29, 288–304.

Chapter 14

Ahmadi, F., Anoosheh, M., Vaismoradi, M., & Safdari, M.-T. (2009). The experience of puberty in adolescent boys: an Iranian perspective. *International Nursing Review* 56, 257–263.

Akers, A. Y., Gold, M. A., Bost, J. E., et al. (2011). Variation in sexual behaviors in a cohort of adolescent females: The role of personal, perceived peer, and perceived family attitudes. *Journal of Adolescent Health* 48, 87–93.

Al Zaabi, O., Heffernan, M., Holroyd, E., & Jackson, M. A. (2019). Islamic parents' attitudes and beliefs towards school-based sexual and reproductive health education programmes in Oman. *Sex Education* 19, 534–550.

American Academy of Pediatrics (2014). School start times for adolescents. *Pediatrics* 134, 642–649.

Archibald, A. B., Graber, J. A., & Brooks-Gunn, J. (2003). Pubertal processes and physiological growth in adolescence. In *Blackwell Handbook of Adolescence* (pp. 24–47). Blackwell Publishing: Malden, MA.

Ashdown-Franks, G., Vancampfort, D., Firth, J. et al. (2019). Association of leisure-time sedentary behavior with fast food and carbonated soft drink consumption among 133,555 adolescents aged 12–15 years in 44 low- and middle-income countries. *International Journal of Behavioral Nutrition and Physical Activity* 16, 35.

Barkley-Levenson, E., & Galván, A. (2014). Neural representation of expected value in the adolescent brain. *Proceedings of the National Academy of Sciences of the United States of America* 111, 1646–1651.

Beers, L. A. S., & Hollo, R. E. (2009). Approaching the adolescent-headed family: A review of teen parenting. *Current Problems in Pediatric and Adolescent Health Care* 39, 216–233.

Belachew, T., Hadley, C., Lindstrom, D., et al. (2011). Food insecurity and age at menarche among adolescent girls in Jimma Zone Southwest Ethiopia: a longitudinal study. *Reproductive Biology and Endocrinology* 9, 125.

Bello, B. M., Fatusi, A. O., Adepoju, O. E., et al. (2017). Adolescent and parental reactions to puberty in Nigeria and Kenya: A cross-cultural and intergenerational comparison. *Journal of Adolescent Health* 61, S35–S41.

Belsky, J., Steinberg, L. D., Houts, R. M., et al. (2007). Family rearing antecedents of pubertal timing. *Child Development* 78, 1302–1321.

Belsky, J., Houts, R. M., & Fearon, R. P. (2010). Infant attachment security and the timing of puberty: Testing an evolutionary hypothesis. *Psychological Science* 21, 1195–1201.

Berkey, C. S., Rockett, H. R., Field, A. E., et al. (2000). Activity, dietary intake, and weight changes in a longitudinal study of preadolescent and adolescent boys and girls. *Pediatrics* 105, E56.

Best, C., & Fortenberry, J. D. (2013). Adolescent sexuality and sexual behavior. In W. O'Donohue, L. Benuto, & T. L. Woodward (Eds.), *Handbook of Adolescent Health Psychology* (pp. 271–291): Springer.

Bethea, C. L., Lu, N. Z., Gundlah, C., & Streicher, J. M. (2002). Diverse actions of ovarian steroids in the serotonin neural system. *Frontiers in Neuroendocrinology* 23, 41–100.

Beyth-Marom, R., Austin, L., Fischhoff, B., et al. (1993). Perceived consequences of risky behaviors: adults and adolescents. *Developmental Psychology* 29, 549.

Bjork, J. M., Knutson, B., Fong, G. W., et al. (2004). Incentive-elicited brain activation in adolescents: similarities and differences from young adults. *Journal of Neuroscience* 24, 1793–1802.

Blakemore, S.-J. (2008). The social brain in adolescence. *Nature Reviews Neuroscience* 9, 267.

Blakemore, S.-J., Burnett, S., & Dahl, R. E. (2010). The role of puberty in the developing adolescent brain. *Human Brain Mapping* 31, 926–933.

Blakemore, S.-J., & Choudhury, S. (2006). Development of the adolescent brain: Implications for executive function and social cognition. *Journal of Child Psychology and Psychiatry* 47, 296–312.

Blakemore, S. J., & Robbins, T. W. (2012). Decision-making in the adolescent brain. *Nature Neuroscience* 15, 1184.

Blanton, R. E., Levitt, J. G., Peterson, J. R., et al. (2004). Gender differences in the left inferior frontal gyrus in normal children. *Neuroimage* 22, 626–636.

Bleakley, A. Khurana, A., Hennessy, M., & Ellithorpe, M. (2018). How patterns of learning about sexual information among adolescents are related to sexual behaviors. *Perspectives on Sexual and Reproductive Health* 50, 15–23.

Boynton-Jarrett, R., Wright, R. J., Putnam, F. W., et al. (2013). Childhood abuse and age at menarche. *Journal of Adolescent Health* 52, 241–247.

Braithwaite, D., Moore, D. H., Lustig, R. H., et al. (2009). Socioeconomic status in relation to early menarche among Black and White girls. *Cancer Causes & Control* 20, 713–720.

Brooks-Gunn, J., & Reiter, E. O. (1990). The role of pubertal processes. In *At the Threshold: The Developing Adolescent* (pp. 16–53). Harvard University Press: Cambridge, MA.

Bunting, L., & McAuley, C. (2004). Teenage pregnancy and motherhood: The contribution of support. *Child & Family Social Work* 9, 207–215.

Cain, N., & Gradisar, M. (2010). Electronic media use and sleep in school-aged children and adolescents: A review. *Sleep Medicine* 11, 735–742.

Calle, E. E., & Kaaks, R. (2004). Overweight, obesity and cancer: epidemiological evidence and proposed mechanisms. *Nature Reviews Cancer* 4, 579.

Calogero, R. M., Tylka, T. L., Mensinger, J. L., et al. (2019). Recognizing the fundamental right to be fat: A weight-inclusive approach to size acceptance and healing from sizeism. *Women & Therapy* 42, 22–44.

Calzo, J. P., Blashill, A. J., Brown, T. A., & Argenal, R. L. (2017). Eating disorders and disordered weight and shape control behaviors in sexual minority populations. *Current Psychiatry Reports* 19, 49.

Cameron, N.O., Muldrow, A.F., & Stefani, W. (2018). The weight of things: Understanding African American women's perceptions of health, body image, and attractiveness. *Qualitative Health Research* 28, 1242–1254.

Carskadon, M. A., Acebo, C., Richardson, G. S., et al. (1997). An approach to studying circadian rhythms of adolescent humans. *Journal of Biological Rhythms* 12, 278–289.

Carskadon, M. A., & Rechtschaffen, A. (2011). Monitoring and staging human sleep. *Principles and Practice of Sleep Medicine* 5, 16–26.

Carskadon, M. A., Wolfson, A. R., Acebo, C., et al. (1998). Adolescent sleep patterns, circadian timing, and sleepiness at a transition to early school days. *Sleep* 21, 871–881.

Casavant, M. J., Blake, K., Griffith, J., et al. (2007). Consequences of use of anabolic androgenic steroids. *Pediatric Clinics of North America* 54, 677–690.

Casey, B. J., Jones, R. M., & Somerville, L. H. (2011). Braking and accelerating of the adolescent brain. *Journal of Research on Adolescence* 21, 21–33.

Caspi, A., Lynam, D., Moffitt, T. E., & Silva, P. A. (1993). Unraveling girls' delinquency: Biological, dispositional, and contextual contributions to adolescent misbehavior. *Developmental Psychology* 29, 19.

Castillo, E. M., & Comstock, R. D. (2007). Prevalence of use of performance-enhancing substances among United States adolescents. *Pediatric Clinics of North America* 54, 663–675.

Celio, M., Karink, N. S., & Steiner, H. (2006). Early maturation as a risk factor for aggression and delinquency in adolescent girls: a review. *International Journal of Clinical Practice* 60, 1254–1262.

Cheng, G., Buyken, A. E., Shi, L., et al. (2012). Beyond overweight: nutrition as an important lifestyle factor influencing timing of puberty. *Nutrition Reviews* 70, 133–152.

Choudhury, S., Charman, T., & Blakemore, S. J. (2008). Development of the teenage brain. *Mind, Brain, and Education* 2, 142–147.

Colrain, I. M., & Baker, F. C. (2011). Changes in sleep as a function of adolescent development. *Neuropsychology Review* 21, 5–21.

Condon, R. G. (1987). *Inuit Youth: Growth and Change in the Canadian Arctic* (Vol. 1). Rutgers University Press: New Brunswick, NJ.

Cooper, C. Saycer, A. A., & Dennison, E. M. (2006). The developmental environment: Clinical perspectives on the effects on the musculoskeletalk systems. In P. Gluckman & M. Hanson (Eds.). *Developmental Origins of Health and Disease* (pp. 392–405). Cambridge University Press: Cambridge, United Kingdom.

Couper, E., Jacobs, R., & Anderson, V. (2002). Adaptive behaviour and moral reasoning in children with frontal lobe lesions. *Brain Impairment* 3, 105–113.

Couturier, J., & Lock, J. (2006). What is recovery in adolescent anorexia nervosa? *International Journal of Eating Disorders* 39, 550–555.

Crone, E. A., & Dahl, R. E. (2012). Understanding adolescence as a period of social–affective engagement and goal flexibility. *Nature Reviews Neuroscience* 13, 636–650.

Cruz, M. L., Shaibi, G. Q., Weigensberg, M. J., et al. (2005). Pediatric obesity and insulin resistance: chronic disease risk and implications for treatment and prevention beyond body weight modification. *Annual Review of Nutrition* 25, 435–468.

Dahl, R. E. (2016). The developmental neuroscience of adolescence: Revisiting, refining, and extending seminal models. *Developmental Cognitive Neuroscience* 17, 101–102.

de Bellis, M. D., Keshavan, M. S., Beers, S. R., et al. (2001). Sex differences in brain maturation during childhood and adolescence. *Cerebral Cortex* 11, 552–557.

Deardorff, J., Ekwaru, J. P., Kushi, L. H., et al. (2011). Father absence, body mass index, and pubertal timing in girls: Differential effects by family income and ethnicity. *Journal of Adolescent Health* 48, 441–447.

Depestele, L., Soenens, B., Lemmens, G. M., et al. (2017). Parental autonomy-support and psychological control in eating disorder patients with and without binge-eating/purging behavior and non-suicidal self-injury. *Journal of Social and Clinical Psychology* 36, 126–141.

DeRose, L. M., & Brooks-Gunn, J. (2006). Transition into adolescence: The role of pubertal processes. In L. Balter & C. S. Tamis-LeMonda (Eds.), *Child Psychology: A Handbook of Contemporary Issues* (pp. 385–414). Psychology Press: New York.

Dewald, J. F., Meijer, A. M., Oort, F. J., et al. (2010). The influence of sleep quality, sleep duration and sleepiness on school performance in children and adolescents: A meta-analytic review. *Sleep Medicine Reviews* 14, 179–189.

Diamond, L. M., & Cribbet, M. R. (2013). Links between adolescent sympathetic and para-sympathetic nervous system functioning and interpersonal behavior over time. *International Journal of Psychophysiology* 88, 339–348.

Doremus-Fitzwater, T. L., Varlinskaya, E. I., & Spear, L. P. (2010). Motivational systems in adolescence: Possible implications for age differences in substance abuse and other risk-taking behaviors. *Brain and Cognition* 72, 114–123.

Dorn, L. D. (2006). Measuring puberty. *Journal of Adolescent Health* 39, 625–626.

Dorn, L. D., Susman, E. J., & Ponirakis, A. (2003). Pubertal timing and adolescent adjustment and behavior: Conclusions vary by rater. *Journal of Youth and Adolescence* 32, 157–167.

Duell, N., Steinberg, L., Chein, J., et al. (2016). Interaction of reward seeking and self-regulation in the prediction of risk taking: A cross-national test of the dual systems model. *Developmental Psychology* 52, 1593–1605.

Edwards, F. (2012). Early to rise? The effect of daily start times on academic performance. *Economics of Education Review* 31, 970–983.

Elias, V. L., Fullerton, A. S., & Simpson, J. M. (2015). Long-term changes in attitudes toward premarital sex in the United States: reexamining the role of cohort replacement. *Journal of Sex Research* 52129–52139.

Fagan, J. (2014). Adolescent parents' partner conflict and parenting alliance, fathers' prenatal involvement, and fathers' engagement with infants. *Journal of Family Issues* 35, 1415–1439.

Fechner, P. Y. (2003). The biology of puberty: New developments in sex differences. In *Gender Differences at Puberty* (pp. 17–28). Cambridge University Press: New York.

Feinberg, I., & Campbell, I. G. (2010). Sleep EEG changes during adolescence: An index of a fundamental brain reorganization. *Brain and Cognition* 72, 56–65.

Finer, L. B., & Philbin, J. M. (2013). Sexual initiation, contraceptive use, and pregnancy among young adolescents. *Pediatrics* 131, 886–891.

Furstenberg Jr, F. (2016). Early childbearing in the new era of delayed adulthood. In *Routledge Handbook of Youth and Young Adulthood* (pp. 229–234).

Galvan, A., Hare, T. A., Parra, C. E., et al. (2006). Earlier development of the accumbens relative to orbitofrontal cortex might underlie risk-taking behavior in adolescents. *Journal of Neuroscience* 26, 6885–6892.

Gangwisch, J. E., Babiss, L. A., Malaspina, D., et al. (2010). Earlier parental set bedtimes as a protective factor against depression and suicidal ideation. *Sleep* 33, 97–106.

Ge, X., Brody, G. H., Conger, R. D., et al. (2002). Contextual amplification of pubertal transition effects on deviant peer affiliation and externalizing behavior among African American children. *Developmental Psychology* 38, 42–54.

Ge, X., Natsuaki, M. N., Jin, R., & Biehl, M. C. (2011). A contextual amplification hypothesis: Pubertal timing and girls' emotional and behavioral problems. In M. Kerr, H. Stattin, R. C. M. E. Engels, et al. (Eds.), *Hot Topics in Developmental Research. Understanding Girls' Problem Behavior: How Girls' Delinquency Develops in the Context of Maturity and Health,*

Co-occurring Problems, and Relationships (pp. 11–29). Wiley-Blackwell: Hoboken, NJ.

Geier, C. F., Terwilliger, R., Teslovich, T., et al. (2010). Immaturities in reward processing and its influence on inhibitory control in adolescence. *Cerebral Cortex* 20, 1613–1629.

Ge, X., Conger, R. D., & Elder Jr, G. H. (1996). Coming of age too early: Pubertal influences on girls' vulnerability to psychological distress. *Child Development* 67, 3386–3400.

Giedd, J. N., Blumenthal, J., Jeffries, N. O., et al. (1999). Brain development during childhood and adolescence: A longitudinal MRI study. *Nature Neuroscience* 2, 861–863.

Giedd, J. N., Lalonde, F. M., Celano, M. J., et al. (2009). Anatomical brain magnetic resonance imaging of typically developing children and adolescents. *Journal of the American Academy of Child and Adolescent Psychiatry* 48, 465–470.

Giedd, J. N. (2009). The teen brain: Primed to learn, primed to take risks. *Cerebrum*, 1–9.

Glass, C. M., Haas, S. A., & Reither, E. N. (2010). The skinny on success: Body mass, gender and occupational standing across the life course. *Social Forces; A Scientific Medium of Social Study and Interpretation* 88, 1777–1806.

Goddard, E., & Treasure, J. (2013). Anxiety and social emotional processing in eating disorders: examination of family trios. *Cognitive Therapy and Research* 37, 890–904.

Goddings, A.-L., & Giedd, J. (2014). Structural brain development during childhood and adolescence. *The Cognitive Neurosciences*, 15–22.

Gogtay, N., Giedd, J. N., Lusk, L., et al. (2004). Dynamic mapping of human cortical development during childhood through early adulthood. *Proceedings of the National Academy of Sciences of the United States of America* 101, 8174–8179.

Gordon-Larsen, P., Adair, L. S., & Popkin, B. M. (2003). The relationship of ethnicity, socioeconomic factors, and overweight in US adolescents. *Obesity Research* 11, 121–129.

Graber, J. A., Seeley, J. R., Brooks-Gunn, J., & Lewinsohn, P. M. (2004). Is pubertal timing associated with psychopathology in young adulthood? *Journal of the American Academy of Child & Adolescent Psychiatry* 43, 718–726.

Gradisar, M., Gardner, G., & Dohnt, H. (2011). Recent worldwide sleep patterns and problems during adolescence: A review and meta-analysis of age, region, and sleep. *Sleep Medicine* 12, 110–118.

Gradisar, M., Wolfson, A. R., Harvey, A. G., et al. (2013). The sleep and technology use of Americans: findings from the National Sleep Foundation's 2011 Sleep in America poll. *Journal of Clinical Sleep Medicine* 9, 1291–1299.

Granillo, T., Jones-Rodriguez, G., & Carvajal, S. C. (2005). Prevalence of eating disorders in Latina adolescents: Associations with substance use and other correlates. *Journal of Adolescent Health* 36, 214–220.

Griffiths, L. J., Parsons, T. J., & Hill, A. J. (2010). Self-esteem and quality of life in obese children and adolescents: a systematic review. *International Journal of Pediatric Obesity* 5, 282–304.

Grolnick, W. S., & Pomerantz, E. M. (2009). Issues and challenges in studying parental control: Toward a new conceptualization. *Child Development Perspectives* 3, 165–170.

Guyer, A. E., Monk, C. S., McClure-Tone, E. B., et al. (2008). A developmental examination of amygdala response to facial expressions. *Journal of Cognitive Neuroscience* 20, 1565–1582.

Hagenauer, M. H., Perryman, J. I., Lee, T. M., & Carskadon, M. A. (2009). Adolescent changes in the homeostatic and circadian regulation of sleep. *Developmental Neuroscience* 31, 276–284.

Haines, J., Rifas-Shiman, S. L., Horton, N. J., et al. (2016). Family functioning and quality of parent-adolescent relationship: cross-sectional associations with adolescent weight-related behaviors and weight status. *International Journal of Behavioral Nutrition and Physical Activity* 13, 1–12.

Gordon-Larsen, P., Adair, L. S., & Popkin, B. M. (2003). The relationship of ethnicity, socioeconomic factors, and overweight in US adolescents. *Obesity Research* 11, 121–129.

Harden, K. P. (2014). A sex-positive framework for research on adolescent sexuality. *Perspectives on Psychological Science* 9, 455–469.

Haynie, D. L. (2003). Contexts of risk? Explaining the link between girls' pubertal development and their delinquency involvement. *Social Forces* 82, 355–397.

Haywood, K. M., & Getchell, N. (2005). *Life Span Motor Development*, 4th ed. Human Kinetics: Champaign, IL.

Higuchi, S., Motohashi, Y., Liu, Y., & Maeda, A. (2005). Effects of playing a computer game using a bright display on presleep physiological variables, sleep latency, slow wave sleep and REM sleep. *Journal of Sleep Research* 14, 267–273.

Hoffman, S. D., & Maynard, R. A. (2008). *Kids Having Kids: Economic Costs & Social Consequences of Teen Pregnancy*. The Urban Institute.

Hysing, M., Pallesen, S., Stormark, K. M., et al. (2015). Sleep and use of electronic devices in adolescence: results from a large population-based study. *BMJ Open* 5, e006748.

Jaccard, J., Dodge, T., & Dittus, P. (2002). Parent-adolescent communication about sex and birth control: A conceptual framework. *New Directions for Child and Adolescent Development* 2002, 9–42.

Janssen, H. G., Davies, I. G., Richardson, L. D., & Stevenson, L. (2018). Determinants of take-away and fast food consumption: a narrative review. *Nutrition Research Reviews* 31, 16–34.

Johnston, L. D., O'Malley, P. M., Bachman, J. G., & Schulenberg, J. E. (2012). *Monitoring the Future National Results on Adolescent Drug Use: Overview of Key Findings, 2011*.

Johnston, L. D., O'Malley, P. M., Bachman, J. G., et al. (2014). *Monitoring the Future National Survey Results on Drug Use, 1975–2013*: Volume I, Secondary school students.

Joy, E., Kussman, A., & Nattiv, A. 2016 update on eating disorders in athletes: A comprehensive narrative review with a focus on clinical assessment and management. *British Journal of Sports Medicine* 50, 154–62.

Kann, L., Kinchen, S., Shanklin, S. L., et al. (2014). Youth risk behavior surveillance—United States, 2013. *Morbidity and Mortality Weekly Report: Surveillance Summaries* 63, 1–168.

Kaplan, D. L., Jones, E. J., Olson, E. C., & Yunzal-Butler, C. B. (2013). Early age of first sex and health risk in an urban adolescent population. *Journal of School Health* 83, 350–356.

Kaplowitz, P. B. (2008). Link between body fat and the timing of puberty. *Pediatrics* 121, S208–S217.

Katzman, D. K. (2005). Medical complications in adolescents with anorexia nervosa: A review of the literature. *International Journal of Eating Disorders* 37, S52–S59.

Kaye, W. (2008). Neurobiology of anorexia and bulimia nervosa. *Physiology & Behavior* 94, 121–135.

Kearney, M. S., & Levine, P. B. (2012). Why is the teen birth rate in the United States so high and why does it matter? *Journal of Economic Perspectives* 26, 141–163.

Kenney, E. L., & Gortmaker, S. L. (2017). United States adolescents' television, computer, videogame, smartphone, and tablet use: Associations with sugary drinks, sleep, physical activity, and obesity. *The Journal of Pediatrics* 182, 144–149.

Kerr, Z. Y., Chandran, A., Nedimyer, A. K., et al. (2019). Concussion incidence and trends in 20 high school sports. *Pediatrics* 144, e20192180.

Keyes, K. M., Maslowsky, J., Hamilton, A., & Schulenberg, J. (2015). The great sleep recession: Changes in sleep duration among US adolescents, 1991–2012. *Pediatrics* 135, 460–468.

Khalsa, S., Portnoff, L.C., McCurdy-McKinnon, D., & Feusner, J. (2017). What happens after treatment? A systematic review of relapse, remission, and recovery in anorexia nervosa. *Journal of Eating Disorders* 5.

Kirby, D., Lepore, G., & Ryan, J. (2007). Sexual risk and protective factors. Factors affecting teen sexual behavior, pregnancy, childbearing and sexually transmitted disease: Which are important?

Klump, K. L., Gobrogge, K. L., Perkins, P. S., et al. (2006). Preliminary evidence that gonadal hormones organize and activate disordered eating. *Psychological Medicine* 36, 539–546.

Kost, K., & Henshaw, S. (2014). US Teenage pregnancies, births and abortions, 2010: National and state trends by age, race and ethnicity. Guttmacher Institute. May 2014.

Kreager, D. A., Staff, J., Gauthier, R., et al. (2016). The double standard at sexual debut: Gender, sexual behavior and adolescent peer acceptance. *Sex Roles* 75, 377–392.

Krueger, A., Dietz, P., Van Handel, M., et al. (2016). Estimates of CDC-funded and national HIV diagnoses: A comparison by demographic and HIV-related factors. *AIDS Behavior* 20, 2961–2965.

LaBotz, M., & Griesemer, B. A. (2016). Use of performance-enhancing substances. *Pediatrics* 138, e20161300.

Lancy, D. F., & Grove, M. A. (2011). "Getting noticed": Middle childhood in cross-cultural perspective. *Human Nature* 22, 281–302.

LeBourgeois, M. K., Hale, L., Chang, A. M., et al. (2017). Digital media and sleep in childhood and adolescence. *Pediatrics* 140, S92.

Lehrer, J. A., Pantell, R., Tebb, K., & Shafer, M.-A. (2007). Forgone health care among U.S. adolescents: Associations between risk characteristics and confidentiality concern. *Journal of Adolescent Health* 40, 218–226.

Lemola, S., Perkinson-Gloor, N., Brand, S., et al. (2015). Adolescents' electronic media use at night, sleep disturbance, and depressive symptoms in the smartphone age. *Journal of Youth and Adolescence* 44, 405–418.

Lenroot, R. K., & Giedd, J. N. (2006). Brain development in children and adolescents: Insights from anatomical magnetic resonance imaging. *Neuroscience and Biobehavioral Reviews* 30, 718–729.

Lindberg, L., Santelli, J., & Desai, S. (2016). Understanding the decline in adolescent fertility in the United States, 2007–2012. *Journal of Adolescent Health* 59, 577–583.

Lohman, B. J., Gillette, M. T., & Neppl, T. K. (2016). Harsh parenting and food insecurity in adolescence: The association with emerging adult obesity. *Journal of Adolescent Health* 59, 123–127.

Loughran, S. P., Wood, A. W., Barton, J. M., et al. (2005). The effect of electromagnetic fields emitted by mobile phones on human sleep. *Neuroreport* 16, 1973–1976.

Lubans, D., Richards, J., Hillman, C. et al. (2016). Physical activity for cognitive and mental health in youth. *Pediatrics* 138 e20161642.

Luppino, F. S., de Wit, L. M., Bouvy, P. F., et al. (2010). Overweight, obesity, and depression: a systematic review and meta-analysis of longitudinal studies. *Archives of General Psychiatry* 67, 220–229.

Macapagal, K, Moskowitz, D. A., Li, D. H., et al. 2018. Hookup app use, sexual behavior, and sexual health among adolescent men who have sex with men in the United States. *Journal of Adolescent Health* 62, 708–715.

Malone, S. K., Ziporyn, T., & Buttenheim, A. M. (2017). Applying behavioral insights to delay school start times. *Sleep Health* 3, 483–485.

Martin, J. A., Hamilton, B. E., Osterman, M. J. K., et al. (2017). *Births: Final Data for 2015.* National Center for Health Statistics: Hyattsville, MD.

Martinez, G., Copen, C. E., & Abma, J. C. (2011). Teenagers in the United States: Sexual activity, contraceptive use, and childbearing, 2006–2010 National Survey of Family Growth. *Vital and Health Statistics. Series* 23, Data from the National Survey of Family Growth 31, 1–35.

Marván, M. L., Vacio, A., García-Yáñez, G., & Espinosa-Hernández, G. (2007). Attitudes toward menarche among Mexican preadolescents. *Women & Health* 46, 7–23.

Masten, C. L., Eisenberger, N. I., Borofsky, L. A., et al. (2009). Neural correlates of social exclusion during adolescence: understanding the distress of peer rejection. *Social Cognitive and Affective Neuroscience* 4, 143–157.

Masten, C. L., Eisenberger, N. I., Borofsky, L. A., et al. (2011). Subgenual anterior cingulate responses to peer rejection: a marker of adolescents' risk for depression. *Development and Psychopathology* 23, 283–292.

Maynard, R. A. (2018). The costs of adolescent childbearing. In *Kids Having Kids* (pp. 285–337). Routledge: London.

Mazzeo, S. E., & Bulik, C. M. (2009). Environmental and genetic risk factors for eating disorders: what the clinician needs to know. *Child and Adolescent Psychiatric Clinics of North America* 18, 67–82.

McCabe, S. E., West, B. T., Veliz, P., et al. (2017). Trends in medical and nonmedical use of prescription opioids among US adolescents: 1976–2015. *Pediatrics* 139.

McMurray, R. G., Harrell, J. S., Deng, S., et al. (2000). The influence of physical activity, socioeconomic status, and ethnicity on the weight status of adolescents. *Obesity Research* 8, 130–139.

Meijer, A. M. (2008). Chronic sleep reduction, functioning at school and school achievement in preadolescents. *Journal of Sleep Research* 17, 395–405.

Mendle, J., Turkheimer, E., & Emery, R. E. (2007). Detrimental psychological outcomes associated with early pubertal timing in adolescent girls. *Developmental Review* 27, 151–171.

Mensinger, J. L., Calogero, R. M., & Tylka T. L. (2016). Internalized weight stigma moderates eating behavior outcomes in women with high BMI participating in a healthy living program. *Appetite* 102, 32–43.

Merikangas, K. R., He, J. P., Burstein, M., et al. (2010). Lifetime prevalence of mental disorders in U.S. adolescents: results from the National Comorbidity Survey Replication-Adolescent Supplement (NCS-A). *Journal of the American Academy of Child and Adolescent Psychiatry* 49, 980–989.

Millstein, S. G., & Halpern–Felsher, B. L. (2002). Judgments about risk and perceived invulnerability in adolescents and young adults. *Journal of Research on Adolescence* 12, 399–422.

Mollborn, S., & Dennis, J. A. (2012). Investigating the life situations and development of teenage mothers' children: Evidence from the ECLS-B. *Population Research and Policy Review* 31, 31–66.

Moore, M. R., & Brooks-Gunn, J. (2002). Adolescent parenthood. In *Handbook of Parenting: Vol. 3: Being and Becoming a Parent,* 2nd ed. (pp. 173–214). Lawrence Erlbaum Associates Publishers: Hillsdale, NJ.

Mosher, W. D., Jones, J., & Abma, J. C. (2012). Intended and unintended births in the United States: 1982–2010. http://ai2-s2-pdfs.s3.amazonaws.com/2cf1/97770f344eb8a638599e1b0fa786b1abefa7.pdf

Mullinax, M., Mathur, S., & Santelli, J. (2017). Adolescent sexual health and sexuality education. In *International Handbook on Adolescent Health and Development* (pp.143–167).

Nabi, G., Amin, M., Sultan, R., & Kamil, M. (2014). Environmental factors and puberty onset: An update. *Journal of Biology and Life Science* 5, 165–174.

Negriff, S., & Subrahmanyam, K. (2020). Is online peer engagement bad for all youth all of the time? The benefits and perils of online peer interactions. In *Online Peer Engagement in Adolescence* (pp. 54–70). Routledge: London.

Negriff, S., & Susman, E. J. (2011). Pubertal timing, depression, and externalizing problems: A framework, review, and examination of gender differences. *Journal of Research on Adolescence* 21, 717–746.

Neumark-Sztainer, D., Wall, M., Guo, J., et al. (2006). Obesity, disordered eating, and eating disorders in a longitudinal study of adolescents: How do dieters fare 5 years later? *Journal of the American Dietetic Association* 106, 559–568.

Nhlekisana, R. O. (2017). From childhood to womanhood: Puberty rites of !XOO girls of Zutshwa. *Marang: Journal of Language and Literature* 29, 31–41.

Nichols, J. F., Rauh, M. J., Lawson, M. J., et al. (2006). Prevalence of the female athlete triad syndrome among high school athletes. *Archives of Pediatrics & Adolescent Medicine* 160, 137–142.

Noland, H., Price, J. H., Dake, J., & Telljohann, S. K. (2009). Adolescents' sleep behaviors and perceptions of sleep. *Journal of School Health* 79, 224–230.

Ogden, C. L., Carroll, M. D., Curtin, L. R., et al. (2010). Prevalence of high body mass index in US children and adolescents, 2007–2008. *JAMA* 303, 242–249.

Ogden, C. L., Carroll, M. D., Kit, B. K., & Flegal, K. M. (2014). Prevalence of childhood and adult obesity in the United States, 2011–2012. *JAMA* 311, 806–814.

Ogden, C. L., Carroll, M. D., & Flegal, K. M. (2014). Prevalence of obesity in the United States. *JAMA* 312, 189–190.

Ottenberg, S. (1994). *Initiations*. Greenwood Press.

Owens, J. A., Dearth-Wesley, T., Herman, A. N., et al. (2017). A quasi-experimental study of the impact of school start time changes on adolescent sleep. *Sleep Health* 3, 437–443.

Ozer, E., Irwin, C. (2009). Adolescent and young adult health: From basic health status to clinical interventions. In R. Lerner (Ed.), *Handbook of Adolescent Psychology*, 3rd ed. (pp. 618–641). Wiley: Hoboken, NJ.

Padmanabhan, A., Geier, C. F., Ordaz, S. J., et al. (2011). Developmental changes in brain function underlying the influence of reward processing on inhibitory control. *Developmental Cognitive Neuroscience* 1, 517–529.

Pagliaccio, D., Luby, J. L., Bogdan, R., et al. (2015). Amygdala functional connectivity, HPA axis genetic variation, and life stress in children and relations to anxiety and emotion regulation. *Journal of Abnormal Psychology* 124, 817.

Parent, A.-S., Teilmann, G., Juul, A., Skakkebaek, N. E., et al. (2003). The timing of normal puberty and the age limits of sexual precocity: Variations around the world, secular trends, and changes after migration. *Endocrine Reviews* 24, 668–693.

Patel, P. H., and Sen, B. (2012). Teen motherhood and long-term health consequences. *Maternal and Child Health Journal* 16, 1063–1071.

Patel, D. R., Yamasaki, A., & Brown, K. (2017). Epidemiology of sports-related musculoskeletal injuries in young athletes in United States. *Translational Pediatrics* 6, 160–166.

Paus, T. (2005). Mapping brain maturation and cognitive development during adolescence. *Trends in Cognitive Sciences* 9, 60–68.

Pazol, K., Daniels, K., Romero, L., et al. (2016). Trends in long-acting reversible contraception use in adolescents and young adults: New Estimates accounting for sexual experience. *Journal of Adolescent Health* 59, 438–442.

Peper, J. S., & Dahl, R. E. (2013). The teenage brain: Surging hormones—brain-behavior interactions during puberty. *Current Directions in Psychological Science* 22, 134–139.

Perper, K., Peterson, K., & Manlove, J. (2010). Diploma attainment among teen mothers. Fact sheet. *Child Trends*.

Pérusse, L., Rankinen, T., Zuberi, A., et al. (2005). The human obesity gene map: the 2004 update. *Obesity Research* 13, 381–490.

Phillips, B., Hening, W., Britz, P., & Mannino, D. (2006). Prevalence and correlates of restless legs syndrome: results from the 2005 National Sleep Foundation Poll. *Chest* 129, 76–80.

Plato (360 BCE). *Laws*, Book 2.

Powell, L. M., & Nguyen, B. T. (2013). Fast-food and full-service restaurant consumption among children and adolescents: effect on energy, beverage, and nutrient intake. *JAMA Pediatrics* 167, 14–20.

Raevuori, A., Hoek, H. W., Susser, E., et al. (2009). Epidemiology of anorexia nervosa in men: a nationwide study of Finnish twins. *PLoS ONE* 4, 1–4.

Raevuori, A., et al. Epidemiology of anorexia nervosa in men: a nationwide study of Finnish twins. *PloS ONE* 4, e4402.

Rathi, N., Riddell, L., & Worsley, A. (2017). Food consumption patterns of adolescents aged 14–16 years in Kolkata, India. *Nutrition Journal* 16, 1–12.

Reagan, P. B., Salsberry, P. J., Fang, M. Z., et al. (2012). African-American/White differences in the age of menarche: Accounting for the difference. *Social Science & Medicine* 75, 1263–1270.

Rilling, J. K., & Sanfey, A. G. (2011). The neuroscience of social decision-making. *Annual Review of Psychology* 62, 23–48.

Robb, A. S., & Dadson, M. J. (2002). Eating disorders in males. *Child and Adolescent Psychiatric Clinics of North America* 11, 399–418.

Robinson, J., Cox, G., Malone, A., et al. (2013). A systematic review of school-based interventions aimed at preventing, treating, and responding to suicide-related behavior in young people. *Crisis*.

Rogol, A. D., Roemmich, J. N., & Clark, P. A. (2002). Growth at puberty. *Journal of Adolescent Health* 31, 192–200.

Romeo, R. D. (2013). The teenage brain: The stress response and the adolescent brain. *Current Directions in Psychological Science* 22, 140–145.

Romo, D. L., Garnett, C., Younger, A. P., et al. (2017). Social media use and its association with sexual risk and parental monitoring among a primarily Hispanic adolescent population. *Journal of Pediatric and Adolescent Gynecology* 30, 466–473.

Rosen, D. S. (2010). Identification and management of eating disorders in children and adolescents. *Pediatrics* 126, 1240–1253.

Rubin, C., Maisonet, M., Kieszak, S., et al. (2009). Timing of maturation and predictors of menarche in girls enrolled in a contemporary British cohort. *Paediatric and Perinatal Epidemiology* 23, 492–504.

Ruedinger, E., & Cox, J. E. (2012). Adolescent childbearing: consequences and interventions. *Current Opinions in Pediatrics* 24, 446–452.

Ryan, R. M. (2015). Nonresident fatherhood and adolescent sexual behavior: A comparison of siblings approach. *Developmental Psychology* 51, 211–223.

Ryan, R. M., Kalil, A., & Ziol-Guest, K. M. (2008). Longitudinal patterns of nonresident fathers' involvement: The role of resources and relations. *Journal of Marriage and Family* 70, 962–977.

Satterwhite, C. L., Torrone, E., Meites, E., et al. (2013). Sexually transmitted infections among us women and men: Prevalence and incidence estimates, 2008. *Sexually Transmitted Diseases* 40, 187–193.

Schlegel, A., & Barry, H. (1980). The evolutionary significance of adolescent initiation ceremonies. *American Ethnologist* 7.

Schlegel, A., & Barry, H. (2017). Pain, fear, and circumcision in boys' adolescent initiation. *Ceremonies. Cross-Cultural Research* 51, 435–463.

Schlegel, A., & Barry Iii, H. (1991). *Adolescence: An Anthropological Inquiry*. Free Press.

Schlomer, G. L., & Cho, H.-J. (2017). Genetic and environmental contributions to age at menarche: Interactive effects of father absence and LIN28B. *Evolution and Human Behavior* 38, 761–769.

Schulz, K. M., & Sisk, C. L. (2016). The organizing actions of adolescent gonadal steroid hormones on brain and behavioral development. *Neuroscience & Biobehavioral Reviews* 70, 148–158.

Shaibi, G. Q., & Goran, M. I. (2008). Examining metabolic syndrome definitions in overweight Hispanic youth: A focus on insulin resistance. *The Journal of Pediatrics* 152, 171–176.

Subrahmanyam, K. (2020). Online behaviors. In S. Hupp & J. Jewell (Eds.), *The Encyclopedia of Child and Adolescent Development*.

Shannon, J. D., Cabrera, N. J., Tamis-LeMonda, C., & Lamb, M. E. (2009). Who stays and who leaves? Father accessibility across children's first 5 years. *Parenting* 9, 78–100.

Sharma, J. C. (1983). The genetic contribution to pubertal growth and development studied by longitudinal growth data on twins. *Annals of Human Biology* 10, 163–171.

Shaw, P., Greenstein, D., Lerch, J., et al. (2006). Intellectual ability and cortical development in children and adolescents. *Nature* 440, 676–679.

Shrewsbury, V., & Wardle, J. (2008). Socioeconomic status and adiposity in childhood: A systematic review of cross-sectional studies 1990–2005. *Obesity* 16, 275–284.

Simon, P. A., Kwan, D., Angelescu, A., et al. (2008). Proximity of fast food restaurants to schools: do neighborhood income and type of school matter? *Preventive Medicine* 47, 284–288.

Singh, A. S., Mulder, C., Twisk, J. W., et al. (2008). Tracking of childhood overweight into adulthood: a systematic review of the literature. *Obesity Reviews* 9, 474–488.

Sinha, A., & Kling, S. (2009). A review of adolescent obesity: Prevalence, etiology, and treatment. *Obesity Surgery* 19, 113–120.

Sisk, C. L. (2016). Hormone-dependent adolescent organization of socio-sexual behaviors in mammals. *Current Opinion in Neurobiology* 38, 63–68.

Sklad, M. (1977). The rate of growth and maturing of twins. *Acta geneticae medicae et gemellologiae* 26, 221–237.

Skoog, T., Stattin, H., Ruiselova, Z., & Özdemir, M. (2013). Female pubertal timing and problem behaviour: The role of culture. *International Journal of Behavioral Development* 37, 357–365.

Slyper, A. H. (2006). The pubertal timing controversy in the USA, and a review of possible causative factors for the advance in timing of onset of puberty. *Clinical Endocrinology* 65, 1–8.

Smith, D. G., Xiao, L., & Bechara, A. (2012). Decision making in children and adolescents: Impaired Iowa Gambling Task performance in early adolescence. *Developmental Psychology* 48, 1180–1187.

Sommer, M., Likindikoki, S., & Kaaya, S. (2014). Tanzanian adolescent boys' transitions through puberty: The importance of context. *American Journal of Public Health* 104, 2290–2297.

Somerville, L. H. (2013). The teenage brain: Sensitivity to social evaluation. *Current Directions in Psychological Science* 22, 121–127.

Speiser, P. W., Rudolf, M. C., Anhalt, H., et al. (2005). Childhood obesity. *The Journal of Clinical Endocrinology & Metabolism* 90, 1871–1887.

Sprecher, S., Harris, G., & Meyers, A. (2008). Perceptions of sources of sex education and targets of sex communication: Sociodemographic and cohort effects. *The Journal of Sex Research* 45, 17–26.

Spruijt-Metz, D. (2011). Etiology, treatment, and prevention of obesity in childhood and adolescence: A decade in review. *Journal of Research on Adolescence* 21, 129–152.

Steinberg, L. (2008). A social neuroscience perspective on adolescent risk-taking. *Developmental Review* 28, 78–106.

Steinberg, L., Albert, D., Cauffman, E., et al. (2008). Age differences in sensation seeking and impulsivity as indexed by behavior and self-report: Evidence for a dual systems model. *Developmental Psychology* 44, 1764–1778.

Steinberg, L., & Monahan, K. C. (2011). Adolescents' exposure to sexy media does not hasten the initiation of sexual intercourse. *Developmental Psychology* 47, 562–576.

Stenner, P. H. D., Bianchi, G., Popper, M., et al. (2006). Constructions of sexual relationships: A study of the views of young people in Catalunia, England and Slovakia and their health implications. *Journal of Health Psychology* 11, 669–684.

Stiles-Shields, C., Rienecke Hoste, R., Doyle, P., & Le Grange, D. (2012). A review of family-based treatment for adolescents with eating disorders. *Reviews on Recent Clinical Trials* 7, 133–140.

Stice, E., Marti, C. N., & Rohde, P. (2013). Prevalence, incidence, impairment, and course of the proposed DSM-5 eating disorder diagnoses in an 8-year prospective community study of young women. *Journal of Abnormal Psychology* 122, 445–457.

Strausz, T., Ahlberg, J., Lobbezoo, F., et al. (2010). Awareness of tooth grinding and clenching from adolescence to young adulthood: a nine-year follow-up. *Journal of Oral Rehabilitation* 37, 497–500.

Sudgot-Borgen, J. (1994). Risk and trigger factors for the development of eating disorders in female athletes. *Medicine & Science in Sports & Exercise* 26, 414–419.

Suleiman, A. B., Galván, A., Harden, K. P., & Dahl, R. E. (2016). Becoming a sexual being: The "elephant in the room" of adolescent brain development. *Developmental Cognitive Neuroscience* 25, 209–220.

Suraev, A. S., Bowen, M. T., Ali, S. O., et al. (2014). Adolescent exposure to oxytocin, but not the selective oxytocin receptor agonist TGOT, increases social behavior and plasma oxytocin in adulthood. *Hormones and Behavior* 65, 488–496.

Talbot, L. S., McGlinchey, E. L., Kaplan, K. A., et al. (2010). Sleep deprivation in adolescents and adults: changes in affect. *Emotion* 10, 831–841.

Tamnes, C. K., Østby, Y., Fjell, A. M., et al. (2009). Brain maturation in adolescence and young adulthood: regional age-related changes in cortical thickness and white matter volume and microstructure. *Cerebral Cortex* 20, 534–548.

Tanner, A. E., Ma, A., Roof, K. A., et al. (2015). The "kaleidoscope" of factors influencing urban adolescent pregnancy in Baltimore, Maryland. *Vulnerable Children and Youth Studies* 10, 257–269.

Tanner, J. M., & Whitehouse, R. H. (1976). Clinical longitudinal standards for height, weight, height velocity, weight velocity, and stages of puberty. *Archives of Disease in Childhood* 51, 170–179.

Teicher, M., Samson, J., Anderson, C., et al. (2016). The effects of childhood maltreatment on brain structure, function and connectivity. *Nature Reviews Neuroscience* 17, 652–666.

Ter Bogt, T. F., van Dorsselaer, S. A., Monshouwer, K., et al. (2006). Body mass index and body weight perception as risk factors for internalizing and externalizing problem behavior among adolescents. *Journal of Adolescent Health* 39, 27–34.

Terman, L. M., & Hocking, A. (1913). The sleep of school children, its distribution according to age, and its relation to physical and mental efficiency. *Journal of Educational Psychology* 4, 199–208.

Thompson, S. M., Hammen, C., & Brennan, P.A. (2016). The impact of asynchronous pubertal development on depressive symptoms in adolescence and emerging adulthood among females. *Journal of Youth and Adolescence* 45, 494–504.

Thorleifsdottir, B., Björnsson, J. K., Benediktsdottir, B., et al. (2002). Sleep and sleep habits from childhood to young adulthood over a 10-year period. *Journal of Psychosomatic Research* 53, 529–537.

Tiggemann, M., & Anesbury, T. (2000). Negative stereotyping of obesity in children: The role of controllability beliefs. *Journal of Applied Social Psychology* 30, 1977–1993.

Toga, A. W., Thompson, P. M., & Sowell, E. R. (2006). Mapping brain maturation. *Focus* 4, 378–390.

Tottenham, N., & Galván, A. (2016). Stress and the adolescent brain: Amygdala-prefrontal cortex circuitry and ventral striatum as developmental targets. *Neuroscience & Biobehavioral Reviews* 70, 217–227.

Trinh, S. L., Lee, J., Halpern, C. T., & Moody, J. (2019). Our buddies, ourselves: The role of sexual homophily in adolescent friendship networks. *Child Development* 90, e132–e147.

U.S. Department of Health and Human Services (2018). *Physical Activity Guidelines for Americans*, 2nd ed. U.S. Department of Health and Human Services: Washington, DC.

Van den Bulck, J. (2007). Adolescent use of mobile phones for calling and for sending text messages after lights out: results from a prospective cohort study with a one-year follow-up. *Sleep* 30, 1220–1223.

Van Dongen, H. P., Rogers, N. L., & Dinges, D. F. (2003). Sleep debt: Theoretical and empirical issues. *Sleep and Biological Rhythms* 1, 5–13.

Van Leijenhorst, L., Moor, B. G., Op de Macks, Z. A., et al. (2010). Adolescent risky decision-making: Neurocognitive development of reward and control regions. *Neuroimage* 51, 345–355.

Vandenbosch, L., & Eggermont, S. (2013). Sexualization of adolescent boys: Media exposure and boys' internalization of appearance ideals, self-objectification, and body surveillance. *Men and Masculinities* 16, 283–306.

Vasilenko, S. A., Lefkowitz, E. S., & Welsh, D. P. (2014). Is sexual behavior healthy for adolescents? A conceptual framework for research on adolescent sexual behavior and physical, mental, and social health. *New Directions for Child and Adolescent Development* 2014, 3–19.

Ver Ploeg, M., Breneman, V., Farrigan, T., et al. (2009). *Access to Affordable and Nutritious Food: Measuring and Understanding Food Deserts and Their Consequences*. United States Department of Agriculture: Washington, DC.

Vikraman, S., Fryar, C. D., & Ogden, C. L. (2015) Caloric intake from fast food among children and adolescents in the United States 2011–2012. NCHS data brief, no. 213. National Center for Health Statistics: Hyattsville, MD.

Vuolo, M., Staff, J., & Mortimer, J. T. (2012). Weathering the great recession: Psychological and behavioral trajectories in the transition from school to work. *Developmental Psychology* 48, 1759.

Walvoord, E. C. (2010). The timing of puberty: Is it changing? Does it matter? *Journal of Adolescent Health* 47, 433–439.

Wang, Y., & Lobstein, T. I. M. (2006). Worldwide trends in childhood overweight and obesity. *International Journal of Pediatric Obesity* 1, 11–25.

Ward, L. M., Erickson, S. E., Lippman, J. R., & Giaccardi, S. (2016). Sexual media content and effects. In *Oxford Research Encyclopedia of Communication*. Oxford University Press: New York.

Watson, N. F., Martin, J. L., Wise, M. S., et al. (2017). Delaying middle school and high school start times promotes student health and performance: An American Academy of Sleep Medicine position statement. *Journal of Clinical Sleep Medicine* 13, 623–625.

Wehkalampi, K., Silventoinen, K., Kaprio, J., et al. (2008). Genetic and environmental influences on pubertal timing assessed by height growth. *American Journal of Human Biology* 20, 417–423.

Weinberg, M. S., Lottes, I. L., & Shaver, F. M. (1995). Swedish or American heterosexual college youth: Who is more permissive? *Archives of Sexual Behavior* 24, 409–437.

Weisfeld, G. (1997). Puberty rites as clues to the nature of human adolescence. *Cross-Cultural Research* 31, 27–54.

Whiting, J. M., Burbank, V. K., & Ratner, M. S. (1986). The duration of maidenhood across cultures. In J. B. Lancaster & B. A. Hamburg (Eds.), *School-Age Pregnancy and Parenthood: Biosocial Dimensions* (pp. 273–302). Aldine de Gruyter: New York.

Widman, L., Choukas-Bradley, S., Helms, S. W., et al. (2014). Sexual communication between early adolescents and their dating partners, parents, and best friends. *The Journal of Sex Research* 51, 731–741.

Widman, L., Noar, S. M., Choukas-Bradley, S., & Francis, D. B. (2014). Adolescent sexual health communication and condom use: A meta-analysis. *Health Psychology* 33, 1113–1124.

Wilson, C. M., Wright, P. F., Safrit, J. T., & Rudy, B. (2010). Epidemiology of HIV infection and risk in adolescents and youth. *Journal of Acquired Immune Deficiency Syndromes* 54, S5–S6.

Wolak, J., Mitchell, K., & Finkelhor, D. (2007). Unwanted and wanted exposure to online pornography in a national sample of youth Internet users. *Pediatrics* 119, 247–257.

Wolfson, A. R., & Carskadon, M. A. (1998). Sleep schedules and daytime functioning in adolescents. *Child Development* 69, 875–887.

Wright, P. J., Malamuth, N. M., & Donnerstein, E. (2012). Research on sex in the media: What do we know about effects on children and adolescents? In *Handbook of Children and the Media*, 2nd ed. (pp. 273–302). Sage Publications, Inc.: Thousand Oaks, CA.

Yang, X., Ram, N., Lougheed, J. P., et al. (2019). Adolescents' emotion system dynamics: Network-based analysis of physiological and emotional experience. *Developmental Psychology* 55, 1982–1993.

Zenk, S. N., & Powell, L. M. (2008). US secondary schools and food outlets. *Health & Place* 14, 336–346.

Zhang, M., Tillman, D. A., & An, S. A. (2017). Global prevalence of sleep deprivation in students and heavy media use. *Education and Information Technologies* 22, 239–254.

Zhao, Y., & Encinosa, W. (2009). Hospitalizations for eating disorders from 1999–2006. HCUP Statistical Brief #70. Agency for Healthcare, Research, and Quality: Rockville, MD.

Chapter 15

Ambady, N., Shih, M., Kim, A., & Pittinsky, T. L. (2001). Stereotype susceptibility in children: Effects of identity activation on quantitative performance. *Psychological Science* 12, 385–390.

Arnett, J. J. (2013). The evidence for generation we and against generation me. *Emerging Adulthood* 1, 5–10.

Aronson, J., Lustina, M. J., Good, C., et al. (1999). When white men can't do math: Necessary and sufficient factors in stereotype threat. *Journal of Experimental Social Psychology* 35, 29–46.

Aronson, J., & Steele, C. M. (2005). Stereotypes and the fragility of academic competence, motivation, and self-concept. In A. J. Elliot & C. S. Dweck (Eds.), *Handbook of Competence and Motivation* (pp. 436–456). Guilford Publications: New York.

Artman, L., Cahan, S., & Avni-Babad, D. (2006). Age, schooling and conditional reasoning. *Cognitive Development* 21, 131–145.

Banerjee, M.; Byrd, C.; Rowley, S. (2018). The relationships of school-based discrimination and ethnic-racial socialization to African American adolescents' achievement outcomes. *Social Science* 7, 208.

Bavelier, D., & Green, C. S. (2016). The brain-boosting power of video games. *Scientific American* 315, 26–31.

Beauchamp, M. H., Dooley, J. J., & Anderson, V. (2013). A preliminary investigation of moral reasoning and empathy after traumatic brain injury in adolescents. *Brain Injury* 27, 896–902.

Benner, A. D. (2011). The transition to high school: Current knowledge, future directions. *Educational Psychology Review* 23, 299.

Benner, A. D., & Wang, Y. (2014). Shifting attendance trajectories from middle to high school: Influences of school transitions and changing school contexts. *Developmental Psychology* 50, 1288.

Benner, A. D. & Wang, Y. (2017). Racial/ethnic discrimination and adolescents' well-being: The role of cross-ethnic friendships and friends' experiences of discrimination. *Child Development* 88, 493–504.

Best, J. R., Miller, P. H., & Jones, L. L. (2009). Executive functions after age 5: Changes and correlates. *Developmental Review* 29, 180–200.

Binder, A. J., and Bound, J. (2019). The declining labor market prospects of less-educated men. *Journal of Economic Perspectives* 33, 163–90.

Bjorklund, D. F. (2012). *Children's Strategies: Contemporary Views of Cognitive Development.* Psychology Press: New York.

Blum-Kulka, S. (2008). Language, communication and literacy: Major steps in the development of literate discourse. In *From Research to Practice in Early Education* (pp. 117–154).

Boom, J., Wouters, H., & Keller, M. (2007). A cross-cultural validation of stage development: A Rasch re-analysis of longitudinal socio-moral reasoning data. *Cognitive Development* 22, 213–229.

Bosco, F. M., Gabbatore, I., & Tirassa, M. (2014). A broad assessment of theory of mind in adolescence: The complexity of mindreading. *Consciousness and Cognition* 24, 84–97.

Brain, C., & Mukherji, P. (2005). *Understanding child psychology.* Nelson Thornes.

Brizio, A., Gabbatore, I., Tirassa, M., & Bosco, F. M. (2015). "No more a child, not yet an adult": Studying social cognition in adolescence. *Frontiers in Psychology* 6, 1011.

Brody, G. H., Chen, Y.-F., Murry, V. M., et al. (2006). Perceived discrimination and the adjustment of African American youths: A five-year longitudinal analysis with contextual moderation effects. *Child Development* 77, 1170–1189.

Bull, R., & Lee, K. (2014). Executive functioning and mathematics achievement. *Child Development Perspectives* 8, 36–41.

Bunting, H., Drew, H., Lasseigne, A., & Anderson-Butcher, D. (2013). Enhancing parental involvement and family resources. In *The School Services Sourcebook: A Guide for School-Based Professionals.* Oxford University Press: New York.

Cassady, J. C. (2004). The influence of cognitive test anxiety across the learning–testing cycle *Learning and Instruction* 14, 569–592.

Chavous, T. M., Rivas-Drake, D., Smalls, C., et al. (2008). Gender matters, too: The influences of school racial discrimination and racial identity on academic engagement outcomes among African American adolescents. *Developmental Psychology* 44, 637–654.

Chen, O., Castro-Alonso, J.C., Paas, F., et al. (2018). Extending cognitive load theory to incorporate working memory resource depletion: Evidence from the spacing effect. *Educational Psychology Review* 30, 483–501.

Chetty, R., Hendren, N., & Katz, L. F. (2016). The effects of exposure to better neighborhoods on children: New evidence from the moving to opportunity experiment. *American Economic Review* 106, 855–902.

Choudhury, S., Blakemore, S. J., & Charman, T. (2006). Social cognitive development during adolescence. *Social Cognitive and Affective Neuroscience* 1, 165–174.

Christenson, S. L., & Thurlow, M. L. (2004). School dropouts: Prevention considerations, interventions, and challenges. *Current Directions in Psychological Science* 13, 36–39.

Baron-Cohen, S. (2004). *The Essential Difference.* Penguin: London, United Kingdom.

Cole, M., Gay, J., Glick, J., & Sharp, D. (1971). *Culture and Cognitive Processes.*

Converse, P. D., Thackray, M., Piccone, K., et al. (2016). Integrating self-control with physical attractiveness and cognitive ability to examine pathways to career success. *Journal of Occupational and Organizational Psychology* 89, 73–91.

Coyle, T. R., Pillow, D. R., Snyder, A. C., & Kochunov, P. (2011). Processing speed mediates the development of general intelligence (g) in adolescence. *Psychological Science* 22, 1265–1269.

Cragg, L., & Gilmore, C. (2014). Skills underlying mathematics: The role of executive function in the development of mathematics proficiency. *Trends in Neuroscience and Education* 3, 63–68.

Craik, F. I. M., & Tulving, E. (1975). Depth of processing and the retention of words in episodic memory. *Journal of Experimental Psychology: General* 104, 268–294.

Damon, W. A., & Steinberg, L. (2006). Adolescent development in interpersonal context. In N. Eisenberg, W. Damon, & R. M. Lerner (Eds.), *Handbook of Child Psychology: Vol. 3, Social, Emotional, and Personality Development,* 6th ed. (pp. 1003–1067). John Wiley & Sons Inc.: Hoboken, NJ.

Daugherty, A. M., & Ofen, N. (2015). That's a good one! Belief in efficacy of mnemonic strategies contributes to age-related increase in associative memory. *Journal of Experimental Child Psychology* 136, 17–29.

Dawson, E., Gilovich, T., & Regan, D. T. (2002). Motivated reasoning and performance on the selection task. *Personality and Social Psychology Bulletin* 28, 1379–1387.

Diemer, M. A., & Rapa, L. J. (2016). Unraveling the complexity of critical consciousness, political efficacy, and political action among marginalized adolescents. *Child Development* 87, 221–238.

Dotterer, A. M., McHale, S. M., & Crouter, A. C. (2009). The development and correlates of academic interests from childhood through adolescence. *Journal of Educational Psychology* 101, 509.

Duckworth, A. (2016). *Grit: The Power of Passion and Perseverance.* Simon and Schuster: New York.

Duckworth, A., & Gross, J. J. (2014). Self-control and grit: Related but separable determinants of success. *Current Directions in Psychological Science* 23, 319–325.

Duckworth, A. L., Quinn, P. D., Lynam, D. R., et al. (2011). Role of test motivation in intelligence testing. *Proceedings of the National Academy of Sciences* 108, 7716–7720.

Duff, D., Tomblin, J. B., & Catts, H. (2015). The influence of reading on vocabulary growth: A case for a matthew effect. *Journal of Speech, Language, and Hearing Research* 58, 853–864.

Dumontheil, I., Küster, O., Apperly, I. A., & Blakemore, S.-J. (2010). Taking perspective into account in a communicative task. *NeuroImage* 52, 1574–1583.

Dweck, C. S. (2002). Messages that motivate: How praise molds students' beliefs, motivation, and performance (in surprising ways). In J. Aronson (Ed.), *Improving Academic Achievement.* Academic Press: New York.

Dweck, C. S., & Leggett, E. L. (1988). A social-cognitive approach to motivation and personality. *Psychological Review* 95, 256–273.

Eagan, M. K., Hurtado, S., Chang, M. J., et al. (2013). Making a difference in science education: The impact of undergraduate research programs. *American Educational Research Journal* 50, 683–713.

Eccles, J. S., Vida, M. N., & Barber, B. (2004). The relation of early adolescents' college plans and both academic ability and task-value beliefs to subsequent college enrollment. *The Journal of Early Adolescence* 24, 63–77.

Elkind, D. (1967). Egocentrism in adolescence. *Child Development* 38, 1025–1034.

Else-Quest, N. M., Hyde, J. S., & Linn, M. C. (2010). Cross-national patterns of gender differences in mathematics: A meta-analysis. *Psychological Bulletin* 136, 103–127.

Fagan, A. A., Wright, E. M., & Pinchevsky, G. M. (2014). The protective effects of neighborhood collective efficacy on adolescent substance use and violence following exposure to violence. *Journal of Youth and Adolescence* 43, 1498–1512.

Flanagan, C., & Levine, P. (2010). Civic engagement and the transition to adulthood. *The Future of Children* 20, 159–179.

Fordham, S., & Ogbu, J. U. (1986). Black students' school success: Coping with the "burden of 'acting white.'" *The Urban Review* 18, 176–206.

Fredricks, J. A., Alfeld, C., & Eccles, J. (2010). Developing and fostering passion in academic and nonacademic domains. *Gifted Child Quarterly* 54, 18–30.

Fredricks, J. A., Blumenfeld, P. C., & Paris, A. H. (2004). School engagement: Potential of the concept, state of the evidence. *Review of Educational Research* 74, 59–109.

Freeman, J., & Simonsen, B. (2015). Examining the impact of policy and practice interventions on high school dropout and school completion rates: A systematic review of the literature. *Review of Educational Research* 85, 205–248.

French, M. T., Homer, J. F., Popovici, I., & Robins, P. K. (2015). What you do in high school matters: High school GPA, educational attainment, and labor market earnings as a young adult. *Eastern Economic Journal* 41, 370–386.

Galdi, S., Cadinu, M., & Tomasetto, C. (2014). The roots of stereotype threat: When automatic associations disrupt girls' math performance. *Child Development* 85, 250–263.

Gay, J., & Cole, M. (1967). *The New Mathematics and an Old Culture: A Study of Learning among the Kpelle of Liberia*. Holt, Rinehart, & Winston: New York.

Gibbs, B. G. (2010). Reversing fortunes or content change? Gender gaps in math-related skill throughout childhood. *Social Science Research* 39, 540–569.

Gibbs, J. C. (2013). *Moral Development and Reality: Beyond the Theories of Kohlberg, Hoffman, and Haidt*. Oxford University Press: New York.

Gilligan, C. (1982). New maps of development: New visions of maturity. *American Journal of Orthopsychiatry* 52, 199.

Good, C., Aronson, J., & Harder, J. A. (2008). Problems in the pipeline: Stereotype threat and women's achievement in high-level math courses. *Journal of Applied Developmental Psychology* 29, 17–28.

Granic, I., Lobel, A., & Engels, R. (2014). The benefits of playing video games. *American Psychologist* 69, 66–78.

Guiso, L., Monte, F., Sapienza, P., & Zingales, L. (2008). Culture, gender, and math. *Science-New York then Washington* 320, 1164.

Hamm, J. V., & Zhang, L. (2010). The schooling context of adolescents' peer relations. In J. L. Meece & J. Eccles (Eds.), *The Handbook of Schools and Schooling Effects on Development* (pp. 518–554). Erlbaum: Hillsdale, NJ.

Hancock, D. R. (2001). Effects of test anxiety and evaluative threat on students' achievement and motivation. *The Journal of Educational Research* 94, 284–290.

Harris-Britt, A., Valrie, C. R., Kurtz-Costes, B., & Rowley, S. J. (2007). Perceived racial discrimination and self-esteem in African American youth: Racial socialization as a protective factor. *Journal of Research on Adolescence* 17, 669–682.

Hatano, G. (1982). Learning to add and subtract: A Japanese perspective. *Addition and Subtraction: A Cognitive Perspective* 211–223.

Hidi, S., & Renninger, K. A. (2006). The four-phase model of interest development. *Educational Psychologist* 41, 111–127.

Huizinga, M., Dolan, C. V., & van der Molen, M. W. (2006). Age-related change in executive function: Developmental trends and a latent variable analysis. *Neuropsychologia* 44, 2017–2036.

Inhelder, B., & Piaget, J. (1958). *The Growth of Logical Thinking from Childhood to Adolescence: An Essay on the Construction of Formal Operational Structures (Developmental Psychology)*. Basic Books: New York.

Jeynes, W. H. (2013). Father involvement, African Americans, and reducing the achievement. In *Father Involvement in Young Children's Lives: A Global Analysis* (pp. 71–87). Springer Science & Business Media: New York.

Kail, R. (1991). Development of processing speed in childhood and adolescence. *Advances in Child Development and Behavior* 23, 151–185.

Kail, R. V., Lervåg, A., & Hulme, C. (2016). Longitudinal evidence linking processing speed to the development of reasoning. *Developmental Science* 19, 1067–1074.

Kalil, A., Levine, J. A., & Ziol-Guest, K. M. (2005). Following in their parents' footsteps: How characteristics of parental work predict adolescents' interest in parents' jobs. In B. Schneider and L. J. Waite (Eds.), *Being Together, Working Apart: Dual-Career Families and the Work-Life Balance* (pp. 422–442). Cambridge University Press: New York.

Kieffer, M. J., & Lesaux, N. K. (2010). Morphing into adolescents: Active word learning for English-language learners and their classmates in middle school. *Journal of Adolescent & Adult Literacy* 54, 47–56.

Killen, M., & Smetana, J. G. (2015). Origins and development of morality. In *Handbook of Child Psychology and Developmental Science, Vol. 3: Socioemotional Processes*, 7th ed. (pp. 701–749). John Wiley & Sons Inc.: Hoboken, NJ.

Klaczynski, P. A., Schuneman, M. J., & Daniel, D. B. (2004). Theories of conditional reasoning: A developmental examination of competing hypotheses. *Developmental Psychology* 40, 559–571.

Kuhn, D. (2018). A role for reasoning in a dialogic approach to critical thinking. *Topoi* 37, 121–128.

Labelle-Chiasson, V., Vera-Estay, E., Dooley, J. J., & Beauchamp, M. H. (2012). The role of intelligence as a cognitive predictor of moral reasoning. *Journal of the International Neuropsychology Society* 18, 206.

Landauer, T. K., & Dumais, S. T. (1997). A solution to Plato's problem: The latent semantic analysis theory of acquisition, induction, and representation of knowledge. *Psychological Review* 104, 211.

Leavell, A. S., Tamis-LeMonda, C. S., Ruble, D. N., et al. (2012). African American, White and Latino fathers' activities with their sons and daughters in early childhood. *Sex Roles* 66, 53–65.

Lee, K., Bull, R., & Ho, R. M. H. (2013). Developmental changes in executive functioning. *Child Development* 84, 1933–1953.

Lee, S. J., & Oyserman, D. (2007). Reaching for the future: The education-focused possible selves of low-income mothers. *New Directions for Adult and Continuing Education*.

Lee, J. O., Kosterman, R., Jones, T. M., et al. (2016). Mechanisms linking high school graduation to health disparities in young adulthood: A longitudinal analysis of the role of health behaviours, psychosocial stressors, and health insurance. *Public Health* 139, 61–69.

Lee, J., Walsh, M. E., Raczek, A. E., et al. (2018). The long-term impact of systemic student support in elementary school: Reducing high-school dropout. *American Educational Research Association* 4.

Lerner, R. M., & Lerner, J. V. (2006). Toward a new vision and vocabulary about adolescence: Theoretical, empirical, and applied bases of a "positive youth development" perspective. In C. S. Tamis-LeMonda (Ed.), *Child Psychology: A Handbook of Contemporary Issues*, 2nd ed. (pp. 445–469). Psychology Press: New York.

Lerner, R. M., Lerner, J. V., Bowers, E., & John Geldhof, G. (2015). *Positive Youth Development and Relational-Developmental-Systems Handbook of Child Psychology and Developmental Science*: John Wiley & Sons, Inc.: Hoboken, NJ.

Lesaux, N. K., Crosson, A. C., Kieffer, M. J., & Pierce, M. (2010). Uneven profiles: Language minority learners' word reading, vocabulary, and reading comprehension skills. *Journal of Applied Developmental Psychology* 31, 475–483.

Leslie, S.-J., Cimpian, A., Meyer, M., & Freeland, E. (2015). Expectations of brilliance underlie gender distributions across academic disciplines. *Science* 347, 262–265.

Levine, S. C., Foley, A., Lourenco, S., et al. (2016). Sex differences in spatial cognition: Advancing the conversation. *Wiley Interdisciplinary Reviews: Cognitive Science* 7, 127–155.

Levin, H. M. (2012). Reconstructing schools in America In W. Tate (Ed.), *Research on Schools, Neighborhoods, and Communities: Toward Civic Responsibility*. Rowman and Littlefield Publishers.

Levine, S. C., Foley, A., Lourenco, S., et al. (2016). Sex differences in spatial cognition: Advancing the conversation. *Wiley Interdisciplinary Reviews: Cognitive Science* 7, 127–155.

Lindberg, S. M., Hyde, J. S., Petersen, J. L., & Linn, M. C. (2010). New trends in gender and mathematics performance: A meta-analysis. *Psychological Bulletin* 136, 1123–1135.

Low, J., & Hollis, S. (2003). The eyes have it: Development of children's generative thinking. *International Journal of Behavioral Development* 27, 97–108.

Luria, A. R. (1976). *Cognitive Development: Its Cultural and Social Foundations* (Trans M. Lopez-Morillas & L. Solotaroff). Harvard University Press: Cambridge, MA.

Malti, T., Killen, M., & Gasser, L. (2012). Social judgments and emotion attributions about exclusion in Switzerland. *Child Development* 83, 697–711.

McFarland, J., Cui, J., Rathbun, A., & Holmes, J. (2018). Trends in high school dropout and completion rates in the United States: 2018. U.S. Department of Education. National Center for Education Statistics.

Midgette, E., Haria, P., & MacArthur, C. (2008). The effects of content and audience awareness goals for revision on the persuasive essays of fifth- and eighth-grade students. *Reading and Writing* 21, 131–151.

Mushoriwa, T. D., Sibanda, J., & Nkambule, H. Z. (2010). Testing generative thinking among Swazi children. *Global Journal of Educational Research* 9, 7–16.

Owens, A., & Candipan, J. (2019). Social and spatial inequalities of educational opportunity: A portrait of schools serving high-and low-income neighbourhoods in US metropolitan areas. *Urban Studies* 56, 3178–3197.

Owens, M., Stevenson, J., Hadwin, J. A., & Norgate, R. (2012). Anxiety and depression in academic performance: An exploration of the mediating factors of worry and working memory. *School Psychology International* 33, 433–449.

Park, D., Yu, A., Baelen, R. N., et al. (2018). Fostering grit: Perceived school goal-structure predicts growth in grit and grades. *Contemporary Educational Psychology* 55, 120–128.

Peske, H. G., & Haycock, K. (2006). Teaching Inequality: How Poor and Minority Students Are Shortchanged on Teacher Quality: A Report and Recommendations by the Education Trust. Education Trust.

Pillow, B. H. (2002). Children's and adults' evaluation of the certainty of deductive inferences, inductive inferences, and guesses. *Child Development* 73, 779–792.

Pinquart, M. (2015). Associations of parenting styles and dimensions with academic achievement in children and adolescents: A meta-analysis. *Educational Psychology Review* 28, 475–493.

Putwain, D., Remedios, R., & Symes, W. (2016). The appraisal of fear appeals as threatening or challenging: frequency of use, academic self-efficacy and subjective value. *Educational Psychology* 36, 1670–1690.

Reilly, D. (2012). Gender, culture, and sex-typed cognitive abilities. *PloS ONE* 7, e39904.

Roeser, R. W., & Eccles, J. S. (2014). Schooling and the mental health of children and in the United States. In *Handbook of Developmental Psychopathology*, 3rd ed. (pp. 163–184). Springer: New York

Rogoff, B., & Chavajay, P. (1995). What's become of research on the cultural basis of cognitive development? *American Psychologist* 50, 859–877.

Ronfeldt, M., Loeb, S., & Wyckoff, J. (2013). How teacher turnover harms student achievement. *American Educational Research Journal* 50, 4–36.

Rosenbaum, J. E. (1991). Black pioneers—do their moves to the suburbs increase economic opportunity for mothers and children? *Housing Policy Debate* 2, 1179–1213.

Rosenbaum, J. E., Kulieke, M. J., & Rubinowitz, L. S. (1988). White suburban schools' responses to low-income black children: Sources of successes and problems. *The Urban Review* 20, 28–41.

Rowley, S., Kurtz-Costes, B., & Cooper, S. M. (2010). The schooling of African American children. In J. L. Meece & J. S. Eccles (Eds.), *Handbook of Research on Schools, Schooling, and Human Development* (pp. 275–292). Routledge: London, United Kingdom.

Rubinstein, J. S., Meyer, D. E., & Evans, J. E. (2001). Executive control of cognitive processes in task switching. *Journal of Experimental Psychology: Human Perception and Performance* 27, 763–797.

Ryan, A. M., Shim, S. S., & Makara, K. A. (2013). Changes in academic adjustment and relational self-worth across the transition to middle school. *Journal of Youth and Adolescence* 42, 1372–1384.

Schwartz, P. D., Maynard, A. M., & Uzelac, S. M. (2008). Adolescent egocentrism: A contemporary view. *Adolescence* 43, 441–448.

Schwerdt, G., & West, M. R. (2013). The impact of alternative grade configurations on student outcomes through middle and high school. *Journal of Public Economics* 97, 308–326.

Sebastian, C. L., Fontaine, N. M., Bird, G., et al. (2012). Neural processing associated with cognitive and affective Theory of Mind in adolescents and adults. *Social Cognitive and Affective Neuroscience* 7, 53–63.

Sebastian, C. L. (2015). Social cognition in adolescence: Social rejection and theory of mind. *Psicología Educativa* 21, 125–131.

Selkirk, L. C., Bouchey, H. A., & Eccles, J. S. (2011). Interactions among domain-specific expectancies, values, and gender: Predictors of test anxiety during early adolescence. *The Journal of Early Adolescence* 31, 361–389.

Shamay-Tsoory, S. G., Harari, H., Aharon-Peretz, J., & Levkovitz, Y. (2010). The role of the orbitofrontal cortex in affective theory of mind deficits in criminal offenders with psychopathic tendencies. *Cortex* 46, 668–677.

Shih, M., Pittinsky, T. L., & Ambady, N. A. (1999). Stereotype susceptibility: Identity salience and shifts in quantitative performance. *Psychological Science* 10, 80–83.

Shin, H., & Ryan, A. M. (2014). Early adolescent friendships and academic adjustment: Examining selection and influence processes with longitudinal social network analysis. *Developmental Psychology* 50, 2462–2472.

Shore, M. F., & Massimo, J. L. (2014). Fifteen years after treatment. A follow-up study of comprehensive vocationally-oriented psychotherapy. *American Journal of Orthopsychiatry* 84, 619–623.

Snow, C. E., & Uccelli, P. (2009). The challenge of academic language. In D. Olson & Torrance (Eds.), *The Cambridge Handbook of Literacy* (pp. 112–133). Cambridge University Press: New York.

Staff, J., & Mortimer, J. T. (2007). Educational and work strategies from adolescence to early adulthood: Consequences for educational attainment. *Social Forces* 85, 1169–1194.

Steele, C. M., & Aronson, J. (1995). Stereotype threat and the intellectual test performance of African Americans. *Journal of Personality and Social Psychology* 69, 797.

Steinberg, L. (2001). We know some things: Parent–adolescent relationships in retrospect and prospect. *Journal of Research on Adolescence* 11, 1–19.

Storage, D., Horne, Z., Cimpian, A., & Leslie, S.-J. (2016). The frequency of "brilliant" and "genius" in teaching evaluations predicts the representation of women and African Americans across fields. *PloS ONE* 11, e0150194.

Sum, A., Khatiwada, I., McLaughlin, J., & Palma, S. (2009). The consequences of dropping out of high school. Center for Labor Market Studies Publications 23.

Sun, L., & Nippold, M. A. (2012). Narrative writing in children and adolescents: Examining the literate lexicon. *Language, Speech, and Hearing Services in Schools* 43, 2–13.

Uccelli, P., Barr, C. D., Dobbs, C. L., et al. (2015). Core academic language skills: An expanded operational construct and a novel instrument to chart school-relevant language proficiency in preadolescent and adolescent learners. *Applied Psycholinguistics* 36, 1077–1109.

Uccelli, P., Demir-Lira, Ö. E., Rowe, M. L., et al. (2018). Children's early decontextualized talk predicts academic language proficiency in mid-adolescence. *Child Development* 90, 1650–1663.

Vartanian, L. R. (2001). Adolescents' reactions to hypothetical peer group conversations: Evidence for an imaginary audience? *Adolescence* 36, 347–380.

Vera-Estay, E., Dooley, J. J., & Beauchamp, M. H. (2015). Cognitive underpinnings of moral reasoning in adolescence: The contribution of executive functions. *Journal of Moral Education* 44, 17–33.

Vetter, N. C., Altgassen, M., Phillips, L., et al. (2013). Development of affective theory of mind across adolescence: Disentangling the role of executive functions. *Developmental Neuropsychology* 38, 114–125.

Wai, J., Cacchio, M., Putallaz, M., & Makel, M. C. (2010). Sex differences in the right tail of cognitive abilities: A 30 year examination. *Intelligence* 38, 412–423.

Wang, M.-T., & Eccles, J. S. (2011). Adolescent behavioral, emotional, and cognitive engagement trajectories in school and their differential relations to educational success. *Journal of Research on Adolescence* 22, 31–39.

Wang, M.-T., & Sheikh-Khalil, S. (2014). Does parental involvement matter for student achievement and mental health in high school? *Child Development* 85, 610–625.

Wang, M. T., & Fredricks, J. A. (2014). The reciprocal links between school engagement, youth problem behaviors, and school dropout during adolescence. *Child Development* 85, 722–737.

Wang, M.-T., Fredricks, J., Ye, F., et al. (2019). Conceptualization and assessment of adolescents' engagement and disengagement in school: A multidimensional school engagement scale. *European Journal of Psychological Assessment* 35, 592–606.

Wentzel, K. R., Battle, A., Russell, S. L., & Looney, L. B. (2010). Social supports from teachers and peers as predictors of academic and social motivation. *Contemporary Educational Psychology* 35, 193–202.

Wentzel, K. R., Russell, S., & Baker, S. (2016). Emotional support and expectations from parents, teachers, and peers predict adolescent competence at school. *Journal of Educational Psychology* 108, 242–255.

Whipp, J. L., & Geronime, L. (2017). Experiences that predict early career teacher commitment to and retention in high-poverty urban schools. *Urban Education* 52, 799–828.

Wigfield, A., & Meece, J. L. (1988). Math anxiety in elementary and secondary school students. *Journal of Educational Psychology* 80, 210.

Wong, C. A., Eccles, J. S., & Sameroff, A. (2003). The influence of ethnic discrimination and ethnic identification on African American adolescents' school and socioemotional adjustment. *Journal of Personality* 71, 1197–1232.

Zeidner, M. (2007). Test anxiety in educational contexts: Concepts, findings. *Emotion in Education* 165.

Chapter 16

Ahmed, S. P., Bittencourt-Hewitt, A., & Sebastian, C. L. (2015). Neurocognitive bases of emotion regulation development in adolescence. *Developmental Cognitive Neuroscience* 15, 11–25.

Anderson, M., & Jiang, J. (2018). Teens, social media & technology 2018. Pew Research Center 31.

Armstrong, E. A., Hamilton, L., & England, P. (2010). Is hooking up bad for young women? *Contexts* 9, 22–27.

Auerbach, R. P., Milner, A. J., Stewart, J. G., & Esposito, E. C. (2015). Identifying differences between depressed adolescent suicide ideators and attemptors. *Journal of Affective Disorders* 186, 127–133.

Bachmann S. (2018). Epidemiology of suicide and the psychiatric perspective. *International Journal of Environmental Research and Public Health* 15, 1425.

Barber, B. L., Stone, M. R., & Eccles, J. S. (2010). Protect, prepare, support, and engage. *Handbook of Research on Schools, Schooling, and Human Development* 336–378.

Bechara, A. (2005). Decision making, impulse control and loss of willpower to resist drugs: a neurocognitive perspective. *Nature Neuroscience* 8, 1458–1463.

Benner, A. D., & Crosnoe, R. (2011). The racial/ethnic composition of elementary schools and young children's academic and socioemotional functioning. *American Educational Research Journal* 48, 621–646.

Berzonsky, M. D., & Adams, G. R. (1999). Re-evaluating the identity status paradigm: Still useful after 35 years. *Developmental Review* 19, 557–590.

Berzonsky, M. D., Cieciuch, J., Duriez, B., & Soenens, B. (2011). The how and what of identity formation: Associations between identity styles and value orientations. *Personality and Individual Differences* 50, 295–299.

Best, P., Manktelow, R., & Taylor, B. (2014). Online communication, social media and adolescent wellbeing: A systematic narrative review. *Children and Youth Services Review* 41, 27–36.

Bhatia, S. K., & Bhatia, S. C. (2007). Childhood and adolescent depression. *American Family Physician* 75, 73–80.

Birkeland, M. S., Breivik, K., & Wold, B. (2014). Peer acceptance protects global self-esteem from negative effects of low closeness to parents during adolescence and early adulthood. *Journal of Youth and Adolescence* 43, 70–80.

Birkeland, M. S., Melkevik, O., Holsen, I., & Wold, B. (2012). Trajectories of global self-esteem development during adolescence. *Journal of Adolescence* 35, 43–54.

Bisson, M. A., & Levine, T. R. (2009). Negotiating a friends with benefits relationship. *Archives of Sexual Behavior* 38, 66–73.

Bleakley, A., Vaala, S., Jordan, A. B., & Romer, D. (2014). The Annenberg Media Environment Survey. Inv*Media and the Well-Being of Children and Adolescents* (pp. 1–19). Oxford University Press: Oxford, United Kingdom.

Boden, J. M., Fergusson, D. M., & Horwood, L. J. (2008). Does adolescent self-esteem predict later life outcomes? A test of the causal role of self-esteem. *Development and Psychopathology* 20, 319–339.

Bolognini, M., Plancherel, B., Laget, J., & Halfon, O. (2003). Adolescent's suicide attempts: Populations at risk, vulnerability, and substance use. *Substance Use & Misuse* 38, 1651–1669.

Bowie, D. (1971). Changes. On *Hunky Dory*. New York: RCA Music Group.

Boyd, D. (2014). *It's Complicated: The Social Lives of Networked Teens.* Yale University Press: New Haven, CT.

Brody, G. H., Lei, M. K., Chae, D. H., et al. (2014). Perceived discrimination among African American adolescents and allostatic load: A longitudinal analysis with buffering effects. *Child Development* 85, 989–1002.

Brody, G. H., Miller, G. E., Yu, T., et al (2016). Supportive family environments ameliorate the link between racial discrimination and epigenetic aging: A replication across two longitudinal cohorts. *Psychological Science* 27, 530–541.

Brown, B. B., & Dietz, E. L. (2009). Informal peer groups in middle childhood and adolescence. In K. E. Rubin, W. M. Bukowski, & B. Laursen, (Eds.), *Handbook of Peer Interactions, Relationships, and Groups* (pp. 361–376).

Brown, C.H., Brincks, A., Huang, S. et al. (2018). Two-year impact of prevention programs on adolescent depression: An integrative data analysis approach. *Prevention Sci* 19, 74–94.

Bukowski, W. M., Laursen, B., & Rubin, K. (Eds.) (2019). *Handbook of Peer Interactions, Relationships, and Groups,* 2nd ed. Gilford Press: New York.

Calzo, J. P., Masyn, K. E., Austin, S. B., et al. (2017). Developmental latent patterns of identification as mostly heterosexual versus lesbian, gay, or bisexual. *Journal of Research on Adolescence* 27, 246–253.

Cao, B., & Lin, W-Y. (2015). How do victims react to cyberbullying on social networking sites? The influence of previous cyberbullying victimization experiences. *Computers in Human Behavior* 52, 458–465.

Card, N. A., & Hodges, E. V. (2006). Shared targets for aggression by early adolescent friends. *Developmental Psychology* 42, 1327–1338.

Carpenter, C. J. (2012). Narcissism on Facebook: Self-promotional and anti-social behavior. *Personality and Individual Differences* 52, 482–486.

Cassidy, J. (2000). Adult romantic attachments: A developmental perspective on individual differences. *Review of General Psychology* 4, 111–131.

Chang, L. Y., Wu, W. C., Wu, C. C., et al. (2017). The role of sleep problems in the relationship between peer victimization and antisocial behavior: A five-year longitudinal study. *Social Science & Medicine* 173, 126–133.

Chein, J., Albert, D., O'Brien, L., et al. (2011). Peers increase adolescent risk taking by enhancing activity in the brain's reward circuitry. *Developmental Science* 14, F1–F10.

Chin, J. W., & Johnson, J. (2011). Making the team: Threats to health and wellness within sport hazing cultures. *International Journal of Health, Wellness & Society,* 1.

Chmielewski, J. F., Tolman, D. L., & Kincaid, H. (2017). Constructing risk and responsibility: A gender, race, and class analysis of news representations of adolescent sexuality. *Feminist Media Studies* 17, 412–425.

Cleary, S. D. (2000). Adolescent victimization and associated suicidal and violent behaviors. *Adolescence* 35, 671–682.

Coleman, J. S. (1961). *The Adolescent Society.* Free Press of Glencoe.

Coley, R. L., Leventhal, T., Lynch, A. D., & Kull, M. (2013). Relations between housing characteristics and the well-being of low-income children and adolescents. *Developmental Psychology* 49, 1775–1789.

Collins, W. A., & Laursen, B. (2004). Parent-adolescent relationships and influences. *Handbook of Adolescent Psychology* 2, 331–362.

Connell, A. M., & Dishion, T. J. (2008). Reducing depression among at-risk early adolescents: Three-year effects of a family-centered intervention embedded in schools. *Journal of Family Psychology* 22, 574–585.

Connolly, J., Craig, W., Goldberg, A., & Pepler, D. (2004). Mixed-gender groups, dating, and romantic relationships in early adolescence. *Journal of Research on Adolescence* 14, 185–207.

Crabbe, R., Pivnick, L. K., Bates, J., et al. (2019). Contemporary college students' reflections on

their high school peer crowds. *Journal of Adolescent Research* 34, 563–596.

Criss, M. M., Lee, T. K., Morris, A. S., et al. (2015). Link between monitoring behavior and adolescent adjustment: An analysis of direct and indirect effects. *Journal of Child and Family Studies* 24, 668–678.

Crocetti, E., Klimstra, T. A., Hale, W. W., et al. (2013). Impact of early adolescent externalizing problem behaviors on identity development in middle to late adolescence: A prospective 7-year longitudinal study. *Journal of Youth and Adolescence* 42, 1745–1758.

Cross, W. E., Seaton, E., Yip, T., et al. (2017) Identity work: Enactment of racial-ethnic identity in everyday life, *Identity* 17, 1–12.

Csikszentmihalyi, M., & Larson, R. (1987). Validity and reliability of the experience-sampling method. *Journal of Nervous and Mental Disease* 175, 526–536.

Csikszentmihalyi, M., & Larson, R. (2014). Validity and reliability of the experience-sampling method. In *Flow and the Foundations of Positive Psychology* (pp. 35–54). Springer: Dordrecht.

Cui, L., Morris, A. S., Harrist, A. W., et al. (2015). Adolescent RSA responses during an anger discussion task: Relations to emotion regulation and adjustment. *Emotion* 15, 360–372.

Curtin, S. C., Warner, M., & Hedegaard, H. (2016). Suicide rates for females and males by race and ethnicity: United States, 1999 and 2014. Center for Disease Control and Prevention.

Davidson (2014). The 7 social media mistakes most likely to cost you your job. *Money,* October 16, 2014.

Deane, C., Vijayakumar, N., Allen, N., et al. (2020). Parenting × brain development interactions as predictors of adolescent depressive symptoms and well-being: Differential susceptibility or diathesis-stress? *Development and Psychopathology* 32, 139–150.

Deo, I. R., & Prelow, H. M. (2018). The role of stressors and academic competence in adolescent depression by race. *Journal of Adolescent and Family Health* 9, 5.

Derefinko, K. J., Peters, J. R., Eisenlohr-Moul, T. A., et al. (2014). Relations between trait impulsivity, behavioral impulsivity, physiological arousal, and risky sexual behavior among young men. *Archives of Sexual Behavior* 43, 1149–1158.

Diamond, L. M. (2008). *Sexual Fluidity.* Harvard University Press: Cambridge, MA.

Diamond, L. M. (2012). The desire disorder in research on sexual orientation in women: Contributions of dynamical systems theory. *Archives of Sexual Behavior* 41, 73–83.

Dishion, T. J., & McMahon, R. J. (1998). Parental monitoring and the prevention of child and adolescent problem behavior: A conceptual and empirical formulation. *Clinical Child and Family Psychology Review* 1, 61–75.

Doornwaard, S. M., Moreno, M. A., & van den Eijnden, R. J., et al. (2014). Young adolescents' sexual and romantic reference displays on Facebook. *Journal of Adolescent Health* 55, 535–541.

Doughty, S. E., McHale, S. M., & Feinberg, M. E. (2015). Sibling experiences as predictors of romantic relationship qualities in adolescence. *Journal of Family Issues,* 36, 589–608.

Drummond, K. D., Bradley, S. J., Peterson-Badali, M., & Zucker, K. J. (2008). A follow-up study of girls with gender identity disorder. *Developmental Psychology* 44, 34–45.

Duell, N., Icenogle, G., & Steinberg, L. (2016). Adolescent decision making and risk taking. In L. Balter & C. Tamis-Lemonda (Eds.), *Child Psychology: A Handbook of Contemporary Issues* (pp. 263–284). Routledge: New York.

Dunn, J. (1983). Sibling relationships in early childhood. *Child Development* 787–811.

Dykas, M. J., Ziv, Y., & Cassidy, J. (2008). Attachment and peer relations in adolescence. *Attachment & Human Development* 10, 123–141.

Egan, K. G., & Moreno, M. A. (2011). Alcohol references on undergraduate males' Facebook profiles. *American Journal of Men's Health* 5, 413–420.

Ellis, W. E., & Zarbatany, L. (2007). Explaining friendship formation and friendship stability: The role of children's and friends' aggression and victimization. *Merrill-Palmer Quarterly* 53, 79–104.

Erath, S. A., Flanagan, K. S., Bierman, K. L., & Tu, K. M. (2010). Friendships moderate psychosocial maladjustment in socially anxious early adolescents. *Journal of Applied Developmental Psychology* 31, 15–26.

Erikson, E. H. (1950). Growth and crises of the "healthy personality." In M. J. E. Senn (Ed.), *Symposium on the Healthy Personality* (pp. 91–146). Josiah Macy, Jr. Foundation.

Erikson, E. H. (1956). The problem of ego identity. *Journal of the American Psychoanalytic Association* 4, 56–121.

Erikson, E.H. 1963. *Youth, Change, and Challenge.* New York: Basic Books.

Escobar-Viera, C. G., Whitfield, D. L., Wessel, C. B., et al. (2018). For better or for worse? A systematic review of the evidence on social media use and depression among lesbian, gay, and bisexual minorities. *JMIR Mental Health* 5, e10496. 1–14.

Espinoza, G., & Juvonen, J. (2011). Perceptions of the school social context across the transition to middle school: Heightened sensitivity among Latino students? *Journal of Educational Psychology* 103, 749–758.

Fairlie, A. M., Wood, M. D., & Laird, R. D. (2012). Prospective protective effect of parents on peer influences and college alcohol involvement. *Psychology of Addictive Behaviors* 26, 30–41.

Falk, C. F., & Heine, S. J. (2015). What is implicit self-esteem, and does it vary across cultures? *Personality and Social Psychology Review* 19, 177–198.

Farruggia, S. P., Chen, C., Greenberger, E., et al. (2004). Adolescent self-esteem in cross-cultural perspective: Testing measurement equivalence and a mediation model. *Journal of Cross-Cultural Psychology*, 35, 719–733.

Feigelman, W., & Gorman, B. S. (2008). Assessing the effects of peer suicide on youth suicide. *Suicide and Life-Threatening Behavior* 38, 181–194.

Fine, M., & Sirin, S. R. (2008). *Muslim American Youth: Understanding Hyphenated Identities through Multiple Methods* (Vol. 12). NYU Press: New York.

Fisher, J. (2017). *Healing the Fragmented Selves of Trauma Survivors: Overcoming Internal Self-alienation.* Taylor & Francis: New York.

Fleischmann, F., Phalet, K., Deboosere, P., & Neels, K. (2012). Comparing concepts of ethnicity in ethnic composition measures: Local community contexts and the educational attainment of the second generation in Belgium. *Journal of Ethnic and Migration Studies* 38, 1513–1531.

Fortunato, L., Young, A. M., Boyd, C. J., & Fons, C. E. (2010). Hook-up sexual experiences and problem behaviors among adolescents. *Journal of Child & Adolescent Substance Abuse* 19, 261–278.

Freud, A. (1958). Child observation and prediction of development: A memorial lecture in honor of Ernst Kris. *The Psychoanalytic Study of the Child* 13, 92–116.

Fuligni, A. J. (2007). Family obligation, college enrollment, and emerging adulthood in Asian and Latin American families. *Child Development Perspectives* 1, 96–100.

Furman, W., Schaffer, L., & Florsheim, P. (2003). *Adolescent Romantic Relationships and Sexual Behavior.* Lawrence Erlbaum Associates: Hillsdale, NJ.

Gabard-Durnam, L. J., Flannery, J., Goff, B., et al. (2014). The development of human amygdala functional connectivity at rest from 4 to 23 years: a cross-sectional study. *Neuroimage* 95, 193–207.

Gartner, R. E., & Sterzing, P. R. (2018). Social ecological correlates of family-level interpersonal and environmental microaggressions toward sexual and gender minority adolescents. *Journal of Family Violence* 33, 1–16.

George, C., Kaplan, N., & Main, M. (1985). The Berkeley adult attachment interview. Unpublished protocol, Department of Psychology, University of California, Berkeley.

Geven, S., Kalmijn, M., & van Tubergen, F. (2016). The ethnic composition of schools and students' problem behaviour in four European countries: the role of friends. *Journal of Ethnic and Migration Studies* 42, 1473–1495.

Giota, K. G., & Kleftaras, G. (2013). The role of personality and depression in problematic use of social networking sites in Greece. *Cyberpsychology: Journal of Psychosocial Research on Cyberspace*, 7.

Greene, M. L., Way, N., & Pahl, K. (2006). Trajectories of perceived adult and peer discrimination among Black, Latino, and Asian American adolescents: Patterns and psychological correlates. *Developmental Psychology* 42, 218–236.

Hadley, A. M., Hair, E. C., & Moore, K. A. (2008). Assessing what kids think about themselves: A guide to adolescent self-concept for out-of-school time program practitioners. *Child Trends* 32, 1–6.

Hafen, C. A., Laursen, B., Burk, W. J., et al. (2011). Homophily in stable and unstable adolescent friendships: Similarity breeds constancy. *Personality and Individual Differences* 51, 607–612.

Hager, A. D., & Leadbeater, B. J. (2016). The longitudinal effects of peer victimization on physical health from adolescence to young adulthood. *Journal of Adolescent Health* 58, 330–336.

Haimson, O. L., Brubaker, J. R., Dombrowski, L., & Hayes, G. R. (2015). Disclosure, stress, and support during gender transition on Facebook. In *Proceedings of the 18th ACM Conference on Computer Supported Cooperative Work & Social Computing* (pp. 1176–1190).

Hankin, B. L. (2005). Childhood maltreatment and psychopathology: Prospective tests of attachment, cognitive vulnerability, and stress as mediating processes. *Cognitive Therapy and Research* 29, 645–671.

Hankin, B. L., Mermelstein, R., & Roesch, L. (2007). Sex differences in adolescent depression: Stress exposure and reactivity models. *Child Development* 78, 279–295.

Hare, T. A., Tottenham, N., Galvan, A., et al. (2008). Biological substrates of emotional reactivity and regulation in adolescence during an emotional go-nogo task. *Biological Psychiatry* 63, 927–934.

Hawk, S. T., Ter Bogt, T. F., Van Den Eijnden, R. J., & Nelemans, S. A. (2015). Too little power, too much information! Power, narcissism, and adolescents' disclosures on social networking sites. *Computers in Human Behavior* 52, 72–80.

Hirschi, T., & Gottfredson, M. (1983). Age and the explanation of crime. *American Journal of Sociology* 89, 552–584.

Hofstede, G. (2011). Dimensionalizing cultures: The Hofstede model in context. *Online Readings in Psychology and Culture* 2.

Holt, M. K., Green, J. G., Tsay-Vogel, M., et al. (2017). Multidisciplinary approaches to research on bullying in adolescence. *Adolescent Research Review* 2, 1–10.

Huang, C. (2010). Internet use and psychological well-being: A meta-analysis. *Cyberpsychology, Behavior, and Social Networking* 13, 241–249.

Johnson, M. D., & Galambos, N. L. (2014). Paths to intimate relationship quality from parent–adolescent relations and mental health. *Journal of Marriage and Family* 76, 145–160.

Juang, L. P., & Cookston, J. T. (2009). Acculturation, discrimination, and depressive symptoms among Chinese American adolescents: A longitudinal study. *The Journal of Primary Prevention* 30, 475–496.

Katzer, C., Fetchenhauer, D., & Belschak, F. (2009). Cyberbullying: Who are the victims? A comparison of victimization in Internet chatrooms and victimization in school. *Journal of Media Psychology* 21, 25–36.

Keenan-Miller, D., Hammen, C., & Brennan, P. (2007). Adolescent psychosocial risk factors for severe intimate partner violence in young adulthood. *Journal of Consulting and Clinical Psychology* 75, 456.

Khurana, A., Bleakley, A., Jordan, A. B., & Romer, D. (2015). The protective effects of parental monitoring and internet restriction on adolescents' risk of online harassment. *Journal of Youth and Adolescence* 44, 1039–1047.

Kiang, L., Yip, T., & Fuligni, A. J. (2008). Multiple social identities and adjustment in young adults from ethnically diverse backgrounds. *Journal of Research on Adolescence* 18, 643–670.

Kieling, C., Baker-Henningham, H., Belfer, M., et al. (2011). Child and adolescent mental health worldwide: evidence for action. *The Lancet* 378, 1515–1525.

Kiesner, J., Poulin, F., & Dishion, T. J. (2010). Adolescent substance use with friends: Moderating and mediating effects of parental monitoring and peer activity contexts. *Merrill-Palmer Quarterly* 56, 529–556.

King, P. E., Ramos, J. S., & Clardy, C. E. (2013). Searching for the sacred: Religion, spirituality, and adolescent development. In K. I. Pargament, J. J. Exline, & J. W. Jones (Eds.), *APA Handbook of Psychology, Religion, and Spirituality (Vol. 1): Context, Theory, and Research* (pp. 513–528). American Psychological Association.

Klimstra, T. A., Luyckx, K., Hale III, W. A., et al. (2010). Short-term fluctuations in identity: Introducing a micro-level approach to identity formation. *Journal of Personality and Social Psychology* 99, 191–202.

Kowalski, R. M., Giumetti, G. W., Schroeder, A. N., Lattanner, M. R. (2014) Bullying in the digital age: A critical review and meta-analysis of cyberbullying research among youth. *Psychological Bulletin*, 140, 1073–1137.

Kroger, J. (2012). The status of identity. In P. Kerig, M. S. Schulz, & S. Hauser (Eds.) *Adolescence and Beyond: Family Processes and Development* (pp. 54–83). Oxford University Press: New York.

Kuss, D. J., & Griffiths, M. D. (2011). Online social networking and addiction—A review of the psychological literature. *International Journal of Environmental Research and Public Health* 8, 3528–3552.

Laible, D. J., Carlo, G., & Roesch, S. C. (2004). Pathways to self-esteem in late adolescence: The role of parent and peer attachment, empathy, and social behaviours. *Journal of Adolescence* 27, 703–716.

Lantagne, A., & Furman, W. (2017). Romantic relationship development: The interplay between age and relationship length. *Developmental Psychology* 53, 1738–1749.

Larson, R. W., Moneta, G., Richards, M. H., & Wilson, S. (2002). Continuity, stability, and change in daily emotional experience across adolescence. *Child Development* 73, 1151–1165.

Lee, K. T. H., Lewis, R. W., Kataoka, S., et al. (2018). Out-of-school time and behaviors during adolescence. *Journal of Research on Adolescence* 28, 284–293.

Leeman, R. F., Hoff, R. A., Krishnan-Sarin, S., et al. (2014). Impulsivity, sensation-seeking, and part-time job status in relation to substance use and gambling in adolescents. *Journal of Adolescent Health* 54, 460–466.

Legate, N., Ryan, R. M., & Rogge, R. D. (2017). Daily autonomy support and sexual identity disclosure predicts daily mental and physical health outcomes. *Personality and Social Psychology Bulletin* 43, 860–873.

Lenhart, A., Smith, A., Anderson, M., et al. (2015). *Teens, Technology and Friendships*. Pew Research Center.

Lennarz, H. K., Lichtwarck-Aschoff, A., Finkenauer, C., & Granic, I. (2017). Jealousy in adolescents' daily lives: How does it relate to interpersonal context and well-being? *Journal of Adolescence* 54, 18–31.

Lindell, A. K., & Campione-Barr, N. (2017). Relative power in sibling relationships across adolescence. *New Directions for Child and Adolescent Development* 2017, 49–66.

Litwiller, B. J., & Brausch, A. M. (2013). Cyber bullying and physical bullying in adolescent suicide: the role of violent behavior and substance use. *Journal of Youth and Adolescence* 42, 675–684.

Liu, C., Ang, R. P., & Lwin, M. O. (2013). Cognitive, personality, and social factors associated with adolescents' online personal information disclosure. *Journal of Adolescence* 36, 629–638.

Loeser, M. K., Whiteman, S. D., & McHale, S. M. (2016). Siblings' perceptions of differential treatment, fairness, and jealousy and adolescent adjustment: A moderated indirect effects model. *Journal of Child and Family Studies* 25, 2405–2414.

Lopez, C. M., Driscoll, K. A., & Kistner, J. A. (2009). Sex differences and response styles: Subtypes of rumination and associations with depressive symptoms. *Journal of Clinical Child & Adolescent Psychology* 38, 27–35.

Luthar, S. S., Small, P. J., & Ciciolla, L. (2018). Adolescents from upper middle class communities: Substance misuse and addiction across early adulthood. *Development and Psychopathology* 30, 315–335.

Lyman, E. L., & Luthar, S. S. (2014). Further evidence on the "costs of privilege": Perfectionism in high-achieving youth at socioeconomic extremes. *Psychology in the Schools* 51, 913–930.

Maciejewski, D. F., van Lier, P. A., Branje, S. J., et al. (2017). A daily diary study on adolescent emotional experiences: Measurement invariance and developmental trajectories. *Psychological Assessment* 29, 35–49.

Madden, M., Cortesi, S., Gasser, U., et al. (2012). Parents, teens, and online privacy. Pew Internet & American Life Project.

Madigan, S., Villani, V., Azzopardi, C., et al. (2018). The prevalence of unwanted online sexual exposure and solicitation among youth: a meta-analysis. *Journal of Adolescent Health* 63, 133–141.

Mahoney, J. L., Vandell, D. L., Simpkins, S., & Zarrett, N. (2009). Adolescent out-of-school activities. *Handbook of Adolescent Psychology* 2, 228–269.

Main, M., & Goldwyn, R. (1994). Adult Attachment Interview scoring and classification manual. Unpublished manuscript, University of California at Berkeley.

Marcia, J. E. (1966). Development and validation of ego-identity status. *Journal of Personality and Social Psychology* 3, 551–558.

Marcia, J. E. (1980). Identity in adolescence. *Handbook of Adolescent Psychology* 9, 159–187.

Marcia, J. E. (2002). Adolescence, identity, and the Bernardone family. *Identity: An International Journal of Theory and Research* 2, 199–209.

Markus, H. R., & Kitayama, S. (2010). Cultures and selves: A cycle of mutual constitution. *Perspectives on Psychological Science* 5, 420–430.

McHale, S. M., & Crouter, A. C. (1996). The family contexts of children's sibling relationships. In G. H. Brody (Ed.), *Advances in Applied Developmental Psychology 10. Sibling Relationships: Their Causes and Consequences* (pp. 173–195). Ablex Publishing.

McHale, S. M., Updegraff, K. A., & Whiteman, S. D. (2012). Sibling relationships and influences in childhood and adolescence. *Journal of Marriage and Family* 74, 913–930.

McLeod, G. F., Horwood, L. J., & Fergusson, D. M. (2016). Adolescent depression, adult mental health and psychosocial outcomes at 30 and 35 years. *Psychological Medicine* 46, 1401–1412.

Meier, A., & Allen, G. (2009). Romantic relationships from adolescence to young adulthood: Evidence from the National Longitudinal Study of Adolescent Health. *The Sociological Quarterly* 50, 308–335.

Meier, E. P., & Gray, J. (2014). Facebook photo activity associated with body image disturbance in adolescent girls. *Cyberpsychology, Behavior, and Social Networking* 17, 199–206.

Miller, P. J., Wang, S. H., Sandel, T., & Cho, G. E. (2002). Self-esteem as folk theory: A comparison of European American and Taiwanese mothers' beliefs. *Parenting: Science and Practice* 2, 209–239.

Millings, A., Buck, R., Montgomery, A., et al. (2012). School connectedness, peer attachment, and self-esteem as predictors of adolescent depression. *Journal of Adolescence* 35, 1061–1067.

Mitchell, K. J., Ybarra, M., & Finkelhor, D. (2007). The relative importance of online victimization in understanding depression, delinquency, and substance use. *Child Maltreatment* 12, 314–324.

Moed, A., Gershoff, E. T., Eisenberg, N., et al. (2015). Parent–adolescent conflict as sequences of reciprocal negative emotion: Links with conflict resolution and adolescents' behavior problems. *Journal of Youth and Adolescence* 44, 1607–1622.

Moilanen, K. L., Shaw, D. S., Criss, M. M., & Dishion, T. J. (2009). Growth and predictors of parental knowledge of youth behavior during early adolescence. *Journal of Early Adolescence* 29, 800–825.

Morgan, E. M., Snelson, C., & Elison-Bowers, P. (2010). Image and video disclosure of substance use on social media websites. *Computers in Human Behavior* 26, 1405–1411.

Moshman, D. (2011). Identity as a theory of oneself. In *Adolescent Rationality and Development* (pp. 151–160). Psychology Press: New York.

Nickerson, A. B., & Slater, E. D. (2009). School and community violence and victimization as predictors of adolescent suicidal behavior. *School Psychology Review* 38, 218–232.

Nischal, A., Tripathi, A., Nischal, A., & Trivedi, J. K. (2012). Suicide and antidepressants: What current evidence indicates. *Mens Sana Monographs* 10, 33–44.

Nurmi, J.-E. (2004). Socialization and self-development: Channeling, selection, adjustment, and reflection. In R. M. Lerner & L. Steinberg (Eds.), *Handbook of Adolescent Psychology* (pp. 85–124). John Wiley & Sons Inc.: Hoboken, NJ

Odum, A. L. (2011). Delay discounting: I'm ak, you're ak. *Journal of the Experimental Analysis of Behavior* 96, 427–439.

Orth, U., Robins, R. W., & Roberts, B. W. (2008). Low self-esteem prospectively predicts depression in adolescence and young adulthood. *Journal of Personality and Social Psychology* 95, 695–708.

Ott, M. Q., Corliss, H. L., Wypij, D., et al. (2011). Stability and change in self-reported sexual orientation identity in young people: Application of mobility metrics. *Archives of Sexual Behavior* 40, 519–532.

Owen, J. J., Rhoades, G. K., Stanley, S. M., & Fincham, F. D. (2010). "Hooking up" among college students: Demographic and psychosocial correlates. *Archives of Sexual Behavior* 39, 653–663.

Padilla-Walker, L. M., Harper, J. M., & Bean, R. A. (2011). Pathways to parental knowledge: The role of family process and family structure. *The Journal of Early Adolescence* 31, 604–627.

Padilla-Walker, L. M., & Christensen, K. J. (2011). Empathy and self-regulation as mediators between parenting and adolescents' prosocial behavior toward strangers, friends, and family. *Journal of Research on Adolescence* 21, 545–551.

Pahl, K., & Way, N. (2006). Longitudinal trajectories of ethnic identity among urban Black and Latino adolescents. *Child Development* 77, 1403–1415.

Panek, E. T., Nardis, Y., & Konrath, S. (2013). Mirror or megaphone? How relationships between narcissism and social networking site use differ on Facebook and Twitter. *Computers in Human Behavior* 29, 2004–2012.

Parker, J. G., Low, C. M., Walker, A. R., & Gamm, B. K. (2005). Friendship jealousy in young adolescents: individual differences and links to sex, self-esteem, aggression, and social adjustment. *Developmental Psychology* 41, 235–250.

Patchin, J. W., & Hinduja, S. (2010). Cyberbullying and self-esteem. *Journal of School Health* 80, 614–621.

Patil, P. A., Porche, M. V., Shippen, N. A., et al. (2018). Which girls, which boys? The intersectional risk for depression by race and ethnicity, and gender in the US. *Clinical Psychology Review* 66, 51–68.

Peach, H. D., & Gaultney, J. F. (2013). Sleep, impulse control, and sensation-seeking predict delinquent behavior in adolescents, emerging adults, and adults. *Journal of Adolescent Health* 53, 293–299.

Phinney, J. S. (1992). The multigroup ethnic identity measure: A new scale for use with diverse groups. *Journal of Adolescent Research* 7, 156–176.

Phinney, J. S. (1996). Understanding ethnic diversity: The role of ethnic identity. *American Behavioral Scientist* 40, 143–152.

Phinney, J. S. (2008). Bridging identities and disciplines: Advances and challenges in understanding multiple identities. *New Directions for Child and Adolescent Development* 2008, 97–109.

Piquero, A. R., Farrington, D. P., & Blumstein, A. (2003). The criminal career paradigm. *Crime and Justice* 30, 359–506.

Primack, B. A., & Escobar-Viera, C. G. (2017). Social media as it interfaces with psychosocial development and mental illness in transitional age youth. *Child and Adolescent Psychiatric Clinics* 26, 217–233.

Puckett, J. A., Woodward, E. N., Mereish, E. H., & Pantalone, D. W. (2015). Parental rejection following sexual orientation disclosure: Impact on internalized homophobia, social support, and mental health. *LGBT Health* 2, 265–269.

Qin, D. (2009). Being "good" or being "popular" gender and ethnic identity negotiations of Chinese immigrant adolescents. *Journal of Adolescent Research* 24, 37–66.

Qin, D. B. (2008). Doing well vs. feeling well: Understanding family dynamics and the psychological adjustment of Chinese immigrant adolescents. *Journal of Youth and Adolescence* 37, 22–35.

Qin, D. B., Chang, T. F., Han, E. J., & Chee, G. (2012). Conflicts and communication between high-achieving Chinese American adolescents and their parents. *New Directions for Child and Adolescent Development* 2012, 35–57.

Qin, D. B., Way, N., & Mukherjee, P. (2008). The other side of the model minority story: The familial and peer challenges faced by Chinese American adolescents. *Youth & Society* 39, 480–506.

Rabinowitz, J. A., Osigwe, I., Drabick, D. A., & Reynolds, M. D. (2016). Negative emotional reactivity moderates the relations between family cohesion and internalizing and externalizing symptoms in adolescence. *Journal of Adolescence* 53, 116–126.

Raskauskas, J., & Stoltz, A. D. (2007). Involvement in traditional and electronic bullying among adolescents. *Developmental Psychology* 43, 564–575.

Reiss, F. (2013). Socioeconomic inequalities and mental health problems in children and adolescents: a systematic review. *Social Science & Medicine* 90, 24–31.

Rhodes, N., Pivik, K., & Sutton, M. (2015). Risky driving among young male drivers: The effects of mood and passengers. *Transportation Research Part F: Traffic Psychology and Behaviour* 28, 65–76.

Rivas-Drake, D., Syed, M., Umaña-Taylor, A., et al. (2014). Feeling good, happy, and proud: A meta-analysis of positive ethnic–racial affect and adjustment. *Child Development* 85, 77–102.

Robers, S. (2015). *Indicators of School Crime and Safety: 2010*. DIANE Publishing.

Romer, D., Duckworth, A. L., Sznitman, S., & Park, S. (2010). Can adolescents learn self-control? Delay of gratification in the development of control over risk taking. *Prevention Science* 11, 319–330.

Rowley, R. L., & Hertzog, J. L. (2016). From holding hands to having a thing to hooking up: framing heterosexual youth relationships. *Marriage & Family Review* 52, 548–562.

Rubin, K. H., Bukowski, W. M., & Bowker, J. C. (2015). Children in peer groups. In *Handbook of Child Psychology and Developmental Science* (pp. 1–48).

Rudolph, K. D., Ladd, G., & Dinella, L. (2007). Gender differences in the interpersonal consequences of early-onset depressive symptoms. *Merrill-Palmer Quarterly*, 461–488.

Russell, S. T., Everett, B. G., Rosario, M., & Birkett, M. (2014). Indicators of victimization and sexual orientation among adolescents: analyses from Youth Risk Behavior Surveys. *American Journal of Public Health* 104, 255–261.

Ryan, C., Russell, S. T., Huebner, D., et al. (2010). Family acceptance in adolescence and the health of LGBT young adults. *Journal of Child and Adolescent Psychiatric Nursing* 23, 205–213.

Saewyc, E. M. (2011). Research on adolescent sexual orientation: Development, health disparities, stigma, and resilience. *Journal of Research on Adolescence* 21, 256–272.

Salk, R. H., Hyde, J. S., & Abramson, L. Y. (2017). Gender differences in depression in representative national samples: meta-analyses of diagnoses and symptoms. *Psychological Bulletin* 143, 783–822.

Samarova, V., Shilo, G., & Diamond, G. M. (2013). Changes over time in parents' acceptance of their Israeli sexual minority adolescents.

Sampasa-Kanyinga, H., & Lewis, R. F. (2015). Frequent use of social networking sites is associated with poor psychological functioning among children and adolescents. *Cyberpsychology, Behavior, and Social Networking* 18, 380–385.

Savin-Williams, R. C. (1996). Ethnic- and sexual-minority youth. In R. C. Savin-Williams & K. M. Cohen (Eds.), *The Lives of Lesbians, Gays, and Bisexuals: Children to Adults* (pp. 152–165). Harcourt Brace College Publishers.

Savin-Williams, R. C. (2019). Developmental trajectories and milestones of sexual-minority youth. In S. Lamb & J. Gilbert (Eds.), *Cambridge Handbooks in Psychology. The Cambridge Handbook of Sexual Development: Childhood and Adolescence* (pp. 156–179). Cambridge University Press: New York.

Savin-Williams, R. C., & Cohen, K. M. (2004). Homoerotic development during childhood and adolescence. *Child and Adolescent Psychiatric Clinics of North America* 13, 529–549.

Savin-Williams, R. C., & Ream, G. L. (2003). Sex variations in the disclosure to parents of same-sex attractions. *Journal of Family Psychology* 17, 429–438.

Schraegle, W. A., & Titus, J. B. (2017). The relationship of seizure focus with depression, anxiety, and health-related quality of life in children and adolescents with epilepsy. *Epilepsy & Behavior* 68, 115–122.

Schwartz, S. J., Donnellan, M. B., Ravert, R. D., et al. (2013). Identity development, personality, and well-being in adolescence and emerging adulthood: Theory, research, and recent advances. In R. M. Lerner, M. A. Easterbrooks, J. Mistry, & I. B. Weiner (Eds.), *Handbook of Psychology: Developmental Psychology* (pp. 339–364). John Wiley & Sons, Inc.: Hoboken, NJ.

Seidman, E., Allen, L., Aber, J. L., et al. (1994). The impact of school transitions in early adolescence on the self-system and perceived social context of poor urban youth. *Child Development* 65, 507–522.

Selkie, E. M., Fales, J. L., & Moreno, M. A. (2016). Cyberbullying prevalence among US middle and high school–aged adolescents: A systematic review and quality assessment. *Journal of Adolescent Health* 58, 125–133.

Selman, R. (2017). *Fostering Friendship: Pair Therapy for Treatment and Prevention*. Routledge: New York.

Sengupta, A., & Chaudhuri, A. (2011). Are social networking sites a source of online harassment for teens? Evidence from survey data. *Children and Youth Services Review* 33, 284–290.

Seymour, B., & Dolan, R. (2008). Emotion, decision making, and the amygdala. *Neuron* 58, 662–671.

Shulman, E. P., Steinberg, L. D., & Piquero, A. R. (2013). The age–crime curve in adolescence and early adulthood is not due to age differences in economic status. *Journal of Youth and Adolescence* 42, 848–860.

Sigurdsson, B., Palsson, S. P., Aevarsson, O., et al. (2015). Validity of Gotland Male Depression Scale for male depression in a community study: The Sudurnesjamenn study. *Journal of Affective Disorders* 173, 81–89.

Smetana, J. G. (2011). Adolescents' social reasoning and relationships with parents: Conflicts and coordinations within and across domains. *Adolescent Vulnerabilities and Opportunities: Constructivist and Developmental Perspectives* 139–158.

Smetana, J. G., Villalobos, M., Rogge, R. D., & Tasopoulos-Chan, M. (2010). Keeping secrets from parents: Daily variations among poor, urban adolescents. *Journal of Adolescence* 33, 321–331.

Smith, A. R., Chein, J., & Steinberg, L. (2013). Impact of socio-emotional context, brain development, and pubertal maturation on adolescent risk-taking. *Hormones and Behavior* 64, 323–332.

Solomon, Y., Warin, J., Lewis, C., & Langford, W. (2002). Intimate talk between parents and their teenage children: democratic openness or covert control? *Sociology* 36, 965–983.

Sousa, C., Herrenkohl, T. I., Moylan, C. A., et al. (2011). Longitudinal study on the effects of child abuse and children's exposure to domestic violence, parent-child attachments, and antisocial behavior in adolescence. *Journal of Interpersonal Violence* 26, 111–136.

Spaeth, M., Weichold, K., & Silbereisen, R. K. (2015). The development of leisure boredom in early adolescence: Predictors and longitudinal associations with delinquency and depression. *Developmental Psychology* 51, 1380–1394.

Spirito, A., Valeri, S., Boergers, J., & Donaldson, D. (2003). Predictors of continued suicidal behavior in adolescents following a suicide attempt. *Journal of Clinical Child and Adolescent Psychology* 32, 284–289.

Steiger, A. E., Allemand, M., Robins, R. W., & Fend, H. A. (2014). Low and decreasing self-esteem during adolescence predict adult depression two decades later. *Journal of Personality and Social Psychology* 106, 325–338.

Steinberg, L. (2005). Cognitive and affective development in adolescence. *Trends in Cognitive Sciences* 9, 69–74.

Steinberg, L. (2008). A social neuroscience perspective on adolescent risk-taking. *Developmental Review* 28, 78–106.

Steinberg, L., Graham, S., O'Brien, L., et al. (2009). Age differences in future orientation and delay discounting. *Child Development* 80, 28–44.

Stocker, C. M., Burwell, R. A., & Briggs, M. L. (2002). Sibling conflict in middle childhood predicts children's adjustment in early adolescence. *Journal of Family Psychology* 16, 50–57.

Suleiman, A. B., Galván, A., Harden, K. P., & Dahl, R. E. (2017). Becoming a sexual being: The "elephant in the room" of adolescent brain development. *Developmental Cognitive Neuroscience* 25, 209–220.

Swearer, S. M., Martin, M., Brackett, M., & Palacios, R. A. (2017). Bullying intervention in adolescence: The intersection of legislation, policies, and behavioral change. *Adolescent Research Review* 2, 23–35.

Szwedo, D. E., Mikami, A. Y., & Allen, J. P. (2012). Social networking site use predicts changes in young adults' psychological adjustment. *Journal of Research on Adolescence* 22, 453–466.

Thompson, E. M., & Morgan, E. M. (2008). "Mostly straight" young women: Variations in sexual behavior and identity development. *Developmental Psychology* 44, 15–21.

Tiggemann, M., & Slater, A. (2014). NetTweens: The internet and body image concerns in preteenage girls. *The Journal of Early Adolescence* 34, 606–620.

Tolman, D. L., & Chmielewski, J. F. (2019). Toward women wanting. *Archives of Sexual Behavior* 48, 1709–1714.

Triandis, H. C. (1995). New directions in social psychology. In *Individualism & Collectivism*. Westview Press.

Tsitsika, A., Janikian, M., Schoenmakers, T. M., et al. (2014). Internet addictive behavior in adolescence: a cross-sectional study in seven European countries. *Cyberpsychology, Behavior, and Social Networking* 17, 528–535.

Twenge, J. M. (2017). *iGen: Why Today's Super-Connected Kids Are Growing Up Less Rebellious, More Tolerant, Less Happy—and Completely Unprepared for Adulthood—and What That Means for the Rest of Us*. Atria: New York.

Twenge, J. M., Spitzberg, B. H., & Campbell, W. K. (2019). Less in-person social interaction with peers among US adolescents in the 21st century and links to loneliness. *Journal of Social and Personal Relationships* 36, 1892–1913.

Uhls, Y. T., Ellison, N. B., & Subrahmanyam, K. (2017). Benefits and costs of social media in adolescence. *Pediatrics* 140, S67–S70.

Umaña-Taylor, A. J., & Guimond, A. B. (2010). A longitudinal examination of parenting behaviors and perceived discrimination predicting Latino adolescents' ethnic identity. *Developmental Psychology* 46, 636–650.

Umaña-Taylor, A. J., Bhanot, R., & Shin, N. (2006). Ethnic identity formation during adolescence: The critical role of families. *Journal of Family Issues* 27, 390–414.

Umaña-Taylor, A. J., O'Donnell, M., Knight, G. P., et al. (2014). Mexican-origin early adolescents' ethnic socialization, ethnic identity, and psychosocial functioning. *The Counseling Psychologist* 42, 170–200.

Umaña-Taylor, A. J., Yazedjian, A., & Bámaca-Gómez, M. (2004). Developing the ethnic identity scale using Eriksonian and social identity perspectives. *Identity: An International Journal of Theory and Research* 4, 9–38.

Umaña-Taylor, A. J., Alfaro, E. C., Bámaca, M. Y., & Guimond, A. B. (2009). The central role of familial ethnic socialization in Latino adolescents' cultural orientation. *Journal of Marriage and Family* 71, 46–60.

Umaña-Taylor, A. J., Quintana, S. M., Lee, R. M., et al (2014). Ethnic and racial identity in the 21st century study group. Ethnic and racial identity during adolescence and into young adulthood: An integrated conceptualization. *Child Development* 85, 21–39.

Vaala, S. E., & Bleakley, A. (2015). Monitoring, mediating, and modeling: Parental influence on adolescent computer and Internet use in the United States. *Journal of Children and Media* 9, 40–57.

van Beusekom, G., Bos, H. M., Overbeek, G., & Sandfort, T. G. (2015). Same-sex attraction, gender nonconformity, and mental health: The protective role of parental acceptance. *Psychology of Sexual Orientation and Gender Diversity* 2, 307.

Vernon, L., Barber, B. L., & Modecki, K. L. (2015). Adolescent problematic social networking and school experiences: The mediating effects of sleep disruptions and sleep quality. *Cyberpsychology, Behavior, and Social Networking* 18, 386–392.

Volk, A. A., Dane, A. V., & Marini, Z. A. (2014). What is bullying? A theoretical redefinition. *Developmental Review* 34, 327–243.

Wang, J., Iannotti, R. J., & Nansel, T. R. (2009). School bullying among adolescents in the United States: Physical, verbal, relational, and cyber. *Journal of Adolescent Health* 45, 368–375.

Weinstein, S. M., & Mermelstein, R. (2007). Relations between daily activities and adolescent mood: The role of autonomy. *Journal of Clinical Child and Adolescent Psychology* 36, 182–194.

Weymouth, B. B., Buehler, C., Zhou, N., & Henson, R. A. (2016). A meta-analysis of parent–adolescent conflict: Disagreement, hostility, and youth maladjustment. *Journal of Family Theory & Review* 8, 95–112.

Wiesner, M., & Kim, H. K. (2006). Co-occurring delinquency and depressive symptoms of adolescent boys and girls: A dual trajectory modeling approach. *Developmental Psychology* 42, 1220–1235.

Wigfield, A., Byrnes, J. P., & Eccles, J. S. (2006). Development during early and middle Adolescence. In P. A. Alexander & P. H. Winne (Eds.), *Handbook of Educational Psychology* (pp. 87–113). Lawrence Erlbaum Associates Publishers: Hillsdale, NJ.

Wilson, R. E., Gosling, S. D., & Graham, L. T. (2012). A review of Facebook research in the social sciences. *Perspectives on Psychological Science* 7, 203–220.

Yap, M. B., Allen, N. B., & Ladouceur, C. D. (2008). Maternal socialization of positive affect: The impact of invalidation on adolescent emotion regulation and depressive symptomatology. *Child Development* 79, 1415–1431.

Ybarra, M. L., Boyd, D., Korchmaros, J. D., & Oppenheim, J. K. (2012). Defining and measuring cyberbullying within the larger context of bullying victimization. *Journal of Adolescent Health* 51, 53–58.

Ybarra, M. L., Diener-West, M., & Leaf, P. J. (2007). Examining the overlap in Internet harassment and school bullying: Implications for school intervention. *Journal of Adolescent Health* 41, S42–S50.

Yeager, D. S. (2017). Dealing with social difficulty during adolescence: The role of implicit theories of personality. *Child Development Perspectives* 11, 196–201.

Yeager, D. S., Fong, C. J., Lee, H. Y., & Espelage, D. L. (2015). Declines in efficacy of anti-bullying programs among older adolescents: Theory and a three-level meta-analysis. *Journal of Applied Developmental Psychology* 37, 36–51.

Zimmerman, G. M., & Messner, S. F. (2010). Neighborhood context and the gender gap in adolescent violent crime. *American Sociological Review* 75, 958–980.

Zweig, J. M., Phillips, S. D., & Lindberg, L. D. (2002). Predicting adolescent profiles of risk: Looking beyond demographics. *Journal of Adolescent Health* 31, 343–353.

Index

infants and back sleeping, 159
types of, 114
Sleep (early childhood)
    developmental cascades from sleep
        deprivation, 322–323
    developmental changes in, 308, *309*
    family context, 310–311
    obesity and, 322–323
    sleep needs, 309–310
Sleep (middle childhood)
    historical trends in children's sleep
        duration, 440
    overweight status and, 452
    school performance, 452
    sleep needs, 440–442
    sleep problems, 442–443
Sleep (adolescence)
    circadian rhythms and melatonin, 576
    overview, 576
    poor-quality sleep, 578–579
    sleep deprivation and sleep debt, 577–578
    technology context, 576, 579–580
Sleep breathing disorders, *443*
Sleep consolidation, 308, *309*
Sleep debt, 578
Sleep deprivation, 322–323, 577–578
Sleep disorders, 442–443
Sleep hyperhydrosis, *443*
Sleep regulation, 308
Sleeping through the night, 117
Sleep-wake cycles, 98, 114
Sleep-wake transition disorders, *443*
Slovakian adolescents, 565
Slow-to-warm-up babies, 261, 262
Slow-wave sleep, 578
Small-for-date infants, 110
Small-group practice, 491
Smart Snacks in School, 438–439
Smell
    perception by infants, 133, 134
    sensory receptors, *128*
Smiling, infants and toddlers, 252–253
Smith, Linda, *12*
SNAP. *See* Supplemental Nutrition Assistance
    Program
Social anxiety, 660
Social cognition (infants and toddlers)
    challenges of studying, 206
    cultural context, 203–204
    defined, 196
    developmental cascades from, 205–206
    home context, 202–203
    methods of assessment, 207
    overview, 196
    understanding others' actions, knowledge,
        and beliefs, 198–202
    understanding others' attention, 196–198
Social cognition (early childhood)
    contexts of, 354–355
    evaluating people's knowledge and
        experience, 349–350
    theory of mind, 350–354
Social cognition (adolescence)
    adolescent egocentrism, 597–598
    moral behavior, 599–600
    moral reasoning, 598–599
    overview, 596
    perspective taking, 596–597
Social comparison, 516
Social desirability bias, 34

Social development (infants and toddlers)
    attachment, 267–275
    developmental cascades, 285–287, *288*
    effects of neglect on, 249–250
    importance of cultivating, 288
    peer relations and the origins of morality,
        275–278
    self-identity, 278–285
Social development (early childhood)
    attachment and care-giver child
        relationship quality, 389–391
    cultural context, 395–396
    family context of social skills and
        aggression, 393–395
    identity development, 396–406
    introduction, 389
    methods of measuring, 418
    moral development, 406–414
    peers and friends, 391–393
    unique role and timing of, 417
Social development (middle childhood)
    cultural context, 539–540
    family and school contexts, 538
    influence of peer relationships on social
        competence, 542–543
    introduction, 503–504, 514
    methods of measuring, 544
    physical activity and, 450
    relationships with parents, 527–530
    relationships with peers, 530–537
    self-identity development, 514–527
    social media context, 538–539
Social development (adolescence)
    developmental cascades from, 661–665
    introduction, 623–624, 650–651
    methods of measuring, 665
    relationships with parents and siblings,
        651–655
    relationships with peers, 655–658
    social media and, 658–661
Social distancing, 313
Social domain theory, 409–413
Social exclusion, pain of, 536–537
Social identification, 398
Social information, communicated by
    emotions, 252
Social interactions
    cascading effects of emotion understanding
        and, 414–415
    cascading effects of infant locomotion on,
        166
    early emotion regulation and, 286
    infant temperament and, 263–264
    language development in early childhood
        and, 371–372
    See also Social relationships
Social isolation, substance use and, 663
Social learning theory
    definition and description of, *12*, 23–24
    on gender identity, 397–398
Social media
    benefits of, 658–659
    cyberbulling, 538–539, 657–658
    dangerous encounters, 661
    disclosing too much information, 660–661
    overuse of, 659–660
    social development in middle childhood
        and, 538–539
    teen views on, *661*
    use of by adolescents, 658–661

Social referencing, 258, 289
Social relationships
    academic performance in middle childhood
        and, 497
    in adolescence, 650–661
    importance of self-esteem in, 541
    theory-of-mind skills in early childhood
        and, 372
    See also Social interactions
Social smiling, 252–253
Socialization, racial and ethnic, 404–406
Societal domain, *409*, 410–411
Society for Research on Child Development,
    46–47
Sociocultural theory
    concept of culture, 28
    cultural learning environment, 28–29
    cultural universals, 30
    definition and overview, *12*, 28
    on language development, 229–230,
        229–0230
    Lev Vygotsky and, *12*, 21–22, 28, 229
Sociodramatic play, 331
Socioeconomic context
    of early childhood illness, injury, and
        maltreatment, 317, *318*
    of early childhood language, literacy, and
        mathematical skills, 364–365
    experience-dependent brain plasticity and,
        79, *80*
    of infant cognitive development, 194–195
    of infant language development, 234–235
    influence on the age at menarche, *559*
Sociograms, 534
Sociometric nomination, 534, 544
Solidity, infant understanding of, 180
Somatic motor association area, *294*
Somatic sensory association area, *294*
Somnolence, disorders of, *443*
So-Moral task, 599, 620
Soroban, *601*
Soul of a Child, The (Preyer), 149
Sound perception
    loudness and pitch, 144
    perceiving music, 144–145
    perceiving speech, 145–146
    perceptual integration, 146–147
    See also Hearing
South Carolina, 320
Spanish-English dual-language learning, 236,
    243
Spatial cognition, 361
Spatial intelligence, 471
Spatial reasoning, 499
Spearman, Charles, 470
Special education, 497–498
Speech perception, by infants, 145–146
Speech sounds
    infant vocalizations and, 213–214
    phonological development, 211–214
Spelke, Elizabeth, *12*
Sperm
    assisted reproduction, 92–93
    conception and, 90, 91, 92
    development, 552
    male reproductive health, 91
Spermarche, 552
Spina bifida, 103
Spinal cord development, 95